The Gendered Society Reader

The Gendered Society Reader

Fifth Edition

Michael Kimmel
STONY BROOK UNIVERSITY, STATE UNIVERSITY OF NEW YORK

Amy Aronson
FORDHAM UNIVERSITY

New York Oxford
OXFORD UNIVERSITY PRESS

Oxford University Press is a department of the University of Oxford. It furthers the University's objective of excellence in research, scholarship, and education by publishing worldwide.

Oxford New York
Auckland Cape Town Dar es Salaam Hong Kong Karachi
Kuala Lumpur Madrid Melbourne Mexico City Nairobi
New Delhi Shanghai Taipei Toronto

With offices in
Argentina Austria Brazil Chile Czech Republic France Greece
Guatemala Hungary Italy Japan Poland Portugal Singapore
South Korea Switzerland Thailand Turkey Ukraine Vietnam

For titles covered by Section 112 of the US Higher Education Opportunity Act, please visit www.oup.com/us/he for the latest information about pricing and alternate formats.

Published by Oxford University Press.
198 Madison Avenue, New York, NY 10016
www.oup.com

ISBN: 978-0-19-992749-4

Printing number: 9 8 7 6 5 4 3 2 1

Printed in the United States of America
on acid-free paper

For Zachary and H. Perry,
godbrothers

CONTENTS

*An asterisk indicates new to the fifth edition.

Introduction

MICHAEL KIMMEL

Every day there's another story about how women and men are different. They say we come from different planets—women from Venus, men from Mars. They say we have different brain chemistries, different brain organization, different hormones. Different bodies, different selves. They say we have different ways of knowing, listen to different moral voices, have different ways of speaking and hearing each other.

You'd think we were different species. In his best-selling book, the pop psychologist John Gray informs us that not only do women and men communicate differently, "but they think, feel, perceive, react, respond, love, need, and appreciate differently" (Gray 1995, 5). It's a miracle of cosmic proportions that we ever understand one another!

Yet here we all are, together, in the same classes, eating in the same dining halls, walking on the same campus, reading the same books, being subject to the same criteria for grading. We live in the same houses, eat the same meals, read the same newspapers, and watch the same TV shows. What gives?

One thing that seems to be happening is that we are increasingly aware of the centrality of gender in our lives. In the past four decades, the pioneering work of feminist scholars, both in traditional disciplines and in women's studies, has made us increasingly aware of the centrality of gender in shaping social life. We now know that gender is one of the central organizing principles around which social life revolves.

This wasn't always the case. Four decades ago, social scientists would have only listed social class and race as the master statuses that defined and proscribed social life. If you wanted to study gender in the 1960s in social science, for example, you would have found one course to meet your needs—"Marriage and the Family"—which was sort of the "Ladies Auxiliary" of the social sciences. There were no courses on gender. But today, gender has joined race and class in our understanding of the foundations of an individual's identity. Gender, we now know, is one of the axes around which social life is organized, and through which we understand our own experiences.

While much of our cultural preoccupation seems to be about the differences between women and men, there are two near-universal phenomena that define the experiences of women and men in virtually every culture we have ever known. First: *Why is it that virtually every single society differentiates people on the basis of gender?* Why are women and men perceived as different in every known society? What are the differences that are perceived? Why is gender at least one—if not the central—basis for the division of labor? And, second: *Why is it that virtually every known society is also based on male domination?* Why does virtually every society divide social, political, and economic resources unequally between the genders? Why is a gendered division of labor also an unequal division of labor? Why are women's tasks and men's tasks valued differently?

Of course, there are dramatic differences among societies regarding the type of gender differences, the levels of gender inequality, and the amount of violence (implied or real) that is necessary to maintain both systems of difference and domination. But the basic facts remain: *virtually every society known to us is founded upon assumptions of gender difference and the politics of gender inequality.*

Most of the arguments about gender difference begin, as does this book, with biology. Women and men *are* biologically different, after all. Our reproductive anatomies are different, as are our reproductive destinies. Our brain structures differ, our brain chemistries differ. Our musculature is different. We have different levels of different hormones circulating through our different bodies. Surely, these add up to fundamental, intractable, and universal differences, and these differences provide the foundation for male domination, don't they?

In these models, biological "sex"—by which we mean the chromosomal, chemical, anatomical apparatuses that make us either male or female—leads inevitably to "gender," by which we mean the cultural and social meanings, experiences, and institutional structures that are defined as appropriate for those males and females.

"Sex" is male and female; "gender" refers to cultural definitions of masculinity and femininity—the meanings of maleness or femaleness.

Biological models of sex difference occupy the "nature" side of the age-old question about whether it is nature or nurture that determines our personalities. Of course, most sensible people recognize that both nature *and* nurture are necessary for gender development. Our biological sex provides the raw material for our development—and all that evolution, different chromosomes, and hormones have to have some effect on who we are and who we become.

But biological sex varies very little, and yet the cultural definitions of gender vary enormously. And it has been the task of the social and behavioral sciences to explore the variations in definitions of gender. Launched originally as critiques of biological universalism, the social and behavioral sciences—anthropology, history, psychology, sociology—have all had an important role to play in our understanding of gender.

What they suggest is that what it means to be a man or a woman will vary in four significant ways. First, the meanings of gender vary from one society to another. What it means to be a man or a woman among aboriginal peoples in the Australian outback or in the Yukon territories is probably very different from what it means to be a man or a woman in Norway or Ireland. It has been the task of anthropologists to specify some of those differences, to explore the different meanings that gender has in different cultures. Some cultures, like our own, encourage men to be stoic and to prove their masculinity, and men in other cultures seem even more preoccupied with demonstrating sexual prowess than American men seem to be. Other cultures prescribe a more relaxed definition of masculinity, based on civic participation, emotional responsiveness, and the collective provision for the community's needs. Some cultures encourage women to be decisive and competitive; others insist that women are naturally passive, helpless, and dependent.

Second, the meanings of masculinity and femininity vary within any one culture over time. What it meant to be a man or a woman in seventeenth-century France is probably very different from what it might mean today. My own research has suggested that the meanings of manhood have changed dramatically from the founding of America in 1776 to the present (see Kimmel 2006). (Although for reasons of space I do not include any historical material in this volume, inquiries into the changing definitions of gender have become an area of increasing visibility.)

Third, the meaning of masculinity and femininity will change as any individual person grows. Following Freudian ideas that individuals face different developmental tasks as they grow and develop, psychologists have examined the ways in which the meanings of masculinity and femininity change over the course of a person's life. The issues confronting a man about proving himself, feeling successful, and the social institutions in which he will attempt to enact those experiences will change, as will the meanings of femininity for prepubescent women, women in child-bearing years, and post-menopausal women, or for women entering the labor market and those retiring from it.

Finally, the meanings of gender will vary *among* different groups of women and men within any particular culture at any particular time. Simply put, not all American men and women are the same. Our experiences are also structured by class, race, ethnicity, age, sexuality, and region of the country. Each of these axes modifies the others. Just because we make gender visible doesn't mean that we make these other organizing principles of social life invisible. Imagine, for example, an older, black, gay man in Chicago and a young, white, heterosexual farm boy in Iowa. Wouldn't they have different definitions of masculinity? Or imagine a twenty-two-year-old heterosexual poor Asian American woman in San Francisco and a wealthy white Irish Catholic lesbian in Boston. Wouldn't their ideas about what it means to be a woman be somewhat different? The interplanetary theory of gender differences collapses all such differences, and focuses *only* on gender. One of the important elements of a sociological approach is to explore the differences *among* men and *among* women, since, as it turns out, these are often more decisive than the differences between women and men.

If gender varies across cultures, over historical time, among men and women within any one culture, and over the life course, that means we really cannot speak of masculinity or femininity as though they were constant, universal essences, common to all women and to all men. Rather, gender is an ever-changing fluid assemblage of meanings and behaviors. In that sense, we must speak of *masculinities* and *femininities,* in recognition of the different definitions of masculinity and femininity that we construct. By pluralizing the terms, we acknowledge that masculinity and femininity mean different things to different groups of people at different times.

At the same time, we can't forget that all masculinities and femininities are not created equal. American men and women must also contend with a dominant definition, a culturally preferred version that is held up as the model against which we are expected to measure ourselves. We thus come to know what it means to be a man or a woman in our culture by setting our definitions in opposition to a set of "others"—racial minorities, sexual minorities. For men, the classic "other" is, of course, women. It often feels imperative that men make it clear—eternally, compulsively, decidedly—that they are not "like" women.

For both women and men, this is the "hegemonic" definition—the one that is held up as the model for all of us. The hegemonic definition of masculinity is "constructed in relation to various subordinated masculinities as well as in relation to women," writes sociologist R. W. Connell (1987, 183). The sociologist Erving Goffman once described this hegemonic definition of masculinity like this:

> In an important sense there is only one complete unblushing male in America: a young, married, white, urban, northern, heterosexual, Protestant, father, of college education, fully employed, of good complexion, weight, and height, and a recent record in sports.... Any male who fails to qualify in any one of these ways is likely to view himself—during moments at least—as unworthy, incomplete, and inferior. (Goffman 1963, 128)

Women also must contend with such an exaggerated ideal of femininity. Connell calls it "emphasized femininity." Emphasized femininity is organized around compliance with gender inequality, and is "oriented to accommodating the interests and desires of men." One sees emphasized femininity in "the display of sociability rather than technical competence, fragility in mating scenes, compliance with men's desire for titillation and ego-stroking in office relationships, acceptance of marriage and child care as a response to labor-market discrimination against women" (Connell 1987, 183, 188, 187). Emphasized femininity exaggerates gender difference as a strategy of "adaptation to men's power" stressing empathy and nurturance; "real" womanhood is described as "fascinating" and women are advised that they can wrap men around their fingers by knowing and playing by "the rules."

The essays in the first four sections of this book recapitulate these disciplinary concerns and also present the development of the sociological argument chronologically. Following Darwin and others, biological evidence was employed in the nineteenth century to assert the primacy of sex differences, and the section on biological differences presents some evidence of distinct and categorical biological differences, and a couple of critiques of that research from a neurobiologist and a psychologist respectively. Cross-cultural research by anthropologists, among them Margaret Mead, perhaps the nation's most historically celebrated cultural anthropologist, offered a way to critique the claims of biological inevitability and universality lodged in those biological arguments. The selections in this section demonstrate how anthropologists have observed those cross-cultural differences and have used such specific cultural rituals as initiation ceremonies or the prevalence of rape in a culture to assess different definitions of gender.

Psychological research also challenged biological inevitability, locating the process of *acquiring* gender within the tasks of the child in his or her family. Achieving successful gender identity was a perilous process, fraught with danger of gender "inversion" (homosexuality) as the early and renowned social psychologist Lewis Terman saw it in his treatise on *Sex and Personality* in 1936. Subsequent psychological research has refined our understanding of how individuals acquire the "sex roles" that society has mapped out for them.

And it falls to the sociologist to explore the variations *among* different groups of women and men, and also to specify the ways in which some versions of masculinity or femininity are held up as the hegemonic models against which all others are arrayed and measured. Sociologists are concerned less with the specification of sex roles, and more with the understanding of *gender relations*—the social and political dynamics that shape our conceptions of "appropriate" sex roles. Thus, sociologists are interested not only in gendered individuals—the ways in which we acquire our gendered identities—but also in gendered institutions—the ways in which those gendered individuals interact with one another in the institutions of our lives that shape, reproduce, and reconstitute gender.

The five central, institutional sections of this book explore how the fundamental institutions of family, education, religion, the workplace, and politics express and normalize gender difference, and, in doing so, reproduce relations of inequality between women and men. Sociologists argue that male domination is reproduced not only by socializing women and men differently, but also by placing them in organizations and institutions in which specifically gendered norms and values predominate and by which both women and men are then evaluated and judged. Gendered individuals do not inhabit gender-neutral social situations; both individuals and institutions bear the mark of gender.

The four central, institutional sections of this book explore how the fundamental institutions of family, education, religion, and the workplace express and normalize gender difference, and, in so doing, reproduce relations of inequality between women and men. In each of these arenas, the debates about gender differences and inequality have been intense, from the questions about the division of household labor, sexual orientation of parents, the effect of religion on gender identity, comparable worth, workplace discrimination, and a variety of other critical policy debates. The essays in these sections will enable the reader to make better sense of these debates and understand the ways in which gender is performed and elaborated within social institutions.

Finally, we turn to our intimate lives, our bodies, and our experiences of friendship, love, and sex. Here differences between women and men do emerge. Men and women have different ways of loving, of caring, and of having sex. And it turns out that this is true whether the women and men are heterosexual or homosexual—that is, gay men and heterosexual men are more similar to each other than they are different; and, equally, lesbians and heterosexual women have more in common than either does with men. On the other hand, the differences between women and men seem to have as much to do with the shifting definitions of love and intimacy, and the social arenas in which we express (or suppress) our emotions, as they do with the differences in our personalities. And there is significant evidence that the gender gap in love and sex and friendship is shrinking as women claim greater degrees of sexual agency and men find their emotional lives (with lovers, children, and friends) impoverished by adherence to hegemonic definitions of masculinity. Men and women do express some differences in our intimate lives, but these differences are hardly of interplanetary cosmic significance. It appears that women and men are not from different planets—not opposite sexes, but neighboring sexes. And we are moving closer and closer to each other.

This may be the most startling finding that runs through many of these essays. What we find consistently is that the differences between women and men do not account for very much of the different experiences that men and women have. Differences *between* women and men are not nearly as great as the differences *among* women or *among* men—differences based on class, race, ethnicity, sexuality, age, and other variables. Women and men enter the workplace for similar reasons, though what they find there often reproduces the differences that "predicted" they would have different motivations. Boys and girls are far more similar to each other in the classroom, from elementary school through college, although everything in the school—from their textbooks, their teachers, their experiences in the playground, the social expectations of their aptitudes and abilities—pushes them to move farther and farther apart.

The most startling conclusion that one reaches from examining the evidence on gender difference is that women and men are not from different planets at all. In the end, we're all Earthlings!

References

Connell, R. W. *Gender and Power.* Stanford, CA: Stanford University Press, 1987.

Goffman, Erving. *Stigma.* Englewood Cliffs, NJ: Prentice-Hall, 1963.

Gray, John. *Men Are from Mars, Women Are from Venus.* New York: Harper Collins, 1995.

Kimmel, Michael. *Manhood in America: A Cultural History*, 3rd edition. New York: Oxford University Press, 2011.

Terman, Lewis and Catherine Cox Miles. *Sex and Personality.* New York: McGraw-Hill, 1936.

Changes to the Fifth Edition:

- The addition of a new section on The Gender of Politics (Part 10).
- Twenty-five new essays, including three new pieces on The Gendered Media, and new coverage of:
  - Non-heterosexual families
  - Adolescent masculinities in the classroom
  - Muslim women
- A new, separate Instructor's Manual/Test Bank is now available for *The Gendered Society Reader* (contact Oxford University Press).

Acknowledgments

The editors wish to thank the following reviewers for their feedback on the fourth edition:

Nancy L. Ashton, Richard Stockton College of New Jersey

Dana Dunn, University of Texas at Arlington

Sara J. Eaton, North Central College Naperville

Helen Emmitt, Centre College

Robert B. Jenkot, Coastal Carolina University

Karen L. Frederick, Saint Anselm College

Jane E. Rose, Purdue University-Westville

Jasmina Sinanovic, CUNY

Deborah Woodman, Algoma University.

PART 1

Anatomy and Destiny

BIOLOGICAL ARGUMENTS ABOUT GENDER DIFFERENCE

Anatomy, many of us believe, is destiny; our constitution of our bodies determines our social and psychological disposition. Biological sex decides our gendered experiences. Sex is temperament. Biological explanations offer perhaps the tidiest and most coherent explanations for both gender difference and gender inequality. The observable differences between males and females derive from different anatomical organization, which make us different as men and women, and those anatomical differences are the origin of gender inequality. These differences, as one biologist put it, are "innate, biologically determined, and relatively resistant to change through the influences of culture."

Biologists rely on three different sets of evidence. Evolutionists, such as sociobiologists and evolutionary psychologists, argue that sex differences derive from the differences in our reproductive anatomies—which compel different reproductive "strategies." Because a female must invest much energy and time in ensuring

Caveman Lawyer" and the affronted caveman of the Geico car insurance ads joke about the ubiquity of caveman narratives. More disturbingly, the Darwinian discourse also crops up when men need an excuse for antisocial behavior. One man, who was caught on amateur video participating in the Central Park group sexual assaults in the summer of 2000, can be heard on video telling his sobbing victim, "Welcome back to the caveman times." How does a man come to think of himself as a caveman when he attacks a woman? What made so many American men decide that it's the DNA, rather than the devil, that makes them do it?

Using the late sociologist Pierre Bourdieu's theory of habitus, or the account of how cultural ideas are taken up in the form of bodily habits and tastes that reinforce behavioral norms and social inequality, I suggest that scientific theories find their way into both popular culture and men's corporeal habits and attitudes. Evolution has become popular culture, where popular culture is more than just media representations but refers to the institutions of everyday life: family, marriage, school, work—all sites where gender and racial knowledges are performed according to images people have available to them in actionable repertoires, scripts, and narratives. As popular culture, evolutionary narratives offer men a way to think of, and embody, male sexuality.

That an evolutionary account of heterosexual male desire has captured the popular imagination is obvious from *Muscle and Fitness* magazine's article on "Man the Visual Animal," which explains why men leer at women. Using a theory of the evolved difference between human male and female sexual psychologies developed by leading evolutionary psychologist Donald Symons, the article offers the following explanation under the subheading "Evolution Happens":

> Not much has changed in human sexuality since the Pleistocene. In his landmark book *The Evolution of Human Sexuality* (Oxford University Press, 1979), Symons hypothesizes that the male's sexual response to visual cues has been so rewarded by evolution that it's become innate.[3]

Such stories provide a means by which heterosexual male readers can experience their sexuality as acultural, primal: "The desire to ogle is your biological destiny."[4]

Evolution may happen (or may have happened), but these stories do not just happen. Their appeal seems to lie precisely in the sense of security provided by the imagined inevitability of heterosexual manhood. In a marketplace of masculine identities the caveman ethos is served up as Viagra for the masculine soul. Just as the 1950s women suffering what Betty Friedan famously called the "feminine mystique" were supposed to seek satisfaction in their Tupperware collections and their feminine figures, men today have been offered a way to think of their masculinity as powerful, productive, even aggressive—in a new economic and political climate where real opportunities to be rewarded for such traits have slipped away.[5]

It's hardly that most men today find themselves raising children at home while female partners bring home the bacon. But, like the 1950s housewife, more men must now find satisfaction despite working below their potential (given that their job skills have lost their position to technology or other labor sources) in a postindustrial service economy that is less rewarding both materially and morally. As journalist Susan Faludi puts it in her book *Stiffed*:

> The fifties housewife, stripped of her connections to a wider world and invited to fill the void with shopping and the ornamental display of her ultrafemininity, could be said to have morphed into the nineties man, stripped of his connections to a wider world and invited to fill the void with consumption and a gym-bred display of his ultramasculinity.[6]

On top of the economic changes affecting men, during the 1990s a growing anti-rape movement also challenged men, taking them to task for the problem of violence against women. More state and federal dollars supported efforts to stop such violence, and men increasingly feared complaints and repercussions for those complaints. The rape trials of Mike Tyson and William Kennedy

Smith, Jr., the increasingly common school shootings (executed overwhelmingly by boys), the sexual harassment of women by men at the Citadel, the media attention given to the notorious Spurr Posse (a gang of guys who sought sex for "points" at almost all costs), the local sexual assault trials of countless high school and college athletic stars, the sexual harassment allegations against Supreme Court Justice nominee Clarence Thomas, and the White House sex scandals involving Bill Clinton meant more men lost ground. Indeed, the 1990s saw relentless—though not necessarily ill-founded—criticism of men's sexual violence and other forms of aggression.

Right-wing leaders were as upset with men as were feminists and other progressives. Those opposing abortion rights argued that sexual intercourse without procreation was undermining male responsibility, and those opposing women's equal-rights legislation argued that women's liberation would only allow men to relinquish their economic obligations to their families, sending women and children into divorce-induced poverty. Considering that critics of men came from both liberal and conservative camps, and from among men as well as women, it seems fair to say that in turn-of-the-century America moral disdain for men, whatever their age, race, or economic rank, had reached an all-time high.

For some men, the response was to cultivate a rude-dude attitude—popularized by Howard Stern, *The Man Show*, and MTV's endless shows about college spring-break vacations. For some others, the response was to face, with a sense of responsibility and urgency, men's animal natures and either accept or reform their caveman ways. While some men were embracing the role of consumers and becoming creatures of ornamentation—the "metrosexuals"—other men revolted against metrosexuality, embracing a can-do virility that Sara Stewart in *The New York Post* referred to as "retrosexuality," or that "cringe-inducing backlash of beers and leers."[7] Caveman masculinity is a form of retrosexuality that seems to carry the authority of objective science.

The popular understanding of men's sexuality as naturally vigorous and irrepressibly heterosexual helps fuel a culture Michael Kimmel[8] labeled "guyland" in his book by that name. Guyland is a social space in addition to a life stage, in which young single men act rough, gruff, sexually aggressive, and anti-gay, and do lewd, rude-dude things—resenting anything intellectual, politically correct, or smacking of either responsibility or women's authority. According to Kimmel, the five main markers of adulthood—leaving home, completing one's education, starting work, getting married, and becoming a parent—no longer happen all at once and so have left young men without a clear social marker of manhood.[9] In this context, the caveman discourse offers guys a *biological* marker of manhood.

Interestingly, feminist philosopher Sandra Lee Bartky made an argument about women's changing status impacting women's bodily comportment, saying that modern Western women began to restrict and constrict their bodies more as they gained institutional and social freedoms.[10] Bartky writes:

> As modern industrial societies change and as women themselves offer resistance to patriarchy, older forms of domination are eroded. But new forms arise, spread, and become consolidated. Women are no longer required to be chaste or modest, to restrict their sphere of activity to the home, or even to realize their properly feminine destiny in maternity: normative femininity is coming more and more to be centered on a woman's body—not its duties and obligations... [but] its presumed heterosexuality and its appearance.[11]

While women are now expected to restrict themselves in a tightly controlled, carefully managed feminine bodily comportment to compensate for their increased freedoms, I would suggest, appropriating Bartky, that we now see men finding their freedom and power in a bodily comportment just the opposite of Bartky's modern feminine woman: Men are boozing and belching their way to a lack of restrictions—to combat the increased restrictions they find in life and law.

Evolutionary theorists offer their ideas not to promote the caveman identity or fuel men's aggression, but in part because they believe the scientific facts about men's nature could help society address, and remedy, the violence and other problems so many have been blaming on men. What these scholars didn't predict is that so many average Joes would take up their ideas for slightly different reasons, namely as a move to feel powerful and domineering in a world squeezing men's resources and demanding that they be civil. Because of the ways caveman discourse appeals to many guys, it's important to consider the caveman story not simply as it is told by evolutionary scholars but as it is taken up throughout popular culture.

The Caveman as Popular Scientific Story

Popular culture is a political Petri dish for Darwinian ideas about sex. Average American guys don't read academic evolutionary science, but many do read about science in popular magazines and in bestselling books about the significance of the latest scientific ideas. As such, it is worth examining—even when magazine writers and television producers intentionally "dumb down" relatively sophisticated academic claims. In this section, I look at the way some popular texts make sense of evolutionary claims about men. Later I suggest that the caveman ideology, much of which centers on men's aggressive heterosexuality, gets embodied and thereby reproduced.[12]

In September of 1999, *Men's Health* magazine featured a caveman fitness program. Readers are shown an exercise routine that corresponds to the physical movements their ancestors would have engaged in: throwing a spear, hauling an animal carcass, honing a stone. A nice-looking, clean-shaven young man is shown exercising, his physical posture mirrored by a scruffy animal-skin-clad caveman behind him in the photo. Each day of the week-long routine is labeled according to the caveman mystique: building the cave home; the hunt; the chase; the kill; the long trek home; prepare for the feast; and rest. That an exercise plan is modeled after man-as-caveman reveals the common assumption that being a caveman is good for a man, a healthy existence.

Another issue of *Men's Health* magazine explains "the sex science facts" to male readers interested in "the biology of attraction." We follow the steps of a mating dance, but don't quite understand that's what we're doing. Indeed, we must learn the evolutionary history of sex to see why men feel the way they do when they notice a beautiful woman walking down the street:

> Of course, out there in the street, you have no thoughts about genetic compatibility or childbearing. Probably the farthest thing from your mind is having a child with that beautiful woman. But that doesn't matter. What you think counts for almost nothing. In the environment that crafted your brain and body, an environment in which you might be dead within minutes of spotting this beauty, the only thing that counted was that your clever neocortex—your seat of higher reason—be turned off so that you could quickly select a suitable mate, impregnate her, and succeed in passing on your genes to the next generation.[13]

The article proceeds to identify the signals of fertility that attract men: youth, beauty, big breasts, and a small waistline. Focusing on the desire for youth in women, the article tells men that "the reason men of any age continue to like young girls is that we were designed to get them pregnant and dominate their fertile years by keeping them that way.... When your first wife has lost the overt signals of reproductive viability, you desire a younger woman who still has them all.[14] And, of course, male readers are reminded that "your genes don't care about your wife or girlfriend or what the neighbors will say.[15]

Amy Alkon's *Winston-Salem Journal* advice column, "The Advice Goddess," uses an evolutionary theory of men's innate loutishness to comfort poor "Feeling Cheated On," who sent a letter complaining that her boyfriend fantasizes about other women during their lovemaking. The Advice Goddess cited a study by Bruce J. Ellis and Donald Symons (whose work was also mentioned in *Muscle & Fitness)* to conclude that "male sexuality is all about variety. Men are hard-wired to want you, the entire girls' dorm next door, and the entire girls' dorm next to that."[16]

Popular magazines tell men that they have a biological propensity to favor women with the faces of 11½-year-old girls (where the eyes and chin are close together) and a waist-to-hip ratio of .7 (where the waist measures 70% that of the hips). Men are told that their sexist double standard concerning appearance is evolutionary. Some of this research is very speculative—for instance, in some studies, men are simply shown photos of women with specific waist-to-hip ratios and then asked, "Would you like to spend the rest of your life with this woman?"—as though such staged answers reveal something about the individuals' real-life choices (or genes). But the results of this research make great copy.

Men's Health magazine in 1999 offered an article called "The Mysteries of Sex.... Explained!" and relied on evolutionary theory, quoting several professors in the field, to explain "why most women won't sleep with you." The article elucidates:

> Stop blaming your wife. The fault lies with Mother Nature, the pit boss of procreation. Neil M. Malamuth, Ph.D., professor of psychology at UCLA, explains. "You're in Las Vegas with 10 grand. Your gambling strategy will depend on which form your money takes. With 10 chips worth $1,000 each, you'd weigh each decision cautiously. With 10,000 $1 chips, you'd throw them around." That's reproductive strategy in a nutshell.[17]

Popular magazine articles like this follow a standard formula. They quote the scientists, reporting on the evolutionary theorists' research, and offer funny anecdotes about male sexuality to illustrate the research findings. This *Men's Health* article continues to account for men's having fetishes: "Men are highly sexed creatures, less interested in relationship but highly hooked on visuals," says David Givens, Ph.D., an anthropologist. "'Because sex carries fewer consequences for men, it's easier for us to use objects as surrogate sexual partners.' Me? I've got my eye on a Zenith, model 39990."[18]

It's not just these popular and often humorous accounts of men that are based in some version of evolutionary theory. Even serious academic arguments rely on evolutionary theories of human behavior. For example, Steven Rhoads, a member of the University of Virginia faculty in public policy, has written *Taking Sex Differences Seriously* (2004), a book telling us why gender equity in the home and the workplace is a feminist pipe dream. Rhoads argues that women are wrong to expect men to take better care of children, do more housework, and make a place for them as equals at work because, he states, "men and women still have different natures and, generally speaking, different preferences, talents and interests."[19] He substantiates much of his argument about the divergent psychological predispositions in men and women with countless references to studies done by evolutionary scholars.

News magazines and television programs have also spent quite a bit of time popularizing evolutionary science and its implications for understanding human sex differences. The ABC News program *Day One* reported in 1995 on evolutionary psychologist David Buss's book, *The Evolution of Desire*.[20] Buss appeared on the show, which elaborated his theory by presenting us with supermodel Cindy Crawford and Barbie (the doll), presumably as representations of what men are wired to find desirable. As Buss explained in the interview, our evolutionary forebrothers who did not prefer women with high cheekbones, big eyes, lustrous hair, and full lips did not reproduce. As Buss put it, those men who happened to like someone who was older, sicker, or infertile "are not our ancestors. We are all the descendants of those men who preferred young healthy women and so as offspring, as descendants of those men, we carry with us their desires."[21] On that same television show, *Penthouse* magazine publisher Bob Guccione was interviewed and explained that men are simply biologically designed to enjoy looking at sexy women: "This may be very politically incorrect but that's the way it is.... It's all part of our ancestral conditioning."[22] Evolutionary narratives clearly work for publishers of pornography marketed to men.

Newsweek's 1996 cover story, "The Biology of Beauty: What Science Has Discovered About Sex Appeal," argues that the beautylust humans exhibit "is often better suited to the Stone Age than to the Information Age; the qualities we find alluring may be powerful emblems of health, fertility and resistance to disease. . . . "[23] Though "beauty isn't all that matters in life," the article asserts, "our weakness for 'biological quality' is the cause of endless pain and injustice."[24]

Sometimes the magazines and TV shows covering the biological basis of sexual desire give a nod to the critics. The aforementioned *Newsweek* article, for instance, quotes feminist writer Katha Pollitt, who insists that "human beings cannot be reduced to DNA packets."[25] And then, as if to affirm Pollitt's claim, homosexuality is invoked as an example of the countless non-adaptive delights we desire: "Homosexuality is hard to explain as a biological adaptation. So is stamp collecting. . . . We pursue countless passions that have no direct bearing on survival."[26] So when there is a nod to ways humans are not hardwired, homosexual desires are framed as oddities having no basis in nature, while heterosexual attraction along the lines of stereotypical heterosexual male fantasy is framed as biological. Heterosexual desire enjoys a *biologically correct* status.

Zoologist Desmond Morris explains how evolutionary theory applies to humans in his 1999 six-part television series, *Desmond Morris' The Human Animal: A Personal View of the Human Species*.[27] The first show in the series draws from his book, *The Naked Ape*, explaining that humans are relatively hairless with little to protect themselves besides their big brains.[28] This is stated as we watch two naked people, one male and one female, walk through a public place where everyone else is dressed in modern-day clothing. Both are white, both are probably 25 to 30 years old, both look like models (the man with well chiseled muscles, a suntan, and no chest hair; the woman thin, yet shapely with larger than average breasts, shaved legs, and a manicured pubic region). This presentation of man and woman in today's aesthetically ideal form as the image of what all of us were once like is *de rigueur* for any popular representation of evolutionary theory applied to human sexuality. No woman is flabby, flat chested, or has body hair; no man has pimples or back hair. These culturally mandated ideal body types are presented as the image of what our human ancestors naturally looked like and desired. In this way and others, such shows posit modern aesthetic standards as states of nature.

Time magazine's 1994 cover story on "Our Cheating Hearts" reports that "the emerging field known as evolutionary psychology" gives us "fresh detail about the feelings and thoughts that draw us into marriage—or push us out."[29] After explaining the basics about men being less discriminating about their sexual partners than women, the article moves on to discuss why people divorce, anticipating resistance to the evolutionary explanation:

> Objections to this sort of analysis are predictable: "But people leave marriages for emotional reasons. They don't add up their offspring and pull out their calculators." But emotions are just evolution's executioners. Beneath the thoughts and feelings and temperamental differences marriage counselors spend their time sensitively assessing are the stratagems of the genes—cold, hard equations composed of simple variables: social status, age of spouse, number of children, their ages, outside romantic opportunities and so on. Is the wife really duller and more nagging than she was 20 years ago? Maybe, but maybe the husband's tolerance for nagging has dropped now that she is 45 and has no reproductive future.[30]

In case *Time* readers react to the new evolutionary psychology as part of a plot to destroy the cherished nuclear family, they are told that "progress will also depend on people using the explosive insight of evolutionary psychology in a morally responsible way. . . . We are potentially moral animals—which is more than any other animal can say—but we are not naturally moral animals. The first step to being moral is to realize how thoroughly we aren't."[31]

While many accounts of evolution's significance for male sexuality seem simply to rationalize sexist double standards and wallow in men's loutishness, a number of pop-Darwinist claims have the moral purpose of liberating men from being controlled by their caveman natures. Their message: men can become enlightened cavemen. These stories make an attempt to liberate men by getting them to see themselves differently. They tell men that they are cavemen with potential. They either make fun of men's putatively natural shortcomings or encourage them to cage the caveman within through a kind of scientific consciousness-raising.

For example, Jeff Hood's book *The Silverback Gorilla Syndrome* uses the logic of let's-face-that-we're-cavemen to get men to become more compassionate and peaceful.[32] Hood, an organizational consultant and nature lover, recognizes the common problems of contemporary Western masculinity: fierce competition in the workplace; a lack of introspection and authentic relationships; and a reliance on cunning and bluffery to maintain one's self-image or position of power. This form of masculinity is an exhausting, life-threatening charade, which costs men their marriages and their health, and threatens the entire planet due to the destruction men wreak on the environment and on other people.

Hood's introduction explains:

> In the course of emerging from the jungles of our primate ancestors, we have stumbled onto, some would say earned, a thing called awareness. This faculty has spawned a body of knowledge leading to science, industry, technology—and ultimately increased comfort and longer lives. But it has also sparked an illusion of separation from the rest of the animal kingdom. Forging ahead in the quest for control over our destiny and our planet, we act as if the laws of nature do not apply to us. We are blind to the many ways in which the dominant attitudes and competitive behavior we have inherited threaten to push us dangerously out of balance with our world. Our saving grace may be to use our awareness instead for tempering the silverback gorilla syndrome that has brought us success at such great cost. This book is an attempt to increase that awareness.[33]

Hood wants to turn men into responsible, compassionate creatures, insisting that awareness of the caveman within—an inner gorilla whom Hood playfully calls "Big G"—is the only way out.

Even well-meaning applications of evolutionary theory like Hood's book, however, fail to question the idea of men's heterosexual, aggressive inner core or evolved psychology. As such, they have a limited ability to move beyond the assumptions that lead so many others to use the same basic theory to rationalize being boorish. Men reformed via an evolutionary consciousness are still going to see themselves as different from, and even superior to, women.

The Caveman as Embodied Ethos

In a culture so attached to scientific authority and explication, it is worth examining the popular appeal of evolutionary theory and its impact on masculine embodiment. The popularity of the scientific story of men's evolved desires—however watered down or distorted the science becomes as enthusiasts popularize it—can tell us something about the appeal and influence of that story.

If the evolutionary stories appeal to many men, and it seems they do indeed, it's because they ring true. Many men feel like their bodies are aggressive. They feel urges, at a physical level, in line with evolutionary theoretical predictions. The men who feel like cavemen do not see their identity as a fiction; it is their bodily reality and seems to be backed by the authority of science.

The work of Pierre Bourdieu provides a tool for understanding how power is organized at the level of unconscious embodiment of cultural forces. I suggest that popular manifestations of scientific evolutionary narratives about men's sexuality have a real material effect on many men. Bourdieu's theory of practice develops the concepts of *habitus* and *field* to describe a reciprocally constitutive relationship between bodily dispositions and dominant power structures. Bourdieu concerned himself primarily with the ways in which socioeconomic class is incorporated at the level of the body, including class-based ways of speaking, postures, lifestyles, attitudes, and tastes.

Significant for Bourdieu is that people acquire tastes that mark them as members of particular social groups and particular social levels.[34] Membership in a particular social class produces and reproduces a class sensibility, what Bourdieu (1990) called "practical sense."[35] Habitus is "a somatized social relationship, a social law converted into an embodied law."[36] The process of becoming competent in the everyday life of a society or group constitutes habitus. Bourdieu's notion of embodiment can be extended to suggest that habitus, as embodied field, amounts to "the pleasurable and ultimately erotic constitution of [the individual's] social imaginary."[37]

Concerning the circulation of evolutionary narratives, we can see men taking erotic pleasure in the formation of male identity and the performance of accepted norms of heterosexual masculinity using precisely these tools of popular evolutionary science. Put differently, pop-Darwinism is a discourse that finds its way into men's bones and boners. The caveman story can become a man's practical sense of who he is and what he desires. This is so because masculinity is a dimension of embodied and performative practical sensibility—because men carry themselves with a bodily comportment suggestive of their position as the dominant gender, and they invest themselves in particular lifestyle practices, consumption patterns, attire, and bodily comportment. Evolutionary narratives thus enter the so-called habitus, and an aestheticized discourse and image of the caveman circulates through popular culture becoming part of natural perception, and consequently is reproduced by those embodying it.

In his study of the overwhelmingly white and male workspace of the Options Exchange floor, sociologist Richard Widick uses Bourdieu's theory to explain the traders' physical and psychical engagement with their work. Widick holds that "the traders' inhabitation and practical mastery of the trading floor achieves the bio-physical psycho-social state of a natural identity."[38] Hence the traders describe their manner as a "trading instinct." In a similar way, American men with what we might call a caveman instinct can be said to have acquired a "pre-reflexive practical sense" of themselves as heterosexually driven.[39]

Bourdieu gives the name "symbolic violence" to that process by which we come to accept and embody power relations without ever accepting them in the conscious sense of knowing them and choosing them. We hold beliefs that don't need to be thought—the effects of which can be "durably and deeply embedded in the body in the form of dispositions."[40] From this perspective, the durable dispositions of evolutionary discourse are apparent in our rape culture, for example, when a member of the group sexual assault in New York tells the woman he's attacking, "Welcome back to the caveman times." Embodying the ideology of irrepressible heterosexual desire makes such aggression appear to be natural.

Bourdieu's theory allows us to see that both cultural and material forces reveal themselves in the lived reality of social relations.[41] We can see on men's bodies the effects of their struggle with slipping economic privilege and a sense of entitlement to superiority over women. If men live out power struggles in their everyday experiences, then caveman masculinity can be seen as an imagined compensation for men's growing sense of powerlessness.[42] To be sure, some men have more social and economic capital than others. Those with less might invest even more in their bodies and appearances.[43]

Sociologist R. W. Connell discusses the significance of naturalizing male power. She states:

> The physical sense of maleness is not a simple thing. It involves size and shape, habits of posture and movement, particular physical skills and the lack of others, the image of one's own body, the way it is presented to other people and the ways they respond to it, the way it operates at work and in sexual relations. In no sense is all this a consequence of XY chromosomes, or even of the possession on which discussions of masculinity have so lovingly dwelt, the penis. The physical sense of maleness grows through a personal history of social practice, a life-history-in-society.[44]

We see and believe that men's power over women is the order of nature because "power is translated not only into mental body-images and fantasies, but into muscle tensions, posture, the feel and texture of the body."[45] Scientific discourse constitutes the field for some men in the constructed figure of the caveman, enabling those men to internalize such an identity. The caveman thus becomes an imaginative projection that is experienced and lived as real biological truth.

In his book, *Cultural Boundaries of Science,* Thomas Gieryn comments on the cultural authority of science, suggesting that "if 'science' says so, we are more often than not inclined to believe it or act on it—and to prefer it to claims lacking this epistemic seal of approval."[46] To his observation I would add that we are also more likely to *live* it. Ideas that count as scientific, regardless of their truth value, become lived ideologies. It's how modern American men have become cavemen and how the caveman ethos enjoys reproductive success.

Cultural anthropologist Paul Rabinow gives the name "biosociality" to the formation of new group and individual identities and practices that emerge from the scientific study of human life.[47] Rabinow offers the example of neurofibromatosis groups whose members have formed to discuss their experiences, educate their children, lobby for their disease, and "understand" their fate. And in the future, he points out, "... [i]t is not hard to imagine groups formed around the chromosome 17, locus 16,256, site 654,376 allele variant with a guanine substitution."[48] Rabinow's concept of biosociality is instructive here; for the discourse of the caveman offers this form of biosociality. The caveman constitutes an identity based on new scientific "facts" about one's biology.

Of course, evolutionary psychologists might insist that men's desires are, in some final instance, biological properties of an internal psyche or sexual psychology. I am suggesting, in line with Bourdieu, that men's desires are always performed in relation to the dominant discourses in circulation within their cultural lifeworlds, either for or against the representations that permeate those lifeworlds. We can see that a significant number of men are putting the pop-Darwinian rhetoric to good use in social interactions. The scientific discourse of the caveman (however unscientific we might regard it by the time it gets to everyday guys reading magazines and watching TV) is corporealized, quite literally incorporated into living identities, deeply shaping these men's experiences of being men.

The Caveman as Ethnicity

I recognize the lure of the caveman narrative. After all, it provides an explanation for patterns we do see and for how men do feel in contemporary society, tells men that they are beings who are the way they are for a specific reason, offers them an answer about what motivates them, and carries the authority of scientific investigation about their biological makeup. Evolutionary theory offers an origin story. Plus, it's fun: thinking of the reasons you might feel a certain way because such feelings might have been necessary for your ancestors to survive a hostile environment back in the Pleistocene can be a satisfying intellectual exercise.

In telling men a story about who they are, naturally, pop-Darwinism has the normalizing, disciplinary effect of forging a common, biological identity among men. Embodying ideology allows men to feel morally exonerated while they reproduce that very ideology. The discourse of male biological unity suppresses many significant differences among men, and of course many ways in which men would otherwise identify with women's tastes and behaviors. The evolutionary explanation of men's sexual behavior is an all-encompassing narrative enabling men to frame their own thoughts and experiences through it. As such it's a *grand narrative,* a totalizing theory explaining men's experiences as though all men act and feel the same ways, and as though the ideas of Western science provide a universal truth about those actions and feelings.

I'm skeptical of this kind of totalizing narrative about male sexuality because evolution applied to human beings does not offer that sort of truth. The application of evolutionary theory to human behavior is not as straightforwardly scientific as it might seem, even for those of us who believe in the theory of evolution by natural selection. It is a partial, political discourse that authorizes certain prevalent masculine behaviors and a problematic acceptance of those behaviors. I think there are better—less totalizing, and differently consequential—discourses out there that describe and explain those same behaviors. I'm also skeptical of men's use of the evolutionary narrative because, at its best, it can only create "soft patriarchs"—kinder, gentler cavemen who resist the putative urges of which evolutionary science makes them aware.[49]

Because evolutionary stories ultimately affirm a vision of men as naturally like one another, and naturally unlike women, caveman masculinity lends itself to becoming an "ethnic option," a way of identifying and living one's manhood. Sociologist Mary C. Waters explains that ethnic identity is actually not "the automatic labeling of a primordial characteristic" but instead is a complex, socially created identity.[50] The caveman as an ethnicity reveals an embrace of biology as a reaction to social constructionist understandings of masculinity, feminist demands on men, and the changing roles of men at work and in families. As an ethnicity, caveman masculinity is seen as not only impossible but undesirable to change.[51]

Did scholars in evolutionary psychology intend to present modern men with such an ethnic option? Of course not. To repeat: Darwinian ideas are often spread by enthusiasts—secondary school teachers, science editors of various newspapers and magazines, and educational television show producers—who take up evolutionary theorists' ideas and convey them to mass audiences. Evolutionary thinking has become popular in part because it speaks to a publicly recognized predicament of men. Changing economic patterns have propelled men's flight from marriage and breadwinning, in conjunction with women's increased (albeit significantly less prosperous) independence. If a man today wants multiple partners with as little commitment as possible, evolutionary rhetoric answers why this is so.

Evolutionary discourse doesn't offer a flattering story about men. But, more significantly, many people don't understand that it's *a story*. Evolution has become not only a grand narrative but a lived ideology. Maleness and femaleness, like heterosexuality and homosexuality, are not simply identities but *systems of knowledge*.[52] And those systems of knowledge inform thinking and acting. Bourdieu's concept of habitus explains the ways in which culture and knowledge, including evolutionary knowledge, implant themselves at the level of the body, becoming a set of attitudes, tastes, perceptions, actions, and reactions. The status of science as objective, neutral knowledge helps make evolution a lived ideology because it feels truthful, natural, real.

Taking the historical and cultural changes affecting men seriously and embracing the diversity among men demand new understandings of masculinity, identity, and science. In gaining such a sociological perspective, men might resist making gender a new ethnicity and instead take a great leap forward to become new kinds of men.

Notes

1. A version of this essay also appears in the new edition of *Men's Lives*, edited by Michael Kimmel and Michael Messner.
2. For defenses of the study of the popularization of scientific discourse, and exemplary studies of the popularization of Darwinian discourse in different eras, see Alfred Kelly, *The Descent of Darwin: The Popularization of Darwinism in Germany, 1860–1914* (Chapel Hill: University of North Carolina Press, 1981) and Alvar Ellegard, *Darwin and the General Reader: The Reception of Darwin's Theory of Evolution in the British Press, 1859–1872* (Chicago: University of Chicago Press, 1990).
3. Mary Ellen Strote, "Man the Visual Animal," *Muscle and Fitness* (February 1994): 166.
4. Ibid., 166.
5. Betty Friedan, *The Feminine Mystique* (New York: Dell Publishing Company, Inc., 1963).
6. Susan Faludi, *Stiffed: The Betrayal of the American Man* (New York: HarperCollins, 1999), 40.
7. Sara Stewart, "Beasty Boys—'Retrosexuals' Call for Return of Manly Men; Retrosexuals Rising," *The New York Post*, July 18, 2006.
8. Michael Kimmel, *Guyland: The Perilous World Where Boys Become Men* (New York: HarperCollins, 2008).
9. Ibid., 24–25.
10. Sandra Lee Bartky, "Foucault, Femininity, and the Modernization of Patriarchal Power," in *The Politics of Women's Bodies*, ed. Rose Weitz (New York: Oxford University Press, 1998), 25–45.
11. Ibid., 41–42.

12. My argument here parallels a study of the pervasive iconography of the gene in popular culture. In *The DNA Mystique: The Gene as a Cultural Icon* (New York: W. H. Freeman, 1995), Dorothy Nelkin and M. Susan Lindee explain that popular culture provides "narratives of meaning" (p. 11). Those narratives filter complex ideas, provide guidance, and influence how people see themselves and evaluate other people, ideas, and policies. In this way, Nelkin and Lindee argue, DNA works as an ideology to justify boundaries of identity and legal rights, as well as to explain criminality, addiction, and personality. Of course, addict genes and criminal genes are misnomers—the definitions of what counts as an addict and what counts as a crime have shifted throughout history. Understanding DNA stories as ideological clarifies why, for example, people made sense of Elvis's talents and shortcomings by referring to his genetic stock (Ibid., 79–80). To call narratives of DNA ideological, then, is *not* to resist the scientific argument that deoxyribonucleic acid is a double-helix structure carrying information forming living cells and tissues, but to look at the way people make sense of DNA and use DNA to make sense of people and events in their daily lives.
13. Laurence Gonzales, "The Biology of Attraction," *Men's Health* 20.7 (2005): 186–93.
14. Ibid., 192.
15. Ibid., 193.
16. Amy Alkon, "Many Men Fantasize During Sex, But It Isn't a Talking Point," *Winston-Salem Journal*, 29 September 2005, p. 34.
17. Greg Gutfeld, "The Mysteries of Sex... Explained!," *Men's Health* April (1999): 76.
18. Ibid., 76.
19. Steven R. Rhoads, *Taking Sex Differences Seriously* (San Francisco: Encounter Books, 2004), 4.
20. David M. Buss, *The Evolution of Desire: Strategies of Human Mating* (New York: Basic Books, 1994).
21. David M. Buss, interview by *Day One*, ABC News.
22. Ibid.
23. Geoffrey Cowley, "The Biology of Beauty," *Newsweek* 127 (1996): 62.
24. Ibid., 64.
25. Ibid., 66.
26. Ibid.
27. *Desmond Morris' The Human Animal: A Personal View of the Human Species* ["Beyond Survival"] directed by Clive Bromhall (Discovery Communication/TLC Video, 1999).
28. Desmond Morris, *The Naked Ape* (New York: Dell Publishing Company, Inc., 1967).
29. Robert Wright, *The Moral Animal: Evolutionary Psychology and Everyday Life* (New York: Pantheon Books, 1994), 45.
30. Ibid., 50.
31. Ibid., 52.
32. Jeff Hood, *The Silverback Gorilla Syndrome: Transforming Primitive Man* (Santa Fe, NM: Adventures in Spirit Publications, 1999).
33. Ibid., 1.
34. Pierre Bourdieu, *Distinction: A Social Critique of the Judgment of Taste* (Cambridge: Harvard University Press, 1984).
35. Pierre Bourdieu, *The Logic of Practice* (Stanford: Stanford University Press, 1990).
36. Pierre Bourdieu, *Masculine Domination* (Stanford: Stanford University Press, 2001).
37. Richard Widick, "Flesh and the Free Market: (On Taking Bourdieu to the Options Exchange)," *Theory and Society* 32 (2003): 679–723, 716.
38. Ibid., 701.
39. Ibid.
40. Bourdieu, *Masculine*, 39
41. Lois McNay, "Agency and Experience: Gender as a Lived Relation," in *Feminism After Bourdieu*, ed. Lisa Adkins and Bev Skeggs (Oxford: Blackwell Publishing, 2004), 177.
42. See McNay, 175–90, for a discussion of emotional compensation and lived experience.
43. See Beverley Skeggs, *Formations of Class and Gender: Becoming Respectable* (London: Sage Publications, 1997), for a study pointing this out about working class women.
44. R. W. Connell, *Gender and Power: Society, the Person and Sexual Politics* (Cambridge: Polity Press, 1987), 84.
45. Ibid., 85.
46. Thomas F. Gieryn, *Cultural Boundaries of Science: Credibility on the Line* (Chicago: The University of Chicago Press, 1999), 1.
47. Paul Rabinow, *Making PCR, A Story of Biotechnology* (Chicago: University of Chicago Press, 1996), 101–2.
48. Ibid., 102.

49. I am appropriating W. Bradford Wilcox's term, from his book *Soft Patriarchs, New Men: How Christianity Shapes Fathers and Husbands* (Chicago: University of Chicago Press, 2004). Wilcox argues that the Christian men's movement known as the Promise Keepers encourages men to spend more time with their wives and children without ever challenging the fundamental patriarchal family structure that places men at the top.

50. Mary C. Waters, *Ethnic Options: Choosing Identities in America* (Berkeley: University of California Press, 1990), 16.

51. See Michael S. Kimmel, *Manhood in America: A Cultural History* (New York: Free Press, 1996), 127–37.

52. Steven Seidman, *Difference Troubles: Queering Social Theory and Sexual Politics* (Cambridge, UK: Cambridge University Press, 1997), 93.

Testosterone Rules

ROBERT M. SAPOLSKY

Face it, we all do it—we all believe in stereotypes about minorities. These stereotypes are typically pejorative and false, but every now and then they have a core of truth. I know, because I belong to a minority that lives up to its reputation. I have a genetic abnormality generally considered to be associated with high rates of certain socially abhorrent behaviors: I am male. Thanks to an array of genes that produce some hormone-synthesizing enzymes, my testes churn out a corrosive chemical and dump the stuff into my bloodstream, and this probably has behavioral consequences. We males account for less than 50 percent of the population, yet we generate a huge proportion of the violence. Whether it is something as primal as having an ax fight in a rain forest clearing or as detached as using computer-guided aircraft to strafe a village, something as condemned as assaulting a cripple or as glorified as killing someone wearing the wrong uniform, if it is violent, we males excel at it.

Why should this be? We all think we know the answer: something to do with those genes being expressed down in the testes. A dozen millennia ago or so, an adventurous soul managed to lop off a surly bull's testicles, thus inventing behavioral endocrinology. It is unclear from the historical records whether the experiment resulted in grants and tenure, but it certainly generated an influential finding: that the testes do something or other to make males aggressive pains in the ass.

That something or other is synthesizing the infamous corrosive chemical, testosterone (or rather, a family of related androgen hormones that I'll call testosterone for the sake of simplicity, hoping the androgen specialists won't take it the wrong way). Testosterone bulks up muscle cells—including those in the larynx, giving rise to operatic basses. It makes hair sprout here and there, undermines the health of blood vessels, alters biochemical events in the liver too dizzying to contemplate, and has a profound impact, no doubt, on the workings of cells in big toes. And it seeps into the brain, where it influences behavior in a way highly relevant to understanding aggression.

Robert M. Sapolsky, "Testosterone Rules," *Discover* (March 1997). Reprinted with the permission of the author.

Genes are the hand behind the scene, directing testosterone's actions. They specify whether steroidal building blocks are turned into testosterone or estrogen, how much of each, and how quickly. They regulate how fast the liver breaks down circulating testosterone, thereby determining how long an androgenic signal remains in the bloodstream. They direct the synthesis of testosterone receptors—specialized proteins that catch hold of testosterone and allow it to have its characteristic effects on target cells. And genes specify how many such receptors the body has, and how sensitive they are. Insofar as testosterone alters brain function and produces aggression, and genes regulate how much testosterone is made and how effectively it works, this should be the archetypal case for studying how genes can control our behavior. Instead, however, it's the archetypal case for learning how little genes actually do so.

Some pretty obvious evidence links testosterone with aggression. Males tend to have higher testosterone levels in their circulation than do females, and to be more aggressive. Times of life when males are swimming in testosterone—for example, after reaching puberty—correspond to when aggression peaks. Among many species, testes are mothballed most of the year, kicking into action and pouring out testosterone only during a very circumscribed mating season—precisely the time when male-male aggression soars.

Impressive though they seem, these data are only correlative—testosterone found on the scene repeatedly with no alibi when some aggression has occurred. The proof comes with the knife, the performance of what is euphemistically known as a subtraction experiment. Remove the source of testosterone in species after species, and levels of aggression typically plummet. Reinstate normal testosterone levels afterward with injections of synthetic testosterone, and aggression returns.

The subtraction and replacement paradigm represents pretty damning proof that this hormone, with its synthesis and efficacy under genetic control, is involved in aggression. "Normal testosterone levels appear to be a prerequisite for normative levels of aggressive behavior" is the sort of catchy, hummable phrase the textbooks would use. That probably explains why you shouldn't mess with a bull moose during rutting season. But it's not why a lot of people want to understand this sliver of science. Does the action of testosterone tell us anything about individual differences in levels of aggression, anything about why some males—some human males—are exceptionally violent? Among an array of males, are the highest testosterone levels found in the most aggressive individuals?

Generate some extreme differences and that is precisely what you see. Castrate some of the well-paid study subjects, inject others with enough testosterone to quadruple the normal human levels, and the high-testosterone males are overwhelmingly likely to be the more aggressive ones. Obviously, extreme conditions don't tell us much about the real world, but studies of the normative variability in testosterone—in other words, seeing what everyone's natural levels are like without manipulating anything—also suggest that high levels of testosterone and high levels of aggression tend to go together. This would seem to seal the case that interindividual differences in levels of aggression among normal individuals are probably driven by differences in levels of testosterone. But that conclusion turns out to be wrong.

Here's why. Suppose you note a correlation between levels of aggression and levels of testosterone among normal males. It could be because (*a*) testosterone elevates aggression; (*b*) aggression elevates testosterone secretion; or (*c*) neither causes the other. There's a huge bias to assume option a, while b is the answer. Study after study has shown that if you examine testosterone levels when males are first placed together in the social group, testosterone levels predict nothing about who is going to be aggressive. The subsequent behavioral differences drive the hormonal changes, rather than the other way around.

Because of a strong bias among certain scientists, it has taken forever to convince them of this point. Suppose you're studying what behavior and hormones have to do with each other. How do you study the behavioral part? You get yourself a notebook, a stopwatch, a pair of binoculars. How do you measure the hormones and analyze the genes that regulate them? You need some gazillion-dollar machines; you muck around with radiation and chemicals, wear a lab coat, maybe even goggles—the whole nine yards. Which toys would you rather get for Christmas? Which facet of science are you going to believe in more? The higher the technology, goes the formula, the more scientific the discipline. Hormones seem to many to be more substantive than behavior, so when a correlation occurs, it must be because hormones regulate behavior, not the other way around.

This is a classic case of what is often called physics envy, a disease that causes behavioral biologists to fear their discipline lacks the rigor of physiology, physiologists to wish for the techniques of biochemists, biochemists to covet the clarity of the answers revealed by molecular geneticists, all the way down until you get to the physicists who confer only with God. Recently, a zoologist friend had obtained blood samples from the carnivores he studies and wanted some hormones in the samples tested in my lab. Although inexperienced with the technique, he offered to help in any way possible. I felt hesitant asking him to do anything tedious, but since he had offered, I tentatively said, "Well, if you don't mind some unspeakable drudgery, you could number about a thousand assay vials." And this scientist, whose superb work has graced the most prestigious science journals in the world, cheerfully answered, "That's okay. How often do I get to do real science, working with test tubes?"

Difficult though scientists with physics envy find it to believe, interindividual differences in testosterone levels don't predict subsequent differences in aggressive behavior among individuals. Similarly, fluctuations in testosterone levels within one individual over time don't predict subsequent changes in the levels of aggression in that one individual—get a hiccup in testosterone secretion one afternoon and that's not when the guy goes postal.

Look at our confusing state: normal levels of testosterone are a prerequisite for normal levels of aggression. Yet if one male's genetic makeup predisposes him to higher levels of testosterone than the next guy, he isn't necessarily going to be more aggressive. Like clockwork, that statement makes the students suddenly start coming to office hours in a panic, asking whether they missed something in their lecture notes.

Yes, it's going to be on the final, and it's one of the more subtle points in endocrinology—what's referred to as a hormone having a "permissive effect." Remove someone's testes and, as noted, the frequency of aggressive behavior is likely to plummet. Reinstate pre-castration levels of testosterone by injecting the hormone, and pre-castration levels of aggression typically return. Fair enough. Now, this time, castrate an individual and restore testosterone levels to only 20 percent of normal. Amazingly, normal pre-castration levels of aggression come back. Castrate and now introduce twice the testosterone levels from before castration, and the same level of aggressive behavior returns. You need some testosterone around for normal aggressive behavior. Zero levels after castration, and down it usually goes; quadruple levels (the sort of range generated in weight lifters abusing anabolic steroids), and aggression typically increases. But anywhere from roughly 20 percent of normal to twice normal and it's all the same. The brain can't distinguish among this wide range of basically normal values.

If you knew a great deal about the genetic makeup of a bunch of males, enough to understand how much testosterone they secreted into their bloodstream, you still couldn't predict levels of aggression among those individuals. Nevertheless, the subtraction and reinstatement data seem to indicate that, in a broad sort of way, testosterone causes aggressive behavior. But that turns out not to be true either, and the implications of this are lost on most people the first thirty times they hear about it. Those implications are important, however—so important that it's worth saying thirty-one times.

Round up some male monkeys. Put them in a group together and give them plenty of time to sort out where they stand with each other—grudges, affiliative friendships. Give them enough time to form a dominance hierarchy, the sort of linear ranking in which number 3, for example, can pass his day throwing around his weight with numbers 4 and 5, ripping off their monkey chow, forcing them to relinquish the best spots to sit in, but numbers 1 and 2 still expect and receive from him the most obsequious brownnosing.

Hierarchy in place, it's time to do your experiment. Take that third-ranking monkey and give him some testosterone. None of this within-the-normal-range stuff. Inject a ton of it, way higher than what you normally see in rhesus monkeys, give him enough testosterone to grow antlers and a beard on every neuron in his brain. And, no surprise, when you check the behavioral data, he will probably be participating in more aggressive interactions than before.

So even though small fluctuations in the levels of the hormone don't seem to matter much, testosterone still causes aggression, right? Wrong. Check out number 3 more closely. Is he raining aggressive terror on everyone in the group, frothing with indiscriminate violence? Not at all. He's still judiciously kowtowing to numbers 1 and 2 but has become a total bastard to numbers 4 and 5. Testosterone isn't causing aggression, it's exaggerating the aggression that's already there.

Another example, just to show we're serious. There's a part of your brain that probably has lots to do with aggression, a region called the amygdala. Sitting near it is the Grand Central Station of emotion-related activity in your brain, the hypothalamus. The amygdala communicates with the hypothalamus by way of a cable of neuronal connections called the stria terminalis. (No more jargon, I promise.) The amygdala influences aggression via that pathway, sending bursts of electrical excitation that ripple down the stria terminalis to the hypothalamus and put it in a pissy mood.

Once again, do your hormonal intervention: flood the area with testosterone. You can inject the hormone into the bloodstream, where it eventually makes its way to the amygdala. You can surgically microinject the stuff directly into the area. In a few years, you may even be able to construct animals with extra copies of the genes that direct testosterone synthesis, producing extra hormone that way. Six of one, half a dozen of the other. The key thing is what doesn't happen next. Does testosterone make waves of electrical excitation surge down the stria terminalis? Does it turn on that pathway? Not at all. If and only if the amygdala is already sending an excited volley down the stria terminalis, testosterone increases the rate of such activity by shortening the resting time between bouts. It's not turning on the pathway, it's increasing the volume of signaling if it is already turned on. It's not causing aggression, it's exaggerating the preexisting pattern of it, exaggerating the response to environmental triggers of aggression.

In every generation, it is the duty of behavioral biologists to try to teach this critical point, one that seems a maddening cliché once you get it. You take that hoary old dichotomy between nature and nurture, between intrinsic factors and extrinsic ones, between genes and environment, and regardless of which behavior and underlying biology you're studying, the dichotomy is a sham. No genes. No environment. Just the interaction between the two.

Do you want to know how important environment and experience are in understanding testosterone and aggression? Look back at how the effects of castration are discussed earlier. There were statements like "Remove the source of testosterone in species after species and levels of aggression typically plummet." Not "Remove the source... and aggression always goes to zero." On the average it declines, but rarely to zero, and not at all in some individuals. And the more social experience an individual had being aggressive prior to castration, the more likely that behavior persists sans cojones. In the right context, social conditioning can more than make up for the complete absence of the hormone.

A case in point: the spotted hyena. These animals are fast becoming the darlings of endocrinologists, sociobiologists, gynecologists, and tabloid writers because of their wild sex reversal system. Females are more muscular and more aggressive than males, and are socially dominant to them, rare traits in the mammalian world. And get this: females secrete more of certain testosterone-related hormones than the males do, producing muscles, aggression, and masculinized private

in the context of competing scientific versions of the evolution of social life, we show how sociologists, as public intellectuals, can challenge these populist and deterministic accounts of human nature. We begin by exploring the impact that evolutionary psychology has had on public apprehensions of society and identity.

The Sociological Importance of Origin Myths

In the average bookshop, popular science occupies a great deal more shelf space than sociology. Here, the bestsellers tend to focus on origins—of the universe or of the human species. It is the latter that concern us here, for they impinge directly on sociological concerns: they do not confine themselves to the origins of the physical characteristics of *Homo sapiens* or even to the supposed behaviour of our Stone-Age ancestors, but offer accounts of what it is to be human. Much of the lay and scientific interest in evolutionary studies of behaviour arises from the expectation that their findings contribute to a better understanding of contemporary human conduct. Thus this form of scientific research has direct political and social impact, making sociological critique all the more urgent.

This approach to the study of humanity originated in the sociobiological revolution of the 1970s, which sparked a serious controversy between the natural and the social sciences (Segerstrale, 2000)[1] and eventually led to a proliferation of different disciplines that attempted to apply biology to culture. At the heart of the "new sociobiological synthesis" and its offspring was a particular twist on the traditional interpretation of Darwinian theory.[2] While earlier accounts had focused on the individual's struggle for survival within its immediate environment (acquiring food, avoiding being eaten), sociobiology turned instead to the struggle between individuals for representation in the next generation. Each individual organism was now assumed to be unconsciously engaging in strategies to maximize its opportunities to mate and to ensure the survival of as many of its own offspring as possible.

It is this focus on sex and reproduction that lies at the heart of the tales of evolutionary psychology, told by scientists and reshaped by the media, packaged for the lay public in pop science, and appropriated as part of the generally available cultural stock of knowledge. To give one example of media reportage of such scientific work, an item appeared on BBC News online on 14 August 2006 proclaiming that: "A woman's sex drive begins to plummet once she is in a secure relationship." We are told that, among a sample of 530 men and women, men's desire for sex with their partners remained constant over time, whereas 60 per cent of women wanted sex "often" at the beginning of the relationship, under 50 per cent after four years and around 20 per cent after 20 years. Apparently, these were evolved differences. The report continues:

> Dr. Dietrich Klusmann...said: 'For men, a good reason their sexual motivation to remain constant would be to guard against being cuckolded by another male.' But women, he said, have evolved to have a high sex drive when they are initially in a relationship in order to form a 'pair bond' with their partner. But, once this bond is sealed a woman's sexual appetite declines, he added.

Further speculation on the evolutionary "functions" of such differences follows, including the suggestion, now increasingly common in this field, that women might be "diverting their sexual interest to other men in order to secure the best combination of genetic material for their offspring" (BBC News online, 2006).

This story, which is fairly typical, offers some clues as to why sociologists fail to take such accounts seriously. Any sociologist could immediately see the logical flaws in the argument, would spot the functionalist teleology underpinning it, question the methodology and be able to advance several alternative interpretations of the data. We might also point out that scientists' reliance on the commonsense assumption that sex cements the pair-bond, another centrepiece of evolutionary psychology (Diamond, 1997), derives from historically specific understandings of intimacy (e.g., Seidman, 1991). The BBC report, unsurprisingly, did not offer any sociological critique, only a comment from another evolutionary psychologist who found the arguments "plausible."

We cannot, however, afford to ignore such accounts simply because we find them absurd. To do so is to abdicate responsibility in a social climate where these stories become part of the "cultural scenarios" that inform everyday knowledge, interaction and individual self-constructions. Species stories on "how we got this way" are readily incorporated into individual narratives on "how I got this way"—and some writers of popular evolutionary psychology actively promote such extrapolations. For example in the introduction to *Why is Sex Fun?*, Diamond claims that:

> [T]his book may help you to understand why your body feels the way it does, and why your beloved is behaving in the way he or she is. Perhaps, too, if you understand why you feel driven to some self-destructive sexual behaviour, that understanding may help you gain distance from your instincts and to deal more intelligently with them. (1997: viii)

Diamond here assumes a self-reflexive reader who is nonetheless a product of his or her instincts. The extent to which such accounts actually inform individuals' self-understanding is an interesting sociological problem, but there is a more pressing problem *for* sociology here: they offer a reductionist, misleading means of self-interpretation, which it is our business to contest.

Evolutionary psychology also offers an impoverished view of culture. Having conceded that culture may be important to human life and part of our unique species characteristics, some have, following Dawkins (1976), introduced the idea of "memes." This concept, elaborated by Susan Blackmore (1999), treated "culture" as the sum total of individual units, which resembled genes: they could be transmitted from one individual to another, they showed variation, and as a result of that variation, some were transmitted more often than others. In this sense, cultural development was not just *like* biological evolution, it *was* evolution: a situation where memes competed frantically with each other for space in human brains. This incorporation of culture into an evolutionary framework displaces sociology—we have, it seems, become an endangered species. We need to defend our own disciplinary interests and also challenge the hegemony of a version of evolutionary theory that enables this appropriation of culture. Indeed the admission that culture plays a part at all ought to give us an opportunity to advance different versions of social and cultural change. Yet sociologists, with a few exceptions, have been reluctant to engage with evolutionary theory of any kind in recent years. We have long dismissed the functionalist methodology underpinning 19th-century accounts of evolutionary progression from one form of social order to the next,[3] and rightly shrink from the eugenicist implications of social Darwinism. However, at a time when creationism, as an aspect of religious fundamentalism, is becoming a political force—especially in the USA—it seems unwise simply to damn evolutionary theory as a whole. The accounts of evolutionary psychology peddled to the public at present not only offer an impoverished understanding of culture, but also of evolutionary theory itself. There are other ways of reading Darwin and interpreting Darwinism.

Only certain kinds of scientific stories, however, get told, and those that are told become simplified when they enter into everyday discourse and popular culture. In characterizing evolutionary psychology as narrative we recognize that any account of the past, biographical, historical or evolutionary is necessarily a reconstruction since we can only ever apprehend the past from the standpoint of the present (Mead, 1932). This is not to say that the past is *merely* a fiction, since the past also provides the conditions for the emergence of the present (Maines, 2001; Mead, 1932). But whereas historians carefully piece together evidence on the conditions of emergence of specific consecutive events, providing a carefully reasoned, if always provisional, representation of the past, evolutionary psychologists make a huge conjectural leap from the present to a reconstructed prehistory. In a society where science has an almost talismanic status, however, such flaws seem to make little difference to the perceived plausibility of the story.

The Siren Songs of Sexual Selection

How it is that such evolutionary accounts of human nature have been so successful at colonizing the popular imagination? At heart, most share two assumptions: first, that human behaviour and society are the products of evolutionary pressure, and second, that human cultural evolution has outstripped biological evolution. In other words, our bodies and instinctive behaviours are identical to those possessed by our hunter-gatherer ancestors, which causes problems when these bodies and instincts must operate in post-industrial societies characterized by abundant food and leisure.[4] A fundamental disjuncture exists, they argue, between our instinctive responses and our current situation, which can create deep unhappiness for individuals faced by conflicting social and biological expectations, and, more devastatingly, the potential for global destruction when biologically based drives meet technological innovation.[5] Here lies the first source of their attraction: they promise to provide a "scientific" account of what is wrong with us, both at the species and the individual level. In a world where many still take "scientific" to be synonymous with "true," and where most are aware that human ingenuity may well contain the seeds of our own destruction, this has undoubted appeal. If one cannot blame divine providence, then it is useful to be able to attribute potential disasters to forces that are beyond individual control. However, there are several other elements that account for the seductive appeal of these evolutionary accounts.

In the first place, these accounts follow a particular structure, the narrative of deep time told as if it were biography, from the beginnings of life on the planet to the emergence of one particular primate species, a teleological reading of the book of life through the lens of human evolution. Ironically enough, given that the publication of Darwin's *Origin of Species* (1859) is commonly cited as the moment where the last shreds of the religious veil shrouding humanity's ultimate insignificance were torn aside, this technique implicitly reassures the reader that the purpose of evolution was to produce humanity. Additionally, however, as Hayden White (1978) observed in relation to historical narrative, the telling of such stories depends on the moralization of reality: since historians cannot include every detail in accounts of events past, they foreground those elements of the story that appear particularly significant for their needs. In the case of evolutionary accounts, although authors differ as to which "defining" human characteristic appeared first (Landau, 1984; Latour and Strum, 1986), the narrative of human development remains largely the same and performs several functions. In the first place, the *biological* evolution of the species is foregrounded—the emergence of binocular vision, of grasping thumbs, of big brains, bipedal walking, and so on. These points are matters of material record, and no one other than a creationist would wish to argue that human bodies are anything but the product of evolution—but having accepted physiological evolution, one is logically led to the question of behavioural evolution.

Narrative structures also contribute to the appeal of these accounts through the imposition of simplicity and the adduction of cause and effect. Cultural complexity and behavioural diversity are sidelined, becoming irrelevant as the "universal" elements of human development are revealed. At the same time, this structure enables these accounts of human evolution to become nearly impregnable to interrogation. As is the case for many other examples of popular science (Curtis, 1994), these stories tend to be presented in a narrative form that closely resembles the popular genre of detective fiction. Implicitly, this use of the narrative coupled with the "mystery/whodunnit" style makes conclusions much harder to challenge. At the outset, the solution to the problem of human behaviour is unknown, but having examined a range of potential suspects (including the soggy red-herrings limply proffered by social scientists), the perpetrator is identified, often through a process of elimination. Since murder is rarely committed by a multiplicity of miscreants, there is no need for a range of different motives for, or causes of, human behaviour to be sought: the criminal has been caught and brought to book. For sociologists, this represents an unacceptably reductionist approach to human diversity: for the audience, it presents a clear-cut explanation for human behaviour that, in its focus on sex and reproduction, resonates firmly with the "special" status of sex in Western culture (Jackson and Scott, 2004).

Analogy and metaphor also contribute to the enduring appeal of these attempts to naturalize human behaviour and society. These accounts often use what generations of sociologists have understood as the "organic analogy" as a way to make the millennia of deep time meaningful to their audience. Frequently, metaphors based in individual human lifespan and the nuclear family are used to emphasize the immediate relevance of the matters under discussion. Persistently, the suggestion is made that, as a species, we are on the cusp of adolescence, poised to step forward into maturity—if we can only find the courage and self-knowledge to face and embrace our biological heritage. Abstract notions of human evolution are rendered immediate by placing them in this familiar and familial context, at the same time as the audience is implicitly praised for its willingness to face the past's consequences and to take adult responsibility for their behaviour.

In contrast, social scientists are shown to cling desperately to out-moded and discredited knowledge. For evolutionary psychologists, this is encapsulated in the Standard Social Science Model (SSSM) of behaviour, which places the theory of the "blank slate" at the heart of the humanistic interpretation of human behaviour (Barkow et al., 1992). That this invented model bears little resemblance to the actual (diverse) explanatory frameworks of social scientists has not prevented some researchers from blaming it for our inability to prevent such crimes as rape and domestic abuse. For example:

> Police officers, lawyers, teachers, parents, counsellors, convicted rapists, potential rapists and children are being taught "rape prevention" measures that will fail because they are based on fundamentally inaccurate notions about human nature... The social science theory of rape is based on empirically erroneous, even mythological ideas about human development, behaviour and psychology. (Thornhill and Palmer, 2000: xii–xiii)

Our unwillingness to embrace our biological past is, allegedly, not just wrong but dangerous and irresponsible.

Notions of time and progress dominate the portrayal of human identity in these accounts, and there is a constant, persistent stress on the need to accept that the past is our present; we cannot understand what is wrong with modernity without understanding how human nature evolved to produce a disjuncture between human biology and human culture. Frequently, these stories about humanity add extra immediacy to their appeal by emphasizing the future dangers that await if we fail to recognize and deal with our animal past—but what is interesting is the way in which those future shocks vary, depending on the pressing problems of the present. So, for example, in the post-war years, Desmond Morris (1967) and Robert Ardrey (1961) emphasized the problem of aggression and territoriality in ape evolution, pointing to the way in which the development of distance weapons (arrows, H-bombs) bypassed the evolved mechanisms that inhibited fatal aggression. By the mid-1990s, Jared Diamond and others focused on the dangers posed by uninhibited environmental exploitation, arguing again that technological innovation and cultural evolution had given us the ability dangerously to over-exploit the eco-system.

It might well be suggested that such changes in the identification of humanity's Achilles heel are to be expected, given that the authors are writing for a general audience, and will naturally choose to focus their attention on publicly prominent themes, whether these be war or biodiversity. Despite the fact that the basic mechanism is the same in both cases (that human cultural evolution has outflanked biological restraint), it remains ironic that the consequences of such allegedly "fixed" weaknesses are changing over time. Even more ironic is the fact that these changes in the interpretation of the "fixed" future of the species and the planet are mirrored in the conflicting interpretations of Darwin and Darwinism within biological thought itself.

It is in these conflicts that sociologists can find the tools with which to unpick what appears to be the univocal chorus proclaiming the identification of biological fixity. Aware as we are of the fragmentary and multiple nature of human identity and the overwhelming cultural diversity that exists on the planet, we cannot manufacture our own "grand narrative" to counter the assertion of human universals. However, we can point to the fact that, popular culture notwithstanding, biologists themselves have fundamental disagreements both with regard to the way that evolution operates and with respect to the nature of the selective pressures that might have influenced the origin and development of human identity and society. Science, as the sociology and history of science has persistently shown over the past four decades, often produces competing versions of "truth."

One Man, Many Faces...

The interpretation of Darwinism that currently dominates the media, we have suggested, is a very particular one in which what matters in the evolutionary game is the number of offspring produced. For the most part, bodies and behaviours are treated as progressively "adapting" over the generations in order to maximize that figure through competition between individuals for access to both resources and sexual partners. But this is not the only approach to the study of evolution, since Darwinism encompasses a number of different perspectives, all of whom insist that they are the true inheritors of Darwin's mantle.

In consequence, popular accounts of evolutionary biology tend to gloss over terms and concepts that are subject to more than one interpretation within biological philosophy and practice. Take the question of "adaptation," for example, a notion fundamental to evolutionary psychology. An "adaptation" is a means through which the individual organism can utilize its environment more effectively. Thus our eyes are an adaptation that enables us to see the world around us. The difficulty, however, comes when the concept of "adaptation" is applied to the understanding of behaviour and bodies. Is everything an adaptation? Certainly this seems to be the assumption made by many of the ultra-Darwinists, but their interpretation has been contested by other scientists. For example, Gould and Lewontin (1979) argued that the problem with sociobiological thinking was its tendency to assume that *everything* was adaptive. Instead, they suggested that many elements of animal bodies and activities might well be "spandrels," characteristics that are neither the product of, nor subject to selection, but the inevitable result of an individual's growth and development. Another area of debate is the question of whether populations are still in the process of evolving. When studying the evolutionary basis of behaviour, should one assume that an adaptation has reached fixity in a population (i.e., is possessed by every member), or whether selection for a particular trait is still ongoing? This issue was central to the controversy surrounding the evolution of infanticide (Rees, 2001), in which each participant was convinced that their interpretation was Darwinistically correct. There may well be as many different accounts of "what Darwin said" as there have historically been interpretations of "what Marx really meant."

Some biologists (Segerstrale, 2000) believe that these differing interpretations are rooted in the political orientation of particular scientists: both Lewontin and Gould were criticized for allowing their left-wing sympathies to intrude on what was a supposedly objective debate. This is ironic, since it is commonly assumed that the importation of biological thought into political discourse was a right-wing habit, as in the racist implications of 19th-century theories of social evolution and the Nazi appropriation of Darwinism (Numbers, 1998; Proctor, 1988). We are very familiar with the ways in which evolution and biology have been adopted and adapted by those on the right of the political spectrum to justify and naturalize the hierarchies that those on the left wish to destabilize and reform. What is less well known, however, is the extent to which they have also been adopted by biologists in support of a reforming agenda. For example, during and after the First World War, the evolutionary philosophy underlying German militarism was identified and critiqued by contemporary American biologists such as Vernon Kellogg and David Starr Jordan. Kellogg's popular writings made the passionate case that the uncritical adoption of the idea of a fatal, inevitable "struggle for existence," and the "survival of the fittest" had produced the perfect justification for war. As an alternative, they pointed to the fact that natural selection was only one source of evolutionary change,[6] and that in fact, since war eradicated the best and brightest of a country's youth, it was functionally dysgenic. In this sense, one could base an ideology of peace within Darwinist selection (Mitman, 1992).

Peter Kropotkin's work on the importance of mutual assistance for survival, along with the early work of Herbert Spencer, provided the basis for a research programme that took cooperation, rather than competition, as the driving force in the evolution of social life.[7] Here, the Darwinian "struggle for existence" was fundamentally a contest between the organism and the environment, rather than between members of the same species for representation in the next generation. From Kroptkin's point of view, the fittest animals were not the strongest, but those which had acquired the habit of working together to achieve their goals. Warder Clyde Allee's research, in the inter-war years, empirically demonstrated the value of cooperation. Using invertebrates, he showed that groups of animals, placed in a hostile environment, survived longer than did isolated individuals. This, he argued, suggested that even at the sub-social level, individuals benefited from group living, and suggested that rather than originating in the hierarchical relationships of the immediate nuclear family, social life could conceivably be rooted in these proto-cooperative—and non-hierarchical—impulses. This argument contrasted sharply with the alternative model of primate social origins promoted by Solly Zuckerman in Britain, whose studies of baboons had led him to insist that sex was the only explanation for sociality (Rees, 2006).

By the 1950s, Allee's programme for cooperationist biology was faltering and the future looked bleak for the biology of the left. The attempt to find democracy's biological base as a counter to the fascist ideologies prevalent during the 1920s and 30s had petered out as communist totalitarianism took hold: where once biologists had emphasized the need for unity, cooperation and potential self-sacrifice, now the metaphors of conflict and competition were treated as central to a healthy democracy and market economy. Once again, the focus of attention was on the individual, and the struggle to survive in a Hobbesian battle of each against all. Emphasizing cooperative collaboration was a threat to the sanctity of the individual's right to liberty and choice, and veered dangerously close to communism. By the late 1960s, the arguments of the last defender of cooperation as crucial to social life had been publicly demolished (Williams, 1966; Wynne-Edwards, 1962). Selection took place, not at the level of the group, but at the level of the gene.

One could treat this focus on cooperation as error, rectified by the self-correcting nature of science. However, biologists have continued to debate the nature of the relationship between conflict and cooperation in evolution, and these debates have become more prominent since the Cold War ended. These researchers have derived their inspiration from a combination of the work of Kropotkin and Darwin—and in particular, Darwin's assertion that "an increase in the number of well-endowed men and advancement in the standard of morality will certainly give an immense advantage to one tribe over another" (1871, quoted in Chapman and Sussman, 2004: 7). In other words, although self-sacrifice on the part of an individual will damage that *individual*, a *society* of cooperative selfsacrificers will, on the whole, be far more successful than would one of selfish competitors (Chapman and Sussman, 2004; Sober and Wilson, 1998).

Taking a slightly different tack, Marc Bekoff has shown that, rather than arising from selfish self-interest (Ridley, 2001), the notions of "morality" and "justice" may have independent evolutionary origins. Most social animals learn adult behaviour through social play, and such play—fundamental to successful maturation—requires honest dealing between individuals. At the most basic level, two animals playing together need to agree that this is "play," rather than an attempt to mate with, fight or eat the other. As a result, a bigger individual cannot "play" with a smaller animal without voluntarily and consistently handicapping herself in some way, nor can a subordinate animal take advantage of a dominant's exposure of belly and throat to bite. Those "machiavellian" individuals who do break the rules soon find themselves excluded from this valuable and clearly enjoyable activity (Bekoff, 2004). In the absence of play, social development is inhibited: willingness and ability to "play fair" is therefore at a premium. On this interpretation, morality and cooperation emerge as desirable factors subject to selective pressure in their own right. Evolutionary accounts such as these, in their emphasis on cooperation and interaction, decentre sexual selection and can make space for a more complex and diverse story to be told. They are thus very different from the pseudo-left accounts, such as that of Singer (1999), which, as Fuller (2006) points out, retain sexual selection at their core.

Conclusion

Nothing in this article should be taken as a criticism of evolutionary biology perse: it is not our business to make such judgements, especially since feminist evolutionary biologists such as Patricia Gowaty (1997) and Sarah Hrdy (2000) are already paying close attention to the impact of assumptions concerning sex, gender and sexuality within their discipline. Our concern is with the unchallenged public circulation of simplified evolutionary accounts of human nature, accounts that are accepted as accurate simply because they are "scientific," and which make the sheer, staggering, and utterly glorious diversity of human beings as individuals and as societies impossible to apprehend. We must demonstrate that sociology gives us far more purchase on this diversity than the mechanistic notion of memes, and that our discipline cannot be reduced to an equally mechanistic "standard model" (SSSM).

We are failing the public if we fail to engage with these accounts. And on this reading, engagement does not mean rejection, but an effort to understand what kind of story is being told and its position within the history of biological thought. Sociologists, after all, are experts in dealing with internal disciplinary disagreements: we should not be surprised to find them in the biological sciences, and nor should we refrain from seeking out debate and dialogue with scientists who have stories to tell that do not follow the dominant theme of competition. If we are to mount a credible challenge to the myth of the "SSSM" we should also recognize that evolutionary thought is not a monolithic entity. We genuinely do not know whether human behaviour and culture are the products of evolutionary selective pressure, although we find it unlikely. But it is crucial to distinguish between those popular accounts that insist on the fixity of human identity and human nature, and those that are, more modestly, and more hopefully, attempting to identify the biological limits to human capacity in order that they may be surmounted. After all, as Katherine Hepburn said to Humphrey Bogart in *The African Queen:* "Nature, Mr Allnut, is what we were put in this world to overcome."

Notes

1. Although attempts to explain human behaviour by reference to humanity's evolved past were in popular circulation for many years before this. See, for example, Ardrey (1961), Sahlins (1977).
2. See Bowler (2003) for a history of evolutionary thought prior to Darwin.
3. Of course neofunctionalism does continue to have some influence.
4. This is another example of the use of the past to explain the present: we are adapted, as a species, to gorge on sugar and fat whenever possible. That instinct, essential for survival in a harsh environment, is producing today's obesity epidemic, since it's hard to avoid sugar and fat in a post-industrial society.
5. So, for example, the conflict between the demands of the labour market and the demands of childbearing; alternatively, the vastly increased risk

of global destruction when wars are fought at a distance.

6. The other sources included geographical isolation, mutation theory and Mendelism. In addition, many characteristics separating species were not considered to be adaptive and therefore were not the product of natural selection. The problem with German theory for American biologists was that it ignored these issues and privileged natural selection (Mitman, 1992).
7. Chicago in the early 20th century also saw another progressive and sociological appropriation of Darwin: that of G.H. Mead. For Mead, Darwin provided a means of countering the individualistic assumption that the individual existed prior to the social and also static conceptions of "human nature" and social organization. Mead saw evolution as a process that continues socially "through the development of a universe of discourse... through communication and participation... in common activities" (1956: 36).

References

Ardrey, R. (1961) *African Genesis: A Personal Investigation into the Animal Origins and Nature of Man*. London: Collins.

Barkow, J., L. Cosmides and J. Tooby (eds) (1992) *The Adapted Mind: Evolutionary Psychology and the Generation of Culture*. Oxford: Oxford University Press.

BBC News online (2006) "Security 'Bad News for Sex Drive'", URL (consulted August 2006): http://news.bbc.co.uk/1/hi/health/4790313.stm?ls

Bekoff, M. (2004) "Wild Justice, Cooperation and Fair Play: Minding Manners, Being Nice and Feeling Good," in A. Chapman and R. Sussman *The Origins and Nature of Sociality*, pp. 53–80. New York: Aldine.

Blackmore, S. (1999) *The Meme Machine*. Oxford: Oxford University Press.

Bowler, P. (2003) *Evolution: The History of an Idea*, 3rd edn. Berkeley: University of California Press.

Chapman, A. and R. Sussman (eds) (2004) *The Origins and Nature of Sociality*. New York: Aldine.

Curtis, R. (1994) "Narrative Form and Normative Force: Baconian Story-Telling in Popular Science," *Social Studies of Science* 24(3): 419–61.

Dawkins, R. (1976) *The Selfish Gene*. Oxford: Oxford University Press.

Diamond, J. (1997) *Why is Sex Fun? The Evolution of Human Sexuality*. London: Weidenfeld and Nicholson.

Fuller, S. (2006) *The New Sociological Imagination*. London: Sage.

Gould, S. and R. Lewontin (1979) "The Spandrels of San Marco and the Panglossian Paradigm: A Critique of the Adaptationist Programme," *Proceedings of the Royal Society of London B* 205: 581–98.

Gowaty, P. (ed.) (1997) *Feminism and Evolutionary Biology: Boundaries, Intersections and Frontiers*. London: Chapman & Hall.

Hrdy, S. (2000) *Mother Nature*. London: Vintage.

Jackson, S. and S. Scott (2004) "Sexual Antinomies in Late Modernity," *Sexualities* 7(2): 233–46.

Landau, M. (1984) *Narratives of Human Evolution*. New Haven, CT: Yale University Press.

Latour, B. and S. Strum (1986) "Human Social Origins: Please Tell Us Another Story," *Journal of Social and Biological Structures* 9: 169–87.

Maines, D. (2001) *The Faultline of Consciousness: A View of Interactionism in Sociology*. New York: Aldine de Gruyter.

Mead, G.H. (1932) *The Philosophy of the Present*. Chicago, IL: Open Court.

Mead, G.H. (1956) "Evolution Becomes a General Idea," in A. Strauss (ed.) *George Herbert Mead on Social Psychology*, pp. 3–18. Chicago, IL: University of Chicago Press.

Mitman, G. (1992) *The State of Nature: Ecology, Community and American Social Thought, 1900–1950*. Chicago, IL: University of Chicago Press.

Morris, D. (1967) *The Naked Ape*. London: Jonathan Cape.

Numbers, R. (1998) *Darwinism Comes to America*. Cambridge, MA: Harvard University Press.

Proctor, R. (1988) *Racial Hygiene: Medicine under the Nazis*. Cambridge, MA: Harvard University Press.

Rees, A. (2001) "Practising Infanticide, Observing Narrative: Controversial Texts in a Field Science," *Social Studies of Science* 31(4): 507–31.

Rees, A. (2006) "Ecology, Biology and Social Life: Explaining the Origins of Primate Sociality," *History of Science* 44(4): 409–34.

Ridley, M. (2001) *The Cooperative Gene*. New York: Free Press.

Sahlins, M. (1977) *The Use and Abuse of Biology: An Anthropological Critique of Sociobiology*. London: Tavistock.

Segerstrale, U. (2000) *Defenders of the Truth: The Battle for Science in the Sociobiology Debates and Beyond*. Oxford: Oxford University Press.

Seidman, S. (1991) *Romantic Longings: Love in America 1839–1980*. New York: Routledge.

Singer, P. (1999) *A Darwinian Left: Politics, Evolution and Cooperation*. London: Weidenfeld and Nicholson.

Sober, E. and D. Wilson (1998) *Unto Others: The Evolution of Altruism*. Cambridge, MA: Harvard University Press.

Thornhill, R. and C. Palmer (2000) *A Natural History of Rape: Biological Bases of Sexual Coercion*. Cambridge, MA: MIT Press.

White, H. (1978) "The Historical Text as Literary Artifact," in H. White *Tropics of Discourse: Essays in Cultural Criticism*, pp. 81–100. Baltimore, MD: Johns Hopkins University Press.

Williams, G.C. (1966) *Adaptation and Natural Selection: A Critique of Some Current Evolutionary Thought*. Princeton, NJ: Princeton University Press.

Wynne-Edwards, V.C. (1962) *Animal Dispersal in Relation to Social Behaviour*. London: Oliver and Boyd.

PART 2

Cultural Constructions of Gender

Biological evidence helps explain the ubiquity of gender difference and gender inequality, but social scientific evidence modifies both the universality and the inevitability implicit in biological claims. Cross-cultural research suggests that gender and sexuality are far more fluid, far more variable, than biological models would have predicted. If biological sex alone produced observed sex differences, Margaret Mead asked in the 1920s and 1930s, why did it produce such *different* definitions of masculinity and femininity in different cultures? In her path-breaking study, *Sex and Temperament in Three Primitive Societies*, Mead began an anthropological tradition of exploring and often celebrating the dramatically rich and varied cultural constructions of gender.

Anthropologists are more likely to locate the origins of gender difference and gender inequality in a sex-based division of labor, the near-universality of and the variations in the ways in which societies organize the basic provision and distribution of material goods. They've found that when women's and men's spheres are most distinctly divided—where women and men do different things in different places—women's status tends to be lower than when men and women share both work and workplaces.

Some researchers have explored the function of various cultural rituals and representations in creating the symbolic justification for gender differences and inequality based on this sex-based division of labor. For example, Gilbert Herdt describes a variety of "coming out" processes in a variety of cultures, thus demonstrating (1) the connections between sexual identity and gender identity and (2) the dramatic variation among those identities. Serena Nanda reminds us that the fluidity of gender in real life is often far richer and more wonderfully varied than the rigid mental categories of biological sex that cultures may impose.

Men as Women and Women as Men: Disrupting Gender

JUDITH LORBER

> This thing here, you call this a person? There is no such thing as a person who is half male half female.
>
> *Meira Weiss forthcoming*

The French writer Colette felt that she was a "mental hermaphrodite" but had "a sturdy and perfectly female body" (Lydon 1991, 28). When she offered to travel with a noted womanizer, he said that he traveled only with women: "Thus when Damien declares that he travels only with women, implying that a woman is what Colette is not, the only linguistically possible conclusion is that she must be a man. But she and we know this not to be the case, despite her willingness to admit to a certain 'virility.' What then, can Colette legitimately call herself?" (29).[1] Cool and rational androgynous women are social men, one step removed from the "mannish lesbian" (Newton 1984). Men who use a highly emotionally charged vocabulary may be judged romantic geniuses, but their masculinity may be somewhat suspect, as was Byron's (Battersby 1989).

The history of a nineteenth-century French hermaphrodite illustrates the impossibility of living socially as both a woman and a man even if it is physiologically possible (Butler 1990, 93–106). Herculine Barbin, who was raised in convents as a girl, after puberty, fell in love with a young woman and had sexual relations with her. At the age of twenty-two, Herculine (usually called Alexina) confessed the homosexuality to a bishop, and after examination by two doctors, was legally recategorized as a man and given a man's name. But Herculine's genitals, as described in two doctors' reports, were ambiguous: a one-and-a-half-inch-long penis, partly descended testicles, and a urethral opening (Foucault 1980, 125–28). One doctor reasoned as follows:

> Is Alexina a woman? She has a vulva, labia majora, and a feminine urethra, independent of a sort of imperforate penis, which might be a monstrously developed clitoris. She has a vagina.... These are completely feminine attributes. Yet, but Alexina has never menstruated; the whole outer part of her body is that of a man, and my explorations do not enable me to find a womb. Her tastes, her inclinations, draw her toward women. At night she has voluptuous sensations that are followed by a discharge of sperm; her linen is stained and starched with it. Finally, to sum up the matter, ovoid bodies and spermatic cords are found by touch in a divided scrotum. These are the real proofs of sex.... Alexina is a man, hermaphroditic, no doubt, but with an obvious predominance of masculine sexual characteristics. (127–28)

But Barbin, now called Abel, did not feel he was fully a man socially because he did not think any woman would marry him, and at the age of thirty he ended a "double and bizarre existence" via suicide. The doctor who performed the autopsy felt that the external genitalia could just as well have been classified as female, and that, with a penis-clitoris capable of erection and a vagina, Barbin was physiologically capable of bisexuality (128–44). But there was no social status of man-woman.

What would have become of Herculine Barbin one hundred years later? Surgery to remove the

---

Judith Lorber, Paradoxes of Gender, (New Haven: Yale University Press, 1994).

testicles, enlarge the vagina, and make the penis smaller? Then hormones to produce breasts and reduce body hair? Or closure of the vaginal opening, release of the testes, cosmetic surgery to enlarge the penis, and administration of testosterone? Having been brought up as a girl, but loving a woman, would Barbin have identified as a "man," a "lesbian," or a "bisexual"? Would the woman who loved him as a woman accept him as a husband? Without surgery or gender reassignment, would Herculine and Sara have been accepted as a lesbian couple today? Without surgery, but with gender reassignment, would Abel and Sara have been accepted as a heterosexual couple? Would Barbin have used a gender-neutral name, dressed in a gender-neutral way? What sex would be on her or his official documents? What kind of work would he or she have done?[2]

One possibility was documented in 1937. A hermaphrodite named Emma, who had a penis-like clitoris as well as a vagina, was raised as a girl. Emma had sexual relationships with a number of girls (heterosexual sex), married a man with whom she also had heterosexual sex, but continued to have women lovers (Fausto-Sterling 1993). She refused to have vaginal closure and live as a man because it would have meant a divorce and having to go to work. Emma was quite content to be a physiological bisexual, possibly because her gender identity was clearly that of a woman.

Anne Fausto-Sterling says that "no classification scheme could more than suggest the variety of sexual anatomy encountered in clinical practice" (1993). In 1992, a thirty-year-old Ethiopian Israeli whose social identity was a man was discovered at his Army physical to have a very small penis and a very small vagina. Exploratory surgery revealed vestigial ovaries and vestigial testicles, a uterus, and fallopian tubes. He was XY, but when he was classified a male at birth it was on the basis of how the external genitalia looked, and the penis took precedence. Because he had been brought up as a man and wanted to have this identity supported physiologically, his penis was enlarged and reconstructed, and the vagina was closed and made into a scrotum.

Testosterone was administered to increase his sexual desire for women.[3]

"Penis and Eggs"

When physiological anomalies occur today in places with sophisticated medical technology, the diagnosis, sex assignment, and surgical reconstruction of the genitalia are done as quickly as possible in order to minimize the intense uncertainty that a genderless child produces in our society (Kessler 1990). Other cultures, however, are more accepting of sex and gender ambiguity.

In the Dominican Republic, there has been a genetic phenomenon in which children who looked female at birth and were brought up as girls produced male hormones at puberty and virilized. Their genitalia masculinized, their voices deepened, and they developed a male physical appearance (Imperato-McGinley et al. 1974, 1979). They are called *guevedoces* (penis at 12) or *machihembra* (first woman, then man) or *guevotes* (penis and eggs). According to one set of reports, sixteen of nineteen who were raised as girls gradually changed to men's social roles—working outside the home, marrying, and becoming heads of households (Imperato-McGinley et al. 1979). One, now elderly, who emigrated to the United States, felt like a man, but under family pressure lived as a woman. One, still in the Dominican Republic, had married as a woman at sixteen, had been deserted after a year, continued to live as a woman, and wanted surgery to be a "normal" woman. Not all those who lived as men had fully functioning genitalia, and all were sterile.

The physicians who studied thirty-three of these male pseudohermaphrodites (biologically male with ambiguous-appearing genitalia at birth) claim that the nineteen who decided without medical intervention that they would adopt men's identities and social roles despite having been raised as girls "appear to challenge both the theory of the immutability of gender identity after three or four years of age and the sex of rearing as the major factor in determining male-gender identity" (Imperato-McGinley et al. 1979, 1236). Their report stresses the effects of the hormonal input and secondary male sex characteristics at puberty, despite the mixture of reactions and gradualness of the gender changeover.

Another physician (Baker 1980) questions whether the pseudohermaphrodites were reared unambiguously as girls, given their somewhat abnormal genitalia at birth, and an anthropologist (Herdt 1990) claims that culturally, the community recognized a third sex category, since they had names for it. Although the medical researchers described the parents' reactions during the course of the virilization as "amazement, confusion, and finally, acceptance rather than hostility" (Imperato-McGinley et al. 1979, 1235–36), their interviews with the pseudohermaphrodites revealed that as children, they had always suffered embarrassment because of their genitalia, and they worried about future harassment whether they chose to live as women or as men. That is, they were never unambiguously girls socially, and their appearance and sterility undercut their claims to be men. Nonetheless, most chose to live as men. Virilization was not total, but it provided the opportunity for the choice of the more attractive social role.[4] According to the medical researchers: "In a domestic setting, the women take care of the household activities, while the affected subjects work as farmers, miners or woodsmen, as do the normal males in the town. They enjoy their role as head of the household" (Imperato-McGinley et al. 1979, 1234).

In Papua New Guinea, where the same recessive genetic condition and marriage to close relatives produces similar male pseudohermaphrodites, the culture does have an intergender category (*kwolu-aatmwol*). Many of these children were identified by experienced midwives at birth and reared anticipatorily as boys (Herdt 1990; Herdt and Davidson 1988). Although the *kwolu-aatmwols* went through boys' rituals as they grew up, their adult status as men was incomplete ritually, and therefore socially, because they were sterile and also because they were embarrassed by the small size of their penises. They rarely allowed themselves to be fellated by adolescent boys, a mark of honor for adult men, although some, as teenagers, in an effort to become more masculine, frequently fellated older men. In their behavior and attitudes, they were masculine. Their identity as adult men was stigmatized, however, because they did not participate in what in Western societies would be homosexual (and stigmatized) sex practices, but in that culture made them fully men (Herdt 1981).

The pseudohermaphrodites who were reared as girls, either because they were not identified or their genital anomalies were hidden, did not switch to living as men when they virilized. Rather, they tried very hard to live as women, but were rejected by the men they married. Only at that point did they switch to men's dress, but they were even more ostracized socially, since they did not undergo any men's rituals. According to Gilbert Herdt and Julian Davidson: "Once exposed, they had no place to hide and no public in which to continue to pose as 'female.' It was only this that precipitated gender role change. Yet this is not change to the male role, because the natives know the subjects are not male; rather they changed from sex-assigned female to turnim-men, male-identified kwolu-aatmwol" (1988, 53).

Thus, neither childhood socialization nor pubescent virilization nor individual preferences was definitive in the adult gender placement of these male pseudohermaphrodites. Their assigned status was problematic men; away from their home villages, they could pass as more or less normal men. One was married, but to a prostitute; he had been "ostentatiously masculine" as an adolescent, was a good provider, and was known as "a fearless womanizer" (Herdt and Davidson 1988).

Switching Genders

Transsexuals have normal genitalia, but identify with the members of the opposite gender. Since there is no mixed or intermediate gender for people with male genitalia who want to live as women or people with female genitalia who want to live as men, transsexuals end up surgically altering their genitalia to fit their gender identity. They also undergo hormone treatment to alter their body shape and hair distribution and to develop secondary sex characteristics, such as breasts or beards. Transsexuals do not change their sex completely (Stoller 1985, 163). Their chromosomes remain the same, and no man-to-woman transsexual has a uterus implant, nor do any women-to-men transsexuals produce sperm. They change gender; thus, the accurate terms are *man-to-woman* and *woman-to-man*, not *male-to-female* and *female-to-male*.

Discussing only men-to-women transsexuals, Richard Docter sees the process as one in which more and more frequent cross-dressing reinforces the desire to completely switch genders:

> The cross-gender identity seems to grow stronger with practice and with social reinforcements of the pseudowoman. In unusual cases, the end result is a kind of revolution within the self system. The balance of power shifts in favor of the cross-gender identity with consequent disorganization and conflict within the self system. One result can be a quest to resolve the tension through sexual reassignment procedures or hormonal feminization. (1988, 3)

Transsexuals, however, have also indicated a sense from an early age of being in the wrong body (Morris 1975). Sexologists and psychiatrists have debated whether this anomalous gender identity is the result of biology, parenting, or retrospective reconstruction.[5]

The social task for transsexuals is to construct a gender identity without an appropriately gendered biography.[6] To create a feminized self, men-to-women transsexuals use the male transvestite's "strategies and rituals" of passing as a woman—clothing, makeup, hair styling, manicures, gestures, ways of walking, voice pitch, and "the more subtle gestures such as the difference in ways men and women smoke cigarettes" and the vocabulary women use (Bolin 1988, 131–41). Creating a new gender identity means creating a paper trail of bank, social security, educational, and job history records; drivers' licenses, passports, and credit cards all have to be changed once the new name becomes legal (pp. 145–46). Then significant others have to be persuaded to act their parts, too. Discussing men-to-women transsexuals, Anne Bolin notes:

> The family is the source of transsexuals' birth and nurturance as males and symbolically can be a source of their birth and nurturance as females. Thus, when their families accept them as females, refer to them by their female names, and use feminine gender references, it is a profound event in the transsexuals' lives, one in which their gender identity as females is given a retroactive credence.... The family is a significant battleground on which a symbolic identity war is waged.... Because an individual can only be a son or daughter [in Western societies], conferral of daughterhood by a mother is a statement of the death of a son. (1988, 94)

The final rite of passage is not only passing as a visibly and legally identifiable gendered person with a bona fide kinship status but passing as a *sexual* person. For Bolin's men-to-women transsexuals, "the most desirable condition for the first passing adventure is at night with a 'genetic girlfriend' in a heterosexual bar" (p. 140).

Some transsexuals become gay or lesbian. In Anne Bolin's study population of seventeen men-to-women transsexuals, only one was exclusively heterosexual in orientation (1988, Fig. 1, 62). Nine were bisexual, and six were exclusively lesbian, including two transsexuals who held a wedding ceremony in a gay church.[7] Justifying the identification as lesbian by a preoperative man-to-woman transsexual who had extensive hormone therapy and had developed female secondary sexual characteristics, Deborah Heller Feinbloom and her co-authors argue that someone "living full-time in a female role must be called a woman, albeit a woman with male genitalia (and without female genitalia)," although potential lovers might not agree (1976, 69).[8] If genitalia, sexuality, and gender identity are seen as a package, then it is paradoxical for someone to change their anatomy in order to make love with someone they could easily have had a sexual relationship with "normally." But gender identity (being a member of a group, women or men) and gender status (living the life of a woman or a man) are quite distinct from sexual desire for a woman or man. It is Western culture's preoccupation with genitalia as the markers of both sexuality and gender and the concept of these social statuses as fixed for life that produces the problem and the surgical solution for those who cannot tolerate the personal ambiguities Western cultures deny.[9]

Gender Masquerades

Transvestites change genders by cross-dressing, masquerading as a person of a different gender for erotic, pragmatic, or rebellious reasons. Since they can put on and take off gender by changing clothes, they disrupt the conventional conflation of sex, sexuality, and gender in Western cultures much more than transsexuals do.

François Timoléon de Choisy was a seventeenth-century courtier, historian, ambassador, and priest who was "indefatigably heterosexual" but a constant cross-dresser. The Abbé de Choisy married women twice, once as a woman, once as a man, and both spouses had children by him. He survived the turmoil of gender ambiguity by going to live in another community or country when the censure got too vociferous (Garber 1992, 255–59). The Chevalier (sometimes Chevalière) d'Eon de Beaumont, a famous cross-dresser who lived in the eighteenth century, seems to have been celibate. Because d'Eon did not have any sexual relationships, English and French bookmakers took serious bets on whether d'Eon was a man or a woman. Physically, he was a male, according to his birth and death certificates, and he lived forty-nine years as a man (259–66). He also lived thirty-four years as a woman, many of them with a woman companion who "was astounded to learn that she was a man" (265). Garber asks: "Does the fact that he was born a male infant and died 'with the male organs perfectly formed' mean that he was, in the years between, a man? A 'very man'" (255)? A man in what sense—physical, sexual, or gendered?

Some men who pass as women and women who pass as men by cross-dressing say they do so because they want privileges or opportunities the other gender has, but they may also be fighting to alter their society's expectations for their own gender. One of her biographers says of George Sand:

> While still a child she lost her father, tried to fill his place with a mother whom she adored, and, consequently, developed a masculine attitude strengthened by the boyish upbringing which she received at the hands of a somewhat eccentric tutor who encouraged her to wear a man's clothes.... For the rest of her life she strove, unconsciously, to recreate the free paradise of her childhood, with the result that she could never submit to a master.... Impatient of all masculine authority, she fought a battle for the emancipation of women, and sought to win for them the right to dispose freely of their bodies and their hearts. (Maurois 1955, 13)[10]

Natalie Davis calls these defiers of the social order disorderly women. Their outrage and ridicule produce a double message; they ask for a restoration of the social order purified of excesses of gender disadvantage, and their own gender inversion also suggests possibilities for change (1975, 124–51).[11]

During the English Renaissance, open cross-dressing on the street and in the theater defied accepted gender categories.[12] In early modern England, the state enforced class and gender boundaries through sumptuary laws that dictated who could wear certain colors, fabrics, and furs. Cross-dressing and wearing clothes "above one's station" (servants and masters trading places, also a theatrical convention) thus were important symbolic subverters of social hierarchies at a time of changing modes of production and a rising middle class (Howard 1988). Since seventeenth-century cross-dressing up-ended concepts of appropriate sexuality, the fashion was accused of feminizing men and masculinizing women: "When women took men's clothes, they symbolically left their subordinate positions. They became masterless women, and this threatened overthrow of hierarchy was discursively read as the eruption of uncontrolled sexuality" (Howard 1988, 424).

The way the gender order got critiqued and then restored can be seen in a famous Renaissance play about a cross-dressing character called the "roaring girl." *The Roaring Girl*, by Thomas Middleton and Thomas Dekker, written in 1608–1611, was based on a real-life woman, Mary Frith, who dressed in men's clothes and was "notorious as a bully, whore, bawd, pickpurse, fortune-teller, receiver [of stolen goods], and forger" (Bullen 1935, 4). She also smoked and drank like a man and was in prison for a time. She lived to the age of seventy-four. In Middleton and Dekker's play, this roaring girl, called Moll Cutpurse, becomes a model of morality. She remains chaste, and thus free of men sexually and economically, unlike most poor women, as she herself points out:

> Distressed needlewomen and trade-fallen wives,
> Fish that must needs bite or themselves be bitten,
> Such hungry things as these may soon be took
> With a worm fastened on a golden hook. (III, i, 96–97)

Her cross-dressing allows her to observe and question the ways of thieves and pickpockets not to learn to be a criminal but to protect herself. She can protect any man who marries her:

> You may pass where you list, through crowd most thick,
> And come off bravely with your purse unpick'd.
> You do not know the benefits I bring with me;
> No cheat dares work upon you with thumb or knife,
> While you've a roaring girl to your son's wife. (V, ii, 159–63)

But she feels she is too independent to be a traditional wife:

> I have no humour to marry; I love to lie a' both sides a' the bed myself: and again, a' th' other side, a wife, you know, ought to be obedient, but I fear me I am too headstrong to obey; therefore I'll ne'er go about it. (II, ii, 37–41)

Her other reason for not marrying is that men cheat, lie, and treat women badly. If they changed, "next day following I'll be married," to which another character in the play responds: "This sounds like doomsday" (V, ii, 226–27), not likely to happen soon.

Despite her gloomy views on men and marriage, Moll helps a young couple marry by pretending to be wooed by the man. His father, who has withheld his consent for his son's original choice, is so outraged that the son is thinking of marrying Moll Cutpurse that he willingly consents to his son's marriage to the woman he had loved all along. Thus, rather poignantly, Moll's independence and street smarts are invidious traits when compared to those of a "good woman." Her cross-dressing is not a defiance of the gender order, but rather places her outside it:

> 'tis woman more than man,
> Man more than woman; and, which to none can hap
> The sun gives her two shadows to one shape;
> Nay, more, let this strange thing walk, stand, or sit,
> No blazing star draws more eyes after it. (I, i, 251–55)

Moll Cutpurse's social isolation means that the gender order does not have to change to incorporate her independence as a woman: "a politics of despair . . . affirms a seemingly inevitable exclusion of marginal genders from the territory of the natural and the real" (Butler 1990, 146).

Affirming Gender

In most societies with only two gender statuses—"women" and "men"—those who live in the status not meant for them usually do not challenge the social institution of gender. In many ways, they reinforce it. Joan of Arc, says Marina Warner (1982) in discussing her transvestism, "needed a framework of virtue, and so she borrowed the apparel of men, who held a monopoly on virtue, on reason and courage, while eschewing the weakness of women, who were allotted to the negative pole, where virtue meant meekness and humility, and nature meant carnality" (147). A masculine woman may be an abomination to tradition, but from a feminist point of view, she is not a successful rebel, for she reinforces dominant men's standards of the good: "The male trappings were used as armor—defensive and aggressive. It . . . attacked men by aping their appearance in order to usurp their functions. On the personal level, it defied men and declared them useless; on the social level, it affirmed male supremacy, by needing to borrow the appurtenances to assert personal needs and desires...; men remain the touchstone and equality a process of imitation" (Warner 1982, 155).[13]

Joan of Arc said she donned armor not to pass as a man, but to be beyond sexuality, beyond gender. She called herself *pucelle*, a maid, but socially, she was neither woman nor man. She was an "ideal androgyne": "She could thereby transcend her sex; she could set herself apart and usurp the privileges of the male and his claims to superiority. At the same time, by never pretending to be other than a woman and a maid, she was usurping a man's function but shaking off the trammels of his sex altogether to occupy a different, third order, neither male nor female, but unearthly, like the angels" (Warner 1982, 145–46).

When Joan was on trial, she was denuded of her knightly armor and accused of female carnality, and then she was burned at the stake—as a woman and a witch. Twenty-five years later, at her rehabilitation trial, and in 1920, when she was declared a saint, she was presented as a sexless virgin, amenorrheic and possibly anorectic.

As a heroine today, Joan of Arc is more likely to be a symbolic Amazon, a woman warrior, than an ideal androgyne, sexless and saintly. The ambiguity of her gender representation was corroborated by one of the first women to enter West Point to be trained with men as an army officer. On her first day in the dining hall, Carol Barkalow "was startled to find among the depictions of history's greatest warriors the muralist's interpretation of Joan of Arc. There she stood in silver armor, alongside Richard the Lion Hearted and William the Conqueror, sword uplifted in one hand, helmet clasped in the other, red hair falling to her shoulders, with six knights kneeling in homage at her feet" (1990, 27). As Barkalow found later, the warrior maid had set little precedent for the acceptance of women as military leaders. The mixed-gender message of the portrait was prescient, for the main problem at West Point seemed to be one of categorization—women army officers were suspect as women when they looked and acted too much like men, but they were a puzzlement as soldiers when they looked and acted like women.

Other Genders

There are non-Western societies that have third and fourth genders that link genitalia, sexual orientation, and gender status in ways quite different from Western cultures. These statuses demonstrate how physical sex, sexuality, and gender interweave, but are separate elements conferring different levels of prestige and stigma.

The Native American berdache is an institutionalized cross-gendered role that legitimates males doing women's work. The berdache can also be a sacred role, and if a boy's dreaming indicates a pull toward the berdache status, parents would not think of dissenting. Although it would seem logical that societies that put a high emphasis on aggressive masculinity, like the Plains Indians, would offer the berdache status as a legitimate way out for boys reluctant to engage in violent play and warfare, berdaches do not occur in all warlike tribes and do occur in some that are not warlike (Williams 1986, pp. 47–49).[14]

Berdaches educate children, sing and dance at tribal events, tend the ill, carry provisions for war parties, and have special ritual functions (Whitehead 1981, 89; Williams 1986, 54–61). Among the Navahos, berdaches not only do women's craft work, but also farm and raise sheep, which are ordinarily men's work: "Beyond this, because they are believed to be lucky in amassing wealth they usually act as the head of their family and have control of the disposal of all the family's property" (Williams 1986, 61).

Berdaches are legitimately homosexual:

> Homosexual behavior may occur between non-berdache males, but the cultures emphasize the berdache as the usual person a man would go to for male sex. With the role thus institutionalized, the berdache serves the sexual needs of many men without competing against the institution of heterosexual marriage. Men are not required to make a choice between being heterosexual or being homosexual, since they can accommodate both desires. Nevertheless, for that minority of men who do wish to make such a choice, a number of cultures allow them the option of becoming the husband to a berdache. (Williams 1986, 108–9)

Since homosexual relationships do not make a man into a berdache, Walter Williams makes a distinction between homosexuality, as sexual relations between two men, and heterogendered sexual relations, between a man and a berdache: "The berdache and his male partner do not occupy the same recognized gender status" (96). Two berdaches do not have sexual relations with each other, nor do they marry. In some cultures, the berdache's husband loses no prestige; in others, he does, coming in for kidding for having an unusual sexual relationship, like a young man married to an older woman (Williams 1986, 113). Sometimes the joking is because the berdache is a particularly good provider. The berdache's husband is not labeled a homosexual, and if a divorce occurs, he can easily make a heterosexual marriage.

The berdache is not the equivalent of the Western male homosexual (Callender and Kochems 1985). The berdache's social status is defined by work and dress and sometimes a sacred calling; the social status of modern western homosexual men is defined by sexual orientation and preference for men as sexual partners (Whitehead 1981, 97–98). The berdache's gender status is not that of a man but of a woman, so their homosexual relationships are heterogendered; homosexual couples in Western society are homogendered.

The Plains Indians had a tradition of *warrior women*, but a cross-gender status for younger women was not institutionalized in most Native American tribes (Blackwood 1984, 37). Harriet Whitehead argues that because men were considered superior in these cultures, it was harder for women to breach the gender boundaries upward than it was for men to breach them downward (1981, 86). Walter Williams speculates that every woman was needed to have children (1986, 244). The tribes that did allow women to cross gender boundaries restricted the privilege to women who claimed they never menstruated (Whitehead 1981, 92). Young women could become men in societies that were egalitarian and tolerant of cross-gendered work activities (Blackwood 1984). Among the Mohave, a girl's refusal to learn women's tasks could lead to her being taught the same skills boys learned and to ritual renaming, nose piercing, and hair styling as a man. At that point, her status as a man allowed her to marry a woman and to do men's work of hunting, trapping, growing crops, and fighting. She was also expected to perform a man's ritual obligations. Because divorce was frequent and children went with the mother, cross-gendered women could rear children. Adoptions were also common. Sexually, cross-gendered women were homosexual, but, like berdaches, their marriages were always heterogendered—they did not marry or have sexual relationships with each other.[15] Among less egalitarian Native American societies, a legitimate cross-gender status, *manly hearted woman*, was available for post-menopausal women who acquired wealth (Whitehead 1981, 90–93). In some African cultures today, a wealthy woman can marry a woman and adopt her children as a father (Amadiume 1987).

Lesbians in Western societies differ from cross-gendered women in Native American and African societies in that they do not form heterogendered couples. Both women in a lesbian couple continue to be identified socially as women; neither becomes a "husband." If they have children, neither becomes a "father," both are mothers to the children (Weston 1991).

Hijras are a group in northern India who consider themselves intersexed men who have become women; many, but not all, undergo ritualistic castration (Nanda 1990). They serve both a legitimate cultural function as ritual performers, and an illegitimate sexual function, as homosexual prostitutes. Sometimes they are considered women, sometimes men, but they are deviant in either status not because of their sexuality but because they don't have children. Hijras are required to dress as women, but they do not imitate or try to pass as ordinary women; rather, they are as deviant as women as they are as men:

> Their female dress and mannerisms are exaggerated to the point of caricature, expressing sexual overtones that would be considered inappropriate for ordinary women in their roles as daughters, wives, and mothers. Hijra performances are

> burlesques of female behavior. Much of the comedy of their behavior derives from the incongruities between their behavior and that of traditional women. They use coarse and abusive speech and gestures in opposition to the Hindu ideal of demure and restrained femininity. Further, it is not at all uncommon to see hijras in female clothing sporting several days growth of beard, or exposing hairy, muscular arms. The ultimate sanction of hijras to an abusive or unresponsive public is to lift their skirts and expose the mutilated genitals. The implicit threat of this shameless, and thoroughly unfeminine, behavior is enough to make most people give them a few cents so they will go away. (Nanda 1986, 38)

Hijras live separately in their own communal households, relating to each other as fictive mothers, daughters, sisters, grandmothers, and aunts. Occupationally, they sing and dance at weddings and births, run bathhouses, work as cooks and servants, and engage in prostitution with men; or they are set up in households by men in long-term sexual relationships. The hijras who Serena Nanda interviewed came from lower class, middle-caste families in small cities and said they had wanted to dress and act as women from early childhood. They left home because of parental disapproval and to protect their siblings' chances for marriage (65).

Hijras worship Bahuchara Mata, a mother-goddess. Shiva is also sometimes worshiped by hijras, for his manifestation in half-man, half-woman form. In the great Indian legend, the *Mahabharata,* one of the heroes, Arjuna, lives for a year in exile as a woman, doing menial work and teaching singing and dancing. Those who were not men and not women were blessed by Ram in the Hindu epic, *Ramayana*. In addition to these Hindu religious connections, Islam is also involved in hijra culture. The founders of the original seven hijra communal "houses," or subgroups, were said to be Muslim, and in keeping with this tradition, modern houses also have Muslim gurus. This religious legitimation and their performance of cultural rituals integrate hijras into Indian society, as does the Indian tradition of creative asceticism. Young, sexually active hijras, however, are seen by the elders as compromising the ascetic sources of their legitimacy.

Hijras seem to resemble transvestite performers (female impersonators or "drag queens") in modern Western society. But transvestite performers do not have roots in Western religious tradition, nor are they castrated. Castrated hijras do not have the same social status as men-to-women transsexuals in Western societies, since transsexuals act as normal women, and hijras do not. In some respects, hijras resemble the castrati of European operatic tradition.

In the seventeenth century, because the Roman Catholic church forbade women to sing in public, women's parts were sung by castrati, boys whose testicles were removed in adolescence so their voices would remain soprano. Throughout the eighteenth century, castrati and women singers both appeared on the operatic stage, often in competition, although the castrati had the advantages of far superior training, respectability, church support, and fame. There was constant gender reversal in casting and plot. Women contraltos sang men's roles in men's clothes (now called "trouser roles"); soprano castrati sang the "leading ladies" in women's costumes (*en travesti*); and both masqueraded in plots of mistaken or hidden identity in the clothes of the role's opposite but their actual gender.

Casanova, in his memoirs, tells of being sexually attracted to a supposed castrato, Bellino, in the early 1740s. This attraction totally confounded his notorious ability to "smell" a woman in his presence, so he was much relieved, when he seduced Bellino (in anticipation of homosexual sex), to find out that Bellino was a woman soprano posing as a eunuch in order to sing in Rome. Of course, she sang women's roles. She had heterosexual sex with Casanova, although this womanizer was just as ready to make love with a man (Ellison 1992).[16]

A third type of institutionalized intermediate gender role are the xaniths of Oman, a strictly gender-segregated Islamic society in which women's sexual purity is guarded by their wearing long, black robes and black face masks when in public and by not mingling with men other than close relatives at home (Wikan 1982, 168–86). Xaniths are homosexual prostitutes who dress in men's clothes but in pastel colors rather than white, wear their hair in neither a masculine nor a feminine style, and have feminine mannerisms. They sing and eat with the women at weddings, mingle freely with women, but they maintain men's legal status. (Women are lifelong minors; they must have a male guardian.) They are not considered full-fledged women because they are prostitutes, and women, in Oman ideology, may engage in sexual acts only with their husbands. The xaniths' social role is to serve as sexual outlets for unmarried or separated men, and thus they protect the sexual purity of women. The men who use them as sexual outlets are not considered homosexual, because supposedly they always take the active role.

Xaniths live alone and take care of their own households, doing both men's work—the marketing—and women's work—food preparation. Being a xanith seems to be a family tradition, in that several brothers will become xaniths. They move in and out of the gender status fairly easily, reverting to manhood when they marry and successfully deflower their brides. To be considered a man, a groom must show bloody evidence of defloration or accuse his bride of not having been a virgin. A xanith, therefore, who shows he has successfully deflowered a virgin bride becomes a man. Just as a female in Oman culture is not a woman until she has intercourse, a male is not a man until he successfully consummates his marriage. A woman, though, can never revert to the virgin state of girlhood, but a man can revert to xanithhood by singing with the women at the next wedding.

In the sense that passive homosexual sex rather than heterogendered behavior is the defining criteria of status, the xanith is closest to the feminized homosexual prostitute in Western culture, but not, according to Wikan, to homosexual men in other Middle Eastern cultures:

> Homosexual practice is a common and recognized phenomenon in many Middle Eastern cultures, often in the form of an institutionalized practice whereby older men seek sexual satisfaction with younger boys. But this homosexual relationship generally has two qualities that make it fundamentally different from that practiced in Oman. First, it is part of a deep friendship or love relationship between two men, which has qualities, it is often claimed, of being purer and more beautiful than love between man and woman.... Second, both parties play both the active and the passive sexual role—either simultaneously or through time. (1982, 177)

One or the Other, Never Both

> Michel Foucault, in the introduction to Barbin's memoirs, says of the concept of "one true sex": Biological theories of sexuality, juridical conceptions of the individual, forms of administrative control in modern nations, led little by little to rejecting the idea of a mixture of the two sexes in a single body, and consequently to limiting the free choice of indeterminate individuals. Henceforth, everybody was to have one and only one sex. Everybody was to have his or her primary, profound, determined and determining sexual identity; as for the elements of the other sex that might appear, they could only be accidental, superficial, or even quite simply illusory. (1980, viii)

Yet, in Western societies, despite our firm belief that each person has one sex, one sexuality, and one gender, congruent with each other and fixed for life, and that these categories are one of only two sexes, two sexualities, and two genders, hermaphrodites, pseudohermaphrodites, transsexuals, transvestites, and bisexuals exhibit a dizzying fluidity of bodies, desires, and social statuses. According to Annie Woodhouse, "punters" are men "who don't want to go to bed with a man, but don't want to go to bed with a real woman either." So they go to bed with men dressed as women (1989, 31). The ambiguous appearance of the women Holly Devor (1989) interviewed was typed as "mannish," and so they had difficulty being considered "opposite" enough for heterosexual relationships. As lesbians, their appearance was not only acceptable, but they could, and did, sexually excite other women when passing as men, as did Deborah Sampson, the woman who fought in the American Revolution in a man's uniform, and Nadezhda Durova, the Russian "cavalry maiden" in the Napoleonic Wars (Durova 1989; Freeman and Bond 1992). Marjorie Garber writes of Yvonne Cook, a man who dresses as a woman, considers herself a lesbian and has a woman lover who dresses as a man (1992, 4).

All these components can change and shift back and forth over days, weeks, months, and years. With unisex clothing, gender can change in minutes, depending on the context and the response of others to gender cues. Bisexuals have long-term serial relationships with women and men, but may define themselves as either heterosexual or homosexual. Transvestites consciously play with sexual and gender categories. Gay men, lesbians, and bisexuals cross Western culture's sexual boundaries but do not always challenge gender norms. Transsexuals, in their quest for "normality," often reaffirm them. Through their "subversive bodily acts," all demonstrate the social constructedness of sex, sexuality, and gender (Butler 1990, 79–141). But they have not disrupted the deep genderedness of the modem Western world. And to maintain genderedness, to uphold gender boundaries, the "impulses toward, or fear of, turning into someone of the opposite sex" that many ordinary, normal people feel, have to be suppressed (Stoller 1985, 152).

The norms, expectations, and evaluation of women and men may be converging, but we have no social place for a person who is neither woman nor man. A man who passes as a woman or a woman as a man still violates strong social boundaries, and when transsexuals change gender, they still cross a great divide. In this sense, Western culture resembles the intensely gendered world of Islam, where all the rules of marriage, kinship, inheritance, purity, modesty, ritual, and even burial are challenged by people of ambiguous sex (Sanders 1991). Rather than allowing the resultant social ambiguity to continue, medieval Islamic jurists developed a set of rules for gendering hermaphrodites: "A person with ambiguous genitalia or with no apparent sex might have been a biological reality, but it had no gender and, therefore, no point of entry into the social world: it was unsocialized" (Sanders 1991, 88). As in modern Western society, a person who was neither woman nor man had no social place and could have no social relationships without disturbing the social order: "What was at stake for medieval Muslims in gendering one ungendered body was, by implication, gendering the most important body: the social body" (89). The social body in modern Western society, both for the individual and the group, is, above all, gendered.

Notes

1. The passage as Colette wrote it is: "At a time when I was, when at least I believed I was insensitive to Damien, I suggested to him that he and I would make a pair of ideal traveling companions, both courteously selfish, easy to please, and fond of long silences....

   'I like to travel only with women,' he answered.

   The sweet tone of his voice scarcely softened the brutality of his words... He was afraid he had hurt my feelings and tried to make up, with something even worse.

   'A woman? You? I know you would like to be one...'" (1933, 75; ellipses in the original).
2. After reclassification, Barbin, who had been a certified and competent schoolteacher, had to look for men's work. Bolin (1988, 156–57) notes a similar problem for men-to-women transsexuals who worked in fields dominated by men.
3. Richard Sadove M.D., personal communication. Dr. Sadove did the reconstructive surgery.
4. Fausto-Sterling 1985, 87–88, Herdt 1990, 437–38.
5. Most of the research is on men-to-women transsexuals. For reviews, see Bolin 1987; Docter 1988. For a scathing critique of transsexual research and practice, see Stoller 1985, 152–70. For a critique of the medical construction of transsexualism as a fixed core identity, see Billings and Urban 1982.
6. See Garfinkel 1967, 116–85, for a detailed account of how Bill-Agnes managed the practical details of passing while constructing a new gendered identity. Raymond (1979) is critical of men-to-women's gender identity because they have not had

the previous experience of women's oppression.

7. Bolin's data on five transsexuals' postoperative sexual relationships indicated that three were bisexual and one was lesbian (181).
8. There have also been relationships between women-to-men and men-to-women transsexuals; these, however, are heterosexual and heterogendered (Money 1988, 93).
9. Actually, the mark of gender identity in Western culture is the penis—the person who has one of adequate size is male and a man; the person who does not, is not-male, not a man. Femaleness and womanhood seem to be more problematic and need more "work" to construct. For an opposite view about masculinity, see Gilmore 1990.
10. Also see Heilbrun 1988, 32–36; L. J. Kaplan 1991, 492–500.
11. Also see Smith-Rosenberg 1985.
12. Dollimore 1986; Greenblatt 1987, 66–93; Howard 1988; Lavine 1986. On the fluidity of representations of bodily sex during the Renaissance, see Laqueur 1990a, 114–34. On the "semiotics of dress" in modern life, see E. Wilson 1985.
13. Also see Wheelwright 1989, 9–15.
14. Bolin lists seventy North and South American Indian tribes that have berdaches (1987, 61n).
15. By the end of the nineteenth century, the adoption of Western sexual and gender mores led to the delegitimation of the female cross-gender status (Blackwood 1984, 39–40), but not the male, according to W. L. Williams (1986).
16. The last known castrato, Alessandro Moreschi (1858–1922), made a series of recordings in 1902 and 1903, the year Pope Pius X formally banned castrati from the papal chapel, but he sang in the Sistine Chapel choir until 1913 (Ellison 1992, 37).

Coming of Age and Coming Out Ceremonies Across Cultures

GILBERT HERDT

Coming of age and being socialized into the sexual lifeways of the culture through ceremonies and initiation rites are common in many cultures of the world. These traditions help to incorporate the individual—previously a child, possibly outside of the moral rules and sexual roles of the adult group—into the public institutions and practices that bring full citizenship. We have seen in prior chapters many examples of these transitions and ceremonial practices, and we are certainly justified in thinking of them as basic elements in the human condition. Coming of age or "puberty" ceremonies around the world are commonly assumed to introduce the young person to sexual life as a heterosexual. In both traditional and modern societies, ritual plays a role in the emergence of sexuality and the support of desires and relationships expected in later life.

Yet not all of this is seamless continuity, and in the study of homosexuality across cultures we must be aware of the gaps and barriers that exist between what is experienced in childhood or adolescence and the roles and customs in adulthood that may negate or oppose these experiences. Ruth Benedict (1938) stresses how development in a society may create cultural discontinuities in this sexual and gender cycle of identities and roles, necessitating rituals. She hints that homosexuality in particular may cause discontinuity of this kind, and the life stories of many gays and lesbians in western society reveal this problem. But in all societies, there is an issue of connecting childhood with adulthood, with the transition from sexual or biological immaturity to sexual maturity. In short, these transitions may create a "life crisis" that requires a social solution—and this is the aim of initiation ceremonies and rites of transition. Rituals may provide for the individual the necessary means to achieve difficult changes in sexual and gender status. Particularly in deeply emotional rituals, the energy of the person can be fully invested or bonded to the newfound group. This may create incredible attachments of the kind we have observed among the ancient Greeks, the feudal Japanese, and the Sambia of New Guinea, wherein the younger boy is erotically involved or partnered with an older male. In the conditions of a warrior society, homoerotic partnerships are particularly powerful when they are geared to the survival of the group.

The transition out of presumptive heterosexuality and secrecy and into the active process of self-identifying as gay or lesbian in the western tradition bears close comparison with these rites of passage. In the process of "coming out"—the current western concept of ritual passage—as gay or lesbian, a person undergoes emotional changes and a transformation in sexuality and gender that are remarkable and perhaps equal in their social drama to the initiation rites of small societies in New Guinea and Africa. Thus, the collective aspirations and desires of the adolescent or child going through the ritual to belong, participate in, and make commitments to communities of his or her own kind take on a new and broader scope.

Coming out is an implicit rite of passage for people who are in a crisis of identity that finds them "betwixt and between" being presumed to be heterosexual and living a totally secret and hidden life as a homosexual. Not until they enter into the gay or lesbian lifeway or the sexual culture of the gay and lesbian community will they begin to learn and be socialized into the rules, knowledge, and social roles and relationships of the new cultures. For many people, this experience is liberating; it is a highly charged, emotional, and dramatic process that changes them into adult gays or lesbians in all areas of their lives—with biological families, with coworkers, with friends or schoolmates, and with a sexual and romantic partner of the same gender, possibly for the rest of their lives.

This transformation in the self and in social relations brings much that is new and sometimes frightening. An alternative moral system is opened up by the rituals. Why people who desire the same gender require a ritual when others in our society do not is painfully clear, Ritual is necessary because of the negative images, stigma, and intense social contamination that continue to exist in the stereotypes and antihomosexual laws of our society. To be homosexual is to be discredited as a full person in society; it is to have a spoiled identity—as a homosexual in society or as a frightened closet homosexual who may be disliked by openly gay and lesbian friends. But perhaps of greatest importance are the repression and social censorship involved: to have one's desires suppressed, to even experience the inner or "true" self as a secret.

It is hard to break through this taboo alone or without the support of a community because doing so exposes the person to all sorts of risk, requires considerable personal resources, and precipitates an emotional vulnerability that for many is very difficult to bear. But that is not all. For some people in our society, homosexuality is a danger and a source of pollution. Once the person's homosexuality is revealed, the stigma can also spread to the family, bringing the pollution of shame and dishonor to father and mother, clan and community. This is the old mask of the evil of homosexuality.... And this is what we have found in a study of these matters in Chicago (Herdt and Boxer 1996).

It is very typical to see an intense and negative reaction of family members to the declaration of same-sex desires by adolescents, even this late in the twentieth century. Society changes slowly and its myths even more slowly. For many people, homosexuality is an evil as frightening to the imagination as the monsters of bad Hollywood movies. Many people find it extremely difficult to deal with homosexuality and may exert strong pressures on their young to hide and suppress their feelings. Consequently, young people may feel that by declaring their same-sex desires, they will betray their families or the traditions of their sexual culture and its lifeways, which privilege marriage and the carrying on of the family name. And the younger person who desires the same gender may be afraid to come out for fear of dishonoring his or her ethnic community in the same way. To prevent these reactions, many people—closet homosexuals in the last century and many who fear the effects today—hide their basic feelings and all of their desires from their friends and families.

Here is where we may learn a lesson from other cultures. The mechanism of ritual helps to teach about the trials and ordeals of passages in other times and places, which in itself is a comfort, for it signals something basic in the human condition. To come out is to openly challenge sexual chauvinism, homophobia, and bias—refusing to continue the stigma and pollution of the past and opening new support and positive role models where before there were none. Through examples from New Guinea, the Mojave, and the Chicago gay and lesbian group, I examine these ideas in the following pages.

Many cultures around the world celebrate coming of age with a variety of events and rituals that introduce the person to sexual life. Indeed, initiation can be an introduction to sexual development and erotic life (Hart 1963). In Aboriginal Australia and New Guinea wherever the precolonial secret societies of the region flourished, the nature of all sexual interaction was generally withheld from prepubertal boys and girls until initiation. It often began their sense of sexual being, even if they had not achieved sexual puberty, since maturation often occurred late in these societies. Many of the Pacific societies actually disapproved of childhood sexual play, for this was felt to disrupt marriage and social regulation of premarital social relations. The Sambia are no different, having delayed sexual education until the initiation of boys and girls in different secret contexts for each. The stories of Sambia boys are clear in associating the awakening of their sexuality in late childhood with their initiation rites and fellatio debut with adolescent bachelor partners. The definition of social reality was thus opened up to same-gender sexuality.

Sambia Boys' Ritual Initiation

The Sambia are a tribe numbering more than two thousand people in the Eastern Highlands of Papua New Guinea. Most elements of culture and social organization are constructed around the nagging destructive presence of warfare in the area. Descent is patrilineal and residence is patrilocal to maximize the cohesion of the local group as a warriorhood. Hamlets are composed of tiny exogamous patriclans that facilitate marriage within the group and exchange with other hamlets, again based on the local politics of warfare. Traditionally, all marriage was arranged; courtship is unknown, and social relationships between the sexes are not only ritually polarized but also often hostile. Like other Highlands societies of New Guinea, these groups are associated with a men's secret society that ideologically disparages women as dangerous creatures who can pollute men and deplete them of their masculine substance. The means of creating and maintaining the village-based secret society is primarily through the ritual initiation of boys beginning at ages seven through ten and continuing until their arranged and consummated marriages, many years later. The warriorhood is guaranteed by collective ritual initiations connecting neighboring hamlets. Within a hamlet, this warriorhood is locally identified with the men's clubhouse, wherein all initiated bachelors reside. Married men frequent the clubhouse constantly; and on occasion (during fight times, rituals, or their wives' menstrual periods) they sleep there. An account of Sambia culture and society has been published elsewhere and need not be repeated here (Herdt 1981).

Sambia sexual culture, which operates on the basis of a strongly essentializing model of sexual development, also incorporates many ideas of social support and cultural creation of the sexual; these ideas derive from the role of ritual and supporting structures of gendered ontologies throughout the life course of men and women. Sexual development, according to the cultural ideals of the Sambia life plan, is fundamentally distinct for men and women. Biological femaleness is considered "naturally" competent and innately complete; maleness, in contrast, is considered more problematic since males are believed incapable of achieving adult reproductive manliness without ritual treatment. Girls are born with female genitalia, a birth canal, a womb, and, behind that, a functional menstrual-blood organ, or *tingu*. Feminine behaviors such as gardening and mothering are thought to be by-products of women's natural *tingu* functioning. As the *tingu* and womb become engorged with blood, puberty and menarche occur; the menses regularly follow, and they are linked with women's child-bearing capacities. According to the canonical male view, all women then need is a penis (i.e., semen) in facilitating adult procreation by bestowing breast milk (transformed from semen), which prepares a woman for nursing her newborn. According to the women's point of view, however, women are biologically competent and can produce their own breast milk—a point of conflict between the two gendered ontologies. This gives rise to a notion that women have a greater internal resilience and health than males and an almost inexhaustible sexual appetite. By comparison, males are not competent biologically until they achieve manhood, and thus they require constant interventions of ritual to facilitate maturation.

The Sambia believe that boys will not "naturally" achieve adult competence without the interventions of ritual, an idea that may seem strange but is actually common throughout New Guinea, even in societies that do not practice boy-inseminating rites (Herdt 1993). Among the Sambia, the practice of age-structured homoerotic relations is a transition into adulthood. The insemination of boys ideally ends when a man marries and fathers a child. In fact, the vast majority of males—more than 90 percent—terminate their sexual relations with boys at that time. Almost all the men do so because of the taboos and, to a lesser degree, because they have "matured" to a new level of having exclusive sexual access to one or more wives, with genital sexual pleasure being conceived of as a greater privilege.

The sexual culture of the Sambia men instills definite and customary lifeways that involves a formula for the life course. Once initiated (before age ten), the boys undergo ordeals to have their "female" traces (left over from birth and from living with their mothers) removed; these ordeals involve painful rites, such as nose-bleedings, that are intended to promote masculinity and aggression. The boys are then in a ritually "clean" state that enables the treatment of their bodies and minds in new ways. These boys are regarded as "pure" sexual virgins, which is important for their insemination. The men believe that the boys are unspoiled because they have not been exposed to the sexual pollution of women, which the men greatly fear. It is thus through oral intercourse that the men receive a special kind of pleasure, unfettered by pollution, and the boys are thought to acquire semen for growth, becoming strong and fertile. All the younger males are thus inseminated by older bachelors, who were once themselves semen recipients.

The younger initiates are semen recipients until their third-stage "puberty" ceremony, around age fifteen. Afterward, they become semen donors to the younger boys. According to the men's sacred lore and the dogmas of their secret society, the bachelors are "married" to the younger recipient males—as symbolized by secret ritual flutes, made of bamboo and believed to be empowered by female spirits that are said to be hostile to women. During this time, the older adolescents are "bisexuals" who may inseminate their wives orally, in addition to the secret insemination of the boys.

Eventually these youths have marriages arranged for them. After they become new fathers, they in turn stop sexual relations with boys. The men's family duties would be compromised by boy relations, the Sambia men say.

The growth of males is believed to be slower and more difficult than that of females. Men say that boys lack an endogenous means for creating manliness. Males do possess a *tingu* (menstrual blood) organ, but it is believed to be "dry" and nonfunctional. They reiterate that a mother's womb, menstrual blood, and vaginal fluids—all containing pollution—impede masculine growth for the boy until he is separated by initiation from mother and the women's world. Males also possess a semen organ (*keriku-keriku*), but unlike the female menstrual blood organ, it is intrinsically small, hard, and empty, containing no semen of its own. Although semen is believed to be the spark of human life and, moreover, the sole precipitant of biological maleness (strong bones and muscles and, later, male secondary-sex traits: a flat abdomen, a hairy body, a mature glans penis), the Sambia hold that the human body cannot naturally produce semen; it must be externally introduced. The purpose of ritual insemination through fellatio is to fill up the *keriku-keriku* (which then stores semen for adult use) and thereby masculinize the boy's body as well as his phallus. Biological maleness is therefore distinct from the mere possession of male genitalia, and only repeated inseminations begun at an early age and regularly continued for years confer the reproductive competence that culminates in sexual development and manliness.

There are four functions of semen exchange: (1) the cultural purpose of "growing" boys through insemination, which is thought to substitute for mother's milk; (2) the "masculinizing" of boys' bodies, again through insemination, but also through ritual ordeals meant to prepare them for warrior life; (3) the provision of "sexual play" or pleasure for the older youths, who have no other sexual outlet prior to marriage; and (4) the transmission of semen and soul substance from one generation of clansmen to the next, which is vital for spiritual and ritual power to achieve its rightful ends (Herdt 1984b). These elements of institutionalized boy-inseminating practices are the object of the most vital and secret ritual teachings in first-stage initiation, which occurs before puberty. The novices are expected to be orally inseminated during the rituals and to continue the practice on a regular basis for years to come. The semen transactions are, however, rigidly structured homoerotically: Novices may act only as fellators in private sexual interactions with older bachelors, who are typically seen as dominant and in control of the same-sex contacts. The adolescent youth is the erotically active party during fellatio, for his erection and ejaculation are necessary for intercourse, and a boy's oral insemination is the socially prescribed outcome of the encounter. Boys must never reverse roles with the older partners or take younger partners before the proper ritual initiations. The violation of such rules is a moral wrong that is sanctioned by a variety of punishments. Boy-inseminating, then, is a matter of sexual relations between unrelated kin and must be seen in the same light as the semen exchanges of delayed sister exchange marriage: Hamlets of potential enemies exchange women and participate in semen exchange of boys, which is necessary for the production of children and the maturation of new warriors.

Ritual initiation for boys is conducted every three or four years for a whole group of boys as an age-set from neighboring villages. This event lasts several months and consists of many ordeals and transitions, some of them frightening and unpleasant, but overall welcomed as the entry into honorable masculinity and access to social power. It culminates in the boys' entry into the men's clubhouse, which is forbidden to women and children. The boys change their identities and roles and live on their own away from their parents until they are grown up and married. The men's house thus becomes their permanent dormitory and secret place of gender segregation.

Sambia girls do not experience initiation until many years later, when they undergo a formal marriage ceremony. Based on what is known, it seems doubtful that the girls undergo a sexual period of same-gender relations like those of the boys, but I cannot be sure because I was not permitted to enter the menstrual hut, where the initiations of girls were conducted. Males begin their ritual careers and the change in their sexual lives early because the transformation expected of the boys is so great. Girls live on with their parents until they are married and achieve their first menstruation, which occurs very late, age nineteen on average for the Sambia and their neighbors. A secret initiation is performed for the girls in the menstrual hut. Only then can they begin to have sexual relations with their husbands and live with them in a new house built by husband and wife.

The first-stage initiation ceremonies begin the events of life crisis and change in identities for the boys. They are young. After a period of time they are removed to the forest, where the most critical rituals begin to introduce them to the secrets of the men's house and the secret society of the men's warriorhood. The key events involve blood-letting rituals and penis-and-flute rites, which we study here from observations of the initiation conducted in 1975 (Herdt 1982). Here the boys experience the revelation of sexuality and the basic elements of their transition into age-structured homoerotic relations.

On the first morning of the secret rituals in the forest, the boys have fierce and painful nose-bleeding rituals performed on them. This is believed to remove the pollution of their mothers and the women's world that is identified with the boys' bodies. But it is also a testing ground to see how brave they are and the degree to which their fathers, older brothers, and the war leaders of the village can rely on the boys not to run and hide in times of war. Afterward, the boys are prepared by their ritual guardian, who is referred to as their "mother's brother," a kind of "male mother," for the main secret teaching that is to follow. They are dressed in the finest warrior decorations, which they have earned the right to wear through the initiation ordeals. And this begins their preparation for the rites of insemination that will follow. Now that their insides have been "cleansed" to receive the magical gift of manhood—semen—they are taken into the sacred chamber of a forest setting, and there they see for the first time the magical flutes, believed to be animated by the female spirit of the flute, which protects the men and the secrecy of the clubhouse and is thought to be hostile to women.

The key ceremony here is the penis-and-flutes ritual. It focuses on a secret teaching about boy insemination and is regarded by the men and boys alike as the most dramatic and awesome of all Sambia rituals. It begins with the older bachelors, the youths with whom the boys will engage in sexual relations later, who enter the chamber dressed up as the "female spirits of the flutes." The flute players appear, and in their presence, to the accompaniment of the wailing flutes, some powerful secrets of the men's cult are revealed. The setting is awesome: a great crowd waiting in silence as the mysterious sounds are first revealed; boys obediently lining up for threatening review by elders; and boys being told that secret fellatio exists and being taught how to engage in it. Throughout the ritual boys hear at close range the flute sounds associated since childhood with collective masculine power and mystery and pride. The flutes are unequivocally treated as phallic—as symbols of the penis and the power of men to openly flaunt their sexuality. The intent of the flutes' revelation is threatening to the boys as they begin to guess its meaning.

I have observed this flute ceremony during two different initiations, and although my western experience differs greatly from that of Sambia, one thing was intuitively striking to me: The men were revealing the *homoerotic meanings* of the sexual culture. This includes a great preoccupation with the penis and with semen but also with the mouth of the boy and penile erection, sexual impulses, homoerotic activities in particular, and the commencement of sexuality in its broadest sense for the boys. If there is a homoerotic core to the secret society of the Sambia, then this is surely where it begins. These revelations come as boys are enjoined to become fellators, made the sharers of ritual secrets, and threatened with death if they tell women or children what they have learned. They have to keep the secret forever.

Over the course of many years I collected the stories of the boys' experiences as they went through these rituals. The boys' comments indicated that they perceived several different social values bound up with the expression of homoerotic instruction in the flute ceremony. A good place to begin is with childhood training regarding shame about one's genitals. Here is Kambo, a boy who was initiated, talking about his own experience: "I thought—not good that they [elders] are lying or just playing a trick. That's [the penis] not for eating.... When I was a child our fathers said, 'This [penis] is not for handling; if you hold it you'll become lazy.' And because of that [at first in the cult house] I felt—it's not for sucking." Childhood experience is a contributing source of shame about fellatio: Children are taught to avoid handling their own genitals. In a wider sense Kambo's remark pertains to the taboo on masturbation, the sexual naïveté of children, and the boys' prior lack of knowledge about their fathers' homosexual activities.

Another key ritual story concerns the nutritive and "growth" values of semen. A primary source of this idea is men's ritual equation of semen with mother's breast milk, as noted before. The initiates take up this idea quickly in their own subjective orientations toward fellatio. (Pandanus nuts, like coconut, are regarded as another equivalent of semen.) The following remark by Moondi is a typical example of such semen identifications in the teachings of the flute ceremony: "The 'juice' of the pandanus nuts,... it's the same as the 'water' of a man, the same as a man's 'juice' [semen]. And I like to eat a lot of it [because it can give me more water],... for the milk of women is also the same as the milk of men. Milk [breast milk] is for when she carries a child—it belongs to the infant who drinks it." The association between semen and the infant's breast food is also explicit in this observation by Gaimbako, a second-stage initiate: "Semen is the same kind as that [breast milk] of women.... It's the very same kind as theirs,... the same as pandanus nuts too.... But when milk [semen] falls into my mouth [during fellatio], I think it's the milk of women." So the boys are taught beliefs that are highly motivating in support of same-gender sexual relations.

But the ritual also creates in boys a new awareness about their subordination to the older men. Kambo related this thought as his immediate response to the penis teaching of the flute ceremony: "I was afraid of penis. It's the same as mine—why should I eat it? It's the same kind; [our penises are] only one kind. We're men, not *different* kinds." This supposition is fundamental and implied in many boys' understandings. Kambo felt that males are of one kind, that is, "one sex," as distinct from females. This implies tacit recognition of the sameness of men, which ironically suggests that they should be not sexually involved but in competition for the other gender. Remember, too, the coercive character of the setting: The men's attempt to have boys suck the flutes is laden with overt hostility, much stronger than the latent hostility expressed in lewd homosexual jokes made during the preceding body decoration. The boys are placed in a sexually subordinate position, a fact that is symbolically communicated in the idiom that the novices are "married" to the flutes. (Novices suck the small flute, which resembles the mature glans penis, the men say.) The men thus place the boys in an invidious state of subordination during which the boys may sense that they are being treated too much like women. Sometimes this makes them panic and creates fear and shame. In time, however, a different feeling about the practice sets in.

Nearly all the novices perform their first act of fellatio during the days of initiation, and their story helps us to understand what happens later in their masculine development. Let me cite several responses of Moondi to this highly emotional act:

> I was wondering what they [elders] were going to do to us. And... I felt afraid. What will they do to us next? But they put the bamboo in and out of the mouth; and I wondered, what are they doing? Then, when they tried out our mouths, I began to understand... that they were talking about the penis. Oh, that little bamboo is the penis of the men.... My whole body was afraid, completely afraid,... and I was heavy, I wanted to cry.
>
> At that point my thoughts went back to how I used to think it was the *aatmwogwambu* [flute

spirit], but then I knew that the men did it [made the sounds]. And... I felt a little better, for before [I thought that] the aatmwogwambu would get me. But now I saw that they [the men] did it.

They told us the penis story.... Then I thought a lot, as my thoughts raced quickly. I was afraid—not good that the men "shoot" me [penetrate my mouth] and break my neck. Aye! Why should they put that [penis] inside our mouths! It's not a good thing. They all hide it [the penis] inside their grass skirts, and it's got lots of hair too!

"You must listen well," the elders said. "You all won't grow by yourselves; if you sleep with the men you'll become a *strong* man." They said that; I was afraid.... And then they told us clearly: semen is inside—and when you hold a man's penis, you must put it inside your mouth—he can give you semen.... It's the same as your mother's breast milk.

"This is no lie!" the men said. "You can't go tell the children, your sisters."... And then later I tried it [fellatio], and I thought: Oh, they told us about *aamoonaalyi* [breast milk; Moondi means semen]—it [semen] is in there.

Despite great social pressures, some boys evince a low interest in the practice from the start, and they seldom participate in fellatio. Some novices feverishly join in. Those are the extremes. The great majority of Sambia boys regularly engage in fellatio for years as constrained by taboo. Homoerotic activities are a touchy subject among males for many reasons. These activities begin with ceremony, it is true, but their occurrence and meaning fan out to embrace a whole secret way of life. What matters is that the boys become sharers of this hidden tradition; and we should expect them to acquire powerful feelings about bachelors, fellatio, semen, and the whole male sexual culture.

One story must stand for many in the way that the Sambia boys grow into this sexual lifeway. One day, while I was talking idly with Kambo, he mentioned singing to himself as he walked in the forest. I asked him what he sang about; and from this innocuous departure point, he said this: "When I think of men's name songs then I sing them: that of a bachelor who is sweet on me; a man of another line or my own line. When I sing the song of a creek in the forest I am happy about that place.... Or some man who sleeps with me—when he goes elsewhere, I sing his song. I think of that man who gave me a lot of semen; later, I must sleep with him. I feel like this: he gave me a lot of water [semen].... Later, I will have a lot of water like him."

Here we see established in Kambo's thought the male emphasis on "accumulating semen" and the powerful homoerotic relationships that accompany it. Even a simple activity like singing can create a mood of subjective association with past fellatio and same-gender relationships with the older males. Kambo's last sentence contains a wish: that he will acquire abundant manliness, like that of the friend of whom he sings.

No issue in recent reviews has inspired more debate than the basic question of whether—or to what extent—sexual feelings and erotic desires are motives or consequences of these cultural practices. Does the Sambia boy desire sexual intercourse with the older male? Is the older male sexually attracted to the boy? Indeed, what does "erotic" or "sexual" mean in this context, and is "desire" the proper concept with which to gauge the ontology? Or do other factors, such as power or kinship, produce the sexual attraction and excitement (conscious or unconscious) necessary to produce arousal and uphold the tradition (Herdt 1991)?

Although Sambia culture requires that men eventually change their focus to marriage and give up boy-inseminating, some of the men continue to practice age-structured relations because they find them so pleasurable. A small number of individual men enjoy inseminating boys too much to give up the practice. They develop favorites among the boys and even resort to payment of meat when they find it difficult to obtain a boy who will service them. In our culture these men would probably be called homosexuals because of their preference for the boys, their desires, and their need to mask their activities within the secret domain of ritual. But such an identity of homosexual or gay does not exist for the Sambia, and we must be careful not to project these meanings onto them, for that would be ethnocentric. We can, however, see how they live and what it means to have such an experience—in the absence of the sexual identity system of western culture.

One of these men, Kalutwo, has been interviewed by me over a long period of time, and his sexual and social history reveals a pattern of broken, childless marriages and an exclusive attraction to boys. As he got older, he would have to "pay" the boys with gifts to engage in sex, but when he was younger, some of the boys were known to be fond of him as well (Herdt and Stoller 1990). Several other males are different from Kalutwo in liking boys but also liking women and being successfully married with children. They would be called bisexual in our society. They seem to enjoy sexual pleasure with women and take pride in making babies through their wives, yet they continue illicitly to enjoy oral sex with boys. But Kalutwo disliked women sexually and generally preferred the closeness, sexual intimacy, and emotional security of young men and boys. As he got older, it was increasingly difficult for him to obtain boys as sexual partners, and this seemed to make him feel depressed. Moreover, as he got older, he was increasingly at odds with his male peers socially and stood out from the crowd, having no wife or children, as expected of customary adult manhood. Some people made fun of him behind his back; so did some of the boys. In a society that had a homosexual role, Kalutwo might have found more social support or comfort and perhaps might have been able to make a different transition into middle age. But his village still accepts him, and he has not been turned away or destroyed—as might have occurred in another time had he lived in a western country.

Perhaps in these cases we begin to understand the culture of male camaraderie and emotional intimacy that created such deeply felt desire for same-gender relations in ancient Greece and Japan, in which sexual pleasures and social intimacies with the same gender were as prized as those of intercourse and family life with women. No difficulty was posed to society or to self-esteem so long as these men met their social and sexual obligations and were honorable in their relations with younger males. We know from the anthropological reports from New Guinea that such individuals existed elsewhere as well, and among the Malekula and Marind-anim tribes, for example, adult married men would continue such relations with boys even after reaching the age of being grandfathers in the group, for this was expected.

Mojave Two-Spirit Initiation

My reading of the gender-transformed role among American Indians has shown the importance of two spirits in Native American society for the broader understanding of alternative sexualities. What I have not established thus far is the development of the role in the life of the individual. Among the Mojave Indians, a special ceremony in late childhood marked a transition into the third-gender role that allowed for homoerotic relations so long as they were between people in different gender roles. The two spirit was the product of a long cultural history that involved myth and ceremonial initiation. The ceremonies were sacred and of such importance that their official charter was established in the origin myths of the tribe, known from time immemorial. The meanings of this transition deserve to be highlighted as another variation on coming of age ceremonies in nonwestern cultures.

The Mojave child was only about ten years old when he participated in the ceremony for determining whether a change to two spirit would occur. Perhaps this seems young for a coming of age ceremony; but it might be that the very degree of change and the special nature of the desires to become a man-woman required a childhood transition. In the Mojave case, it was said that a Mojave boy could act "strangely" at the time, turning away from male tasks and refusing the toys of his own sex. The parents would view this as a sign of personal and gender change. Recall that mothers had dreams that their sons would grow up to become two spirits. No doubt this spiritual sign helped to lend religious support for the ceremony. At any rate these signs of gender change were said by the Mojave to express the "true" intentions of the child to change into a man-woman. Nahwera, a Mojave elder, stated: "When there is a desire in a child's heart to become a transvestite that child will act different. It will let people become aware of that desire" (Devereux 1937, 503). Clearly, the child was beginning to act on desires that transgressed his role and required an adjustment, through ritual, to a new kind of being and social status in the culture.

Arrangements for the ceremony were made by the parents. The boy was reported to have been "surprised" by being offered "female apparel," whereon the relatives waited nervously to see his response. Devereux reported that this was considered both an initiation and an ultimate test of the child's true desires. "If he submitted to it, he was considered a genuine homosexual.... If the boy acted in the expected fashion during the ceremony he was considered an initiated homosexual, if not, the gathering scattered, much to the relief of the boy's family" (Devereux 1937, 508). The story suggests that the parents in general may have been ambivalent about this change and may not have wanted it. Nevertheless, true to Mojave culture, they accepted the actions of the boy and supported his decision to become a two-spirit person. The Mojave thus allowed a special combination of a child's ontological being and the support of the family to find its symbolic expression in a ready-made institutionalized cultural practice. It only awaited the right individual and circumstances for the two-spirit person to emerge in each community in each generation.

Both the Sambia example of age-structured relations and the Mojave illustration of gender-transformed homosexuality reveal transitions in late childhood up to age ten. What is magical about age ten? It may be that certain critical developmental changes begin to occur around this time—desires and attractions that indicate the first real sexuality and growing sense of becoming a sexual person. In fact, our study in Chicago revealed that nine and one-half years for boys and ten years for girls were the average age when they were first attracted to the same gender (Herdt and Boxer 1996).

Coming Out—Gay and Lesbian Teens in America

Ours is a culture that defines male and female as absolutely different and then goes to great lengths to deny having done so; American culture reckons "heterosexual" and "homosexual" as fundamentally distinctive kinds of "human nature" but then struggles to find a place for both. Although such gender dimorphism is common in the thinking of nonwestern peoples, the latter idea is rare in, even absent from, many cultures—including our own cultural ancestors, the ancient Greeks. The Greeks described people's sexual behaviors but not their being as homosexual or heterosexual. As we have seen, the Greeks did not place people in categories of sexuality or create sexual classifications that erased all other cultural and personality traits. In our society today this kind of thinking is common and permeates the great symbolic types that define personal being and social action in most spheres of our lives. For many heterosexuals, their worldview and life course goals remain focused on the greatest ritual of reproduction: the church-ordained marriage. And this leads to parenting and family formation. Many think of this ritual process as "good" in all of its aspects. Others see same-gender desire as an attack on that reproductive and moral order, a kind of crisis of gender and sexuality that requires the assertion of a mythical "family values," descended from nineteenth-century ideals, that are seldom relevant to heterosexuals today, let alone to gays and lesbians.

Coming out is another form of ritual that intensifies change in a young person's sexual identity development and social being. It gives public expression to desires long felt to be basic to the person's sexual nature but formerly hidden because of social taboos and homophobia. The process leads to many events that reach a peak in the person's young adult years, especially in the development of gay or lesbian selves, roles, and social relations. Coming out continues to unfold across the entire course of life: There is never really an end to the process for the simple reason that as gay or lesbian people age and their social situations change, they continue to express in new, relevant ways what it means to be gay or lesbian. Such a social and existential crisis of identity—acted out on the stage of the lesbian and gay community—links the social drama of American youths' experiences with those of tribal initiations, such as those of the Sambia and Mojave, played out in the traditional communities. Of course, these two kinds of drama are different and should not be confused, but they share the issues of handling same-gender desires in cultural context.

Two different processes are involved. First is the secretive act of "passing" as heterosexual, involving the lone individual in largely hidden social networks and secret social spaces.... In many towns and cities, especially unsophisticated and traditionally conservative areas of the country, the possibilities are only now emerging for gay/lesbian identification and social action. Second is the coming out in adolescence or young adulthood.

Initially the gay or lesbian grows up with the assumption of being heterosexual. As an awareness of same-gender desires emerges, a feeling of having to hide these desires and pretend otherwise, of acting straight, leads to many moments of secrecy. Later, however, sexual and social experiences may yield a divergent awareness and a desire to be open. What follows is a process of coming out—typically begun in urban centers, sometimes in high school, sometimes later, after the young person has left home for college, work, or the service—that leads to self-identification as gay or lesbian. Through these ritual steps of disclosure all kinds of new socialization and opportunities emerge, including entrance into the gay and lesbian community.

Being and doing gay life are provisioned by the rituals of coming out, and they open significant questions for thinking about youths in search of positive same-gender roles. American teenagers may seem less exotic to the gay or lesbian reader; but they are more of an oddity to the heterosexual adult community as they come out. To many in our own society, these youths look "queer" and "strange" and "diseased," attitudes that reflect historical stereotypes and cultural homophobia.

The growing visibility of the lesbian and gay movement in the United States has made it increasingly possible for people to disclose their desires and "come out" at younger ages. Over the past quarter century, the evidence suggests that the average age of the declaration of same-gender desires has gotten earlier—a lot earlier, as much as ten years earlier than it was in the 1970s—and is for the first time in history a matter of adolescent development. It is not a matter for everyone, of course, but increasingly for those who become aware and are lucky to have the opportunities to begin a new life. In our study of gay and lesbian self-identified youths in Chicago, we found that the average age for boys and girls' "coming out" was sixteen. But we also found that the earliest awareness of same-gender attraction begins at about age ten, which suggests that the desires are a part of the deeper being of the gay or lesbian person.

Gay and lesbian teenagers are growing up with all of the usual problems of our society, including the political, economic, and social troubles of our country, as well as the sexual and social awakening that typifies the adolescent experience. I have already noted how American society and western cultures in general have changed in the direction of more positive regard for gays. This does not mean, however, that the hatred and homophobia of the past are gone or that the secrecy and fear of passing have faded away. People still fear, and rightly so, the effects of coming out on their lives and safety, their well-being and jobs, their social standing and community prestige. These youths are opting to come out as openly lesbian or gay earlier in the life course than ever before in our society. Yet they experience the troubles of feeling themselves attracted to the same gender, with its taboos and sorrows of stigma and shame, not knowing what to do about it. Fortunately, the gay and lesbian culture provides new contexts of support; these youths have institutions and media that talk about it; they learn from adult role models that they can live relatively happy and rewarding lives with their desires.

We can study how one group of adolescents in Chicago has struggled with these issues while preparing for socialization and coming out in the context of the lesbian and gay community. The study of gay, lesbian, and bisexual youths in Chicago was located in the largest gay social services agency of the city, Horizons Community

Services. Horizons was created in the early 1970s out of the gay liberation movement, and by 1979 it had founded a gay and lesbian youth group, one of the first in the United States. The agency is based in the gay neighborhood of the city, and it depends on volunteers and the goodwill and interest of friends of the agency. In recent years the youths have led the Gay and Lesbian Pride Day Parade in Chicago and have become a symbol of social and political progress in gay culture in the city.

The Horizons study was organized around the youth group, for ages thirteen to twenty, but the average age of the youths interviewed in depth was about eighteen. We interviewed a total of 202 male and female youths of all backgrounds from the suburbs and inner city, white and black and brown. Many people of color and of diverse ethnic subcultures in Chicago have experienced racism and many forms of homophobia, and these have effectively barred their coming out. The group tries to find a place for all of these diverse adolescents; no one is turned away. Group meetings are coordinated by lesbian and gay adults, esteemed role models of the teens. They facilitate a discussion of a variety of topics, particularly in matters of the coming out process, such as fears and homophobic problems at school or home, and issues of special interest to the teens. The youth group has an active social life as well, hosting parties and organizing social events, such as the annual alternative gay and lesbian prom, held on the weekend of high school proms in Chicago, for the youth members.

Protecting teens from the risk of infection from AIDS is another key goal of Horizons' sponsorship of the youth group. AIDS has become an increasingly important element of the youth group discussions. "Safe sex" is promoted through educational material and special public speakers. In general, the socialization rituals of the group prepare the youths for their new status in the gay and lesbian community, and the rituals culminate in marching in the Gay and Lesbian Pride Day Parade every June.

The lesbian or gay youth is in the throes of moving through the symbolic "death" of the heterosexual identity and role and into the "rebirth" of their social being as gay. As a life crisis and a passage between the past and future, the person is betwixt and between normal social states, that is, between the heterosexual worlds of parents and the cultural system of gay and lesbian adults. To the anthropologist, the youths are symbolically exiting what was once called "homosexuality" and entering what is now called "gay and lesbian." To the psychologist, their transition is from dependence and internalized homophobia to a more open and mature competence and pride in the sexual/gender domains of their lives. The transformative power contained in the rituals of coming out as facilitated by Horizons helps in the newfound development of the person. But it also helps in the lives of everyone touched by a youth who is coming out. As long as this process is blocked or resisted, the pull back into passing as heterosexual is very tempting.

Back in the 1960s,... coming out was a secret incorporation into the closet "homosexual" community. Studies at the time showed that the more visible contexts of engaging in same-sex contacts might lead to de facto coming out, but these were generally marginal and dangerous places, such as public toilets, where victimization and violence could occur. To come out in secret bars, the military, toilets, or bus depots did not create a positive identification with the category of gay/lesbian. There was generally no identity that positively accorded with gay or lesbian self-esteem as we think of it today. Thus, we can understand how many people found it revolutionary to fight back against homophobia and begin to march openly in parades in the 1970s. Nevertheless, the change was uneven and difficult.

People who continue to pass as straight when they desire people of the same gender and may in fact have sexual relations with them present a perplexing issue—not only for lesbians and gay men but also for society as a whole. This kind of person, through secrecy and passing, serves as a negative role model of what not to be. Alas, there are many movie stars, celebrities, and sports heroes who live closeted lives of this kind—until they are discovered or "outed" by someone. Many youths are frightened or intimidated when they discover adults they know and love, such as teachers, uncles, family friends, or pastors, who pass as heterosexual but have been discovered to desire the same gender. Adolescents can be angered to discover that a media person they admire has two lives, one publicly heterosexual and one privately homosexual. This is a cultural survival of the nineteenth-century system of closet homosexuality, with its hide-and-seek games to escape the very real dangers of homophobia. In contrast, positive role models provided by the largely white middle-class adult advisers at Horizons are the crucial source for learning how to enter the gay and lesbian community.

Cultural homophobia in high school is a powerful force against coming out. Learning to hide one's desires is crucial for the survival of some youths, especially at home and at school, the two greatest institutions that perpetuate homophobia in the United States. Our informants tell us that standard slurs to put people down in the schools remain intact. To be slurred as a "dyke" or a "faggot" is a real blow to social esteem. But "queer" is the most troubling epithet of all. To be targeted as a "queer" in high school is enormously troubling for the youths, somehow more alienating and isolating, an accusation not just of doing something "different" but of being something "unnatural." One seventeen-year-old eleventh grade boy remarked to us that he was secretive at school. "I'm hidden mostly—cause of the ways they'll treat you. Okay, there are lots of gangs.... They find out you're [what they call] a faggot and they beat on you and stuff. If they ask me I say it's none of their business." The role of secrecy, passing, and hiding continues the homophobia. Ironically, as Michelle Fine (1988, 36) notes in her study of black adolescent girls in New York City high schools, it was the gay and lesbian organization in the school that was the most open and safe environment in which young African-American girls could access their own feelings. They could, with the support of the lesbian and gay teenage group, start to become the agents of their *own* desires. Our study has shown that in Chicago most lesbian or gay youths have experienced harassment in school; and when this is combined with harassment and problems at home, it signals a serious mental health risk, especially for suicide. And the risk of suicide before lesbian or gay youths come to find the support of the Horizons group is very great.

The ritual of coming out means giving up the secrecy of the closet. This is a positive step toward mental health, for life in the closet involves not only a lot of hiding but also a good deal of magical thinking, which may be detrimental to the person's well-being. By magical thinking, I mean mainly contagious beliefs about homosexuality such as the common folk ideas of our culture that stereotype homosexuality as a disease that spreads, as well as the historical images of homosexuality as a mental illness or a crime against nature. These magical beliefs support homophobia and warn about the dangers of going to a gay community organization, whispering how the adolescent might turn into a monster or sex fiend or be raped or murdered or sold into slavery.

Another common contagious fear is the belief that by merely contacting other gays, the adolescent's "sin or disease" will spread to the self and will then unwittingly spread to others, such as friends and siblings. One of the common magical beliefs of many adults and parents is that the youth has merely to avoid other gays and lesbians in order to "go straight." This is surely another cultural "leftover" from the dark myth of homosexuality as evil.... If the adolescent will only associate with straights, the parent feels, this strange period of "confusion" will pass, and he or she will become heterosexual like everyone else. Such silly stereotypes are strongly associated with the false notion that all gay or lesbian teens are simply "confused," which was promoted by psychologists in the prior generation. This belief is based on the cultural myth that same-sex desires are "adolescent" desires of a transient nature that may be acquired or learned but can go away; and if the self ignores them, the desire for the opposite sex will grow in their place. Magical fears of contracting AIDS is a new and most powerful deterrent to coming out among some youths. Many youths fear their initial social contact with anyone gay because they think they might contagiously contract AIDS by being gay or lesbian or by interacting socially with gays.

The gender difference in the experience of coming out as a male or a female highlights the cultural pressures that are still exerted on teens to conform to the norm of heterosexuality in our society. Girls typically have more heterosexual experience in their histories, with two-thirds of the girls having had significant heterosexual contact before they came to Horizons. Since the age of our sample was about eighteen, it is easy to see that relatively early on, between the ages of thirteen and seventeen, girls were being inducted into sexual relations with boys. We face here the problem of what is socially necessary and what is preferred. Only one-third of the boys had had heterosexual experience, and fully two-fifths of them had had no sexual experience with girls. Note also that for many of the boys, their sexual contacts with girls were their lesbian-identified friends at the Horizons youth group. The boys tended to achieve sexual experiences earlier than the girls, by age sixteen, at which point the differences in development had evened out. Both genders were beginning to live openly lesbian or gay lives.

Clearly, powerful gender role pressures are exerted on girls to conform to the wishes of parents, siblings, peers, and boyfriends. Some of this, to use a phrase by Nancy Chodorow (1992) about heterosexuality as a compromise formation, results in a compromise of their desires, even of their personal integrity, in the development of their sexual and self-concept. But as we know from the work of Michele Fine (1992), who studied adolescent sexuality among African-American girls in the New York City schools, females were not able to explore and express their desires until they located a safe space that enabled them to think out loud. In fact, they could not become the agents of their own desires until they had located the gay and lesbian youth group in the high school! There, some of them had to admit, contrary to their stereotypes, they found the gay youths more accepting and open of variations than any of their peers or the adults. The lesson here is that when a cultural space is created, people can explore their own desires and better achieve their own identities and sociosexual goals in life.

We have found that four powerful magical beliefs exist in the implicit learning of homophobia and self-hatred among gay and lesbian youths. First is the idea that homosexuals are crazy and heterosexuals are sane. Unlearning this idea involves giving up the assumption of heterosexual normalcy in favor of positive attitudes and role models. Second is the idea that the problem with same-gender desires is in the self, not in society. Unlearning this belief means recognizing cultural homophobia and discovering that the problem with hatred lies not in the self but in society. Third is the magical belief that to have same-gender desires means giving up gendered roles as they were previously known and acting as a gender-transformed person, a boy acting or dressing as a girl, a girl living as a boy, or either living as an androgyne. There is nothing wrong with these transformations. What we have seen in the cross-cultural study, however, is that there are a variety of ways to organize same-gender desires. The old ways of gender inversion from the nineteenth century are only one of these. Unlearning gender reversal means accepting one's own gendered desires and enactments of roles, whatever these are, rather than living up to social standards—either in the gay or straight community.

Fourth is the belief that if one is going to be gay, there are necessary goals, rules, roles, and political and social beliefs that must be performed or expressed. This idea goes against the grain of American expressive individualism, in which we feel that each one of us is unique and entitled to "know thyself" as the means of social fulfillment. The key is that there is not one perfect way to be gay; there are many divergent ways. Nor is there any single event, or magic pill, that will enable the process of coming out. It is a lifelong process, as long as it takes to live and find a fulfilling social and spiritual lifeway in our culture.

Lesbian and gay youths have shown that coming out is a powerful means of confronting the unjust, false, wrongful social faces and values of prejudice in our culture. Before being out, youths are asking, "What can we be?" or "How can we fit into this society?" Emerging from the secrecy, these youths are making new claims on society to live up to its own standards of justice. The rituals of coming out are a way of unlearning and creating new learning about living with same-gender desires and creating a positive set of relationships around them. Surely the lesson of the gay movement is that hiding desires and passing as something other than what one is are no less injurious to the normal heart and the healthy mind of gay youths than was, say, passing as a Christian if one was a Jew in Nazi Germany or passing as white in the old South or in South Africa under apartheid.

Lesbian and gay youths are challenging society in ways that are no less revolutionary than discriminations based on skin color, gender, or religion. A new of kind of social and political activism has arisen; it goes beyond AIDS/HIV, but builds on the grief and anger that the entire generation feels about the impact of the pandemic on gay and lesbian culture. Some call this new generation queer. But others prefer lesbian or gay or bisexual or transgendered. Perhaps the word is less important than the commitment to building a rich and meaningful social world in which all people, including lesbians and gays, have a place to live and plan for the future.

We have seen in this chapter how a new generation of lesbian- and gay-identified youths has utilized transition rituals to find a place in the gay and lesbian community. It was the activism and social progress of the lesbian and gay culture that made this huge transformation possible. The emergence of a community enabled the support of youth groups and other institutions for the creation of a new positive role model and self-concept. Youths are beginning to take up new status rights and duties, having a new set of cultural ideas to create the moral voice of being gay, bisexual, lesbian, or queer. The rituals, such as the annual Gay and Lesbian Pride Day Parade, make these newly created traditions a lived reality; they codify and socialize gay and lesbian ideals, knowledge, and social roles, bonding past and future in a timeless present that will enable these youths to find a place in a better society.

References

Benedict, Ruth. 1938. "Continuities and discontinuities in cultural conditioning." *Psychiatry* 1:161–167.

Chodorow, Nancy J. 1992. "Heterosexuality as a Compromise Formation: Reflections on the Psychoanalytic Theory of Sexual Development." *Psychoanalysis and Contemporary Thought* 15:267–304.

Devereux, George. 1937. "Institutionalized Homosexuality Among the Mohave Indians." *Human Biology* 9:498–527.

Fine, Michelle. 1988. "Sexuality, Schooling, and Adolescent Females: The Missing Discourse of Desire." *Harvard Education Review* 58:29–53.

Hart, C. W. M. 1963. "Contrasts Between Prepubertal and Postpubertal Education." In *Education and Culture,* ed. G. Spindler, pp. 400–425. New York: Holt, Rinehart and Winston.

Herdt, Gilbert. 1981. *Guardians of the Flutes: Idioms of Masculinity.* New York: McGraw-Hill.

———. 1982. "Fetish and Fantasy in Sambia Initiation." In *Rituals of Manhood,* ed. G. Herdt., pp. 44–98. Berkeley and Los Angeles: University of California Press.

———. 1984b. "Semen Transactions in Sambia Culture." In *Ritualized Homosexuality in Melanesia,* ed. G. Herdt, pp. 167–210. Berkeley and Los Angeles: University of California Press.

———. 1991. "Representations of Homosexuality in Traditional Societies: An Essay on Cultural Ontology and Historical Comparison, Part II." *Journal of the History of Sexuality* 2:603–632.

———. 1993. "Introduction." In *Ritualized Homosexuality in Melanesia,* ed. G. Herdt, pp. vii–xliv. Berkeley and Los Angeles: University of California Press.

———, and Andrew Boxer. 1996. *Children of Horizons: How Gay and Lesbian Youth Are Forging a New Way Out of the Closet.* Boston: Beacon Press.

———, and Robert J. Stoller. 1990. *Intimate Communications: Erotics and the Study of Culture.* New York: Columbia University Press.

Cultural Patterns and Sex/Gender Diversity

SERENA NANDA

Sex/Gender Diversity Across Cultures

Roles transcending sex/gender binaries are clearly a widespread cultural phenomenon. Sex/gender variation exists in many different cultural contexts and takes many different forms. Many societies regard sex/gender variants as merely natural, albeit unusual, phenomena (Geertz 1975), while other societies accommodate sex/gender variants through the construction of alternative sex/gender roles (Herdt l996; Nanda 2000). Native American cultures appear to be particularly associated with multiple genders, for both men and women (Lang 1998; Roscoe 1996; Williams 1986). These roles (formerly called *berdache*, now called *two-spirit*) varied greatly: in some cultures the alternative sex/gender roles were assigned to hermaphrodites, in others they were associated with sexual orientation or practice, in others with cross-dressing, and in still others, with occupation, or a combination of all of these, but in any case regarded as alternative and autonomous genders with a status equal to that of men or women. Gender variant individuals, in MesoAmerica (see Marcos 2002) as well as in Native American societies, did not become members of the "opposite" sex or gender, but rather enacted alternative gender roles that were distinguished from both man and woman. These roles often comprised a "mixture" of masculine and feminine qualities, expressed in the wearing of a combination of men's and women's clothing or in other activities.

While most recorded alternative gender roles are associated with males, others, like the "sworn virgin" of the Balkans (Grémaux 1996), the *tombois* of Indonesia (Blackwood 1998; Blackwood and Wieringa 1998), the *sadhin* of India (Humes 1996; Phillimore 1991), or the Mohave *hwame* (Devereux 1937) are associated with females. While other roles, like the Hawaiian *mahu*, the Thai kathoey, or the Indonesian *bissu* (Boellstorff 2005) originally applied to both males and females, they now refer mainly to feminine males (see Costa and Matzner 2007).

Culture and the Homosexual/Heterosexual Divide

The cross-cultural data strongly challenges the Western understanding of an exclusive homosexual/heterosexual divide, which associates sexual orientation with essentialized identities. The culturally constructed homosexual/heterosexual divide is not universal and has frequently been inappropriately imposed on other cultures. Sexuality (sexual desire and practice) in many cultures is not viewed as either permanent or as an important component in gender, or it may be associated with other elements of culture in ways that stand in great contrast to our own. In Brazil and Oman, for example, sexual practice, not sexual orientation, is the key element in the sex/gender system (see Parker 1995; Wikan 1977); in still other cultures, sexual orientation has little or no relevance to gender identity. While many male alternative gender roles are associated with gendered sexuality, in Thailand and in Indonesia, for example, these roles are differentiated from the Western concept of "gay" and the male same-sex relations characteristic of such roles are defined as heterogenderal rather than homosexual (Boellstorff 2004).

Among the Sambia of New Guinea, male same-sex practice is not related to sexual orientation and identity, but is part of a male initiation ritual considered essential for the development of adult masculinity (Herdt 1981). The Sambia believe that women, unlike men, are innately fertile and mature naturally without external aid, whereas males do not naturally mature as fast or as competently as females. Males cannot attain puberty or secondary sex characteristics such as body hair, or become "strong men" without semen; since the Sambia believe that male bodies do not naturally produce semen, it must be externally and artificially introduced into the body through the initiation ritual. In this ritual, boys consume semen from adult men through fellatio, which produces maleness. Only repeated inseminations of this kind are considered capable of conferring on the young boy the reproductive competence that results in manliness and fatherhood.

Even in cultures where alternative sex/gender roles and identities involve sexual relations with men, same-sex practice is not in itself, a sufficient condition of alternative gender status. Indeed, contrary to the Euro-American system, in which sexual orientation and practice comes closest to defining the alternative gender of "homosexual," in many other cultures, only the male partner taking the (passive) female role is considered gender variant; the man taking the insertive male sexual role is not even culturally acknowledged as different. Even in Western culture, the current exclusive binary homosexual/heterosexual divide has waxed and waned in different eras and emerged in its contemporary form only in the last several hundred years. In pre-modern Europe homosexuality was not a criteria of gender, and "the homosexual," as a sex/gender category did not exist (Trumbach 1996).

Same-sex desire in women is often not culturally acknowledged, for example in Suriname, although intimate relations between women are known to be commonplace (Wekker 1999). In other societies, such as Lesotho, female/female sexual relations are a regular feature of a growing girl's development that may cease in later life and may also be a normal feature of relations between adult women. These same-sex desires and practices have no cultural relevance to feminine gender identities or adult gender roles (Kendall 1999, citing Gay 1985). "Mummy-baby" relationships between younger and older girls and women involve mentoring on issues of sex and courtship and also involve intimacy and romance, such as the exchange of love letters and sexual relations. As the girls get older, they may become "mummies" to their own "babies" but begin to have boyfriends as well. The intensity of "mummy-baby" relationships usually ends with marriage when women become more focused on domestic responsibilities.

Further, while the American concept, "homosexual" includes both men and women with a same-sex orientation regardless of other aspects of their gender role performance, in much of the world sexual orientation is only culturally acknowledged as relevant in gender identity for those men and women who enact their role "opposites," i.e., effeminate homosexual men or masculine lesbian women. In West Sumatra, Indonesia, in contrast to the West, women's same-sex desires do not determine their gender roles or gender identities. Whereas both partners in a female-female relationship in the United States are labeled lesbians, in Sumatra, two females in a sexual relationship are viewed as occupying different gender roles. Their relationship is called *cowok-cewek* (guy/girl): a cowok is expected to exhibit masculine behavior and dress, exhibit manly qualities such as bravery, and desire sex only with women, while a cewek is expected to dress and comport herself as a woman, have sexual desires for men, and show feminine abilities to cook and keep house. Cowoks express masculine gender identities, while cewaks express feminine gender identities; the Western concept of lesbian as based on same-sex orientation is absent in this Indonesian understanding (Blackwood 1998; Boellstorff 2005).

Social Attitudes Toward Sex/Gender Diversity

While in many contemporary societies individuals exhibiting non-normative or transgressive gender behaviors and/or identities may be treated with ridicule, fear, or disrespect, traditionally such individuals were often believed to have sacred powers and superior skills, and they occupied special prestigious social roles. The *hijras* of India, for example, are considered auspicious and traditionally have a presence at weddings and the birth of a child, conferring fertility on a family (Reddy 2005; Nanda 1999; Nanda 2012). In many Native American societies, two-spirit persons received special recognition as healers and shamans, and were go-betweens in arranging marriages, for which their mixed gender roles particularly suited them (Williams 1986). In Brazil, also, individuals on the margins because of their sex/gender status are associated with powerful ritual capacities (Fry 1995; Wafer 1991). It is not surprising that transgressive sex/gender individuals, who undermine social conventions and cause social disorder, should be linked to prodigious magical and other powers.

In pre-contact Hawaii, also, feminine men and masculine women, called mahu (literally, hermaphrodite), were not only accepted, but were valued caregivers for children and the elderly and were considered highly skilled in traditional arts. Male mahu particularly were associated with teaching hula and chants and were keepers of cultural tradition. As the term mahu changed to refer to male-to-female transgendered people as well as effeminate and gender-normative gay men, it became increasingly a term of derision, but more recently, with the renaissance of Hawaiian culture, it is taking on its older meanings. Mahu oral histories indicate that some transgendered Native Hawaiians now increasingly experience themselves, and are viewed by others, as especially skilled in traditional Hawaiian cultural patterns like hula, lei-making, chanting, singing, and sewing. As mahu, they express a strong responsibility to pass these skills on to future generations (Matzner 2001).

In Thailand, Brazil, the Philippines, and other cultures, the association of alternative gendered males with sex work has resulted in negative public images and to some extent hostile treatment of alternatively gendered individuals by the state, though they may also achieve prestige through their ability to transform themselves into glamorous and stylish women (Kulick 1998; Jackson 1999), a persona that is particularly associated with entertainment and beauty contests (Johnson 1997; Besnier 2002; 2011).

The importance of accommodating differently gendered persons into civic life is an explicit issue of national debate in Indonesia. One of the several gender-variant roles in Indonesia, the waria (Boellstorff 2004; 2005; Graham 2006), are highly visible and defined by their public performances as entertainers. Like the bakla of the Philippines or the Thai kathoey, the waria widely engage in sex work, but they also work in beauty salons (Boellstorff 2004). Like transgendered persons in all cultures, the waria are much concerned with respect and with being regarded as full citizens of their nation. Toward this end, they promote their work in bridal salons, where they have established expertise in creating wedding costumes, make-up, and hair styles that project a "true Indonesian image" that transcends the many ethnic and regional divisions in the nation. Thus, the waria importantly contribute to furthering the unity of the Indonesian nation. This contribution is recognized by the state, which provides financial and other assistance to waria in the fields of beauty and bridal culture. However, in Indonesia and Malaysia, both Muslim nations, the Islamic emphasis on the importance of marriage and family life takes precedence over other gender values, which puts restraints on the expression of various kinds of alternative sex/gender roles (Peletz 2009).

Sex/Gender Systems and the Cultural Idea of the Person

A significant cultural pattern that shapes a society's attitudes toward sex/gender variation is the culturally constructed idea of the person.[1] Thus, while the sex/gender systems of other societies may be useful in providing more positive sex/gender identities for transgendered persons in our own society, these cultural values are not easily transferable to the West, with its emphasis on the expression of a person's individuality trumping collective or community gender values. In other cultures, gender identity is not as central, stable, or uniform as it is in Western culture, where it competes with other identities, such as age, ethnicity, kinship status, and class as a significant basis for self identification and action. And it is important to keep in mind that the impact of modernization and globalization are changing traditional concepts of the person, impacting sex/gender variant individuals as well as others in society (Besnier 2011).

In fact, in spite of the traditional American view that gender identity is, or should be, constant over a lifetime, research reveals that alternative sex/gender identities are varied among individuals, may change over a lifetime; and are associated with different degrees of negatively experienced internal conflict, even in the United States, whose views of the person are more restricted and less flexible than in other societies (Valentine 2007).

In India, for example, despite a clear gender demarcation between men and women, gender transformations occur in Indian mythology and are also permitted and occur in society. One of my hijra consultants, Salima, a hermaphrodite and a "born" hijra, referred to other hijras as "converts," a term that nicely illustrates the Indian view that people can either retain the gender they were born into or they can change their gender, just as one converts to a different religion. These possibilities for gender transformation are related to Hindu concepts of the person. Because Hinduism explicitly recognizes that humans achieve their ultimate goals by following many different paths, it affords the individual temperament the widest latitude in behavior, including what Western psychology might call compulsive extremes (Lannoy 1975:119). This results in a greater tolerance for individual diversity, especially in matters of sexuality, than does Western culture. It is within this framework of the Indian concept of the person that hijras—as neither man nor woman—can find meaning in their ambiguous gender (Nanda 1996).

In Oman, also, accommodating attitudes regarding the alternative sex/gender role of the *xanith*—a mixture of man and woman—are rooted in the Omani construction of the person. The xanith, who are known for playing the female sexual role, are reclassified as men for all social purposes if they marry and prove their sexual potency as males, no matter how effeminate they remain (Wikan 1977). While a male taking the female in sex is stigmatized, Omanis acknowledge that the sexual deviant cannot be suppressed, and they let him practice his deviance in peace. The xanith is given a publicly acknowledged social status and participates in the full life of the society in his specialized role. Omani culture views the world as imperfect. People are created with dissimilar natures and are likewise imperfect. Thus, the sexually passive, effeminate male is acknowledged and reclassified as a xanith.

Native American societies in North America, though culturally very different, appear to give a wide scope to individual sex/gender differences, institutionalizing them in social roles, rather than driving them underground (Whitehead 1981). Unlike the United States, with its emphasis on the individual psyche, these societies seem less concerned in general with why individuals become the way they are or why they change from one role to another; indeed, changes in sexuality and gender identity over a lifetime may be viewed as quite natural (Lang 1999). George Devereux (1937) noted that the Mohave believed that there is an element of predestination or fate involved in gender transformations and suggested that this inhibits negative moral evaluations or sanctions on gender variant individuals.

In Tahiti, too, as in Polynesia generally, community response to alternative sex/gender roles are rooted in cultural ideas about the person. Traditionally oriented Tahitians, for example, considered the mahu a natural phenomenon and had little interest in how or why the mahu developed. Nor is the mahu subject to any negative moral evaluations or sanctions. People say that the mahu "is born like that," and he is simply accepted. In Tahiti generally, people are reluctant to generalize about the quality of an individual's character based on his or her membership in a gender category; such reluctance inhibits generalizations about ordinary men and women as well as mahu (Levy 1973). In Tahiti, the self is seen as a natural state of being and not easily changeable, which inhibits not only a curiosity about the cause of becoming a mahu, but any desire to correct or cure him, although this ready acceptance does not hold true in all of Polynesia (Besnier 2002).

Thai culture presents another interesting contrast to the American emphasis on the unity of the self and the integration of its public and private components, as this impacts on sex/gender variation, particularly the "coming out" of American homosexuals. In Thailand the public expression of one's "true self" is not as valued as it is in the West. "Coming out" as a gay man in Thailand brings shame or "loss of face," without the compensation of the high value on "being oneself" so essential in American culture. Another contrast between American culture regarding "coming out" and Filipino culture is commented on by *baklas* (sex/gender variants) who have migrated to the United States. To them, coming out in the United States has a dramatic aspect that is both puzzling and sad, in contrast to their own society where "nobody cares." "Perhaps" one bakla notes, "... American families are very cruel ... the whites, my God, shedding tears, leaving the family. The stories are always so sad" (Manalansan 2003).

In fact, in our own society there is a changing climate regarding not just homosexuality but also other forms of sex/gender variation. American culture has moved from an emphasis on an exclusive binary sex/gender system, under which transsexualism—a person of one sex becoming a person of the opposite sex—has been challenged by transgenderism, a view of sex/gender variation as a continuum that can accommodate individuals with many different sex/gender identities[2] (Valentine 2007; Bolin 1996). The anthropological research on sex/gender diversity in other cultures has been an important support of the contemporary transgender movement. By itself, a cross-cultural perspective will not do away with the trans- and homo-phobia that makes the lives of countless individuals throughout the world so difficult. But anthropological understandings of both the similarities and differences among individuals and among cultures offers people everywhere a sense of inclusion in our common humanity.

Acknowledgments

Deep thanks to all my colleagues whose field studies of cross-cultural sex/gender systems have made such an important contribution to understanding human sex/gender diversity.

Notes

1. An excellent discussion of the pitfalls of essentialism regarding cultural concepts of the person is found in the introduction to Besnier (2011).
2. Despite the many cultural and even legal supports of transsexualism in the United States, some judges are still skeptical, holding that both science and the courts have not resolved the issue of whether transsexuals are more appropriately defined in terms of their birth sex status or their post-operative sex/gender status [*In re Marshall G. Gardiner, deceased.* (2002)]. (Norgren and Nanda 2006).

References

Besnier, Niko. 2011. *On the Edge of the Global: Modern Anxieties in a Pacific Island Nation.* Stanford, CA: Stanford University Press.

Besnier, Niko. 2002. Transgenderism, Locality and the Miss Galaxy Beauty Pageant in Tonga. *American Ethnologist* 29:534–566.

Blackwood, E. 1998. *Tombois* in West Sumatra: Constructing masculinity and erotic desire. *Cultural Anthropology, 13*, 491–513.

Blackwood, E., & Wieringa, S. 1998. Eds. *Female desires: Same-sex relations and transgender practices across cultures.* New York: Columbia University Press.

Boellstorff, T. (2004). Playing back the nation: *Waria*, Indonesian transvestites. *Cultural Anthropology, 19*, pp. 159–195.

Boellstorff, T. 2005. *The Gay archipelago.* Princeton, NJ: Princeton University Press.

Bolin, A. 1996. Transcending and transgendering: Male-to-female transsexuals, dichotomy and diversity. In G. Herdt (Ed.). *Third sex third gender: Beyond sexual dimorphism in culture and history* (pp. 447–485). New York: Zone Books.

Costa, LeeRay, and Andrew Matzner. 2007. *Male bodies, women's souls: Personal narratives of Thailand's transgendered youth.* Binghamton, NY: Haworth Press.

Devereux, G. 1937. Institutionalized homosexuality of the Mohave Indians. *Human Biology, 9,* pp. 498–587.

Fry, P. 1995. Male homosexuality and Afro-Brazilian possession cults. In S. O. Murray (Ed.). *Latin American male homosexualities* (pp. 193–220). Albuquerque: University of New Mexico.

Geertz, C. 1975. Common sense as a cultural system. *Antioch Review, 33* (1): pp. 5–26.

Graham, S. 2006. *Challenging gender norms: The five genders of Indonesia.* Belmont, CA: Wadsworth.

Grémaux, R. 1996. Woman becomes man in the Balkans. In G. Herdt (Ed.). *Third sex third gender: Beyond sexual dimorphism in culture and history* (pp. 241–284). New York: Zone Books.

Herdt, G. 1981. *Guardians of the flute: Idioms of masculinity.* New York: McGraw-Hill.

Herdt, G. 1996. (Ed.) *Third sex third gender: Beyond sexual dimorphism in culture and history.* New York: Zone Books.

Humes, C.A. 1996. Becoming male: Salvation through gender modification in Hinduism and

Buddhism. In S.P. Ramet (Ed.). *Gender reversals and gender cultures: Anthropological and historical perspectives* (pp. 123-137). London: Routledge.

Jackson, P. 1999. *Lady boys, tom boys, rentboys: Male and female homosexualities in contemporary Thailand.* Binghamton, NY: Haworth Press.

Jacobs, S., Thomas, W., & Lang, S. 1997. Eds. *Two-Spirit people: Native American gender identity, sexuality, and spirituality.* Urbana: University of Illinois Press.

Johnson, M. 1997. *Beauty and power: Transgendering and cultural transformation in the Southern Philippines.* New York: Berg.

Kendall (no first name or initial given). 1999. Women in Lesotho and the (Western) construction of homophobia. In E. Blackwood & S. Wieringa (Eds.). *Female desires: Same-sex relations and transgender practices across cultures* (pp. 157–180). New York: Columbia University Press.

Kulick, D. 1998. *Travesti: Sex, gender and culture among Brazilian transgendered prostitutes.* Chicago: University of Chicago Press.

Lang, S. 1998. *Men as women, women as men: Changing gender in native American cultures.* (J. L. Vantine, Trans.). Austin: University of Texas Press.

Lang, S. 1999. Lesbians, men-women, and two-spirits: Homosexuality and gender in Native American cultures. In E. Blackwood & S. E. Wieringa (Eds). *Female desires: Same-sex relations and transgender practices across cultures* (pp. 91–118). New York: Columbia University Press.

Lannoy, R. 1975. *The speaking tree.* New York: Oxford University Press.

Levy, R. 1973. *Tahitians: Mind and Experience in the Society Islands.* Chicago: University of Chicago Press.

Manalansan, M.F. 2003. *Global divas: Filipino gay men in the diaspora.* Durham, NC: Duke University Press.

Marcos, S. 2002. Beyond binary categories: Mesoamerican religious sexuality. In S. Ellingson & M.C. Green (Eds.). Religion and sexuality in cross-cultural perspective (pp. 111–136). New York: Routledge.

Matzner, A. 2001. *'O au no keia: Voices from Hawai'i's mahu and transgender communities.* Philadelphia, PA: X Libris.

Nanda, Serena. 2012. The Hijras: An alternative gender in India. In *Annual Editions: Anthropology.* New York: McGraw-Hill.

Nanda, S. 1996. Hijras: An alternative sex and gender role in India. In G. Herdt. (Ed.). *Third sex third gender: Beyond sexual dimorphism in culture and history* (pp. 373–418). New York: Zone Books.

Nanda, S. 1999. *Neither man nor woman: The hijras of India* (2nd ed.). Belmont, CA: Wadsworth.

Nanda, S. 2000. *Gender diversity: Crosscultural variations.* Prospect Heights, IL: Waveland.

Norgren, J., & S. Nanda. 2006. *American cultural pluralism and law* (3rd ed.). Westport, CT: Praeger/Greenwood.

Parker, R. C. 1995. Changing Brazilian constructions of homosexuality. In S. O. Murray (Ed.). *Latin American male homosexualities* (pp. 241–55). Albuquerque: University of New Mexico Press.

Peletz, M. 2009. *Gender pluralism: Southeast Asia since early modern times.* New York: Routledge.

Phillimore, P. l991. Unmarried women of the Dhaula Dhar: Celibacy and social control in Northwest

India. *Journal of Anthropological Research* 47(3): 331–350.

Reddy, Gayatri. 2005. *With respect to sex: Negotiating hijra identity in south India.* Chicago: University of Chicago Press.

Roscoe, W. 1996. How to become a berdache: Toward a unified analysis of gender diversity. In G. Herdt (Ed.). *Third sex, third gender: Beyond sexual dimorphism in culture and history* (pp. 329–372). New York: Zone Books.

Trumbach, R. 1996. London's sapphists: From three sexes to four genders in the making of modern culture. In G. Herdt (Ed.). *Third sex third gender: Beyond sexual dimorphism in culture and history* (pp. 111–136). New York: Zone Books.

Valentine, D. 2007. *Imagining transgender: An ethnography of a category.* Durham, NC: Duke University Press.

Wafer, J. 1991. *The taste of blood: Spirit possession in Brazilian candomble.* Philadelphia: University of Pennsylvania Press.

Wekker, G. 1999. "What's Identity got to do with it?": Rethinking identity in light of the *Mati* work in Suriname. In E. Blackwood and S. Wieringa (Eds.). *Female desires: Same-sex relations and transgender practices across cultures.* New York: Columbia University Press.

Whitehead, H. 1981. The bow and the burden strap: A new look at institutionalized homosexuality in Native North America. In S.B. Ortner & H. Whitehead (Eds.). *Sexual meanings: The cultural construction of gender and sexuality* (pp. 80–115). Cambridge: Cambridge University Press.

Wikan, U. 1977. Man becomes woman: Transsexualism in Oman as a key to gender roles. *Man*, N.S. *12*, pp. 304–319.

Williams, W. 1986. *The spirit and the flesh.* Boston: Beacon Press.

PART 3

The Psychology of Sex Roles

Even if biology were destiny, the founder of psychoanalysis Sigmund Freud argued, the process by which biological males and females become gendered men and women does not happen naturally nor inevitably. Gender identity, he argued, is an achievement—the outcome of a struggle for boys to separate from their mothers and identify with their fathers, and of a parallel and complementary struggle for girls to reconcile themselves to their sexual inadequacy and therefore maintain their identification with their mothers.

Subsequent generations of psychologists have attempted to specify the content of that achievement of gender identity, and how it might be measured. In the early 1930s, Lewis Terman, one of the country's most eminent social psychologists, codified gender identity into a set of attitudes, traits, and behaviors that enabled researchers to pinpoint exactly where any young person was on a continuum between masculinity and femininity. If one had successfully acquired the "appropriate" collection of traits and attitudes, one (and one's parents) could rest assured that one would continue to develop "normally." Gender nonconformity—boys who scored high on the femininity side of the continuum or girls who scored high on the masculine side—was a predictor, Terman argued, for sexual nonconformity.

Homosexuality was the sexual behavioral outcome of a gender problem, of men who had not successfully mastered masculinity or women who had not successfully mastered femininity.

In this section Janet Shibley Hyde reviews all the studies of gender difference in psychology—traits, attitudes, and behaviors—and finds few, if any, really big differences. It turns out that the empirical research reveals that we're all from planet Earth.

Despite these similarities, an enormous cultural and psychological edifice is concerned with creating, sustaining, and reproducing gender difference, and then convincing us that it's natural, inevitable, and biologically based. C. J. Pascoe, for example, shows how homophobic teasing and bullying serve as a sort of policing device to make sure that boys (and to a lesser extent girls) remain conformists to gender norms. The article by Deborah L. Tolman observes how socialization creates the very differences we believe we observe and thus sustain the inequalities we think are so natural.

The Gender Similarities Hypothesis

JANET SHIBLEY HYDE

The mass media and the general public are captivated by findings of gender differences. John Gray's (1992) *Men Are from Mars, Women Are from Venus,* which argued for enormous psychological differences between women and men, has sold over 30 million copies and been translated into forty languages (Gray, 2005). Deborah Tannen's (1991) *You Just Don't Understand: Women and Men in Conversation* argued for the *different cultures hypothesis:* that men's and women's patterns of speaking are so fundamentally different that men and women essentially belong to different linguistic communities or cultures. That book was on the *New York Times* bestseller list for nearly four years and has been translated into twenty-four languages (AnnOnline, 2005). Both of these works, and dozens of others like them, have argued for the *differences hypothesis:* that males and females are, psychologically, vastly different. Here, I advance a very different view—the *gender similarities hypothesis* (for related statements, see Epstein, 1988; Hyde, 1985; Hyde & Plant, 1995; Kimball, 1995).

The Hypothesis

The gender similarities hypothesis holds that males and females are similar on most, but not all, psychological variables. That is, men and women, as well as boys and girls, are more alike than they are different. In terms of effect sizes, the gender similarities hypothesis states that most psychological gender differences are in the close-to-zero ($d \leq 0.10$) or small ($0.11 < d < 0.35$) range, a few are in the moderate range ($0.36 < d < 0.65$), and very few are large ($d = 0.66$–1.00) or very large ($d > 1.00$).

Although the fascination with psychological gender differences has been present from the dawn of formalized psychology around 1879 (Shields, 1975), a few early researchers highlighted gender similarities. Thorndike (1914), for example, believed that psychological gender differences were too small, compared with within-gender variation, to be important. Leta Stetter Hollingworth (1918) reviewed available research on gender differences in mental traits and found little evidence of gender differences. Another important reviewer of gender research in the early 1900s, Helen Thompson Woolley (1914), lamented the gap between the data and scientists' views on the question:

> The general discussions of the psychology of sex, whether by psychologists or by sociologists show such a wide diversity of points of view that one feels that the truest thing to be said at present is that scientific evidence plays very little part in producing convictions. (p. 372)

The Role of Meta-Analysis in Assessing Psychological Gender Differences

Reviews of research on psychological gender differences began with Woolley's (1914) and Hollingworth's (1918) and extended through Maccoby and Jacklin's (1974) watershed book *The Psychology of Sex Differences,* in which they reviewed more than 2,000 studies of gender differences in a wide variety of domains, including

---

Janet Shibley Hyde, "The Gender Similarities Hypothesis" from *American Psychologist* 60, no. 6 (September 2005): 581–592.

abilities, personality, social behavior, and memory. Maccoby and Jacklin dismissed as unfounded many popular beliefs in psychological gender differences, including beliefs that girls are more "social" than boys; that girls are more suggestible; that girls have lower self-esteem; that girls are better at rote learning and simple tasks, whereas boys are better at higher level cognitive processing; and that girls lack achievement motivation. Maccoby and Jacklin concluded that gender differences were well established in only four areas: verbal ability, visual-spatial ability, mathematical ability, and aggression. Overall, then, they found much evidence for gender similarities. Secondary reports of their findings in textbooks and other sources, however, focused almost exclusively on their conclusions about gender differences (e.g., Gleitman, 1981; Lefrançois, 1990).

Shortly after this important work appeared, the statistical method of meta-analysis was developed (e.g., Glass, McGaw, & Smith, 1981; Hedges & Olkin, 1985; Rosenthal, 1991). This method revolutionized the study of psychological gender differences. Meta-analyses quickly appeared on issues such as gender differences in influenceability (Eagly & Carli, 1981), abilities (Hyde, 1981; Hyde & Linn, 1988; Linn & Petersen, 1985), and aggression (Eagly & Steffen, 1986; Hyde, 1984, 1986).

Meta-analysis is a statistical method for aggregating research findings across many studies of the same question (Hedges & Becker, 1986). It is ideal for synthesizing research on gender differences, an area in which often dozens or even hundreds of studies of a particular question have been conducted.

Crucial to meta-analysis is the concept of effect size, which measures the magnitude of an effect—in this case, the magnitude of gender difference. In gender meta-analyses, the measure of effect size typically is *d* (Cohen, 1988):

$$d = \frac{M_M - M_F}{S_W},$$

where M_M is the mean score for males, M_F is the mean score for females, and s_w is the average within-sex standard deviation. That is, *d* measures how far apart the male and female means are in standardized units. In gender meta-analysis, the effect sizes computed from all individual studies are averaged to obtain an overall effect size reflecting the magnitude of gender differences across all studies. In the present article, I follow the convention that negative values of *d* mean that females scored higher on a dimension, and positive values of *d* indicate that males scored higher.

Gender meta-analyses generally proceed in four steps: (a) The researcher locates all studies on the topic being reviewed, typically using databases such as PsycINFO and carefully chosen search terms. (b) Statistics are extracted from each report, and an effect size is computed for each study. (c) A weighted average of the effect sizes is computed (weighting by sample size) to obtain an overall assessment of the direction and magnitude of the gender difference when all studies are combined. (d) Homogeneity analyses are conducted to determine whether the group of effect sizes is relatively homogeneous. If it is not, then the studies can be partitioned into theoretically meaningful groups to determine whether the effect size is larger for some types of studies and smaller for other types. The researcher could ask, for example, whether gender differences are larger for measures of physical aggression compared with measures of verbal aggression.

The Evidence

To evaluate the gender similarities hypothesis, I collected the major meta-analyses that have been conducted on psychological gender differences. They are listed in Table 1, grouped roughly into six categories: those that assessed cognitive variables, such as abilities; those that assessed verbal or nonverbal communication; those that assessed social or personality variables, such as aggression or leadership; those that assessed measures of psychological well-being, such as self-esteem; those that assessed motor behaviors, such as throwing distance; and those that assessed miscellaneous constructs, such as moral reasoning. I began with meta-analyses reviewed previously by Hyde and Plant (1995), Hyde and Frost (1993), and Ashmore (1990). I updated these lists with more recent meta-analyses and, where possible, replaced older meta-analyses with more up-to-date meta-analyses that used larger samples and better statistical methods.

Hedges and Nowell (1995; see also Feingold, 1988) have argued that the canonical method of meta-analysis—which often aggregates data from many small convenience samples—should be augmented or replaced by data from large probability samples, at least when that is possible (e.g., in areas such as ability testing). Test-norming data as well as data from major national surveys such as the National Longitudinal Study of Youth provide important information. Findings from samples such as these are included in the summary shown in Table 1, where the number of reports is marked with an asterisk.

Inspection of the effect sizes shown in the rightmost column of Table 1 reveals strong evidence for the gender similarities hypothesis. These effect sizes are summarized in Table 2. Of the 128 effect sizes shown in Table 1, 4 were unclassifiable because the meta-analysis provided such a wide range for the estimate. The remaining 124 effect sizes were classified into the categories noted earlier: close-to-zero ($d \leq 0.10$), small ($0.11 < d < 0.35$), moderate

Table 1. Major Meta-Analyses of Research on Psychological Gender Differences

Study and Variable	Age	No. of Reports	*d*
Cognitive Variables			
Hyde, Fennema, & Lamon (1990)			
Mathematics computation	All	45	−0.14
Mathematics concepts	All	41	−0.03
Mathematics problem solving	All	48	+0.08
Hedges & Nowell (1995)			
Reading comprehension	Adolescents	5*	−0.09
Vocabulary	Adolescents	4*	+0.06
Mathematics	Adolescents	6*	+0.16
Perceptual speed	Adolescents	4*	−0.28
Science	Adolescents	4*	+0.32
Spatial ability	Adolescents	2*	+0.19
Hyde, Fennema, Ryan, et al. (1990)			
Mathematics self-confidence	All	56	+0.16
Mathematics anxiety	All	53	−0.15
Feingold (1988)			
DAT spelling	Adolescents	5*	−0.45
DAT language	Adolescents	5*	−0.40
DAT verbal reasoning	Adolescents	5*	−0.02
DAT abstract reasoning	Adolescents	5*	−0.04
DAT numerical ability	Adolescents	5*	−0.10
DAT perceptual speed	Adolescents	5*	−0.34
DAT mechanical reasoning	Adolescents	5*	+0.76
DAT space relations	Adolescents	5*	+0.15
Hyde & Linn (1988)			
Vocabulary	All	40	−0.02
Reading comprehension	All	18	−0.03
Speech production	All	12	−0.33

(continued)

Table 1. *(continued)*

Study and Variable	Age	No. of Reports	d
Cognitive Variables			
Linn & Petersen (1985)			
Spatial perception	All	62	+0.44
Mental rotation	All	29	+0.73
Spatial visualization	All	81	+0.13
Voyer et al. (1995)			
Spatial perception	All	92	+0.44
Mental rotation	All	78	+0.56
Spatial visualization	All	116	+0.19
Lynn & Irwing (2004)			
Progressive matrices	6–14 years	15	+0.02
Progressive matrices	15–19 years	23	+0.16
Progressive matrices	Adults	10	+0.30
Whitley et al. (1986)			
Attribution of success to ability	All	29	+0.13
Attribution of success to effort	All	29	−0.04
Attribution of success to task	All	29	−0.01
Attribution of success to luck	All	29	−0.07
Attribution of failure to ability	All	29	+0.16
Attribution of failure to effort	All	29	+0.15
Attribution of failure to task	All	29	−0.08
Attribution of failure luck	All	29	−0.15
Communication			
Anderson & Leaper (1998)			
Interruptions in conversation	Adults	53	+0.15
Intrusive interruptions	Adults	17	+0.33
Leaper & Smith (2004)			
Talkativeness	Children	73	−0.11
Affiliative speech	Children	46	−0.26
Assertive speech	Children	75	+0.11
Dindia & Allen (1992)			
Self-disclosure (all studies)	—	205	−0.18
Self-disclosure to stranger	—	99	−0.07
Self-disclosure to friend	—	50	−0.28
LaFrance et al. (2003)			
Smiling	Adolescents and adults	418	−0.40
Smiling: Aware of being observed	Adolescents and adults	295	−0.46
Smiling: Not aware of being observed	Adolescents and adults	31	−0.19

Table 1. *(continued)*

Study and Variable	Age	No. of Reports	*d*
	Communication *(continued)*		
McClure (2000)			
Facial expression processing	Infants	29	−0.18 to −0.92
Facial expression processing	Children and adolescents	89	−0.13 to −0.18
	Social and Personality Variables		
Hyde (1984, 1986)			
Aggression (all types)	All	69	+0.50
Physical aggression	All	26	+0.60
Verbal aggression	All	6	+0.43
Eagly & Steffen (1986)			
Aggression	Adults	50	+0.29
Physical aggression	Adults	30	+0.40
Psychological aggression	Adults	20	+0.18
Knight et al. (2002)			
Physical aggression	All	41	+0.59
Verbal aggression	All	22	+0.28
Aggression in low emotional arousal context	All	40	+0.30
Aggression in emotional arousal context	All	83	+0.56
Bettencourt & Miller (1996)			
Aggression under provocation	Adults	57	10.17
Aggression under neutral conditions	Adults	50	+0.33
Archer (2004)			
Aggression in real-world settings	All	75	+0.30 to +0.63
Physical aggression	All	111	+0.33 to +0.84
Verbal aggression	All	68	+0.09 to +0.55
Indirect aggression	All	40	−0.74 to +0.05
Stuhlmacher & Walters (1999)			
Negotiation outcomes	Adults	53	+0.09
Walters et al. (1998)			
Negotiator competitiveness	Adults	79	10.07
Eagly & Crowley (1986)			
Helping behavior	Adults	99	+0.13
Helping: Surveillance context	Adults	16	+0.74
Helping: No surveillance	Adults	41	−0.02
Oliver & Hyde (1993)			
Sexuality: Masturbation	All	26	+0.96

(continued)

Table 1. *(continued)*

Study and Variable	Age	No. of Reports	d
Social and Personality Variables *(continued)*			
Sexuality: Attitudes about casual sex	All	10	+0.81
Sexual satisfaction	All	15	−0.06
Attitudes about extramarital sex	All	17	+0.29
Murnen & Stockton (1997)			
Arousal to sexual stimuli	Adults	62	+0.31
Eagly & Johnson (1990)			
Leadership: Interpersonal style	Adults	153	−0.04 to −0.07
Leadership: Task style	Adults	154	0.00 to −0.09
Leadership: Democratic vs. autocratic	Adults	28	+0.22 to +0.34
Eagly et al. (1992)			
Leadership: Evaluation	Adults	114	+0.05
Eagly et al. (1995)			
Leadership effectiveness	Adults	76	−0.02
Eagly et al. (2003)			
Leadership: Transformational	Adults	44	−0.10
Leadership: Transactional	Adults	51	−0.13 to +0.27
Leadership: Laissez-faire	Adults	16	+0.16
Feingold (1994)			
Neuroticism: Anxiety	Adolescents and adults	13*	−0.32
Neuroticism: Impulsiveness	Adolescents and adults	6*	−0.01
Extraversion: Gregariousness	Adolescents and adults	10*	−0.07
Extraversion: Assertiveness	Adolescents and adults	10*	+0.51
Extraversion: Activity	Adolescents and adults	5	+0.08
Openness	Adolescents and adults	4*	+0.19
Agreeableness: Trust	Adolescents and adults	4*	−0.35
Agreeableness: Tendermindedness	Adolescents and adults	10*	−0.91
Conscientiousness	Adolescents and adults	4	−0.18
Psychological Well-Being			
Kling et al. (1999, Analysis I)			
Self-esteem	All	216	+0.21
Kling et al. (1999, Analysis II)			
Self-esteem	Adolescents	15*	+0.04 to +0.16
Major et al. (1999)			
Self-esteem	All	226	+0.14
Feingold & Mazzella (1998)			
Body esteem	All	—	+0.58
Twenge & Nolen-Hoeksema (2002)			
Depression symptoms	8–16 years	310	+0.02

Table 1. *(continued)*

Study and Variable	Age	No. of Reports	d
Psychological Well-Being *(continued)*			
Wood et al. (1989)	Adults	17	−0.03
Life satisfaction	Adults	22	−0.07
Happiness			
Pinquart & Sörensen (2001)			
Life satisfaction	Elderly	176	+0.08
Self-esteem	Elderly	59	+0.08
Happiness	Elderly	56	−0.06
Tamres et al. (2002)			
Coping: Problem-focused	All	22	−0.13
Coping: Rumination	All	10	−0.19
Motor Behaviors			
Thomas & French (1985)			
Balance	3–20 years	67	+0.09
Grip strength	3–20 years	37	+0.66
Throw velocity	3–20 years	12	+2.18
Throw distance	3–20 years	47	+1.98
Vertical jump	3–20 years	20	+0.18
Sprinting	3–20 years	66	+0.63
Flexibility	5–10 years	13	−0.29
Eaton & Enns (1986)			
Activity level	All	127	+0.49
Miscellaneous			
Thoma (1986)			
Moral reasoning: Stage	Adolescents and adults	56	−0.21
Jaffee & Hyde (2000)			
Moral reasoning: Justice orientation	All	95	+0.19
Moral reasoning: Care orientation	All	160	−0.28
Silverman (2003)			
Delay of gratification	All	38	−0.12
Whitley et al. (1999)			
Cheating behavior	All	36	+0.17
Cheating attitudes	All	14	+0.35
Whitley (1997)			
Computer use: Current	All	18	+0.33
Computer self-efficacy	All	29	+0.41
Konrad et al. (2000)			
Job attribute preference: Earnings	Adults	207	+0.12
Job attribute preference: Security	Adults	182	−0.02
Job attribute preference: Challenge		63	+0.05

(continued)

Table 1. (*continued*)

Study and Variable	Age	No. of Reports	d
Miscellaneous			
Job attribute preference: Physical work environment	Adults	96	−0.13
Job attribute preference: Power	Adults	68	+0.04

Note: Positive values of *d* represent higher scores for men and/or boys; negative values of *d* represent higher scores for women and/or girls. Asterisks indicate that data were from major, large national samples. Dashes indicate that data were not available (i.e., the study in question did not provide this information clearly). No. = number; DAT = Differential Aptitude Test.

Table 2. Effect Sizes (n = 124) for Psychological Gender Differences, Based on Meta-Analyses, Categorized by Range of Magnitude

	Effect Size Range				
Effect Sizes	**0–0.10**	**0.11–0.35**	**0.36–0.65**	**0.66–1.00**	**>1.00**
Number	37	59	19	7	2
% of total	30	48	15	6	2

(0.36 < *d* < 0.65), large (*d* = 0.66–1.00), or very large (> .1.00). The striking result is that 30% of the effect sizes are in the close-to-zero range, and an additional 48% are in the small range. That is, 78% of gender differences are small or close to zero. This result is similar to that of Hyde and Plant (1995), who found that 60% of effect sizes for gender differences were in the small or close-to-zero range.

The small magnitude of these effects is even more striking given that most of the meta-analyses addressed the classic gender differences questions—that is, areas in which gender differences were reputed to be reliable, such as mathematics performance, verbal ability, and aggressive behavior. For example, despite Tannen's (1991) assertions, gender differences in most aspects of communication are small. Gilligan (1982) has argued that males and females speak in a different moral "voice," yet meta-analyses show that gender differences in moral reasoning and moral orientation are small (Jaffee & Hyde, 2000).

The Exceptions

As noted earlier, the gender similarities hypothesis does not assert that males and females are similar in absolutely every domain. The exceptions—areas in which gender differences are moderate or large in magnitude—should be recognized.

The largest gender differences in Table 1 are in the domain of motor performance, particularly for measures such as throwing velocity (*d* = 2.18) and throwing distance (*d* = 1.98) (Thomas & French, 1985). These differences are particularly large after puberty, when the gender gap in muscle mass and bone size widens.

A second area in which large gender differences are found is some—but not all—measures of sexuality (Oliver & Hyde, 1993). Gender differences are strikingly large for incidences of masturbation and for attitudes about sex in a casual, uncommitted relationship. In contrast, the gender difference in reported sexual satisfaction is close to zero.

Across several meta-analyses, aggression has repeatedly shown gender differences that are moderate in magnitude (Archer, 2004; Eagly & Steffen, 1986; Hyde, 1984, 1986). The gender difference in physical aggression is particularly reliable and is larger than the gender difference in verbal aggression. Much publicity has been given to gender differences in relational aggression, with girls scoring higher (e.g., Crick & Grotpeter, 1995). According to the Archer (2004) meta-analysis, indirect or

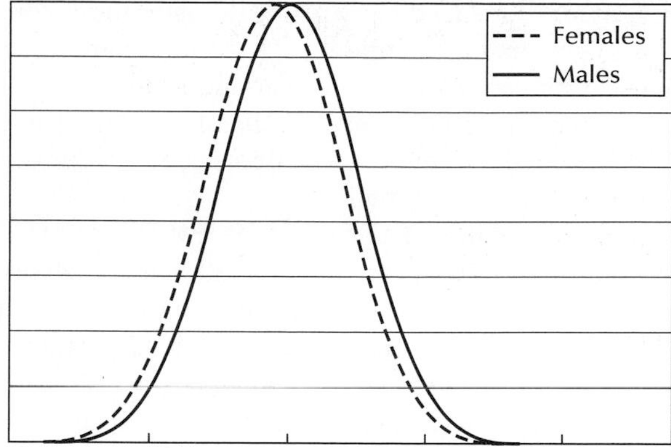

Figure 1. Graphic Representation of a 0.21 Effect Size
Note: Two normal distributions that are 0.21 standard deviations apart (i.e., d = 0.21). This is the approximate magnitude of the gender difference in self-esteem, averaged over all samples, found by Kling et al. (1999). From "Gender Differences in Self-Esteem: A Meta-Analysis," by K. C. Kling, J. S. Hyde, C. J. Showers, and B. N. Buswell, 1999, *Psychological Bulletin*, 125, p. 484. Copyright © 1999 by the American Psychological Association.

relational aggression showed an effect size for gender differences of −0.45 when measured by direct observation, but it was only −0.19 for peer ratings, −0.02 for self-reports, and −0.13 for teacher reports. Therefore, the evidence is ambiguous regarding the magnitude of the gender difference in relational aggression.

The Interpretation of Effect Sizes

The interpretation of effect sizes is contested. On one side of the argument, the classic source is the statistician Cohen (1969, 1988), who recommended that 0.20 be considered a small effect, 0.50 be considered medium, and 0.80 be considered large. It is important to note that he set these guidelines before the advent of meta-analysis, and they have been the standards used in statistical power analysis for decades.

In support of these guidelines are indicators of overlap between two distributions. For example, Kling, Hyde, Showers, and Buswell (1999) graphed two distributions differing on average by an effect size of 0.21, the effect size they found for gender differences in self-esteem. This graph is shown in Figure 1. Clearly, this small effect size reflects distributions that overlap greatly—that is, that show more similarity than difference. Cohen (1988) developed a U statistic that quantifies the percentage of nonoverlap of distributions. For d = 0.20, U = 15%; that is, 85% of the areas of the distributions overlap. According to another Cohen measure of overlap, for d = 0.20, 54% of individuals in Group A exceed the 50th percentile for Group B.

For another way to consider the interpretation of effect sizes, d can also be expressed as an equivalent value of the Pearson correlation, r (Cohen, 1988). For the small effect size of 0.20, r = .10, certainly a small correlation. A d of 0.50 is equivalent to an r of .24, and for d = 0.80, r = .37.

Rosenthal (1991; Rosenthal & Rubin, 1982) has argued the other side of the case—namely, that seemingly small effect sizes can be important and make for impressive applied effects. As an example, he took a two-group experimental design in which one group is treated for cancer and the other group receives a placebo. He used the method of binomial effect size display (BESD) to illustrate the consequences. Using this method, for example, an r of .32 between treatment and outcome, accounting for only 10% of the variance, translates into a survival rate of 34% in the placebo group and 66% in the treated group. Certainly, the effect is impressive.

How does this apply to the study of gender differences? First, in terms of costs of errors in scientific decision making, psychological gender differences are quite a different matter from curing cancer. So, interpretation of the magnitude of effects must be heavily conditioned by the costs of making Type I and Type II errors for the particular question under consideration. I look forward to statisticians developing indicators that take these factors into account. Second, Rosenthal used the *r* metric, and when this is translated into *d*, the effects look much less impressive. For example, a *d* of 0.20 is equivalent to an *r* of 0.10, and Rosenthal's BESD indicates that that effect is equivalent to cancer survival increasing from 45% to 55%—once again, a small effect. A close-to-zero effect size of 0.10 is equivalent to an *r* of .05, which translates to cancer survival rates increasing only from 47.5% to 52.5% in the treatment group compared with the control group. In short, I believe that Cohen's guidelines provide a reasonable standard for the interpretation of gender differences effect sizes.

One caveat should be noted, however. The foregoing discussion is implicitly based on the assumption that the variabilities in the male and female distributions are equal. Yet the greater male variability hypothesis was originally proposed more than a century ago, and it survives today (Feingold, 1992; Hedges & Friedman, 1993). In the 1800s, this hypothesis was proposed to explain why there were more male than female geniuses and, at the same time, more males among the mentally retarded. Statistically, the combination of a small average difference favoring males and a larger standard deviation for males, for some trait such as mathematics performance, could lead to a lopsided gender ratio favoring males in the upper tail of the distribution reflecting exceptional talent. The statistic used to investigate this question is the variance ratio (VR), the ratio of the male variance to the female variance. Empirical investigations of the VR have found values of 1.00–1.08 for vocabulary (Hedges & Nowell, 1995), 1.05–1.25 for mathematics performance (Hedges & Nowell), and 0.87–1.04 for self-esteem (Kling et al., 1999). Therefore, it appears that whether males or females are more variable depends on the domain under consideration. Moreover, most VR estimates are close to 1.00, indicating similar variances for males and females. Nonetheless, this issue of possible gender differences in variability merits continued investigation.

Developmental Trends

Not all meta-analyses have examined developmental trends and, given the preponderance of psychological research on college students, developmental analysis is not always possible. However, meta-analysis can be powerful for identifying age trends in the magnitude of gender differences. Here, I consider a few key examples of meta-analyses that have taken this developmental approach (see Table 3).

At the time of the meta-analysis by Hyde, Fennema, and Lamon (1990), it was believed that gender differences in mathematics performance were small or nonexistent in childhood and that the male advantage appeared beginning around the time of puberty (Maccoby & Jacklin, 1974). It was also believed that males were better at high-level mathematical problems that required complex processing, whereas females were better at low-level mathematics that required only simple computation. Hyde and colleagues addressed both hypotheses in their meta-analysis. They found a small gender difference favoring girls in computation in elementary school and middle school and no gender difference in computation in the high school years. There was no gender difference in complex problem solving in elementary school or middle school, but a small gender difference favoring males emerged in the high school years (d = 0.29). Age differences in the magnitude of the gender effect were significant for both computation and problem solving.

Kling et al. (1999) used a developmental approach in their meta-analysis of studies of gender differences in self-esteem, on the basis of the assertion of prominent authors such as Mary Pipher (1994) that girls' self-esteem takes a nosedive at the beginning of adolescence. They found that the magnitude of the gender difference did grow larger from childhood to adolescence: In childhood (ages 7–10), d = 0.16; for early adolescence (ages 11–14), d = 0.23;

Table 3. Selected Meta-Analyses Showing Developmental Trends in the Magnitude of Gender Differences

Study and Variable	Age (years)	No. of Reports	*d*
Hyde, Fennema, & Lamon (1990)			
Mathematics: Complex problem solving	5–10	11	0.00
	11–14	21	−0.02
	15–18	10	+0.29
	19–25	15	+0.32
Kling et al. (1999)			
Self-esteem	7–10	22	+0.16
	11–14	53	+0.23
	15–18	44	+0.33
	19–22	72	+0.18
	23–59	16	+0.10
	>60	6	−0.03
Major et al. (1999)			
Self-esteem	5–10	24	+0.01
	11–13	34	+0.12
	14–18	65	+0.16
	19 or older	97	+0.13
Twenge & Nolen-Hoeksema (2002)			
Depressive symptoms	8–12	86	−0.04
	13–16	49	+0.16
Thomas & French (1985)			
Throwing distance	3–8	—	+1.50 to +2.00
	16–18	—	+3.50

Note: Positive values of *d* represent higher scores for men and/or boys; negative values of *d* represent higher scores for women and/or girls. Dashes indicate that data were not available (i.e., the study in question did not provide this information clearly). No. = number.

and for the high school years (ages 15–18), $d = 0.33$. However, the gender difference did not suddenly become large in early adolescence, and even in high school the difference was still not large. Moreover, the gender difference was smaller in older samples; for example, for ages 23–59, $d = 0.10$.

Whitley's (1997) analysis of age trends in computer self-efficacy is revealing. In grammar school samples, $d = 0.09$, whereas in high school samples, $d = 0.66$. This dramatic trend leads to questions about what forces are at work transforming girls from feeling as effective with computers as boys do to showing a large difference in self-efficacy by high school.

These examples illustrate the extent to which the magnitude of gender differences can fluctuate with age. Gender differences grow larger or smaller at different times in the life span, and meta-analysis is a powerful tool for detecting these trends. Moreover, the fluctuating magnitude of gender differences at different ages argues against the differences model and notions that gender differences are large and stable.

The Importance of Context

Gender researchers have emphasized the importance of context in creating, erasing, or even reversing psychological gender differences (Bussey &

Bandura, 1999; Deaux & Major, 1987; Eagly & Wood, 1999). Context may exert influence at numerous levels, including the written instructions given for an exam, dyadic interactions between participants or between a participant and an experimenter, or the sociocultural level.

In an important experiment, Lightdale and Prentice (1994) demonstrated the importance of gender roles and social context in creating or erasing the purportedly robust gender difference in aggression. Lightdale and Prentice used the technique of deindividuation to produce a situation that removed the influence of gender roles. *Deindividuation* refers to a state in which the person has lost his or her individual identity; that is, the person has become anonymous. Under such conditions, people should feel no obligation to conform to social norms such as gender roles. Half of the participants, who were college students, were assigned to an individuated condition by having them sit close to the experimenter, identify themselves by name, wear large name tags, and answer personal questions. Participants in the deindividuation condition sat far from the experimenter, wore no name tags, and were simply told to wait. All participants were also told that the experiment required information from only half of the participants, whose behavior would be monitored, and that the other half would remain anonymous. Participants then played an interactive video game in which they first defended and then attacked by dropping bombs. The number of bombs dropped was the measure of aggressive behavior.

The results indicated that in the individuated condition, men dropped significantly more bombs ($M = 31.1$) than women did ($M = 26.8$). In the deindividuated condition, however, there were no significant gender differences and, in fact, women dropped somewhat more bombs ($M = 41.1$) than men ($M = 36.8$). In short, the significant gender difference in aggression disappeared when gender norms were removed.

Steele's (1997; Steele & Aronson, 1995) work on stereotype threat has produced similar evidence in the cognitive domain. Although the original experiments concerned African Americans and the stereotype that they are intellectually inferior, the theory was quickly applied to gender and stereotypes that girls and women are bad at math (Brown & Josephs, 1999; Quinn & Spencer, 2001; Spencer, Steele, & Quinn, 1999; Walsh, Hickey, & Duffy, 1999). In one experiment, male and female college students with equivalent math backgrounds were tested (Spencer et al., 1999). In one condition, participants were told that the math test had shown gender difference in the past, and in the other condition, they were told that the test had been shown to be gender fair—that men and women had performed equally on it. In the condition in which participants had been told that the math test was gender fair, there were no gender differences in performance on the test. In the condition in which participants expected gender differences, women underperformed compared with men. This simple manipulation of context was capable of creating or erasing gender differences in math performance.

Meta-analysts have addressed the importance of context for gender differences. In one of the earliest demonstrations of context effects, Eagly and Crowley (1986) meta-analyzed studies of gender differences in helping behavior, basing the analysis in social-role theory. They argued that certain kinds of helping are part of the male role: helping that is heroic or chivalrous. Other kinds of helping are part of the female role: helping that is nurturant and caring, such as caring for children. Heroic helping involves danger to the self, and both heroic and chivalrous helping are facilitated when onlookers are present. Women's nurturant helping more often occurs in private, with no onlookers. Averaged over all studies, men helped more ($d = 0.34$). However, when studies were separated into those in which onlookers were present and participants were aware of it, $d = 0.74$. When no onlookers were present, $d = 20.02$. Moreover, the magnitude of the gender difference was highly correlated with the degree of danger in the helping situation; gender differences were largest favoring males in situations with the most danger. In short, the gender difference in helping behavior can be large, favoring males, or close to zero, depending on the social context in which the behavior is measured. Moreover, the pattern of gender differences is consistent with social-role theory.

Anderson and Leaper (1998) obtained similar context effects in their meta-analysis of gender differences in conversational interruption. At the time of their meta-analysis, it was widely believed that men interrupted women considerably more than the reverse. Averaged over all studies, however, Anderson and Leaper found a *d* of 0.15, a small effect. The effect size for intrusive interruptions (excluding back-channel interruptions) was larger: 0.33. It is important to note that the magnitude of the gender difference varied greatly depending on the social context in which interruptions were studied. When dyads were observed, $d = 0.06$, but with larger groups of three or more, $d = 0.26$. When participants were strangers, $d = 0.17$, but when they were friends, $d = -0.14$. Here, again, it is clear that gender differences can be created, erased, or reversed, depending on the context.

In their meta-analysis, LaFrance, Hecht, and Paluck (2003) found a moderate gender difference in smiling ($d = -0.41$), with girls and women smiling more. Again, the magnitude of the gender difference was highly dependent on the context. If participants had a clear awareness that they were being observed, the gender difference was larger ($d = -0.46$) than it was if they were not aware of being observed ($d = -0.19$). The magnitude of the gender difference also depended on culture and age.

Dindia and Allen (1992) and Bettencourt and Miller (1996) also found marked context effects in their gender meta-analyses. The conclusion is clear: The magnitude and even the direction of gender differences depend on the context. These findings provide strong evidence against the differences model and its notions that psychological gender differences are large and stable.

Costs of Inflated Claims of Gender Differences

The question of the magnitude of psychological gender differences is more than just an academic concern. There are serious costs of overinflated claims of gender differences (for an extended discussion of this point, see Barnett & Rivers, 2004; see also White & Kowalski, 1994). These costs occur in many areas, including work, parenting, and relationships.

Gilligan's (1982) argument that women speak in a different moral "voice" than men is a well-known example of the differences model. Women, according to Gilligan, speak in a moral voice of caring, whereas men speak in a voice of justice. Despite the fact that meta-analyses disconfirm her arguments for large gender differences (Jaffee & Hyde, 2000; Thoma, 1986; Walker, 1984), Gilligan's ideas have permeated American culture. One consequence of this overinflated claim of gender differences is that it reifies the stereotype of women as caring and nurturant and men as lacking in nurturance. One cost to men is that they may believe that they cannot be nurturant, even in their role as father. For women, the cost in the workplace can be enormous. Women who violate the stereotype of being nurturant and nice can be penalized in hiring and evaluations. Rudman and Glick (1999), for example, found that female job applicants who displayed agentic qualities received considerably lower hireability ratings than agentic male applicants ($d = 0.92$) for a managerial job that had been "feminized" to require not only technical skills and the ability to work under pressure but also the ability to be helpful and sensitive to the needs of others. The researchers concluded that women must present themselves as competent and agentic to be hired, but they may then be viewed as interpersonally deficient and uncaring and receive biased work evaluations because of their violation of the female nurturance stereotype.

A second example of the costs of unwarranted validation of the stereotype of women as caring nurturers comes from Eagly, Makhijani, and Klonsky's (1992) meta-analysis of studies of gender and the evaluation of leaders. Overall, women leaders were evaluated as positively as men leaders ($d = 0.05$). However, women leaders portrayed as uncaring autocrats were at a more substantial disadvantage than were men leaders portrayed similarly ($d = 0.30$). Women who violated the caring stereotype paid for it in their evaluations. The persistence of the stereotype of women as nurturers leads to serious costs for women who violate this stereotype in the workplace.

The costs of overinflated claims of gender differences hit children as well. According to stereotypes, boys are better at math than girls are (Hyde, Fennema, Ryan, Frost, & Hopp, 1990). This stereotype is proclaimed in mass media headlines (Barnett & Rivers, 2004). Meta-analyses, however, indicate a pattern of gender similarities for math performance. Hedges and Nowell (1995) found a *d* of 0.16 for large national samples of adolescents, and Hyde, Fennema, and Lamon (1990) found a *d* of −0.05 for samples of the general population (see also Leahey & Guo, 2000). One cost to children is that mathematically talented girls may be overlooked by parents and teachers because these adults do not expect to find mathematical talent among girls. Parents have lower expectations for their daughters' math success than for their sons' (Lummis & Stevenson, 1990), despite the fact that girls earn better grades in math than boys do (Kimball, 1989). Research has shown repeatedly that parents' expectations for their children's mathematics success relate strongly to outcomes such as the child's mathematics self-confidence and performance, with support for a model in which parents' expectations influence children (e.g., Frome & Eccles, 1998). In short, girls may find their confidence in their ability to succeed in challenging math courses or in a mathematically oriented career undermined by parents' and teachers' beliefs that girls are weak in math ability.

In the realm of intimate heterosexual relationships, women and men are told that they are as different as if they came from different planets and that they communicate in dramatically different ways (Gray, 1992; Tannen, 1991). When relationship conflicts occur, good communication is essential to resolving the conflict (Gottman, 1994). If, however, women and men believe what they have been told—that it is almost impossible for them to communicate with each other—they may simply give up on trying to resolve the conflict through better communication. Therapists will need to dispel erroneous beliefs in massive, unbridgeable gender differences.

Inflated claims about psychological gender differences can hurt boys as well. A large gender gap in self-esteem beginning in adolescence has been touted in popular sources (American Association of University Women, 1991; Orenstein, 1994; Pipher, 1994). Girls' self-esteem is purported to take a nosedive at the beginning of adolescence, with the implication that boys' self-esteem does not. Yet meta-analytic estimates of the magnitude of the gender difference have all been small or close to zero: $d = 0.21$ (Kling et al., 1999, Analysis I), $d = 0.04$–0.16 (Kling et al., 1999, Analysis II), and $d = 0.14$ (Major, Barr, Zubek, & Babey, 1999). In short, self-esteem is roughly as much a problem for adolescent boys as it is for adolescent girls. The popular media's focus on girls as the ones with self-esteem problems may carry a huge cost in leading parents, teachers, and other professionals to overlook boys' self-esteem problems, so that boys do not receive the interventions they need.

As several of these examples indicate, the gender similarities hypothesis carries strong implications for practitioners. The scientific evidence does not support the belief that men and women have inherent difficulties in communicating across gender. Neither does the evidence support the belief that adolescent girls are the only ones with self-esteem problems. Therapists who base their practice in the differences model should reconsider their approach on the basis of the best scientific evidence.

Conclusion

The gender similarities hypothesis stands in stark contrast to the differences model, which holds that men and women, and boys and girls, are vastly different psychologically. The gender similarities hypothesis states, instead, that males and females are alike on most—but not all—psychological variables. Extensive evidence from meta-analyses of research on gender differences supports the gender similarities hypothesis. A few notable exceptions are some motor behaviors (e.g., throwing distance) and some aspects of sexuality, which show large gender differences. Aggression shows a gender difference that is moderate in magnitude.

It is time to consider the costs of overinflated claims of gender differences. Arguably, they cause harm in numerous realms, including women's opportunities in the workplace, couple conflict and communication, and analyses of self-esteem problems among adolescents. Most important, these claims are not consistent with the scientific data.

References

American Association of University Women. (1991). *Shortchanging girls, shortchanging America: Full data report*. Washington, DC: Author.

Anderson, K. J., & Leaper, C. (1998). Meta-analyses of gender effects on conversational interruption: Who, what, when, where, and how. *Sex Roles, 39*, 225–252.

AnnOnline. (2005). *Biography: Deborah Tannen*. Retrieved January 10, 2005, from http://www.annonline.com.

Archer, J. (2004). Sex differences in aggression in real-world setting: A meta-analytic review. *Review of General Psychology, 8*, 291–322.

Ashmore, R. D. (1990). Sex, gender, and the individual. In L. A. Pervin (Ed.), *Handbook of personality: Theory and research* (pp. 486–526). New York: Guilford Press.

Barnett, R., & Rivers, C. (2004). *Same difference: How gender myths are hurting our relationships, our children, and our jobs*. New York: Basic Books.

Bettencourt, B. A., & Miller, N. (1996). Gender differences in aggression as a function of provocation: A meta-analysis. *Psychological Bulletin, 119*, 422–447.

Brown, R. P., & Josephs, R. A. (1999). A burden of proof: Stereotype relevance and gender differences in math performance. *Journal of Personality and Social Psychology, 76*, 246–257.

Bussey, K., & Bandura, A. (1999). Social cognitive theory of gender development and differentiation. *Psychological Review, 106*, 676–713.

Cohen, J. (1969). *Statistical power analysis for the behavioral sciences*. New York: Academic Press.

———. (1988). *Statistical power analysis for the behavioral sciences* (2nd ed.). Hillsdale, NJ: Erlbaum.

Crick, N. R., & Grotpeter, J. K. (1995). Relational aggression, gender, and social-psychological adjustment. *Child Development, 66*, 710–722.

Deaux, K., & Major, B. (1987). Putting gender into context: An interactive model of gender-related behavior. *Psychological Review, 94*, 369–389.

Dindia, K., & Allen, M. (1992). Sex differences in self-disclosure: A meta-analysis. *Psychological Bulletin, 112*, 106–124.

Eagly, A. H., & Carli, L. L. (1981). Sex of researchers and sex-typed communications as determinants of sex differences in influenceability: A meta-analysis of social influence studies. *Psychological Bulletin, 90*, 1–20.

Eagly, A. H., & Crowley, M. (1986). Gender and helping behavior: A meta-analytic review of the social psychological literature. *Psychological Bulletin, 100*, 283–308.

Eagly, A. H., Johannesen-Schmidt, M. C., & van Engen, M. L. (2003). Transformational, transactional, and laissez-faire leadership styles: A meta-analysis comparing women and men. *Psychological Bulletin, 129*, 569–591.

Eagly, A. H., & Johnson, B. T. (1990). Gender and leadership style: A meta-analysis. *Psychological Bulletin, 108*, 233–256.

Eagly, A. H., Karau, S. J., & Makhijani, M. G. (1995). Gender and the effectiveness of leaders: A meta-analysis. *Psychological Bulletin, 117*, 125–145.

Eagly, A. H., Makhijani, M. G., & Klonsky, B. G. (1992). Gender and the evaluation of leaders: A meta-analysis. *Psychological Bulletin, 111*, 3–22.

Eagly, A. H., & Steffen, V. (1986). Gender and aggressive behavior: A meta-analytic review of the social psychological literature. *Psychological Bulletin, 100*, 309–330.

Eagly, A. H., & Wood, W. (1999). The origins of sex differences in human behavior: Evolved dispositions versus social roles. *American Psychologist, 54*, 408–423.

Eaton, W. O., & Enns, L. R. (1986). Sex differences in human motor activity level. *Psychological Bulletin, 100*, 19–28.

Epstein, C. F. (1988). *Deceptive distinctions: Sex, gender, and the social order*. New Haven, CT: Yale University Press.

Feingold, A. (1988). Cognitive gender differences are disappearing. *American Psychologist, 43*, 95–103.

———. (1992). Sex differences in variability in intellectual abilities: A new look at an old controversy. *Review of Educational Research, 62*, 61–84.

———. (1994). Gender differences in personality: A meta-analysis. *Psychological Bulletin, 116*, 429–456.

Feingold, A., & Mazzella, R. (1998). Gender differences in body image are increasing. *Psychological Science, 9*, 190–195.

Frome, P. M., & Eccles, J. S. (1998). Parents' influence on children's achievement-related perceptions. *Journal of Personality and Social Psychology, 74*, 435–452.

Gilligan, C. (1982). *In a different voice: Psychological theory and women's development*. Cambridge, MA: Harvard University Press.

Glass, G. V., McGaw, B., & Smith, M. L. (1981). *Meta-analysis in social research*. Beverly Hills, CA: Sage.

Gleitman, H. (1981). *Psychology*. New York: Norton.

Gottman, J. (1994). *Why marriages succeed or fail*. New York: Simon & Schuster.

Gray, J. (1992). *Men are from Mars, women are from Venus: A practical guide for improving communication and getting what you want in your relationships*. New York: HarperCollins.

———. (2005). *John Gray, Ph.D. is the best-selling relationship author of all time*. Retrieved January 10, 2005, from http://www.marsvenus.com.

Hedges, L. V., & Becker, B. J. (1986). Statistical methods in the meta-analysis of research on gender differences. In J. S. Hyde & M. C. Linn (Eds.), *The psychology of gender: Advances through meta-analysis* (pp. 14–50). Baltimore: Johns Hopkins University Press.

Hedges, L. V., & Friedman, L. (1993). Sex differences in variability in intellectual abilities: A reanalysis of Feingold's results. *Review of Educational Research, 63*, 95–105.

Hedges, L. V., & Nowell, A. (1995, July 7). Sex differences in mental test scores, variability, and numbers of high-scoring individuals. *Science, 269*, 41–45.

Hedges, L. V., & Olkin, I. (1985). *Statistical methods for meta-analysis*. San Diego, CA: Academic Press.

Hollingworth, L. S. (1918). Comparison of the sexes in mental traits. *Psychological Bulletin, 15*, 427–432.

Hyde, J. S. (1981). How large are cognitive gender differences? A meta-analysis using w^2 and *d*. *American Psychologist, 36*, 892–901.

———. (1984). How large are gender differences in aggression? A developmental meta-analysis. *Developmental Psychology, 20*, 722–736.

———. (1985). *Half the human experience: The psychology of women* (3rd ed.). Lexington, MA: Heath.

———. (1986). Gender differences in aggression. In J. S. Hyde & M. C. Linn (Eds.), *The psychology of gender: Advances through meta-analysis* (pp. 51–66). Baltimore: Johns Hopkins University Press.

Hyde, J. S., Fennema, E., & Lamon, S. (1990). Gender differences in mathematics performance: A meta-analysis. *Psychological Bulletin, 107*, 139–155.

Hyde, J. S., Fennema, E., Ryan, M., Frost, L. A., & Hopp, C. (1990). Gender comparisons of mathematics attitudes and affect: A meta-analysis. *Psychology of Women Quarterly, 14*, 299–324.

Hyde, J. S., & Frost, L. A. (1993). Meta-analysis in the psychology of women. In F. L. Denmark & M. A. Paludi (Eds.), *Psychology of women: A handbook of issues and theories* (pp. 67–103). Westport, CT: Greenwood Press.

Hyde, J. S., & Linn, M. C. (1988). Gender differences in verbal ability: A meta-analysis. *Psychological Bulletin, 104*, 53–69.

Hyde, J. S., & Plant, E. A. (1995). Magnitude of psychological gender differences: Another side to the story. *American Psychologist, 50*, 159–161.

Jaffee, S., & Hyde, J. S. (2000). Gender differences in moral orientation: A meta-analysis. *Psychological Bulletin, 126*, 703–726.

Kimball, M. M. (1989). A new perspective on women's math achievement. *Psychological Bulletin, 105*, 198–214.

———. (1995). *Feminist visions of gender similarities and differences*. Binghamton, NY: Haworth Press.

Kling, K. C., Hyde, J. S., Showers, C. J., & Buswell, B. N. (1999). Gender differences in self-esteem: A meta-analysis. *Psychological Bulletin, 125*, 470–500.

Knight, G. P., Guthrie, I. K., Page, M. C., & Fabes, R. A. (2002). Emotional arousal and gender differences in aggression: A meta-analysis. *Aggressive Behavior, 28*, 366–393.

Konrad, A. M., Ritchie, J. E., Lieb, P., & Corrigall, E. (2000). Sex differences and similarities in job attribute preferences: A meta-analysis. *Psychological Bulletin, 126*, 593–641.

LaFrance, M., Hecht, M. A., & Paluck, E. L. (2003). The contingent smile: A meta-analysis of sex differences in smiling. *Psychological Bulletin, 129*, 305–334.

Leahey, E., & Guo, G. (2000). Gender differences in mathematical trajectories. *Social Forces, 80*, 713–732.

Leaper, C., & Smith, T. E. (2004). A meta-analytic review of gender variations in children's language use: Talkativeness, affiliative speech, and assertive speech. *Developmental Psychology, 40*, 993–1027.

Lefrançois, G. R. (1990). *The lifespan* (3rd ed.). Belmont, CA: Wadsworth.

Lightdale, J. R., & Prentice, D. A. (1994). Rethinking sex differences in aggression: Aggressive behavior in the absence of social roles. *Personality and Social Psychology Bulletin, 20*, 34–44.

Linn, M. C., & Petersen, A. C. (1985). Emergence and characterization of sex differences in spatial ability: A meta-analysis. *Child Development, 56*, 1479–1498.

Lummis, M., & Stevenson, H. W. (1990). Gender differences in beliefs and achievement: A cross-cultural study. *Developmental Psychology, 26*, 254–263.

Lynn, R., & Irwing, P. (2004). Sex differences on the progressive matrices: A meta-analysis. *Intelligence, 32*, 481–498.

Maccoby, E. E., & Jacklin, C. N. (1974). *The psychology of sex differences*. Stanford, CA: Stanford University Press.

Major, B., Barr, L., Zubek, J., & Babey, S. H. (1999). Gender and self-esteem: A meta-analysis. In W. B. Swann, J. H. Langlois, & L. A. Gilbert (Eds.), *Sexism and stereotypes in modern society: The gender science of Janet Taylor Spence* (pp. 223–253). Washington, DC: American Psychological Association.

McClure, E. B. (2000). A meta-analytic review of sex differences in facial expression processing and their development in infants, children, and adolescents. *Psychological Bulletin, 126*, 424–453.

Murnen, S. K., & Stockton, M. (1997). Gender and self-reported sexual arousal in response to sexual stimuli: A meta-analytic review. *Sex Roles, 37*, 135–154.

Oliver, M. B., & Hyde, J. S. (1993). Gender differences in sexuality: A meta-analysis. *Psychological Bulletin, 114*, 29–51.

Orenstein, P. (1994). *Schoolgirls: Young women, self-esteem, and the confidence gap*. New York: Anchor Books.

Pinquart, M., & Sörensen (2001). Gender differences in self-concept and psychological well-being in old age: A meta-analysis. *Journal of Gerontology: Psychological Sciences., 56B*, P195–P213.

Pipher, M. (1994). *Reviving Ophelia: Saving the selves of adolescent girls*. New York: Ballantine Books.

Quinn, D. M., & Spencer, S. J. (2001). The interference of stereotype threat with women's generation of mathematical problem-solving strategies. *Journal of Social Issues, 57*, 55–72.

Rosenthal, R. (1991). *Meta-analytic procedures for social research* (Rev. ed.). Newbury Park, CA: Sage.

Rosenthal, R., & Rubin, D. B. (1982). A simple, general purpose display of magnitude of experimental effect. *Journal of Educational Psychology, 74*, 166–169.

Rudman, L. A., & Glick, P. (1999). Feminized management and backlash toward agentic women: The hidden costs to women of a kinder, gentler image of middle managers. *Journal of Personality and Social Psychology, 77*, 1004–1010.

Shields, S. A. (1975). Functionalism, Darwinism, and the psychology of women: A study in social myth. *American Psychologist, 30*, 739–754.

Silverman, I. W. (2003). Gender differences in delay of gratification: A meta-analysis. *Sex Roles, 49*, 451–463.

Spencer, S. J., Steele, C. M., & Quinn, D. M. (1999). Stereotype threat and women's math performance. *Journal of Experimental Social Psychology, 35*, 4–28.

Steele, C. M. (1997). A threat in the air: How stereotypes shape intellectual identity and performance. *American Psychologist, 52*, 613–629.

Steele, C. M., & Aronson, J. (1995). Stereotype threat and the intellectual test performance of African Americans. *Journal of Personality and Social Psychology, 69*, 797–811.

Stuhlmacher, A. C., & Walters, A. E. (1999). Gender differences in negotiation outcome: A meta-analysis. *Personnel Psychology, 52*, 653–677.

Tamres, L. K., Janicki, D., & Helgeson, V. S. (2002). Sex differences in coping behavior: A meta-analytic review and an examination of relative coping. *Personality and Social Psychology Review, 6*, 2–30.

Tannen, D. (1991). *You just don't understand: Women and men in conversation*. New York: Ballantine Books.

Thoma, S. J. (1986). Estimating gender differences in the comprehension and preference of moral issues. *Developmental Review, 6*, 165–180.

Thomas, J. R., & French, K. E. (1985). Gender differences across age in motor performance: A meta-analysis. *Psychological Bulletin, 98*, 260–282.

Thorndike, E. L. (1914). *Educational psychology* (Vol. 3). New York: Teachers College, Columbia University.

Twenge, J. M., & Nolen-Hoeksema. S. (2002). Age, gender, race, socioeconomic status, and birth cohort differences on the Children's Depression Inventory: A meta-analysis. *Journal of Abnormal Psychology, 111*, 578–588.

Voyer, D., Voyer, S., & Bryden, M. P. (1995). Magnitude of sex differences in spatial abilities: A meta-analysis and consideration of critical variables. *Psychological Bulletin, 117*, 250–270.

Walker, L. J. (1984). Sex differences in the development of moral reasoning: A critical review. *Child Development, 55*, 677–691.

Walsh, M., Hickey, C., & Duffy, J. (1999). Influence of item content and stereotype situation on gender differences in mathematical problem solving. *Sex Roles, 41*, 219–240.

Walters, A. E., Stuhlmacher, A. F., & Meyer, L. L. (1998). Gender and negotiator competitiveness: A meta-analysis. *Organizational Behavior and Human Decision Processes, 76*, 1–29.

White, J. W., & Kowalski, R. M. (1994). Deconstructing the myth of the nonaggressive woman: A feminist analysis. *Psychology of Women Quarterly, 18*, 487–508.

Whitley, B. E. (1997). Gender differences in computer-related attitudes and behavior: A meta-analysis. *Computers in Human Behavior, 13*, 1–22.

Whitley, B. E., McHugh, M. C., & Frieze, I. H. (1986). Assessing the theoretical models for sex differences in causal attributions of success and failure. In J. S. Hyde & M. C. Linn (Eds.), *The psychology of gender: Advances through meta-analysis* (pp. 102–135). Baltimore: Johns Hopkins University Press.

"Dude, You're a Fag": Adolescent Masculinity and the Fag Discourse

C. J. PASCOE

> "There's a faggot over there! There's a faggot over there! Come look!" yelled Brian, a senior at River High School, to a group of 10-year-old boys. Following Brian, the 10-year-olds dashed down a hallway. At the end of the hallway Brian's friend, Dan, pursed his lips and began sashaying towards the 10-year-olds. He minced towards them, swinging his hips exaggeratedly and wildly waving his arms. To the boys Brian yelled, "Look at the faggot! Watch out! He'll get you!" In response the 10-year-olds raced back down the hallway screaming in terror.
>
> *(From author's fieldnotes)*

The relationship between adolescent masculinity and sexuality is embedded in the specter of the faggot. Faggots represent a penetrated masculinity in which "to be penetrated is to abdicate power" (Bersani, 1987: 212). Penetrated men symbolize a masculinity devoid of power, which, in its contradiction, threatens both psychic and social chaos. It is precisely this specter of penetrated masculinity that functions as a regulatory mechanism of gender for contemporary American adolescent boys.

Feminist scholars of masculinity have documented the centrality of homophobic insults to masculinity (Lehne, 1998; Kimmel, 2001) especially in school settings (Wood, 1984; Smith, 1998; Burn, 2000; Plummer, 2001; Kimmel, 2003). They argue that homophobic teasing often characterizes masculinity in adolescence and early adulthood, and that anti-gay slurs tend to primarily be directed at other gay boys.

This article both expands on and challenges these accounts of relationships between homophobia and masculinity. Homophobia is indeed a central mechanism in the making of contemporary American adolescent masculinity. This article both critiques and builds on this finding by (1) pointing to the limits of an argument that focuses centrally on homophobia, (2) demonstrating that the fag is not only an identity linked to homosexual boys[1] but an identity that can temporarily adhere to heterosexual boys as well and (3) highlighting the racialized nature of the fag as a disciplinary mechanism.

"Homophobia" is too facile a term with which to describe the deployment of "fag" as an epithet. By calling the use of the word "fag" homophobia—and letting the argument stop with that point—previous research obscures the gendered nature of sexualized insults (Plummer, 2001). Invoking homophobia to describe the ways in which boys aggressively tease each other overlooks the powerful relationship between masculinity and this sort of insult. Instead, it seems incidental in this conventional line of argument that girls do not harass each other and are not harassed in this same manner.[2] This framing naturalizes the relationship between masculinity and homophobia, thus obscuring the centrality of such harassment in the formation of a gendered identity for boys in a way that it is not for girls.

"Fag" is not necessarily a static identity attached to a particular (homosexual) boy. Fag talk and fag imitations serve as a discourse with which boys discipline themselves and each other through joking relationships.[3] Any boy can temporarily become a fag in a given social space or interaction. This does not mean that those boys who identify as or are perceived to be homosexual are not subject to intense harassment. But becoming a fag has as much to do with failing at the masculine tasks of competence, heterosexual prowess and strength or in anyway revealing weakness or femininity, as it does with a sexual identity. This fluidity of the fag identity is what makes the specter of the fag such a powerful disciplinary mechanism. It is fluid enough that boys police most of their behaviors out of fear of having the fag identity permanently adhere and definitive enough so that boys recognize a fag behavior and strive to avoid it.

The fag discourse is racialized. It is invoked differently by and in relation to white boys' bodies than it is by and in relation to African-American boys' bodies. While certain behaviors put all boys at risk for becoming temporarily a fag, some behaviors can be enacted by African-American boys without putting them at risk of receiving the label. The racialized meanings of the fag discourse suggest that something more than simple homophobia is involved in these sorts of interactions. An analysis of boys' deployments of the specter of the fag should also extend to the ways in which gendered power works through racialized selves. It is not that this gendered homophobia does not exist in African-American communities. Indeed, making fun of "Negro faggotry seems to be a rite of passage among contemporary black male rappers and filmmakers" (Riggs, 1991: 253). However, the fact that "white women and men, gay and straight, have more or less colonized cultural debates about sexual representation" (Julien and Mercer, 1991: 167) obscures varied systems of sexualized meanings among different racialized ethnic groups (Almaguer, 1991; King, 2004).

Theoretical Framing

The sociology of masculinity entails a "critical study of men, their behaviors, practices, values and perspectives" (Whitehead and Barrett, 2001: 14). Recent studies of men emphasize the multiplicity of masculinity (Connell, 1995) detailing the ways in which different configurations of gender practice are promoted, challenged or reinforced in given social situations. This research on how men do masculinities has explored gendered practices in a wide range of social institutions, such as families (Coltrane, 2001), schools (Skelton, 1996; Parker, 1996; Mac and Ghaill, 1996; Francis and Skelton, 2001), workplaces (Cooper, 2000), media (Craig, 1992), and sports (Messner, 1989; Edly and Wetherel, 1997; Curry, 2004). Many of these studies have developed specific typologies of masculinities: gay, Black, Chicano, working class, middle class, Asian, gay Black, gay Chicano, white working class, militarized, transnational business, New Man, negotiated, versatile, healthy, toxic, counter, and cool masculinities, to name a few (Messner, 2004). In this sort of model the fag could be (and often has been) framed as a type of subordinated masculinity attached to homosexual adolescent boys' bodies.

Heeding Timothy Carrigan's admonition that an "analysis of masculinity needs to be related as well to other currents in feminism" (Carrigan et al., 1987: 64), in this article I integrate queer theory's insights about the relationships between gender, sexuality, identities and power with the attention to men found in the literature on masculinities. Like the sociology of gender, queer theory destabilizes the assumed naturalness of the social order (Lemert, 1996). Queer theory is a "conceptualization which sees sexual power as embedded in different levels of social life" and interrogates areas of the social world not usually seen as sexuality (Stein and Plummer, 1994). In this sense queer theory calls for sexuality to be looked at not only as a discrete arena of sexual practices and identities, but also as a constitutive element of social life (Warner, 1993; Epstein, 1996).

While the masculinities' literature rightly highlights very real inequalities between gay and straight men (see for instance Connell, 1995), this emphasis on sexuality as inhered in static identities attached to male bodies, rather than major organizing principles of social life (Sedgwick, 1990), limits scholars' ability to analyze the myriad ways in which sexuality, in part, constitutes gender. This article does not seek to establish that there are homosexual boys and heterosexual boys and the homosexual ones are marginalized. Rather this article explores what happens to theories of gender if we look at a *discourse* of sexualized identities in addition to focusing on seemingly static identity categories inhabited by men. This is not to say that gender is reduced only to sexuality, indeed feminist scholars have demonstrated that gender is embedded in and constitutive of a multitude of social structures—the economy, places of work, families and schools. In the tradition of post-structural feminist theorists of race and gender who look at "border cases" that explode taken-for-granted binaries of race and gender (Smith, 1994), queer theory is another tool which enables an integrated analysis of sexuality, gender and race.

As scholars of gender have demonstrated, gender is accomplished through day-to-day interactions (Fine, 1987; Hochschild, 1989; West and Zimmerman, 1991; Thorne, 1993). In this sense, gender is the "activity of managing situated conduct in light of normative conceptions of attitudes and activities appropriate for one's sex category" (West and Zimmerman, 1991: 127). Similarly, queer theorist Judith Butler argues that gender is accomplished interactionally through "a set of repeated acts within a highly rigid regulatory frame that congeal over time to produce the appearance of substance, of a natural sort of being" (Butler, 1999: 43). Specifically she argues that gendered beings are created through processes of citation and repudiation of a "constitutive outside" (Butler, 1993: 3) in which is contained all that is cast out of a socially recognizable gender category. The "constitutive outside" is inhabited by abject identities, unrecognizably and unacceptably gendered selves. The interactional accomplishment of gender in a Butlerian model consists, in part, of the continual iteration and repudiation of this abject identity. Gender, in this sense, is "constituted through the force of exclusion and abjection, on which produces a constitutive outside to the subject, an abjected outside, which is, after all, 'inside' the subject as its own founding repudiation" (Butler, 1993: 3). This repudiation creates and reaffirms a "threatening specter" (Butler, 1993: 3) of failed, unrecognizable gender, the existence of which must be continually repudiated through interactional processes.

I argue that the "fag" position is an "abject" position and, as such, is a "threatening specter" constituting contemporary American adolescent masculinity. The fag discourse is the interactional process through which boys name and repudiate this abjected identity. Rather than analyzing the fag as an identity for homosexual boys, I examine uses of the discourse that imply that any boy can become a fag, regardless of his actual desire or self-perceived sexual orientation. The threat of the abject position infuses the faggot with regulatory power. This article provides empirical data to illustrate Butler's approach to gender and indicates that it might be a useful addition to the sociological literature on masculinities through highlighting one of the ways in which a masculine gender identity is accomplished through interaction.

Method

Research Site

I conducted fieldwork at a suburban high school in north-central California which I call River High.[4] River High is a working class, suburban 50-year-old high school located in a town called Riverton. With the exception of the median household income and racial diversity (both of which are elevated due to Riverton's location in California), the town mirrors national averages in the percentages of white-collar workers, rates of college attendance, and marriages, and age composition (according to the 2000 census). It is a politically moderate to conservative, religious community. Most of the students' parents commute to surrounding cities for work.

On average, Riverton is a middle-class community. However, students at River are likely to refer to the town as two communities: "Old Riverton" and "New Riverton." A busy highway and railroad tracks bisect the town into these two sections. River High is literally on the "wrong side of the tracks," in Old Riverton. Exiting the freeway, heading north to Old Riverton, one sees a mix of 1950s-era ranch-style homes, some with neatly trimmed lawns and tidy gardens, others with yards strewn with various car parts, lawn chairs and appliances. Old Riverton is visually bounded by smoke-puffing factories. On the other side of the freeway New Riverton is characterized by wide sidewalk-lined streets and new walled-in home developments. Instead of smokestacks, a forested mountain, home to a state park, rises majestically in the background. The teens from these homes attend Hillside High, River's rival.

River High is attended by 2,000 students. River High's racial/ethnic breakdown roughly represents California at large: 50 percent white, 9 percent African-American, 28 percent Latino and 6 percent Asian (as compared to California's 46, 6, 32, and 11 percent respectively, according to census data and school records). The students at River High are primarily working class.

Research

I gathered data using the qualitative method of ethnographic research. I spent a year and a half conducting observations, formally interviewing 49 students at River High (36 boys and 13 girls), one male student from Hillside High, and conducting countless informal interviews with students, faculty and administrators. I concentrated on one school because I explore the richness rather than the breadth of data (for other examples of this method see Willis, 1981; MacLeod, 1987; Eder et al., 1995; Ferguson, 2000).

I recruited students for interviews by conducting presentations in a range of classes and hanging around at lunch, before school, after school and at various events talking to different groups of students about my research, which I presented as "writing a book about guys." The interviews usually took place at school, unless the student had a car, in which case he or she met me at one of the local fast food restaurants where I treated them to a meal. Interviews lasted anywhere from half an hour to two hours.

The initial interviews I conducted helped me to map a gendered and sexualized geography of the school, from which I chose my observation sites. I observed a "neutral" site—a senior government classroom, where sexualized meanings were subdued. I observed three sites that students marked as "fag" sites—two drama classes and the Gay/Straight Alliance. I also observed two normatively "masculine" sites—auto-shop and weightlifting.[5] I took daily fieldnotes focusing on how students, faculty and administrators negotiated, regulated and resisted particular meanings of gender and sexuality. I attended major school rituals such as Winter Ball, school rallies, plays, dances and lunches. I would also occasionally "ride along" with Mr. Johnson (Mr. J.), the school's security guard, on his battery-powered golf cart to watch which, how and when students were disciplined. Observational data provided me with more insight to the interactional processes of masculinity than simple interviews yielded. If I had relied only on interview data,

I would have missed the interactional processes of masculinity which are central to the fag discourse.

Given the importance of appearance in high school, I gave some thought as to how I would present myself, deciding to both blend in and set myself apart from the students. In order to blend in I wore my standard graduate student gear—comfortable, baggy cargo pants, a black t-shirt or sweater and tennis shoes. To set myself apart I carried a messenger bag instead of a back-pack, didn't wear makeup, and spoke slightly differently than the students by using some slang, but refraining from uttering the ubiquitous "hecka" and "hella."

The boys were fascinated by the fact that a 30-something white "girl" (their words) was interested in studying them. While at first many would make sexualized comments asking me about my dating life or saying that they were going to "hit on" me, it seemed eventually they began to forget about me as a potential sexual/romantic partner. Part of this, I think, was related to my knowledge about "guy" things. For instance, I lift weights on a regular basis and as a result the weightlifting coach introduced me as a "weight-lifter from U.C. Berkeley" telling the students they should ask me for weight-lifting advice. Additionally, my taste in movies and television shows often coincided with theirs. I am an avid fan of the movies "Jackass" and "Fight Club," both of which contain high levels of violence and "bathroom" humor. Finally, I garnered a lot of points among boys because I live off a dangerous street in a nearby city famous for drug deals, gang fights, and frequent gun shots.

What Is a Fag?

"Since you were little boys you've been told, 'hey, don't be a little faggot,'" explained Darnell, an African-American football player, as we sat on a bench next to the athletic field. Indeed, both the boys and girls I interviewed told me that "fag" was the worst epithet one guy could direct at another. Jeff, a slight white sophomore, explained to me that boys call each other fag because "gay people aren't really liked over here and stuff." Jeremy, a Latino junior, told me that this insult literally reduced a boy to nothing, "To call someone gay or fag is like the lowest thing you can call someone. Because that's like saying that you're nothing."

Most guys explained their or others' dislike of fags by claiming that homophobia is just part of what it means to be a guy. For instance Keith, a white soccer-playing senior, explained, "I think guys are just homophobic." However, it is not just homophobia, it is a *gendered* homophobia. Several students told me that these homophobic insults only applied to boys and not girls. For example, while Jake, a handsome white senior, told me that he didn't like gay people, he quickly added, "Lesbians, okay that's *good*." Similarly Cathy, a popular white cheerleader, told me "Being a lesbian is accepted because guys think 'oh that's cool.'" Darnell, after telling me that boys were told not to be faggots, said of lesbians, "They're [guys are] fine with girls. I think it's the guy part that they're like ewwww!" In this sense it is not strictly homophobia, but a gendered homophobia that constitutes adolescent masculinity in the culture of this school. However, it is clear, according to these comments, that lesbians are "good" because of their place in heterosexual male fantasy not necessarily because of some enlightened approach to same-sex relationships. It does however, indicate that using only the term homophobia to describe boys' repeated use of the word "fag" might be a bit simplistic and misleading.

Additionally, girls at River High rarely deployed the word "fag" and were never called "fags." I recorded girls uttering "fag" only three times during my research. In one instance, Angela, a Latina cheerleader, teased Jeremy, a well-liked white senior involved in student government, for not ditching school with her, "You wouldn't 'cause you're a faggot." However, girls did not use this word as part of their regular lexicon. The sort of gendered homophobia that constitutes adolescent masculinity does not constitute adolescent femininity. Girls were not called dykes or lesbians in any sort of regular or systematic way. Students did tell me that "slut" was the worst thing a girl could be called. However, my fieldnotes indicate that the word "slut" (or its synonym "ho") appears one time for every eight times the word "fag" appears. Even when it does occur, "slut" is rarely deployed as a direct insult against another girl.

Highlighting the difference between the deployment of "gay" and "fag" as insults brings the gendered nature of this homophobia into focus. For boys and girls at River High "gay" is a fairly common synonym for "stupid." While this word shares the sexual origins of "fag," it does not *consistently* have the skew of gender-loaded meaning. Girls and boys often used "gay" as an adjective referring to inanimate objects and male or female people, whereas they used "fag" as a noun that denotes only un-masculine males. Students used "gay" to describe anything from someone's clothes to a new school rule that the students did not like, as in the following encounter:

> In auto-shop Arnie pulled out a large older version black laptop computer and placed it on his desk. Behind him Nick said "That's a gay laptop! It's five inches thick!"

A laptop can be gay, a movie can be gay or a group of people can be gay. Boys used "gay" and "fag" interchangeably when they refer to other boys, but "fag" does not have the non-gendered attributes that "gay" sometimes invokes.

While its meanings are not the same as "gay," "fag" does have multiple meanings which do not necessarily replace its connotations as a homophobic slur, but rather exist alongside. Some boys took pains to say that "fag" is not about sexuality. Darnell told me "It doesn't even have anything to do with being gay." J. L., a white sophomore at Hillside High (River High's cross-town rival), asserted "Fag, seriously, it has nothing to do with sexual preference at all. You could just be calling somebody an idiot you know?" I asked Ben, a quiet, white sophomore who wore heavy metal t-shirts to auto-shop each day, "What kind of things do guys get called a fag for?" Ben answered "Anything... literally, anything. Like you were trying to turn a wrench the wrong way, 'dude, you're a fag.' Even if a piece of meat drops out of your sandwich, 'you fag!'" Each time Ben said "you fag" his voice deepened as if he were imitating a more masculine boy. While Ben might rightly *feel* like a guy could be called a fag for "anything... literally, anything," there are actually specific behaviors which, when enacted by most boys, can render him more vulnerable to a fag epithet. In this instance Ben's comment highlights the use of "fag" as a generic insult for incompetence, which in the world of River High, is central to a masculine identity. A boy could get called a fag for exhibiting any sort of behavior defined as non-masculine (although not necessarily behaviors aligned with femininity) in the world of River High: being stupid, incompetent, dancing, caring too much about clothing, being too emotional or expressing interest (sexual or platonic) in other guys. However, given the extent of its deployment and the laundry list of behaviors that could get a boy in trouble it is no wonder that Ben felt like a boy could be called "fag" for "anything."

One-third (13) of the boys I interviewed told me that, while they may liberally insult each other with the term, they would not actually direct it at a homosexual peer. Jabes, a Filipino senior, told me

> I actually say it [fag] quite a lot, except for when I'm in the company of an actual homosexual person. Then I try not to say it at all. But when I'm just hanging out with my friends I'll be like, "shut up, I don't want to hear you any more, you stupid fag."

Similarly J. L. compared homosexuality to a disability, saying there is "no way" he'd call an actually gay guy a fag because

> There's people who are the retarded people who nobody wants to associate with. I'll be so nice to those guys and I hate it when people make fun of them. It's like, "bro do you realize that they can't help that?" And then there's gay people. They were born that way.

According to this group of boys, gay is a legitimate, if marginalized, social identity. If a man is gay, there may be a chance he could be considered masculine by other men (Connell, 1995). David, a handsome white senior dressed smartly in khaki pants and a white button-down shirt, said, "Being gay is just a lifestyle. It's someone you choose to sleep with. You can still throw around a football and be gay." In other words there is a possibility, however slight, that a boy can be gay and masculine. To be a fag is, by definition, the opposite of masculine, whether or not the word is deployed with sexualized or non-sexualized meanings. In explaining this to me, Jamaal, an African-American junior, cited the explanation of popular rap artist, Eminem,

> Although I don't like Eminem, he had a good definition of it. It's like taking away your title. In an interview they were like, "you're always capping on gays, but then you sing with Elton John." He was like "I don't mean gay as in gay."

This is what Riki Wilchins calls the "Eminem Exception. Eminem explains that he doesn't call people 'faggot' because of their sexual orientation but because they're weak and unmanly" (Wilchins, 2003). This is precisely the way in which this group of boys at River High uses the term "faggot." While it is not necessarily acceptable to be gay, at least a man who is gay can do other things that render him acceptably masculine. A fag, by the very definition of the word, indicated by students' usages at River High, cannot be masculine. This distinction between "fag" as an unmasculine and problematic identity and "gay" as a possibly masculine, although marginalized, sexual identity is not limited to a teenage lexicon, but is reflected in both psychological discourses (Sedgwick, 1995) and gay and lesbian activism.

Becoming a Fag

"The ubiquity of the word faggot speaks to the reach of its discrediting capacity" (Corbett, 2001: 4). It is almost as if boys cannot help but shout it out on a regular basis—in the hallway, in class, across campus as a greeting, or as a joke. In my fieldwork I was amazed by the way in which the word seemed to pop uncontrollably out of boys' mouths in all kinds of situations. To quote just one of many instances from my fieldnotes:

> Two boys walked out of the P.E. locker room and one yelled "fucking faggot!" at no one in particular.

This spontaneous yelling out of a variation of fag seemingly apropos of nothing happened repeatedly among boys throughout the school.

The fag discourse is central to boys' joking relationships. Joking cements relationships between boys (Kehily and Nayak, 1997; Lyman, 1998) and helps to manage anxiety and discomfort (Freud, 1905). Boys invoked the specter of the fag in two ways: through humorous imitation and through lobbing the epithet at one another. Boys at River High imitated the fag by acting out an exaggerated "femininity," and/or by pretending to sexually desire other boys. As indicated by the introductory vignette in which a predatory "fag" threatens the little boys, boys at River High link these performative scenarios with a fag identity. They lobbed the fag epithet at each other in a verbal game of hot potato, each careful to deflect the insult quickly by hurling it toward someone else. These games and imitations make up a fag discourse which highlights the fag not as a static but rather as a fluid identity which boys constantly struggle to avoid.

In imitative performances the fag discourse functions as a constant reiteration of the fag's existence, affirming that the fag is out there; at any moment a boy can become a fag. At the same time these performances demonstrate that the boy who is invoking the fag is *not* a fag. By invoking it so often, boys remind themselves and each other that at any point they can become fags if they are not sufficiently masculine.

> Mr. McNally, disturbed by the noise outside of the classroom, turned to the open door saying "We'll shut this unless anyone really wants to watch sweaty boys playing basketball." Emir, a tall skinny boy, lisped "I wanna watch the boys play!" The rest of the class cracked up at his imitation.

Through imitating a fag, boys assure others that they are not a fag by immediately becoming masculine again after the performance. They mock their own performed femininity and/or same-sex desire, assuring themselves and others that such an identity is one deserving of derisive laughter. The fag identity in this instance is fluid, detached from Emir's body. He can move in and out of this "abject domain" while simultaneously affirming his position as a subject.

Boys also consistently tried to put another in the fag position by lobbing the fag epithet at one another.

> Going through the junk-filled car in the auto-shop parking lot, Jay poked his head out and asked "Where are Craig and Brian?" Neil, responded with "I think they're over there," pointing, then thrusting his hips and pulling his arms back and forth to indicate that Craig and Brian might be having sex. The boys in auto-shop laughed.

This sort of joke temporarily labels both Craig and Brian as faggots. Because the fag discourse is so familiar, the other boys immediately understand that Neil is indicating that Craig and Brian are having sex. However these are not necessarily identities that stick. Nobody actually thinks Craig and Brian are homosexuals. Rather the fag identity is a fluid one, certainly an identity that no boy wants, but one that a boy can escape, usually by engaging in some sort of discursive contest to turn another boy into a fag. However, fag becomes a hot potato that no boy wants to be left holding. In the following example, which occurred soon after the "sex" joke, Brian lobs the fag epithet at someone else, deflecting it from himself:

> Brian initiated a round of a favorite game in auto-shop, the "cock game." Brian quietly, looking at Josh, said, "Josh loves the cock," then slightly louder, "Josh loves the cock." He continued saying this until he was yelling "JOSH LOVES THE COCK!" The rest of the boys laughed hysterically as Josh slinked away saying "I have a bigger dick than all you mother fuckers!"

These two instances show how the fag can be mapped, momentarily, on to one boy's body and how he, in turn, can attach it to another boy, thus deflecting it from himself. In the first instance Neil makes fun of Craig and Brian for simply hanging out together. In the second instance Brian goes from being a fag to making Josh into a fag, through the "cock game." The "fag" is transferable. Boys move in and out of it by discursively creating another as a fag through joking interactions. They, somewhat ironically, can move in and out of the fag position by transforming themselves, temporarily, into a fag, but this has the effect of reaffirming their masculinity when they return to a heterosexual position after imitating the fag.

These examples demonstrate boys invoking the trope of the fag in a discursive struggle in which the boys indicate that they know what a fag is—and that they are not fags. This joking cements bonds between boys as they assure themselves and each other of their masculinity through repeated repudiations of a non-masculine position of the abject.

Racing the Fag

The fag trope is not deployed consistently or identically across social groups at River High. Differences between white boys' and African-American boys' meaning making around clothes and dancing reveal ways in which the fag as the abject position is racialized.

Clean, oversized, carefully put together clothing is central to a hip-hop identity for African-American boys who identify with hip-hop culture.[6] Richard Majors calls this presentation of self a "cool pose" consisting of "unique, expressive and conspicuous styles of demeanor, speech, gesture, clothing, hairstyle, walk, stance and handshake," developed by African-American men as a symbolic response to institutionalized racism (Majors, 2001: 211). Pants are usually several sizes too big, hanging low on a boy's waist, usually revealing a pair of boxers beneath. Shirts and sweaters are similarly oversized, often hanging down to a boy's knees. Tags are frequently left on baseball hats worn slightly askew and sit perched high on the head. Meticulously clean, unlaced athletic shoes with rolled up socks under the tongue complete a typical hip-hop outfit.

This amount of attention and care given to clothing for white boys not identified with hip-hop culture (that is, most of the white boys at River High) would certainly cast them into an abject, fag position. White boys are not supposed to appear to care about their clothes or appearance, because only fags care about how they look. Ben illustrates this:

> Ben walked in to the auto-shop classroom from the parking lot where he had been working on a particularly oily engine. Grease stains covered his jeans. He looked down at them, made a face and walked toward me with limp wrists, laughing and lisping in a high pitch sing-song voice "I got my good panths all dirty!"

Ben draws on indicators of a fag identity, such as limp wrists, as do the boys in the introductory vignette to illustrate that a masculine person certainly would not care about having dirty clothes. In this sense, masculinity, for white boys, becomes the carefully crafted appearance of not caring about appearance, especially in terms of cleanliness.

However, African-American boys involved in hip-hop culture talk frequently about whether or not their clothes, specifically their shoes, are dirty:

> In drama class both Darnell and Marc compared their white Adidas basketball shoes. Darnell mocked Marc because black scuff marks covered his shoes, asking incredulously "Yours are a week old and they're dirty—I've had mine for a month and they're not dirty!" Both laughed.

Monte, River High's star football player, echoed this concern about dirty shoes when looking at the fancy red shoes he had lent to his cousin the week before, told me he was frustrated because after his cousin used them, the "shoes are hella scuffed up." Clothing, for these boys, does not indicate a fag position, but rather defines membership in a certain cultural and racial group (Perry, 2002).

Dancing is another arena that carries distinctly fag associated meanings for white boys and masculine meanings for African-American boys who participate in hip-hop culture. White boys often associate dancing with "fag." J. L. told me that guys think "'nSync's gay" because they can dance. 'nSync is an all white male singing group known for their dance moves. At dances white boys frequently held their female dates tightly, locking their hips together. The boys never danced with one another, unless engaged in a round of "hot potato." White boys often jokingly danced together in order to embarrass each other by making someone else into a fag:

> Lindy danced behind her date, Chris. Chris's friend, Matt, walked up and nudged Lindy aside, imitating her dance moves behind Chris. As Matt rubbed his hands up and down Chris's back, Chris turned around and jumped back startled to see Matt there instead of Lindy. Matt cracked up as Chris turned red.

However dancing does not carry this sort of sexualized gender meaning for all boys at River High. For African-American boys dancing demonstrates membership in a cultural community (Best, 2000). African-American boys frequently danced together in single sex groups, teaching each other the latest dance moves, showing off a particularly difficult move or making each other laugh with humorous dance moves. Students recognized K. J. as the most talented dancer at the school. K. J. is a sophomore of African-American and Filipino descent who participated in the hip-hop culture of River High. He continually wore the latest hip-hop fashions. K. J. was extremely popular. Girls hollered his name as they walked down the hall and thrust urgently written love notes folded in complicated designs into his hands as he sauntered to class. For the past two years K. J. won first place in the talent show for dancing. When he danced at assemblies the room reverberated with screamed chants of "Go K.J.! Go K.J.! Go K.J.!" Because dancing for African-American boys places them within a tradition of masculinity, they are not at risk of becoming a fag for this particular gendered practice. Nobody called K. J. a fag. In fact in several of my interviews boys of multiple racial/ethnic backgrounds spoke admiringly of K. J.'s dancing abilities.

Implications

These findings confirm previous studies of masculinity and sexuality that position homophobia as central to contemporary definitions of adolescent masculinity. These data extend previous research by unpacking multilayered meanings that boys deploy through their uses of homophobic language and joking rituals. By attending to these meanings I reframe the discussion as one of a fag discourse, rather than simply labeling this sort of behavior as homophobia. The fag is an "abject" position, a position outside of masculinity that actually constitutes masculinity. Thus, masculinity, in part becomes the daily interactional work of repudiating the "threatening specter" of the fag.

The fag extends beyond a static sexual identity attached to a gay boy. Few boys are permanently identified as fags; most move in and out of fag positions. Looking at "fag" as a discourse rather than a static identity reveals that the term can be invested with different meanings in different social spaces. "Fag" may be used as a weapon with which to temporarily assert one's masculinity by denying it to others. Thus "fag" becomes a symbol around which contests of masculinity take place.

The fag epithet, when hurled at other boys, may or may not have explicit sexual meanings, but it always has gendered meanings. When a boy calls another boy a fag, it means he is not a man, not necessarily that he is a homosexual. The boys in this study know that they are not supposed to call homosexual boys "fags" because that is mean. This, then has been the limited success of the mainstream gay rights movement. The message absorbed by some of these teenage boys is that "gay men can be masculine, just like you." Instead of challenging gender inequality, this particular discourse of gay rights has reinscribed it. Thus we need to begin to think about how gay men may be in a unique position to challenge gendered as well as sexual norms.

This study indicates that researchers who look at the intersection of sexuality and masculinity need to attend to the ways in which racialized identities may affect how "fag" is deployed and what it means in various social situations. While researchers have addressed the ways in which masculine identities are racialized (Connell, 1995; Ross, 1998; Bucholtz, 1999; Davis, 1999; Price, 1999; Ferguson, 2000; Majors, 2001) they have not paid equal attention to the ways in which "fag" might be a racialized epithet. It is important to look at when, where and with what meaning "the fag" is deployed in order to get at how masculinity is defined, contested, and invested in among adolescent boys.

Research shows that sexualized teasing often leads to deadly results, as evidenced by the spate of school shootings in the 1990s (Kimmel, 2003). Clearly the fag discourse affects not just homosexual teens, but all boys, gay and straight. Further research could investigate these processes in a variety of contexts: varied geographic locations, sexualized groups, classed groups, religious groups and age groups.

Acknowledgments

The author would like to thank Natalie Boero, Leslie Bell, Meg Jay and Barrie Thorne for their comments on this article. This work was supported by the Center for the Study of Sexual Culture at University of California, Berkeley.

Notes

1. While the term "homosexual" is laden with medicalized and normalizing meanings, I use it instead of "gay" because "gay" in the world of River High has multiple meanings apart from sexual practices or identities.
2. Girls do insult one another based on sexualized meanings. But in my own research I found that girls and boys did not harass girls in this manner with the same frequency that boys harassed each other through engaging in joking about the fag.
3. I use discourse in the Foucauldian sense, to describe truth producing practices, not just text or speech (Foucault, 1978).
4. The names of places and respondents have been changed.
5. Auto-shop was a class in which students learned how to build and repair cars. Many of the students in this course were looking into careers as mechanics.
6. While there are several white and Latino boys at River High who identify with hip-hop culture, hip-hop is identified by the majority of students as an African-American cultural style.

References

Almaguer, Tomas (1991) "Chicano Men: A Cartography of Homosexual Identity and Behavior," *Differences* 3: 75–100.

Bersani, Leo (1987) "Is the Rectum a Grave?" *October* 43: 197–222.

Best, Amy (2000) *Prom Night: Youth, Schools and Popular Culture*. New York: Routledge.

Bucholtz, Mary (1999) "'You Da Man': Narrating the Racial Other in the Production of White Masculinity," *Journal of Sociolinguistics* 3/4: 443–60.

Burn, Shawn M. (2000) "Heterosexuals' Use of 'Fag' and 'Queer' to Deride One Another: A Contributor to Heterosexism and Stigma," *Journal of Homosexuality* 40: 1–11.

Butler, Judith (1993) *Bodies that Matter*. New York: Routledge.

———. (1999) *Gender Trouble*. New York: Routledge.

Carrigan, Tim, Connell, Bob and Lee, John (1987) "Toward a New Sociology of Masculinity," in Harry Brod (ed.) *The Making of Masculinities: The New Men's Studies*, pp. 188–202. Boston, MA: Allen & Unwin.

Coltrane, Scott (2001) "Selling the Indispensable Father," paper presented at *Pushing the Boundaries Conference: New Conceptualizations of Childhood and Motherhood*, Philadelphia.

Connell, R. W. (1995) *Masculinities*. Berkeley: University of California Press.

Cooper, Marianne (2000) "Being the 'Go-To Guy': Fatherhood, Masculinity and the Organization of Work in Silicon Valley," *Qualitative Sociology* 23: 379–405.

Corbett, Ken (2001) "Faggot = Loser," *Studies in Gender and Sexuality* 2: 3–28.

Craig, Steve (1992) *Men, Masculinity and the Media*. Newbury Park: Sage.

Curry, Timothy J. (2004) "Fraternal Bonding in the Locker Room: A Profeminist Analysis of Talk About Competition and Women," in Michael Messner and Michael Kimmel (eds.) *Men's Lives*. Boston, MA: Pearson.

Davis, James E. (1999) "Forbidden Fruit, Black Males' Constructions of Transgressive Sexualities in Middle School," in William J. Letts IV and James T. Sears (eds.) *Queering Elementary Education: Advancing the Dialogue About Sexualities and Schooling*, pp. 49 ff. Lanham, MD: Rowan & Littlefield.

Eder, Donna, Evans, Catherine and Parker, Stephen (1995) *School Talk: Gender and Adolescent Culture*. New Brunswick, NJ: Rutgers University Press.

Edly, Nigel and Wetherell, Margaret (1997) "Jockeying for Position: The Construction of Masculine Identities," *Discourse and Society* 8: 203–17.

Epstein, Steven (1996) "A Queer Encounter," in Steven Seidman (ed.) *Queer Theory/Sociology*, pp. 188–202. Cambridge, MA: Blackwell.

Ferguson, Ann (2000) *Bad Boys: Public Schools in the Making of Black Masculinity*. Ann Arbor: University of Michigan Press.

Fine, Gary (1987) *With the Boys: Little League Baseball and Preadolescent Culture*. Chicago, IL: University of Chicago Press.

Foucault, Michel (1978) *The History of Sexuality, Volume I*. New York: Vintage Books.

Francis, Becky and Skelton, Christine (2001) "Men Teachers and the Construction of Heterosexual Masculinity in the Classroom," *Sex Education* 1: 9–21.

Freud, Sigmund (1905) *The Basic Writings of Sigmund Freud* (translated and edited by A. A. Brill). New York: The Modern Library.

Hochschild, Arlie (1989) *The Second Shift*. New York: Avon.

Julien, Isaac and Mercer, Kobena (1991) "True Confessions: A Discourse on Images of Black Male Sexuality," in Essex Hemphill (ed.) *Brother to Brother: New Writings by Black Gay Men*, pp. 167–73. Boston, MA: Alyson Publications.

Kehily, Mary Jane and Nayak, Anoop (1997) "Lads and Laughter: Humour and the Production of Heterosexual Masculinities," *Gender and Education* 9: 69–87.

Kimmel, Michael (2001) "Masculinity as Homophobia: Fear, Shame, and Silence in the Construction of Gender Identity," in Stephen Whitehead and Frank Barrett (eds.) *The Masculinities Reader*, pp. 266–87. Cambridge: Polity.

———. (2003) "Adolescent Masculinity, Homophobia, and Violence: Random School Shootings, 1982–2001," *American Behavioral Scientist* 46: 1439–58.

King, D. L. (2004) *Double Lives on the Down Low*. New York: Broadway Books.

Lehne, Gregory (1998) "Homophobia Among Men: Supporting and Defining the Male Role," in Michael Kimmel and Michael Messner (eds.) *Men's Lives*, pp. 237–49. Boston, MA: Allyn and Bacon.

Lemert, Charles (1996) "Series Editor's Preface," in Steven Seidman (ed.) *Queer Theory/Sociology*. Cambridge, MA: Blackwell.

Lyman, Peter (1998) "The Fraternal Bond as a Joking Relationship: A Case Study of the Role of Sexist Jokes in Male Group Bonding," in Michael Kimmel and Michael Messner (eds.) *Men's Lives*, pp. 171–93. Boston, MA: Allyn and Bacon.

Mac and Ghaill, Martain (1996) "What about the Boys—School, Class and Crisis Masculinity," *Sociological Review* 44: 381–97.

MacLeod, Jay (1987) *Ain't No Makin It: Aspirations and Attainment in a Low Income Neighborhood*. Boulder, CO: Westview Press.

Majors, Richard (2001) "Cool Pose: Black Masculinity and Sports," in Stephen Whitehead and Frank Barrett (eds.) *The Masculinities Reader*, pp. 208–17. Cambridge: Polity.

Messner, Michael (1989) "Sports and the Politics of Inequality," in Michael Kimmel and Michael Messner (eds.) *Men's Lives*. Boston, MA: Allyn and Bacon.

———. (2004) "On Patriarchs and Losers: Rethinking Men's Interests," paper presented at Berkeley *Journal of Sociology* Conference, Berkeley.

Parker, Andrew (1996) "The Construction of Masculinity Within Boys' Physical Education," *Gender and Education* 8: 141–57.

Perry, Pamela (2002) *Shades of White: White Kids and Racial Identities in High School*. Durham, NC: Duke University Press.

Plummer, David C. (2001) "The Quest for Modern Manhood: Masculine Stereotypes, Peer Culture and the Social Significance of Homophobia," *Journal of Adolescence* 24: 15–23.

Price, Jeremy (1999) "Schooling and Racialized Masculinities: The Diploma, Teachers and Peers in the Lives of Young, African-American Men," *Youth and Society* 31: 224–63.

Riggs, Marlon (1991) "Black Macho Revisited: Reflections of a SNAP! Queen," in Essex Hemphill (ed.) *Brother to Brother: New Writings by Black Gay Men*, pp. 153–260. Boston, MA: Alyson Publications.

Ross, Marlon B. (1998) "In Search of Black Men's Masculinities," *Feminist Studies* 24: 599–626.

Sedgwick, Eve K. (1990) *Epistemology of the Closet*. Berkeley: University of California Press.

———. (1995) "Gosh, Boy George, You Must Be Awfully Secure in Your Masculinity!" in Maurice Berger, Brian Wallis and Simon Watson (eds.) *Constructing Masculinity*, pp. 11–20. New York: Routledge.

Skelton, Christine (1996) "Learning to Be Tough: The Fostering of Maleness in One Primary School," *Gender and Education* 8: 185–97.

Smith, George W. (1998) "The Ideology of 'Fag': The School Experience of Gay Students," *The Sociological Quarterly* 39: 309–35.

Smith, Valerie (1994) "Split Affinities: The Case of Interracial Rape," in Anne Herrmann and Abigail Stewart (eds.) *Theorizing Feminism*, pp. 155–70. Boulder, CO: Westview Press.

Stein, Arlene and Plummer, Ken (1994) " 'I Can't Even Think Straight': 'Queer' Theory and the Missing Sexual Revolution in Sociology," *Sociological Theory* 12: 178 ff.

Thorne, Barrie (1993) *Gender Play: Boys and Girls in School*. New Brunswick, NJ: Rutgers University Press.

Warner, Michael (1993) "Introduction," in Michael Warner (ed.) *Fear of a Queer Planet: Queer Politics and Social Theory*, pp. vii–xxxi. Minneapolis: University of Minnesota Press.

West, Candace and Zimmerman, Don (1991) "Doing Gender," in Judith Lorber (ed.) *The Social Construction of Gender*, pp. 102–21. Newbury Park: Sage.

Whitehead, Stephen and Barrett, Frank (2001) "The Sociology of Masculinity," in Stephen Whitehead and Frank Barrett (eds.) *The Masculinities Reader*, pp. 472–6. Cambridge: Polity.

Wilchins, Riki (2003) "Do You Believe in Fairies?" *The Advocate*, 4 February.

Willis, Paul (1981) *Learning to Labor: How Working Class Kids Get Working Class Jobs*. New York: Columbia University Press.

Wood, Julian (1984) "Groping Toward Sexism: Boy's Sex Talk," in Angela McRobbie and Mica Nava (eds.) *Gender and Generation*. London: Macmillan Publishers.

It's Bad for Us Too: How the Sexualization of Girls Impacts the Sexuality of Boys, Men, and Women

DEBORAH L. TOLMAN

Introduction

Emerging evidence suggests that the sexualization of girls has particular negative consequences on girls' development into healthy adult sexuality (see Lamb, this volume; see also Impett, Schooler, & Tolman, 2006; Ward, 2002; Ward & Rivadeneyra, 1999; Tolman, 2000; Zurbriggen & Morgan, 2006). While it creates problems for girls, it may be less obvious that the sexualization of girls impacts the sexuality of women, men and boys. In this chapter, I will present the evidence for and theorize how it is indeed bad for boys', men's and women's sexuality as well. The sexual objectification of women itself been reshaped by the saturation of society in sexualized images of girls. From a developmental perspective, imposing adult sexuality onto girls has a boomerang effect on men's and boys' expectations about what women and their sexuality are or should be like, and on women's conceptions of, beliefs about, and experiences of their own sexuality.

The chapter is separated into three sections. The first section is dedicated to the impact of the sexualization of girls on boys' sexuality development and men's sexuality.[1] The second section will cover the impact on adult women's sexuality. The third and final section addresses a striking recent phenomenon and subject of vociferous debate in both popular culture and academia in response to the Report: the question of whether the sexualization of girls may be a route to positive sexuality and sexual empowerment for young women (Else-Quest & Hyde, 2009; Lerum & Dworkin, 2009a, 2009b; Vanvesenbeek, 2009).

Impact on Boys and Men

The sexualization of girls and women is endemic in the sexual socialization of boys and in the subsequent sexuality of men. One of the definitions of sexualization outlined in the Report is sexual objectification. The sexualization of girls has affected the ways in which women are sexually objectified, bootstrapping girlhood into the forms that women's sexual objectification now takes, what Gail Dines (2009) has called "childification" of women in these portrayals. In still images, videos, and movies, the imposition of adult sexuality onto girls serves to normalize it, diminishing the sense of shock or concern that such images might have generated in the past. She also notes that such images are more pervasive with the technological development of computer-generated images of sexualized girls in pornography, a work-around to laws that prevent those under 18 to participate in its production, producing "barely legal" models, all of which are disseminated as what "real women" are or should be like. I will review the media research on how the sexualization of girls affects male sexuality and its development and then consider research informing our understanding of its impact on adult men's sexuality and intimate relationships.

Impact on Boys' and Men's Media: Sexualization of Girls in Old and New Technologies

The confluence of the sexualization of girls and its impact on the sexual objectification of women occurs in sexualized media aimed at boys and men,

Deborah L. Tolman, "It's Bad for Us Too: How the Sexualization of Girls Impacts the Sexuality of Boys, Men, and Women." From *The Sexualization of Girls and Girlhood*, ed. Zurbriggen and Roberts. 2012. Oxford University Press.

as both producing and providing contexts for the development of male sexuality and its expression. The pervasiveness and popularity of these sexually saturated genres continues to expand, in form and accessibility, in media comprised of print, network and cable television, movies, and new more interactive technologies, including the Internet and video gaming. Dines (2009) analyzes how the sexualization of girls is part and parcel of the current landscape of pornography in multiple venues, including the Internet, magazines (in particular "lad mags" such as *Maxim*), but such images are no longer confined to the admittedly ineffectively regulated arena of official pornography. What has been called the "pornification" of mainstream culture is a disturbing trend that not only increases sexualized images of girls and women geometrically but also normalizes the sexualization of girls and generates unreal and unattainable notions of "normal" women (see also Jensen, 2007; Paul, 2005). That is, the "spilling" of pornographic imagery out of formalized pornography into mainstream venues, such as music videos, cable television and iPhone apps (Diaz, 2009), suggests the importance of considering media effects research on pornography as salient to everyday interactions with a broad array of media.

Video games are an especially problematic new arena in which the sexual objectification of women has been documented. Research has demonstrated that virtually the only way women are portrayed is as sex objects, even in the rare instance that a woman is the heroine or star of the game (Burgess, Stermer & Burgess, 2007). The interplay between sexualization and violence is particularly disturbing in this medium, as the user of games is actually "doing" (virtually) the actions that are being portrayed; the interactive quality is cause for concern (Dill & Dill, 1998; Dill & Thill, 2007). Yao, Mahood & Linz (2010), Dill & Dill (1998), and Dietz (1998) found that video games are powerful agents of socialization, and that male participants who played a sexually explicit vs. a nonsexual game were much more likely to view and treat women as sex objects. In particular, Dill & Dill (1998) found that a preponderance of games, especially those most popular with younger teenage males, emphasizes masculinity as tied to power, dominance, and aggression over women, coupled with images of femininity as tied to inferiority, sexual objectification and enjoyment of or attraction to male sexual aggression. While there is not yet an extensive empirical literature, this growing body of evidence regarding relatively mild or "soft" portrayals as in video games constitutes cause for concern (Ezzell, 2009).

While boys are exposed to images of men "consuming" women's bodies as objects of their desire in G-rated movies (Martin & Kazyak, 2009), they are bombarded as never before with sexualized images of girls and women on the Internet. This pervasiveness has produced a new phenomenon: boys (and girls) as young as 10 years old are inadvertently but regularly exposed to pornographic images and video (Davies, 2004; Greenfield, 2004). In addition, ubiquitous pornographic images on the Internet—both pretend and real—have yielded more intentional viewing (e.g., in 2006, 90% of boys and 70% of girls aged 13 and 14 had accessed sexually explicit media at least once in the previous year (cited in Ezzell, 2009)). The phenomenon of tweens and young teens viewing these images is not limited to individuals seeking out this content by themselves. Young people's exposure is also on the rise due to the skyrocketing popularity of Internet-based social networking (such as Facebook and MySpace) that has become a regular part of boys' and girls' everyday lives. Insidious effects of this daily dosage of sexualized images constituting "business as usual" is that it both normalizes and numbs. In the context of such networks, young people construct components of this sexualized environments themselves (Greenfield, 2004), posting pictures of sexed-up girls and youthful-looking sexy women depicted as filled with desire for the young men who are looking at them. Constant interactive engagement with such portraits may be yielding an inadvertent and problematic sex education for boys (and girls).

There is no doubt that viewing pornography is part of the informal (and often only) sexuality education of the vast majority of boys, who have ever-easier access to these ever-younger sexually objectified females. Research demonstrates that some young men who watch pornography begin to derive sexual pleasure *only* from viewing pornography and from sexually objectifying women (Paul, 2005; see also Kimmel, 2008). Paul (2005) observed that the pervasiveness of more violent and humiliating pornography not only creates specific conditions for individual men to require an intensified level of sexual objectification but also infuses "enabling conditions" for male violence against girls and women (see also Attwood, 2005b). In what ways might adolescent boys' easier access to and likely increased use of such pornography to facilitate masturbation be shaping the sexuality development of boys and young men?

Research into this phenomenon has documented negative impacts with younger men, including unreal expectations of women's desires and behaviors, scripts to enable "breaking" women's resistance, intensification of sexual objectification of women, seeing sex with partners as boring, habituation and desensitization and normalization of aggressive sexuality (Attwood, 2005b; Jensen, 2007; Paul, 2007). Linz, Donnerstein & Penrod (1988) established the desensitization effects of sexually degrading explicit and non-explicit films on beliefs about rape and the sexual objectification of women. The notion that "the more extreme, the more interesting the depiction is" is perpetuated by YouTube and the many vehicles outside of the official pornography industry that are unregulated and possibly unregulatable, in which such portrayals are pervasive.

Impact on Male Sexuality and Intimate Relationships

Objectifying another person is premised on the absence of empathy (Herman, 1992). A number of researchers have described how losing or not developing the capacity to empathize is problematic for, and undermining of, relationship building and maintenance (Kimmel, 2006; Kindlon & Thompson, 1998), which diminishes the humanity of boys and men themselves (Brooks, 1995). Studies of adult men's sexuality and difficulties with intimacy and in intimate relationships, and with younger men's interactions with and attitudes about young women as sexual and romantic partners, are beginning to suggest such patterns (Burn & Ward, 2005; England, Shafer & Fogarty, 2007; Loftus, 2002; Weaver, Masland & Zillmann, 1984), and research suggests these patterns may differ by race and class (i.e., Stephens & Phillips, 2003; Weekes, 2002). There is evidence that men who are exposed to soft core porn or mainstream sexualized images of girls are more likely to find their own partners less attractive and intimacy more difficult (Kendrick & Gutierres, 1980; Schooler & Ward, 2006). Several experimental studies have shown that exposure to pornography leads men to indicate less satisfaction with their intimate partners' attractiveness, sexual performance, and level of affection and to express greater desire for sex without emotional involvement (Zillmann & Bryant, 1988). The infusing of the sexualization of girls into pornography is likely to intensify these reactions and expectations.

One of the central ways that boys and men establish and maintain masculinity is through the sexual objectification of women. The pressure to prove manhood begins in earnest in puberty (Pleck, Sonenstein & Ku, 1993; Tolman, Spencer, Rosen-Reynoso & Porche, 2003; Tolman, 2006), and the closest targets are the girls around them (Quinn, 2002). If boys are engaging with more and more mainstreamed and violent formal and informal pornography at younger ages through more interactive media, such sources may be how boys are learning sexual scripts and what is sexually exciting. Unreal portrayals of girls being sexually ravenous and ready at all times, who have bodies that are physically impossible to achieve or maintain in terms of the size and look of sexual parts, thinness, and looking perennially young, without comparable exposure to other images of girls and women, may be creating expectations and "sexual maps" that are not viable in real relationships. The growing phenomenon of boys and young men taping or web casting sexual assaults on women (i.e., Dobbin, 2008; see also Ezzell, 2009), reflecting the sense of normalization that is surrounding these behaviors, also raises the specter of spectatoring—are boys learning to watch rather than to experience their sexuality? Is their sexual experience about sexual feelings or is it becoming intertwined with an increasing need to feel in control in a world that feels more and more out of control?

Kimmel (2008) observes how the sexual objectification of young women has been normalized for young men in what they do as well as what they see; in the guise of bonding, Kimmel found that young men are working hard to prove their masculinity to themselves and one another. He recounts how young men sexualize and objectify young women as a group activity (see also Tolman, et al., 2003), characterized by intensified expressions of aggression and violence that bode poorly for the development of intimacy, vulnerability, or mutuality with women as intimate and sexual partners into adulthood (Burn & Ward, 2005; Kimmel, 2008). Stombler (1994) recorded such behavior as fundamental to fraternity life. As Levy (2005) points out, women's collusion or participation in this process may yield more attributions of sexuality to women's behaviors than intended and render dating a context in which men may oversexualize women (Lindgren, Hoda & George, 2007; Rudman & Borgida, 1995). The antithetical adherence to a strong sexual double standard by both men and women, even as women are incited by ostensibly "normal" circumstances to appear "slutty" or "pornified" (Levy, 2005; Sweeney, 2008; see below), may in fact make pathways to healthy adult sexuality ever more obscure, confusing and littered with obstacles for young men (O'Sullivan & Majerovich, 2008).

There is some research indicating that young men report their wish for women to be the initiators in sexual and relational encounters, to share the "burden" of risk of rejection with women (Dworkin & O'Sullivan, 2007) rather than have women be only objects of their desire. However, at the same time, there is ample evidence that young women are also held accountable to a standard of femininity that reserves an ironically safer place for them as appealing only if they are not overly aggressive initiators of sexual interactions (McRobbie, 2009). The tighter tightrope that the dual desire of young men to have more egalitarian scripts regarding initiation (and risk of rejection) with persistent pressure to treat young women as sexual objects may be confusing and undermine intimacy for both men and women (Levy, 2005; Bogle, 2008).

Impact on Adult Women

The sexualization of girls means that the impetus to be sexually attractive and desirable, to become a "good" sexual object, exerts a shaping force long before adult sexuality emerges. It also means that sexual objectification itself is looking younger. Women are not socialized to embrace their sexuality as part of themselves but to be "good girls" (who grow up to be "good women"), who are not supposed to have strong sexual feelings, needs, or wishes of their own. In fact, these two dimensions of female sexual socialization are intertwined, as objects do not have feelings (Tolman & Debold, 1993). I will review two arenas of effects: the impact of the "youthification" of female sexual desirability on women and the impact of being socialized as an increasingly "youthified" sexual object rather than a mature sexual being on sexual functioning and on negotiating sexuality in heterosexual relationships. I will then illuminate how these impacts are exploited with the example of the fitness industry, creating and then relieving while further complicating the pressure to stay (and equate) young, "healthy," and attractive.

Youthification of Female Sexual Desirability

The sexualization of girls is problematic for girls on many fronts, as this book and the Report attest, including inappropriately imposing adult sexuality on them. The inappropriate sexuality in the case of adult women, however, is the "youthification" of female sexuality, the pervasiveness and cultural imposition of a youthful ideal of beauty (sexual appeal) and also the sexualization of young female bodies as a narrow ideal. In an era when young and younger is the new sexier and sexier, aging itself becomes a risk not because of an increase in sexual dysfunction but because of exclusion from the category of sexually attractive (Tasker & Negra, 2007). Youthification of sexual attractiveness poses unnatural and unattainable limits on available images and embodiments for women as they inevitably age. Women being fearful that getting older disqualifies them from being sexually appealing (to some men) may not be groundless.

Studies demonstrate that exposure to pornography leads to some men's diminished interest in their real-life partners and unrealistic expectations for their partners' appearance and sexual behavior (i.e., Kendrick & Gutierres, 1980). The "youthification" of sexual objectification as an effect of the sexualization of girls intensifies and imparts another dimension to women's anxiety about aging and having a thin, youthful-looking body (Dittmar & Howard, 2004).

Middle age and older women, whose naturally aging bodies contrast more and more with the omnipresence of young "sexy" bodies, have become vulnerable target consumer groups for many cosmetic surgeries designed to make their bodies look sexier by making them look younger, eliminating and undoing the aging process. Cosmetic surgeries as a new option for achieving that forever younger sexy body has become normalized through reality makeover shows (Banet-Weiser & Portwood-Stacer, 2006), though in actual reality it is accessible only to a privileged few who can afford extraordinarily expensive procedures not covered by insurance. Data from the American Society of Plastic Surgeons show that common procedures designed to keep women's bodies looking young and sexually attractive have been steadily increasing. Between 2000 and 2005, annual rates of Botox injections rose from roughly three quarters of a million to almost 4 million, amounting to a 388% increase. In the same 5-year period, there was also a 115% increase in tummy tucks annually and a 283% increase in buttock lifts (American Society of Plastic Surgeons, 2006b). Evidence that these procedures reflect adult women's attempts to retain a sexy young body is in the age differentials for these procedures: the rates for women 35–50 years of age who receive breast lifts, buttock lifts, tummy tucks, and liposuction are approximately double those of women 19–34 years of age (American Society of Plastic Surgeons, 2006a). These surgeries are not medically indicated, can have negative medical side effects, and can even be fatal (Chalker, 2009). Some of these procedures actually reduce sexual sensations and the ability to express emotions, i.e., breast and Botox procedures (Braun, 2010).

The notion of a young and sexy female body has spread to the genitals themselves, as in the recent emergence of "vaginal rejuvenation" and a new industry of other female cosmetic genital surgeries, such as labiaplasty (the cutting back of "overly large" labia) which are solely for aesthetics, that promise more beautiful, tighter, and more appealing genitals (Braun, 2005, 2010; Tiefer, 2008). Women who have received cosmetic labiaplasty range in age from early teens (requests as young as 10) through to 50s or 60s, with those in their 20s and 30s predominating (cited in Braun, 2010). These surgeries have no established medical indications or regulations and can produce (an underreported) lack of sensation and pain. Risks are also underreported and outcome reports have been problematized as scientifically unsound and conducted more as consumer satisfaction than clinical outcome surveys (Liao et al., 2007, cited in Braun, 2010).

Aging female bodies are not the only ones left out of the category "sexually attractive/desirable woman," which has become more exclusionary, marginalizing, obfuscating or pushing and leaving out large numbers of other women who do not look young, supple, girlish or White and heterosexual (i.e., elderly (Loe, 2004), fat (Levy, 2005), disabled (Gill, 2008; Rousso, 1994), lesbian (Hill & Fischer, 2008), women of color (Gill, 2008; Ward, 2004)). Very particular young, thin and highly sexualized celebrity African-American and Latina women pepper the cultural visual landscape (Stephens & Phillips, 2003; Ward, Hansbrough & Walker, 2005). However, these primarily young, thin and light-skinned women's bodies do not represent the bodies of most African-American and Latina women (Ward & Rivadeneyra, 2002). Several analyses have suggested that being excluded from the category "object of male sexual desire" in society, including being older, larger, darker, disabled or not fitting into bodily conventions of sexy or attractive, could be a "protective" factor for those women (Gill, 2009; McRobbie, 2009; Tolman, 2002), but the denial of this aspect of one's humanity, including for those who derive esteem or pleasure from being admired, could have other negative consequences.

Impact on Women's Sexual Relationships and Sexual Functioning

Sexualization can induce negative feelings in girls about their bodies in adolescence, which ultimately may lead to sexual problems in adulthood (Graham, Saunders, Milhausen & McBride, 2004; Wiederman, 2000). Some studies indicate that women with high body dissatisfaction engage in less sexual activity and are especially apprehensive about sexual situations in which their bodies can be seen; conversely, women who feel more positively about and comfortable with their bodies are more comfortable with their own sexual feelings (Ackard, Kearney-Cooke & Peterson, 2000; Trapnell, Meston & Gorzalka, 1997; Wiederman, 2000). Women who report more body dissatisfaction report a later onset of masturbation (Wiederman & Pryor, 1997) and are less likely to receive (but not to perform) oral sex (Wiederman & Hurst, 1998). Schooler, Ward, Merriwether & Caruthers (2005) found that greater levels of body discomfort and body self-consciousness each predicted lower levels of sexual assertiveness, sexual experience, and condom use self-efficacy, as well as higher levels of sexual risk-taking. When self-objectification was experimentally induced in one study, women reported decreased interest in the physical aspects of sex (Roberts & Gettman, 2004). Cosmetic surgeries for "vaginal rejuvenation" may be contributing to physiological sexual problems (Braun, 2010; Tiefer, 2008).

Such findings demonstrate that the interplay between being sexualized as girls and socialized into sexual objects may inhibit women's ability to advocate for, or even acknowledge, their own sexual feelings or pleasure in adulthood. A woman who has been socialized to separate from her experiences of sexual arousal and desire may find it difficult to be aware of her desires, assert her desires, or feel entitled to satisfaction in sexual situations (Brotto, Heiman & Tolman, 2009). Empirical evidence that young women do opt to let events unfold based on their (male) partner's wants and interests supports these concerns (Cotton et al., 2004; Morgan & Zurbriggen, 2007). The historical hypersexualization of African-American girls and women (Collins, 2000; hooks, 1992), recently intensified in the media (Ward, Hansbrough & Walker, 2005), results in African-American young women not feeling entitled to protection from STIs and pregnancy or to sexual pleasure (Burson, 1998; Belgrave, Van Oss Marin & Chambers, 2000).

There is recent evidence that sexual objectification has negative impacts on women's sexual functioning. Sanchez & Kiefer (2007) found that body shame in women was more strongly linked to greater sexual problems than in men, including lower sexual arousability, ability to reach orgasm and having less pleasure from physical intimacy, which was mediated by sexual self-consciousness, regardless of relationship status or age. Donaghue (2009) found negative implications of body dissatisfaction for women's sexual self-schemas. Yamamiya, Cash & Thompson (2006) found that women feeling bad their bodies during sex with a partner was associated with lower sexual self-efficacy, more ambivalence in sexual decision-making and more emotional disengagement. Another study found that self-objectification was related to self-consciousness during sexual activity and decreased sexual functioning via body shame and appearance anxiety for women, with women in an exclusive relationship reporting relatively less self-consciousness during sexual activity (Steer & Tiggemann, 2008; see also Sanchez & Broccoli, 2008). Focusing attention during sexual encounters on how one looks rather than how one feels can see also lead to diminished sexual pleasure (Wiederman, 2000, 2001).

"Moving Targets:" Exploitation of the Impact on Women's Sexuality

The sexualization of girls and the ensuing "youthified" sexual objectification of women has worked its way into the multi-billion dollar fitness industry for women by subtly co-opting sexualizing activities, preying on women's latest anxieties about being sexually attractive or "good enough" sexual objects and on women's disconnection from their bodies as a way to sell. By using the language of "empowerment" while obfuscating yet exploiting its sexualizing associations, this fitness fad is exemplified by the promotion of strip tease as exercise and performing fitness activities in stiletto heels, and the immense popularity of pole dancing as a route to fitness (i.e., Pilates "on the pole" (Dunn-Camp, 2007)).

In an interview study in which Whitehead & Kurz (2009) identified ways that young women make sense of pole dancing, they found that embracing it as "fun" fitness activity was predicated on distancing the activity from its associations with unwanted or "dirty" sexual objectification and from women who pole dance to make money as sexual objects for male customers. In another interview study, researchers found that women engaging in bodily movement that has sexual connotations outside of a sexual context enabled them to feel "in control" and to enjoy their bodily movements in the context of a fitness class (Melamed, under review). However, their participation in a practice of sexual objectification, divorced from women's sexual feelings or pleasure, is premised on their explicit denial of the origins of the practice in sex work. If women must distance themselves from the "dirty" associations they describe about "real" pole dancing, then why pole dance for fitness rather than engage in other bodily practices as a source of personal power? The women said that they felt what their instructors promised, empowered, "amazing" and youthful but only by desexualizing and not experiencing this practice as sexual. The elephant in the room is the pole itself.

Pole dancing as a physical fitness activity underscores and reifies how *looking* youthfully sexy trumps *feeling* sexy or even sexual, while ironically taking advantage of the disconnection which so many women experience from their bodies in the wake of their sexual socialization and the sexualization of girls. If pole dancing were a route to sexual empowerment for women themselves, shouldn't there be directions for how to use the pole for women's own sexual pleasure?

Impact on Young Women: Sexual Objectification as Sexual Empowerment?

One current public discussion that has been linked to the sexualization of girls is that it could be a positive reflection of a new acceptance of young women's sexuality: that young women and society have transcended the sexual double standard that denies active female sexuality (Lerum & Dworkin, 2009a, 2009b). Indeed, in recent and frequent depictions of young women, their sexuality is everywhere. In advertisements, in movies, on television (network as well as cable and especially in the guise of "reality" TV), they appear to flaunt their bodies by choice to show off their unabashed sexuality; coy flirtation has given way to in-your-face sexy. Young women voluntarily shaking booty and flashing waxed privates, laughing along with the admiring male crowds captured on reality programs, such as the wildly successful franchise *Girls Gone Wild*, could be interpreted as a new day dawning for young women's sexuality. It has been asserted that women's sexual agency—sexual assertiveness, taking the initiative, shedding a demure seductive look for portrayals of sexual voraciousness more reminiscent of their male counterparts than their female foremothers, say and know what they want as much as the next guy—is the new expected norm for young women and that it is synonymous with sexual empowerment (Gill, 2008; Lerum & Dworkin, 2009a, 2009b). In this final section, I will review the relevant literature and provide a critical lens for approaching this question.

Recent Research: Complicating Pictures of Empowerment with the Objectification of Women's Sexual Agency

The most recent research suggests that young women continue to be negatively affected by sexualized portrayals of young, lithe women, in particular leading them not to feelings of sexual empowerment but to more constrained and stereotypical notions about gender roles and sexual roles, i.e., that women are sexual objects (Ward, 2002; Zurbriggen & Morgan, 2006). Ward & Averitt (2005) reported that heavier reading of popular men's magazines and stronger identification with popular male TV characters was associated with undergraduate (male and female) virgins' expectation that their first experience with sexual intercourse would be more negative. Among undergraduate women, more frequent viewing of reality dating television programs was correlated with greater acceptance of a sexual double standard and the belief that dating is a game and that men and women are adversaries (Zurbriggen & Morgan, 2006; see also Ward, 2002). Roberts & Gettman (2004) found that after exposure to objectifying words found on magazine covers, young women expressed reduced interest in sexual relationships. Young women have been found to have ambivalent and contradictory responses to viewing pornography, for instance disliking it but finding it sexually arousing (Ciclitera, 2004).

Even given this evidence that the sexual double standard still "operates" to organize young women's sexuality, the power and ubiquity of a sense that young women are now unabashed and unadulterated in their sexual aggression requires attention. I suggest that it has become more difficult than ever to analyze these questions *as young women's sexual agency itself has been objectified.* That is, rather than sexual agency being anchored in women knowing what they feel and acting on it, it is now the latest command performance: to appear to have sexual agency. This phenomenon has occurred at the same time in images of sexy and sexual young women and in young women's engagement with their own sexuality. This perspective is supported by the work of communications researchers who have identified how new images of women's sexual agency are used in advertising (Gill, 2008; McRobbie, 2009). While such research does not investigate the impact of media, it does provide avenues for reading "between the lines" of the proliferation of images of sexy, assertive young women.

These researchers observe how fashion, consumerism, bodily pleasure, and sexuality are talked about and portrayed in order to crystallize women into a new market by proffering "new" female sexualities (which are in fact a commodification of old sexualities (Attwood, 2005a, 2006; Harris, 2004; see also McRobbie, 2009)). Farvid & Braun (2006), in a content analysis of portrayals of male and female sexuality in *Cosmopolitan* (US) and *Cleo* (UK) magazines, observed pervasive contradictory messages directed towards young women (be sexually confident but don't speak your mind directly, be "subtle" about sexual communication to get him to pleasure you without bruising his ego), yielding what they call "pseudo liberation and sexual empowerment" (p. 306). Gill (2008) has noted that the "girl" version of sexual empowerment includes being "hot" constituted by a narrow set of bodily and comportment characteristics and is not accompanied by young women's (or television producer's) demands that men bare it all for women to enjoy. These researchers ask whether these portrayals and how young people are making sense of them constitute a parody of female sexual power rather than its expression.

McRobbie (2009) notes that what she calls the performance of being a sexy and assertive young women must be tempered with a kind of soft femininity that precludes masculine sexual aggression in order for it to be of interest. Alternatively, Gill (2009) suggests that white, heterosexual women have shifted from sexual objectification to "sexual subjectification," that is, rather than being shown as passive objects of desire, these young women (and only these young women) are portrayed as being active "subjects" of their own sexuality. However, rather than being "liberating," such portraits may constitute a new set of limiting mandates about how young women should express or appear to express their sexuality that is anchored in the "midriff bearing," actively desiring young woman, requiring a toned but not too strong body that looks youthful but should not be too physically capable. To support this analysis, she shows how another new image of female sexuality evident in advertising, the "hot lesbian," is completely disconnected from lesbian sexuality itself and being used to sell products not to lesbians but to men. These media analysts argue that these new depictions of gender relations visually posit that the solution to male bad behavior is for women to be badder; portrayals of the desirable, desiring young women to always be "up for it" reflects how advertisers have recuperated and commodified a kind of feminist consciousness and offered it back to women sanitized of its political critique of gender relations, male sexual violence against women and heteronormativity (Gill, 2008, 2009; Harris, 2004; McRobbie, 2009).

Young Women's Sexual Empowerment?: Choice, Contradiction and the Absence of Embodied Sexual Desire

While images are one significant arena where ideas about young women's sexuality circulate, the contested question on the table is whether or how young women have taken up being sexual objects as an "ironic" new form of sexual agency. Given that in the not-too-distant past, being sexually assertive and being positioned as a sexual object were to be avoided at all costs, it seems remarkable that such a profound 180-degree turnaround of female sexuality has occurred. However, new media cycles and the speed with which new images, forms and performances sweep through social networks may make such quick transformations possible in ways that are unprecedented. Are women being acknowledged and not suffering consequences for being sexual on their own terms, agents of their own sexuality, if you will, empowered to be sexually assertive or to pursue their own sexual feelings on their own behalf?

One simple assertion is that it is what it seems—young women voluntarily stripping for crowds and the camera, even masturbating on camera, having fun like and with the guys by being sexual free agents, is unequivocal evidence of sexual empowerment—the power to choose to engage in any sexual action. Another simple analysis is that young women have been sold and bought a bill of goods that what they want is to be as raunchy as guys and the "girl version" is to make the choice to be fantastic (literally, to bring heterosexual male sexual fantasies to life) and that they are being duped into believing they have achieved sexual freedom. A third way to evaluate this conundrum is anchored in a set of psychological questions about young women's experience of this ostensible sexual empowerment. These psychological questions are about the place of dissociation and embodied desire—sexual and emotional—in sexual empowerment. By dissociation, I mean a literal disconnection from one's feelings, both emotional and physical. Embodied sexual desire is the experience of sexual feelings, passions, desire and arousal in one's own body; that is, desire not only as what one wants at an intellectual or cognitive level but as bodily experience.

While there is virtually no peer-reviewed research to date that enables an evaluation of these interpretations, there is one very rich and thorough source that enables investigation of these three interpretations. Ariel Levy has named the infusion of highly sexualized media into the mainstream "raunch culture" (Levy, 2005), an outcome of the pornification of culture that has already been discussed. Her journalistic investigations provide an account of how this culture gained ascendance, who produces it, what roles young women are playing in it, and what young women say about their experiences participating in it. She offers some pointed analyses that go beneath the surface of portrayals and actual performances of young women's sexuality that reveal the only sexual agency we know, male sexual agency. In trying to make sense of "raunch culture," Levy discovered a kind of double-speak in the uncritical embrace of sexual object turned sexual actor status by these young women. She and others (Gill, 2009; Harris, 2004; McRobbie, 2009) observe that being a "great sexual object" who also acts like a porn star is a performance rather than the embodiment of a new form of female sexuality, which in the past has been desired but condemned but that now accrues attention, popularity and new versions of old experiences of power—the power to turn men on, the power to tease men who are bursting at the seams at the sight of their sexual fantasies come to life, and the power to accept or reject them.

Specifically, Levy noted widespread absence of any discussion of female sexual pleasure (save for the pleasure of feeling power over a "vulnerable" other), a consistent lack of or explicit denial of feeling sexual, rather, only enjoyment of being perceived as sexy, the pervasiveness of alcohol in all of the settings she observed (including the production of "reality" TV), and the still-present and even eroticized threat and reality of male sexual violence that makes it all more exciting unless it happens. Young women did not describe their wanting or demanding what felt good or right to them sexually, as the new sexual empowerment is about doing—performing—rather than feeling, adopting a girl version of sexuality as conquest that, when queried, seems less about sexual agency and more to do with other rewards—being admired as fantastic sexual objects to the point of embodying the pornographic, which Levy found was ultimately embarrassing, humiliating or the undesired endpoint of sexual experiences. This seemingly limited and disembodied sexuality is complemented and intensified by how young men are (more than ever) sexually socialized to be disconnected consumers of these very young women.

Levy identifies the paucity of choice and missing multiplicity of ideas about what sexuality and sexual expression are or might be—for women and even for men if unencumbered by persistent gender inequality—and how the current landscape obscures that limit while at the same time holding it in place. It is difficult to evaluate claims of acting on or acting out sexual choices when, as Farvid & Braun (2006) note, these sexual choices are invisibly limited. That is, women are partaking at a very sparse buffet without a sense of what is not on the menu or their right or wish to want those choices. As Braun (2010) observes, "if social control is enacted through advertising and media, which creates the guise of free choice . . . free choice becomes culturally circumscribed" (see also Harris, 2004). That is, more than ever, "free choice" is limited to what's on sale, but the ways in which these choices are a subset of the range of choices women have as sexual beings are in fact regulatory—and that is not visible to the naked or untrained eye. Corsianos (2007) contends that the production of what looks like choice in the content of mainstream pornography contributes to the constraint on sexual choice itself.

Levy concludes "we are afraid of real female power . . . to figure out what we internally want from sex instead of mimicking whatever popular culture holds up to us as sexy" (pp. 199–200). In the wide range of anecdotal accounts she collected, the theme of young women going for sexy looks and acting sexy while at the same time expressing discomfort or lack of interest in being sexual (thinking about the way they are experienced rather than what they are experiencing) reflects the strong hold that sexual objectification has over what might constitute one's sexuality. In her interviews, young women narrated their embrace of "the male sexual gaze" as the only apparent option for sexual agency, conveying "if you can't beat them, join them" mentality (see Thompson, this volume, for supportive and contradictory views).

This line of thinking suggests the need *to distinguish between embodied sexuality and performances of sexuality that are now portrayed as sexual freedom.* The spectre of disembodiment that echoes in available accounts by young women and analyses of portrayals in advertising and the media raises a red flag about the role of sexual objectification in sexual empowerment. Even orgasm—the one form of women's sexual pleasure that is acknowledged, albeit itself objectified—appears to be more about doing a good performance than one's own pleasure, evidenced by one young woman Levy observed after she did a masturbation scene for *Girls Gone Wild*, who was concerned that she had not done it right, because she had taken too long to produce her orgasm.

Teasing apart the complex, contradictory and commercial dimensions of the "new sexual empowerment" and raising challenges about what is missing from it—women's embodied sexual pleasure as an anchor to sexual subjectivity, real choices that flesh out rather than laminate female sexual agency—within or perhaps missing from the lived experiences of real young women is a vital next step for public discourse, education, and research. With the exception of Levy's account, research and analysis addressing the question of young women's sexual empowerment reflect dissections of images rather than real young women's experiences. The question of how they make sense of "sexual empowerment" remains up for grabs: Is it authentic or what does it mean to have to be (or appear to be) sexual in a new kind of way that forefronts appearance but makes irrelevant whether or not a woman's desire is real or embodied? Investigating younger and older women's negotiations of embodiment and pressures to disembody may provide a way of navigating questions about and analyses of sexual empowerment that appear to defy, diffuse, defuse, or obfuscate young women's sexuality under the newest "youthified" regime of pervasive sexual objectification.

Conclusion

In this chapter, I have reviewed what we know about the consequences of the sexualization of girls and the current youthified forms of sexual objectification of women for boys', and men's and women's sexuality. In some ways, this is a literature that awaits development, and the leads we have currently underscore the urgency for such a research agenda. What may be most problematic and challenging is the way that these representations and, increasingly, enactments of sexual objectification seem more and more to be "normal" in general and what real people's sexuality is supposed to be like. Media literacy campaigns that reveal the commercial interests embedded in the depiction and simultaneous cooptation and commercialization of female sexual agency as the latest product to consume, crave, create and maintain are needed, as is "choice education." Young people deserve the tools to discern and challenge the limited choices that put forth as a sparse menu for sexuality that barely offers any sense of it as part of our humanity and to demand more and better options for how they are represented and how they can be.

For women, boys, and men, sexual objectification as sexuality is continuous with education that fails to teach children and teenagers to differentiate their sexual desires from their desire for attention, to differentiate being sexual from being sexy, and to distinguish sex as consumption from sex as experience. Gill (2009) argues that being for or against sexualization is less useful than breaking it out as a multifaceted not homogeneous process. Sexual rights for girls and women, including rights to pleasure, knowledge and the freedom to enact what one does and does not desire (Tolman & Costa, 2010) is predicated on an understanding of and refusal to embrace the divisions left standing among women and girls predicated on their sexual behavior regardless of what is motivating it.

In all of this stew of sexual objectification and inappropriate sexualization, however, it is important to keep in mind that boys, men, women and girls themselves are not empty vessels into which images and constructions of girls and women as (only) sexual objects and sexualized body parts are deposited. Media, feminist and psychological theories posit individuals as at least potentially "active agents" in determining how they will make sense of and "consume" what these various cultural contexts provide, underscoring avenues for critique, resistance and change, both individual and social. Not all boys are trolling the Internet for porn, playing video games with interactive options for sexualized violence, nor are all men disengaged from their emotional lives; not all young women are baring it all for cameras or want to, and not all women buy into (literally and figuratively) the impossible portrayals that define sexy or deny feeling sexual.

Author Note

The author wishes to thank Rachel Liebert for assistance in research, Christin Bowman and Amy Baker for assistance in preparing the manuscript, and the editors and anonymous reviewer for their feedback and guidance.

Note

1. While there is evidence that the sexual objectification and self-objectification of boys' and men's bodies are on the rise, this line of argument is not included in this chapter because it falls outside of its scope. While boys' and men's focus on their appearance may be a subject of increased concern, it is also neither a socially mandated nor a pervasive part of their self-identity on a broad scale (boys and men are without question more than their bodies, albeit male adolescent anxieties can certainly be about their physical development) as is the case with girls and women.

References

Ackard, D. M., Kearney-Cooke, A., & Peterson, C. B. (2000). Effect of body image and self-image on women's sexual behaviors. *International Journal of Eating Disorders, 28*(4), 422–429.

American Society of Plastic Surgeons. (2006a). 2005 cosmetic surgery age distributions 18 or younger. Retrieved September 5, 2006, from www.plasticsurgery.org/public_education/loader.cfm?url=/commonspot/security/getfile.cfm&PageID=17849

American Society of Plastic Surgeons. (2006b). 2006 cosmetic surgery age distribution: 19–34 and 35–50. Retrieved September 8, 2006, from www.plasticsurgery.org/ public_education/loader.cfm?url=/commonspot/security/getfile.cfm&PageID=17850

Attwood, F. (2005a). Fashion and passion: Marketing sex to women. *Sexualities, 8*(4), 392–406.

Attwood, F. (2005b). What do people do with porn? Qualitative research into the consumption, use and experience of pornography and other sexually explicit media. *Sexuality & Culture, 9*(2), 65–86.

Attwood, F. (2006). Sexed up: Theorizing the sexualization of culture. *Sexualities, 79*(1), 77–94.

Aubrey, J. S. (2006). Effects of sexually objectifying media on self-objectification and body surveillance in undergraduates: Results of a 2-year panel study. *Journal of Communication, 56*(2), 366–386.

Banet-Weiser, S., & Portwood-Stacer, L. (2006). 'I just want to be me again!': Beauty pageants, reality television and post-feminism. *Feminist Theory, 7*(2), 255–272.

Belgrave, F. Z., Van, O. M., & Chambers, D. B. (2000). Culture, contextual, and intrapersonal predictors of risky sexual attitudes among urban African American girls in early adolescence. *Cultural Diversity and Ethnic Minority Psychology, 6*(3), 309–322.

Bogle, K. A. (2008). *Hooking up: Sex, dating and relationships on campus*. New York: New York University Press.

Braun, V. (2010). Female genital cosmetic surgery: A critical review of current knowledge and contemporary debates. *Journal of Women's Health, 19*(7), 1393–1407.

Braun, V. (2005). In search of (better) sexual pleasure: Female genital 'cosmetic' surgery. *Sexualities, 8*(4), 407–424.

Brooks, G. R. (1995). *The centerfold syndrome: How men can overcome objectification and achieve intimacy with women*. San Francisco: Jossey-Bass.

Brotto, L. A., Heiman, J. R., & Tolman, D. L. (2009). Narratives of desire in mid-age women with and without arousal difficulties. *Journal of Sex Research, 46*(5), 387–398.

Burn, S. M., & Ward, A. Z. (2005). Men's conformity to traditional masculinity and relationship satisfaction. *Psychology of Men and Masculinities, 6*, 254–263.

Burgess, M. C. R., Stermer, S. P., & Burgess, S. R. (2007). Sex, lies, and video games: The portrayal of male and female characters on video game covers. *Sex Roles, 57*(5–6), 419–433.

Burson, J. A. (1998). AIDS, sexuality and African-American adolescent females. *Child and Adolescent Social Work Journal, 15*(5), 357–365.

Chalker, R. (2009). *The 'perfect' porn vulva: More women demanding cosmetic genital surgery*. Retrieved February 20, 2010, from http://www.alternet.org/sex/141479/the_%5C%27perfect%5C%27_porn_vulva:_more_women_demanding_cosmetic_genital_surgery/

Ciclitira, K. (2004). Pornography, women and feminism: Between pleasure and politics. *Sexualities, 7*(3), 281–301.

Collins, P. H. (2000). *Black feminist thought*. New York: Routledge.

Corsianos, M. (2007). Mainstream pornography and "women": Questioning sexual agency. *Critical Sociology, 33*(5–6), 863–885.

Cotton, S., Mills, L., Succop, P. A., Biro, F. M., & Rosenthal, S. L. (2004). Adolescent girls' perceptions of the timing of their sexual initiation: 'Too young' or 'just right'? *Journal of Adolescent Health, 34*(5), 453–458.

Davies, G. (2004). Over half of children see net porn. *Times Educational Supplement* (4595), 9. Retrieved February 25, 2010, from Education Research Complete database.

Diaz, J. (2009). First Apple-approved iPhone porn app. Retrieved February 25, 2010, from http://gizmodo.com/5302365/first-apple+approved-iphone- porn-app/gallery/

Dietz, T. L. (1998). An examination of violence and gender role portrayals in video games: Implications for gender socialization and aggressive behavior. *Sex Roles, 38*(5–6), 425–442.

Dill, K. E., & Dill, J. C. (1998). Video game violence: A review of the empirical literature. *Aggression and Violent Behavior, 3*(4), 407–428.

Dill, K. E., & Thill, K. P. (2007). Video game characters and the socialization of gender roles: Young people's perceptions mirror sexist media depictions. *Sex Roles, 57*(11–12), 851–864.

Dines, G. (2009). Childified women: How the mainstream porn industry sells child pornography to men. In S. Olfman (Ed.), *The sexualization of childhood*. (pp. 121–142). Westport, CT: Praeger Publishers/Greenwood Publishing Group.

Dittmar, H., & Howard, S. (2004). Thin-ideal internalization and social comparison tendency as moderators of media models' impact on women's body-focused anxiety. *Journal of Social and Clinical Psychology, 23*, 768–791.

Dobbin, M. (2008). *Victim slams YouTube over rape footage*. Retrieved January 22, 2010, from http://www.theage.com.au/news/technology/rape-victim-slams-youtube-for-footage/2008/03/05/1204402501579.html

Donaghue, N. (2009). Body satisfaction, sexual self-schemas and subjective well-being in women. *Body Image, 6*(1), 37.

Dunn-Camp, S. (2007). Pole-ates? Teaser takes on new meaning in this sexy new twist on the method. *Pilates Style Magazine*, May/June, p. 21.

Dworkin, S. L., & O'Sullivan, L. (2007). 'It's less work for us and it shows us she has good taste': Masculinity, sexual initiation, and contemporary sexual scripts. In M. Kimmel (Ed.), *The sexual self: The construction of sexual scripts* (pp. 105–121). Nashville: Vanderbilt University Press.

Else-Quest, N., & Hyde, J. (2009). The missing discourse of development: Commentary on Lerum and Dworkin. *Journal of Sex Research, 46*(4), 264–267.

England, P., Schafer, E. F., & Fogarty, A. (2007). Hooking up and forming romantic relationships on today's college campuses. In M. Kimmel & A. Aronson (Eds.), *The gendered society reader*. New York: Oxford University Press.

Ezzell, M. (2009). Pornography, lad mags, video games, and boys: Reviving the canary in the cultural coal mine. In S. Olfman (Ed.), *The sexualization of childhood* (pp. 7–32). Westport, CT: Praeger/Greenwood.

Farvid, P., & Braun, V. (2006). Most of us guys are raring to go anytime, anyplace, anywhere: Male and female sexuality in *Cleo* and *Cosmo. Sex Roles, 55*(5–6), 295–310.

Gill, R. (2009). Beyond the "sexualization of culture" thesis: An intersectional analysis of "sixpacks," "midriffs" and "hot lesbians" in advertising. *Sexualities, 12*, 137.

Gill, R. (2008). Empowerment/sexism: Figuring female sexual agency in contemporary advertising. *Feminism & Psychology, 18*(1), 35–60.

Greenfield, P. M. (2004). Inadvertent exposure to pornography on the internet: Implications of peer-to-peer file-sharing networks for child development and families. *Journal of Applied Developmental Psychology, 25*(6), 741–750.

Graham, C. A., Sanders, S. A., Milhausen, R. R., & McBride, K. R. (2004). Turning on and turning off: A focus group study of the factors that affect women's sexual arousal. *Archives of Sexual Behavior, 33*(6), 527–538.

Harris, A. (Ed.). (2004). *All about the girl: Culture, power, and identity*. New York: Routledge.

Herman, J. L. (1992). *Trauma and recovery: The aftermath of violence—From domestic abuse to political terror*. New York: Basic Books.

Hill, M. S., & Fischer, A. R. (2008). Examining objectification theory: Lesbian and heterosexual women's experiences with sexual- and self-objectification. *The Counseling Psychologist, 36*, 745–776.

hooks, b. (1992). *Black looks: Race and representation*. Cambridge, MA: South End Press.

Impett, E. A., Schooler, D., & Tolman, D. L. (2006). To be seen and not heard: Femininity ideology and adolescent girls' sexual health. *Archives of Sexual Behavior, 35*(6), 129–142.

Jensen, R. (2007). *Getting off: Pornography and the end of masculinity*. Cambridge, MA: South End Press.

Kenrick, D. T., & Guttieres, S. E. (1980). Contrast effects and judgments of physical attractiveness: When beauty becomes a social problem. *Journal of Personality and Social Psychology, 38*, 131–140.

Kimmel, M. (2008). *Guyland: The perilous world where boys become men*. New York: Harper.

Kindlon, D., & Thompson, M. (1999). *Raising Cain: Protecting the emotional life of boys*. New York: Ballantine Books.

Lerum, K., & Dworkin, S. L. (2009a). "Bad girls rule": An interdisciplinary feminist commentary on the report of the APA task force on the sexualization of girls. *Journal of Sex Research, 46*(3), 1–14.

Lerum, K., & Dworkin, S. L. (2009b). Toward the interdisciplinary dialogue on youth, sexualization, and health. *Journal of Sex Research, 46*(4), 271–273.

Levy, A. (2005). *Female chauvinist pigs: Women and the rise of raunch culture*. New York: Free Press.

Lindgren, K. P., Shoda, Y., & George, W. H. (2007). Sexual or friendly? Associations about women, men and self. *Psychology of Women Quarterly, 31*(2), 190–201.

Linz, D. G., Donnerstein, E., & Penrod, S. (1988). Effects of long-term exposure to violent and sexually degrading depictions of women. *Journal of Personality and Social Psychology, 55*(5), 758–768.

Loe, M. (2004). Sex and the senior woman: Pleasure and danger in the Viagra era. *Sexualities, 7*, 303–326.

Loftus, D. (2002). *Watching sex: How men really respond to pornography*. New York: Thunder's Mouth.

Martin, K. A., & Kazyak, E. (2009). Hetero-romantic love and heterosexiness in children's G-rated films. *Gender & Society, 23*(3), 315–336.

Melamed, S. (under review). Self-subjectification and simulating erotic dance: Women's experience in pole dance fitness class.

McRobbie, A. (2009). *The aftermath of feminism: Gender, culture, and social change*. London: Sage.

Morgan, E. M., & Zurbriggen, E. L. (2007). Wanting sex and wanting to wait: Young adults' accounts of sexual messages from first significant dating partners. *Feminism & Psychology, 17*(4), 515–541.

O'Sullivan, L. F., & Majerovich, J. (2008). Difficulties with sexual functioning in a sample of male and female late adolescent and young adult university students. *Canadian Journal of Human Sexuality, 17*(3), 109–121.

Paul, P. (2005). *Pornified: How pornography is damaging our lives, our relationships, and our families*. New York: Holt.

Pleck, J., Sonenstein, F., & Ku, L. (1993). Masculinity ideology: Its impact on adolescent males' heterosexual relationships. *Journal of Social Issues, 49*(3), 11–29.

Quinn, B. A. (2002). Sexual harassment and masculinity: The power and meaning of "girl watching". *Gender Society, 16*, 386–402.

Roberts, T., & Gettman, J. Y. (2004). Mere exposure: Gender differences in the negative effects of priming a state of self-objectification. *Sex Roles, 51*(1–2), 17–27.

Rousso, H. (1994). Daughters with disabilities: Defective women or minority women. In J. Irvine (Ed.), *Sexual cultures and the construction of adolescent identities* (pp. 139–171). Philadelphia: Temple University Press.

Rudman, L. A., & Borgida, E. (1995). The afterglow of construct accessibility: The behavioral consequences of priming men to view women as sexual objects. *Journal of Experimental Social Psychology, 31*(6), 493–517.

Sanchez, D. T., & Broccoli, T. L. (2008). The romance of self-objectification: Does priming romantic relationships induce states of self-objectification among women? *Sex Roles, 59*(7–8), 545–554.

Sanchez, D. T., & Kiefer, A. K. (2007). Body concerns in and out of the bedroom: Implications for sexual pleasure and problems. *Archives of Sexual Behavior, 36*(6), 808.

Schooler, D., Ward, L. M., Merriwether, A., & Caruthers, A. S. (2005). Cycles of shame: Menstrual shame, body shame, and sexual decision-making. *Journal of Sex Research, 42*(4), 324–334.

Schooler, D., & Ward, L. M. (2006). Average Joes: Men's relationships with media, real bodies and sexuality. *Psychology of Men and Masculinity, 7*, 27–41.

Steer, A., & Tiggemann, M. (2008). The role of self-objectification in women's sexual functioning. *Journal of Social & Clinical Psychology, 27*(3), 205–225.

Stephens, D. P., & Phillips, L. D. (2003). Freaks, gold diggers, divas, and dykes: The sociohistorical development of adolescent African American women's sexual script. *Sexuality & Culture: An Interdisciplinary Quarterly, 7*(1), 3–49.

Stombler, M. (1994). 'Buddies' or 'slutties': The collective sexual reputation of fraternity little sisters. *Gender & Society. Special Issue: Sexual identities/sexual communities, 8*(3), 297–323.

Sweeney, B. N. (2008). Dangerous and out of control? College men, masculinity, and subjective experiences of sexuality. *Dissertation Abstracts International: Section A: Humanities and Social Sciences, 68*(9A), 4094.

Tasker, Y., & Negra, D. (Eds.). (2007). *Interrogating postfeminism: Gender and the politics of popular culture*. Durham, NC: Duke University Press.

Tiefer, L. (2008). Female genital cosmetic surgery: Freakish or inevitable? Analysis from medical marketing, bioethics, and feminist theory. *Feminism & Psychology, 18*(4), 466–479.

Tolman, D. (2000). Object lessons: Romance, violation, and female adolescent sexual desire. *Journal of Sex Education & Therapy, 25*(1), 70.

Tolman, D. L. (2002). *Dilemmas of desire: Teenage girls talk about sexuality*. Cambridge, MA: Harvard University Press.

Tolman, D. L. (2006). In a different position: Conceptualizing female adolescent sexuality within compulsory heterosexuality. *New Directions for Child and Adolescent Development, 2006*(112), 71–89.

Tolman, D. L., & Debold, E. (1993). Conflicts of body and image: Female adolescents, desire, and the no-body body. In P. Fallon, M. Katzman, & S. Wooley

(Eds.), *Feminist perspectives on eating disorders* (pp. 301–317). New York: Guilford Press.

Tolman, D. L., Spencer, R., Rosen-Reynoso, M., & Porche, M. V. (2003). Sowing the seeds of violence in heterosexual relationships: Early adolescents narrate compulsory heterosexuality. *Journal of Social Issues, 59*(1), 159–178.

Tolman, D. L., & Costa, S. H. (2010). Sexual rights for young women: Lessons from developing countries. In P. Aggleton & R. Parker (Eds.), *Routledge handbook of sexuality, health and human rights,* (pp. 389–398). New York: Routledge.

Trapnell, P. D., Meston, C. M., & Gorzalka, B. B. (1997). Spectatoring and the relationship between body image and sexual experience: Self-focus or self-valence? *Journal of Sex Research, 34*(3), 267–278.

Vanwesenbeeck, I. (2009). The risks and rights of sexualization: An appreciative commentary on Lerum and Dworkin's "bad girls rule." *Journal of Sex Research, 46*(4), 268–270.

Ward, L. M. (2002). Does television exposure affect emerging adults' attitudes and assumptions about sexual relationships? Correlational and experimental confirmation. *Journal of Youth & Adolescence, 31*, 1–15.

Ward, L. M. (2004). Wading through the stereotypes: Positive and negative associations between media use and black adolescents' conceptions of self. *Developmental Psychology, 40*, 284–294.

Ward, L. M., & Averitt, L. (2005). *Associations between media use and young adults' perceptions of first intercourse. course*. Paper presented at the annual meeting of the National Communication Association, Boston.

Ward, L. M., Hansbrough, E., & Walker, E. (2005). Contributions of music video exposure to black adolescents' gender and sexual schemas. *Journal of Adolescent Research, 20*(2), 143–166.

Ward, L. M., & Rivadeneyra, R. (1999). Contributions of entertainment television to adolescents' sexual attitudes and expectations: The role of viewing amount versus viewer involvement. *The Journal of Sex Research, 36*(3), 237–249.

Ward, L. M., & Rivandeneyra, R. (2002, August). *Dancing, strutting and bouncing in cars: The women of music videos*. Paper presented at the annual meeting of the American Psychological Association, Chicago.

Weaver, J., Masland, J. L., & Zillmann, D. (1984). Effect of erotica on young men's aesthetic perception of their female sexual partners. *Perceptual and Motor Skills, 58*, 929–930.

Weekes, D. (2002). Get your freak on: How black girls sexualise identity. *Sex Education, 2*(3), 251–262.

Whitehead, K., & Kurz, T. (2009). 'Empowerment' and the pole: A discursive investigation of the reinvention of pole dancing as a recreational activity. *Feminism & Psychology, 19*(2), 224–244.

Wiederman, M. W. (2000). Women's body image self-consciousness during physical intimacy with a partner. *Journal of Sex Research, 37*(1), 60–68.

Wiederman, M. W. (2001). "Don't look now": The role of self-focus in sexual dysfunction. *The Family Journal: Counseling and Therapy for Couples and Families, 9*, 210–214.

Wiederman, M. W., & Hurst, S. R. (1998). Body size, physical attractiveness, and body image among young adult women: Relationships to sexual experience and sexual esteem. *Journal of Sex Research, 35*(3), 272–281.

Wiederman, M., & Pryor, T. (1997). Body dissatisfaction and sexuality among women with bulimia nervosa. *International Journal of Eating Disorders, 21*, 361–365.

Yamamiya, Y., Cash, T. F., & Thompson, J. K. (2006). Sexual experiences among college women: The differential effects of general versus contextual body images on sexuality. *Sex Roles, 55*(5–6), 421–427.

Yao, M., Mahood, C., & Linz, D. (2010). Sexual priming, gender stereotyping, and likelihood to sexually harass: Examining the cognitive effects of playing a sexually-explicit video game. *Sex Roles, 62*(1/2), 77–88.

Zillmann, D., & Bryant, J. (1988). Pornography's impact on sexual satisfaction. *Journal of Applied Social Psychology, 18*, 438–453.

Zurbriggen, E. L., & Morgan, E. M. (2006). Who wants to marry a millionaire? Reality dating television programs, attitudes toward sex, and sexual behaviors. *Sex Roles, 54*, 1–17.

PART

4

The Social Construction of Gender Relations

To sociologists, the psychological discussion of sex roles—that collection of attitudes, traits, and behaviors that are normative for either boys or girls—exposes the biological sleight of hand that suggests that what is normative—enforced, socially prescribed—is actually normal. But psychological models themselves do not go far enough, unable to fully explain the variations *among* men or women based on class, race, ethnicity, sexuality, age, or to explain the ways in which one gender consistently enjoys power over the other. And, most importantly to sociologists, psychological models describe how individuals acquire sex role identity, but then assume that these gendered individuals enact their gendered identities in institutions that are gender-neutral.

Sociologists have taken up each of these themes in exploring (1) how the institutions in which we find ourselves are also gendered, (2) the ways in which those psychological prescriptions for gender identity reproduce *both* gender difference and male domination, and (3) the ways in which gender is accomplished and expressed in everyday interaction.

Cynthia Fuchs Epstein took the occasion of her presidential address to the American Sociological Association to survey the various interpersonal and institutional mechanisms of women's near-universal subordination.

Taking a different approach toward similar ends, Candace West and her two collaborators, in two separate essays, make clear that gender is not a property of the individual, something that one *has*, but rather is a process that one *does* in everyday interaction with others. And that what one is doing is not simply doing gender, but also doing difference, which in our society also means doing inequality.

Doing Gender

CANDACE WEST AND DON H. ZIMMERMAN

In the beginning, there was sex and there was gender. Those of us who taught courses in the area in the late 1960s and early 1970s were careful to distinguish one from the other. Sex, we told students, was what was ascribed by biology: anatomy, hormones, and physiology. Gender, we said, was an achieved status: that which is constructed through psychological, cultural, and social means. To introduce the difference between the two, we drew on singular case studies of hermaphrodites and anthropological investigations of "strange and exotic tribes."

Inevitably (and understandably), in the ensuing weeks of each term, our students became confused. Sex hardly seemed a "given" in the context of research that illustrated the sometimes ambiguous and often conflicting criteria for its ascription. And gender seemed much less an "achievement" in the context of the anthropological, psychological, and social imperatives we studied—the division of labor, the formation of gender identities, and the social subordination of women by men. Moreover, the received doctrine of gender socialization theories conveyed the strong message that while gender may be "achieved," by about age five it was certainly fixed, unvarying, and static—much like sex.

Since about 1975, the confusion has intensified and spread far beyond our individual classrooms. For one thing, we learned that the relationship between biological and cultural processes was far more complex—and reflexive—than we previously had supposed. For another, we discovered that certain structural arrangements, for example, between work and family, actually produce or enable some capacities, such as to mother, that we formerly associated with biology. In the midst of all this, the notion of gender as a recurring achievement somehow fell by the wayside.

Our purpose in this article is to propose an ethnomethodologically informed, and therefore distinctively sociological, understanding of gender as a routine, methodical, and recurring accomplishment. We contend that the "doing" of gender is undertaken by women and men whose competence as members of society is hostage to its production. Doing gender involves a complex of socially guided perceptual, interactional, and micropolitical activities that cast particular pursuits as expressions of masculine and feminine "natures."

When we view gender as an accomplishment, an achieved property of situated conduct, our attention shifts from matters internal to the individual and focuses on interactional and, ultimately, institutional arenas. In one sense, of course, it is individuals who "do" gender. But it is a situated doing, carried out in the virtual or real presence of others who are presumed to be oriented to its production. Rather than as a property of individuals, we conceive of gender as an emergent feature of social situations: both as an outcome of and a rationale for various social arrangements and as a means of legitimating one of the most fundamental divisions of society.

To advance our argument, we undertake a critical examination of what sociologists have meant by *gender*, including its treatment as a role enactment in the conventional sense and as a "display" in Goffman's (1976) terminology. Both *gender role*

Candace West and Don H. Zimmerman, "Doing Gender" from *Gender & Society* 1, no. 2 (June 1987): 125–151.

and *gender display* focus on behavioral aspects of being a woman or a man (as opposed, for example, to biological differences between the two). However, we contend that the notion of gender as a role obscures the work that is involved in producing gender in everyday activities, while the notion of gender as a display relegates it to the periphery of interaction. We argue instead that participants in interaction organize their various and manifold activities to reflect or express gender, and they are disposed to perceive the behavior of others in a similar light.

To elaborate our proposal, we suggest at the outset that important but often overlooked distinctions be observed among *sex, sex category,* and *gender. Sex* is a determination made through the application of socially agreed upon biological criteria for classifying persons as females or males. The criteria for classification can be genitalia at birth or chromosomal typing before birth, and they do not necessarily agree with one another. Placement in a *sex category* is achieved through application of the sex criteria, but in everyday life, categorization is established and sustained by the socially required identificatory displays that proclaim one's membership in one or the other category. In this sense, one's sex category presumes one's sex and stands as proxy for it in many situations, but sex and sex category can vary independently; that is, it is possible to claim membership in a sex category even when the sex criteria are lacking. *Gender,* in contrast, is the activity of managing situated conduct in light of normative conceptions of attitudes and activities appropriate for one's sex category. Gender activities emerge from and bolster claims to membership in a sex category.

We contend that recognition of the analytical independence of sex, sex category, and gender is essential for understanding the relationships among these elements and the interactional work involved in "being" a gendered person in society. While our primary aim is theoretical, there will be occasion to discuss fruitful directions for empirical research following from the formulation of gender that we propose.

We begin with an assessment of the received meaning of gender, particularly in relation to the roots of this notion in presumed biological differences between women and men.

Perspectives on Sex and Gender

In Western societies, the accepted cultural perspective on gender views women and men as naturally and unequivocally defined categories of being with distinctive psychological and behavioral propensities that can be predicted from their reproductive functions. Competent adult members of these societies see differences between the two as fundamental and enduring—differences seemingly supported by the division of labor into women's and men's work and an often elaborate differentiation of feminine and masculine attitudes and behaviors that are prominent features of social organization. Things are the way they are by virtue of the fact that men are men and women are women—a division perceived to be natural and rooted in biology, producing in turn profound psychological, behavioral, and social consequences. The structural arrangements of a society are presumed to be responsive to these differences.

Analyses of sex and gender in the social sciences, though less likely to accept uncritically the naive biological determinism of the view just presented, often retain a conception of sex-linked behaviors and traits as essential properties of individuals. The "sex differences approach" is more commonly attributed to psychologists than to sociologists, but the survey researcher who determines the "gender" of respondents on the basis of the sound of their voices over the telephone is also making trait-oriented assumptions. Reducing gender to a fixed set of psychological traits or to a unitary "variable" precludes serious consideration of the ways it is used to structure distinct domains of social experience.

Taking a different tack, role theory has attended to the social construction of gender categories, called "sex roles" or, more recently, "gender roles" and has analyzed how these are learned and enacted. Beginning with Linton (1936) and continuing through the works of Parsons (Parsons 1951; Parsons and Bales 1955) and Komarovsky (1946, 1950), role theory has emphasized the social and dynamic aspect of role construction and enactment.

But at the level of face-to-face interaction, the application of role theory to gender poses problems of its own. Roles are *situated* identities—assumed and relinquished as the situation demands—rather than *master identities,* such as sex category, that cut across situations. Unlike most roles, such as "nurse," "doctor," and "patient" or "professor" and "student," gender has no specific site or organizational context.

Moreover, many roles are already gender marked, so that special qualifiers—such as "female doctor" or "male nurse"—must be added to exceptions to the rule. Thorne (1980) observes that conceptualizing gender as a role makes it difficult to assess its influence on other roles and reduces its explanatory usefulness in discussions of power and inequality. Drawing on Rubin (1975), Thorne calls for a reconceptualization of women and men as distinct social groups, constituted in "concrete, historically changing—and generally unequal—social relationships" (Thorne 1980, p. 11).

We argue that gender is not a set of traits, nor a variable, nor a role, but the product of social doings of some sort. What then is the social doing of gender? It is more than the continuous creation of the meaning of gender through human actions. We claim that gender itself is constituted through interaction. To develop the implications of our claim, we turn to Goffman's (1976) account of "gender display." Our object here is to explore how gender might be exhibited or portrayed through interaction, and thus be seen as "natural," while it is being produced as a socially organized achievement.

Gender Display

Goffman contends that when human beings interact with others in their environment, they assume that each possesses an "essential nature"—a nature that can be discerned through the "natural signs given off or expressed by them" (1976, p. 75). Femininity and masculinity are regarded as "prototypes of essential expression—something that can be conveyed fleetingly in any social situation and yet something that strikes at the most basic characterization of the individual" (1976, p. 75). The means through which we provide such expressions are "perfunctory, conventionalized acts" (1976, p. 69), which convey to others our regard for them, indicate our alignment in an encounter, and tentatively establish the terms of contact for that social situation. But they are also regarded as expressive behavior, testimony to our "essential natures."

Goffman (1976, pp. 69–70) sees *displays* as highly conventionalized behaviors structured as two-part exchanges of the statement-reply type, in which the presence or absence of symmetry can establish deference or dominance. These rituals are viewed as distinct from but articulated with more consequential activities, such as performing tasks or engaging in discourse. Hence, we have what he terms the "scheduling" of displays at junctures in activities, such as the beginning or end, to avoid interfering with the activities themselves. Goffman (1976, p. 69) formulates *gender display* as follows:

> If gender be defined as the culturally established correlates of sex (whether in consequence of biology or learning), then gender display refers to conventionalized portrayals of these correlates.

These gendered expressions might reveal clues to the underlying, fundamental dimensions of the female and male, but they are, in Goffman's view, optional performances. Masculine courtesies may or may not be offered and, if offered, may or may not be declined (1976, p. 71). Moreover, human beings "themselves employ the term 'expression,' and conduct themselves to fit their own notions of expressivity" (1976, p. 75). Gender depictions are less a consequence of our "essential sexual natures" than interactional portrayals of what we would like to convey about sexual natures, using conventionalized gestures. Our human nature gives us the ability to learn to produce and recognize masculine and feminine gender displays—"a capacity [we] have by virtue of being persons, not males and females" (1976, p. 76).

Upon first inspection, it would appear that Goffman's formulation offers an engaging sociological corrective to existing formulations of gender. In his view, gender is a socially scripted dramatization of the culture's *idealization* of feminine and masculine natures, played for an audience that is well schooled in the presentational idiom. To continue the metaphor, there are scheduled performances presented in special locations, and like plays, they constitute introductions to or time out from more serious activities.

There are fundamental equivocations in this perspective. By segregating gender display from the serious business of interaction, Goffman obscures the effects of gender on a wide range of human activities. Gender is not merely something that happens in the nooks and crannies of interaction, fitted in here and there and not interfering with the serious business of life. While it is plausible to contend that gender displays—construed as conventionalized expressions—are optional, it does not seem plausible to say that we have the option of being seen by others as female or male.

It is necessary to move beyond the notion of gender display to consider what is involved in doing gender as an ongoing activity embedded in everyday interaction. Toward this end, we return to the distinctions among sex, sex category, and gender introduced earlier.

Sex, Sex Category, and Gender

Garfinkel's (1967, pp. 118–40) case study of Agnes, a transsexual raised as a boy who adopted a female identity at age 17 and underwent a sex reassignment operation several years later, demonstrates how gender is created through interaction and at the same time structures interaction. Agnes, whom Garfinkel characterized as a "practical methodologist," developed a number of procedures for passing as a "normal, natural female" both prior to and after her surgery. She had the practical task of managing the fact that she possessed male genitalia and that she lacked the social resources a girl's biography would presumably provide in everyday interaction. In short, she needed to display herself as a woman, simultaneously learning what it was to be a woman. Of necessity, this full-time pursuit took place at a time when most people's gender would be well-accredited and routinized. Agnes had to consciously contrive what the vast majority of women do without thinking. She was not "faking" what "real" women do naturally. She was obliged to analyze and figure out how to act within socially structured circumstances and conceptions of femininity that women born with appropriate biological credentials come to take for granted early on. As in the case of others who must "pass," such as transvestites, Kabuki actors, or Dustin Hoffman's "Tootsie," Agnes's case makes visible what culture has made invisible—the accomplishment of gender.

Garfinkel's (1967) discussion of Agnes does not explicitly separate three analytically distinct, although empirically overlapping, concepts—sex, sex category, and gender.

Sex

Agnes did not possess the socially agreed upon biological criteria for classification as a member of the female sex. Still, Agnes regarded herself as a female, albeit a female with a penis, which a woman ought not to possess. The penis, she insisted, was a "mistake" in need of remedy (Garfinkel 1967, pp. 126–27, 131–32). Like other competent members of our culture, Agnes honored the notion that there are "essential" biological criteria that unequivocally distinguish females from males. However, if we move away from the commonsense viewpoint, we discover that the reliability of these criteria is not beyond question. Moreover, other cultures have acknowledged the existence of "cross-genders" and the possibility of more than two sexes.

More central to our argument is Kessler and McKenna's (1978, pp. 1–6) point that genitalia are conventionally hidden from public inspection in everyday life; yet we continue through our social rounds to "observe" a world of two naturally, normally sexed persons. It is the *presumption* that essential criteria exist and would or should be there if looked for that provides the basis for sex categorization. Drawing on Garfinkel, Kessler and McKenna argue that "female" and "male" are cultural events—products of what they term the "gender attribution process"—rather than some collection of traits, behaviors, or even physical attributes. Illustratively they cite the child who, viewing a picture of someone clad in a suit and a tie, contends, "It's a man, because he has a pee-pee" (Kessler and McKenna 1978, p. 154). Translation: "He must have a pee-pee [an essential characteristic] because I see the *insignia* of a suit and tie." Neither initial sex assignment (pronouncement at birth as a female or male) nor the actual existence of essential criteria for that assignment (possession of a clitoris and vagina or penis and testicles) has much—if anything—to do with the identification of sex category in everyday life. There, Kessler and McKenna note, we operate with a moral certainty of a world of two sexes. We do not think, "Most persons with penises are men, but some may not be" or "Most persons who dress as men have penises." Rather, we take it for granted that sex and sex category are congruent—that knowing the latter, we can deduce the rest.

Sex Categorization

Agnes's claim to the categorical status of female, which she sustained by appropriate identificatory displays and other characteristics, could be *discredited* before her transsexual operation if her possession of a penis became known and after by her surgically constructed genitalia. In this regard, Agnes had to be continually alert to actual or potential threats to the security of her sex category. Her problem was not so much living up to some prototype of essential femininity but preserving her categorization as female. This task was made easy for her by a very powerful resource, namely, the process of commonsense categorization in everyday life.

The categorization of members of society into indigenous categories such as "girl" or "boy," or "woman" or "man," operates in a distinctively social way. The act of categorization does not involve a positive test, in the sense of a well-defined set of criteria that must be explicitly satisfied prior to making an identification. Rather, the application of membership categories relies on an "if-can" test in everyday interaction. This test stipulates that if people *can be seen* as members of relevant categories, *then categorize them that way.* That is, use the category that seems appropriate, except in the presence of discrepant information or obvious features that would rule out its use. This procedure is quite in keeping with the attitude of everyday life, which has us take appearances at face value unless we have special reason to doubt. It should be added that it is precisely when we have special reason to doubt that the issue of applying rigorous criteria arises, but it is rare, outside legal or bureaucratic contexts, to encounter insistence on positive tests.

Agnes's initial resource was the predisposition of those she encountered to take her appearance (her figure, clothing, hair style, and so on) as the undoubted appearance of a normal female. Her further resource was our cultural perspective on the properties of "natural, normally sexed persons." Garfinkel (1967, pp. 122–28) notes that in everyday life, we live in a world of two—and only two—sexes. This arrangement has a moral status, in that we include ourselves and others in it as "essentially, originally, in the first place, always have been, always will be, once and for all, in the final analysis, either 'male' or 'female'" (Garfinkel 1967, p. 122).

Consider the following case:

> This issue reminds me of a visit I made to a computer store a couple of years ago. The person who answered my questions was truly a *salesperson.* I could not categorize him/her as a woman or a man. What did I look for? (1) Facial hair: She/he was smooth skinned, but some men have little or no facial hair. (This varies by race, Native Americans and Blacks often have none.) (2) Breasts: She/he was wearing a loose shirt that hung from his/her shoulders. And, as many women who suffered through a 1950s' adolescence know to their shame, women are often flat-chested. (3) Shoulders: His/hers were small and round for a man, broad for a woman. (4) Hands: Long and slender fingers, knuckles a bit large for a woman, small for a man. (5) Voice: Middle range, unexpressive for a woman, not at all the exaggerated tones some gay males affect. (6) His/her treatment of me: Gave off no signs that would let me know if I were of the same or different sex as this person. There were not even any signs that he/she knew his/her sex would be difficult to categorize and I wondered about that even as I did my best to hide these questions so I would not embarrass him/her while we talked of computer paper. I left still not knowing the sex of my salesperson, and was disturbed by that unanswered question (child of my culture that I am). (Diane Margolis, personal communication)

What can this case tell us about situations such as Agnes's or the process of sex categorization in general? First, we infer from this description that the computer salesclerk's identificatory display was ambiguous, since she or he was not dressed or adorned in an unequivocally female or male fashion. It is when such a display *fails* to provide grounds for categorization that factors such as facial hair or tone of voice are assessed to determine membership in a sex category. Second, beyond the fact that this incident could be recalled after "a couple of years," the customer was not only "disturbed" by the ambiguity of the salesclerk's category but also assumed that to acknowledge this ambiguity would be embarrassing to the salesclerk. Not only do we want to know the sex category of those around us (to see it at a glance, perhaps), but we presume that others are displaying it for us, in as decisive a fashion as they can.

Gender

Agnes attempted to be "120 percent female" (Garfinkel 1967, p. 129), that is, unquestionably in all ways and at all times feminine. She thought she could protect herself from disclosure before and after surgical intervention by comporting herself in a feminine manner, but she also could have given herself away by overdoing her performance. Sex categorization and the accomplishment of gender are not the same. Agnes's categorization could be secure or suspect, but did not depend on whether or not she lived up to some ideal conception of femininity. Women can be seen as unfeminine, but that does not make them "unfemale." Agnes faced an ongoing task of being a woman—something beyond style of dress (an identificatory display) or allowing men to light her cigarette (a gender display). Her problem was to produce configurations of behavior that would be seen by others as normative gender behavior.

Agnes's strategy of "secret apprenticeship," through which she learned expected feminine decorum by carefully attending to her fiancé's criticisms of other women, was one means of masking incompetencies and simultaneously acquiring the needed skills (Garfinkel 1967, pp. 146–47). It was through her fiancé that Agnes learned that sunbathing on the lawn in front of her apartment was "offensive" (because it put her on display to other men). She also learned from his critiques of other women that she should not insist on having things her way and that she should not offer her opinions or claim equality with men (Garfinkel 1967, pp. 147–48). (Like other women in our society, Agnes learned something about power in the course of her "education.")

Popular culture abounds with books and magazines that compile idealized depictions of relations between women and men. Those focused on the etiquette of dating or prevailing standards of feminine comportment are meant to be of practical help in these matters. However, the use of any such source *as a manual of procedure* requires the assumption that doing gender merely involves making use of discrete, well-defined bundles of behavior that can simply be plugged into interactional situations to produce recognizable enactments of masculinity and femininity. The man "does" being masculine by, for example, taking the woman's arm to guide her across a street, and she "does" being feminine by consenting to be guided and not initiating such behavior with a man.

Agnes could perhaps have used such sources as manuals, but, we contend, doing gender is not so easily regimented. Such sources may list and describe the sorts of behaviors that mark or display gender, but they are necessarily incomplete. And to be successful, marking or displaying gender must be finely fitted to situations and modified or transformed as the occasion demands. Doing gender consists of managing such occasions so that, whatever the particulars, the outcome is seen and seeable in context as gender-appropriate or, as the case may be, gender-*in*appropriate, that is, *accountable.*

Gender and Accountability

As Heritage (1984, pp. 136–37) notes, members of society regularly engage in "descriptive accountings of states of affairs to one another," and such accounts are both serious and consequential. These descriptions name, characterize, formulate, explain, excuse, excoriate, or merely take notice of some circumstance or activity and thus place it within some social framework (locating it relative to other activities, like and unlike).

Such descriptions are themselves accountable, and societal members orient to the fact that their activities are subject to comment. Actions are often designed with an eye to their accountability, that is, how they might look and how they might be characterized. The notion of accountability also encompasses those actions undertaken so that they are specifically unremarkable and thus not worthy of more than a passing remark, because they are seen to be in accord with culturally approved standards.

Heritage (1984, p. 179) observes that the process of rendering something accountable is interactional in character:

> [This] permits actors to design their actions in relation to their circumstances so as to permit others, by methodically taking account of circumstances, to recognize the action for what it is.

The key word here is *circumstances.* One circumstance that attends virtually all actions is the sex category of the actor. As Garfinkel (1967, p. 118) comments:

> [T]he work and socially structured occasions of sexual passing were obstinately unyielding to [Agnes's] attempts to routinize the grounds of daily activities. This obstinacy points to the *omnirelevance* of sexual status to affairs of daily life as an invariant but unnoticed background in the texture of relevances that compose the changing actual scenes of everyday life. (Italics added)

If sex category is omnirelevant (or even approaches being so), then a person engaged in virtually any activity may be held accountable for performance of that activity as a *woman* or a *man,* and their incumbency in one or the other sex category can be used to legitimate or discredit their other activities. Accordingly, virtually any activity can be assessed as to its womanly or manly nature. And note, to "do" gender is not always to live up to normative conceptions of femininity or masculinity; it is to engage in behavior *at the risk of gender assessment.* While it is individuals who do gender, the enterprise is fundamentally interactional and institutional in character, for accountability is a feature of social relationships and its idiom is drawn from the institutional arena in which those relationships are enacted. If this be the case, can we ever *not* do gender? Insofar as a society is partitioned by "essential" differences between women and men and placement in a sex category is both relevant and enforced, doing gender is unavoidable.

Resources for Doing Gender

Doing gender means creating differences between girls and boys and women and men, differences that are not natural, essential, or biological. Once the differences have been constructed, they are used to reinforce the "essentialness" of gender. In a delightful account of the "arrangement between the sexes," Goffman (1977) observes the creation of a variety of institutionalized frameworks through which our "natural, normal sexedness" can be enacted. The physical features of social setting provide one obvious resource for the expression of our "essential" differences. For example, the sex segregation of North American public bathrooms distinguishes "ladies" from "gentlemen" in matters held to be fundamentally biological, even though both "are somewhat similar in the question of waste products and their elimination" (Goffman 1977, p. 315). These settings are furnished with dimorphic equipment (such as urinals for men or elaborate grooming facilities for women), even though both sexes may achieve the same ends through the same means (and apparently do so in the privacy of their own homes). To be stressed here is the fact that:

> The *functioning* of sex-differentiated organs is involved, but there is nothing in this functioning that biologically recommends segregation; that arrangement is a totally cultural matter . . . toilet segregation is presented as a natural consequence of the difference between the sex-classes when in fact it is a means of honoring, if not producing, this difference. (Goffman 1977, p. 316)

Standardized social occasions also provide stages for evocations of the "essential female and male natures." Goffman cites organized sports as one such institutionalized framework for the expression of manliness. There, those qualities that ought "properly" to be associated with masculinity, such as endurance, strength, and competitive spirit, are celebrated by all parties concerned—participants, who may be seen to demonstrate such traits, and spectators, who applaud their demonstrations from the safety of the sidelines (1977, p. 322).

Assortative mating practices among heterosexual couples afford still further means to create and maintain differences between women and men. For example, even though size, strength, and age tend to be normally distributed among females and males (with considerable overlap between them), selective pairing ensures couples in which boys and men are visibly bigger, stronger, and older (if not "wiser") than the girls and women with whom they are paired. So, should situations emerge in which greater size, strength, or experience is called for, boys and men will be ever ready to display it and girls and women, to appreciate its display.

Gender may be routinely fashioned in a variety of situations that seem conventionally expressive to begin with, such as those that present "helpless" women next to heavy objects or flat tires. But, as Goffman notes, heavy, messy, and precarious concerns can be constructed from *any* social situation, "even though by standards set in other settings, this may involve something that is light, clean, and safe" (Goffman 1977, p. 324). Given these resources, it is clear that any interactional situation sets the stage for depictions of "essential" sexual natures. In sum, these situations "do not so much allow for the expression of natural differences as for the production of that difference itself" (Goffman 1977, p. 324).

Many situations are not clearly sex categorized to begin with, nor is what transpires within them obviously gender relevant. Yet any social encounter can be pressed into service in the interests of doing gender. Thus, Fishman's (1978) research on casual conversations found an asymmetrical "division of labor" in talk between hetero-sexual intimates. Women had to ask more questions, fill more silences, and use more attention-getting beginnings in order to be heard. Her conclusions are particularly pertinent here:

> Since interactional work is related to what constitutes being a woman, with what a woman is, the idea that it is work is obscured. The work is not seen as what women do, but as part of what they are. (Fishman 1978, p. 405)

We would argue that it is precisely such labor that helps to constitute the essential nature of women as women in interactional contexts.

Individuals have many social identities that may be donned or shed, muted or made more salient, depending on the situation. One may be a friend, spouse, professional, citizen, and many other things to many different people—or, to the same person at different times. But we are always women or men—unless we shift into another sex category. What this means is that our identificatory displays will provide an ever-available resource for doing gender under an infinitely diverse set of circumstances.

Some occasions are organized to routinely display and celebrate behaviors that are conventionally linked to one or the other sex category. On such occasions, everyone knows his or her place in the interactional scheme of things. If an individual identified as a member of one sex category engages in behavior usually associated with the other category, this routinization is challenged. Hughes (1945, p. 356) provides an illustration of such a dilemma:

> [A] young woman . . . became part of that virile profession, engineering. The designer of an airplane is expected to go up on the maiden flight of the first plane built according to the design. He [sic] then gives a dinner to the engineers and workmen who worked on the new plane. The dinner is naturally a stag party. The young woman in question designed a plane. Her co-workers urged her not to take the risk—for which, presumably, men only are fit—of the maiden voyage. They were, in effect, asking her to be a lady instead of an engineer. She chose to be an engineer. She then gave the party and paid for it like a man. After food and the first round of toasts, she left like a lady.

On this occasion, parties reached an accommodation that allowed a woman to engage in presumptively masculine behaviors. However, we note that in the end, this compromise permitted demonstration of her "essential" femininity, through accountably "ladylike" behavior.

Hughes (1945, p. 357) suggests that such contradictions may be countered by managing interactions on a very narrow basis, for example, "keeping the relationship formal and specific." But the heart of the matter is that even—perhaps, especially—if the relationship is a formal one, gender is still something one is accountable for. Thus a woman physician (notice the special qualifier in her case) may be accorded respect for her skill and even addressed by an appropriate title. Nonetheless, she is subject to evaluation in terms of normative conceptions of appropriate attitudes and activities for her sex category and under pressure to prove that she is an "essentially" feminine being, despite appearances to the contrary. Her sex category is used to discredit her participation in important clinical activities, while her involvement in medicine is used to discredit her commitment to her responsibilities as a wife and mother. Simultaneously, her exclusion from the physician colleague community is maintained and her accountability *as a woman* is ensured.

In this context, "role conflict" can be viewed as a dynamic aspect of our current "arrangement between the sexes" (Goffman 1977), an arrangement that provides for occasions on which persons of a particular sex category can "see" quite clearly that they are out of place and that if they were not there, their current troubles would not exist. What is at stake is, from the standpoint of interaction, the management of our "essential" natures, and from the standpoint of the individual, the continuing accomplishment of gender. If, as we have argued, sex category is omnirelevant, then any occasion, conflicted or not, offers the resources for doing gender.

We have sought to show that sex category and gender are managed properties of conduct that are contrived with respect to the fact that others will judge and respond to us in particular ways. We have claimed that a person's gender is not simply an aspect of what one is, but, more fundamentally, it is something that one does, and *does* recurrently, in interaction with others.

What are the consequences of this theoretical formulation? If, for example, individuals strive to achieve gender in encounters with others, how does a culture instill the need to achieve it? What is the relationship between the production of gender at the level of interaction and such institutional arrangements as the division of labor in society? And, perhaps most important, how does doing gender contribute to the subordination of women by men?

Research Agendas

To bring the social production of gender under empirical scrutiny, we might begin at the beginning, with a reconsideration of the process through which societal members acquire the requisite categorical apparatus and other skills to become gendered human beings.

Recruitment to Gender Identities

The conventional approach to the process of becoming girls and boys has been sex-role socialization. In recent years, recurring problems arising from this approach have been linked to inadequacies inherent in role theory *per se*—its emphasis on "consensus, stability and continuity" (Stacey and Thorne 1985, p. 307), its historical and depoliticizing focus (Thorne 1980, p. 9; Stacey and Thorne 1985, p. 307), and the fact that its "social" dimension relies on "a general assumption that people choose to maintain existing customs" (Connell 1985, p. 263).

In contrast, Cahill (1982, 1986a, 1986b) analyzes the experiences of preschool children using a social model of recruitment into normally gendered identities. Cahill argues that categorization practices are fundamental to learning and displaying feminine and masculine behavior. Initially, he observes, children are primarily concerned with distinguishing between themselves and others on the basis of social competence. Categorically, their concern resolves itself into the opposition of "girl/boy" classification versus "baby" classification (the latter designating children whose social behavior is problematic and who must be closely supervised). It is children's concern with being seen as socially competent that evokes their initial claims to gender identities:

> During the exploratory stage of children's socialization...they learn that only two social identities are routinely available to them, the identity of "baby," or, depending on the configuration of their external genitalia, either "big boy" or "big girl." Moreover, others subtly inform them that the identity of "baby" is a discrediting one. When, for example, children engage in disapproved behavior, they are often told "You're a baby" or "Be a big boy."

> In effect, these typical verbal responses to young children's behavior convey to them that they must behaviorally choose between the discrediting identity of "baby" and their anatomically determined sex identity. (Cahill 1986a, p. 175)

Subsequently, little boys appropriate the gender ideal of "efficaciousness," that is, being able to affect the physical and social environment through the exercise of physical strength or appropriate skills. In contrast, little girls learn to value "appearance," that is, managing themselves as ornamental objects. Both classes of children learn that the recognition and use of sex categorization in interaction are not optional, but mandatory.

Being a "girl" or a "boy" then, is not only being more competent than a "baby," but also being competently female or male, that is, learning to produce behavioral displays of one's "essential" female or male identity. In this respect, the task of four- to five-year-old children is very similar to Agnes's:

> For example, the following interaction occurred on a preschool playground. A 55-month-old boy (D) was attempting to unfasten the clasp of a necklace when a preschool aide walked over to him.
>
> A: Do you want to put that on?
> D: No. It's for girls.
> A: You don't have to be a girl to wear things around your neck. Kings wear things around their necks. You could pretend you're a king.
> D: I'm not a king. I'm a boy. (Cahill 1986a, p. 176)

As Cahill notes of this example, although D may have been unclear as to the sex status of a king's identity, he was obviously aware that necklaces are used to announce the identity "girl." Having claimed the identity "boy" and having developed a behavioral commitment to it, he was leery of any display that might furnish grounds for questioning his claim.

In this way, new members of society come to be involved in a *self-regulating process* as they begin to monitor their own and others' conduct with regard to its gender implications. The "recruitment" process involves not only the appropriation of gender ideals (by the valuation of those ideals as proper ways of being and behaving) but also *gender identities* that are important to individuals and that they strive to maintain. Thus gender differences, or the sociocultural shaping of "essential female and male natures," achieve the status of objective facts. They are rendered normal, natural features of persons and provide the tacit rationale for differing fates of women and men within the social order.

Additional studies of children's play activities as routine occasions for the expression of gender-appropriate behavior can yield new insights into how our "essential natures" are constructed. In particular, the transition from what Cahill (1986a) terms "apprentice participation" in the sex-segregated worlds that are common among elementary school children to "bona fide participation" in the heterosocial world so frightening to adolescents is likely to be a keystone in our understanding of the recruitment process.

Gender and the Division of Labor

Whenever people face issues of *allocation*—who is to do what, get what, plan or execute action, direct or be directed, incumbency in significant social categories such as "female" and "male" seems to become pointedly relevant. How such issues are resolved conditions the exhibition, dramatization, or celebration of one's "essential nature" as a woman or man.

Berk (1985) offers elegant demonstration of this point in her investigation of the allocation of household labor and the attitudes of married couples toward the division of household tasks. Berk found little variation in either the actual distribution of tasks or perceptions of equity in regard to that distribution. Wives, even when employed outside the home, do the vast majority of household and child-care tasks. Moreover, both wives and husbands tend to perceive this as a "fair" arrangement. Noting the failure of conventional sociological and economic theories to explain this seeming contradiction, Berk contends that something more complex is involved than rational arrangements for the production of household goods and services:

> Hardly a question simply of who has more time, or whose time is worth more, who has more skill or more power, it is clear that a complicated relationship between the structure of work imperatives and

> the structure of normative expectations attached to work as *gendered* determines the ultimate allocation of members' time to work and home. (Berk 1985, pp. 195–96)

She notes, for example, that the most important factor influencing wives' contribution of labor is the total amount of work demanded or expected by the household; such demands had no bearing on husbands' contributions. Wives reported various rationales (their own and their husbands') that justified their level of contribution and, as a general matter, underscored the presumption that wives are essentially responsible for household production.

Berk (1985, p. 201) contends that it is difficult to see how people "could rationally establish the arrangements that they do solely for the production of household goods and services"—much less, how people could consider them "fair." She argues that our current arrangements for the domestic division of labor support *two* production processes: household goods and services (meals, clean children, and so on) and, at the same time, gender. As she puts it:

> Simultaneously, members "do" gender, as they "do" housework and child care, and what [has] been called the division of labor provides for the joint production of household labor and gender; it is the mechanism by which both the material and symbolic products of the household are realized. (1985, p. 201)

It is not simply that household labor is designated as "women's work," but that for a woman to engage in it and a man not to engage in it is to draw on and exhibit the "essential nature" of each. What is produced and reproduced is not merely the activity and artifact of domestic life, but the material embodiment of wifely and husbandly roles, and derivatively, of womanly and manly conduct. What are also frequently produced and reproduced are the dominant and subordinate statuses of the sex categories.

How does gender get done in work settings outside the home, where dominance and subordination are themes of overarching importance? Hochschild's (1983) analysis of the work of flight attendants offers some promising insights. She found that the occupation of flight attendant consisted of something altogether different for women than for men:

> As the company's main shock absorbers against "mishandled" passengers, their own feelings are more frequently subjected to rough treatment. In addition, a day's exposure to people who resist authority in a woman is a different experience than it is for a man.... In this respect, it is a disadvantage to be a woman. And in this case, they are not simply women in the biological sense. They are also a highly visible distillation of middle-class American notions of femininity. They symbolize Woman. Insofar as the category "female" is mentally associated with having less status and authority, female flight attendants are more readily classified as "really" females than other females are. (Hochschild 1983, p. 175)

In performing what Hochschild terms the "emotional labor" necessary to maintain airline profits, women flight attendants simultaneously produce enactments of their "essential" femininity.

Sex and Sexuality

What is the relationship between doing gender and a culture's prescription of "obligatory heterosexuality"? As Frye (1983, p. 22) observes, the monitoring of sexual feelings in relation to other appropriately sexed persons requires the ready recognition of such persons "before one can allow one's heart to beat or one's blood to flow in erotic enjoyment of that person." The appearance of heterosexuality is produced through emphatic and unambiguous indicators of one's sex, layered on in ever more conclusive fashion (Frye 1983, p. 24). Thus, lesbians and gay men concerned with passing as heterosexuals can rely on these indicators for camouflage; in contrast, those who would avoid the assumption of heterosexuality may foster ambiguous indicators of their categorical status through their dress, behaviors, and style. But "ambiguous" sex indicators are sex indicators nonetheless. If one wishes to be recognized as a lesbian (or heterosexual woman), one must first establish a categorical status as female. Even as popular images portray lesbians as "females who are not feminine" (Frye 1983, p. 129), the accountability of persons for their "normal, natural sexedness" is preserved.

Nor is accountability threatened by the existence of "sex-change operations"—presumably, the most radical challenge to our cultural perspective on sex and gender. Although no one coerces transsexuals into hormone therapy, electrolysis, or surgery, the alternatives available to them are undeniably constrained:

> When the transsexual experts maintain that they use transsexual procedures only with people who ask for them, and who prove that they can "pass," they obscure the social reality. Given patriarchy's prescription that one must be *either* masculine or feminine, free choice is conditioned. (Raymond 1979, p. 135, italics added)

The physical reconstruction of sex criteria pays ultimate tribute to the "essentialness" of our sexual natures—as women *or* as men.

Gender, Power, and Social Change

Let us return to the question: Can we avoid doing gender? Earlier, we proposed that insofar as sex category is used as a fundamental criterion for differentiation, doing gender is unavoidable. It is unavoidable because of the social consequences of sex-category membership: the allocation of power and resources not only in the domestic, economic, and political domains but also in the broad arena of interpersonal relations. In virtually any situation, one's sex category can be relevant, and one's performance as an incumbent of that category (i.e., gender) can be subjected to evaluation. Maintaining such pervasive and faithful assignment of lifetime status requires legitimation.

But doing gender also renders the social arrangements based on sex category accountable as normal and natural, that is, legitimate ways of organizing social life. Differences between women and men that are created by this process can then be portrayed as fundamental and enduring dispositions. In this light, the institutional arrangements of a society can be seen as responsive to the differences—the social order being merely an accommodation to the natural order. Thus if, in doing gender, men are also doing dominance and women are doing deference, the resultant social order, which supposedly reflects "natural differences," is a powerful reinforcer and legitimator of hierarchical arrangements. Frye observes:

> For efficient subordination, what's wanted is that the structure not appear to be a cultural artifact kept in place by human decision or custom, but that it appear *natural*—that it appear to be quite a direct consequence of facts about the beast which are beyond the scope of human manipulation.... That we are trained to behave so differently as women and men, and to behave so differently toward women and men, itself contributes mightily to the appearance of extreme dimorphism, but also, the *ways* we act as women and men, and the *ways* we act toward women and men, mold our bodies and our minds to the shape of subordination and dominance. We do become what we practice being. (Frye 1983, p. 34)

If we do gender appropriately, we simultaneously sustain, reproduce, and render legitimate the institutional arrangements that are based on sex category. If we fail to do gender appropriately, we as individuals—not the institutional arrangements—may be called to account (for our character, motives, and predispositions).

Social movements such as feminism can provide the ideology and impetus to question existing arrangements, and the social support for individuals to explore alternatives to them. Legislative changes, such as that proposed by the Equal Rights Amendment, can also weaken the accountability of conduct to sex category, thereby affording the possibility of more widespread loosening of accountability in general. To be sure, equality under the law does not guarantee equality in other arenas. As Lorber (1986, p. 577) points out, assurance of "scrupulous equality of categories of people considered essentially different needs constant monitoring." What such proposed changes can do is provide the warrant for asking why, if we wish to treat women and men as equals, there needs to be two sex categories at all.

The sex category/gender relationship links the institutional and interactional levels, a coupling that legitimates social arrangements based on sex category and reproduces their asymmetry in face-to-face interaction. Doing gender furnishes the interactional scaffolding of social structure, along with a built-in mechanism of social control. In appreciating the institutional forces that maintain distinctions between women and men, we must not lose sight of the interactional validation of those distinctions that confers upon them their sense of "naturalness" and "rightness."

Social change, then, must be pursued both at the institutional and cultural level of sex category and at the interactional level of gender. Such a conclusion is hardly novel. Nevertheless, we suggest that it is important to recognize that the analytical distinction between institutional and interactional spheres does not pose an either/or choice when it comes to the question of effecting social change. Reconceptualizing gender not as a simple property of individuals but as an integral dynamic of social orders implies a new perspective on the entire network of gender relations:

> [T]he social subordination of women, and the cultural practices which help sustain it; the politics of sexual object-choice, and particularly the oppression of homosexual people; the sexual division of labor, the formation of character and motive, so far as they are organized as femininity and masculinity; the role of the body in social relations, especially the politics of childbirth; and the nature of strategies of sexual liberation movements. (Connell 1985, p. 261)

Gender is a powerful ideological device, which produces, reproduces, and legitimates the choices and limits that are predicated on sex category. An understanding of how gender is produced in social situations will afford clarification of the interactional scaffolding of social structure and the social control processes that sustain it.

References

Berk, Sarah F. 1985. *The Gender Factory: The Apportionment of Work in American Households.* New York: Plenum.

Cahill, Spencer E. 1982. "Becoming Boys and Girls." Ph.D. dissertation, Department of Sociology, University of California, Santa Barbara.

———. 1986a. "Childhood Socialization as Recruitment Process: Some Lessons from the Study of Gender Development." Pp. 163–86 in *Sociological Studies of Child Development,* edited by P. Adler and P. Adler. Greenwich, CT: JAI Press.

———. 1986b. "Language Practices and Self-Definition: The Case of Gender Identity Acquisition." *The Sociological Quarterly* 27:295–311.

Connell, R.W. 1985. "Theorizing Gender." *Sociology* 19:260–72.

Fishman, Pamela. 1978. "Interaction: The Work Women Do." *Social Problems* 25:397–406.

Frye, Marilyn. 1983. *The Politics of Reality: Essays in Feminist Theory.* Trumansburg, NY: The Crossing Press.

Garfinkel, Harold. 1967. *Studies in Ethnomethodology.* Englewood Cliffs, NJ: Prentice-Hall.

Goffman, Erving. 1976. "Gender Display." *Studies in the Anthropology of Visual Communication* 3:69–77.

———. 1977. "The Arrangement Between the Sexes." *Theory and Society* 4:301–31.

Heritage, John. 1984. *Garfinkel and Ethnomethodology.* Cambridge, England: Polity Press.

Hochschild, Arlie R. 1983. *The Managed Heart. Commercialization of Human Feeling.* Berkeley: University of California Press.

Hughes, Everett C. 1945. "Dilemmas and Contradictions of Status." *American Journal of Sociology* 50:353–59.

Kessler, Suzanne J., and Wendy McKenna. 1978. *Gender: An Ethnomethodological Approach.* New York: Wiley.

Komarovsky, Mirra. 1946. "Cultural Contradictions and Sex Roles." *American Journal of Sociology* 52:184–89.

———. 1950. "Functional Analysis of Sex Roles." *American Sociological Review* 15:508–16.

Linton, Ralph. 1936. *The Study of Man.* New York: Appleton-Century.

Lorber, Judith. 1986. "Dismantling Noah's Ark." *Sex Roles* 14:567–80.

Parsons, Talcott. 1951. *The Social System.* New York: Free Press.

———, and Robert F. Bales. 1955. *Family, Socialization and Interaction Process.* New York: Free Press.

Raymond, Janice G. 1979. *The Transsexual Empire.* Boston: Beacon.

Rossi, Alice. 1984. "Gender and Parenthood." *American Sociological Review* 49:1–19.

Rubin, Gayle. 1975. "The Traffic in Women: Notes on the 'Political Economy' of Sex." Pp. 157–210 in *Toward an Anthropology of Women*, edited by R. Reiter. New York: Monthly Review Press.

Stacey, Judith, and Barrie Thorne. 1985. "The Missing Feminist Revolution in Sociology." *Social Problems* 32:301–16.

Thorne, Barrie. 1980. "Gender... How Is It Best Conceptualized?" Unpublished manuscript.

Doing Difference

CANDACE WEST AND SARAH FENSTERMAKER

Few persons think of math as a particularly feminine pursuit. Girls are not supposed to be good at it and women are not supposed to enjoy it. It is interesting, then, that we who do feminist scholarship have relied so heavily on mathematical metaphors to describe the relationships among gender, race, and class.[1] For example, some of us have drawn on basic arithmetic, adding, subtracting, and dividing what we know about race and class to what we already know about gender. Some have relied on multiplication, seeming to calculate the effects of the whole from the combination of different parts. And others have employed geometry, drawing on images of interlocking or intersecting planes and axes.

To be sure, the sophistication of our mathematical metaphors often varies with the apparent complexity of our own experiences. Those of us who, at one point, were able to "forget" race and class in our analyses of gender relations may be more likely to "add" these at a later point. By contrast, those of us who could never forget these dimensions of social life may be more likely to draw on complex geometrical imagery all along; nonetheless, the existence of so many different approaches to the topic seems indicative of the difficulties all of us have experienced in coming to terms with it.

Not surprisingly, proliferation of these approaches has caused considerable confusion in the existing literature. In the same book or article, we may find references to gender, race, and class as "intersecting systems," as "interlocking categories," and as "multiple bases" for oppression. In the same anthology, we may find some chapters that conceive of gender, race, and class as distinct axes and others that conceive of them as concentric ones. The problem is that these alternative formulations have very distinctive, yet unarticulated, theoretical implications. For instance, if we think about gender, race, and class as additive categories, the whole will never be greater (or lesser) than the sum of its parts. By contrast, if we conceive of these as multiples, the result could be larger or smaller than their added sum, depending on where we place the signs.[2] Geometric metaphors further complicate things, since we still need to know where

Candace West and Sarah Fenstermaker, "Doing Difference" from *Gender & Society* 9, no. 1 (February 1995): 8–37.

those planes and axes go after they cross the point of intersection (if they are parallel planes and axes, they will never intersect at all).

Our purpose in this article is not to advance yet another new math but to propose a new way of thinking about the workings of these relations. Elsewhere (Berk 1985; Fenstermaker, West, and Zimmerman 1991; West and Fenstermaker 1993; West and Zimmerman 1987), we offered an ethnomethodologically informed, and, hence, distinctively sociological, conceptualization of gender as a routine, methodical, and ongoing accomplishment. We argued that doing gender involves a complex of perceptual, interactional, and micropolitical activities that cast particular pursuits as expressions of manly and womanly "natures." Rather than conceiving of gender as an individual characteristic, we conceived of it as an emergent property of social situations: both an outcome of and a rationale for various social arrangements and a means of justifying one of the most fundamental divisions of society. We suggested that examining how gender is accomplished could reveal the mechanisms by which power is exercised and inequality is produced.

Our earlier formulation neglected race and class; thus, it is an incomplete framework for understanding social inequality. In this article, we extend our analysis to consider explicitly the relationships among gender, race, and class, and to reconceptualize "difference" as an ongoing interactional accomplishment. We start by summarizing the prevailing critique of much feminist thought as severely constrained by its white middle-class character and preoccupation. Here, we consider how feminist scholarship ends up borrowing from mathematics in the first place. Next, we consider how existing conceptualizations of gender have contributed to the problem, rendering mathematical metaphors the only alternatives. Then, calling on our earlier ethnomethodological conceptualization of gender, we develop the further implications of this perspective for our understanding of race and class. We assert that, while gender, race, and class—what people come to experience as organizing categories of social difference—exhibit vastly different descriptive characteristics and outcomes, they are, nonetheless, comparable as mechanisms for producing social inequality.

White Middle-Class Bias in Feminist Thought

What is it about feminist thinking that makes race and class such difficult concepts to articulate within its own parameters? The most widely agreed upon and disturbing answer to this question is that feminist thought suffers from a white middle-class bias. The privileging of white and middle-class sensibilities in feminist thought results from both who did the theorizing and how they did it. White middle-class women's advantaged viewpoint in a racist and class-bound culture, coupled with the Western tendency to construct the self as distinct from "other," distorts their depictions of reality in predictable directions (Young 1990). The consequences of these distortions have been identified in a variety of places, and analyses of them have enlivened every aspect of feminist scholarship (see, for example, Aptheker 1989; Collins 1990; Davis 1981; Hurtado 1989; Zinn 1990).

For example, bell hooks points out that feminism within the United States has never originated among the women who are most oppressed by sexism, "women who are daily beaten down, mentally, physically, and spiritually—women who are powerless to change their condition in life" (1984, 1). The fact that those most victimized are least likely to question or protest is, according to hooks (1984), a consequence of their victimization. From this perspective, the white middle-class character of most feminist thought stems directly from the identities of those who produce it.

Aída Hurtado notes further the requisite time and resources that are involved in the production of feminist writing: "without financial assistance, few low-income and racial/ethnic students can attend universities; without higher education, few working-class and ethnic/racial intellectuals can become professors" (1989, 838). Given that academics dominate the production of published feminist scholarship, it is not surprising that feminist theory is dominated by white, highly educated women (see also hooks 1981; Joseph and Lewis 1981).

Still others (Collins 1990; Davis 1981; Lorde 1984; Moraga and Anzalduá 1981; Zinn, Cannon, Higginbotham, and Dill 1986) point to the racism and classism of feminist scholars themselves. Maxine Baca Zinn and her colleagues observe that, "despite white, middle-class feminists' frequent expressions of interest and concern over the plight of minority and working-class women, those holding the gate-keeping positions at important feminist journals are as white as are those at any mainstream social science or humanities publication" (1986, 293).

Racism and classism can take a variety of forms. Adrienne Rich contends that, although white (middle-class) feminists may not consciously believe that their race is superior to any other, they are often plagued by a form of "white solipsism"—thinking, imagining, and speaking "as if whiteness described the world," resulting in "a tunnel-vision which simply does not see nonwhite experience or existence as precious or significant, unless in spasmodic, impotent guilt reflexes, which have little or no long-term, continuing usefulness" (1979, 306). White middle-class feminists, therefore, may offer conscientious expressions of concern over "racism-and-classism," believing that they have thereby taken into consideration profound differences in women's experience; simultaneously, they can fail to see those differences at all (Bhavnani, 2003).

There is nothing that prevents any of these dynamics from coexisting and working together. For example, Patricia Hill Collins (1990) argues that the suppression of Black feminist thought stems both from white feminists' racist and classist concerns and from Black women intellectuals' consequent lack of participation in white feminist organizations. Similarly, Cherríe Moraga (1981) argues that the "denial of difference" in feminist organizations derives not only from white middle-class women's failure to "see" it but also from women of color's and working-class women's reluctance to challenge such blindness. Alone and in combination with one another, these sources of bias do much to explain why there has been a general failure to articulate race and class within the parameters of feminist scholarship; however, they do not explain the attraction of mathematical metaphors to right the balance. To understand this development, we must look further at the logic of feminist thought itself.

Mathematical Metaphors and Feminist Thought

Following the earlier suggestion of bell hooks (1981; see also Hull, Scott, and Smith 1982), Elizabeth Spelman contends that, in practice, the term "women" actually functions as a powerful false generic in white feminists' thinking:

> The "problem of difference" for feminist theory has never been a general one about how to weigh the importance of what we have in common against the importance of our differences. To put it that way hides two crucial facts: First, the description of what we have in common "as women" has almost always been a description of white middle-class women. Second, the "difference" of this group of women—that is, their being white and middle-class—has never had to be "brought into" feminist theory. To bring in "difference" is to bring in women who aren't white and middle class. (1988, 4)

She warns that thinking about privilege merely as a characteristic of individuals—rather than as a characteristic of modes of thought—may afford us an understanding of "what privilege feeds but not what sustains it" (1988, 4).

What are the implications of a feminist mode of thought that is so severely limited? The most important one, says Spelman, is the presumption that we can effectively and usefully isolate gender from race and class. To illustrate this point, she draws on many white feminists who develop their analyses of sexism by comparing and contrasting it with "other" forms of oppression. Herein she finds the basis for additive models of gender, race, and class, and "the ampersand problem":

> de Beauvoir tends to talk about comparisons between sex and race, or between sex and class, or between sex and culture... comparisons between sexism and racism, between sexism and classism, between sexism and anti-Semitism. In the work of Chodorow and others influenced by her, we observe a readiness to look for links between sexism and other forms of oppression as distinct from sexism. (1988, 115)

Spelman notes that in both cases, attempts to add "other" elements of identity to gender, or "other" forms of oppression to sexism, disguise the race (white) and class (middle) identities of those seen as "women" in the first place. Rich's "white solipsism" comes into play again, and it is impossible to envision how women who are not white and middle class fit into the picture.

Although Spelman (1988) herself does not address mathematical metaphors based on multiplication, we believe that her argument is relevant to understanding how they develop. For example, take Cynthia Fuchs Epstein's (1973) notion of the "positive effect of the multiple negative" on the success of Black professional women. According to Epstein, when the "negative status" of being a woman is combined with the "negative status" of being Black, the result is the "positive status" of Black professional women in the job market. Baca Zinn and her colleagues contend that the very idea of this "multiple negative" having a positive effect "could not have survived the scrutiny of professional Black women or Black women students" (1986, 293). They suggest that only someone who was substantially isolated from Black women and their life experiences could have developed such a theory (and, presumably, only someone similarly situated could have promoted its publication in an established mainstream sociology journal).

Spelman's (1988) analysis highlights the following problem: if we conceive of gender as coherently isolatable from race and class, then there is every reason to assume that the effects of the three variables can be multiplied, with results dependent on the valence (positive or negative) of those multiplied variables; yet, if we grant that gender cannot be coherently isolated from race and class in the way we conceptualize it, then multiplicative metaphors make little sense.

If the effects of "multiple oppression" are not merely additive nor simply multiplicative, what are they? Some scholars have described them as the products of "simultaneous and intersecting systems of relationship and meaning" (Andersen and Collins 1992, xiii; see also Almquist 1989; Collins 1990; Glenn 1985). This description is useful insofar as it offers an accurate characterization of persons who are simultaneously oppressed on the basis of gender, race, and class, in other words, those "at the intersection" of all three systems of domination; however, if we conceive of the basis of oppression as more than membership in a category, then the theoretical implications of this formulation are troubling. For instance, what conclusions shall we draw from potential comparisons between persons who experience oppression on the basis of their race and class (e.g., working-class men of color) and those who are oppressed on the basis of their gender and class (e.g., white working-class women)? Would the "intersection of two systems of meaning in each case be sufficient to predict common bonds among them"? Clearly not, says June Jordan: "When these factors of race, class and gender absolutely collapse is whenever you try to use them as automatic concepts of connection." She goes on to say that, while these concepts may work very well as indexes of "commonly felt conflict," their predictive value when they are used as "elements of connection" is "about as reliable as precipitation probability for the day after the night before the day" (1985, 46).

What conclusions shall we draw from comparisons between persons who are said to suffer oppression "at the intersection" of all three systems and those who suffer in the nexus of only two? Presumably, we will conclude that the latter are "less oppressed" than the former (assuming that each categorical identity set amasses a specific quantity of oppression). Moraga warns, however, that "the danger lies in ranking the oppressions. *The danger lies in failing to acknowledge the specificity of the oppression*" (1981, 29).

Spelman (1988, 123–25) attempts to resolve this difficulty by characterizing sexism, racism, and classism as "interlocking" with one another. Along similar lines, Margaret Andersen and Patricia Hill Collins (1992, xii) describe gender, race, and class as "interlocking categories of experience." The image of interlocking rings comes to mind, linked in such a way that the motion of any one of them is constrained by the others. Certainly, this image is more dynamic than those conveyed by additive, multiplicative, or geometric models: we can see where the rings

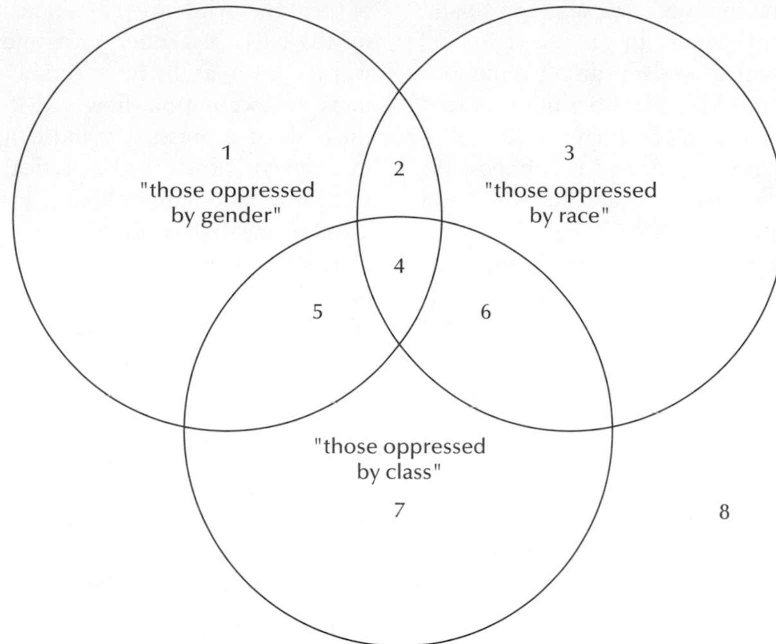

Figure 1. Oppressed People.

Note: 1 = White upper- and middle-class women; 2 = Upper- and middle-class women of color; 3 = Upper- and middle-class men of color; 4 = Working-class women of color; 5 = White working-class women; 6 = Working-class men of color; 7 = White working-class men; 8 = White upper- and middle-class men. This figure is necessarily oversimplified. For example, upper- and middle-class people are lumped together, neglecting the possibility of significant differences between them.

are joined (and where they are not), as well as how the movement of any one of them would be restricted by the others, but note that this image still depicts the rings as separate parts.

If we try to situate particular persons within this array, the problem with it becomes clear. We can, of course, conceive of the whole as "oppressed people" and of the rings as "those oppressed by gender," "those oppressed by race," and "those oppressed by class" (see Figure 1). This allows us to situate women and men of all races and classes within the areas covered by the circles, save for white middle- and upper-class men, who fall outside them. However, what if we conceive of the whole as "experience"[3] and of the rings as gender, race, and class (see Figure 2)?

Here, we face an illuminating possibility and leave arithmetic behind: no person can experience gender without simultaneously experiencing race and class. As Andersen and Collins put it, "While race, class and gender can be seen as different axes of social structure, individual persons experience them simultaneously" (1992, xxi).[4] It is this simultaneity that has eluded our theoretical treatments and is so difficult to build into our empirical descriptions (for an admirable effort, see Segura 1992). Capturing it compels us to focus on the actual mechanisms that produce social inequality. How do forms of inequality, which we now see are more than the periodic collision of categories, operate together? How do we see that all social exchanges, regardless of the participants or the outcome, are simultaneously "gendered," "raced," and "classed"?

To address these questions, we first present some earlier attempts to conceptualize gender. Appreciation for the limitations of these efforts,

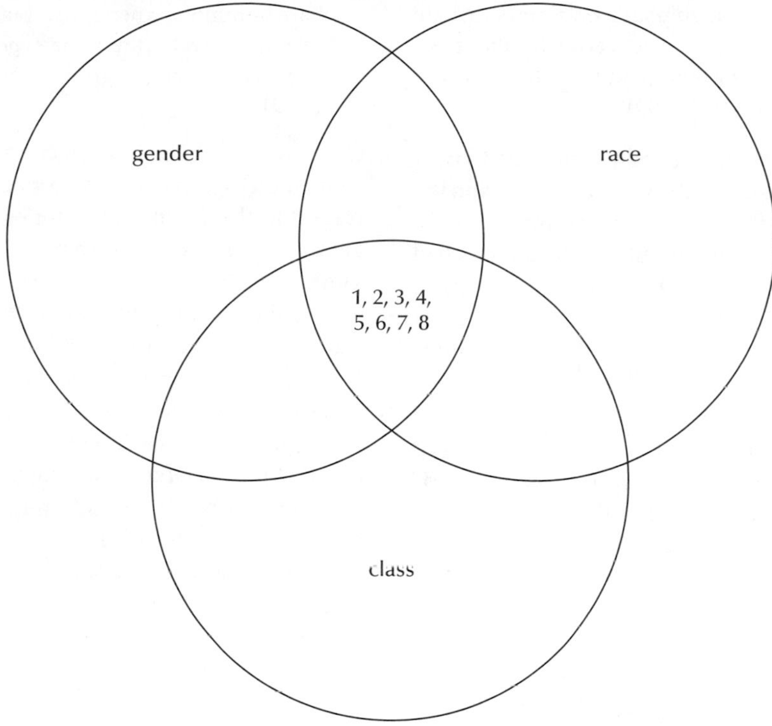

Figure 2. Experience.

Note: 1 = White upper- and middle-class women; 2 = Upper- and middle-class women of color; 3 = Upper- and middle-class men of color; 4 = Working-class women of color; 5 = White working-class women; 6 = Working-class men of color; 7 = White working-class men; 8 = White upper- and middle-class men. This figure is necessarily oversimplified. For example, upper- and middle-class people are lumped together, neglecting the possibility of significant differences between them.

we believe, affords us a way to the second task: reconceptualizing the dynamics of gender, race, and class as they figure simultaneously in human institutions and interaction.

Traditional Conceptualizations of Gender

To begin, we turn to Arlie Russell Hochschild's "A Review of Sex Roles Research," published in 1973. At that time, there were at least four distinct ways of conceptualizing gender within the burgeoning literature on the topic: (1) as sex differences, (2) as sex roles, (3) in relation to the minority status of women, and (4) in relation to the caste/class status of women. Hochschild observes that each of these conceptualizations led to a different perspective on the behaviors of women and men:

> What is to type 1 a feminine trait such as passivity is to type 2 a role element, to type 3 is a minority characteristic, and to type 4 is a response to powerlessness. Social change might also look somewhat different to each perspective; differences disappear, deviance becomes normal, the minority group assimilates, or power is equalized. (1973, 1013)

Nona Glazer observes a further important difference between the types Hochschild identified, namely, where they located the primary source of inequality between women and men:

> The *sex difference* and [*sex*] *roles* approaches share an emphasis on understanding factors that characterize individuals. These factors may be inherent to each sex or acquired by individuals in the course of socialization. The *minority group* and *caste/class*

approaches share an emphasis on factors that are external to individuals, a concern with the structure of social institutions, and with the impact of historical events. (1977, 103)

In retrospect, it is profoundly disturbing to contemplate what the minority group approach and the class/caste approach implied about feminist thinking at the time. For example, Juliet Mitchell launched "Women: The Longest Revolution" with the claim that "[t]he situation of women is different from that of any other social group . . . within the world of men, their position is comparable to that of an oppressed minority" (1966, 11). Obviously, if "women" could be compared to "an oppressed minority," they had to consist of someone other than "oppressed minorities" themselves (cf. Hacker 1951).

Perhaps because of such theoretical problems, feminist scholars have largely abandoned the effort to describe women as a caste, as a class, or as a minority group as a project in its own right (see, for example, Aptheker 1989; Hull, Scott, and Smith 1982). What we have been left with, however, are two prevailing conceptualizations: (1) the sex differences approach and (2) the sex roles approach. And note, while the minority group and caste/class approaches were concerned with factors external to the individual (e.g., the structure of social institutions and the impact of historical events), the approaches that remain emphasize factors that characterize the individual (Glazer 1977).

Arguably, some might call this picture oversimplified. Given the exciting new scholarship that focuses on gender as something that is socially constructed, and something that converges with other inequalities to produce difference among women, have we not moved well beyond "sex differences" and "sex roles"? A close examination of this literature suggests that we have not. For example, Collins contends that

> [w]hile race and gender are both socially constructed categories, constructions of gender *rest on clearer biological criteria* than do constructions of race. Classifying African-Americans into specious racial categories is considerably more difficult than noting the *clear biological differences* distinguishing females from males . . . Women do share common experiences, but the experiences are not generally the same type as those affecting racial and ethnic groups. (1990, 27, emphasis added)

Of course, Collins is correct in her claim that women differ considerably from one another with respect to the distinctive histories, geographic origins, and cultures they share with men of their same race and class. The problem, however, is that what unites them as women are the "clear biological criteria distinguishing females from males." Here, Collins reverts to treating gender as a matter of sex differences (i.e., as ultimately traceable to factors inherent to each sex), in spite of her contention that it is socially constructed. Gender becomes conflated with sex, as race might speciously be made equivalent to color.

Consider a further example. Spelman launches her analysis with a discussion of the theoretical necessity of distinguishing sex from gender. She praises de Beauvoir (1953) for her early recognition of the difference between the two and goes on to argue,

> It is one thing to be biologically female, and quite another to be shaped by one's culture into a "woman"—a female with feminine qualities, someone who does the kinds of things "women" not "men" do, someone who has the kinds of thoughts and feelings that make doing these things seem an easy expression of one's feminine nature. (1988, 124)

How, then, does Spelman conceive of the social construction of woman? She not only invokes "sexual roles" to explain this process (1988, 121–23) but also speaks of "racial roles" (1988, 106) that affect the course that the process will take. Despite Spelman's elegant demonstration of how "woman" constitutes a false generic in feminist thought, her analysis takes us back to "sex roles" once again.

Our point here is not to take issue with Collins (1990) or Spelman (1988) in particular; it would be a misreading of our purpose to do so. We cite these works to highlight a more fundamental difficulty facing feminist theory in general: new conceptualizations of the bases of gender inequality still rest on old conceptualizations of gender

(West and Fenstermaker 1993, 151). For example, those who rely on a sex differences approach conceive of gender as inhering in the individual, in other words, as the masculinity or femininity of a person. Elsewhere (Fenstermaker, West, and Zimmerman, 1991; West and Fenstermaker 1993; West and Zimmerman 1987), we note that this conceptualization obscures our understanding of how gender can structure distinctive domains of social experience (see also Stacey and Thorne 1985). "Sex differences" are treated as the explanation instead of the analytic point of departure.

Although many scholars who take this approach draw on socialization to account for the internalization of femininity and masculinity, they imply that by about five years of age these differences have become stable characteristics of individuals—much like sex (West and Zimmerman 1987, 126). The careful distinction between sex and gender, therefore, is obliterated, as gender is reduced effectively to sex (Gerson 1985).[5] When the social meanings of sex are rerooted in biology, it becomes virtually impossible to explain variation in gender relations in the context of race and class. We must assume, for example, that the effects of inherent sex differences are either added to or subtracted from those of race and class. We are led to assume, moreover, that sex differences are more fundamental than any other differences that might interest us (see Spelman 1988, 116–19, for a critical examination of this assumption)—unless we also assume that race differences and class differences are biologically based (for refutations of this assumption, see Gossett 1965; Montagu 1975; Omi and Winant 1986; and Stephans 1982).

Those who take a sex roles approach are confounded by similar difficulties, although these may be less apparent at the outset. What is deceptive is role theory's emphasis on the specific social locations that result in particular expectations and actions (Komarovsky 1946, 1992; Linton 1936; Parsons 1951; Parsons and Bales 1955). In this view, the actual enactment of an individual's "sex role" (or, more recently, "gender role") is contingent on the individual's social structural position and the expectations associated with that position. The focus is on gender as a role or status, as it is learned and enacted. In earlier work (Fenstermaker, West, and Zimmerman 1991; West and Fenstermaker 1993; West and Zimmerman 1987), we have noted several problems with this approach, including its inability to specify actions appropriate to particular "sex roles" in advance of their occurrence, and the fact that sex roles are not situated in any particular setting or organizational context (Lopata and Thorne 1978; Thorne 1980). The fact that "sex roles" often serve as "master statuses" (Hughes 1945) makes it hard to account for how variations in situations produce variations in their enactment. Given that gender is potentially omnirelevant to how we organize social life, almost any action could count as an instance of sex role enactment.

The most serious problem with this approach, however, is its inability to address issues of power and inequality (Connell 1985; Lopata and Thorne 1987; Thorne 1980). Conceiving of gender as composed of the "male role" and the "female role" implies a separate-but-equal relationship between the two, one characterized by complementary relations rather than conflict. Elsewhere (Fenstermaker, West, and Zimmerman 1991; West and Fenstermaker 1993; West and Zimmerman 1987), we illustrate this problem with Barrie Thorne and her colleagues' observation that social scientists have not made much use of role theory in their analyses of race and class relations. Concepts such as "race roles" and "class roles" have seemed patently inadequate to account for the dynamics of power and inequality operating in those contexts.

As many scholars have observed, empirical studies of the "female role" and "male role" have generally treated the experiences of white middle-class persons as prototypes, dismissing departures from the prototypical as instances of deviance. This is in large part what has contributed to the charges of white middle-class bias we discussed earlier. It is also what has rendered the sex role approach nearly useless in accounting for the diversity of gender relations across different groups.

Seeking a solution to these difficulties, Joan Acker has advanced the view that gender consists of something else altogether, namely, "patterned, socially produced distinctions between female and male, feminine and masculine... [that occur] in the course of participation in work organizations as well as in many other locations and relations" (1992b, 250). The object here is to document the "gendered processes" that sustain "the pervasive ordering of human activities, practices and social structures in terms of differentiations between women and men" (1992a, 567).

We agree fully with the object of this view and note its usefulness in capturing the persistence and ubiquity of gender inequality. Its emphasis on organizational practices restores the concern with "the structure of social institutions and with the impact of historical events" that characterized earlier class/caste approaches, and facilitates the simultaneous documentation of gender, race, and class as basic principles of social organization. We suggest, however, that the popular distinction between "macro" and "micro" levels of analysis reflected in this view makes it possible to empirically describe and explain inequality without fully apprehending the common elements of its daily unfolding. For example, "processes of interaction" are conceptualized apart from the "production of gender divisions," that is, "the overt decisions and procedures that control, segregate, exclude, and construct hierarchies based on gender, and often race" (Acker 1992a, 568). The production of "images, symbols and ideologies that justify, explain, and give legitimacy to institutions" constitutes yet another "process," as do "the [mental] internal processes in which individuals engage as they construct personas that are appropriately gendered for the institutional setting" (Acker 1992a, 568). The analytic "missing link," as we see it, is the mechanism that ties these seemingly diverse processes together, one that could "take into account the constraining impact of entrenched ideas and practices on human agency, but [could] also acknowledge that the system is continually construed in everyday life and that, under certain conditions, individuals resist pressures to conform to the needs of the system" (Essed 1991, 38).

In sum, if we conceive of gender as a matter of biological differences or differential roles, we are forced to think of it as standing apart from and outside other socially relevant, organizing experiences. This prevents us from understanding how gender, race, and class operate simultaneously with one another. It prevents us from seeing how the particular salience of these experiences might vary across interactions. Most important, it gives us virtually no way of adequately addressing the mechanisms that produce power and inequality in social life. Instead, we propose a conceptual mechanism for perceiving the relations between individual and institutional practice, and among forms of domination.

An Ethnomethodological Perspective

Don Zimmerman concisely describes ethnomethodological inquiry as proposing "that the properties of social life which seem objective, factual, and transsituational, are actually managed accomplishments or achievements of local processes" (1978, 11). In brief, the "objective" and "factual" properties of social life attain such status through the situated conduct of societal members. The aim of ethnomethodology is to analyze situated conduct to understand how "objective" properties of social life achieve their status as such.

The goal of this article is not to analyze situated conduct per se but to understand the workings of inequality. We should note that our interest here is not to separate gender, race, and class as social categories but to build a coherent argument for understanding how they work simultaneously. How might an ethnomethodological perspective help with this task? As Marilyn Frye observes,

> For efficient subordination, what's wanted is that the structure not appear to be a cultural artifact kept in place by human decision or custom, but that it appear natural—that it appear to be quite a direct consequence of facts about the beast which are beyond the scope of human manipulation. (1983, 34)

Gender

Within Western societies, we take for granted in everyday life that there are two and only two sexes (Garfinkel 1967, 122). We see this state of affairs as "only natural" insofar as we see persons as "essentially, originally and in the final analysis either 'male' or 'female'" (Garfinkel 1967, 122). When we interact with others, we take for granted that each of us has an "essential" manly or womanly nature—one that derives from our sex and one that can be detected from the "natural signs" we give off (Goffman 1976, 75).

These beliefs constitute the normative conceptions of our culture regarding the properties of normally sexed persons. Such beliefs support the seemingly "objective," "factual," and "transsituational" character of gender in social affairs, and in this sense, we experience them as exogenous (i.e., as outside of us and the particular situation we find ourselves in). Simultaneously, however, the meaning of these beliefs is dependent on the context in which they are invoked—rather than transsituational, as implied by the popular concept of "cognitive consensus" (Zimmerman 1978, 8–9). What is more, because these properties of normally sexed persons are regarded as "only natural," questioning them is tantamount to calling ourselves into question as competent members of society.

Consider how these beliefs operate in the process of sex assignment—the initial classification of persons as either females or males (West and Zimmerman 1987, 131–32). We generally regard this process as a biological determination requiring only a straightforward examination of the "facts of the matter" (cf. the description of sex as an "ascribed status" in many introductory sociology texts). The criteria for sex assignment, however, can vary across cases (e.g., chromosome type before birth or genitalia after birth). They sometimes do and sometimes do not agree with one another (e.g., hermaphrodites), and they show considerable variation across cultures (Kessler and McKenna 1978). Our *moral conviction* that there are two and only two sexes (Garfinkel 1967, 116–18) is what explains the comparative ease of achieving initial sex assignment. This conviction accords females and males the status of unequivocal and "natural" entities, whose social and psychological tendencies can be predicted from their reproductive functions (West and Zimmerman 1987, 127–28). From an ethnomethodological viewpoint, sex is socially and culturally constructed rather than a straightforward statement of the biological "facts."

Now, consider the process of sex categorization—the ongoing identification of persons as girls or boys and women or men in everyday life (West and Zimmerman 1987, 132–34). Sex categorization involves no well-defined set of criteria that must be satisfied to identify someone; rather, it involves treating appearances (e.g., deportment, dress, and bearing) as if they were indicative of underlying states of affairs (e.g., anatomical, hormonal, and chromosomal arrangements). The point worth stressing here is that, while sex category serves as an "indicator" of sex, it does not depend on it. Societal members will "see" a world populated by two and only two sexes, even in public situations that preclude inspection of the physiological "facts." From this perspective, it is important to distinguish sex category from sex assignment and to distinguish both from the "doing" of gender.

Gender, we argue, is a situated accomplishment of societal members, the local management of conduct in relation to normative conceptions of appropriate attitudes and activities for particular sex categories (West and Zimmerman 1987, 134–35). From this perspective, gender is not merely an individual attribute but something that is accomplished in interaction with others. Here, as in our earlier work, we rely on John Heritage's (1984, 136–37) formulation of accountability: the possibility of describing actions, circumstances, and even descriptions of themselves in both serious and consequential ways (e.g., as "unwomanly" or "unmanly"). Heritage points out that members of society routinely characterize activities in ways that take notice of those activities (e.g., naming, describing, blaming, excusing, or merely acknowledging them) and place them in a social framework (i.e., situating them in the context of other activities that are similar or different).

The fact that activities can be described in such ways is what leads to the possibility of conducting them with an eye to how they might be assessed (e.g., as "womanly" or "manly" behaviors). Three important but subtle points are worth emphasizing here. One is that the notion of accountability is relevant not only to activities that conform to prevailing normative conceptions (i.e., activities that are conducted "unremarkably," and, thus, do not warrant more than a passing glance) but also to those activities that deviate. The issue is not deviance or conformity; rather, it is the possible evaluation of action in relation to normative conceptions and the likely consequence of that evaluation for subsequent interaction. The second point worth emphasizing is that the process of rendering some action accountable is an interactional accomplishment. As Heritage explains, accountability permits persons to conduct their activities in relation to their circumstances—in ways that permit others to take those circumstances into account and see those activities for what they are. "[T]he intersubjectivity of actions," therefore, "ultimately rests on a symmetry between the *production* of those actions on the one hand and their *recognition* on the other" (1984, 179)—both in the context of their circumstances.[6] And the third point we must stress is that, while individuals are the ones who do gender, the process of rendering something accountable is both interactional and institutional in character: it is a feature of social relationships, and its idiom derives from the institutional arena in which those relationships come to life. In the United States, for example, when the behaviors of children or teenagers have become the focus of public concern, the Family and Motherhood (as well as individual mothers) have been held accountable to normative conceptions of "essential" femininity (including qualities like nurturance and caring). Gender is obviously much more than a role or an individual characteristic: it is a mechanism whereby situated social action contributes to the reproduction of social structure (West and Fenstermaker 1993, 158).

Womanly and manly natures thusly achieve the status of objective properties of social life (West and Zimmerman 1987). They are rendered natural, normal characteristics of individuals and, at the same time, furnish the tacit legitimation of the distinctive and unequal fates of women and men within the social order. If sex categories are potentially omnirelevant to social life, then persons engaged in virtually any activity may be held accountable for their performance of that activity as women or as men, and their category membership can be used to validate or discredit their other activities. This arrangement provides for countless situations in which persons in a particular sex category can "see" that they are out of place, and if they were not there, their current problems would not exist. It also allows for seeing various features of the existing social order—for example, the division of labor (Berk 1985), the development of gender identities (Cahill 1986), and the subordination of women by men (Fenstermaker, West, and Zimmerman 1991)—as "natural" responses. These things "are the way they are" by virtue of the fact that men are men and women are women—a distinction seen as "natural," as rooted in biology, and as producing fundamental psychological, behavioral, and social consequences.

Through this formulation, we resituate gender, an attribute without clear social origin or referent, in social interaction. This makes it possible to study how gender takes on social import, how it varies in its salience and consequence, and how it operates to produce and maintain power and inequality in social life. Below, we extend this reformulation to race, and then, to class. Through this extension, we are not proposing an equivalence of oppressions. Race is not class, and neither is gender; nevertheless, while race, class, and gender will likely take on different import and will often carry vastly different social consequences in any given social situation, we suggest that how they operate may be productively compared. Here, our focus is on the social mechanics of gender, race, and class, for that is the way we may perceive their simultaneous workings in human affairs.

Race

Within the United States, virtually any social activity presents the possibility of categorizing the participants on the basis of race. Attempts to establish race as a scientific concept have met with little success (Gosset 1965; Montagu 1975; Omi and Winant 1986; Stephans 1982). There are, for example, no biological criteria (e.g., hormonal, chromosomal, or anatomical) that allow physicians to pronounce race assignment at birth, thereby sorting human beings into distinctive races.[7] Since racial categories and their meanings change over time and place, they are, moreover, arbitrary.[8] In everyday life, nevertheless, people can and do sort out themselves and others on the basis of membership in racial categories.

Michael Omi and Howard Winant argue that the "seemingly obvious, 'natural' and 'common sense' qualities" of the existing racial order "themselves testify to the effectiveness of the racial formation process in constructing racial meanings and identities" (1986, 62). Take, for instance, the relatively recent emergence of the category "Asian American." Any scientific theory of race would be hard pressed to explain this in the absence of a well-defined set of criteria for assigning individuals to the category. In relation to ethnicity, furthermore, it makes no sense to aggregate in a single category the distinctive histories, geographic origins, and cultures of Cambodian, Chinese, Filipino, Japanese, Korean, Laotian, Thai, and Vietnamese Americans. Despite important distinctions among these groups, Omi and Winant contend, "the majority of Americans cannot tell the difference" between their members (1986, 24). "Asian American," therefore, affords a means of achieving racial categorization in everyday life.

Of course, competent members of U.S. society share preconceived ideas of what members of particular categories "look like" (Omi and Winant 1986, 62). Remarks such as "Odd, you don't look Asian" testify to underlying notions of what "Asians" ought to look like. The point we wish to stress, however, is that these notions are not supported by any scientific criteria for reliably distinguishing members of different "racial" groups. What is more, even state-mandated criteria (e.g., the proportion of "mixed blood" necessary to legally classify someone as Black)[9] are distinctly different in other Western cultures and have little relevance to the way racial categorization occurs in everyday life. As in the case of sex categorization, appearances are treated as if they were indicative of some underlying state.

Beyond preconceived notions of what members of particular groups look like, Omi and Winant suggest that Americans share preconceived notions of what members of these groups are like. They note, for example, that we are likely to become disoriented "when people do not act 'Black,' 'Latino' or indeed 'white' " (1986, 62). From our ethnomethodological perspective, what Omi and Winant are describing is the accountability of persons to race category. If we accept their contention that there are prevailing normative conceptions of appropriate attitudes and activities for particular race categories and if we grant Heritage's (1984, 179) claim that accountability allows persons to conduct their activities in relation to their circumstances (in ways that allow others to take those circumstances into account and see those activities for what they are), we can also see race as a situated accomplishment of societal members. From this perspective, race is not simply an individual characteristic or trait but something that is accomplished in interaction with others.

To the extent that race category is omnirelevant (or even verges on this), it follows that persons involved in virtually any action may be held accountable for their performance of that action as members of their race category. As in the case of sex category, race category can be used to justify or discredit other actions; accordingly, virtually any action can be assessed in relation to its race categorical nature. The accomplishment of race (like gender) does not necessarily mean "living up" to normative conceptions of attitudes and activities appropriate to a particular race category; rather, it means engaging in action at the risk of race assessment. Thus, even though individuals are the ones who accomplish race, "the enterprise is fundamentally interactional and institutional in character, for accountability is a feature of social relationships and its idiom is drawn from the institutional arena in which those relationships are enacted" (West and Zimmerman 1987, 137).

The accomplishment of race renders the social arrangements based on race as normal and natural, that is, legitimate ways of organizing social life. In the United States, it can seem "only natural" for counselors charged with guiding high school students in their preparation for college admission to advise Black students against advanced courses in math, chemistry, or physics "because Blacks do not do well" in those areas (Essed 1991, 242). The students may well forgo such courses, given that they "do not need them" and "can get into college without them." However, Philomena Essed observes, this ensures that students so advised will enter college at a disadvantage in comparison to classmates and creates the very situation that is believed to exist, namely, that Blacks do not do well in those areas. Small wonder, then, that the proportion of U.S. Black students receiving college degrees remains stuck at 13 percent, despite two decades of affirmative action programs (Essed 1991, 26). Those Black students who are (for whatever reason) adequately prepared for college are held to account for themselves as "deviant" representatives of their race category and, typically, exceptionalized (Essed 1991, 232). With that accomplishment, institutional practice and social order are reaffirmed.

Although the distinction between "macro" and "micro" levels of analysis is popular in the race relations literature too (e.g., in distinguishing "institutional" from "individual" racism or "macro-level" analyses of racialized social structures from "micro-level" analyses of identity formation), we contend that it is ultimately a false distinction. Not only do these "levels" operate continually and reciprocally in "our lived experience, in politics, in culture [and] in economic life" (Omi and Winant 1986, 67), but distinguishing between them "places the individual outside the institutional, thereby severing rules, regulations and procedures from the people who make and enact them" (Essed 1991, 36). We contend that the accountability of persons to race categories is the key to understanding the maintenance of the existing racial order.

Note that there is nothing in this formulation to suggest that race is necessarily accomplished in isolation from gender. To the contrary, if we conceive of both race and gender as situated accomplishments, we can see how individual persons may experience them simultaneously. For instance, Spelman observes that,

> [i]nsofar as she is oppressed by racism in a sexist context and sexism in a racist context, the Black woman's struggle cannot be compartmentalized into two struggles—one as a Black and one as a woman. Indeed, it is difficult to imagine why a Black woman would think of her struggles this way except in the face of demands by white women or by Black men that she do so. (1988, 124)

To the extent that an individual Black woman is held accountable in one situation to her race category, and in another, to her sex category, we can see these as "oppositional" demands for accountability. But note, it is a *Black woman* who is held accountable in both situations.

Contrary to Omi and Winant's (1986, 62) use of hypothetical cases, on any particular occasion of interaction, we are unlikely to become uncomfortable when "people" do not act "Black," "people" do not act "Latino," or when "people" do not act "white." Rather, we are likely to become disconcerted when particular Black *women* do not act like Black *women*, particular Latino *men* do not act like Latino *men*, or particular white *women* do not act like white *women*—in the context that we observe them. Conceiving of race and gender as ongoing accomplishments means we must locate their emergence in social situations, rather than within the individual or some vaguely defined set of role expectations.[10]

Despite many important differences in the histories, traditions, and varying impacts of racial and sexual oppression across particular situations, the mechanism underlying them is the same. To the extent that members of society know their actions are accountable, they will design their actions in relation to how they might be seen and described by others. And to the extent that race category (like sex category) is omnirelevant to social life, it provides others with an ever-available resource for interpreting those actions. In short, inasmuch as our society is divided by "essential" differences between members of different race categories and categorization by race is both relevant and mandated, the accomplishment of race is unavoidable (cf. West and Zimmerman 1987, 137).

For example, many (if not most) Black men in the United States have, at some point in their lives, been stopped on the street or pulled over by police for no apparent reason. Many (if not most) know very well that the ultimate grounds for their being detained is their race and sex category membership. Extreme deference may yield a release with the command to "move on," but at the same time, it legitimates the categorical grounds on which the police (be they Black or white) detained them in the first place. Indignation or outrage (as might befit a white man in similar circumstances) is likely to generate hostility, if not brutality, from the officers on the scene (who may share sharply honed normative conceptions regarding "inherent" violent tendencies among Black men). Their very survival may be contingent on how they conduct themselves in relation to normative conceptions of appropriate attitudes and activities for Black men in these circumstances. Here, we see both the limited rights of citizenship accorded to Black men in U.S. society and the institutional context (in this case, the criminal justice system) in which accountability is called into play.

In sum, the accomplishment of race consists of creating differences among members of different race categories—differences that are neither natural nor biological (cf. West and Zimmerman 1987, 137). Once created, these differences are used to maintain the "essential" distinctiveness of "racial identities" and the institutional arrangements that they support. From this perspective, racial identities are not invariant idealizations of our human natures that are uniformly distributed in society. Nor are normative conceptions of attitudes and activities for one's race category templates for "racial" behaviors. Rather, what is invariant is the notion that members of different "races" *have* essentially different natures, which explain their very unequal positions in our society.[11]

Class

This, too, we propose, is the case with class. Here, we know that even sympathetic readers are apt to balk: gender, yes, is "done," and race, too, is "accomplished," but class? How can we reduce a system that "differentially structures group access to material resources, including economic, political and social resources" (Andersen and Collins 1992, 50) to "a situated accomplishment"? Do we mean to deny the material realities of poverty and privilege? We do not. There is no denying the very different material realities imposed by differing relations under capital; however, we suggest that these realities have little to do with class categorization—and ultimately, with the accountability of persons to class categories—in everyday life.

For example, consider Shellee Colen's description of the significance of maids' uniforms to white middle-class women who employ West Indian immigrant women as child care workers and domestics in New York City. In the words of Judith Thomas, one of the West Indian women Colen interviewed,

> She [the employer] wanted me to wear the uniform. She was really prejudiced. She just wanted that the maid must be identified...She used to go to the beach every day with the children. So going to the beach in the sand and the sun and she would have the kids eat ice cream and all that sort of thing...I tell you one day when I look at myself, I was so dirty...just like I came out from a garbage can. (1986, 57)

At the end of that day, says Colen, Thomas asked her employer's permission to wear jeans to the beach the next time they went, and the employer gave her permission to do so. When she did wear jeans, and the employer's brother came to the beach for a visit, Thomas noted,

> I really believe they had a talk about it, because in the evening, driving back from the beach, she said "Well, Judith, I said you could wear something else to the beach other than the uniform [but] I think you will have to wear the uniform because they're very informal on this beach and they don't know who is guests from who isn't guests." (1986, 57)

Of the women Colen interviewed (in 1985), not one was making more than $225 a week, and Thomas was the only one whose employer was paying for medical insurance. All (including Thomas) were supporting at least two households: their own in New York, and that of their kin back in the West Indies. By any objective social scientific criteria, then, all would be regarded as members of the working-class poor; yet, in the eyes of Thomas's employer (and, apparently, the eyes of others at the beach), Thomas's low wages, long hours, and miserable conditions of employment were insufficient to establish her class category. Without a uniform, she could be mistaken for one of the guests and, hence, not be held accountable as a maid.

There is more to this example, of course, than meets the eye. The employer's claim notwithstanding, it is unlikely that Thomas, tending to white middle-class children who were clearly not her own, would be mistaken for one of the guests at the beach. The blue jeans, however, might be seen as indicating her failure to comply with normative expectations of attitudes and behaviors appropriate to a maid and, worse yet, as belying the competence of her employer (whose authority is confirmed by Thomas displaying herself as a maid). As Evelyn Nakano Glenn notes in another context, "the higher standard of living of one woman is made possible by, and also helps to perpetuate, the other's lower standard of living" (1992, 34).

Admittedly, the normative conceptions that sustain the accountability of persons to class category are somewhat different from those that sustain accountability to sex category and race category. For example, despite earlier attempts to link pauperism with heredity and thereby justify the forced sterilization of poor women in the United States (Rafter 1992), scientists today do not conceive of class in relation to the biological characteristics of a person. There is, moreover, no scientific basis for popular notions of what persons in particular class categories "look like" or "act like." But although the dominant ideology within the United States is no longer based explicitly on Social Darwinism (see, for example, Gossett 1965, 144–75) and although we believe, in theory, that anyone can make it, we as a society still hold certain truths to be self-evident. As Donna Langston observes:

> If hard work were the sole determinant of your ability to support yourself and your family, surely we'd have a different outcome for many in our society. We also, however, believe in luck and on closer examination, it certainly is quite a coincidence that the "unlucky" come from certain race, gender and class backgrounds. In order to perpetuate racist, sexist and classist outcomes, we also have to believe that the current economic distribution is unchangeable, has always existed, and probably exists in this form throughout the known universe, i.e., it's "natural." (1991, 146)

Langston pinpoints the underlying assumptions that sustain our notions about persons in relation to poverty and privilege—assumptions that compete with our contradictory declarations of a meritocratic society, with its readily invoked exemplar, Horatio Alger. For example, if someone is poor, we assume it is because of something *they* did or did not do: they lacked initiative, they were not industrious, they had no ambition, and so forth. If someone is rich, or merely well-off, it must be by virtue of *their own* efforts, talents, and initiative. While these beliefs certainly *look* more mutable than our views of women's and men's "essential" natures or our deep-seated convictions regarding the characteristics of persons in particular race categories, they still rest on the assumption that a person's economic fortunes derive from qualities of the person. Initiative is thus treated as inherent among the haves, and laziness is seen as inherent among the have-nots.[12] Given that initiative is a prerequisite for employment in jobs leading to upward mobility in this society, it is hardly surprising that "the rich get richer and the poor get poorer." As in the case of gender and race, profound historical effects of entrenched institutional practice result, but they unfold one accomplishment at a time.

To be sure, there are "objective" indicators of one's position within the system of distribution that differentially structure our access to resources. It is possible to sort members of society in relation to these indicators, and it is the job of many public agencies (e.g., those administering aid to families with dependent children, health benefits, food stamps, legal aid, and disability benefits) to do such sorting. In the process, public agencies allocate further unequal opportunities with respect to health, welfare, and life chances; however, whatever the criteria employed by these agencies (and these clearly change over time and place), they can be clearly distinguished from the accountability of persons to class categories in everyday life.

As Benjamin DeMott (1990) observes, Americans operate on the basis of a most unusual assumption, namely, that we live in a classless society. On the one hand, our everyday discourse is replete with categorizations of persons by class. DeMott (1990, 1–27) offers numerous examples of television shows, newspaper articles, cartoons, and movies that illustrate how class "will tell" in the most mundane of social doings. On the other hand, we believe that we in the United States are truly unique "in escaping the hierarchies that burden the rest of the developed world" (DeMott 1990, 29). We cannot see the system of distribution that structures our unequal access to resources. Because we cannot see this, the accomplishment of class in everyday life rests on the presumption that everyone is endowed with equal opportunity and, therefore, that real differences in the outcomes we observe must result from individual differences in attributes like intelligence and character.

For example, consider the media's coverage of the trial of Mary Beth Whitehead, the wife of a sanitation worker and surrogate mother of Baby M. As DeMott (1990, 96–101) points out, much of this trial revolved around the question of the kind of woman who would agree to bear and sell her child to someone else. One answer to this question might be "the kind of woman" who learned early in life that poverty engenders obligations of reciprocal sacrifice among people—even sacrifice for those who are not their kin (cf. Stack 1974). Whitehead was one of eight children, raised by a single mother who worked on and off as a beautician. Living in poverty, members of her family had often relied on "poor but generous neighbors" for help and had provided reciprocal assistance when they could. When William and Betsy Stern (a biochemist and a pediatrician) came to her for help, therefore, Whitehead saw them as "seemingly desperate in their childlessness, threatened by a ruinous disease (Mrs. Stern's self-diagnosed multiple sclerosis), [and] as people in trouble, unable to cope without her" (DeMott 1990, 99). Although she would be paid for carrying the pregnancy and although she knew that they were better off financially than she was, Whitehead saw the Sterns as "in need of help" and, hence, could not do otherwise than to provide it. DeMott explains:

> She had seen people turn to others helplessly in distress, had herself been turned to previously; in her world failure to respond was unnatural. Her class experience, together with her own individual nature, made it natural to perceive the helping side of surrogacy as primary and the commercial side as important yet secondary. (1990, 98)

Another answer to the "what kind of woman" question might be Whitehead's lack of education about the technical aspects of artificial insemination (DeMott 1990, 100). A high school dropout, she thought that this procedure allowed clinicians to implant both a man's sperm and a woman's egg in another woman's uterus, thereby making it possible for infertile couples to have their own genetic children. It was not until just before the birth that Whitehead learned she would be the one contributing the egg and, subsequently, would not be bearing their child but her own. Under these circumstances, it would certainly seem "natural" for her to break her contract with the Sterns at the point of learning that it required her to give them her baby.

The media coverage of Whitehead's trial focused neither on class-based understandings of altruism nor on class-associated knowledge of sexual reproduction; rather, it focused on the question of Whitehead's character:

> The answers from a team of expert psychologists were reported in detail. Mrs. Whitehead was described as "impulsive, egocentric, self-dramatic, manipulative and exploitative." One member of the team averred that she suffered from a "schizotypal personality disorder." [Another] gave it as his opinion that the defendant's ailment was a "mixed personality disorder," and that she was "immature, exhibitionistic, and histrionic."... [U]nder the circumstances, he did not see that "there were any 'parental rights';" Mrs. Whitehead was "a surrogate uterus"... "and not a surrogate mother." (DeMott 1990, 96)

Through these means, "the experts" reduced Whitehead from a woman to a womb, and, therefore, someone with no legitimate claim to the child she had helped to conceive. Simultaneously, they affirmed the right of Betsy Stern to be the mother—even of a child she did not bear. As Whitehead's attorney put it in his summation, "What we are witnessing, and what we can predict will happen, is that one class of Americans will exploit another class. And it will always be the wife of the sanitation worker who must bear the children for the pediatrician" (Whitehead and Schwartz-Nobel 1989, 160, cited in DeMott 1990, 97). The punch line, of course, is that our very practices of invoking "essential differences" between classes support the rigid system of social relations that disparately distributes opportunities and life chances. Without these practices, the "natural" relations under capital might well seem far more malleable.

The accomplishment of class renders the unequal institutional arrangements based on class category accountable as normal and natural, that is, as legitimate ways of organizing social life (cf. West and Zimmerman 1987). Differences between members of particular class categories that are created by this process can then be depicted as fundamental and enduring dispositions.[13] In this light, the institutional arrangements of our society can be seen as responsive to the differences—the social order being merely an accommodation to the natural order.

In any given situation (whether or not that situation can be characterized as face-to-face interaction or as the more "macro" workings of institutions), the simultaneous accomplishments of class, gender, and race will differ in content and outcome. From situation to situation, the salience of the observables relevant to categorization (e.g., dress, interpersonal style, skin color) may seem to eclipse the interactional impact of the simultaneous accomplishment of all three. We maintain, nevertheless, that, just as the mechanism for accomplishment is shared, so, too, is their simultaneous accomplishment ensured.

Conclusion: The Problem of Difference

As we have indicated, mathematical metaphors describing the relations among gender, race, and class have led to considerable confusion in feminist scholarship. As we have also indicated, the conceptualizations of gender that support mathematical metaphors (e.g., "sex differences" and "sex roles") have forced scholars to think of gender as something that stands apart from and outside of race and class in people's lives.

In putting forth this perspective, we hope to advance a new way of thinking about gender, race, and class, namely, as ongoing, methodical, and situated accomplishments. We have tried to demonstrate the usefulness of this perspective for understanding how people experience gender, race, and class simultaneously. We have also tried to illustrate the implications of this perspective for reconceptualizing "the problem of difference" in feminist theory.

What are the implications of our ethnomethodological perspective for an understanding of relations among gender, race, and class? First, and perhaps most important, conceiving of these as ongoing accomplishments means that we cannot determine their relevance to social action apart from the context in which they are accomplished (Fenstermaker, West, and Zimmerman 1991; West and Fenstermaker 1993). While sex category, race category, and class category are potentially omnirelevant to social life, individuals inhabit many different identities, and these may be stressed or muted, depending on the situation. For example, consider the following incident described in detail by Patricia Williams, a law professor who, by her own admission, "loves to shop" and is known among her students for her "neat clothes":[14]

> Buzzers are big in New York City. Favored particularly by smaller stores and boutiques, merchants throughout the city have installed them as screening devices to reduce the incidence of robbery: if the face at the door looks desirable, the buzzer is pressed and the door is unlocked. If the face is that of an undesirable, the door stays pressed and the door is locked. I discovered [these buzzers] and their meaning one Saturday in 1986. I was shopping in Soho and saw in a store window a sweater that I wanted to buy for my mother. I pressed my round brown face to the window and my finger to the buzzer, seeking admittance. A narrow-eyed white teenager, wearing running shoes and feasting on bubble gum glared out, evaluating me for signs that would pit me against the limits of his social understanding. After about five minutes, he mouthed "we're closed," and blew pink rubber at

me. It was two Saturdays before Christmas, at one o'clock in the afternoon; there were several white people in the store who appeared to be shopping for things for *their* mothers. (1991, 44)

In this incident, says Williams, the issue of undesirability revealed itself as a racial determination. This is true in a comparative sense; for example, it is unlikely that a white woman law professor would have been treated this way by this salesperson and likely that a Latino gang member would have. This is also true in a legal sense; for example, in cases involving discrimination, the law requires potential plaintiffs to specify whether or not they were discriminated against on the basis of sex *or* race or some other criterion. We suggest, however, that sex category and class category, although muted, are hardly irrelevant to Williams's story. Indeed, we contend that one reason readers are apt to find this incident so disturbing is that it did not happen to a Latino gang member but to a Black woman law professor. Our point is not to imply that anyone should be treated this way but to show that one cannot isolate Williams's race category from her sex category or class category and fully understand this situation. We would argue, furthermore, that how class and gender are accomplished in concert with race must be understood through that specific interaction.

A second implication of our perspective is that the accomplishment of race, class, and gender does not require categorical diversity among the participants. To paraphrase Erving Goffman, social situations "do not so much allow for the expression of natural differences as for the production of [those] difference[s themselves]" (1977, 72). Some of the most extreme displays of "essential" womanly and manly natures may occur in settings that are usually reserved for members of a single sex category, such as locker rooms or beauty salons (Gerson 1985). Some of the most dramatic expressions of "definitive" class characteristics may emerge in class-specific contexts (e.g., debutante balls). Situations that involve more than one sex category, race category, and class category may highlight categorical membership and make the accomplishment of gender, race, and class more salient, but they are not necessary to produce these accomplishments in the first place. This point is worth stressing, since existing formulations of relations among gender, race, and class might lead one to conclude that "difference" must be present for categorical membership and, thus, dominance to matter.

A third implication is that, depending on how race, gender, and class are accomplished, what looks to be the same activity may have different meanings for those engaged in it. Consider the long-standing debates among feminists (e.g., Collins 1990; Davis 1971; Dill 1988; Firestone 1970; Friedan 1963; hooks 1984; Hurtado 1989; Zavella 1987) over the significance of mothering and child care in women's lives. For white middle-class women, these activities have often been seen as constitutive of oppression in that they are taken as expressions of their "essential" womanly natures and used to discredit their participation in other activities (e.g., Friedan 1963). For many women of color (and white working-class women), mothering and child care have had (and continue to have) very different meanings. Angela Davis (1971, 7) points out that, in the context of slavery, African American women's efforts to tend to the needs of African American children (not necessarily their own) represented the only labor they performed that could not be directly appropriated by white slave owners. Throughout U.S. history, bell hooks observes,

> Black women have identified work in the context of the family as humanizing labor, work that affirms their identity as women, as human beings showing love and care, the very gestures of humanity white supremacist ideology claimed black people were incapable of expressing. (1984, 133–34)

Looking specifically at American family life in the nineteenth century, Bonnie Thornton Dill (1988) suggests that being a poor or working-class African American woman, a Chinese American woman, or a Mexican American woman meant something very different from being a Euro-American woman. Normative, class-bound conceptions of "woman's nature" at that time included tenderness, piety, and nurturance—qualities that legitimated the confinement of middle-class Euro-American women to the domestic sphere and that promoted such confinement as the goal of working-class and poor immigrant Euro-American families' efforts.

> For racial-ethnic women, however, the notion of separate spheres served to reinforce their subordinate status and became, in effect, another assault. As they increased their work outside the home, they were forced into a productive sphere that was organized for men and "desperate" women who were so unfortunate or immoral that they could not confine their work to the domestic sphere. In the productive sphere, however, they were denied the opportunity to embrace the dominant ideological definition of "good" wife and mother. (Dill 1988, 429)

Fourth and finally, our perspective affords an understanding of the accomplishment of race, gender, or class as constituted in the context of the differential "doings" of the others. Consider, for example, the very dramatic case of the U.S. Senate hearings on Clarence Thomas's nomination to the Supreme Court. Wherever we turned, whether to visual images on a television screen or to the justificatory discourse of print media, we were overwhelmed by the dynamics of gender, race, and class operating in concert with one another. It made a difference to us as viewers (and certainly to his testimony) that Clarence Thomas was a Black *man* and that he was a *Black* man. It also made a difference, particularly to the African American community, that he was a Black man who had been raised in poverty. Each categorical dimension played off the others and off the comparable but quite different categorizations of Anita Hill (a "self-made" Black woman law professor, who had grown up as one of 13 children). Most white women who watched the hearings identified gender and men's dominance as the most salient aspects of them, whether in making sense of the Judiciary Committee's handling of witnesses or understanding the relationship between Hill and Thomas. By contrast, most African American viewers saw racism as the most salient aspect of the hearings, including white men's prurient interest in Black sexuality and the exposure of troubling divisions between Black women and men (Morrison 1992). The point is that how we label such dynamics does not necessarily capture their complex quality. Foreground and background, context, salience, and center shift from interaction to interaction, but all operate interdependently.

Of course, this is only the beginning. Gender, race, and class are only three means (although certainly very powerful ones) of generating difference and dominance in social life.[15] Much more must be done to distinguish other forms of inequality and their workings. Empirical evidence must be brought to bear on the question of variation in the salience of categorical memberships, while still allowing for the simultaneous influence of these memberships on interaction. We suggest that the analysis of situated conduct affords the best prospect for understanding how these "objective" properties of social life achieve their ongoing status as such and, hence, how the most fundamental divisions of our society are legitimated and maintained.

Notes

1. In this article, we use "race" rather than "ethnicity" to capture the commonsensical beliefs of members of our society. As we will show, these beliefs are predicated on the assumption that different "races" can be reliably distinguished from one another.
2. Compare, for example, the very different implications of "Double Jeopardy: To Be Black and Female" (Beale 1970) and "Positive Effects of the Multiple Negative: Explaining the Success of Black Professional Women" (Epstein 1973).
3. In this context, we define "experience" as participation in social systems in which gender, race, and class affect, determine, or otherwise influence behavior.
4. Here, it is important to distinguish an individual's experience of the dynamics of gender, race, and class as they order the daily course of social interaction from that individual's sense of identity as a member of gendered, raced, and classed categories. For example, in any given interaction, a woman who is Latina and a shopkeeper may experience the simultaneous effects of gender, race, and class, yet identify her experience as only "about" race, only "about" gender, or only "about" class.

5. The ambivalence that dogs the logic of social constructionist positions should now be all too familiar to feminist sociologists. If we are true to our pronouncements that social inequalities and the categories they reference (e.g., gender, race, and class) are not rooted in biology, then we may at some point seem to flirt with the notion that they are, therefore, rooted in nothing. For us, biology is not only not destiny but also not the only reality. Gender, race, and class inequalities are firmly rooted in the ever-present realities of individual practice, cultural conventions, and social institutions. That's reality enough, when we ponder the pernicious and pervasive character of racism, sexism, and economic oppression.
6. That persons may be held accountable does not mean that they necessarily will be held accountable in every interaction. Particular interactional outcomes are not the point here; rather, it is the possibility of accountability in any interaction.
7. To maintain vital statistics on race, California, for instance, relies on mothers' and fathers' self-identifications on birth certificates.
8. Omi and Winant (1986, 64–75) provide numerous empirical illustrations, including the first appearance of "white" as a term of self-identification (circa 1680), California's decision to categorize Chinese people as "Indian" (in 1854), and the U.S. Census's creation of the category "Hispanic" (in 1980).
9. Consider Susie Guillory Phipps's unsuccessful suit against the Louisiana Bureau of Vital Records (Omi and Winant 1986, 57). Phipps was classified as "Black" on her birth certificate, in accord with a 1970 Louisiana law stipulating that anyone with at least one-thirty-second "Negro blood" was "Black." Her attorney contended that designating a race category on a person's birth certificate was unconstitutional and that, in any case, the one-thirty-second criterion was inaccurate. Ultimately, the court upheld Louisiana's state law quantifying "racial identity" and thereby affirmed the legal principle of assigning persons to specific "racial" groups.
10. This would be true if only because outcomes bearing on power and inequality are so different in different situations. Ours is a formulation that is sensitive to variability, that can accommodate, for example, interactions where class privilege and racism seem equally salient, as well as those in which racism interactionally "eclipses" accountability to sex category.
11. As Spelman observes, 'The existence of racism does not require that there are races; it requires the belief that there are races" (1988, 208, n. 24).
12. A devil's advocate might argue that gender, race, and class are fundamentally different because they show different degrees of "mutability" or latitude in the violation of expectations in interaction. Although class mobility is possible, one might argue, race mobility is not; or, while sex change operations can be performed, race change operations cannot. In response, we would point out that the very notion that one cannot change one's race—but can change one's sex and manipulate displays of one's class—only throws us back to biology and its reassuring, but only apparent, immutability.
13. Although we as a society believe that some people may "pull themselves up by their bootstraps" and others may "fall from grace," we still cherish the notion that class will reveal itself in a person's fundamental social and psychological character. We commonly regard the self-made man, the welfare mother, and the middle-class housewife as distinct categories of persons, whose attitudes and activities can be predicted on categorical grounds.
14. We include these prefatory comments about shopping and clothes for those readers who, on encountering this description, asked, "What does she look like?" and "What was she wearing?" Those who seek further information will find Williams featured in a recent fashion layout for *Mirabella* magazine (As Smart as They Look 1993).
15. We cannot stress this strongly enough. Gender, race, and class are obviously very salient social accomplishments in social life, because so many features of our cultural institutions and daily discourse are organized to perpetuate the categorical distinctions on which they are based. As Spelman observes, "the more a society has invested in its members' getting the categories right, the more occasions there will be for reinforcing them, and the fewer occasions there will be for questioning them" (1988, 152). On any given occasion of interaction, however, we may also be held accountable to other categorical memberships (e.g., ethnicity,

nationality, sexual orientation, place of birth), and, thus, "difference" may then be differentially constituted.

References

Acker, Joan. 1992a. Gendered institutions: From sex roles to gendered institutions. *Contemporary Sociology* 21:565–69.

———. 1992b. Gendering organizational theory. In *Gendering Organizational Theory*, edited by Albert J. Mills and Peta Tancred. London: Sage.

Almquist, Elizabeth. 1989. The experiences of minority women in the United States: Intersections of race, gender, and class. In *Women: A feminist perspective*, edited by Jo Freeman. Mountain View, CA: Mayfield.

Andersen, Margaret L., and Patricia Hill Collins. 1992. Preface to *Race, class and gender*, edited by Margaret L. Andersen and Patricia Hill Collins. Belmont, CA: Wadsworth.

Aptheker, Bettina. 1989. *Tapestries of life: Women's work, women's consciousness, and the meaning of daily experience*. Amherst: University of Massachusetts Press.

As smart as they look. *Mirabella*, June 1993, 100–111.

Beale, Frances. 1970. Double jeopardy: To be Black and female. In *The Black woman: An anthology*, edited by Toni Cade (Bambara). New York: Signet.

Berk, Sarah Fenstermaker. 1985. *The gender factory: The apportionment of work in American households*. New York: Plenum.

Bhavnani, Kum-Kum. 2003. Talking racism and the editing of women's studies. In *Introducing women's studies*, edited by Diane Richardson and Vicki Robinson. New York: Macmillan.

Cahill, Spencer E. 1986. Childhood socialization as recruitment process: Some lessons from the study of gender development. In *Sociological studies of child development*, edited by Patricia Adler and Peter Adler. Greenwich, CT: JAI.

Colen, Shellee. 1986. "With respect and feelings": Voices of West Indian child care and domestic workers in New York City. In *All American women*, edited by Johnetta B. Cole. New York: Free Press.

Collins, Patricia Hill. 1990. *Black feminist thought*. New York: Routledge.

Connell, R. W. 1985. Theorizing gender. *Sociology* 19:260–72.

Davis, Angela. 1971. The Black woman's role in the community of slaves. *Black Scholar* 3:3–15.

———. 1981. *Women, race and class*. New York: Random House.

de Beauvoir, Simone. 1953. *The second sex*. New York: Knopf.

DeMott, Benjamin. 1990. *The imperial middle: Why Americans can't think straight about class*. New Haven, CT: Yale University Press.

Dill, Bonnie Thornton. 1988. Our mothers' grief: Racial ethnic women and the maintenance of families. *Journal of Family History* 13:415–31.

Epstein, Cynthia Fuchs. 1973. Positive effects of the double negative: Explaining the success of Black professional women. In *Changing women in a changing society*, edited by Joan Huber. Chicago: University of Chicago Press.

Essed, Philomena. 1991. *Understanding everyday racism: An interdisciplinary theory*. Newbury Park, CA: Sage.

Fenstermaker, Sarah, Candace West, and Don H. Zimmerman. 1991. Gender inequality: New conceptual terrain. In *Gender, family and economy: The triple overlap*, edited by Rae Lesser Blumberg. Newbury Park, CA: Sage.

Firestone, Shulamith. 1970. *The dialectic of sex*. New York: Morrow.

Friedan, Betty. 1963. *The feminine mystique*. New York: Dell.

Frye, Marilyn. 1983. *The politics of reality: Essays in feminist theory*. Trumansburg, NY: Crossing Press.

Garfinkel, Harold. 1967. *Studies in ethnomethodology*. Englewood Cliffs, NJ: Prentice-Hall.

Gerson, Judith. 1985. *The variability and salience of gender: Issues of conceptualization and measurement*. Paper presented at the annual meeting of the American Sociological Association, Washington, DC, August.

Glazer, Nona. 1977. A sociological perspective: Introduction. In *Woman in a man-made world*, edited by Nona Glazer and Helen Youngelson Waehrer. Chicago: Rand McNally.

Glenn, Evelyn Nakano. 1985. Racial ethnic women's labor: The intersection of race, gender and class oppression. *Review of Radical Political Economics* 17:86–108.

———. 1992. From servitude to service work: Historical continuities in the racial division of paid reproductive labor. *Signs: Journal of Women in Culture and Society* 18:1–43.

Goffman, Erving. 1976. Gender display. *Studies in the Anthropology of Visual Communication* 3:69–77.

———. 1977. The arrangement between the sexes. *Theory and Society* 4:301–31.

Gossett, Thomas. 1965. *Race: The history of an idea in America*. New York: Schocken Books.

Hacker, Helen Mayer. 1951. Women as a minority group. *Social Forces* 30:60–69.

Heritage, John. 1984. *Garfinkel and ethnomethodology*. Cambridge, England: Polity.

Hochschild, Arlie Russell. 1973. A review of sex role research. *American Journal of Sociology* 78: 1011–29.

hooks, bell. 1981. *Ain't I a woman: Black women and feminism*. Boston: South End.

———. 1984. *From margin to center*. Boston: South End.

Hughes, Everett C. 1945. Dilemmas and contradictions of status. *American Journal of Sociology* 50:353–59.

Hull, Gloria T., Patricia Bell Scott, and Barbara Smith, eds. 1982. *All the women are white, all the Blacks are men, but some of us are brave*. Old Westbury, NY: Feminist Press.

Hurtado, Aída. 1989. Relating to privilege: Seduction and rejection in the subordination of white women and women of color. *Signs: Journal of Women in Culture and Society* 14:833–55.

Jordan, June. 1985. Report from the Bahamas. In *On call: Political essays*. Boston: South End.

Joseph, Gloria, and Jill Lewis, eds. 1981. *Common differences*. Garden City, NY: Anchor.

Kessler, Suzanne J., and Wendy McKenna. 1978. *Gender: An ethnomethodological approach*. New York: Wiley.

Komarovsky, Mirra. 1946. Cultural contradictions and sex roles. *American Journal of Sociology* 52:184–89.

———. 1992. The concept of social role revisited. *Gender & Society* 6:301–12.

Langston, Donna. 1991. Tired of playing monopoly? In *Changing our power: An Introduction to women's studies*, 2d ed., edited by Jo Whitehorse Cochran, Donna Langston, and Carolyn Woodward. Dubuque, IA: Kendall-Hunt.

Linton, Ralph. 1936. *The study of man*. New York: Appleton-Century.

Lopata, Helena Z., and Barrie Thorne. 1987. On the term "sex roles." *Signs: Journal of Women in Culture and Society* 3:718–21.

Lorde, Audre. 1984. *Sister outsider*. Trumansburg, NY: Crossing.

Montagu, Ashley, ed. 1975. *Race & IQ*. London: Oxford University Press.

Mitchell, Juliet. 1966. Women: The longest revolution. *New Left Review* 40:11–37.

Moraga, Cherríe. 1981. La güera. In *This bridge called my back: Radical writing by women of color*, edited by Cherríe Moraga and Gloria Anzalduá. New York: Kitchen Table Press.

Moraga, Cherríe, and Gloria Anzaiduá, eds. 1981. *This bridge called my back: Writings by radical women of color*. Watertown, MA: Persephone.

Morrison, Toni, ed. 1992. *Race-ing justice, engendering power: Essays on Anita Hill, Clarence Thomas, and the construction of social reality*. New York: Pantheon.

Omi, Michael, and Howard Winant. 1986. *Racial formation in the United States from the 1960s to the 1980s*. New York: Routledge & Kegan Paul.

Parsons, Talcott. 1951. *The social system*. New York: Free Press.

Parsons, Talcott, and Robert F. Bales. 1955. *Family, socialization and interaction process*. New York: Free Press.

Rafter, Nichole H. 1992. Claims-making and socio-cultural context in the first U.S. eugenics campaign. *Social Problems* 39:17–34.

Rich, Adrienne. 1979. Disloyal to civilization: Feminism, racism, gynephobia. In *On lies, secrets, and silence*. New York: Norton.

Segura, Denise A. 1992. Chicanas in white collar jobs: "You have to prove yourself more." *Sociological Perspectives* 35:163–82.

Spelman, Elizabeth V. 1988. *Inessential woman: Problems of exclusion in feminist thought*. Boston: Beacon Press.

Stacey, Judith, and Barrie Thorne. 1985. The missing feminist revolution in sociology. *Social Problems* 32:301–16.

Stack, Carol B. 1974. *All our kin: Strategies for survival in a Black community*. New York: Harper & Row.

Stephans, Nancy. 1982. *The idea of race in science*. Hamden, CT: Archon.

Thorne, Barrie. 1980. Gender... How is it best conceptualized? Unpublished manuscript, Department of Sociology, Michigan State University, East Lansing.

West, Candace, and Sarah Fenstermaker. 1993. Power, inequality and the accomplishment of gender: An ethnomethodological view. In *Theory on gender/feminism on theory*, edited by Paula England. New York: Aldine.

West, Candace, and Don H. Zimmerman. 1987. Doing gender. *Gender & Society* 1:125–51.

Williams, Patricia. 1991. *The alchemy of race and rights*. Cambridge, MA: Harvard University Press.

Young, Iris Marion. 1990. Impartiality and the civic public. In *Throwing like a girl and other essays in feminist philosophy*. Bloomington: Indiana University Press.

Zavella, Patricia. 1987. *Women's work and Chicano families: Cannery workers of the Santa Clara Valley*. Ithaca, NY: Cornell University Press.

Zimmerman, Don H. 1978. Ethnomethodology. *American Sociologist* 13:6–15.

Zinn, Maxine Baca. 1990. Family, feminism and race in America. *Gender & Society* 4:68–82.

Zinn, Maxine Baca, Lynn Weber Cannon, Elizabeth Higginbotham, and Bonnie Thornton Dill. 1986. The costs of exclusionary practices in women's studies. *Signs: Journal of Women in Culture and Society* 11:290–303.

Great Divides: The Cultural, Cognitive, and Social Bases of the Global Subordination of Women

CYNTHIA FUCHS EPSTEIN

The world is made up of great divides—divides of nations, wealth, race, religion, education, class, gender, and sexuality—all constructs created by human agency. The conceptual boundaries that define these categories are always symbolic and may create physical and social boundaries as well (Gerson and Peiss 1985; Lamont and Molnar 2002). Today, as in the past, these constructs not only order social existence, but they also hold the capacity to create serious inequalities, generate conflicts, and promote human suffering. In this address, I argue that the boundary based on sex creates the most fundamental social divide—a divide that should be a root issue in all sociological analysis if scholars are to adequately understand the social dynamics of society and the influential role of stratification. The work of many sociologists contributes to this claim, although I can only refer to some of them in the context of a single article.

The conceptual boundaries that determine social categories are facing deconstruction throughout our profession. Once thought stable and real in the sense that they are descriptive of biological or inherited traits, social categories such as race and ethnicity are contested today by a number of scholars (Barth 1969; Brubaker 2004; Duster 2006; Telles 2004). Indeed, sociologists are questioning the underlying reasoning behind

Cynthia Fuchs Epstein, "Great Divides: The Cultural, Cognitive, and Social Bases of the Global Subordination of Women" from *American Sociological Review*, 72 (February 2007): 1–22.

categorical distinctions, noting their arbitrariness, and further, the ways in which they tend to be "essentializing and naturalizing" (Brubaker 2004:9).[1] Yet, not many of these critical theorists have included *gender* in this kind of analysis.[2] Where they have, such work tends to be relegated to, if not ghettoized within, the field of "gender studies."[3]

Of course, the categories of race, ethnicity, and gender are real in the sense that—as W. I. Thomas put it in his oft-quoted observation—"if men *[sic]* define situations as real, they are real in their consequences (cited in Merton [1949] 1963:421). Categorization on the basis of observable characteristics often serves as a mobilizing strategy for action against (or for) people assigned to the category and may even force them into a grouplike state (Bourdieu 1991; Brubaker 2004). Alternatively, categorization may create conformity to a stereotype—in the process known as "the self-fulfilling prophecy" (Merton [1949] 1963). But it is one thing for individuals to engage in categorical thinking, and another for social scientists to accept a category with its baggage of assumptions. Today, many social scientists use popular understandings of race, ethnicity, and gender as if they were descriptive of inherent or acquired stable traits, and they treat them as established variables that describe clusters of individuals who share common traits. In this manner, social scientists are no different from the lay public, who, in their everyday activities and thinking, act as if categories are reliable indicators of commonalities in a population.

The consequences of such categorization may be positive or negative for those in a given category. For example, people of color face far more suspicion from the police than do whites, and favored male professors benefit from the evaluation that they are smart and knowledgeable while comparatively favored female professors tend to be evaluated as nice (Basow 1995). Yet, unlike the basis on which social *groups* may be defined, categories include individuals who may never know one another or have any interaction with each other. However, they may all share selected physical traits or relationships. Skin color, hair texture, genitals, place of birth, and genealogy are among the determinants of categories.

I consider *gender* to be the most basic and prevalent category in social life throughout the world, and in this address, I explore the life consequences that follow from this designation for the female half of humanity. Gender is, of course, based on biological sex, as determined by the identification of an individual at birth as female or male by a look at their genitals. This first glance sets up the most basic divide in all societies—it determines an individual's quality of life, position on the social hierarchy, and chance at survival. The glance marks individuals for life and is privileged over their unique intelligence, aptitudes, or desires. Of course, persons who are transgendered, transsexual, or hermaphrodites[4] do not fit this dichotomous separation, but there is little recognition of categories based on sex other than male and female in almost every society (Butler 1990; Lorber 1994, 1996).

Sex Division and Subordination

The sexual divide is the most persistent and arguably the deepest divide in the world today. Of course, it is only one of many great divides. Boundaries mark the territories of human relations. They are created by "cultural entrepreneurs"[5] who translate the concepts into practice—rulers behind the closed doors of palaces and executive offices; judges in courtrooms; priests, rabbis, and mullahs; leaders and members of unions and clubs; and teachers, parents, and the people in the street. The great divides of society are enforced by persuasion, barter, custom, force, and the threat of force (Epstein 1985). The extent to which boundaries are permeable and individuals can escape categorization, and thus, their assignment to particular social roles and statuses, is a function of a society's or an institution's stability and capacity to change. The ways in which boundaries may be transgressed make up the story of social change and its limits. They are the basis for human freedom.

Of all the socially created divides, the gender divide is the most basic and the one most resistant to social change. As I have suggested before (Epstein 1985, 1988, 1991b, 1992), dichotomous categories, such as those that distinguish between blacks and whites; free persons and slaves; and men and women, are always invidious. This dichotomous categorization is also particularly powerful in maintaining the advantage of the privileged category. With regard to the sex divide, the male sex is everywhere privileged—sometimes the gap is wide, sometimes narrow. Some individuals and small clusters of women may succeed in bypassing the negative consequences of categorization, and in some cases they may even do better educationally or financially than the men in their group. Among women, those from a privileged class, race, or nationality may do better than others. But worldwide, in every society, women as a category are subordinated to men.

I further suggest that the divide of biological sex constitutes a marker around which all major institutions of society are organized. All societal institutions assign roles based on the biological sex of their members. The divisions of labor in the family, local and global labor forces, political entities, most religious systems, and nation-states are all organized according to the sexual divide.

Cultural meanings are also attached to the categories of female and male, which include attributions of character and competence (Epstein 1988, see Ridgeway 2006 for a review). These situate individuals assigned to each category in particular social and symbolic roles. There is some overlap in the roles to which females and males are assigned, but in all societies sex status is the major determinant—it is the master status that determines the acquisition of most other statuses.

Of course, biological sex does prescribe humans' reproductive roles (e.g., child bearer, inseminator). But there is no biological necessity for a woman to become a mother, even though only women can become biological mothers, and a man may or may not choose to become a biological father. Therefore, we can conclude that *all* social statuses and the roles attached to them are *socially* prescribed. Further, norms prescribe (or proscribe) detailed behavior fixed to all social roles. And, because statuses are universally ranked, the statuses women are permitted to acquire usually are subordinate to men's statuses. Furthermore, women's roles are universally paired with roles assigned to men, to the family, in the workplace, and in the polity. Virtually no statuses are stand-alone positions in society; all are dependent on reciprocal activities of those who hold complementary statuses. These too are socially ranked and usually follow the invidious distinctions that "male" and "female" evoke. Almost no statuses are free from gender-typing.

These observations lead me to proposals that I believe are essential for comprehensive sociological analysis today, and to call for the elimination of the boundary that has separated so-called gender studies from mainstream sociology.[6]

Given the ubiquitous nature of sex-typing of social statuses, and social and symbolic behavior, I propose that the dynamics of gender segregation be recognized as a primary issue for sociological analysis and attention be paid to the mechanisms and processes of sex differentiation and their roles in group formation, group maintenance, and stratification.[7] I further suggest that

- Females' and males' actual and symbolic roles in the social structure are a seedbed for group formation and group boundary-maintenance.
- All societies and large institutions are rooted in the differentiation and subordination of females.
- The more group solidarities are in question in a society, the stronger the differentiation between males and females and the more severe is women's subjugation.

The enforcement of the distinction is achieved through cultural and ideological means that justify the differentiation. This is despite the fact that, unlike every other dichotomous category of people, females and males are necessarily bound together, sharing the same domiciles and most often the same racial and social class statuses. Analyses of these relationships are difficult given the ways in which they are integrated with each other and the extent to which they are basic in all institutions.

There is, of course, variation in societies and the subgroups within them, and a continuum exists in the severity of female subordination. Indeed, subordination is not a static process and it varies from almost complete to very little. The process is dynamic in shape and degree. Women gain or lose equality depending on many elements—the state of an economy, the identity politics of groups or nations, the election of conservative or liberal governments, the need for women's labor in the public and private sectors, the extent of their education, the color of their skin,[8] the power of fundamentalist religious leaders in their societies, and their ability to collaborate in social movements. But even in the most egalitarian of societies, the invidious divide is always a lurking presence and it can easily become salient.

It is important to note that women's inequality is not simply another case of social inequality, a view I have held in the past (Epstein 1970). I am convinced that societies and strategic subgroups within them, such as political and work institutions, *maintain their boundaries* their very social organization—through the use of invidious distinctions made between males and females.[9] Everywhere, women's subordination is basic to maintaining the social cohesion and stratification systems of ruling and governing groups—male groups—on national and local levels, in the family, and in all other major institutions. Most dramatically, this process is at work today in the parts of the world where control of females' behavior, dress, and use of public space have been made representations of orthodoxies in confrontation with modernism, urbanism, and secular society. But even in the most egalitarian societies, such as the United States, women's autonomy over their bodies,[10] their time, and their ability to decide their destinies is constantly at risk when it intrudes on male power.

The gender divide is not determined by biological forces. *No society or subgroup leaves social sorting to natural processes.* It is through social and cultural mechanisms and their impact on cognitive processes that social sorting by sex occurs and is kept in place—by the exercise of force and the threat of force, by law, by persuasion, and by embedded cultural schemas that are internalized by individuals in all societies. Everywhere, local cultures support invidious distinctions by sex. As Jerome Bruner (1990) points out in his thoughtful book, *Acts of Meaning,* normatively oriented institutions—the law, educational institutions, and family structures—serve to enforce folk psychology, and folk psychology in turn serves to justify such enforcement. In this address, I shall explore some spheres in which the process of sex differentiation and the invidious comparisons between the sexes are especially salient.

The Position of Women in the United States and in the Profession of Sociology

It is fitting that my presidential address to the 101st meeting of the American Sociological Association should begin with an analytic eye on our profession. I became the ninth woman president in the ASA's 101 years of existence. The first woman president, Dorothy Swaine Thomas, was elected in 1952, the second, Mirra Komarovsky, almost 20 years later—two women presidents in the first seven decades of the existence of the association. Seven others have been chosen in the 23 years since.[11]

We nine women are symbolic of the positive changes in the position of women in the United States. Our case is situated at the high end of the continuum of women's access to equality. Similarly, our profession has devoted much research attention to women's position in society, though the findings of scholars on the subject are often not integrated with the profession's major theoretical and empirical foci. Many radical voices in the discipline refer to "gender issues" only ritualistically. This is so even though sociological research on gender is one of the major examples of "public sociology" of the past 40 years.

When I was a sociology graduate student at Columbia University in the 1960s, there were no women on the sociology faculty, as was the case at most major universities. The entire bibliography on women in the workplace, assembled for my thesis (1968) on women's exclusion from the legal profession, was exhausted in a few pages. However, it included Betty Friedan's ([1963] 1983) *The Feminine Mystique,* with its attack on Talcott Parsons's (1954) perspective on the functions of the nuclear family and his observation that women's role assignment in the home had exceedingly positive functional significance in that it prevented competition with their husbands (p. 191).[12] She also attacked Freud's ([1905] 1975) theories that women's biology is their destiny, that their feelings of inferiority are due to "penis envy," and his contention "that the woman has no penis often produces in the male a lasting depreciation of the other sex" (Freud 1938:595, footnote 1).

Friedan contributed to both the knowledge base of the social sciences and to the status of women. I believe she did more than any other person in modern times to change popular perceptions of women and their place in the world. While not the first to identify the dimensions of women's inequality,[13] Friedan put theory into practice, building on the attention she received when *The Feminine Mystique* was published. At a moment made ripe by the sensibilities of the civil rights movement and the growing participation of women in the labor force, she took up a challenge posed to her by Pauli Murray, the African American lawyer and civil rights activist, to create "an NAACP for women."[14] With the encouragement and participation of a small but highly motivated group of women in government, union offices, and professional life—white women, African American women, and women from Latin-American backgrounds (a fact that has gone unnoticed far too long)—and with the participation of the third woman ASA president, Alice Rossi, Friedan founded the National Organization for Women in 1966. Working through NOW, Friedan set out to provide political support for implementation of Title VII of the Civil Rights Act of 1964, which prohibited discrimination on the basis of sex as well as race, color, religion, and national origin. The changes accomplished by the organizational work of Friedan, and a number of other activists[15] and scholars,[16] were nothing short of a social revolution. It is a revolution of interest to sociologists not only for its creation of women's rights in employment and education but because *it became a natural field experiment establishing that there was no natural order of things relegating women to "women's work" and men to "men's work."* Yet, like most revolutions it was limited in its accomplishment of its stated goals and its principles are constantly under attack.

But the revolution did motivate research. There has been an explosion of scholarship on the extent of sex divides on macro and micro levels. Social scientists have documented in hundreds of thousands of pages of research the existence and consequences of subtle and overt discrimination against women of all strata and nationalities and the institutionalization of sexism.

The number of studies of the differentiation of women's and girls' situations in social life has grown exponentially in the 40 years since the beginning of the second wave of the women's movement. This work has pointed to women's and girls' vulnerabilities in the home and the workplace; their lower pay and lesser ability to accumulate wealth; their exploitation in times of war and other group conflicts; and the conditions under which an ethos of hyper-masculinity[17] in nations and subgroups controls women's lives. Some of the work of sociologists and of our colleagues in related disciplines has persuaded legislators and judges in many countries to acknowledge the inequalities and harsh treatment girls and women face. Pierre Sané, the Assistant Secretary General of UNESCO, has noted the synergy between social research and human rights activities, and he stresses in international meetings[18] that women's rights must be regarded as human rights and enforced by law.

Let us remember that the "woman question" as a serious point of inquiry for the social sciences is relatively new. In the past, wisdom on this subject came primarily from armchair ideologists, philosophers, legislators, judges, and religious leaders. With few exceptions,[19] these theorists asserted that women's subordinate position was for good reason—divine design, or for those not religiously inclined, *nature* mandated it. Today, a new species of theorists hold to this ideology—fundamentalist leaders in many nations, churches and religious sects in particular—but also scholars, some in the United States, in fields such as sociobiology and evolutionary psychology (e.g., Alexander 1979; Barash 1977; Trivers 1972; Wilson 1975). This was perhaps predictable, if my thesis is correct, because women had started to intrude into male ideological and physical turf in the academy and elsewhere in society, upsetting the practices of male affiliation. The prejudices that pass as everyday common sense also support this ideology, often with backing from sophisticated individuals responsible for making policies that affect girls and women.[20] They have been joined by some well-meaning women social scientists—a few possessing iconic status[21]—who have affirmed stereotypes about females' nature on the basis of poor or no data.[22]

Female Subordination in Global Context

The "woman question" is not just one among many raised by injustice, subordination, and differentiation. It is basic. The denigration and segregation of women is a major mechanism in reinforcing male bonds, protecting the institutions that favor them, and providing the basic work required for societies to function. To ignore this great social divide is to ignore a missing link in social analysis.

I will not illustrate my thesis about the persistence of the worldwide subordination of the female sex with pictures, graphs, or charts. Instead I call on readers' imaginations to picture some of the phenomena that illustrate my thesis. Imagine most women's lifetimes of everyday drudgery in households and factories; of struggles for survival without access to decent jobs. Imagine the horror of mass rapes by armed men in ethnic conflicts, and of rapes that occur inside the home by men who regard sexual access as their right.[23] Imagine also women's isolation and confinement behind walls and veils in many societies. Some examples are harder to imagine—for example, the 100 million women missing in the world, first brought to our attention by the economist Amartya Sen (1990), who alerted us to the bizarre sex ratios in South Asia, West Asia, and China. He pointed to the abandonment and systematic undernourishment of girls and women and to the poor medical care they receive in comparison to males. International human rights groups have alerted us to the selective destruction of female fetuses. It is estimated that in China and India alone, 10,000,000 females were aborted between 1978 and 1998 (Rao 2006). Also hidden are the child brides who live as servants in alien environments and who, should their husbands die, are abandoned to live in poverty and isolation. And there are the millions of girls and women lured or forced into sex work. In the Western world, only the occasional newspaper article brings to view the fact that African women face a 1 in 20 chance of dying during pregnancy (half a million die each year).[24] The persistent segregation of the workplace, in even the most sophisticated societies, in which girls and women labor in sex-labeled jobs that are tedious, mind-numbing, and highly supervised, is out of view. Unseen too are the countless beatings, slights, and defamations women and girls endure from men, including intimates, every day all over the world.

Insistence and Persistence on "Natural Differences"

These patterns are largely explained in the world as consequences stemming from natural causes or God's will. Here, I limit analysis mainly to the view of *natural causation* as the *master narrative*—the narrative that attributes role division of the sexes to biology. Some believe that early socialization cements the distinction. It is clear that strong religious beliefs in the natural subordination of women determine the role women must play in societies.

Biological explanation is the master narrative holding that men and women are naturally different and have different intelligences, physical abilities, and emotional traits. This view asserts that men are naturally suited to dominance and women are naturally submissive. The narrative holds that women's different intellect or emotional makeup is inconsistent with the capacity to work at prestigious jobs, be effective scholars, and lead others. Popularized accounts of gender difference have generated large followings.[25]

But the set of assumptions about basic differences are discredited by a body of reliable research. Although there seems to be an industry of scholarship identifying sex differences, it is important to note that scholarship showing only tiny or fluctuating differences, or none at all, is rarely picked up by the popular press. Most media reports (e.g., Brooks 2006, Tierney 2006) invariably focus on sex differences, following the lead of many journals that report tiny differences in distributions of males and females as significant findings (Epstein 1991a, 1999b). Further, the media rarely report the fact that a good proportion of the studies showing any differences are based on small numbers of college students persuaded to engage in experiments conducted in college laboratories and not in real world situations. Or, in the case of studies indicating the hormonal relationship between men's aggression and women's presumed lack of it, a number of studies are based on the behavior of laboratory animals. Other studies compare test scores of students in college, rarely reporting variables such as the class, race, and ethnicity of the population being studied. Even in these settings, the systematic research of social scientists has proved that males and females show almost no difference or shifting minor differences in measures of cognitive abilities (Hyde 2005) and emotions.[26] And there may be more evidence for similarity than even the scholarly public has access to, because when studies find no differences, the results might not be published in scholarly publications. The Stanford University cognitive psychologist Barbara Tversky (personal communication) notes that when she has sought to publish the results of experiments on a variety of spatial tasks that show no gender differences, journal editors have demanded that she and her collaborators take them out because they are null findings. Even so, we can conclude that under conditions of equality, girls and women perform and achieve at test levels that are the same as or similar to males—and, in many cases, they perform better.[27]

The American Psychological Association has reported officially that males and females are more alike than different when tested on most psychological variables. The APA's finding is based on Janet Hyde's 2005 analysis of 46 meta-analyses conducted recently in the United States. They conclude that gender roles and social context lead to the few differences. Further, they report that sex differences, though believed to be immutable, fluctuate with age and location.[28] Women manifest similar aggressive feelings although their expression of them is obliged to take different forms (Frodi, Macaulay, and Thome 1977). A 2006 report from the National Academy of Sciences found that after an exhaustive review of the scientific literature, including studies of brain structure and function, it could find no evidence of any significant biological factors causing the underrepresentation of women in science and mathematics.[29] Sociologists too have found women's aspirations are linked to their opportunities (Kaufman and Richardson 1982). I observe that like men, women want love, work, and recognition.

So, given similar traits, do women prefer dead-end and limited opportunity jobs; do they wish to work without pay in the home or to be always subject to the authority of men? In the past, some economists thought so. The Nobel Laureate Gary Becker (1981) proposed that women make rational choices to work in the home to free their husbands for paid labor. A number of other scholars follow the rational-choice model to explain women's poorer position in the labor force. Not only has the model proven faulty (England 1989, 1994), but history has proven such ideas wrong. The truth is that men have prevented the incursions of women into their spheres except when they needed women's labor power, such as in wartime, proving that women were indeed a reserve army of labor. As I found in my own research, when windows of opportunity presented themselves, women fought to join the paid labor force at every level, from manual craft work to the elite professions. Men resisted, seeking to preserve the boundaries of their work domains—from craft unionists to the top strata of medical, legal, and legislative practice (Chafe 1972; Epstein 1970, [1981] 1993; Frank 1980; Honey 1984; Kessler-Harris 1982; Lorber 1975, 1984; Milkman 1987; O'Farrell 1999; Rupp 1978).

Social and economic changes in other parts of the West, and in other parts of the world, provide natural field experiments to confirm this data from the United States. In the West, where women have always been employed in the unpaid, family workforce, a revolution in women's interest and participation in the paid workplace spiraled after the First World War. In the United States, from 1930 to 1970 the participation of married women ages 35 to 44 in the labor force moved from 10 percent to 46 percent and today it is 77 percent (Goldin 2006). The opening of elite colleges and universities to women students after the 1960s led progressively to their increased participation in employment in the professions and other top jobs. This was the direct result of a concerted effort to use the Civil Rights Act of 1964 to force the opening of these sectors. Ruth Bader Ginsburg and her associates in the

Women's Rights Project of the ACLU fought and won important battles in the Supreme Court and Judge Constance Baker Motley, the first African American woman to become a federal judge, ruled that large law firms had to recruit women on the same basis as men to comply with the equal treatment promised by the Civil Rights Act.

Yet even as the ideology of equality became widespread and brought significant changes, the worldwide status of women remained subordinate to that of men. Stable governments and a new prosperity led to something of a revolution in women's statuses in the United States and other countries in the West, notably in Canada with its new charter prohibiting discrimination. There was also an increase in women's employment in the paid labor force in the 15 countries of the European Union, including those countries that traditionally were least likely to provide jobs for women, although the statistics do not reveal the quality of the jobs (Norris 2006). And, of course, women's movements have been instrumental in making poor conditions visible. In countries of the Middle East, the East, and the Global South, women are beginning to have representation in political spheres, the professions, and commerce, although their percentage remains quite small. Women's lot rises or falls as a result of regime changes and economic changes and is always at severe risk.[30] But nowhere are substantial numbers of women in political control; nowhere do women have the opportunity to carry out national agendas giving women truly equal rights.[31]

Structural gains, accompanied by cultural gains, have been considerable in many places. Most governments have signed on to commitments to women's rights, although they are almost meaningless in many regimes that egregiously defy them in practice. And, of course, in many societies women have fewer rights than do men and find themselves worse off than they were a generation ago.[32]

In no society have women had clear access to the best jobs in the workplace, nor have they anywhere achieved economic parity with men. As Charles and Grusky (2004) document in their recent book, *Occupational Ghettos: The Worldwide Segregation of Women and Men,* sex segregation in employment persists all over the world, including in the United States and Canada. Women workers earn less than men even in the most gender-egalitarian societies. Charles and Grusky suggest that the disadvantage in employment is partly because women are clustered in "women's jobs"—jobs in the low-paid service economy or white-collar jobs that do not offer autonomy. These are typically occupational ghettos worldwide. While Charles and Grusky observe that women are crowded into the nonmanual sector, women increasingly do work in the globlized manufacturing economy—for example, in assembly line production that supplies the world with components for computers or in the clothing sweatshops in Chinatowns in the United States and around the world (Bose and Acosta-Belen 1995; Zimmerman, Litt, and Bose 2006; see also Bao 2001; Lee 1998; Salzinger 2003).

Many women in newly industrializing countries experienced a benefit from employment created by transnational corporations in the 1980s and '90s. They received income and independence from their families, but they remained in sex-segregated, low-wage work, subject to cutbacks when corporations sought cheaper labor markets. As to their suitability for heavy labor, it is common to see (as I have personally witnessed) women hauling rocks and stones in building sites in India and other places. Throughout the world, where water is a scarce commodity it is women who carry heavy buckets and vessels of water, usually on foot and over long distances, because this has been designated as a woman's job and men regard it as a disgrace to help them. Apparently, in much of the world, the guiding principle of essentialism labels as women's jobs those that are not physically easier, necessarily, but rather those that are avoided by men, pay little, and are under the supervision of men.

Of course, women have moved into some male-labeled jobs. As I noted in my book on the consequences of sex boundaries, *Deceptive Distinctions* (1988), the amazing decades of the 1970s and '80s showed that women could do work—men's work—that no one, including themselves, thought they could and they developed interests no one thought they had, and numbers of men welcomed them, or at least tolerated them.

My research shows that women may cross gender barriers into the elite professions that retain their male definition, such as medicine and law (Epstein [1981] 1993), when there is legal support giving them access to training and equal recruitment in combination with a shortage of personnel. Women made their most dramatic gains during a time of rapid economic growth in the Western world.

I first started research on women in the legal profession in the 1960s, when women constituted only 3 percent of practitioners (Epstein [1981] 1993). When I last assessed their achievements (Epstein 2001), women composed about 30 percent of practicing lawyers and about half of all law students. The same striking changes were happening in medicine (they are now almost half of all medical students [Magrane, Lang, and Alexander 2005]), and women were moving into legal and medical specialties once thought to be beyond their interests or aptitudes, such as corporate law and surgery. Yet, even with such advances they face multiple glass ceilings (Epstein et al. 1995). Only small percentages have attained high rank.[33] And it should come as no surprise that men of high rank,[34] the popular media (Belkin 2003), and right-wing commentators (Brooks 2006; Tierney, 2006) insist that it is women's own choice to limit their aspirations and even to drop out of the labor force. But this has not been women's pattern. Most educated women have continuous work histories. It is true, however, that many women's ambitions to reach the very top of their professions are undermined. For one thing, they generally face male hostility when they cross conventional boundaries and perform "men's work."[35] For another, they face inhospitable environments in male-dominated work settings in which coworkers not only are wary of women's ability but visibly disapprove of their presumed neglect of their families. Women generally face unrelieved burdens of care work in the United States, with few social supports (Coser 1974; Gornick 2003; Williams 2000). And they face norms that this work demands their *personal* attention—a *female's attention.*

Even in the most egalitarian societies, a myriad of subtle prejudices and practices are used by men in gatekeeping positions to limit women's access to the better, male-labeled jobs and ladders of success, for example, partnership tracks in large law firms (Epstein et al. 1995) Alternative routes for women, "Mommy tracks" have been institutionalized—touted as a benefit—but usually result in stalled careers (Bergmann and Helburn 2002). Husbands who wish to limit their own work hours to assist working wives usually encounter severe discrimination as well. Individual men who are seen as undermining the system of male advantage find themselves disciplined and face discrimination (Epstein et al. 1999, Williams 2000). In the United States this may lead to the loss of a promotion or a job. In other places in the world, the consequences are even more dire.[36]

In the current "best of all worlds," ideologies of difference and, to use Charles Tilly's (1998) concept, "exploitation and opportunity hoarding" by men in control keep the top stratum of law and other professions virtually sex segregated. Gatekeepers today don't necessarily limit entry, as that would place them in violation of sex discrimination laws in the United States or put them in an uncomfortable position, given modern Western ideologies of equality. But powerful men move only a small percentage of the able women they hire (often hired in equal numbers with men) upward on the path toward leadership and decision making, especially in professions and occupations experiencing slow growth. Most rationalize, with the approval of conventional wisdom, that women's own decisions determine their poor potential for achieving power.

Inequality in the workplace is created and reinforced by inequality in education. Newspaper headlines reported that more women than men get B.A.s in the United States today (Lewin 2006a) "leaving men in the dust." But a report a few days later noted that the increase is due to older women going back to school, and that women's degrees are in traditional women's fields (Lewin 2006b).

But women's performance and acceptance in the world of higher education in the United States is the good news! Consider the rest of the world. In many countries girls are denied *any* education. Consider, for example, the case of Afghanistan, where the Taliban still are attempting to resume power. In July 2006, they issued warnings to parents that girls going to school may get acid thrown in their faces or be murdered (Coghlan 2006).

Consider that in Southern Asia 23.5 million girls do not attend school and in Central and West Africa virtually half of all girls are also excluded (Villalobos 2006). While poverty contributes to poor educational opportunities for boys as well as girls in many parts of the world, girls' restrictions are far greater. Some fundamentalist societies permit women to get a higher education, but this is to prepare them for work in segregated conditions where they serve other women.

The sex segregation of labor as measured by sophisticated sociologists and economists does not even acknowledge women's labor *outside* the wage-earning structure. Women and girls labor behind the walls of their homes, producing goods that provide income for their families, income they have no control over. Thus, millions of girls and women are not even counted in the labor force, although they perform essential work in the economy (Bose, Feldberg, and Sokoloff 1987).[37]

In addition, females can be regarded as a commodity themselves. They are computed as a means of barter in tribal families that give their girls (often before puberty) to men outside their tribe or clan who want wives to produce children and goods. Men also trade their daughters to men of other tribes as a form of compensation for the killing of a member of another tribe or other reasons.[38] Harmony is re-equilibrated through the bodies of females.

There is much more to report about the roles and position of women in the labor force world-wide—my life's work—but there are other spheres in which females everywhere are mired in subordinate roles. Chief among them are the family and the social and cultural structures that keep women both segregated and in a state of symbolic and actual "otherness," undermining their autonomy and dignity. Nearly everywhere, women are regarded as "others."[39]

Mechanisms Creating "Otherness"

To some extent, women are subject to the process of social speciation—a term that Kai Erikson (1996) introduced (modifying the concept of pseudospeciation offered by Erik Erikson) to refer to the fact that humans divide into various groups who regard themselves as "the foremost species" and then feel that others ought to be kept in their place by "conquest or the force of harsh custom" (Erikson 1996:52). Harsh customs and conquest certainly ensure the subordination of girls and women. I shall consider some of these below.

Kin Structures

In many societies brides are required to leave their birth homes and enter as virtual strangers into the homes of their husbands and their husbands' kin. Because of the practice of patrilocality they usually have few or no resources—human or monetary. Marrying very young, they enter these families with the lowest rank and no social supports. About one in seven girls in the developing world gets married before her 15th birthday according to the Population Council, an international research group (Bearak 2006). Local and international attempts to prevent this practice have been largely unsuccessful.[40]

In exploring the actual and symbolic segregation of women I have been inspired by the work of Mounira Charrad in her 2001 prize-winning book *States and Women's Rights: The Making of Postcolonial Tunisia, Algeria, and Morocco.* The work of Val Moghadam (2003) and Roger Friedland (2002) also informs this analysis. Writing of the relative status of women, Charrad points to the iron grip of patrilineal kin groups in North African societies. She notes how Islamic family law has legitimized the extended male-centered patrilineage that serves as the foundation of kin-based solidarities within tribal groups so that state politics and tribal politics converge. This supports the patriarchal power not only of husbands, but also of all male kin over women so that the clan defines its boundaries through a family law that rests on the exploitation of women. Her study shows how Islamic family law (Sharia) provides a meaningful symbol of national unity in the countries of the Maghreb. This has changed in Tunisia, but it remains the case for other societies—Iraq, Saudi Arabia, Jordan, Kuwait, Afghanistan, southeastern Turkey, parts of Iran, and southern Egypt. As Moghadam (2003) points out, the gender dimension of the Afghan conflict is prototypical of other conflicts today. During periods of strife, segregation and subordination of women becomes a sign of cultural identity. We see it clearly in the ideologies of Hamas and Hezbollah, Iran, Chechnya, and other Islamic groups and societies, and in the ideologies of fundamentalist Christian and Jewish groups. Representations of women are deployed during processes of revolution and state building to preserve group boundaries within larger societies with competing ideologies, and when power is being reconstituted, linking women either to modernization and progress or to cultural rejuvenation and religious orthodoxy.

Few social scientists have paid attention to the role of kin structures and their accompanying conceptual structures in the minds of players in national and international politics, but I believe this negligence persists at our peril as we experience conflicts between kin-based collectivities in the world.

Of course, human sexuality has much to do with the cultural sex divide. The fact that men desire women sexually, and that women also desire men, means that they are destined to live together no matter what the culture and family structures in which they live. And sexuality could, and can, create equality through bonds of connection and affection. As William Goode (1959) points out in an important but perhaps forgotten paper, "The Theoretical Importance of Love," love is a universal emotion. As such it threatens social structures because the ties between men and women could be stronger than the bonds between men. Thus, everywhere the affiliations made possible by love are contained in various ways.

In societies in which marriage is embedded in a larger kin structure beyond the nuclear family, the practices and rules of domicile and the conventions around it have the potential to undermine the possibility of a truly affective marital tie, one that could integrate women in the society. A couple may face a wall of separation—apartheid in the home in separate parts of the compound or house. Or, they may be community-bound or home-bound in fundamentalist religious groups within larger secular societies such as the United States (e.g., the Jewish Satmar community in New York [where women are not permitted to drive] [Winston 2005] or some Christian fundamentalist communities where women are required to home-school their children).

I shall now focus on some other symbolic uses of sex distinctions that facilitate the subordination of women.

Honor

Females are designated as carriers of honor in many societies. Their "virtue" is a symbolic marker of men's group boundaries. As we know from Mary Douglas (1966) and others, we can think about any social practice in terms of purity and danger. In many societies, females are the designated carriers of boundary distinctions. Their conformity to norms is regarded as the representation of the dignity of the group, while males typically have much greater latitude to engage in deviant behavior. To achieve and maintain female purity, women's behavior is closely monitored and restricted. As Friedland (2002) writes, religious nationalists direct "their attention to the bodies of women—covering, separating and regulating" (p. 396) them, in order "to masculinize the public sphere, to contain the erotic energies of heterosexuality within the family seeking to masculinize collective representations, to make the state male, a virile collective subject, the public status of women's bodies is a critical site and source for religious nationalist political mobilization" (p. 401).

The idea that girls must remain virgins until they marry or their entire family will suffer dishonor is used as a mechanism for women's segregation and subordination all over the world. It is also used as justification for the murder of many young women by male family members claiming to cleanse the girls' supposed dishonor from the family.[41] In particular, we see this at play in parts of the Middle East and among some Muslim communities in the diaspora.

When a woman strays from her prescribed roles, seeks autonomy, or is believed to have had sex with a man outside of marriage, killing her is regarded as a reasonable response by her very own relatives, often a father or brother. In Iraq, at last count, since the beginning of the present war, there have been 2,000 honor killings (Tarabay 2006), and United Nations officials estimate 5,000 worldwide (BBC 2003). In the summer of 2006, the *New York Times* reported that in Turkey, a society becoming more religiously conservative, girls regarded as errant because they moved out of the control of their parents or chose a boyfriend, thus casting dishonor on the family, are put in situations in which they are expected and pressured to commit suicide. Suicide spares a family the obligation to murder her and face prosecution (Bilefsky 2006). Elsewhere, such murders are barely noted by the police.

Female circumcision is also intended to preserve women's honor. In many areas of the African continent, girls are subjected to genital cutting as a prelude to marriage and as a technique to keep them from having pleasure during sex, which, it is reasoned, may lead them to an independent choice of mate.

Conferring on women the symbolism of sexual purity as a basis of honor contributes to their vulnerability. In today's genocidal warfare, the mass rape of women by marauding forces is not just due to the sexual availability of conquered women. Rape is used as a mechanism of degradation. If the men involved in the Bosnian and Darfur massacres regarded rape as an atrocity and a *dishonor* to their cause, it could not have been used so successfully as a tool of war. Further, we know that the Bosnian and Sudanese rape victims, like women who have been raped in Pakistan, India, and other places, are regarded as defiled and are shunned, as are the babies born of such rapes.

Clothing as a Symbolic Tool for Differentiation

The chador and veil are tools men use to symbolize and maintain women's honor. Although men, with some exceptions,[42] wear Western dress in much of the world, women's clothing is used to symbolize their cultures' confrontations with modernity, in addition to clothing's symbolic roles. Presumably worn to assure modesty and to protect women's honor, the clothing prescribed, even cultural relativists must admit, serves to restrict women's mobility. Hot and uncomfortable, women cannot perform tasks that require speed and mobility, and it prevents women from using motorbikes and bicycles, the basic means of transportation in poor societies. Distinctive clothing is not restricted to the Third World. Fundamentalist groups in Europe and the United States also mandate clothing restrictions for women.[43]

Of course, clothing is used to differentiate women and men in all societies. In the past, Western women's clothing was also restrictive (e.g., long skirts and corsets) and today, as women have moved toward greater equality, women and men are permitted to wear similar garb (such as jeans and t-shirts). Of course, fashion prescribes more sexually evocative (thus distinctive) clothing for women than it does for men.

Time and Space

How can we speak of the otherness and subordination of women without noting the power of the variables of time and space in the analysis? In every society the norms governing the use of time and space are gendered (Epstein and Kalleberg 2004). People internalize feelings about the proper use of time and space as a result of the normative structure. Worldwide, the boundaries of time and space are constructed to offer men freedom and to restrict women's choices. In most of the world, women rise earlier than do men and start food preparation; they eat at times men don't. Further, sex segregation of work in and outside the home means a couple's primary contact may be in the bedroom. If women intrude on men's space they may violate a taboo and be punished for it. Similarly, men who enter into women's spaces do so only at designated times and places. The taboo elements undermine the possibility of easy interaction, the opportunity to forge friendships, to connect, and to create similar competencies. In the Western world, working different shifts is common (Presser 2003), which also results in segregation of men and women.

There are rules in every society, some by law and others by custom, that specify when and where women may go, and whether they can make these journeys alone or must appear with a male relative. Some segregation is to protect men from women's temptations (e.g., Saudi Arabia, Iran, the Satmar sect in Monsey, NY) and some to protect women from men's sexual advances (e.g., Mexico, Tokyo, Mumbai). But the consequence is that men overwhelmingly are allotted more space and territorialize public space.

A common variable in the time prescription for women is surveillance; women are constrained to operate within what I am calling *role zones.* In these, their time is accounted for and prescribed. They have less *free* time. In our own Western society, women note that the first thing to go when they attempt to work and have children is "free time." Free time is typically enjoyed by the powerful, and it gives them the opportunity to engage in the politics of social life. Most people who work at a subsistence level, refugees, and those who labor in jobs not protected by the authority of the dominant group, don't have free time either. Slave owners own the time of their slaves.

A Theory of Female Subordination

All of this leads me to ask a basic sociological question. Why does the subordination of women and girls persist no matter how societies change in other ways? How does half the world's population manage to hold and retain power over the other half? And what are we to make of the women who comply?

The answers lie in many of the practices I have described and they remain persuasive with a global perspective. I propose an even more basic explanation for the persistence of inequality, and often a reversion to inequality, when equality seems to be possible or near attainment. In *Deceptive Distinctions* (1988) I proposed the theory that the division of labor in society assigns women the most important survival tasks—reproduction and gathering and preparation of food. All over the world, women do much of the reproductive work, ensuring the continuity of society. They do this both in physical terms and in symbolic terms. Physically, they do so through childbirth and child care. They do much of the daily work any social group needs for survival. For example, half of the world's food, and up to 80 percent in developing countries, is produced by women (Food and Agriculture Organization of the United Nations n.d.; Women's World Summit Foundation 2006). They also prepare the food at home, work in the supermarkets, behind the counters, and on the conveyor belts that package it. In their homes and in schools, they produce most preschool and primary school education. They take care of the elderly and infirm. They socialize their children in the social skills that make interpersonal communication possible. They are the support staffs for men. This is a good deal—no, a great deal—for the men.

Controlling women's labor and behavior is a mechanism for male governance and territoriality. Men's authority is held jealously. Men legitimate their behavior through ideological and theological constructs that justify their domination. Further, social institutions reinforce this.[44]

I shall review the mechanisms:

We know about the use and threat of force (Goode 1972).[45] We know as well about the role of law and justice systems that do not accord women the same rights to protection, property, wealth, or even education enjoyed by men. We know that men control and own guns and the means of transport, and they often lock women out of membership and leadership of trade unions, political parties, religious institutions, and other powerful organizations. We know too that huge numbers of men feel justified in threatening and punishing females who deviate from male-mandated rules in public and private spaces. That's the strong-arm stuff.

But everywhere, in the West as well as in the rest of the world, women's segregation and subjugation is also done *culturally* and through *cognitive* mechanisms that reinforce existing divisions of rights and labor and award men authority over women. Internalized cultural schemas reinforce men's views that their behavior is legitimate and persuade women that their lot is just. The media highlight the idea that women and men think differently and naturally gravitate to their social roles.[46] This is more than just "pluralistic ignorance" (Merton [1948] 1963). Bourdieu ([1979] 1984) reminds us that dominated groups often contribute to their own subordination because of perceptions shaped by the conditions of their existence—the dominant system made of binary oppositions! Using Eviatar Zerubavel's (1997) term, "mindscapes" set the stage for household authorities and heads of clans, tribes, and communities to separate and segregate women in the belief that the practice is inevitable and right. Such mindscapes also persuade the females in their midst to accept the legitimacy and inevitability of their subjection, and even to defend it, as we have seen lately in some academic discourses.

The mindscapes that legitimate women's segregation are the cognitive translations of ideologies that range the spectrum from radical fundamentalism to difference feminism; all are grounded in cultural-religious or pseudoscientific views that women have different emotions, brains, aptitudes, ways of thinking, conversing, and imagining. Such mindsets are legitimated every day in conventional understandings expressed from the media, pulpits, boardrooms, and in departments of universities. Psychologists call them schemas (Brewer and Nakamura 1984)—culturally set definitions that people internalize. Gender operates as a cultural "superschema" (Roos and Gatta 2006) that shapes interaction and cues stereotypes (Ridgeway 1997). Schemas that define femaleness and maleness are basic to all societies. Schemas also define insiders and outsiders and provide definitions of justice and equality.

In popular speech, philosophical musings, cultural expressions, and the banter of everyday conversation, people tend to accept the notion of difference. They accept its inevitability and are persuaded of the legitimacy of segregation, actual or symbolic. Thus, acceptance of difference perspectives—the idea that women often have little to offer to the group, may result in rules that forbid women from speaking in the company of men (in a society governed by the Taliban) or may result in senior academics' selective deafness to the contributions of a female colleague in a university committee room.

Conclusion

In conclusion I want to reiterate certain observations:

Intrinsic qualities are attributed to women that have little or nothing to do with their actual characteristics or behavior. Because those attributions are linked to assigned roles their legitimation is an ongoing project. Changing these ideas would create possibilities for changing the status quo and threaten the social institutions in which men have the greatest stake and in which some women believe they benefit.

Is women's situation different from that of men who, by fortune, color of skin, or accident of birth also suffer from exploitation by the powerful? I am claiming *yes,* because they carry not only the hardships—sometimes relative hardships—but the ideological and cognitive overlay that defines their subordination as legitimate and normal. Sex and gender are the organizing markers in all societies. In no country, political group, or community are men defined as lesser human beings than their *female* counterparts. But almost everywhere women are so defined.

Why is this acceptable? And why does it persist?

So many resources are directed to legitimating females' lower place in society. So few men inside the power structure are interested in inviting them in. And so many women and girls accept the Orwellian notion that restriction is freedom, that suffering is pleasure, that silence is power.[47]

Of course this is not a static condition, nor, I hope, an inevitable one. Women in the Western world, and in various sectors of the rest of the world, have certainly moved upward in the continuum toward equality. Thirty-five years ago I noted how women in the legal profession in the United States were excluded from the informal networks that made inclusion and mobility possible. Now, noticeable numbers have ventured over the barriers. Similarly, there has been a large increase in the numbers of women who have entered the sciences,[48] business, medicine, and veterinary medicine (Cox and Alm 2005). This has changed relatively swiftly. Women didn't develop larger brains—nor did their reasoning jump from left brain to right brain or the reverse. Nor did they leave Venus for Mars. Rather, they learned that they could not be barred from higher education and they could get appropriate jobs when they graduated. The problem is no longer one of qualifications or entry but of promotion and inclusion into the informal networks leading to the top. But the obstacles are great.

In his review of cognitive sociological dynamics, DiMaggio (1997) reminds us of Merton's notion of "pluralistic ignorance," which is at work when people act with reference to shared collective opinions that are empirically incorrect. There would not be a firm basis for the subordinate condition of females were there not a widespread belief, rooted in folk culture, in their essential difference from males in ability and emotion. This has been proven time and time again in research in the "real" world of work and family institutions (e.g., Epstein et al. 1995) and laboratory observations (Berger, Cohen, and Zelditch 1966; Frodi et al. 1977; Ridgeway and Smith-Lovin 1999).

We know full well that there are stories and master social narratives accepted by untold millions of people that have no basis in what social scientists would regard as evidence. The best examples are the basic texts of the world's great religions. But there are also societywide beliefs of other kinds. Belief systems are powerful. And beliefs that are unprovable or proven untrue often capture the greatest number of believers. Sometimes, they are simply the best stories.

We in the social sciences have opened the gates to a better understanding of the processes by which subordinated groups suffer because the use of *categories* such as race and ethnicity rank human beings so as to subordinate, exclude, and exploit them (Tilly 1998). However, relatively few extend this insight to the category of gender or sex. The sexual divide so defines social life, and so many people in the world have a stake in upholding it, that it is the most resistant of all categories to change. Today, Hall and Lamont (forthcoming; Lamont 2005) are proposing that the most productive societies are those with porous boundaries between categories of people. Perhaps there is an important incentive in a wider understanding of this idea. Small groups of men may prosper by stifling women's potential, but prosperous nations benefit from women's full participation and productivity in societies. Societies might achieve still more if the gates were truly open.

Sociologists historically have been committed to social change to achieve greater equality in the world, in both public and private lives. But in this address I challenge our profession to take this responsibility in our scholarship and our professional lives; to observe, to reveal, and to strike down the conceptual and cultural walls that justify inequality on the basis of sex in all of society's institutions—to transgress this ever-present boundary—for the sake of knowledge and justice.

Acknowledgments

Direct correspondence to Cynthia Fuchs Epstein, Department of Sociology, Graduate Center, City University of New York, 365 Fifth Avenue, New York, NY 10016 (cepstein@gc.cuny.edu). I thank Mitra Rastegar for superb research assistance. I am grateful also to Howard Epstein for dedicated editorial help over many incarnations of this paper and to Kathleen Gerson, Jerry Jacobs, Brigid O'Farrell, Valentine Moghadam, Carol Sanger, and Hella Winston for helpful comments on versions of the address to the ASA.

Notes

1. Brubaker also cites the contributions of Rothbart and Taylor 1992; Hirshfield 1996; and Gil-White 1999 to this perspective.
2. Duster (2006) does include gender.
3. For example, see Epstein 1988; Lorber 1994; Connell 1987; Ridgeway 2006; Bussey and Bandura 1999; Tavris 1992.
4. I have used these commonly used terms, but alternative words such as "trans" and "intersex" are deemed more appropriate by some scholars and advocates.
5. I offer this concept following Becker (1963) who writes of "moral entrepreneurs;" Brubaker (2004) who writes of "ethnopolitical entrepreneurs;" and Fine (1996) who writes of "reputational entrepreneurs."
6. A number of sociologists have specifically called for a greater integration of feminist theory and studies within the mainstream of American sociology (e.g., Chafetz 1984, 1997; Laslett 1996; Stacey and Thome 1985).
7. I am not the first to make this plea (e.g., see Acker 1973; Blumberg 1978; Chafetz 1997).
8. There is, of course, a growing body of scholarship on women of color. See for example, Baca Zinn and Dill (1996); Collins (1998); and Hondagneu-Sotelo (2003).
9. Martin (2004) and Lorber (1994) both consider gender to be a social institution.
10. The most obvious example is the right to have an abortion, which through *Roe v. Wade* (1973) withdrew from the states the power to prohibit abortions during the first six months of pregnancy. In 1989, *Webster* v. *Reproductive Health Services* gave some of that power back. Since that time, President Bush and other legislators proposed a constitutional amendment banning abortions, giving fetuses more legal rights than women. This remains a deeply contested issue in American

politics (Kaminer 1990). The National Women's Law Center has expressed concern that the current Supreme Court cannot be counted on to preserve women's "hard-won legal gains, especially in the areas of constitutional rights to privacy and equal protection" (2006). In many other places in the world women are not protected by their governments. In 2005, the World Health Organization found that domestic and sexual violence is widespread. Amnesty International reports tens of thousands of women are subjected to domestic violence, giving as examples Republic of Georgia and Bangladesh where, when women go to the authorities after being strangled, beaten, or stabbed, they are told to reconcile with their husbands (Lew and Moawad 2006).

11. Information from ASA: http://www.asanet.org/governance/pastpres.html. The current president, Frances Fox Piven, brings the number of women presidents to 10 in 102 years.
12. It is curious that his further observation that the relationship was also "an important source of strain" (p. 191) has rarely been acknowledged, although Friedan did note this in *The Feminine Mystique*.
13. These include (but of course, the list is incomplete) John Stuart Mill and Harriet Taylor, Mary Wollstonecraft, Elizabeth Cady Stanton, Lucretia Mott, Sojourner Truth, Charlotte Perkins Gilman, Emmeline Pankhurst, W.E.B. DuBois, Emma Goldman, and in the years just preceding Friedan's book, Simone de Beauvoir (1949), to whom she dedicated *The Feminine Mystique*, and Mirra Komarovsky (1946; [1953] 2004).
14. I interviewed Friedan in 1999 about the origins of NOW for an article I was writing for *Dissent* (Epstein 1999a).
15. One was Gloria Steinem, who worked with Friedan to establish the National Women's Political Caucus. Steinem became a notable public speaker on behalf of women's rights and established the national magazine *MS.*, which reports on serious women's issues.
16. Friedan recruited me as well in the formation of the New York City Chapter of NOW in 1966. Through her auspices I presented a paper on the negative social consequences for women of segregated help-wanted ads in newspapers at hearings of the EEOC in 1967 on Guidelines for Title VII of the Civil Rights Act and to establish guidelines for the Office of Federal Contract Compliance in 1968.
17. For work on men see especially the work of Kimmel (1996); Connell (1987); Collinson, Knights, and Collinson (1990); and Collinson and Hearn (1994).
18. The most recent was The International Forum on the Social Science-Policy Nexus in Buenos Aires February 20 to 24, 2006.
19. For example, John Stuart Mill (1869) *The Subjection of Women*.
20. A pinpointed policy was enacted recently. Seeking to override a 1972 federal law barring sex discrimination in education (Title IX of the Civil Rights Act of 1964), the Bush administration is giving public school districts new latitude to expand the number of single-sex classes and single-sex schools (Schemo 2006). My own review of studies on the impact of segregated education shows no benefits (Epstein 1997; Epstein and Gambs 2001).
21. Here I refer to a number of "standpoint" theorists such as Belenky et al. (1986), Smith (1990), Hartstock (1998), and of course Carol Gilligan (1982) whose initial study showing a difference in boys' and girls' moral values and moral development was based on eight girls and eight boys in a local school and 27 women considering whether to have an abortion. See also Helen Fisher (1982), an evolutionary anthropologist. These views typically assert that women are naturally more caring, more accommodating, and averse to conflict.
22. See my analysis of this literature in Epstein (1988).
23. For more horrors see Parrot and Cummings (2006).
24. Perhaps the best known eye into this world is that of Nicholas Kristof, the *New York Times* writer, whose Op Ed articles chronicle the horrors faced by women in Africa and the inaction of Western societies to redress them (for example, the United States cut off funding to the United Nations Population Fund, an agency that has led the effort to reduce maternal deaths, because of false allegations it supports abortion) (Kristof 2006).
25. The works of John Gray (1992), the author of *Men Are from Mars, Women Are from Venus* and spin-off titles have sold over 30 million copies in the United States. See also Deborah Tannen's (1990) *You Just Don't Understand* on the presumed inability of

men and women to understand each other on various dimensions, repudiated by the work of the linguistic scholar Elizabeth Aries (1996).

26. There has been a recent flurry over reported differences in male and female brains (cf. Brizendine 2006; Bell et al. 2006) and reports of a 3 to 4 percentage difference in IQ. The brain studies are usually based on very small samples and the IQ studies on standardized tests in which the differences reported are at the very end of large distributions that essentially confirm male/female similarities (see Epstein 1988 for a further analysis).
27. A 2006 *New York Times* report shows that women are getting more B.A.s than are men in the United States. However, in the highest income families, men age 24 and below attend college as much as, or slightly more than their sisters, according to the American Council on Education. The article also reports that women are obtaining a disproportionate number of honors at elite institutions such as Harvard, the University of Wisconsin, UCLA, and some smaller schools such as Florida Atlantic University (Lewin 2006a). A comparison of female and male math scores varies with the test given. Females score somewhat lower on the SAT-M but differences do not exist on the American College Test (ACT) or on untimed versions of the SAT-M (Bailey n.d.).
28. Girls even perform identically in math until high school when they are channeled on different tracks. In Great Britain, they do better than males, as noted in the ASA statement contesting the remarks of then Harvard President Lawrence Summers questioning the ability of females to engage in mathematics and scientific research (American Sociological Association 2005; see also Boaler and Sengupta-Irving 2006).
29. The panel blamed environments that favor men, continuous questioning of women's abilities and commitment to an academic career, and a system that claims to reward based on merit but instead rewards traits that are socially less acceptable for women to possess (Fogg 2006).
30. Hartmann, Lovell, and Werschkul (2004) show how, in the recession of March to November 2001, there was sustained job loss for women for the first time in 40 years. The economic downturn affected women's employment, labor force participation, and wages 43 months after the start of the recession.
31. In Scandinavian countries, women have achieved the most political representation: Finland (37.5 percent of parliament seats), Norway (36.4 percent of parliament seats), Sweden (45.3 percent of parliament seats), and Denmark (38 percent of parliament seats) (U.N. Common Database 2004; Dahlerup n.d.). Of course, women in some societies still do not have the right to vote, and in a few, like Kuwait, where they have just gotten the vote, it is unclear whether they have been able to exercise it independently.
32. This is the case in Egypt, Iran, Iraq, Gaza, and Lebanon as fundamentalist groups have gained power, even in those regimes that are formally secular.
33. The current figure for women partners in large law firms (those with more than 250 lawyers) in the United States is 17 percent, although women are one-half of the recruits in these firms (National Association for Law Placement cited in O'Brien 2006; Nicholson 2006).
34. A national survey of 1,500 professors (as yet unpublished) at all kinds of institutions in the United States conducted by Neil Gross of Harvard and Solon Simmons of George Mason University shows that most professors don't agree that discrimination—intentional or otherwise—is the main reason that men hold so many more positions than do women in the sciences (Jaschik 2006).
35. In studies of jobs dominated by men that are seen as requiring traits that distinguish men as superior to women in intellect or strength, it is reported that men's pride is punctured if women perform them (see Chetkovich 1997 on firefighters; Collinson, Knights, and Collinson 1990 on managers).
36. For example, when the magazine publisher Ali Mohaqeq returned to Afghanistan in 2004 after a long exile he was imprisoned for raising questions about women's rights in the new "democracy." Afghan courts claimed his offense was to contravene the teachings of Islam by printing essays that questioned legal discrimination against women (Witte 2005).
37. Women have been unpaid workers on family farms or in small businesses, taking in boarders, and doing factory outwork (see Bose et al. 1987 for the United States; Bose and Acosta-Belen 1995 for Latin America; and Hsiung 1996 for Taiwan).
38. There are numerous references on the Web to the use of women given in marriage to another tribe

or group in the reports of Amnesty International, for example in Papua New Guinea, Afghanistan, Pakistan, and Fiji.

39. The characterization of women as "other" was most notably made by Simone de Beauvoir ([1949] 1993) in her book, *The Second Sex.*
40. Struggles between human rights activists in and out of government and fundamentalist regimes have shifted upward and downward on such matters as raising the age of marriage of girls. For example, attempts by Afghanistan's King Abanullah in the 1920s to raise the age of marriage and institute education for girls enraged the patriarchal tribes who thwarted his regime. Fifty years later a socialist government enacted legislation to change family law to encourage women's employment, education, and choice of spouse. The regime failed in the early 1990s due to internal rivalries and a hostile international climate (Moghadam 2003:270) and the Taliban took power. In the early 1990s they exiled women to their homes, denied them access to education and opportunities to work for pay, and even denied them the right to look out of their windows.
41. A United Nations (2002) report found that there were legislative provisions "allowing for partial or complete defense" in the case of an honor killing in: Argentina, Bangladesh, Ecuador, Egypt, Guatemala, Iran, Israel, Jordan, Lebanon, Peru, Syria, Turkey, Venezuela, and the Palestinian National Authority (of course law does not equal practice). For example, in Pakistan and Jordan honor killings are outlawed but they occur nevertheless.
42. In demonstrations in societies led by religious leaders, men typically wear Western style shirts and trousers although their leaders typically choose clerics' robes and turbans. Leaders of countries outside the "Western" orbit often choose distinctive dress—robes, beards, open neck shirts, and other costumes for ceremonial occasions or to make political statements.
43. Hella Winston (personal communication, September 30, 2006) told me that in the orthodox Jewish community of New Square in New York State, a recent edict by the Rabbi reminded women they were to wear modest dress, specifying that "sleeves must be to the end of the bone, and [to] not wear narrow clothing or short clothing." They were not to ride bikes or speak loudly.
44. Where religious laws govern such areas of civic life as family relations, inheritance, and punishment for crimes, for example, they invariably institutionalize women's subordinate status.
45. As one of many possible examples: when hundreds of women gathered in downtown Tehran on July 31, 2006 to protest institutionalized sex discrimination in Iran (in areas such as divorce, child custody, employment rights, age of adulthood, and court proceedings where a woman's testimony is viewed as half of a man's), 100 male and female police beat them. Reports also noted a tightening of the dress code and segregation on buses and in some public areas such as parks, sidewalks, and elevators. Another demonstration on March 8, 2006 was dispersed as police dumped garbage on the heads of participants (Stevens 2006).
46. The recent book by Louann Brizendine (2006), which asserts that the female and male brains are completely different, offering such breezy accounts as "woman is weather, constantly changing and hard to predict" and "man is mountain," has been on the top 10 on the Amazon.com book list and led to her prominent placement on ABC's 20/20 and morning talk shows. Thanks to Troy Duster for passing this on.
47. For example, a recent poll cited in the *New York Times* (June 8, 2006) indicates that a majority of women in Muslim countries do not regard themselves as unequal (Andrews 2006). Of course, this attitude is widespread throughout the world, including Western societies.
48. Comparing percentages of women attaining doctorates in the sciences from 1970–71 to 2001–2002 the increases were: Engineering .2–17.3; Physics 2.9–15.5; Computer Science 2.3–22.8; Mathematics 7.6–29.

References

Acker, Joan. 1973. "Women and Social Stratification: A Case of Institutional Sexism." Pp. 174–82 in *Changing Women in a Changing Society,* edited by Joan Huber. Chicago, IL: University of Chicago Press.

Alexander, Richard D. 1979. *Darwinism and Human Affairs.* Seattle, WA: University of Washington Press.

American Sociological Association. 2005. "ASA Council Statement on the Causes of Gender Differences in Science and Math Career Achievement"

(February 28). Retrieved September 21, 2006 (http://www2.asanet.org/footnotes/mar05/indexthree.html).

Andrews, Helena. 2006. "Muslim Women Don't See Themselves as Oppressed, Survey Finds." *New York Times,* June 7, p. A9.

Aries, Elizabeth. 1996. *Men and Women in Interaction: Reconsidering the Differences.* New York: Oxford University Press.

Baca Zinn, Maxine and Bonnie Thornton Dill. 1996. "Theorizing Difference from Multiracial Feminism." *Feminist Studies* 22:321–31.

Bailey, Justin P. n. d. "Men are from Earth, Women are from Earth: Rethinking the Utility of the Mars/Venus Analogy." Retrieved September 28, 2006 (www.framingham.edu/joct/pdf/J.Bailey.1.pdf).

Bao, Xiaolan. 2001. *Holding Up More Than Half the Sky: Chinese Women Garment Workers in New York City, 1948–92.* Urbana, IL and Chicago, IL: University of Illinois Press.

Barash, David P. 1977. *Sociobiology and Behavior.* New York: Elsevier.

Barth, Frederik, 1969. "Introduction." Pp. 9–38 in *Ethnic Groups and Boundaries: The Social Organization of Cultural Difference,* edited by Frederik Barth. London, England: Allen & Unwin.

Basow, Susan A. 1995. "Student Evaluation of College Professors: When Gender Matters." *Journal of Educational Psychology* 87:656–65.

BBC. 2003. "Speaking Out Over Jordan 'Honour Killings.'" Retrieved September 21, 2006 (http://news.bbc.co.uk/2/hi/middle_east/2802305.stm).

Bearak, Barry. 2006. "The Bride Price." *New York Times Magazine,* July 9, p. 45.

Beauvoir.Simone de. [1949] 1993. *The Second Sex.* New York: Alfred A. Knopf.

Becker, Gary. 1981. *A Treatise on the Family.* Cambridge, MA: Harvard University Press.

Becker, Howard. 1963. *Outsiders: Studies in the Sociology of Deviance.* New York: The Free Press.

Belenky, Mary Field, Blythe Clinchy, Nancy Goldberger, and Jill Tarule. 1986. *Women's Ways of Knowing: The Development of Self, Voice, and Mind.* New York: Basic Books.

Belkin, Lisa. 2003. "The Opt-Out Revolution." *New York Times Magazine,* October 26, p. 42.

Bell, Emily C., Morgan C. Willson, Alan H. Wilman, Sanjay Dave, and Peter H. Silverstone. 2006. "Males and Females Differ in Brain Activation During Cognitive Tasks." *NeuroImage* 30:529–38.

Berger, Joseph, Bernard P. Cohen, and Morris Zelditch Jr. 1966. "Status Characteristics and Expectation States." Pp. 29–46 in *Sociological Theories in Progress,* vol. I, edited by Joseph Berger, Morris Zelditch Jr., and Bo Anderson. Boston, MA: Houghton Mifflin.

Bergmann, Barbara R. and Suzanne Helburn. 2002. *America's Child Care Problem: The Way Out.* New York: Palgrave, St. Martin's Press.

Bilefsky, Dan. 2006. "How to Avoid Honor Killing in Turkey? Honor Suicide." *New York Times,* July 16 section 1, p. 3.

Blumberg, Rae Lesser. 1978. *Stratification: Socioeconomic and Sexual Inequality.* Dubuque, IA: Brown.

Boaler, Jo and Tesha Sengupta-Irving. 2006. "Nature, Neglect & Nuance: Changing Accounts of Sex, Gender and Mathematics." Pp. 207–20 in *Gender and Education, International Handbook,* edited by C. Skelton and L. Smulyan. London, England: Sage.

Bose, Christine E. and Edna Acosta-Belén. 1995. *Women in the Latin American Development Process.* Philadelphia, PA: Temple University Press.

Bose, Christine E., Roslyn Feldberg, and Natalie Sokolof. 1987. *Hidden Aspects of Women's Work.* New York: Praeger.

Bourdieu, Pierre. [1979] 1984. *Distinctions: A Social Critique of the Judgment of Taste.* Cambridge, MA: Harvard University Press.

———. 1991. "Identity and Representation: Elements for a Critical Reflection on the Idea of Region." Pp. 220–28 in *The Logic of Practice,* edited by P. Bourdieu. Stanford, CA: Stanford University Press.

Brewer, William F. and Glenn Nakamura. 1984. "The Nature and Functions of Schemas." Pp. 119–60 in *Handbook of Social Cognition,* vol. 1, edited by R. S. Wyer and T. K. Srull. Hillsdale, NJ: Erlbaum.

Brizendine, Louann. 2006. *The Female Brain.* New York: Morgan Road Books.

Brooks, David. 2006. "The Gender Gap at School." *New York Times,* June 11, section 4, p. 12.

Brubaker, Rogers. 2004. *Ethnicity Without Groups.* Cambridge, MA: Harvard University Press.

Bruner, Jerome. 1990. *Acts of Meaning: Four Lectures on Mind and Culture.* Cambridge, MA: Harvard University Press.

Bussey, Kay and Albert Bandura. 1999. "Social Cognitive Theory of Gender Development and Differentiation." *Psychological Review* 106:676–713.

Butler, Judith. 1990. *Gender Trouble*. New York: Routledge.

Chafe, William H. 1972. *The American Woman: Her Changing Social, Economic and Political Roles: 1920–1970*. Oxford, England: Oxford University Press.

Chafetz, Janet Saltzman. 1984. *Sex and Advantage: A Comparative Macro-Structural Theory of Sex Stratification*. Totowa, NJ: Roman & Allanhyeld.

———. 1997. "Feminist Theory and Sociology: Underutilized Contribution for Mainstream Theory." *Annual Review of Sociology* 23:97–120.

Charles, Maria and David Grusky. 2004. *Occupational Ghettos: The Worldwide Segregation of Women and Men*. Stanford, CA: Stanford University Press.

Charred, Mounira. 2001. *States and Women's Rights: The Making of Postcolonial Tunisia, Algeria and Morocco*. Berkeley, CA: The University of California Press.

Chetkovich, Carol. 1997. *Real Heat: Gender and Race in the Urban Fire Service*. New York: Routledge.

Coghlan, Tom. 2006. "Taliban Use Beheadings and Beatings to Keep Afghanistan's Schools Closed." *The Independent*, July 11. Retrieved July 11, 2006 (http://news.independent.co.uk/world/asia/article1171369.ece).

Collins, Patricia Hill. 1998. *Fighting Words: Black Women and the Search for Justice*. Minneapolis, MN: University of Minnesota Press.

Collinson, David L. and Jeff Hearn. 1994. "Naming Men as Men: Implications for Work, Organization and Management." *Gender, Work and Organization* 1:2–22.

Collinson, David L., David Knights, and Margaret Collinson. 1990. *Managing to Discriminate*. London, England: Routledge.

Connell, R. W. 1987. *Gender and Power: Society, the Person and Sexual Politics*. Stanford, CA: Stanford University Press.

Coser, Rose Laub. 1974. "Stay Home Little Sheba: On Placement, Displacement and Social Change." *Social Problems* 22:470–80.

Cox, W. Michael and Richard Alm. 2005. "Scientists are Made, Not Born." *New York Times*, February 25, p. A25.

Dahlerup, Drude. n.d. "The World of Quotas." *Women in Politics: Beyond Numbers*. International Institute for Democracy and Electoral Assistance. Retrieved September 21, 2006 (http://archive.idea.int/women/parl/ch4c.htm).

DiMaggio, Paul. 1997. "Culture and Cognition." *Annual Review of Sociology* 23:263–87.

Douglas, Mary. 1966. *Purity and Danger: An Analysis of Concepts of Pollution and Taboo*. London, England: Routledge & Kegan Paul.

Duster, Troy. 2006. "Comparative Perspectives and Competing Explanations: Taking on the Newly Configured Reductionist Challenge to Sociology." *American Sociological Review* 71:1–15.

England, Paula. 1989. "A Feminist Critique of Rational-Choice Theories: Implications for Sociology." *The American Sociologist* 20:14–28.

———. 1994. "Neoclassical Economists' Theories of Discrimination." Pp. 59–70 in *Equal Employment Opportunity*, edited by P. Burstein. New York: Aldine De Gruyter.

Epstein, Cynthia Fuchs. 1968. "Women and Professional Careers: The Case of Women Lawyers." Ph.D. Dissertation, Department of Sociology, Columbia University, New York.

———. 1970. *Woman's Place: Options and Limits in Professional Careers*. Berkeley, CA: University of California Press.

———. [1981] 1993. *Women in Law*. Urbana, IL: University of Illinois Press.

———. 1985. "Ideal Roles and Real Roles or the Fallacy of the Misplaced Dichotomy." Pp. 29–51 in *Research in Social Stratification and Mobility*, edited by Robert V. Robinson. Greenwich, CT: JAI Press Inc.

———. 1988. *Deceptive Distinctions*. New Haven, CT and New York: Yale University Press and Russell Sage Foundation.

———. 1991a. "What's Wrong and What's Right With the Research on Gender." *Sociological Viewpoints* 5:1–14.

———. 1991b. "The Difference Model: Enforcement and Reinforcement in the Law." Pp. 53–71 in *Social Roles and Social Institutions: Essays in Honor of Rose Laub Coser*, edited by J. Blau and N. Goodman. Boulder, CO: Westview.

———. 1992. "Tinkerbells and Pinups: The Construction and Reconstruction of Gender Boundaries at Work." Pp. 232–56 in *Cultivating Differences: Symbolic Boundaries and the Making of Inequality*, edited by M. Lamont and M. Founder. Chicago, IL: University of Chicago Press.

———. 1997. "Multiple Myths and Outcomes of Sex Segregation." *New York Law School Journal of Human Rights* XIV: Part One, 185–210, Symposium.

———. 1999a. "The Major Myth of the Women's Movement." *Dissent* 46(4):83–86.

———. 1999b. "Similarity and Difference: The Sociology of Gender Distinctions." Pp. 45–61 in *Handbook of the Sociology of Gender,* edited by J. S. Chafetz. New York: Kluwer Academic/Plenum Publishers.

———. 2001. "Women in the Legal Profession at the Turn of the Twenty-First Century: Assessing Glass Ceilings and Open Doors." *Kansas Law Review* 49:733–60.

Epstein, Cynthia Fuchs and Deborah Gambs. 2001. "Sex Segregation in Education." Pp. 983–90 in *Encyclopedia of Gender,* vol. 2, edited by Judith Worell. Philadelphia, PA: Elsevier.

Epstein, Cynthia Fuchs and Arne Kalleberg, eds. 2004. *Fighting for Time: Shifting Boundaries of Work and Social Life.* New York: Russell Sage Foundation.

Epstein, Cynthia Fuchs, Robert Sauté, Bonnie Oglensky, and Martha Gever. 1995. "Glass Ceilings and Open Doors: The Mobility of Women in Large Corporate Law Firms." *Fordham Law Review* LXTV:291–449.

Epstein, Cynthia Fuchs, Carroll Seron, Bonnie Oglensky, and Robert Sauté. 1999. *The Part Time Paradox: Time Norms, Professional Life, Family and Gender.* New York and London: Routledge.

Erikson, Kai. 1996. "On Pseudospeciation and Social Speciation." Pp. 51–58 in *Genocide: War and Human Survival,* edited by C. Strozier and M. Flynn. Lanham, MD: Rowman & Littlefield.

Fine, Gary Alan. 1996. "Reputational Entrepreneurs and the Memory of Incompetence: Melting Supporters, Partisan Warriors, and Images of President Harding." *The American Journal of Sociology* 101:1159–93.

Fisher, Helen. 1982. *The Sex Contract: The Evolution of Human Behavior.* New York: William Morrow.

Fogg, Piper. 2006. "Panel Blames Bias for Gender Gap." *The Chronicle,* September 29. Retrieved October 24, 2006 (http://chronicle.com/weekly/v53/i06/06a01301.htm).

Food and Agriculture Organization of the United Nations. n.d. "Gender and Food Security: Agriculture." Retrieved August 5, 2006 (http://www.fao.org/gender/en/agri-e.htm).

Frank, Marian. 1980. *The Life and Times of "Rosie the Riveter."* A study guide for the video *Rosie the Riveter,* Connie Field, director. Los Angeles, CA: Direct Cinema.

Freud, Sigmund. 1938. *The Basic Writings of Sigmund Freud.* Translated by A. A. Brill. New York: Modern Library.

———. [1905] 1975. *Three Essays on the Theory of Sexuality.* New York: Basic Books.

Friedan, Betty. [1963] 1983. *The Feminine Mystique.* New York: W.W. Norton.

Friedland, Roger. 2002. "Money, Sex and God: The Erotic Logic of Religious Nationalism." *Sociological Theory* 20:381–425.

Frodi, Ann, Jacqueline Macaulay, and Pauline Robert Thorne. 1977. "Are Women Always Less Aggressive than Men? A Review of the Experimental Literature." *Psychological Bulletin* 84:634–60.

Gerson, Judith and Kathy Peiss. 1985. "Boundaries, Negotiation and Consciousness: Reconceptualizing Gender Relations." *Social Problems* 32:317–31.

Gilligan, Carol. 1982. *In a Different Voice: Psychological Theory and Women's Development.* Cambridge, MA: Harvard University Press.

Gil-White, Francisco. 1999. "How Thick is Blood? The Plot Thickens . . . : If Ethnic Actors Are Primordialists, What Remains of the Circumstantialist/Primordialist Controversy?" *Ethnic and Racial Studies* 22:789–820.

Goldin, Claudia. 2006. "The Quiet Revolution That Transformed Women's Employment, Education and Family." *American Economic Association Papers and Proceedings* 96:7–19.

Goode, William J. 1959. "The Theoretical Importance of Love" *American Sociological Review* 24:38–47.

———. 1972. "The Place of Force in Human Society." *American Sociological Review* 37:507–19.

Gornick, Janet 2003. *Families that Work: Policies for Reconciling Parenthood and Employment.* New York: Russell Sage Foundation.

Gray, John. 1992. *Men are from Mars, Women are from Venus.* New York: HarperCollins.

Hall, Peter and Michele Lamont. Forthcoming. *Successful Societies* (working title).

Hartmann, Heidi, Vicky Lovell, and Misha Werschkul. 2004. "Women and the Economy: Recent Trends in Job Loss, Labor Force Participation and Wages." Briefing Paper, Institute for Women's Policy Research. IWPR Publication B235.

Hartstock, Nancy. 1988. *The Feminist Standpoint Revisited, and Other Essays.* Boulder, CO: Westview Press.

Hirschfeld, Lawrence A. 1996. *Race in the Making: Cognition, Culture and the Child's Construction of Human Kinds.* Cambridge, MA: MIT Press.

Hondagneu-Sotelo, Pierrette, ed. 2003. *Gender and U.S. Immigration: Contemporary Trends.* Berkeley, CA: University of California Press.

Honey, Maureen. 1984. *Creating Rosie the Riveter: Class, Gender and Propaganda during World War 2.* Boston, MA: University of Massachusetts Press.

Hsiung, Ping-Chun. 1996. *Living Rooms as Factories: Class, Gender and the Satellite Factory System in Taiwan.* Philadelphia, PA: Temple University Press

Hyde, Janet Shibley. 2005. "The Gender Similarities Hypothesis." *American Psychologist* 60:581–92.

Jaschik, Scott 2006. "Bias or Interest?" *Inside Higher Ed,* September 20. Retrieved September 28 (http://insidehighered.com/layout/set/print/news/2006/09/20/women).

Kaminer, Wendy. 1990. *A Fearful Freedom: Women's Flight from Equality.* Reading, MA: Addison-Wesley.

Kaufman, Debra R. and Barbara Richardson. 1982. *Achievement and Women: Challenging the Assumptions.* New York: The Free Press.

Kessler-Harris, Alice. 1982. *Women Have Always Worked: A Historical Overview.* Old Westbury, CT: Feminist Press.

Kimmel, Michael. 1996. *Manhood in America.* New York: The Free Press.

Komarovsky, Mirra. 1946. "Cultural Contradictions and Sex Roles." *The American Journal of Sociology* 52:184–89.

———. [1953] 2004. *Women in the Modern World: Their Education and Their Dilemmas.* Walnut Creek, CA: AltaMira Press.

Kristof, Nicholas. 2006. "Save My Wife." *New York Times,* September 17, opinion section, p. 15.

Lamont, Michele. 2005. "Bridging Boundaries: Inclusion as a Condition for Successful Societies." Presented at the Successful Societies Program of the Canadian Institute for Advanced Research, October, Montebello, Quebec, Canada.

Lamont, Michele and Virag Molnar. 2002. "The Study of Boundaries in the Social Sciences." *Annual Review of Sociology* 28:167–95.

Laslett, Barbara. 1996. *Gender and Scientific Authority.* Chicago, IL: University of Chicago Press.

Lee, Ching Kwan. 1998. *Gender and the South China Miracle: Two Worlds of Factory Women.* Berkeley, CA: University of California Press.

Lew, Irene and Nouhad Moawad. 2006. "Cheers & Jeers of the Week: Breast Cancer Strategies; Domestic Abuse Unnoticed." *Women's eNews,* September 30. Retrieved October 2, 2006 (http://www.womensenews.org/article.cfm/dyn/aid/2907/context/archive).

Lewin, Tamar. 2006a. "At College's, Women are Leaving Men in the Dust." *New York Times,* July 9, p. A1.

———. 2006b. "A More Nuanced Look at Men, Women and College." *New York Times,* July 12, p. B8.

Lorber, Judith. 1975. "Women and Medical Sociology: Invisible Professionals and Ubiquitous Patients." Pp. 75–105 in *Another Voice,* edited by Marcia Millman and Rosabeth Moss Kanter. Garden City, NY: Doubleday/Anchor.

———. 1984. *Women Physicians: Careers, Status, and Power.* New York: Tavistock Publications.

———. 1994. *Paradoxes of Gender.* New Haven, CT: Yale University Press.

———. 1996. "Beyond the Binaries: Depolarizing the Categories of Sex, Sexuality and Gender." *Sociological Inquiry* 66:143–59.

Magrane, Diane, Jonathan Lang, and Hershel Alexander. 2005. *Women in U.S. Academic Medicine: Statistics and Medical School Benchmarking.* Washington, DC: Association of American Medical Colleges.

Martin, Patricia Yancey. 2004. "Gender as Social Institution." *Social Forces* 82:1249–73.

Merton, Robert K. [1949] 1963. *Social Theory and Social Structure.* Glencoe, IL: The Free Press.

Milkman, Ruth. 1987. *Gender at Work: The Dynamics of Job Segregation by Sex During World War II.* Urbana, IL: University of Illinois Press.

Moghadam, Valentine. 2003. *Modernizing Women: Gender and Social Change in the Middle East.* 2d ed. London, England: Lynne Rienner.

O'Brien, Timothy. 2006. "Why Do So Few Women Reach the Top of Big Law Firms?" *New York Times,* March 19, p. B27.

O'Farrell, Brigid. 1999. "Women in Blue Collar and Related Occupations at the End of the Millenium." *Quarterly Review of Economics and Finance* 39:699–722.

National Women's Law Center. 2006. "New Report Analyzes What's at Stake for Women During Upcoming Supreme Court Term." Press Release. September 27. Retrieved October 2,

2006 (http://www.nwlc.org/details.cfm?id=2857§ion=newsroom).

Nicholson, Lisa H. 2006. "Women and the 'New' Corporate Governance: Making In-Roads to Corporate General Counsel Positions: It's Only a Matter of Time?" *Maryland Law Review* 65:625–65.

Norris, Floyd. 2006. "A Statistic That Shortens the Distance to Europe." *New York Times,* September 30, p. C3.

Parsons, Talcott. 1954. "The Kinship System of the Contemporary United States." Pp. 189–94 in *Essays in Sociological Theory.* Glencoe, IL: The Free Press.

Parrot, Andrew and Nina Cummings. 2006. *Forsaken Females: The Global Brutalization of Women.* Lanham, MD: Rowman and Littlefield.

Presser Harriet. 2003. *Working in a 24/7 Economy: Challenges for American Families.* New York: Russell Sage Foundation.

Rao, Kavitha. 2006. "Missing Daughters on an Indian Mother's Mind." *Women's eNews,* March 16. Retrieved October 23, 2006 (http://www.womensenews.org/article.cfm?aid=2672).

Ridgeway, Cecilia L. 1997. "Interaction and the Conservation of Gender Inequality: Considering Employment." *American Sociological Review* 62:218–35.

———. 2006. "Gender as an Organizing Force in Social Relations: Implications for the Future of Inequality." Pp. 245–87 in *The Declining Significance of Gender?* edited by Francine D. Blau and Mary C. Brinton. New York: The Russell Sage Foundation.

Ridgeway, Cecilia L. and Lynn Smith-Lovin. 1999. "The Gender System and Interaction." *Annual Review of Sociology* 25:19–216.

Roos, Patricia and Mary L. Gatta. 2006. "Gender Inquiry in the Academy." Presented at the Annual Meeting of the American Sociological Association, August 14, Montreal, Canada.

Rothbart, Myron and Marjorie Taylor. 1992. "Category Labels and Social Reality: Do We View Social Categories as Natural Kinds?" Pp. 11–36 in *Language, Interaction and Social Cognition,* edited by Gun R. Semin and Klaus Fiedler. London, England: Sage.

Rupp, Leila. 1978. *Mobilizing Women for War: German and American Propaganda, 1939–1945.* Princeton, NJ: Princeton University Press.

Salzinger, Leslie. 2003. *Genders in Production: Making Workers in Mexico's Global Factories.* Berkeley, CA: University of California Press.

Schemo, Diana Jean. 2006. "Change in Federal Rules Backs Single-Sex Public Education." *New York Times,* October 25, p. A16.

Sen, Amartya. 1990. "More than 100 Million Women are Missing." *New York Review of Books,* 37(20). Retrieved January 25, 2006 (http://ucatlas.ucsc.edu/gender/Sen100M.html).

Smith, Dorothy. 1990. *The Conceptual Practices of Power: A Feminist Sociology of Knowledge.* Boston, MA: Northeastern University Press.

Stacey, Judith and Barrie Thorne. 1985. 'The Missing Feminist Revolution in Sociology." *Social Problems* 32:301–16.

Stevens, Alison. 2006. "Iranian Women Protest in Shadow of Nuclear Face-off." *Women's eNews,* June 16. Retrieved September 28, 2006 (http://www.womensenews.org/article.cfm/dyn/aid/2780).

Tannen, Deborah. 1990. *You Just Don't Understand: Women and Men in Conversation.* New York: Morrow.

Tarabay, Jamie. 2006. "Activists Seek to Protect Iraqi Women from Honor Killings." *NPR Morning Edition,* May 18. Retrieved June 6, 2006 (http://www.npr.org/templates/story/story.php?storyId=5414315).

Tavris, Carol. 1992. *The Mismeasure of Woman: Why Women are not the Better Sex, the Inferior Sex or the Opposite Sex.* New York: Touchstone.

Telles, Edward. 2004. *Race in Another America: The Significance of Skin Color in Brazil.* Princeton, NJ: Princeton University Press.

Tierney, John. 2006. "Academy of P.C. Sciences." New *York Times,* September 26, p. A23.

Tilly, Charles. 1998. *Durable Inequality.* Berkeley, CA: University of California Press.

Trivers, Robert L. 1972. "Parental Investment and Sexual Selection." Pp. 136–79 in *Sexual Selection and the Descent of Man, 1871–1971,* edited by B. Campbell. Chicago, IL: Aldine.

United Nations. 2002. *Working Towards the Elimination of Crimes against Women Committed in the Name of Honor, Report of the Secretary General.* United Nations General Assembly, July 2. Retrieved October 23, 2006 (http://www.unhchr.ch/huridocda/huridoca.nsf/AllSymbols/985168F508EE799FC1256C52002AE5A9/%24File/N0246790.pdf).

U.N. Common Database. 2004. "Gender Equality: Indicator: Seats in Parliament Held by Women–2004." Retrieved September 21, 2006 (http://globalis.gvu.unu.edu/indicator.cfm?IndicatorID=63&country=IS#rowIS).

Villalobos, V. Munos. 2006. "Economic, Social and Cultural Rights: Girls' right to education." Report submitted by the Special Rapporteur on the right to education. United Nations Commission on Human Rights, Economic and Social Council. Retrieved September 28, 2006 (http://www.crin.org/docs/SR_Education_report.pdf).

Williams, Joan. 2000. *Unbending Gender: Why Family and Work Conflict and What to Do About It.* New York: Oxford University Press.

Wilson, Edward O. 1975. *Sociobiology: The New Synthesis.* Cambridge, MA: Belknap Press of Harvard University Press.

Winston, Hella. 2005. *Unchosen: The Hidden Lives of Hasidic Rebels.* Boston, MA: Beacon Press.

Witte, Griff. 2005. "Post-Taliban Free Speech Blocked by Courts, Clerics: Jailed Afghan Publisher Faces Possible Execution." *Washington Post,* December 11, p. A24.

Women's World Summit Foundation. 2006. "World Rural Women's Day: 15 October: Introduction." Retrieved September 28, 2006 (http://www.woman.ch/women/2-introduction.asp).

Zerubavel, Eviatar. 1997. *Social Mindscapes: An Invitation to Cognitive Sociology.* Cambridge, MA: Harvard University Press.

Zimmerman Mary K., Jacquelyn S. Litt, and Christine E. Bose. 2006. *Global Dimensions of Gender and Care Work.* Stanford, CA: Stanford University Press.

PART

5

The Gendered Family

The current debates about the "crisis" of the family—a traditional arrangement that some fear is collapsing under the weight of contemporary trends ranging from relaxed sexual attitudes, increased divorce, and women's entry into the labor force, to rap music and violence in the media—actually underscore how central the family is to the reproduction of social life—and to gender identity. If gender identity were biologically "natural," we probably wouldn't need such strong family structures to make sure that everything turned out all right.

Though the "typical" family of the 1950s television sitcom—breadwinner father, housewife/mother, and 2.5 happy and well-adjusted children—is the empirical reality for less than 10 percent of all households, it remains the cultural ideal against which contemporary family styles are measured. Andrew J. Cherlin surveys the new American family and finds an exciting, not threatening diversity.

Following Cherlin, two different articles examine the changing nature of the family. Caryn E. Medved and William K. Rawlins look at the role reversals in some contemporary heterosexual families, in which the woman is the breadwinner and the man is the stay-at-home dad. What happens to gender relations? Does this make families more egalitarian?

And what happens when the parents are “gender-equals”—that is, children are being raised by a gay or lesbian couple? Judith Stacey and Timothy J. Biblarz approach the issue from a more macrolevel, looking at the outcomes for children. It turns out that what children need is a lot of love, support, and time—and that those qualities know no gender or sexual orientation.

American Marriage in the Early Twenty-First Century

ANDREW J. CHERLIN

The decline of American marriage has been a favorite theme of social commentators, politicians, and academics over the past few decades. Clearly the nation has seen vast changes in its family system—in marriage and divorce rates, cohabitation, childbearing, sexual behavior, and women's work outside the home. Marriage is less dominant as a social institution in the United States than at any time in history. Alternative path ways through adulthood—childbearing outside of marriage, living with a partner without ever marrying, living apart but having intimate relationships—are more acceptable and feasible than ever before. But as the new century begins, it is also clear that despite the jeremiads, marriage has not faded away. In fact, given the many alternatives to marriage now available, what may be more remarkable is not the decline in marriage but its persistence. What is surprising is not that fewer people marry, but rather that so *many* still marry and that the desire to marry remains widespread. Although marriage has been transformed, it is still meaningful. In this article I review the changes in American marriage, discuss their causes, compare marriage in the United States with marriage in the rest of the developed world, and comment on how the transformation of marriage is likely to affect American children in the early twenty-first century.

Changes in the Life Course

To illuminate what has happened to American marriage, I begin by reviewing the great demographic changes of the past century including changes in age at marriage, the share of Americans ever marrying, cohabitation, nonmarital births, and divorce.

Recent Trends

Figure 1 shows the median age at marriage—the age by which half of all marriages occur—for men and women from 1890 to 2002. In 1890 the median age was relatively high, about twenty-six for men and twenty-two for women. During the first half of the twentieth century the typical age at marriage dropped—gradually at first, and then precipitously after World War II. By the 1950s it had reached historic lows: roughly twenty-three for men and twenty for women. Many people still think of the 1950s as the standard by which to compare today's families, but as Figure 1 shows, the 1950s were the anomaly: during that decade young adults married earlier than ever before or since. Moreover, nearly all young adults—about 95 percent of whites and 88 percent of African Americans—eventually married.[1] During the 1960s, however, the median age at marriage began to climb, returning to and then exceeding that prevalent at the start of the twentieth century. Women, in particular, are marrying substantially later today than they have at any time for which data are available.

What is more, unmarried young adults are leading very different lives today than their earlier counterparts once did. The late-marrying young women and men of the early 1900s typically lived at home before marriage or paid for room and board in someone else's home. Even when they

Andrew J. Cherlin, "American Marriage in the Early Twenty-First Century" from *The Future of Children* 15, no. 2 (Fall 2005): 3–55.

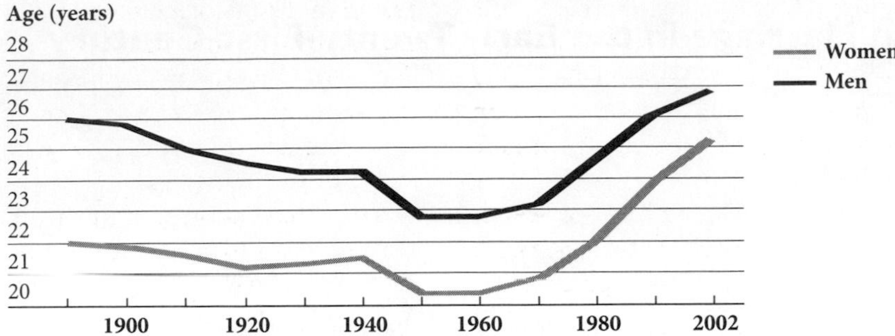

Figure 1. Median Age at Marriage, 1890–2002.

Source: U.S. Bureau of the Census, "Estimated Median Age at First Marriage, by Sex: 1890 to Present," 2003, www.census.gov/population/socdemo/hh-fam/tabMS-2.pdf (accessed July 23, 2004).

were courting, they lived apart from their romantic interests and, at least among women, the majority abstained from sexual intercourse until they were engaged or married. They were usually employed, and they often turned over much of their paycheck to their parents to help rear younger siblings. Few went to college; most had not even graduated from high school. As recently as 1940, only about one-third of adults in their late twenties had graduated from high school and just one in sixteen had graduated from college.[2]

Today's unmarried young adults are much more likely to be living independently, in their own apartments. Five out of six young adults graduate from high school, and about one-third complete college.[3] They are more likely than their predecessors to spend their wages on themselves. Their sexual and intimate lives are also very different from those of earlier generations. The vast majority of unmarried young adults have had sexual intercourse. In fact, most women who married during the 1990s first had intercourse five years or more before marrying.[4]

About half of young adults live with a partner before marrying. Cohabitation is far more common today than it was at any time in the early- or mid-twentieth century (although it was not unknown among the poor and has been a part of the European family system in past centuries). Cohabitation today is a diverse, evolving phenomenon. For some people, it is a prelude to marriage or a trial marriage. For others, a series of cohabiting relationships may be a long-term substitute for marriage. (Thirty nine percent of cohabiters in 1995 lived with children of one of the partners.) It is still rare in the United States for cohabiting relationships to last long—about half end, through marriage or a breakup, within a year.[5]

Despite the drop in marriage and the rise in cohabitation, there has been no explosion of nonmarital births in the United States. Birth rates have fallen for unmarried women of all reproductive ages and types of marital status, including adolescents. But because birth rates have fallen faster for married women than for unmarried women, a larger share of women who give birth are unmarried. In 1950, only 4 percent of all births took place outside of marriage. By 1970, the figure was 11 percent; by 1990, 28 percent; and by 2003, 35 percent. In recent years, then, about one-third of all births have been to unmarried women—and that is the statistic that has generated the most debate.[6] Of further concern to many observers is that about half of all unmarried first-time mothers are adolescents. Academics, policymakers, and private citizens alike express unease about the negative consequences of adolescent childbearing, both for the parents and for the children, although whether those consequences are due more to poverty or to teen childbearing per se remains controversial.

When people think of nonmarital or "out-of wedlock" childbearing, they picture a single parent. Increasingly, however, nonmarital births are occurring to cohabiting couples—about 40 percent according to the latest estimate.[7] One study of unmarried women giving birth in urban hospitals found that about half were living with the fathers of their children.

Couples in these "fragile families," however, rarely marry. One year after the birth of the child, only 15 percent had married, while 26 percent had broken up.[8]

Marriage was not an option for lesbians and gay men in any U.S. jurisdiction until Massachusetts legalized same-sex marriage in 2004. Cohabitation, however, is common in this group. In a 1992 national survey of sexual behavior, 44 percent of women and 28 percent of men who said they had engaged in homosexual sex in the previous year reported that they were cohabiting.[9] The Census Bureau, which began collecting statistics on same-sex partnerships in 1990, does not directly ask whether a person is in a romantic same-sex relationship; rather, it gives people the option of saying that a housemate is an "unmarried partner" without specifying the nature of the partnership. Because some people may not wish to openly report a same-sex relationship to the Census Bureau, it is hard to determine how reliable these figures are. The bureau reports, however, that in 2000, 600,000 households were maintained by same-sex partners. A substantial share—33 percent of female partnerships and 22 percent of male partnerships—reported the presence of children of one or both of the partners.[10]

As rates of entry into marriage were declining in the last half of the twentieth century, rates of exit via divorce were increasing—as they have been at least since the Civil War era. At the beginning of the twentieth century, about 10 percent of all marriages ended in divorce, and the figure rose to about one-third for marriages begun in 1950.[11] But the rise was particularly sharp during the 1960s and 1970s, when the likelihood that a married couple would divorce increased substantially. Since the 1980s the divorce rate has remained the same or declined slightly. According to the best estimate, 48 percent of American marriages, at current rates, would be expected to end in divorce within twenty years.[12] A few percent more would undoubtedly end in divorce after that. So it is accurate to say that unless divorce risks change, about half of all marriages today would end in divorce. (There are important class and racial-ethnic differences, which I will discuss below.)

The combination of more divorce and a greater share of births to unmarried women has increased the proportion of children who are not living with two parents. Figure 2 tracks the share of children living, respectively, with two parents, with one parent, and with neither parent between 1968 and 2002. It shows a steady decline in the two-parent share and a corresponding increase in the one-parent share. In 2002, 69 percent of children were living with two parents, including families where one biological (or adoptive) parent had remarried. Not counting step- or adoptive families, 62 percent, according to the most recent estimate in 1996, were living with two biological parents.[13] Twenty-seven percent of American children were living with one parent; another 4 percent, with neither parent.[14] Most in the latter group were living with relatives, such as grandparents.

Where do all these changes leave U.S. marriage patterns and children's living arrangements in the early twenty first century? As demographers have noted, many of the above trends have slowed over the past decade, suggesting a "quieting" of family change.[15] Marriage remains the most common living arrangement for raising children. At any one time, most American children are being raised by two parents. Marriage, however, is less dominant in parents' and children's lives than it once was. Children are more likely to experience life in a single-parent family, either because they are born to unmarried mothers or because their parents divorce. And children are more likely to experience instability in their living arrangements as parents form and dissolve marriages and partnerships. Although children are less likely to lose a parent through death today than they once were, the rise in nonmarital births and in divorce has more than compensated for the decline in parental death.[16] From the adult perspective, the overall drop in birth rates and the increases in nonmarital childbearing and divorce mean that,

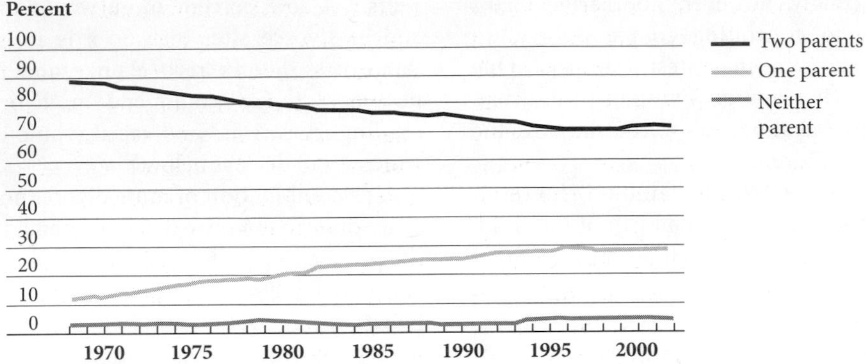

Figure 2. Living Arrangements of U.S. Children, 1968–2002.

Source: U.S. Bureau of the Census, "Living Arrangements of Children under 18 Years Old: 1960 to Present," 2003, www.census.gov/population/socdemo/hh-fam/tabCH-1.pdf (accessed July 23, 2004).

at any one time, fewer adults are raising children than in the past.

Class and Racial-Ethnic Divergence

To complete this portrait of American marriage one must take note of class and racial-ethnic variations, for the overall statistics mask contrasting trends in the lives of children from different racial-ethnic groups and different social classes. In fact, over the past few decades, the family lives of children have been diverging across class and racial-ethnic lines.[17] A half-century ago, the family structures of poor and non-poor children were similar: most children lived in two-parent families. In the intervening years, the increase in single-parent families has been greater among the poor and near-poor.[18] Women at all levels of education have been postponing marriage, but less-educated women have postponed childbearing less than better-educated women have. The divorce rate in recent decades appears to have held steady or risen for women without a college education but fallen for college-educated women.[19] As a result, differences in family structure according to social class are much more pronounced than they were fifty years ago.

Consider the share of mothers who are unmarried. Throughout the past half-century, single motherhood has been more common among women with less education than among well-educated women. But the gap has grown over time. In 1960, 14 percent of mothers in the bottom quarter of the educational distribution were unmarried, as against 4.5 percent of mothers in the top quarter—a difference of 9.5 percentage points. By 2000, the corresponding figures were 43 percent for the less-educated mothers and 7 percent for the more educated—a gap of 36 percentage points.[20] Sara McLanahan argues that societal changes such as greater opportunities for women in the labor market, a resurgence of feminist ideology, and the advent of effective birth control have encouraged women to invest in education and careers. Those who make these investments tend to delay childbearing and marriage, and they are more attractive in the marriage market.[21] Put another way, women at the top and bottom of the educational distribution may be evolving different reproductive strategies. Among the less educated, early childbearing outside of marriage has become more common, as the ideal of finding a stable marriage and then having children has weakened, whereas among the better educated, the strategy is to delay childbearing and marriage until after investing in schooling and careers.

One result of these developments has been growth in better-educated, dual-earner married-couple families. Since the 1970s these families have enjoyed much greater income growth than have breadwinner-homemaker families or single-parent families. What we see today, then, is a growing group of more fortunate children who tend to live with two parents whose incomes are adequate or ample and a growing group of less fortunate children who live with financially pressed single parents. Indeed, both groups at the extremes—the most and the least fortunate children—have been expanding over the past few decades, while the group of children in the middle has been shrinking.[22]

The family lives of African American children have also been diverging from those of white non-Hispanic children and, to a lesser extent, Hispanic children. African American family patterns were influenced by the institution of slavery, in which marriage was not legal, and perhaps by African cultural traditions, in which extended families had more influence and power compared with married couples. As a result, the proportion of African American children living with single parents has been greater than that of white children for a century or more.[23] Nevertheless, African American women married at an earlier age than did white women through the first half of the twentieth century.[24]

But since the 1960s, the decline of marriage as a social institution has been more pronounced among African Americans than among whites. The best recent estimates suggest that at current rates only about two-thirds of African American women would be expected ever to marry.[25] Correspondingly, the share of African American children born outside of marriage has risen to 69 percent.[26] In fact, about three-fifths of African American children may never live in a married-couple family while growing up, as against one-fifth of white children.[27] The greater role of extended kin in African American families may compensate for some of this difference, but the figures do suggest a strikingly reduced role of marriage among African Americans.

The family patterns of the Hispanic population are quite diverse. Mexican Americans have higher birth rates than all other major ethnic groups, and a greater share of Mexican American births than of African American births is to married women.[28] Moreover, Mexican American families are more likely to include extended kin.[29] Consequently, Mexican Americans have more marriage-based, multigenerational households than do African Americans. Puerto Ricans, the second largest Hispanic ethnic group and the most economically disadvantaged, have rates of nonmarital childbearing second only to African Americans.[30] But Puerto Ricans, like many Latin Americans, have a tradition of consensual unions, in which a man and woman live together as married but without approval of the church or a license from the state. So it is likely that more Puerto Rican "single" mothers than African American single mothers are living with partners.

Explaining the Trends

Most analysts would agree that both economic and cultural forces have been driving the changes in American family life over the past half-century. Analysts disagree about the relative weight of the two, but I will assume that both have been important.

Economic Influences

Two changes in the U.S. labor market have had major implications for families.[31] First, demand for workers increased in the service sector, where women had gained a foothold earlier in the century while they were shut out of manufacturing jobs. The rising demand encouraged women to get more education and drew married women into the workforce—initially, those whose children were school-aged, and later, those with younger children. Single mothers had long worked, but in 1996 major welfare reform legislation further encouraged work by setting limits on how long a parent could receive public assistance. The increase in women's paid work, in turn, increased demand for child care services and greatly increased the number of children cared for outside their homes.

The second work-related development was the decline, starting in the 1970s, in job opportunities for men without a college education. The flip side of the growth of the service sector was the decline in manufacturing. As factory jobs moved overseas and industrial productivity increased through automated equipment and computer-based controls, demand fell for blue-collar jobs that high school–educated men once took in hopes of supporting their families. As a result, average wages in these jobs fell. Even during the prosperous 1990s, the wages of men without a college degree hardly rose.[32] The decline in job opportunities had two effects. It decreased the attractiveness of non-college educated men on the marriage market—made them less "marriageable" in William Julius Wilson's terms—and thus helped drive marriage rates down among the less well educated.[33] It also undermined the single-earner "family wage system" that had been the ideal in the first half of the twentieth century and increased the incentive for wives to take paying jobs.

Cultural Developments

But economic forces, important as they were, could not have caused all the changes in family life noted above. Declines in the availability of marriageable men, for example, were not large enough to account, alone, for falling marriage rates among African Americans.[34] Accompanying the economic changes was a broad cultural shift among Americans that eroded the norms both of marriage before childbearing and of stable, lifelong bonds after marriage.

Culturally, American marriage went through two broad transitions during the twentieth century. The first was described famously by sociologist Ernest Burgess as a change "from institution to companionship."[35] In institutional marriage, the family was held together by the forces of law, tradition, and religious belief. The husband was the unquestioned head of the household. Until the late nineteenth century, husband and wife became one legal person when they married—and that person was the husband. A wife could not sue in her own name, and her husband could dispose of her property as he wished. Until 1920 women could not vote; rather, it was assumed that almost all women would marry and that their husbands' votes would represent their views. But as the forces of law and tradition weakened in the early decades of the twentieth century, the newer, companionate marriage arose. It was founded on the importance of the emotional ties between wife and husband—their companionship, friendship, and romantic love. Spouses drew satisfaction from performing the social roles of breadwinner, homemaker, and parent. After World War II, the spouses in companionate marriages, much to everyone's surprise, produced the baby boom: they had more children per family than any other generation in the twentieth century. The typical age at marriage fell to its lowest point since at least the late nineteenth century, and the share of all people who ever married rose. The decade of the 1950s was the high point of the breadwinner-homemaker, two-, three-, or even four-child family.

Starting around 1960, marriage went through a second transition. The typical age at marriage returned to, and then exceeded, the high levels of the early 1900s. Many young adults stayed single into their mid- to late twenties or even their thirties, some completing college educations and starting careers. Most women continued working for pay after they married. Cohabitation outside marriage became much more acceptable. Childbearing outside marriage became less stigmatized. The birth rate resumed its long decline and sank to an all-time low. Divorce rates rose to unprecedented levels. Same-sex partnerships found greater acceptance as well.

During this transition, companionate marriage waned as a cultural ideal. On the rise were forms of family life that Burgess had not foreseen, particularly marriages in which both husband and wife worked outside the home and single-parent families that came into being through divorce or through childbearing outside marriage. The roles of wives and husbands became more flexible and open to negotiation. And a more individualistic perspective on the rewards of marriage took root. When people evaluated how satisfied they were with their marriages, they began to think more in terms of developing their own sense of self and less in terms of gaining satisfaction through building a family and playing the roles of spouse and parent. The result was a transition from the companionate marriage to what we might call the individualized marriage.[36]

The Current Context of Marriage

To be sure, the "companionate marriage" and the "individualized marriage" are what sociologists refer to as ideal types. In reality, the distinctions between the two are less sharp than I have drawn them. Many marriages, for example, still follow the companionate ideal. Nevertheless, as a result of the economic and cultural trends noted above, marriage now exists in a very different context than it did in the past. Today it is but one among many options available to adults choosing how to shape their personal lives. More forms of marriage and more alternatives to it are socially acceptable. One may fit marriage into life in many ways: by first living with a partner, or sequentially with several partners, without explicitly considering whether to marry; by having children with one's eventual spouse or with someone else before marrying; by (in some jurisdictions) marrying someone of the same gender and building a shared marital world with few guidelines to rely on. Within marriage, roles are more flexible and negotiable, although women still do more of the household work and childrearing.

The rewards that people seek through marriage and other close relationships have also shifted. Individuals aim for personal growth and deeper intimacy through more open communication and mutually shared disclosures about feelings with their partners. They may insist on changes in a relationship that no longer provides them with individualized rewards. They are less likely than in the past to focus on the rewards gained by fulfilling socially valued roles such as the good parent or the loyal and supportive spouse. As a result of this changing context, social norms about family and personal life count for less than they did during the heyday of companionate marriage and far less than during the era of institutional marriage. Instead, personal choice and self-development loom large in people's construction of their marital careers.

But if marriage is now optional, it remains highly valued. As the practical importance of marriage has declined, its symbolic importance has remained high and may even have increased.[37] At its height as an institution in the mid-twentieth century, marriage was almost required of anyone wishing to be considered a respectable adult. Having children outside marriage was stigmatized, and a person who remained single through adulthood was suspect. But as other lifestyle options became more feasible and acceptable, the need to be married diminished. Nevertheless, marriage remains the preferred option for most people. Now, however, it is not a step taken lightly or early in young adulthood. Being "ready" to marry may mean that a couple has lived together to test their compatibility, saved for a down payment on a house, or possibly had children to judge how well they parent together. Once the foundation of adult family life, marriage is now often the capstone.

Although some observers believe that a "culture of poverty" has diminished the value of marriage among poor Americans, research suggests that the poor, the near-poor, and the middle class conceive of marriage in similar terms. Although marriage rates are lower among the poor than among the middle class, marriage as an ideal remains strong for both groups. Ethnographic studies show that many low-income individuals subscribe to the capstone view of marriage. In a study of low-income families that I carried out with several collaborators, a twenty-seven-year-old mother told an ethnographer:[38]

> I was poor all my life and so was Reginald. When I got pregnant, we agreed we would marry some day in the future because we loved each other and wanted to raise our child together. But we would not get married until we could afford to get a house and pay all the utility bills on time. I have this thing about utility bills. Our gas and electric got turned off all the time when we were growing up and we wanted to make sure that would not happen when we got married. That was our biggest worry.... We worked together and built up savings and then we got married. It's forever for us.

The poor, the near-poor, and the middle class also seem to view the emotional rewards of marriage in similar terms. Women of all classes value companionship in marriage: shared lives, joint childrearing, friendship, romantic love, respect, and fair treatment. For example, in a survey conducted in twenty-one cities, African Americans were as likely as non-Hispanic whites to rate highly the emotional benefits of marriage, such as friendship, sex life, leisure time, and a sense of security; and Hispanics rated these benefits somewhat higher than either group.[39] Moreover, in the "fragile families" study of unmarried low- and moderate-income couples who had just had a child together, Marcia Carlson, Sara McLanahan, and Paula England found that mothers and fathers who scored higher on a scale of relationship supportiveness were substantially more likely to be married one year later.[40] Among the items in the scale were whether the partner "is fair and willing to compromise" during a disagreement, "expresses affection or love," "encourages or helps," and does not insult or criticize. In a 2001 national survey of young adults aged twenty to twenty-nine conducted by the Gallup Organization for the National Marriage Project, 94 percent of never-married respondents agreed that "when you marry, you want your spouse to be your soul mate, first and foremost." Only 16 percent agreed that "the main purpose of marriage these days is to have children." [41]

As debates over same-sex marriage illustrate, marriage is also highly valued by lesbians and gay men. In 2003 the Massachusetts Supreme Court struck down a state law limiting marriage to opposite-sex couples, and same-sex marriage became legal in May 2004 (although opponents may eventually succeed in prohibiting it through a state constitutional amendment). Advocates for same-sex marriage argued that gay and lesbian couples should be entitled to marry so that they can benefit from the legal rights and protections that marriage brings. But the Massachusetts debate also showed the symbolic value of marriage. In response to the court's decision, the state legislature crafted a plan to enact civil unions for same-sex couples. These legally recognized unions would have given same-sex couples most of the legal benefits of marriage but would have withheld the status of being married. The court rejected this remedy, arguing that allowing civil unions but not marriage would create a "stigma of exclusion," because it would deny to same-sex couples "a status that is specially recognized in society and has significant social and other advantages." That the legislature was willing to provide legal benefits was not sufficient for the judges, nor for gay and lesbian activists, who rejected civil unions as second-class citizenship. Nor would it be enough for mainstream Americans, most of whom are still attached to marriage as a specially recognized status.

Putting U.S. Marriage in International Perspective

How does the place of marriage in the family system in the United States compare with its place in the family systems of other developed nations? It turns out that marriage in the United States is quite distinctive.

A Greater Attachment to Marriage

Marriage is more prevalent in the United States than in nearly all other developed Western nations. Figure 3 shows the total first marriage rate for women in the United States and in six other developed nations in 1990. (Shortly after 1990, the U.S. government stopped collecting all the information necessary to calculate this rate.) The total first marriage rate provides an estimate of the proportion of women who will ever marry.[42] It must be interpreted carefully because it yields estimates that are too low if calculated at a time when women are postponing marriage until older ages, as they were in 1990 in most countries. Thus, all the estimates in Figure 3 are probably too low. Nevertheless, the total first marriage rate is useful in comparing countries at a given time point, and I have selected the nations in Figure 3 to illustrate the variation in this rate in the developed world. The value of 715 for the United States—the highest of any country—implies that 715 out of 1,000 women were expected to marry. Italy had a relatively high value, while France and Sweden had the lowest. In between were Britain, Canada, and Germany.

Not only is marriage stronger demographically in the United States than in other developed countries, it also seems stronger as an ideal. In the World Values Surveys conducted between 1999 and 2001, one question asked of

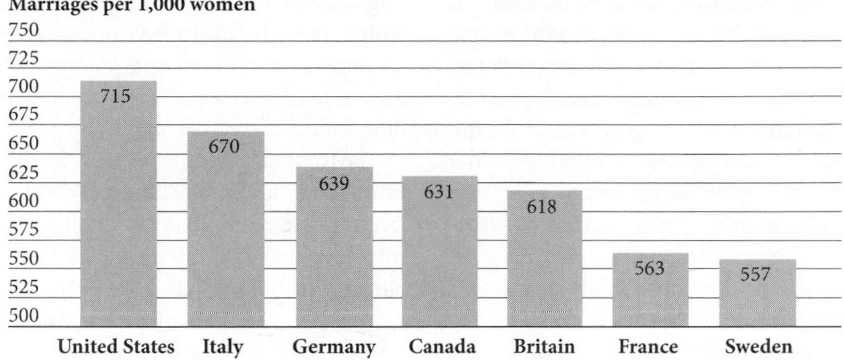

Figure 3. Total First Marriage Rates of Women, Selected European and English-Speaking Countries, 1990.

Sources: Alain Monnier and Catherine de Guibert-Lantoine, "The Demographic Situation of Europe and Developed Countries Overseas: An Annual Report," *Population; An English Selection* 8 (1996): 235–50; U.S. National Center for Health Statistics, "Advance Report of Final Marriage Statistics, 1989 and 1990," *Monthly Vital Statistics Report* 43, no. 12, supp. (Government Printing Office, 1995).

adults was whether they agreed with the statement, "Marriage is an outdated institution." Only 10 percent of Americans agreed—a lower share than in any developed nation except Iceland. Twenty-two percent of Canadians agreed, as did 26 percent of the British, and 36 percent of the French.[43] Americans seem more attached to marriage as a norm than do citizens in other developed countries.

This greater attachment to marriage has a long history. As Alexis de Tocqueville wrote in the 1830s, "There is certainly no country in the world where the tie of marriage is more respected than in America or where conjugal happiness is more highly or worthily appreciated."[44] Historian Nancy Cott has argued that the nation's founders viewed Christian marriage as one of the building blocks of American democracy. The marriage-based family was seen as a mini-republic in which the husband governed with the consent of the wife.[45] The U.S. government has long justified laws and policies that support marriage. In 1888, Supreme Court Justice Stephen Field wrote, "marriage, as creating the most important relation in life, as having more to do with the morals and civilization of a people than any other institution, has always been subject to the control of the legislature."[46]

The conspicuous historical exception to government support for marriage was the institution of slavery, under which legal marriage was prohibited. Many slaves nevertheless married informally, often using public rituals such as jumping over a broomstick.[47] Some scholars also think that slaves may have retained the kinship patterns of West Africa, where marriage was more a process that unfolded over time in front of the community than a single event.[48] The prospective husband's family, for example, might wait until the prospective wife bore a child to finalize the marriage.

The distinctiveness of marriage in the United States is also probably related to greater religious participation. Tocqueville observed, "there is no country in the world where the Christian religion retains a greater influence over the souls of men than in America."[49] That statement is still true with respect to the developed nations today: religious vitality is greatest in the United States.[50] For instance, in the World Values Surveys, 60 percent of Americans reported attending religious services at least monthly, as against 36 percent of Canadians, 19 percent of the British, and 12 percent of the French.[51] Americans look to religious institutions for guidance on marriage and family life more than do the citizens of most Western countries.

Sixty-one percent of Americans agreed with the statement, "Generally speaking, do you think that the churches in your country are giving adequate answers to the problems of family life?" Only 48 percent of Canadians, 30 percent of the British, and 28 percent of the French agreed.[52]

Moreover, family policies in many European nations have long promoted births, whereas American policies generally have not. This emphasis on pronatalism has been especially prominent in France, where the birth rate began to decline in the 1830s, decades before it did in most other European nations.[53] Since then, the French government has been concerned about losing ground in population size to potential adversaries such as Germany.[54] (The Germans felt a similar concern, which peaked in the Nazis' pronatalist policies of the 1930s and early 1940s.)[55] As a result, argues one historian, French family policy has followed a "parental logic" that places a high priority on supporting parents with young children—even working wives and single parents.[56] These policies have included family allowances prorated by the number of children, maternity insurance, and maternity leave with partial wage replacement. In contrast, policies in Britain and the United States followed a "male breadwinner logic" of supporting married couples in which the husband worked outside the home and the wife did not.[57] Pronatalist pressure has never been strong in the United States, even though the decline in the U.S. birth rate started in the early 1800s, because of the nation's openness to increasing its population through immigration.

More Transitions Into and Out of Marriage

In addition to its high rate of marriage, the United States has one of the highest rates of divorce of any developed nation. Figure 4 displays the total divorce rate in 1990 for the same countries shown in Figure 3. The total divorce rate, which provides an estimate of the number of marriages that would end in divorce, has limits similar to those of the total marriage rate but is likewise useful in international comparisons.[58] Figure 4 shows that the United States had a total divorce rate of 517 divorces per 1,000 marriages, with just over half of all marriages ending in divorce. Sweden had the second highest total divorce rate, and other Scandinavian countries had similar levels. The English-speaking countries of Britain and Canada were next, followed by France and Germany. Italy had a very low level of predicted divorce.

Both entry into and exit from marriage are indicators of what Robert Schoen has called a country's "marriage metabolism": the number of marriage- and divorce-related transitions that adults and their children undergo.[59] Figure 5, which presents the sum of the total first marriage rate and the total divorce rate, shows that the United States has by far the highest marriage metabolism of any of the developed countries in question.[60] Italy, despite its high marriage rate, has the lowest metabolism because of its very low divorce rate. Sweden, despite its high divorce rate, has a lower metabolism than the United States because of its lower marriage rate. In other words, what makes the United States most distinctive is the combination of high marriage and high divorce rates—which implies that Americans typically experience more transitions into and out of marriages than do people in other countries.

A similar trend is evident in movement into and out of cohabiting unions. Whether in marriage or cohabitation, Americans appear to have far more transitions in their live-in relationships. According to surveys from the mid-1990s, 5 percent of women in Sweden had experienced three or more unions (marriages or cohabiting relationships) by age thirty-five. In the rest of Europe, the comparable figure was 1 to 3 percent.[61] But in the United States, according to a 1995 survey, 9 percent of women aged thirty-five had experienced three or more unions, nearly double the Swedish figure and far higher than that of other European nations.[62] By 2002, the U.S. figure had climbed to 12 percent.[63] No other comparable nation has such a high level of multiple marital and cohabiting unions.

American children are thus more likely to experience multiple transitions in living arrangements than are children in Europe. Another study using the same comparative data from the mid-1990s reported that 12 percent of American children had lived in three or more parental partnerships by age

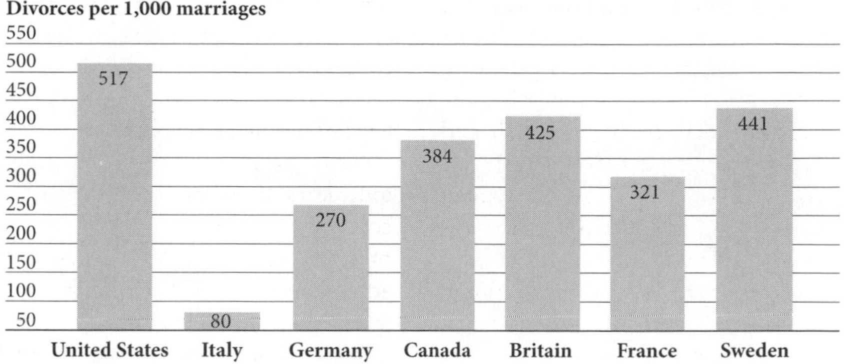

Figure 4. Total Divorce Rates, Selected European and English-Speaking Countries, 1990.

Sources: Monnier and de Guibert-Lantoine, "The Demographic Situation of Europe and the Developed Countries Overseas" (see Figure 3); U.S. National Center for Health Statistics, "Advance Report of Final Divorce Statistics, 1989 and 1990," *Monthly Vital Statistics Report* 43, no. 9, supp. (Government Printing Office, 1995).

fifteen, as against 3 percent of children in Sweden, which has the next highest figure.[64] As transitions out of partnerships occur, children experience a period of living in a single-parent family. And although American children, in general, are more likely to live in a single-parent family while growing up than are children elsewhere, the trend differs by social class. As Sara McLanahan shows in a comparison of children whose mothers have low or moderate levels of education, American children are much more likely than those in several European nations to have lived with a single mother by age fifteen. The cross-national difference is less pronounced among children whose mothers are highly educated.[65]

Also contributing to the prevalence of single-parent families in the United States is the relatively large share of births to unmarried, noncohabiting women—about one in five.[66] In most other developed nations with numerous nonmarital births, a greater share of unmarried mothers lives with the fathers of their children. In fact, the increases in nonmarital births in Europe in recent decades largely reflect births to cohabiting couples rather than births to single parents.[67] As noted, the United States is seeing a similar trend toward births to cohabiting couples, but the practice is still less prevalent in the United States than in many European nations.

Greater Economic Inequality

Children in the United States experience greater inequality of economic well-being than children in most other developed nations. One recent study reported that the gap between the cash incomes of children's families in the lowest and highest 10 percent was larger in the United States than in twelve other developed countries.[68] The low ranking of the United States is attributable both to the higher share of births to single parents and to the higher share of divorce. But even when the comparison is restricted to children living in single-parent families, children in the United States have the lowest relative standard of living. For example, one comparative study reported that 60 percent of single-mother households in the United States were poor, as against 45 percent in Canada, 40 percent in the United Kingdom, 25 percent in France, 20 percent in Italy, and 5 percent in Sweden.[69] The differences are caused by variations both in the income earned by single parents and in the generosity of government cash transfers. In other words, having a high share of single-parent families predisposes the United States to have a higher poverty rate, but other countries compensate better for single parenthood through a combination of social welfare spending and supports for employed parents, such as child care.

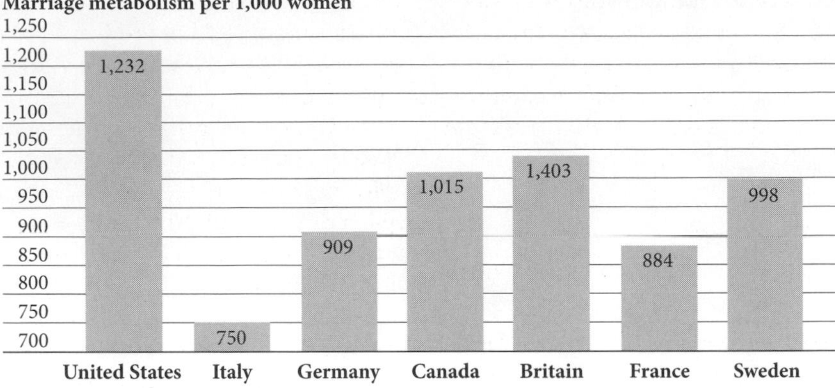

Figure 5. Marriage Metabolism, Selected European and English-Speaking Countries, 1990.

Sources: See Figures 3 and 4.

More Controversy over Gay and Lesbian Partnerships

Other developed countries tend to be more open to gay and lesbian partnerships than is the United States. Two European nations, Belgium and the Netherlands, have legalized same-sex marriage. By 2005, courts in seven Canadian provinces had ruled that laws restricting marriage to opposite-sex couples were discriminatory, and the Canadian federal government had introduced a bill to legalize gay marriage nationwide. Many other developed nations, including all the Scandinavian countries and Germany, have amended their family laws to include legal recognition of same-sex partnerships.[70]

France enacted its somewhat different form of domestic partnership, the *pacte civil de solidarité* (PACS), in 1999. Originally conceived in response to the burden placed on gay couples by the AIDS epidemic, the 1999 legislation was not restricted to same-sex partnerships.[71] In fact, it is likely that more opposite-sex partners than same-sex partners have chosen this option.[72] The PACS does not provide all the legal benefits of marriage. It is a privately negotiated contract between two persons who are treated legally as individuals unless they have children. Even when they have children, the contract does not require one partner to support the other after a dissolution, and judges are reluctant to award joint custody. Moreover, individuals in a same-sex PACS do not have the right to adopt children or to use reproductive technology such as in vitro fertilization.

For the most part, the issue of marriage has been less prominent in European than in North American debates about same-sex partnerships. To this point, no serious movement for same-sex marriage has appeared in Britain.[73] The French debate, consistent with the nation's child-oriented social policies, has focused more on the kinship rights and relationships of the children of the partners than on whether the legal form of partnership should include marriage.[74] In 2004, the mayor of Bègles, France, created a furor—similar to that seen in the United States following the granting of marriage licenses in San Francisco—by marrying a gay couple. But marriage remains less central to the politics of same-sex partnerships in France and elsewhere in Europe than it is in North America.

Marriage Transformed

Marriage remains an important part of the American family system, even if its dominance has diminished. Sentiment in favor of marriage appears to be stronger in the United States than elsewhere in the developed world, and the share of adults who are likely to marry is higher—as is, however, their propensity to get divorced. Increasingly, gay and lesbian activists are arguing, with some success, that they, too, should be allowed to marry. Even poor and near-poor Americans, who are statistically less likely to marry, hold to marriage as an ideal. But the contemporary ideal differs from that of the past in two important ways.

The Contemporary Ideal

First, marriage is now more optional in the United States than it has ever been. Until recently, family formation rarely occurred out-side of marriage. Now, to a greater extent than ever before, one can choose whether to have children on one's own, in a cohabiting relationship, or in a marriage. Poor and working-class Americans have radically separated the timing of childbearing and marriage, with many young adults having children many years before marrying. At current rates, perhaps one-third of African Americans will never marry. To be sure, some of the increase in seemingly single-parent families reflects a rise in the number of cohabiting couples who are having children, but these cohabiting relationships often prove unstable. How frequently the option of marriage becomes a reality depends heavily on one's race, ethnicity, or social class. African Americans and less well-educated Americans, for example, still value marriage highly but attain it less frequently than whites and better-educated Americans.

Second, the rewards of marriage today are more individualized. Being married is less a required adult role and more an individual achievement—a symbol of successful self-development. And couples are more prone to dissolve a marriage if their individualized rewards seem inadequate. Conversely, marriage is less centered on children. Today, married couples in the United States are having fewer children than couples have had at any time in the nation's history except during the Great Depression.

The changes in marriage, however, have not been solely cultural in origin. It is still the norm that a man must be able to provide a steady income to be seen as a good prospect for marriage. He no longer need earn all the family's income, but he must make a substantial, stable contribution. As the labor market position of young men without a college education has eroded, their attractiveness in the marriage market has declined. Many of their potential partners have chosen to have children outside marriage early in adulthood rather than to wait for the elusive promise of finding a spouse. Moreover, the introduction of the birth control pill and the legalization of abortion have allowed young women and men to become sexually active long before they think about marriage.

When the American family system is viewed in international perspective, it is most distinctive for the many transitions into and out of marital and cohabiting unions. Americans are more likely to experience multiple unions over the course of their lives than are Europeans. Moreover, cohabiting relationships in the United States still tend to be rather short, with a median duration (until either marriage or dissolution) of about one year. The median duration of cohabiting unions is about four years in Sweden and France and two or more years in most other European nations.[75] All this means that American children probably face greater instability in their living arrangements than children anywhere else in the developed world. Recent research has suggested that changes in family structure, regardless of the beginning and ending configurations, may cause problems for children.[76] Some of these apparent problems may reflect preexisting family difficulties, but some cause-and-effect association between instability and children's difficulties probably exists. If so, the increase in instability over the past decades is a worrisome trend that may not be receiving the attention it deserves.

Positive Developments

This is not to suggest that all the trends in marriage in America have been harmful to children. Those who live with two parents or with one well-educated parent may be doing better than comparable children a few decades ago. As noted, income growth has been greater in dual-career families, and divorce rates may have fallen among the college educated. In addition, the time spent with their parents by children in two-parent families has gone up, not down, and the comparable time spent by children with single parents has not changed, even though mothers' work outside the home has increased.[77] Working mothers appear to compensate for time spent outside the home by cutting back on housework and leisure—and, for those who are married, relying on modest but noticeable increases in husbands' housework—to preserve time with children.[78]

Meanwhile, the decline in fertility means that there are fewer children in the home to compete for their parents' attention. Middle-class parents engage in an intensive childrearing style that sociologist Annette Lareau calls "concerted cultivation": days filled with organized activities and parent-child discussions designed to enhance their children's talents, opinions, and skills.[79] While some social critics decry this parenting style, middle-class children gain skills that will be valuable to them in higher education and in the labor market. They learn how to communicate with professionals and other adults in positions of authority. They develop a confident style of interaction that Lareau calls "an emerging sense of entitlement," compared with "an emerging sense of constraint" among working-class and lower-class youth.

Marriage and Public Policy

Because marriage has been, and continues to be, stronger in the United States than in much of Europe, American social welfare policies have focused more on marriage than have those of many European countries. That emphasis continues. George W. Bush's administration advocates marriage-promotion programs as the most promising way to assist families. No European country has pursued a comparable policy initiative. Moreover, the issue of gay marriage has received more attention in the United States than in most of Europe. This greater emphasis on marriage in public policy reflects the history and culture of the United States. Policies that build on and support marriage are likely to be popular with American voters because they resonate with American values. Europe's more generous public spending on children, regardless of their parents' marital status, is rooted in concerns about low population growth that have never been strong in the United States. Such public spending on single-parent families also reflects the lesser influence of religion in Europe. So it is understandable that American policymakers wishing to generate support for new family policy initiatives might turn to marriage-based programs.

Yet the relatively high value placed on marriage in the United States coexists with an unmatched level of family instability and large numbers of single-parent families. This, too, is part of the American cultural heritage. The divorce rate appears to have been higher in the United States than in most of Europe since the mid-nineteenth century.[80]

This emblematic American pattern of high marriage and divorce rates, cohabiting unions of short duration, and childbearing among unpartnered women and men makes it unrealistic to think that policymakers will be able to reduce rates of multiple unions and of single parenthood in the United States to typical European levels. Consequently, a family policy that relies too heavily on marriage will not help the many children destined to live in single-parent and cohabiting-parent families—many of them economically disadvantaged—for some or all of their formative years. Only assistance directed to needy families, regardless of their household structure, will reach them. Such policies are less popular in the United States, as the widespread disdain for cash welfare and the popularity of the 1996 welfare reform legislation demonstrate. Moreover, some American policymakers worry that programs that support all parents without regard to partnership status may decrease people's incentive to marry.[81] The dilemma for policymakers is how to make the trade-off between marriage-based and marriage-neutral programs. A careful balance of both is needed to provide adequate support to American children.

Notes

1. W. C. Rodgers and A. Thornton, "Changing Patterns of First Marriage in the United States," *Demography* 22 (1985): 265–79; Joshua R. Goldstein and Catherine T. Kenney, "Marriage Delayed or Marriage Forgone? New Cohort Forecasts of First Marriage for U.S. Women," *American Sociological Review* 66 (2001): 506–19.

2. U.S. Bureau of the Census, "Percent of People 25 Years Old and Over Who Have Completed High School or College, by Race, Hispanic Origin and Sex: Selected Years 1940 to 2002," 2003, table A-2, www.census.gov/population/socdemo/education/tabA-2.pdf (accessed June 24, 2004).
3. Ibid.
4. U.S. National Center for Health Statistics, "Fertility, Family Planning, and Women's Health: New Data from the 1995 National Survey of Family Growth," *Vital and Health Statistics* 23, no. 19 (1997), available at www.cdc.gov/nchs/data/series/sr_23/sr23_019.pdf (accessed July 13, 2004).
5. Larry L. Bumpass and Hsien-Hen Lu, "Trends in Cohabitation and Implications for Children's Family Contexts in the United States," *Population Studies* 54 (2000): 29–41. They note that 49 percent of women aged thirty to thirty-four years old in the 1995 National Survey of Family Growth reported ever cohabiting.
6. U.S. National Center for Health Statistics, "Number and Percent of Births to Unmarried Women, by Race and Hispanic Origin: United States, 1940–99," *Vital Statistics of the United States, 1999,* vol. 1, *Natality*, table 1-17 (available at www.cdc.gov/nchs/data/statab/t991x17.pdf [accessed January 12, 2005]); and U.S. National Center for Health Statistics, "Births: Preliminary Data for 2002," *National Vital Statistics Report* 53, no. 9, www.cdc.gov/nchs/data/nvsr/nvsr53/nvsr53_09.pdf (accessed January 12, 2005). For 2003, the figures were 34.6 percent overall, 23.5 percent for non-Hispanic whites, 68.5 percent for non-Hispanic blacks, and 45 percent for Hispanics.
7. Ibid.
8. Marcia Carlson, Sara McLanahan, and Paula England, "Union Formation in Fragile Families," *Demography* 41 (2004): 237–61.
9. Dan Black and others, "Demographics of the Gay and Lesbian Population in the United States: Evidence from Available Systematic Data," *Demography* 37 (2000): 139–54.
10. U.S. Bureau of the Census, "Married-Couple and Unmarried-Partner Households: 2000" (Government Printing Office, 2003).
11. Andrew Cherlin, *Marriage, Divorce, Remarriage* (Harvard University Press, 1992).
12. Matthew Bramlett and William D. Mosher, *Cohabitation, Marriage, Divorce and Remarriage in the United. States,* series 22, no. 2 (U.S. National Center for Health Statistics, Vital and Health Statistics, 2002), available at www.cdc.gov/nchs/data/series/sr_23/sr23_022.pdf (accessed June 2003).
13. U.S. Bureau of the Census. "Detailed Living Arrangements of Children by Race and Hispanic Origin, 1996," 2001, www.census.gov/population/socdemo/child/p70-74/tab01.pdf (accessed June 28, 2004). The data are from the 1996 Survey of Income and Program Participation, wave 2.
14. Some of the one-parent families contain an unmarried cohabiting partner, whom the Census Bureau normally does not count as a "parent." According to the 1996 estimates cited in the previous note, about 2.5 percent of children live with a biological or adoptive parent who is cohabiting.
15. Lynne Casper and Suzanne M. Bianchi, *Continuity and Change in the American Family* (Thousand Oaks, Calif.: Sage, 2002).
16. David Ellwood and Christopher Jencks, "The Uneven Spread of Single-Parent Families: What Do We Know? Where Do We Look for Answers?" in *Social Inequality,* edited by Kathryn M. Neckerman (New York: Russell Sage Foundation, 2004), pp. 3–118.
17. Sara McLanahan, "Diverging Destinies: How Children Are Faring under the Second Demographic Transition," *Demography* 41 (2004): 607–27.
18. Ellwood and Jencks, "The Uneven Spread of Single-Parent Families" (see note 16).
19. Steven P. Martin, "Growing Evidence for a 'Divorce Divide'? Education and Marital Dissolution Rates in the U.S. since the 1970s," Working Paper on Social Dimensions of Inequality (New York: Russell Sage Foundation, 2004).
20. McLanahan, "Diverging Destinies" (see note 17).
21. Ibid.
22. Isabel Sawhill and Laura Chadwick, *Children in Cities: Uncertain Futures* (Brookings, 1999); and Donald J. Hernandez, *America's Children: Resources from Family, Government, and Economy* (New York: Russell Sage Foundation, 1993).
23. S. Philip Morgan and others, "Racial Differences in Household and Family Structure at the Turn of the Century," *American Journal of Sociology* 98 (1993): 798–828.
24. Cherlin, *Marriage, Divorce, Remarriage* (see note 11).

25. Goldstein and Kenney, "Marriage Delayed or Marriage Forgone?" (see note 1).
26. U.S. National Center for Health Statistics, "Births: Preliminary Data" (see note 6).
27. Bumpass and Lu, "Trends in Cohabitation" (see note 5).
28. U.S. National Center for Health Statistics, "Revised Birth and Fertility Rates for the 1990s and New Rates for the Hispanic Populations, 2000 and 2001: United States," *National Vital Statistics Reports* 51, no. 12 (Government Printing Office, 2003); and U.S. National Center for Health Statistics, "Births: Final Data for 2000," *National Vital Statistics Report* 50, no. 5 (Government Printing Office, 2002).
29. Frank D. Bean and Marta Tienda, *The Hispanic Population of the United States* (New York: Russell Sage Foundation, 1987).
30. U.S. National Center for Health Statistics, "Births: Final Data for 2000" (see note 28).
31. McLanahan, "Diverging Destinies" (see note 17).
32. Elise Richer and others, *Boom Times a Bust: Declining Employment among Less-Educated Young Men* (Washington: Center for Law and Social Policy, 2003); available at www.clasp.org/DMS/Documents/ 1058362464.08/Boom_Times.pdf (accessed July 13, 2004).
33. William J. Wilson, *The Truly Disadvantaged: The Inner City, the Underclass, and Public Policy* (University of Chicago Press, 1987).
34. Robert D. Mare and Christopher Winship, "Socioeconomic Change and the Decline in Marriage for Blacks and Whites," in *The Urban Underclass,* edited by Christopher Jencks and Paul Peterson (Brookings, 1991), pp. 175–202; and Daniel T. Lichter, Diane K. McLaughlin, and David C. Ribar, "Economic Restructuring and the Retreat from Marriage," *Social Science Research* 31 (2002): 230–56.
35. Ernest W. Burgess and Harvey J. Locke, *The Family: From Institution to Companionship* (New York: American Book Company, 1945).
36. Andrew J. Cherlin, "The Deinstitutionalization of American Marriage," *Journal of Marriage and the Family* 66 (2004): 848–61.
37. Ibid.
38. Linda Burton of Pennsylvania State University directed the ethnographic component of the study. For a general description, see Pamela Winston and others, "Welfare, Children, and Families: A Three-City Study Overview and Design," 1999, www.jhu.edu\-welfare\overviewanddesign.pdf (accessed July 10, 2004).
39. M. Belinda Tucker, "Marital Values and Expectations in Context: Results from a 21-City Survey," in *The Ties That Bind: Perspectives on Marriage and Cohabitation,* edited by Linda J. Waite (New York: Aldine de Gruyter, 2000), pp. 166–87.
40. Carlson, McLanahan, and England, "Union Formation" (see note 8).
41. Barbara Dafoe Whitehead and David Popenoe, "Who Wants to Marry a Soul Mate?" in *The State of Our Unions, 2001,* The National Marriage Project, Rutgers University, pp. 6–16, 2001, available at marriage.rutgers.edu/Publications/SOOU/NMPAR2001.pdf (accessed February 12, 2004).
42. The estimate assumes that the age-specific marriage rates in the year of calculation (in this case, 1990) will remain unchanged in future years. Since this assumption is unrealistic, the total marriage rate is unlikely to predict the future accurately. But it does demonstrate the rate of marriage implied by current trends.
43. Ronald Inglehart and others, *Human Beliefs and Values: A Cross-Cultural Sourcebook Based on the 1999–2002 Values Surveys* (Mexico City: Siglo Veinciuno Editores, 2004).
44. Alexis de Tocqueville, *Democracy in America,* vol. 1 (New York: Knopf, Everyman's Library, 1994), p. 304.
45. Nancy Cott, *Public Vows: A History of Marriage and the Nation* (Harvard University Press, 2000).
46. Quoted in ibid., pp. 102–03.
47. Herbert G. Gutman, *The Black Family in Slavery and Freedom, 1750–1925* (New York: Pantheon, 1976).
48. Jacqueline Jones, *Labor of Love, Labor of Sorrow: Black Women and the Family from Slavery to the Present* (New York: Basic Books, 1985).
49. Tocqueville, *Democracy in America* (see note 44), p. 303.
50. Grace Davie, "Patterns of Religion in Western Europe: An Exceptional Case," in *The Blackwell Companion to the Sociology of Religion,* edited by Richard K. Fenn (Oxford: Blackwell, 2001), pp. 264–78; and Seymour Martin Lipset, "American Exceptionalism Reaffirmed," *Tocqueville Review* 10 (1990): 3–35.

51. Inglehart and others, *Human Beliefs and Values* (see note 43).
52. Ibid.
53. See the discussion in Ron J. Lesthaeghe, *The Decline of Belgian Fertility, 1800–1970* (Princeton University Press, 1977), p. 304.
54. Alisa Klaus, "Depopulation and Race Suicide: Maternalism and Pronatalist Ideologies in France and the United States," in *Mothers of a New World: Maternalist Politics and the Origins of the Welfare State,* edited by Seth Koven and Sonya Michel (New York: Routledge, 1993), pp. 188–212.
55. Paul Ginsborg, "The Family Politics of the Great Dictators," in *Family Life in the Twentieth Century,* edited by David I. Kertzer and Marzio Barbagli (Yale University Press, 2003), pp. 188–97.
56. Susan Pedersen, *Family, Dependence, and the Origins of the Welfare State: Britain and. France, 1914–1945* (Cambridge University Press, 1993).
57. Ibid.
58. The total divorce rate is formed by summing duration-specific divorce rates prevalent in the year of observation—in this case, 1990. It therefore assumes that the duration-specific rates of 1990 will remain the same in future years. It shares the limits of the total marriage rate (see note 42).
59. Robert Schoen and Robin M. Weinick, "The Slowing Metabolism of Marriage: Figures from 1988 U.S. Marital Status Life Tables," *Demography* 39 (1993): 737–46. Schoen and Weinick used life table calculations to establish the marriage and divorce probabilities for American men and women. Unfortunately, only total marriage rates and total divorce rates are available for other countries. Consequently, I calculated a total divorce rate for the United States from published duration-specific divorce rates for 1990. I then summed the total first marriage rate and total divorce rate for the United States and the other countries displayed in Figure 4. Although this procedure is not as accurate as using rates generated by life tables, the difference is unlikely to alter the relative positions of the countries in the figure.
60. Strictly speaking, I should use the total divorce rate for people in first marriages (as opposed to including people in remarriages), but the available data do not allow for that level of precision.
61. Alexia Fürnkranz-Prskawetz and others, "Pathways to Stepfamily Formation in Europe: Results from the FFS," *Demographic Research* 8 (2003): 107–9.
62. Author's calculation from the 1995 National Survey of Family Growth microdata file.
63. Author's calculation from the 2002 National Survey of Family Growth microdata file.
64. Patrick Heuveline, Jeffrey M. Timberlake, and Frank F. Furstenberg Jr., "Shifting Childrearing to Single Mothers: Results from 17 Western Countries," *Population and Development Review* 29 (2003): 47–71. The figures quoted appear in note 6.
65. McLanahan, "Diverging Destinies" (see note 17).
66. About one-third of all births are to unmarried mothers, and Bumpass and Lu report that about 60 percent of unmarried mothers in 1995 were not cohabiting (0.33 × 0.60 = 0.198). Bumpas and Lu, "Trends in Cohabitation" (see note 5).
67. Kathleen Kiernan, "European Perspectives on Nonmarital Childbearing," in *Out of Wedlock: Causes and Consequences of Nonmarital Fertility,* edited by Lawrence L. Wu and Barbara Wolfe (New York: Russell Sage Foundation, 2001), pp. 77–108.
68. Lars Osberg, Timothy M. Smeeding, and Jonathan Schwabish, "Income Distribution and Public Social Expenditure: Theories, Effects, and Evidence," in *Social Inequality,* edited by Kathryn M. Neckerman (New York: Russell Sage Foundation, 2004), pp. 821–59.
69. Poverty was defined as having a family income of less than half of the median income for all families. Bruce Bradbury and Markus Jäntti, "Child-Poverty across the Industrialized World: Evidence from the Luxembourg Income Study," in *Child Well-Being, Child Poverty and Child Policy in Modern Nations: What Do We Know?* edited by Koen Vleminckx and Timothy M. Smeeding (Bristol, England: Policy Press, 2000), pp. 11–32.
70. Marzio Barbagli and David I. Kertzer, "Introduction," and Paulo Ronfani, "Family Law in Europe," in *Family Life in the Twentieth Century,* edited by David I. Kertzer and Marzio Barbagli (Yale University Press, 2003), respectively, pp. xi–xliv and 114–51.
71. Claude Martin and Irene Théry, "The Pacs and Marriage and Cohabitation in France,"

International Journal of Law, Policy and the Family 15 (2001): 135–58.

72. Patrick Festy, "The 'Civil Solidarity Pact' (PACS) in France: An Impossible Evaluation," *Population et Sociétés*, no. 369 (2001): 1–4.
73. John Eekelaar, "The End of an Era?" *Journal of Family History* 28 (2003): 108–22.
74. Eric Fassin, "Same Sex, Different Politics: 'Gay Marriage' Debates in France and the United States," *Popular Culture* 13 (2001): 215–32.
75. Kathleen Kiernan, "Cohabitation in Western Europe," *Population Trends* 96 (Summer 1999): 25–32.
76. See, for example, Lawrence L. Wu and Brian C. Martinson, "Family Structure and the Risk of Premarital Birth," *American Sociological Review* 59 (1993): 210–32; Jake M. Najman and others, "Impact of Family Type and Family Quality on Child Behavior Problems: A Longitudinal Study," *Journal of the American Academy of Child and Adolescent Psychiatry* 36 (1997): 1357–65.
77. John F. Sandberg and Sandra D. Hofferth, "Changes in Children's Time with Parents, U.S. 1981–1997," *Demography* 38 (2001): 423–36.
78. Suzanne M. Bianchi, "Maternal Employment and Time with Children: Dramatic Change or Surprising Continuity?" *Demography* 37 (2000): 401–14.
79. Annette Lareau, *Unequal Childhoods: Class, Race, and Family Life* (University of California Press, 2003).
80. Goren Therborn, *Between Sex and Power: Family in the World, 1900–2000* (London: Routledge, 2004).
81. This proposition is similar to what David Ellwood has called the "assistance-family structure conundrum." David T. Ellwood, *Poor Support: Poverty and the American Family* (New York: Basic Books, 1988).

At-Home Fathers and Breadwinning Mothers: Variations in Constructing Work and Family Lives

CARYN E. MEDVED AND WILLIAM K. RAWLINS

> *At times I used to dream about when they are older [and] I will be able to write; when they are older, the house will get cleaned lickety split . . . I do the dishes and I do the laundry and all the mundane household stuff [but] now I don't get to cuddle and watch Sesame Street.*

The above excerpt is from an interview with Bob, an at-home father, reminiscing about the memorable times he used to spend with his daughters when they were younger. Bob is married to Julie, a senior manager working at a large firm in the Midwest. He continues, "There was always a realization between us that she was like the, I guess, the corporate person," and he humorously adds, "I have a lot of patience with kids, but with adults, less so." Alternative ways of composing and talking about work and family life as evidenced in Bob and Julie's story are slowly making their way into

Caryn E. Medved and William K. Rawlins, "At-Home Fathers and Breadwinning Mothers: Variations in Constructing Work and Family Lives." *Women & Language* 34 (September 2011): 9–39.

mainstream U.S. culture (Kershaw, 2009; Morgan, 2011; Stout, 2010). The number of couples reporting to be primarily or solely financially dependent on a wife's income range from 12% of women who earn more than 60% of the family's income to just under 3% who report being entirely dependent on a wife's earnings (Bureau of Labor Statistics, 2010; Raley, Mattingly, & Bianchi, 2006). The U.S. also saw a 200% increase in the number of reported at-home fathers between 1994 and 2005 (U.S. Census Bureau, 2006). Further, men were disproportionately affected early on during the recent recession as the most significant layoffs hit male-dominated industries (Şahin, Song, & Hobijn, 2010; see also Boushey, 2011). The Pew Research Center also reports that women continue to outpace men in education and earnings growth (Fry & Cohn, 2010). Undoubtedly, substantial changes in the discourse and related practices of marriage and earning are underway.

Investigations of dual-earner couples' experiences have dominated work and family studies over the past few decades (e.g., Buzzanell, 1997; Hochschild, 1989; Hood, 1983; Medved, 2004; Potuchek, 1997; Risman & Johnson-Sumerford, 1998; Stone, 2007). This research documents the work and family choices and conflicts of dual-earner couples that now represent 47.8% of married couples in the U.S. (Bureau of Labor Statistics, 2011). Scholars also have turned their attention to alternative work and family arrangements including the experiences of: (a) at-home fathers (e.g., Doucet, 2004; Radin, 1988; Rochelen, Suizzo, Kelley, & Scaringi, 2008; Smith, 1998; Smith, 2009; Vavrus, 2002) and (b) breadwinning mothers (Drago, Black, & Wooden, 2005; Medved, 2009a; Meisenbach, 2010; Winslow-Bowe, 2006). Yet to our knowledge no significant efforts have been made to study the social construction and coordination of meaning and identity in the lives of *both husbands and wives* transposing post-World War II gendered marital work and family roles. We know little about *how* these supposed role reversing or reverse traditional couples do and/or undo gender through language and social interaction (Deutsch, 2007; West & Zimmerman, 1987). Illustrating the different ways these couples communicatively construct their unique approaches to work and family is this study's key contribution to the gender and communication literature; we provide a glimpse into varied examples of working out social change at the micro-level. Given that language and social interaction are crucial sites where the definitions and daily practices of masculinities and femininities along with their historic associations with the public and private spheres are reproduced, adapted, resisted and/or transformed, we are led to listen and learn from these couples' stories.

As a background for telling their stories, we first briefly review research on dual-earning couples' marital negotiations, professional women's workforce opting out, as well as stay-at-home fathering experiences. Second, we describe our theoretical approach to the study of gender and language (e.g., Deutsch, 2007; Ferree, Lorber, & Hess, 2000; Gerson & Piess, 1985; Potuchek, 1992). Third, we present our findings from exploratory, indepth interviews with ten at-home father and breadwinning mother couples. Specifically, we identify five homemaking-moneymaking stances among these couples: reversing, conflicting, collaborating, improvising, and sharing. We illustrate each of these five stances through a composite narrative, each developed from one of the couples' interview transcripts. Finally, we discuss our study's implications as well as future research directions.

Review of Literature

Dual-Earner Couples' Negotiations

Marital structures and communication strategies are often-studied sites for the (re) negotiation of gender. The post-World War II rise of the middle-class, White, dual-earner couple brought gender issues center stage for scholars and feminist activists alike. The category "dual-earner" has always encompassed a wide array of earning arrangements ranging from dual labor force participation regardless of income level to professional dual *careers* couples and even asymmetrical earnings with "wives as senior partners" (Atkinson & Boles, 1984; Halpern & Cheung, 2008; see also Rosenfeld, Bowen, & Richman, 1995, on communication strategies for dual-career couples). Various theoretical perspectives have been evoked to explore these couples' experiences and negotiations, including social exchange (Becker, 1993), economic bargaining (Bittman, England, Folbre, Sayer, & Matheson, 2003), feminist and gender construction (Buzzanell, 1997; Hochschild, 1989; Medved, 2004; Potuchek, 1992; Risman, 1999; Zvonkovic, Greaves, Schmiege, & Hall, 1996), and integrated theoretical perspectives (Alberts, Tracy, & Trethewey, 2010).

We know that increases in dual-career women's incomes do not inevitably or neatly translate into greater marital power. Gender and other social and discursive forces, not simply earning differentials, need to be taken into account to understand divisions of household labor (e.g., Alberts et al., 2010; Offer & Schneider, 2011; Risman & Johnson-Sumerford, 1998), and marital decision making and satisfaction (Bodi, Mikula, & Riederer, 2010; Zvonkovic et al., 1996). Even when market hours are fairly equal, wives still do more housework than their husbands (Tichenor, 2005). What spouses consider a fair division of labor remains gendered and complexly related to marital satisfaction (Wilkie, Ferree, & Ratcliff, 1998). Generally speaking, as dual-career women's incomes rise, women do less and men perform more housework (Bittman et al., 2003). Yet men at the extremes of the income range slightly *reduce* their participation in housework (Hochschild, 1989). Finally, higher income-earning women, at times, use communication strategies that downplay their financial contributions and refrain from exercising the traditional masculine link between money and power (Potuchek, 1997). What is less understood is how couples negotiate gender and identity when husbands effectively opt out or remain out of the workforce after layoffs and wives remain tied to paid labor. How does this context shape how these couples make sense out of work and family? Key to understanding this process of negotiation is exploring how these couples talk about their approaches to caring and earning.

Labor Force Decision Making and Opting Out

Stone (2007) found that while only a minority of professional women plan ahead to leave their careers for full-time motherhood, many exit due to frustration with both organizational as well as spousal flexibility and support, along with intensive mothering pressures (see also Hays, 1996; Medved & Kirby, 2005; Warner, 2005). Stone argues that these women do not make this choice lightly and voice concerns about likely problems with career re-entry in professional positions. Many fail to plan for potential unintended consequences of financial dependency such as the possibility of divorce or husbands' job loss or disability (Bennetts, 2007). Gerson's (1985) arguments remain relevant as she contends that women's workforce decisions are products of: (a) "pushing" women out of the workforce (i.e., desires for traditional motherhood, lack of spousal assistance, lack of supportive work environments, falling career aspirations); as well as (b) "pulling" them into paid labor (i.e., career aspirations, ambivalence toward motherhood, financial necessity). She notes that "women [may] . . . resemble men who find themselves in jobs they would prefer to leave, except for one important difference . . . few men enjoy the traditional, although shrinking, female option of trading paid work for domestic work" (p. 19). Meaning construction in the lives of men (and their wives) who *do* trade career for domestic work is the focus of the present study. Further, we believe that to richly understand this inherently communicative process, we must investigate and juxtapose *both* men and women's interrelated accounts of labor force participation and exit. Just as life course theorists argue that work and family is constituted by "linked lives" (Elder, 1995), we argue that marital identities, at times are also linked identities and must be explored as joint-constructions or co-constructions.

Stay-at-Home Fathering

Bridges, Etaugh, and Barnes-Farrell (2002) report that stay-at-home fathers are judged more harshly than stay-at-home mothers for ostensibly sacrificing their families' financial security. In other words, they are sanctioned for engaging in caregiving and *not* breadwinning per conventional gender expectations (Riggs, 1997). For their parts, working mothers are perceived as less communal (i.e., sensitive, warm, nurturing, and dedicated to family) and less effective as parents than fathers. Even so, Wentworth and Chell (2001) explain that "male cross-gender behavior is treated more harshly than female cross-gender behavior" (p. 640). They suggest "there is a stronger link between gender roles and perceived sexuality for men than for women" (p. 640). Although we must not forget that the sexuality of powerful career women is also challenged (Jamison, 1997), a man performing household labor or childcare may be perceived minimally as "less of a man," perhaps even threatening to children or homosexual (Murray, 1996). In an early study of primary caregiving fathers, Radin (1988) reported that men did not persist in at-home roles for extended periods of time due to gendered pressures to conform. Radin, however, found four commonalities among men who *did* remain in full-time caregiving roles for more than two years (versus reverting to traditional patterns) including: (a) viewing their own fathers as inattentive, (b) being in their 30s and/or with prior career experience, (c) enjoying the support of extended family members, and (d) having a small family. Rochlen and colleagues' (2008) work also found that men exit paid work when (a) their wives have a high value for career, (b) they see full-time parenting as an opportunity, and (c) caregiving aligns with their preference or personality. Both at-home mothering and fathering couples report similar levels of marital satisfaction, but women in either arrangement report higher levels of stress and exhaustion than men (Zimmerman, 2000).

In a study of 70 Canadian at-home fathers, Doucet (2004) reported that although stay-at-home fathers take on primary childcare responsibilities, they do not entirely forgo traditional masculine sources of work-related identity. At-home fathers report engaging in various kinds of work, including unpaid community work, part-time home-based employment, and self-provisioning work (e.g., landscaping, carpentry, woodworking, car repair). Doucet also found that among the various forms of masculinity displayed in at-home fathers' narratives, hegemonic forms of masculinity remained widespread (see also Vavrus, 2002). These men often mentioned feeling social pressure to earn and feeling isolated from the "real world" of paid labor, as well as the need to socialize with other men on common masculine conversational ground. Smith (1998) found that "hegemonic conceptions of who ought to be minding the children and house subvert or thwart [at-home father's] attempts to validate themselves and these practices" (p. 138).

In sum, we know that gender and power are intertwined with dual-career couples' negotiation of childcare, domestic labor, and labor force participation. Men's power and privilege in the home persists to a certain extent, despite women's increased contributions to household income. Yet lived moments of "undoing gender" cannot be discounted and warrant investigation (Deutsch, 2007). What is less well known is how couples engaging in gender atypical arrangements—particularly primary breadwinning mothers married to at-home fathers come to understand, enact, and potentially resist or rework conventional gendered tasks and identities through language and social interaction. Given the relatively uncharted and exploratory nature of this study, we frame this investigation around one central research question: *How do stay-at-home fathers and breadwinning mothers articulate their stances toward moneymaking and homemaking?*

Doing, Undoing, and Reworking Gender

Gender operates on multiple, dynamic, and interdependent levels (e.g., Ashcraft & Mumby, 2003; Deutsch, 2007; Ferree, Lorber, & Hess, 2000; Gerson & Piess, 1985). We take up social constructionist and feminist arguments that the interactive and discursive expressions of gender are complexly intertwined with their structural and institutional manifestations (Deutsch, 2007; Holmer-Nadesan, 1996). Studying the discourse of these couples concurrently gives us (a) insight into their ongoing negotiations and coordination of gendered tasks and identities, as well as (b) examples of how available language shapes and is reshaped by what these couples see as possible performances of homemaking and moneymaking. We "do gender" in everyday discourse and related practices in the context of larger cultural and structural forces (West & Zimmerman, 1987). Equally important, we can *undo* and rework gender through our language and social interactions (Butler, 1990; Buzzanell, 1995; Denker, 2009; Medved, 2009b). We must not only explore the ways we perpetuate modern gendered assumptions about caregiving and wage-earning, but also the ways we resist and 'break the bowls' of gender (Lorber, 2005). We also need to pay attention to dissembling binaries; that is exploring the various enactments of gender in-between simply doing and undoing, public and private, or masculine and feminine (Connell, 1995; Deutsch, 2007; Geuss, 2003; Medved, 2007). Multiple masculinities and femininities exist as interdependent discourses, co-constructed identities, and lived experiences. Gender role prescriptions still exist although they are not as static or fixed as in the past. Instead, they persist in ongoing interplay with gendered identities, understandings of selves and as coconstructed processes in marital relationships (Sveningsson & Alversson, 2003). Sometimes gendered social change is subtle and can only be seen in small acts and words at the margins of our lived experiences. Further, fathering and housework are feminist issues (Silverstein, 1996) just as are women's access to and success in the workplace (Buzzanell, 1995). We embrace these theoretical assumptions about language and gender in the five stories below that (re)present varying gendered co-constructions of homemaking-moneymaking tasks and identities.

Investigative Practices

The texts examined in this study were collected through semi-structured interviews with eight married couples from a large metropolitan area and mid-sized town in the Midwest, and two couples from the east coast of the United States. Separate interviews were conducted with each husband and wife; sixteen of our interviews were conducted face-to-face and audio-recorded by one of the authors (Hertz, 1995). We interviewed four participants over the phone with two individuals' insights audio-taped and the others' preserved in detailed notes. Each interview lasted between one and two hours. All audio recordings were transcribed by a professional service, resulting in 495 typed pages.

Participants

All the stay-at-home fathering couples (SAHFC) were white, middle to upper-middle class, heterosexual couples with at-home fathers and breadwinning mothers, including one couple who had recently returned to a traditional arrangement. All were recruited through the authors' professional and social networks and flyers posted in local areas. Men volunteering to participate self-selected as a "stay-at-home" father. That is, they considered themselves primary childcare providers who had left full-time careers (or were on an extended hiatus) and were dependent on spousal income. While the label SAHFC is not ideal, it provides a clear description of what characteristics differentiate these couples from dual-career or traditional male breadwinning couples. In line with past research, these at-home fathers often still participated in part-time volunteer work or limited at-home paid labor (Doucet, 2004). On average, the couples had been married about 10 years (range = 5 to 18) with various numbers and ages of children (Appendix 1). The interviewed women's occupations included: management consultant, banker, lawyer, non-profit manager, online business manager, graduate student/program assistant, and sales manager. The amount of time these couples had spent in their current work and family arrangements averaged three years, ranging from three months to seven years. Given our goals, social constructionist underpinnings, and research question, we sought married couples who have lived this unique relational situation and were willing to share their stories.

Analysis of Interviews

An inductive, interpretive analysis of interview discourse was the most appropriate method given the nature of this study (Strauss and Corbin, 1990). Our goal was *not* to assess whether or not SAHFC were more or less happy or equal partners in the division of labor. Rather, our aim was to develop a grounded, interpretive awareness of participants' communicative construction of work and family in this unique marital relationship. Further, we chose to portray the complexity and texture of their lives and choices using narrative form.

Each author first independently read the entire corpus of transcripts and began to flesh out his/her own understandings of what was going on across these individuals' stories (Lindlof & Taylor, 1995; Patton, 1990). Then we shared these initial conceptions and came to some common understandings of issues to examine more systematically when studying the transcripts a second time. Key themes and insights were then indexed and organized in separate analytical memos. We then shared the memos and began to develop provisional categories to describe both commonalities and differences across the individuals' and couples' talk. Next, an array of orientations toward domestic labor and paid employment began to emerge. That is, we started grouping couples together whose discourse reflected a similar stance toward homemaking and moneymaking (Rawlins, 1984, 1992, 1998). By "stance" we mean a common position toward action and an emotional and/or intellectual point of view shared by sets of participating couples. As we further explored the stories of couples *within each cluster* we identified three facets of their experiences that were described similarly: (a) task responsibility, (b) identity adoption, and (c) role eligibility (see Appendix 2).

First, *task responsibility* describes variations in how members of a couple reflect categorically on their daily routines, responsibilities, and tasks as a couple/family using gendered and fixed conceptions as opposed to describing active adoption of alternative possibilities and conceiving the nature of their responsibilities as negotiated and flexible. Task responsibility, in short, focuses on their articulations of who does what, for how long, and why, in the marriage. The second way in which these narrative clusters seemed to diverge from each other relates to the couples' expressed identification with their unique work and family arrangement. Portrayals of *identity adoption* characterize performances of identities that maintain and/or are based on pre-determined gendered roles and tasks in contrast to sustained performances of identities based on co-created practices and responsibilities. By identities, we mean talk of self-understandings or answers to the question, "Who am I?" as embedded in the language of our participants (Sveningsson & Alvesson, 2003). Discourses of identity adoption for SAHFCs convey a sense of "who are we" in relation to "what we do" in marriage. A final insight emerging from our reading of these transcripts was how they portrayed gender in relation to work and family role eligibilities. By role, we mean the socially defined expectations associated with performing specific activities. Role eligibility focuses on couples' articulation of who is allowed to do what in the marriage. Variation in *role eligibility* occurred in the ways that couples' discourse reflected stereotyped and unequal eligibilities for men and women to perform homemaking and moneymaking roles as opposed to allowing for negotiated and equal eligibilities for spouses to perform domestic and paid labor.

We decided to report our findings in the form of five narratives carefully developed to illustrate the array of stances portrayed in and across our participants' discourse. Each narrative was constructed as a composite story of one couple's separately conducted interviews (Hertz, 1995). Rather than disassembling these ten couples' stories into a series of themes or sound bites taken out of their rich narrative context, we chose one couple's story to represent each stance toward homemaking and moneymaking. In addition to illustrating a given couple's experiences, we offer each of these narratives to convey within the limits of a journal article format a possible way of articulating marital selves and tasks in this unconventional relational context. While we were struck by the similarities of husbands' and wives' accounts within specific couples, we also tried to include any diverging views within our representations. We term the stances toward homemaking and moneymaking portrayed in the five representative narratives: (a) reversing, (b) conflicting, (c) collaborating, (d) improvising, and (e) sharing.

Five Homemaking-Moneymaking Stances

Before presenting the five stances, we briefly mention four factors that were commonly described as occasioning these ten couples' decisions to live as at-home fathering families (see also Doucet, 2004). First, both parents wanted their children to be raised in their own home by one or both of them; they wanted hands-on responsibility for their kids' daily lives. Second, except for one case of equal earnings, in every couple, the mother's paid work brought the family greater income and benefits than the father's earnings prior to his movement into full-time caregiving. Third, every father except one had greater flexibility in his work schedule than the mother, again, prior to his taking on full-time caregiving duties. A fourth occasioning factor is that of temperament. These men and women described the father's temperament as conducive to spending extended periods of time with their child(ren) and being relatively unthreatened by homemaking work and identities. We will return to these issues in our final discussion section, but for now, here are the stances.

Stance One: Reversing

We label this first stance *reversing* to indicate the performance of gender nontraditional homemaking and moneymaking tasks. Reversing, in this context, means to exchange duties though not necessarily to alter or transform their meanings and associated identities or eligibilities. Simply put, the sex of the person performing the task is reversed but its meaning stays intact in these couples' articulations. The couple illustrating the *reversing* stance had been married for eight years with a fifteen-month-old daughter. When Bethany was born, Scott and Alicia were both employed. Even so, Alicia observed, "When I was younger, I thought I'd have more children and be home. . . . The most important job you can do is stay at home." In Scott's words, "She wanted to take on that role." But they knew they could save money if she worked more after their daughter's birth because as a management consultant, "Alicia has always been the one who has made more in the relationship." Following Alicia's maternity leave, Scott had a five-month paid family leave; following this, Alicia quit her job to stay home full-time.

Home on leave with Bethany, Scott still tried doing work via email, occasionally taking her with him into the office, and attempting consulting and conference calls from home. He also tried to "squeeze work in" at night. Alicia remarked, "His ideas about what a father does were based on his father. . . . You always should have a job." Although he accomplished some work during his leave, he had an "identity crisis," according to Alicia. He felt tremendous anxiety about not staying connected with his occupation. It was "horrible," she said. "We idealized the idea of him being at home; we thought it seemed so great, but it didn't work out that way." Meanwhile, Alicia's work was too challenging, mainly in relation to breastfeeding and travel. Her employer "tried" to accommodate her but, in Scott's words, "Alicia wanted to be home." She was ambivalent about work and felt guilty not being with her daughter. She would pump breast milk at work, and at night it was Scott's job to thaw the frozen bottles and feed Bethany. Alicia wanted Scott to have the chance to care for Bethany, but she also wanted to be a "mother."

Determining household tasks was a challenge for this couple when switching work roles. Steve asked: When the man is doing the more feminine chores, what happens to the more masculine tasks like raking leaves, etc.? Alicia said their negotiations over these issues became "his work versus my work but trying to keep Bethany in the forefront." She would "walk through the door" and start to care for their daughter, and from then on Scott would need to do his paid work. Due to exhaustion, "Later on we developed a list of who does what." Alicia said she always knew she would quit her job, it was a matter of when. And while Scott considers his time as an at-home father "a very profound experience," he thinks Bethany "needed" her mom at home and Alicia needed to be there. He's become more of a believer in a mother and child's biological connection and is devoting increasing amounts of time to his paying job.

Through this *reversing narrative*, we see a SAHFC organizing their activities and identities according to prescribed gender roles and traditionally gendered images of parenting, despite living in an alternative work arrangement (i.e., mother is primary earner and father is primary childcare provider). Homemaking work is described categorically and, by and large, as feminine or women's work; moneymaking work is viewed as a masculine or a predominantly male domain regardless of the sex of the person performing it. Becoming a SAHFC therefore involves transitory *role* reversals rather than the adoption of new identities; this stance still presupposes natural and gender-linked parenting roles. We term this stance "reversing" because the categorical reflections and identities associated with at-home parenting and outside-of-the-home moneymaking remain intact while often at odds with the gendered self-conceptions of the persons performing these labors. The commonsense notion of role reversal applies most straightforwardly here related to the husband's and wife's performances of unconventional duties without the reconfiguration of identities. Further, unequal eligibilities to perform homemaking and moneymaking roles persist based on traditionally determined societal gender alignments. As a result, this attempt to live according to preset—although reverse-gendered—duties and roles while still maintaining traditionally gendered personal identities and self-understandings was associated with a range of related tensions that rendered it a transitory option at best.

Stance Two: Conflicting

Stance two is termed *conflicting* in that couples articulate contradictory meanings for the performance of unconventional work and family tasks, identities, and eligibilities. The conflicting approach simultaneously reflects both openness and discontent with the division of task responsibilities. And, while their narratives acknowledge that elements of their identities and perceived eligibilities are different than gendered prescriptions, their meaning-making is fraught with tension. The SAHFC couple illustrating the *conflicting* stance had been married for eighteen years with a nine-year-old son and a seven-year-old daughter. Both Mike and Sue were employed full-time when their nanny of four years left. Mike said they already decided he would "back out of working full time" to "cover" their kids. With Sue's "higher earnings," Mike termed it "the path of least resistance . . . also, optimizing the financial part" of their situation. For her part, Sue recalled she had just been unexpectedly laid off and was interviewing at the time; her husband " . . . took a very pragmatic view as opposed to the more emotional view that I think I had at the time, where he's looking at it saying you're very marketable. . . . You need to go out there and find a job. Right? We've already committed to me being home. Right?"

Mike described "more blurred" distinctions between the family's parental roles for their children, "especially since they see that I'm still—when I'm home—I'm still working." He was proud of his "routine" and "groove" with the kids and that he was "the turn-to guy a lot of times when stuff is going on." Sue affirmed, "He's got good natural instincts to be taking care of the kids" and "has a great relationship with them." Yet she also revealed that "going to college, I assumed that I would work for a couple of years" to "pay off" her education and then she would "quit and I would be at home raising kids." Given their atypical work and family situation, however, she thought her kids would "grow up" with different attitudes toward women in the workplace, hoping they would be "more open-minded about what are some of the different options." At the same time she was trying to make sure "they don't get the message that [my paid] work is more important than them, even though I have to spend more of my time there."

Mike's biggest challenge as the at-home parent was "organizing everything," including the kids' chores, activities, and what is expected of them. Yet for him "the biggest other challenge" involved his own career issues, noting, "The part-time guy" has to accept "that one career role is gonna be subordinate to another." Mike's identity seemed strongly connected to his part-time paid work as a financial planning consultant. He frequently described "covering more of the kid stuff" in matter-of-fact terms and portrayed a traditional male's preoccupation with earning money despite protecting the needs of Sue's "full-time gig" and managing his schedule to do "the family thing in the afternoon" when the children returned home from school. Even so, he hoped that increasing his financial planning business would make it "much harder" for him to "flex" his time around everyone else's while equalizing his and Sue's incomes and time spent at home. Mike looked to the future and explained, "a year from now I hope that I say that it's much harder . . . because my [work] demands have gone up." While "it works out pretty well" for now, Mike wanted more time for paid work.

Mike and Sue each described household chores as contested in traditionally gendered ways. Mike commented, "She's much more concerned about how clean the house is," and added, "She'll come home and be grumbly about the house being messy and no one will care about that but her." In turn, Sue observed, "I believe I have primary responsibility for dishes and laundry, but he would probably not agree." She continued, "Lately he's done a lot more laundry then he used to. In the past it was when I would come home and I'd lose it, the next day he'd do laundry, right? But, you know, he's kinda starting to see that pattern and wanting to avoid it." These accounts suggest disputed power arrangements where, besides being the primary income provider, the woman is somehow responsible for domestic matters. Sue remarked that often she "can't get this job done because I have to go off and do my other day job, right?"

Despite their shared perceptions of Mike's at-home parenting potential early in their marriage, Sue had not anticipated the consequences to her of their current family arrangement:

> We always knew that if and when we were to have kids . . . that he would be very good at staying home . . . But it was never real at that point, right? And I guess I had always grown up assuming—you know, I had a stay-at-home mom. . . . I assumed I would work for a couple of years to kind of pay off college, if you will, make it worth the while, you know, and then quit and I would be home raising the kids. I never really assumed that I'd be a long-term career woman.

In recent years she switched to a job "that has allotted me much more balance in my life, but I'm clearly not paid as much nor do I have as much advancement opportunity." She summarized, "I understand the rules of the game, but I don't like them, but yet I'm still there playing it." Mike contrasted Sue's identity needs with his, "She doesn't have the kind of attachment some people do to her job and her career in a self-esteem kind of standpoint . . . she doesn't identify herself as what she is. . . . It's not about her. . . . Like some people would say, like me." Mike repeatedly narrated a stereotypical vision blending the past and present of gendered predicaments in corporate America; many successful women want "to just get out of it" and are verbal about it. In contrast, he believed that then and now dissatisfied men "hold more of that inside." Sue echoed these sentiments in describing their own arrangement's challenges, "So the biggest one that's probably—it's like the iceberg where I only see the little tip—is Mike's—Mike's self-esteem. And then, you know, the next one is just my emotional well-being." She depicted their situation in terms mirroring Mike's general discussion, "I think it weighs on him heavily to not be, you know, earning more money . . . and I think to some degree he's not gonna complain to me about anything that's going on in his life because I bring—I wear my stress on my sleeve, so why would he want to add to that?"

The narratives of couples we consider *conflicting* presuppose many facets of traditional feminine and masculine roles and subject positions associated with homemaking and money making even as these couples worked together to negotiate alternative arrangements. To the extent that traditionally gendered discourses, roles, and identities implicitly or explicitly informed their alternative arrangements of parenting, housework, and/or paid labor that challenged such regimes, they experienced conflict. These conflicts reflect inequities and asymmetrical eligibilities historically associated with gendered labor in the home, such as the woman working "a second shift." They also involve conflicted self-images derived from not being able to do what one had hoped to do or perceives one is supposed to do with one's time and talents as a traditionally gendered person/mother/father. As such, neither partner feels fully reconciled to their domestic and paid labor-related identities even as they successfully manage their day-to-day routines.

Stance Three: Collaborating

The homemaking/moneymaking stance we call *collaborating* highlights an approach to work and family that recognizes existing gender prescriptions while, at the same time, expresses a desire to transcend these very same gendered work and family meanings. By collaborating, we mean that a SAHFC articulates an approach to work and life that both holds onto and lets go of conventional gendered meanings and practices. The couple whose story exemplifies the *collaborating* stance had been married for sixteen years with a seven-year-old son, Hank. Lisa and Ty each described their shared "conscious decision" to have a child and for Ty to stay home with him. Their rationale was based on Lisa's higher income and medical benefits from banking and the flexibility of Ty's paid work as a musician. Ty wryly framed his early realizations about doing full-time child-care in terms of gendered positions on knowledge, "It's not a hundred percent true, but men generally like to know or think they know what they're doing all the time. They avoid things that they don't know what they're doing, or they just pretend it doesn't exist." Even so, implicating himself, he described his own need to learn and address demands of childcare:

> So, when it comes to domestic stuff and baby stuff, it's so much easier to just say, I don't know anything about that. And you don't want to know anything about it. It's like if you don't know anything about it, nobody expects you to do it . . . I'm going to be here and if he throws up all over the place or has an explosion in a snowsuit and fills it up with poop, and you're out strolling around—you know, "Mommy, Mommy." There's no mommy there. It's just you.

He noted with gender-bending creativity, "For the biggest part of those early years, I was the man-mom."

For her part, Lisa sincerely felt that Ty "won the prize and got to stay home." Yet when asked how being the primary breadwinner affected their marriage, she replied, "Well, I don't know that it has affected it. That's always been my role. But I think it kind of works for us." She added, "Also I think Ty's not threatened by it. I think that some men have such an ego that they could never have a wife who is the breadwinner. They're too busy beating on their chests; they can't have someone else bringing home the bacon. But he's not that way." In terms of her paid work, Lisa mentioned liking "problem solving," creative challenges, and the opportunities to figure out numerical puzzles in the banking world. She was pleased about her self-sufficiency and her ability to provide income. Even so, she also felt it was difficult to "feel like you're being a good parent and doing good at your job, I think. Especially the parent part. I just feel like I miss a lot. . . . There's not enough time and this child is growing up so fast." Because of her devotion to parenting, Lisa enjoyed her extended opportunities to be home with their son during her maternity leave and the two years she "worked from home." In fact, despite her second thoughts from a financial standpoint, she elected to spend the severance pay she was once awarded to support a full year at home taking care of Hank with Ty. Both parents emphasized choosing how they would live and being at home to raise their son over "materialistic" concerns.

The couple described household labor as equitably distributed based on personal preferences and availability. Ty explained that he enjoys cooking and would do that "regardless of anything." In his view other housework depended on Lisa's paid work, "on what had been going on with her on the job front and how exhausting or time consuming her job was." He described a period during Hank's early childhood, "that lasted about four years; she was gone before he woke up in the morning and got home sometimes in time just to go up and kiss him goodnight and maybe put him down at that point." At present, they have negotiated other patterns, "So, for instance, right now she does the laundry. She does grocery shopping. Although I do the day-to-day grocery shopping, she does the big grocery shopping. . . . She does more than half of the cleaning I would say, although I participate in that." Lisa's account of how they divided housework resonated closely with Ty's, "I think that it's determined a lot just by availability. . . . I think it's just more of what we need to do and who has the time to do it." She reflected, "I don't really think we've ever pointed a finger and said, 'Oh no, that's your job. You need to do it.' We've never done that. We've just kind of worked it out."

Like the other collaborating couples we interviewed, Ty and Lisa repeatedly expressed sensitivity to and respect for what the other was experiencing at various points by assuming identities and responsibilities of child-raising and bread-winning that often challenged traditionally gendered accounts. Their stories were sprinkled with bittersweet recognition of the limits their own negotiated choices placed upon their time and personally desired activities—but more often with ironically reflexive accounts of humorous situations that defied stereotyped options for parenting and occupational identities. Ty recalled how they mutually recognized "the sitcom moment" they found themselves reenacting with Lisa returning from the office just after Ty botched a dinner recipe at the end of his already trying day at home. He noted, "I'm not sure how couples deal with that 'cause it's kind of how does she come in and comfort me without it being patronizing? You know what I mean? How does the man blow off steam for something like the domestic travails of the day?"

Lisa and Ty each expressed summary satisfaction with the family and occupational arrangements they have accomplished together. Lisa stated, "I just think that we know it's not just one person's responsibility to raise a child or to have a home, or even working. . . . I just think that we know that we're a team and we know how important this child is to us and how important it is to him to have a stable, healthy, loving environment." In sum, like the other collaborating couples, Lisa and Ty expressed awareness of societal prescriptions for gender roles but were able to navigate jointly these rules in order to construct and minimize role-based tensions.

This narrative demonstrates how the *collaborating* stance involves a SAHFC acknowledging traditional feminine and masculine roles and subject positions associated with homemaking and moneymaking while negotiating collaboratively their own arrangements. These couples described gendered expectations for parents and breadwinners yet were able to distance themselves at times from the injunctions of traditionally gendered roles even as they were sensitive to their influence. At times, couples achieved this dual perspective through ironically appropriating gender-prescribed roles. They also portrayed themselves "as a team," emphasizing their equality and respect for their own choices and responsibilities. Such language seemed self-consciously to shape and reflect the couple's co-created discursive space, activities, and understandings of the risks and benefits of their ongoing choices. Consequently, their narratives embodied noticeably more acceptance and celebration of their mutual and individual contributions than conflict as well as a desire to surpass their current identities as at-home fathers and breadwinning mothers.

Stance Four: Improvising

A fourth stance that emerged from our readings of these texts articulates an approach to work and family life that attempts to improvise meaning without taking gender as the primary frame for tasks, identities, or eligibilities. The *improvising* stance disavows gendered assumptions and senses of self, at times replacing these assumptions with the language of personal preference or personality. The couple illustrating the *improvising* stance had been married for eight years with eightand five-year-old daughters. Bob and Julie's first daughter required eye surgery and the couple was switching from breast- to bottle-feeding when Julie accepted a job with excellent benefits and exciting career prospects in a city where a renowned pediatric eye surgeon practiced. Bob left his job in a bookstore, and after their move, stayed home to care for their first child when Julie returned to work. Bob stated, "We were adamant that a stranger was not going to take care of our children." Julie added that "Bob was born to do this" and that "he has more patience." In contrast, she had always seen herself "working to get promoted" in a corporate job. Bob concurred that "there was always a realization between us that she was like the, I guess the corporate person. That is where her interests lie. That is what she is good at." He stated, "I have a lot of patience with kids, but with adults, less so . . . Julie loves kids, but playing 'super friends' for half an hour doesn't really appeal to her."

Traditionally gendered vocabularies and roles assumed minimal importance in this couple's descriptions of their family life and their respective identities. Rather, Bob spoke of himself and his domestic work in light of its specific demands, his own convictions, activities, and emotions. He related, "I wanted kids, and it seemed very natural for me to be home with them. . . . Like I love taking care of them. I love being responsible."

Bob was ambivalent about their second child nearing school age. On one hand, he thought it may give him more time to finish renovating their home and to pursue writing. On the other, it marked a change in the childcare activities so important to his sense of self. He observed:

> At times I used to dream about when they are older I will be able to write; when they are older, the house will get done lickety split. But, you know, that time is such a—you know, I do the dishes and I do the laundry and all the mundane household stuff, [but] now I don't get to cuddle and watch *Sesame Street*. . . . And we still read, but that seems less, the more and more independent they get, the less and less it is with me.

At another point in the interview, he candidly noted the importance of full-time at-home fathering work to his identity, saying, "So much of your self esteem and your, how you look at yourself as an adult, . . . is your work in the world. What is it that you do? [T]hey are my job." For her part, Julie maintained, "Having kids hasn't changed my ambition." As senior manager of direct-to-consumer business at a large firm, she saw her operation as the "glue" between merchandising, the website and catalogue business, and the customers. The rewarding part of her job was that she could see quickly "the results of what they do." She wanted to continue to advance in her career.

Bob and Julie clearly divided their respective work responsibilities so that he performed most of the homemaking and Julie the moneymaking labor. Still, certain domestic issues have arisen between them that they both attributed respectfully to differing personal priorities rather than attributing these issues to gender-related power disparities, unspoken entitlements, or obligations. Although he disrupted their living space, Julie acknowledged that Bob's efforts to renovate their house on top of doing most of the housework and childcare involved "major, major" work. Even so, she said, "Sometimes I'd come home and household chores or dishes or dinner wasn't done because he's been working on the house." At times, laundry and chores have been "issues" for her. She acknowledged Bob does the laundry, noting, "I think I've done one or two loads since we've been married." Yet sometimes she would be "frustrated" because items she wanted to wear to work weren't clean. She stated, "I want to be able to come home and relax." Often tired and stressed from work, she has learned there are things she can't control at home. Julie realized that Bob just has different priorities for his time than she does. Bob seemed to understand Julie's concerns and described these issues in similar terms, although from his perspective: "She will get frustrated. She comes home or she wants this one top and it is not washed. And she is like, 'Well, why haven't you done laundry?' And I am like, 'Well, we are not out of clothes.' She is like, 'Yeah, but . . . I want to wear it again.' I am like, 'Well, you have other clothes in your closet.' " For Bob, all of these tasks are part of his responsibility for "pretty much . . . everything at home." So his different priorities emerge from within the overall context of homemaking. He observed, "Yeah, and the housework for me is not as big a priority and honestly it is tough to find time. The kids will be like, 'Read me a story,' and the dishes are piled up." He added, "That is always my priority because I mean, it seems just natural to me, like what is more important washing dishes or your kid?"

The couple described their marriage as distinctive and involving friendship with open communication, equality, mutual support, and room for differences. Bob stated:

> Julie and I have, I would say, a very equal relationship. . . . We recognize that as good friends as we are and as much as we are working towards the same goals and everything, that we are different and there are times that those differences drive each other crazy. You know, differences in communication and outlook and that. But, we really have, I would say, remarkably few disagreements just because we try to avoid the miscommunication and things of that nature.

Julie succinctly characterized their marriage, "We're open and honest. We make sure that if something is bothering us, we tell each other. We're best friends." In her opinion, some of their friends "want to be us" since "they've come to know Bob and how we do things."

Their story embodies the *improvising* stance, which involves a SAHFC challenging and, at times actively disavowing, traditional feminine and masculine roles and subject positions associated with homemaking and moneymaking by mutually negotiating and performing alternative arrangements. These couples' descriptions of their expectations for themselves as parents and breadwinners actively displaced and refigured traditionally gendered roles and naturalized assumptions through fluid improvisation. They accepted their counter-stereotypical performance of tasks and mostly viewed this condition as non-problematic. Regarding each other as friends, they valued their subjective experiences and took for granted their equal and negotiated eligibilities to perform homemaking and moneymaking activities.

Stance Five: Sharing

Our final stance centers on *sharing* as constructed through the language of co-providing and co-caring. This stance reflects a consciousness for both creating new meanings and living work and family life differently. The couple exemplifying the *sharing* orientation to domestic and paid labor had been married for five years with a three-year-old son at the time of their interviews. Thomas self-selected to be interviewed because he considered himself equal to his wife as a primary childcare provider in their family. They moved to their present home in order for Sandra to pursue a doctorate, with Tom deciding to commence his doctoral studies soon after. In discussing their lives together, Tom observed, "We always envisioned being, you know, integrally related in our child's life. . . . And in a weird way we always envisioned both of us being fully working people and being parents as well." Even so, Sandra has perceived no familial models and little institutional support for their co-parenting efforts, placing most of the burdens on the two of them to develop their own practices and identities as co-parents. She celebrated how Tom "purposefully" relinquished his identity as their primary breadwinner and saw the symbolic commitment to equality "most clearly manifested in the choice of our name. We took each other's last name."

They have had to pursue energetically their goals for themselves as scholars and their own standards as co-parents of their three-year-old son, Gary. Tom stated, "We're both the primary caregiver in the family." He described the negotiated and constantly evolving nature of their daily lives: "We don't have traditional work schedules. And so, I mean I'm certainly with Gary full-time. I'm with him multiple hours every day . . . sometimes I'll have class in the evening and Sandra's working from eight in the morning till ten at night at her job. So it's a really fluid, goofy schedule." Sandra echoed this depiction, noting that their requests for teaching assignments and course schedules always accommodate the other person. She called their efforts "schedule manipulation" accomplished for financial reasons, and "because we feel powerful doing what we're doing."

The spirit of shared power and cooperative adaptation permeated this couple's narratives as co-parents and homemakers. Tom related, "When he was first born . . . I would drive him to the university twice a day so he could breastfeed. And we would go sit on the edge of campus in our car. And that's when she and I would get to talk. Because we were committed to his breastfeeding and her being able to see him." Sandra observed, "A distinct quality between us is, well, I can say mutual respect." She declared that the "work" they have devoted together to "Gary first and then school" added a deep and edifying sense of friendship to their already loving marriage. She remarked, "And we have worked out the most intense friendship over this child that we're more intimate allies than I think we ever could have been."

The *sharing* narrative demonstrates considerable marital fluidity and responsiveness to each other's lived contingencies in organizing employment and childcare activities. Both individuals participated in wage-earning and care-providing and considered each other no less primary in either respect. Such a couple works consciously to sustain co-constructed values and identities for themselves as co-parents. Their shared participation in homemaking and moneymaking work occurs irrespective of gendered presuppositions or role-based discourses. There is continual negotiation of schedules and tasks arising from both persons' symmetrical eligibilities to embrace homemaking and moneymaking responsibilities. We term this stance "sharing" because of the necessarily common convictions and practices required to create and sustain this equal stance as active co-parents and co-providers in the face of numerous discourses, power arrangements, and social responses threatening its viability. The potential conflicts associated with this stance derive from the ongoing necessity of (re)negotiating the co-parents' own practices and identities, perceived time constraints, and cultivating legitimizing discourses for others who question their arrangement's integrity.

Discussion and Implications

In framing our study, we asked, *how do stay-at-home fathers and breadwinning mothers articulate their stances toward moneymaking and homemaking?* Analyzing our participants' discourses, we found these couples orchestrating their private and public lives differently depending on how they jointly framed tasks, identities, and role eligibilities. While some couples temporarily sojourned and retained traditionally gendered associations for their activities and selves, others keenly reconstituted historical alignments between femininity and care as well as masculinity and economic provision. Other couples relegated gender to a relatively minimal role in their articulations of daily life. We have (re)presented their diverse efforts through five stances: reversing, conflicting, collaborating, improvising, and sharing. Following Deutsch (2007), we adopt a perspective on "doing gender" (West & Zimmerman, 1987; West & Fenstermaker, 1995) that attempts to tease out not only how gender is perpetuated through language and social interaction but also how it is *adapted and even disassembled* in subtle and not so subtle ways. Further, across these five stances, we vividly illustrate different micro-level approaches to "working out" social change with respect to work and family roles, identities and tasks. In our final section, we examine these stances more deeply with respect to the social construction of masculinities and femininities and its potential to segue into transformative social change, as well as directions for future research. Here we mainly focus on gender while recognizing that our insights are bound by class, race, and sexuality (Ferree, Lorber, & Hess, 2000; Johnson, 2001).

The language of "role reversal" has captured popular imagination with respect to stay-at-home fathers and breadwinning mothers (e.g., Harris, 2009). In some ways, the reversing stance exemplified by Scott and Alicia's early parenting experiences most straightforwardly depicts gender maintenance through both language and behaviors that appear to preserve traditional gendered assumptions of caregiving and paid employment. At the time of the interview, presupposed differences in biology and socialization seemed to trump the economics of their situation (assuming that earning more money is the valued economic outcome). Within a six-month period of time, Scott's identity crisis led to his move back into full-time paid employment. Like other professional women electing to opt out (Stone, 2007), Alicia's desire to "mother" and her difficulties managing work responsibilities motivated her shift into the central caregiver role. In the reversing stance, traditional distinctions remain between masculinity and public sphere participation as well as femininity and private sphere constructions.

While observing their reproduction of hegemonic forms of masculinity and femininity, we also must respect their situation's complexity and ongoing identity struggles. For most of their marriage, Alicia had earned more money than Scott; her role as primary wage-earner can be seen as part of women's growing structural access to workplace opportunities as well as Scott's willingness to embrace marriage as the secondary earner. Thus, during early marriage and the relatively short time of their reversal, they jointly constructed and lived moments of social change that cannot be discounted in their relational biography. And, while Scott and Alicia reverted to conventional societal gendered roles, they ostensibly made this decision by choice. Future research needs to probe constructions of choice and/or agency with respect to marital work and life arrangements along with their political implications (see also Stone, 2007; Williams, 2000). Scott, for example, spoke of the profundity of his experience choosing to be home with his newborn daughter. While his time as an at-home father might have been relatively short, its personal and relational impact could be far-reaching. Perhaps Scott's caregiving experiences shifted his own understandings and/or performances of masculinity, regardless of his choice to return to paid employment. Further, other men in his workplace might have seen Scott take time off to care for his daughter and, as a result, considered this option in their own lives (Medved, Okimoto, & Ryan, 2010). The importance of role models as signaling or opening up social change must not be undervalued. We see in this first snapshot how existing gendered assumptions about work and family life can be reproduced through SAHFC's communication strategies, even in the context of reversing the performance of caring and earning duties while still holding out the potential for social change.

The conflicting stance illustrates how couples performing gender atypical duties can simultaneously experience the colliding forces of frustration *and* satisfaction, gender maintenance *and* resistance, as well as gender consciousness *and* a lack of gender awareness. These couples often articulated relational tensions or moments when the reality of their choices, duties, and identities clashed with how they wistfully thought their lives would progress, or the inflexibility of employment structures. For instance, like Sue, successful women's greater earning power may be framed as trapping couples (or individual wives or husbands) into enacting work and family lives that contradict or confuse their experiences of an authentic self. Sue's and Mike's narratives express both frustration about being constrained by Sue's ability to earn a greater income at the time of the interview as well as joy and competence in carrying out their respective tasks. She also noted Mike's discomfort over not contributing more significantly to the family income. This conflicting couple wanted the opportunity to change their arrangement but felt constrained by the conditions of their financial situation. Masculinities and femininities are portrayed in this stance as complex, contradictory, and dynamic constructions in relation to caring and earning.

Before we default to marking the conflicting stance as also simply perpetuating hegemonic forms of gender, we must recognize that conflict has always been part of social change—the very feelings of discomfort expressed by conflicting couples illustrate the social constructionist perspective in action. Unconventional gendered arrangements involving conflictual interactions can evidence social change, including real moments of relational renegotiation. Indeed, identity construction under such circumstances itself is a struggle at times; and, through Mike and Sue's (as well as all of our participants') words, we can see the struggle more vividly. Change at all levels isn't simply an either/or proposition, but a *process* of becoming or doing and undoing that we richly see in Mike and Sue's struggles and successes. Both the reversing and conflicting stances portray examples of difficult interactions occurring as these couples wrestle with shifting discourses and practices of work and family. The antagonistic sound of their conflicting narrative can be contrasted with another SAHC story framing change as collaboration.

The collaborating stance illustrates the concurrent *holding onto* and *letting go* of masculinities and femininities in relation to homemaking and moneymaking. Ty's and Lisa's abilities both to acknowledge and parody traditional gendered assumptions about who "ought" to do particular tasks and how they "should" be performed provides an insightful example of the strategic use of irony in everyday talk and action (see also Risman & Johnson-Sumerford, 1998). As demonstrated by Trethewey (1999), irony is a "lived" strategy individuals may use in managing the "both/and" quality of life. Together, this couple bridged the exigencies of role eligibility and identity, often doing so communicatively in ways that allowed both historical constructions and current enactments of gender to co-exist. They did not seek resolution of this tension or wholesale transformation of gender but appeared to live with it and use it as a source of insight. Ty, for instance, insightfully invoked irony when he explained how he was both constrained by his understandings of appropriately masculine emotion yet also able to laugh when his well-planned dinner went awry in what he called a "sitcom" moment. Although not easy, he recognized the futility of holding tightly to this narrow view of being a man. Irony permitted Ty (and allows us) to see how seemingly incongruous alternatives (maintaining versus transforming gendered assumptions of care and paid labor) can actually co-exist in various ways.

While collaboration seems a sophisticated and gentile way to manage conflicting gendered selves, conventional masculinity and femininity remain part of the interpretive frame. The locus of conflict, or perhaps tension, in the collaborating stance seems to be more internal than relational, in contrast to the first two homemaking and moneymaking stances. Thus, we need to ask whether ironic collaboration can create enough "gender vertigo" to dismantle traditional forms of gender and power (Risman, 1999). Can irony sufficiently weaken the link between sex category and gendered divisions of labor? Or, to seriously affect social change, must masculinities and femininities be disassembled, fade into the background, or be degendered in interactions (Lorber, 2005)?

Case in point: the improvising stance as viewed through Bob and Julie's narrative seems to let go of gender accountability in their work and family lives. Following Deutsch (2007), we agree that "under some conditions, [gender] may be so irrelevant that it is not even accessed" (p. 116). Perhaps more realistically in the present analysis, we could say that gender assumed a less important role in Julie and Bob's communication about work and family life than it is often afforded. Bob articulated a sense of self and relationship with Julie grounded in the language of friendship, and Julie explained that Bob was born to be their daughter's primary caregiver. Gender's assumed master status appears to be subsumed in their language of non-hierarchical relations, personal preference, and differing sex-typical abilities. Improvising couples didn't appear, actively or explicitly, to resist gender conventions; rather they seemed not to take them into account in their framing of work and family life. In the improvising stance, we see the undoing of gender most clearly through its relative absence. Bob and Julie minimized traditional masculinities and femininities in assigning duties and crafting selves. Even more interesting is their use of biological and/or natural language to justify *sex atypical* work and family roles. Bob is constructed as born to do caregiving and the more natural one to be at home full-time with their two girls. Most often, biological language is argued by gender theorists to only *reinforce* oppression and inequity between men and women. What are the personal or political implications of positioning some men as more natural caregivers than women (Silverstein, 1996)? And, does the absence of gendered discourse necessarily equate to its transgression? This stance portrays another way of framing and performing alternative forms of work and family life that raises fascinating questions about SAHFC arrangements and social change across identities, roles, institutions, and discourses.

Of course, the improvising stance comes with its own unique challenges. Tensions emerged, for instance, when Julie got frustrated that Bob did not do laundry the way she wanted it done; Bob retorted that it was his job and he would "do laundry like a guy." Although Bob still used gender to mark his performance of household labor, he owned the task as gender appropriate and even uniquely performed by men versus defining it as "woman's work." Here we see the language of equal role eligibilities producing relational tension (i.e., Julie wanted laundry done her way) but a very different type of tension is constructed than evidenced in discourses of unequal role eligibilities (i.e., if Sue perceived that women still need to perform the "second shift" of household labor). It is not the mere existence of tension that is most instructive about these couples' experiences, but the negotiated nature of these tensions as revealed through close examination of their discourse. While clear divisions of labor existed, Bob and Julie's tensions arose from *how* work should be done rather than *who* should do particular kinds of work. The question then arises whether difference always means inequality (Deutsch, 2007). Bob and Julie's situation seems to illustrate one example when differences, sex atypical as they are, do not seem to beget inequality. Does Bob's masculine identity rooted in the daily travails of caregiving evidence maternal thinking (Ruddick, 1995) or changing norms of masculinity (Anderson, 2009; Morman & Floyd, 2002)? And, did Bob and Julie (as well as other couples participating in this study), at an earlier point in time, struggle differently with constructing their unconventional identities and, if so, how?

Finally, the sharing stance explicitly and consciously resists traditional masculinities and femininities in both word and deed while also contesting separate but equal allocations of labor. Empowerment through overt resistance is articulated in Tom and Sandra's account of sharing work and family tasks and identities, perhaps more so than in the other four stances. Here we see the post-feminist ideal of equal and fully participative divisions of labor as well as external markers of gender change such as taking each other's names (see also Risman & Johnson-Sumerford, 1998). Tensions arise in this stance due to the lack of role models and resistance to existing work and family structures. Here we see public attempts at reworking gender and creating new forms of language and behavior at the relational level. At the same time, Tom and Sandra also perform microacts of resistance by manipulating employment structures to accommodate their desires to share work and family. Theirs is not an easy path; it is one fraught with challenges but expressed as empowering for both of them. Active resistance through gender consciousness is only one means of social change. Future research needs to explore effective and ineffective communication strategies and behavioral practices that aid SAHFCs in their attempts to realize potentially transformative changes in social institutions (see also Kirby, Golden, Medved, Jorgenson, & Buzzanell, 2003; Williams, 2000).

Conclusions and Next Steps

What can we learn from this study of variations in couples' homemaking and moneymaking stances? First, by documenting (and providing our interpretations of) the subtle differences in the performance and articulation of gender in the lives of these couples, we illustrate varieties of masculinities and femininities at play in their work and family lives. Scott, Mike, Ty, Bob, and Tom share with us shades and adaptations of masculinities, differentially caught up in interdependent webs of caregiving, wage earning, heterosexuality, and identity. Likewise, Alicia's enactment of being a woman, successful employee, wife and mother is but one rendering of femininity with similarities and differences from Sue, Lisa, Julie, and Sandra.

Second, the stories embodying these five homemaking-moneymaking stances reinforce that no one right way or single model for success in doing or undoing gender exists. A communication approach to exploring gendered work and family social change recognizes the criticality of process over form or, at minimum, their intimate interaction. The key contribution of this study is to illustrate that ostensibly identical work and family arrangements are lived very differently when we dig deeper into the various ways SAHFCs communicatively frame their work and family lives. We agree with Gerson's (2010) assertion that we must get "beyond drawing simple—and overly deterministic—associations between forms and outcome [but rather] we need to explore the forces that shape [work] and family" (p. 216), including often overlooked discursive, relational, and interactional forces.

Third, both the co-constructed and contextual natures of these performances come to the forefront. Could Bob take on the identity of natural, full-time caregiver and gatekeeper of laundry without Julie's symmetrical performance as the determined, non-domestic career woman? If Tom wasn't willing to engage fully in caregiving, wage-earning, and identity transformation, could Sandra claim her empowered shared marital identity? And, isn't Mike's identity struggle also part and parcel of Sue's struggles to craft a coherent, if only transient, sense of self? We believe that these narratives richly display how SAHFCs as relational partners co-construct a life and "participate together in the process of making sense of their local circumstances" (Bochner & Ellis, 1995, p. 201). These performances are also likely to change over time through the couples' ongoing negotiation of individually and mutually experienced contingencies emerging in their home and work lives. Today, more likely than in the past, families move in and out of assorted family forms and earning/caring arrangements, thereby making critical the present focus on processes of negotiation and renegotiation (Gerson, 2010).

Extending this line of scholarship beyond the issues outlined above, future research should investigate the experiences and attitudes of larger and more diverse samples of couples. We wonder what other stances (or modifications of the five offered in this analysis) might be developed through exploring a larger corpus of discourse and related data such as division of labor diaries or extensive participant-observation field notes. What additional tensions or struggles would their stories reflect? Over time, do couples living the conflicted stance ever articulate feeling reconciled or comfortable in their reversal? If not, (why) do they remain as SAHFC? When and why do reversing couples decide they need to make a change? Additional research also should include the voices of couples from an extensive socio-economic range and various racial and ethnic backgrounds. Choosing to stay-at-home may be a function of economics and not an option for many couples. We also know that historical and contemporary gender roles and identities in African American and Hispanic (Broman, 1991) marriages as well as gay and lesbian relationships (Moore, 2008) may differ at times from White and heterosexual Americans.

There are also important practical implications of this study. Couples also may use this information as a resource in their own decision-making. Couples must listen carefully to how spouses talk about the idea of transposing roles prior to making that decision or in the midst of related conflicts. Spouses might listen for ways husbands or wives talk about who they are or could be as earners or caregivers (identity adoption), their views on who should be doing particular types of work (role eligibility), and what types of work they see men and women legitimately doing (task responsibility). Keying into such language is not easy but might give couples one more tool to make good decisions or better diagnose the potential challenges or frustrations they may experience (or are experiencing) in taking on these types of arrangements.

In closing, our analysis of the five homemaking and moneymaking stances detailed in this study provides a unique glimpse into the diverse ways SAHFCs negotiate gendered tasks, identities, and roles related to caring and earning. In the midst of unconventional ways of composing their lives, these couples' narratives illustrate the variety of subtle and critical communicative processes that facilitate and constrain gendered social change. Their stories show us what it means to redraw the boundaries of our work and family lives.

Appendix 1
Participating Couples

Reversing	Conflicting	Collaborating	Improvising	Sharing
Scott/Alicia Married: 8 yrs. SAHFC: 5 mos. Children: 2	Mike/Sue Married: 18 yrs. SAHFC: 4 yrs. Children: 2	Ty/Lisa Married: 16 yrs. SAHFC: 7 yrs. Children: 1	Bob/Julie Married: 8 yrs. SAHFC: 6 yrs. Children: 2	Tom/Sandra Married: 5 yrs. SAHFC: 3 yrs. Children: 1
	John/Liz Married: 14 yrs. SAHFC: 4 yrs. Children: 5	Matt/Ellen Married: 7 yrs. SAHFC: 1 yr. Children: 1	Milt/Denise Married: 12 yrs. SAHFC: 8 mos. Children: 2	
		Jay/Gail Married: 5 yrs. SAHFC: 3 mos. Children: 2		
		Tim/Annie Married: 8 yrs. SAHFC: 1 yr. Children: 2		

Appendix 2
Homemaking-Moneymaking Stances

	Reversing	Conflicting	Collaborating	Improvising	Sharing
Task Responsibility	Fixed by categorical, gendered, conceptions; temporarily exchanged	Informed by traditionally gendered conceptions, yet blurred and compounded by partners working in both spheres	Recognized traditionally gendered, conceptions while negotiating together their own arrangements	Mutually negotiated practices that appropriate, challenge, and disavow traditionally gendered discourses	Fluid responsiveness to each other's needs; joint participation in paid work and childcare
Identity Adoption	Maintains traditional or predetermined and gendered images of parenting and paid work	Sustained yet unsettled by ongoing practices in tension with traditional roles	Ongoing, mutually supported members of a "team" selectively and incompletely transcending gender role expectations	Jointly sustained performances of gender-atypical identities as parents and providers	Co-constructed, shared, and sustained by flexibly engaging in co-parenting and co-providing
Role Eligibility	Unequal, based on fixed, gender stereotypes	Asymmetrical, presupposing traditionally gendered roles while performing alternative arrangements	Jointly negotiated, contingent upon each partner's talents, availability, and preferences while acknowledging traditional roles	Asymmetrical, based on each partner's gender-atypical preferences and perceived "fit" with role performance	Equal and mutually negotiated

References

Alberts, J. K., Tracy, S. J., & Trethewey, A. (2010). An integrated theory of the division of domestic labor: Threshold level, social organizing, and sensemaking. *Journal of Family Communication, 11*, 21–28.

Anderson, E. (2009). *Inclusive masculinity: The changing nature of masculinities*. New York, NY: Routledge.

Ashcraft, K. L., & Mumby, D. K. (2003). *Reworking gender: A feminist communicology of organization*. Thousand Oaks, CA: Sage.

Atkinson, M.P., & Boles, J. (1984). WASP (Wives as Senior Partners). *Journal of Marriage and the Family, 46*, 681–670.

Becker, G. S. (1993). *A treatise on the family*. Cambridge, MA: Harvard University Press.

Bennetts, L., (2007). *The feminine mistake: Are we giving up too much?* New York, NY: Hyperion.

Berk, S. F. (1985). *The gender factory: The apportionment of work in American households*. New York, NY: Plenum.

Bittman, M., England, P., Folbre, N., Sayer, L., & Matheson, G. (2003). When does gender trump money? Bargaining and time in household work. *American Journal of Sociology, 109*, 186–214.

Bochner, A. P., & Ellis, C. (1995). Telling and living: Narrative co-construction and the practices of interpersonal relationships. In W. Leeds-Hurwitz (Ed.), *Social approaches to communication* (pp. 201–213). New York, NY: The Guilford Press.

Bodi, O., Mikula, G., & Reiderer, B. (2010). Long-term effects between perceived justice in the division of domestic work and women's relationship satisfaction. *Social Psychology, 41*, 57–65.

Boushey, H. (2011, January 25). The end of the mansession: Now it's the women who are the economy's big losers. *Slate Magazine*. Retrieved from http://www.slate.com

Bridges, J. S., Etaugh, C., & Barnes-Farrell, J. (2002). Trait judgments of stay-at-home and employed parents: A function of social role and/or shifting standards? *Psychology of Women Quarterly, 26*, 140–150.

Broman, C. L. (1991). Gender, work-family roles, and psychological well-being of blacks. *Journal of Marriage and Family, 53*(2), 509–521.

Bureau of Labor Statistics. (2011). *Employment characteristics of families summary*. Retrieved from http://www.bls.gov/news.release/famee.nro.htm

Bureau of Labor Statistics. (2010). Personal communication from Mary Bowler, Division of Labor Force Statistics. Washington D.C.

Butler, J. (1990). *Gender trouble: Feminism and the subversion of identity*. New York, NY: Routledge.

Buzzanell, P. M. (1995). Reframing the glass ceiling as a socially constructed process. Implications for understanding and change. *Communication Monographs, 4*, 327–354.

Buzzanell, P. M. (1997). Toward an emotion-based feminist framework for research on dual career couples. *Women & Language, 20*, 40–48.

Connell, R. W. (1995). *Masculinities*. Berkeley, CA: University of California Press.

Denker, K. J. (2009) Doing gender in the academy: The challenges for women in the academic organization. *Women & Language, 32*, 103–112.

Deutsch, F. M. (2007). Undoing gender. *Gender & Society*, 2, 106–127.

Doucet, A. (2004). "It's almost like I have a job, but I don't get paid": Fathers at home reconfiguring work, care, and masculinity. *Fathering, 2*, 277–303.

Drago, R., Black, D., & Wooden, M. (2005). Female breadwinner families: Their existence, persistence, and sources. *Journal of Sociology, 41*, 343–362.

Elder, G. H., Jr. (1995). The life course paradigm: Social change and individual development. In P. Moen, G. H. Elder, Jr., & K. Lüscher (Eds.), *Examining lives in context: Perspectives on the ecology of human development* (pp. 101–139). Washington DC: APA Press.

Ferree, M. M., Lorber, J., & Hess, B. B. (2000). Introduction. In M.M. Ferree, J. Lorber, B. B. Hess (Eds.) *Revisioning gender* (pp. xv–xxxvi). Walnut Creek, CA: Altamira Press.

Fry, R., & Cohn, D. (2010, January 19). New economics of marriage: The rise of wives. Pew Center for Research. Retrieved from http://pewresearch.org/pubs/1466/economics-marriage-rise-of-wives

Gerson, K. (1985). *Hard choices: How women decide about work, career, and motherhood*. Berkley, CA: University of California Press.

Gerson, K. (2010). *The unfinished revolution: How a new generation is reshaping family, work, and gender in America*. New York, NY: Oxford University Press.

Gerson, K., & Peiss, J.M. (1985). Boundaries, negotiation, consciousness: Reconceptualizing gender relations. *Social Problems, 32*, 317–331.

Geuss, R. (2003). *Public goods, private goods*. Princeton, NJ: Princeton University Press.

Halpern, D. F., & Cheung, F. M. (2008). *Women at the top: Powerful leaders tell us how to combine work and family*. Sussex, UK: Wiley-Blackwell.

Harris, D. (2009). Recession prompts gender role reversal. Retrieved from http://abcnews.go.com

Hays, S. (1996). *The cultural contradictions of motherhood*. New Haven, CT: Yale University Press.

Hertz, R. (1995). Separate but simultaneous interviewing of husbands and wives: Making sense of their stories. *Qualitative Inquiry, 1*, 429–451.

Hochschild, A. R. (1989). *The second shift: Working parents and the revolution at home*. New York, NY: Viking.

Holmer-Nadesan, M. (1996). Organizational identity and space of action. *Organizational Studies, 17*, 49–81.

Hood, J. C. (1983). *Becoming a two-job family*. New York, NY: Viking.

Jamison, K. H. (1997). *Beyond the double binds: Women and leadership*. New York, NY: Oxford University Press.

Johnson, F. (2001). Ideological undercurrents in the semantic notion of 'working mother.' *Women & Language, 24*, 21–28.

Kirby, E. L., Golden, A. A., Medved, C. E., Jorgenson, J., & Buzzanell, P. M. (2003). An organizational challenge to the discourse of work and family research: From problematics to empowerment. In P. Kalbfleish (Ed.), *Communication Yearbook 27* (pp. 1–43). Mahwah, NJ: Lawrence Erlbaum.

Kershaw, S. (2009, April 23). Mr. Moms (By Way of Fortune 500). *New York Times*. Retrieved from http://www.nytimes.com

Lindlof, T. R., & Taylor, B. C. (1995). *Qualitative communication research*. Thousand Oaks, CA: Sage Publications.

Lorber, J. (2005). *Breaking the bowls: Degendering and feminist change*. New York, NY: Norton.

Medved, C. E. (2009a). Constructing breadwinning-mother identities: Moral, personal and political positioning. *Women's Studies Quarterly, 37*, 136–154.

Medved, C. E. (2009b). Crossing and transforming occupational and household gendered divisions of labor. C. Beck (Ed.), *Communication Yearbook 33* (pp. 300–341). New York, NY: Routledge.

Medved, C. E. (2007). Special Issue Introduction. Investigating family labor in communication studies: Threading across historical and contemporary discourses. *Journal of Family Communication, 7*, 225–243.

Medved, C. E. (2004). The everyday accomplishment of work and family: Accounting for practical actions and commonsense rules in everyday routines. *Communication Studies, 55*, 128–154.

Medved, C. E., & Kirby, E. L. (2005). Family CEOs: A feminist analysis of corporate mothering discourses. *Management Communication Quarterly, 18*, 435–478.

Medved, C. E., Okimoto, C., & Ryan, R. (2010). A qualitative analysis of explanations for the emergence of reverse traditional work and family arrangements. A paper presented at the Eastern Sociological Society Convention, Philadelphia, PA.

Meisenbach, R. J. (2010). The female breadwinner: Phenomenological experience and gendered identity in work/family spheres. *Sex Roles, 62*, 2–19.

Moore, M. R. (2008). Gendered power relations among women: A study of household decision making in Black, lesbian stepfamilies. *American Sociological Review, 73*, 335–356.

Morgan, C. (2011, Winter). Role reversal. *Rebel*, 65–70.

Morman, M. T., & Floyd, K. (2002). A 'changing culture of fatherhood': Effects on affectionate communication, closeness, and satisfaction in men's relationships with their fathers and their sons. *Western Journal of Communication, 66*, 395–412.

Murray, S. B. (1996). "We all love Charles": Men in child care and the social construction of gender. *Gender & Society, 10*, 368–385.

Offer, S., & Schneider, B. (2011). Revisiting the gender gap in time-use patterns: Multitasking and well-being among mothers and fathers in dual-earner families. *American Sociological Review, 76*(6), 809–833.

Patton, M. Q. (1990). *Qualitative evaluation and research methods* (2nd ed.). Newbury Park, CA: Sage.

Potuchek, J. L. (1992). Employed wives' orientations to breadwinning: A gender theory analysis. *Journal of Marriage and the Family, 54*, 48–58.

Potuchek, J. L. (1997). *Who supports the family? Gender and breadwinning in dualearner marriages.* Stanford, CA: Stanford University Press.

Radin, N. (1988). Primary care giving fathers of long duration. In P. Bronstein & C. P Cowan (Eds.), *Fatherhood today: Men's changing role in the family* (pp. 127–143). New York, NY: John Wiley & Sons.

Raley, S. B., Mattingly, M. J., & Bianchi, S. M. (2006). How dual are dual-income couples? Documenting change from 1970 to 2001. *Journal of Marriage and the Family, 68*, 11–28.

Rawlins, W. K. (1984). Interpretive stance in gender-role research. *Women's Studies in Communication, 7*, 69–72.

Rawlins, W. K. (1992). *Friendship matters: Communication, dialectics, and the life course.* New Brunswick, NJ: Aldine Transaction.

Rawlins, W. K. (1998). From ethnographic occupations to ethnographic stances. In J. S. Trent (Ed.), *Communication: Views from the helm for the 21st century* (pp. 359–362). Boston, MA: Allyn and Bacon.

Riggs, J. M. (1997). Mandates for mothers and fathers: Perceptions of breadwinners and care givers. *Sex Roles, 37*, 565–580.

Risman, B. J. (1999). *Gender vertigo: American families in transition.* New Haven, CT: Yale University Press.

Risman, B. J., & Johnson-Sumerford, D. (1998). Doing it fairly: A study of post-gender marriages. *Journal of Marriage and Family, 60*, 23–40.

Rochlen, A. B., Suizzo, M., Kelley, R. A., & Scaringi, V. (2008). "I'm just providing for my family:" A qualitative study of stay-at-home fathers. *Psychology of Men and Masculinity, 9*, 17–28.

Rosenfeld, L. B., Bowen, G. L., & Richman, J. M. (1995). Communication in three types of dual-career marriages. In M. A. Fitzpatrick & A. L. Vangelisti (Eds.), *Explaining family interactions* (pp. 257–289). Thousand Oaks, CA: Sage

Ruddick, S. (1995). *Maternal thinking: Towards a politics of peace.* Boston, MA: Beacon Press.

Şahin, A., Song, J., & Hobijn, B. (2010, February). *The unemployment gender gap during the current recession.* Federal Reserve Bank of New York. Retrieved from http://www.newyorkfed.org/research/economists/sahin/GenderGap.pdf

Silverstein, L. B. (1996). Fathering is a feminist issue. *Psychology of Women Quarterly, 20*, 3–37.

Smith, C. D. (1998). "Men don't do this sort of thing": A case study of the social isolation of househusbands. *Men and masculinities, 1*, 138–172.

Smith, J. A. (2009). *The Daddy shift: How stay-at-home dads, breadwinning moms, and shared parenting are transforming the American family.* Boston, MA: Beacon Press.

Stamp, P. (1985). Research note: Balance of financial power in marriage: An exploratory study of breadwinning wives. *Sociological Review, 33*, 546–557.

Stone, P. (2007). *Opting out?: Why women really quit careers and head home.* Berkeley, CA: University of California Press.

Stout, H. (2010, September). What's the new status symbol for alpha women? A stay at home husband. *Marie Claire*, 148, 150, 152.

Strauss, A., & Corbin, J. (1990). *The basics of qualitative research: Techniques and procedures for developing grounded theory* (2nd ed.). Thousand Oaks, CA: Sage.

Sveningsson, S., & Alvesson, M. (2011). Managing managerial identities: Organizational fragmentation, discourse, and identity struggle. *Human Relations, 56*, 1163–1193.

Tichenor, V. (2005). Maintaining men's dominance: Negotiating identity and power when she earns more. *Sex Roles, 53*, 191–205.

Trethewey, A. (1999). Isn't it ironic: Using irony to explore the contradictions of organizational life. *Western Journal of Communication, 63*, 140–167.

U.S. Census Bureau (2005, September 21). SHP-1. Parents and children in stay-at-home parent family groups. Current Population Survey (CPS). Retrieved from www.census.gov

Varvus, M. D. (2002). Domesticating patriarchy: Hegemonic masculinity and television's "Mr. Mom." *Critical Studies in Media Communication, 19*, 352–375.

Warner, J. (2005). *Perfect madness: Mothering in the age of anxiety.* New York, NY: Penguin.

Wentworth, D. K., & Chell, R. M. (2001). The role of househusband and housewife as perceived by a college population. *The Journal of Psychology, 135*, 639–650.

West, C., & Zimmerman, D. (1987). Doing gender. *Gender & Society, 1*, 125–151.

West, C., & Fenstermaker, S. (1995). Doing difference. *Gender & Society, 9*, 8–37.

part than usual in how they design, conduct, and interpret their studies. Of course, we recognize that this is equally true for those who criticize such studies (including Wardle [1997], Lerner and Nagai [2000], and ourselves). The inescapably ideological and emotional nature of this subject makes it incumbent on scholars to acknowledge the personal convictions they bring to the discussion. Because we personally oppose discrimination on the basis of sexual orientation or gender, we subject research claims by those sympathetic to our stance to a heightened degree of critical scrutiny and afford the fullest possible consideration to work by scholars opposed to parenting by lesbians and gay men.

The Case Against Lesbian and Gay Parenthood

Wardle (1997) is correct that contemporary scholarship on the effects of parental sexual orientation on children's development is rarely critical of lesbigay parenthood. Few respectable scholars today oppose such parenting. However, a few psychologists subscribe to the view that homosexuality represents either a sin or a mental illness and continue to publish alarmist works on the putative ill effects of gay parenting (e.g., Cameron and Cameron 1996; Cameron, Cameron, and Landess 1996). Even though the American Psychological Association expelled Paul Cameron, and the American Sociological Association denounced him for willfully misrepresenting research (Cantor 1994; Herek 1998, 2000), his publications continue to be cited in amicus briefs, court decisions, and policy hearings. For example, the chair of the Arkansas Child Welfare Agency Review Board repeatedly cited publications by Cameron's group in her testimony at policy hearings, which, incidentally, led to restricting foster child placements to heterosexual parents (Woodruff 1998).

Likewise, Wardle (1997) draws explicitly on Cameron's work to build his case against gay parent rights. Research demonstrates, Wardle maintains, that gay parents subject children to disproportionate risks; that children of gay parents are more apt to suffer confusion over their gender and sexual identities and are more likely to become homosexuals themselves; that homosexual parents are more sexually promiscuous than are heterosexual parents and are more likely to molest their own children; that children are at greater risk of losing a homosexual parent to AIDS, substance abuse, or suicide, and to suffer greater risks of depression and other emotional difficulties; that homosexual couples are more unstable and likely to separate; and that the social stigma and embarrassment of having a homosexual parent unfairly ostracizes children and hinders their relationships with peers. Judges have cited Wardle's article to justify transferring child custody from lesbian to heterosexual parents.[1]

Wardle (1997), like other opponents of homosexual parenthood, also relies on a controversial literature that decries the putative risks of "fatherlessness" in general. Thus, Wardle cites books by Popenoe (1993, 1996), Blankenhorn (1995), and Whitehead (1993) when he argues:

> [C]hildren generally develop best, and develop most completely, when raised by both a mother and a father and experience regular family interaction with both genders' parenting skills during their years of childhood. It is now undeniable that, just as a mother's influence is crucial to the secure, healthy, and full development of a child, [a] paternal presence in the life of a child is essential to the child emotionally and physically. (p. 860)

Wardle, like Blankenhorn, extrapolates (inappropriately) from research on single-mother families to portray children of lesbians as more vulnerable to everything from delinquency, substance abuse, violence, and crime, to teen pregnancy, school dropout, suicide, and even poverty.[2] In short, the few scholars who are opposed to parenting by lesbians and gay men provide academic support for the convictions of many judges, journalists, politicians, and citizens that the sexual orientation of parents matters greatly to children, and that lesbigay parents represent a danger to their children and to society. Generally, these scholars offer only limited, and often implicit, theoretical explanations for the disadvantages of same-sex parenting—typically combining elements of bio-evolutionary theory with social and cognitive learning theories (e.g., Blankenhorn 1995). Cameron et al. (1996) crudely propose that homosexuality is a "learned pathology" that parents pass on to children through processes of modeling, seduction, and "contagion." The deeply rooted hetero-normative convictions about what constitutes healthy and moral gender identity, sexual orientation, and family composition held by contributors to this literature hinders their ability to conduct or interpret research with reason, nuance, or care.

The Case for Lesbian and Gay Parenthood

Perhaps the most consequential impact that heterosexism exerts on the research on lesbigay parenting lies where it is least apparent—in the far more responsible literature that is largely sympathetic to its subject. It is easy to expose the ways in which the prejudicial views of those directly hostile to lesbigay parenting distort their research (Herek 1998). Moreover, because antigay scholars regard homosexuality itself as a form of pathology, they tautologically interpret any evidence that children may be more likely to engage in homoerotic behavior as evidence of harm. Less obvious, however, are the ways in which heterosexism also hampers research and analysis among those who explicitly support lesbigay parenthood. With rare exceptions, even the most sympathetic proceed from a highly defensive posture that accepts heterosexual parenting as the gold standard and investigates whether lesbigay parents and their children are inferior.

This sort of hierarchical model implies that *differences* indicate *deficits* (Baumrind 1995). Instead of investigating whether (and how) differences in adult sexual orientation might lead to meaningful differences in how individuals parent and how their children develop, the predominant research designs place the burden of proof on lesbigay parents to demonstrate that they are not less successful or less worthy than heterosexual parents. Too often scholars seem to presume that this approach precludes acknowledging almost any differences in parenting or in child outcomes. A characteristic review of research on lesbian-mother families concludes:

> [A] rapidly growing and highly consistent body of empirical work has failed to identify significant differences between lesbian mothers and their heterosexual counterparts or the children raised by these groups. Researchers have been unable to establish empirically that detriment results to children from being raised by lesbian mothers. (Falk 1994:151)

Given the weighty political implications of this body of research, it is easy to understand the social sources of such a defensive stance. As long as sexual orientation can deprive a gay parent of child custody, fertility services, and adoption rights, sensitive scholars are apt to tread gingerly around the terrain of differences. Unfortunately, however, this reticence compromises the development of knowledge not only in child development and psychology, but also within the sociology of sexuality, gender, and family more broadly. For if homophobic theories seem crude, too many psychologists who are sympathetic to lesbigay parenting seem hesitant to theorize at all. When researchers downplay the significance of any findings of differences, they forfeit a unique opportunity to take full advantage of the "natural laboratory" that the advent of lesbigay-parent families provides for exploring the effects and acquisition of gender and sexual identity, ideology, and behavior.

This reticence is most evident in analyses of sexual behavior and identity—the most politically sensitive issue in the debate. Virtually all of the published research claims to find no differences in the sexuality of children reared by lesbigay parents and those raised by nongay parents—but none of the studies that report this finding attempts to theorize about such an implausible outcome. Yet it is difficult to conceive of a credible theory of sexual development that would not expect the adult children of lesbigay parents to display a somewhat higher incidence of homoerotic desire, behavior, and identity than children of heterosexual parents. For example, biological determinist theory should predict at least some difference in an inherited predisposition to same-sex desire; a social constructionist theory would expect lesbigay parents to provide an environment in which children would feel freer to explore and affirm such desires; psychoanalytic theory might hypothesize that the absence of a male parent would weaken a daughter's need to relinquish her pre-oedipal desire for her mother or that the absence of a female parent would foster a son's pre-oedipal love for his father that no fear of castration or oedipal crisis would interrupt. Moreover, because parents determine where their children reside, even one who subscribed to J. Harris's (1998) maverick theory—that parents are virtually powerless when compared with peers to influence their children's development—should anticipate that lesbigay parents would probably rear their children among less homophobic peers.

Bem's (1996) "exotic becomes erotic" theory of sexual orientation argues that in a gender-polarized society, children eroticize the gender of peers whose interests and temperaments differ most from their own. Most children thereby become heterosexual, but boys attracted to "feminine" activities and girls who are "tomboys" are apt to develop homoerotic desires. The impact of parental genes and child-rearing practices remains implicit because parents contribute genetically to the temperamental factors Bem identifies as precursors to a child's native activity preferences, and parental attitudes toward gender polarization should affect the way those innate preferences translate into children's cognition and play. In fact, the only "theory" of child development we can imagine in which a child's sexual development would bear no relationship to parental genes, practices, environment, or beliefs would be an arbitrary one.[3] Yet this is precisely the outcome that most scholars report, although the limited empirical record does not justify it.

Over the past decade, prominent psychologists in the field began to call for less defensive research on lesbian and gay family issues (G. Green and Bozett 1991; Kitzinger and Coyle 1995; Patterson 1992). Rethinking the "no differences" doctrine, some scholars urge social scientists to look for potentially beneficial effects children might derive from such distinctive aspects of lesbigay parenting as the more egalitarian relationships these parents appear to practice (Patterson 1995; also see Dunne 2000). More radically, a few scholars (Kitzinger 1987, 1989; Kitzinger and Coyle 1995) propose abandoning comparative research on lesbian and heterosexual parenting altogether and supplanting it with research that asks "why and how are lesbian parents oppressed and how can we change that?" (Clarke 2000:28, paraphrasing Kitzinger 1994:501). While we perceive potential advantages from these agendas, we advocate an alternative strategy that moves beyond hetero-normativity without forfeiting the fruitful potential of comparative research. Although we agree with Kitzinger and Coyle (1995) and Clarke (2000) that the social obstacles to lesbian (and gay) parenthood deserve rigorous attention, we believe that this should supplement, not supplant, the rich opportunity planned lesbigay parenthood provides for the exploration of the interactions of gender, sexual orientation, and biosocial family structures on parenting and child development. Moreover, while we welcome research attuned to potential strengths as well as vulnerabilities of lesbigay parenting, we believe that knowledge and policy will be best served when scholars feel free to replace a hierarchical model, which assigns "grades" to parents and children according to their sexual identities, with a more genuinely pluralist approach to family diversity. Sometimes, to bowdlerize Freud's famous dictum, a difference *really is* just a difference!

Problems with Concepts, Categories, and Samples

The social effects of heterosexism constrain the character of research conducted on lesbigay parenting in ways more profound than those deriving from the ideological stakes of researchers. First, as most researchers recognize, because so many individuals legitimately fear the social consequences of adopting a gay identity, and because few national surveys have included questions about sexual orientation, it is impossible to gather reliable data on such basic demographic questions as how many lesbians and gay men there are in the general population, how many have children, or how many children reside (or have substantial contact) with lesbian or gay parents. Curiously, those who are hostile to gay parenting tend to minimize the incidence of same-sex orientation, while sympathetic scholars typically report improbably high numerical estimates. Both camps thus implicitly presume that the rarer the incidence, the less legitimate would be lesbigay claims to rights. One could imagine an alternative political logic, however, in which a low figure might undermine grounds for viewing lesbigay parenting as a meaningful social threat. Nonetheless, political anxieties have complicated the difficulty of answering basic demographic questions.

Since 1984, most researchers have statically reproduced numbers, of uncertain origin, depicting a range of from 1 to 5 million lesbian mothers, from 1 to 3 million gay fathers, and from 6 to 14 million children of gay or lesbian parents in the United States (e.g., Patterson 1992, 1996).[4] More recent estimates by Patterson and Freil (2000) extrapolate from distributions observed in the National Health and Social Life Survey (Laumann et al. 1995). Depending upon the definition of parental sexual orientation employed, Patterson and Freil suggest a current lower limit of 800,000 lesbigay parents ages 18 to 59 with 1.6 million children and an upper limit of 7 million lesbigay parents with 14 million children. However, these estimates include many "children" who are actually adults. To estimate the number who are dependent children (age 18 or younger), we multiplied the child-counts by .66, which is the proportion of dependent children among all offspring of 18- to 59-year-old parents in the representative National Survey of Families and Households (Sweet and Bumpass 1996).[5] This adjustment reduces the estimates of current dependent children with lesbigay parents to a range of 1 to 9 million, which implies that somewhere between 1 percent and 12 percent of all (78 million) children ages 19 and under in the United States (U.S. Census Bureau 1999) have a lesbigay parent. The 12-percent figure depends upon classifying as a lesbigay parent anyone who reports that even the idea of homoerotic sex is appealing, while the low (1 percent) figure derives from the narrower, and in our view more politically salient, definition of a lesbigay parent as one who self-identifies as such (also see Badgett 1998; Black, Maker, et al. 1998).

Across the ideological spectrum, scholars, journalists and activists appear to presume that the normalization of lesbigay sexuality should steadily increase the ranks of children with lesbian and gay parents. In contrast, we believe that normalization is more likely to reduce the proportion of such children. Most contemporary lesbian and gay parents procreated within heterosexual marriages that many had entered hoping to escape the social and emotional consequences of homophobia. As homosexuality becomes more legitimate, far fewer people with homoerotic desires should feel compelled to enter heterosexual marriages, and thus fewer should become parents in this manner.

On the other hand, with normalization, intentional parenting by self-identified lesbians and gay men should continue to increase, but it is unlikely to do so sufficiently to compensate for the decline in the current ranks of formerly married lesbian and gay parents. Thus, the proportion of lesbian parents may not change much. Many women with homoerotic desires who once might have married men and succumbed to social pressures to parent will no longer do so; others who remained single and childless because of their homoerotic desires will feel freer to choose lesbian maternity. It is difficult to predict the net effect of these contradictory trends. However, as fewer closeted gay men participate in heterosexual marriages, the ranks of gay fathers should thin. Even if gay men were as eager as lesbians are to become parents, biology alone sharply constrains their ability to do so. Moreover, there is evidence that fewer men of any sexual orientation actually desire children as strongly as do comparable women (cf. Groze 1991; Shireman 1996), and most demographic studies of sexual orientation find a higher incidence of homosexuality among men than women (Kinsey et al. 1948; Kinsey et al. 1953; Laumann et al. 1994; Michael et al. 1994). Thus, although the ranks of intentional paternity among gay men should increase, we do not believe this will compensate for the declining numbers of closeted gay men who will become fathers through heterosexual marriages. Hence the estimate of 1 to 12 percent of children with a lesbigay parent may represent a peak interval that may decline somewhat with normalization.

A second fundamental problem in sampling involves the ambiguity, fluidity, and complexity of definitions of sexual orientation. "The traditional type of surveys on the prevalence of 'homosexuality,'" remarks a prominent Danish sociologist, "are already in danger of becoming antiquated even before they are carried out; the questions asked are partially irrelevant; sexuality is not what it used to be" (Bech 1997:211). What defines a parent (or adult child) as lesbian, gay, bisexual, or heterosexual? Are these behavioral, social, emotional, or political categories? Historical scholarship has established that sexual identities are modern categories whose definitions vary greatly not only across cultures, spaces, and time, but even among and within individuals (Katz 1995; Seidman 1997). Some gay men, for example, practice celibacy; some heterosexual men engage in "situational" homosexual activity. Some lesbians relinquish lesbian identities to marry; some relinquish marriage for a lesbian identity. What about bisexual, transsexual, or transgendered parents, not to mention those who repartner with individuals of the same or different genders? Sexual desires, acts, meanings, and identities are not expressed in fixed or predictable packages.

Third, visible lesbigay parenthood is such a recent phenomenon that most studies are necessarily of the children of a transitional generation of self-identified lesbians and gay men who became parents in the context of heterosexual marriages or relationships that dissolved before or after they assumed a gay identity. These unique historical conditions make it impossible to fully distinguish the impact of a parent's sexual orientation on a child from the impact of such factors as divorce, re-mating, the secrecy of the closet, the process of coming out, or the social consequences of stigma. Only a few studies have attempted to control for the number and gender of a child's parents before and after a parent decided to identify as lesbian or gay. Because many more formerly married lesbian mothers than gay fathers retain custody of their children, most research is actually on post-divorce lesbian motherhood. A few studies compare heterosexual and gay fathers after divorce (Bigner and Jacobsen 1989, 1992). If fewer self-identified lesbians and gay men will become parents through heterosexual marriages, the published research on this form of gay parenthood will become less relevant to issues in scholarly and public debates.

Fourth, because researchers lack reliable data on the number and location of lesbigay parents with children in the general population, there are no studies of child development based on random, representative samples of such families. Most studies rely on small-scale, snowball and convenience samples drawn primarily from personal and community networks or agencies. Most research to date has been conducted on white lesbian mothers who are comparatively educated, mature, and reside in relatively progressive urban centers, most often in California or the Northeastern states.[6]

Although scholars often acknowledge some of these difficulties (Bozett 1989; Patterson and Friel 2000; Rothblum 1994), few studies explicitly grapple with these definitional questions. Most studies simply rely on a parent's sexual self-identity at the time of the study, which contributes unwittingly to the racial, ethnic, and class imbalance of the populations studied. Ethnographic studies suggest that "lesbian," "gay," and "bisexual" identity among socially subordinate and nonurban populations is generally less visible or less affirmed than it is among more privileged white, educated, and urban populations (Boykin 1996; Cantu 2000; Carrier 1992; Greene and Boyd-Franklin 1996; Hawkeswood 1997; Lynch 1992; Peterson 1992).

Increasingly, uncloseted lesbians and gay men actively choose to become parents through diverse and innovative means (Benkov 1994). In addition to adoption and foster care, lesbians are choosing motherhood using known and unknown sperm donors (as single mothers, in intentional co-mother couples, and in complex variations of biosocial parenting). Both members of a lesbian couple may choose to become pregnant sequentially or simultaneously. Pioneering lesbian couples have exchanged ova to enable both women to claim biological, and thereby legal, maternal status to the same infant (Bourne 1999). It is much more difficult (and costly) for gay men to choose to become fathers, particularly fathers of infants. Some (who reside in states that permit this) become adoptive or foster parents; others serve as sperm donors in joint parenting arrangements with lesbian or other mothers. An affluent minority hire women as "surrogates" to bear children for them.

The means and contexts for planned parenthood are so diverse and complex that they compound the difficulties of isolating the significance of parental sexual orientation. To even approximate this goal, researchers would need to control not only for the gender, number, and sexual orientation of parents, but for their diverse biosocial and legal statuses. The handful of studies that have attempted to do this focus on lesbian motherhood. The most rigorous research designs compare donor-insemination (DI) parenthood among lesbian and heterosexual couples or single mothers (e.g., Chan, Brooks, et al. 1998; Flaks et al. 1995). To our knowledge, no studies have been conducted exclusively on lesbian or gay adoptive parents or compare the children of intentional gay fathers with children in other family forms. Researchers do not know the extent to which the comparatively high socioeconomic status of the DI parents studied accurately reflects the demographics of lesbian and gay parenthood generally, but given the degree of effort, cultural and legal support, and, frequently, the expense involved, members of relatively privileged social groups would be the ones most able to make use of reproductive technology and/or independent adoption.

In short, the indirect effects of heterosexism have placed inordinate constraints on most research on the effects of gay parenthood. We believe, however, that the time may now be propitious to begin to reformulate the basic terms of the enterprise.

Reconsidering the Psychological Findings

Toward this end, we examined the findings of 21 psychological studies (listed at the bottom of Table 1) published between 1981 and 1998 that we considered best equipped to address sociological questions about how parental sexual orientation matters to children. One meta-analysis of 18 such studies (11 of which are included among our 21) characteristically concludes that "the results demonstrate no differences on any measures between the heterosexual and homosexual parents regarding parenting styles, emotional adjustment, and sexual orientation of the child(ren)" (Allen and Burrell 1996:19). To evaluate this claim, we selected for examination only studies that: (1) include a sample of gay or lesbian parents and children and a comparison group of heterosexual parents and children; (2) assess differences between groups in terms of statistical significance; and (3) include findings directly relevant to children's development. The studies we discuss compare relatively advantaged lesbian parents (18 studies) and gay male parents (3 studies) with a roughly matched sample of heterosexual parents. Echoing the conclusion of meta-analysts Allen and Burrell (1996), the authors of all 21 studies almost uniformly claim to find no differences in measures of parenting or child outcomes. In contrast, our careful scrutiny of the findings they report suggests that on some dimensions—particularly those related to gender and sexuality—the sexual orientations of these parents matter somewhat more for their children than the researchers claimed.[7]

The empirical findings from these studies are presented in Tables 1 and 2. Table 1 summarizes findings on the relationship between parental sexual orientation and three sets of child "outcome" variables: (1) gender behavior/gender preferences, (2) sexual behavior/sexual preferences, and (3) psychological well-being. Table 2 summarizes findings on the relationship between parental sexual orientation and other attributes of parents, including: (1) behavior toward children's gender and sexual development, (2) parenting skills, (3) relationships with children, and (4) psychological well-being. Positive signs (+) indicate a statistically significant higher level of the variable for lesbigay parents or their children, while negative signs (–) indicate a higher level for heterosexual parents or their children. Zero (0) indicates no significant difference.

While Table 1 reports the results of all 21 studies, our discussion here emphasizes findings from six studies we consider to be best designed to isolate whatever unique effects parents' sexual

Table 1. Findings on the Associations between Parents' Sexual Orientations and Selected Child Outcomes: 21 Studies, 1981 to 1998

Variable Measured	Direction of Effect
Gender Behavior/Preferences	
Girls' departure from traditional gender role expectations and behaviors—in dress, play, physicality, school activities, occupational aspirations (Hoeffer 1981; Golombok et al. 1983; R. Green et al. 1986; Steckel 1987; Hotvedt and Mandel 1982).	0/+
Boys' departure from traditional gender role expectations and behaviors—in dress, play, physicality, school activities, occupational aspirations (Hoeffer 1981; Golombok et al. 1983; R. Green et al. 1986; Steckel 1987; Hotvedt and Mandel 1982).	0/+
Boys' level of aggressiveness and domineering disposition (Steckel 1987).	-
Child wishes she/he were the other sex. (Green et al. 1986).	0
Sexual Behavior/Sexual Preferences	
Young adult child has considered same-sex sexual relationship(s); has had same-sex sexual relationship(s) (Tasker and Golombok 1997).	+
Young adult child firmly self-identifies as bisexual, gay, or lesbian (Tasker and Golombok 1997).	0
Boys' likelihood of having a gay sexual orientation in adulthood, by sexual orientation of father (Bailey et al. 1995).	(+)
Girls' number of sexual partners from puberty to young adulthood (Tasker and Golombok 1997).	+
Boys' number of sexual partners from puberty to young adulthood (Tasker and Golombok 1997).	(-)
Quality of intimate relationships in young adulthood (Tasker and Golombok 1997).	0
Have friend(s) who are gay or lesbian (Tasker and Golombok 1997).	+
Self-Esteem and Psychological Well-Being	
Children's self-esteem, anxiety, depression, internalizing behavioral problems, externalizing behavioral problems, total behavioral problems, performance in social arenas (sports, friendships, school), use of psychological counseling, mothers' and teachers' reports of children's hyperactivity, unsociability, emotional difficulty, conduct difficulty, other behavioral problems (Golombok, Spencer, and Rutter 1983; Huggins 1989; Patterson 1994; Flaks et al. 1995; Tasker and Golombok 1997; Chan, Raboy, and Patterson 1998; Chan, Brooks, et al. 1998).	0
Daughters' self-reported level of popularity at school and in the neighborhood (Hotvedt and Mandel 1982).	+
Mothers' and teachers' reports of child's level of affection, responsiveness, and concern for younger children (Steckel 1987).	+
Experience of peer stigma concerning own sexuality (Tasker and Golombok 1997).	+
Cognitive functioning (IQ, verbal, performance, and so on) (Flaks et al. 1995; R. Green et al. 1986).	0
Experienced problems gaining employment in young adulthood (Tasker and Golombok 1997).	0

Sources: The 21 studies considered in Tables 1 and 2 are, in date order: Hoeffer (1981); Kweskin and Cook (1982); Miller, Jacobsen, and Bigner (1982); Rand, Graham, and Rawlings (1982); Golombok, Spencer, and Rutter (1983); R. Green et al. (1986); M. Harris and Turner (1986); Bigner and Jacobsen (1989); Hotvedt and Mandel (1982); Huggins (1989); Steckel (1987); Bigner and Jacobsen (1992); Jenny, Roesler. and Poyer (1994); Patterson (1994); Bailey et al. (1995); Flaks et al. (1995); Brewaeys et al. (1997); Tasker and Golombok (1997); Chan, Raboy, and Patterson (1998); Chan, Brooks, et al. (1998); and McNeill, Rienzi, and Kposowa (1998).

+ = significantly higher in lesbigay than in heterosexual parent context.
0 = no significant difference between lesbigay and heterosexual parent context.
- = significantly lower in lesbigay than heterosexual parent context.
( ) = borders on statistical significance.
0/+ = evidence is mixed.

orientations might have on children. Four of these—Flaks et al. (1995), Brewaeys et al. (1997); Chan, Raboy, and Patterson (1998); and Chan, Brooks, et al. (1998)—focus on planned parenting and compare children of lesbian mothers and heterosexual mothers who conceived through DI. This focus reduces the potential for variables like parental divorce, re-partnering, coming out, and so on to confound whatever effects of maternal sexual orientation may be observed. The other two studies—R. Green et al. (1986) and Tasker and Golombok (1997)—focus on children born within heterosexual marriages who experienced the divorce of their biological parents before being raised by a lesbian mother with or without a new partner or spouse. Although this research design heightens the risk that in statistical analyses the effect of maternal sexual orientation may include the effects of other factors, distinctive strengths of each study counterbalance this limitation. R. Green et al. (1986) rigorously attempt to match lesbian mothers and heterosexual mothers on a variety of characteristics, and they compare the two groups of mothers as well as both groups of children on a wide variety of dimensions.[8] Tasker and Golombok (1997) offer a unique long-term, longitudinal design. Their data collection began in 1976 on 27 heterosexual single mothers and 39 of their children (average age 10) and 27 lesbian mothers and 39 of their children (also average age 10) in England. Follow-up interviews with 46 of the original children were conducted 14 years later, allowing for a rare glimpse at how children with lesbian mothers and those with heterosexual mothers fared over their early life courses into young adulthood.

Children's Gender Preferences and Behavior

The first panel of Table 1 displays findings about the relationship between the sexual orientation of parents and the gender preferences and behaviors of their children. The findings demonstrate that, as we would expect, on some measures meaningful differences have been observed in predictable directions. For example, lesbian mothers in R. Green et al. (1986) reported that their children, especially daughters, more frequently dress, play, and behave in ways that do not conform to sex-typed cultural norms. Likewise, daughters of lesbian mothers reported greater interest in activities associated with both "masculine" and "feminine" qualities and that involve the participation of both sexes, whereas daughters of heterosexual mothers report significantly greater interest in traditionally feminine, same-sex activities (also see Hotvedt and Mandel 1982). Similarly, daughters with lesbian mothers reported higher aspirations to nontraditional-gender occupations (Steckel 1987). For example, in R. Green et al. (1986), 53 percent (16 out of 30) of the daughters of lesbians aspired to careers such as doctor, lawyer, engineer, and astronaut, compared with only 21 percent (6 of 28) of the daughters of heterosexual mothers.

Sons appear to respond in more complex ways to parental sexual orientations. On some measures, like aggressiveness and play preferences, the sons of lesbian mothers behave in less traditionally masculine ways than those raised by heterosexual single mothers. However, on other measures, such as occupational goals and sartorial styles, they also exhibit greater gender conformity than do daughters with lesbian mothers (but they are not more conforming than sons with heterosexual mothers) (R. Green et al. 1986; Steckel 1987).[9] Such evidence, albeit limited, implies that lesbian parenting may free daughters and sons from a broad but uneven range of traditional gender prescriptions. It also suggests that the sexual orientation of mothers interacts with the gender of children in complex ways to influence gender preferences and behavior. Such findings raise provocative questions about how children assimilate gender culture and interests—questions that the propensity to downplay differences deters scholars from exploring.[10]

Consider, for example, the study by R. Green et al. (1986) that, by our count, finds at least 15 intriguing, statistically significant differences in gender behavior and preferences among children (4 among boys and 11 among girls) in lesbian and heterosexual single-mother homes. Yet the study's abstract summarizes: "Two types of single-parent households [lesbian and heterosexual mothers] and their effects on children ages 3–11 years were compared.... No significant differences were found between the two types of households for boys and few significant differences for girls" (p. 167).[11]

Similarly, we note an arresting continuum of data reported, but ignored, by Brewaeys et al. (1997, table 4). Young boys (ages 4 to 8) conceived through DI in lesbian co-mother families scored the lowest on a measure of sex-typed masculine behaviors (the PSAI-preschool activities inventory, rated by parents), DI boys in heterosexual two-parent families were somewhat more sex-typed, while "naturally" conceived boys in heterosexual two-parent families received the highest sex-typed masculine scores. By our calculation, the difference in the magnitude of scores between DI boys with lesbian co-mothers and conventionally conceived sons with heterosexual parents is sufficient to reach statistical significance, even though the matched groups contained only 15 and 11 boys, respectively. Rather than exploring the implications of these provocative data, the authors conclude: "No significant difference was found between groups for the mean PSAI scores for either boys or girls" (Brewaeys et al. 1997:1356).

Children's Sexual Preferences and Behavior

The second panel of Table 1 shifts the focus from children's gender behavior and preferences to their sexual behavior and preferences, with particular attention to thought-provoking findings from the Tasker and Golombok (1997) study, the only comparative study we know of that follows children raised in lesbian-headed families into young adulthood and hence that can explore the children's sexuality in meaningful ways. A significantly greater proportion of young adult children raised by lesbian mothers than those raised by heterosexual mothers in the Tasker and Golombok sample reported having had a homoerotic relationship (6 of the 25 young adults raised by lesbian mothers—24 percent—compared with 0 of the 20 raised by heterosexual mothers). The young adults reared by lesbian mothers were also significantly more likely to report having thought they might experience homoerotic attraction or relationships. The difference in their openness to this possibility is striking: 64 percent (14 of 22) of the young adults raised by lesbian mothers report having considered same-sex relationships (in the past, now, or in the future), compared with only 17 percent (3 of 18) of those raised by heterosexual mothers. Of course, the fact that 17 percent of those raised by heterosexual mothers also report some openness to same-sex relationships, while 36 percent of those raised by lesbians do not, underscores the important reality that parental influence on children's sexual desires is neither direct nor easily predictable.

If these young adults raised by lesbian mothers were more open to a broad range of sexual possibilities, they were not statistically more likely to self-identify as bisexual, lesbian, or gay. To be coded as such, the respondent not only had to currently self-identify as bisexual/lesbian/gay, but also to express a commitment to that identity in the future. Tasker and Golombok (1997) employ a measure of sexual identity with no "in-between" categories for those whose identity may not yet be fully fixed or embraced. Thus, although a more nuanced measure or a longer period of observation could yield different results, Golombok and Tasker (1996) choose to situate their findings within the "overall no difference" interpretation:

> The commonly held assumption that children brought up by lesbian mothers will themselves grow up to be lesbian or gay is not supported by the findings of the study: the majority of children who grew up in lesbian families identified as heterosexual in adulthood, and there was no statistically significant difference between young adults from lesbian and heterosexual family backgrounds with respect to sexual orientation. (p. 8)

This reading, while technically accurate, deflects analytic attention from the rather sizable differences in sexual attitudes and behaviors that the study actually reports. The only other comparative study we found that explores intergenerational resemblance in sexual orientation is Bailey et al. (1995) on gay fathers and their adult sons. This study also provides evidence of a moderate degree of parent-to-child transmission of sexual orientation.

Tasker and Golombok (1997) also report some fascinating findings on the number of sexual partners children report having had between puberty and young adulthood. Relative to their counterparts with heterosexual parents, the adolescent and young adult girls raised by lesbian mothers appear to have been more sexually adventurous and less chaste, whereas the sons of lesbians evince the opposite pattern—somewhat less sexually adventurous and more chaste (the finding was statistically significant for the 25-girl sample but not for the 18-boy sample). In other words, once again, children (especially girls) raised by lesbians appear to depart from traditional gender-based norms, while children raised by heterosexual mothers appear to conform to them. Yet this provocative finding of differences in sexual behavior and agency has not been analyzed or investigated further.

Both the findings and nonfindings discussed above may be influenced by the measures of sexual orientation employed. All of the studies measure sexual orientations as a dichotomy rather than as a continuum. We have no data on children whose parents do not identify their sexuality neatly as one of two dichotomous choices, and we can only speculate about how a more nuanced conceptualization might alter the findings reported. Having parents less committed to a specific sexual identity may free children to construct sexualities altogether different from those of their parents, or it may give whatever biological predispositions exist freer reign to determine eventual sexual orientations, or parents with greater ambiguity or fluidity of sexual orientation might transmit some of this to their children, leading to greater odds of sexual flexibility.

Children's Mental Health

Given historic social prejudices against homosexuality, the major issue deliberated by judges and policy makers has been whether children of lesbian and gay parents suffer higher levels of emotional and psychological harm. Unsurprisingly, therefore, children's "self-esteem and psychological well-being" is a heavily researched domain. The third panel of Table 1 shows that these studies find no significant differences between children of lesbian mothers and children of heterosexual mothers in anxiety, depression, self-esteem, and numerous other measures of social and psychological adjustment. The roughly equivalent level of psychological well-being between the two groups holds true in studies that test children directly, rely on parents' reports, and solicit evaluations from teachers. The few significant differences found actually tend to favor children with lesbian mothers (see Table 1).[12] Given some credible evidence that children with gay and lesbian parents, especially adolescent children, face homophobic teasing and ridicule that many find difficult to manage (Tasker and Golombok 1997; also see Bozett 1989:148; Mitchell 1998), the children in these studies seem to exhibit impressive psychological strength.

Similarly, across studies, no relationship has been found between parental sexual orientation and measures of children's cognitive ability. Moreover, to our knowledge no theories predict such a link. Thus far, no work has compared children's *long-term* achievements in education, occupation, income, and other domains of life.[13]

Links between parental sexual orientation, parenting practices, and parent/child relationships may indicate processes underlying some of the links between parents' sexual orientation and the child outcomes in Table 1. Table 2 presents empirical findings about the parents themselves and the quality of parent-child relationships.

Parental Behavior toward Children's Gender and Sexual Development

The scattered pieces of evidence cited above imply that lesbigay parenting may be associated with a broadening of children's gender and sexual repertoires. Is this because lesbigay parents actively attempt to achieve these outcomes in their children? Data in the first panel of Table 2 provide little evidence that parents' own sexual orientations correlate strongly with their preferences concerning their children's gender or sexual orientations. For example, the lesbian mothers in Kweskin and Cook (1982) were no more likely than heterosexual mothers to assign masculine and feminine qualities to an "ideal" boy or girl, respectively, on the well-known Bern Sex Role Inventory. However, mothers did tend to desire gender-traits in children that resembled those they saw in themselves, and the lesbians saw themselves as less feminine-typed than did the heterosexual mothers. This suggests that a mother's own gender identity may mediate the connection between maternal sexual orientation and maternal gender preferences for her children.

Also, in some studies lesbian mothers were less concerned than heterosexual mothers that their children engage in gender "appropriate" activities and play, a plausible difference most researchers curiously downplay. For example, Hoeffer's (1981) summary reads:

> Children's play and activity interests as indices of sex-role behavior were compared for a sample of lesbian and heterosexual single mothers and their children. More striking than any differences were the similarities between the two groups of children on acquisition of sex-role behavior and between the two groups of mothers on the encouragement of sex-role behavior. (p. 536)

Yet from our perspective, the most interesting (and statistically significant) finding in Hoeffer (1981, table 4) is one of difference. While the heterosexual single mothers in the sample were significantly more likely to prefer that their boys engage in masculine activities and their girls in feminine ones, lesbian mothers had no such interests. Their preferences for their children's play were gender-neutral.

Differences in parental concern with children's acquisition of gender and in parenting practices that do or do not emphasize conformity to sex-typed gender norms are understudied and underanalyzed. The sparse evidence to date based on self-reports does not suggest strong differences between lesbigay and heterosexual parents in this domain.

Parenting Practices: Developmental Orientations and Parenting Skills

The second panel of Table 2 displays findings about parenting skills and child-rearing practices—developmental orientations, parental control and support, parent/child communication, parental affection, time spent with children—that have been shown to be central for many aspects of children's development (introversion/extroversion, success in school, and so on) (Baumrind 1978, 1980). The many findings of differences here coalesce around two patterns. First, studies find the nonbiological lesbian co-mothers (referred to as lesbian "social mothers" in Brewaeys et al. [1997]) to be more skilled at parenting and more involved with the children than are stepfathers. Second, lesbian partners in the two-parent families studied enjoy a greater level of synchronicity in parenting than do heterosexual partners.

For example, the lesbian birth mothers and heterosexual birth mothers who conceived through DI studied by Flaks et al. (1995) and Brewaeys et al. (1997) scored about the same on all measures of parenting. However, the DI lesbian social mothers scored significantly higher than the DI heterosexual fathers on measures of parenting skills, practices, and quality of interactions with children. DI lesbian social mothers also spent significantly more time than did DI heterosexual fathers in child-care activities including disciplinary, control, and limit-setting activities. In fact, in the Brewaeys et al. (1997) study, lesbian social mothers even scored significantly higher on these measures than did biological fathers in heterosexual couples who conceived conventionally. Similarly, in Chan, Raboy, and Patterson (1998), whereas the lesbian birth mothers and co-mother partners evaluated their children's emotional states and social behaviors in almost exactly the same way, heterosexual mothers and fathers evaluated their children differently: Fathers identified fewer problems in the children than did mothers (a similar pattern is observed in Chan, Brooks, et al. 1998, table 4).

These findings imply that lesbian co-parents may enjoy greater parental compatibility and achieve particularly high quality parenting skills, which may help explain the striking findings on parent/child relationships in the third panel of Table 2. DI lesbian social mothers report feeling closer to the children than do their heterosexual male counterparts. The children studied report feeling closer to DI lesbian social mothers as

Table 2. Findings on the Associations between Parents' Sexual Orientations, Other Attributes of Parents, and Parent-Child Relationships: 21 Studies, 1981 to 1998

Variable Measured	Direction of Effect
Parental Behavior toward Children's Gender and Sexual Development	
Mother prefers child engages in gender-appropriate play activities (Hoeffer 1981; R. Green et al. 1986; M. Harris and Turner 1986).	0/-
Mother classifies the ideal child as masculine (if boy) and feminine (if girl) (Kweskin and Cook 1982).	0
Mother prefers that child be gay or lesbian when grown up (Golombok et al. 1983; Tasker and Golombok 1997).	0
Child believes that mother would prefer that she/he has lesbigay sexual orientation (Tasker and Golombok 1997).	+
Parenting Practices: Developmental Orientations and Parenting Skills	
Mother's developmental orientation in child rearing and parenting skill (Miller et al. 1982; McNeill et al. 1998; Flaks et al. 1995).	0/+
Spouse/partner's developmental orientation in child rearing and parenting skill (Flaks et al. 1995; Brewaeys et al. 1997).	+
Spouse/partner's desire for equal/shared distribution of childcare (Chan, Brooks, et al. 1998).	+
Degree to which mother and spouse/partner share child-care work (Brewaeys et al. 1997; Chan, Brooks, et al. 1998).	+
Similarity between mother's and spouse/partner's parenting skills (Flaks et al. 1995).	+
Similarity between mother's and spouse/partner's assessment of child's behavior and well-being (Chan, Raboy, and Patterson 1998; Chan, Brooks, et al. 1998).	+
Mother allowed adolescent child's boyfriend/girlfriend to spend the night (Tasker and Golombok 1997).	0
Residential Parent/Child Relationships	
Mother's rating of quality of relationship with child (Golombok et al. 1983; M. Harris and Turner 1986; Brewaeys et al. 1997; McNeill et al. 1998).	0
Mother's likelihood of having a live-in partner post-divorce (Kweskin and Cook 1982; R. Green et al. 1986).	+
Spouse/partner's rating of quality of relationship with child (Brewaeys et al. 1997).	+
Child's report of closeness with biological mother growing up (Tasker and Golombok 1997; Brewaeys et al. 1997).	0
Child's report of closeness with biological mother's partner/spouse growing up (Tasker and Golombok 1997; Brewaeys et al. 1997).	0/+
Child felt able to discuss own sexual development with parent(s) while growing up (Tasker and Golombok 1997).	+
Nonresidential Parent/Child Relationships	
(Non-custodial) father's level of involvement with children, limit setting, and developmental orientation in child rearing (Bigner and Jacobsen 1989, 1992).	0/+
Mother's encouragement of child's contact with nonresidential father (Hotvedt and Mandel 1982).	0
Divorced mother's contact with children's father in the past year (Golombok et al. 1983).	+
Child's frequency of contact with nonresidential father (Golombok et al. 1983).	+
Child's positive feelings toward nonresidential father (Hotvedt and Mandel 1982; Tasker and Golombok 1997).	0/(+)

(continued)

Table 2. (*continued*)

Variable Measured	Direction of Effect
Parent's Self-Esteem and Psychological Well-Being	
Mother's level of depression, self-esteem (Rand et al. 1982; R. Green et al. 1986; Chan, Raboy and Patterson 1998; Golombok et al. 1983).	0/+
Mother's level of leadership, independence, achievement orientation (R. Green et al. 1986; Rand et al. 1982).	0/+
Mother's use of sedatives, stimulants, in- or out-patient psychiatric care in past year (Golombok et al. 1983).	0
Mother ever received psychiatric care in adult life? (Golombok et al. 1983).	+
Mother's level of self-reported stress associated with single-parenthood (R. Green et al. 1986).	0

Sources: See Table 1.

+ = significantly higher in lesbigay than in heterosexual parent context.
0 = no significant difference between lesbigay and heterosexual parent context.
- = significantly lower in lesbigay than heterosexual parent context.
( ) = borders on statistical significance.
0/+ = evidence is mixed.

well as to lesbian stepmothers than to either DI fathers or stepfathers (measures of emotional closeness between birth mothers and children did not vary by mother's sexual orientation). Children of lesbian mothers also report feeling more able than children of heterosexual parents to discuss their sexual development with their mothers and their mothers' partners (Tasker and Golombok 1997; also see Mitchell 1998:407). If lesbian social mothers and stepmothers have more parenting awareness and skill, on average, than heterosexual DI fathers or stepfathers, and if they spend more time taking care of children, they may be more likely to earn the children's affection and trust.

We believe (as do Brewaeys et al. 1997; Chan et al. 1998; Flaks et al. 1995) that the comparative strengths these lesbian co-parents seem to exhibit have more to do with gender than with sexual orientation. Female gender is probably the source of the positive signs for parenting skill, participation in child rearing, and synchronicity in child evaluations shown in the comparisons in Table 2. Research suggests that, on average, mothers tend to be more invested in and skilled at child care than fathers, and that mothers are more apt than fathers to engage in the kinds of child-care activities that appear to be particularly crucial to children's cognitive, emotional, and social development (Furstenberg and Cherlin 1991; Simons and Associates 1996). Analogously, in these studies of matched lesbian and heterosexual couples, women in every category—heterosexual birth mother, lesbian birth mother, nonbiological lesbian social mother—all score about the same as one another but score significantly higher than the men on measures having to do with the care of children.[14]

In our view, these patterns reflect something more than a simple "gender effect," however, because sexual orientation is the key "exogenous variable" that brings together parents of same or different genders. Thus, sexual orientation and gender should be viewed as *interacting* to create new kinds of family structures and processes—such as an egalitarian division of child care—that have fascinating consequences for all of the relationships in the triad and for child development (also see Dunne 1999, 2000; Patterson 1995). Some of the evidence suggests that two women co-parenting may create a synergistic pattern that brings more egalitarian, compatible, shared parenting and time spent with children, greater understanding of children, and closeness and communication between parents and children. The genesis of this pattern cannot be understood on the basis of either sexual orientation or gender alone. Such findings raise fruitful comparative questions for future research about family dynamics among two parents of the same or different gender who do or do not share similar attitudes, values, and behaviors.

We know little thus far about how the sexual orientation of nonresidential fathers may be related to their relationships with their children (the fourth panel of Table 2) (and even less about that for custodial fathers). The Bigner and Jacobsen studies (1989, 1992) find similarity in parenting and in father/child relations among heterosexual nonresidential fathers and gay nonresidential fathers. Bozett (1987a, 1987b, 1989) found that in a small sample of children with gay fathers, most children had very positive feelings toward their fathers, but they also worried that peers and others might presume that they, too, had a gay sexual orientation (Bozett did not include a control group of children with heterosexual fathers).

Parental Fitness

The bottom panel of Table 2 demonstrates that evidence to date provides no support for those, like Wardle (1997), who claim that lesbian mothers suffer greater levels of psychological difficulties (depression, low self-esteem) than do heterosexual mothers. On the contrary, the few differences observed in the studies suggest that these lesbian mothers actually display somewhat higher levels of positive psychological resources.

Research on a more diverse population, however, might alter the findings of difference and similarity shown in Table 2. For example, the ethnographic evidence suggests that people of color with homoerotic practices often value racial solidarity over sexual solidarity. Boykin, Director of the National Black Gay and Lesbian Leadership Forum, cites a 1994 University of Chicago study which found that among people who engage in homoerotic activity, whites, urbanites, and those with higher education were more likely to consider themselves gay or lesbian (Boykin 1996:36). If, as it appears, racial/ethnic solidarities deter disproportionate numbers of people of color from coming out, they might suffer greater psychological and social costs from living in the closet or, conversely, might benefit from less concern over their sexual identities than do white gay parents. We also do not know whether lesbian couples of different racial/ethnic and social class contexts would display the same patterns of egalitarian, compatible co-parenting reported among the white lesbian couples.

No Differences of Social Concern

The findings summarized in Tables 1 and 2 show that the "no differences" claim does receive strong empirical support in crucial domains. Lesbigay parents and their children in these studies display no differences from heterosexual counterparts in psychological well-being or cognitive functioning. Scores for lesbigay parenting styles and levels of investment in children are at least as "high" as those for heterosexual parents. Levels of closeness and quality of parent/child relationships do not seem to differentiate directly by parental sexual orientation, but indirectly, by way of parental gender. Because every relevant study to date shows that parental sexual orientation per se has no measurable effect on the quality of parent-child relationships or on children's mental health or social adjustment, there is no evidentiary basis for considering parental sexual orientation in decisions about children's "best interest." In fact, given that children with lesbigay parents probably contend with a degree of social stigma, these similarities in child outcomes suggest the presence of compensatory processes in lesbigay-parent families. Exploring how these families help children cope with stigma might prove helpful to all kinds of families.

Most of the research to date focuses on social-psychological dimensions of well-being and adjustment and on the quality of parent/child relationships. Perhaps these variables reflect the disciplinary preferences of psychologists who have conducted most of the studies, as well as a desire to produce evidence directly relevant to the questions of "harm" that dominate judicial and legislative deliberations over child custody. Less research has explored questions for which there are stronger theoretical grounds for expecting differences—children's gender and sexual behavior and preferences. In fact, only two studies (R. Green et al. 1986; Tasker and Golombok 1997) generate much of the baseline evidence on potential connections between parents' and child's sexual and gender identities. Evidence in these and the few other studies that focus on these variables does not support the "no differences" claim. Children with lesbigay parents appear less traditionally gender-typed and more likely to be open to homoerotic relationships. In addition, evidence suggests that parental gender and sexual identities interact to create distinctive family processes whose consequences for children have yet to be studied.

How the Sexual Orientation of Parents Matters

We have identified conceptual, methodological, and theoretical limitations in the psychological research on the effects of parental sexual orientation and have challenged the predominant claim that the sexual orientation of parents does not matter at all. We argued instead that despite the limitations, there is suggestive evidence and good reason to believe that contemporary children and young adults with lesbian or gay parents do differ in modest and interesting ways from children with heterosexual parents. Most of these differences, however, are not causal, but are indirect effects of parental gender or selection effects associated with heterosexist social conditions under which lesbigay-parent families currently live.

First, our analysis of the psychological research indicates that the effects of parental gender trump those of sexual orientation (Brewaeys et al. 1997; Chan, Brooks, et al. 1998; Chan, Raboy, and Patterson 1998; Flaks et al. 1995). A diverse array of gender theories (social learning theory, psychoanalytic theory, materialist, symbolic interactionist) would predict that children with two same-gender parents, and particularly with co-mother parents, should develop in less gender-stereotypical ways than would children with two heterosexual parents. There is reason to credit the perception of lesbian co-mothers in a qualitative study (Dunne, 2000) that they "were redefining the meaning and content of motherhood, extending its boundaries to incorporate the activities that are usually dichotomized as mother and father" (p. 25). Children who derive their principal source of love, discipline, protection, and identification from women living independent of male domestic authority or influence should develop less stereotypical symbolic, emotional, practical, and behavioral gender repertoires. Indeed, it is the claim that the gender mix of parents has no effect on their children's gender behavior, interests, or development that cries out for sociological explanation. Only a crude theory of cultural indoctrination that posited the absolute impotence of parents might predict such an outcome, and the remarkable variability of gender configurations documented in the anthropological record readily undermines such a theory (Bonvillain 1998; Brettell and Sargent 1997; Ortner and Whitehead 1981). The burden of proof in the domain of gender and sexuality should rest with those who embrace the null hypothesis.

Second, because homosexuality is stigmatized, selection effects may yield correlations between parental sexual orientation and child development that do not derive from sexual orientation itself. For example, social constraints on access to marriage and parenting make lesbian parents likely to be older, urban, educated, and self-aware—factors that foster several positive developmental consequences for their children. On the other hand, denied access to marriage, lesbian co-parent relationships are likely to experience dissolution rates somewhat higher than those among heterosexual co-parents (Bell and Weinberg 1978; Weeks, Heaphy, and Donovan forthcoming, chap. 5). Not only do same-sex couples lack the institutional pressures and support for commitment that marriage provides, but qualitative studies suggest that they tend to embrace comparatively high standards of emotional intimacy and satisfaction (Dunne 2000; Sullivan 1996; Weeks et al. forthcoming). The decision to pursue a socially ostracized domain of intimacy implies an investment in the emotional regime that Giddens (1992) terms "the pure relationship" and "confluent love." Such relationships confront the inherent instabilities of modern or postmodern intimacy, what Beck and Beck-Gersheim (1995) term "the normal chaos of love." Thus, a higher dissolution rate would be correlated with but not causally related to sexual orientation, a difference that should erode were homophobia to disappear and legal marriage be made available to lesbians and gay men.

Most of the differences in the findings discussed above cannot be considered deficits from any legitimate public policy perspective. They either favor the children with lesbigay parents, are secondary effects of social prejudice, or represent "just a difference" of the sort democratic societies should respect and protect. Apart from differences associated with parental gender, most of the presently observable differences in child "outcomes" should wither away under conditions of full equality and respect for sexual diversity. Indeed, it is time to recognize that the categories "lesbian mother" and "gay father" are historically transitional and conceptually flawed, because they erroneously imply that a parent's sexual orientation is the decisive characteristic of her or his parenting. On the contrary, we propose that homophobia and discrimination are the chief reasons why parental sexual orientation matters at all. Because lesbigay parents do not enjoy the same rights, respect, and recognition as heterosexual parents, their children contend with the burdens of vicarious social stigma. Likewise, some of the particular strengths and sensitivities such children appear to display, such as a greater capacity to express feelings or more empathy for social diversity (Mitchell 1998; O'Connell 1994), are probably artifacts of marginality and may be destined for the historical dustbin of a democratic, sexually pluralist society.

Even in a utopian society, however, one difference seems less likely to disappear: The sexual orientation of parents appears to have a unique (although not large) effect on children in the politically sensitive domain of sexuality. The evidence, while scanty and underanalyzed, hints that parental sexual orientation is positively associated with the possibility that children will be more likely to attain a similar orientation—and theory and common sense also support such a view. Children raised by lesbian co-parents should and do seem to grow up more open to homoerotic relationships. This may be partly due to genetic and family socialization processes, but what sociologists refer to as "contextual effects" not yet investigated by psychologists may also be important. Because lesbigay parents are disproportionately more likely to inhabit diverse, cosmopolitan cities—Los Angeles, New York and San Francisco—and progressive university communities—such as Santa Cruz, Santa Rosa, Madison, and Ann Arbor (Black, Gates, et al. 2000)—their children grow up in comparatively tolerant school, neighborhood, and social contexts, which foster less hostility to homoeroticism. Sociology could make a valuable contribution to this field by researching processes that interact at the individual, family, and community level to undergird parent-child links between gender and sexuality.

Under homophobic conditions, lesbigay parents are apt to be more sensitive to issues surrounding their children's sexual development and to injuries that children with nonconforming desires may experience, more open to discussing sexuality with their children, and more affirming of their questions about sexuality (Mitchell 1998; Tasker and Golombok 1997). It therefore seems likely, although this has yet to be studied, that their children will grow up better informed about and more comfortable with sexual desires and practices. However, the tantalizing gender contrast in the level of sexual activity reported for sons versus daughters of lesbians raises more complicated questions about the relationship between gender and sexuality.

Even were heterosexism to disappear, however, parental sexual orientation would probably continue to have some impact on the eventual sexuality of children. Research and theory on sexual development remain so rudimentary that it is impossible to predict how much difference might remain were homosexuality not subject to social stigma. Indeed, we believe that if one suspends the hetero-normative presumption, one fascinating riddle to explain in this field is why, even though children of lesbigay parents appear to express a significant increase in homoeroticism, the majority of all children nonetheless identify as heterosexual, as most theories across the "essentialist" to "social constructionist" spectrum seem (perhaps too hastily) to expect. A nondefensive look at the anomalous data on this question could pose fruitful challenges to social constructionist, genetic, and bio-evolutionary theories.

We recognize the political dangers of pointing out that recent studies indicate that a higher proportion of children with lesbigay parents are themselves apt to engage in homosexual activity. In a homophobic world, anti-gay forces deploy such results to deny parents custody of their own children and to fuel backlash movements opposed to gay rights. Nonetheless, we believe that denying this probability capitulates to heterosexist ideology and is apt to prove counterproductive in the long run. It is neither intellectually honest nor politically wise to base a claim for justice on grounds that may prove falsifiable empirically. Moreover, the case for granting equal rights to nonheterosexual parents should not require finding their children to be identical to those reared by heterosexuals. Nor should it require finding that such children do not encounter distinctive challenges or risks, especially when these derive from social prejudice. The U.S. Supreme Court rejected this rationale for denying custody when it repudiated discrimination against interracially married parents in *Palmore* v. *Sidoti* in 1984: "[P]rivate biases may be outside the reach of the law, but the law cannot, directly or indirectly, give them effect" (quoted in Polikoff 1990:569–70). Inevitably, children share most of the social privileges and injuries associated with their parents' social status. If social prejudice were grounds for restricting rights to parent, a limited pool of adults would qualify.

One can readily turn the tables on a logic that seeks to protect children from the harmful effects of heterosexist stigma directed against their parents. Granting legal rights and respect to gay parents and their children should lessen the stigma that they now suffer and might reduce the high rates of depression and suicide reported among closeted gay youth living with heterosexual parents. Thus, while we disagree with those who claim that there are no differences between the children of heterosexual parents and children of lesbigay parents, we unequivocally endorse their conclusion that social science research provides no grounds for taking sexual orientation into account in the political distribution of family rights and responsibilities.

It is quite a different thing, however, to consider this issue a legitimate matter for social science research. Planned lesbigay parenthood offers a veritable "social laboratory" of family diversity in which scholars could fruitfully examine not only the acquisition of sexual and gender identity, but the relative effects on children of the gender and number of their parents as well as of the implications of diverse biosocial routes to parenthood. Such studies could give us purchase on some of the most vexing and intriguing topics in our field, including divorce, adoption, step-parenthood, and domestic violence, to name a few. To exploit this opportunity, however, researchers must overcome the hetero-normative presumption that interprets sexual differences as deficits, thereby inflicting some of the very disadvantages it claims to discover. Paradoxically, if the sexual orientation of parents were to matter less for political rights, it could matter more for social theory.

Acknowledgments

We are grateful for the constructive criticisms on early versions of this article from: Celeste Atkins, Amy Binder, Phil Cowan, Gary Gates, Adam Green, David Greenberg, Oystein Holter, Celia Kitzinger, Joan Laird, Jane Mauldon, Dan McPherson, Shannon Minter, Valory Mitchell, Charlotte Patterson, Anne Peplau, Vernon Rosario, Seth Sanders, Alisa Steckel, Michael Wald, and the reviewers and editors of *ASR*. We presented portions of this work at: UCLA Neuropsychiatric Institute Symposium on Sexuality; the Feminist Interdisciplinary Seminar of the University of California, Davis; and the Taft Lecture Program at the University of Cincinnati.

Notes

1. In *J.B.F.* v. *JM.F.* (Ex parte J.M.F. 1970224, So. 2d 1190, 1988 Ala. LEXIS 161 [1998]), for example, Alabama's Supreme Court quoted Wardle's (1997) essay to justify transferring custody of a child from her lesbian mother to her heterosexual father.
2. The extrapolation is "inappropriate" because lesbigay-parent families have never been a comparison group in the family structure literature on which these authors rely (cf. Downey and Powell 1993; McLanahan 1985).

3. In March 2000, Norwegian sociologist Oystein Holter (personal communication) described Helmut Stierlin's "delegation" theory (published in German)—that children take over their parents' unconscious wishes. Holter suggests this theory could predict that a child who grows up with gay parents under homophobic conditions might develop "contrary responses." We are unfamiliar with this theory but find it likely that under such conditions unconscious wishes of heterosexual and nonheterosexual parents could foster some different "contrary responses."
4. These estimates derive from an extrapolation of Kinsey data claiming a roughly 10 percent prevalence of homosexuality in the adult male population. Interestingly, Michael et al.'s (1994) revisiting of Kinsey (Kinsey, Pomeroy, and Martin 1948; Kinsey, Pomeroy, Martin, and Gebhard 1953) suggests that Kinsey himself emphasized that different measures of sexual orientation yield different estimates of individuals with same-sex sexual orientations in the population. Had scholars read Kinsey differently, they might have selected his figure of 4 percent of the men in his sample who practiced exclusive homosexual behavior from adolescence onward, rather than the widely embraced 10 percent figure. In fact, the 10 percent number is fundamentally flawed: Kinsey found that of the 37 percent of the white men in his sample who had at least one sexual experience with another man in their lifetime, only 10 percent of them (i.e., 3.7 percent of the entire white male sample) had exclusively same-sex sexual experiences for any three-year period between ages 16 and 55.
5. This assumes that the ratio of number of dependent children to total offspring among current lesbigay parents will be roughly the same as that for all parents and children.
6. The field is now in a position to take advantage of new data sources. For example, the 1990 U.S. census allows (albeit imperfectly) for the first time the identification of gay and lesbian couples, as will the 2000 census (Black, Gates, et al. 2000). From 1989 to the present, the U.S. General Social Surveys (http://www.icpsr.umich.edu/GSS/index.html) have also allowed for the identification of the sexual orientation of respondents, as does the National Health and Social Life Survey (Laumann et al. 1995).
7. We chose to display the specific findings in each of the quantitative studies, rather than to conduct a meta-analysis, because at this stage of knowledge not enough studies are targeted to the same general "outcome" to enable a meta-analysis to reveal systematic patterns. The single meta-analysis that has been done (Allen and Burrell 1996) reached the typical "no difference" conclusion, but its conclusions were hampered by this very problem. The small number of studies available led Allen and Burrell to pool studies focused on quite different parent and child "outcomes," heightening the risk that findings in one direction effectively offset findings in another.
8. Belcastro et al. (1993) point out that R. Green et al. (1986) did not successfully match heterosexual and lesbian single-mother families on the dimension of household composition. While 39 of R. Green et al.'s 50 lesbian single-mother households had a second adult residing in them by one-plus years post-divorce, only 4 of the 40 heterosexual single mothers did so. R. Green et al. (1986) note this difference, but do not discuss its implications for findings; nor do Belcastro et al. (1993).
9. Many of these studies use conventional levels of significance (e.g., $|t|>1.96$, $p<.05$, two-tailed tests) on minuscule samples, substantially increasing their likelihood of failing to reject the null hypothesis. For example, Hoeffer's (1981) descriptive numbers suggest a greater preference for masculine toys among boys with heterosexual mothers than those with lesbian mothers, but sampling only 10 boys in each group makes reaching statistical significance exceedingly difficult. Golombok, Spencer, and Rutter's (1983, table 8) evidence of a greater average tendency toward "femininity" among daughters raised by heterosexual mothers than those raised by lesbian single mothers does not reach statistical significance in part because their tabular crosscutting leads to very small cell counts (to meet conventional criteria the differences between groups would have to be huge in such cases). Single difference-tests that maximize cell counts (e.g., the percentage of children—male or female—in each group who report gender-role behavior that goes against type) might well yield significant results. Recent research on model selection shows that to find the best model in large samples, conventional levels

of significance need to be substantially tightened, but that for very small samples conventional levels can actually be too restrictive (Raftery 1995).

10. Much qualitative work, particularly by lesbian feminist scholars, has been exploring these issues. For example Wells (1997) argues that, unlike what she refers to as "patriarchal families," lesbian co-mother families rear sons to experience rather than repress emotions and instill in daughters a sense of their potential rather than of limits imposed by gender. From a quantitative perspective, this is a "testable" hypothesis that has sizable theoretical implications but which researchers in the field do not seem to be pursuing.
11. The R. Green et al. (1986) research was conducted in a context in which custody cases often claimed that lesbian motherhood would create gender identity disorder in children and that lesbian mothers themselves were unfit. It is understandable that their summary reassures readers that the findings point to more similarities than differences in both the mothers and their children.
12. Patterson (1994) found that children ages 4 to 9 with lesbian mothers expressed more stress than did those with heterosexual mothers, but at the same time they also reported a greater sense of overall well-being. Patterson speculates that children from lesbian-mother families may be more willing to express their feelings—positive and negative—but also that the children may actually experience more social stress at the same time that they gain confidence from their ability to cope with it.
13. The only empirical evidence reported is Tasker and Golombok's (1997) finding of no differences in unemployment rates among young adults that are associated with their parents' sexual orientations. However, some of the children studied were still in school, and the authors provide no information on occupations attained to assess differences in long-term occupational achievements.
14. Chan, Brooks, et al. (1998:415) make interesting connections between these kinds of findings and the theoretical perspectives developed in Chodorow (1978) and Gilligan (1982).

References

Allen, Mike and Nancy Burrell. 1996. "Comparing the Impact of Homosexual and Heterosexual Parents on Children: Meta-Analysis of Existing Research." *Journal of Homosexuality* 32:19–35.

Badgett, M. V. Lee. 1998. "The Economic Well-Being of Lesbian, Gay, and Bisexual Adults' Families." Pp. 231–48 in *Lesbian, Gay and Bisexual Identities in Families: Psychological Perspectives*, edited by C.J. Patterson and A.R. D'Augelli. New York: Oxford University Press.

Bailey, J. Michael, David Bobrow, Marilyn Wolfe, and Sarah Mikach. 1995. "Sexual Orientation of Adult Sons of Gay Fathers." *Developmental Psychology* 31:124–29.

Baumrind, Diana. 1978. "Parental Disciplinary Patterns and Social Competence in Children." *Youth and Society* 9:239–75.

———. 1980. "New Directions in Socialization Research." *American Psychologist* 35:639–52.

———. 1995. "Commentary on Sexual Orientation: Research and Social Policy Implications." *Developmental Psychology* 31:130–36.

Bech, Henning. 1997. *When Men Meet: Homosexuality and Modernity.* Chicago, IL: University of Chicago Press.

Beck, Ulrich and Elisabeth Beck-Gersheim. 1995. *The Normal Chaos of Love.* London, England: Polity.

Belcastro, Philip A., Theresa Gramlich, Thomas Nicholson, Jimmie Price, and Richard Wilson. 1993. "A Review of Data Based Studies Addressing the Affects [*sic*] of Homosexual Parenting on Children's Sexual and Social Functioning." *Journal of Divorce and Remarriage* 20:105–22.

Bell, Alan P. and Martin S. Weinberg. 1978. *Homosexualities: A Study of Diversity among Men and Women.* New York: Simon and Schuster.

Benkov, Laura. 1994. *Reinventing the Family: Lesbian and Gay Parents.* New York: Crown.

Bem, Daryl J. 1996. "Exotic Becomes Erotic: A Developmental Theory of Sexual Orientation." *Psychological Review* 103:320–35.

Bigner, Jerry J. and R. Brooke Jacobsen. 1989. "Parenting Behaviors of Homosexual and Heterosexual Fathers." *Journal of Homosexuality* 18:73–86.

———. 1992. "Adult Responses to Child Behavior and Attitudes toward Fathering: Gay and Nongay Fathers." *Journal of Homosexuality* 23:99–112.

Black, Dan A., Gary Gates, Seth Sanders, and Lowell Taylor. 2000. "Demographics of the Gay and Lesbian Population in the United States: Evidence from Available Systematic Data Sources." *Demography* 37:139–54.

Black, Dan A., Hoda R. Maker, Seth G. Sanders, and Lowell Taylor. 1998. "The Effects of Sexual Orientation on Earnings." Working paper, Department of Economics, Gatton College of Business and Economics, University of Kentucky, Lexington, KY.

Blankenhorn, David. 1995. *Fatherless America: Confronting Our Most Urgent Social Problem.* New York: Basic.

Bonvillain, Nancy. 1998. *Women and Men: Cultural Constructs of Gender.* 2d ed. Upper Saddle River, NJ: Prentice Hall.

Bourne, Amy E. 1999. "Mothers of Invention." *San Francisco Daily Journal,* May 21, pp. 1, 9.

Boykin, Keith. 1996. *One More River to Cross: Black and Gay in America.* New York: Anchor.

Bozett, Frederick W. 1987a. "Children of Gay Fathers." Pp. 39–57 in *Gay and Lesbian Parents,* edited by F. W. Bozett. New York: Praeger.

———. 1987b. "Gay Fathers." Pp. 3–22 in *Gay and Lesbian Parents,* edited by F. W. Bozett. New York: Praeger.

———. 1989. "Gay Fathers: A Review of the Literature." Pp. 137–62 in *Homosexuality and the Family,* edited by F. W. Bozett. New York: Haworth Press.

Brettell, Caroline B. and Carolyn F. Sargent, eds. 1997. *Gender in Cross-Cultural Perspective.* 2d ed. Upper Saddle River, NJ: Prentice Hall.

Brewaeys, A., I. Ponjaert, E. V. Van Hall, and S. Golombok. 1997. "Donor Insemination: Child Development and Family Functioning in Lesbian Mother Families." *Human Reproduction* 12:1349–59.

Cameron, Paul and Kirk Cameron. 1996. "Homosexual Parents." *Adolescence* 31:757–76.

Cameron, Paul, Kirk Cameron, and Thomas Landess. 1996. "Errors by the American Psychiatric Association, the American Psychological Association, and the National Educational Association in Representing Homosexuality in Amicus Briefs about Amendment 2 to the U.S. Supreme Court." *Psychological Reports* 79:383–404.

Cantor, David. 1994. *The Religious Right: The Assault on Tolerance and Pluralism in America.* New York: Anti-Defamation League.

Cantu, Lionel. 2000. "Entre Hombres/Between Men: Latino Masculinities and Homosexualities." Pp. 224–46 in *Gay Masculinities,* edited by P. Nardi. Thousand Oaks, CA: Sage.

Carrier, Joseph. 1992. "Miguel: Sexual Life History of a Gay Mexican American." Pp. 202–24 in *Gay Culture in America: Essays from the Field,* edited by G. Herdt. Boston, MA: Beacon.

Chan, Raymond W., Risa C. Brooks, Barbara Raboy, and Charlotte J. Patterson. 1998. "Division of Labor among Lesbian and Heterosexual Parents: Associations with Children's Adjustment." *Journal of Family Psychology* 12:402–19.

Chan, Raymond W., Barbara Raboy, and Charlotte J. Patterson. 1998. "Psychosocial Adjustment among Children Conceived Via Donor Insemination by Lesbian and Heterosexual Mothers." *Child Development* 69:443–57.

Chodorow, Nancy. 1978. *The Reproduction of Mothering: Psychoanalysis and the Sociology of Gender.* Berkeley, CA: University of California Press.

Clarke, Victoria. 2000. "Sameness and Difference in Research on Lesbian Parenting." Working paper, Women's Studies Research Group, Department of Social Sciences, Loughborough University, Leicestershire, UK.

Downey, Douglas B. and Brian Powell. 1993. "Do Children in Single-Parent Households Fare Better Living with Same-Sex Parents?" *Journal of Marriage and the Family* 55:55–72.

Dunne, Gillian A. 1999. "What Difference Does 'Difference' Make? Lesbian Experience of Work and Family Life." Pp. 189–221 in *Relating Intimacies,* edited by J. Seymour and P. Bagguley. New York: St. Martin's.

———. 2000. "Opting into Motherhood: Lesbians Blurring the Boundaries and Transforming the Meaning of Parenthood and Kinship." *Gender and Society* 14:11–35.

Falk, Patrick J. 1994. "The Gap Between Psychosocial Assumptions and Empirical Research in Lesbian-Mother Child Custody Cases." Pp. 131–56 in *Redefining Families: Implications for Children's Development,* edited by A. E. Gottfried and A. W. Gottfried. New York: Plenum.

Flaks, David K., Ilda Ficher, Frank Masterpasqua, and Gregory Joseph. 1995. "Lesbians Choosing Motherhood: A Comparative Study of Lesbian and Heterosexual Parents and Their Children." *Developmental Psychology* 31:105–14.

Furstenberg, Frank F., Jr. and Andrew J. Cherlin. 1991. *Divided Families.* Cambridge, MA: Harvard University Press.

Gallagher, Maggie. "The Gay-Parenting Science." *New York Post,* March 30, p. 3.

Giddens, Anthony. 1992. *The Transformation of Intimacy: Sexuality, Love and Eroticism in Modern Societies.* Stanford, CA: Stanford University Press.

Gilligan, Carol. 1982. *In a Different Voice: Psychological Theory and Women's Development.* Cambridge, MA: Harvard University Press.

Golombok, Susan, Ann Spencer, and Michael Rutter. 1983. "Children in Lesbian and Single-Parent Households: Psychosexual and Psychiatric Appraisal." *Journal of Child Psychology and Psychiatry* 24:551–72.

Golombok, Susan and Fiona Tasker. 1996. "Do Parents Influence the Sexual Orientation of Their Children? Findings From a Longitudinal Study of Lesbian Families." *Developmental Psychology* 32:3–11.

Green, Richard, Jane Barclay Mandel, Mary E. Hotvedt, James Gray and Laurel Smith. 1986. "Lesbian Mothers and Their Children: A Comparison with Solo Parent Heterosexual Mothers and Their Children." *Archives of Sexual Behavior* 15:167–84.

Green, G. Dorsey and Frederick W. Bozett. 1991. "Lesbian Mothers and Gay Fathers." Pp. 197–214 in *Homosexuality: Research Implications for Public Policy,* edited by J. C. Gonsiorek and J. D. Weinrich. Newbury Park, CA: Sage.

Greene, Beverly and Nancy Boyd-Franklin. 1996. "African-American Lesbians: Issues in Couple Therapy." Pp. 251–71 in *Lesbians and Gays in Couples and Families: A Handbook for Therapists,* edited by J. Laird and R. J. Green. San Francisco, CA: Jossey-Bass.

Groze, Vic. 1991. "Adoption and Single Parents: A Review." *Child Welfare* 70:321–32.

Harris, Judith Rich. 1998. *The Nurture Assumption: Why Children Turn Out the Way They Do.* New York: Free Press.

Harris, Mary B. and Pauline H. Turner. 1986. "Gay and Lesbian Parents." *Journal of Homosexuality* 12:101–13.

Hawkeswood, William. 1997. *One of the Children: Gay Black Men in Harlem.* Berkeley, CA: University of California Press.

Herek, Gregory M. 1998. "Bad Science in the Service of Stigma: A Critique of the Cameron Group's Survey Studies." Pp. 223–55 in *Stigma and Sexual Orientation: Understanding Prejudice against Lesbians, Gay Men, and Bisexuals,* edited by G. M. Herek. Thousand Oaks, CA: Sage.

———. 2000. "Paul Cameron Fact Sheet" (Copyright 1997–2000 by G. M. Herek). Retrieved (http://psychology.ucdavis.edu/rainbow/html/facts_cameron_sheet.html).

Hoeffer, Beverly. 1981. "Children's Acquisition of Sex-Role Behavior in Lesbian-Mother Families." *American Journal of Orthopsychiatry* 51:536–44.

Hotvedt, Mary E. and Jane Barclay Mandel. 1982. "Children of Lesbian Mothers." Pp. 275–91 in *Homosexuality, Social, Psychological, and Biological Issues,* edited by W. Paul. Beverly Hills, CA: Sage.

Huggins, Sharon L. 1989. "A Comparative Study of Self-Esteem of Adolescent Children of Divorced Lesbian Mothers and Divorced Heterosexual Mothers." Pp. 123–35 in *Homosexuality and the Family,* edited by F. W. Bozett. New York: Haworth.

Jenny, Carole, Thomas A. Roesler, and Kimberly L. Poyer. 1994. "Are Children at Risk for Sexual Abuse by Homosexuals?" *Pediatrics* 94:41–44.

Katz, Jonathan Ned. 1995. *The Invention of Heterosexuality.* New York: Dutton.

Kinsey, Alfred C., Wardell B. Pomeroy, and Clyde E. Martin. 1948. *Sexual Behavior in the Human Male.* Philadelphia, PA: W. B. Saunders.

Kinsey, Alfred C., Wardell B. Pomeroy, Clyde E. Martin, and Paul H. Gebhard. 1953. *Sexual Behavior in the Human Female.* Philadelphia, PA: W. B. Saunders.

Kitzinger, Celia. 1987. *The Social Construction of Lesbianism.* London, England: Sage.

———. 1989. "Liberal Humanism as an Ideology of Social Control: The Regulation of Lesbian Identities." Pp. 82–98 in *Texts of Identity,* edited by J. Shorter and K. Gergen. London, England: Sage.

———. 1994. "Should Psychologists Study Sex Differences? Editor's Introduction: Sex Differences Research: Feminist Perspectives." *Feminism and Psychology* 4:501–506.

Kitzinger, Celia and Adrian Coyle. 1995. "Lesbian and Gay Couples: Speaking of Difference." *The Psychologist* 8:64–69.

Kweskin, Sally L. and Alicia S. Cook. 1982. "Heterosexual and Homosexual Mothers' Self-Described

Sex-Role Behavior and Ideal Sex-Role Behavior in Children." *Sex Roles* 8:967–75.

Laumann, Edward O., John H. Gagnon, Robert T. Michael, and Stuart Michaels. 1994. *The Social Organization of Sexuality: Sexual Practices in the United States.* Chicago, IL: University of Chicago Press.

———. 1995. *National Health and Social Life Survey, 1992* [MRDF]. Chicago IL: University of Chicago and National Opinion Research Center [producer]. Ann Arbor, MI: Inter-university Consortium for Political and Social Research [distributor].

Lerner, Robert and Althea K. Nagai. 2000. "Out of Nothing Comes Nothing: Homosexual and Heterosexual Marriage Not Shown to be Equivalent for Raising Children." Paper presented at the Revitalizing the Institution of Marriage for the 21st Century conference, Brigham Young University, March, Provo, UT.

Lynch, F. R. 1992. "Nonghetto Gays: An Ethnography of Suburban Homosexuals." Pp. 165–201 in *Gay Culture in America: Essays from the Field,* edited by G. Herdt. Boston, MA: Beacon.

McLanahan, Sara S. 1985. "Family Structure and the Reproduction of Poverty." *American Journal of Sociology* 90:873–901.

McNeill, Kevin P., Beth M. Rienzi, and Augustine Kposowa. 1998. "Families and Parenting: A Comparison of Lesbian and Heterosexual Mothers." *Psychological Reports* 82:59–62.

Michael, Robert T., John H. Gagnon, Edward O. Laumann, and Gina Bari Kolata. 1994. *Sex in America: A Definitive Survey.* Boston, MA: Little Brown.

Miller, Judith Ann, R. Brooke Jacobsen, and Jerry J. Bigner. 1982. "The Child's Home Environment for Lesbian vs. Heterosexual Mothers: A Neglected Area of Research." *Journal of Homosexuality* 7:49–56.

Mitchell, Valory. 1998. "The Birds, the Bees... and the Sperm Banks: How Lesbian Mothers Talk with Their Children about Sex and Reproduction." *American Journal of Orthopsychiatry* 68:400–409.

O'Connell, Ann. 1994. "Voices from the Heart: The Developmental Impact of a Mother's Lesbianism on Her Adolescent Children." *Smith College Studies in Social Work* 63:281–99.

Ortner, Sherry and Harriet Whitehead. 1981. *Sexual Meanings: The Cultural Construction of Gender and Sexuality.* Cambridge, England: Cambridge University Press.

Patterson, Charlotte J. 1992. "Children of Lesbian and Gay Parents." *Child Development* 63:1025–42.

———. 1994. "Children of the Lesbian Baby Boom: Behavioral Adjustment, Self-Concepts and Sex Role Identity." Pp, 156–75 in *Lesbian and Gay Psychology: Theory, Research, and Clinical Applications,* edited by B. Green and G. M. Herek. Thousand Oaks, CA: Sage.

———. 1995. "Families of the Lesbian Baby Boom: Parents' Division of Labor and Children's Adjustment." *Developmental Psychology* 31:115–23.

———. 1996. "Lesbian and Gay Parents and Their Children." Pp. 274–304 in *The Lives of Lesbians, Gays, and Bisexuals: Children to Adults,* edited by R. C. Savin-Williams and K, M. Cohen. Fort Worth, TX: Harcourt Brace College Publishers.

Patterson, Charlotte J. and Lisa V. Freil. 2000. "Sexual Orientation and Fertility." In *Infertility in the Modern World: Biosocial Perspectives,* edited by G. Bentley and N. Mascie-Taylor. Cambridge, England: Cambridge University Press.

Peterson, John. 1992. "Black Men and Their Same-Sex Desires and Behaviors." Pp. 147–64 in *Gay Culture in America: Essays From the Field,* edited by G. Herdt. Boston, MA: Beacon.

Polikoff, Nancy D. 1990. "This Child Does Have Two Mothers: Redefining Parenthood to Meet the Needs of Children in Lesbian-Mother and Other Nontraditional Families." *Georgetown Law Journal* 78:459–575.

Popenoe, David. 1993. "American Family Decline, 1960–1990: A Review and Appraisal." *Journal of Marriage and the Family* 55:527–41.

———. 1996. *Life without Father.* New York: Free Press.

Price, Deb. 1999. "Middle Ground Emerges for Gay Couples." *Detroit News,* October 4.

Raftery, Adrian E. 1995. "Bayesian Model Selection in Social Research (with Discussion)." *Sociological Methodology* 25:111–95.

Rand, Catherine, Dee L. R. Graham and Edna I. Rawlings. 1982. "Psychological Health and Factors the Court Seeks to Control in Lesbian Mother Custody Trials." *Journal of Homosexuality* 8:27–39.

Rothblum, Ester D. 1994. "'I Only Read About Myself on Bathroom Walls': The Need for Research on the Mental Health of Lesbians and Gay Men.'"

Journal of Consulting and Clinical Psychology 62:213–20.

Seidman, Steven. 1997. *Difference Troubles: Queering Social Theory and Sexual Politics.* New York: Cambridge University Press.

Shireman, Joan F. 1996. "Single Parent Adoptive Homes." *Children and Youth Services Review* 18:23–36.

Simons, Ronald L. and Associates. 1996. *Understanding Differences between Divorced and Intact Families: Stress, Interactions, and Child Outcome.* Thousand Oaks, CA: Sage.

Steckel, Alisa. 1987. "Psychosocial Development of Children of Lesbian Mothers." Pp. 75–85 in *Gay and Lesbian Parents,* edited by F. W. Bozett. New York: Praeger.

Sullivan, Maureen. 1996. "Rozzie and Harriet?: Gender and Family Patterns of Lesbian Coparents." *Gender and Society* 10:747–67.

Sweet, James and Larry Bumpass. 1996. *The National Survey of Families and Households—Waves 1 and 2: Data Description and Documentation.* Center for Demography and Ecology, Univeristy of Wisconsin–Madison, Madison, WI (http://www/ssc.wisc.edu/nsfh/home. htm).

Tasker, Fiona L. and Susan Golombok. 1997. *Growing Up in a Lesbian Family.* New York: Guilford.

U.S. Census Bureau. 1999. "Population Estimates Program." Population Division, Washington, DC. Retrieved January 5, 2000 (http://www.census.gov/population/estimates/nation/intfile2–1.txt, and natdoc.txt).

Wald, Michael S. 1999. "Same-Sex Couples: Marriage, Families, and Children, An Analysis of Proposition 22, The Knight Initiative." Stanford Institute for Research on Women and Gender, Stanford University, Stanford, CA.

Wardle, Lynn D. 1997. "The Potential Impact of Homosexual Parenting on Children." *University of Illinois Law Review* 1997:833–919.

Weeks, Jeffrey, Brian Heaphy, and Catherine Donovan. Forthcoming. *Families of Choice and Other Life Experiments: The Intimate Lives of Non-Heterosexuals.* Cambridge, England: Cambridge University Press.

Wells, Jess. 1997. *Lesbians Raising Sons.* Los Angeles, CA: Alyson Books.

Whitehead, Barbara Dafoe. 1993. "Dan Quayle Was Right." *Atlantic Monthly,* April, vol. 271, pp. 47–50.

Woodruff, Robin. 1998. Testimony re: "Subcommittee Meeting to Accept Empirical Data and Expert Testimony Concerning Homosexual Foster Parents." Hearing at the Office of the Attorney General, September 9, 1998. Little Rock, AK. Available from the authors on request.

PART 6

The Gendered Classroom

Along with the family, educational institutions—from primary schools to secondary schools, colleges, universities, and professional schools—are central arenas in which gender is reproduced. Students learn more than the formal curriculum—they learn what the society considers appropriate behavior for men and women. And for adults, educational institutions are gendered workplaces, where the inequalities found in other institutions are also found.

From the earliest grades, students' experiences in the classroom differ by gender. Boys are more likely to interrupt, to be called upon by teachers, and to have any misbehavior overlooked. Girls are more likely to remain obedient and quiet and to be steered away from math and science.

All three of the contributions to this section are based on field research. The researchers sat down and talked with boys and girls about what they thought, how they understood both gender difference and gender inequality. Wayne Martino's portraits of middle schoolers are surprising in their gender conformity, especially for the boys. He finds that these discourses are what lie behind boy's difficulties in school, not some putative feminist agenda to keep boys down. Steven Roberts suggests the way that class plays into boys' educational experiences. And Diane Reay takes on the new research on girls' aggression and finds that while both boys and girls can be mean and aggressive, there is a wider range of acceptable identities for girls than there may be for boys. Perhaps thanks to feminism, which did, after all, open up a wider array of possible futures for women, young girls have a wider range of identities from which to choose.

"Spice Girls," "Nice Girls," "Girlies," and "Tomboys": Gender Discourses, Girls' Cultures, and Femininities in the Primary Classroom

DIANE REAY

This article attempts to demonstrate that contemporary gendered power relations are more complicated and contradictory than any simplistic binary discourse of "the girls versus the boys" suggests (Heath, 1999). Although prevailing dominant discourses identify girls as "the success story of the 1990s" (Wilkinson, 1994), this small-scale study of a group of 7-year-old girls attending an inner London primary school suggests that, particularly when the focus is on the construction of heterosexual femininities, it is perhaps premature always to assume that "girls are doing better than boys." While girls may be doing better than boys in examinations, this article indicates that their learning in the classroom is much broader than the National Curriculum and includes aspects that are less favourable in relation to gender equity. Although masculinities are touched on in this article, this is only in as far as they relate to girls. This deliberate bias is an attempt to refocus on femininities at a time when masculinities appear to be an ever-growing preoccupation within education.

However, although the subjects of this research are 14 girls, the position the article takes is that femininities can only be understood relationally. There is a co-dependence between femininities and masculinities which means that neither can be fully understood in isolation from the other. The article therefore explores how a particular group of primary-aged girls is positioned, primarily in relation to dominant discourses of femininity but also in relation to those of masculinity. There is also an attempt to map out their relationships to transgressive but less prevalent discourses of femininity, which in a variety of ways construct girls as powerful. The findings from such a small-scale study are necessarily tentative and no generalised assertions are made about girls as a group. Rather, the aim is to use the girls' narratives and their experiences in school and, to a lesser extent, those of the boys, to indicate some ways in which the new orthodoxy, namely that girls are doing better than boys, does not tell us the whole story about gender relations in primary classrooms.

The last decade has seen a growing popular and academic obsession with boys' underachievement both in the UK and abroad (Katz, 1999; Smithers, 1999). However, as Lyn Yates points out, much of the "underachieving boys' discourse fails either to deal adequately with power or to see femininity and masculinity as relational phenomena" (Yates, 1997). For instance, within the explosion of concern with masculinities in academia, there has been little focus on the consequences for girls of "boys behaving badly." As Gaby Weiner and her colleagues argue:

> new educational discourses have silenced demands for increased social justice for girls and women characterised by increasing resistance to policies and practices focusing specifically on them. (Weiner et al., 1997, p. 15)

Diane Reay, "'Spice Girls,' 'Nice Girls,' 'Girlies,' and 'Tomboys': Gender Discourses, Girls' Cultures, and Femininities in the Primary Classroom" from Gender and Education 13, no. 2 (2001): 153–166.

Jill Blackmore describes attempts by some male academics in Australia to develop programmes for boys which seek to depict boys as powerless in the face of the progress and success of feminism and girls, and, indeed, as victims of their own male psychology (Blackmore, 1999). Jane Kenway writes more broadly of "the lads' movement" in Australia; a general resurgence of concern that boys and men are getting an unfair deal (Kenway, 1995). In Britain, there has been a growing alarm about "boys doing badly" that preoccupies both mainstream and feminist academics alike (Epstein et al., 1998). What gets missed out in these current concerns is the specificity of the "failing boy" and the ways in which other groups of males continue to maintain their social advantage and hold on to their social power (Arnot et al., 1999; Lucey & Walkerdine, 1999). It is within this context of contemporary preoccupation with boys that this article attempts to problematise issues surrounding gender equity and, in particular, to challenge the view that in millennial Britain it is boys rather than girls who are relatively disadvantaged.

The Research Study

The article is based on data from a 1-year study, conducted over the academic year 1997/98, of children in a Year 3 class in an inner-city primary school. 3R comprised 26 children, 14 girls and 12 boys. There were five middle-class children, three girls and two boys, all white apart from Amrit who was Indian. The 21 working-class children were more ethnically mixed. As well as one Somalian and two boys of mixed parentage, there were four Bengali children, three boys and one girl. The social class attribution of the children was based on parental occupations but was also confirmed by information provided by the class teacher. Fifteen of the children were entitled to free school meals. The school is surrounded by 1960s and 1970s public housing estates from which most of its intake is drawn, and indeed, 14 of the children in 3R lived on one of these five estates.

I spent one day a week over the course of the year engaged in participant observation in both the classroom and the playground, amassing over 200 pages of field notes. Additionally, I interviewed all the children, both individually and in focus groups. I also carried out group work activities in which children both wrote and drew on a range of topics from playground games to best friends. As James et al. point out:

> Talking with children about the meanings they themselves attribute to their paintings or asking them to write a story allows children to engage more productively with our research questions using the talents which they possess. (James et al., 1998, p. 189)

The unequal relationship between researcher and researched is compounded when the researcher is an adult and the researched a child. In order to mitigate at least some of the power differentials I organised workshops for the children in which I taught simple questionnaire design and interviewing techniques. The children then compiled their own questionnaires so that they could interview each other. These interviews, as well as those I conducted, 84 overall, were tape-recorded and transcribed. The class teacher and I also collected sociogram data, which enabled us to map out the children's friendship networks and work relationships.

Gender Discourses

Many writers on education have attempted to provide a variety of conceptual tools in order to understand educational contexts and processes (Ball, 1994; Maclure, 1994). A key debate amongst educational researchers has been between structuralist and post-structuralist approaches. Although often these two conceptual approaches are seen as opposing perspectives, in this article, I use and combine what I perceive to be the strengths of both positions to illuminate the ways in which girls both construct themselves, and are constructed, as feminine (see also, Walkerdine, 1991, 1997; Williams, 1997; Walkerdine et al., 2000 for similar approaches). As Davies et al. (1997) assert, power is both located in the structural advantage of individuals and also exercised partly through the construction of discourses.

Multiple discourses contribute not only to how researchers appreciate the conditions of childhood but also to how children come to view themselves

(James et al., 1998). Post-structuralist feminists have explored extensively the ways in which different discourses can position girls (Davies, 1993; Hey, 1997; Walkerdine, 1997). It is important to recognise that there are many competing gender discourses, some of which have more power and potency than others for particular groups of girls (Francis, 1998). Such processes of discursive recognition, of feeling a better fit within one discourse than another (Francis, 1999), are influenced by social class. Similarly, gender discourses are taken up differentially by different ethnic groupings. It is also important to stress that girls can position themselves differently in relation to gender discourses according to the peer group context they find themselves in. For example, it soon became evident in my research that girls assume different positions depending on whether they are in single- or mixed-sex contexts. As Gee and his colleagues assert:

> There are innumerable discourses in modern societies: different sorts of street gangs, elementary schools and classrooms, academic disciplines and their sub-specialities, police, birdwatchers, ethnic groups, genders, executives, feminists, social classes and sub-classes, and so on and so-forth. Each is composed of some set of related social practices and social identities (or positions). Each discourse contracts complex relations of complicity, tension and opposition with other discourses. (Gee et al., 1996, p. 10)

I found similar "complex relations of complicity, tension and opposition" in relation to the nexus of gender discourses that these girls draw on. Yet, any local discursive nexus is framed by a wider social context within which, as Valerie Hey (1997) points out, there is a lack of powerful public discourses for girls, leaving them caught between schooling which denies difference and compulsory heterosexuality which is fundamentally invested in producing it. If this gives the impression of a fluid situation in relation to how contemporary girls position themselves as female, there is also substantial evidence of continuities in which, at least for the girls in this research, conformist discourses continue to exert more power than transgressive or transformative ones.

Masculinities in the Classroom: Setting the Context

Although the main focus of this article is how gender discourses position girls at school, in order to understand femininities in this primary classroom, the ways in which masculinities are being played out cannot be ignored. I want to start with two short excerpts from boys. Josh and David, two white, middle-class, 7-year-old boys, interviewed each other about what they like most and least about being a boy:

> J: David, what do you like most about being a boy?
> D: Well, it must be that it's much easier to do things than being a girl, that's what I think. You get to do much better things.
> J: So you think you find being a boy more interesting than being a girl? Is that what you're saying?
> D: Yes because it's boring being a girl.
> J: OK, and what do you like least about being a boy?
> D: Well, I don't know, I can't think of anything.
> J: Well, can't you think really—there must be something.
> D: I'll think [long pause]. Well, it's easier to hurt yourself.
> D: OK What do you like most about being a boy?
> J: I'd probably say that it's better being a boy because they have more interesting things to do and it's more exciting for them in life I find.
> D: Yes, I see. What do you like least about being a boy?
> J: Ohh I'd probably say not being so attractive as girls probably I'd say they're much more attractive than boys.

Josh and David were the only middle-class boys in a Year 3 class of predominantly working-class children. Existing research has found that the culturally exalted form of masculinity varies from school to school and is informed by the local community (Skelton, 1997; Connolly, 1998). These two boys were adjusting to a predominantly working-class, inner-city peer group in which dominant local forms of masculinity were sometimes difficult for both to negotiate, but in particular, for David (for one thing, he did not like football). They both also found the low priority given to academic work among the other boys problematic. Even so, they were clear that it was still better being a boy.

Both boys, despite their social class positioning, were popular among the peer group. In particular, Josh commanded a position of power and status in the peer group which was virtually unchallenged (see also Reay, 1990). Sociogram data collected from all the children in the class positioned him as the most popular child, not only with the working-class boys in the class but also with the girls. David's positioning is more difficult to understand. His particular variant of middle-class masculinity was far less acceptable to his working-class peers than Josh's. He was studious and hated games. In the exercise where children drew and described their favourite playground activity, David sketched a single figure with a bubble coming out of his head with "thoughts" inside. He annotated it with "I usually like walking about by myself and I'm thinking." However, within the confines of the classroom, for much of the time, he retained both status and power, paradoxically through a combination of being male and clever. When the girls were asked to nominate two boys and two girls they would most like to work with, David was the second most popular male choice after Josh. However, he was the most popular choice with the other boys. The complex issues as to why these two boys were popular when their masculinities did not fit the dominant one within the male peer group are beyond the brief of this article. Rather, what is salient is the relevance of their positioning within the peer group for the group of girls who are the article's main protagonists.

Although the focus has been on "the others" within masculinity, black and white working-class boys (Willis, 1977; Sewell, 1997), it is the association of normativity with white, middle-class masculinity that seems most difficult for girls to challenge effectively. Disruptive, failing boys' behaviour has given girls an unexpected window of opportunity through which some variants of femininities can be valorised over specific pathologised masculinities, particularly within the arena of educational attainment. Both girls and boys were aware of discourses which position girls as more mature and educationally focused than boys and regularly drew on them to make sense of gender differences in the classroom (see also Pattman & Phoenix, 1999). What seems not to have changed is the almost unspoken acceptance of white, middle-class masculinity as the ideal that all those "others"—girls as well as black and white working-class boys—are expected to measure themselves against. Popular discourses position both masculinity and the middle classes as under siege, suggesting an erosion of both male and class power bases (Bennett, 1996; Coward, 1999). While there have been significant improvements in the direction of increasing equity, particularly in the area of gender, the popularity of Josh and David, combined with the uniform recognition among the rest of the peer group that they were the cleverest children in the class, suggests that popular discourses may mask the extent to which white, middle-class male advantages in both the sphere of education and beyond continue to be sustained.

However, 10 of the 12 boys in 3R were working class. The "failing boys" compensatory culture of aggressive "laddism" (Jackson, 1998) had already started to be played out at the micro-level of this primary classroom. The working-class, white and mixed race boys were more preoccupied with football than the academic curriculum (see also Skelton, 1999). When they were not playing football in the playground, they would often be surreptitiously exchanging football cards in the classroom. Alongside regular jockeying for position within the male peer group, which occasionally escalated into full-blown fights, there was routine, casual labelling of specific girls as stupid and dumb. The three Bengali boys at the bottom of this particular male peer group hierarchy compensated by demonising, in particular, the three middle-class girls. Their strategy echoes that of the subordinated youth in Wight's (1996) study, where in order to gain the approval and acceptance of their dominant male peers, they endeavoured to become active subjects in a sexist discourse which objectified girls.

Sugar and Spice and All Things Nice?

3R had four identifiable groups of girls—the "nice girls," the "girlies," the "spice girls" and the "tomboys" (see Figure 1).

The latter two groups had decided on both their own naming as well as those of the "girlies" and the "nice girls," descriptions which were generally seen as derogatory by both girls and boys. "Girlies" and "nice girls" encapsulate "the limited and limiting discourse of conventional femininity" (Brown, 1998), and in this Year 3 class, although there was no simple class divide, the "nice girls" were composed of Donna, Emma and Amrit, the only three middle-class girls in 3R, plus a fluctuating group of one to two working-class girls. The "nice girls," seen by everyone, including themselves, as hard-working and well behaved, exemplify the constraints of a gendered and classed discourse which afforded them the benefits of culture, taste and cleverness but little freedom. Prevalent discourses which work with binaries of mature girls and immature boys and achieving girls and underachieving boys appear on the surface to be liberating for girls. However, the constraints were evident in the "nice girls'" self-surveillant, hypercritical attitudes to both their behaviour and their schoolwork; attitudes which were less apparent amongst other girls in the class. It would appear that this group of 7-year-old, predominantly middle-class girls had already begun to develop the intense preoccupation with academic success that other researchers describe in relation to middle-class, female, secondary school pupils (Walkerdine et al., 2000).

Contemporary work on how masculinities and femininities are enacted in educational contexts stresses the interactions of gender with class, race and sexuality (Mac an Ghaill, 1988; Hey, 1997; Connolly, 1998). Sexual harassment in 3R (a whole gamut of behaviour which included uninvited touching of girls and sexualised name-calling) was primarily directed at the "girlies" and was invariably perpetuated by boys who were subordinated within the prevailing masculine hegemony either because of their race or social class. However, while sexual harassment was an infrequent occurrence, identifying the "nice girls" as a contaminating presence was not. In the playground, the three working-class Bengali boys were positioned as subordinate to the white and Afro-Caribbean boys; for example, they were often excluded from the football games on the basis that they were not skilful enough. These three boys constructed the "nice girls" as a polluting,

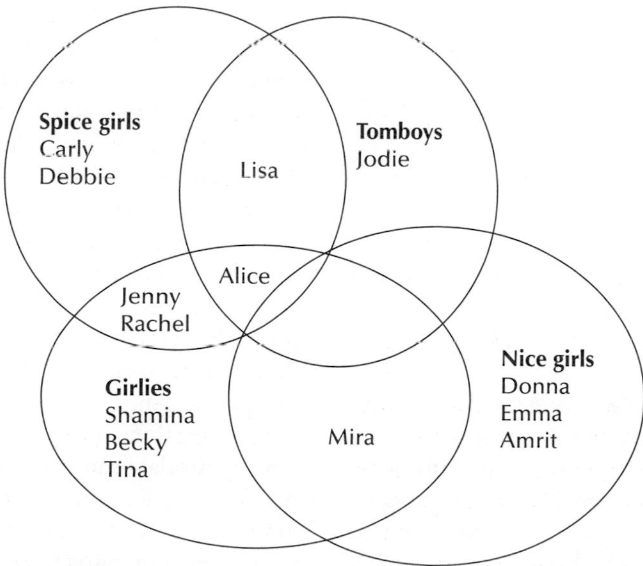

Figure 1. Girl Groups in 3R.

contagious "other." They would regularly hold up crossed fingers whenever one of these girls came near them. As a direct result, the "nice girls" began to use the classroom space differently, taking circuitous routes in order to keep as far away from these boys as possible. Barrie Thorne (1993) found similar gender practices in which girls were seen as "the ultimate source of contamination." Like the girls in Thorne's research, the "nice girls" did not challenge the boys but rather developed avoidance strategies which further circumscribed their practices.

Being one of the "nice girls" had derogatory connotations for working-class girls as well as working-class boys. Alice, in particular, was adamant that she could not contemplate them as friends because they were "too boring," while in one of the focus group discussions, Jodie, Debbie and Carly all agreed that "no one wants to be a nice girl." Their views reflect the findings of feminist research which position "being nice" as specific to the formulation of white, middle-class femininity (Jones, 1993; Griffin, 1995; Kenway et al., 1999). For a majority of the working-class girls in the class, being a "nice girl" signified an absence of the toughness and attitude that they were aspiring to.

This is not to construct the "nice girls" as passive in relation to other groups in the class. They often collaborated with Josh and David on classwork and were vocal about the merits of their approach to schoolwork over those of other girls in the class:

> EMMA: The other girls often mess around and be silly, that's why Alice and Lisa never get their work finished.
> DONNA: Yes we're more sensible than they are.
> EMMA: And cleverer.

However, the dominant peer group culture in the classroom was working class and, while this had little impact on the popularity of Josh and David, it did have repercussions for the status and social standing of the "nice girls" within the peer group.

"The limited and limiting discourse of conventional femininity" also had a powerful impact on the "girlies," a group of three working-class girls (two white and one Bengali). Kenway et al., (1999) write about "the sorts of femininities which unwittingly underwrite hegemonic masculinity" (p. 120). Certainly, the "girlies," with their "emphasised femininity" (Connell, 1987, p. 187), were heavily involved in gender work which even at the age of 7 inscribed traditional heterosexual relations. Paul Connolly (1998) describes the ways in which sexual orientation and relations defined through boyfriends and girlfriends seems to provide an important source of identity for young children. This was certainly the case for the "girlies." These girls were intensely active in the work of maintaining conventional heterosexual relationships through the writing of love letters, flirting and engaging in regular discussions of who was going out with who. They were far more active in such maintenance work than the boys.

Both the "girlies" and the "nice girls" were subject to "discourses of denigration" circulating among the wider peer group (Blackmore, 1999, p. 136). In individual interviews, many of the boys and a number of the other girls accounted for the "nice girls'" unpopularity by describing them as "boring" and "not fun to be with," while the "girlies" were variously described by boys as "stupid" and "dumb." While the boys were drawing on a male peer group discourse which positioned the "girlies" as less intelligent than they were, the "girlies" were far from "stupid" or "dumb." Although not as scholarly as the "nice girls," they were educationally productive and generally achieved more highly than their working-class male counterparts. Rather, the working-class discourse of conventional femininity within which they were enmeshed operated to elide their academic achievement within the peer group.

Discourses of conventional femininity also seemed to have consequences for the two Asian girls in the class. Amrit, who was Indian, was from a middle-class background while Shamina was Bengali and working class. Yet, both girls, despite their class differences, shared a high degree of circumscription in relation to the range of femininities available to them in the school context. As Shamina explained, "the spice girls and the tomboys are naughty. I am a good girl." In contrast to the other girls in the girls' focus group discussion, who all claimed to enjoy playing football, both Shamina and Amrit asserted that "football was a boys' game," and Amrit said, "It's not worth bothering with football. It's too boring. Me and my friends just sit on the benches and talk."

Heidi Mirza (1992) argues that the cultural construction of femininity among African-Caribbean girls fundamentally differs from the forms of femininity found among their white peers. In the case of Amrit and Shamina, there were substantial areas of overlap rather than fundamental differences. However, neither managed to carve out spaces in which to escape gender subordination from the boys in the ways that the "spice girls" and the "tomboys," both all-white groups, did. Racism and its impact on subjectivities may well be an issue here. Although it is impossible to make generalisations on the basis of two children, ethnicity, as well as class, appears to be an important consideration in the possibilities and performance of different femininities.

Membership of the "spice girls" revolved around two white, working-class girls, Carly and Debbie. Jenny, Rachel, Alice and Lisa were less consistently members of the group. Lisa and Alice would sometimes claim to be "tomboys" while Jenny and Rachel, when playing and spending time with the "girlies," and especially when Carly and Debbie were in trouble with adults in the school, would realign themselves as "girlies." Very occasionally, when she had quarrelled both with Carly and Debbie, and with Jodie, the one consistent tomboy among the girls, Alice too would reinvent herself as a "girlie."

Although there were many overlaps between both the practices and the membership of the "girlies" and the "spice girls," aspects of the "spice girls" interaction with the boys appeared to transgress prevailing gender regimes, while the "girlies' " behaviour followed a far more conformist pattern. Yet, the "spice girls" were, for much of the time, also active in constructing and maintaining traditional variants of heterosexuality. Their espousal of "girl power" did not exclude enthusiastic partaking of the boyfriend/girlfriend games. There was much flirting, letter writing, falling in and out of love and talk of broken hearts. However, they also operated beyond the boundaries of the "girlies'" more conformist behaviour when it came to interaction with the boys. Debbie and Carly, the most stalwart members of the "spice girls," both described the same activity—rating the boys—as their favourite playground game. As Carly explained, "you follow the boys around and give them a mark out of ten for how attractive they are."

The "spice girls" adherence to so-called girl power also allowed them to make bids for social power never contemplated by the "girlies" or the "nice girls." During a science lesson which involved experiments with different foodstuffs, including a bowl of treacle, Carly and Debbie jointly forced David's hand into the bowl because, as Carly asserted, "he is always showing off, making out he knows all the answers." This incident, which reduced David to tears and shocked the other children, served to confirm the class teacher in her view that the two girls "were a bad lot." The "girls with attitude" stance that Carly and Debbie so valued and their philosophy of "giving as good as they got" were reinterpreted by adults in the school as both inappropriate and counterproductive to learning. Paul Connolly (1998) points out that girls' assertive or disruptive behaviour tends to be interpreted more negatively than similar behaviour in boys, while Robin Lakoff (1975) has described how, when little girls "talk rough" like the boys do, they will normally be ostracised, scolded or made fun of. For the "spice girls," "doing it for themselves" in ways which ran counter to traditional forms of femininity resulted in them being labelled at various times by teachers in the staffroom as "real bitches," "a bad influence" and "little cows." The tendency Clarricoates found in 1978 for girls' misbehaviour to be "looked upon as a character defect, whilst boys' misbehaviour is viewed as a desire to assert themselves" was just as evident in teachers' discourses more than 20 years later.

Debbie and Carly were doubly invidiously positioned in relation to the "girls as mature discourse." They were perceived to be "too mature," as "far too knowing sexually" within adult discourses circulating in the school but they were also seen, unlike the boys and the majority of the girls in 3R, as "spiteful" and "scheming little madams" for indulging in behaviour typical of many of the boys. There were several incidents in the playground of sexual harassment of girls by a small group of boys. Most of the adults dismissed these as "boys mucking about." However, Carly and Debbie's attempts to invert regular processes of gender objectification, in which girls are routinely the objects of a male gaze, were interpreted by teachers as signs of "an unhealthy preoccupation with sex." Their predicament exemplifies the dilemma for girls of "seeking out empowering places within regimes alternatively committed to denying subordination or celebrating it" (Hey, 1997, p. 132). In this classroom, girls like Carly and Debbie seemed to tread a fine line between acceptable and unacceptable "girl power" behaviour. Overt heterosexuality was just about on the acceptable side of the line but retaliatory behaviour towards the boys was not.

Valerie Walkerdine (1997) describes how playful and assertive girls come to be understood as overmature and too precocious. Girls like Debbie and Carly, no less than the girls in Walkerdine's advertisements, occupy a space where girls have moved beyond being "nice" or "girlie." Rather, as sexual little women, they occupy a space where they can be bad. As Walkerdine points out, while it is certainly a space in which they can be exploited, it provides a space of power for little girls, although one which is also subject to discourses of denigration. The forms that denigration take are very different to those experienced by the "nice girls" or the "girlies" but become apparent in teachers' judgments of the two girls' behaviour.

"It's Better Being a Boy"—The Tomboys

The most intriguing case in my research was that of the "tomboys." The "tomboys" in Becky Francis's research study were depicted by another girl in the class as traitors to girlhood:

> Rather than rejecting the aspiration to maleness because it is "wrong" or "unnatural," Zoe argues that "girls are good enough," implying that her girlfriends want to be boys because they see males as superior, and that she is defending girlhood against this sexist suggestion. (Francis, 1998, p. 36)

As I have touched on earlier in the article, in 3R, there was a general assumption among the boys that maleness, if not a superior subject positioning, was a more desirable one. While, in particular the "spice girls," but also at various times both the "girlies" and "nice girls" defended girlhood against such claims, their stance was routinely undermined by the position adopted by the tomboys.

Jodie was the only girl in the class who was unwavering in her certainty that she was not a girl but a "tomboy," although a couple of the other girls in the class for periods of time decided that they were also "tomboys":

> JODIE: Girls are crap, all the girls in this class act all stupid and girlie.
> DIANE: So does that include you?
> JODIE: No, cos I'm not a girl, I'm a tomboy.

On the one hand, Jodie could be viewed as a budding "masculinised new woman at ease with male attributes" (Wilkinson, 1999, p. 37). Yet, her rejection of all things feminine could also be seen to suggest a degree of shame and fear of femininity. Jodie even managed to persuade Wayne and Darren, two of the boys in the class, to confirm her male status. Both, at different times, sought me out to tell me Jodie was "really a boy." It is difficult to know how to theorise such disruptions of normative gender positionings. Jodie's stance combines elements of resistance with recognition. She clearly recognised and responded to prevailing gender hierarchies which situate being male with having more power and status. Jodie appears to operate at the boundaries where femininity meets masculinity. She is what Barrie Thorne (1993) calls "active at the edges."

However, while Thorne reports that it was rarely used among her fourth and fifth graders, the term "tomboy" is frequently used in 3M as a marker of respect by both boys and girls. Being a "tomboy" seems to guarantee male friendship and male respect. Several of the working-class girls in the class, like Alice, appeared to move easily from taking up a position as a "tomboy" through to assuming a "girls with attitude" stance alongside Debbie and Carly to becoming a "girlie" and back again. One week Alice would come to school in army fatigues with her hair scraped back, the next, in Lycra with elaborately painted nails and carefully coiffured hair. However, Alice was unusual among the girls in ranging across a number of subject positions. For most of the girls, although they had choices, those choices seemed heavily circumscribed and provided little space for manoeuvre.

The regulatory aspects of the "girlies" and the "nice girls'" self-production as feminine were very apparent, yet the conformity of the "tomboys" to prevailing gender regimes was far more hidden. While it is important to recognise the transgressive qualities of identifying and rejecting traditional notions of femininity in Jodie's behaviour, the empowering aspects of being a "tomboy" also masked deeply reactionary features embedded in assuming such a gender position. Implicit in the concept of "tomboy" is a devaluing of traditional notions of femininity, a railing against the perceived limitations of being female. This is particularly apparent in Jodie's comments:

> JODIE: I don't really have any friends who are girls cos they don't like doing the things I like doing. I like football and stuff like that.
> DIANE: Don't girls like football?
> JODIE: Yeah, some of them, but they're no good at it.

Perhaps, in part, it is Jodie's obsession with football that contributes to her contradictory gender positionings. As Christine Skelton (1999) points out, there is a close association between football and hegemonic masculinities and, therefore, if Jodie is to be seen as "a football star," she needs to assume a male rather than a female subject positioning.

But there is another possible reading in which Jodie's preoccupation with football facilitates, rather than is the cause of, her flight from femininity. Michelle Fine and Pat Macpherson define girls' identification with football as "both a flight from femininity…and an association of masculinity with fairness, honesty, integrity and strength" (Fine & Macpherson, 1992, p. 197). The girls in their study would call each other boys as a compliment: "Girls can be good, bad or—best of all—they can be boys" (p. 200) and this was definitely a viewpoint Jodie adhered to. Jodie's individualised resistance can be set alongside Carly and Debbie's joint efforts to disrupt prevailing gender orders among the peer group. Yet, paradoxically, Jodie, no less than the "girlies," seemed engaged in a process of accommodating the boys. The means of accommodation may differ but the compliance with existing gender regimes remains. Madeline Arnot (1982) writes of the ways in which boys maintain the hierarchy of social superiority of masculinity by devaluing the female world. In 3R, Jodie was also involved in this maintenance work. Although her practices are not rooted in subordination to the boys, she is still acquiescent in prevailing gender hierarchies. Her practices, no less than those of the "girlies" and the "nice girls," are confirmatory of male superiority.

Connell writes that "it is perfectly logical to talk about masculine women or masculinity in women's lives, as well as men's" (Connell, 1995, p. 163). However, so-called "masculine" girls do not seem to disrupt but rather appear to endorse existing gender hierarchies. All the girls at various times were acting in ways which bolstered the boys' power at the expense of their own. Even Jodie's performance of a surrogate masculinity works to cement rather than transform the gender divide. As a consequence, the radical aspects of transgressive femininities like those of Jodie's are undermined by their implicit compliance with gender hierarchies. Being one of the boys seems to result in greater social power but it conscripts Jodie into processes Sharon Thompson (1994) identifies as "raging misogyny." In my field notes, there are 16 examples of Jodie asserting that "boys are better than girls." Jodie's case is an extreme example of the ways in which girls' ventriloquising of the dominant culture's denigration of femininity and female relations can serve to disconnect them from other girls (Brown, 1998).

Conclusion

Performing gender is not straightforward; rather, it is confusing. The seduction of binaries such as male:female, boy:girl often prevents us from seeing the full range of diversity and differentiation existing within one gender as well as between categories of male and female. Both the girls and boys in 3R were actively involved in the production of gendered identities, constructing gender through a variety and range of social processes (Kerfoot & Knight, 1994). Yet, within this "gender work," social and cultural differences generate the particular toolkit of cultural resources individual children have available to them. There is a multiplicity of femininities and masculinities available in this primary classroom. But this is not to suggest that these children have myriad choices of which variant of femininity and masculinity to assume. They do not. Class, ethnicity and emergent sexualities all play their part, and constrain as well as create options.

Pyke argues that:

> Hierarchies of social class, race and sexuality provide additional layers of complication. They form the structural and cultural contexts in which gender is enacted in everyday life, thereby fragmenting gender into multiple masculinities and femininities. (Pyke, 1996, p. 531)

Yet, despite the multiple masculinities and femininities manifested in 3R, there is evidence of hegemonic masculinity in this classroom no less than outside in the wider social world. Within such a context, it makes sense for girls to seek to resist traditional discourses of subordinate femininity. Yet, attempting to take up powerful positions through articulation with, and investment in, dominant masculinities serves to reinforce rather than transform the gender divide. As a consequence, the prevailing gender order is only occasionally disrupted, in particular by the spice girls through their sex play and objectification of a number of the boys and also, paradoxically, through their working-class status. Unlike the "nice girls" whose activities are circumscribed through being positioned by the boys as a contagious, polluting other, the "spice girls'" positioning as "rough" in relation to sensitive middle-class boys allows them to take up a "polluting" assignment (Douglas, 1966) and use it as a weapon to intimidate the boys.

The girls' struggle to make meaning of themselves as female constitutes a struggle in which gendered peer group hierarchies such as those in 3R position boys as "better" despite a mass of evidence to show they are neither as academically successful nor as well behaved as girls in the classroom. Peer group discourses constructed girls as harder working, more mature and more socially skilled. Yet, all the boys and a significant number of the girls, if not subscribing to the view that boys are better, adhered to the view that it is better being a boy. There are clearly confusions within the gender work in this classroom. To talk of dominant femininity is to generate a contradiction in terms because it is dominant versions of femininity which subordinate the girls to the boys. Rather, transgressive discourses and the deviant femininities they generate like Jodie's "tomboy" and Debbie and Carly's espousal of "girl power" accrue power in both the male and female peer group, and provide spaces for girls to escape gender subordination by the boys.

On the surface, gender relations in this classroom are continually churned up and realigned in a constant process of recomposition. But beneath, at a more subterranean level of knowing and making sense, both boys and girls seem to operate with entrenched dispositions in which being a boy is still perceived to be the more preferable subject positioning. Despite the contemporary focus, both within and without the classroom, on "girl power" (Arlidge, 1999), as Jean Anyon (1983) found almost 20 years ago, it appears that girls' subversions and transgressions are nearly always contained within, and rarely challenge, the existing structures. For much of the time, girls are "trapped in the very contradictions they would transcend." Girls' contestation may muddy the surface water of gender relations, but the evidence of this classroom indicates that the ripples only occasionally reach the murky depths of the prevailing gender order. Within both the localised and dominant discourses that these children draw on, being a boy is still seen as best by all the boys and a significant number of the girls.

Children may both create and challenge gender structures and meanings. However, for much of the time for a majority of the girls and boys in 3R, gender either operates as opposition or hierarchy or most commonly both at the same time. As Janet Holland and her colleagues found in relation to the adolescents in their study, the girls just as much as the boys in this class were "drawn into making masculinity powerful" (Holland et al., 1998, p. 30). The contemporary orthodoxy that girls are doing better than boys masks the complex messiness of gender relations in which, despite girls' better educational attainment, within this peer group, the prevalent view is still that it's better being a boy.

Despite the all-pervading focus on narrow, easily measured, learning outcomes in British state schooling, learning in classrooms is much wider than test results suggest. While test results indicate that girls are more successful educationally than boys, it appears that in this primary classroom girls and boys still learn many of the old lessons of gender relations which work against gender equity. Sue Heath (1999, p. 293) argues that there is a need for school-based work that sensitively addresses issues of gender identity and masculinities within a pro-feminist framework. There is also an urgent need for work that addresses the construction and performance of femininities.

References

Anyon, J. (1983) Intersections of gender and class: accommodation and resistance by working-class and affluent females to contradictory sex-role ideologies, in: S. Walker & L. Barton (Eds.) *Gender, Class and Education* (Lewes, Falmer Press).

Arlidge, J. (1999) Girl power gives boys a crisis of confidence, *Sunday Times*, 14 March.

Arnot, M. (1982) Male hegemony, social class and women's education, *Journal of Education*, 16, pp. 64–89.

Arnot, M., David, M. & Weiner, G. (1999) *Closing the Gender Gap: postwar education and social change* (Cambridge, Polity Press).

Ball, S. J. (1994) *Educational Reform* (Buckingham, Open University Press).

Bennett, C. (1996) The boys with the wrong stuff, *Guardian*, 6 November.

Blackmore, J. (1999) *Troubling Women: feminism, leadership and educational change* (Buckingham, Open University Press).

Brown, L. M. (1998) *Raising Their Voices: the politics of girls' anger* (Cambridge, MA, Harvard University Press).

Clarricoates, K. (1978) Dinosaurs in the classroom: a re-examination of some aspects of the "hidden" curriculum in primary schools, *Women's Studies International Forum*, 1, pp. 353–364.

Connell, R. W. (1987) *Gender and Power* (Sydney, Allen & Unwin).

———. (1995) *Masculinities* (Cambridge, Polity Press).

Connolly, P. (1998) *Racism, Gender Identities and Young Children* (London, Routledge).

Coward, R. (1999) The feminist who fights for the boys, *Sunday Times*, 20 June.

Davies, B. (1993) *Shards of Glass* (Sydney, Allen & Unwin).

Davies, P., Williams, J. & Webb, S. (1997) Access to higher education in the late twentieth century: policy, power and discourse, in: J. Williams (Ed.) *Negotiating Access to Higher Education* (Buckingham, Open University Press).

Douglas, M. (1966) *Purity and Danger: an analysis of concepts of pollution and taboo* (London, Routledge & Kegan Paul).

Epstein, D., Elwood, J., Hey, V. & Maw, J. (1998) *Failing Boys? Issues in Gender and Achievement* (Buckingham, Open University Press).

Fine, M. & Macpherson, P. (1992) Over dinner: feminism and adolescent female bodies, in: M. Fine (Ed.) *Disruptive Voices: the possibilities of feminist research* (Ann Arbor, MI, University of Michigan Press).

Francis, B. (1998) *Power Plays: primary school children's construction of gender, power and adult work* (Stoke-on-Trent, Trentham Books).

———. (1999) Modernist reductionism or post-structuralist relativism: can we move on? An evaluation of the arguments in relation to feminist educational research, *Gender and Education*, 11, pp. 381–394.

Heath, S. (1999) Watching the backlash: the problematisation of young women's academic success in 1990's Britain, *Discourse*, 20, pp. 249–266.

Hey, V. (1997) *The Company She Keeps: an ethnography of girls' friendship* (Buckingham, Open University Press).

Holland, J., Ramazanoglu, C., Sharpe, S. & Thomson, R. (1998) *The Male in the Head: young people, heterosexuality and power* (London, Tufnell Press).

Gee, J. P., Hull, G. & Lankshear, C. (1996) *The New Work Order* (London, Allen & Unwin).

Griffin, C. (1995) Absences that matter: constructions of sexuality in studies of young women friendship groups, paper presented at the *Celebrating Women's Friendship Conference*, Alcuin College, University of York, 8 April.

Jackson, D. (1998) Breaking out of the binary trap: boys' underachievement, schooling and gender relations, in: D. Epstein, J. Elwood, V. Hey & J. Maw (Eds.) *Failing Boys? Issues in Gender and Achievement* (Buckingham, Open University Press).

James, A., Jenks, C. & Prout, A. (1998) *Theorising Childhood* (Cambridge, Polity Press).

Jones, A. (1993) Becoming a "girl": post-structuralist suggestions for educational research, *Gender and Education*, 5, pp. 157–166.

Katz, A. (1999) Crisis of the "low can-do" boys, *Sunday Times*, 21 March.

Kenway, J. (1995) Masculinities in schools: under siege, on the defensive and under reconstruction, *Discourse*, 16, pp. 59–79.

Kenway, J. & Willis, S. with Blackmore, J. & Rennie, L. (1999) *Answering Back: girls, boys and feminism in schools* (London, Routledge).

Kerfoot, D. & Knight, D. (1994) Into the realm of the fearful: identity and the gender problematic, in: H. L. Radtke & H. J. Stam (Eds.) *Power/Gender: social relations in theory and practice* (London, Sage).

Lakoff, R. T. (1975) *Language and Woman's Place* (New York, Harper & Row).

Lucey, H. & Walkerdine, V. (1999) Boys' underachievement: social class and changing masculinities, in: T. Cox (Ed.) *Combating Educational Disadvantage* (London, Falmer Press).

Mac an Ghaill, M. (1988) *Young, Gifted and Black: student–teacher relations in the schooling of black youth* (Buckingham, Open University Press).

Maclure, M. (1994) Language and discourse: the embrace of uncertainty, *British Journal of Sociology of Education*, 15, pp. 283–300.

Mirza, S. H. (1992) *Young, Female and Black* (London, Routledge).

Pattman, R. & Phoenix, A. (1999) Constructing self by constructing the "other": 11–14 year old boys' narratives of girls and women, paper presented at the Gender and Education Conference, University of Warwick, 29–31 March.

Pyke, K. D. (1996) Class-based masculinities: the interdependence of gender, class and interpersonal power, *Gender & Society*, 10, pp. 527–549.

Reay, D. (1990) Working with boys, *Gender and Education*, 2, pp. 269–282.

Sewell, T. (1997) *Black Masculinities and Schooling: how black boys survive modern schooling* (Stoke-on-Trent, Trentham Books).

Skelton, C. (1997) Primary boys and hegemonic masculinities, *British Journal of Sociology of Education*, 18, pp. 349–369.

———. (1999) "A passion for football": dominant masculinities and primary schooling, paper presented to the British Educational Research Association Conference, University of Sussex, 2–5 September.

Smithers, R. (1999) Self-esteem the key for macho boys who scorn "uncool" school, *Guardian*, 16 March.

Thompson, S. (1994) What friends are for: on girls' misogyny and romantic fusion, in: J. Irvine (Ed.) *Sexual Cultures and the Construction of Adolescent Identities* (Philadelphia, PA, Temple University Press).

Thorne, B. (1993) *Gender Play: girls and boys in school* (Buckingham, Open University Press).

Walkerdine, V. (1991) *Schoolgirl Fictions* (London, Verso).

———. (1997) *Daddy's Girl: young girls and popular culture* (London, Macmillan).

Walkerdine, V., Lucey, H. & Melody, J. (2000) Class, attainment and sexuality in late twentieth-century Britain, in: C. Zmroczer & P. Mahony (Eds.) *Women and Social Class: international feminist perspectives* (London: UCL Press).

Weiner, G., Arnot, M. & David, M. (1997) Is the future female? Female success, male disadvantage and changing gender patterns in education, in: A. H. Halsey, P. Brown, H. Lauder & A. Stuart-Wells (Eds.) *Education: culture, economy and society* (Oxford, Oxford University Press).

Wight, D. (1996) Beyond the predatory male: the diversity of young Glaswegian men's discourses to describe heterosexual relationships, in: L. Adkins & V. Merchant (Eds.) *Sexualising the Social: power and the organisation of sexuality* (London, Macmillan).

Wilkinson, H. (1994) *No Turning Back: generations and the genderquake* (London, Demos).

———. (1999) The Thatcher legacy: power feminism and the birth of girl power, in: N. Walters (Ed.) *On the Move: feminism for a new generation* (London, Virago).

Williams, J. (Ed.) (1997) *Negotiating Access to Higher Education* (Buckingham, Open University Press).

Willis, P. (1977) *Learning to Labour: how working class kids get working class jobs* (Farnborough, Saxon House).

Yates, L. (1997) Gender equity and the boys debate: what sort of challenge is it? *British Journal of Sociology of Education*, 18, pp. 337–348.

Policing Masculinities: Investigating the Role of Homophobia and Heteronormativity in the Lives of Adolescent School Boys

WAYNE MARTINO

In this paper I draw on Michel Foucault's works (1978, 1984a, 1987) for analyzing the pervasive role that sexuality plays in determining certain traditional views of masculinity at a Catholic high school in Perth, Western Australia. Attention is drawn to the social practices through which the boys learn to fashion particular forms of gendered subjectivity that are policed within regimes of compulsory heterosexuality (see Beckett, 1998; Epstein, 1994, 1997; Epstein & Johnson, 1998; Flood, 1997; Laskey & Beavis, 1996; Pallotta-Chiarolli, 1995; Rich, 1980; Unks, 1995).

Another dimension addressed here is the focus on the specific capacitiesthat several boys have for questioning the effects of particular forms of masculinity in their lives. Many of these boys who become the brunt of other boys' abusive treatment appear to have developed certain skills for reflecting about dominant or hegemonic forms of masculinity (see Martino, 1997, 1988a, 1999b; McLean, 1996). This paper's focus on white, middle-class boys and their willingness to engage in critical discourses of masculinity contributes to the research on masculinities and schooling (Connell, 1989; Epstein, 1997; 1998; Epstein & Johnson, 1998; Frank, 1993; Gilbert & Gilbert, 1998; Kessler, Ashenden, Connell, & Dowsett, 1985; Mac an Ghaill, 1994; Nayak & Kehily, 1996; Skelton, 1997; Walker, 1988). While already existing research explores how adolescent boys make sense of their experiences of masculinity, this paper traces how several boys explain what they understand about the category of "masculinity" (Coleman, 1990).

A Foucauldian Framework for Analyzing Masculinities

The concept of "regimes of practice," in its application to investigating the ways in which adolescent boys enact various masculinities, is informed by a Foucauldian analytics of self-fashioning techniques and modalities of power involved in the production of subjectivity (see Foucault, 1978, 1980a, 1988a). For example, Foucault (1987) claims:

> What I wanted to know was *how the subject constituted himself* (sic), in such and such a determined

The Journal of Men's Studies, Vol. 8, No. 2, Winter 2000, pp. 213–236.

> form, as a mad subject or as a normal subject, through a certain number of practices which were games of truth, applications of power, etc. I had to reject a certain *a priori* theory of the subject in order to make this analysis of the relationships which can exist between the constitution of the subject or different forms of the subject and games of truth, practices of power and so forth. (p. 121; italics added)

Foucault is careful here to situate this focus on "how the subject constitute[s] himself" within a field or game of truth/power relations. Hence, different forms of the subject cannot be separated from a regime of practices through which power is channeled and particular truths established. In short, the formation of subjectivity is understood in terms of the cultural techniques for working on and fashioning the gendered self, which are made available within existing regimes of practice. In this paper it is such a conceptualization of subjectivity that informs an analysis of the social practices through which boys learn to enact particular stylized forms of masculinity. This leads to an investigation of what Foucault (1978) terms "polymorphous techniques of power" in relation to examining the formation of adolescent masculinities. The ways in which modalities of power are channeled through normalizing regimes of practice to permeate individual modes of behavior and to incite particular forms of desire become the analytic focus:

> . . . my main concern will be to locate the forms of power, the channels, and the discourses it permeates in order to reach the most tenuous and individual modes of behavior, the paths that give it access to the rare or scarcely perceivable forms of desire, how it penetrates and controls everyday pleasure—all this entailing effects that may be those of refusal, blockage, and invalidation, but also incitement and intensification: in short the "polymorphous techniques of power." (Foucault, 1978, p. 11)

It is this intensification and incitement of particular forms of desire within specific regimes of practice that shape the way adolescent boys relate, not only to themselves as gendered subjects, but to one another. And it is in this sense that sexuality is accorded a pivotal role in this paper in terms of investigating the ways in which adolescent boys learn to police their masculinities within regimes of self-surveillance.

Foucault (1884a), for example, highlights that sexuality must be treated as "the correlation of a domain of knowledge, a type of normativity and a mode of relation to the self":

> . . . it means trying to decipher how, in Western societies, a complex experience is constituted from and around certain forms of behavior: an experience which conjoins a field of study (*connaissance*) (with its own concepts, theories, diverse disciplines), a collection of rules (which differentiate the permissible from the forbidden, natural from monstrous, normal from pathological, what is decent from what is not, etc.), *a mode of relation between the individual and himself* (which enables him to recognize himself as a sexual subject amid others). (pp. 333–334; italics in original)

Here, Foucault emphasizes that he is concerned with investigating the deployment of sexuality within a normalizing regime of practices in which the individual is incited to relate to him/herself as a particular kind of subject. And Foucault highlights the pivotal role that sexuality plays in deciphering who we are as particular kinds of subjects. He illustrates how the specification of sexual behavior is tied to disciplinary regimens in which certain concepts, theories, and rules for governing conduct are formed according to an assemblage of historically contingent norms for regulating the boundaries of acceptable and desirable forms of heteronormative masculinity (see Epstein, 1997; Frank, 1987, 1990, 1993). Forms of masculinity in this paper, therefore, are treated as "a type of normativity and a mode of relation to the self," understood in terms of an ensemble of self-fashioning practices that are linked to normalizing judgements and techniques for producing culturally and historically specific forms of subjectivity.

Thus, for Foucault, studying human experience involves describing a collection of rules that are related to establishing a type of normalizing relation to the self within a regime of practices in which sexuality functions as a means of self-regulating individuals and placing them under a particular kind of surveillance. Hence, the experience of adolescent boys is understood in terms of a regime of practices—in their historical and cultural deployment—within which particular forms of gendered subjectivity are constituted.

Attention, therefore, is drawn in this paper to how adolescent boys constitute themselves as males of particular types. In focusing on the ways in which boys learn to relate to themselves, consideration is given to the categories of thought and modes of thinking that they adopt and apply to themselves in fashioning a particular style of masculinity. This leads to the formulation of particular kinds of questions regarding the enactment of masculinity such as: How do adolescent boys fashion for themselves a particular form of subjectivity or masculinity? What practices do they engage in to decipher "who they are"? How are certain desires formed within a regime of knowledge-power relations that serve as an index of their masculinity? In other words, what enables the adolescent boy to recognize himself as a proper incumbent of certain categories of masculinity? (see also Coleman, 1990). These are some of the questions that are addressed in this paper.

The Research Method

The interviews included in this paper were part of my doctoral research into the construction of adolescent masculinities at a Catholic, co-educational high school in Perth, Western Australia. The school draws on a mainly white, middle-class population. Having been a teacher at the school and having taught many, though not all, of the boys interviewed, it was easy to find research participants. Letters of consent, describing the nature of the research and what it would involve, were given to the boys aged 15 years who were part of a Year 10 group at this school and to several Year 12 students, aged 17, who heard about the research. Their parents were also required to sign a letter of consent. The Year 10 cohort, however, was chosen as a major focus of the study because I had noticed how these boys congregated into distinctive peer-group cultures with the footballers/surfies establishing their presence by dominating a space on the oval where approximately thirty of them would play football.

The fact that the researcher was acquainted with the boys in this study, however, might pose some concerns. While students might feel more comfortable with and trust a researcher they know with more personal information, they could also provide specific responses they think the researcher wants from them. Furthermore, some of the boys who had taken classes with the researcher might have acquired a vocabulary and an understanding with which to articulate specific issues. Consequently, the boys might be more aware of the researcher's language use, tone, and inflection so that they could "read" the many meanings and intentions behind the questions posed to them. Despite these limitations, however, arguably certain benefits accrued by virtue of the researcher-participants classroom involvements in terms of the boys feeling comfortable and open to express their thoughts and opinions without the fear that their masculinity would be questioned. In fact, many of the boys stated that they would not have felt comfortable discussing their lives at school and their peer relationships with someone they did not know very well or like.

It is important to emphasize that the selection of interview data is always going to be governed by particular norms. In this case, the focus is on those boys who, in one sense, were positioned and positioned themselves against the norms of compulsory heterosexuality and homophobic regulation policed by the dominant group of "footballers" at this school. This is not to deny that there are potential power relations involved in this research situation. A deliberate attempt, in fact, is made to include the comments of several boys from various peer groups whoquestioned or rejected the norms of the "cool masculinity" enacted by the dominant group of footballers/surfies. In this way, the effects of a regime of normalizing practices in which compulsory heterosexuality becomes naturalized and taken for granted are mapped (Angelides, 1994; Beckett, 1998; Epstein, 1994; Steinberg, Epstein, & Johnson, 1997). However, attention is also drawn to the practices of self-surveillance and regulation adopted by those boys who are not members of the footballer group but who still engage in homophobic discourse to police their masculinities. In this sense, the particular skills and capacities of these boys for questioning masculinities in schooling contexts are identified, with the implications and possibilities for critical practice being made explicit.

What is emphasized here is the need to make explicit the role that particular norms might play in the selection and interpretation of the data that, it is argued, are inescapable since no position exists outside of power relations (see Foucault, 1978, 1984a). The prevalence of homophobic comments and name calling at this particular school, where certain boys were labeled gay or "poofs," led to my desire to investigate the heteronormative regimes of practice operating in these students' lives. Initially, boys and girls from one English class I taught were asked to participate in the research. After the first round of interviews, I decided to focus only on the boys so that a more detailed exploration of the complexities involved in the ways they enacted their masculinity could be conducted. The initial interview involved students just talking about their lives at school, their friends, and any problems they experienced as boys or girls. Subsequent follow-up interviews asked for clarification about particular comments and issues that had been raised in the initial interview. In later interviews, I asked the boys explicitly to discuss their understandings of "masculinity." The reason for this was to produce data that would enable me to analyze their attempts at defining masculinity.

Ethical Issues

Inevitably, as Mac an Ghaill (1994) has pointed out, ethical issues and dilemmas will arise in a study where young people are incited to disclose information about their lives and experiences. The fact that many of the students already knew me and related to me meant that they felt quite comfortable and safe talking about a range of personal issues. The consequence of this was that the interviews often became a "safe space" for the boys to express their feelings with the risk of the research often slipping into "a form of therapy" (Mac an Ghaill, 1994, p. 174). In light of this slippage, decisions had to be made about what could be reported or published. In these circumstances, permission from the student was always sought beforehand, and every attempt was made to ensure that they could not be identified. The boys were also provided with transcripts of their interviews that they were free to edit as they saw fit. Attempts were also made to regularly follow up on the boys, particularly those who had discussed serious problems, with the view to encouraging them to visit the school counselor, which several of them did.

Regulatory Practices and Peer Group Masculinities

At the school where this research was conducted, a dominant group consisting of approximately thirty boys regularly occupied a space on the oval where they played football (see Martino, 1999a). This group wielded considerable power and was identified as the "footballers." While it is important to avoid categorizing these boys as a homogenous group, it is important nonetheless to stress that all the boys interviewed identified them as a distinctive peer group—known as the "footballer/surfie kind of guys." Thus, these boys had a recognizable identity and presence at the school and were perceived to wield power. This is not to deny, though, that within the "footballers" there were hierarchies of power operating, as Steve testifies (see Martino, 1997, 1999a).

Steve,[1] a former member of the footballer group, rejected these boys because of the abusive treatment he received from them. Many of the "footballers" thought that Steve, who was a team captain, had a "big head" and consequently became a target for their abuse. What is interesting is that his own experiences of marginalization enabled him to reject the footballers' homophobic practices directed at other boys. When I ask him to explain his relations to other peer groups at school, he stated that "we don't hassle other people." This led him to describe the different groups he observed at school, while focusing on the power of the "footballers" to police other boys through practices of homophobic denigrations.

> STEVE: . . . there's sort of Smith and his mates [the "footballers"]—all their group . . . hangs around the oval. And then there's ours [Steve's group]. And a group that hangs around the basketball court. And then there's another group, [which] Smith's group thinks [are] "faggots."
>
> WM: They think who's a "faggot"?
>
> STEVE: The fourth group, which is Murray, Rob Murray, and Friedman.
>
> WM: So how do you know that they [Steve's group] think they're "faggots"?
>
> STEVE: 'Cause I used to hang around with them.
>
> WM: So they used to talk about them?
>
> STEVE: Yeah.
>
> WM: Why? What leads them to label them in that way, do you think?
>
> STEVE: Maybe because the other group they hang around—they're girls and boys. So they like sit around in a circle. They'll sit around with girls and everything whereas Smith and all that, they'd sit around [with] just boys and then the girls would be off somewhere else, so they used to think these guys had a bit of feminine side to 'em, so they'd tell them they're "poofters" or something like that.
>
> WM: What made them make that judgement—because the girls were there—they talked to girls?
>
> STEVE: I dunno. Well Ryan, he's got a sort of a "poofter" voice, which everyone picks up and gives him shit about.
>
> WM: And he's a part of that group?
>
> STEVE: Yeah . . . and then there's Friedman, well, he was, there was a rumor going around that he got kicked out, or he left X school because he got caught wanking himself or something like that—I'm not quite sure. So everyone labeled him as a "faggot." But I talk to him all the time, he's all right. We associate with this group all the time, so it's all right.
>
> WM: So you're saying these guys who talk and sit with the girls get treated badly by just that one group, by the "footballers"?
>
> STEVE: Yeah, they're teased, yeah.

What is interesting is that Ryan and Friedman are members of two distinct groups. Ryan has a small group of friends who are all girls, but Steve places him in the same group as the "handballers" (of which Friedman is a member)—those boys who are distinguished as "non-footballers"—who also sometimes sit and talk to girls during the break. Perhaps this is beside the point because Ryan, and other boys who form part of the "handballer" group, are targeted by the "footballers" on the basis of their assumed homosexuality. They are differentiated by the "footballers" on a number of counts, but primarily in terms of their engagement in handball and their association with girls. This leads them to be viewed as "having a bit of a feminine side to them" and forms the basis for attributions of homosexuality. Moreover, Ryan is considered to have a "poofy voice" and Friedman also has a reputation from a previous school because he "got caught wanking himself." This data draws attention to the regime of homophobic practices and strategies of surveillance that the powerful boys [foot ballers] use to police sex/gender boundaries. What is equally significant is Steve's questioning of these practices and his rejection of the rules for designating what constitutes appropriate or desirable masculinity as enacted through practices of homophobic othering and differentiation.

It is interesting, however, that Steve, while rejecting the abusive "footballers' " homophobic practices, also engages in homophobic discourse. For instance, he claims that despite the fact that Friedman was labeled a "faggot," "he was all right," and that he talked to him all the time, pointing to the role that Steve himself plays in policing his own masculinity within the limits prescribed by the norms of compulsory heterosexuality. This research, therefore, raises the issue of the need to investigate further these self-policing practices by probing boys' attitudes toward alternative sexualities and how Steve would feel if Dave were, in fact, gay.

Despite the limits of the normalizing practices in which Steve is negotiating and policing his own masculinity, his comments in relation to Dave appear to indicate that he is appealing to a sense of justice and to giving people "a fair go." This has implications for discussing issues of dominant forms of heterosexual masculinity with schoolboys that will be discussed later (see McLean, 1995).

Dave: Working at the Limits of Heterosexual Masculinities

Dave Friedman, the "handballer," who Steve mentioned above as being targeted by the "footballers," talks at length about the homophobic harassment he received at the hands of a particular group of boys while attending another school, a Catholic boys-only school. Interestingly, the "footballers" at the boys-only school are friends with Smith's footballers. So word spreads to his new school about his *reputation* as a "poofter" even before he arrives. And the reason he left the first school was due to escalating levels of homophobic harassment. What follows is Dave's account of life at the Catholic boys-only school.

> DAVE: There were these guys, and they hassled me . . . they targeted me and another guy . . . there might have been a couple of others, but it was largely associated with the fact that a lot of the things we did were perhaps stereotypical of what they saw as being related to homosexuality.
>
> WM: Like?
>
> DAVE: Like at the time I did ballet, and the guy I knew, his posture and manner and everything he did was supposedly leading towards something such that they [footballers] suspect that he would turn out homosexual. So, they abused him for that, and me for that. I remember a couple of others, I can't remember what they did, but I remember distinctly that they were harassed for being homosexual. Well, they weren't, but they were seen as homosexual, whether they had a girlfriend or not, it was just that they paid no attention to sort of the facts.

Dave's attention is drawn to a regime of normalizing practices in which homophobic strategies are used against boys who are identified as homosexual on the basis of their posturing, manner, or activities like ballet. Thus, there are certain mannerisms and performative practices involving body posturing, as well as the kind of voice a boy has, which lead particular boys to be labeled as gay (see Nayak & Kehily, 1996; Walker, 1988). Furthermore, such practices are imbricated in the way that many boys learn to establish their masculinities, at the level of performativity, through processes of differentiation in which indicators of homosexuality are readily recognizable as markers of deviance from a heterosexual norm, and hence an appropriate masculinity (see Beckett, 1998; Connell, 1987, 1995; Epstein, 1994; McLean, 1996; Redman, 1996; Steinberg et al., 1997; Willis, 1977).

It is also important to note that Dave, like Steve, also engages in homophobic discourse or a form of heterosexism when he claims that boys were being harassed for being homosexual but then qualifies his comment by the assertion that they "weren't," which once again poses the question of how he would respond if they were. Would the homophobic taunting then be seen as legitimate? Once again this data points to the significant ways in which the marginalized boys also police and enact their masculinities within a regime of normalizing practices and compulsory heterosexuality.

However, what is interesting is the way that Dave develops an understanding of what motivates other boys to behave in this way. In fact, he uses the interview to try to account for the reasons as to why he is marginalized by the dominant group. Firstly, he attributes such practices to the bullies' own lack of confidence in themselves:

> Socially . . . they stuck to one group, and they all drew on each other for support because I don't think they could have really survived on their own, and to get energy, I think, for confidence building. They didn't have any confidence [in] themselves, and they take pleasure in bringing other people down, tall poppy syndrome. They take other people down, which gives them a sense of satisfaction and everything, because the people they hang around with weren't really their friends.

> I really doubt that they were friends, but they were drawn together by a common sense of lower self-esteem, and they needed support and they drew themselves together, and they were able to profit from hurting other people.

Secondly, he attributes their behavior to innate drives or energies and lack of maturity. In fact, he mentions the influence of girls in quelling boys' tendency to display this kind of violence:

> But a lot of boys didn't behave like that; they just went along with the leaders of the pack. A lot of them had influence from females from outside the school, which I think with them they reach a higher maturity at a younger age, so I think they did have influences there, but really I think with boys its in their own nature. You see boys grow up; you've got Adolf Hitler and that type of thing. They have a lot of energy in them that can be expelled either positively or negatively, and I think girls tend to be an energy that can nullify it, that if it is destructive they can stop it from going over the top. I mean because it is girls that make it seem as socially unacceptable; they condemn that type of behavior, like violent, real racist, prejudiced attitudes, that type of thing.

Here Dave tends to attribute the boys' behavior to innate drives that predispose them to act in violent ways. This is reinforced in his reference to the boys' energy that must be "expelled either positively or negatively." What is particularly interesting is that Dave explicitly mentions the role of girls in terms of their higher level of maturity that is implicitly tied to their tendency to "nullify" the violence that is enacted by boys against other boys. He appears to be drawing attention to the different norms for governing the conduct of girls who police boys' bullying practices through a condemnation of violent behaviors. This highlights the differences he encountered between the boys-only school and the coeducational school he now attends in terms of the varying levels and overt enactment of homophobic violence in each school setting. In fact, he appears to be suggesting that such a "culture" of violence was officially endorsed and socially sanctioned in the boys-only Catholic school he attended:

> DAVE: I remember from, say, Year 5 that there were these very strong, very anti-homosexual feelings; everyone was very much against it. Maybe because, knowing that in the school, at this private Catholic school, the all-boys school, it was felt that obviously it was not socially acceptable and that it was very bad to feel like that. If you were a homosexual, it was very bad, it was against what society is meant to be. The values that they experienced, it said that homosexuals were just a lower form.
>
> WM: So how did they know if someone was homosexual?
>
> DAVE: No, they don't. They assume, if they like the person, they won't press it, if they don't like the person, which is usually the case, that is if they show any sign of weakness or compassion, then other people jump to conclusions and bring them down. So really it's a survival of the fittest. It's not very good to be sensitive. If you have no feeling and compassion or anything like that, you would survive in a place like that.
>
> WM: It's not too good.
>
> DAVE: This is my own personal point of view. Maybe it's a bit extremist, but it's just the way I see what happened to me in that environment. And now that I'm out of that environment, I've had a chance to analyze it and sort of observe it. I'm not viewing it with any emotions, but seeing it analytically—this is what they do and how they do it.

Thus Dave not only uses the confessional space of the interview as a form of therapy, but also as a means by which he is able to make some sense of his experiences. Here the regulatory behavior of the boys in terms of cutting down the "tall poppies" intersects with gendered regimes of practice in which particular forms of masculinity are regulated. Attention is drawn to a regime of bullying practices in which those boys who are sensitive or who display "any sign of weakness" risk becoming targets of homophobic violence at the hands of a "pack" of other boys who acquire and maintain a status at the top of a pecking order of masculinities (see Connell, 1987, 1995). This is highlighted in Dave's reference to the "survival of the fittest," which once again signals that he is drawing on a particular body of gendered knowledge that is grounded in a form of biological determinism to account for the behavior of his peers. Such behaviors, which involve enacting a form of power, are interpreted, in this particular case, as instances of boys publicly enacting and performing a stylized form of heterosexual masculinity (see Dixon, 1997; Epstein, 1997; Haywood, 1993; Nayak & Kehily, 1996; Parker, 1996; Redman, 1996; Skelton, 1997).

Many of the boys interviewed focused on the ways in which sexuality is used to police sex/gender boundaries and highlight some of the specific occasions on which it occurs in their peer groups. What is particularly interesting about Dave's final comment in the excerpt above is that it draws attention to how he is making sense of his experiences at his previous school. It is being physically removed from that environment, he indicates, which enables him to develop capacities for analyzing how particular modalities of power are operationalized within certain normalizing regimes of practice.

Dave is then asked about what life is like for him at his current school and whether he has experienced this kind of harassment there. While he claims that he has not encountered forms of violence and abuse on the same level, he does mention how the "footballers," when he first came to the school, targeted him in this way. He talks about how the "footballers" knew some of the boys from his previous school and continued the homophobic abuse that his former peers had enacted against him. However, in this co-educational community, Dave highlights the extent to which the perpetration of such forms of violence was modified by the influence of the girls.

Despite the fact that levels of homophobic violence at his present school were not as great as in his previous educational setting, due primarily to what Dave considers girls' feminizing influence in a co-educational context, he still draws attention to the perpetration of such practices, particularly by the "footballers":

WM: How did they give you crap?

DAVE: It was again for my dancing. A lot of stuff like "ballet boy," I don't know; they were very unimaginative. Just a lot to do with being a woman; being homosexual was a big thing again because of dancing. That was the main problem!

WM: Who was doing that here?

DAVE: It was a large group at that time in Year 9. . . . I was condemned by that big group of footballers who had characters like Carl Roberts, Miles Teller, John Green and a few others.

WM: So is that the big group on the oval?

DAVE: Yeah.

Here Dave highlights the role of normalizing practices that involve designating ballet or dance as a feminized activity. Once again, the policing of heterosexual masculinities is framed in terms of identifying sex-inappropriate practices, which then form the basis for imputing homosexuality. It is not so much dance "itself" that poses a problem, but its *association* with the "feminine." This link is produced through a regime of practices that is imbricated in regulatory technologies of the gendered self (see Haywood, 1993; Laskey & Beavis, 1996; Mason & Tomsen, 1997; Martino, 1998b, Parker, 1996; Steinberg et al., 1997). What is emphasized by Dave and many of the boys interviewed is that the "footballers" perpetrated such sex-based harassment that functions as a means by which the latter are able to gain a "cool" or tough status as "masculine" subjects within a hierarchical peer group network (see Kessler et al., 1985; Mac an Ghaill, 1994; Walker, 1988; Willis, 1977). Thus, a certain demeanor, defined in these terms, becomes identifiable for the researcher as a particular stylized form of heterosexual masculinity that is embodied at the level of performativity (see Nayak & Kehily, 1996; Steinberg et al., 1997).

WM: So how do you see that group on the oval?

DAVE: I'd see them as a group that thinks themselves the most popular.

WM: Popular? How are they popular?

Dave: Socially acceptable, I think, compared to the other groups whom they see as maybe inferior to them in their social acceptability.

WM: What makes them popular do you think? Is it the things they do, their interests, the way you see them behaving?

Dave: I think it was for the boys their *masculinity*. . . . You had practically everyone in that group doing football, drinking beer, smoking, anything rebellious yet within the lines ruled by society as acceptable. They also talked about the women they had . . . they believed they had good looks . . . they ignored other people. I think this accounts for the whole group, they ignored others who were not in their rank, and they always kept to themselves. They considered themselves good looking and had a lot of girlfriend/boyfriend relationships, and having sex was big talk. The younger you were when you had it the first time, the better.

What is interesting is the normative ties that Dave establishes between the category of "masculinity" and a range of social practices. For Dave, displaying masculinity for these boys is linked to asserting publicly their heterosexuality by boasting about their sexual exploits with girls (see Hite, 1980; Holland, Ramazanoglu, & Sharpe, 1993; Kehily & Nayak, 1997; Wood, 1984). He also highlights the extent to which these boys bolstered such a stylized form of heterosexual masculinity through social practices that involved playing football, smoking, and drinking. On the basis of engaging in such practices and "having good looks," these boys were perceived to acquire a high-status masculinity.

Dave also mentions a group of popular girls who always talked about the "footballers" in their group and discusses their role in enforcing this model of masculinity:

Dave: The girls also talked about it [sex] by themselves and about the boys . . . they had top ten lists for the boys.

WM: The girls had top ten lists?

Dave: Yeah, that group of popular girls, yeah. They judged the boys on good looks and their masculinity and how manly they were. It was sort of like you had the men as the roosters with them preening their feathers and going around the school kicking dirt into the face of other people and you had the girls watching to see who was the strongest, the most dominant. And the boys also would accept that male figure as the most manly of them all, the most socially acceptable, and they would look up to him. The girls would acknowledge that and also view him with the same attitude as the guys did, but it was constantly changing, though.

Here, Dave indicates how the practices of a group of girls contributed to the boys' acquisition of a particular stylized masculinity and, hence, social status. The girls' role in reinforcing a heterosexual masculinity is emphasized. Moreover, attention is drawn to the performative dimension of this masculinity by the comparison of the boys to "roosters preening their feathers." This is indicative of the boys posturing their bodies to establish a particular heterosexual masculinity that is on display, not only for the girls, but for other boys as well. The analogy is significant because it highlights the extent to which these boys learn to acquire a particular demeanor, which is readily recognizable and identifiable as an instance of displaying a stylized heterosexual masculinity (see Butler, 1990).

What is also important to note is that Dave's reference to the "footballers" as "kicking the dirt in the face of other people" describes another aspect of these boys' demeanor that is explainable in terms of their own sense of social superiority and embodied power over other boys:

WM: The "kicking of dirt in the face of other people," can you explain what you mean by that?

Dave: I think that's more ignorance of other people. That those not in their group they pay no attention to and consider them not to be worthy of their attention. They're

> just totally ignored, and they feel that they don't need to interact with them at all or need to be with them at any time. . . . Also Manual Arts for these boys is a big thing, woodwork, metalwork, that type of thing, technical drawing . . . alcohol, sex, really manly things like ropemanship, callused hands, that type of thing, they find these things important . . . a lot of people are drawn into that category. You still have a lot of nice people who have a lot of potential who are drawn into this category. They're trying to be like that. I just really hope that they get out of it because a lot of people have potential in other areas, and they'rewasting their time, I think.

The desirability of enacting such a form of heterosexual masculinity is further emphasized when Dave explains what he means when he describes these boys as *displaying their masculinity*:

> WM: Can you talk to me about what you understand about displaying masculinity? Like you referred to that group of guys as having masculine attitudes. Can you explain what you mean by that?
>
> DAVE: I'm not sure, but what I see as a *masculine* attitude is that they value certain things like bodily physical strength and attractiveness like they have to be physically attractive to the opposite sex as in they have to be very strong, handsome, charming . . . able to get attention of the opposite sex readily and easily whenever they wanted. They also have to be sport orientated, very sporty, very fit, able to do any sport and do it well. Intelligent, well it's not always good to not have a brain so they definitely want a bit of intelligence, but they don't put too much emphasis on being brainy; it's more like not being too thick or stupid.

Dave's comments here draw attention to the stylized demeanor of the "footballers." The requirements for displaying a particular heterosexual masculinity are spelt out in terms of demonstrating physical strength, being able to attract the opposite sex readily, and engaging actively in sports. Moreover, Dave claims that boys need to balance not appearing too stupid, while avoiding presenting themselves as too intelligent, because both positions contravene the normalizing boundaries within which a high-status masculinity is enacted (see Gilbert & Gilbert, 1998; Martino, 1999b).

James: The Pervasive Role of Homophobic Practices

The effects of such practices in which sexuality is deployed as a means of policing gender boundaries for boys is also highlighted by James, aged 17, who had been harassed on the basis of his imputed homosexuality. In fact, his interview is used to describe a regime of social relations and practices in which heterosexual masculinities are policed through the deployment of homophobic strategies that are bodily and verbally enacted (see Butler, 1996; Flood, 1997; Mills, 1996; Nayak & Kehily, 1996; Ward, 1995). James had been the brunt of homophobic abuse and used the interview to make sense of why he had been targeted. He recounts a series of experiences involving encounters with various boys on the bus that he caught to and from school.

On his way to school one morning, a group of boys from one of the local high schools started calling James names. Initially, he was targeted as an "art boy" because he was carrying an art file. But the harassment escalated, and they began calling him "fag boy." Moreover, he claims that what exacerbated the harassment was the fact that one of his friends, Andrew, who always caught the bus with him, was a Year 9 boy, aged 14. He describes Andrew in the following way:

> To me he is like my little brother because I don't have a little brother. He just comes over whenever he wants and does whatever he wants; he's good to be around. Even though people might think why hang around with a 14 year old, but I don't really care because he is like a good friend, and he like catches the bus. He always follows me around sometimes.

The homophobic harassment persisted, and Andrew also became implicated in the abuse that is directed at James, with their sexuality questioned. The boys at the back of the bus continued to target James and Andrew, calling them names and throwing objects at both. James indicated that he became very angry and tried to ignore the harassment. Eventually he took another bus to avoid being targeted. However, on this other bus, another group of Year 10 students from his own school started to harass him in much the same way as the previous group of boys.

In his interview, James questioned why he was the target of homophobic practices. He attempted to understand these boys' behavior.

> I mean like I don't even know these people, and they call me "art boy" because I've got my file. No matter how many people are there at the bus stop, they always do it, no matter what, and I don't know why. I mean I don't know why these people insist on labeling, singling me out; they don't even know me. Maybe I look like a fag or something, or I deserve to be called a fag because I do art; hey, I just can't stand it. The thing that really irritates [me] is the fact that the bus is full of all these students from other schools as well and you can see them. They just look out for me, and they just go, "Yeah, those guys must be right!" They just look at you while the idiots at the back are abusing you, and they just look and think, "What's going on?" or you know, "Oh, yeah, he looks like a fag," or they just look at you blankly. They don't really give a shit, and you think one of them might turn around and say, you know, "What the hell are you doing that for? You don't even know him."

What is significant here again is James's deployment of homophobic discourse in self-monitoring and policing a particular form of hegemonic heterosexual masculinity. For instance, he makes the comment that maybe he deserves to be called "a fag" because he studies art, which raises issues about his own internalized homophobia. This data once again highlights the need for educators to develop strategies for questioning the role that homophobia plays in the regulation and formation of masculinities in the lives of boys at school.

James is also calling for support in a situation in which he feels quite helpless and angry. This call for help, which is underscored by an appeal to a sense of justice that he believes should motivate others to act on his behalf, is also reflected in his reference to the need for bus drivers to address the problem:

> Almost every day when I catch the bus in the afternoon, I mean the bus I catch now in the afternoon, there is hardly anyone on it. I like to catch a bus; now when I go home from school I just like to be on my own. I hate it when there's groups of people coming my way. I get very intimidated because of all this shit. . . . I get really intimidated easily now . . . you think the bus driver might have done something like stop the bus and say don't do that; don't hang your heads out of the window. I mean one driver did, but it's never the same driver, but one driver did once, and I thought, "Oh, shit, they're going to get off and big mouth me or something and say, 'it's your fault, fag boy.' " . . . It's that sort of shit that is bloody irritating; you know, just because I've got a file and I do art, I'm a fag boy. I mean, it's probably stupid in a way that we all consider them "cool." We don't actually think they're "cool," but because they're in their group with their friends, they think they're cool.

This interview with James draws attention to the regime of normalizing practices in which sex/gender boundaries are policed for adolescent boys.

Bruce: Practices of Self-Surveillance and the Gendered Dimension of Displaying Emotion

Bruce's interviews also highlight this regime of normalizing practices. He comments on the norms governing the public display of traditional forms of masculinity that emphasize the avoidance of communicating on an emotional level in peer group situations. He reads this capacity as "feminine" and claims that this is because girls are "more in touch with their emotions":

> Girls are kind of more open. I guess if guys . . . opened up to one another, . . . they might find out that they're all really the same, and that they could accept one another. Say, I open up my emotions to people, and some guys, still they'll reject you. They

don't want you to say that the guy is in touch with his "feminine side," I guess. I say "feminine side" because females can get in touch with their emotions, and they're not afraid to talk about them, while a lot of guys are.

Here, Bruce identifies a particular mode of relating that is organized around quite specific norms for governing gender-specific conduct. On one level, he seems to be suggesting that enacting a particular currency of heterosexual masculinity involves an avoidance of emotions. This is reinforced through engaging in sexist practices as a principal mode of relating to other boys (see Easthope, 1986; Haywood, 1993; Holland et al., 1993; Parker, 1996; Segal, 1990; Simpson, 1994; Willis, 1977; Wood, 1984).

Bruce continues to elaborate on a generalized rule for behaving or relating, which he reads as an instance of heterosexual masculinity. The rule that boys should not show their emotions is also one that he identifies as constraining the way in which he would like to be able to relate to his male friends:

WM: So why do you think guys are afraid to express their emotions?

BRUCE: Rejection.

WM: Rejection from their friends?

BRUCE: Yeah, well I think it all comes back to rejection.

WM: What would they be rejected for, then? Why would they be rejected?

BRUCE: Um, for showing their emotions because this attitude of masculinity and this stereotype has been built up for so long, passed on from their fathers; it just keeps getting passed on generation after generation.

WM: So it's not really just a stereotype thing, is that what you're saying, that it's kind of quite "real"?

BRUCE: It's "real," definitely, with a lot of people. I'm not saying everyone's like that, but you will find a lot of it in most people. Even I must admit, um, I feel uncomfortable say, giving my best friend a big hug in front of other guys.

WM: Why?

BRUCE: Um, because that's not accepted by them; they reject that kind of idea of showing your emotions because you like this person, even though it's platonic. There's nothing sexual about it; it's just that you really like this person. You can't show that because it's like that's reserved for the opposite sex. You don't do that kind of thing; that's showing your emotions too much, and that's how we've been conditioned into being after so long, whereas females, they hug each other all the time. That's the way they are because they're friends and they like each other; they're not afraid to do that, and other females condone that. They don't reject it. So I guess there's a lot less prejudice when it comes to a showing of emotions in the female side than the male side; they're still very, I don't know, closed. They're like that little town on *Shame*, the little closed community within themselves. They're not allowed to show the real them; they have to hide that. I guess that could be attributed to years ago when the male was the breadwinner, the woman stayed at home, and that power that goes along with men and by showing your true emotions, that kind of doesn't. It doesn't reflect your power, I guess, you could say. One of the attitudes and emotions that go along with power is that you are very, you're hard, you're cold, you strive to achieve, you, um, I don't know, it's hard to express. Powerful people aren't usually real kind, friendly, open people if you know what I mean.

Bruce links boys' avoidance of expressing emotion to an "attitude of masculinity," which has been "passed on from their fathers." In so doing, he emphasizes the pivotal role of fathers and adult men in establishing norms for governing their son's behavior as gendered subjects. Moreover, what is significant is that Bruce has developed quite specific capacities for reading masculinity and is applying them to his own practices and those of other boys. For example, his reference to the Australian film, *Shame*, which dealt with the pack rape of a 16-year-old girl in an outback town, is pertinent in this respect. This film was studied in an English class conducted by the researcher where issues around masculinity were discussed at length. Bruce is drawing on these understandings to make sense of his own lived experiences of masculinity. He reiterates the extent to which specific norms govern regimes of practices for boys in terms of policing sex/gender boundaries (see Flood, 1997; Laskey & Beavis, 1996; McLean, 1996; Steinberg et al., 1997).

Conclusion

Foucault's work (1978, 1984a, 1987) has been particularly useful in serving as an interpretive frame for analyzing the normalizing regimes of practice through which various masculinities are enacted. The data included in this paper have been used to draw attention to several boys' understanding and rejection of certain norms governing the production of a particular form of hegemonic heterosexual masculinity (Boulden, 1996; Butler, 1996; Epstein & Johnson, 1998; Frank, 1987; Martino, 1998b; McLean, 1996). It has also highlighted the powerful role that sexuality plays in terms of how these boys police and monitor their masculinities within heteronormative regimes of internalized homophobia. The willingness of these boys to question such norms on another level, however, appears to be related to their own active positioning against the "footballers," who are in the business of policing acceptable forms of masculinity through a regime of homophobic practices. It is important to highlight that not all Anglo-Australian boys necessarily embrace hegemonic masculinity in all its various forms. Dave, through his subjection to a regime of homophobic practices enacted by hegemonic boys at the schools he attended, demonstrates capacities for questioning these normalizing practices. Steve, while not being a target of homophobic harassment himself, is also critical of the "footballers"' behavior because he, too, has been rejected and treated unfairly by them. Bruce, while not appearing to have been treated unfairly, is starting to reflect on what he perceives to be the limits and constraints imposed on him by a set of norms governing the production of hegemonicheterosexual masculinity.

However, what needs to be highlighted is that these boys (except for Bruce), while questioning the homophobic practices of the "footballers," are themselves still caught up in normalizing regimes for policing heterosexual masculinity. This raises crucial questions about the pivotal role that sexuality plays in the formation and regulation of gendered subjectivity for all these boys.

The implications of this are significant in signaling a move forward in attempting to address issues of masculinity and homophobia in schools. As Britzman (1995) argues, crucial questions about how normality is constructed and naturalized need to be addressed in schools (see Martino, 1999b). In light of the research documented in this paper, it is indisputable that we have to find ways to help students to problematize the whole idea of what is considered to be natural and given and how we have come to understand ourselves in these terms. These questions, as illustrated in this paper, are directly related to how many boys come to understand themselves as appropriately masculine (see Epstein, 1998; Jackson, 1998; Martino, 1999a). However, the boys' willingness to talk about their experiences and issues of masculinity at school is noteworthy and may well serve as a platform for further addressing questions and issues of homophobia. Moreover, the whole idea of being treated fairly and with respect emerges as a strong force in these boys' accounts of their experiences at school. With Bruce, these issues are also present as he grapples with the regimes of compulsory heterosexuality that prescribe the limits of acceptable masculinity within peer group cultures at school (Mac an Ghail, 1994; Walker, 1988). In light of their comments, it would appear that addressing issues of masculinity within a social justice framework that appeals to students' sense of justice may well have productive consequences in addressing issues of power and masculinities in schools (see Nickson, 1996).

Several boys, however, claimed that they had never been given the opportunity to discuss such issues. As Shaun, another one of the interviewees claims, "There's no opportunity for guys to get down and think about what they're doing and why they are doing it and stuff like that."

This sentiment is also reiterated by Eric, who asserts that:

> . . . everything is seen as one type of male stereotype, but it's a particular version of masculinity. You have to be interested in sports, you have to like girls and all the rest of it, and it is always fed to you from day one, and you've never actually seen the other version of masculinity . . . and all of a sudden you just see this other version of masculinity, and you've never like, you know, through your education, you've never been told about it. . . .

In light of these comments that explicitly advocate the need for more open discussion about what constitutes masculinity, there are definite possibilities for engaging boys in actively exploring the impact and effects of heteronormative and homophobic currencies of masculinity on their lives. However, professional development for teachers and whole school approaches to dealing with gender issues are necessary in order to create a culture that is committed to interrogating those discourses that naturalize masculinity and in so doing present it as an unalterable given that is driven by "some kind of biological determinism" or essence (Jackson & Salisbury, 1996, p. 104; see also Gender Equity Taskforce, 1997; Gilbert & Gilbert, 1998; House of Representatives Standing Committee, 1994; Martino, 1998b). These discourses continue to be articulated in Australia within the popularist literature on boys (Biddulph, 1994, 1997) and, as Salisbury and Jackson (1996) argue, inform and shape many teachers' perceptions of boys' conduct in schools. In light of this and current research into boys and schooling, it is imperative that such interventions be executed in the best interests of both girls and boys. By opening spaces for discussion about masculinity and how it becomes normalized in schools, it would appear, in light of what the boys have to say in this paper, that possibilities for successfully implementing a critical practice designed to encourage students to question the role that homophobia and heteronormativity play in their lives can be initiated. By appealing to students' sense of justice within a framework that stresses mutual respect and care for others, discussions can be conducted in schools that are designed to involve students in critically evaluating masculinities and their normalizing effects (Martino, 1995, 1998a).

Note

1. The boys' names used in this paper are pseudonyms. All names have been changed to ensure anonymity and to guarantee confidentiality.

References

Angelides, S. (1994). The queer intervention: Sexuality, identity, and cultural politics. *Melbourne Journal of Politics, 22*, 66–88.

Armstrong, N. (1988). The gender bind: Women and the disciplines. *Genders, 3*, 1–23.

Beckett, L. (1998). *Everyone is special: A handbook for teachers on sexuality education*. Brisbane: Association of Women Educators.

Biddulph, S. (1994). *Manhood*. Sydney: Finch Publishing.

Biddulph, S. (1997). *Raising boys*. Sydney: Finch Publishing.

Boulden, K. (1996). Keeping a straight face: Schools, students and homosexuality—Part 2. In L. Laskey & C. Beavis (Eds.), *Schooling and sexualities: Teaching for a positive sexuality* (pp. 175–185). Geelong: Deakin University for Education and Change.

Britzman, D. (1995). Is there a queer pedagogy? Or stop reading straight. *Educational Theory, 45*, 151–165.

Butler, J. (1990). *Gender trouble: Feminism and the subversion of identity*. London: Routledge.

Butler, J. (1995). The poof paradox: Homogeneity and silencing in three Hobart high schools. In L. Laskey & C. Beavis (Eds.), *Schooling and sexualities: Teaching for a positive sexuality* (pp. 131–149). Geelong: Deakin University for Education and Change.

Coleman, W. (1990). Doing masculinity/doing theory. In J. Hearn & D. Morgan (Eds.), *Men, masculinities and social theory* (pp. 186–199). London: Unwin Hyman.

Connell, R. W. (1995). *Masculinities*. Sydney: Allen & Unwin.

Connell, R. W. (1987). *Gender and power*. Cambridge: Polity Press.

Dixon, C. (1997). Pete's tool: Identity and sex-play in the design and technology classroom. *Gender and Education, 9*, 89–104.

Easthope, A. (1986). *What a man's gotta do: The masculine myth in popular culture*. London: Paladin.

Epstein, D. (1994). *Challenging lesbian and gay inequalities in education*. Buckingham & Philadelphia: Open University Press.

Epstein, D. (1997). Boyz' own stories: Masculinities and sexualities in schools. *Gender and Education, 9*, 105–115.

Epstein, D. (1998). Real boys don't work: "Underachievement," masculinity and the harassment of "sissies." In D. Epstein, J. Elwood, V. Hey, & J. Maw (Eds.), *Failing boys?* (pp. 96–108). Buckingham: Open University Press.

Epstein, D., & Johnson, R. (1998). *Schooling sexualities*. Buckingham: Open University Press.

Flood, M. (1997). *Homophobia and masculinities among young men (Lessons in becoming a straight man)*. Paper presented at O'Connell Education Centre, Canberra, 22 April.

Foucault, M. (1978). *The history of sexuality: Volume 1*. (R. Hurley, Trans.). New York: Vintage.

Foucault, M. (1980). *Michel Foucault: Power/knowledge: Selected interviews and other writings 1972–1977*. C. Gordon (Ed.). Sussex: Harvester.

Foucault, M. (1984a). Preface to *The history of sexuality*, Volume II. In P. Rabinow (Ed.), *The Foucault reader* (pp. 333–339). London: Penguin.

Foucault, M. (1984b, August 7). Michel Foucault: An interview: Sex, power and the politics of identity. *The Advocate, 400*(58), 26–58.

Foucault, M. (1987). The ethic of care for the self as a practice of freedom. *Philosophy and Social Criticism, 12*, 113–131.

Foucault, M. (1988). Technologies of the self. In L. Martin, H. Gutman, & P. Hutton (Eds.), *Technologies of the self* (pp. 16–49). Amberst, MA: The University of Massachusetts Press.

Frank, B. (1987). Hegemonic heterosexual masculinity. *Studies in Political Economy, 24*, 159–170.

Frank, B. (1993). Straight/strait jackets for masculinity: Educating for real men. *Atlantis, 18*(1 & 2), 47–59.

Gender Equity Taskforce. (1997). *Gender equity: A framework for Australian schools*. Canberra: Ministerial Council for Employment, Education, Training and Youth Affairs.

Gilbert, R., & Gilbert, P. (1998). *Masculinity goes to school*. Sydney: Allen & Unwin.

Haywood, C. (1993). *Using sexuality: An exploration into the fixing of sexuality to make male identities in a mixed sex sixth form*. Unpublished master's thesis, University of Warwick, UK.

Hite, S. (1981). *The Hite report on male sexuality*. New York: Knopf.

Holland, J., Ramazanoglu, C., & Sharpe, S. (1993). *Wimp or gladiator: Contradictions in acquiring masculine sexuality*. London: Tufnell Press.

House of Representatives Standing Committee. (1994). *Sticks and stones: Report on violence in Australian schools*. Canberra: Australian Government Publishing Service.

Jackson, D. (1998). Breaking out of the binary trap: Boys' underachievement, schooling and gender relations. In D. Epstein, J. Elwood, V. Hey, & J. Maw (Eds.), *Failing boys?* (pp. 77–95). Buckingham: Open University Press.

Jackson, D., & Salisbury, J. (1996). Why should secondary schools take working with boys seriously? *Gender and Education, 8*, 103–115.

Kehily, M., & Nayak, A. (1997). "Lads and laughter": Humor and the production of heterosexual hierarchies. *Gender and Education, 9*, 69–87.

Kessler, S., Ashenden, D., Connell, R., & Dowsett, G. (1985). Gender relations in secondary schooling. *Sociology of Education, 58*, 34–88.

Laskey, L., & Beavis, C. (1996). *Schooling and sexualities*. Geelong: Deakin University.

Mac an Ghaill, M. (1994). *The making of men*. Buckingham: Open University Press.

Martino, W. (1994). Masculinity and learning: Exploring boys' underachievement and underrepresentation in subject English, *Interpretations, 27*, 22–57.

Martino, W. (1995). Deconstructing masculinity in the English classroom: A site for reconstituting gendered subjectivity. *Gender and Education, 7*, 205–220.

Martino, W. (1997). "A bunch of arseholes": Exploring the politics of masculinity for adolescent boys in schools. *Social Alternatives, 16*, 39–43.

Martino, W. (1998a). "Dickheads," "poofs," "try hards," and "losers": Critical literacy for boys in the English classroom, *English in Aotearoa, 35*, 31–57.

Martino, W. (1998b). "It's all a bit of a mess really!": Addressing homophobia in schools. In L. Becket

(Ed.), *Everyone is special!* (pp. 33–39). Brisbane: Association of Women Educators.

Martino, W. (1999a). "Cool boys," "party animals," "squids," and "poofters": Interrogating the dynamics and politics of adolescent masculinities in school. *British Journal of the Sociology of Education, 20*(2), 239–263.

Martino, W. (1999b). "It's ok to be gay": Interrupting straight thinking in the English classroom. In W. Letts & J. Sears (Eds.), *Queering elementary education* (pp. 137–149). Colorado: Rowan & Littlefield.

Mason, G., & Tomsen, S. (1997). *Homophobic violence.* Sydney: The Hawkins Press.

McLean, C. (1996). Men, masculinity and heterosexuality. In L. Laskey & C. Beavis (Eds.), *Schooling and sexualities: Teaching for a positive sexuality* (pp. 25–35). Geelong: Deakin University, Centre for Education and Change.

McLean, C. (1995). "What about the boys?" *South Australian Education of Girls and Female Students' Association Journal, 4*(3), 15–25.

Mills, M. (1996). "Homophobia kills": A disruptive moment in the educational politics of legitimization. *British Journal of Sociology of Education, 17*(3), 315–326.

Nayak, A., & Kehily, M. (1996). Playing it straight: Masculinities, homophobias and schooling. *Journal of Gender Studies, 5*(2), 211–230.

Nickson, A. (1996). Keeping a straight face: Schools, students and homosexuality—Part 1. In L. Laskey & C. Beavis (Eds.), *Schooling and sexualities: Teaching for a positive sexuality* (pp. 161–174). Geelong: Deakin University for Education and Change.

Pallotta-Chiarolli, M. (1995). "Can I write the word GAY in my essay?": Challenging homophobia in single sex boys' schools. In R. Browne & R. Fletcher (Eds.), *Boys in schools: Addressing the issues.* Lane Cove: Finch Publishing.

Parker, A. (1996). The construction of masculinity within boys' physical education. *Gender and Education, 8*(2), 114–157.

Redman, P. (1996). Curtis loves Ranjit: Heterosexual masculinities, schooling and pupils' sexual cultures. *Educational Review, 48*(2), 175–182.

Rich, A. (1980). Compulsory heterosexuality and lesbian experience. *Signs, 54*, 631–60.

Segal, L. (1990). *Slow motion: Changing masculinities, changing men.* London: Virago Press.

Simpson, M. (1994). *Male impersonators: Men performing masculinity.* New York: Routledge.

Skelton, C. (1997). Primary boys and hegemonic masculinities. *British Journal of the Sociology of Education, 18*(3), 349–369.

Steinberg, D. L., Epstein, D., & Johnson, R. (1997). *Border patrols: Policing the boundaries of heterosexuality.* London: Cassell.

Theobald, M. (1987). Humanities, science and the female mind: An historical perspective. *Unicorn, 13*(3), 162–165.

Thomas, K. (1990). *Gender and subject in higher education.* Buckingham: The Society for Research into Higher Education and Open University Press.

Unks, G. (1995). *The gay teen.* London: Routledge.

Walker, J. C. (1988). *Louts and legends.* Sydney: Allen & Unwin.

Ward, N. (1995). "Pooftah," "wanker," "girl": Homophobic harassment and violence in schools. In *Girls & boys: Challenging perspective, building partnerships. Proceedings of the Third Conference of the Ministerial Advisory Committee on Gender Equity* (pp. 82–93). Brisbane: Ministerial Advisory Committee on Gender Equity.

Willis, P. (1977). *Learning to labour: How working class kids get working class jobs.* Westmead: Saxon House.

Wood, J. (1984). Groping towards sexism: Boys' sex talk. In A. McRobbie & M. Nava (Eds.), *Gender and generation* (pp. 54–84). London: Macmillan.

"I Just Got On With It": The Educational Experiences of Ordinary, Yet Overlooked, Boys

STEVEN ROBERTS

Introduction

Since Willis' (1977) seminal contribution to our understanding of male pupil (counter) cultures, theorisations of boys' educational disengagement have often involved representations of macho, resistant, typically working-class, male behaviour (for example, Mac an Ghaill 1994; McDowell 2003). The dominance of these discourses has led to disproportionate academic attention given to 'laddishness' (Ashley 2009). Even when this anti-hero is discussed in reference to its 'other'—the working-class high-performer, or 'ear 'ole' in Willis' parlance—boys' educational outcomes and experiences are often measured and depicted dichotomously. This polarised understanding neglects significant variation in attainment and educational experiences between boys, with researchers often overlooking what might be described as 'ordinary kids.'

The notion of 'ordinary kids' is far from novel, as academic literature from the 1980s attests (for example, Brown 1987; Jenkins 1983; Pye 1988). Yet, recently 'ordinariness' has largely epitomised something of a 'missing middle' in research into young peoples' lives (Roberts 2011), particularly when examining young people's experiences of education. How ordinariness interacts with, informs, enhances, and/or restricts learning has not been a priority; instead, many researchers have operated with discrete dualisms in their attempts to make sense of educational outcomes, inequalities and developments. For instance, boys are positioned against girls, achievers versus underachievers, the working classes in opposition to the middle classes, or we have used contradistinctions of good and bad qualifications, vocational or academic courses, resistant or conformist attitudes, and so on.

Perhaps these 'middle-ground' groups, who neatly fall neither one side nor the other of such categorical divides, are not interesting or spectacular. Perhaps they are politically and socially unproblematic, 'safe' and unable to enlighten us further. However, overlooking the experiences of such young people, for whatever reasons, ensures that our knowledge is more of a patchwork than a coherent whole. Far from filling the vacuum, using qualitative data from interviews with ordinary, 'moderately qualified' young men, this article follows Kettley's (2007, 2010) lead in contributing to the development of a more holistic understanding of male educational experiences and attitudes.

Starting with compulsory secondary schooling, the respondents' narratives problematise the polarised manner in which boys' educational effort and attainment is often described. Their experiences also challenge the dominant theories of (masculine) resistance that attempt to explain working-class educational failure and allow for a deconstruction of the 'trouble with boys' discourse that pervades contemporary popular media and political representations (see McDowell 2003, 60–75). Secondly, the article critically analyses the respondents' post-compulsory educational choices and experiences. By analysing experiences at different levels of education, the respondents' accounts reveal how social *and* cultural processes impact their orientation

Steven Roberts, "'I Just Got On With It': The Educational Experiences of Ordinary, Yet Overlooked, Boys." *British Journal of Sociology in Education* 33 (March 2012): 203–21.

to formalised learning and its attendant consequences on their 'horizons for action' (Hodkinson, Sparkes, and Hodkinson 1996). Contrary to typically conceived dichotomous notions of resistance and conformity, these orientations appear to be distinctively middle-ground. Such orientations are, however, not entirely modern phenomena. Consequently, the notion of 'alienated instrumentalism' (Brown 1987) is explored and developed as a means of explaining the existence of this often overlooked middle-ground position, but also its persistence over time.

Bad Boys and Good Girls?

Before outlining the study details, this section establishes a context for the discussion by deconstructing the idea that boys' educational underachievement should be of particular concern.

The thrust of policy initiatives and media attention in recent years has been, and continues to be, strongly directed towards the underachievement of boys. McDowell (2003), among others, has previously noted how the UK summertime is often awash with newspaper headlines illustrating how girls continue to leave boys lagging behind academically. Recent summers have not been particularly different, with Winifred Robinson's article in the *Daily Mail* in August 2009, subtitled 'Why Boys are the True Victim of Discrimination,' offering a good case in point.

Such rhetoric and broad generalisations can manifest a distorted sense of reality where all boys are positioned as failures *vis-à-vis* the success enjoyed by all girls (Epstein et al. 1998; Francis and Skelton 2005). This idea is clearly problematic, and also unfounded. Walkerdine, Lucey, and Melody (2001), for instance, argue that women from working-class families are commonly faced with situations such as early exit or underperformance at school, early motherhood and low-paid insecure jobs in contrast to the relative uniformity of the educational performance and general lives of their middle-class contemporaries. Of further significance, the tendency to associate boys with underachievement and girls with high achievement leads to a situation where the high-achieving boy is cast as countering gender norms, but the underperforming girl is often overlooked altogether (Jones and Myhill 2004; Ingram 2009).

The numerical reality is that, seen as low achievers,[1] boys outnumber girls by three to two (Cassen and Kingdon 2007)—but this masks the complex impact of ethnicity. While nearly one-half of all underachievers are white British males, the gender disparity is wider for some ethnic groups, such as Bangladeshi and Black-African (Reay 2009). Given these ethnic groups tend to be among the poorest in the United Kingdom and that such white boys often come from disadvantaged backgrounds, what appears to be a question of gender is in fact more a question of class, and the intersection of both. Ashley (2009, 181) neatly summarises the disproportionate fascination with the actions of boys, stating that 'gender often has a smaller effect size than race or social class, yet it is boys to whom the media often turn first for good stories.'

In discussions of gender and class, then, such variables should not be analysed independently. In sociological analysis, the intersection of these two social characteristics has long been an important feature of attempts to explain male educational disengagement. The seminal contribution in this field is Willis' (1977) classic study of working-class schoolboys. Their working-class masculinity positioned the boys as being counter-school, resistant to and rejecting of 'legitimate' authority. Representations of macho male behaviour have also been theorised as the basis for boys' rejection of educational values by the likes of Mac an Ghaill (1994) and McDowell (2003). The relative strengths of these studies are well documented, but their limitations are, perhaps, often overlooked. The dominance of 'lads' discourses that have been provided by such research has led to two significant and interrelated problems: first, the disproportionate academic attention given to 'laddishness' can lionise or celebrate a mythical and anti-hero status (Quinn et al. 2006; Ashley 2009); and, secondly, the dualistic focus that often derives from this has consequences for wider research.[2] For example, even when problematising the dualistic concepts of 'troublesome boys' and 'compliant girls,' Jones and Myhill (2004) used a dichotomous framework, identifying simply 'high-performing/low-performing girls' and 'high-performing/low-performing boys.' Such dichotomies are also found in Whitehead's (2003) research into masculinity and motivation and in Ingram's (2009) exploration of the working-class 'institutional habitus,' which both use conceptual frameworks based on broad polar opposites of academic 'failure' and 'success.' The accounts in this article provide an example of rather differentiated experience; by exhibiting an 'in-between'/moderate level of engagement they illustrate the need to move beyond dualistic understandings and the attendant limitations of studying only 'discrete aspects of educational attainment' (Kettley 2007, 201).

Methods, Sample and Context

The data presented here derives from a research project investigating the transition to adulthood of 24 young men living in the county of Kent, in the South East of England. The respondents were 'moderately qualified' young men, aged between 18 and 24, and were all front-line retail-sector employees. Being 'moderately qualified' was used heuristically to help avoid a focus on the previously mentioned dualisms such as those having 'good' or 'bad' qualifications (labels typically associated with having 'five or more' or 'less than five' GCSE passes at grade C or above) and, therefore, included respondents with qualifications ranging from some Level II (GCSE passes at grade C or above) to various Level III subjects and courses. None had experienced higher education and all reported no future aspirations of tertiary-level engagement. Using the occupation of their head of household, just over two-thirds of the respondents might be described as working class (corresponding to the lower half of the National Statistics Socio-economic Classification). Ethnically, all classified themselves as white, and, although not by design, this reflects the rather homogeneous ethnic composition of the research location.

Respondents were independently interviewed during the summer and autumn of 2009. Most interviews lasted around an hour, but occasionally much longer (one interview lasted two and a half hours). Interviews were audio-recorded, fully transcribed and thematically coded. Educational experiences and attitudes were a substantially explored feature of the study. While 'the in-depth interview does not simply give the respondents' "point of view," but can also illuminate the structural causes that have contributed to particular life choices and outcomes' (Crompton 2008, 1222), it is equally important to recognise that interviews are accounts of events, or even representations, rather than factual statements. However, for some, truth claims are important, the account in itself is also of interest, especially if it sheds light on how the event was felt or made sense of by the individual (Heath et al. 2009, 88).

The paper now illustrates the ways the young men portrayed, first, their compulsory schooling, and then their post-compulsory educational experiences. It should be noted that, in using the biographical approach, rather than being asked by the researcher to position themselves in relation to the behaviour/attitude of others, the categories they discussed were established through their own words. To retain respondent anonymity, pseudonyms are used throughout.

'I Was Kind of Always in the Middle': Ordinary Experiences of Secondary School

The neat categorical divisions regularly applied to school experiences were far from evident in this study. Instead, the respondents reflected upon their compulsory schooling with a degree of ambivalence and, despite largely sharing similar working-class backgrounds, they positioned themselves in something of a middle-ground position in relation to the extremes of resistance and conformity exemplified by conscientious 'ear oles' or the counter-school culture embodied by 'lads':

> I was bang on in the middle . . . I don't wanna be stereotypical, but you have obviously got your sensible, if I can I use the word, geek . . . then you got your real trouble makers, and then you got your group in the middle . . . that's the group that I hanged around with. (Jake)
>
> I was kind of always in the middle—you look on the classic teen movies, you got the geeks, the

> jocks and the guys that are in-between. Started in between them and just got on with it really. (Damian)

This self-awareness of an in-between status is important because it recognises that 'laddish' or 'swotty' behaviour both continues to exist and be acknowledged, but also that these should be seen as extremes of a continuum of potential behaviours, rather than discrete and separate categories. For example, despite nearly all respondents describing their experience in this way, being situated in this in-between position meant different things to different respondents and translated itself into various behaviours. Most respondents talked about enjoying the social aspects of school, hanging around with friends, and so forth, and this often involved 'messing around' (Tim), 'mucking about' (Peter) and, like Willis' boys, 'having a laugh' (Robbie, Pat, Dave). The ways in which the respondents went about having a laugh might be deemed to be a 'laddish' form of resistance. However, such acts of disruption during the school day varied dramatically across the sample. These separate exchanges with Peter and Danny, for instance, highlight this:

> PETER: Tried not to [misbehave], but there was always some days where you thought 'I probably shouldn't have done that.'
>
> RESEARCHER: What's the worst thing you did at school?
>
> PETER: Playing football with another student (in classroom during a break), bouncing it off our head and all that, and I smashed a light and it came down and hit the other lad's head. We got pretty done for that.
>
> DANNY: Few harsh comments or something. We made a lot of teachers cry.
>
> RESEARCHER: Were you part of that?
>
> DANNY: Sometimes. I started to bunk off in my last year as well, which was a bit silly to be honest. I'd say it was [to hang out with] friends to be honest . . . They [were] influencing me into a different world . . . experimentation shall we say . . . like, smoking weed.

Between the two extremes of playing truant or 'bunking off' to smoke cannabis and accidentally breaking the lights with the football while 'mucking about,' the large majority of the young men reminisced about how they were a little bit 'mouthy' or 'cheeky,' rather than recounting incidents where they had misbehaved or demonstrated a relentless and outright resistance to school:

> I was the class joker, you'd never believe it. I didn't really misbehave, it was just the inability to stop talking, then obviously that gets you into trouble. (Tim)
>
> I was never naughty, but I was more cheeky . . . If I got told off I would switch on, but if I could push my boundaries, I would. (Jake)
>
> I wouldn't say I was disruptive but I wasn't well behaved, I was kind of like the cheeky chappy, making a laugh but doing my work at the same time, kind of knowing when to draw the line, I wouldn't push teachers too far. (Damian)

Beyond this apparently middle-ground (mis) behaviour, Jake and Damian's comments highlight an interesting and commonplace issue; the young men often recalled times when they had 'pushed the boundaries,' yet they still responded to the direction to re-engage with their work. This 'mucking about' was not a staple part of their school experience. It was certainly something that many of them enjoyed remembering and subsequently talking about, but largely their school days were made up of 'getting on with it,' perhaps punctuated by occasional attempts at having a laugh in its various forms. Even where responses were more fitting of a typically resistant masculine disaffection with school, they remained tempered in comparison with the counter-school culture expressed so vividly by Willis' 'lads.' These comments from those who reflected upon school with least affection clearly illustrate this:

> I used to hate school really. I didn't like anything academic. I only went to school to play for the rugby team or cricket team; that was the only reason I wanted to go to school . . . I was too lazy, or I just did enough I never did, like, extra. So I did what I could and then relaxed. (Gavin)

> It wasn't learning so much, it was just sort of the get up and go part of it to go to school . . . But just sitting down in English just didn't interest me at all . . . I was quite a good person to be honest with you. Just didn't knuckle down enough, I wouldn't go out and start fights or nothing. (Bobby)

This theme of not starting fights which Bobby mentions is particularly interesting. Physical violence, fighting and bullying formed substantial parts of the pursuit of 'mad laughs' for boys in Macdonald and Marsh's (2005, 53) research, as it did for the 'hard lads' identified by McDowell (2003, 117). This attitude and its attendant value were also noted earlier by Willis (1977, 36), who posited that 'violence, with its connotations of masculinity, spread throughout the group.' In the present study, bullying and intimidation was recognised, and often freely discussed, but was almost exclusively perceived as an activity that was observed from afar. Distancing oneself from an act that is largely socially abhorrent to adults may have been more easily achieved through a retrospective lens. However, whereas Willis' ethnography captured the essence and meaning of bullying at its moment of action, respondents in MacDonald and Marsh's (2005, 53) study recalled their school days with the benefit of a few years hindsight and sometimes still identified themselves as bullies and also acknowledged the function such behaviour had served. With this in mind, it seems that we have no reason to doubt that the recollections of physicality in the current study were as respondents conveyed.

The recollections were cut in two particular ways. Largely, the young men framed acts of bullying and intimidation as something of which they were aware but that was performed by others. Secondly, and only occasionally, this overlapped into an awareness of potentially being bullied, with just one respondent admitting to being the victim of bullying:

> Some of my friends, you may have considered bullies because they picked on the less popular kids or made unpopular kids less popular, but I was never too fussed about that, never bothered about status, you know. I just got on with what I wanted to do really. (Jason)
>
> Some kids were picked on and stuff, but it didn't seem very regular. I remember some of the bigger kids had reputations for being a bit nasty . . . But I never really got picked on at all. (Pat)

Given the significance allotted to physicality in the literature regarding masculinity and school disengagement or underperformance among boys (for example, Willis 1977; Swain 2004; Ringrose and Renold 2010), positioning oneself as separate from much of the anti-social behaviour that occurred, such as bullying, starting fights or causing trouble for teachers, might be a little surprising. Such remarks can obviously be skewed by seeing one's own actions through a rose-tinted lens of nostalgia, or be symptomatic of not wanting to reveal previous misdemeanours. Whatever the facts, however, the construction of this past reality and what it now means to the respondents are both equally as interesting as they reveal how the individuals made sense of the incidents (Heath et al. 2009). Throughout the sample, the revelations contest, to some extent, the idea that fighting and physicality 'become permanent possibilities for the alleviation of boredom' (Willis 1977, 34). If 'violence and the judgement of violence is the most basic axis of . . . ascendance over conformists' (Willis 1977, 34), then what we see here is that it is a form of resistance that applies or appeals to some students but not others. It may be 'one way to make the mundane suddenly *matter*' (Willis 1977, 34; original emphasis), yet it is not the only way. For the self-professed 'inbetweeners' at least, it is the extreme and largely non-preferred method of circumventing the mundane.

Such behaviour also needs to be understood in conjunction with the respondents' academic attitudes. Overwhelmingly, the young men's narratives were permeated with comments that did not correspond to academic disaffection:

> I was anti-school because I didn't wanna go to school, but I wanted to get the grades . . . obviously, you don't wanna go to school. (Tim)
>
> I had mixed feelings . . . There were some subjects I was pretty good at, like the sciences, um, and maths and I never had to particularly try with

> those at GCSE, and I liked being good at that sort of thing. (Luke)

Wanting the grades, 'switching on' when it was necessary, doing just enough, and so forth, reveal a certain degree of compliance. Yet, to label these young men as conformists in a bi-polar model of attainment and experience would be inaccurate and misleading. In some ways, the dominant informal culture among pupils revealed here seemed to have both *produced* and *restricted* a degree of non-conformity/conformity. As Ingram (2009) notes with regards to resistant cultures among boys, 'agents who occupy similar positions and who [are] placed in similar conditions and subjected to similar conditionings, have every likelihood of having similar dispositions and interests and therefore of producing similar practices and adopting similar stances' (Bourdieu 1984, 725). Understood in this way, this amalgam of 'mixed feelings' was a driving force behind collectively wanting to 'just get on with it,' while also occasionally 'having a laugh.' Consequently, being situated at the mid-point range of experience becomes a very explicable position.

These school histories illustrate that the working-class representations of machismo portrayed by Willis and others are just one part of a wider canvas of experience. Indeed, this is reminiscent of Jenkins' (1983) critique of cultural reproduction through the contrasting experience of 'lads' and 'ordinary kids.' Illustrating the fluidity of social boundaries, Jenkins' study highlights how ideal-type taxonomies overlook the complex ways in which young men can be 'lads' at some points and 'ordinary' at others. The weakness of such taxonomies is further made clear by considering the manner in which Mac an Ghaill's (1994) categories of 'macho lads,' 'academic achievers' and 'new enterprisers' also neglect any real middle-ground. While Mac an Ghaill's 'macho lads' have a clear correspondence with Willis' 'lads,' the latter two categories are claimed to 'incorporate more adequately both the changing occupational and educational realities . . . and the different aspirations of students' (O'Donnell and Sharpe 2000, 46). 'Academic achievers' is a category that, in many ways, is self-explanatory. The 'new enterprisers,' however, Mac an Ghaill (1994, 63) suggests are working-class males who have identified an opportunity for upward social mobility through the new vocationalised curriculum. The moderate level of qualifications, the moderate misbehaviour, the lack of such obvious instrumentalism (see below) and the absence of upward mobility during their labour market experience to date suggest that such categories are incongruent with the young men in this research.

Making Sense of 'Middle-Ground' Behaviour: Alienated Instrumentalism?

Challenging Willis' polarised model, Brown (1987) positioned a majority of young people, boys and girls, as being ordinary kids who 'neither simply accept nor reject school, but comply with it' (1987, 31)—a notion seemingly fitting for the present study's respondents. Similar to O'Donnell and Sharpe's (2000) study, boredom and/or wanting to move on did not manifest itself as the contempt for school conveyed in other research. The young men did not see their school days as articulated by Willis' working-class dualism of 30 years ago, or even in the manner described by some young men more recently in McDowell's (2003) study of white, working-class masculinity. Instead, they articulated a middling position, trading off relative behavioural conformity with a relative lack of academic conformity in terms of 'not trying too hard.' This resonates with the 'alienated instrumentalism' exhibited by Brown's (1987, 1990) 'ordinary' kids. However, whereas Brown acknowledged that 'modest levels of academic achievement appeared to provide access to the sorts of jobs pupils wanted' (1990, 95), the present respondents did not know what employment they wanted at that stage of their life. None, for example, had considered that their GCSE choices were based on an aspired career path, as indicated here:

> No, I just took them cos I enjoyed them . . . I had been doing them up until GCSEs and then from like 13 lessons you then took your top 3 and then your basic maths English and sciences. (Carl)
>
> I took economics partly cos I liked the teacher [laughs] . . . He liked my brother and my brother

> thought he was good, so . . . I thought yeah why not. And to be honest I didn't know what else to do. (James)

Brown also suggests that ordinary kids, faced with limited opportunities for doing jobs they aspired to do, justify relative compliance in pursuing qualifications as a means of getting 'any job' (1987, 67). This understanding is problematised by the overwhelming lack of weight attributed to qualifications by the present respondents in relation to obtaining retail work. Jez, for example, was the exception perceiving his GCSEs as providing any competitive advantage to date.

The element of the instrumentalist orientation that fitted more squarely with the ordinary experiences with both the students of the 1980s and today was that working for qualifications, doing at least *something*, was of moral and social worth. In fact, it was something that was 'normal':

> My teachers obviously, like, always said I could do better, but I wanted to push myself, a bit, as much as I could have done. (Peter)
>
> You don't really wanna be [at] the bottom do you? You have to go to school and do something, that's just how it is. Sometimes you made an effort, cos you don't wanna be a complete fucking bum. (Pat)

From this perspective, *levels* of attainment are not the ultimate goal. This is emphasised by Dave, who despite finishing with just one of his nine GCSE passes at grade C or above, insisted that he 'pretty much liked school' and 'enjoyed all the subjects.'

Analogous with Brown, to have left school *completely* empty-handed would have been a waste of time. Therefore, for ordinary kids, then and now, responses such as 'just getting on with it' (Dave), and 'doing it cos that's what you're there to do' (Peter) underpin conformist, *yet instrumental*, attitudes towards school 'and [make] the everyday actions of school life possible' (Brown 1987, 96). Importantly, however, this instrumentalism is not tied to 'certain historical conditions in which the reward structure of the school and the labour market correspond sufficiently to allow pupils to predict the likely outcome of efforts in school' as much as Brown (1987, 123) suggested in the 1980s. The employment structure has since (dramatically) changed, and the relationship between qualifications and obtaining entry-level retail work, for example, was deemed spurious by these respondents. Their relatively conformist efforts at school are, therefore, built on something different; none of the young men put in such effort to achieve a job in retail, but encountered and engaged with a normalised discourse of academic effort on the basis that it was simply what was done. This is reflected in comments such as 'school's school, it's alright, so-so' (Tim) and 'you just didn't like what you didn't like about it' (Luke).

Why they might act in this way becomes of particular intrigue. However, rather than being truly remarkable, the respondents' sentiments outlined above, and repeated in different guises throughout the interviews, are a representation of what Brown called the 'invisible majority.' It could be argued that this relative conformity is further evidence of working-class kids being cultural dupes (Willis 1977) or that they have been acculturated (Ingram 2009). Yet, despite their ambivalence, their responses seem to indicate active agency, in that they deliberately distanced themselves from both 'troublemakers' and 'swots.' This was combined with an attitude and behaviour that could easily be associated with working class-based notions of moral and social worth (Sayer 2005) that reflect something about their dignity, their own character (Senett 1998).

MacDonald and Marsh (2005) have argued that understanding local context is crucial in explaining differential levels of educational disengagement. In their study in the North East of England, for example, an abundance of traditional working-class jobs being replaced by a relative paucity of employment prospects is highlighted as being critical for the comparatively higher level of anti-school sentiment versus that found by O'Donnell and Sharpe's (2000) London-based study. Indeed, for MacDonald and Marsh (2005, 65), where the rich tradition of working-class job prospects in the locality they studied had once served to ensure a 'begrudging acceptance of the instrumental value of schooling,' the jobs available nowadays, such as 'serving in cake shops or stacking supermarket shelves,' did not require educational engagement. The problem with this explanation is that the respondents in the present study are engaged in these very kinds of jobs, as are many other young men with low-to-moderate qualification profiles (Roberts 2011). De-industrialisation was much more acute in the North East relative to the South East of England. However, the types of contemporary local employment opportunities in both localities were largely understood in the same negative way, yet educational disengagement was far less sharp among the Kent respondents.

From these accounts, it appears that alienated instrumentalism is not as static a frame of reference as indicated by Brown in 1980s. In the present study, the young men's accounts of compulsory schooling clearly imply a varied reality of experience. This follows Jenkins' (1983) reasoning, described above, that one can be either a lad or ordinary at different times. Indeed, such accounts were also identified by MacDonald and Marsh (2005, 56), who indicate that '[s]ometimes the same individuals recounted narratives of school that contained *both* instrumental engagement and complete disaffection.' As has been shown here, a further form of school experience is plausible—one where limited engagement and limited disaffection occur and provide the basis for an ordinary, but fluid, school experience.

Post-16 'Choices'

This section develops Brown's notion of alienated instrumentalism and how it operates for contemporary young men in post-compulsory settings. Before proceeding, it is not enough to categorise the respondents as having typically conceived 'good' (five or more A–C grades) or 'bad' (less than five A–C grades) GCSEs. The respondents' clutch of qualifications presented them with differing options. For example, Pat, who achieved four A–C grades, was not given the option of staying on at school to undertake A-levels, but this qualification haul ensured he was accepted by a local further education college to do A-levels. Similarly, Dave insisted that, despite obtaining just one A–C GCSE grade, his enrolment on a college course in computing was contingent upon having demonstrated at least *some* effort in his GCSEs, declaring that 'cos in ICT I got quite a good grade at GCSE level, so the course I went for, I got an interview straight away.'

Such qualifications, then, partly configured the respondent's 'horizons for action' (Hodkinson, Sparkers, and Hodkinson 1996) as they finished their compulsory education. These horizons are determined partly by the availability of external opportunities and partly by internal subjective perceptions of what seems possible and, importantly, 'what might be appropriate' (Hodkinson 1998, 304). This concept enables the young men's decisions to be better understood because it allows us to see that, rather than being a totally technical, rational, calculated decision, their post-16 options were pursued as part of 'the socially constructed and historically derived common base of knowledge, values and norms for action that people grow into and come to take as a natural way of life' (Hodkinson 1998, 304).

So, what choices did these young men make? All but two respondents immediately enrolled in post-compulsory education—and one of these two enrolled within a year of leaving school. This engagement with post-compulsory education varied across qualification level, subject matter and completion rate. Given the relationship between social class and educational choices and pathways (for example, Reay et al. 2001; Reay and Ball 1998; Edwards et al. 1997), it is no great surprise that, of those who undertook Alevels, all except one were from non-manual backgrounds. The horizon for action available to these young men, therefore, is likely to have led them towards an academic route. It also ensured that more vocational pathways were unattractive, but also actually perceived as a non-option. This happens because 'horizons for action both limit and enable our view of the world and the choices we can make within it' (Hodkinson 1998, 304). Concomitantly, those who pursued vocational courses were largely from manual backgrounds and this often had as seemingly an important influence on their choices as did their qualification levels. Tim, for instance, whose father is a plumber, achieved nine A–C GSCE grades yet left school to pursue a vocational course. Similarly, Jez, who described his parents as 'workers, working class but not necessarily poor,' obtained all A–C passes in his GCSEs but signed up to a Business Studies college course, before dropping out within a week and committing himself to retail work. Here, he explains how his options unfolded and how he made sense of them:

> When I turned 16 mum said I got the option of college and not paying rent, or going out and earning money and stuff. So I decided to just go and earn money. Just cos I didn't have much money when I was younger, so I always wanted my own money and to be able to do my own things. (Jez)

Beyond understanding how one's horizon for action can influence the choice of educational programme, it is also important to understand the decision to participate in post-compulsory education in the first place. Despite exhibiting largley alienated-instrumentalist attitudes to school—attitudes that could justifiably lead them to consider the available employment possibilities—in the first instance, further education was deemed the appropriate next step for the majority. We might, therefore, expect that the decision to continue in education was technically rational, leaning closer towards an instrumental orientation, with a consequence that the alienated element of such a frame of reference would diminish. Indeed, this is what MacDonald and Marsh (2005, 56) reveal happened to some of their sample, suggesting that '[some] informants described a process of instrumental accommodation in the latter years of compulsory education . . . [or] were currently attending Further Education college after earlier dismal experiences.' For the present respondents, however, 'dismal' experiences and/or episodes of disengagement had not occurred. Accordingly, the reality, once again, is that their decisions about, experiences of, and efforts towards post-compulsory education reflect something of a middle-ground as opposed to pure instrumentalism.

Their decisions were 'pragmatically rational' (Hodkinson 1998, 304); that is, partly rational and partly intuitive in respect of the opportunities that confronted them. Consequently, almost all respondents felt they ought to 'get something behind me' (Christian) or 'get something under my belt' (Bobby), while at the same time often acknowledging that 'it meant I wouldn't have to do anything else for a couple of years' (Luke) or that 'it seemed easy, instead of me bumming around' (Danny). In deciding to stay on, the respondents followed the majority trend, which saw more than 78% of 16–18 year olds participate in post-16 education at the end of 2007 (DCSF 2008).

Although never specifically articulated in such a manner, it could be argued that many respondents chose subjects that reflected a sense of appropriate (working-class) masculine achievement. Connecting subject choice with aspired occupations in this manner, however, was mixed across the sample. A more apparent relationship might be expected between qualification type and having a relatively fixed career strategy among those undertaking vocational courses. However, across the qualification and subject range, those who did not configure a relationship between their post-16 choices and their potential careers varied in their level of educational engagement:

> I was gonna stay on [at school] but school was a bit rubbish, so I left, and er, my mum said 'oh yeah you know, you like sports so why don't you go do sports science' so I did. And then it went from there, parental instinct. (Tim discussing his BTEC in Sports Science)
>
> I chose to stay on cos I thought I would try and see where it would lead me, and just give it a go and I just done it . . . I thought about starting work, but I thought I was a bit too young to, like, get into it. (Peter discussing his A-levels)
>
> [I thought] I might as well do it. Like, see if I can go anywhere with it . . . I was influenced by my friends, cos some of my friends were doing business. (Danny on undertaking a BTEC in Business)
>
> I think I chose subjects I thought I enjoyed the most. In the end I hated economics, cos I was probably too lazy to make an effort . . . I was never that certain about what I wanted to do. (James considering his A-level choices)

Whether or not the respondents' choice of course correlated with an aspired occupational outcome, a rather consistent experience of post-compulsory education was evident. While the misbehaviour from their compulsory school days had declined, this was not necessarily the result of increased effort. The general theme throughout the post-compulsory years was that a degree of alienated instrumentalism was still very much at play. For instance, Gavin suggested that he 'worked a bit harder but was still lazy.' This attitude was summed up by Danny, who commented that:

> I'd bunk off here and there. But that was what college was like, we'd all meet up, go in the morning and sometimes not come back after lunch cos we'd be in the pub, but *that's just what everyone does.* (Researcher's emphasis)

Further education often seemed to be a normal, indeed expected, next step. Alienation, it would seem, might be best used to describe their frame of reference towards the *labour market* at this moment in their life. For example, as indicated above by Luke, being involved in education was a form of *avoiding* the labour market for another two years. These comments belie the idea that being given the 'choice' of post-compulsory education might result in increased effort. Paradoxically, alienation persists at this level even though the respondents chose to stay on in education. This is strongly reflected by the fact that several respondents dropped out of their programme of study. Some, in fact, were involved in multiple enrolment and subsequent drop-out. Tim, for example, obtained nine A–C grades then undertook a college course in sports science, dropped out after about 15 months, then started a college course in music technology, which he subsequently quit within eight months.

In post-compulsory education, then, these young men largely continued to 'get on with it,' being neither particularly resistant nor conforming to the extent where they exerted additional effort to maximise their attainment. They had *personally* opted for this form of study, and, as such, the alienated part of the 'alienated instrumentalist' frame of reference might appear to be contradictory. Nonetheless, it is something that was apparent in the young men's accounts of their choices and experiences at this level. Another potential explanation for why they chose to continue to participate in education rests with the Foucault-inspired theorisation of power and freedom outlined by Rose (1999). Rose's concept of 'governance through freedom' lends itself as an explanatory tool in understanding the respondents' choices because it reveals an additional layer of complexity in one's horizon for action. It refers to a form of governance that is achieved by shaping people's conduct and the ways in which they construct themselves in an active fashion. People act upon themselves without direct state intervention or force, but through the exercise of freedom and personal choice. Moreover, this type of governance shapes individuals' aspirations and needs and forges alignments between the aspirations and calculations of ruling and 'independent authorities' or 'political aims' and the 'personal aspirations' of free citizens (Rose 1999, 49).

Rose (1999) argues that, in liberal societies, individuals are required to take responsibility and to regulate themselves in a manner that confirms they are freely choosing individuals—however, their actions need to be in line with what is defined as possible. Understood in this way, the decision to stay on is influenced by—and at the same time supports and reinforces—a normalised discourse of post-compulsory participation. As can be seen from the comments above, the young men were sometimes uncertain of why they made their decision to stay on, but still framed this decision as a choice that they had *freely* made. It is an option, however, which reflects a degree of conformity—their continued participation might be deemed to be a result of governance through freedom.

Conclusion

This article has revealed some diversity in young men's compulsory and post-compulsory educational experiences. It may well be the case that 'social constructionist accounts of gendered behaviour which relate to achievement are established and convincing' (Francis and Skelton 2005, 134), but such understandings do not account for social groups in their entirety. This is made clear in McCormack's (2011) portrayal of substantially attenuated forms of homophobic behaviour in secondary schools. Where it is traditionally conceived that heterosexual boys engage in such practices to maintain masculine identity (for example, Ellis and High 2004; Vicars 2006), McCormack illustrates that such traditional understandings of hetero-masculinity appears to have limited 'cultural sway' (2011, 339) in some contemporary school environments. Similarly critiquing caricatured stereotypes, the narratives in this article problematise notions of masculine resistance, facilitating a move beyond the dichotomous terminology of disaffection and engagement and towards a more holistic picture of educational experience.

Although specific attention was not given to pedagogy or educational delivery, there was no sense that masculinity was diluted by an adherence to feminine approaches to learning (Francis and Skelton 2005.) This understanding in itself is built upon an unhelpful dichotomous understanding; in this situation the young men did not entirely embrace the pursuit of high academic achievement. Resistance, misbehaviour and disaffection appear to form part of a fluid, wider canvass of experience that often includes relative conformity—just as noted by Jenkins (1983). Curiously, however, such accounts tend to be overlooked in political and media discourses, which instead favour a focus on male underachievement and resistance *vis-à-vis* the success and conformity of their female counterparts. Policy remedies that correspond to such discourses are likely to only be suited to dealing with the most disaffected boys/young men, if at all.

The 'ordinary' experiences outlined by the young men in this research were different. They were characterised by a certain degree of ambivalence. In fact, these accounts reflect a modified version of the alienated-instrumentalism previously described by Brown (1987, 1990). The young men did not become totally disaffected. Eventually they moved into low-level work unrelated to their educational engagement, without ever necessarily feeling like they had wasted their time at school. Ultimately, they considered at least some effort in education to be of social and moral worth.

Such alienated instrumentalism continued to form the main frame of reference when the respondents took up positions in post-compulsory education. It might reasonably be expected that, in electing particular courses, the young men might have been more instrumental in their attitudes than they were at school, but this was not the case. Avoiding the labour market and, more importantly, the idea that one simply went to college or continued in education because that was the 'normal' step to take was a dominant feature of their narratives. For most of the respondents, there was no direct link between programme choice and occupational aspiration, and this was the case even when choosing vocational qualifications. With this in mind, Rose's (1999) formulation of governance through freedom has been noted as a potential framework to explain ongoing post-compulsory education.

Whatever the reason, this latter finding has implications for the impending changes to the UK education system which, by 2015, will extend the compulsory participation age to 18. Pushing students into subject streams based on what they want to do for a career might not be as easy as it seems, or even as effective as hoped, if young people honestly do not know in their own minds what they want to do. Instead, among this sample at least, rather than being perceived as an opportunity for upward social mobility, education is recognised as being a normal step in the transition from youth to adulthood, something that does not necessarily promote a sense of resistance or particular enjoyment. These accounts are a necessary addition to what is already often researched if we are to fully comprehend educational disengagement/engagement.

Notes

1. Here low achievement was measured at four levels: no passes at all in GCSE/ GNVQ examinations; nothing better than a 'D' in any examination; no pass in at least one of English or mathematics; and having not achieved at least five passes at any grade, including English and mathematics.
2. Mac an Ghaill does, however, go beyond a dualistic account to offer a more nuanced assessment of masculinity. This is detailed later in the paper.

References

Ashley, M. 2009. Time to confront Willis's lads with a ballet class? A case study of educational orthodoxy and white working-class boys. *British Journal of Sociology of Education* 30: 179–91.

Bourdieu, P. 1984. *Distinction: A social critique of the judgement of taste*. London: Routledge & Kegan Paul.

Brown, P. 1987. *Schooling ordinary kids: Inequality, unemployment and the new vocationalism*. London: Tavistock.

Brown, P. 1990. Schooling and economic life in the UK. In *Childhood, youth and social change: A comparative perspective*, ed. L. Chisholm, P. Buchner, and H. H. Kruger, 85–103. Basingstoke: The Farmer Press.

Cassen, R., and G. Kingdon. 2007. *Tackling low educational achievement*. York: Joseph Rowntree Foundation.

Crompton, R. 2008. 40 years of sociology: Some comments. *Sociology* 42: 1218–27.

DCSF. 2008. Post 16 participation rate at highest level ever. www.dcsf.gov.uk/pns/DisplayPN.cgi?pn_id=2008_0119 (accessed December 12, 2009).

Edwards, T., C. Taylor Fitz-Gibbon, F. Hardman, R. Hayward, and N. Meagher. 1997. *Separate but equal? A-levels and GNVQs*. London: Routledge.

Ellis, V., and S. High. 2004. Something more to tell you. *British Educational Research Journal* 30: 213–25.

Epstein, D., J. Elwood, V. Hey, and J. Maw, eds. 1998. *Failing boys?* Buckingham: Open University Press.

Francis, B., and C. Skelton. 2005. *Reassessing gender and achievement: Questioning key contemporary debates*. Abingdon: Routledge.

Heath, S., R. Brooks, E. Cleaver, and E. Ireland. 2009. *Researching young people's lives*. London: Sage.

Hodkinson, P. 1998. How young people make career decisions. *Education and Training* 37: 3–8.

Hodkinson, P., A.C. Sparkes, and H. Hodkinson. 1996. *Triumphs and tears: Young people, markets and the transition from school to work*. London: David Fulton.

Ingram, N. 2009. Working-class boys, educational success and the misrecognition of working-class culture. *British Journal of Sociology of Education* 30: 421–34.

Jenkins, R. 1983. *Lads, citizens, and ordinary kids: Working class youth lifestyles in Belfast*. London: Routledge and Kegan Paul.

Jones, S., and D. Myhill. 2004. 'Troublesome boys' and 'complaint girls': Gender identity and perceptions of achievement and underachievement. *British Journal of Sociology of Education* 25: 547–61.

Kettley, N. 2007. *Educational attainment and society*. London: Continuum.

Kettley, N. 2010. *Theory building in educational research*. London: Continuum.

Mac an Ghaill, M. 1994. *The making of men: Masculinities sexualities and schooling*. Buckingham: Open University Press.

MacDonald, R., and J. Marsh. 2005. *Disconnected youth? Growing up in Britain's poor neighbourhoods*. London: Palgrave.

McCormack, M. 2011. The declining significance of homohysteria for male students in three sixth forms in the south of England. *British Educational Research Journal* 37, no. 2: 337–53.

McDowell, L. 2003. *Redundant masculinities? Employment change and white working class youth*. London: Blackwell.

O'Donnell, M., and S. Sharpe. 2000. *Uncertain masculinities*. London: Routledge.

Pye, J. 1988. *Invisible children: Who are the real losers in school?* Oxford: Oxford University Press.

Quinn, J., L. Thomas, K. Slack, L. Casey, W. Thexton, and J. Noble. 2006. Lifting the hood: Lifelong learning and young, white, provincial working-class masculinities. *British Educational Research Journal* 32: 735–50.

Reay, D. 2009. Making sense of white working class underachievement. In *Who cares about the white working class?*, ed. K.P. Sveinsson, 22–7. London: The Runnymeade Trust.

Reay, D., and S.J. Ball. 1998. 'Making their minds up': Family dynamics of school choice. *British Educational Research Journal* 24: 431–48.

Reay, D., J. Davies, M. David, and S.J. Ball. 2001. Choices of degree or degrees of choice?: Class, 'race' and the higher education choice process *Sociology* 35: 855–74.

Ringrose, J., and E. Renold. 2010. Normative cruelties and gender deviants: The performative effects of bully discourses for girls and boys in school. *British Educational Research Journal* 36: 573–96.

Roberts, S. 2011. Beyond NEET and tidy pathways: Considering the missing middle of youth studies. *Journal of Youth Studies* 14: 21–39.

Rose, N. 1999. *Powers of freedom: Reframing political thought*. Cambridge: Cambridge University Press.

Sayer, A. 2005. *The moral significance of class*. Cambridge: Cambridge University Press.

Sennett, R. 1998. *The corrosion of character: The consequences of work in the New Capitalism*. London: W.W. Norton.

Swain, J. 2004. The resources and strategies that 10–11 year-old boys use to construct masculinities in the school setting. *British Educational Research Journal* 30: 167–85.

Vicars, M. 2006. Who are you calling queer? *British Educational Research Journal* 32: 347–61.

Walkerdine, V., H. Lucey, and J. Melody. 2001. *Growing up girl: Psychosocial explorations of gender and class*. Basingstoke: Palgrave.

Whitehead, J.M. 2003. Masculinity, motivation and academic success: A paradox. *Teacher Development: An International Journal* 7: 287–309.

Willis, P. 1977. *Learning to labour: Why working class kids get working class jobs*. Farnborough: Saxon House.

PART 7

The Gender of Religion

The first time people put in an appearance in the Bible, it's gendered. "Male and female created He them" is the ungrammatical but somehow authoritative way the King James Bible puts it in Genesis (1:27). And this has always been a justification for a divinely ordained binary division between males and females.

But how can we be so sure? After all, it doesn't say "male *or* female"—as if one had to be only one and not the other. In fact, it might even mean that "He" created each of us as "male and female"—a divinely inspired androgyny.

We needn't necessarily subscribe to these positions to recognize two important things about religion and its relation to gender. First, religion, itself, at least in the Western world, is preoccupied with gender (Eastern religions are far less obsessed with gender). Indeed, prescribing the proper relationships between women and men is one of the Bible's chief preoccupations. And, second, that all such prescriptive elements are subject to multiple interpretations.

The institutional articulation of proper interpretations of doctrine—the fact that religious "experts" tell us what these rather vague prescriptive notions actually mean in everyday life—makes these timeless Biblical truths quite responsive to immediate, concrete, historical needs. For centuries, the institution of the church used certain Biblical passages to justify the utter subordination of women. Whether articulated by Dan Brown or feminist theologians, the Biblically inspired but utterly political persecution of independent women is an indelible stain on the history of religious institutions. Shahra Razavi and Anne Jenichen explain this complex institutional and doctrinal relationship.

Whether in doctrine or in institutional practices, women's second-class status has generated significant resistance from women. And yet, ironically, women are far more religious than men, far more likely to go to church, and far more likely to say that God has a place in daily conversations. Just as the institution of religion is gendered, so too are the individuals who are religious. Gendered people navigate gendered institutions, and J. Edward Sumerau explores the ways in which different groups of religious women and men navigate these institutions.

Each generation finds the texts it needs to justify the world as that generation finds it. Today, as the formerly fixed prescriptions of the proper relationships between women and men are being challenged everywhere in the world, new generations of the observant are pointing to different, if equally canonical, texts to justify their position. Jen'Nan Ghazal Read and John P. Bartkowski show how a new generation of American-born, second-generation Muslim students are re-embracing the veil (much to their parents' shock!) as a way to connect to a global Islamic community that they have actually never known.

To Veil or Not to Veil? A Case Study of Identity Negotiation Among Muslim Women in Austin, Texas

JEN'NAN GHAZAL READ AND JOHN P. BARTKOWSKI

In light of expanded social opportunities for women in Western industrialized countries, scholars have turned their attention to the status of women in other parts of the world. This burgeoning research literature has given rise to a debate concerning the social standing of Muslim women in the Middle East. On one hand, some scholars contend that Muslim women occupy a subordinate status within many Middle Eastern countries. Some empirical evidence lends support to this view, as many researchers have highlighted the traditional and gendered customs prescribed by Islam—most notably, the veiling and shrouding of Muslim women (Afshar 1985; Fox 1977; Odeh 1993; Papanek 1973; see Dragadze 1994 for review).

On the other hand, a growing number of scholars now argue that claims about the oppression and subjugation of veiled Muslim women may, in many regards, be overstated (Brenner 1996; El-Guindi 1981, 1983; El-Solh and Mabro 1994; Fernea 1993, 1998; Gocek and Balaghi 1994; Hessini 1994; Kadioglu 1994; Kandiyoti 1991, 1992; Webster 1984). Scholars who have generated insider portraits[1] of Islamic gender relations have revealed that Muslim women's motivations for veiling can vary dramatically. Some Muslim women veil to express their strongly held convictions about gender difference, others are motivated to do so more as a means of critiquing Western colonialism in the Middle East. It is this complexity surrounding the veil that leads Elizabeth Fernea (1993, 122) to conclude that the veil (or *hijab*[2]) "means different things to different people within [Muslim] society, and it means different things to Westerners than it does to Middle Easterners" (see also Abu-Lughod 1986; Walbridge 1997).

Our study takes as its point of departure the conflicting meanings of the veil among both Muslim religious elites and rank-and-file Islamic women currently living in the United States. In undertaking this investigation, we supplement the lone study (published in Arabic) that compares the gender attitudes of veiled and unveiled women (see L. Ahmed 1992 for review). That study, based largely on survey data collected from university women living in the Middle East, demonstrates that while veiled women evince somewhat conservative gender attitudes, the vast majority of them support women's rights in public life and a substantial proportion subscribe to marital equality. We seek to extend these suggestive findings by using in-depth, personal interviews, because data from such interviews are more able to capture the negotiation of cultural meanings by veiled and unveiled respondents, as well as the nuances of these women's gender identities (Mishler 1986).

The importance of our study is further underscored by the influx of Muslims into the United States during recent decades and the increasing prominence of Muslim Americans and Islamic women on the domestic scene (G. Ahmed 1991; Ghanea Bassiri 1997; Haddad 1991a, 1991b; Hermansen 1991). Although

Jen'Nan Ghazal Read and John P. Bartkowski, "To Veil or Not to Veil? A Case Study of Identity Negotiation Among Muslim Women in Austin, Texas" from *Gender & Society* 14, No. 3 (June 2000): 395–417.

population estimates of Muslim Americans vary (ranging from 5 to 8 million), many observers consider Islam to be one of the fastest growing religions in the United States (Johnson 1991; Stone 1991). Moreover, recent research indicates that a majority of Muslims in the United States are university graduates firmly situated within the American middle class (Haddad 1991b). Yet, even as this religious subculture has enjoyed such rapid growth and economic privilege throughout much of the West, Muslims in the United States and abroad have become the target of pejorative stereotypes (Bozorgmehr, Der-Martirosian, and Sabagh 1996; Haddad 1991a, 1991b). Caricatures that portray Islamic women as submissive and backward have become more pervasive within recent years (L. Ahmed 1992; Esposito 1998), but recent research on Muslim women living in the United States has called such unflattering depictions into question (Hermansen 1991). Such research has revealed that Muslim American women creatively negotiate their gender, religious, and ethnic identities in light of dominant U.S. social norms and modernist discourses that often define these women as "other."

Our investigation therefore aims to enrich this growing research literature, while critically evaluating negative stereotypes about Muslim women. After outlining our theoretical perspective, we review the debates that currently characterize Muslim elite discourse concerning the veil. Then, to discern the impact of these broad cultural disputes on the gender identities of women of Islam located in the United States, we analyze interview data collected from a sample of religiously active Muslim women—both veiled and unveiled—currently living in Austin, Texas. Our analysis highlights salient points of ideological divergence, as well as unanticipated points of congruence, between these veiled and unveiled Muslim women concerning this controversial cultural practice.

Theory and Context: Discourse, Identity, and the Landscape of Islam

How can scholars effectively explore the interconnections between broad-based cultural constructions of gender on one hand and the more circumscribed (inter)subjective negotiation of gender relations on the other? In an effort to address these issues, a large number of contemporary feminist theorists and gender scholars have begun to examine discourse as one important medium through which gender is constructed (e.g., Bartkowski 1997a, 1997b, 1998, 2000; Currie 1997; Todd and Fisher 1988; Wodak 1997). Our study is informed by these theoretical insights and by feminist standpoint theories and notions of subjectivity that take seriously women's agency, as well as their bodily practices and everyday experiences, in the negotiation of their gender identities (e.g., Currie 1997; Davis 1997; Hollway 1995; Mahoney and Yngvesson 1992; Smith 1987; West and Fenstermaker 1995; see Mann and Kelley 1997 for review).

Theories of discourse suggest that cultural forms (e.g., gender, religion, ethnicity) are best understood as *constructed*, *contested*, and *intersecting* social phenomena. First, the meanings attributed to the Muslim veil are not endemic to the veil itself; rather, they are produced through cultural discourse and vast networks of social relationships. Social practices that imbue the veil with cultural significance include the rhetoric of religious elites who equate veiling with religious devotion, as well as the actual ostracism of unveiled Muslim women from some Islamic institutions. Second, theories of discourse call attention to the contested character of cultural forms. Cultural symbols are capable of being interpreted in a variety of different ways and often become a site of struggle and contestation. Divergent interpretations of the same cultural practice may be advanced by groups who share a common religious heritage. As evidenced in our analysis below, various factions of Muslim elites offer strikingly different interpretations of the veil and the Qur' anic passages pertaining to this cultural practice. Finally, theories of discourse attune researchers to the multidimensional and overlapping character of cultural forms. Discourses are not discrete ideologies; rather, they are culturally specific modes of understanding the world that intersect with competing viewpoints. As we reveal below, religiously active Muslim women living in the United States are exposed not only to the internecine gender debates waged within Islamic circles mentioned above. These women also construct their gender identities in light of non-Muslim discourses of gender and ethnicity prevalent in late-twentieth-century America.

As noted, we complement these insights with feminist notions of standpoint, subjectivity, and bodily practice. Taken together, these theoretical perspectives suggest that discursive regimes provide social actors with important symbolic resources for identity negotiation and for the legitimation of everyday social and bodily practices (see, e.g., Dellinger and Williams 1997; Stombler and Padavic 1997 for recent empirical treatments). Current gender scholarship construes identity negotiation as a *process* and everyday *practice* that is fraught with ambiguity, contradiction, and struggle. These perspectives stand in bold contrast to more static psychological conceptualizations *of personality* as divorced from lived experience and bodily practice. Therefore, we are careful to recognize how competing discourses of the veil enable veiled Muslim women to legitimate their decision to veil on a variety of grounds—from explicitly antifeminist rationales to feminist justifications for veiling. Yet, at the same time, we reveal how the respondents use their everyday experiences to lend a practical edge to their understanding of the veil and their perceptions of themselves as Muslim women.

The most germane aspects of Muslim theology for this study concern two sets of Islamic sacred texts, the Qur'an and the hadiths (e.g., Munson 1988). The Qur'an is held in high esteem by virtually all Muslims. Not unlike the "high view" of the Bible embraced by various conservative Christian groups, many contemporary Muslims believe that the Qur'an is the actual Word of God that was ably recorded by Muhammed during the early portion of the seventh century. In addition to the Qur'an, many Muslims also look to the hadiths for moral and spiritual guidance in their daily lives. The hadiths, second-hand reports of Muhammed's personal traditions and lifestyle, began to be collected shortly after his death because of the difficulty associated with applying the dictates of the Qur'an to changing historical circumstances. The full collection of these hadiths has come to be known as the *sunna*. Along with the Qur'an, the hadiths constitute the source of law that has shaped the ethics and values of many Muslims.

Within Islam, the all-male Islamic clergy (variously called *faghihs*, *imams*, *muftis*, *mullahs*, or *ulumas*) often act as interpretive authorities who are formally charged with distilling insights from the Qur'an or hadiths and with disseminating these scriptural interpretations to the Muslim laity (Munson 1988). Given that such positions of structural privilege are set aside for Muslim men, Islam is a patriarchal religious institution. Yet, patriarchal institutions do not necessarily produce homogeneous gender ideologies, a fact underscored by the discursive fissures that divide Muslim religious authorities and elite commentators concerning the veil.

Competing Discourses of the Veil in Contemporary Islam

Many Muslim clergy and Islamic elites currently prescribe veiling as a custom in which "good" Muslim women should engage (Afshar 1985; Al-Swailem 1995; Philips and Jones 1985; Siddiqi 1983). Proponents of veiling often begin their defense of this cultural practice by arguing that men are particularly vulnerable to corruption through unregulated sexual contact with women (Al-Swailem 1995, 27–29; Philips and Jones 1985, 39–46; Siddiqi 1983). These experts contend that the purpose of the hijab or veil is the regulation of such contact:

> The society that Islam wants to establish is not a sensate, sex-ridden society.... The Islamic system of *Hijab* is a wide-ranging system which protects the family and closes those avenues that lead toward illicit sex relations or even indiscriminate contact between the sexes in society.... To protect her virtue and to safeguard her chastity from lustful eyes and covetous hands, Islam has provided for purdah which sets norms of dress, social get-together... and going out of the four walls of one's house in hours of need. (Siddiqi 1983, vii–viii)

Many expositors of the pro-veiling discourse call attention to the uniquely masculine penchant for untamed sexual activity and construe the veil as a God-ordained solution to the apparent disparities in men's and women's sexual appetites. Women are therefore deemed responsible for the management of men's sexuality (Al-Swailem 1995, 29). Some contend that the Muslim woman who veils should be sure that the hijab covers her whole body (including the palms of her hands), should be monotone in color ("so as not to be attractive to draw the attentions to"), and should be opaque and loose so as not to reveal "the woman's shape or what she is wearing underneath" (Al-Swailem 1995, 24–25).

Pro-veiling Muslim luminaries also defend veiling on a number of nonsexual grounds. The veil, according to these commentators, serves as (1) a demonstration of the Muslim woman's unwavering obedience to the tenets of Islam; (2) a clear indication of the essential differences distinguishing men from women; (3) a reminder to women that their proper place is in the home rather than in pursuing public-sphere activities; and (4) a sign of the devout Muslim woman's disdain for the profane, immodest, and consumerist cultural customs of the West (e.g., Al-Swailem 1995, 27–29; Siddiqi 1983, 140, 156). In this last regard, veiling is legitimated as an anti-imperialist statement of ethnic and cultural distinctiveness.

Nevertheless, the most prominent justifications for veiling entail, quite simply, the idea that veiling is prescribed in the Qur'an (see Arat 1994; Dragadze 1994; Hessini 1994; Sherif 1987; Shirazi-Mahajan 1995 for reviews). Several Muslim clergy place a strong interpretive emphasis on a Qur'anic passage (S. 24:31) that urges women "not [to] display their beauty and adornments" but rather to "draw their head cover over their bosoms and not display their ornament." Many of these same defenders of the veil marshal other Qur'anic passages that bolster their pro-veiling stance: "And when you ask them [the Prophet's wives] for anything you want ask them from before a screen (*hijab*); that makes for greater purity for your hearts and for them" (S. 33:53); "O Prophet! Tell your wives and daughters and the believing women that they should cast their outer garments over themselves, that is more convenient that they should be known and not molested" (S. 33:59).

In addition to these Qur'anic references, pro-veiling Muslim clergy highlight hadiths intended to support the practice of veiling (see Sherif 1987 for review). Many pro-veiling Muslim clergy maintain that the veil verse was revealed to Muhammad at a wedding five years before the Prophet's death. As the story goes, three tactless guests overstayed their welcome after the wedding and continued to chat despite the Prophet's desire to be alone with his new wife. To encourage their departure, Muhammad drew a curtain between the nuptial chamber and one of his inconsiderate companions while ostensibly uttering "the verse of the hijab" (S. 33:53, cited above). A second set of hadiths claim that the verse of hijab was prompted when one of the Prophet's companions accidentally touched the hand of one of Muhammad's wives while eating dinner. Yet a third set of hadiths suggests that the verse's objective was to stop the visits of an unidentified man who tarried with the wives of the Prophet, promising them marriage after Muhammad's death.

In stark contrast to the pro-veiling apologias discussed above, an oppositional discourse against veiling has emerged within Islamic circles in recent years. Most prominent among these opponents of veiling are Islamic feminists (Al-Marayati 1995; Mernissi 1991; Shaheed 1994, 1995; see contributions in Al-Hibri 1982; Gocek and Balaghi 1994; see AbuKhalil 1993; An-Na'im 1987; Anees 1989; Arat 1994; Badran 1991; Fernea 1998 for treatments of Islamic feminism and related issues). Although Islamic feminists are marginalized from many of the institutional apparatuses available to the all-male Muslim clergy, they nevertheless exercise considerable influence via the dissemination of dissident publications targeted at Islamic women and through grassroots social movements (Fernea 1998; Shaheed 1994). Fatima Mernissi (1987, 1991), arguably the most prominent Muslim feminist, is highly critical of dominant gender conceptualizations that construe veiling as the ultimate standard by which the spiritual welfare and religious devoutness of Muslim women should be judged. In *The Veil and the Male Elite: A Feminist Interpretation of*

Women's Rights in Islam, Mernissi (1991, 194) queries her readers:

> What a strange fate for Muslim memory, to be called upon in order to censure and punish [Islamic women]! What a strange memory, where even dead men and women do not escape attempts at assassination, if by chance they threaten to raise the *hijab* [veil] that covers the mediocrity and servility that is presented to us [Muslim women] as tradition. How did the tradition succeed in transforming the Muslim woman into that submissive, marginal creature who buries herself and only goes out into the world timidly and huddled in her veils? Why does the Muslim man need such a mutilated companion?

Mernissi and other Muslim commentators who oppose veiling do so on a number of grounds. First, Mernissi seeks to reverse the sacralization of the veil by linking the hijab with oppressive social hierarchies and male domination. She argues that the veil represents a tradition of "mediocrity and servility" rather than a sacred standard against which to judge Muslim women's devotion to Allah. Second, antiveiling Muslim commentators are quick to highlight the historical fact that veiling is a cultural practice that originated from outside of Islamic circles (see Schmidt 1989). Although commonly assumed to be of Muslim origin, historical evidence reveals that veiling was actually practiced in the ancient Near East and Arabia long before the rise of Islam (Esposito 1995; Sherif 1987; Webster 1984). Using this historical evidence to bolster their antiveiling stance, some Muslim feminists conclude that because the veil is not a Muslim invention, it cannot be held up as the standard against which Muslim women's religiosity is to be gauged.

Finally, Islamic feminists such as Mernissi (1991, chap. 5) point to the highly questionable scriptural interpretations on which Muslim clergy often base their pro-veiling edicts (see Hessini 1994; Shirazi-Mahajan 1995). Dissident Islamic commentators call attention to the fact that the Qur'an refers cryptically to a "curtain" and never directly instructs women to wear a veil. Although proponents of veiling interpret Qur'anic edicts as Allah's directive to all Muslim women for all time, Islamic critics of veiling counter this interpretive strategy by placing relatively greater weight on the "occasions of revelation" (*asbab nuzul al Qur'an*)—that is, the specific social circumstances under which key Qur'anic passages were revealed (Mernissi 1991, 87–88, 92–93; see Sherif 1987). It is with this interpretive posture that many Islamic feminists believe the veil verse (S. 33:53) to be intended solely for the wives of Muhammad (Mernissi 1991, 92; see Sherif 1987). Muslim critics of veiling further counter many of the pro-veiling hadith citations by arguing that they are interpretations of extrascriptural texts whose authenticity is highly questionable (Mernissi 1991, 42–48; see Sherif 1987; Shirazi-Mahajan 1995). Finally, critics of hijab point to select verses in the Qur'an that invoke images of gender egalitarianism, including one passage that refers to the "vast reward" Allah has prepared for both "men who guard their modesty and women who guard their modesty" (S. 33:35).

The Veil and Gender Identity Negotiation Among Muslim Women in Austin

To this point, we have drawn comparisons between pro veiling edicts that link devout, desexualized Muslim womanhood to the practice of veiling and antiveiling discourses that reject this conflation of hijab and women's religious devotion. We now attempt to gauge the impact of these debates on the gender identities of a sample of 24 Muslim women—12 of whom veil, 12 of whom do not. All women in our sample define themselves as devout Muslims (i.e., devoted followers of Muhammad who actively practice their faith). These women were recruited through a combination of snowball and purposive sampling. Taken together, the respondents identify with a range of different nationalities (e.g., Iranian, Pakistani, Kuwaiti) and Muslim sects (e.g., Sunni, Shi'i, Ahmadia). Nineteen women have lived 10 or more years in the United States, while five women in our sample have immigrated in the past 5 years. Their ages range from 21 to 55 years old, and they occupy a range of social roles (e.g., college students, professional women, homemakers). Consistent with the demographic characteristics of

U.S. Muslim immigrants at large (Haddad 1991b), our sample is composed of middle-class women with some postsecondary education (either a college degree or currently attending college). Class homogeneity among the respondents is also partly a product of the locale from which the sample was drawn, namely, a university town. Consequently, this study extends cross-cultural scholarship on the intersection of veiling, ethnicity, and nationality for middle-class Muslim women living in Western and largely modernized societies (e.g., Bloul 1997; Brenner 1996; Hatem 1994).

In-depth interviews with these Muslim women were conducted by the first author during 1996 and 1997. The interview questionnaire covered a range of topics, including the women's practical experiences with veiling, the meaning of the veil to them, their reasons for wearing or not wearing the veil and the impact of this decision on their social relationships, their perceptions about the significance of the veil in their country of origin, and the importance of Islamic beliefs and devotional activities (e.g., prayer, scriptural study) to these women. In light of our topic's sensitivity, as well as cultural differences between our respondents and the first author (a non-Muslim unveiled woman), the interviews were not audiotaped. Because many of the women were forthright about their opposition to participating in a study based on tape-recorded interviews, the tenor, depth, and candor of these interviews would have been seriously inhibited if conversations were tape-recorded. Consequently, with the women's consent, handwritten notes were recorded during the course of each interview. Immediately after the interview, these notes were then elaborated into a more detailed set of transcripts. Each transcript was initially evaluated as an independent conversation concerning the significance of the veil and its relationship to the respondent's religious and gender identity. Emergent themes from each interview were flagged and coded during this stage of the analysis. Then, during a second stage of analysis, we compared the themes that emerged from interviews conducted with each of the two different subgroups of Muslim women (veiled and unveiled).

Interview data collected from these women, identified below by pseudonyms, are designed to address several interrelated issues: What does the veil itself and the practice of veiling mean to these women? Among the women who veil, why do they do so? Among the women who do not veil, how have they arrived at the decision to remain unveiled? Finally, how does each group of our respondents feel about women who engage in the "opposite" cultural practice?

Veiled Contradictions: Perceptions of Hijab and Gender Practices Among Veiled Muslim Women

Religious Edicts and Social Bonds

In several respects, the veiled respondents' accounts of wearing hijab conform to the pro-veiling gender discourse explicated above. Many of the veiled women invoke various sorts of religious imagery and theological edicts when asked about their motivations for veiling. One respondent in her early twenties, Huneeya, states flatly: "I wear the hijab because the Qur'an says it's better [for women to be veiled]." Yet another veiled woman, Najette, indicates that hijab "makes [her] more special" because it symbolizes her commitment to Islam. Mona says outright: "The veil represents submission to God," and Masouda construes the veil as a "symbol of worship" on the part of devout Muslim women to Allah and the teachings of the Prophet Muhammad. Not surprisingly, many veiled women contend that veiling is commanded in the Qur'an.

Of course, this abundance of theological rationales is not the only set of motivations that the veiled women use to justify this cultural practice. For many of the veiled respondents, the scriptural edicts and the religious symbolism surrounding the veil are given palpable force through their everyday gender practices and the close-knit social networks that grow out of this distinctive cultural practice. Indeed, narratives about some women's deliberate choice to begin veiling at a particular point in their lives underscore how religious edicts stand in tension with the women's strategic motivations. Several women recount that they began to veil because they had friends who did so or because they felt more closely connected to significant others through this cultural practice. Aisha, for example, longed to wear the veil while she attended high school in the Middle East approximately three decades ago. Reminiscent of issues faced by her teen counterparts in the United States, Aisha's account suggests that high school was a crucial time for identity formation and the cultivation of peer group relationships. The veil served Aisha as a valuable resource in resolving many of the dilemmas she faced 30 years ago as a maturing high school student. She decided to begin veiling at that time after hearing several prominent Muslim speakers at her school "talk[ing] about how good veiling is." The veil helped Aisha not only to form meaningful peer relationships at that pivotal time in her life (i.e., adolescence) but also continues to facilitate for her a feeling of connectedness with a broader religious community of other veiled Muslim women. During her recent trip to Egypt during the summer, Aisha says that the veil helped her "to fit in" there in a way that she would not have if she were unveiled.

Several other respondents also underscore the significance of Islamic women's friendship networks that form around the veil, which are particularly indispensable because they live in a non-Muslim country (i.e., the United States). In recounting these friendship circles that are cultivated around hijab in a "foreign" land, our veiled respondents point to an important overlay between their gender identities (i.e., good Muslim women veil) and their ethnic identities (i.e., as Middle Easterners). The common foundation on which these twin identities are negotiated is distinctively religious in nature. Hannan touts the personal benefits of veiling both as a *woman*—"the veil serves as an identity for [Islamic] women"—and as a *Muslim:* "[Because I veil,] Muslim people know I am Muslim, and they greet me in Arabic." This interface between gender and ethnicity is also given voice by Aisha, whose initial experiences with the veil were noted above. Aisha maintains, "The veil differentiates Muslim women from other women. When you see a woman in hijab, you know she's a Muslim." Much like the leading Muslim commentators who encourage Islamic women to "wear" their religious convictions (literally, via the veil) for all to see, these veiled respondents find comfort in the cultural and ethnic distinctiveness that the veil affords them. In this way, hijab is closely connected with their overlapping religious-gender-ethnic identities and links them to the broader community (*ummah*) of Islamic believers and Muslim women.

Gender Difference and Women's "Emancipation"

In addition to providing religious rationales for wearing the veil, many of the women who wear hijab also invoke the discourse of masculine-feminine difference to defend the merits of veiling. For several women, the idea of masculine hyper-sexuality and feminine vulnerability to the male sex drive is crucial to this essentialist rationale for veiling. Despite the fact that veiled women were rather guarded in their references to sex, their nods in that direction are difficult to interpret in any other fashion. In describing the veil's role in Islam and in the lives of Muslim men and women (such as herself), Sharadda states, "Islam is natural and men need some things naturally. If we abide by these needs [and veil accordingly], we will all be happy." She continues, "If the veil did not exist, many evil things would happen. Boys would mix with girls, which will result in evil things."

Similarly, Hannan describes what she perceives to be women's distinctive attributes and their connection to the veil: "Women are like diamonds; they are so precious. They should not be revealed to everyone—just to their husbands and close kin." Like Qur'anic references to women's "ornaments," Hannan is contrasting the "precious" diamond-like feminine character to the ostensibly less refined, less distinctive masculine persona. Interestingly, it is by likening women to diamonds that Hannan rhetorically inverts traditional gender hierarchies that privilege "masculine" traits over their "feminine" counterparts. In the face of those who would denigrate feminine qualities, Hannan reinterprets the distinctiveness of womanhood as more "precious" (i.e., more rare and valuable) than masculine qualities. Women's inherent difference from men, then, is perceived to be a source of esteem rather than denigration.

It is important to recognize, however, that the respondents who invoke this rhetoric of gender difference are not simply reproducing the pro-veiling discourse advanced by Muslim elites. Despite their essentialist convictions, many of the veiled respondents argue that the practice of wearing hijab actually liberates them from men's untamed, potentially explosive sexuality and makes possible for them various sorts of public-sphere pursuits. So, whereas pro-veiling Islamic elites often reason that women's sexual vulnerability (and, literally, their fragile bodily "ornaments") should restrict them to the domestic sphere, many of the veiled women in this study simply do not support this view of domesticized femininity. To the contrary, these women—many of whom are themselves involved in occupational or educational pursuits—argue that the veil is a great equalizer that enables women to work alongside of men. In the eyes of Hannan, women's "preciousness" should not be used to cajole them to remain in the home: "Women who wear the hijab are not excluded from society. They are freer to move around in society because of it."

Rabbab, who attends to various public-sphere pursuits, offers a similar appraisal. She argues that the face veil (hijab) is an invaluable aid for Muslim women who engage in extradomestic pursuits. In advancing this claim, Rabbab uses women who veil their whole bodies (such body garments are called *abaya*) as a counterpoint of excessive traditionalism. When asked what the veil means to her personally, as well as to Muslim women and Islamic culture at large, she says,

> It depends on the extent of the hijab [that is worn]....Women who wear face veils and cover their whole bodies [with abaya] are limited to the home. They are too dependent on their husbands. How can they interact when they are so secluded?...[However,] taking away the hijab [i.e., face veil] would make women have to fight to be taken seriously [in public settings]....With hijab, men take us more seriously.

This hijab-as-liberator rationale for veiling was repeated by many of the veiled women who pursued educational degrees in schools and on college campuses where young predatorial men ostensibly rove in abundance. Aisha, a 41-year-old former student, recounts how the veil emancipated her from the male gaze during her school years:

> There was a boy who attended my university. He was very rude to all of the girls, always whistling and staring at them. One day, I found myself alone in the hallway with him. I was very nervous because I had to walk by him. But because I was wearing the hijab, he looked down when I walked past. He did not show that respect to the unveiled girls.

Drawing on experiences such as these, Aisha concludes succinctly: "The veil gives women advantages....They can go to coeducational schools and feel safe." A current student, Najette, says that the veil helps her to "feel secure" in going about her daily activities. Finally, the account of a young female student who is 22 years of age sheds further light on the hijab's perceived benefits in the face of men's apparent propensity to objectify women: "If you're in hijab, then someone sees you and treats you accordingly. I feel more free. Especially men, they don't look at your appearance—they appreciate your intellectual abilities. They respect you." For many of the veiled women in this study, the respect and protection afforded them by the hijab enables them to engage in extradomestic pursuits that would ironically generate sharp criticism from many pro-veiling Muslim elites.

The Discontents of Hijab and Tolerance for the Unveiled

While the foregoing statements provide clear evidence of these women's favorable feelings about hijab, many of the veiled women also express mixed feelings about this controversial cultural symbol. It was not uncommon for the veiled respondents to recount personal difficulties that they have faced because of their decision to wear hijab. Some dilemmas associated with the veil emanate from the fact that these women live in a secular society inhabited predominantly by Christians rather than Muslims. Najette, the same respondent who argued that veiling makes her feel "special," was quick to recognize that this esteem is purchased at the price of being considered "weird" by some Americans who do not understand her motivations for veiling. For women like her, engaging in a dissident cultural practice underscores Najette's cultural distinctiveness in a way that some people find refreshing and others find threatening.

Such points of tension surrounding the veil are evident not only in cross-cultural encounters such as that mentioned above. Even within Muslim circles, the practice of veiling has generated enough controversy to produce rifts among relatives and friends when some of the veiled respondents appear publicly in hijab. Huneeya, a student who veils because she wishes to follow Qur'anic edicts and enjoys being treated as an intellectual equal by her male peers, highlighted just this point of friction with her family members, all of whom except her are "against hijab. [My family members] think it is against modernity."

For some women, the tensions produced within intimate relationships by the veil move beyond the realm of intermittent family squabbles. One veiled respondent, Asma, revealed that extended family difficulties surrounding the veil have caused her to alter the practice of veiling itself, if only temporarily. Her recent experiences underscore the complex machinations of power involved in the contested arenas of family relations and friendships where veiling is concerned. Asma moved to the United States with her husband only two years ago. Asma was quite conscientious about veiling. She relished the sense of uniqueness and cultural distinctiveness afforded to her by the hijab while living in a non-Muslim country. Yet, recent summer-long visits from her mother-in-law presented her with a dilemma. Asma's mother-in-law had arranged the marriage between her son and daughter-in-law. At the time, the mother-in-law greatly appreciated the conservative religious values embraced by her future daughter-in-law, evidenced in Asma's attentiveness to wearing the veil. Yet, since that time, Asma's mother-in-law had undergone a conversion of sorts concerning the practice of veiling. Quite recently, Asma's mother-in-law stopped wearing the veil and wanted her daughter-in-law to follow suit by discarding the veil as well. Indeed, this mother-in-law felt that Asma was trying to upstage her by using the veil to appear more religiously devout than her elder. Asma's short-term solution to this dilemma is to submit to the wishes of her mother-in-law during her summer visits to the United States. Consequently, for two months each summer, Asma discards her veil. Yet, this solution is hardly satisfactory to her and does not placate Asma's veiled friends who think less of her for unveiling:

> I feel very uncomfortable without the veil. The veil keeps us [Muslim women] from getting mixed up in American culture. But I don't want to make my mother-in-law feel inferior, so I take it off while she is here. I know my friends think I am a hypocrite.

Although Asma is sanctioned by her friends for unveiling temporarily during her mother-in-law's visit, our interview data suggest that the preponderance of veiled women in this study harbor no ill will toward their Muslim sisters who choose not to veil. Despite these veiled women's enthusiastic defenses of hijab, they are willing to define what it means to be a good Muslim broadly enough to include Islamic women who do not veil. When asked, for instance, what she thought being a good Muslim entails, one of our veiled respondents (Najette) states simply: "You must be a good person and always be honest." Echoing these sentiments, Masouda suggests, "Your attitude towards God is most important for being a good Muslim—your personality. You must be patient, honest, giving." Even when asked point-blank if veiling makes a woman a good Muslim, another veiled respondent answers, "Hijab is not so important for being a good Muslim. Other things are more important, like having a good character and being honest." One respondent even took on a decidedly ecumenical tone in detaching veiling from Islamic devotion: "Being a good Muslim is the same as being a good Christian or a good Jew—treat others with respect and dignity. Be considerate and open-minded." In the end, then, these women in hijab are able to distinguish between what veiling means to them at a personal level (i.e., a sign of religious devotion) versus what the veil says about Muslim women in general (i.e., a voluntary cultural practice bereft of devotional significance). These veiled women's heterogeneous lived experiences with the hijab—both comforting and uncomfortable, affirming and tension producing, positive and negative—seem to provide them with a sensitivity to cultural differences that often seems lacking in the vitriolic debates about veiling currently waged by leading Muslims.

Islamic Feminism Modified: Perceptions of Hijab and Gender Practices Among the Unveiled

Patriarchal Oppression and Religious Fanaticism

Just as veiled women draw on the pro-veiling discourse to defend the wearing of hijab, the unveiled women in this study often justify their abstention from this cultural practice by invoking themes from the antiveiling discourse. Several of these unveiled women argue quite straightforwardly that the veil reinforces gender distinctions that work to Muslim women's collective disadvantage. According to many of the unveiled women, the veil was imposed on Muslim women because of Middle Eastern men's unwillingness to tame their sexual caprice and because of their desire to dominate women. Rabeeya, for example, contends that Muslim women are expected to veil because "Middle Eastern men get caught up in beauty. The veil helps men control themselves." Offering a strikingly similar response, Najwa argues that "men can't control themselves, so they make women veil." Using the same critical terminology—that is, *control*—to make her point, Fozia has an even less sanguine view of the veil's role in Islam. When asked about the significance of the veil in Muslim societies, she states flatly: "The veil is used to control women." In short, many of the unveiled respondents view hijab in much the same way as elite Islamic feminists; that is, as a mechanism of patriarchal control.

Comments such as these suggest points of congruence between the veiled and unveiled respondents' understandings of hijab. Both groups of women seem to agree that hijab is closely related to men's sexuality. Recall that some of the veiled women contrast masculine hypersexuality to a desexualized view of femininity. Such women conclude that the veil is the God-ordained corrective for men's inability to control their own sexual impulses. Likewise, as evidenced in several statements from unveiled women, they link the veil to men's apparent inability (or, better, unwillingness) to contain their sexual desires. However, whereas several of the veiled women see masculine hypersexuality as natural and view the veil as a divine remedy for such sexual differences, many of the unveiled women reject these views. The unveiled respondents seem less willing to accept the notion that categorical gender differences should translate into a cultural practice that (literally and figuratively) falls on the shoulders of women. In a key point of departure from their sisters who wear hijab, the unveiled women in this study trace the origin of the veil not to God but rather to men's difficulties in managing their sexuality (again, "men can't control themselves, so they make women veil"). In men's attempt to manage their sexual impulses, so the account goes, they have foisted the veil on women. Very much in keeping with feminist discourses that take issue with such gendered double standards, the unveiled women conclude that it is unfair to charge women with taming men's sexuality.

Apart from these issues of social control and sexuality, several of the unveiled respondents also invoke themes of religious devotion and ethnic identity when discussing the significance of the veil for Muslims in general and for themselves (as unveiled Islamic women) in particular. Recall that leading Muslims who support veiling often highlight the religious and ethnic distinctiveness of hijab; however, prominent Muslim feminists counter that veiling did not originate with Islam and should not be understood as central to women's religious devoutness or ethnic identities (as non-Westerners). Echoing these Muslim feminist themes, several of the unveiled respondents seek to sever the veil from its religious and ethnic moorings. Fozia says that Muslim "women are made to believe that the veil is religious. In reality, it's all political," while Fatima asserts, "The veil is definitely political. It is used by men as a weapon to differentiate us from Westerners." Yet another respondent, Mah'ha, argues that it is only "fanatical" and "strict"

Muslims who use the veil to draw sharp distinctions between Middle Easterners and Westerners. These remarks and others like them are designed to problematize the conflation of religious devotion, ethnic distinctiveness, and hijab evidenced in the pro-veiling discourse. Whereas the dominant discourse of veiling measures women's devotion to Islamic culture against hijab, many of the unveiled respondents imply—again, via strategic terms such as *political*, *fanatical*, and *strict*—that religious devotion and ethnic identification are good only in proper measure.

This rhetorical strategy allows these unveiled women to claim more moderate (and modern) convictions over and against those whose devotion to Allah has in their view been transmogrified into political dogmatism, religious extremism, and racial separatism. The unveiled women in our study do not eschew religious commitment altogether, nor are they in any way ashamed of their ethnic heritage. To the contrary, the unveiled respondents champion religious commitment (again, in good measure) and are proud to count themselves among the followers of Muhammad. Yet, they are quick to illustrate that their devotion to Allah and their appreciation of their cultural heritage are manifested through means that do not include the practice of veiling. Amna, for example, says, "Religious education makes me feel like a more pious Muslim. I read the Qur'an weekly and attend Friday prayer sermons," while Rabeeya states, "Being a good Muslim means believing in one God; no idolatry; following the five pillars of Islam; and believing in Muhammad." Concerning the issue of ethnoreligious identity, the basic message articulated by many of the unveiled women can be stated quite succinctly: A Muslim woman can be true to her cultural and religious heritage without the veil. Samiya, a 38-year-old unveiled woman, says as much: "Muslim society doesn't exist on the veil. Without the veil, you would still be Muslim." Therefore, many of the unveiled women believe that the veil is of human (actually, male) origin rather than of divine making. And it is this very belief about the veil's this-worldly origins that enables many of the unveiled women to characterize themselves as devout followers of Muhammad who honor their cultural heritage even though they have opted not to veil.

Standing on Common Ground: Tolerance for the Other Among Unveiled Women

Finally, we turn our attention to the subjective contradictions that belie the prima facie critical reactions of our unveiled respondents toward the veil. Interestingly, just as the veiled women are reluctant to judge harshly their unveiled counterparts, these unveiled women who eschew hijab at a personal level nevertheless express understanding and empathy toward their Middle Eastern sisters who veil. At several points during interview encounters, the unveiled respondents escape the polemical hold of the antiveiling discourse by building bridges to their sisters who engage in a cultural practice that they themselves eschew.

First, several respondents imply that it would be wrong to criticize veiled women for wearing hijab when it is men—specifically, male Muslim elites—who are to blame for the existence and pervasiveness of the veil in Islamic culture. Amna, who does not veil, takes on a conciliatory tone toward women who do so by conceding that "the veil helps women in societies where they want to be judged solely on their character and not on their appearances." How is it that such statements, which sound so similar to the justifications for wearing hijab invoked by veiled women, emanate from the unveiled respondents? The strongly antipatriarchal sentiments of the unveiled women (described in the preceding section) seem to exonerate veiled women from charges of gender traitorism. Recall that many of the unveiled respondents, in fact, locate the origin of the veil in *men's* sexual indiscretion and in *men's* desire to control women: "Middle Eastern *men* get caught up in beauty. The veil helps *men* control *themselves*" (Rabeeya); "*Men* can't control *themselves*, so *they* make women veil" (Najwa); "The veil is *used to control women*. The women are *made to believe* that the veil is religious" (Fozia) (emphasis added). Ironically, it is the very antipatriarchal character of these statements that simultaneously enables the unveiled women to express their stinging criticism of the veil itself while proclaiming tolerance and respect for Islamic women who wear the veil. Indeed, since many of the unveiled respondents construe hijab to be a product of *patriarchal* oppression and assorted *masculine* hang-ups (e.g., struggles with sexuality, a preoccupation with domination and control), veiled women cannot legitimately be impugned for wearing hijab.

Second, many of the unveiled respondents are willing to concede that despite their own critical views of the veil, hijab serves an important cultural marker for Islamic women other than themselves. When asked about the role of the veil among Muslim women she knows in the United States, Rabeeya recognizes that many of her veiled Islamic sisters who currently live in America remain "very, very tied to their culture. Or they are trying to be. They [veil because they] want to feel tied to their culture even when they are far away from home." Because she herself is a devout Islamic woman living in a religiously pluralistic and publicly secularized society, Rabeeya is able to empathize with other Muslim women residing in the United States who veil in order to shore up their cultural identity. Similarly, Sonya draws noteworthy distinctions between her personal antipathy toward veiling and veiled women's attraction to hijab: "Some Muslim women need the veil to identify themselves with the Muslim culture. I don't feel that way."

Finally, several of the unveiled women in our study seem to express tolerance and empathy for their sisters in hijab because, at one time or another in the past, they themselves have donned the veil. Two of the unveiled respondents, for example, are native Iranians who are currently living in the United States. When these women return to Iran, they temporarily don the veil. Najwa, one of these women, explains, "As soon as we cross the Iranian border, I go to the bathroom on the airplane and put on the hijab." The experiences of our other native-born Iranian woman, Fatima, speak even more directly to the practical nuances that undergird unveiled women's tolerance for their veiled counterparts. On one hand, Fatima is highly critical of the veil, which has been the legally required dress for women in Iran during the past two decades. Referring to this fact, she impugns the veil as a "political... weapon" used by religious elites to reinforce invidious distinctions between Westerners and Middle Easterners. Yet, on the other hand, her personal experiences with hijab lead her to reject the stereotype that women who veil are "backward": "Progress has nothing to do with veiling. Countries without veiling can be very backwards... I have nothing against veiling. I feel very modern [in not veiling], but I respect those who veil." Like so many of her unveiled sisters, then, Rabeeya is critical of the veil as a religious icon but is unwilling to look down on Islamic women who wear hijab.

Conclusion and Discussion

This study has examined how a sample of Muslim women living in Austin, Texas, negotiate their gender identities in light of ongoing Islamic disputes about the propriety of veiling. Interview data with 12 veiled and 12 unveiled women reveal that many of them draw upon the pro-veiling and antiveiling discourses of Muslim elites, respectively, to justify their decisions about the veil. At the same time, the women highlight various subjective contradictions manifested in many of their accounts of veiling. Women who veil are not typically disdainful toward their unveiled Muslim sisters, and unveiled women in our sample seem similarly reluctant to impugn their veiled counterparts. Such findings were unanticipated in light of elite Muslim debates about the propriety of veiling.

What are we to make of the fact that the acrimony manifested between elite Muslim proponents and opponents of veiling is largely absent from these women's accounts of the veil? Several possible answers to this question emerge from our investigation. First, both the veiled and unveiled women in our study clearly exercise agency in crafting their gender identities. Drawing on themes of individualism and tolerance for diversity, the women are able to counterpose their own "choice" to veil or to remain unveiled on one hand with the personal inclinations of their sisters who might choose a path that diverges from their own. In this way, the respondents fashion gender identities that are malleable and inclusive enough to navigate through the controversy surrounding the veil.

Second, the social context within which the women are situated seems to provide them with resources that facilitate these gender innovations. As noted above, our sample is composed of middle-class, well-educated Muslim women. We suspect that the progressive, multicultural climate of Austin and the human capital enjoyed by the women foster greater empathy between the veiled respondents and their unveiled counterparts. This degree of tolerance between veiled and unveiled Muslim women evinced in our study may be decidedly different for Islamic women living in other parts of the United States, other Western nations, or particular countries in the Middle East where the veil is a more publicly contested symbol.

Consequently, this study lends further credence to the insight that culture is not simply produced from "above" through the rhetoric of elites to be consumed untransformed by social actors who are little more than judgmental dopes. While the proveiling and antiveiling discourses have carved out distinctive positions for veiled Muslim women and their unveiled counterparts within the late twentieth century, the respondents in our study are unique and indispensable contributors to contemporary Islamic culture. It is these women, rather than the often combative elite voices within Islamic circles, who creatively build bridges across the contested cultural terrain of veiling; who forge ties of tolerance with their sisters, veiled and unveiled; and who help foster the sense of community (*ummah*) that is so esteemed by Muslims around the world. Convictions about Islamic culture and community take on new meaning as they are tested in the crucible of Muslim women's everyday experiences. These findings parallel those that have emerged from other studies of politicized issues in the contemporary United States, including debates about abortion, family decision making, and women's paid labor force participation (Bartkowski 1997b, 1999; Gallagher and Smith 1999; Hunter 1994). These studies have revealed that the contemporary "culture wars" over gender are often waged by a select few—namely, elite ideologists and vanguard activists—whose views do not wholly correspond with the local standpoints of actual women at whom such rhetoric is targeted.

Several avenues for future research emerge from this study. First, observational research exploring the actual interactions between veiled and unveiled Muslim women in the United States is warranted. While our study suggests a level of ideological tolerance among veiled and unveiled Muslim women for "sisters who choose otherwise," the question remains: Does this ideological tolerance lead to practical collaboration among veiled and unveiled Muslim women, particularly if they are frequenting the same mosque? Because our study focuses on *perceptions* of veiling and *cognitive meanings* attributed to the veil, we are unable to answer such vexing questions about the actual *practice* of gender. One recent ethnographic study highlights how Muslim women with divergent views of the veil can, under some circumstances, forge meaningful community ties with one another (Walbridge 1997). Nevertheless, additional research is needed to clarify the specific circumstances under which such collaboration between veiled and unveiled women may be facilitated and those contexts under which such connections might be inhibited.

Second, our study pays short shrift to the patriarchal institutional structure that remains prevalent within so many mosques and Muslim communities located in the United States. By drawing on interview data with Muslim women rather than ethnographic observations from Austin mosques, our study is unable to assess the prospects for structural changes in gender relations within these religious institutions. We have emphasized the agency of Muslim women in recrafting Islamic culture and suggest that power is not monopolized by the all-male Muslim religious leaders charged with leading the Islamic laity. Nevertheless, we would be remiss if we failed to acknowledge the structural advantage enjoyed by all-male Muslim clerics for potential agenda setting within mosques and other Muslim religious institutions (cf. Kandiyoti 1988). Will the critiques of leading Islamic feminists—and the egalitarian sensibilities of some Muslim American women—present an effective challenge to the long-standing institutionalization of male authority within these religious organizations? In light of the growing literature on gendered organizations (e.g., Acker

1990; Britton 1997), this question undoubtedly deserves attention from gender scholars and researchers of Muslim communities.

Finally, there are some telling points of convergence between gender relations in contemporary Islam, Orthodox Judaism, and conservative Protestantism. Given the spate of recent studies which suggest that gender is negotiated by conservative Protestants and Orthodox Jews (e.g., Bartkowski 1997b, 1999, 2000; Brasher 1998; Davidman 1993; Gallagher and Smith 1999; Griffith 1997; Manning 1999; Stacey 1990), what parallels might exist between the gendered experiences of Muslim women and their conservative Protestant or Orthodox Jewish counterparts? And, in what ways might the gender practices and the enactment of specific definitions of the religiously "devout woman" (whether Muslim, evangelical, or Orthodox Jew) diverge? No research of which we are aware has compared the processes of identity negotiation among Muslim women with those manifested in other conservative religious contexts.[3] When interpreted in light of the emerging literature on gender negotiation within conservative Protestantism and Orthodox Judaism, our findings suggest that there is much to be gained by drawing more detailed cross-cultural comparisons between the gendered experiences of such women, as well as the culturally specific "patriarchal bargains" (Kandiyoti 1988) with which these groups of women are confronted. In the end, arriving at a richer understanding of gender negotiation in those contexts where we might least expect to find it can shed new light on the transformation of gender relations as we begin the millennium.

Acknowledgments

Earlier versions of this article were presented at the 1998 meetings of the Southern Sociological Society in Atlanta, Georgia, and the 1999 meetings of the American Sociological Association in Chicago, Illinois. Special thanks to Susan Marshall and Faegheh Shirazi-Mahajan for their guidance and comments throughout this project. This article has benefited from the insightful comments of James Fraser, Helen Regis, Debra Umberson, and Christine Williams. We wish to acknowledge the assistance of Amer Al-Saleh in securing select documentary data for this study. All interpretations presented here are our own.

Notes

1. The merits of this insider or "emic" perspective are also clearly evidenced by a growing body of research that highlights the heterogeneous and contested character of gender relations among conservative Protestants (e.g., Bartkowski 1997a, 1997b, 1998, 1999, 2000; Gallagher and Smith 1999; Griffith 1997; Stacey 1990) and Orthodox Jews (Davidman 1993), an issue to which we return in the final section of this article.
2. For stylistic convenience, we often refer to the veil as *hijab*.
3. Gerami (1996) provides one exception to this general neglect of interreligious comparisons, although her analyses are largely survey based. Comparisons between Orthodox Jewish American women and their Muslim counterparts might be particularly telling in light of these women's similar experiences as devout, largely middle-class non-Christians living in the United States.

References

AbuKhalil, As'ad. 1993. Toward the study of women and politics in the Arab world: The debate and the reality. *Feminist Issues* 13:3–23.

Abu-Lughod, Lila. 1986. *Veiled sentiments*. Berkeley: University of California Press.

Acker, Joan. 1990. Hierarchies, jobs, bodies: A theory of gendered organizations. *Gender & Society* 4:139–58.

Afshar, Haleh. 1985. The legal, social and political position of women in Iran. *International Journal of the Sociology of Law* 13:47–60.

Ahmed, Gutbi Mahdi. 1991. Muslim organizations in the United States. In *The Muslims of America*, edited by Y. Y. Haddad. Oxford, UK: Oxford University Press.

Ahmed, Leila. 1992. *Women and gender in Islam: Historical roots of a modern debate*. New Haven, CT: Yale University Press.

Al-Hibri, Azizah, ed. 1982. *Women and Islam*. Oxford, UK: Pergamon.

Al-Marayati, Laila. 1995. Voices of women unsilenced—Beijing 1995 focus on women's health and issues of concern for Muslim women. *UCLA Women's Law Journal* 6:167.

Al-Swailem, Sheikh Abdullah Ahmed. 1995. Introduction. In *A comparison between veiling and unveiling*, by Halah bint Abdullah. Riyadh, Saudi Arabia: Dar-es-Salaam.

Anees, Munawar Ahmad. 1989. Study of Muslim women and family: A bibliography. *Journal of Comparative Family Studies* 20:263–74.

An-Na'im, Abdullahi. 1987. The rights of women and international law in the Muslim context. *Whittier Law Review* 9:491.

Arat, Yesim. 1994. Women's movement of the 1980s in Turkey: Radical outcome of liberal Kemalism? In *Reconstructing gender in the Middle East: Tradition, identity, and power*, edited by F. M. Gocek and S. Balaghi. New York: Columbia University Press.

Badran, Margot. 1991. Competing agendas: Feminists, Islam and the state in 19th and 20th century Egypt. In *Women, Islam & the state*, edited by D. Kandiyoti. Philadelphia: Temple University Press.

Bartkowski, John P. 1997a. Debating patriarchy: Discursive disputes over spousal authority among evangelical family commentators. *Journal for the Scientific Study of Religion* 36:393–410.

———. 1997b. Gender reinvented, gender reproduced: The discourse and negotiation of spousal relations within contemporary Evangelicalism. Ph.D. diss., University of Texas, Austin.

———. 1998. Changing of the gods: The gender and family discourse of American Evangelicalism in historical perspective. *The History of the Family* 3:97–117.

———. 1999. One step forward, one step back: "Progressive traditionalism" and the negotiation of domestic labor within Evangelical families. *Gender Issues* 17:40–64.

———. 2000. Breaking walls, raising fences: Masculinity, intimacy, and accountability among the promise keepers. *Sociology of Religion* 61:33–53.

Bloul, Rachel A. 1997. Victims or offenders? "Other" women French sexual politics. In *Embodied practices: Feminist perspectives on the body*, edited by K. Davis. Thousand Oaks, CA: Sage.

Bozorgmehr, Mehdi, Claudia Der-Martirosian, and Georges Sabagh. 1996. Middle Easterners: A new kind of immigrant. In *Ethnic Los Angeles*, edited by R. Waldinger and M. Bozorgmehr. New York: Russell Sage Foundation.

Brasher, Brenda E. 1998. *Godly women: Fundamentalism and female power*. New Brunswick, NJ: Rutgers University Press.

Brenner, Suzanne. 1996. Reconstructing self and society: Javanese Muslim women and the veil. *American Ethnologist* 23:673–97.

Britton, Dana M. 1997. Gendered organizational logic: Policy and practice in men's and women's prisons. *Gender & Society* 11:796–818.

Currie, Dawn H. 1997. Decoding femininity: Advertisements and their teenage readers. *Gender & Society* 11:453–57.

Davidman, Lynn. 1993. *Tradition in a rootless world: Women turn to Orthodox Judaism*. Berkeley: University of California Press.

Davis, Kathy, ed. 1997. *Embodied practices: Feminist perspectives on the body*. Thousand Oaks, CA: Sage.

Dellinger, Kirsten, and Christine L. Williams. 1997. Makeup at work: Negotiating appearance rules in the workplace. *Gender & Society* 11:151–77.

Dragadze, Tamara. 1994. Islam in Azerbaijan: The position of women. In *Muslim women's choices: Religious belief and social reality*, edited by C. F. El-Solh and J. Mabro. New York: Berg.

El-Guindi, Fadwa. 1981. Veiling Infitah with Muslim ethic: Egypt's contemporary Islamic movement. *Social Problems* 28:465–85.

———. 1983. Veiled activism: Egyptian women in the contemporary Islamic movement. *Mediterranean Peoples* 22/23:79–89.

El-Solh, Camillia Fawzi, and Judy Mabro, eds. 1994. *Muslim women's choices; Religious belief and social reality*. New York: Berg.

Esposito, John L., ed. 1995. *The Oxford encyclopedia of the modern Islamic world*. New York: Oxford University Press.

———. 1998. Women in Islam and Muslim societies. In *Islam, gender, and social change*, edited by Y. Y. Haddad and J. L. Esposito. New York: Oxford University Press.

Fernea, Elizabeth W. 1993. The veiled revolution. In *Everyday life in the Muslim Middle East*, edited by D. L. Bowen and E. A. Early. Bloomington: Indiana University Press.

———. 1998. *In search of Islamic feminism: One woman's journey*. New York: Doubleday.

Fox, Greer L. 1977. "Nice girl": Social control of women through a value construct. *Signs: Journal of Women in Culture and Society* 2:805–17.

Gallagher, Sally K., and Christian Smith. 1999. Symbolic traditionalism and pragmatic egalitarianism: Contemporary Evangelicals, families, and gender. *Gender & Society* 13:211–233.

Gerami, Shahin. 1996. *Women and fundamentalism: Islam and Christianity*. New York: Garland.

Ghanea Bassiri, Kambiz. 1997. *Competing visions of Islam in the United States: A study of Los Angeles*. London: Greenwood.

Gocek, Fatma M., and Shiva Balaghi, eds. 1994. *Reconstructing gender in the Middle East: Tradition, identity, and power*. New York: Columbia University Press.

Griffith, R. Marie. 1997. *God's daughters: Evangelical women and the power of submission*. Berkeley: University of California Press.

Haddad, Yvonne Yazbeck. 1991a. American foreign policy in the Middle East and its impact on the identity of Arab Muslims in the United States. In *The Muslims of America*, edited by Y. Y. Haddad. Oxford, UK: Oxford University Press.

———. 1991b. Introduction. In *The Muslims of America*, edited by Y. Y Haddad. Oxford, UK: Oxford University Press.

Hatem, Mervat F. 1994. Egyptian discourses on gender and political liberalization: Do secularist and Islamist views really differ? *Middle East Journal* 48:661–76.

Hermansen, Marcia K. 1991. Two-way acculturation: Muslim women in America between individual choice (liminality) and community affiliation (communitas). In *The Muslims of America*, edited by Y. Y. Haddad. Oxford, UK: Oxford University Press.

Hessini, Leila. 1994. Wearing the hijab in contemporary Morocco: Choice and identity. In *Reconstructing gender in the Middle East: Tradition, identity, and power*, edited by F. M. Gocek and S. Balaghi. New York: Columbia University Press.

Hollway, Wendy. 1995. Feminist discourses and women's heterosexual desire. In *Feminism and discourse*, edited by S. Wilkinson and C. Kitzinger. London: Sage.

Hunter, James Davison. 1994. *Before the shooting begins: Searching for democracy in America's culture war*. New York: Free Press.

Johnson, Steven A. 1991. Political activity of Muslims in America. In *The Muslims of America*, edited by Y. Y. Haddad. Oxford, UK: Oxford University Press.

Kadioglu, Ayse. 1994. Women's subordination in Turkey: Is Islam really the villain? *Middle East Journal* 48:645–60.

Kandiyoti, Deniz. 1988. Bargaining with patriarchy. *Gender & Society* 2:274–90.

———, ed. 1991. *Women, Islam & the state*. Philadelphia: Temple University Press.

———. 1992. Islam and patriarchy: A comparative perspective. In *Women in Middle Eastern history: Shifting boundaries in sex and gender*, edited by N. R. Keddie and B. Baron. New Haven, CT: Yale University Press.

Mahoney, Maureen A., and Barbara Yngvesson. 1992. The construction of subjectivity and the paradox of resistance: Reintegrating feminist anthropology and psychology. *Signs: Journal of Women in Culture and Society* 18:44–73.

Mann, Susan A., and Lori R. Kelley. 1997. Standing at the crossroads of modernist thought: Collins, Smith, and the new feminist epistemologies. *Gender & Society* 11:391–408.

Manning, Cristel. 1999. *God gave us the right: Conservative Catholic, Evangelical Protestant, and Orthodox Jewish women grapple with feminism*. New Brunswick, NJ: Rutgers University Press.

Memissi, Fatima. 1987. *Beyond the veil*. Rev. ed. Bloomington: Indiana University Press.

———. 1991. *The veil and the male elite: A feminist interpretation of women's rights in Islam*. Translated by Mary Jo Lakeland. New York: Addison-Wesley.

Mishler, Elliot G. 1986. *Research interviewing: Context and narrative*. Cambridge, MA: Harvard University Press.

Munson, Henry Jr. 1988. *Islam and revolution in the Middle East*. New Haven, CT: Yale University Press.

Odeh, Lama Abu. 1993. Post-colonial feminism and the veil: Thinking the difference. *Feminist Review* 43:26–37.

Papanek, Hanna. 1973. Purdah: Separate worlds and symbolic shelter. *Comparative Studies in Society and History* 15:289–325.

Philips, Abu Ameenah Bilal, and Jameelah Jones. 1985. *Polygamy in Islam*. Riyadh, Saudi Arabia: International Islamic Publishing House.

Schmidt, Alvin J. 1989. *Veiled and silenced: How culture shaped sexist theology*. Macon, GA: Mercer University Press.

Shaheed, Farida. 1994. Controlled or autonomous: Identity and the experience of the network, women living under Muslim laws. *Signs: Journal of Women in Culture and Society* 19:997–1019.

———. 1995. Networking for change: The role of women's groups in initiating dialogue on women's issues. In *Faith and freedom: Women's human rights in the Muslim world*, edited by M. Afkhami, New York: Syracuse University Press.

Sherif, Mostafa H. 1987. What is hijab? *The Muslim World* 77:151–63.

Shirazi-Mahajan, Faegheh. 1995. A dramaturgical approach to hijab in post-revolutionary Iran. *Journal of Critical Studies of the Middle East* 7 (fall): 35–51.

Siddiqi, Muhammad Iqbal. 1983. *Islam forbids free mixing of men and women*. Lahore, Pakistan: Kazi.

Smith, Dorothy E. 1987. *The everyday world as problematic: A feminist sociology*. Boston: Northeastern University Press.

Stacey, Judith. 1990. *Brave new families*. New York: Basic Books.

Stombler, Mindy, and Irene Padavic. 1997. Sister acts: Resisting men's domination in Black and white fraternity little sister programs. *Social Problems* 44:257–75.

Stone, Carol L. 1991. Estimate of Muslims living in America. In *The Muslims of America*, edited by Y. Y. Haddad. Oxford, UK: Oxford University Press.

Todd, Alexandra Dundas, and Sue Fisher, eds. 1988. *Gender and discourse: The power of talk*. Norwood, NJ: Ablex.

Walbridge, Linda S. 1997. *Without forgetting the imam: Lebanese Shi'ism in an American community*. Detroit, MI: Wayne State University Press.

Webster. Sheila K. 1984. Harim and hijab: Seclusive and exclusive aspects of traditional Muslim dwelling and dress. *Women's Studies International Forum* 7:251–57.

West, Candace, and Sarah Fenstermaker. 1995. Doing difference. *Gender & Society* 9:8–37.

Wodak, Ruth, ed. 1997. *Discourse and gender*. Thousand Oaks, CA: Sage.

"That's What a Man Is Supposed to Do": Compensatory Manhood Acts in an LGBT Christian Church

J. EDWARD SUMERAU

An emerging line of research shows that lesbian, gay, bisexual, and transgendered (LGBT) Christians face significant conflict between their sexual and religious identities (McQueeney 2009; Moon 2004; Thumma 1991; Wilcox 2003, 2009; Wolkomir 2006). Implications of these studies include that LGBT Christians draw on the "cultural toolkits" (Swidler 1986) of Christian and queer culture to create "safe spaces" for the processes of ideological, identity, and emotion work necessary for resolving their identity conflicts. They also suggest gay men are more likely to face such conflict (Rodriguez and Ouellette 2000a), and LGBT Christian organizations often become male dominated in terms of leadership, culture, and demographics over time (Wilcox 2009). While these studies have invigorated our understanding of LGBT Christian culture, they have thus far left the "politics of masculinity" (Messner 1997) among gay Christian men unexplored. How do gay Christian men construct identities as men, and what consequences do these actions have for the reproduction of inequality?

I examine these questions through an ethnographic study of a southeastern LGBT Christian organization. Specifically, I analyze how a group of gay Christian men, responding to sexist,

J. Edward Sumerau, "'That's What a Man Is Supposed to Do': Compensatory Manhood Acts in an LGBT Christian Church." *Gender & Society* 26 (June 2012): 461–87.

heterosexist, and religious stigma, as well as the acquisition of a new pastor, constructed "compensatory manhood acts," which refer to acts whereby subordinated men signify masculine selves by emphasizing elements of hegemonic masculinity (Schrock and Schwalbe 2009). In so doing, I synthesize and extend analyses of LGBT Christian cultures and masculinities by demonstrating how gay Christian men signify masculine selves, and the consequences these actions have for the reproduction of inequality. Importantly, it is not my intention to generalize my findings to the larger population of LGBT Christian churches. Rather, I use the data from this case to elaborate strategies of compensatory manhood acts subordinated groups of men may use in various social settings when they seek to compensate for their subordination in relation to other men and signify masculine selves (see Schwalbe et al. 2000).

The Social Construction of Masculinities

Over the past three decades, sociologists have demonstrated that men construct, enact, and negotiate a wide variety of masculinities shaped by both their social locations within interlocking systems of oppression, and local, regional, and global conceptions of what it means to be a man (see, e.g., Connell and Messerschmidt 2005; Messner 1997; Schrock and Schwalbe 2009). Rather than as a physical or personality trait embedded within male bodies, these studies conceptualize masculinities as collective forms of practice, belief, and interaction, which reproduce the subordination of women to men, and some men to others. These studies also show how the social construction of masculinities reproduces sexism (Kimmel 1996), heterosexism (Pascoe 2007), classism (Eastman and Schrock 2008), racism (Chen 1999), and ageism (Slevin and Linneman 2010). Overall, these studies suggest that understanding the reproduction of large-scale systems of inequality requires interrogating the social construction of masculinities.

Interrogating masculinities requires analyzing how men signify masculine selves. Following Goffman (1977), this process involves the dramaturgical work men do to establish and affirm the identity man (see also West and Zimmerman 1987). We may thus conceptualize masculine selves as the result of putting on a convincing "manhood act" (Schwalbe 2005). Schrock and Schwalbe (2009, 289) define "manhood acts" as "the identity work males do to claim membership in the dominant gender group, to maintain the social reality of the group, to elicit deference from others, and to maintain privileges vis-à-vis women." Whereas the elements of a convincing manhood act may vary historically and culturally and across different social settings, Schrock and Schwalbe (2009) argue that all such acts aim to signify a masculine self by exerting control over and resisting being controlled by others (see also Johnson 2005).

Interrogating masculinities, however, also requires making sense of "hegemonic masculinity" (Connell 1987, 1995; Connell and Messerschmidt 2005), or the most honored way to be a man in a given cultural or historical context. Even though very few men may enact the most honored version of manhood in a given culture or time, the hegemonic ideal typically carries enough symbolic weight to pervade the entire culture and provide the yardstick by which all performances of manhood are judged (Chen 1999; Connell 1987; Schrock and Schwalbe 2009). As Erving Goffman (1963, 128) observed:

> In an important sense there is only one unblushing male in America: a young, married, white, urban, northern, heterosexual, Protestant father of college education, fully employed, of good complexion, weight, and height, and a recent record in sports. Every American male tends to look out upon the world from this perspective.

As such, all blushing males, such as the gay men at the heart of this study, may feel the need to find ways to compensate for their subordination vis-à-vis the hegemonic ideal.

Historically, one strategy of compensation available to subordinated groups of men living within systems of oppression and privilege is the imitation of the hegemonic ideal (Connell 1995; Johnson 2005; Kimmel 1996). Since such systems are dominated by, identified with, and centered on the most honored way of being a man (Johnson 2005), this requires enacting and/or affirming the beliefs, values, characteristics, and practices of hegemonic masculinity (Chen 1999; Connell 1995; Kimmel 1996). At times, these men may engage in "compensatory manhood acts"—emphasizing and/or exaggerating elements of hegemonic masculinity to compensate for their subordination and signify masculine selves (Schrock and Schwalbe 2009).

Previous research has documented compensatory manhood acts in many social contexts. Some of the men in Snow and Anderson's (1987, 1362) study of the homeless, for example, used "fanciful identity assertions" to define their future or ideal selves as sexual, desirable, and powerful men capable of possessing female trophies. As one man stated, "Chicks are going to be all over us when we come back into town with our new suits and Corvettes. We'll have to get some cocaine too. Cocaine will get you women every time." Similarly, ethnographers have shown how male racial minorities (Anderson 1999; Chen 1999; Ferguson 2001), poor and working-class men (Eastman and Schrock 2008; MacLeod 1995; Schrock and Padavic 2007), and female-to-male transsexuals (Schilt 2006; Schilt and Westbrook 2009) engage in exaggerated displays of masculinity to compensate for their subordination in relation to the hegemonic ideal. In each case, subordinated men unable to enact the most honored form of manhood engage in compensatory manhood acts to differentiate themselves from women, and bolster their claims to privileges conferred on men in a patriarchal society.

Researchers have also documented how some men who identify as gay reject heterosexuality as an index of manhood while emphasizing conventional notions of masculinity. Specifically, these studies have shown how gay men compensate for their subordination and signify masculine selves by emphasizing larger bodies and muscularity (Hennen 2005), athletic ability (Anderson 2011), sexual risk-taking (Collins 2009; Green and Halkitis 2006), brotherhood and the devaluation of women (Yeung and Stombler 2000; Yeung, Stombler, and Wharton 2006), the punishment of male performances of femininity (Asencio 2011), youthfulness (Slevin and Linneman 2010), and expressions of "macho" fashion (Mosher, Levitt, and Manley 2006). Similarly, Wolkomir (2009, 507) showed how gay men in mixed-orientation marriages emphasized their ability to provide for their wives and children: "A man takes care of his wife and family, and I could still do that." Whether they stressed physical, sexual, or paternal prowess, gay men in each of these studies emphasized elements of the hegemonic ideal to signify creditable masculine selves.

Previous research has also revealed the importance of evaluating socially constructed notions of Christian manhood. Sociologists of religion, for example, have shown how heterosexual Christian men redefine notions of male headship and spousal authority (Bartkowski 2001; Gallagher and Smith 1999) and make sense of competing discourses of instrumental and affective masculinity (Bartkowski and Xu 2000; Gallagher and Wood 2005) by drawing on a combination of Christian and hegemonic notions of masculine authority. Similarly, scholars have revealed how heterosexual men in Christian subcultures (Wilkins 2009) and conservative Christian movements (Heath 2003; Robinson and Spivey 2007) emphasize immutable differences between women and men to reproduce masculine privilege. Whereas these studies suggest heterosexual Christian men may interpret manhood in a variety of ways, they also reveal that these efforts rely heavily on differentiating Christian men from women and other men.

Studies of gay Christian men, however, have generally neglected masculinities. Rather, these studies typically focus on how gay Christian men manage the emotional (Wolkomir 2006) and identity-based (Thumma 1991) dilemmas surrounding sexual and religious identity integration. When researchers have incorporated gender into their analyses, they have limited their focus to how notions of Black (McQueeney 2009; Pitt 2010) and Latino (Rodriguez and Ouellette 2000b) masculinities impact strategies of identity integration. Instead of evaluating the impact of gender on identity integration, the present study examines how gay Christian men draw on gendered, sexual, and religious discourses to construct compensatory manhood acts.

Finally, it is important to note that sociologists have tied the accomplishment of compensatory manhood acts to the reproduction of inequality (Schrock and Schwalbe 2009). Studies have shown, for example, how working-class men use violence to maintain control over women in heterosexual relationships (Pyke 1996). Similarly, researchers have shown how African American (Anderson 1999), working-class (MacLeod 1995), and homosexual (Yeung, Stombler, and Wharton 2006) men construct compensatory manhood acts in ways that unintentionally reproduce their own subordination. Although the gay Christian men I studied are in some ways unique, their example reveals how the construction of compensatory manhood acts is not only about resisting subordination but is also a means through which men may claim organizational power.

Setting and Method

Data for this study derive from participant observation in a church affiliated with the United Fellowship of Metropolitan Community Churches (UFMCC). The UFMCC is an international denomination composed of more than 300 congregations. It promotes an inclusive doctrine based on "the recognition of the inherent value of each individual regardless of sexual orientation, race, class, gender, gender identification, age, or abilities" (UFMCC 2009). The church examined here developed in 1993 when LGBT Christians who felt excluded by churches in their community formed two Bible study groups. Over the next 15 years, these groups expanded into a regular church that purchased its own property and held weekly services.

My involvement with Shepherd Church (all names are pseudonyms) began when I contacted their office and explained my interest in studying the organization. At the time, I was seeking a setting to study the development of local religious and LGBT organizations over time. The representative I spoke with explained that since they were currently without a pastor, I would need to propose my research interests to the board. At their next board meeting, I introduced myself as a bisexual, white, atheist male raised in a working-class Baptist home, and presented members with a proposal for my study, professional references, and some articles I wrote while working as a journalist. Two weeks later, the members granted my request to study the church.

Over the next 36 months, I observed and participated in worship services (190), board meetings (30), Bible studies (45), choir practices (10), outreach efforts (5), and social events (105) with members of Shepherd Church. I also collected newsletters, newspaper pieces, emails, hymnals, pamphlets, and publications by the congregation and the denomination. On average, I spent about one to three hours with members during each visit conducting informal interviews before and after each activity. Throughout my fieldwork, I tape-recorded every meeting and took shorthand notes whenever possible. Afterward, I used these resources to compose detailed field notes, transcribed audio recordings in full, and took notes on any materials gathered in the field (for gender and sexual demographics in Shepherd Church over time, see Table 1).

I also conducted 20 life history interviews with members of the church. Interviews lasted between three and four hours, and I tape-recorded and transcribed each one in full. Apart from using an interview guide that consisted of a list of orienting questions about members' religious and social background and involvement in the church, the interviews were unstructured. My sample consisted of eight white lesbian women, two African American lesbian women, and ten white gay men including the new pastor. Each respondent held informal and/or formal positions of power in the church at some point during my study. All respondents held middle- and upper-middle-class jobs, and all but one had been raised in Protestant churches.

It is important to note that the racial and class characteristics of Shepherd Church may have played a role in the men's construction of masculinities (for race and class demographics in Shepherd Church, see Table 2). Although studies of LGBT Christians have thus far left the construction of race, class, and gender identities unexplored, they have found that cultural notions of race, class, and gender impact the identity integration strategies of

TABLE 1. Gender and Sexual Characteristics of Shepherd Church over Time

Demographic Category	Subgroup Characteristics	Population at Time of Pastor's Arrival	Population One Year after Pastor's Arrival
Women	Lesbian	59 (60%)	15 (33%)
	Transsexual	3 (3%)	0 (0%)
	Heterosexual	4 (4%)	0 (0%)
	Total	66 (67%)	15 (33%)
Men	Gay	25 (26%)	30 (67%)
	Transsexual	3 (3%)	0 (0%)
	Bisexual	2 (2%)	0 (0%)
	Heterosexual	2 (2%)	0 (0%)
	Total	32 (33%)	30 (67%)
Total church	Total	98 (100%)	45 (100%)

Christian sexual minorities (see, e.g., McQueeney 2009; Pitt 2010; Rodriguez and Ouellette 2000b). In the case of Shepherd Church, the congregation was mostly white (88%) and middle- to upper-middle-class (90%) prior to the arrival of the pastor. These men's construction of compensatory manhood acts may well have benefited from their locations in privileged racial and class categories.

Regional and religious factors may also have impacted the compensatory strategies of these men. Their surrounding community, for example, consisted of a minimal LGBT public presence, well-organized local and state anti-gay political groups, and a religious atmosphere dominated by conservative Protestants. Further, the vast majority of these men were raised in the southeast and came from conservative Protestant backgrounds. In a similar fashion, the newly acquired pastor was a white, middle-class man raised in the Southern Baptist tradition, and had, prior to openly coming out as gay, held prominent positions in conservative Baptist churches in Virginia. These men's construction of compensatory manhood acts may thus have been influenced by their collective regional and religious interpretations of Christian manhood.

My analysis developed in an inductive fashion. Following the arrival of the new pastor, many men began emphasizing the importance of being Christian men. Drawing on elements of "grounded theory" (Charmaz 2006), I began coding my data for changes taking place in the church, and meanings of gender, sexuality, and Christianity promoted by the members, which revealed patterns that I sorted into thematic categories. Further, I examined the masculinities literature, and began to see the discourses mobilized by the pastor and gay men as part of the process through which they compensated for their subordination and signified masculine selves. Building on this insight, I generated labels to capture how they constructed compensatory manhood acts by (1) emphasizing paternal stewardship; (2) stressing emotional control and inherent rationality; and (3) defining intimate relationships in a Christian manner.

Problematizing Gay Christian Manhood

Prior to the arrival of the new pastor, women and men ran Shepherd Church in an egalitarian manner (see, e.g., Sumerau 2010; Sumerau and Schrock 2011). Specifically, they took turns leading worship services and Bible studies, holding formal positions of power, and delivering sermons and musical performances. Further, they stressed equal representation, sought to include all members in organizational decisions, and affirmed racial, gendered, classed, and sexual diversity in the church, thereby collectively establishing an LGBT Christian space that was growing in terms

TABLE 2. Race and Class Characteristics of Shepherd Church over Time

Race/Ethnic Category	Social Class Category	Population at Time of Pastor's Arrival	Population One Year after Pastor's Arrival
White	Upper class	12 (12%)	3 (7%)
	Middle class	58 (59%)	17 (38%)
	Lower class	18 (18%)	18 (40%)
	Total	88 (90%)	38 (84%)
Black	Middle class	2 (2%)	1 (2%)
	Lower class	3 (3%)	5 (11%)
	Total	5 (5%)	6 (13%)
Hispanic	Middle class	1 (1%)	1 (2%)
	Lower class	4 (4%)	0 (0%)
	Total	5 (5%)	1 (2%)
Total church	Total	98 (100%)	45 (100%)

of population and finances at the time of the pastor's arrival.

During this period of rapid growth, the vast majority of members expressed concerns about being taken seriously in the larger religious community. Specifically, they believed they needed to acquire the services of an ordained pastor in order to be a legitimate church. As a result, they began holding meetings and conference calls with the denomination. In response, the denomination selected three candidates, and the members had the opportunity to either veto or approve each candidate. Importantly, all three candidates were white, middle-class, gay men raised and trained in conservative Protestantism. After vetoing the first two candidates, the congregation approved and installed the final candidate.

The new pastor, however, brought a different image for the church. Specifically, he emphasized notions of Christian manhood predicated on masculine authority (see, e.g., Bartkowski 2001). As he explained to a group of men during his first week in the church:

> I think you have done well here with the lesbians running things, but inclusive doesn't mean anything goes. This is still a Christian church, and that means we have to act accordingly, and be responsible Christian men. Like a father does with his children, each of you needs to be the strong, dependable blocks we build this church on, and, like in a family, you have to model this behavior for the rest of the church.

Similar to members of the Promise Keepers (Heath 2003), the new pastor viewed masculine authority as a central element of both Christian manhood and a truly Christian organization.

The new pastor's arrival thus facilitated a dramatic transformation in Shepherd Church. Specifically, most of the gay men collaborated with the pastor to construct compensatory manhood acts. Four of the gay men, the majority of the lesbian women (44 of 59), and all of the bisexual, heterosexual, and transgendered women and men, however, began departing the organization in the months following the pastor's arrival. Rather than conform to the new "politics of masculinity" (Messner 1997) in the church, they formed a new Bible study group where they continued to promote their egalitarian version of Christianity.

It is important to note that the pastor's notion of Christian manhood may have been especially salient to the gay men at Shepherd Church because of painful experiences each of them faced in the course of their lives. Raised in conservative Christian churches, they all learned from an early age to base their sense of themselves as good people on their ability to be Christian men. Their development of homosexual identities, however, placed these claims in jeopardy. As a result, they experienced feelings of guilt, shame, and fear. As Michael recalled:

> I was supposed to grow up and be a man—be responsible for a wife and a family and my church. How was I supposed to do that? I remember feeling like my life was over. I had heard what those gay people were like; I wasn't like that: I was a good Christian man.

For Michael and the other gay men, being a Christian man was a "moral identity" (Katz 1975; McQueeney 2009). Each of these attributes signified his worth, character, and value as a person. Being gay, however, created the possibility that he was not a good person.

The men's experiences were especially traumatic because their identification as homosexuals violated what they believed were valid scriptural interpretations of the sanctity of heterosexual marriage and traditional, complementary gender roles (see Ammerman 1987; Bartkowski 2001). Specifically, most conservative Christian churches defined homosexuals as sinners and abominations in the eyes of God. As Marcus explained one morning after church:

> Growing up you heard about "those gay people" and how they were ruining the world, but it didn't really sink in until I realized I was one of "those people." Then, whoa man, I spent so many nights crying, praying and asking why God would do this to me. Why did I have to be damned? Why couldn't I be good, just why?

For Marcus and the others, identifying as gay was similar to receiving a death sentence, and deemed their Christian identities invalid. As others have noted (see, e.g., Wilcox 2003), they joined an LGBT church in search of a "safe space" to express their Christian *and* sexual identities.

Their painful experiences, however, were not limited to their sexual and religious identities. Raised in conservative Christian churches, they also learned from an early age that God's will is expressed in a divine mandate requiring women's submission and men's leadership for the promotion of an ideal Christian society (see also Wolkomir 2006). Specifically, they learned that real men headed churches and families by leading, protecting, and providing for their wives, children, and fellow Christians (Ammerman 1987). As Micah noted:

> I still get it every time I go home: "When you going to grow up and be a man, boy?" and "What kind of man don't have no wife or kids?" Oh, and "When you goin' to grow out of the gay stuff?" It's hard sometimes because that's what a man is supposed to do right—raise a family, take care of a wife. What does that say about me?

For Micah and many others, identifying as homosexual generated a direct attack on their manhood. Similar to men in "bear" groups (Hennen 2005) and gay fraternities (Yeung, Stombler, and Wharton 2006), they sought to claim masculine selves denied to them in the larger social world. In the following sections, I examine how the new pastor and the gay men who remained at Shepherd Church accomplished this by constructing compensatory manhood acts.

Constructing Gay Christian Manhood

What follows is an analysis of how the gay men at Shepherd Church constructed compensatory manhood acts. First, I examine how they constructed compensatory manhood acts by emphasizing paternal stewardship over the church and the LGBT community. Specifically, this strategy involved defining themselves as fatherly guides and financial providers. Then, I show how they constructed compensatory manhood acts by stressing emotional control and inherent rationality to differentiate themselves from women and effeminate men. Finally, I analyze how they constructed compensatory manhood acts by defining intimate relationships in a Christian manner, thus emphasizing responsible sexual conduct, monogamy, and immutable sexual natures. While these strategies allowed them to signify masculine selves, they also reproduced the superiority of men at the expense of women and sexual minorities.

Emphasizing Paternal Stewardship

On his arrival, the new pastor stressed resisting stereotypical depictions of homosexual men as selfish and irresponsible children. As he stated in his first sermon, the members of Shepherd Church could resist such stereotypes by being good stewards of their church:

> We all know how others try to clobber us gay guys by saying we're anti-family or irresponsible children who only want to play. Well, we know different, and part of our job as men is to show the world we are good providers and leaders in our communities.

Importantly, the gay men at Shepherd Church were already intimately familiar with these cultural depictions of homosexual men. As Troy explained during one Bible Study:

> You know how they see us, right? They talk about us like we're kids. We're too busy doing our makeup and partying to raise a family or support our partners or any of the other things real men do with their time or, more likely, with their money.

Seeking to refute such depictions, they constructed compensatory manhood acts by emphasizing paternal stewardship. Specifically, they defined themselves as fatherly guides and financial providers for women and other sexual minorities.

These gay men constructed identities as Christian men by defining themselves as fatherly guides providing the necessary leadership for their communities to survive. This tactic involved defining other sexual minorities as children requiring supervision. As Matthew noted:

> It's like being a father to your own kids. Many of these folks that come here and to other community events are fresh out of the closet, and, like children, they have no clue how to look out for themselves. That's where we come in. We can come to them like parents, provide them with the wisdom and experience we have, and they'll be better for it.

In a similar fashion, Tommy explained, during a Bible study, "Well, it's understandable that a lot of these little ones don't realize all the fighting and struggles we went through building this community. They just need some good fatherly teaching." Echoing others, Matthew and Tommy emphasized the importance of sharing the "wisdom and experience" they possessed with the "kids" or "children" that "have no clue" how to exist within an LGBT community. Similar to members of the Promise Keepers (Heath 2003), they constructed compensatory manhood acts by defining themselves as fatherly guides capable of providing for less informed others.

The gay men at Shepherd Church also constructed compensatory manhood acts by defining women as selfish creatures in need of fatherly guidance. As Micah noted:

> It's not a bad thing, just how they are, but the lesbians jumping beds and relationships so often that they often lose sight of what matters. It's just how they are. We have to kind of pick up the slack. It's not that they're bad people, but they need some strong guidance.

Similarly, Dante observed, "It's not a lesbian thing, I don't think. My mom's that way. Women are kind of flighty, I guess, and that's okay because, like in a family, the men can make sure things run smooth." Echoing others, Dante and Micah defined "women" as "kind of flighty" and in need of the guidance "men" could provide. Similar to gay men in mixed-orientation marriages (Wolkomir 2009), they defined women as subordinates in need of their guidance and direction.

After the pastor's arrival, these gay men also began defining themselves as financial providers. Specifically, this strategy involved differentiating between male providers and others:

> Tommy says, "I think it's important to remember this is our church, and we have a responsibility to take care of it." Speaking up, Maria says, "Well, anyone can help with the cleaning. Alice and I have been doing it the last couple weeks, and it's important." The Pastor holds out his hand, and says, "That is good work ya'll are doing, Maria, but more importantly, like the check John and Michael put in this morning, is the financial well-being of the church. I mean, we can worship in some dirt, but we need for all of us to come together to take care of finances and be real stewards for our father's house."

In moments like this, they defined "financial" provision as the primary form of Christian stewardship. Whereas "anyone" could "help with the cleaning," they downplayed these traditionally feminine activities and emphasized the "financial well-being" of the church.

Importantly, the gay men at Shepherd Church often explicitly invoked gender when discussing financial provision without women around. As Marcus explained, "Well, it's a man job to bring in the money, and so it's okay that the lesbians don't kick in as much cash, but it's disappointing sometimes, but that's what men are supposed to do, right?" Marcus and others defined bringing in money as an activity that "men are supposed to do" while asserting that "the lesbians" often did not do so anyway. Similarly, they often defined financial provision as an essential element of manhood. As the Pastor observed, "It's important to recognize women trying to contribute, but it's more important to make sure the men understand it's their job, their responsibility, their calling from God." Echoing leaders of the ex-gay movement (Robinson and Spivey 2007), the pastor defined financial provision as a "calling," a "responsibility," and a "job" men receive from God, and emphasized "making sure the men understand" God's plan. On the contrary, congregational logs revealed that women often contributed more money than men. Importantly, none of the men ever mentioned this. In a culture where breadwinning is interpreted as evidence of a masculine self (see Kimmel 1996), the men may have ignored this information to preserve their compensatory manhood acts from possible challenges.

Overall, the gay men at Shepherd Church constructed compensatory manhood acts by emphasizing paternal stewardship over the church and the larger LGBT community. In so doing, however, they reproduced cultural notions of male supremacy by defining women and other sexual minorities as irresponsible children incapable of taking care of themselves (see Kimmel 1996). Similar to leaders of the ex-gay Christian movement (Robinson and Spivey 2007), men active in the Promise Keepers (Heath 2003), and gay men in mixed-orientation marriages (Wolkomir 2009), they constructed identities as men by reproducing the supremacy of fatherly guidance, male headship, and breadwinning. As such, their compensatory manhood acts reproduced the elevation of men at the expense of women and sexual minorities.

Stressing Emotional Control and Inherent Rationality

On his arrival, the new pastor also stressed resisting stereotypical depictions of homosexual men as overly emotional and effeminate. As he stated in the first Bible study I attended where only men were present, the gay men at Shepherd Church could resist such stereotypes by controlling their emotions and drawing on their inherent rationality:

> It's important to talk about how we go about handling our emotions during these changing times. As men, we all know that the media seems to guess we are all weepy and girly like women, but we know, probably better than most, that our Father blessed us with an inherent rationality that we can draw on in times of struggle, and it's important for us all to do this and keep our emotions in check as we make necessary changes for the church.

Importantly, the gay men at Shepherd Church were already well versed in the importance of emotional control. As Michael noted in an interview:

> Sometimes, life can be hell. People will be really nasty when they hear you're a gay. Sissy, wimp, and fag are, like, words, but fists and damnation leave some deep marks. As a man, it's hard to control your feelings and deal with the pain; it's hard, but it's important.

Similarly, Troy recalled, "It was like in high school, if you lost control, even for a second let a tear slip, or your voice crack, you were automatically a queeny bitch." Seeking to refute depictions of overly emotional, effeminate homosexual men, they constructed compensatory manhood acts by stressing emotional control and inherent rationality.

These gay men constructed identities as men by stressing emotional control. This strategy often involved making references to Biblical figures that suffered unfairly while remaining composed and faithful to God. As the pastor argued during one Bible study:

> "Now, you have to remember that it wasn't easy," the pastor says while Tommy passes the candy jar around the table. "I mean, Paul had it rough, and he could have sat down on the edge of the cliff and cried "Woe is me!" I don't think anyone would have blamed him, just like no one might blame some of us after the discrimination our people have faced." As he finishes speaking, four men offer "amens." Smiling, the pastor continues, "What we have to remember, like Paul did, is that God is with us, and we will be okay and make it through if we don't give up, don't give in. Part of that is keeping our emotions, our grief, our tears in check—there is no time for tears when you're working for God!"

Similarly, Daniel noted, "It's like a fight, you can't wimp out like some sissy or little girl. When things are hard, and they can be really hard, you just have to have faith and fight on." Echoing these sentiments, Jamie observed, "We all learned crying and whining is for queens. Real men have to stand up, not take stuff from bigots and idiots." As these statements reveal, the gay men at Shepherd Church defined emotional control as central to manhood, and the expression of emotions as something that only a "sissy or little girl" would do. Similar to mixed-martial arts fighters (see Vaccarro, Schrock, and McCabe 2011), these men thus constructed compensatory manhood acts by defining the expression of emotions as inherently unmanly.

They also constructed compensatory manhood acts by explicitly defining emotional display as feminine and differentiating themselves from women. As Donny stated:

> "The way those women were just a-crying, I can't imagine acting like that," he says while nudging my arm. Puzzled, I ask, "You do realize Manny was crying as loud as any of the women?" Smiling, he responds, "I said 'those women,' didn't I? You've met Manny before, if that ain't a true-blue queen I don't know who is, probably has more right to the title 'woman' than any of the others with all the whining and carrying on he does."

Similarly, Martin explained after a worship service, "I swear, those queens, the lesbian ones and the gay ones, give us such a bad name. Look at them crying over photos and such, you wouldn't catch me dead doin' that, damn girls." Echoing Donny and others, Martin considered that "crying" in the presence of others was something that "damn girls" and "queens" did, which gave real gay men a "bad name." Further, as Donny's comments suggest, this type of behavior could disqualify males from the identity "man." Similar to some men in batterer intervention programs (Schrock and Padavic 2007), these gay men constructed compensatory manhood acts by defining emotional control as masculine and emotional expression as feminine.

These gay men also constructed identities as men by stressing inherent rationality. Specifically, they stressed the rational nature of men while accusing lesbians of falling victim to emotions. The following field note provides a typical example:

> Troy turns to James and I, and says, "You hear Jamie saying there's a new sheriff in town now that he's on the board," and James responds, "Well, I don't know what you think, but I got to say, good, it's just like bringing in the pastor. We need real leadership, no more of this lesbian drama and funny business. We need to focus on what really matters and how we can grow as a church." Chuckling and handing me a drink, Troy says, "Well, I can agree there. Sometimes they just, I don't know, things get so heated, so crazy, it seems like we need to make decisions with more composure or something."

Similarly, the pastor noted, "I don't know. I've dealt with lesbians before, but these just seem to take everything so personal. Real decision making needs to leave all those feelings at the door." As these examples reveal, these gay men stressed leaving "feelings" and "personal" concerns out of the "real decision making" while equating female leadership with "drama," "funny business," and "heated" or "crazy" decision making lacking "composure." Similar to how lawyers (Pierce 1995) define rationality as masculine, they constructed compensatory manhood acts by suggesting they, and not women, possessed the inherent rationality necessary to lead the church.

Further, they claimed men's inherent rationality made them naturally more suited for leadership. As Tommy noted, "Men are just built to make decisions, like my own talents for taking care of things; that's just something inside me." Similarly, Martin noted, "I think sometimes the drama gets the best of women, but it's not their fault, they're not built like us, and that's just how it is. Men just seem to know how to handle the important stuff." Micah also observed, "Sometimes I think maybe God did just make us different. I know a lot of people have left because they liked it better with the ladies running things, but it seems so much smoother, like a well-oiled machine now." These gay men thus stressed their own inherent ability to lead, and defined their God-given rationality as greater than the "drama" of the "ladies." Similar to how ex-gay Christian advocates define masculinity as a God-given good to rationalize the use of intervention therapies (Robinson and Spivey 2007), they constructed identities as men by symbolically positioning themselves above supposedly irrational women.

The gay men at Shepherd Church thus constructed compensatory manhood acts by stressing emotional control and inherent rationality. Similar to men in batterer intervention programs (Schrock and Padavic 2007), law firms (Pierce 1995), gay and ex-gay Christian support groups (Wolkomir 2006), ex-gay ministries (Robinson and Spivey 2007), and mixed-martial arts groups (Vaccarro, Schrock, and McCabe 2011), they constructed identities as men by reproducing a long-held cultural mandate that "real men" control their emotions (see Kimmel 1996). Whereas these strategies allowed them to construct identities as men, they relied on depictions of women as emotionally unstable and incapable of leadership, reproducing the subordination of women by perpetuating stereotypical depictions of immutable differences between feminine and masculine emotional subjectivity (see Schwalbe et al. 2000).

Defining Intimate Relationships in a Christian Manner

On his arrival, the new pastor also emphasized resisting cultural depictions of homosexual men as sexually promiscuous. As he told a group of men at the first fellowship dinner he attended, they could accomplish this by following Christian principles:

> As gay men, we have to be careful about our relationships. There are those out there just looking to clobber us and call us sickos, but if we model respectable, Christian, monogamous, and committed relationships, in time those same people will welcome us into the fold like states that have begun to recognize gay marriages.

Importantly, these gay men were already acutely aware of these issues. As Barney explained:

> It's all over the place, this silly belief that all we do is screw and screw and screw. Now, don't get me wrong, I'm a man so I definitely like to screw. But we're not all roaming around looking in every corner for a piece of tail—that's just crazy!

Seeking to refute such depictions, these gay men constructed compensatory manhood acts by defining intimate relationships in a Christian manner. Although they could have interpreted Christian principles regarding intimate relationships in a variety of ways (see Gallagher and Wood 2005), they defined Christian intimacy in ways that symbolically positioned themselves above supposedly promiscuous lesbians, bisexuals, and polyamorous others (see also Wilkins 2009).

The gay men at Shepherd Church constructed compensatory manhood acts by emphasizing responsible sexual conduct. This was especially true for single men, and men who had recently come out of the closet. Typically, they focused on using protection and viewing sex as part of a quest for a long-term relationship. As the new pastor explained in an interview:

> Like any other man, the boys coming out of the closet feel like they gotta get their numbers up. But what's important for them to know is it's not about being gay, it's about becoming responsible gay Christian men. It's not about who you sleep with, but how you do it. It's about building relationships, healthy exchanges between caring adults that could lead to more than a hook-up, and it's about being safe.

Similarly, Martin noted during a social gathering, "Oh, we can be as nasty as anyone, but the point is finding that special someone, not just out doing everything for the sake of doing it." As these illustrations reveal, these gay men emphasized forming "healthy, committed, adult relationships" that "could possibly lead" to something more serious, and "being safe" in regard to diseases and hook-ups. At the same time, they echoed elements of hegemonic masculinity by asserting that, "like any other man," all gay men would naturally seek to "get their numbers up."

Since single men were in much shorter supply in the church, the primary way these gay men constructed compensatory manhood acts involved emphasizing monogamy. Similar to some conservative Christian interpretations of heterosexual marriage (see Bartkowski 2001), this strategy involved defining monogamous homosexuality as the ultimate expression of God's will. Specifically, church members began holding holy unions, relationship workshops, couples retreats, and major anniversary festivities for committed couples after the arrival of the new pastor. As Michael observed during an anniversary celebration, "One thing about being back in the church is the opportunity to live right, settle down with a partner, and make a home together just like God intends." Similarly, Dante explained during a Bible study, "The whole point of this life, or the way I read the Bible, is to find someone special, someone you feel fits you right, and build a committed relationship." Echoing other men in the church as well as many heterosexual Christians, these gay men constructed compensatory manhood acts by defining monogamy as the way to "live right," and "the whole point of this life" according to the "Bible."

Whereas the dual emphasis on responsible sexual conduct and homosexual monogamy challenged dominant Christian conceptions of homosexuality, gay men at Shepherd Church also constructed compensatory manhood acts by using these discourses to denigrate promiscuity on the part of lesbian, gay, and bisexual others. The following field note excerpt offers an example:

> Barney asks, "So what does a lesbian bring to a second date?" I say, "What?" Chuckling erupts as Barney says, "A moving van," and slaps me on the back. Allan adds, "Don't get me wrong, the lesbian drama is a lot of fun, but sometimes I wish they would grow up." Patrick adds, "Well, it's just weird, the way women hop from relationship to relationship, from bed to bed; makes me wonder if there is something about the cunt that causes all the heterosexual adultery out there." Grinning at the laughter, he continues, "Men just aren't like that, we get around and then find a partner; women just go crazy, on to the next every two weeks or so. It's freakin' scary!" Softly, Martin adds, "It's just un-Christian, I think, and maybe that's why they have so many troubles, the lot of them."

In exchanges like these, gay men denigrated lesbians for failing to obtain long-term monogamous relationships. While these men were obviously aware of stereotypical depictions of lesbians, they reinterpreted such depictions to proclaim their own superiority. Rather than simply as an example of getting their numbers up, they defined lesbian serial monogamy as evidence of immaturity and immorality. Similarly, many men expressed dismay and even disgust at the dating practices of lesbians. As Troy explained, "It's just odd, hopping around the way they do. It's just unseemly, and it makes the rest of us look bad." Echoing others, Troy felt the way lesbians "hop from relationship to relationship, from bed to bed" made gay men "look bad," and, like Patrick and Martin, he felt the way "women just go crazy" was "just unseemly" and "un-Christian." Similar to how some boys use language to turn girls into props for signifying heterosexuality (Pascoe 2007) and some female rugby players use notions of femininity to distance themselves from lesbians (Ezzell 2009), these men used their definition of monogamy to turn lesbians into props for constructing compensatory manhood acts.

These gay men also constructed compensatory manhood acts by emphasizing immutable sexual natures. Specifically, this strategy involved defining bisexual and polyamorous desires as a sign of weakness or an inability to accept one's sexuality. As Micah explained in an interview:

> In my experience, bisexuality doesn't exist. Don't get me wrong, I messed with a girl or two before I accepted that I was gay. But I feel like bisexual is

just for before they realize if they are gay or straight. I think you're just born one way or another.

For Micah and many others, bisexuality was not a possibility. Most of the men felt they had been "born" gay, and just did not "realize" it until a certain point in their lives. As the pastor observed: "Bisexuality is tricky; I mean, I was just talking to Dana and, I don't know, sometimes I think ya'll need to get off the fence, but other times I don't know." Echoing the pastor, these gay men often spoke of bisexual and polyamorous others as "on the fence" or "in between" sexualitics. Similar to many Christian treatments of homosexuality (see Moon 2004), they sanctified immutable sexual natures by dismissing alternate sexual desires and practices.

Because of the emphasis on immutable sexualities, bisexual and polyamorous members often faced the same conflicts lesbian women and gay men face in other churches. As Dana, a bisexual man, noted, "They're as bad as the Baptists. They want me to join the opposite team, but it's the same damn message—narrow-minded bullshit." Further, many gay men spoke of "accepting your God-given sexuality" and your "sexual nature." As Martin noted at a gathering:

> I think people need to be honest with themselves. We're all born gay or straight. We all know this. God doesn't mention other options in the Bible, and why should we expect otherwise? The point is to find a partner, a companion, a lover, and how are you supposed to do that playing both sides of the field? It seems weird to associate with the bisexuals, and poly-whatevers in politics. It makes the rest of us look like freaks.

Echoing Christian notions of immutable sexual natures, Martin and others stressed an obligation to follow the sexual design laid down by "God" in the "Bible," and to recognize that "we're all born gay or straight" so we should not "expect otherwise" or "associate" with "bisexuals," "poly-whatevers," or other "freaks." Similar to ex-gay Christian depictions of homosexuals and feminists (Robinson and Spivey 2007), these gay men constructed compensatory manhood acts by differentiating themselves from unnatural deviants unwilling to submit to the demands of God.

In sum, the gay men at Shepherd Church constructed compensatory manhood acts by defining intimate relationships in a Christian manner. In so doing, however, they reproduced narrow definitions of sexuality often used to justify the subordination of sexual minorities in mainstream Christianity (see, e.g., Wilcox 2009; Wolkomir 2006). Further, they accomplished this by turning women into scapegoats, and symbolically positioning the sexual desires of gay men above those of lesbians, bisexuals, and polyamorous people. As such, their construction of compensatory manhood acts ultimately reproduced sexist and heterosexist notions of sexuality.

Conclusion

The gay men at Shepherd Church learned from an early age to base their perceptions of themselves as good people on their ability to be Christian men. Their development of homosexual identities, however, placed these claims in jeopardy. While they could have rejected dominant notions of manhood, as they all once had and those who left the church continued to do, the arrival of a new pastor provided them with an opportunity to go in a different direction. As a result, they worked with the pastor to construct compensatory manhood acts—emphasizing elements of hegemonic masculinity to compensate for their subordination and signify masculine selves. Specifically, they did so by emphasizing paternal stewardship, stressing emotional control and inherent rationality, and defining intimate relationships in a Christian manner.

While their construction of compensatory manhood acts allowed them to successfully compensate for their subordination and signify masculine selves, it also reproduced cultural notions that facilitate the subordination of women and alternative sexualities. By characterizing women as overly emotional and incapable of handling leadership positions, for example, they reproduced conventional gendered discourses used to justify masculine authority in occupational (Padavic 1991), religious (Robinson and Spivey 2007), and legal (Pierce 1995) settings. Similarly, their promotion of immutable sexual natures reproduced rhetoric (see, e.g., Moon 2004) used to deny equal rights to LGBT people. Whereas religious researchers have sought to understand why LGBT churches tend to become male dominated in terms of leadership, demographics, and culture (see, e.g., Wilcox 2009), these findings reveal that part of this answer may lie in the "politics of masculinity" (Messner 1997) promoted in these social settings.

These findings also support research on the impact of cultural notions of masculinity on gay Christian men (see, e.g., McQueeney 2009; Pitt 2010; Rodriguez and Ouellette 2000b), and extend this research by revealing how gay Christian men draw on conventional notions of gender, sexuality, and religion to construct compensatory manhood acts. Specifically, the gay Christian men at Shepherd Church drew on notions of Christian manhood to deflect cultural stigma against homosexual men, fashion creditable masculine selves, and claim gender-based privilege in their local organization. Similar to leaders of conservative Christian groups, such as the Promise Keepers (Heath 2003) and the ex-gay ministries (Robinson and Spivey 2007), they promoted a "politics of masculinity" (Messner 1997) characterized by the elevation of men at the expense of women and other sexual minorities. Whereas researchers have generally treated LGBT and conservative Christian groups as purely oppositional forces (see, e.g., Wolkomir 2006), the case of Shepherd Church suggests that in some cases these organizations may share more similarities than previously thought. These findings thus reveal the importance of examining and comparing the social construction of masculinities in specific religious settings.

These findings also extend previous treatments of compensatory manhood acts by drawing our attention to the ways subordinated men may use such actions to claim power over women and effeminate men. Whereas previous studies have shown how subordinated men construct compensatory manhood acts to claim power over women in intimate relationships (Pyke 1996), they have generally focused on how such actions unintentionally reproduce subordinated men's *own* disadvantage (see, e.g., Anderson 1999; MacLeod 1995; Yeung, Stombler, and Wharton 2006). The gay Christian men at Shepherd Church, however, constructed compensatory manhood acts in ways that explicitly defined women and other sexual minorities as inferior beings. While these actions did in fact reproduce cultural notions that facilitate the oppression of gay men, they also reproduced societal patterns of gender inequality by justifying the superiority of men within the context of their church. These findings thus reveal the importance of addressing not only how subordinated men compensate for their disadvantage at the societal level but also how such actions may ultimately result in the oppression of women and sexual minorities in local settings.

These findings also reveal the necessity of examining how subordinated men construct compensatory manhood acts in ways that simultaneously deflect stigma *and* claim organizational power over women. Whereas previous studies of subordinated men generally focus on *either* attempts to deflect stigma or efforts to claim privileges over women, the case of Shepherd Church reveals that these may often be interrelated results of the construction of compensatory manhood acts. Further, examples of this interrelation may be seen in many arenas where subordinated men seek to resist controlling images while bolstering claims to male privilege. African American men during the Civil Rights movement, for example, sought to de-stigmatize cultural notions of Black men while devaluing the contributions of African American women (see, e.g., Collins 2000). In a similar fashion, poor and working-class men may fashion themselves as hard workers while denigrating women who enter their occupational domains (see, e.g., Padavic 1991). Unraveling the ways subordinated men may accomplish these interrelated goals, however, requires asking questions beyond the scope of the present study. Researchers could, for example, examine how subordinated men accomplish these goals in nonreligious settings, such as social movement organizations, occupations, and schools. Further, researchers could examine what role women might play in the construction of compensatory manhood acts as well as the ways women may resist such acts. Finally, researchers should explore the ways that cultural notions of race, class, age, and/or nationality might play a role in these actions.

These findings also demonstrate the importance of examining when and where subordinated men are more likely to engage in strategies of compensation. Previous studies have, for example, conceptualized men's strategies of compensation as—seemingly automatic—responses to marginalization vis-à-vis the hegemonic ideal (see, e.g., Connell and Messerschmidt 2005; Schrock and Schwalbe 2009). In the case of Shepherd Church, however, all the gay men experienced marginalization in relation to the most honored form of manhood, and yet none of them constructed compensatory manhood acts prior to the arrival of the new pastor. Rather than merely a reaction to religious and/or sexual marginalization, their construction of compensatory manhood acts relied on the establishment of organizational leadership conducive to the elevation of men at the expense of women. Whereas future research may reveal important variations, these findings suggest that subordinated men may be more likely to construct compensatory manhood acts when they find themselves in settings where organizational leaders promote and affirm masculine authority and privilege (see also Dellinger 2004).

To fully understand the reproduction of gender and sexual inequality, we must analyze how subordinated men construct identities as men and the consequences of these actions (Schrock and Schwalbe 2009). Specifically, this will require critically investigating how men who belong to marginalized social groups interpret notions of manhood as well as the factors that lead some men to act in ways that reproduce the elevation of men at the expense of women and sexual minorities. As the case of Shepherd Church reveals, the construction of compensatory manhood acts relies on both the adoption of notions of male supremacy and organizational conditions conducive to the subordination of women. Unraveling and comparing the variations in compensatory manhood acts and, more generally, the multitude of ways men collaborate to signify, interpret, and affirm the oppression of women and sexual minorities, may deepen our understanding of the reproduction of inequality as well as possibilities for social change.

References

Ammerman, Nancy T. 1987. *Bible believers: Fundamentalists in the modern world*. New Brunswick, NJ: Rutgers University Press.

Anderson, Elijah. 1999. *Code of the Street: Decency, violence and the moral life of the inner city*. New York: Norton.

Anderson, Eric. 2011. Updating the outcome: Gay athletes, straight teams, and coming out in educationally based sports teams. *Gender & Society* 25:250–68.

Asencio, Marysol. 2011. Locas, respect, and masculinity: Gender conformity in migrant Puerto Rican gay masculinities. *Gender & Society* 25:335–54.

Bartkowski, John. 2001. *Remaking the Godly marriage: Gender negotiation in evangelical families*. New Brunswick, NJ: Rutgers University Press.

Bartkowski, John, and Xiaohe Xu. 2000. Distant patriarchs or expressive dads? The discourse and practice of fathering in conservative Protestant families. *Sociological Quarterly* 41:465–85.

Charmaz, Kathy C. 2006. *Constructing grounded theory: A practical guide through qualitative analysis*. Thousand Oaks, CA: Sage.

Chen, Anthony S. 1999. Lives at the center of the periphery, lives at the periphery of the center: Chinese American masculinities and bargaining with hegemony. *Gender & Society* 13:584–607.

Collins, Dana. 2009. "We're there and queer": Homonormative mobility and lived experience among gay expatriates in Manila. *Gender & Society* 23:465–93.

Collins, Patricia Hill. 2000. *Black feminist thought: Knowledge, consciousness, and the politics of empowerment*. New York: Routledge.

Connell, R. W. 1987. *Gender and power*. Stanford, CA: Stanford University Press.

Connell, R. W. 1995. *Masculinities*. Los Angeles: University of California Press.

Connell, R. W., and James W. Messerschmidt. 2005. Hegemonic masculinity: Rethinking the concept. *Gender & Society* 19:829–59.

Dellinger, Kirsten. 2004. Masculinities in "safe" and "embattled" organizations: Accounting for pornographic and feminist magazines. *Gender & Society* 18:545–66.

Eastman, Jason T., and Douglas P. Schrock. 2008. Southern rock musicians' construction of white trash. *Race, Gender & Class* 15:205–19.

Ezzell, Matthew B. 2009. "Barbie dolls" on the pitch: Identity work, defensive othering, and inequality in women's rugby. *Social Problems* 56:111–31.

Ferguson, Ann Arnett. 2001. *Bad boys: Public schools in the making of Black masculinity*. Ann Arbor: University of Michigan Press.

Gallagher, Sally K., and Christian Smith. 1999. Symbolic traditionalism and pragmatic egalitarianism: Contemporary evangelicals, family, and gender. *Gender & Society* 13:211–33.

Gallagher, Sally K., and Sabrina L. Wood. 2005. Godly manhood going wild?: Transformations in conservative Protestant masculinity. *Sociology of Religion* 66:135–60.

Goffman, Erving. 1963. *Stigma: Notes on the management of spoiled identity*. Englewood Cliffs, NJ: Prentice-Hall.

Goffman, Erving. 1977. The arrangement between the sexes. *Theory and Society* 4:301–31.

Green, Adam I., and Perry N. Halkitis. 2006. Crystal methamphetamine and sexual sociality in an urban gay subculture: An elective affinity. *Culture, Health & Sexuality* 8:317–33.

Heath, Melanie. 2003. Soft-boiled masculinity: Renegotiating gender and racial ideologies in the Promise Keepers movement. *Gender & Society* 17:423–44.

Hennen, Peter. 2005. Bear bodies, bear masculinity: Recuperation, resistance, or retreat? *Gender & Society* 19:25–43.

Johnson, Allan G. 2005. *The gender knot: Unraveling our patriarchal legacy*. Philadelphia: Temple University Press.

Katz, Jack. 1975. Essences as moral identities: Verifiability and responsibility in imputations of deviance and charisma. *American Journal of Sociology* 80:1369–90.

Kimmel, Michael. 1996. *Manhood in America: A cultural history*. New York: Free Press.

MacLeod, Jay. 1995. *Ain't no makin' it: Aspirations and attainment in a low-income neighborhood*. Boulder, CO: Westview.

McQueeney, Krista. 2009. "We are God's children, y'all": Race, gender, and sexuality in lesbian-and-gay-affirming congregations. *Social Problems* 56:151–73.

Messner, Michael A. 1997. *The politics of masculinities: Men in movements*. Thousand Oaks, CA: Sage.

Moon, Dawne. 2004. *God, sex, and politics: Homosexuality and everyday theologies*. Chicago, IL: University of Chicago Press.

Mosher, Chad M., Heidi M. Levitt, and Eric Manley. 2006. Layers of leather: The identity formation of Leathermen as a process of transforming meanings of masculinity. *Journal of Homosexuality* 51:93–123.

Padavic, Irene. 1991. The re-creation of gender in a male workplace. *Symbolic Interaction* 14:279–94.

Pascoe, C. J. 2007. *Dude, you're a fag: Masculinity and sexuality in high school*. Berkeley: University of California Press.

Pierce, Jennifer. 1995. *Gender trials: Emotional lives of contemporary law firms*. Berkeley: University of California Press.

Pitt, Richard N. 2010. "Still looking for my Jonathan": Gay Black men's management of religious and sexual identity conflicts. *Journal of Homosexuality* 57:39–53.

Pyke, Karen D. 1996. Class-based masculinities: The interdependence of gender, class, and interpersonal power. *Gender & Society* 10:527–49.

Robinson, Christine M., and Sue E. Spivey. 2007. The politics of masculinity and the Ex-Gay movement. *Gender & Society* 21:650–75.

Rodriguez, Eric M., and Suzanne C. Ouellette. 2000a. Gay and lesbian Christians: Homosexual and religious identity integration in the members and participants of a gay-positive church. *Journal for the Scientific Study of Religion* 39:333–47.

Rodriguez, Eric M., and Suzanne C. Ouellette. 2000b. Religion and masculinity in Latino gay lives. In *Gay masculinities*, edited by Peter M. Nardi. Thousand Oaks, CA: Sage.

Schilt, Kristen. 2006. Just one of the guys? How transmen make gender visible at work. *Gender & Society* 20:465–90.

Schilt, Kristen, and Laurel Westbrook. 2009. Doing gender, doing heternormativity: "Gender normals," transgender people, and the social maintenance of heterosexuality. *Gender & Society* 23:440–64.

Schrock, Douglas, and Michael Schwalbe. 2009. Men, masculinity, and manhood acts. *Annual Review of Sociology* 35:277–95.

Schrock, Douglas P., and Irene Padavic. 2007. Negotiating hegemonic masculinity in a batterer intervention program. *Gender & Society* 21:625–49.

Schwalbe, Michael. 2005. Identity stakes, manhood acts, and the dynamics of accountability. In *Studies in symbolic interaction, number 28*, edited by Norman Denzin. New York: Elsevier.

Schwalbe, Michael, Sandra Godwin, Daphne Holden, Douglas Schrock, Shealy Thompson, and Michelle Wolkomir. 2000. Generic processes in the reproduction of inequality: An interactionist analysis. *Social Forces* 79:419–52.

Slevin, Kathleen F., and Thomas J. Linneman. 2010. Old gay men's bodies and masculinities. *Men and Masculinities* 12:483–507.

Snow, David, and Leon Anderson. 1987. Identity work among the homeless: The verbal construction and avowal of personal identities. *American Journal of Sociology* 92:1336–71.

Sumerau, J. Edward. 2010. Constructing an inclusive congregational identity in a metropolitan community church. Unpublished master's thesis, Florida State University, Tallahassee.

Sumerau, J. Edward, and Douglas P. Schrock. 2011. "It's important to show your colors": Counter-heteronormative embodiment in a metropolitan community church." In *Embodied resistance: Breaking the rules, challenging the norms*, edited by Chris Bobel and Samantha Kwan. Nashville, Tennessee: Vanderbilt University Press.

Swidler, Ann. 1986. Culture in action: Symbols and strategies. *American Sociological Review* 51: 273–86.

Thumma, Scott. 1991. Negotiating a religious identity: The case of the gay evangelical. *Sociological Analysis* 52:333–47.

UFMCC (United Fellowship of Metropolitan Community Churches). 2009. Mission statement, press kit, and informational bulletins. http://www.mccchurch. org (accessed summer 2009).

Vaccarro, Christian, Douglas P. Schrock, and Janice McCabe. 2011. Managing emotional manhood: Fighting and fostering fear in mixed martial arts. *Social Psychology Quarterly*.

West, Candace, and Don Zimmerman. 1987. Doing gender. *Gender & Society* 1:125–51.

Wilcox, Melissa. 2003. *Coming out in Christianity: Religion, identity, and community*. Bloomington: Indiana University Press.

Wilcox, Melissa M. 2009. *Queer women and religious individualism*. Bloomington: Indiana University Press.

Wilkins, Amy C. 2009. Masculinity dilemmas: Sexuality and intimacy talk among Christians and Goths. *Signs* 34:343–68.

Wolkomir, Michelle. 2006. *Be not deceived: The sacred and sexual struggles of gay and ex-gay Christian men*. New Brunswick, NJ: Rutgers University Press.

Wolkomir, Michelle. 2009. Making heteronormative reconciliations: The story of romantic love, sexuality, and gender in mixed-orientation marriages. *Gender & Society* 23:494–519.

Yeung, King-To, and Mindy Stombler. 2000. Gay and Greek: The identity paradox of gay fraternities. *Social Problems* 47:134–52.

Yeung, King-To, Mindy Stombler, and Renee Wharton. 2006. Making men in gay fraternities: Resisting and reproducing multiple dimensions of hegemonic masculinity. *Gender & Society* 20:5–31.

The Unhappy Marriage of Religion and Politics: Problems and Pitfalls for Gender Equality

SHAHRA RAZAVI AND ANNE JENICHEN

The past three decades have witnessed the rising political prominence of religious actors and movements. While religious attachments and practices may have weakened in some countries (most notably, Western Europe), on a worldwide basis they seem to have persisted, if not intensified.[1] Moreover, religious arguments continue to be actively invoked in politics across a wide range of countries, both developed and developing. This alleged 'de-privatisation'[2] of religion has raised fundamental questions about the predictions of sweeping secularisation as the inevitable companion to modernisation and development.

The assertiveness of religion has coincided with a number of other transformations. First has been the introduction and rise to hegemony of a highly contested economic model ('neoliberalism'), introduced from the mid-1970s under conditions of harsh stabilisation and structural adjustment. A second, more welcome, development has been the greater emphasis on democracy and rights in the post-cold war era, which has given particular prominence to women's rights as well as human rights more broadly.[3] In much of the world, however, the positive developments in political and legal rights have not been matched by improvements in social justice, as income inequalities have increased and poverty remained stubbornly in place. Some argue that the failed promises of the modern, secular state to produce both democracy and development have in many regions prompted the search for alternative discourses of power and authenticity to challenge the dominant Western agenda.[4] Apart from the dynamics emanating from the national and local or grassroots level, the role of transnational networks of finance and the proliferation of diaspora communities over the past three decades have also contributed to the rise and influence of religious actors and movements in many contexts.[5]

Feminists wonder where this leaves gender equality. To put it crudely, has the presence of religion within the political arena made it harder for women to pursue equality with men? This is one of the central questions animating this special issue. The volume brings together 11 papers, spanning different regional contexts, from Asia (India, Pakistan) to Africa (Nigeria) and the Middle East (Iran, Israel, Turkey), and from the Americas (Chile, Mexico, US) to Eastern and Central Europe (Poland, Serbia), encompassing countries with populations belonging to diverse religious traditions including Christianity, Hinduism, Judaism and Islam. The case studies explore how religion and politics have interfaced in different national settings, and the implications of this nexus for gender equality and feminist politics, that is, how women as actors—both individually and collectively—have contested (or reinforced) hegemonic norms and representations that may be inimical to their gender interests.[6]

This article is structured as follows: after the introduction, some of the key conceptual premises informing the volume are elaborated. The next section then looks at how religious precepts have been mobilised for nationalist and ethnic politics, and

---

Shahra Razavi and Anne Jenichen, "The Unhappy Marriage of Religion and Politics: Problems and Pitfalls for Gender Equality." *Third World Quarterly* 31 (2010):833–50.

the latter's implications for gender inequality; particular attention is given to the ways in which the struggle for gender equality can be compromised where it is used (or feared to be used) as a pretext for majoritarian ethnic or religious supremacy. This is followed by an analysis of how religion has been used to reinforce authoritarian state tendencies, especially where the state claims its legitimacy in the name of religion. The article then turns to some of the new democracies, where processes of democratisation have both empowered feminist groups seeking reform of the 'private sphere' and simultaneously strengthened religious institutions that are opposed to key elements of the feminist agenda. The article draws to a close by reflecting on some of the dilemmas facing feminist action and alliance building in a context where conservative religious forces are assertive and where the struggle for gender equality coincides with other justice claims.

Questioning the 'Private–Public' Divide and Rethinking the Political Sphere

In rethinking the relevance of secularism and theories of secularisation, José Casanova introduced an early and useful differentiation between secularisation as institutional differentiation, secularisation as the decline of religiosity, and secularisation as the privatisation of religion.[7] One of the key arguments emerging from his influential analysis was that the 'de-privatisation' of modern religion was empirically irrefutable and morally defensible. He further argued that only the presence of religion in the public sphere of civil society, where religious actors engage in open public debate on a range of common public concerns and issues, would be compatible with democratic principles. In his later work he questioned whether 'the secular separation of religion from political society or even from the state' are necessary or sufficient conditions for democratic politics as long as both the state and religious institutions adhere to the rule of law and do not violate democratic rules—Alfred Stepan's concept of 'twin tolerations.'[8]

To begin with, was religion ever a purely 'private' matter, as the term 'deprivatisation' implies—cordoned off from the state by a wall of separation, and contained within the private sphere of personal belief? Even in Western Europe, the stronghold of secularism, religions have contributed considerably to the shaping of welfare and abortion regimes.[9] Several of the papers in this volume question whether religion was absent from the actually existing secularisms that took hold in the 20th century, themselves highly diverse and developed in relation to particular religious formations (be it Protestantism in the US, Hinduism in India or Sunni Islam in Turkey) and shaped by critical historical conditions.[10] Modernist and secularist pretensions notwithstanding, few 'secularist' states were willing to risk their political survival by radically interfering in matters of the family, marriage and personal laws, which were widely seen as the domain of religious authorities. The price paid for this pragmatic non-interference was state endorsement of gender inequality in family and personal status, and sometimes also criminal, laws.[11] Hence in many nominally secularised states, such as Israel and India, religious precepts continued to hold sway.

Furthermore, is the notion of 'twin separations' sufficient to protect the rights and needs of women and men, believers and non-believers against discrimination? As Anne Phillips rightly argues, viewing the relationship between religion and politics in quasi-corporatist terms—as a relationship between democratic political institutions, on the one hand, and religious communities and authorities, on the other—pays far too little attention to the ways in which each of these may misrepresent or coerce their individual members (women, non-believers and believers).[12] Hence the relationship needs to be viewed also through the lens of *individual rights and needs*, rather than assuming that individuals' interests are simply represented by the principles and practices as defined by religious as well as political leaders and spokespersons.

Given the way in which women are positioned as 'bearers of culture' (including religion and tradition), their deportment, dress code and sexuality are often rendered markers of the 'good society' envisaged by different groups. Religious authorities commonly insist on regulating relationships of the private domain, including sexuality, biological and social reproduction, marriage, gender roles and definitions of what constitutes a 'proper' family. Such regulations, premised on some transcendent principle, are steeped in patriarchal and heteronormative assumptions, and often work to women's disadvantage. As the contributions to this issue attest, 'private' issues, such as the right to divorce, permissible forms of sexuality, access to contraception and abortion have become sites of intense contestation between conservative religious actors who see religious moral principles as 'natural', absolute and non-negotiable (valid for all times and places), and feminist and other human rights advocates who argue for democratic, pluralist and rights-based alternatives. 'The private' is indeed political, and has become increasingly politicised.

One important prism for analysing the relationship between religion and the state is through the legal framework. Yet religions shape gender (in) equality through multiple channels of state action, not only legal ones, including through public health (Chile, Mexico, Poland, the US), education (Iran, Pakistan, Poland, Turkey), and welfare policies and programmes, even where there is formal legal separation between religion and the state.

Beyond the state an important arena is that of political parties. In some countries political parties are openly religious in name and ideological and policy orientation (eg Pakistan, Iran, Israel), while in others religious issues are channelled into political parties through alliances with religious interest groups (eg the US, India) or with the Church (eg Poland, Serbia, Chile, Mexico). Religion can also have a more diffuse presence, as prospective politicians demonstrate their political legitimacy by demonstrating their personal religiosity (eg Nigeria, the US).

Outside the formal arena of politics lies the arena of civil society and associational life where people organise (in lobby groups, NGOs, trade unions) and mobilise (in social movements, coalitions and campaigns) to pressure and persuade governments and citizens on a wide range of issues. However, seeing the arena of public debate and contestation as a power-free zone where participants deliberate as equal peers is suspect. While in most countries counter-hegemonic discourses and counter-publics are able to articulate new social visions, breaking taboos on gender roles, family forms and sexuality, their voices are often muffled by conservative forces that command greater access to resources and state protection, if not assistance. Sometimes the dividing line is not even clear, as many think-tanks and NGOs enjoy state support and patronage. It would be dangerous therefore to rely on civil society exclusively to produce egalitarian visions and projects, as it can easily reproduce existing social hierarchies and exclusions.[13]

The interface between politics and religion is frequently examined from a perspective that is exclusively centred on state power dynamics and formal political institutions. However, much of the 'informal power' of religion lies in the way its ideas and norms are diffused outside the formal political arena, through everyday effects that shape people's attitudes and lives.[14] As Farida Shaheed (this volume) argues, the conventional approach is inadequate because of the difficulty of separating out the realms of 'the social' from 'the political,' and 'the public' from 'the private' everyday life. And as Charmaine Pereira and Jibrin Ibrahim caution, the indirect effects of state laws can be even more pernicious and difficult to challenge than the laws themselves. As several contributions in this volume show (Pakistan, Turkey, Serbia, Poland), some of the more insidious and lasting changes that religious actors introduce are in terms of practices and meanings that reshape people's minds and become unquestioned social norms—or 'common sense' in Gramscian terms.[15] When such norms are discriminatory or reduce women's opportunities, they are of serious concern. Where such norms are contrary to social practices they can also initiate resistance—day-to-day defiance of the Islamic dress code by young women on the streets of Tehran, or young couples in Chile and Poland defying Catholic dogma on sexual abstinence before marriage.

There is unmistakably a recent narrowing of agendas of various (though by no means all) religious actors and movements, not only Islamist, around an exclusive moral, ideological and identity-based politics. Many such movements capitalise on gender issues to demand a greater public role for themselves as moral guardians of the nation promising justice and redress. In this context we pose a set of questions: what is the form and significance of the resurgence of religious forces in different contexts and what has it entailed in terms of gender equality? As we show, the causes/significance of religious assertiveness and the form it takes are context-specific, and therefore defy broad-brush explanations.

Religion, Nationalism and Ethno-Political Conflict

Historically religion has played an important part in the formation of most nation-states.[16] Here we focus on the postcolonial and post-Soviet moments, when the ambivalence of nationalist projects has become more apparent. In many such instances the exclusionary effects of ethnic nationalisms, often leading to the marginalisation of religious or other minorities and even to violent conflict, have prevailed over its liberating effects. By promoting a sense of community and belonging, nationalism often breeds intolerance and hatred towards an 'alien other' which is to be excluded. Religion, as a powerful source of identity, is frequently utilised both to promote intragroup cohesion and to mobilise inter-group differences and conflict. It can serve as a source of legitimacy for national leaders who are developing new political institutions, or who are trying to bolster their legitimacy in times of crisis. In addition, dominant religious institutions can also have a strong bearing (often more than political parties) on citizens' political choices and are therefore important allies in the assertion of (secular) political power.[17]

For women there is much at stake in how religion becomes mobilised for nationalist struggles. While nationalism can prompt feminist consciousness and pave the way for the emergence of indigenous feminist movements, feminist agendas have all too often been regarded as secondary, their implementation frequently suspended until after the success of the 'larger national cause,' and in the end abandoned altogether.[18] Nationalist discourses designate women as 'bearers of the collective,' assigning men the role of governing the nation and its state, while women are assigned responsibility for its biological and cultural reproduction. Any reform of this gender-based division presents a threat to the nationalist bid for protection and unification of the community, thereby rendering feminist politics a menace to the nationalist project.[19] Religion can further amplify these dynamics by providing a 'divine' grounding for them.

The case studies on Serbia, India, Israel and Nigeria in this issue illustrate the exclusionary dynamics of ethnic nationalisms, and reveal their discriminatory and muting impact on women, their rights and feminist politics. Rada Drezgić in her contribution demonstrates how Milošević, himself an atheist, mobilised the Serbian Orthodox Church and Serb religious sentiments to rally support for his political agenda in the process of Serbian nation-state formation (beginning with the death of Tito in 1980). During the disintegration of the former Yugoslavia and the associated wars of secession in the early 1990s, religious affiliation became a crucial element in ethnonational differentiation, while women's bodies were appropriated for the biological survival of post-Yugoslav nations and the preservation of their ethnic 'purity,' resulting in systematic rapes and forced pregnancies as part of the war strategy of 'ethnic cleansing.' Since then pro-natalist and anti-abortion discourses have flourished, threatening women's reproductive rights and equality in Serbia, although the presence of a relatively strong feminist movement and socialist 'pro-choice' tradition have thus far prevented a radical overturning of abortion legislation. Nevertheless, the continuing nationalist discourse assigning women nurturing and reproductive roles has begun to show its effect, for instance by gradually reversing the 'modernisation' of the domestic division of labour between the sexes. And there is little reason for optimism according to Drezgić: since Milošević was toppled in 2000 the public and political influence of the conservative Serbian Orthodox Church has grown, as weak and unstable ruling coalitions and politicians have sought to bolster their position and enhance their legitimacy by allying themselves with it.

In her contribution Zoya Hassan discusses the rise of the nationalist *Hindutva* movement in India, which equates the nation with the majority Hindu community, as a result of attempts by political leaders, both secular and religiously inclined, to curry favour with religious leaders in order to marshal political support. However, the most important issue, she argues, is not the growth of religious politics *per se*, but the inordinate play of identity politics (primarily based on caste and religion), to the extent that ordinary Indians no longer have access to public institutions except on the basis of religious and social identities. In Israel, as illustrated by Ruth Halperin-Kaddari & Yaacov Yagdar, the Zionist movement started out as a secular ideology intended to emancipate 'its' people from the influence of all oppressions, including religious ones. Yet the state of Israel was officially created as a 'Jewish state,' in which religious symbols and discourses, along with the 'right of return,' served to unite the Jewish nation, eventually resulting in an ethnic democracy in which non-Jewish citizens can only be granted 'second-class citizenship.'

In several states with religiously diverse populations, such as India, Israel and Nigeria, the state 'communalises' religion by according religious authorities and institutions semi-autonomy from the otherwise non-religious national legal regime. This mainly concerns the area of personal status laws.[20] The articles on India and Israel in this volume, therefore, pay particular attention to the exclusive religious jurisdiction over family law and its discriminatory effects on women. They furthermore demonstrate how the conflict between the (Hindu and Jewish, respectively) majority and the (primarily Muslim) minority populations have muted feminist attempts to reform the personal status laws. In India the Hindu right has instrumentalised efforts to introduce a Uniform Civil Code (UCC) for its own nationalist purposes, fuelling Muslim fears of the imposition of a 'Hindu,' officially disguised as 'universal,' code. Feminist organisations that were originally supportive of the UCC thus had to distance themselves from it. In Israel, given the close link between religion and nationalism, as well as the overshadowing reality of the ongoing Arab–Israeli conflict, feminists, Jewish and Muslim/Arab alike, who challenge religions' exclusive jurisdiction, face accusations of betraying their 'community,' as well as jeopardising its identity and even security. However, while Ruth Halperin-Kaddari and Yaacov Yadgar emphasise the importance of reform of personal status matters from within religious communities, Hasan cautions that such an approach risks freezing identities within religious boundaries.

The exclusionary nature of religiously buttressed nationalism often leads to violent conflict between ethno-religious groups.[21] Competing religious identities can legitimate conflict, and violent conflict in turn can make people more conscious of their religious identity and more committed to it. This has not only been the case in the former Yugoslavia, Israel and India, but also in Nigeria, where politicians have consistently used (ethno-) religious mobilisation to fuel social exclusion and conflict. Although Islam and Christianity are often represented in terms of a conflictual relationship to one another, Charmaine Pereira and Jibrin Ibrahim draw attention to areas of convergence between the two religions: the common referencing of women's bodies and sexuality and the need to control both. Indicative of this convergence is the proposed bill on 'Public Nudity, Sexual Intimidation and Other Related Matters' in 2008, which, across religious divides, aims at the 'Restoration of Human Dignity.' However, it primarily targets women's autonomy, while allowing unauthorised individuals to determine for themselves how women should be dressed, resulting in reported assaults on women who, allegedly, are 'indecently' dressed.

Religion at the Service of the State: Bolstering Authoritarianism

The capacity of civil society to produce contestation and democratic change becomes particularly constrained where religious actors and scripts gain a strong foothold in the political and social arenas. Nowhere is this clearer than in Iran and Pakistan, analysed in the papers by Homa Hoodfar and Shadi Sadr, and Farida Shaheed, respectively.

In both countries the state defines itself as Islamic, and conservative readings of *Shari'a* inform the legal domain. As Lisa Hajjar observes, where religious law becomes the law of the land, and where state power is exercised in the name of religion, 'defense of religion can be conflated with defense of the state, and critiques or challenges can be regarded and treated as heresy and apostasy.'[22] Authoritarianism is thereby bolstered. Hoodfar and Sadr go even further and argue that, in the case of Iran, the larger obstacle to gender equality has more to do with the authoritarian nature of the state, rather than the actual or potential compatibility (or lack thereof) of religious traditions or practices with democratic principles. Islamist women's rights activists in Iran have presented 'woman-friendly' readings of Islamic texts which challenge the conservative interpretation of *Shari'a* and which could have been adopted by the Islamic state. Instead, the ruling elite has pursued its ambition of building an Islamic society based on its own gender vision, and this has increasingly meant the relegation of *Shari'a* to a backseat.

The fact that in both Pakistan and Iran it is Islam that has been fused so closely with authoritarian state practices may raise questions about its alleged incompatibility with human rights, democracy and gender equality (notwithstanding the fact that authoritarian states such as Franco's Spain and Latin American military dictatorships were all Christian and Catholic, rather than Muslim[23]). In polemical assertions about the 'civilisational clash' between Islam and Christianity the former is often construed as monolithic and hostile to human rights and oppressive towards women. Tragically the terrorist attacks of recent years perpetrated by Muslim militants and the barbaric treatment of women by regimes such as the Taliban in Afghanistan have reinforced such readings. The tendency to homogenise Islamic politics, however, conceals a wide diversity of ideas and movements. The Iraqi sociologist, Sami Zubaida, for example, identifies three broad tendencies within political Islam, which include what he calls 'conservative Islam,' often associated with authoritarian states, radical and militant variants, typically pursued by militant youth, and the more reformist orientations which seek to Islamise state and society in the context of social reform and democratisation.[24]

The history and politics of the state—that is their specific experiences and legacies of colonial or imperial domination, nation-building projects and challenges of ethnic and regional diversity, as well as geopolitical factors—have been very different in Iran and Pakistan. This has coloured the manner in which they were Islamicised. In Iran this happened through a popular anti-authoritarian revolution in 1979, while Pakistan's *raison-d'etre* as a state created for Indian Muslims brought religion into politics from its inception. But religion was given a major boost after a military coup brought General Zia ul-Huq to power (also in 1979 and when Pakistan was being used as a conduit for Western military assistance to the Mujahideen fighting against the USSR in Afghanistan). These countries' diverse historical and political trajectories have also given the struggles for democracy and gender equality their distinct characters, strategies and challenges.

Iran—a country where the 'prophetic' role assumed by religious authorities in opposition to a dictatorial regime was transformed into a 'priestly' one as religion was institutionalised within politics and fused with the state[25]—continues to provide important insights into the limits and contradictions of merging religion with the state. Not only is the political role of religious authorities a highly contested one, but the need for 'separation of religion and state' is being voiced by both secular forces as well as by 'believers' from within the heart of the Islamic establishment. These advocates of 'reform' (*eslahat*) have included male lay intellectuals, some notable clerical authorities, and a number of feminists with an Islamic orientation.

In both countries Islamisation projects have used the state's legal, punitive, administrative and ideological instruments to impose an anti-democratic, discriminatory and misogynistic template on society. They have brutally closed down spaces for contestation and nurtured state-sponsored militias and foot soldiers—some of whom are women (the Al-Hafsa women in Pakistan, the female preachers trained by the Office of the Supreme Leader in Iran)—to 'guide,' 'educate' and proselytise the population. While

Islamisation may have been engineered 'in the pursuit of greater power alignments' (Shaheed this issue), power is never devoid of ideas, ideology or culture. Within the current Islamist political sociability and discourse 'women-asculture'[26] has come to occupy a central position. As the paper on Nigeria rightly observes, in principle the expansion of *Shari'a* could have addressed a number of areas in economic and social development, such as provisions for the collection and distribution of *zakat* (the charity tithe), or the implementation of regulations prohibiting usury. Instead, the emphasis in Nigeria, as in Iran and Pakistan, has been on punishments for sexual offences and alcohol consumption, accompanied by an emphasis on public morality, as expressed through the impositions placed on women.

Three salient observations emerge from our contributors' analyses. First, the obsessive preoccupation with sexuality, gender and 'the family' and efforts by the state to regulate them has given the 'woman question' an immediacy and urgency that has been historically unprecedented. Blatant discrimination has in turn incensed a wide spectrum of women activists and fuelled, at least in Iran, one of the most dynamic and innovative women's movements in the country's history—one that has worked both 'outside' and 'inside' the state, using diverse strategies and discourses and increasingly coalescing around a concrete and pragmatic set of shared objectives.

The second point alluded to in Homa Hoodfar and Shadi Sadr's analysis is the danger that pro-democracy movements run in parallel with the longer-standing struggles of women's rights for reform and democratisation, rather than making women's claims for equality a central part of their struggle for democracy. While a great deal of rethinking and realignment has been taking place on women's issues among women rights activists of diverse outlooks in the preceding decades, gender seems to be all but non-existent as a category of thinking among the emerging group of (male) dissident intellectuals struggling for a more democratic polity. Contributing to this process has been, with few notable exceptions, the absence of women from the presumably more general democracy debates at the level of leadership (even if women are present in the body of the movement, on the streets and in protests). The implicit understanding seems to be that democracy is a gender-neutral category, and that struggles for citizenship rights are 'naturally inclusive of women.'

The third point, underlined by Farida Shaheed, is the need for human rights and women's rights advocates to utilise a vocabulary and sociocultural agenda that has greater social resonance by embedding their claims within society's more liberal and popular traditions and idioms. The international human rights discourse perhaps lacks the resonance that notions of 'justice' and fairness have. Moreover, the failure to present a credible agenda for combating economic and social deprivation that responds to popular concerns and anxieties about increasing inequality, unemployment and insecurity cedes the ground to the morally conservative elements who exploit such anxieties with their populist rhetoric of 'Islamic justice.' We will return to this issue in the final section of the article.

Religion, Democratisation and the 'Democratic Paradox'

Women's groups and movements have in recent decades both contributed to national processes of democratisation and benefited from such processes to democratically voice their demands *vis-à-vis* the state. Yet democracy has complex effects or 'built-in paradoxes and contradictions.'[27] At the same time that it has in some contexts empowered feminist groups seeking reform, it has also strengthened religious institutions that are opposed to some elements of the feminist agenda. In the context of electoral competition, contending political parties need allies to defeat their opponents and religious organisations are often good alliance partners as they are able to tap into a sizeable social network.[28] A well known illustration analysed in Elizabeth Bernstein and Janet Jakobsen's contribution is the political coalition between conservative evangelical groups and secular neoliberals of the Republican Party in the US. This coalition supported Republican dominance in electoral politics and gave a major boost to conservative policies on issues of gender and sexuality both domestically and internationally.

Even nominally secular political parties and politicians, as several of our contributions suggest, have not hesitated in using religion for political or electoral purposes, and in the process provided the necessary foundations for its continued life and growth. A case in point is India, one of the oldest democracies in the developing world, where, as Zoya Hasan shows, the Congress Party's attempts to play the 'religious card'—calculated to undercut the popularity of its rivals and please communally minded Muslims and Hindus at different moments—ended up giving a massive boost to the Hindu right in the 1980s.

Where religious groups and institutions have played an important role in contesting authoritarian regimes, this has made it difficult for women's rights advocates to oppose them in the 'new' democracies that replaced the authoritarian system. The country studies on Chile by Virginia Guzmán, Ute Seibert and Silke Staab and on Poland by Jacqueline Heinen and Stéphane Portet show how the Catholic Church has reconfigured its alliances and adopted new strategies and discourses in opposition to policies for sex education in schools (in both countries) and reproductive rights (emergency contraception in Chile, abortion in Poland), seeking to subvert feminist demands for the democratisation of the private sphere. As Blofield observed, the representatives of the Catholic Church in Chile continue to 'collect the debt' of their predecessors by capitalising on their defence of human rights during the dictatorship, now (re)defined as the right to life from conception, to privacy and to parental primacy in decisions over a child's education.[29]

Despite equally strong support from the Vatican and links to political parties, youth movements and think-tanks in both contexts, the hegemony of the Church seems to have been more effectively challenged in Chile. The negative association between feminism and the discredited socialist regime has tainted feminist organising in Poland and weakened its capacity to withstand the assault on women's reproductive rights. The relative success of the women's movement in Chile, on the other hand, may be in large part the result of the continued support that 'women friendly' policies have enjoyed from two successive left-leaning governments (of Ricardo Lagos and Michele Batchelet between 2000 and 2009) in a presidential system where the executive has ample opportunity to define the political agenda. The fact that political parties are in general more programmatic in Chile, and the left parties more candid in their opposition to the Catholic dogma, seems to have facilitated their capacity to respond to public opinion, which in both countries appears to favour less church involvement in dictating sexual practices. In Poland, however, the political landscape has been very unstable since the fall of socialism, marked by short-lived coalition governments and weakly institutionalised political parties; the left-leaning parties, even if they would like to limit the Church's incursions into the public sphere, tend to avoid any direct confrontation with it for fear of the electoral consequences.

In Mexico and Turkey the relationship between religion and politics has been historically more conflictive and their secularisms more 'assertive,'[30] as the contributions by Ana Amuchastegui, Guadalupe Cruz, Evelyn Aldaz and Maria Consuela Mejía, and Yeşim Arat, respectively, show. In Mexico state–Church relations were indelibly marked by a revolutionary movement (in 1917) that expropriated property owned by the Church, and denied it legal existence through the Constitution, while outlawing political parties from having any religious or denominational references. In Turkey the shift from an Islamic monarchy to a republican nation-state (in 1923) abolished the caliphate, expropriated the property of pious foundations and brought Sunni Islam under the aegis of the state (in the form of the General Directorate of Religious Affairs), turning clerical figures into state personnel, while banning political parties from using religion as a political platform.[31]

In the context of increasing democratisation gathering pace over the past decade, ruling parties have had to share power with political contestants, some of whom have strong religious roots: the ruling National Action Party (PAN) in Mexico, and the Justice and Development Party (AKP) in Turkey being prime examples.[32] In this context private sphere issues relating to women's bodily integrity and deportment, and sexual and reproductive rights have become the arena of intense contestation. The dominance of religious parties in government notwithstanding, women's rights advocates and their allies have succeeded in pushing through some landmark pieces of legislation—the Reform of the Penal Code (2002–04) in Turkey,[33] the inclusion of emergency contraception in public health services (2004) in Mexico and the decriminalisation of abortion in Mexico City (2008)—in great part thanks to their energetic campaigns and effective strategies.

Yet the wave of re-criminalisation of abortion across Mexican federal states since 2008 is a stark reminder of the fragility of some of these gains. What is most disconcerting here is the role played by the 'secularist' political party, the Institutionalised Revolutionary Party (PRI), in promoting recriminalisation in an effort to win the support of the Catholic Church for short-term electoral purposes (in view of the forthcoming local and national elections in 2012). In Turkey meanwhile the return of AKP to power in 2007 with a clear majority and with the prospect of accession to the European Union looking increasingly dim, seems to have bolstered the Party's incentives to respond to its socially conservative constituencies. While a great deal has been said about the AKP's efforts to circumvent the (undemocratic) ban on the headscarf through Constitutional amendment, what Arat's article highlights are the more insidious ways in which conservative attitudes and discriminatory practices are spreading within both political and civic society.

Regardless of the precise causality, what is disconcerting is the spread of conservative attitudes within both political and civic society, and the boost that this is likely to give to conservative practices that restrict women's options—an issue that is often left out of the discussions on gender equality in Turkey that are exclusively focused on the headscarf issue. This underlines one of the key themes emerging from this volume: it is not enough to look at developments in the institutionalised public spheres; equally, if not more, pertinent for women's rights and their real options is what goes on in the social and private spheres of everyday life.

Feminist Politics: Creating Alliances for Justice and Democracy

The contributions to this issue demonstrate that there is much at stake for women and their rights to equality, autonomy and bodily integrity in how religion and politics intertwine. There are many instances across the world and across religious traditions, of religious groups and authorities having raised their voice to condemn social injustice and human rights abuses, often in alliance with secular forces; from liberation theologians in Latin America to the Catholic opposition in the US to nuclear war and economic injustice in the 1980s, to the Iranian clerics who oppose orthodox interpretations of Islam.[34] Although religiously influenced social movements have historically been progressive as well as conservative, most of them did not focus on gender equality as their major concern. On the contrary, not infrequently women's rights advocates have found their demands for greater democracy and equality in the 'private' domain of family law, reproduction and sexuality being virulently opposed by those who adopt a religious/moral discourse and claim to be speaking on behalf of religious 'communities.'

As real as this conflict is, it should not be taken to suggest a dividing line between feminism and religion. As several contributions to this volume have suggested, there is very often opposition and debate within the 'religious' camp, as well as diversity of views and positions among feminists, as exemplified by the presence of feminists who promote gender-egalitarian interpretations of religion and other feminists who see religion as deeply problematic for gender equality.

Feminist: Struggles from Within Religious Communities and Frameworks

The resurgence of religion in the public sphere represents a particular challenge to feminist struggles. Not only are claims of 'divine truth' justifying discriminatory practices against women hard to challenge, but the struggle for women's rights and gender equality, as illustrated in the preceding sections, is also often closely tied up, and inseparable from, broader struggles for social and economic justice, ethnic/racial equality and recognition, and national self-determination *vis-à-vis* imperial/global domination. In the Global South the effort to promote universal human rights norms has often pitted women's rights advocates against those who use religion to resist cultural imperialism and Western-style individualism (which they claim is alien to their societies).[35] In multi-religious contexts mobilisation against women's rights violations often inadvertently involves mobilising sentiments based on religious differences. This politicisation of religion and its entanglement with various other disadvantages and discriminations makes it hard, if not impossible, to advocate women's rights without feeding into other struggles and identity conflicts. Therefore, many support an approach of 'internal reform' as the most appropriate, if not the only, way to make religious communities and their political impacts more woman-friendly.[36]

In contexts where secular spaces are limited, such as in theocracies like Iran, or where ethno-religious conflicts have created tensions between feminist and communal claims, such as in Israel and India, feminists who work from within religious communities and/or who invoke religious precepts and interpretations to advocate gender justice have played a crucial role. They often popularise woman-centred interpretations of religious texts, stimulate public debate and force religious authorities into conversations about the rights of women, and sometimes even pave the way for legal and political reforms. However, the degree to which such alternative, 'discursive politics'[37] can get a public hearing or even influence state policy is limited. Particularly in authoritarian settings many governments have acted to repress scholars, activists, and organisations advocating women's rights, even if such advocacy seeks to show compatibility with religion.[38] In settings heated by ethno-religious conflicts women's rights advocates are often played off against the nationalist bid for protection and unification of the community (however defined), as the articles on India and Israel illustrate.

It is therefore questionable whether internal reform movements can offer a more promising avenue for egalitarian change. When we consider the significant social authority of many religions, and the power they can wield against dissident voices, it is too optimistic to rely simply on reform from within. It is also unhelpful to set up an opposition between internally and externally generated change, or to represent one avenue as superior to the other.[39] The dividing line between the two may also be porous, as those who work for 'internal reform' very often draw on the ideas and arguments of 'external' advocates for change. Alliances between feminists of different religious and secular communities are therefore imperative. Discrimination and oppression of their alternative voices have incensed many religious and secular women and have spurred them in many contexts to collaborate. In Iran reformist women have increasingly reached out and joined secularist women in various campaigns, resulting not only in a more 'pragmatic feminism,'[40] but also in mutual learning. Clearly 'reformist or women-centred interpretation of religious laws should be considered not as an alternative to secular and democratic demands but as a component of more holistic social change.'[41]

In India, for example, an alliance of Muslim women's groups with the Indian women's movement, together with movements for secularism, democracy and human rights, has been crucial in broad-basing the struggle for women's rights, which now goes beyond personal laws to promote gender equality. However, given the exclusionary nature of nationalist and identity politics in multi-religious states, such alliances are often not easily built. In Israel, for instance, women's rights activists within the Muslim community have resisted appeals from Jewish women's rights activists to join forces in demanding the promulgation of secular civil family laws as an alternative to communal law, because this would give the state more authority over the community without addressing the problem of state discrimination.[42] Feminists from the Muslim community have preferred to reform Muslim family laws from within, as accomplished in 2001 when the Family Courts Law was amended, reducing the exclusive jurisdiction of *Shari'a* courts.

Gender Justice and Economic Justice

The connections between economic and social justice, on the one hand, and gender justice, on the other, are clear in women's lives: legal rights to abortion and bodily integrity mean very little where quality public health services remain out of reach; and the formal rights to divorce and child custody can remain trapped on paper if women do not have the financial wherewithal to support their dependants.[43] An enabling environment for women's substantive rights therefore requires both a rights-based agenda that guarantees individual rights and autonomy, as well as an economic agenda that upholds social and economic rights.

Feminist groups and movements, often in alliance with leftist parties, unions and other civil society groups, have drawn attention to the unequalising tendencies of the neoliberal agenda, while demanding redistributive measures to redress the economic/social injustices of unfettered globalisation. However, those who promote issues of social justice (poverty, inequality) are not always supportive of women's rights agendas, especially in the arena of reproduction and sexuality. This complicates feminist efforts at alliance building.

At the international level such fissures were apparent in the UN conferences of the 1990s: the conservative alliance led by a group of conservative states and largely religious NGOs that virulently opposed the women's rights agenda (especially with respect to reproduction), was also critical of the agenda of economic liberalisation that Northern governments were pursuing. The Vatican, in particular, voiced concerns about North–South inequality and poverty while opposing women's rights' agendas.[44]

At the national level, too, those who champion a social justice agenda and are critical of 'globalisation' and 'imperialism' may hold deeply patriarchal views of the family; the Iranian President Ahmadinejad and the Pakistani *jihadists* being clear examples of such a tendency. While there are serious questions about the extent to which these advocates have turned, or are even able to turn, their 'anti-imperialist' slogan into a redistributive economic agenda, they can clearly not be considered potential allies given their deeply regressive views on gender equality.

An example of feminist alliance building with religious actors in the US which has not been able to produce progressive outcomes, if assessed from a critical feminist perspective, is discussed by Janet Jakobsen and Elizabeth Bernstein on anti-trafficking policies. The feminist–evangelical alliance has been enabled by a rightward shift of some feminists towards neo-conservatism and a 'law and order' agenda, and the leftward sweep of some evangelical Christians away from divisive issues such as abortion and gay marriage towards a 'new internationalist,' social-justice theology. This has considerably shaped the prevailing political framework on trafficking, both in the US and abroad. It has shifted the debate away from a broad definition of trafficking as inclusive of all forms of labour towards a definition that focuses primarily upon forced prostitution. This shift is intertwined with a move towards a neoliberal framework for understanding both the problem and its potential solutions, resulting not only in the increased criminalisation of sex workers, but also in the deportation of migrant sex workers as well as the funnelling of survivors into dead-end, minimum-wage jobs which increases the likelihood that they will pursue similarly risky livelihood strategies in the future.

Transnational Alliances

The case studies in this issue also attest to the role of international connections and forces in shaping feminist activism at the national level. The growing size and influence of an international women's movement that is linked through both regional and international networks (eg Women Living Under Muslim Laws, Catholics for Choice, Development Alternatives with Women for a New Era), and the cluster of UN summits held in the 1990s which provided NGOs and women's movements with a public forum for debate over wide-ranging policy issues relating to women's rights, have informed national debates and advocacy work (on reproductive rights, personal status laws) in many contexts. In addition, in countries where governments have signed on to key UN conventions (such as the Convention on the Elimination of all forms of Discrimination Against Women—CEDAW), are subject to the scrutiny of human rights bodies (such as the European Court of Human Rights) or seek accession to regional bodies (such as the EU), women's rights activists can use these processes to bring pressure to bear on their governments to change the national legal or policy frameworks—even if the outcomes are not always as positive as activists hoped (eg Poland). This is all the more imperative in a context where conservative religious forces are able to utilise the transnational flows of ideas, influence and finance to consolidate their position within the national contexts where they operate.

Notes

This special issue draws on a research project carried out by the United Nations Research Institute for Social Development (UNRISD) and the Heinrich Böll Foundation (HBF); the country studies on Poland, Serbia and Turkey were partially funded by the UNIFEM Office for Central and Eastern Europe, and three thematic papers complementing the country studies, which are being published separately, were funded by UNFPA. We are grateful to all the contributing authors for their patience in responding to our multiple rounds of questions and comments. We would like to thank Deniz Kandiyoti for her insightful comments on an earlier version of this article, although remaining faults remain our responsibility. We would also like to thank Ji-Won Seo for her excellent research assistance in putting together this special issue.

1. P Norris & R Inglehart, *Sacred and Secular: Religion and Politics Worldwide*, Cambridge: Cambridge University Press, 2004.
2. J Casanova, *Public Religions in the Modern World*, Chicago, IL: University of Chicago Press, 1994.
3. M Molyneux & S Razavi, 'Introduction', in Molyneux & Razavi, *Gender Justice, Development and Rights*, Oxford: Oxford University Press, 2002, pp 1–42.
4. M Juergensmeyer, *The New Cold War? Religious Nationalism Confronts the Secular State*, Berkeley, CA: University of California Press, 1993; and D Westerlund, *Questioning the Secular State: The Worldwide Resurgence of Religion in Politics*, London: Hurst, 1996.
5. The role of both the US (under the presidencies of Ronald Reagan and George W Bush) and Saudi Arabia in funding faith-based organisations (evangelical and Wahabi respectively) in different parts of the world should not be underestimated. The proliferation of diaspora communities in Western Europe and North America has been another source of support and funding for faith-based groups, including Hindu fundamentalist groups in India. For useful references see, M Tadros, *Gender Conundrums of Faith-Based Organisations Delivering Welfare Services*, Programme Paper GD No11, UNRISD, Geneva, 2010.
6. M Molyneux, 'Mobilisation without emancipation? Women's interests, the state and revolution in Nicaragua', *Feminist Studies*, 11(2), 1985, pp 227–254.
7. Casanova, *Public Religions in the Modern World*.
8. J Casanova, 'Religion, politics and gender equality: public religions revisited', in J Casanova & A Phillips, *A Debate on the Public Role of Religion and its Social and Gender Implications*, UNRISD Programme Paper GD No 5, 2009.
9. KJ Morgan, *Working Mothers and the Welfare State: Religion and the Politics of Work–Family Policies in Western Europe and the United States*, Stanford, CA: Stanford University Press, 2006; and M Minkenberg, 'Religion and public policy: institutional, cultural, and political impact on the shaping of abortion policies in Western democracies', *Comparative Political Studies*, 35(2), pp. 221–247.
10. A Kuru, 'Passive and assertive secularism: historical conditions, ideological struggles, and state policies toward religion', *World Politics*, 59(4), 2007, pp 568–594; and J Jakobsen & A Pellegrini (eds), *Secularisms*, Durham, NC: Duke University Press, 2008.
11. D Kandiyoti (ed), *Women, Islam and the State*, Philadelphia, PA: Temple University Press, 1991.
12. A Phillips, 'Religion: ally, threat or just religion', in J Casanova & A Phillips, *A Debate on the Public Role of Religion and its Social and Gender Implications*, UNRISD Programme Paper GD No 5, 2009.
13. A Phillips, 'Does feminism need a conception of civil society?', in S Chambers & W Kymlicka (eds),

Alternative Conceptions of Civil Society, Princeton, NJ: Princeton University Press, 2002.

14. *Ibid.*
15. Antonio Gramsci defined 'common sense' as 'the generic form of thought common to a particular period and a particular popular environment'. See A Gramsci, Q Hoare & GN Smith (eds), *Selections from the Prison Notebooks of Antonio Gramsci*, London: Lawrence and Wishart, 1971, p 323.
16. On the relationship between religion and nationalism, see C Jaffrelot, 'Religion and nationalism', in PB Clarke (ed), *The Oxford Handbook of the Sociology of Religion*, Oxford: Oxford University Press, pp 406–417; and B-AJ Rieffer, 'Religion and nationalism: understanding the consequences of a complex relationship', *Ethnicities*, 3(2), 2003, pp 215–242.
17. S Bruce, *Politics and Religion*, Cambridge: Polity Press, 2003; and Rieffer, 'Religion and nationalism'.
18. RS Herr, 'The possibility of nationalist feminism', *Hypatia*, 18(3), 2003, pp 135–160.
19. N Yuval-Davis, *Gender and Nation*, London: Sage, 1997; and J Nagel, 'Masculinity and nationalism: gender and sexuality in the making of nations', *Ethnic and Racial Studies*, 21(2), 1998, pp 242–269.
20. L Hajjar, 'Religion, state power and domestic violence in Muslim societies: a framework for comparative analysis', *Law and Social Inquiry*, 29(1), 2004, pp. 1–38.
21. The influence of religious nationalist groups on violent conflicts, as compared to the influence of non-religious nationalist groups, has increased since the 1980s. J Fox, 'The rise of religious nationalism and conflict: ethnic conflict and revolutionary wars, 1945–2001', *Journal of Peace Research*, 41(6), 2004, pp 715–731. Although the total number of armed conflicts about identity is decreasing, those which involve religious differences seem to be more intractable. T Ellingsen, 'Toward a revival of religion and religious clashes?', *Terrorism and Political Violence*, 17(3), 2005, pp 305–332.
22. L Hajjar, 'Religion, state power and domestic violence in Muslim societies', p 27.
23. J Casanova, 'Catholic and Muslim politics in comparative perspective', *Taiwan Journal of Democracy*, 1(2), 2005, pp 89–108.
24. S Zubaida, 'Culture, international politics and Islam: debating continuity and change', in W Brown, S Bromley & S Athreye (eds), *A World of Whose Making? Ordering the International: History, Change and Transformation*, London: Pluto Press/Open University, 2004. See also M Ayoob, *The Many Faces of Political Islam: Religion and Politics in the Muslim World*, Ann Arbor, MI: University of Michigan Press, 2008.
25. The contrast between 'prophetic' (moral critique of the state) and 'priestly' (anti-democratic, reinforcing inequalities) roles of religion is taken from TG Jelen & C Wilcox, 'Religion: the one, the few and the many', in Jelen & Wilcox (eds), *Religion and Politics in Comparative Perspective: The One, the Few and the Many*, Cambridge: Cambridge University Press, 2002, pp 1–24.
26. A Najmabadi, '(Un)veiling feminism', in Jakobsen & Pellegrini, *Secularisms*, p 52.
27. L Diamond, 'Three paradoxes of democracy', *Journal of Democracy*, 1(3), 1990, pp 48–60.
28. M Htun & SL Weldon, 'When and why do governments promote women's rights? Toward a comparative politics of states and sex equality', paper prepared for the American Political Science Association conference, Chicago, 29 August–2 September 2007.
29. M Blofield, *The Politics of 'Moral Sin': A Study of Abortion and Divorce in Catholic Chile since 1990*, Santiago: FLASCO, 2001.
30. Kuru, 'Passive and assertive secularism'.
31. T Parla & A. Davison, 'Secularism and laicism in Turkey', in Jakobsen & Pellegrini, *Secularisms*, pp 58–75. Parla and Davison, however, argue that Kemalism was committed not to secularism, but rather to a partial and limited form of laicism insofar as it supported the official establishment and interpretation of the religious tradition of the majority of the population.
32. Kandiyoti, however, argues that the military coup of 1980 marks a watershed in the further dilution of state secularism. In January 1980 a major stabilisation and structural adjustment package was put in place under the auspices of the World Bank and IMF, while the military regime abolished trade unions and established tight state control over other institutions. The restructuring of the state by a praetorian elite safeguarding its interests needed a corresponding state ideology. The military leaders who were in alliance with the right-of-centre political spectrum, most

particularly with the proponents of Turkish-Islam Synthesis promoted by the Intellectuals' Hearth (founded in 1970), sought to manufacture public consent for the consolidation of military power using Islam. This prompted an official transition from secularism to religion-based nationalism. D. Kandiyoti, 'Secularism contested: debate and dissent in Turkey', Lecture delivered at the London School of Economics (LSE), 15 February 2010.

33. For a detailed analysis of the campaign on the Penal Code, see P Ilkkaracan, 'Re/forming laws to secure women's rights in Turkey: the campaign on the Penal Code', in J Gaventa & R McGee (eds), *Citizen Action and National Policy Reform*, London: Zed Books, 2010, pp 195–216.
34. RS Appleby, *The Ambivalence of the Sacred: Religion, Violence, and Reconciliation*, Lanham, MD: Rowman & Littlefield, 2000; and J Haynes, 'Religion and democratizations', *Democratization*, Special Issue, 16(6), 2009, pp 1041–1057.
35. Hajjar, 'Religion, state power and domestic violence in Muslim societies'.
36. Casanova, *Religion, Politics and Gender Equality*.
37. 'Discursive politics' seeks to reinterpret, reformulate, rethink, and rewrite the norms and practices of society and the state. It relies heavily, but not exclusively, on language. Its vehicles are speech and print (conversations, debate, conferences, essays, stories, newsletters and books). MF Katzenstein, 'Discursive politics and feminist activism in the Catholic Church', in MM Feree & PY Martin (eds), *Feminist Organizations: Harvest of the New Women's Movement*, Philadelphia, PA: Temple University Press, 1995, pp 35–52.
38. Hajjar, 'Religion, state power and domestic violence in Muslim societies'; and S Razavi, 'Islamic politics, human rights and women's claims for equality in Iran', *Third World Quarterly*, 27(7), 2006, pp 1223–1237.
39. A Phillips, *Religion*, p 53.
40. P Paidar, *Gender of Democracy: The Encounter between Feminism and Reformism in Contemporary Iran*, UNRISD Programme Paper DGHR No 6, 2001.
41. N Thoidi, cited in V Moghadam, 'Islamic feminism and its discontents: towards a resolution of the debate', *Signs: Journal of Women in Culture and Society*, 27(4), 2002, p 1147.
42. Hajjar, 'Religion, state power and domestic violence in Muslim societies', p 21.
43. R Petchesky, *Global Prescriptions: Gendering Health and Human Rights*, London: UNRISD/Zed Books, 2003.
44. G Sen & S Correa, 'Gender justice and economic justice: reflections on the five year reviews of the UN conferences of the 1990s', paper prepared for UNIFEM for the five-year review of the Beijing Platform for Action, 1999, at http://www.dawn.org.fj/global/health/gender_justice.html, accessed 30 May 2001.

PART

8

The Gendered Workplace

Perhaps the most dramatic social change in industrial countries in the twentieth century has been the entry of women into the workplace. The nineteenth-century ideology of "separate spheres"—the breadwinner husband and the homemaker wife—has slowly and steadily evaporated. While only 20 percent of women and only 4 percent of married women worked outside the home in 1900, more than three-fourths did so by 1995, including 60 percent of married women. In the first decade of the next century, 80 percent of the new entrants into the labor force will be women, minorities, and immigrants.

Despite the collapse of the doctrine of separate spheres—work and home—the workplace remains a dramatically divided world, where women and men rarely do the same jobs in the same place for the same pay. Occupational sex segregation, persistent sex discrimination, wage disparities—all these are problems faced by working women. Paula England provides a bird's-eye overview of where workplace equality has proved most successful and those areas in which women's progress is stalled.

Even women who are seeking to get ahead by entering formerly all-male fields frequently bump into the "glass ceiling"—a limit on how high they can rise in any organization. On the other hand, men who do "women's work"—taking occupations such as nurse, nursery school teacher, librarian—not only avoid the glass ceiling but actually glide up a "glass escalator"—finding greater opportunities at the higher, better paying levels of their professions than women. Adia Harvey Wingfield makes clear that the glass escalator is also a racialized ride—and that men of color may have a different set of experiences entirely.

Kristen Schilt and Matthew Wiswall make clear that gender becomes most visible when it changes. Among transgendered people, male-to-female transgendered people face significantly more discrimination after their transition; female to male transgendered people face significantly less. The gender you are is more important than the gender you were. Changing gender is also changing social status.

The Gender Revolution: Uneven and Stalled

PAULA ENGLAND

We sometimes call the sweeping changes in the gender system since the 1960s a "revolution." Women's employment increased dramatically (Cotter, Hermsen, and England 2008); birth control became widely available (Bailey 2006); women caught up with and surpassed men in rates of college graduation (Cotter, Hermsen, and Vanneman 2004, 23); undergraduate college majors desegregated substantially (England and Li 2006); more women than ever got doctorates as well as professional degrees in law, medicine, and business (Cotter, Hermsen, and Vanneman 2004, 22–23; England et al. 2007); many kinds of gender discrimination in employment and education became illegal (Burstein 1989; Hirsh 2009); women entered many previously male-dominated occupations (Cotter, Hermsen, and Vanneman 2004, 10–14); and more women were elected to political office (Cotter, Hermsen, and Vanneman 2004, 25). As sweeping as these changes have been, change in the gender system has been uneven—affecting some groups more than others and some arenas of life more than others, and change has recently stalled. My goal in this article is not to argue over whether we should view the proverbial cup as half empty or half full (arguments I have always found uninteresting) but, rather, to stretch toward an understanding of why some things change so much more than others. To show the uneven nature of gender change, I will review trends on a number of indicators. While the shape of most of the trends is not in dispute among scholars, the explanations I offer for the uneven and halting nature of change have the status of hypotheses rather than well-documented conclusions.

I will argue that there has been little cultural or institutional change in the devaluation of traditionally female activities and jobs, and as a result, women have had more incentive than men to move into gender-nontraditional activities and positions. This led to asymmetric change; women's lives have changed much more than men's. Yet in some subgroups and arenas, there is less clear incentive for change even among women; examples are the relatively low employment rates of less educated women and the persistence of traditionally gendered patterns in heterosexual romantic, sexual, and marital relationships.

I also argue, drawing on work by Charles and Bradley, that the type of gender egalitarianism that did take hold was the type most compatible with American individualism and its cultural and institutional logics, which include rights of access to jobs and education and the desideratum of upward mobility and of expressing one's "true self" (Charles forthcoming; Charles and Bradley 2002, 2009). One form this gender egalitarianism has taken has been the reduction of discrimination in hiring. This has made much of the gender revolution that has occurred possible; women can now enter formerly "male" spheres. But co-occurring with this gender egalitarianism, and discouraging such integration is a strong (if often tacit) belief in gender essentialism—the notion that men and women are innately and fundamentally different in interests and skills (Charles forthcoming; Charles and Bradley 2002, 2009; Ridgeway 2009). A result of these co-occurring logics is that women are most likely to challenge gender boundaries when there is no path of upward mobility without doing so, but

Paula England, "The Gender Revolution: Uneven and Stalled." *Gender & Society* 24 (2010): 148–67.

otherwise gender blinders guide the paths of both men and women.

Devaluation of "Female" Activities and Asymmetric Incentives for Women and Men to Change

Most of the changes in the gender system heralded as "revolutionary" involve women moving into positions and activities previously limited to men, with few changes in the opposite direction. The source of this asymmetry is an aspect of society's valuation and reward system that has not changed much—the tendency to devalue and badly reward activities and jobs traditionally done by women.

Women's Increased Employment

One form the devaluation of traditionally female activities takes is the failure to treat child rearing as a public good and support those who do it with state payments. In the United States, welfare reform took away much of what little such support had been present. Without this, women doing child rearing are reliant on the employment of male partners (if present) or their own employment. Thus, women have had a strong incentive to seek paid employment, and more so as wage levels rose across the decades (Bergmann 2005). As Figure 1 shows, women's employment has increased dramatically. But change has not been continuous, as the trend line flattened after 1990 and turned down slightly after 2000 before turning up again. This turndown was hardly an "opt-out revolution," to use the popular-press term, as the decline was tiny relative to the dramatic increase across 40 years (Kuperberg and Stone 2008; Percheski 2008). But the stall after 1990 is clear, if unexplained.

Figure 1 also shows the asymmetry in change between men's and women's employment; women's employment has increased much more than men's has declined. There was nowhere near one man leaving the labor force to become a full-time homemaker for every woman who entered, nor did men pick up household work to the extent women added hours of employment (Bianchi, Robinson, and Milkie 2006). Men had little incentive to leave employment.

Among women, incentives for employment vary. Class-based[1] resources, such as education, affect these incentives. At first glance, we might expect

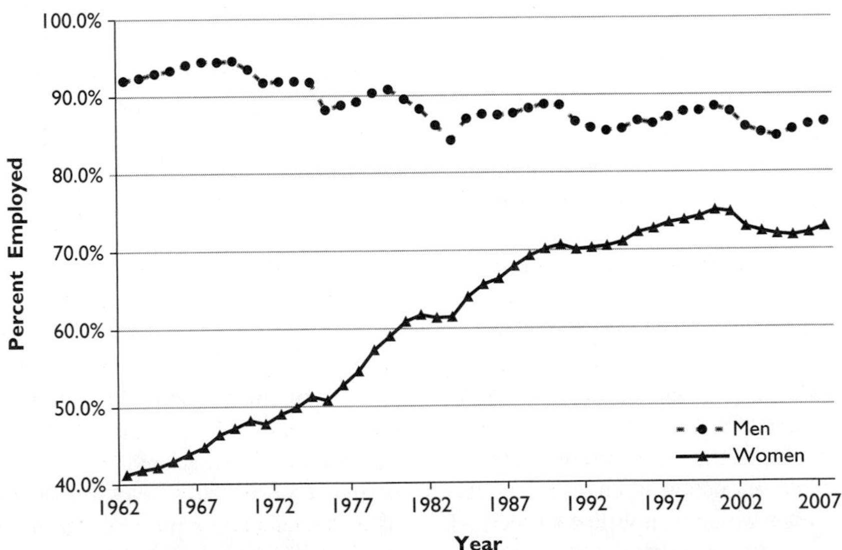

Figure 1. Percentage of U.S. Men and Women Employed, 1962–2007
Source: Cotter, Hermsen, and Vanneman (2009).
Note: Persons are considered employed if they worked for pay anytime during the year. Refers to adults aged 25 to 54.

less educated women to have higher employment rates than their better-educated peers because they are less likely to be married to a high-earning man. Most marriages are between two people at a similar education level (Mare 1991), so the less educated woman, if she is married, typically has a husband earning less than the husband of the college graduate. Her family would seem to need the money from her employment more than the family headed by two college graduates. Let us call this the "need for income" effect. But the countervailing "opportunity cost" factor is that well-educated women have more economic incentive for employment because they can earn more (England, Garcia-Beaulieu, and Ross 2004). Put another way, the opportunity cost of staying at home is greater for the woman who can earn more. Indeed, the woman who did not graduate from high school may have potential earnings so low that she could not even cover child care costs with what she could earn. Thus, in typical cases, for the married college graduate, her own education encourages her employment, while her husband's high earnings discourage it. The less educated woman typically has a poor husband (if any), which encourages her employment, while her own low earning power discourages her employment.[2] It is an empirical question whether the "need for income" or "opportunity cost" effect predominates.

Recent research shows that the opportunity-cost effect predominates in the United States and other affluent nations. England, Gornick, and Shafer (2008) use data from 16 affluent countries circa 2000 and show that, in all of them, among women partnered with men (married or cohabiting), those with more education are more likely to be employed. Moreover, there is no monotonic relationship between partner's earnings and a woman's employment; at top levels of his income, her employment is deterred. But women whose male partners are at middle income levels are more likely to be employed than women whose partners have very low or no earnings, the opposite of what the "need for income" principle suggests.

In the United States, it has been true for decades that well-educated women are more likely to be employed, and the effect of a woman's own education has increased, while the deterring effect of her husband's income has declined (Cohen and Bianchi 1999). For example, in 1970, 59 percent of college graduate women, but only 43 percent of those with less than a high school education, were employed sometime during the year. In 2007, the figures were 80 percent for college graduates and 47 percent for less than high school (the relationship of education and employment was monotonic such that those with some college and only high school were in between college graduates and high school dropouts) (figures are author's calculation from data in Cotter, Hermsen, and Vanneman 2009).[3]

Women Moving into "Male" Jobs and Fields of Study

The devaluation of and underpayment of predominantly female occupations is an important institutional reality that provides incentives for both men and women to choose "male" over "female" occupations and the fields of study that lead to them. Research has shown that predominantly female occupations pay less, on average, than jobs with a higher proportion of men. At least some of the gap is attributable to sex composition because it persists in statistical models controlling for occupations' educational requirements, amount of skill required, unionization, and so forth. I have argued that this is a form of gender discrimination—employers see the worth of predominantly female jobs through biased lenses and, as a result, set pay levels for both men and women in predominantly female jobs lower than they would be if the jobs had a more heavily male sex composition (England 1992; Kilbourne et al. 1994; England and Folbre 2005). While the overall sex gap in pay has diminished because more women have moved into "male" fields (England and Folbre 2005), there is no evidence that the devaluation of occupations because they are filled with women has diminished (Levanon, England, and Allison 2009). Indeed, as U.S. courts have interpreted the law, this type of between-job discrimination is not even illegal (England 1992, 225–51; Steinberg 2001), whereas it is illegal to pay women less than men in the same job, unless based on factors such as seniority, qualifications, or performance. Given this, both men and women continue to have a pecuniary incentive to choose male-dominated occupations. Thus, we should not be surprised that desegregation of occupations has largely taken the form of women moving into male-dominated fields, rather than men moving into female-dominated fields.

Consistent with the incentives embedded in the ongoing devaluation of female fields, desegregation of fields of college study came from more women going into fields that were predominantly male, not from more men entering "female" fields. Since 1970, women increasingly majored in previously male-dominated, business-related fields, such as business, marketing, and accounting; while fewer chose traditionally female majors like English, education, and sociology; and there was little increase of men's choice of these latter majors (England and Li 2006, 667–69). Figure 2 shows the desegregation of fields of bachelor's degree receipt, using the index of dissimilarity (D), a scale on which complete segregation (all fields are all male or all female) is 100 and complete integration (all fields have the same proportion of women as women's proportion of all bachelor's degrees in the given year) is 0. It shows that segregation dropped significantly in the 1970s and early 1980s, but has been quite flat since the mid-1980s. Women's increased integration of business fields stopped then as well (England and Li 2006).

Women have also recently increased their representation in formerly male-dominated professional degrees, getting MDs, MBAs, and law degrees in large numbers. Women were 6 percent of those getting MDs in 1960, 23 percent in 1980, 43 percent in 2000, and 49 percent in 2007; the analogous numbers for law degrees (JDs) were 3, 30, 46, and 47 percent, and for MBAs (and other management first-professional degrees), 4, 22, 39, and 44 percent (National Center for Education Statistics 2004–2008). There was no marked increase in the proportion of men in female-dominated graduate professional programs such as library science, social work, or nursing (National Center for Education Statistics 2009).

As women have increasingly trained for previously male-dominated fields, they have also integrated previously male-dominated occupations in management and the professions in large numbers (Cotter, Hermsen, and Vanneman 2004, 10–13). Women may face discrimination and coworker resistance when they attempt to integrate these fields, but they have a strong pecuniary incentive to do so. Men lose money and suffer cultural disapproval when they choose traditionally

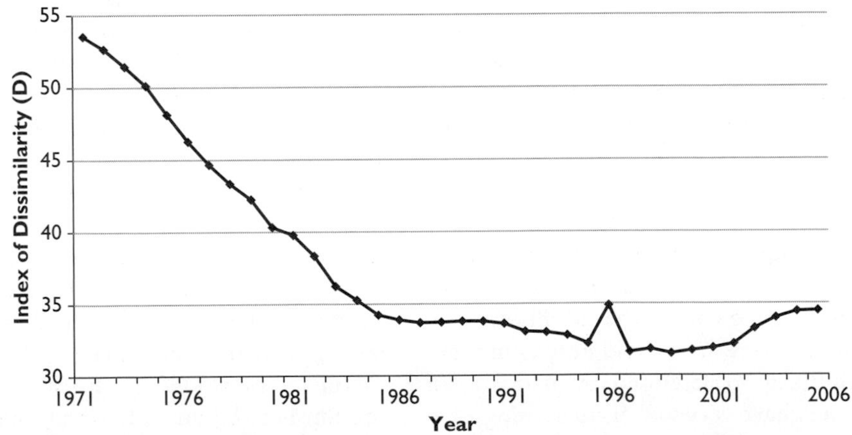

Figure 2. Sex Segregation of Fields of Study for U.S. Bachelor Degree Recipients, 1971–2006

Source: Author's calculations from the National Center for Education Statistics (NCES) 1971–2003 and NCES 2004–2007.

female-dominated fields; they have little incentive to transgress gender boundaries. While some men have entered female-intensive retail service jobs after losing manufacturing jobs, there is little incentive for voluntary movement in this direction, making desegregation a largely one-way street.

What about employers' incentives? There is some debate about whether, absent equal employment legislation, employers have an incentive to engage in hiring and placement discrimination or are better off simply hiring gender-blind (for debate, see Jackson 1998; England 1992, 54–68). Whichever is true, legal enforcement of antidiscrimination laws has imposed some costs for hiring discrimination (Hirsh 2009), and this has probably reduced discrimination in hiring, contributing to desegregation of jobs.

The "Personal" Realm

"The personal is political" was a rallying cry of 1960s feminists, urging women to demand equality in private as well as public life. Yet conventions embodying male dominance have changed much less in "the personal" than in the job world. Where they have changed, the asymmetry described above for the job world prevails. For example, parents are more likely to give girls "boy" toys such as Legos than they are to give dolls to their sons. Girls have increased their participation in sports more than boys have taken up cheerleading or ballet. Women now commonly wear pants, while men wearing skirts remains rare. A few women started keeping their birth given surname upon marriage (Goldin and Shim 2004), with little adoption by men of women's last names. Here, as with jobs, the asymmetry follows incentives, albeit nonmaterial ones. These social incentives themselves flow from a largely unchanged devaluation of things culturally defined as feminine. When boys and men take on "female" activities, they often suffer disrespect, but under some circumstances, girls and women gain respect for taking on "male" activities.

What is more striking than the asymmetry of gender change in the personal realm is how little gendering has changed at all in this realm, especially in dyadic heterosexual relationships. It is still men who usually ask women on dates, and sexual behavior is generally initiated by men (England, Shafer, and Fogarty 2008). Sexual permissiveness has increased, making it more acceptable for both heterosexual men and women to have sex outside committed relationships. But the gendered part of this—the double standard—persists stubbornly; women are judged much more harshly than men for casual sex (Hamilton and Armstrong 2009; England, Shafer, and Fogarty 2008). The ubiquity of asking about height in Internet dating Web sites suggests that the convention that men should be taller than their female partner has not budged. The double standard of aging prevails, making women's chances of marriage decrease with age much more than men's (England and McClintock 2009). Men are still expected to propose marriage (Sassler and Miller 2007). Upon marriage, the vast majority of women take their husband's surname. The number of women keeping their own name increased in the 1970s and 1980s but little thereafter, never exceeding about 25 percent even for college graduates (who have higher rates than other women) (Goldin and Shim 2004). Children are usually given their father's surname; a recent survey found that even in cases where the mother is not married to the father, 92 percent of babies are given the father's last name (McLanahan forthcoming). While we do not have trend data on all these personal matters, my sense is that they have changed much less than gendered features of the world of paid work.

The limited change seen in the heterosexual personal realm may be because women's incentive to change these things is less clear than their incentive to move into paid work and into higher-paying "male" jobs. The incentives that do exist are largely noneconomic. For example, women may find it meaningful to keep their birth-given surnames and give them to their children, and they probably enjoy sexual freedom and initiation, especially if they are not judged adversely for it. But these noneconomic benefits may be neutralized by the noneconomic penalties from transgressing gender norms and by the fact that some have internalized the norms. When women transgress gender barriers to enter "male" jobs, they too may be socially penalized for violating norms, but for many this is offset by the economic gain.

Co-occurring Logics of Women's Rights to Upward Mobility and Gender Essentialism

I have stressed that important change in the gender system has taken the form of women integrating traditionally male occupations and fields of study. But even here change is uneven. The main generalization is shown by Figure 3, which divides all occupations by a crude measure of class, calling professional, management, and nonretail sales occupations "middle class," and all others "working class" (including retail sales, assembly work in manufacturing, blue-collar trades, and other nonprofessional service work). Using the index of dissimilarity to measure segregation, Figure 3 shows that desegregation has proceeded much farther in middle-class than working-class jobs. Middle-class jobs showed dramatic desegregation, although the trend lessened its pace after 1990. By contrast, working-class jobs are almost as segregated as they were in 1950! Women have integrated the previously male strongholds of management, law, medicine, and academia in large numbers. But women have hardly gained a foothold in blue-collar, male-dominated jobs such as plumbing, construction, truck driving, welding, and assembly in durable manufacturing industries such as auto and steel (Cotter, Hermsen, and Vanneman 2004, 12–14). This is roughly the situation in other affluent nations as well (Charles and Grusky 2004). This same class difference in trend can be seen if we compare the degree of segregation among those who have various levels of education; in the United States, sex segregation declined much more dramatically since 1970 for college graduates than any other group (Cotter, Hermsen, and Vanneman 2009, 2004, 13–14).

Why has desegregation been limited to high-level jobs? The question has two parts: why women did not integrate blue-collar male jobs in significant numbers, and why women did integrate professional and managerial jobs in droves. Why one and not the other? Many factors were undoubtedly

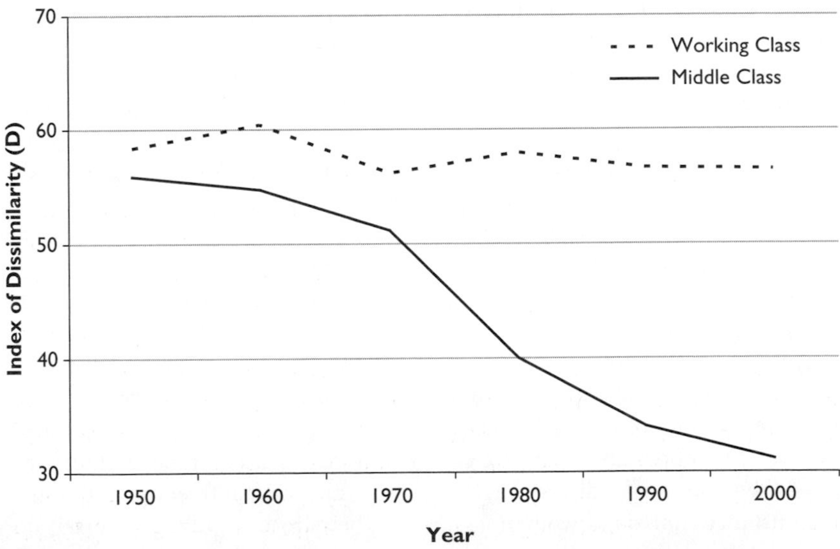

Figure 3. Sex Segregation of Middle-Class and Working-Class Occupations in the United States, 1950–2000

Source: Cotter, Hermsen, and Vanneman (2004, 14).

Note: Middle-class occupations include professional, management, and nonretail sales. All others are classified as working-class occupations.

at work,[4] but I will focus on one account, which borrows from Charles and Bradley (Charles forthcoming; Charles and Bradley 2002, 2009). In the United States and many Western societies today, a certain kind of gender egalitarianism has taken hold ideologically and institutionally. The logic is that individuals should have equal rights to education and jobs of their choice. Moreover, achievement and upward mobility are generally valued. There is also a "postmaterialist" aspect to the culture which orients one to find her or his "true self." The common ethos is a combination of "the American dream" and liberal individualism. Many women, like men, want to "move up" in earnings and/or status, or at least avoid moving down. But up or down relative to what reference group? I suggest that the implicit reference group is typically those in the previous generation (or previous birth cohorts) of one's own social class background and one's own sex. For example, women might see their mothers or aunts as a reference, or women who graduated with their level of education ten years ago. Persons of the same-sex category are the implicit reference group because of strong beliefs in gender essentialism, that notion that men and women are innately and fundamentally different (Charles forthcoming; Ridgeway 2009). While liberal individualism encourages a commitment to "free choice" gender egalitarianism (such as legal equality of opportunity), ironically, orienting toward gender-typical paths has probably been encouraged by the emerging form of individualism that stresses finding and expressing one's "true self." Notions of self will in fact be largely socially constructed, pulling from socially salient identities. Because of the omnipresent nature of gender in the culture (Ridgeway 2009; West and Zimmerman 1987), gender often becomes the most available material from which to construct aspirations and may be used even more when a job choice is seen as a deep statement about self (Charles and Bradley 2009).

Given all this, I hypothesize that if women can move "up" in status or income relative to their reference group while still staying in a job typically filled by women, then because of gender beliefs and gendered identities, they are likely to do so. If they cannot move up without integrating a male field, and demand is present and discrimination not too strong, they are more likely to cross the gender boundary. Applying this hypothesis, why would women not enter male blue-collar fields? To be sure, many women without college degrees would earn much more in the skilled blue-collar crafts or unionized manufacturing jobs than in the service jobs typically filled by women at their education levels—jobs such as maid, child care worker, retail sales clerk, or assembler in the textile industry. So they have an economic incentive to enter these jobs. But such women could also move "up" to clerical work or teaching, higher status and better paying but still traditionally female jobs. Many take this path, often getting more education.

In contrast, consider women who assumed they would go to college and whose mothers were in female-dominated jobs requiring a college degree like teacher, nurse, librarian, or social worker. For these women, to move up in status or earnings from their reference group options requires them to enter traditionally male jobs; there are virtually no heavily female jobs with higher status than these female professions. These are just the women, usually of middle-class origins, who have been integrating management, law, medicine, and academia in recent decades. For them, upward mobility was not possible within traditional boundaries, so they were more likely to integrate male fields.

In sum, my argument is that one reason that women integrated male professions and management much more than blue-collar jobs is that the women for whom the blue-collar male jobs would have constituted "progress" also had the option to move up by entering higher-ranking female jobs via more education. They thus had options for upward mobility without transgressing gender boundaries not present for their middle-class sisters.

Even women entering male-typical occupations, however, sometimes choose the more female-intensive subfields in them. In some cases, ending up in female-intensive subfields results from discrimination, but in others it may result from the gender essentialism discussed above. An example is the movement of women into doctoral study and into the occupation of "professor." This development brought women into a new arena. But within

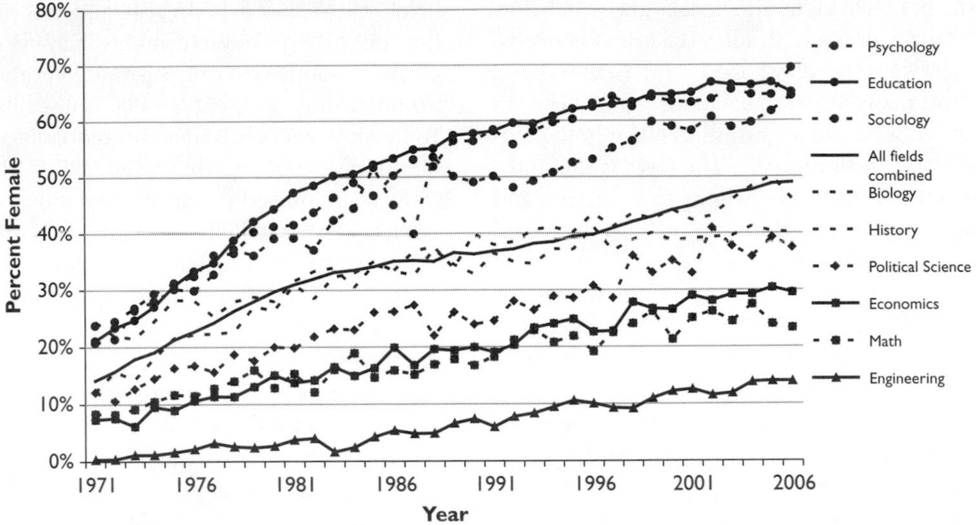

Figure 4. Percentage of All Doctoral Degree Recipients Who Were Women in Selected Large Fields, 1971–2006

Source: Author's calculations from the National Center for Education Statistics (NCES) 1971–2003 and NCES 2004–2007.

Note: All fields combined refers to all fields of doctoral study, not only the nine fields shown here. Engineering refers to doctoral degrees in E.E. Psychology excludes clinical psychology.

this arena, there was virtually no desegregation of fields of doctoral study from 1970 on (England et al. 2007, 32).[5] Women have gone from being only 14 percent of those who get doctorates in 1971 to nearly half. But, conditional on getting a doctoral degree, neither women nor men have changed the fields of study they choose much (England et al. 2007). This can be seen in Figure 4, which shows the percentage women were of nine large fields of study in each year from 1971 to 2006. The percentage female in every field went up dramatically, reflecting the overall increase in women getting doctorates. But the rank order of fields in their percentage female changed little. The fields with the highest percentage of women today are those that already had a high percentage of women decades ago relative to other fields.

What explains the failure of fields of doctoral study—and thus academic departments—to desegregate? Following the line of argument above, I suggest that the extreme differentiation of fields of academic study allowed many women moving "up" to doctoral study and an academic career to do so in fields that seemed consistent with their (tacitly gendered) notions of their interests and "true selves." Women academics in the humanities and social sciences thus find themselves in the more female subunits (disciplines) of a still largely male-dominated larger unit (the professorate).

Conclusion

Change in the gender system has been uneven, changing the lives of some groups of people more than others and changing lives in some arenas more than others. Although many factors are at play, I have offered two broad explanations for the uneven nature of change.

First, I argued that, because of the cultural and institutional devaluation of characteristics and activities associated with women, men had little incentive to move into badly rewarded, traditionally female activities such as homemaking or female-dominated occupations. By contrast, women had powerful economic incentives to move into the traditionally male domains of paid employment and male-typical occupations; and when hiring discrimination declined, many did. These incentives varied by class, however; the incentive to go to work for pay is much stronger for women who can earn more; thus employment levels have been higher for well-educated women. I also noted a lack of change in the gendering of the personal realm, especially of heterosexual romantic and sexual relationships.

Second, I explored the consequences of the co-occurrence of two Western cultural and institutional logics. Individualism, encompassing a belief in rights to equal opportunity in access to jobs and education in order to express one's "true self," promotes a certain kind of gender egalitarianism. It does not challenge the devaluation of traditionally female spheres, but it encourages the rights of women to upward mobility through equal access to education and jobs. To be sure, this ideal has been imperfectly realized, but this type of gender egalitarianism has taken hold strongly. But co-occurring with it, somewhat paradoxically, are strong (if tacit) beliefs in gender essentialism—that men and women are innately and fundamentally different in interests and skills (Charles forthcoming; Charles and Bradley 2002, 2009; Ridgeway 2009). Almost no men and precious few women, even those who believe in "equal opportunity," have an explicit commitment to undoing gender differentiation for its own sake. Gender essentialism encourages traditional choices and leads women to see previous cohorts of women of their social class as the reference point from which they seek upward mobility. I concluded that the co-occurrence of these two logics—equal opportunity individualism and gender essentialism—make it most likely for women to move into nontraditional fields of study or work when there is no possible female field that constitutes upward mobility from the socially constructed reference point. This helps explain why women integrated male-dominated professional and managerial jobs more than blue-collar jobs. Women from working-class backgrounds, whose mothers were maids or assemblers in nondurable manufacturing, could move up financially by entering blue-collar "male" trades but often decide instead to get more education and move up into a female job such as secretary or teacher. It is women with middle-class backgrounds, whose mothers were teachers or nurses, who cannot move up without entering a male-dominated career, and it is just such women who have integrated management, law, medicine, and academia. Yet even while integrating large fields such as academia, women often gravitate toward the more female-typical fields of study.

As sociologists, we emphasize links between parts of a social system. For example, we trace how gender inequality in jobs affects gender inequality in the family, and vice versa (England and Farkas 1986). Moreover, links between parts of the system are recognized in today's prevailing view in which gender is itself a multilevel system, with causal arrows going both ways from macro to micro (Risman 2004). All these links undoubtedly exist, but the unevenness of gender-related change highlights how loosely coupled parts of the social system are and how much stronger some causal forces for change are than others. For example, because it resonated with liberal individualism well, the part of the feminist message that urged giving women equal access to jobs and education made considerable headway and led to much of what we call the gender revolution. But even as women integrated employment and "male" professional and managerial jobs, the part of feminism challenging the devaluation of traditionally female activities and jobs made little headway. The result is persistently low rewards for women who remain focused on mothering or in traditionally female jobs and little incentive for men to make the gender revolution a two-way street.

While discussing the uneven character of gender change, I also noted that the type of gender change with the most momentum—middle-class women entering traditionally male spheres—has recently stalled (Cotter, Hermsen, and Vanneman 2004, 2009). Women's employment rates stabilized, desegregation of occupations slowed down, and desegregation of fields of college study stopped. Erosion of the sex gap in pay slowed as well (Cotter, Hermsen, and Vanneman 2009).

While the reason for the stalling is unclear, like the unevenness of change, the stalling of change reminds us how contingent and path-dependent gender egalitarian change is, with no inexorable equal endpoint. Change has been as much unintended consequence of larger institutional and cultural forces as realization of the efforts of feminist organizing, although the latter has surely helped.[6] Indeed, given the recent stalling of change, future feminist organizing may be necessary to revitalize change.

Notes

1. In this article, I use the term *class* to cover both categoric notions of class and gradational notions of socioeconomic position. Often I use education or occupation as imperfect but readily available indicators of class.
2. A complementary hypothesis about why employment rates are lower for less educated women is that, compared to women with more education, they place a higher value on motherhood and find less intrinsic meaning in the jobs they can get. In this vein, Edin and Kefalas (2005) argue that low-income women place a higher value on motherhood because they have so few alternative sources of meaning. However, Ferree (1976) found that working-class women were happier if employed; they worked for the money but also gained a sense of competence, connectedness, and self-determination from their jobs. McQuillan et al. (2008) find that neither education nor careerism is associated with the value placed on motherhood. Overall, there is no clear conclusion on class differences in how women value motherhood and jobs.
3. Women's employment is higher at higher education levels, but it is not clear if the gender gap in employment is less at higher education levels. This is because men's employment is also affected by education. For example, in 2007, 94 percent of men with a college education, but only 74 percent of those with less than high school, were employed sometime during the year (Cotter, Hermsen, and Vanneman 2009). How gender inequality in employment varies by education depends on the metric used to measure inequality. Inequality is smaller at high education levels if the ratio of women's to men's proportion employed is used, but not if the difference between men's and women's log odds of employment is used (author calculations from Cotter, Hermsen, and Vanneman 2009; results not shown).
4. One important additional factor is that blue-collar male jobs have been contracting (Morris and Western 1999), so integrating them would have been more difficult even if women had wanted to do so. Moreover, male coworkers may fight harder to harass and keep women out of blue-collar than professional and managerial jobs; lacking class privilege, blue-collar men may feel a stronger need than more privileged men to defend their gender privilege. Finally, it is possible that the Equal Employment Opportunity Commission had an institutional bias toward bringing cases challenging discrimination in high-level managerial and professional positions, particularly when they became concerned with the "glass ceiling." This could explain why Burstein (1989) found more discrimination cases in high-level jobs.
5. England et al. (2007) showed no nontrivial change in segregation of doctoral degrees through 2002. Using the same source (National Center for Education Statistics 2004–2007), I have computed the index of dissimilarity, which shows that the lack of change continued through 2006 (results not shown).
6. Risman (2009) reminds us that that our own teaching has probably had an effect on keeping feminism alive, as today's young feminists often say that the college classroom was where they began to identify as feminists.

References

Bailey, Martha J. 2006. More power to the pill: The impact of contraceptive freedom on women's life cycle labor supply. *Quarterly Journal of Economics* 121:289–320.

Bergmann, Barbara. 2005. *The economic emergence of women*. 2nd ed. New York: Basic Books.

Bianchi, Suzanne, John P. Robinson, and Melissa A. Milkie. 2006. *Changing rhythms of American family life*. New York: Russell Sage Foundation.

Burstein, Paul. 1989. Attacking sex discrimination in the labor market: A study in law and politics. *Social Forces* 67:641–65.

Charles, Maria. Forthcoming. A world of difference: International trends in women's economic status. *Annual Review of Sociology*.

Charles, Maria, and Karen Bradley. 2002. Equal but separate: A cross-national study of sex segregation in higher education. *American Sociological Review* 67:573–99.

Charles, Maria, and Karen Bradley. 2009. Indulging our gendered selves: Sex segregation by field of study in 44 countries. *American Journal of Sociology*. 114:924–76.

Charles, Maria, and David B. Grusky. 2004. *Occupational ghettos: The worldwide segregation of women and men*. Stanford, CA: Stanford University Press.

Cohen, Philip N., and Suzanne M. Bianchi. 1999. Marriage, children, and women's employment: What do we know? *Monthly Labor Review* 122:22–31.

Cotter, David A., Joan M. Hermsen, and Paula England. 2008. Moms and jobs: Trends in mothers' employment and which mothers stay home. In *American families: A multicultural reader*, 2nd ed., edited by Stephanie Coontz, with Maya Parson and Gabrielle Raley, 379–86. New York: Routledge.

Cotter, David A., Joan M. Hermsen, and Reeve Vanneman. 2004. *Gender inequality at work*. New York: Russell Sage Foundation.

Cotter, David A., Joan M. Hermsen, and Reeve Vanneman. 2009. End of the gender revolution website. http://www.bsos.umd.edu/socy/vanneman/endofgr/default.html (accessed December 14, 2009).

Edin, Kathryn, and Maria Kefalas. 2005. *Promises I can keep: Why poor women put motherhood before marriage*. Berkeley: University of California Press.

England, Paula 1992. *Comparable worth: Theories and evidence*. New York: Aldine.

England, Paula, Paul Allison, Su Li, Noah Mark, Jennifer Thompson, Michelle Budig, and Han Sun. 2007. Why are some academic fields tipping toward female? The sex composition of U.S. fields of doctoral degree receipt, 1971–2002. *Sociology of Education* 80:23–42.

England, Paula, and George Farkas. 1986. *Households, employment, and gender: A social, economic, and demographic view*. New York: Aldine.

England, Paula, and Nancy Folbre. 2005. Gender and economic sociology. In *The handbook of economic sociology*, edited by N. J. Smelser and R. Swedberg, 627–49. New York: Russell Sage Foundation.

England, Paula, Carmen Garcia-Beaulieu, and Mary Ross. 2004. Women's employment among Blacks, whites, and three groups of Latinas: Do more privileged women have higher employment? *Gender & Society* 18 (4): 494–509.

England, Paula, Janet C. Gornick, and Emily Fitzgibbons Shafer. 2008. Is it better at the top? How women's employment and the gender earnings gap vary by education in sixteen countries. Paper presented at the 2008 annual meeting of the American Sociological Association.

England, Paula, and Su Li. 2006. Desegregation stalled: The changing gender composition of college majors, 1971–2002. *Gender & Society* 20:657–77.

England, Paula, and Elizabeth Aura McClintock. 2009. The gendered double standard of aging in U.S. marriage markets. *Population and Development Review* 35:797–816.

England, Paula, Emily Fitzgibbons Shafer, and Alison C. K. Fogarty. 2008. Hooking up and forming romantic relationships on today's college campuses. In *The gendered society reader*, 3rd ed., edited by Michael Kimmel and Amy Aronson, 531–46. New York: Oxford University Press.

Ferree, Myra Marx. 1976. Working-class jobs: Paid work and housework as sources of satisfaction. *Social Problems* 23 (4): 431–41.

Goldin, Claudia, and Maria Shim. 2004. Making a name: Women's surnames at marriage and beyond. *Journal of Economic Perspectives* 18:143–60.

Hamilton, Laura, and Elizabeth A. Armstrong. 2009. Gendered sexuality in young adulthood: Double binds and flawed options. *Gender & Society* 23:589–616.

Hirsh, C. Elizabeth. 2009. The strength of weak enforcement: The impact of discrimination charges on sex and race segregation in the workplace. *American Sociological Review* 74 (2): 245–71.

Jackson, Robert Max. 1998. *Destined for equality: The inevitable rise of women's status*. Cambridge, MA: Harvard University Press.

Kilbourne, Barbara Stanek, Paula England, George Farkas, Kurt Beron, and Dorothea Weir. 1994. Returns to skills, compensating differentials, and gender bias: Effects of occupational characteristics on the wages of white women and men. *American Journal of Sociology* 100:689–719.

Kuperberg, Arielle, and Pamela Stone. 2008. The media depiction of women who opt out. *Gender & Society* 2:497–517.

Levanon, Asaf, Paula England, and Paul Allison. 2009. Occupational feminization and pay: Assessing causal dynamics using 1950–2000 census data. *Social Forces* 88:865–92.

Mare, Robert D. 1991. Five decades of educational assortative mating. *American Sociological Review* 56:15–32.

McLanahan, Sara. Forthcoming. Children in fragile families. In *Families in an unequal society*, edited by Marcia Carlson and Paula England. Stanford, CA: Stanford University Press.

McQuillan, Julia, Arthur L. Greil, Karina M. Shreffler, and Veronica Tichenor. 2008. The importance of motherhood among women in the contemporary United States. *Gender & Society* 22:477–96.

Morris, Martina, and Bruce Western. 1999. Inequality in earnings at the close of the twentieth century. *Annual Review of Sociology* 25:623–57.

National Center for Education Statistics. 1971–2003. *Digest of education statistics*. Washington, DC: Government Printing Office.

National Center for Education Statistics. 2004–2007. Table numbers by year: 2004: 253, 2005: 252, 2006: 58, 2007: 264, 2008: 279. http://nces.ed.gov/programs/digest (accessed December 14, 2009).

Percheski, Christine. 2008. Opting out? Cohort differences in professional women's employment rates from 1960 to 2000. *American Sociological Review* 73:497–517.

Ridgeway, Cecilia L. 2009. Framed before we know it: How gender shapes social relations. *Gender & Society* 23:145–60.

Risman, Barbara J. 2004. Gender as a social structure: Theory wrestling with activism. *Gender & Society* 18:429–50.

Risman, Barbara J. 2009. From doing to undoing: Gender as we know it. *Gender & Society* 23:81–84.

Sassler, Sharon, and Amanda Miller. 2007. Waiting to be asked: Gender, power and relationship progression among cohabiting couples. Presented at the annual meeting of the American Sociological Association, New York, August.

Steinberg, Ronnie J. 2001. Comparable worth in gender studies. In *International encyclopedia of the social and behavioral sciences*, vol. 4, edited by Neil J. Smelser and Paul B. Baltes. Cambridge: Cambridge University Press.

West, Candace, and Donald H. Zimmerman. 1987. Doing gender. *Gender & Society* 1:125–51.

Racializing the Glass Escalator: Reconsidering Men's Experiences with Women's Work

ADIA HARVEY WINGFIELD

Sociologists who study work have long noted that jobs are sex segregated and that this segregation creates different occupational experiences for men and women (Charles and Grusky 2004). Jobs predominantly filled by women often require "feminine" traits such as nurturing, caring, and empathy, a fact that means men confront perceptions that they are unsuited for the requirements of these jobs. Rather than having an adverse effect on their occupational experiences, however, these assumptions facilitate men's entry into better paying, higher status positions, creating what Williams (1995) labels a "glass escalator" effect.

The glass escalator model has been an influential paradigm in understanding the experiences of men who do women's work. Researchers have identified this process among men nurses, social workers, paralegals, and librarians and have cited its pervasiveness as evidence of men's consistent advantage in the workplace, such that even in jobs where men are numerical minorities they are likely to enjoy higher wages and faster promotions (Floge and Merrill 1986; Heikes 1991; Pierce 1995; Williams 1989, 1995). Most of these studies implicitly assume a racial homogenization of men workers in women's professions, but this supposition is problematic for several reasons. For one, minority men are not only present but are actually overrepresented in certain areas of reproductive work that have historically been dominated by white women (Duffy 2007). Thus, research that focuses primarily on white men in women's professions ignores a key segment of men who perform this type of labor. Second, and perhaps more important, conclusions based on the experiences of white men tend to overlook the ways that intersections of race and gender create different experiences for different men. While extensive work has documented the fact that white men in women's professions encounter a glass escalator effect that aids their occupational mobility (for an exception, see Snyder and Green 2008), few studies, if any, have considered how this effect is a function not only of gendered advantage but of racial privilege as well.

In this article, I examine the implications of race–gender intersections for minority men employed in a female-dominated, feminized occupation, specifically focusing on Black men in nursing. Their experiences doing "women's work" demonstrate that the glass escalator is a racialized as well as gendered concept.

Theoretical Framework

In her classic study *Men and Women of the Corporation*, Kanter (1977) offers a groundbreaking analysis of group interactions. Focusing on high-ranking women executives who work mostly with men, Kanter argues that those in the extreme numerical minority are tokens who are socially isolated, highly visible, and adversely stereotyped. Tokens have difficulty forming relationships with colleagues and often are excluded from social networks that provide mobility. Because of their low numbers, they are also highly visible as people who

Adia Harvey Wingfield, "Racializing the Glass Escalator: Reconsidering Men's Experiences with Women's Work" from *Gender and Society* 23, No. 1 (February 2009): 5–26.

are different from the majority, even though they often feel invisible when they are ignored or overlooked in social settings. Tokens are also stereotyped by those in the majority group and frequently face pressure to behave in ways that challenge and undermine these stereo- types. Ultimately, Kanter argues that it is harder for them to blend into the organization and to work effectively and productively, and that they face serious barriers to upward mobility.

Kanter's (1977) arguments have been analyzed and retested in various settings and among many populations. Many studies, particularly of women in male-dominated corporate settings, have supported her findings. Other work has reversed these conclusions, examining the extent to which her conclusions hold when men were the tokens and women the majority group. These studies fundamentally challenged the gender neutrality of the token, finding that men in the minority fare much better than do similarly situated women. In particular, this research suggests that factors such as heightened visibility and polarization do not necessarily disadvantage men who are in the minority. While women tokens find that their visibility hinders their ability to blend in and work productively, men tokens find that their conspicuousness can lead to greater opportunities for leadership and choice assignments (Floge and Merrill 1986; Heikes 1991). Studies in this vein are important because they emphasize organizations—and occupations—as gendered institutions that subsequently create dissimilar experiences for men and women tokens (see Acker 1990).

In her groundbreaking study of men employed in various women's professions, Williams (1995) further develops this analysis of how power relationships shape the ways men tokens experience work in women's professions. Specifically, she introduces the concept of the glass escalator to explain men's experiences as tokens in these areas. Like Floge and Merrill (1986) and Heikes (1991), Williams finds that men tokens do not experience the isolation, visibility, blocked access to social networks, and stereotypes in the same ways that women tokens do. In contrast, Williams argues that even though they are in the minority, processes are in place that actually facilitate their opportunity and advancement. Even in culturally feminized occupations, then, men's advantage is built into the very structure and everyday interactions of these jobs so that men find themselves actually struggling to remain in place. For these men, "despite their intentions, they face invisible pressures to move up in their professions. Like being on a moving escalator, they have to work to stay in place" (Williams 1995, 87).

The glass escalator term thus refers to the "subtle mechanisms in place that enhance [men's] positions in [women's] professions" (Williams 1995, 108). These mechanisms include certain behaviors, attitudes, and beliefs men bring to these professions as well as the types of interactions that often occur between these men and their colleagues, supervisors, and customers. Consequently, even in occupations composed mostly of women, gendered perceptions about men's roles, abilities, and skills privilege them and facilitate their advancement. The glass escalator serves as a conduit that channels men in women's professions into the uppermost levels of the occupational hierarchy. Ultimately, the glass escalator effect suggests that men retain consistent occupational advantages over women, even when women are numerically in the majority (Budig 2002; Williams 1995).

Though this process has now been fairly well established in the literature, there are reasons to question its generalizability to all men. In an early critique of the supposed general neutrality of the token, Zimmer (1988) notes that much research on race comes to precisely the opposite of Kanter's conclusions, finding that as the numbers of minority group members increase (e.g., as they become less likely to be "tokens"), so too do tensions between the majority and minority groups. For instance, as minorities move into predominantly white neighborhoods, increasing numbers do not create the likelihood of greater acceptance and better treatment. In contrast, whites are likely to relocate when neighborhoods become "too" integrated, citing concerns about property values and racialized ideas about declining neighborhood quality (Shapiro 2004). Reinforcing, while at the same time tempering, the findings of research on men in female-dominated occupations, Zimmer (1988, 71) argues that relationships between tokens and the majority depend on understanding the underlying power relationships between these groups and "the status and power differentials between them." Hence, just as men who are tokens fare better than women, it also follows that the experiences of Blacks and whites as tokens should differ in ways that reflect their positions in hierarchies of status and power.

The concept of the glass escalator provides an important and useful framework for addressing men's experiences in women's occupations, but so far research in this vein has neglected to examine whether the glass escalator is experienced among all men in an identical manner. Are the processes that facilitate a ride on the glass escalator available to minority men? Or does race intersect with gender to affect the extent to which the glass escalator offers men opportunities in women's professions? In the next section, I examine whether and how the mechanisms that facilitate a ride on the glass escalator might be unavailable to Black men in nursing.[1]

Relationships with Colleagues and Supervisors

One key aspect of riding the glass escalator involves the warm, collegial welcome men workers often receive from their women colleagues. Often, this reaction is a response to the fact that professions dominated by women are frequently low in salary and status and that greater numbers of men help improve prestige and pay (Heikes 1991). Though some women workers resent the apparent ease with which men enter and advance in women's professions, the generally warm welcome men receive stands in stark contrast to the cold reception, difficulties with mentorship, and blocked access to social networks that women often encounter when they do men's work (Roth 2006; Williams 1992). In addition, unlike women in men's professions, men who do women's work frequently have supervisors of the same sex. Men workers can thus enjoy a gendered bond with their supervisor in the context of a collegial work environment. These factors often converge, facilitating men's access to higher-status positions and producing the glass escalator effect.

The congenial relationship with colleagues and gendered bonds with supervisors are crucial to riding the glass escalator. Women colleagues often take a primary role in casting these men into leadership or supervisory positions. In their study of men and women tokens in a hospital setting, Floge and Merrill (1986) cite cases where women nurses promoted men colleagues to the position of charge nurse, even when the job had already been assigned to a woman. In addition to these close ties with women colleagues, men are also able to capitalize on gendered bonds with (mostly men) supervisors in ways that engender upward mobility. Many men supervisors informally socialize with men workers in women's jobs and are thus able to trade on their personal friendships for upward mobility. Williams (1995) describes a case where a nurse with mediocre performance reviews received a promotion to a more prestigious specialty area because of his friendship with the (male) doctor in charge. According to the literature, building strong relationships with colleagues and supervisors often happens relatively easily for men in women's professions and pays off in their occupational advancement.

For Black men in nursing, however, gendered racism may limit the extent to which they establish bonds with their colleagues and supervisors. The concept of gendered racism suggests that racial stereotypes, images, and beliefs are grounded in gendered ideals (Collins 1990, 2004; Espiritu 2000; Essed 1991; Harvey Wingfield 2007). Gendered racist stereotypes of Black men in particular emphasize the dangerous, threatening attributes associated with Black men and Black masculinity, framing Black men as threats to white women, prone to criminal behavior, and especially violent. Collins (2004) argues that these stereotypes serve to legitimize Black men's treatment in the criminal justice system through methods such as racial profiling and incarceration, but they may also hinder Black men's attempts to enter and advance in various occupational fields.

For Black men nurses, gendered racist images may have particular consequences for their relationships with women colleagues, who may view Black men nurses through the lens of controlling images and gendered racist stereotypes that emphasize the danger they pose to women. This may take on a heightened significance for white women nurses, given stereotypes that suggest that Black men are especially predisposed to raping white women. Rather than experiencing the congenial bonds with colleagues that white men nurses describe, Black men nurses may find themselves facing a much cooler reception from their women coworkers.

Gendered racism may also play into the encounters Black men nurses have with supervisors. In cases where supervisors are white men, Black men nurses may still find that higher-ups treat them in ways that reflect prevailing stereotypes about threatening Black masculinity. Supervisors may feel uneasy about forming close relationships with Black men or may encourage their separation from white women nurses. In addition, broader, less gender-specific racial stereotypes could also shape the experiences Black men nurses have with white men bosses. Whites often perceive Blacks, regardless of gender, as less intelligent, hardworking, ethical, and moral than other racial groups (Feagin 2006). Black men nurses may find that in addition to being influenced by gendered racist stereotypes, supervisors also view them as less capable and qualified for promotion, thus negating or minimizing the glass escalator effect.

Suitability for Nursing and Higher-Status Work

The perception that men are not really suited to do women's work also contributes to the glass escalator effect. In encounters with patients, doctors, and other staff, men nurses frequently confront others who do not expect to see them doing "a woman's job." Sometimes this perception means that patients mistake men nurses for doctors; ultimately, the sense that men do not really belong in nursing contributes to a push "*out* of the most feminine-identified areas and *up* to those regarded as more legitimate for men" (Williams 1995, 104). The sense that men are better suited for more masculine jobs means that men workers are often assumed to be more able and skilled than their women counterparts. As Williams writes (1995, 106), "Masculinity is often associated with competence and mastery," and this implicit definition stays with men even when they work in feminized fields. Thus, part of the perception that men do not belong in these jobs is rooted in the sense that, as men, they are more capable and accomplished than women and thus belong in jobs that reflect this. Consequently, men nurses are mistaken for doctors and are granted more authority and responsibility than their women counterparts, reflecting the idea that, as men, they are inherently more competent (Heikes 1991; Williams 1995).

Black men nurses, however, may not face the presumptions of expertise or the resulting assumption that they belong in higher-status jobs. Black professionals, both men and women, are often assumed to be less capable and less qualified than their white counterparts. In some cases, these negative stereotypes hold even when Black workers outperform white colleagues (Feagin and Sikes 1994). The belief that Blacks are inherently less competent than whites means that, despite advanced education, training, and skill, Black professionals often confront the lingering perception that they are better suited for lower-level service work (Feagin and Sikes 1994). Black men in fact often fare better than white women in blue-collar jobs such as policing and corrections work (Britton 1995), and this may be, in part, because they are viewed as more appropriately suited for these types of positions.

For Black men nurses, then, the issue of perception may play out in different ways than it does for white men nurses. While white men nurses enjoy the automatic assumption that they are qualified, capable, and suited for "better" work, the experiences of Black professionals suggest that Black men nurses may not encounter these reactions. They may, like their white counterparts, face the perception that they do not belong in nursing. Unlike their white counterparts, Black men nurses may be seen as inherently less capable and therefore better suited for low-wage labor than a professional, feminized occupation such as nursing. This perception of being less qualified means that they also may not be immediately assumed to be better suited for the higher-level, more masculinized jobs within the medical field.

As minority women address issues of both race and gender to negotiate a sense of belonging in masculine settings (Ong 2005), minority men may also face a comparable challenge in feminized fields. They may have to address the unspoken racialization implicit in the assumption that masculinity equals competence. Simultaneously, they may find that the racial stereotype that Blackness equals lower qualifications, standards, and competence clouds the sense that men are inherently more capable and adept in any field, including the feminized ones.

Establishing Distance from Femininity

An additional mechanism of the glass escalator involves establishing distance from women and the femininity associated with their occupations. Because men nurses are employed in a culturally feminized occupation, they develop strategies to disassociate themselves from the femininity associated with their work and retain some of the privilege associated with masculinity. Thus, when men nurses gravitate toward hospital emergency wards rather than obstetrics or pediatrics, or emphasize that they are only in nursing to get into hospital administration, they distance themselves from the femininity of their profession and thereby preserve their status as men despite the fact that they do "women's work." Perhaps more important, these strategies also place men in a prime position to experience the glass escalator effect, as they situate themselves to move upward into higher-status areas in the field.

Creating distance from femininity also helps these men achieve aspects of hegemonic masculinity, which Connell (1989) describes as the predominant and most valued form of masculinity at a given time. Contemporary hegemonic masculine ideals emphasize toughness, strength, aggressiveness, heterosexuality, and, perhaps most important, a clear sense of femininity as different from and subordinate to masculinity (Kimmel 2001; Williams 1995). Thus, when men distance themselves from the feminized aspects of their jobs, they uphold the idea that masculinity and femininity are distinct, separate, and mutually exclusive. When these men seek masculinity by aiming for the better paying or most technological fields, they not only position themselves to move upward into the more acceptable arenas but also reinforce the greater social value placed on masculinity. Establishing distance from femininity therefore allows men to retain the privileges and status of masculinity while simultaneously enabling them to ride the glass escalator.

For Black men, the desire to reject femininity may be compounded by racial inequality. Theorists have argued that as institutional racism blocks access to traditional markers of masculinity such as occupational status and economic stability, Black men may repudiate femininity as a way of accessing the masculinity—and its attendant status—that is denied through other routes (hooks 2004; Neal 2005). Rejecting femininity is a key strategy men use to assert masculinity, and it remains available to Black men even when other means of achieving masculinity are unattainable. Black men nurses may be more likely to distance themselves from their women colleagues and to reject the femininity associated with nursing, particularly if they feel that they experience racial discrimination that renders occupational advancement inaccessible. Yet if they encounter strained relationships with women colleagues and men supervisors because of gendered racism or racialized stereotypes, the efforts to distance themselves from femininity still may not result in the glass escalator effect.

On the other hand, some theorists suggest that minority men may challenge racism by rejecting hegemonic masculine ideals. Chen (1999) argues that Chinese American men may engage in a strategy of repudiation, where they reject hegemonic masculinity because its implicit assumptions of whiteness exclude Asian American men. As these men realize that racial stereotypes and assumptions preclude them from achieving the hegemonic masculine ideal, they reject it and dispute its racialized underpinnings. Similarly, Lamont (2000, 47) notes that working-class Black men in the United States and France develop a "caring self" in which they emphasize values such as "morality, solidarity, and generosity." As a consequence of these men's ongoing experiences with racism, they develop a caring self that highlights work on behalf of others as an important tool in fighting oppression. Although caring is associated with femininity, these men cultivate a caring self because it allows them to challenge racial inequality. The results of these studies suggest that Black men nurses may embrace the femininity associated with nursing if it offers a way to combat racism. In these cases, Black men nurses may turn to pediatrics as a way of demonstrating sensitivity and therefore combating stereotypes of Black masculinity, or they may proudly identify as nurses to challenge perceptions that Black men are unsuited for professional, white-collar positions.

Taken together, all of this research suggests that Black men may not enjoy the advantages experienced by their white men colleagues, who ride a glass escalator to success. In this article, I focus on the experiences of Black men nurses to argue that the glass escalator is a racialized as well as a gendered concept that does not offer Black men the same privileges as their white men counterparts.

Data Collection and Method

I collected data through semi structured interviews with 17 men nurses who identified as Black or African American. Nurses ranged in age from 30 to 51 and lived in the southeastern United States. Six worked in suburban hospitals adjacent to major cities, six were located in major metropolitan urban care centers, and the remaining five worked in rural hospitals or clinics. All were registered nurses or licensed practical nurses. Six identified their specialty as oncology, four were bedside nurses, two were in intensive care, one managed an acute dialysis program, one was an orthopedic nurse, one was in ambulatory care, one was in emergency, and one was in surgery. The least experienced nurse had worked in the field for five years; the most experienced had been a nurse for 26 years. I initially recruited participants by soliciting attendees at the 2007 National Black Nurses Association annual meetings and then used a snowball sample to create the remainder of the data set. All names and identifying details have been changed to ensure confidentiality (see Table 1).

Table 1. Respondents

Name	Age	Specialization	Years of Experience	Years at Current Job
Chris	51	Oncology	26	16
Clayton	31	Emergency	6	6
Cyril	40	Dialysis	17	7
Dennis	30	Bedside	7	7 (months)
Evan	42	Surgery	25	20
Greg	39	Oncology	10	3
Kenny	47	Orthopedics	23	18 (months)
Leo	50	Bedside	20	18
Ray	36	Oncology	10	5
Ryan	37	Intensive care	17	11
Sean	46	Oncology	9	9
Simon	36	Oncology	5	5
Stuart	44	Bedside	6	4
Terrence	32	Bedside	10	6
Tim	39	Intensive care	20	15 (months)
Tobias	44	Oncology	25	7
Vern	50	Ambulatory care	7	7

I conducted interviews during the fall of 2007. They generally took place in either my campus office or a coffee shop located near the respondent's home or workplace. The average interview lasted about an hour. Interviews were tape-recorded and transcribed. Interview questions primarily focused on how race and gender shaped the men's experiences as nurses. Questions addressed respondents' work history and current experiences in the field, how race and gender shaped their experiences as nurses, and their future career goals. The men discussed their reasons for going into nursing, the reactions from others on entering this field, and the particular challenges, difficulties, and obstacles Black men nurses faced. Respondents also described their work history in nursing, their current jobs, and their future plans. Finally, they talked about stereotypes of nurses in general and of Black men nurses in particular and their thoughts about and responses to these stereotypes. I coded the data according to key themes that emerged: relationships with white patients versus minority patients, personal bonds with colleagues versus lack of bonds, opportunities for advancement versus obstacles to advancement.

The researcher's gender and race shape interviews, and the fact that I am an African American woman undoubtedly shaped my rapport and the interactions with interview respondents. Social desirability bias may compel men to phrase responses that might sound harsh in ways that will not be offensive or problematic to the woman interviewer. However, one of the benefits of the interview method is that it allows respondents to clarify comments diplomatically while still giving honest answers. In this case, some respondents may have carefully framed certain comments about working mostly with women. However, the semistructured interview format nonetheless enabled them to discuss in detail their experiences in nursing and how these experiences are shaped by race and gender. Furthermore, I expect that shared racial status also facilitated a level of comfort, particularly as respondents frequently discussed issues of racial bias and mistreatment that shaped their experiences at work.

Findings

The results of this study indicate that not all men experience the glass escalator in the same ways. For Black men nurses, intersections of race and gender create a different experience with the mechanisms that facilitate white men's advancement in women's professions. Awkward or unfriendly interactions with colleagues, poor relationships with supervisors, perceptions that they are not suited for nursing, and an unwillingness to disassociate from "feminized" aspects of nursing constitute what I term *glass barriers* to riding the glass escalator.

Reception from Colleagues and Supervisors

When women welcome men into "their" professions, they often push men into leadership roles that ease their advancement into upper-level positions. Thus, a positive reaction from colleagues is critical to riding the glass escalator. Unlike white men nurses, however, Black men do not describe encountering a warm reception from women colleagues (Heikes 1991). Instead, the men I interviewed find that they often have unpleasant interactions with women coworkers who treat them rather coldly and attempt to keep them at bay. Chris is a 51-year-old oncology nurse who describes one white nurse's attempt to isolate him from other white women nurses as he attempted to get his instructions for that day's shift:

> She turned and ushered me to the door, and said for me to wait out here, a nurse will come out and give you your report. I stared at her hand on my arm, and then at her, and said, "Why? Where do you go to get your reports?" She said, "I get them in there." I said, "Right. Unhand me." I went right back in there, sat down, and started writing down my reports.

Kenny, a 47-year-old nurse with 23 years of nursing experience, describes a similarly and particularly painful experience he had in a previous job where he was the only Black person on staff:

> [The staff] had nothing to do with me, and they didn't even want me to sit at the same area where they were charting in to take a break. They wanted

> me to sit somewhere else.... They wouldn't even sit at a table with me! When I came and sat down, everybody got up and left.

These experiences with colleagues are starkly different from those described by white men in professions dominated by women (see Pierce 1995; Williams 1989). Though the men in these studies sometimes chose to segregate themselves, women never systematically excluded them. Though I have no way of knowing why the women nurses in Chris's and Kenny's workplaces physically segregated themselves, the pervasiveness of gendered racist images that emphasize white women's vulnerability to dangerous Black men may play an important role. For these nurses, their masculinity is not a guarantee that they will be welcomed, much less pushed into leadership roles. As Ryan, a 37-year-old intensive care nurse says, "[Black men] have to go further to prove ourselves. This involves proving our capabilities, *proving to colleagues that you can lead,* be on the forefront" (emphasis added). The warm welcome and subsequent opportunities for leadership cannot be taken for granted. In contrast, these men describe great challenges in forming congenial relationships with coworkers who, they believe, do not truly want them there.

In addition, these men often describe tense, if not blatantly discriminatory, relationships with supervisors. While Williams (1995) suggests that men supervisors can be allies for men in women's professions by facilitating promotions and upward mobility, Black men nurses describe incidents of being overlooked by supervisors when it comes time for promotions. Ryan, who has worked at his current job for 11 years, believes that these barriers block upward mobility within the profession:

> The hardest part is dealing with people who don't understand minority nurses. People with their biases, who don't identify you as ripe for promotion. I know the policy and procedure, I'm familiar with past history. So you can't tell me I can't move forward if others did. [How did you deal with this?] By knowing the chain of command, who my supervisors were. Things were subtle. I just had to be better. I got this mostly from other nurses and supervisors. I was paid to deal with patients, so I could deal with [racism] from them. I'm not paid to deal with this from colleagues.

Kenny offers a similar example. Employed as an orthopedic nurse in a predominantly white environment, he describes great difficulty getting promoted, which he primarily attributes to racial biases:

> It's almost like you have to, um, take your ideas and give them to somebody else and then let them present them for you and you get no credit for it. I've applied for several promotions there and, you know, I didn't get them.... When you look around to the, um, the percentage of African Americans who are actually in executive leadership is almost zero percent. Because it's less than one percent of the total population of people that are in leadership, and it's almost like they'll go outside of the system just to try to find a Caucasian to fill a position. Not that I'm not qualified, because I've been master's prepared for 12 years and I'm working on my doctorate.

According to Ryan and Kenny, supervisors' racial biases mean limited opportunities for promotion and upward mobility. This interpretation is consistent with research that suggests that even with stellar performance and solid work histories, Black workers may receive mediocre evaluations from white supervisors that limit their advancement (Feagin 2006; Feagin and Sikes 1994). For Black men nurses, their race may signal to supervisors that they are unworthy of promotion and thus create a different experience with the glass escalator.

Strong relationships with colleagues and supervisors are a key mechanism of the glass escalator effect. For Black men nurses, however, these relationships are experienced differently from those described by their white men colleagues. Black men nurses do not speak of warm and congenial relationships with women nurses or see these relationships as facilitating a move into leadership roles. Nor do they suggest that they share gendered bonds with men supervisors that serve to ease their mobility into higher-status administrative jobs. In contrast, they sense that racial bias makes it difficult to develop ties with coworkers and makes superiors unwilling to promote them. Black men nurses thus experience this aspect of the glass escalator differently from their white men colleagues. They find that relationships with colleagues and supervisors stifle, rather than facilitate, their upward mobility.

Perceptions of Suitability

Like their white counterparts, Black men nurses also experience challenges from clients who are unaccustomed to seeing men in fields typically dominated by women. As with white men nurses, Black men encounter this in surprised or quizzical reactions from patients who seem to expect to be treated by white women nurses. Ray, a 36-year-old oncology nurse with 10 years of experience, states,

> Nursing, historically, has been a white female's job [so] being a Black male it's a weird position to be in.... I've, several times, gone into a room and a male patient, a white male patient has, you know, they'll say, "Where's the pretty nurse? Where's the pretty nurse? Where's the blonde nurse?"... "You don't have one. I'm the nurse."

Yet while patients rarely expect to be treated by men nurses of any race, white men encounter statements and behaviors that suggest patients expect them to be doctors, supervisors, or other higher-status, more masculine positions (Williams 1989, 1995). In part, this expectation accelerates their ride on the glass escalator, helping to push them into the positions for which they are seen as more appropriately suited.

(White) men, by virtue of their masculinity, are assumed to be more competent and capable and thus better situated in (nonfeminized) jobs that are perceived to require greater skill and proficiency. Black men, in contrast, rarely encounter patients (or colleagues and supervisors) who immediately expect that they are doctors or administrators. Instead, many respondents find that even after displaying their credentials, sharing their nursing experience, and, in one case, dispensing care, they are still mistaken for janitors or service workers. Ray's experience is typical:

> I've even given patients their medicines, explained their care to them, and then they'll say to me, "Well, can you send the nurse in?"

Chris describes a somewhat similar encounter of being misidentified by a white woman patient:

> I come [to work] in my white uniform, that's what I wear—being a Black man, I know they won't look at me the same, so I dress the part—I said good evening, my name's Chris, and I'm going to be your nurse. She says to me, "Are you from housekeeping?"... I've had other cases. I've walked in and had a lady look at me and ask if I'm the janitor.

Chris recognizes that this patient is evoking racial stereotypes that Blacks are there to perform menial service work. He attempts to circumvent this very perception through careful self-presentation, wearing the white uniform to indicate his position as a nurse. His efforts, however, are nonetheless met with a racial stereotype that as a Black man he should be there to clean up rather than to provide medical care.

Black men in nursing encounter challenges from customers that reinforce the idea that men are not suited for a "feminized" profession such as nursing. However, these assumptions are racialized as well as gendered. Unlike white men nurses who are assumed to be doctors (see Williams 1992), Black men in nursing are quickly taken for janitors or housekeeping staff. These men do not simply describe a gendered process where perceptions and stereotypes about men serve to aid their mobility into higher-status jobs. More specifically, they describe interactions that are simultaneously raced *and* gendered in ways that reproduce stereotypes of Black men as best suited for certain blue-collar, unskilled labor.

These negative stereotypes can affect Black men nurses' efforts to treat patients as well. The men I interviewed find that masculinity does not automatically endow them with an aura of competency. In fact, they often describe interactions with white women patients that suggest that their race minimizes whatever assumptions of capability might accompany being men. They describe several cases in which white women patients completely refused treatment. Ray says,

> With older white women, it's tricky sometimes because they will come right out and tell you they

> don't want you to treat them, or can they see someone else.

Ray frames this as an issue specifically with older white women, though other nurses in the sample described similar issues with white women of all ages. Cyril, a 40-year-old nurse with 17 years of nursing experience, describes a slightly different twist on this story:

> I had a white lady that I had to give a shot, and she was fine with it and I was fine with it. But her husband, when she told him, he said to me, I don't have any problem with you as a Black man, but I don't want you giving her a shot.

While white men nurses report some apprehension about treating women patients, in all likelihood this experience is compounded for Black men (Williams 1989). Historically, interactions between Black men and white women have been fraught with complexity and tension, as Black men have been represented in the cultural imagination as potential rapists and threats to white women's security and safety—and, implicitly, as a threat to white patriarchal stability (Davis 1981; Giddings 1984). In Cyril's case, it may be particularly significant that the Black man is charged with giving a shot and therefore literally penetrating the white wife's body, a fact that may heighten the husband's desire to shield his wife from this interaction. White men nurses may describe hesitation or awkwardness that accompanies treating women patients, but their experiences are not shaped by a pervasive racial imagery that suggests that they are potential threats to their women patients' safety.

This dynamic, described primarily among white women patients and their families, presents a picture of how Black men's interactions with clients are shaped in specifically raced and gendered ways that suggest they are less rather than more capable. These interactions do not send the message that Black men, because they are men, are too competent for nursing and really belong in higher-status jobs. Instead, these men face patients who mistake them for lower-status service workers and encounter white women patients (and their husbands) who simply refuse treatment or are visibly uncomfortable with the prospect. These interactions do not situate Black men nurses in a prime position for upward mobility. Rather, they suggest that the experience of Black men nurses with this particular mechanism of the glass escalator is the manifestation of the expectation that they should be in lower-status positions more appropriate to their race and gender.

Refusal to Reject Femininity

Finally, Black men nurses have a different experience with establishing distance from women and the feminized aspects of their work. Most research shows that as men nurses employ strategies that distance them from femininity (e.g., by emphasizing nursing as a route to higher-status, more masculine jobs), they place themselves in a position for upward mobility and the glass escalator effect (Williams 1992). For Black men nurses, however, this process looks different. Instead of distancing themselves from the femininity associated with nursing, Black men actually embrace some of the more feminized attributes linked to nursing. In particular, they emphasize how much they value and enjoy the way their jobs allow them to be caring and nurturing. Rather than conceptualizing caring as anathema or feminine (and therefore undesirable), Black men nurses speak openly of caring as something positive and enjoyable.

This is consistent with the context of nursing that defines caring as integral to the profession. As nurses, Black men in this line of work experience professional socialization that emphasizes and values caring, and this is reflected in their statements about their work. Significantly, however, rather than repudiating this feminized component of their jobs, they embrace it. Tobias, a 44-year-old oncology nurse with 25 years of experience, asserts.

> The best part about nursing is helping other people, the flexibility of work hours, and the commitment to vulnerable populations, people who are ill.

Simon, a 36-year-old oncology nurse, also talks about the joy he gets from caring for others. He contrasts his experiences to those of white men nurses he knows who prefer specialties that involve less patient care:

> They were going to work with the insurance industries, they were going to work in the ER where it's a touch and go, you're a number literally. I don't get to know your name, I don't get to know that you have four grandkids, I don't get to know that you really want to get out of the hospital by next week because the following week is your birthday, your 80th birthday and it's so important for you. I don't get to know that your cat's name is Sprinkles, and you're concerned about who's feeding the cat now, and if they remembered to turn the TV on during the day so that the cat can watch *The Price Is Right*. They don't get into all that kind of stuff. OK, I actually need to remember the name of your cat so that tomorrow morning when I come, I can ask you about Sprinkles and that will make a world of difference. I'll see light coming to your eyes and the medicines will actually work because your perspective is different.

Like Tobias, Simon speaks with a marked lack of self-consciousness about the joys of adding a personal touch and connecting that personal care to a patient's improvement. For him, caring is important, necessary, and valued, even though others might consider it a feminine trait.

For many of these nurses, willingness to embrace caring is also shaped by issues of race and racism. In their position as nurses, concern for others is connected to fighting the effects of racial inequality. Specifically, caring motivates them to use their role as nurses to address racial health disparities, especially those that disproportionately affect Black men. Chris describes his efforts to minimize health issues among Black men:

> With Black male patients, I have their history, and if they're 50 or over I ask about the prostate exam and a colonoscopy. Prostate and colorectal death is so high that that's my personal crusade.

Ryan also speaks to the importance of using his position to address racial imbalances:

> I really take advantage of the opportunities to give back to communities, especially to change the disparities in the African American community. I'm more than just a nurse. As a faculty member at a major university, I have to do community hours, services. Doing health fairs, in-services on research, this makes an impact in some disparities in the African American community. [People in the community] may not have the opportunity to do this otherwise.

As Lamont (2000) indicates in her discussion of the "caring self," concern for others helps Chris and Ryan to use their knowledge and position as nurses to combat racial inequalities in health. Though caring is generally considered a "feminine" attribute, in this context it is connected to challenging racial health disparities. Unlike their white men colleagues, these nurses accept and even embrace certain aspects of femininity rather than rejecting them. They thus reveal yet another aspect of the glass escalator process that differs for Black men. As Black men nurses embrace this "feminine" trait and the avenues it provides for challenging racial inequalities, they may become more comfortable in nursing and embrace the opportunities it offers.

Conclusions

Existing research on the glass escalator cannot explain these men's experiences. As men who do women's work, they should be channeled into positions as charge nurses or nursing administrators and should find themselves virtually pushed into the upper ranks of the nursing profession. But without exception, this is not the experience these Black men nurses describe. Instead of benefiting from the basic mechanisms of the glass escalator, they face tense relationships with colleagues, supervisors' biases in achieving promotion, patient stereotypes that inhibit caregiving, and a sense of comfort with some of the feminized aspects of their jobs. These "glass barriers" suggest that the glass escalator is a racialized concept as well as a gendered one. The main contribution of this study is the finding that race and gender intersect to determine which men will ride the glass escalator. The proposition that men who do women's work encounter undue opportunities and advantages appears to be unequivocally true only if the men in question are white.

This raises interesting questions and a number of new directions for future research. Researchers might consider the extent to which the glass escalator is not only raced and gendered but sexualized as well. Williams (1995) notes that straight men are often treated better by supervisors than are gay men and that straight men frequently do masculinity by strongly asserting their heterosexuality to combat the belief that men who do women's work are gay. The men in this study (with the exception of one nurse I interviewed) rarely discussed sexuality except to say that they were straight and were not bothered by "the gay stereotype." This is consistent with Williams's findings. Gay men, however, may also find that they do not experience a glass escalator effect that facilitates their upward mobility. Tim, the only man I interviewed who identified as gay, suggests that gender, race, and sexuality come together to shape the experiences of men in nursing. He notes,

> I've been called awful things—you faggot this, you faggot that. I tell people there are three *Fs* in life, and if you're not doing one of them it doesn't matter what you think of me. They say, "Three *Fs*?" and I say yes. If you aren't feeding me, financing me, or fucking me, then it's none of your business what my faggot ass is up to.

Tim's experience suggests that gay men—and specifically gay Black men— in nursing may encounter particular difficulties establishing close ties with straight men supervisors or may not automatically be viewed by their women colleagues as natural leaders. While race is, in many cases, more obviously visible than sexuality, the glass escalator effect may be a complicated amalgam of racial, gendered, and sexual expectations and stereotypes.

It is also especially interesting to consider how men describe the role of women in facilitating—or denying—access to the glass escalator. Research on white men nurses includes accounts of ways white women welcome them and facilitate their advancement by pushing them toward leadership positions (Floge and Merrill 1986; Heikes 1991; Williams 1992, 1995). In contrast, Black men nurses in this study discuss white women who do not seem eager to work with them, much less aid their upward mobility. These different responses indicate that shared racial status is important in determining who rides the glass escalator. If that is the case, then future research should consider whether Black men nurses who work in predominantly Black settings are more likely to encounter the glass escalator effect. In these settings, Black men nurses' experiences might more closely resemble those of white men nurses.

Future research should also explore other racial minority men's experiences in women's professions to determine whether and how they encounter the processes that facilitate a ride on the glass escalator. With Black men nurses, specific race or gender stereotypes impede their access to the glass escalator; however, other racial minority men are subjected to different race or gender stereotypes that could create other experiences. For instance, Asian American men may encounter racially specific gender stereotypes of themselves as computer nerds, sexless sidekicks, or model minorities and thus may encounter the processes of the glass escalator differently than do Black or white men (Espiritu 2000). More focus on the diverse experiences of racial minority men is necessary to know for certain.

Finally, it is important to consider how these men's experiences have implications for the ways the glass escalator phenomenon reproduces racial and gendered advantages. Williams (1995) argues that men's desire to differentiate themselves from women and disassociate from the femininity of their work is a key process that facilitates their ride on the glass escalator. She ultimately suggests that if men reconstruct masculinity to include traits such as caring, the distinctions between masculinity and femininity could blur and men "would not have to define masculinity as the negation of femininity" (Williams 1995, 188). This in turn could create a more equitable balance between men and women in women's professions. However, the experiences of Black men in nursing, especially their embrace of caring, suggest that accepting the feminine aspects of work is not enough to dismantle the glass escalator and produce more gender equality in women's professions. The fact that Black men nurses accept and even enjoy caring does not minimize the processes that enable *white* men to ride the glass escalator. This suggests that undoing the glass escalator requires not only blurring the lines between masculinity and femininity but also challenging the processes of racial inequality that marginalize minority men.

Acknowledgments

Special thanks to Kirsten Dellinger, Mindy Stombler, Ralph LaRossa, Cindy Whitney, Laura Logan, Dana Britton, and the anonymous reviewers for their insights and helpful feedback. Thanks also to Karyn Lacy, Andra Gillespie, and Isabel Wilkerson for their comments and support.

Note

1. I could not locate any data that indicate the percentage of Black men in nursing. According to 2006 census data, African Americans compose 11 percent of nurses, and men are 8 percent of nurses (http://www.census.gov/compendia/statab/tables/08s0598.pdf). These data do not show the breakdown of nurses by race and sex.

References

Acker, Joan. 1990. Hierarchies, jobs, bodies: A theory of gendered organizations. *Gender & Society* 4:139–58.

Britton, Dana. 1995. *At work in the iron cage.* New York: New York University Press.

Budig, Michelle. 2002. Male advantage and the gender composition of jobs: Who rides the glass escalator? *Social Forces* 49 (2): 258–77.

Charles, Maria, and David Grusky. 2004. *Occupational ghettos: The worldwide segregation of women and men.* Palo Alto, CA: Stanford University Press.

Chen, Anthony. 1999. Lives at the center of the periphery, lives at the periphery of the center: Chinese American masculinities and bargaining with hegemony. *Gender & Society* 13:584–607.

Collins, Patricia Hill. 1990. *Black feminist thought.* New York: Routledge.

———. 2004. *Black sexual politics.* New York: Routledge.

Connell, R. W. 1989. *Gender and power.* Sydney, Australia: Allen and Unwin.

Davis, Angela. 1981. *Women, race, and class.* New York: Vintage.

Duffy, Mignon. 2007. Doing the dirty work: Gender, race, and reproductive labor in historical perspective. *Gender & Society* 21:313–36.

Espiritu, Yen Le. 2000. *Asian American women and men: Labor, laws, and love.* Walnut Creek, CA: AltaMira.

Essed, Philomena. 1991. *Understanding everyday racism.* New York: Russell Sage.

Feagin, Joe. 2006. *Systemic racism.* New York: Routledge.

Feagin, Joe, and Melvin Sikes. 1994. *Living with racism.* Boston: Beacon Hill Press.

Floge, Liliane, and Deborah M. Merrill. 1986. Tokenism reconsidered: Male nurses and female physicians in a hospital setting. *Social Forces* 64:925–47.

Giddings, Paula. 1984. *When and where I enter: The impact of Black women on race and sex in America.* New York: HarperCollins.

Harvey Wingfield, Adia. 2007. The modern mammy and the angry Black man: African American professionals' experiences with gendered racism in the workplace. *Race, Gender, and Class* 14 (2): 196–212.

Heikes, E. Joel. 1991. When men are the minority: The case of men in nursing. *Sociological Quarterly* 32:389–401.

hooks, bell. 2004. *We real cool.* New York: Routledge.

Kanter, Rosabeth Moss. 1977. *Men and women of the corporation.* New York: Basic Books.

Kimmel, Michael. 2001. Masculinity as homophobia. In *Men and masculinity,* edited by Theodore F. Cohen. Belmont, CA: Wadsworth.

Lamont, Michelle. 2000. *The dignity of working men.* New York: Russell Sage.

Neal, Mark Anthony. 2005. *New Black man.* New York: Routledge.

Ong, Maria. 2005. Body projects of young women of color in physics: Intersections of race, gender, and science. *Social Problems* 52 (4): 593–617.

Pierce, Jennifer. 1995. *Gender trials: Emotional lives in contemporary law firms.* Berkeley: University of California Press.

Roth, Louise. 2006. *Selling women short: Gender and money on Wall Street.* Princeton, NJ: Princeton University Press.

Shapiro, Thomas. 2004. *Hidden costs of being African American: How wealth perpetuates inequality.* New York: Oxford University Press.

Snyder, Karrie Ann, and Adam Isaiah Green. 2008. Revisiting the glass escalator: The case of gender segregation in a female dominated occupation. *Social Problems* 55 (2): 271–99.

Williams, Christine. 1989. *Gender differences at work: Women and men in non-traditional occupations.* Berkeley: University of California Press.

———. 1992. The glass escalator: Hidden advantages for men in the "female" professions. *Social Problems* 39 (3): 253–67.

———. 1995. *Still a man's world: Men who do women's work.* Berkeley: University of California Press.

Zimmer, Lynn. 1988. Tokenism and women in the workplace: The limits of gender neutral theory. *Social Problems* 35 (1): 64–77.

Before and After: Gender Transitions, Human Capital, and Workplace Experiences

KRISTEN SCHILT AND MATTHEW WISWALL

Introduction

When economics professor Donald McCloskey announced he was becoming Deirdre, the chair of his department joked that working as a woman would mean getting a pay cut (McCloskey 1999). While the chair's comment was made in jest, it speaks to a larger and long-standing question of what role gender plays in workplace outcomes. Social scientists have long documented the relationship between an employee's gender and his or her opportunities for advancement in pay and authority. While the gender gap in earnings has narrowed for men and women in comparable occupations, men continue to outpace women in salaries, promotions, and workplace authority (Valian 1999; Padavic and Reskin 2002, Blau and Kahn 2006). Yet, as existing surveys cannot measure gender bias directly or capture all the relevant characteristics of men and women, the source of these workplace disparities remains unknown.

As McCloskey's story illustrates, the workplace experiences of transgender people—individuals who transition from one recognized gender category to another—offer an innovative way to explore the importance of gender in the workplace.[1] People who undergo gender transitions are estimated to makeup only .01% of the United States population, with equal numbers of men becoming women—a group we refer to as MTFs (male-to-female)—and women becoming men—a group we refer to as FTMs (female to male).[2] Yet, we argue that the experience of a person who works both as a man and as a woman can illuminate the subtle ways that gender inequality is socially produced in the workplace. While transgender people have the same human capital and pre-labor market gender socialization after their gender transitions, their workplace experiences often change radically. Existing autobiographical and scholarly research demonstrates that for many MTFs, becoming women brings a loss of authority and pay, as well as

Kristen Schilt and Matthew Wiswall, "Before and After: Gender Transitions, Human Capital, and Workplace Experiences" from *The B.E. Journal of Economic Analysis & Policy* 8, No. 1 (2008): article 9. Reprinted with permission of The Berkeley Electronic Press.

workplace harassment and, in many cases, termination (Bolin 1988; Griggs 1998; McCloskey 1999; Schilt 2006a). On the other hand, for many FTMs, becoming men can bring an increase in workplace authority, reward, and respect, as well as new job opportunities and promotions (Griggs 1998; Schilt 2006b). The *before* and *after* workplace experiences of transgender people, then, can make visible the hidden processes that produce workplace gender inequality.

In this article, we use the pre- and post-gender transition workplace experiences of MTFs and FTMs to examine the persistence of gendered workplace disparities. Drawing on survey data about transgender employment experiences, we demonstrate that gender transitions bring important changes in workplace outcomes. In becoming women, MTFs experience significant losses in hourly earnings. In contrast, FTMs experience no change in earnings or small positive increases in earnings from becoming men. These findings suggest that regardless of childhood gender socialization and prior human capital accumulation, becoming women for MTFs creates a workplace penalty that FTMs do not generally encounter when they become men. And, while MTFs may benefit from being men at work before their gender change, they cannot always take this gender advantage with them into womanhood. We view these findings as evidence that the gender gap in workplace outcomes does not entirely reflect omitted variables, such as unobserved human capital. Rather, the change in post-transition MTFs' earnings suggests that the labor market is not gender neutral.

Theories of Workplace Gender Inequality

A fundamental question in the social sciences is why women continue to lag behind men in salary, promotion, and authority. Although prior research attributes much of the gender wage gap to measurable differences in education, occupations, and labor force attachment, these factors still do not entirely explain all of the gender gap in earnings (Goldin 1990; Paglin and Rufolo 1990; Fuller and Schoenberger 1991; Groshen 1991; Wood, Corcoran and Courant 1993; Brown and Corcoran 1997; Altonji and Blank 1999; Blau and Kahn 2006). Although white-collar men and women with equal qualifications can begin their careers in similar positions in the workplace, men tend to advance faster, creating a gendered promotion gap (Valian 1999; Padavic and Reskin 2002). Even in female-dominated professions, such as nursing and teaching, men outpace women in advancement to positions of authority (Williams 1995). Similar patterns exist among blue-collar professions, as women are often denied sufficient training for advancement in manual trades, passed over for promotions, or subjected to sexual harassment (Miller 1997; Yoder and Aniakudo 1997; Byrd 1999).

There are several conflicting theories to explain these remaining gender gaps.[3] "Omitted variables" theories argue that differences in the types of unobserved human capital accumulated by men and women and/or differences in preferences for certain types of occupations and work settings account for the workplace gender gap. To the extent these differences are not measured in our data, we cannot control for these factors and the currently estimated gender gaps in earnings suffer from omitted variable bias. "Discrimination theories," in contrast, posit that women and men with the same levels of human capital and who hold equivalent jobs or occupations experience different labor market outcomes due to gender discrimination on the part of employers.

Omitted Variable Theories

Omitted variable theories argue that observed differences in workplace outcomes are due to gender differences in human capital accumulation and childhood socialization. As women are more likely to take time off from work for childrearing and family obligations, they obtain less education and work experience on average than men. Men, in contrast, invest much more in their job training and education, giving them more human capital on average than women. Observed differences in labor market outcomes by gender therefore stem at least partly from these disparities in skills and experience. Men are rewarded more than women because they have more human capital.

The patterns of these gender differences in human capital accumulation can be shaped by childhood gender socialization. Children receive messages from a variety of socialization agents—parents, peers, teachers, the media—about what types of behaviors are appropriate for boys and girls (Marini 1989; Subich et al. 1989; Kimmel 2000). This pre-labor market socialization can affect human capital accumulation before men and women even enter the labor force by creating gender-specific preferences for types of occupations (Corcoran and Corcoran 1985). Women learn that feminine traits include caring and nurturing. They then are more likely to seek out jobs that reinforce these traits, explaining their predominance in the "helping" professions, such as nursing and elementary school teaching. Men, on the other hand, are socialized to seek out high paying jobs that carry a great deal of authority to reinforce their sense of masculinity (Gould 1974; Kimmel 2000). This masculine socialization accounts for the predominance of men in blue-collar occupations, as well as high-powered professional occupations. As women are socialized to put family obligations first, women workers are more likely than men to seek out jobs that provide more flexibility for family schedules, but carry lower earnings and fewer opportunities for advancement. Women may also avoid higher paying blue-collar jobs, as these types of occupations as generally viewed as "unfeminine" (Paap 2005).

Discrimination Theories

Discrimination theories point to employer discrimination as the cause of the observed gender differences in workplace outcomes. Taste discrimination, originally formulated in the context of racial discrimination (Becker 1971), posits that employers have explicit preferences for hiring workers that have characteristics with no relation to worker productivity. Employers may engage in what has been termed "homosocial reproduction," hiring workers who reflect their own identities and characteristics (Bird 1996). As white men are more likely to be in control of the hiring process, this means a preference for other white men (Williams 1995; Bird 1996; Padavic and Reskin 2002). Another more widely cited form of discrimination, statistical discrimination, occurs when employers base hiring, promotion, and compensation on worker stereotypes because of incomplete information about worker productivity (Phelps 1972; Arrow 1973; Bowlus and Eckstein 2002; Moro and Norman 2004).

An extensive empirical literature documents that employers have preconceptions as to what types of characteristics the workers who fill specific jobs should carry (Acker 1990; Williams 1995; Moss and Tilly 2001; Padavic and Reskin 2002; Martin 2003). "Feminine" characteristics, such as caring and sympathy, are typically preferred for jobs that involve a large amount of customer service interaction (Hochschild 1983; Leidner 1993). "Masculine" characteristics, such as rationality and competitiveness, are typically preferred for managerial positions (Kanter 1977; Acker 1990), even within female-dominated professions (Williams 1995). These same general patterns of gender segregation in work tasks are also found in high paying professions, such as in the legal profession (Wood et al. 1993; Valian 1999). This attribution of gender to jobs reproduces sex segregation so that, within the same work settings, women tend to be clustered with other women in lower paying jobs, while men are clustered at the top with greater pay, authority, and autonomy (Padavic and Reskin 2002).

While these gender stereotypes have important repercussions for men and women's labor market outcomes, it is difficult to quantify their importance for several reasons. First, while men and women with similar measured education and workplace experiences can be compared in a multivariate analysis, differences in outcomes can be attributed to unmeasured characteristics of workers rather than to systematic gender bias. Second, gendered expectations about what types of jobs women and men are suited for are strengthened by existing occupational segregation. The fact that there are more women nurses and more men doctors comes to be seen as proof that women are better suited for "helping" professions and men for "rational" professions. The normalization of these disparities as inevitable differences obscures the actual operation of men's advantages and therefore makes it difficult to document them empirically.

Finally, men's advantages in the workplace are not a function of one simple process but rather a complex interplay between many factors, such as human capital differences, differences in employers' expectations about skills and abilities by gender, and differences between men and women in family and childcare obligations. It may be difficult to understand the interplay of these multiple factors by merely examining existing observed workplace outcomes.

Using Gender Transitions to Study the Workplace Gender Gap

In this article we propose a unique test of the role of gender in the workplace. Consider an idealized experiment in which a random sample of adults wake up and have unexpectedly undergone a gender transition overnight. Omitted variable theories predict that there should be no change in labor market outcomes, as the skills and backgrounds of the workers remain the same. Discrimination theories, on the other hand, predict that these workers would experience a reversal in labor market outcomes. To test these theories, we designed a before and after panel study that uses the experiences of transgender workers as an approximation to this idealized experiment. With this unique panel data, we can net out the unobserved differences along with observed differences. We would predict that, even after controlling for observed and unobserved differences, women who become men (FTMs) would experience a gain in earnings in relative to men who become women (MTFs). This method is a natural extension of previous methods that use panel data to eliminate time invariant unobservable variables in earnings models. The main innovation of our article is that by focusing on gender transitions, we take a variable of interest that is typically considered invariant—gender—and make it time varying in a within-person panel.

The remainder of this article is organized as follows. The next section provides a brief overview of the existing scholarly research on the before and after workplace experiences of transgender people. Next, we outline the survey design and our original data collection. We then discuss the econometric specifications and results. We conclude with a discussion of the results that puts the quantitative findings in a fuller context by using related qualitative research.

The Gender Transition Process and Workplace Outcomes

A set of guidelines developed in 1979 by the Harry Benjamin International Gender Dysphoria Association—now known as the World Professional Association for Transgender Health (WPATH)—regulates the medicalized process of transitioning from one gender to another. The guidelines, referred to as the Standards of Care, stipulate a set path for a client seeking to change his or her gender.[4] First, this client is instructed to undergo a minimum of three months of therapy (though the time limit is at the discretion of the therapist). If the therapist agrees that medical transition is the appropriate pathway, an open letter to medical personnel is written that recommends this client for hormone treatment—estrogen for MTFs and testosterone for FTMs. Some clients, however, choose not to take hormones for a variety of personal, cultural, and health-related reasons. Therapists also can write a second letter addressed to surgeons that recommends their client for surgical interventions. For MTFs, these interventions can include facial feminizing surgery, vaginoplasty (genital surgery), breast augmentation, and tracheal shaves. For FTMs, these interventions can include chest reconstruction surgery, phalloplasty or metadioplasty (genital surgeries), and hysterectomy (see Griggs 1998 and Green 2004 for more detail on surgeries). While a gender transition often is synonymous with "sexual reassignment surgery" or genital surgery in popular conceptions, however, there is a great deal of variation in which surgeries, if any, transgender people choose to adopt during their transitions (see Griggs 1998; Rubin 2003; Green 2004).

While there is little historical data on gender transitions and workplace outcomes, some information on occupations before and after transitions can be gleaned from the first wave of research on transgender people that emerged in the social sciences in the 1970s and 1980s. In that time period, both MTFs and FTMs tended to be in their twenties, as older clients were viewed as bad candidates for transition as they were already too established in their work and personal lives (Kando 1973; Lothstein 1983). Many pre-transition FTMs worked in male-dominated fields, such as construction, or more gender-neutral fields, such as retail (Feinbloom 1976; Sorensen 1981; Lothstein 1983). In contrast, many pre-transition MTFs worked in female-dominated fields, such as modeling, hairdressing, and secretarial work (Benjamin 1966; Hore, Nicolle, and Calnan 1975; Perkins 1983; Rakic, Starcevic, Maric, and Kelin 1996). MTFs who did work in professional jobs as men were encouraged to move into more "feminine" careers post-transition that were seen as better suited for their new gender. Executives, then, became secretaries—a change that resulted in a large pay cut (Bolin 1988). In the 1990s, however, the demographics of people seeking gender transitions shifted somewhat, as more middle-aged MTFs who were already established in professional careers began seeking access to gender transitions (Lawrence 2003). And, with the aid of the growing transgender rights movement (Frye 2000), FTMs and MTFs increasingly started to make the choice to openly transition and remain in the same job—regardless of the gender stereotyping of their occupations (Schafer 2001).

Researchers who followed up with post-transition individuals reported mixed success for MTFs in the labor market. In one of the earliest studies, Lauband Fisk (1974)—a plastic surgeon and psychiatrist who operated the Stanford Gender Clinic—rated post-operative MTFs on their "economic adjustment" using a four point grading scale. They found that 10 of 18 MTFs interviewed had improved scores following their surgery. Other researchers, however, found an increase in the numbers of MTFs who went on disability after their transition, and who had difficulty maintaining employment (Sorensen 1981a; Lindemalm, Korlin, and Uddenberg 1986). FTMs also reported mixed workplace outcomes. While many of them remained in the same jobs post-transition, there were problems with acceptance, particularly if they were not on hormones and thus did not have an undisputed masculine appearance (Sorensen 1981b). Other studies, however, described FTMs as more satisfied with their work lives post-transition than their MTF counterparts (Kuiper and Cohen-Kettenis 1988). More recent qualitative data suggests that some MTFs leave high-paying professional jobs for lower-paying retail jobs because of employment discrimination (Griggs 1998). When they do remain in "masculine" professions, some MTFs report a devaluation of their skills and abilities by co-workers and employers (Schilt and Connell 2007). Many FTMs, in contrast, report gaining authority and respect at work once they look like men, even when they remain in the same jobs (Griggs 1998; Schilt 2006). To date, however, there still is little information on how gender transitions impact the before and after salaries of transgender people.

Data Collection

Survey Design and Administration

This article draws on survey data from a sample of transgender workers collected in 2004–2005 by the authors. To allow for comparability between the data on the general population and this transgender population, survey questions were modeled after the 2002 Current Population Survey (CPS). Our transgender survey was constructed as a three period panel. The survey asked respondents to provide hours, occupation, industry, and earnings information for jobs held at three distinct points in their lives: the last job held before they underwent any procedures to change their gender, the first job held after their gender transition, and their most recent job. For the last job held before their gender transition, respondents were asked, "Please think back to the last time you worked for pay (full or part time) BEFORE you underwent any procedures to change your gender that would have been noticeable to your supervisors or co-workers."[5] For the second period of the panel, respondents were asked about their workplace experiences immediately after their transition. Specifically, we asked, "Please answer these questions thinking about the first job you held for pay (part or full time) in which you were hired in your current gender." For the third period, respondents answered a similar question about their current main job.

Respondents were asked to self-report a date for each of these time periods (e.g., the last day worked before their transition), and retrospectively report their employment and earnings information as of that date. For most respondents, there was little (less than 1 year) or no gap between their report for the "immediately after" and "most recent" job. Because there is less non-response for the questions corresponding to the job held immediately *after* the gender change, we use this information to contrast to the period *before* the gender change.[6]

For each period, respondents were asked to report how much they "usually earn" at their "main job." We constructed an hourly earnings variable based on reported earnings and the number of weeks and hours the respondent reported that he or she usually worked at this main job. Because earnings were reported for several different calendar periods, the hourly earnings are adjusted for inflation using the Consumer Price Index (CPI-U series). All earnings in the paper are reported in 2004 dollars.

Our survey supplemented the earnings and employment questions with a battery of questions specific to the transgender population. Respondents were asked about their decisions regarding the use of surgical and hormonal treatments to change their gender, their beliefs about how well they passed in their new gender, and how much face-to-face contact they had with co-workers and customers.

Collecting a random sample of transgender people is not possible, as the population is small, widely dispersed, and often hidden. Additionally, there is no way to gather a random sample of the population of transgender people through traditional means (mailings, telephone calls, etc.). Instead, the survey was handed out at transgender conferences—conferences organized by transgender people around transgender issues—and made available on-line through a website advertisement. As most transgender conferences charge a registration fee, our sample is skewed more toward the middle-class. However, we purposefully included one conference that was free to the public to try to obtain a broader class representation.

The survey was handed out to voluntary participants at three transgender conferences: Transunity in Los Angeles, California in June 2004, Gender Odyssey in Seattle, Washington, in September 2004, and the International Foundation for Gender Education in Austin, Texas, in April 2005. Most of the respondents completed the survey on site, but a few of them mailed the survey to the authors later. In addition, the survey was posted online at the website *transacademics.org*, and readers were asked to email or mail completed surveys to the authors.

Transgender Sample

Of the 64 returned surveys, 54 were from respondents who attended one of the three conferences. The remaining ten surveys were obtained by email or mail from non-conference attendees. Because we are concerned with changes in workplace experiences before and after gender transitions, we included only respondents who were employed and reported positive earnings before and after their gender change in the analysis. This excludes all individuals who never held a job before their gender transition and individuals who were employed before their gender transition but were now unemployed.

Including only individuals who were employed before and after limits the final sample to 43 respondents: 16 MTFs and 27 FTMs. The original MTF and FTM composition among all of the 64 returned surveys was similar (27 MTF and 37 FTM). The higher proportion of FTMs is due to the conferences we attended. The Gender Odyssey conference at which 25 surveys were completed is almost exclusively a conference for FTMs.

Descriptive Statistics

Table 1 shows descriptive statistics for our transgender sample. To provide a comparison to the general population, we also report the same descriptive statistics for a sample of the general population taken from the March 2003 Current Population Survey (CPS).[7] Examining Table 1, two important differences between the CPS sample and our pre-transition transgender sample stand out. First,

Table 1. Descriptive Statistics Before Gender Change

	All Males	MTF	All Females	FTM
Mean Age	40.0	39.6	40.2	30.0
(std. error)	(0.072)	(2.57)	(0.074)	(2.18)
Median Age	40	39	40	29
Percent White	83.7	72.2	80.7	72.0
Percent College Degree	28.6	50.0	28.5	64.0
Percent Private Sector Job	81.2	77.8	78.9	56.0
Percent Government Job	13.1	16.7	18.7	32.0
Percent Self-Employed	5.6	5.6	2.4	12.0
Percent White Collar Occupation	47.8	61.1	72.1	64.0
Mean Hourly Earnings (Col. Deg.)	35.67	31.88	24.33	22.38
(std. error)	(1.15)	(5.09)	(0.32)	(3.82)
Mean Hourly Earnings (No Col. Deg.)	18.47	21.87	13.89	12.59
(std. error)	(0.48)	(5.09)	(0.18)	(5.09)
Observations	52,420	18	42,259	25

Notes: All Males and All Females refer to the sample of working adults from the 2003 Current Population Survey (CPS). CPS statistics are calculated using sample weights. Male-to-Female (MTF) and Female-to-Male (FTM) are transgender survey respondents who reported working. Data for transgender workers is for the period before their gender change. Age is the age at the time the respondent completed the survey. Hourly earnings are reported in 2004 dollars.

while MTFs are on average about the same age as the general male population, FTMs are on average about 10 years younger than the general female population and 10 years younger on average than MTFs. As discussed below, we interpret this as evidence that MTFs attempt to preserve their male advantage at work for as long as possible, whereas FTMs may seek to shed their female gender identity more quickly. A second important difference is that both MTFs and FTMs are twice as likely to have a college degree as the general population. This difference likely reflects that our sample was collected from transgender conference attendees. Being alerted to these conferences means having internet access, as well as the means to travel—all indicators of a higher socio-economic class associated with higher levels of education.

On other dimensions, the transgender sample and general population sample are more comparable. Both populations are between 70 and 80 percent white. The composition of types of employment (private, government, and self-employment) for pre-transition MTFs is similar to that of all men. Reflecting the higher level of education among the MTF sample, more MTFs are employed in white-collar occupations than the general male population. There are a higher proportion of pre-transition FTMs employed in the government sector than in the general female population.

The bottom rows of Table 1 compare mean hourly earnings for the pre-transition transgender sample with earnings for the general population, conditional on education.[8] College educated MTFs earn on average $31.88 per hour before their gender transitions, compared to $35.67 for all college educated males. College educated FTMs earn $22.38 per hour before their gender transitions, compared to $24.33 for all college educated females. Non-college educated MTFs earn on average $21.87 before their gender transitions, compared to $18.47 for all non-college educated males. For non-college educated FTMs, mean hourly wages are $12.59 before transition, compared to $13.89 for all non-college educated females.

Econometric Specification

This section describes how our transgender data can be used to examine the long-standing issue of gender differences in earnings. Below, we interpret the earnings results in more detail and examine these results in the context of other employment outcomes.

Given the structure of our data collection, we consider a two period model in which the first period, denoted t = b, is the period at which the respondent was last employed before his or her gender transition. The second period t = a is the period in which earnings are observed after the gender transition. Note that each survey respondent potentially can provide a different calendar time for the before and after periods. Wages are deflated for each of these different calendar times and we include an indicator of the number of years between the before and after periods in the regression models.

Log hourly earnings for individual i in each of the two periods (t = b,a) are assumed to take the following form:

$$\ln W_{it} = \gamma_t + \delta male_{it} + X_{it}'\beta + \alpha_i + \varepsilon_{it}, \qquad (1)$$

where γ_t is the intercept for the log earnings before and after the gender transition, $male_{it}$ is a dummy variable for whether the individual is male in gender in period t, X_{it} is a vector of time varying observable characteristics, such as age and education, α_i is an individual specific fixed effect reflecting the remaining unobserved differences across individuals, and ε_{it} represents the remaining residual error.

We take the difference in earnings between the after period (t = a) and before period (t = b) in (1) to eliminate the α_i fixed effects:

$$\Delta \ln W_i = \Delta\gamma + \delta\Delta male_i + \Delta X_i'\beta + \Delta\varepsilon_i, \qquad (2)$$

where $\Delta \ln W_i = \ln W_{ia} - \ln W_{ib}$ is the change in log earnings between the after and before periods. $\Delta\gamma = \gamma_a - \gamma_b$ is the intercept for the first difference and indicates the change in log earnings following the gender transition. As we discuss in more detail below, if there is an earnings penalty related to non-normative appearance for transgender people, then we expect $\Delta\gamma$ to be negative. $\Delta X_i = X_{ia} - X_{ib}$ is the change in the vector of time varying observable variables, such as the increase in age between the two periods.

$\Delta male_i = male_{ia} - male_{ib}$ is the difference in gender following the gender transition, where $\Delta male_i = +1$ for FTMs, and $\Delta male_i = -1$ for MTFs. We take a positive value for δ to indicate an earnings premium for male gender. The unique feature of our transgender data is that there is within person variation in gender that can be separately identified from the individual specific fixed effect. In traditional panel data, where $\Delta male_i = 0$ for all i, the effect of gender and unobservable characteristics correlated with gender represented by α_i cannot be separately identified.

Results

Table 2 reports the results from estimating (2) using OLS where the dependent variable is the difference in log hourly earnings before and after the gender transition. The first model includes only an intercept $\Delta\gamma$ and the change-to-male variable $\Delta male_i$. In this specification, the intercept $\Delta\gamma$ is estimated at −0.107 (with a *p*-value of 0.08), and the coefficient on the change-to-male variable is estimated at 0.206 (with a *p*-value of 0.001). These estimates imply that male-to-female respondents ($\Delta male_i = -1$) lose about 31 percent of their earnings after their gender transition (−0.107 − 0.206 = 0.313). Female to male respondents ($\Delta male_i = 1$) are estimated to gain about 10 percent in earnings following their gender transition (−0.107 + 0.206 = 0.099).

Model 2 in Table 2 adds the number of years between the self-reported before and after earnings observations. The average number of years between these two periods was 2.8 years, with a median of 2 years and a standard deviation of 4.1 years. The main effect of this variable is small and not statistically significant at the 10 percent level. Including this variable reduces the intercept and the change-to-male variables only slightly.

Model 3 in Table 2 adds three time varying covariates to the specification: i) a variable for whether a respondent reports obtaining a college degree (0 if no change, 1 if no college degree before but a college degree after), ii) a variable indicating that the respondent changed to a white collar job from a blue collar job (−1 if white collar before and blue collar after, 0 if no change, 1 if blue collar

Table 2. Earnings Before and After Gender Change

Variables	1	2	3
Intercept	−0.107 (0.060)	−0.097 (0.073)	−0.154 (0.090)
Change-to-Male (Δmale$_i$)	0.206 (0.060)***	0.205 (0.061)**	0.169 (0.063)*
Difference in Years Before and After	—	−0.003 (0.014)	0.014 (0.030)
Gain College Degree	—	—	0.014 (0.265)
Change to White Collar Job	—	—	0.128 (0.184)
Change to Private Sector Job	—	—	−0.258 (0.153)
Observations	43	43	43
R-Squared	0.226	0.227	0.344
Adjusted R-Squared	0.207	0.189	0.235

Notes: Standard errors in parentheses. The dependent variable is the difference in log hourly earnings: log hourly earnings after the gender change minus log hourly earnings before the gender change. *Change to Male* (Δmale$_i$) equals +1 for Female-to-Male respondents and −1 for Male-to-Female. *Gain College Degree* equals 1 if the respondent earned a 4-year college degree between the before period and the after period, and 0 otherwise. *Change to White Collar Job* equals +1 for individuals who move from blue collar jobs before to white collar jobs after, 0 for those who do not change, and −1 for individuals who move from white collar to blue collar jobs. *Change to Private Sector Job* is defined similarly. Model 3 also includes missing variable flags. *$p < 0.05$; **$p < 0.01$; ***$p < 0.001$ (two-tailed tests).

before and white collar after), and iii) a variable for whether the respondent changed to a private sector job from a public sector job (−1 if private before and public after, 0 if no change, 1 if public before and private after). This specification also includes three missing variable flags, one for each of the included additional variables.[9] Of the three additional variables included in Model 3, only the change to a private sector job is statistically significant from zero at the 10 percent level. The coefficient estimate indicates that transgender people who switched to private sector jobs lost 25.8 percent of their previous earnings. Given the selection into job types, it is unclear how to interpret this finding.

Including these additional control variables in Model 3 increases the estimated transgender wage penalty ($\Delta\gamma$) from a loss of 9.7 percent of hourly earnings in Model 2 to 15.4 percent in Model 3. This may indicate that transgender people are adapting to workplace appearance discrimination by switching to job types that are less discriminatory. Not controlling for these characteristics in Models 1 and 2 masks the larger transgender earnings penalty that is revealed in Model 3. In addition, the gain to becoming male (the coefficient on Δmale$_i$) is estimated to be 16.9 percent in Model 3. This is still large and statistically significant (p-value 0.020), but is smaller than the gain estimated in Models 1 and 2. In Model 3, becoming men for FTMs brings a small increase in overall earnings ($-0.154 + 0.169 = 0.015$), while becoming women for MTFs brings a large reduction in earnings of about 32 percent ($-0.154 - 0.169 = -0.323$).

It is important to note that for most of the sample these multivariate regressions only capture the immediate change in earnings following a gender transition. A longitudinal study of transgender employment over a longer period may reveal more substantial changes. As we discuss in the next section, interview evidence indicates that FTMs experience more subtle changes in their labor market opportunities after becoming men as they gain increased authority and respect in the workplace. MTFs on the other hand experience a decline in these same areas, and more MTFs than FTMs report experiencing harassment and discriminatory promotion and retention decisions (Griggs 1998; Schilt 2006a; Schilt and Connell 2007). We suspect that over time these changes would affect earnings even more substantially than we are able to document here.

Discussion

Although our sample of transgender people is not a random sample from the general population, we argue that studying gender transitions leads to important insights into how gender impacts workplace outcomes. While MTFs and FTMs change their outward gender, their skills, abilities, and gender socialization remain the same.[10] The substantial loss of earnings experienced by MTFs, but not FTMs, suggests that omitted variables theories do not fully account for the role of gender in the workplace.

Endogenous Gender Transitions

An issue with interpreting the identification of the earnings gains to becoming men is that people considering gender transitions may endogenously choose whether or not to transition based on their anticipated earnings from this change. For example, MTFs who expect to experience economic losses due to working as women may be less likely to make this transition. On the other hand, FTMs who expect to gain from working as men may be more likely to make this transition. This implies that the transgender population we surveyed is not representative of the actual population of all potential transgender people, as it does not include individuals who want to change their gender but do not because the labor market penalty is too high. If gender transitions are endogenous, this would bias downward the transgender penalty (the intercept $\Delta\gamma$ estimated in (2)) and bias upward the earnings gains to becoming men (the δ parameter in (2)).

Speaking to this potential bias, we find evidence, documented below, that suggests that the age at transition is influenced by earnings considerations, as MTFs are considerably older on average at the time of their transitions than FTMs. Thus, it may be that MTFs are waiting to transition at a later age because they want to maintain "male" earnings for as long as possible. FTMs, in contrast, may be transitioning earlier because they anticipate they will earn more once they enter the workforce as men. There is some evidence to support this interpretation. Bolin (1988) and Griggs (1998) find, for example, that some MTFs live as women but continue to work as men because they do not want to move to "women's work" or experience employment discrimination. Most of them do eventually make the workplace transition, however, as their increasingly feminized appearance becomes harder to account for at work. In a follow-up study of transgender people who have been accepted for surgery but have not yet undergone a transition, "hesitating" MTFs cite economic concerns, along with health concerns and family concerns, as a justification for their delay (Kockott and Fahrner 1987). This group, however, also is identified as the least psychologically adjusted (compared to those who do transition or to those who still plan to in the near future), suggesting this hesitation is not a tenable position over time.

The importance of living in their desired gender is underscored by the findings that on average both MTFs and FTMs who do transition sacrifice substantial earnings. In Table 2, the transgender penalty (the intercept) is estimated to be large for both MTFs and FTMs. The penalty for the gender transition is large enough that it nearly offsets the gains to becoming men for FTMs, so that for FTMs there is essentially no change in earnings on average after their transitions. This willingness to give up earnings in order to live in their desired gender is supported by qualitative data in which interviewed FTMs expect employment discrimination but decide to transition anyway (Schilt 2006a). We interpret this evidence as suggestive that, while there is a population of people who may not transition for a variety of reasons, most transgender people do eventually transition.

Timing of Transition

One of the more salient patterns evident in the transgender sample is the stark difference in the timing of the gender transition: MTFs transition on average 9.6 years after FTMs. As seen in Table 1, MTFs on average remain in their male gender until age 40, whereas FTMs on average transition at age 30. This later age at transition is consistent with the hypothesis that MTFs seek to preserve working as men as long as possible. We argue that this difference suggests that some MTFs anticipate that their pre-transition human capital will not receive the same value after they become women. As women workers, however, FTMs may feel that they have less to lose and potentially more to gain from making the transition to become men at work.

Table 3 explores whether this difference in age at transition is robust to the inclusion of control variables. The dependent variable for the regression models in Table 3 is the age at which the respondent was last employed before beginning his or her gender transition. The regression models are estimated on the pooled FTM and MTF samples. Model 1 includes an intercept and a dummy variable for FTMs. The estimated intercept replicates the MTF average age at gender transition reported in Table 1. The estimated coefficient on the FTM dummy variable for Model 1 is −9.60, indicating that FTMs transition 9.6 years earlier than MTFs. This coefficient estimate is statistically significant at the 1 percent level.

Models 2–4 in Table 3 add various covariates to the regression model as controls for education, demographics, and pre-transition employment. Looking across the regression models in Table 3, the estimated coefficient on the FTM dummy variable remains statistically significant at the 5 percent level or higher. In Model 2, inclusion of dummy variables for college degree, white race, and white-collar employment before gender change increases the estimated difference between the age at gender change for FTMs and MTFs to −10.36, indicating that FTMs change their gender 10.36 years earlier than MTFs. Model 3 in Table 3 adds a dummy variable (*Same Job Before and After*), which indicates whether the respondent continued to be employed

Table 3. Age at Gender Change

Variables	1	2	3	4
Intercept	39.56***	30.68***	28.34***	28.12***
	(2.57)	(3.77)	(3.80)	(4.33)
FTM	−9.60**	−10.36***	−8.91**	−7.74*
	(3.36)	(2.94)	(2.97)	(2.94)
College Degree	—	10.62	8.03	9.76
		(3.84)	(4.04)	(3.79)
White Race	—	6.32	4.56	3.36
		(3.23)	(3.25)	(3.03)
White Collar Before Job	—	−0.66	0.09	−2.07
		(3.97)	(4.02)	(3.90)
Same Job Before and After	—	—	6.85*	2.42
			(3.15)	(3.29)
Years Worked at Before Job	—	—	—	0.67*
				(0.26)
Observations	43	43	43	43
R-Squared	0.166	0.414	0.482	0.585
Adjusted R-Squared	0.145	0.352	0.396	0.488

Notes: Standard errors in parentheses. FTM is Female-to-Male. The dependent variable is the age at which the transgender respondents reported completing their gender change. *p <0.05; **p< 0.01; ***p < 0.001 (two-tailed tests). Models 2–4 include missing variable flags.

in the same job following his or her gender transition. Inclusion of this variable reduces the estimated coefficient on the FTM dummy variable to −8.91, but it is still significantly different from 0 at the 1 percent level.

Interestingly, the estimated coefficient on the *Same Job Before and After* variable indicates that transgender people who keep the same job following their gender change wait nearly 7 additional years to change their gender than transgender people who get new jobs after transition. To see whether or not this finding reflects strategic behavior to delay a gender transition until stable employment is attained, Model 4 adds to the regression model the number of years respondents report holding their jobs before their gender transition (*Years Worked at Before Job*). The estimated coefficient on this variable is 0.67 and is statistically significant at the 5 percent level. This indicates that both MTFs and FTMs who have accumulated valuable workplace experience in a particular job choose to delay their gender transitions, possibly to avoid disruption to their employment. Taken together, Models 3 and 4 provide additional evidence that the age at gender change is strategically chosen to avoid workplace losses and employment discrimination anticipated to accompany gender transitions.

Other Employment Outcomes

Looking beyond earnings, MTFs in our sample seem to experience a wider range of workplace hardships in becoming women than FTMs experience in becoming men. Survey respondents were provided a blank space to write comments about their workplace experiences. Five FTMs elected to write comments. All five praised their workplaces for their tolerance and acceptance. One respondent in a blue-collar job wrote: "My transition went extremely smoothly. I was shocked at how smooth. No one even talks about it and it had no effect on my pay. If anything, I have been better accepted at work because people don't see me as a dyke like before." The two MTFs who wrote comments, in contrast, emphasized workplace dilemmas. One respondent who transitioned in a blue-collar job she had worked in for twenty years as a man wrote that the women's restroom she used was "booby trapped," and mean notes were left on her desk telling her to quit. Another MTF wrote: "I was 'laid off' from my 10 year management position for having a 'bad attitude.' " She noted that she was laid off the first week that she began coming to work dressed in women's clothing. These comments certainly are not a systematic sample. However, they suggest that MTFs cannot take their masculine workplace advantage with them into womanhood.

Further supporting our argument that a workplace gender penalty often accompanies the move from male-to-female, Schilt (2006a) finds that MTFs experience a much wider range of obstacles to openly transitioning and remaining in the same jobs than their FTM counterparts. In a content analysis of news stories and legal cases about transgender employment from 1977–2005, Schilt shows that many MTFs experience harassment and often termination once they begin their gender transitions, even when they transition in jobs they have held for many years. Some of the most virulent harassment is experienced by MTFs in blue-collar occupations. This is an unsurprising finding, as blue-collar occupations are associated with homophobia and sexism (Welsh 1999). However, what is interesting about this blue-collar context is that in these news stories and legal cases, MTFs reported fitting into this masculine workplace culture prior to their gender transition. That pre-transition MTFs conformed to and benefited from masculine workplace gender norms in blue-collar occupations suggests that they have a great deal to lose when they become women, even though they retain their human capital and prior male socialization. We argue that the losses which accompany becoming women accounts for why MTFs in our sample may delay transitioning, as well as why some MTFs live full-time as women outside of the workplace but continue to work as men for as long as possible (Griggs 1998).

In contrast, Schilt (2006a) found that FTMs experience fewer obstacles to open workplace transitions than their MTF counterparts. In in-depth interviews with FTMs in California, Schilt (2006b) found that many of her respondents experienced an increase in authority, reward, and respect at work once they began working as men—even when they remained in the same jobs they had as women. While FTMs were subjected to feminine gender socialization as children, and had the same skills and abilities as they had as women workers, becoming men brought positive workplace outcomes.[11] Not being male-socialized may mean that FTMs benefit less than male-born men, as male-born men may be socialized to be more aggressive about seeking workplace rewards (Padavic and Reskin 2002). However, many FTMs generally are not penalized for their gender transitions, even though they, like MTFs, are making a "discredited identity" (Goffman 1963) public. Placing our survey data in context with this previous research suggests that being a man garners more workplace rewards than being a woman, even net of all other omitted variables.

Is It Gender or Appearance?

In analyzing the before and after gender change workplace experiences of transgender people, an important question is whether their workplace outcomes are due to changes in gender or changes in appearance. Prior research suggests that the appearance and attractiveness of workers does affect their labor market outcomes (Biddle and Hamermesh 1994; Biddle and Hamermesh 1998). Since transgender people can undergo a number of changes to their physical appearance in the process of their transition, they may be adversely affected by a non-normative appearance. The effects of hormone therapy, the physical structure of male bodies, and the different level of appearance scrutiny of men and women can cause MTFs to face more difficulties passing in their new gender than their FTM counterparts. With the use of testosterone, many FTMs develop thicker facial and body hair, deeper voices, and male-pattern baldness (Rubin 2003; Green 2004). With these masculine appearance cues, they are read as men in interactions often within a few weeks of beginning hormone therapy. Estrogen has fewer feminizing effects on male bodies. MTFs may experience some breast growth, but they do not stop growing facial hair or develop higher voices (Griggs 1998). Estrogen cannot alter physical characteristics that are typically interpreted as masculine, such as height over six feet, visible Adam's apples, and big hands and feet. MTFs can use feminine appearance cues as passing aids, such as feminine clothing, but these often cannot override masculine body cues.

This difference in post-gender change appearance is clearly evident in our survey data. Fifty-six percent of FTM respondents describe themselves as "always" passing as men. In contrast, 17 percent of MTFs describe themselves as "always" passing as women. Some MTFs who had been transitioned for over ten years still described themselves as only passing "sometimes." Some of the adverse employment outcomes for MTFs which we document above may be attributable to their changed appearance rather than to their changed gender.

However, we argue that gender is still likely a leading cause of the before and after differences we document for transgender workers. Ethnographic research suggests that men express concern about their MTF colleagues' work abilities *as women*, not because of their appearance (Schilt and Connell 2007). Demonstrating this anxiety, one MTF who had co-owned a business with two other men was asked, post-transition, if she was still going to be able to run a company if she was always "thinking about nail polish" (Schilt and Connell 2007:606). Additionally, as many FTMs pass successfully as men within a short time of beginning hormone therapy, we can more confidently argue that the workplace benefits they experience are related to becoming men.

Conclusion

This study uses the pre- and post-transition experiences of transgender workers as a novel way to explore the factors that contribute to the persistence of gendered workplace disparities. As existing surveys can neither measure discrimination directly nor measure all the relevant characteristics of men and women, we use the before and after workplace outcomes for transgender people as a unique test of omitted variables theories of workplace gender inequality. The statistical analysis shows that transgender people in our sample are relatively comparable to the general population before their gender transitions in many dimensions, although, notably, transgender people are more educated.

Analyzing the earnings of transgender workers before and after their gender changes, we find that MTFs experience a substantial and statistically significant decrease in earnings while FTMs experience either no change or a slight increase. These findings suggest that the male gender carries a workplace benefit that cannot be carried over in a gender transition. That MTFs cannot take male privilege with them into womanhood may account for their significantly later age at transition than their FTM counterparts.

There are a number of limitations to this study. The small size of our sample reduces the precision of our statistical findings and precludes extensive multivariate analysis. A second limitation is our inability to control for the non-normative appearance of post-transition transgender people. Because of this limitation, the outcomes we document for gender transitions may be conflated with appearance discrimination. In an ideal experiment, we could compare a group of transgender people who definitely pass as women with a group who do not to gain a deeper understanding of how appearance interacts with gender to affect workplace outcomes. A third limitation of our study is that gender transitions do not occur overnight as in the ideal experiment, but may in fact take several years.

Future research can build upon this study in several ways. First, replicating this study with a longitudinal study of transgender workers that tracks earnings and other workplace outcomes long after initial transitions could illuminate whether these gains and losses associated with gender changes plateau or expand. Second, future studies could extend the analysis of before and after workplace outcomes beyond earnings and more traditionally measured workplace outcomes. As we discuss above, many of the forms of gender inequality are subtle, but can become apparent in an in-depth, qualitative examination of the experiences of transgender workers.

The experience of Ben Barres, an FTM neurobiology professor at Stanford, underscores the importance of these subtle forms of gender inequality. As a woman who excelled in math and science, Barres recounts constantly having her intellectual abilities questioned and undermined (Begley 2006). As a man, however, audiences who do not know about his gender change tell him that his scholarly research is much better than that of "his sister." Barres' experiences show how socially constructed beliefs about men and women's natural abilities cloud perceptions and evaluations, thus producing gendered workplace disparities. Our study demonstrates that the workplace experiences of transgender people are a fruitful way to explore these long-standing debates about gender and work, as they clearly illuminate the impact of subtle assumptions about inevitable gender differences on men and women's workplace outcomes.

Notes

1. "Transgender" is an umbrella term that encompasses a wide variety of people who cross socially constructed gender boundaries in some way (Meyerowitz 2002). For instance, people who choose to undergo gender transitions via hormone therapy and genital surgery can be referred to as transgender, as can individuals who cross-dress on occasion. For the purposes of our paper, we are using the term "transgender" to refer to individuals who are working in a gender other than that which they were assigned at birth. Some of our respondents transition medically using hormones and surgical body modifications, while others do not. We discuss this further in the section on appearance discrimination and workplace outcomes.
2. The total percentage of transgender people and the gender breakdown of that percentage are widely contested. The .01% was estimated by the number of people seeking genital surgery. This estimation is flawed, however, as many FTMs and MTFs do not undergo genital surgery (Meyerowitz 2002; Green 2004). Additionally, as MTFs have sought out institutionalized services more frequently than FTMs, there long has been an assumption that there are more men becoming women than vice versa. Transgender community estimates, however, place the percentage as much higher (see Conway 2001 for a discussion of this percentage) and argue for a more equal gender breakdown (Califia 1998; Meyerowitz 2003).
3. Blau, Brinton, and Grusky (2006) provide a recent review of some of the major theories.

4. The actual text of these standards is available at http://wpath.org/Documents2/socv6.pdf.
5. Measuring the start of a gender transition is difficult. Many transgender people feel that they have been in the process of transitioning since childhood, as they might adopt appearance and behavior cues of their destination gender long before they decide to undergo any physical body modifications. The phrasing of this question was designed to create a uniform starting point for transition, i.e., the point at which transgender people seek to have their new gender recognized by their co-workers and employers.
6. Although recall bias for past earnings is a concern, it is not clear that this would bias the results in terms of the differences between FTMs and MTFs in any particular direction.
7. Our CPS sample includes all adults age 18 or older who report working at least 1 hour the past year for pay. The demographic, education, occupation, and industry questions in this survey are nearly identical to those in our transgender survey. For the CPS data, we construct as closely as possible an equivalent measure of hourly earnings using reported hours worked during the year and usual hours worked per week. Earnings for the CPS comparison sample are adjusted for inflation and expressed in 2004 dollars.
8. To address the difference in the distribution of ages in the transgender sample relative to the general population, we calculate average hourly earnings using the distribution of ages in the CPS data to weight the transgender sample to be representative of the general population. In results available on request, we find that mean hourly earnings for the transgender sample change only slightly using the age-weighted sample.
9. Sample distribution of these variables: gain degree (3 gain degree, 39 no change, 1 missing), change to white collar (4 change to white collar, 36 no change, 2 change to blue collar, 1 missing), change to private sector (2 change to private sector, 34 no change, 6 change to public sector, 1 missing).
10. In some cases, transgender people lose some of their human capital, as they cannot always take their work and education history with them into their new gender if they intend to successfully pass. However, as more transgender people are openly identifying as transgender, this has become less of an issue. Additionally, FTMs might be expected to suffer most from this, as they can more easily find jobs as "just men" because they pass more successfully in their new gender than MTFs (Griggs 1998; Schilt 2006a). Yet, as we show in this study, even if this is occurring, FTMs experience a gain in earnings relative to MTFs.
11. As some evidence on the heterogeneity of the outcomes for transgender people, Schilt (2006) shows that FTMs who were white benefited more than FTMs who were black, Latino, or Asian.

References

Acker, J. 1990. "Hierarchies, jobs, bodies: A theory of gendered organizations." *Gender & Society* 4 (2): 139–158.

Altonji, J. G. and R. M. Blank. 1999. "Race and gender in the labor market." In *Handbook of labor economics, vol. 3*, edited by O. Ashenfelter and D. Card. New York: Elsevier Sci.

Arrow, K. 1973. "The theory of discrimination." In *Discrimination in labor markets*, edited by O. Ashenfelter and A. Rees. Princeton: Princeton University Press.

Becker, G. S. 1971. *The economics of discrimination*, 2nd Edition. Chicago: University of Chicago Press, originally published 1957.

Begley, S. 2006. "He, once she, offers own view on science spat." *The Washington Post*. July 13: BI.

Benjamin, H. 1966. *The transsexual phenomenon*. New York: Warner Books.

Biddle, J. E., and D. Hamermesh. 1994. "Beauty and the labor market." *American Economic Review* 84 (5): 1174–94.

———. 1998. "Beauty, productivity, and discrimination: Lawyers' looks and lucre." *Journal of Labor Economics* 16 (1): 172–201.

Bird, S. 1996. "Welcome to the men's club: Homosociality and the maintenance of hegemonic masculinity." *Gender & Society* 10 (2): 120–32.

Blau, F. D., and L. M. Kahn. 2006. "The gender pay gap: Going, going... but not gone." In *The declining significance of gender?*, edited by F. D. Blau, M. C. Brinton, and D. B. Grusky. New York: Russell Sage Foundation.

Bolin, A. 1988. *In search of Eve: Transsexual rites of passage*. South Hadley, MA: Bergin & Garvey.

Bowlus, A., and Z. Eckstein. 2002. "Discrimination and skill differences in an equilibrium search model." *International Economic Review* 43 (4): 1309–45.

Brown, C., and M. Corcoran. 1997. "Sex-based differences in school content and the male/female wage gap." *Journal of Labor Economics* 15 (3): 431–65.

Byrd, B. 1999. "Women in carpentry apprenticeship: A case study." *Labor Studies Journal* 24 (3): 3–22.

Califia, P. 1997. *Sex changes: The politics of transgender*. San Francisco: Clevis Press.

Conway, L. 2001. "How frequently does transsexualism occur?" Accessed online on February 9, 2008 at http://ai.eecs.umich.edu/people/conway/TS/TSprevalence.html.

Corcoran, M. E., and P. N. Courant. 1985. "Sex role socialization and labor market outcomes." *American Economic Review, Papers and Proceedings* 75 (2): 275–78.

Feinbloom, D. 1976. *Transvestites and transsexuals*. New York: Delta Books.

Fuller, R., and R. Schoenberger. 1991. "The gender salary gap: Do academic achievement, internship experience, and. college major make a difference?" *Social Science Quarterly* 72: 715–26.

Goffman, E. 1963. *Stigma*. New York: Prentice Hall.

Goldin, C. 1990. *Understanding the gender gap: An economic history of American women*. New York: Oxford University Press.

Gould, R. 1974. "Measuring masculinity by the size of a paycheck." In *Men & masculinity*, edited by J. Pleck and J. Sawyer. Englewood Cliffs, NJ: Prentice Hall.

Green, J. 2004. *Becoming a visible man*. Nashville: Vanderbilt University Press.

Griggs, C. 1998. *S/he: Changing sex and changing clothes*. New York: Berg.

Groshen, E. L. 1991. "The structure of the female/male wage differential." *Journal of Human Resources* 26: 457–72.

Hochschild, A. R. 1983. *The managed heart: Commercialization of human feeling*. Berkeley: University of California Press.

Hore, B. D., F. V. Nicolle, and J. S. Calnan. 1975. "Male transsexualism in England: Sixteen cases with surgical intervention." *Archives of Sexual Behavior* 4 (1): 81–88.

Kando, T. 1973. *Sex change: The achievement of gender identity among feminized transsexuals*. Springfield, IL: Charles C. Thomas Publisher.

Kanter, R. M. 1977. *Men and women of the corporation*. New York: Basic Books.

Kimmel, M. 2000. *The gendered society*. New York: Oxford University Press.

Kockott, G., and E. M. Fahrner. 1987. "Transsexuals who have not undergone surgery: A follow-up study." *Archives of Sexual Behavior* 16 (6): 511–23.

Kuiper, B., and P. T. Cohen-Kettenis. 1988. "Sex reassignment surgery: A study of 141 Dutch transsexuals." *Archives of Sexual Behavior* 17: 439–57.

Laub, D., and N. Fisk. 1974. "A rehabilitation program for gender dysphoria syndrome and surgical sex change." *Plastic and Reconstructive Surgery* 53: 388–403.

Lawrence, A. 2003. "Factors associated with satisfaction or regret following male-to-female sex reassignment surgery." *Archives of Sexual Behavior* 32:299–315.

Leidner, R. 1993. *Fast food, fast talk: Service work and the routinization of everyday life*. Berkeley: University of California Press.

Lindemalm, G., D. Korlin, and N. Uddenberg. 1986. "Long-term follow-up of 'sex change' in 13 male-to-female transsexuals." *Archives of Sexual Behavior* 15: 187–210.

Lothstein, L. 1983. *Female-to-male transsexualism: Historical, clinical and theoretical issues*. Boston: Routledge & Kegan Paul.

Marini, M. 1989. "Sex differences in earnings in the United States." *Annual Review of Sociology* 15: 348–80.

Martin, P. Y. 2003. "'Said and done' versus 'saying and doing': Gendering practices, practicing gender at work." *Gender & Society* 17 (3): 342–66.

McCloskey, D. 1999. *Crossing: A memoir*. Chicago: University of Chicago Press.

Meyerowitz, J. 2002. *How sex changed: A history of transsexuality in the United States*. Cambridge, MA: Harvard University Press.

Miller, L. 1997. "Not just weapons of the weak: Gender harassment as a form of protest for army men." *Social Psychology Quarterly* 60 (1): 32–51.

Moro, A., and P. Norman. 2004. "A general equilibrium model of statistical discrimination." *Journal of Economic Theory* 114: 1–30.

Moss, P., and C. Tilly, 2001. *Stories employers tell: Race, skill, and hiring in America*. New York: Russell Sage.

Paap, K. 2005. *Working construction*. New York: Cornell University Press.

Padavic, I., and B. Reskin. 2002. *Women and men at work*, 2nd ed. Thousand Oaks: Pine Forge Press.

Paglin, M., and A. M. Rufolo. 1990. "Heterogeneous human capital, occupation choice, and male-female earnings differences." *Journal of Labor Economics* 8: 123–44.

Perkins, R. 1983. *The 'drag queen' scene: Transsexuals in Kings Cross*. Sydney: George Allen & Unwin.

Phelps, E. S. 1972. "The statistical theory of racism and sexism." *American Economic Review* 62 (4): 659–61.

Rakic, Z., V. Starcevic, J. Maric, and K. Kelin. 1996. "The outcome of sex reassignment surgery in Belgrade: 32 patients of both sexes." *Archives of Sexual Behavior* 25: 515–25.

Rubin, H. 2003. *Self made men: Identity and embodiment among transsexual men*. Nashville, TN: Vanderbilt University Press.

Schafer, S. 2001. "More transgenders start new life with old jobs." *Times-Picayune* (February 4). Living: 15.

Schilt, K. 2006a. "Just one of the guys? How female-to-male transsexuals make gender inequality at work visible." Ph.D. dissertation, Department of Sociology, University of California–Los Angeles.

———. 2006b. "Just one of the guys? How transmen make gender visible at work." *Gender & Society* 20 (4): 465–490.

Schilt, K., and C. Connell. 2007. "Do workplace gender transitions make gender trouble?" *Gender, Work and Organization* 14(6): 596–618.

Sorensen, T. 1981a. "Follow-up study of operated transsexual males." *Acta Psychiatria Scandanavica* 63: 486–503.

———. 1981b. "Follow-up study of operated transsexual females." *Acta Psychiatria Scandanavica* 64: 50–64.

Subich, L., G. Barret, D. Doverspike, and R. Alexander. 1989. "The effects of sex role related factors on occupational choice and salary." In *Pay equity: Empirical inquiries*, edited by R. Michael, H. Hartmann, and B. O'Farrell. Washington, DC: National Academy Press: 45–62.

Valian, V. 1999. *Why so slow?: The advancement of women*. Cambridge, MA: MIT Press.

Welsh, S. 1999. "Gender and sexual harassment." *Annual Review of Sociology* 25: 169–90.

Williams, C. 1995. *Still a man's world: Men who do women's work*. Berkeley: University of California Press.

Wood, R. G., M. E. Corcoran, and P. N. Courant. 1993. "Pay differentials among the highly paid: The male-female earnings gap in lawyers' salaries." *Journal of Labor Economics* 11 (3): 417–41.

Yoder, J., and P. Aniakudo. 1997. "Outsider within the firehouse: Subordination and difference in the social interactions of African American women firefighters." *Gender and Society* 11 (3): 324–41.

PART

9

The Gendered Media

Do the media *cause* violence, or do the media simply reflect the violence that already exists in our society? Think of how many times we have heard variations of this debate: Does gangsta rap or violent video games or violent movies or violent heavy metal music lead to increased violence? Does violent pornography lead men to commit rape? Or do these media merely remind us of how violent our society already is?

And how do the various media contribute to our understanding of gender? What role do the various media play in the maintenance of gender difference or gender inequality?

Like other social institutions, the media are a gendered institution. The media (1) reflect already existing gender differences and gender inequalities, (2) construct those very gender differences, and (3) reproduce gender inequality by making those differences seem "natural" and not socially produced in the first place. Part of its function of maintaining inequality is to first create the differences, and then to attempt to conceal its authorship so that those differences seem to flow from the nature of things.

Media reflect already existing gender differences and inequalities by targeting different groups of consumers with different messages that assume prior existing differences. In a sense, women and men don't use or consume the same media—there are women's magazines and men's magazines, chick flicks and action movies, chick lit and lad lit, pornography and romance novels, soap operas and crime procedurals, guy video games and girl video games, blogs, and 'zines—and, of course, advertising that is intricately connected to each of these different formats. As with other institutions, there are "his" and "hers" media.

The essays in this part explore the media as a gendered set of institutions, and they also discuss the way the media are a socializing agent that genders people through media representations. Miranda A. H. Horvath and her colleagues shed light on the age-old question of whether the media can be said to "cause" behaviors (obviously they are "mediated"—that is sort of the point), while Shira Chess and Miles White look at the ways in which media representations shape the self-understandings of young women (of all races) and young black men, respectively.

"Lights on at the End of the Party": Are Lads' Mags Mainstreaming Dangerous Sexism?

MIRANDA A. H. HORVATH, PETER HEGARTY, SUZANNAH TYLER, AND SOPHIE MANSFIELD

> 'It's not our job to educate people.... Men's magazines if anything are the opposite of that—we're the good time. If you mention to people about gonorrhoea and syphilis it ruins the fun. It's lights on at the end of the party' (Martin Daubney, 2007).

Many social scientists think that repeated exposure to magazine content influences perceptions of social reality (Gerbner, Gross, Morgan, & Signorielli, 1994; Gerbner, Gross, Morgan, Signorielli, & Shanahan, 2002). Magazine content can lead to the development of new schemas (Huesmann, 1997, 1998) and the priming of old ones (Ward, 2003). The influence of magazines on behaviour is particularly important with regard to the sexual practices of young people, because adolescents cite magazines as their favoured and most dependable resource for sexual information (Treise & Gotthoffer, 2002; Walsh & Ward, 2010; see also Papadopoulos, 2010). Such influences can be negative; young boys are more likely to identify women as sex objects when they have been exposed to sexualized media than when they have not been so exposed (Peter & Valkenburg, 2007).

The present research builds on such findings by examining some kinds of sexist views that can be easily found in the pages of contemporary *lads' mags* aimed at young male readers. Lads' mags are relatively new media that are readily found alongside other mainstream magazines in newsagents and supermarkets across the United Kingdom, United States, and Australia (Coy & Horvath, 2011). Lads' mags initially captured a diverse market characterized by the desire for more traditional upmarket lifestyle magazines for men (e.g., *GQ, Esquire*). Cheaper weeklies such as *Zoo* and *Nuts* have since appeared with lower production values and with content about less globally famous female celebrities (Mooney, 2008). However, over the last 10–15 years, the distinctions between genres have lessened with even the more upmarket titles becoming increasingly reliant on (hetero) sexualized imagery and a more 'hedonistic predatory construction of masculinity' (Coy & Horvath, 2011, p. 145; see also Attwood, 2005; Benwell, 2004; Crewe, 2003; Stevenson, Jackson, & Brooks, 2003).

While psychologists have often studied how pornography socializes derogatory attitudes towards women among young male viewers (e.g., Bensimon, 2007; Mackay & Covell, 1997; Malamuth, Addison, & Koss, 2000), the lack of total nudity in lads' mags prevents lads' mags from being classified as pornographic (Krassas, Blauwkamp, & Wesselink, 2003). Yet, researchers who have analysed the contents of lads' mags in depth have concluded that magazines such as *Maxim* and *Stuff* script sex such that women are sexual objects, whose sexual satisfaction is of secondary importance to men's (Krassas *et al.*, 2003). Women are often depicted in lads' mags in states of undress, as victims of sexual coercion and male dominance, and in faux lesbian erotic poses, as in pornography, aimed at the straight male viewer (Taylor, 2005). Lads' mags often advise young men to get drunk, fake sincerity to young women, and zone in on 'vulnerable

Miranda A. H. Horvath, Peter Hegarty, Suzannah Tyler, and Sophie Mansfield, "'Lights on at the End of the Party': Are Lads' Mags Mainstreaming Dangerous Sexism?" *British Journal of Psychology* (2011).

women' for 'sexual conquest' (Krassas *et al.*, 2001, 2003; see also Farvid & Braun, 2006; Lambaise, 2007; Taylor, 2005). Cover lines and images in lads' mags advocate easy sex without intimacy (Johnson, 2007). Lads' mags present traditional gender role expectations that women ought to satisfy men sexually (Viki & Abrams, 2002). They present sex and relationship issues through silence, inappropriate advice, or humour (Johnson, 2007). Thus, if taken at face value, lads' mags appear likely to teach young men sexist attitudes and practices (Horvath, Coy, & Murray, 2010) as more sexually explicit pornography is known to do (Bensimon, 2007; Mackay & Covell, 1997; Malamuth *et al.*, 2000).

Editors of lads' mags often urge people not to take their magazines' contents at face value. For example, Martin Daubney, the former editor of popular UK lads' mag *Loaded* dismissed the possibility that magazines do or should educate young people about sex. Sexist content in lads' mags is often characterized as merely 'ironic' (Benwell, 2003; McKay, Mikosza, & Hutchins, 2005) allowing editors to negate the possibility that their magazines influence readers, and to counter-argue that their critics have simply missed the intended joke (Jackson, Stevenson, & Brooks, 2001). However, the definition of 'irony' is inherently subjective; the same comment can be attributed a literal intended meaning or an ironic intended meaning. Irony is not gender-neutral; men are more likely to use irony than women, and the same comment is more likely to be interpreted as ironic if attributed to a man than a woman (Colston & Lee, 2004; Katz, Blasko, & Kazmerski, 2004). Sexist humour may be interpreted as harmless irony by some men and not by others. For example, men who are more sexist find sexist jokes funnier (Eyssel & Bohner, 2007) and disparaging humour about women creates a context in which the expression of sexism becomes the social norm (Ford & Ferguson, 2004; Romero-Sánchez, Durán, Carretero-Dios, Megias, & Moya, 2010). For these reasons, editors' claims about the social consequences of the content of lads' mags ought not themselves to be taken at face value.

Indeed, on occasion, the advice offered to readers of lads' mags has been so unambiguously violent in its prescriptions as to prompt controversy and retraction. In May 2010 the celebrity agony uncle, Danny Dyer, in the UK-based lads' mag *Zoo*, advised a 23-year-old man who wrote to ask for advice about how to get over a past relationship to 'cut your ex's face, and then no one will want her' (Busfield & Sweney, 2010). Dyer was forced to apologize, and *Zoo* staff blamed the advice on a 'production error' (Busfield & Sweney, 2010). Because sexist ironic humour in lads' mags can address such real-world issues as rape, human trafficking, and prostitution (Lanis & Covell, 1995), we asked the question of whether lads' mags may affect readers' norms, making extreme forms of sexism appear more acceptable to them.

Like the editors of lads' mags who blame egregious sexism on production errors, or minimize its effects as mere ironic humour, rapists are known to use 'techniques of neutralization' that justify and motivate their actions (Gilbert & Webster, 1982). For example, rapists learn a culturally derived vocabulary of motive that diminishes their responsibility, and normalizes their behaviour. Rapists blame women for their own victimization by describing women as seductresses, by claiming that 'no' means 'yes', by arguing that most women eventually 'relax and enjoy it' and by insisting that nice girls do not get raped (Scully & Marolla, 1984). As men who have mastered this vocabulary of diminished responsibility, convicted rapists have much to tell us about how sexual violence becomes possible and how it gets normalized (Scully, 1990). In other words, it appears that lads' mags and rapists might share the commonality of using techniques to neutralize derogatory sexism. However, we should not lose sight of the fact that when rapists are convicted they are unlikely to remain legitimate sources of social influence. In contrast, lads' mags are a normalized legitimate source of information, available in the marketplace, and only sometimes positioned on the 'top shelf' (Mooney, 2008, p. 250; Taylor, 2005).

The present research addressed the possibility that lads' mags may be normalizing sexist opinions that would otherwise be perceived as illegitimate;

the normalizations of violence against women voiced by convicted rapists. Each of the two studies addresses a hypothesis relevant to this research question. In Study 1, we tested the hypothesis that attributing derogatory sexist comments to lads' mags makes it easier for young men to identify with such content. In Study 2, we tested the hypothesis that young women and men will struggle to distinguish the strategies of legitimation voiced by convicted rapists and similar descriptions of women presented as harmless humour in lads' mags. Jointly, these studies inform the question of whether such advice as Danny Dyer's was truly exceptional, or if the legitimate 'mainstream' lads' mags genre more routinely contains examples of blatant sexist views in its pages such that its range of content is difficult to completely distinguish from the talk of convicted rapists.

Study 1: Identification with Lads' Mags and Rapists' Opinions About Women

Study 1 aimed to determine whether young men would identify more with sexist quotes about women when those quotes were attributed to lads' mags rather than to convicted rapists. We measured young men's identification with quotes about women drawn from contemporary lads' mags and from interviews with convicted rapists. We predicted that men would identify more with quotes of both sorts under conditions where those quotes were attributed to lads' mags rather than to rapists.

We also predicted that more sexist men would identify with quotes drawn from both sources overall. Of course, convicted rapists say many things in interviews that are not inherently sexist, and lads' mags contain much content that is unrelated to sexism also. We included both the Ambivalent Sexism Inventory (ASI, Glick & Fiske, 1996) and the Acceptance of Modern Myths about Sexual Aggression Scale (AMMSA, Gerger, Kley, Bohner, & Siebler, 2007) to further validate our assumption that identification with the quotes we selected would be evidence of sexism. The ASI measures both negatively valenced (hostile) and positively valenced (benevolent) sexist beliefs about women, and previous research has shown that hostile sexists endorse rape myths to a greater extent (Yamawaki, 2007) and that hostile sexist men find it easier to identify with a rapist in a story about acquaintance rape because they assume that the victim really wanted sex (Abrams, Viki, Masser, & Bohner, 2003). While benevolent sexists are quicker to blame the victim of an acquaintance rape for her own fate (Abrams *et al.*, 2003) and to recommend a more lenient penalty for a man who commits acquaintance rape (Viki, Abrams, & Masser, 2004), we aimed to select quotes that were derogatory towards women and predicted that endorsement of those quotes would be particularly well predicted by hostile sexism.

We also included a measure of rape myths; 'descriptive or prescriptive beliefs about rape (i.e., about its causes, context, consequences, perpetrators, victims and their interaction) that serve to deny, downplay or justify sexual violence that men commit against women' (Bohner, 1998, p. 14). The array of scales developed to measure rape myth acceptance (RMA) (e.g., Burt, 1980; Costin, 1985; Field, 1978; Payne, Lonsway, & Fitzgerald, 1999) have tended to use blatant and colloquial items formulations, producing severely positively skewed distributions (Gerger *et al.*, 2007). The AMSSA is a more subtle measure of RMA that builds on the recognition that sexism is typically expressed in subtle ways that can be disavowed later on in modern societies (Glick & Fiske, 1996; Swim, Aikin, Hall, & Hunter, 1995).

Method

Participants

An opportunistic sample of 92 men aged 18–46 years ($M = 22.70$; $SD = 4.09$) from a UK university was recruited face-to-face at public campus venues ($n = 45$) via a recruitment e-mail ($n = 41$) and recruitment posters ($n = 6$). Participants identified their race/ethnicity in their own words as 'White British' ($n = 54$), 'White' ($n = 22$), British ($n = 5$), 'British Indian' ($n = 2$), 'English' ($n = 2$), and one each as 'Asian', 'Black', 'Black African', 'British', 'Caucasian', 'White Asian', and 'White European'. The men described their relationship status as single ($n = 42$), 'in a relationship' ($n = 44$), 'engaged' ($n = 2$), or 'married' ($n = 4$), and their sexual orientation as heterosexual ($n = 90$) or bisexual ($n = 2$).

Table 1. Quotes Sourced from Lads' Mags and from Convicted Rapists Used as Stimuli in Studies 1 and 2

Quotes sourced from convicted rapists	
1	There's a certain way you can tell that a girl wants to have sex . . . The way they dress, they flaunt themselves.
2	Some girls walk around in short-shorts . . . showing their body off . . . It just starts a man thinking that if he gets something like that, what can he do with it? . . .
3	What burns me up sometimes about girls is dick-teasers. They lead a man on and then shut him off right there.
4	You know girls in general are all right. But some of them are bitches . . . The bitches are the type that . . . need to have it stuffed to them hard and heavy.
5	You'll find most girls will be reluctant about going to bed with somebody or crawling in the back seat of a car . . . But you can usually seduce them, and they'll do it willingly.
6	Girls ask for it by wearing these mini-skirts and hotpants . . . they're just displaying their body . . . Whether they realise it or not they're saying, 'Hey, I've got a beautiful body, and it's yours if you want it.'
7	Some women are domineering, but I think it's more or less the man who should put his foot down. The man is supposed to be the man. If he acts the man, the woman won't be domineering.
8	I think if a law is passed, there should be a dress code. . . . When girls dress in those short skirts and things like that, they're just asking for it.
Quotes sourced from lads' mags	
1	A girl may like anal sex because it makes her feel incredibly naughty and she likes feeling like a dirty slut. If this is the case, you can try all sorts of humiliating acts to help live out her filthy fantasy.
2	Mascara running down the cheeks means they've just been crying, and it was probably your fault . . . but you can cheer up the miserable beauty with a bit of the old in and out.
3	Filthy talk can be such a turn on for a girl . . . no one wants to be shagged by a mouse. . . . A few compliments won't do any harm either . . . 'I bet you want it from behind you dirty whore'. . . .
4	Escorts . . . they know exactly how to turn a man on. I've given up on girlfriends. They don't know how to satisfy me, but escorts do.
5	There's nothing quite like a woman standing in the dock accused of murder in a sex game gone wrong. . . . The possibility of murder does bring a certain frisson to the bedroom.
6	You do not want to be caught red-handed . . . go and smash her on a park bench. That used to be my trick.
7	Girls love being tied up . . . it gives them the chance to be the helpless victim.
8	I think girls are like plasticine, if you warm them up you can do anything you want with them.

Materials

The materials consisted of a questionnaire with several pages. The first page assessed identification with derogatory views about women expressed in lads' mags and by convicted rapists. We limited our search for the *lads' mags items* to a total of 12 editions of four different lads' mags with the highest circulation figures in the United Kingdom, which were published between January and March 2010; *Nut's, Zoo, Loaded*, and *FHM* (circulation data derived from www.abc.org.uk). We extracted eight short quotes from editorials and articles. We selected the eight *convicted rapist items* from verbatim interview transcripts with convicted incarcerated rapists in the United States contained in the book *The Rapist File: Interviews with Convicted Rapists* (Sussman & Bordwell, 2000). All quotes are listed verbatim in Table 1. Each of the 16 items was presented as a 7-point Likert item, which asked men to indicate their identification with the quote from 1 (*do not identify at all*) to 7 (*identify strongly*). We averaged participants' identification with quotes from each source to form reliable measures of identification with the lads' mags and convicted rapist items (Cronbach's α = .81, 0.88, respectively).

Participants completed one of three different versions of this questionnaire that established the experimental design of this study. In the *correctly attributed* version of the questionnaire, all 16 quotes were correctly identified as having been sourced from lads' mags or from interviews with convicted rapists. In the *incorrectly attributed* version, the quotes drawn from lads' mags were attributed to convicted rapists and the quotes drawn from convicted rapists were attributed to lads' mags. The *unattributed* version did not indicate the source of any of the quotes. These three conditions allowed us to test our principal prediction that men would identify more any given quote when that quote was attributed to lads' mags, and less when that quote was attributed to convicted rapists.

The identification items were followed by several measures that did not vary by experimental condition. The first of these was the ASI (Glick & Fiske, 1996), including 11 items measuring *Hostile Sexism* (e.g., 'Women are too easily offended') and 11 items measuring *Benevolent Sexism* (e.g., 'A good woman should be set on a pedestal by her man'). Participants indicated their agreement with each item from zero (*disagree strongly*) to five (*agree strongly*). We averaged participants' agreement with the items to form reliable measures of hostile and benevolent sexism, with higher scores indicating higher sexism (Cronbach's $\alpha = .88, .82$, respectively). Next, the 30 items of the *AMMSA* that measured contemporary myths about sexual violence were presented (e.g., 'Because the fascination caused by sex is disproportionately large, our society's sensitivity to crimes in this area is disproportionate as well', Eyssel & Bohner, 2008; Gerger *et al.*, 2007). Items were presented as 7-point Likert items ranging from 1 (*completely disagree*) to 7 (*completely agree*). Again we averaged scores to form a reliable measure, with higher scores indicating higher myth acceptance (Cronbach's $\alpha = .95$). The third scale presented was a four-item measure of the *Perceived Legitimacy of Lads' Mags* designed for this study. Participants indicated their agreement with Likert items ranging from 0 (*disagree strongly*) to 5 (*agree strongly*). This scale was reliable (Cronbach's $\alpha = 0.86$) and its four items read as follows:

> Lad's mags are a positive way of learning about sexual relationships.
>
> Reading lad's mags is something every young male should do.
>
> Lad's mags' have provided me with accurate and informative information about the opposite sex.
>
> Lad's mags' educate young men accurately on society's gender roles.

Finally, participants reported their gender, age, race/ethnicity, relationships status, and sexual orientation.

Procedure

Male volunteer participants met the female experimenter in a private room in the psychology department of a UK university. Participants were randomly assigned the *correctly attributed, incorrectly attributed*, or *unattributed* condition, and were presented with the materials including the relevant identification questionnaire. The participants then completed the questionnaire in private and submitted it to a locked box. Upon submitting their completed materials, the participants were verbally debriefed, thanked, and presented with an information sheet.

Results

Our hypotheses assumed that identification with both sorts of quotes would be indicative of sexism. To check this assumption, we examined the relationship between identification with quotes drawn from each source and with measures of sexism. Identification with the quotes drawn from lads' mags and from rapists were both highly correlated with hostile sexism, $r(91) = .59$, $.57$, respectively, both $p < .001$, benevolent sexism, $r(91) = .23, p < .05, r(91) = .30, p < .01$, respectively, AMMSA scores, $r(91) = .57, .61$, respectively, both $p < .001$, and our own measure of the *Perceived Legitimacy of Lads' Mags*, $r(91) = .49, .58$, respectively, both $p < .001$. Identification with each sort of quote was equivalently correlated with each measure of sexism (all Fisher's $Z < 1$). Consistent with our assumption that the quotes represented explicitly derogatory content, identification with both kinds of quotes was more strongly correlated with hostile sexism than with benevolent sexism (Fisher's $Z = 2.87, 2.17$ for rapist and lads' mags items, respectively, $p < .001, p = .03$, respectively, both two-tailed).

Identification

The main hypothesis of this study was that men would identify more with a quote when it was attributed to lads' mags, and identify less when that same quote was attributed to convicted rapists. Accordingly, we conducted a 3 × 2 mixed model ANOVA with quote source (lads' mags vs. convicted rapists') as a within-subjects factor and the attribution manipulation as a between-subjects factor (correctly attributed vs. unattributed vs. incorrectly attributed, see Figure 1). Overall, there was no significant main effect of our attribution manipulation: men identified with the items to the same degree in the correctly labelled, unlabelled, and incorrectly labelled conditions ($Ms = 2.84, 2.75, 2.75$, respectively), $F < 1$. There was however a significant main effect of quote source, surprisingly, men identified significantly more with quotes that were genuinely drawn from interviews with convicted rapists than with quotes that were genuinely drawn from lads' mags ($M = 3.23, 2.33$, respectively; $SD = 1.28, 0.99$), $F(1, 89) = 113.74$, $p < .001$, $\eta^2_p = .56$. We discuss this unexpected finding further below.

A significant interaction between the attribution manipulation and the quote source confirmed our main hypothesis, $F(2, 89) = 15.48$, $p < .001$, $\eta^2_p = .26$. Figure 1 shows two linear trends demonstrating that men identified most with both kinds of quotes when attributed to lads' mags, and least when attributed to convicted rapists. Tukey's *post hoc* tests ($\alpha = .05$) showed that men identified more with the quotes drawn from lads' mags when those quotes were correctly attributed than when they were incorrectly attributed. Identification with quotes from lads' mags that were not attributed was intermediately between these two but not significantly different from either. Tukey's tests revealed that identification with the quotes drawn from convicted rapists did not significantly differ by condition.

Discussion

In Study 1, sexist men, particularly hostile sexist men who endorsed modern rape myths, identified most frequently with the quotes we drew from interviews with convicted rapists and contemporary lads' mags. These findings are telling in light of earlier research that hostile sexist men are also quicker to identify with rapist protagonists in vignette studies (Abrams *et al.*, 2003). Previous authors have noted that sexist content is common

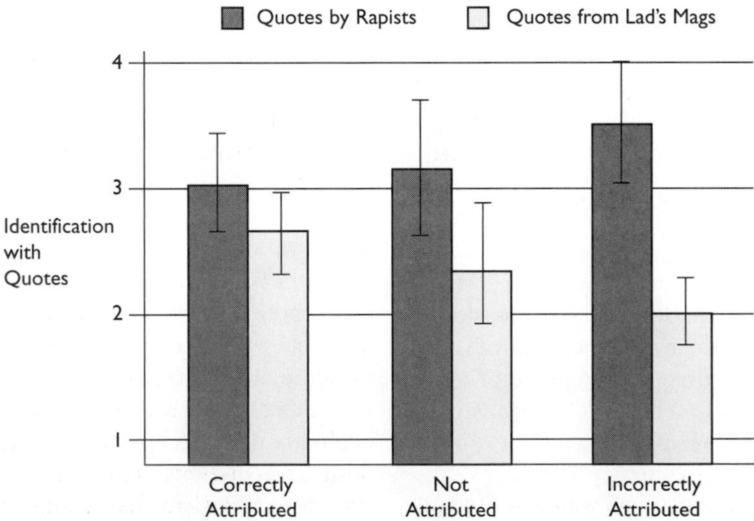

Figure 1. Mean Identification with Quotes by Source and Attribution Condition, Study 1.

Note. Error bars represent standard deviations.

in lads' mags (e.g., Taylor, 2005), but Study 1 shows that young men who are more sexist identify most with the sexist views that can easily be found in such magazines.

Confirming our main prediction, young men identified more with hostile sexist quotes about women when those quotes were *attributed* to lads' mags. The effect of the attribution manipulation was significant for the quotes drawn from lads' mags, but not for the quotes drawn from rapists. This finding is consistent with the possibility that lads' mags might normalize hostile sexism, because sexism appears more acceptable to young men when lads' mags appear to be its source. Unexpectedly, the participants also identified *more* with the rapists' quotes than the lads' mags quotes. Jointly these findings suggest the possibility that the legitimation strategies that rapists deploy when they talk about women are more familiar to these young men than we had anticipated. They also suggest that young men might be unable to correctly detect the source of hostile quotes drawn from lads' mags and convicted rapists. Discussion of explanations for these findings are in the general discussion but it should be noted here that it is plausible the only reason for the main effect we found could be that the quotes we used from convicted rapists were less 'severe' than those extracted from the lads' mags. Study 2 examined the extent to which people could tell the difference between quotes drawn from the two sources.

Study 2: Telling the Difference Between Lads' Mags and Rapists' Views About Women

Study 2 aimed to discern whether and how young women and men tell the difference between the content we draw from lads' mags and content drawn from interviews with convicted rapists. Study 1 suggested that young men identified with the views of convicted rapists more than they would have liked to have acknowledged. In Study 2, women and men were asked to identify the quotes' sources and to rank and categorize them according to whether or not they were derogatory towards women.

Method

Participants

Twenty women and 20 men (M age = 23.23, SD = 3.46, range = 19–30 years) participated as volunteers. The participants identified their race/ethnicity as White British (n = 38) or Mixed Race (n = 2); reported their relationship status as single (n = 13), in a relationship but unmarried (n = 16), engaged to be married (n = 6), or married (n = 5); and reported their sexual identity as heterosexual (n = 40). All participants who were approached consented to take part, and none withdrew from the study at any point.

Materials

The principal experimental materials were 16 laminated cards, each of which presented one of the 16 quotes used in Study 1 on one side and a unique identifying number on the reverse side. The measure of *Perceived Legitimacy of Lads' Mags* and demographic questionnaire used in Study 1 were also used. A dictaphone recorded participants' speech during the sorting tasks and the debriefing.

Procedure

Participants were recruited following the procedures for snowball sampling described by Breakwell, Hammond, Fife-Schaw, and Smith (2006). Specifically, personal contacts of the researcher were asked to introduce the experimenter to people whom they knew and who were unknown to the researcher, who might also be willing to participate as volunteers. Potential participants were informed that the study concerned 'attitudes towards women that some men might hold', that they would be required to read and consider quotations about women that some people may find offensive, and that they would have to carry out three card sorting tasks.

All participants took part during individual testing sessions in a private room in a university psychology department in the United Kingdom. Once the participant had completed a consent form, the experimenter briefed her or him that there were no right or wrong answers to the questions, and that the participant could voice comments, thoughts, and opinions throughout the procedure, and that

Table 2. Perceived Degradingness and Source Attributions of All Quotes by Sorting Task (Study 2)[1]

	Degradingness				Correct Attribution	
	Mean Rank		Proportion			
Source	Lads' Mags	Rapists	Lads' Mags	Rapists	Lads' Mags	Rapists
1	12.15	7.65	.90	.78	.48	.55
2	9.15	6.15	.93	.65	.55	.63
3	8.20	5.90	.70	.50	.78	.48
4	4.45	11.20	.43	.95	.78	.73
5	9.12	7.53	.48	.70	.30	.50
6	11.22	6.72	.88	.75	.30	.63
7	10.05	8.55	.68	.65	.23	.43
8	8.85	9.10	.83	.83	.63	.78
Mean	9.15	7.85	.73	.73	.58	.53

Note. See Table 1 for verbatim quotes. Rank, mean degradingness rank of quote; proportion, proportion of participating categorizing quote as degrading; correct attribution, proportion of participants correctly detecting the quote's source.

these would be tape-recorded and analysed. The experimenter also reminded the participant of the procedures for assuring the confidentiality and anonymity of their data, and the tape recording began when the participants were ready to start the study.

The experimenter scattered the 16 laminated cards displaying the quotes from Study 1 on a table in front of the participant. The experimenter described the quotes as things that some men had said about women, and asked each participant to carry out three sorting tasks. In the first *degrading continuum* participants placed the quotes in order from the most degrading towards women to the least degrading. Second, participants carried out the *degrading split* task, by categorizing the cards into two groups; those that they considered degrading towards women, and those that they considered not degrading towards women. Finally, the experimenter briefed the participants that some of the quotes were from convicted rapists and others were from popular lads' mags, and asked participants to complete the *source detection* task. In this task, participants guessed which quotes had been derived from each source, and their guesses were recorded. Next, the experimenter prompted the participant to verbally explain their categorization of the quotes in each of the two piles with the prompts 'What is it about these quotes that made you think they came from lads' mag?' and 'What is it about these quotes that made you think they came from convicted rapists?' After the participant completed each of the three tasks, the experimenter recorded the rank accorded to each quote, or the category in which it had been placed, using the cards' identification numbers. Participants than completed the measure of *Perceived Legitimacy of Lads' Mags* and the demographic questionnaire, were debriefed verbally, and were thanked for their participation.

Results

Our presentation of the results is divided into two sections. First, we report the statistical analysis of the three card sorting tasks. Next, we describe some themes that emerged from participants' guesses during the source detection task. The first two sorting tasks tested the hypothesis that the two kinds of quotes would be perceived as equally degrading towards women. The mean rank attributed to each quote during the degrading continuum task ranged from 1 to 16 and is shown in Table 2. Higher scores represented a perception of greater degradingness. The mean rank accorded to the eight lads' mag quotes was, on average, higher than the mean rank accorded to the eight rapist quotes (*Ms* = 9.15,

7.85, respectively, both $SD = 1.37$). A one-sample t-test showed that both these means were significantly different from the mid-point of the ranking scale, 8.5, both $t(39) = 3.01$, $p = .005$. In other words, the participants ranked the quotes drawn from lads' mags to be more degrading to women than the quotes drawn from convicted rapists. The proportion of participants who categorized each quote as degrading during the degrading split task is also shown in Table 2. The participants categorized an average of 11.65 quotes as derogatory and 4.35 quotes as non-derogatory, and categorized an equal number of quotes from lads' mags and from convicted rapists as derogatory ($M = 5.85$, 5.80, respectively, $SD = 1.42$, 1.82).

Finally, we examined if the participants could correctly identify the source of the quotes. Participants attributed slightly fewer quotes to lads' mags than to convicted rapists ($M = 7.63$, 8.38, respectively, both $SD = 2.47$). Across the experiment as a whole, the participants guessed correctly only 56.1% of the time when they attributed a quote to a lads' mag and only 55.4% of the time when they attributed a quote to a convicted rapist. Although participants' guesses were better than chance predictions ($t(39) = 2.58$, $p < .001$), the high error rate nonetheless suggests that participants experienced considerable difficulty in distinguishing between quotes from the two sources. Participants categorized the statements similarly irrespective of their gender, exposure to lads' mags, and attitudes towards lads' mags. Women and men did not differ in the number of quotes from either source that they categorized as degrading, attributed to convicted rapists or to lads' mags, or attributed accurately, all $t < 1$, all $p > .34$. Nineteen men and 10 women reported that they had read a lads' mag. Readers and non-readers correctly identified an equivalent number of quotes from rapists and from lads' mags, both $t < 1$. Finally, as in Study 1, we calculated participants' scores on the measure of *Perceived Legitimacy of Lads' Mags* (Cronbach's $\alpha = .75$). There was no relationship between attitudes and any of the following; the mean rank of rapists' and lads' mags' quotes on the degradingness continuum; the number of each type of quote categorized as degrading; or the number of each quote whose source was correctly identified, all $r(39) < .21$, all $p > .20$.

Thematic Analysis

We analysed participants' verbatim explanations of their guesses next by transcribing the tape recordings we made during the performance of the sorting tasks and subjecting them to thematic analysis (Braun & Clarke, 2006). The analysis aimed to determine first whether participants expressed difficulty in making the judgements, and second, the range of ideas that they drew upon to make those judgements. Several participants report difficulty in categorizing the quotes (e.g., 'In general there is nothing that stands out as a lads' mag piece and nothing that stands out as a criminal . . . I am just shocked by how similar some of them are'. Male Participant).

Participants drew upon different ideas to explain how they approached the task. Many participants drew upon the idea that lads' mags printed views that fell within the range of what men might 'normally' say while those attributed to rapists were too offensive, or too violent to fall within this category. Participants also drew on the ideas that lads' mags give *advice* to young men, and are humorous. Others drew upon the ideas that rapists use 'techniques of neutralization' to excuse their actions (Gilbert & Webster, 1982), and that rapists lack understanding of how to interpret sexual refusal (Frith, 2009). Illustrative quotations from participants are shown in Table 3. Finally, we aimed to see if participants expressed evaluations of the quotes themselves. While most participants described the quotes negatively or neutrally, explicit agreement with victim-blaming ideas was evident in a few instances ($N = 5$, e.g., ' . . . some girls do lead men on . . . the way they dress all the time, in really short skirts . . . and really really low tops, so what do they expect? They want men to look at them though don't they?' Female Participant). As many participants reported difficulty, these quotes ought not to be interpreted as evidence of participants' actual cognitive processes. Moreover, participants may have been primed to think about sexism particularly by the experimental task. As such, the thematic analysis should be read as suggestive of

Table 3. Themes in Explanations of Attributions of Quotes to Lads' Mags and Convicted Rapists

Theme	N	Example
		Explanations of attributions of quotes to lads' mags
Advice giving	24	'This is exactly the message they try and promote in lads' mags ... the types of blokes who read them want to know how to be in control'. (M)
Normal male conversation	23	'These are conversations that you would expect boys to have'. (F)
Atypical of rapists	20	'I think if you assume a rapist you think the worst. So that's why the worst ones are in the other pile'. (F)
Humour	13	'Their use of words, their vocabulary and general attitudes towards sex and girls ... they are just making jokes of everything'. (F)
		Explanations of attributions of quotes to convicted rapists
Violence	24	'These ones seem to be a bit over the top, and they tend to be more violent as well. There is more of a sense of anger and entitlement behind some of these ...'. (M)
Excusing	17	'They had the sort of ... they deserved it kind of thing ... these seem to be reasons why they might have committed an offence ... to put the woman in the wrong and make their actions sound less ... bad ...'. (M)
Too offensive for lads' mags	12	'That's pretty sick really and disgusting, so I would never think that it would be from a lads' mag, because that's just too horrible and twisted'. (F)
Mistaken communication	7	'I've always thought as rapists as men that don't understand signals from women, or think that they can just take what they want ... misinterpret certain things that mean women want them . . . saying no but really they mean yes'. (F)

some culturally available ideas that young people can draw upon when they are demanded to explain their judgements about the distinction between the contents of lads' mags and the things that convicted rapists say (c.f., Nisbett & Wilson, 1977).

Discussion

It is far from easy to tell the difference between the quotes we sampled from lads' mags and those sampled from convicted rapists. Indeed, many participants reported their own difficulty in making such determinations. Other participants described lads' mags as normal, funny, and advice giving, but not too violent or offensive.

In light of the participants' own high error rates when classifying the quotes, these ideas appear to be poor descriptions of the contents of such magazines. Indeed, contrary to the participants' self-reported basis for their judgements, the quotes from lads' mags and rapists were categorized as derogatory with equal frequency and the quotes from lads' mags were ranked as more derogatory than those from convicted rapists. Thus, as in Study 1, Study 2 demonstrates how young people may hold erroneous theories that lads' mags do not contain extreme derogatory sexism.

General Discussion

Are the quotes we drew from interviews with convicted rapists and lads' mags similar or different? It seems possible to draw quotes from contemporary lads' mags as easily as from interviews with convicted rapists with which particularly hostile sexist men identify (Study 1). The young men in Study 1 identified more with the quotes genuinely drawn from rapists speech than lads' mags, but identified *less* with the quotes attributed to rapists than attributed to lads' mags, suggesting that they tried to avoid identifying with criminals, but underestimated the overlap in content between convicted rapists and lads' mags. Similarly, in Study 2, young women and men voiced difficulty in identifying the sources of these quotes. To discern the difference between them, they voiced theories about what is normal and what is extreme. However, overall these participants guessed the quotes correctly only about 55% of the time. Contrary to their own theories, the participants judged the contents of lads' mags to be equally, or more, derogatory than that of convicted rapists.

Jointly, the two studies show that the quotes were perceived as different from each other, but that it would be ill-advised to conclude—as some Study-2 participants did—that the content of lads' mags is simply less 'extreme' than the legitimization strategies voiced by convicted rapists. We think that there are two possible explanations of the surprising finding in Study 1 that men identified more with the quotes drawn from convicted rapists. First, in Study 2, the quotes drawn from lads' mags were actually ranked as *more* derogatory, and so men who aimed to appear non-sexist may have been more likely to avoid identification with the quotes from lads' mags than the quotes from convicted rapists. The surprising finding that lads' mags quotes were actually more derogatory than convicted rapist quotes may also explain why the manipulation in Study 1 had a stronger effect on identification with the lads' mags quotes. Second, the quotes may have differed in ways that were not strictly relevant to their derogatory content, but which affected identification for other reasons. The lads' mags quotes appeared to us, and to some participants in Study 2, to be offering advice. As the convicted rapists quotes were drawn from interviews rather than edited print media, they are also somewhat more unrehearsed in their language. Such factors that we did not anticipate or measure here because they were not central to our hypotheses about lads' mags may have affected identification in Study 1.[2]

Both studies demonstrate how young people may be assuming, in line with cultural discourse, that a boundary can be detected between the overlapping discourse of lads' mags and convicted rapists, such that the former is 'normal' and the latter is 'extreme'. Both studies suggest that it is harder to tell the difference than this folk theory suggests. This folk theory may serve as a poor guide because of the existence of a 'continuum of sexual violence' (Kelly, 1988) that includes a wide range of behaviours including threats of violence, sexual harassment, coercive sex, rape, and incest. Kelly (1988) emphasized that the boundaries between categories of sexual violence are fuzzy, and that the continuum does not imply either linear progression or progressive seriousness (Brown & Walklate, 2011). Similarly, other researchers have argued that contrary to the belief that male sexual aggression is unusual or strange (Groth, 1971), rape is learned behaviour (Bart, 1979) and many men hold attitudes or beliefs that may lead them to commit a sexually aggressive act (Scully, 1990). In line with this conceptual framing, our studies show that the ways in which convicted rapists and lads' mags discuss female sexuality are similar enough to each other to be frequently confused and distinctions between them are blurred.

We are not the first to describe the sexist contents of contemporary magazines aimed at young men. However, our studies go beyond past research on lads' mags' because we have not only described what lads' mags *are*, but have also demonstrated how young people make sense of them. While magazine editors deny their publications are a source of social influence, our studies suggest that the 'mainstream' status of such magazines allows them to legitimize views about women that young men might otherwise consider unacceptable. In other words, the status of lads' mags as legitimate mainstream publications may lend their contents performative force (Butler, 1997) to bring about change in the range of sexist opinions with which young men will identify. People are sometimes threatened when their views overlap with those of groups they dislike (Pool, Wood, & Leck, 1998). Here, young people struggled to correctly attribute the sources of the quotes (Study 2) and young men identified more with the quotes when they were attributed to lads' mags (Study 1). Jointly, these two findings suggest that sexist talk about women in lads' mags may be something more than ineffectual harmless ironic fun; these magazines' very status as 'mainstream' publications may afford them the power to normalize very egregious sexist beliefs about women.

Indeed, one participant in Study 2 described the quotes presented to him as 'sort of degrading in a way that can be seen to be acceptable if they put it in a glossy magazine'. He continued: 'not that a lads' mag would condone raping someone, but they try to use language that makes it sound like a consensual type of thing'. Without being aware of our hypothesis, this participant voiced a version of that hypothesis when he assumed that lads' mags normalize degrading sexism, and use language about women's 'consent' to do so. This participant went further than we do by suggesting that lads' mags *deliberately* use linguistic strategies to make their sexist content appear less extreme. Unlike this male participant, we have no basis for an argument that the editors of lads' mags deliberately beguile their readers into accepting sexist content. Rather the findings of Studies 1 and 2 suggest that the justification of such sexism as mere irony is insufficient.

Concluding Thought

Since conducting these experiments in 2010, the mainstream status of lads' mags has entered a state of flux. In February 2011, most major supermarket chains and petrol stations in the United Kingdom agreed to move lads' mags to the top shelf, out of the eye line of children (Object, 2011). Not all sales outlets in the United Kingdom have signed up to the agreement and these changes have not yet come fully into force. The current policy debate about how lads' mags are to be sold centres on the possible harm that their contents might do to children. We hope that our results inform policy debates by shifting attention to the possible dangers that lads' mags might pose to their intended audience of young men, and to the young women with whom those men socialize.

Notes

1. Inspection of the means in Table 2 suggests that the participants did not simply use the perceived degradingness of the quotes to attribute their source. Quotes ranked high on the degradingness continuum were categorized as degrading by more participants overall, $r(15) = .70$, $p < .001$. However, the frequency with which quotes were attributed to convicted rapists was only non-significantly correlated with both measures of degradingness, $r(15) = .42, .31$, respectively, both two-tailed $p > .27$. While these findings must be regarded with caution due to small sample size, they are consistent with the interpretation of the unexpected main effect of the quotes source in Study 1; participants conceive of differences between the content of rapists' talk and lads' mags quotes about women other than the relative degradingness of each.
2. We would like to thank the anonymous reviewer who brought this explanation to our attention and urged us to think more deeply about these matters.

References

Abrams, D., Viki, G. T. N., Masser, B., & Bohner, G. (2003). Perceptions of stranger and acquaintance rape: The role of benevolent and hostile sexism in victim blame and rape proclivity. *Journal of Personality and Social Psychology, 84*, 111–125. doi:10.1037/0022–3514.84.1.111

Attwood, F. (2005). 'Tits and ass and porn and fighting'. Male heterosexuality in magazines for men. *International Journal of Cultural Studies, 8*, 83–100. doi:10.1177/1367877905050165

Bart, P. (1979). Rape as a paradigm of sexism in society—Victimization and its discontents. *Women's Studies International Quarterly, 2*, 347–357.

Bensimon, P. (2007). The role of pornography in sexual offending. *Sexual Addiction & Compulsion, 14*, 95–117. doi:10.1080/10720160701310468

Benwell, B. (2003). Masculinity and men's lifestyle magazines. In B. Benwell (Ed.), *Masculinity and men's lifestyle magazines*. Oxford: Blackwell Publishing.

Benwell, B. (2004). Ironic discourse: Evasive masculinity in men's lifestyle magazines. *Men and Masculinities, 7*, 3–21. doi:10.1177/1097184X03257438

Bohner, G. (1998). *Vergewaltigungsmythen: Sozialpsychologische Untersuchungen u "ber ta" terentlastend e undopferfeind liche Überzeugungen im Bereich sexueller Gewalt* (*Rape myths: Social-psychological studies on beliefs that exonerate the assailant and blame the victim of sexual violence*). Landau: Verlag Empirische Pädagogik.

Braun, V., & Clarke, V. (2006). Using thematic analysis in psychology. *Qualitative Research in Psychology, 3*, 77–101. doi:10.1191/1478088706qp063oa

Breakwell, G. M., Hammond, S., Fife-Schaw, C., & Smith, J. A. (2006). *Research methods in psychology* (3rd ed.). London: Sage.

Brown, J., & Walklate, S. (2011). *Handbook on sexual violence*. London: Routledge.

Burt, M. R. (1980). Cultural myths and supports for rape. *Journal of Personality and Social Psychology, 38*, 217–230. doi:10.1037/0022-3514.38.2.217

Busfield, S., & Sweney, M. (2010). *Danny Dyer advises Zoo reader to 'cut his ex's face'*. Retrieved from http://www.guardian.co.uk/media/2010/may/05/danny-dyer-zoo-magazine

Butler, J. (1997). *Excitable speech: A politics of the performative*. New York: Routledge.

Colston, H. L., & Lee, S. Y. (2004). Gender differences in verbal irony use. *Metaphor and Symbol, 19*, 289–306.

Costin, F. (1985). Beliefs about rape and women's social roles. *Archives of Sexual Behavior, 14*, 319–325. doi:10.1007/. BF01550847

Coy, M., & Horvath, M. A. H. (2011). Lads' mags, young men's attitudes towards women and acceptance of myths about sexual aggressions. *Feminism & Psychology, 21*, 144–150. doi:10.1177/0959353509359145

Crewe, B. (2003). *Representing men: Cultural production and producers in the men's magazine market*. Oxford: Berg.

Daubney, M. (2007). *Lad's mags score own goal*. Retrieved from http://www.drpetra.co.uk/blog/lad%E2%80%99s-mags-score-own-goal/

Eyssel, F., & Bohner, G. (2007). The rating of sexist humor under time pressure as an indicator of spontaneous sexist attitudes. *Sex Roles, 57*, 651–660. doi:101007/s11199-007-9302-5

Eyssel, F., & Bohner, G. (2008). Modern rape myths: The acceptance of modern myths about Sexual Aggression Scale. In M. A. Morrison & T. G. Morrison (Eds.), *The Psychology of modern prejudice* (pp. 261–276). Hauppauge, NY: Nova Science Publishers.

Farvid, P., & Braun, V. (2006). 'Most of Us Guys are Raring to Go Anytime, Anyplace, Anywhere': Male and female sexuality in Cleo and Cosmo. *Sex Roles*, 55, 295–310. doi:10.1007/s11199-006-9084-1

Field, H. S. (1978). Attitudes toward rape: A comparative analysis of police, rapists, crisis counselors, and citizens. *Journal of Personality and Social Psychology, 36*, 156–179.

Ford, T. E., & Ferguson, M. A. (2004). Social consequences of disparagement human: A prejudiced norm theory. *Personality and Social Psychology Review, 8*, 79–94. doi:10.1207/S15327957PSPR0801_4

Frith, H. (2009). Sexual scripts, sexual refusals and rape. In M. A. H. Horvath & J. Brown (Eds.), *Rape: Challenging contemporary thinking*. Collumption: Willan.

Gerbner, G., Gross, L., Morgan, M., & Signorielli, N. (1994). Growing up with television: The cultivation perspective. In J. Bryant & D. Zillmann (Eds.), *Media effects: Advances in theory and research* (pp. 17–42). Hillsdale, NJ: Erlbaum.

Gerbner, G., Gross, L., Morgan, M., Signorielli, N., & Shanahan, J. (2002). Growing up with television: Cultivation processes. In J. Bryant & D. Zillmann (Eds.), *Media effects: Advances in theory and research* (pp. 43–68). Mahwah, NJ: Erlbaum.

Gerger, H., Kley, H., Bohner, G., & Siebler, F. (2007). The acceptance of modern myths about sexual aggression scale: Development and validation in German and English. *Aggressive Behavior, 33*, 422–440. doi:10.1002/ab.20195

Gilbert, L., & Webster, P. (1982). *Bound by love*. Boston, MA: Beacon Press.

Glick, P., & Fiske, S. T. (1996). The ambivalent sexism inventory: Differentiating hostile and benevolent sexism. *Journal of Personality and Social Psychology, 70*, 491–512. doi:10.1037/0022-3514.70.3.491

Groth, N. (1971). *Men who rape*. New York: Plenum Press.

Horvath, M. A. H., Coy, M., & Murray, R. (2010). *Exploring the links between consumption of 'lads mags' and young men's perceptions of women, sexuality and sexual aggression*. Paper presented at the 20th Conference of the European Association of Psychology and Law, Gothenburg, Sweden. 15–18 June.

Huesmann, L. R. (1997). Observational learning of violent behavior. In A. Raine, P. A. Brennen, D. P. Farrington, & S. A. Mednick (Eds.), *Biosocial bases of violence* (pp. 69–88). New York: Plenum.

Huesmann, L. R. (1998). The role of social information processing and cognitive schema in the acquisition and maintenance of habitual aggressive behavior. In R. G. Geen & E. Donnerstein (Eds.), *Human aggression: Theories, research, and implications for social policy* (pp. 73–109). New York: Academic Press.

Jackson, P., Stevenson, N., & Brooks, K. (2001). *Making sense of men's magazines*. Cambridge, UK: Polity Press.

Johnson, S. (2007). Promoting easy sex without genuine intimacy: Maxim and cosmopolitan cover lines and cover images. In M. Galician & D. L. Merskin (Eds.). *Critical thinking about sex, love, and romance in the mass media* (pp. 55–74). Mahwah, NJ: Lawrence Erlbaum Associates Publishers.

Katz, A. N., Blasko, D. G., & Kazmerski, V. A. (2004). Saying what you don't mean: Social influences on sarcastic language processing. *Current Directions in Psychological Science, 13*, 186–189. doi:10.1111/j.0963-7214.2004.00304.x

Kelly, L. (1988). *Surviving sexual violence*. Minneapolise, MN: University of Minnesota Press.

Krassas, N. R., Blauwkamp, J. M., & Wesselink, P. (2001). Boxing Helena and corseting Eunice: Sexual rhetoric in cosmopolitan and Playboy magazines. *Sex Roles, 44*, 751–771.

Krassas, N. R., Blauwkamp, J. M., & Wesselink, P. (2003). Master your Johnson: Sexual rhetoric in Maxim and Stuff magazines. *Sexuality & Culture, 7*, 98–119. doi:10.1007/s12119-003-1005-7

Lambaise, J. (2007). Promoting sexy images: Case study scrutinizes Maxim's cover formula for building quick circulation and challenging competitors. *Journal of Promotion Management, 13*, 111–125. doi:10.1300/J057v13n01_08

Lanis, K., & Covell, K. (1995). Images of women in advertisements: Effects on attitudes related to sexual aggression. *Sex Roles, 32*, 639–649.

MacKay, N. J., & Covell, K. (1997). The impact of women in advertisements on attitudes toward women. *Sex Roles, 36*, 573–583.

Malamuth, N. M., Addison, T., & Koss, M. (2000). Pornography and sexual aggression: Are there reliable effects and can we understand them? *Annual Review of Sex Research, 11*, 26–91.

McKay, J., Mikosza, J., & Hutchins, B. (2005). "Gentlemen, the lunchbox has landed": Representations of masculinities and men's bodies in the popular media. In M. S. Kimmel, J. Hearn, & R. W. Connell (Eds.), *Handbook of studies on men and masculinities* (pp. 270–288). Thousand Oaks, CA: SAGE.

Mooney, A. (2008). Boys will be boys. *Feminist Media Studies, 8*(3), 247–265. doi:10.1080/14680770802217287

Nisbett, R. E., & Wilson, T. D. (1977). Telling more than we can know: Verbal reports on mental processes. *Psychological Review, 84*, 231–259. doi:10.1037/0033-295X.84.3.231

Object (2011). *Major retailers to place Lads' Mags 'on Top Shelf'*. Retrieved from http://www. object.org.uk/component/content/article/3-news/119-lads-mags-to-go-on-top-shelf

Papadopoulos, L. (2010). *Sexualisation of young people: Review*. Retrieved from http://www.homeoffice.gov.uk/documents/Sexualisation-young-people?view=Binary

Payne, D. L., Lonsway, K. A., & Fitzgerald, L. F. (1999). Rape myth acceptance: Exploration of its structure and its measurement using the Illinois Rape Myth Acceptance Scale. *Journal of Research in Personality, 33*, 27–68. doi:10.1006/jrpe. 1998.2238

Peter, J., & Valkenburg, P. M. (2007). Adolescents' exposure to a sexualised media environment and notions of women as sex objects. *Sex Roles, 56*, 381–395. doi:10.1007/s11199-006-9176-y

Pool, G. J., Wood, W., & Leck, K. (1998). The self-esteem motive in social influence: Agreement with valued majorities and disagreement with derogated minorities. *Journal of Personality and Social Psychology, 75*, 967–975. doi:10.1037/0022-3514.75.4.967

Romero-Sánchez, M., Durán, M., Carretero-Dios, H., Megias, J. L., & Moya, M. (2010). Exposure to sexist humour and rape proclivity: The moderator effect of aversiveness ratings. *Journal of Interpersonal Violence, 25*, 2339–2350. doi:10.1177/0886260509354884

Scully, D. (1990). *Understanding sexual violence: A study of convicted rapists*. London: Harper Collins.

Scully, D., & Marolla, J. (1984). Convicted rapists' vocabulary of motive: Excuses and justifications. *Social Problems, 31*, 530–544. doi:10.1177/0957926594005001006

Stevenson, N., Jackson, P., & Brooks, K. (2003). Reading men's lifestyle magazines: Cultural power and the information society. In B. Benwell (Ed.), *Masculinity and men's lifestyle magazines*. Oxford: Blackwell.

Sussman, L., & Bordwell, S. (2000). *The rapist file: Interviews with convicted rapists*. Lincoln: Universe, Incorporated.

Swim, J. K., Aiken, K. J., Hall, U. S., & Hunter, B. A. (1995). Sexism and racism: Old-fashioned and modern prejudices. *Journal of Personality and Social Psychology, 68*, 199–214. doi:10.1037/0022-3514.68.2.199

Taylor, L. D. (2005). All for him: Articles about sex in American lad magazines. *Sex Roles, 52*, 153–163. doi:10.1007/s11199-005-1291-7

Treise, D., & Gotthoffer, A. (2002). Stuff you couldn't ask your parents: Teens talking about using magazines for sex information. In J.D. Brown, J. R. Steele, & K. Walsh-Childers (Eds.), *Sexual teens, sexual media: Investigating media's influence on adolescent sexuality* (pp. 173–189). Mahwah, NJ: Erlbaum.

Viki, G. T., & Abrams, D. (2002). But she was unfaithful: Benevolent sexism and reactions to rape victims who violate traditional gender role expectations. *Sex Roles, 47*, 289–293. doi:10.1023/A:1021342912248

Viki, G. T., Abrams, D., & Masser, B. (2004). Evaluating stranger and acquaintance rape: The role of benevolent sexism in perpetrator blame and recommended sentence length. *Sex Roles, 28*, 295–303. doi:10.1023/B:LAHU.0000029140.72880.69

Walsh, J. L., & Ward, L. M. (2010). Magazine reading and involvement in young adults' sexual health knowledge, efficacy, and behaviours. *Journal of Sex Research, 47*, 285–300. doi:10.1080/00224490902916009

Ward, L. M. (2003). Understanding the role of entertainment media in the sexual socialization of American youth: A review of empirical research. *Developmental Review, 23*, 347–388. doi:10.1016/S0273-2297(03)00013-3

Yamawaki, N. (2007). Rape perception and the function of ambivalent sexism and gender-role traditionality. *Journal of Interpersonal Violence, 22*, 406–423. doi:10.1177/0886260506297210

A 36-24-36 Cerebrum: Productivity, Gender, and Video Game Advertising

SHIRA CHESS

Introduction

Until only recently, video games were often understood to be created by and for masculine audiences (Fron, Fullerton, Morie, & Pearce, 2007a; Ray, 2004; Cassell & Jenkins, 1999). Now, in the past few years, an influx of console video games (particularly for the Nintendo DS and Nintendo Wii systems) have been increasingly marketed to a demographic previously ignored by the gaming industry: adult females. These games and their marketing can help shed light on larger issues including gendered stereotypes about women and video games, implying division and hierarchy between masculine and feminine gamer audiences. In this sense, video games are marketed in a remarkably different way to adult women than they are to traditional (masculine) audiences—in a way that emphasizes productivity over play. Additionally, this productivity often employs traditional expectations of feminine practices—suggesting that women's play might best correlate with beauty, fitness, and family values.

Shira Chess, "A 36-24-36 Cerebrum: Productivity, Gender, and Video Game Advertising." *Critical Studies in Media Communication* 28 (August 2011): 230–52.

The focus of this analysis is specifically on magazine advertising aimed at women audiences. An obvious question might be: why focus on magazine advertising? On first glance this area might appear to be a dead end, with a quickly changing magazine industry (Troland, 2005) that is being overrun by other forms of media and advertising. But it is the very wavering nature of the magazine industry that makes it a compelling space to study new media, gender, and leisure. In his article, "Seeing ahead: Underpinnings for what is next for magazine publishing," Thomas R. Troland (2005) writes, "We are a *Women's Business*. Women buy magazines more than men. Much more than men. And women's lives, roles, needs and expectations have changed immensely during the past forty years" (p. 9). Thus, one reason for this study might be the video game industry's deft targeting of women audiences, *despite* the changing terrain. Because there is already a gendered skew inherent inboth of these forms of media—video games as well as magazines—their combination seems well worth investigation.

In many ways, video games might seem like the last thing many people would expect to be advertised in many women's special interest magazines.[1] What is most compelling here is the use of older paradigms (traditional magazine advertising focusing on traditional values such as family and health) with an attempt to foster new interests in technology, play, and new media. Because video games are also quickly changing, and rapidly opening to more feminine audiences, these magazines provide a bridge for understanding complicated spaces in media both new and old.

Gender, advertising, and ideologies are all part of an inseparable and symbiotic relationship, where advertising very often reinforces and reaffirms gender roles and stereotypes already a part of dominant ideologies. Advertisements help reinforce normative gender roles already present from products and cultures. In the following, I outline several theories about both gender and video games, and gender and productivity. Using that as a theoretical backdrop, I discuss ways that games are marketed to women audiences and the problematic nature of these advertisements. As illustration, I examine several Nintendo DS and Wii advertisements that employ strategies and themes of gendered productivity, using tropes such as time management, beauty, family, and weight loss.

Gender and Video Games

As already noted, until recently video games were often looked at as having a masculine bias. Much of the early research on video games and gender was limited to the question, "how do we get little girls to play video games?" Books such as, *From Barbie to Mortal Kombat* helped to pave the way for discussions of the gendered nature of the video game industry (Cassell & Jenkins, 1999), but focused on girls rather than women. This area of study created a direct link between a lack of video game play and subsequent lower interest levels in math, science, and technology (Cassell & Jenkins, 1999). To that end, research on girls and gaming was in the best interest of game companies hoping to open the market and both feminist academics and activists attempted to gain a more substantial foothold for women in technology careers.

Thus began what was subsequently known as the "Pink Games Movement" of the mid-90s, in which video games specifically aimed at young girls flooded the market. Several video game companies attempted to analyze the success of the most popular game for girls at the time: *Barbie Fashion Designer*. At the same time, entrepreneurial feminist companies such as Brenda Laurel's Purple Moon games tried to introduce feminist theories into video game design (Laurel, 2001). Subsequent studies focused on these specific games, attempting to determine how to recreate the few successes and learn from failures for future "pink games."

For instance, the success of the game *Barbie Fashion Designer* prompted Kaveri Subrahmanyam and Patricia Greenfield (1999) to conclude that the most logical way to garner girl audiences would be to repurpose preferences from other kinds of media surmising that girls' interests lie in areas such as "the drama of human relationships" (p. 54), as well as the use of role-play. In their essay, "Retooling play: Dystopia, dysphoria, and difference," Suzanne de Castell and Mary Bryson (1999) take a more critical and cultural approach, suggesting that most of the supposed preferences of young girls for video games are primarily dictated by culturally learned behavior, rather than biology. Castell and Bryson also suggest that perhaps gender expectations play a larger role in video game design than actual desire. They explain, "[. . .] girls desires have far less to do with what girls want than with what kind of girl adults, whether in education or in the marketplace, want to produce" (p. 251).

Yet, despite all of these attempts, video games are still perceived, by-and-large, to be riddled with masculinity. In his book *Die tryin': Video games, masculinity, culture*, Derek Burrill (2008) discusses ways that video games are playgrounds for the construction and performance of masculinity. He refers to this phenomenon as "digital boyhood" and explains, "It is a space and experience where the digital boy can 'die tryin', tryin' to win, tryin' to beat the game, and tryin' to *prove* his manood (and therefore his place within the patriarchy, the world of capital, and the Law)" (p. 2, author's emphasis). So while some things might have changed in recent years, they have not changed enough to affect the perception of video games as having a masculine bias. Similarly Henry Jenkins (1999) asserts that video games are characterized by masculine play styles, and marked specifically by "traditional boy culture" (p. 270). Speaking specifically of games aimed at boys (as opposed to men) Jenkins cites characteristics such as independence, daring, mastery, hierarchical structures, aggressive, and scatological as being inherent design characteristics of many video games that might have specific appeal to masculine audiences. Burrill posits that video games presume that "the player is always already male" (2008, p. 138). And while women do play many video games, that does not eradicate the perceptions and reputations of perceived masculinity.

Along these lines, the Ludica Group (a collective of gender game researchers from a variety of disciplines) have begun focusing on some of the cultural logic within the gaming industry (Fron et al., 2007a), and have discussed the hegemonies of masculine play (Fron et al., 2007b). They explain:

> The power elite of the game industry is a predominately white, and secondarily Asian, male-dominated corporate and creative elite that represents a select group of large, global publishing companies in conjunction with a handful of massive chain retail distributors. This hegemonic elite determines which technologies will be deployed, and which will not; which games will be made, and by which designers; which players are important to design for, and which play styles will be supported, (p. 1)

The Ludica Group's research considers how deeply marginalized feminine play is within the gaming industry, as well as how several layers of cultural influence (industry, games, media) help to support this system. Thus, it is not simply gamers, developers, or (for that matter) magazine advertisers that are complicit in this system of exclusionary masculinity, but a larger culture that ultimately defines video game play as almost inherently masculine. While games may be changing and becoming more inclusive, one can still see a perception of alterity and otherness to how women gamers are perceived by the industry.

Typical video game magazines generally cater to an expected masculine audience, often employing route stereotypes of femininity: either sexualizing them or showing them as victims. Two recent studies, both appearing in the journal *Sex Roles*, specifically examined video game magazines and gender roles. In their article, "Gender differences in video game characters' roles, appearances, and attire as portrayed in video game magazines," Monica K. Miller and Alicia Summers (2007) primarily focus on content analysis of the magazine article, rather than the advertising. They ultimately assert that there is a vast difference between male and female characters in video games and how they are presented in magazines: males tending to be more heroic, powerful, and wearing military attire, as opposed to female characters who played more tertiary roles, were less powerful, and wore more revealing clothing (Miller & Summers, 2007). In a similar vein, Karen E. Dill and Kathryn P. Thill's (2007) "Video game characters and the socialization of gender roles: young people's perceptions mirror sexist media depictions," includes advertisements in their study of video game magazines (although not exclusively). They ultimately conclude, "Character images tell blatantly sexist stories about gender, and research is just beginning to reveal and analyze those stories" (p. 861). These analyses provide an apt comparison with advertisements for video games that appear in women's general interest magazines. While typical video game advertisements tend to sexualize and fetishize their depictions of femininity, the subsequent advertisements that appear in women's general interest magazines focus their pitches on real world productivity through self-help.

In their essay "The hegemony of play," the Ludica Group briefly discusses some of the issues with video game advertising. It explains, "Many videogame advertisements tend to disenfranchise and alienate women, further contributing to the self-fulfilling prophecy that 'women don't play games"' (Fron et al., 2007a, p. 316). In this essay, the Ludica Group also discusses Nintendo setting their sights on a different kind of gamer (women), in their more recent advertising campaigns, and that this represents signs of "subtle but tectonic shifts." While, admittedly, the advertising campaigns that I discuss in the following are targeted at women audiences, I would argue that the generalizations and essentializations about feminine play do not necessarily escape the "hegemonies of play," entirely. Instead, by using tropes of productivity and self-help, these advertisements help to reinforce gender expectations of how women are expected to play. My analysis of advertising campaigns for video games aimed at women audiences illustrates how hegemonies of play are larger than game design, or even the gaming industry. Further, these hegemonies are not just about masculinity in the gaming industry, but also about how femininity is portrayed, parsed, and understood in terms of video game play. This confluence of topics exceeds video game studies, alsoexamining broader themes of how gendered productivity conflates play with leisure activities.

Productivity, Self-Help, and Gender

Only recently have scholars begun to examine the role of productivity in video games. On the surface, productivity seems like it would be the antithesis of play. In actuality, productivity functions in several ways. For example, scholars such as Postigo (2007) and Taylor (2008) have looked at the productivity inherent in game modifications (mods)—software designed by players to enhance and improve game play and interfaces in massively multiplayer online games. Taylor (2006) has also looked at the productivity in what she refers to as "power gaming" or "instrumental play." Taylor explains that, with intense gaming experiences (which only certain players are prone towards), efficiency plays a much more important role than fun. To a similar effect, Sotamaa (2007) talks about the productivity in Machinema, or movies made by using game interfaces. Finally, Wirman (2007) draws comparisons between fan-related productivity and the productive nature of Taylor's power gamers. In a presentation at the Digital Games Research Association, Wirman also suggests that a certain amount of productivity is an inherent part of all video game play. According to Wirman, "[. . .] productivity is a precondition for a game as a cultural text" (p. 379). Wirman's notion of productivity primarily focuses on in-game productivity as well as the gaming community at large, as opposed to the extra-game productivity discussed later.

More often than not, the productive play discussed in the following takes the form of self-help, often promising the player that production in the game world will benefit and improve the player in the real world. Research on self-help has a significant history, the scope of which is slightly greater than that of this article. What is clear is that self-help is often highly gendered and helps to form and reinforce gender roles. This includes famous relationship-themed books such as *Women who love too much*, as well as popular talk shows such as *Oprah Winfrey* and *Donahue*: all of which primarily target women audiences. There are also several links between the women's self-help industry and the feminist movement which, according to some, can be traced back to Betty Friedan's famous book *The feminine mystique* (Simonds, 1992; Taylor, 1996). More recent feminists have been critical of the self-help industry, often referring to it as feminist backlash (Faludi, 1991) and so-called "victim feminism" (Wolf, 2002).

Regardless of whether activists and researchers see self-help as being productive or destructive to women, few dispute its gendered themes and targeting of feminine audiences. In *Women and self-help culture: Reading between the lines* (1992) Wendy Simonds explains that self-help allows women the opportunity to "try on" new concepts of self. She elaborates:

> A process that aptly characterizes self-help ideology is the makeover, which has special salience for women in this culture. If you don't like it, change it; dress up your assets and hide the ugly parts. The message being conveyed by media that tell women how to make ourselves over is not covert: self-help books, magazines, television, and advertisements all encourage women to see ourselves as mutable, correctable, a product of various influences in constant flux. [. . .] In self-help literature (as well as other media), men, in contrast, are rarely variable—no matter how much women might wish they were. (p. 224)

As such, the intransigence of femininity is a gendered signal which is at the root of self-help literature. In a similar way, the video game advertising aimed at women audiences preaches mutability in areas such as time management, beauty, family, and fitness. By looking at how self-help topics such as beauty and time management are present in video game advertisements I am able to illustrate how gender, leisure, and productivity interact through self-help. In effect, the advertisements that follow reinforce the masculine hegemony of play. Thus, while simultaneously inviting women into these play spaces, they also ghettoize them into these essentializing forms of play.

Women, Video Games, and Magazine Advertising

While one might not ordinarily suspect that video games would be advertised in magazines such as *Good Housekeeping* and *Real Simple*, there have been a surprisingly increasing number of such advertisements in recent years. Primarily, the objects promoted in these ads have been for one of two newer Nintendo systems: the handheld gaming system the Nintendo DS Lite, and the home console system the Nintendo Wii. Since approximately spring 2006, Nintendo has begun advertising these systems in venues where women might encounter them. The following does not analyze the specific games in detail, but rather analyzes ways that these games are advertised and sold to this new demographic. By collapsing play with productivity, there is something larger being sold about how women are expected to play. In turn, video games are able to maintain status as masculine play spaces, reinforcing subtext that women should only play in specific circumstances.

Nintendo DS Lite: Doing Something with Your Nothing

The Nintendo DS (standing for Dual Screen) was unusually positioned to enter a more feminized video game market from its inception. The DS Lite, released in June of 2006, is a handheld (portable) game system with two screens: the upper screen has visual output, while the lower has a touch screen which can be manipulated with a built-in stylus. The small system was quickly positioned by Nintendo as a potential "accessory" and one Nintendo executive was quoted in a news article saying, "It definitely should be part of every purse [. . .] you have your cellphone, your iPod, and your DS Lite" (quoted in Harris, 2006, p. F15). Thus, from its inception, the DS Lite began to use various marketing methods to target feminine audiences. The DS Lite entered the market with the slogan, "Lighter, Brighter" and was immediately advertised in a variety of magazines, on billboards in commuter zones, and on television commercial spots: each showing women playing with the handheld game system (Harris, 2006, p. F15).

Some of the earlier advertisements used the slogan "Do Something with Your Nothing," which appeared in several women's magazines. While these advertisements offer the least of the self-help pitches, they are an excellent example of how productivity is seamlessly stitched into video game advertisements aimed at women audiences. One of the advertisements in this series (Figure 1), which appeared in the September 2006 issue of *Oprah Magazine*, shows three people—two women and one man—in a waiting room. One of the women is playing with a Nintendo DS (and smiling) while the other man and the woman are slumped over in their seats, clearly bored while waiting to be called. The advertisement's main text suggests, "The average wait in a doctor's office is 23.4 minutes. Do something with your nothing." The advertisement is targeting a feminine readership, and suggesting a proper time and place for video game play. While the woman playing the video game is the focus of the ad (wearing a much brighter red than the other two people in the waiting room), the other woman is a secondary focus—slumped over the side of her seat, and decidedly less happy than the woman who is playing. The man is set back further than the two women in this advertisement, and is more about background: the advertisement is highlighting the women.

This advertisement is telling us about the kind of play that had begun to be promoted to women during the summer of 2006. Targeting non-players, the suggestion is to play in order to fill all available time. The woman in red in this advertisement is being chastised to "do something with [her] nothing" (as, to some extent, are those women who are reading the magazine). The chastising headline of "Do something with your nothing" is bossy, reeking of self-help parlance: the ad is literally telling readers what to do. This coincides with what Simonds (1992) referred to as suggesting that women are "mutable" and "correctable."

Figure 1. Nintendo DS Doctor Office Advertisement (*Oprah Magazine*, September 2006).

Many advertisements, obviously, take this tone. But the advice-giving, here, is not about concrete consumable products such as laundry detergent or lipstick—it suggests behavior modification in a way that turns non-productive time into productive time through play.

Thus, the advertisement does not highlight the value of play, but rather it insists on the value of productivity: all time must be spent in some productive way. The "Do Something with your Nothing" campaign set an important trend where video games are not advertised to women for their play-potential but for their value as ways to use up any excess time in a woman's schedule. While perhaps not the most common topic in self-help literature, Arlie Russell Hochschild (2001) suggests that the "time industry" is particularly meant to appeal to working women and their difficulties in managing personal time between home and families. Hochschild explains, "It is women who feel more acutely the need to save time and women who are more tempted by the goods and services of the growing 'time industry.' They are the ones who shop for time" (p. 230). Time management products help to reinforce themes of productivity through a form of self-help. The advertisement is advising readers of the magazines—primarily women—that video games might be a neat means of making use of all available time. As such, "Do Something with Your Nothing" provides a perfect entry point for showcasing how video game advertising aimed at feminine audiences might be used to privilege productivity over play. Despite potentially expanding the market, the advertisement reinforces the hegemony of the video game industry, by distinctly suggesting women's play needs to have real-world productivity.

Specific Nintendo DS games have also reinforced gendered themes, pitching productivity as a goal for feminine play. A perfect example can be seen in two advertisements for the brain improvement game *Brain Age: Train Your Brain in Minutes a Day* which ran in May and June of 2006 in both men's and women's magazines. The first advertisement (Figure 2) appeared in magazines including *Real Simple, Oprah Magazine*, and *People Magazine*. The second advertisement (Figure 3) appeared in magazines such as *Wired Magazine* and *Time Magazine*. As a contrast, the two ads are compelling both for their similarities and their vast differences. Both advertisements privilege productivity over play, but visuals and languagewithin the advertisements gives evidence to how this productivity is gendered through self-help. Additionally, both reinforce cultural expectations about who is entitled to play video games.

The Brain Age advertisements are long-copy: structured like advertorials (giving the impression of being more of an informational magazine article than an advertisement). Both have a person (one a woman and one a man) playing the game in the left-hand corner of the ad. The advertising copy is structured similarly on both pages, and in some places the advertising copy is identical in both advertisements. It is the similarities of these ads that make the highly gendered differences so compelling, highlighting how games are marketed differently to men and women.

The advertisements are composed of almost equal amounts of image and text. The text is key to understanding how gendered play is constructed. The title of the masculine advertisement (in all caps) reads, "CAN YOU USE A VIDEO GAME TO REWIRE YOUR BRAIN?" which suggests a highly technologically focused message. Written in all caps, the text is yelling at the audience. Conversely, the feminine headline uses a subtler and softer statement (not a question): "What the Japanese have discovered about the fountain of youth." While both headlines suggest self-improvement, the headline for the advertisement with the woman immediately infers beauty, self-care, and health, while the masculine advertisement discusses video games, technology, and the brain. It is significant to note that the phrase "video game" is never used at all in the feminine version of the advertisement. This opening helps to establish the feminine advertisement as being more about self-care (in a self-help context) than about play. At the same time, it reinforces that femininity is not an expected part of the video game audience. The advertisements, in turn, help to reestablish expectations about the hegemony of video game play.

Figure 2. Brain Age Advertisement (*Real Simple Magazine*, June 2006).

In effect, the feminine advertisement suggests that taking care of one's brain is part of the daily beauty regimen that all women should be partaking in. At one point it concludes that "A 36–24–36 cerebrum is just a few exercises away." This striking phrase manages to not only equate mental fitness with physical fitness, but does so by using sexist imagery to describe an "ideal" of feminine beauty. The masculine advertisement, conversely, suggests that playing this game might help men become more competitive with their co-workers. Both advertisements preach a kind of productivity (a "do something with your nothing," if you will) but the feminine implications of health and beauty suggest more about self-maintenance, while the masculine advertisement suggests a more playful form of agonism—similar to typical video game advertising.

It is notable how this switch from focusing on the body rather than the mind, follows much played gender stereotypes of Cartesian logic: women signify body while men signify mind. Of this duality, Susan Bordo writes in *Unbearable weight* (1993), "For if, whatever the specific historical content of the duality, *the body* is the negative term, and if woman *is* the body, then women *are* that negativity, whatever it may be: distraction from knowledge, seduction away from God, capitulation to sexual desire, violence or aggression, failure of will, even death" (p. 5). In a similar vein, the two comparable advertisements show a division of how women and men are expected to interpret this software. Despite

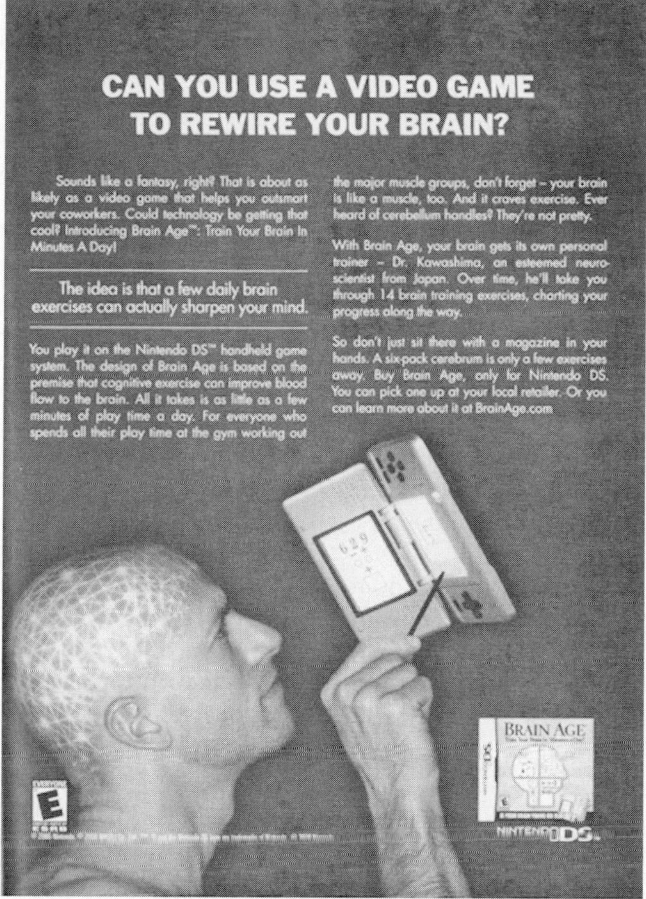

Figure 3. Brain Age Advertisement (*Wired Magazine*, May 2006).

being clearly a brain game, women are encouraged to use it in order enhance physical self-help. This kind of advertisement reinforces negative images about women, vanity, and physical self-help over a much nobler mental self-help pitched in the masculine advertisement.

This self-help pitch reinforces Simmonds earlier quote that women are expected to be mutable to project their femininity. In *Where the girls are: Growing up female with the mass media* Susan Douglas (1995) explains that in recent years, beauty self-help has privileged a kind of narcissism where self-care for women is often commercially linked to women's liberation. She explains: "The ability to spend time and money on one's appearance was a sign of personal success and breaking away from the old roles and rules that had held women down in the past. Break free from those old conventions, the ads urged, and get *truly* liberated: put yourself first" (p. 246). Mutability, in these terms, always seems to involve self-help products to aid in the process of becoming more beautiful. And, of course, these products do not need to be only cosmetics or creams: the Brain Age advertisement seems to rhetorically ask, "why can't beauty come from video games?" At the same time, by not using the phrase "video game" the advertisement is also careful to not disrupt pre-established expectations about who is entitled to be part of video game play.

Visually these advertisements reinforce what their text says outright: that play and technology is a masculine domain that can only be entered into by women under the guise of beauty and self-care. Lighting is a key factor in how these advertisements are constructed. Both in the masculine and feminine advertisements the heads of the models have light attached to them—the man's head is lit up like it is wired with circuitry, while the woman's head produces a haloed effect. There is a harder light against the darker page in the masculine ad, making it appear more serious—and more game-like. Conversely, the softness of the feminine ad allows it to appear non-threatening—it is the head and face, rather than the brain that is being stressed in this advertisement. This use of coloring, light, and darkness in both ads helps to reinforce the messages each advertisement is attempting to convey.

How the models are positioned in the advertisements also helps to reinforce these messages. While both models are featured in profile, the woman's head is looking slightly downward at the DS, while the man's head and eyes are looking up at the technology he's reaching for with his arm. The positioning of each model's head evokes what Erving Goffman refers to in *Gender advertisements* (1988) on "the ritual of subordination." He explains, "A classic stereotype of deference is that of lowering oneself physically in some form or other of prostration. Correspondingly, holding the body erect and the head high is stereotypically a mark of unashamedness, superiority, and disdain" (p. 40). While the advertisements each only feature one person, the relative positioning of each is compelling. The man's body implies the "unashamedness and superiority" suggested by Goffman, while the woman's is lowered implying deference. The woman is cradling the Nintendo DS in her hand, which evokes what Goffman refers to as the "feminine touch." Alternatively, the placement of the man's hand relative to the Nintendo DS emphasizes the technology more than the human. In this version of the ad, the technology is suspended in midair, with the man's hand (and stylus) reaching up to it. The man does not appear to be threatened by the midair technology; although by looking up at it he is shown as dominated by the Nintendo DS. The floating Nintendo ultimately gives the masculine ad a futuristic tone: he is looking upward at the technology of the future, and the technology is suspended in air in an impossible way. The man's positioning shows him as dominated by the DS, while the woman is the dominant figure in her advertisement. Interpretations of these positions are far from straightforward. While the man is allowed to be challenged by a superior technology, the woman is shown dominating it as though it were an older technology (a book). These placements presume and attempt to forecast an audience response based on stereotyping gender and technology.

Ultimately, these advertisements are striking because of how they construct gender in relation with play—particularly technological play. While both advertisements suggest the aforementioned productive role within the context of play, the advertisement intended for women audiences removes technology from the equation, relying far more on stereotypes of women being overly concerned with beauty and self-care. By using self-help themes that reinforce these tropes, there is an underlying suggestion that women would not be interested in play for the sake of play, nor, for that matter, play for the sake of *mental* self-improvement. As such, the advertisement plays on fears of women and aging, while simultaneously remaining ambivalent about women as video game players.

Nintendo Wii: Gender and Family Play Time

While the Nintendo DS uses productivity and practicality to convince feminine audiences to play more, advertising campaigns for the Nintendo Wii often use different techniques. The Nintendo Wii was released in November 2006 as an entirely new kind of gaming system. Instead of typical joysticks and game controllers, this system uses a Wii remote and motion sensors so that the player's movements are directly mimicked by on-screen play. Thus, when playing a tennis game, the player must swing the Wii remote like a racket, and other games have similarly intuitive controls. By changing the interface of the typical console video game system, many felt that Nintendo was trying to appeal to a larger, non-gamer market, including a more feminine audience (Shields, 2008).

While not all Wii campaigns are aimed at women, I will show how the ones that many targeted at feminine audiences use a specific theme: the use of play to bring the family together. These advertisements suggest that playing the Wii with one's family is productive, fun, and will garner love from all family members. Rather than promoting play as singular "me" time or time fillers as the advertisements for the Nintendo DS did, these advertisements suggest family Wii-time as a means of closing generational gaps. At the same time, they maintain technological play as alien territory to women—reestablishing expectations of video games as a masculine territory.

In many ways, this campaign resembles some of the methods that have been used to market food to women. In *Food is love: Advertising and gender roles in modern America* (2007), Katherine Parkin discusses how the advertising of food was used to infer family values, and often to create bonds between family members. She writes:

> Advertisers wanted consumers to believe that their food products had the ability to create connections and continuity between the perceived constancy of the past and the chaos of the present. Moreover, they wanted women to assume responsibility for creating traditions in their family's history. (p. 44)

Thus, while there are several distinctions between food advertising and advertising for the Wii gaming system, both use similar tactics to suggest that the use of the product will create memories, love, and the togetherness of traditional family values. These Nintendo Wii campaigns have attempted to suggest that *play is love*.

According to Margaret Hofer (2003) in *The games we played*, the suggestion that game play reinforces family values began with game manufacturers in the late 1800s. She explains that a catalogue for McLoughlin Brothers in 1895 suggests:

> Games are a necessity in every family, and parents should see to it that their children are well supplied with them. They not only amuse, but serve to instruct and educate them. They tend to make happy firesides, and keep children at home instead of compelling them to seek amusement away from the family circle. (p. 53)

Slightly updated for current times, Nintendo, in its attempts to market its game system to women, uses similar advertising tactics that suggest that the perfect family can be created through community play. While this, unto itself, is certainly not a problem, it essentializes feminine play to productive play and legitimizes it by suggesting that playing with one's family is one of the only acceptable forms of feminine play.

An excellent example of this kind of advertising occurred in the "My Wii story" advertising campaign, which launched in summer of 2007. Through the Nintendo website (http://www.mywiistory.com),[2] people were invited to write in stories about the transformative powers of the Nintendo Wii and how it has helped their lives and families. While both sexes wrote in to "My Wii story," the majority of the submissions were made by women. Several selected stories were turned into magazine advertisements—often appearing in women's special interest magazines and all written by women players. In effect, these advertisements are not necessarily promoting that women play more, but rather, that they use play as a means of connecting their families (and connecting with their families). This form of marketing is deftly used to market towards women audiences. In some ways, this family-centric self-help is what Arlie Russell Hochschild (2003) refers to as "emotional labor." She explains, "This labor requires one to induce or suppress feeling in order to sustain the outward countenance that produces the proper state of mind in others" (p. 7). Further, Hochschild suggests, "As traditionally more accomplished managers of feeling in private life, women more than men have put emotional labor on the market, and they know more about its personal costs" (p. 11). The "My Wii story" campaign often capitalizes on this feminine propensity for feeling more obligations of emotional labor. Self-help advertisements using this technique focus video game pitches on a sense that it is a woman's obligation to keep the family together.

In large part, these advertisements use anecdotes and personal experience as persuasive tools. Figure 4 shows one of the "My Wii story" posts that became a magazine advertisement (and ran

Figure 4. My Wii Story Advertisement (*Martha Stewart Living*, September 2007).

in *Martha Stewart: Living* in September 2007 and February 2008). All of the "My Wii stories" in magazines start off with a testimonial quote about what they like about the Wii gaming system. Below each of these testimonial quotes is a woman's signature—a personal advocacy of the product.

The advertisement in Figure 4 uses the aforementioned Play is Love theme within the testimonial of the "My Wii story" author, Nancy Ponthier. In this testimonial, Wii play is even more directly associated with family togetherness—the main picture shows a mother playfully hugging her son, while negotiating the Wii remote. Her headline quote says, "It's the first video game I've really enjoyed playing." This advertisement, like other "My Wii stories," draws a sharp distinction between "typical" video games and the Nintendo Wii system. Making this remark establishes that while video games are not generally part of the feminine playscape, the Wii system is particularly poised to meet the needs of this different audience. It does not suggest that video games are not masculine; only that *this* video game system in *this* circumstance is not masculine. Nancy Ponthier's testimonial continues:

> We really like playing together as a family, so we quickly moved it from my son's room to the living room. We even like making Mii characters together. They're funny and we get a kick out of describing each other. I took a crack at making my own Mii. Then my kids told me it wasn't "pretty enough" and made it better. I thought that was sweet. They were just so happy I was interested in a video game.

In addition to the Play is Love theme that Nancy Ponthier implies through this story, the children recreating her Mii to make it "prettier" reinforces the theme that a Nintendo Wii will bring the family closer. In effect the causal statement, "I thought that was sweet. They were just so happy I was interested in a video game" implies that her children might love her *slightly* more for playing video games. Additionally, just as with the advertisement for Brain Age, this remark deftly plays into women insecurities about beauty and self-care. In the case of "My Wii story," it is a suggestion of emotional labor. In purchasing a Wii, Nancy Ponthier makes no claims to play for the sake of play; she is playing in order to engender a better relationship with her children. And in that, the subtext becomes more like emotional labor than play. Just as Dill and Thill (2007) suggested that masculine video game magazines fetishize femininity, these advertisements, too, turn femininity into fetish. In contrast with Dill and Thill, though, rather than fetishizing in overtly sexual ways, these advertisements establish feminine video game play is maternal. A hegemony of play is still being established here, and women players are still being presented as *other* in comparison to video game masculinity.

Other "My Wii stories" printed in magazines carry very similar themes that essentialize feminine play, turning it into family play. Women's play, thus, becomes translated into productivity, facilitating family play, and a form of emotional labor—not necessarily playing for their own personal enjoyment, but in order to gain the love of their families and create a common language between family members. As such, the testimonial tone of the advertisement (bearing similarities to traditional self-help) promotes productivity over play.

Fitness and Exergame Advertising

In recent years fitness has begun to play an increasingly important role in video games. Early exercise games (or exergames) such as *Dance Dance Revolution* (a game which involves a colorful floor mat which players must use to emulate on-screen patterns) and *Yourself! Fitness* (a game where the player designs a traditional exercise routine, but has no off-screen and on-screen interactivity) were the first forays into this unlikely territory of mixing video game play with exercise and fitness. In *Persuasive games* (2007), Ian Bogost discusses the varying rhetorics of these different kinds of play, making some compelling analysis of which rhetorical styles work best in fitness play. At the same time, Bogost's argument ignores the rhetorics of gender within the space of exergames. While he astutely acknowledges that class informs the structural and spatial issues embedded in exergames by reminding readers that only those who can afford larger living spaces are equipped to properly play them, he does not acknowledge that issues of weight, aerobics, and exercise are inherently imbued with themes that are thematically intended to attract feminine audiences, and prey on gender stereotypes.

Both Wii Fit and EA Sports Active suggest overall healthy lifestyle choices—combinations of sensible diets and varying kinds of exercise. At the same time, though, their game mechanics and the accompanying advertising can often broach the topics of body image and self-help. In *Femininity and domination* (1990), Sandra Lee Bartky writes of the difficulties that many women have between self- and body-image, explaining that, while on the one hand women are entrained to narcissism, on the other hand they have little control over the body image they are being encouraged to produce. According to Bartky, "women experience a twofold alienation in the production of our own persons: The beings we are to be are mere bodily beings; nor can we control the shape and nature these bodies are to take" (p. 42). Similar claims have been made by Naomi Wolf in *The beauty myth* (2002) and Jean Kilbourne in *Can't buy my love* (1999), both of whom discuss how media images of overly thin women have helped to produce eating disorders such as Anorexia Nervosa and Bulimia. Susan Bordo writes in *Unbearable weight* (1993) that the slender body is always gendered and "never neutral" (p. 204) and is a "contemporary ideal of specifically *female* attractiveness" (p. 205, author's emphasis). Thus, given the gendered nature of images about weight loss and slenderness, it seems unsurprising that recent video games targeting feminine audiences have taken on themes of fitness. The self-help and productive themes of the games ultimately foster contradictory messages about work and play within game spaces for women.

Because body image can be seen as such a trigger-issue for many women's insecurities, it seems small coincidence that an influx of recent games has been using this theme to garner more feminine audiences.

The following considers two advertising campaigns for exergames aimed at feminine audiences: Wii Fit and EA Sports Active. Wii Fit is an exercise game played using the Nintendo Wii and a unique "balance board," which came out in May 2008, and like other Nintendo Wii games has quickly begun to target more feminine audiences, advertising in magazines such as *Oprah Magazine* and *Good Housekeeping*. Similarly, EA Sports Active was released in May 2009, and immediately started targeting the same audience. While both games preach overall healthy lifestyles, the advertising campaigns use varying methods to suggest *productive* lifestyles that include these active games. Moreover, they often tap into women's body image issues within their suggestions of self-help.

In many ways, the name Wii Fit is telling unto itself: while "fit" relates to "fitness" it also can be interpreted as the "fit" of one's clothing, or a desire to "fit in" to what is considered the social norm of weight. Anne Becker remarks that for women in the Western world, "[. . .] the anxiety of misrecognition ('I don't fit in') faced by the majority of spectators is more often translated into identification ('I want to be like that')" (Becker & Burwell, quoted in Kilbourne, 1999). As such, Wii Fit might be just as much about fitting in to a desired body image as it is about physical fitness.

The first Wii Fit magazine advertisement (which appeared in *Oprah Magazine* and *Good Housekeeping* in June 2008) creates themes of accessibility and neutrality, showing that the game can be played by anyone regardless of age, race, or sex. The advertisement headline (Figure 5) asks at the top of the page, "How will it move you?" Below this question are 20 separate bodies: the ad shows 20 different people, of different ages, races, and sexes, in different positions on the Wii balance board. All of the players are wearing a homogenizing white (although different articles of clothing), and each shows movement: none appear to be standing still. Similar to the women's advertisement for Brain Age (Figure 2), the advertisement for Wii Fit never uses the phrase "video game": it almost entirely focuses its pitch on fitness and movement. As the text at the bottom of the advertisement explains, "Fitness has a fun side, but if you want to play, you gotta move." In many ways, this advertisement is suggesting little more than diversity, and is far less gendered than the majority of advertisements already discussed.

But a more recent advertisement for Wii Fit (Figure 6) renegotiates this sense of equality, and employs far more gendered stereotypes about women, play, and productivity. This advertisement appeared in the April 2009 issue of *Real Simple Magazine*.[3] The first page of the advertisement shows a list of potential chores and ways to use everyday tasks to be productive and stay in shape. Specifically, the ad encourages active date nights, ways to "make your household chores work for you," and to "create family memories." The advertisement suggests a complicated relationship between work and play. The phrase, "Working out shouldn't feel like work" suggests that the game is, in fact, work (or in the very least, productive). In this way, the Wii Fit advertisement very deftly plays into issues of women and fitness, while at the same time playing on issues of gender and self-help. Like the Brain Age advertisement (Figure 2), it is constructed similarly to articles in the magazine (*Real Simple*) creating an advertorial style of advice giving.

The second page of the advertisement continues similar themes, opening with the line, "The Gym. Now in convenient living room size." It continues by suggesting that this game (like other Wii games) can help engender cross-generational communication and more family time. While the image on this page shows a woman playing the game alone, the advertising copy primarily focuses on encouraging family relationships. While the focus of the previous advertising page is more about personal self-help, the subsequent page is more about social issues within the family, not unlike the "My Wii story" advertisement (Figure 4).

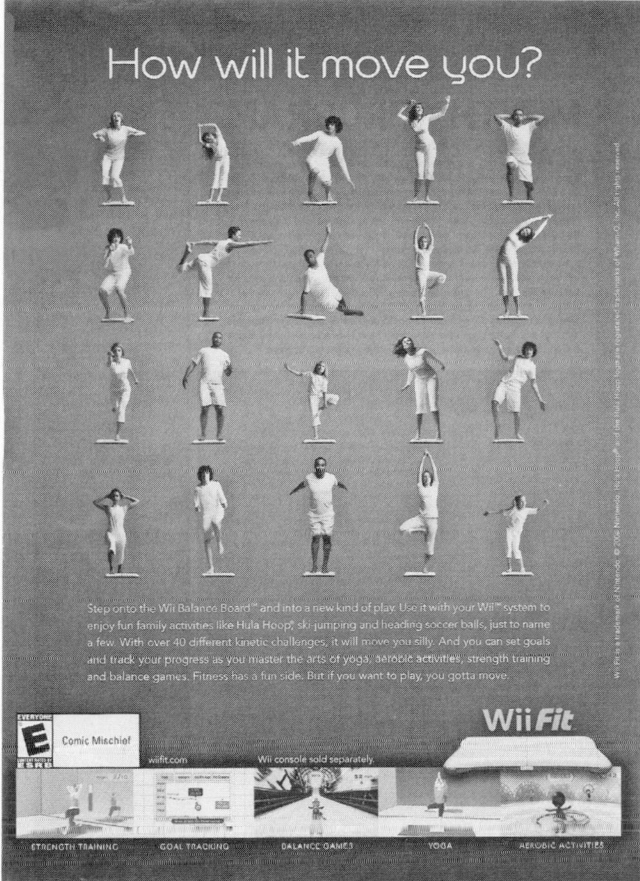

Figure 5. *Wii Fit* Advertisement (*Good Housekeeping*, July 2008).

Advertisements for EA Sports Active used a campaign that further knitted productivity with issues of gender and body image. Advertisements for this exergame used slogans reporting reasons to be "active." For example, one advertisement reports, "I'm active for the terrible twos" while others report, "I'm active for swimsuit season" and "I'm active for my skinny jeans." The advertisements are fairly simple with very little copy, and each has a woman in the center intently playing the game. The slogans of these advertisements are what is most striking, as their reasons for being active (or "productive" one might posit) use entirely gendered stereotypes—a mother chasing after a toddler, certainly, but also the body image issues in obsessing about "swimsuit season" and "skinny jeans." The advertisement for "swimsuit season," which appeared in the June 2009 issue of *Real Simple* employs this gendered productive strategy.[4] In this advertisement, a woman of indeterminate age wearing skimpy shorts, a t-shirt, and a cropped haircut is posed—presumably in a stance from the game. A light sheen on her body suggests that she has been sweating (therefore suggesting that the workout has been successful). Her body pose, while perhaps from the game, almost appears to be a bodybuilder pose, particularly showing off her muscular legs and arms. Despite working out, she is smiling slightly. The woman in this advertisement does, indeed, appear that she will do just fine for "swimsuit season."

Figure 6. Wii Fit Advertisement (*Real Simple Magazine*, April 2009).

The use of productivity as a gendered theme in this advertisement, as well as the other EA Sports Active ads is apparent. The suggestion of the slogan, "I'm active for . . . " is almost enthymematic in its supposition that it is not good enough to be active (or to play) simply to play, but that it is necessary to be active for something specifically productive. While, perhaps, used by many women, the phrases "skinny jeans" and "swimsuit season" become further problematic as they imply an ideal body type for women. With the exception of the first Wii Fit advertisement (Figure 5), most of the exergames advertisements suggest that it is worthwhile to play if one is focusing their efforts on productively improving one's body. One would be hard-pressed to not see the EA Sports Active ads, or suggestions by Wii Fit to "make household chores work for you" as being play rather than work. In conflating domestic work and play, these advertisements suggest an inequality between masculine and feminine video game play. Rather than breaking the hegemony of play, these exergames help to fortify gender roles and expectations.

Conclusion

A recent television commercial for Madden 09 shows two men talking on the phone in the middle of the night, trying to convince one another that they have not yet purchased the game. As the commercial runs, both men are clearly lying: one is already playing the game while the other is opening the game's box. The commercial shows no other family members and no neglecting of domestic (or work) responsibilities. And while the two characters in the commercial *are* lying about having purchased the game, the underlying implication is that this is about competitiveness. For instance, when one man insists he had been sleeping the other remarks, "Hey have you ever had a dream about getting destroyed by me in Madden . . . because that's going to be a reality very shortly." The commercial, ostensibly, creates a permission slip where men are permitted (even expected!) to play at any time, even in the middle of the night.

The Madden 09 commercial sits in stark contrast to the above video game advertisements aimed at women audiences. These advertisements problematize the so-called "tectonic shifts" (Fron et al., p. 316) where women are slowly being welcomed into the already established masculine terrain. While, indeed, advertisements are bringing new audiences into the video game sphere, they are offering a different kind of video game play. This illustrates a larger problem that also exceeds to boundaries of video games—it pushes into issues of women's leisure and how they "play," with or without emerging technologies.

For a long time much of the research on gender and gaming seemed to be asking the question, "How do we get women and girls to play more video games?" While this was certainly a valid question 15 years ago, given changes to the gaming industry it might be time to rethink this question. It might now be more relevant to instead ask "how" and "why" women and girls play. This article has taken some preliminary steps in considering how gender expectations become enfolded into video game play, and how advertising reflects these norms. Specifically, the examples above use productivity through self-help as a primary means to engage a (perhaps) reticent audience of women players and warm them to the idea of video games. While audiences need to be broadened if they are to become more gender inclusive, it is necessary to look at how these games are being advertised, and the cultural gender essentializations that are embedded within them that may only promote specific kinds of video game play.

Researchers need to start considering the implications of gender and productive play. While some might consider advertising video games in women's special interest magazines is a positive move, it is important to survey how play is being marketed to women, and the implications of this marketing. By maintaining previously established hegemonies, gender stereotypes, and blockades between women and video games, new players will continue to ghettoize women players, ultimately treating them as "other" in the broader video game industry.

Notes

1. In fact, while conducting this research, the most common response I got (from both academics and non-academics) was, "I would have never thought video games were advertised in *Good Housekeeping*!"
2. This website is no longer active, and is currently listed as "under construction."
3. Although this advertisement exceeded the timespan of my magazine survey, its relevance to the topic made it essential to include in this study.
4. The advertisement is available in the June 2009 issue of *Real Simple Magazine*. Please email the author at shira.chess@gmail.com for copies of the advertisement.

References

Bartky, S. L. (1990). *Femininity and domination*. New York, NY: Routledge.

Bogost, I. (2007). *Persuasive games: The expressive power of videogames*. Cambridge, MA: MIT Press.

Bordo, S. (1993). *Unbearable weight: Feminism, western culture, and the body*. Berkeley: University of California Press.

Burrill, D. (2008). *Die tryin': Video games, masculinity, culture*. New York, NY: Peter Lang.

Cassell, J., & Jenkins, H. (1999). Chess for girls: Feminism and computer games. In J. Cassell & H. Jenkins (Eds.), *From Barbie to Mortal Kombat* (pp. 2–45). Cambridge, MA: MIT Press.

de Castell, S., & Bryson, M. (1999). Retooling play: Dystopia, dysphoria, and difference. In J. Cassell & H. Jenkins (Eds.), *From Barbie to Mortal Kombat* (pp. 232–261). Cambridge, MA: MIT Press.

Dill, K. E. & Thill, K. P. (2007). Video game characters and the socialization of gender roles: Young people's perceptions mirror sexiest media depictions. *Sex Roles, 57*, 851–864.

Douglas, S. (1995). *Where the girls are: Growing up female with the mass media*. Michigan, MA: Three Rivers Press.

Faludi, S. (1991). *Backlash: The undeclared war against American women*. New York, NY: Doubleday.

Friedan, B. (2001). *The feminine mystique*. New York, NY: W.W. Norton & Company. (Original work published in 1963.)

Fron, J., Fullerton, T., Morie, J., & Pearce, C. (2007a). A game of one's own: Towards a new gendered poetics of digital space. Proceedings from perthDAC.

Fron, J., Fullerton, T., Morie, J., & Pearce, C. (2007b). The hegemony of play. Proceedings from Digital Games Research Association (DiGRA).

Goffman, E. (1988). *Gender advertisements*. New York, NY: Harper Collins.

Harris, M. (2006, October 6). Feminization of gaming: Nintendo makes moves on underserved female consumer. *Edmonton Journal*, p. F15.

Hochschild, A. R. (2001). *The time bind: When work becomes home and home becomes work*. New York, NY: Holt.

Hochschild, A. R. (2003). *The managed heart: Commercialization of human feeling*. Berkeley: University of California Press.

Hofer, M. K. (2003). *The games we played*. New York, NY: Princeton Architectural Press.

Jenkins, H. (1999). Complete freedom of movement: Video games as gendered play spaces. In J. Cassell & H. Jenkins (Eds.), *From Barbie to Mortal Kombat* (pp.262–247). Cambridge, MA:MIT Press.

Kilbourne, J. (1999). *Can't buy my love: How advertising changes the way we think and feel*. New York, NY: Touchstone.

Laurel, B. (2001). *Utopian entrepreneur*. Cambridge, MA: MIT Press.

Miller, M. K., & A. Summers. (2007). Gender differences in video game characters' roles, appearances, and attire as portrayed in video game magazines. *Sex Roles, 57*, 733–742.

Norwood, R. (1990). *Women who love too much*. New York: Pocket Books.

Parkin, K. (2007). *Food is love: Advertising and gender roles in modern America*. Philadelphia, PA: University of Pennsylvania Press.

Postigo, H. (2007). Of mods and modders: Chasing down the value of fan-based digital game modifications. *Games & Culture, 2*(4), 300–313.

Ray, S. G. (2004). *Gender inclusive game design: Expanding the market*. Hingham, MA: Charles River Media.

Shields, M. (2008). Game on. *Mediaweek, 18*(27), 14–16.

Simonds, W. (1992). *Women and self-help culture: Reading between the lines*. Piscataway, NJ: Rutgers University Press.

Sotamaa, O. (2007). Let me take you to the movies: Productive players, commodification, and transformative play. *Convergence, 13*(4), 383–401.

Subrahmanyam, K., & Greenfield, P. (1999). Computer games for girls: What makes them play? In J. Cassell & H. Jenkins (Eds.), *From Barbie to Mortal Kombat* (pp. 46–71). Cambridge, MA: MIT Press.

Taylor, T. L. (2006). Play *between worlds: Exploring online game culture*. Cambridge, MA: MIT Press.

Taylor, T. L. (2008). Becoming a player: Networks, structure, and imagined futures. In Y. Kafai, C. Heter, J. Denner, & J. Sun (Eds.), *Beyond Barbie and Mortal Combat* (pp. 51–66). Cambridge, MA: MIT Press.

Taylor, V. (1996). *Rock-a-by baby: Feminism, self-help, and postpartum depression*. New York, NY: Routledge.

Troland, T. R. (2005). Seeing ahead: Underpinnings for what is next for magazine publishing. *Publishing Research Quarterly, 20*(4), 3–13.

Wirman, H. (2007). "I am not a fan, I just play a lot"—If power gamers aren't fans, who are? *Proceedings from Digital Games Research Association (DiGRA)* (pp. 377–385).

Wolf, N. (2002). *The beauty myth: How images of beauty are used against women.* New York, NY: Harper Perennial.

Real Niggas: Black Men, Hard Men, and the Rise of Gangsta Culture

MILES WHITE

The first time I recall hearing gangsta rap was in 1988, in the dormitory room of a private, predominantly white liberal arts college in the Southwest where I was belatedly earning my bachelor's degree in English literature. N.W.A.'s album *Straight Outta Compton* had recently dropped, and a small group of male students whom I knew fairly well were gathered around a CD player giving it the kind of attention one would give a highly anticipated sporting event. I had found my way into the room by following the sound of some seriously funkified music that reminded me of old school bands from back in the day. These kids, all privileged upper-middle-class white students in their late teens who came from safe suburban neighborhoods, were listening to N.W.A.'s "Fuck Tha Police," which sounded to me like a street riot with machine gun fire. I had never heard of the group, or for that matter gangsta rap, but then neither had most of these kids, except for the one who had brought the CD. The language and scenarios filling the room rendered me speechless. It was not that I had not heard this kind of language on records before, littered with the words *nigger, motherfucker*, and *bitch*, but only on comedic party records, and never in the presence of whites. The kind of language I was listening to was the black working-class folk vernacular I grew up hearing in night clubs, juke joints, house parties, and other places where black folk congregated, partied, and talked trash to each other. I was not the only person in the room who was speechless at what I was hearing, but the nature of our various silences could not have been more different. I was probably visibly unnerved by the violence, the graphic depictions of "cops dying in L.A.," and the enraged voices of some seriously pissed off black men seemingly running amok. These kids, all much younger than me but who all knew me as the resident assistant in the dormitory, looked up at me vacant-eyed but said nothing, going back to the music, totally entranced. No one seemed chagrined even a little by the fact that a black man had just entered the room in the middle of the racial mayhem unfolding in our midst. I was of no

Miles White, *From Jim Crow to Jay-Z: Race, Rap, and the Performance of Masculinity*. University of Illinois Press (2011).

consequence. The real niggas were jumping out of the loudspeakers.

The underground success of N.W.A. and *Straight Outta Compton* set in motion a sea of change in American popular music and culture, and I was unwittingly watching it unfold in its nascent stages—white adolescent males fascinated by young black men weaving narratives of ghetto violence and shootouts with cops told in the most graphic of language. Its tone, use of language, and delivery of vocal rhymes was like nothing I had heard before, at least not as music. *Straight Outta Compton* flipped hip-hop music on its head and began the bumrushing of the American pop music mainstream, the aftershocks of which would exile political and socially conscious styles of hip-hop to the commercial abyss. N.W.A. would have the most profound and lasting impact on the direction of hip-hop music and its cultural milieu for the remainder of the century and into the next, and as such lays credible claim to being the most important rap group ever formed. N.W.A. began the mainstreaming of hardcore styles of gangsta rap that would reintroduce into popular culture historical representations of black males as the hypermasculine brutes and hypersexual bucks turned street-hardened gangbangers and drug dealers, told in graphic ghetto narratives involving casual black-on-black violence, drug trafficking, misogyny, and gunplay. These were bad men. Bad because they were dangerous, took what they wanted, and didn't give a fuck. Bad because they were young black men with guns shooting up the place. N.W.A.'s representation of the reformulated black brute as hardcore rapper was seen by adolescent youth as a real antisocial hell raiser, not just another rock 'n' roll bad boy wannabe. For young males—blacks, whites, indeed of many racial and ethnic stripes—hardcore rap transformed black males from the 'hood into totemic performers of a powerful masculine authenticity and identity at a time in which there appeared to be few real men left.

Bad Men, Bad Niggers, and the World's Most Dangerous Group

N.W.A.'s street swagger only increased with the public backlash that erupted over *Straight Outta Compton*, but the *niggas with attitude* they acted out in their music and representation of black masculinity bear little resemblance to the bad man of African American folklore who was after all something of a heroic figure. Instead, N.W.A. played to the trope of the bad nigger, the social outlaw who was abhorred not only by whites, but also by blacks who knew very well that their survival depended upon getting along with whites. All concerned saw the bad nigger as a troublemaker upsetting the delicate social order.

In his book *From Trickster to Badman*, John W. Roberts makes a careful distinction between the black bad man and bad nigger in African American folkloric tradition and suggests that folk heroic traditions are typically enacted by members of subordinated groups as a counter-hegemonic act of subversion and resistance. The black bad man figure is truly heroic in the classic sense of that term because he seeks the good of those in his community and works toward that even if he is seen by whites as a troublemaker. The bad nigger, on the other hand, exerts his power by resisting all social and moral control, and tends to be viewed as a threat by other blacks since he acts in his own self-interest even if this hurts his community. Antebellum slaves who were labeled bad niggers did not simply provoke confrontation with whites by disregarding the rules of their masters and risking retribution that might also be visited upon the entire community, but were just as likely to unleash rage and violence on other blacks. Such figures were not necessarily seen as heroic by other slaves even if they stood up to white authority. After emancipation, "whites continued to view almost any black person who challenged their authority or right to define black behavior and social roles" as a bad nigger type who could be socially sanctioned or killed,[1] but these kinds of men were rarely outlaws.

Roberts characterizes Stagger Lee, the most well-known of these folkloric characters, as a bad nigger figure because he is not redeemed by his ties to the community nor does he act in their best interests. As such, the bad nigger figure is an outsider in both communities, or worse, he is an outlaw and criminal "whose very existence threatens the well-being of the society as a whole."[2] Issues surrounding social and legal control would greatly influence how African American outlaw figures would come to be viewed in society as opposed to Anglo-American outlaw figures. Roberts argues that they must be viewed differently since whites have had the luxury of viewing the law as supporting their interests and rights while African Americans have found themselves perpetually outside the law and disproportionately prosecuted. The failure of Reconstruction and the institution of Jim Crow laws in the Deep South would greatly influence conceptions of black males in the late nineteenth century. To whites, few if any distinctions were made between black males who stood up to segregation's multitude of injustices or who worked to overthrow them. What defines the bad man is that he does not abandon his own humanity in the face of inhumanity and retains the values of community, decency, fairness; he wishes for harmonious relations while he fights to usher these qualities into the world in which he lives. The bad nigger cares only for his own survival regardless of the consequences to himself or those who share his lot, and disregards the punishments for transgressing the social order they have to shoulder even if he does not. What the controversy surrounding N.W.A. revealed among blacks was how a range of considerations, including class, gender, and generational differences as well as social location, determines how these characters are interpreted at any given moment in history. For most whites, except for many adolescent males who have always found within blackness the tools of rebellion, N.W.A. merely confirmed historical fear of black males, especially those seen as exacting retribution for past grievances. In either case, N.W.A.'s representation of black maleness stood outside the boundaries of acceptable social behavior, even as performance art.

The Sweet Science: Black Masculinity and the Performance of Aggression

The sport of prizefighting is an instructive metaphor for hardcore rap performance and the performance of masculinity and also offers some interesting parallels between these two representations of folkloric figures. Like hardcore rappers, black prizefighters engage a cultural practice that circumscribes them in terms of violence and social transgression. In this most macho of sports, some of its greatest figures over the last century have been black males who have occasionally transcended the sport and offered iconic models of powerful masculinity. For a multitude of reasons they have tended to be seen as heroic figures, or demonized, or both. The heavyweight boxer Muhammad Ali became perhaps the most reviled and revered contemporary embodiment of the folk heroic figure in the bad man mold and felt so himself inasmuch as he positioned himself as the people's champion, identifying with the struggles and ambitions of working-class blacks. Inside the ring, the fact that Ali could and did regularly brutalize white males who thought themselves his better must have been unsettling to many whites who thought the same. Outside the ring he displayed the intelligence of the street through homespun folk poetry, plain talk, and mother wit. More important, perhaps, he exercised control of his own representation of himself. Ali's outspokenness on a range of issues from the war in Vietnam to his right to worship as he pleased demonized him for many and endeared him to others. For blacks who looked up to him, he was something of a bad man because he dared to stand up to white authority and prevail within the same institutions of power that had been the tools of black oppression. To many working-class whites as well as those in institutions of state power, he certainly fit their imaginings of the bad nigger, a fact he only exacerbated when he dropped his "slave name" Cassius Clay and became a Muslim. This may have met the disapproval of many middle-class blacks as well, but he was not ostracized for it because his allegiance to community and to the fight for social justice was seen as authentic and unwavering, which allowed him to be embraced as a heroic figure by working-class and middle-class blacks alike.

Jack Johnson, on the other hand, a dominating figure in the sport from 1908 to 1915 and the first black man to win the prized heavyweight title, has quite a different legacy. He was, in the estimation of biographer Al-Tony Gilmore, truly the archetype of the twentieth-century bad nigger because he frequently challenged white expectations of black social behavior. Johnson openly flaunted his taste for flashy clothes, fast cars, and white women, but cared as little for what white authority thought of him as for what other blacks thought as well. For middle-class blacks and intellectuals he was a particular source of consternation because they were bound to defend his right as a free black man to behave as he wished even though they violently opposed him. In his biography *Bad Nigger! The National Impact of Jack Johnson*, Gilmore recalls that the African American educator Booker T. Washington publicly criticized Johnson, remarking that certain of his actions "are repudiated by the great majority of right-thinking people of the Negro race."[3]

Johnson's success, visibility, and refusal to accept the limitations of white expectation were seen as threats to the social order by both races. Convicted in 1913 under the federal Mann Act, a law created three years earlier with him in mind—he was the first person prosecuted under it, for actions committed before it was passed—Johnson was sentenced to prison but fled the country for several years, eventually returning to serve his time of a year and a day.[4] Johnson may have suffered persecution for exercising individual personal freedoms, but he was generally not seen as a heroic figure by most blacks during his lifetime. Johnson may well have regarded himself as something of a social provocateur in his own manner of doing so, but he did so by deliberately playing to type, appearing to relish taunting whites with the role they created for him, but in so doing he also ostracized himself from many in the black community who might otherwise have celebrated his professional accomplishments. Both Johnson and Ali shared the fact that their personal lives became spectacle as hypervisible black males who risked their bodies in the performance of ritualized violence. In rejecting the norms of black behavior for their times, however, they both put themselves beyond the social control of whites, and as a consequence were severely sanctioned.

Much of hardcore rap is rendered in terms of the pugilistic since it is also an arena where black males perform ritualized aggression and metaphoric violence through language. The representation of black males at the core of both endeavors centers around the spectacularized performance of the body and displays of powerful masculinity as well as a certain kind of emotional positioning that allows them to inflict suffering on another without remorse. In his article "Muscle, 'Hard Men' and 'Iron' Mike Tyson: Reflections on Desire, Anxiety and the Embodiment of Masculinity," Tony Jefferson describes this emotional positioning as "the interiorized quality extracted from risking the body in performance."[5] It is the boxer above all other sportsmen, argues Jefferson, who "remains the supreme emblem of the hard man, thus explaining boxing's macho status in the sports hierarchy."[6] Risking the body in performance is something hardcore rap performers do figuratively in a variety of performance contexts. Street-level freestyle competitions called battle rapping is the arena where up and coming rappers face off in verbal duels that mimic the spectacle of hand-to-hand combat between competing opponents, where one risks humiliation in a culture where ubermasculinity is prized. Boxing and battle rapping both involve demonstrations of masculine strength and aggression, the ability to absorb punishment and still retaliate, to overcome one's opponent by beating him down. The appeal of hardcore rap and the macho posturing characteristic of battling rapping is like boxing, masculine desire as voyeurism, part fantasy, part fetish. Jefferson confesses a fascination with Tyson's ring aggression and ability to inflict pain, something he finds himself incapable of. "In that," he writes, "I am probably like many men: drawn in by the discourse of hardness; utterly incapable of living it."[7]

The ability to identify with and embody hardness, Jefferson suggests, owes to a set of social and psychic congruencies not shared by every man. Jefferson portrays Tyson, another former heavyweight champion who was alternately revered and reviled, as the embodiment of the hard man but also as a man who allowed himself to be ultimately transformed into a beast whose public trajectory arched from a celebrated bad man to convicted rapist and bad nigger within the span of a few short years. He sees Tyson as occupying a nexus of social and emotional neglect that forged in him a quality of hardness and "a compelling satisfaction in or desire to inflict punishment" that overrides the threat of having the same punishment inflicted upon him, so that he does not fear risking his body in the performance of a brutal act.[8] Like boxing, hardcore rap portrays masculine figures risking themselves in heroic performance of verbal violence, which accounts for the aggressive nature of its lyricism and much of its macho posturing. The black male as outlaw that draws on the trope of the bad nigger may be seen alternatively as villain or folk antihero, but seldom is he viewed as a role model. N.W.A. changed that in a rather perverted sort of way.

Representations of the black male as unapologetically black, masculine, and powerful—the urban rapper-gangsta as the new *black brute cum street thug*—was a new kind of figure in American popular music. The hardcore gangsta and thug rap (re)centered the black male body into an affective economy of racial desire that, like African American blackface minstrel performers in the nineteenth century, commodified pejorative representations of themselves because satisfying demand for such images proved to be a lucrative trade. It also performed a "crucial hegemonic function, invoking the black male body as a powerful cultural sign of sexuality as well as a sign of the dangerous."[9] With the arrival of hardcore styles of rap performance, representations of black males and the display of hypermasculine black masculinity forged on the streets of the inner city began to change not simply the nature of hip-hop music, but youth perceptions of masculinity and social behavior on the street. Consequently, the rise of gangsta rap in the late 1980s and early 1990s also saw black middle-class social leaders like C. Delores Tucker aligning with white conservatives in calling for sanctions against hardcore rappers as representing the worst element within the black community.

Gangsta rap reintroduced ruptures in a black community already fractured along class lines in the wake of the civil rights era when upwardly mobile blacks who were able to get out of the inner city got out, leaving behind the poorest of poor blacks. Middle-class African Americans may have had to fight hegemonic oppression and "the image in the white mind that every black person is a potential 'bad nigger,'"[10] but disenfranchised blacks of the economic underclass often find themselves aligned against both white oppression and middle-class black sentiment. The gangsta rapper and real gang members on the street, who are often the same, feel no moral obligations to those who have left them behind. In risking themselves in performance, however, both the street hustler and those who rap about him have become romanticized figures for adolescent male rebellion. Hardcore rap music's move from an insurgent black street music into the popular mainstream is illustrative of the fact that the more rap was packaged in terms of gun-toting gangstas the bigger its suburban audiences became.

Criminal Minded: The Allure of the Bad Nigger as Noble Outlaw

The music, culture, and iconography of hardcore gangsta rap are certainly contradictory, allowing opposing readings suggesting at times resistance to marginalization while perpetuating stereotypes rooted both in popular culture and in institutions that instantiate and legitimate notions of social deviance into imaginings around race and blackness. James Messerschmidt, in his study of adolescent gender and violence, finds that the evolution of criminology is implicated in the ways in which the human body has become linked to perceptions of violence over time and expressed in terms of both gender and racial difference. Messerschmidt examines the work of Adolphe Quetelet (1796–1874), who studied French crime statistics along with social factors like age, sex, and race, and who came "to identify the body as being somehow related to 'deviance,'" proposing that there was a "criminal man" who possessed "corporeal deviations" from what he labeled "average man."[11] Quetelet concluded that society was "threatened by the criminal body, and the body of the criminal was conceived as a sign of social dangerousness and deviation" from the normal.[12]

This deviation or deviance would later become *racialized* by Casare Lombroso (1835–1909), a founder of the science of criminal anthropology, who argues in his book *Criminal Man* that many of the bodily characteristics found in "savages and among the colored races are also to be found in habitual delinquents."[13] Lombroso defined the body, particularly the head and face, as signatures of the socially dangerous and ushered in the new science of criminology by focusing on the visible body to demarcate a corporeal difference between the criminal and the noncriminal. Messerschmidt concludes from this that bodies "are active in the production and transmission of *intersubjective* gendered meanings"[14] that are read and interpreted by other bodies. This idea has implications for thinking about performance and authenticity since notions of authenticity are often read as having to do with cultural, ethnic, or racial agency. Authenticity in terms of racial performance may be judged in terms of accountability, since "adequate participation in social life depends upon the successful presenting, monitoring, and interpreting of bodies."[15]

A spectacular example of a failed accountability in hip-hop may be seen in the case of the white rapper Vanilla Ice, who boasted about his impoverished upbringing and involvement in gang activities in order to establish street credibility as a white rap artist. When this fabrication was uncovered, Ice's reputation as a competent social agent was severely compromised. In street parlance he was "fronting," pretending to be something he was not, and so failed the test of accountability and authenticity. The white rapper Eminem, on the other hand, has more successfully played up his impoverished background and rough childhood growing up near blacks, for the same ends. He therefore has genuine accountability and credibility as a social actor that allows him to perform a kind of racialized social portraiture that signals to others his authentic intimacy with urban street culture and black masculinity. Working with former N.W.A. producer Dr. Dre gave him a kind of street credibility by association, and a number of skirmishes with the legal system including assault and weapons charges worked in his favor to paint him as a bona fide bad ass.

The Vanilla Ice episode in particular exposes how fantasies around gang violence or criminal behavior put the performance of aggression into play for those wishing to be viewed as authentic actors in the hardcore genre. Compelling tales of risk, aggression, violence, and death become privileged by rappers who may have lived the life and those that have not, so that the controlled and licensed aggression of the boxing ring is played in much the same way in the "musickal" performance, as fantasy aggression and so much braggadocio. The most prized credentials a hardcore rapper can have, street credibility and respect in addition to microphone skills, are bestowed on rappers who actually have risked their bodies in performance by engaging in violence or criminality. Sometimes it can be unclear who has crossed that line and who has not, but hardcore rap performers measure themselves by this new standard of macho and try to come off as "hard" to gain the street credibility and record sales that such representations can bestow. Rap performers since the late 1980s "have frequently been caught in a bind with respect to self-presentation, for the image of 'unabashed badness' and sexual transgression . . . sold extremely well in the twentieth century."[16] As a result, many young black males no longer challenge the demonizing stereotype of the black brute, but instead claim criminal histories as marks of distinction and authenticity that give them a legitimacy that white males, at least in the rap game, seldom possess.

If there is a redeeming note to the contemporary gangsta/thug rapper and an alternate reading of him that transcends his complicity in perpetuating the bad nigger/brute stereotype, it is in the very flaunting of black masculinity in provocative and subversive ways that resist the historical policing and containment of black male bodies, a reading that in retrospect makes Jack Johnson appear more of a socio-political provocateur than he may have been given credit for. In her book *Lockstep and Dance: Images of Black Men in Popular Culture*, Linda Tucker has suggested how black men in the United States "function within a prison writ large" structured by various methods of containment ranging from the penal system to representational practices "that criminalize their images, and render them silent and, depending on the context, either threatening or comic, hypervisible or invisible."[17] It is through various performative gestures that may be read as subversive and oppositional that black men resist this containment by acting in ways that make containment if not impossible, then certainly more difficult to maintain. The mediation of technology has made it impossible to contain urban black men to the ghettoized zones of control where they had been relegated. The language and narratives in hard and hardcore rap styles resist containment because they speak back in intemperate voices and interrogate the moral authority of those who have constructed and maintained the existence of the socio-economic ghettos that they inhabit. Technologies of visual mediation allow for the resistance and inversion of the controlling gaze so the objectified black subject confronts, re-objectifies, and interrogates his observer. The twentieth-century view of the black as a tragic figure and kneeling victim, then, competes in America with an alternative view—of the hardcore rapper as a complex and problematic model of black masculinity, perhaps heroically so, arguably making him a bad man after all.

Drawing on the work of the Martinique poet and playwright Aimé Cesaire, whose 1939 book-length poem *Cahier d'un retour au pays natal* (Notebook of a Return to My Native Land) describes the narrator's return to the poverty of his childhood homeland and his identification with his degraded fellow Martinicans, Adam Lively suggests that by "embracing his blackness—not a noble blackness but the ignoble blackness, the niggerhood that is forced on him by prejudice—[Cesaire] is transfigured."[18] Cesaire's poem ultimately looks "to the future, to the 'mauvais negre,' the 'bad nigger' of the future who unlike the good nigger, the Uncle Tom, of the past will be set free by his negritude, his niggerhood."[19] Cesaire's poem from another time and place captures with persuasive clarity the oppositional ethos of the contemporary urban gangsta/thug figure, his defiance to containment and his perhaps impassioned identification with the word *nigga*. When hardcore and thug rappers self-identify as "niggas," there is inherent in it a sense of inverting this rhetorical pejorative; self-defining themselves by it but subverting both its meaning and spelling (from the conventional racial epithet "nigger") converts the existential wound that induces shame and emasculation into a signifying trope of racial power, community, and resistance.

The rapper Ice Cube, for instance, probes and takes on white fear and anxiety around the black male body by proclaiming himself "the nigga you love to hate," from his provocative 1990 album *Amerikkka's Most Wanted*. Ice Cube's persona moves between the nihilistic street violence and misogynist impulses of the bad nigger and that of the bad man—a gangland outlaw turned political-minded social activist with an attitude. Because he knows it has the power to intimidate, Ice Cube wields the black male body as a weapon of retribution and transgression, turning centuries of ambivalence, fear, and derision back on his tormentors. Ice Cube assumes the subjectivity of the condemned black characters in Jean Genet's 1958 stage drama *Les Negres*, who strive for authenticity "through becoming wholly and excessively what they are—thieves, murderers, prisoners, the guilty, Negroes, 'niggers.' " For Genet, "the black man is, as [Jean-Paul] Sartre puts it, 'driven toward authenticity' " in that, insulted and enslaved, he nonetheless "draws himself up, he gathers up the word 'nigger' that has been thrown at him like a stone, he asserts himself as black, in the face of the white, with pride.' Genet's *Negres* achieve their pride by becoming, in a ritualized context, the fears and projections of the white audience. They wear the masks."[20] Genet, who aligned himself with the Black Panthers in the 1960s, had a penchant for portraying blacks as heroic criminals and prisoners in his autobiographical novels, and "was drawn to the idea of blacks embodying the alienated and dispossessed in modern society."[21] *Les Negres*, he suggests, "uses ritual, mask and parody to enact the appropriation and exorcism of prejudice. Blackness is no longer a political strategy, but an aesthetic act," and negritude was "a rite of passage leading the participants to a new state of consciousness."[22]

On the single "Amerikkka's Most Wanted," Ice Cube ritually gathers up his "niggerization" and hurls it back at his critics with his venomous first line "payback's a motherfucking nigga," which is to say that *payback is not just about getting paid, it's about niggas like me up in your face all day.* As revenge fantasy, "Amerikkka's Most Wanted" finds its power in a performative mas(k) ulinity that is not only aggrieved, but that situates Ice Cube within a community of black men who are fearless and aggressive, and who often express themselves in violent ways, the more violent, the more "authentic." For "real niggas" vulnerability is not an option. It is an emotional state reserved for their "feminine" counterparts—the gender-inclusive 'bitches" that include gay men and women, white middle-class morality, middle-class African Americans, inauthentic rappers posing as hardcore, and other "fake ass niggas." In "The Nigga You Love to Hate," Ice Cube taunts the hidden fears of whites with the line "The damn scum that you all hate/Just think if niggas decide to retaliate," which strikes at the heart of hundreds of years of policing of the black male body. In perhaps his most defiantly political statement, he addresses the prison writ large and the systematic containment of young black males who are overrepresented in the judicial and penal systems at a cost of millions of dollars while the educational uplift of a growing number of inner-city black males appears a lost battle: "You wanna sweep a nigga like me up under the rug/Kicking shit called street knowledge. Why more niggas in the pen than in college?"

Showdown in the Terrordome: N.W.A. versus Public Enemy

Rap music's transition from party music into a kind of hardcore urban street-geist was not coincidental. Hardcore rap's popularity and appeal to white youth was a matter of creating a market demand and then filling that demand, a marketing strategy designed in the early 1980s by "a tightly knit group of mostly young, middle-class, black New Yorkers, in close concert with white record producers, executives, and publicists"—whose strategy rested in "its evocation of an age-old image of blackness: a foreign, sexually charged, and criminal underworld against which the norms of white society are defined, and by extension, through which they may be defied."[23] Narratives of hardness as music and as masculine representation emerge in the early 1980s with Run-DMC and later with LL Cool J. Some of Run-DMC's more political work like "It's Like That" from 1982 finds them working the terrain of the bad man, but it would be Chuck D of Public Enemy who most truly fit the heroic bad man mold. Like Run-DMC, Chuck D affected a street look and attitude that was hard-edged but that did not rely on flirting with representations of deviance or criminality. His projection of masculine power and narrative flow were used to circulate messages of socio-political empowerment and positive self-awareness that were well received by blacks and whites alike. Public Enemy would be the first group to improve on Run-DMC's urban rage and racial alienation, producing music that was more confrontational and abrasive.

The arrival of N.W.A. and Public Enemy would both signal the end of Run-DMC's reign as the dominant group in rap performance. Although they could not be more different, both groups arrived on the scene at about the same time, dropping albums in 1988 in the midst of the crack cocaine epidemic—Public Enemy hitting stride with *It Takes A Nation of Millions to Hold Us Back* and N.W.A. releasing *Straight Outta Compton.* Both groups were hard hitting, controversial, and uncompromising in their music, lyricism, and representations of black masculinity. It was music essentially made by urban black youth for other urban black youth, but both attracted sizable white followings. Both groups would also break up prematurely, but their influence on popular music would be gauged by how the industry changed after them. N.W.A. would ultimately have the most profound and lasting impact on hip-hop culture by defining West Coast hardcore gangsta rap as a new musical subgenre, while Public Enemy's socio-political music proved in the long run to be commercially unprofitable after their early and controversial demise.

Public Enemy's music was an eloquent rendering of black rage as black noise set to rhythm, 1960s revolutionary rhetoric packaged into a 1980s digital smack-down engineered by its production team the Bomb Squad. More dense and dissonant than Run-DMC's stripped-down sound, Public Enemy's production prioritized dense layering of numerous sampled loops of music combined with ambient sounds that created a cacophony of warring textures, the sonic equivalent of a race riot. Chuck D's pugilistic rhetorical jabs introduced uncompromisingly pointed commentary on race and the historical socio-political oppression of blacks in the United States. Over the range of several brilliant albums, Public Enemy rendered Run-DMC instantly anachronistic, operating in a politicized theater of militant black nationalist politics where Chuck D assertively talked back to white power. Public Enemy was the only group challenging N.W.A.'s coming dominance over the future of hip-hop culture until it self-destructed in 1989 when the group's minister of information, Professor Griff, made anti-Semitic remarks that went public. Griff was fired from the group only to be brought back. They disbanded, later to reunite, but the damage was done. The group suffered a blow to its credibility from which it would never fully recover. Public Enemy, like Run-DMC, contributed to the evolution of rapcore, a hybrid of rap and metal that can be heard in the music of the groups Rage Against the Machine, Kid Rock, Linkin Park, Limp Bizkit, Insane Clown Posse, and others, but the long-term influence of the group would not match the impact of N.W.A. in shifting the milieu of hip-hop culture and rap performance irrevocably from the hard to the hardcore. In the aftermath of the controversy, record companies apparently decided that highly politicized rap was bad for business. The political, nation-conscious rap that Public Enemy had defined was ultimately made commercially irrelevant, relegated to an alternative lifestyle on the margins of hip-hop culture as it began to mainstream on the strength of N.W.A.'s bad nigger street swagger.

Crack Nation: The Rise of Hardcore Gangsta Culture and Music

The intersection of hip-hop culture, street gang culture, and drug culture created by crack cocaine in the 1980s made for a perfect storm of confluences that within a few short years—from Schoolly D's "P.S.K. What Does it Mean?" in 1985 to Dr. Dre's *The Chronic* in 1992—saw hardcore gangsta rap evolve as a subgenre of hip-hop music and quickly move into the mainstream of American popular music, where it has mutated into a number of geographical styles. Crack cocaine's intrusion into the formation of hardcore music and culture is not often discussed by music scholars, but it is nonetheless a critical discussion. The intrusion of the Cross Bronx Expressway through working-class areas of the South Bronx was a catastrophic event that precipitated the socio-cultural shifts and ruptures out of which hip-hop formed in the 1970s. Likewise, the rapid saturation of crack cocaine into inner-city ghettos must also be seen as an event with even more far-reaching consequences because it became a catastrophe of national proportions, affecting the lives of millions of mostly poor inner-city black people. It also profoundly helped to change hip-hop from a benign, party-oriented music and culture into one that was regarded as largely malevolent. In another contradiction for a musical culture that finds no shortage of them, it is inconceivable that hip-hop would have become the multibillion-dollar industry it has without the popularity of hardcore and the seminal performers that it has produced over the last several decades, including Ice-T, N.W.A., Snoop Dogg, Tupac Shakur, the Notorious B.I.G., Jay-Z, 50 Cent, and others. If there is a dark upside to the crack cocaine epidemic that raged through black communities beginning in the 1980s, arguably this is it, but it came at a tremendous cost and benefited relatively few people compared to the many more lives it destroyed.

The multimillion-dollar crack cocaine industry that swept through the inner-city streets of Los Angeles, Chicago, New York, and other large urban cities across the country in the late 1980s and early 1990s affected inner-city black populations harder than others because cocaine was largely distributed by street gangs who lived in those neighborhoods. By the early 1980s, the inner-city streets had already turned decidedly meaner than they had been in the 1970s, particularly for slum dwellers, and would soon become open drug markets and shooting galleries of internecine gang violence. Crack was primarily produced and distributed on the street by organized street units loosely affiliated with the Bloods and the Crips, two of the largest street gangs in the United States. Any number of regional groups, some highly organized such as Detroit's Young Boys Incorporated and the Chambers Brothers as well as many lesser-known gangs, distributed all around the country. On the West Coast, various factions of these gangs fought running street battles over lucrative open air drug markets located in urban neighborhoods using automatic weapons purchased with drug profits.

Conspiracy theories circulated that the U.S. Central Intelligence Agency (CIA) had deliberately and secretly dumped crack into urban neighborhoods as a plan of targeted genocide aimed at eradicating black people. There does not appear to be credible evidence that the CIA intentionally employed such a vicious policy, but there is abundant evidence that convincingly suggests crack cocaine showed up on the streets of black America as a by-product of CIA activities, specifically, the Iran-Contra scandal during the Reagan administration in the early 1980s. There is also ample information, publicly available, which suggests that officials in the U.S. intelligence community fully knew about the influx of cocaine into the United States as a result of these activities. It is now a matter of record that the U.S. government had been secretly and illegally selling arms to Iran during its long-running war with Iraq and using those proceeds to secretly and illegally fund anticommunist rebels fighting to overthrow the leftist Sandinista government in the small Central American nation of Nicaragua. The operation became the focus of extended congressional hearings in 1987 and resulted in the convictions of fourteen high-ranking officials in the Reagan administration, including Secretary of State Caspar Weinberger, National Security Agency chief John Poindexter, and his assistant, Oliver North.[24] What is now known is that many of the planes flying supplies to the Contra rebels flew back into the United States stacked with kilos of cocaine supplied by Colombian drug cartels that were distributed to black inner-city drug lords on both coasts.

In August 1996, the *San Jose Mercury News* began running a series of investigative articles on these events, identifying a Nicaraguan national by the name of Oscar Danilo Blandon, an official in the Nicaraguan government before it was overthrown by the Sandinista regime, as a central figure in the drug trafficking operation. The story, written by investigative reporter Gary Webb, was published two years later as a book entitled *Dark Alliance: The CIA, the Contras, and the Crack Cocaine Explosion*. Although Webb was discredited by the U.S. government and a number of mainstream newspapers for what they called faulty reporting, Reagan administration officials eventually admitted they knew the Contras were running drugs into the United States.[25] Other federal investigations went further. Reports by the inspector general for the U.S. Justice Department and the CIA inspector general granted that Webb's allegations had substantial merit—that there was a CIA connection between the Colombian cocaine and the crack that flooded the streets of the black inner cities in the 1980s.[26]

Much of this information is now in the public domain and available in the National Archives in Washington, D.C., as well as in a number of articles and books about the episode that largely corroborate the most damming accusations in Webb's account.[27] I have chosen to avoid the controversy surrounding Webb's book, and instead, reference similar information that appeared in the 2005 book *Freakonomics: A Rogue Economist Explores the Hidden Side of Everything*, written by University of Chicago economist Steven D. Levitt and Stephen J. Dubner, a writer for *The New York Times*. These authors, whose information has not been disputed by the government or national news media, report that Blandon acknowledges that CIA officials knew of his drug-related activities in support of raising money for the anti-Sandinista campaign. Whether that was true or not, "what *is* demonstrably true is that Oscar Danilo Blandon helped establish a link—between Colombian cocaine cartels and inner-city crack merchants—that would alter American history. By putting massive amounts of cocaine into the hands of street gangs, Blandon and others like him gave rise to a devastating crack boom. And gangs like the Black Gangster Disciple Nation were given new reason to exist."[28]

The authors of *Freakonomics* conclude that "black Americans were hurt more by crack cocaine than by any other single cause since Jim Crow"[29] since it affected such a large segment of people across a range of critical areas that help define a group's progress in a society. Within a very short time span—widespread crack use appeared in the early 1980s, spiked in 1985, and continued to escalate until 1989, when it peaked—infant mortality rose dramatically. The number of blacks sent to prison quickly tripled, and "the homicide rate among young urban blacks [thirteen to seventeen years old] *quadrupled* [emphasis in original text]. Suddenly, it was just as dangerous to live in parts of Chicago or St. Louis or Los Angeles as it was to live in Bogota.[30] The authors do not try and make a connection between crack dealers, street gang members, and hardcore rap music, but they don't need to—hardcore rappers who came up as street hustlers making their fortunes slinging rock in the 'hood (and some who perhaps did not) have provided firsthand commentary on the central role of cocaine in hardcore styles of rap over much of the last quarter century. The history of crack cocaine in hardcore rap's takeover of hip-hop culture is documented in hundreds of songs dating back almost twenty years, chronicling the birth of a street culture of drugs and drug-related gang violence that had a transforming if not defining effect on hip-hop music and culture.

The epidemic of crack circulating through black inner-city neighborhoods profoundly impacted many young black urban men and their attitudes around masculinity and interpersonal relations whether they were involved in trafficking or not, since many of them grew up in what amounted to militarized war zones. The crack trade produced "a remarkable level of gun violence, particularly among young black men, who made up the bulk of street-level crack dealers" during the peak epidemic years between 1985 and 1989.[31] The terms *gangbanger* and *drive-by* quickly became household words as a result of the unprecedented rise in urban gang violence; these themes began to appear in hip-hop songs that casually depicted street-level scenarios involving drug trafficking and gun-related homicides. The realism of such scenarios derives from the fact that since only top gang members made large sums of money in the crack trade, many street-level dealers desperate to advance "were willing to kill their rivals to do so, whether the rival belonged to the same gang or a different one. There were also gun battles over valuable drug-selling corners."[32] Typically, homicides at the height of the epidemic involved shootouts between rival crack dealers over money, territory, drugs, respect, some imagined slight, or a hundred other reasons, and where innocent bystanders were often caught in the crossfire. The result was a huge increase in violent street crime related to gangs and drugs, with one study finding that more than 25 percent of the homicides in New York City in 1988 were related to the crack cocaine trade.[33]

Whether young black males in these areas were dealing drugs, involved in gangs, or just innocent bystanders, mistrust and the adoption of hardness as a mask and a kind of street attitude became daily armor in a culture where they learned to view each other warily, since any of them were now potential assailants, targets, drug fiends, or undercover narc cops. The level of deceit, distrust, macho posturing, and violence became endemic to inner-city street culture and would eventually show up in songs that mirrored the ruptures, rifts, and ensuing "beefs" between rival gang members, hustlers, rappers, and sometimes entire organizations. The apotheosis of this phenomenon came with the highly public acrimony that developed between two of the most important hardcore rappers the music has produced, Tupac Shakur of Los Angeles' Death Row records and Notorious B.I.G. of New York's Bad Boy label. Much about the conflicts between these two men was personal and never a full blown East Coast-West Coast feud as many in the media would have it, but the dissension nonetheless ended in the assassination of both men by unknown assailants. As the line between the real and artifice became increasingly imperceptible, most of the critical records and artists that would define hardcore gangsta rap music and create a new cultural milieu around it appeared between the years 1985 and 1989, during the height of the epidemic and in the aftermath of Iran-Contra. The different ways in which hardness manifests as a critical metaphor throughout this history—as rock (street slang for crack cocaine), as attitude, as masculinity, as language, as ghetto narrative, as sound, and as imagery—suggest how critically the convergence of drugs and gangs altered the tone of the music and urban street culture. Representations of urban black males in recorded music, graphic art, magazine ads, music videos, feature films, and video games began to reformulate around notions of hardness and hard masculinity as defined by urban street culture and that began to be reflected in clothing, adornment, facial expression, body posture, and the tenor of casual interpersonal interactions. Hip-hop albums that referenced hustling, crack cocaine trafficking, gang culture, and gun violence would show up throughout the late 1980s and the 1990s and into the 2000s, and spread from the East and West coasts to other geographical regions of the country, creating a number of competing styles of hardcore rap performance.

The group that was the epicenter of this thematic narrative shift, however, was N.W.A., whose albums *Panic Zone* (1987), *N.W.A. and the Posse* (1987), and *Straight Outta Compton* (1988) contained numerous references to crack dealers and street trafficking, none more nefarious than the graphically profane "Dopeman," which appeared on all three albums. Eazy-E, co-founder of N.W.A. and Ruthless Records, was himself a street level crack dealer in Compton and South Central Los Angeles who used the profits to fund recording projects for both himself (his own solo debut album *Eazy-Duz-It* was released in 1988) and N.W.A. These groundbreaking if infamous albums put them at the very nexus of the confluence between the drug trade and the formation of hardcore rap music, contextualized within inner-city street gang culture and its ethos of masculine behavior and translated into performance art rendered in the register of the real.

Roc Nation: Jay-Z and the Takeover of the American Dream

The apotheosis of the contemporary hardcore "crack rap" performer is unquestionably the Brooklyn-born lyrical genius Jay-Z, a former New York City drug figure turned multimillionaire entertainment mogul whose repertoire is filled with songs and lyrics that boast of his rise from "bricks to billboards" and "grams to Grammys," and who has built an empire from slinging crack in the 'hood one rock at a time. The double entendre implied in Jay-Z's Roc-A-Fella Records seems almost obscene in its celebration of capitalist excess enjoyed by the few made possible by the exploitation of the many. There is certainly irony in the fact that the label and Jay-Z's related brands—Roc-A-Wear and Roc Nation—are mainstream success stories given the scourge with which they are so blatantly associated. It is complex. It is contradictory. It is part of the story of hip-hop, which Jay-Z himself discusses candidly in his memoir *Decoded*.[34] In it, he vividly describes the allure of the hustler's life and compares that to the life of the hardcore rapper, whose narratives have so often intertwined beginning in the 1980s. As he sees it, "the story of the rapper and the story of the hustler are like rap itself, two kinds of rhythm working together, having a conversation with each other, doing more together than they could do apart."[35]

Jay-Z was not the first rapper to insert drug references into his songs; he is only one of a number of hardcore performers who, beginning with the autobiographical styles of Schoolly D and Ice-T in the 1980s and Tupac Shakur and the Notorious B.I.G. in the 1990s, inserted themselves into larger than life 'hood tales and drew from their own experiences as street hustlers and gang affiliates. Jay-Z also happens to have been the most successful and articulate rap artist of his generation, single-handedly reframing the ghetto fabulous street thug as the penthouse glamorous Mafioso impresario. In many ways, Jay-Z offers an instructive subject for studying the mediascape I describe in the previous chapter since he has been such a transformational figure in the evolution of contemporary hip-hop since the 1990s. His music is intensely experiential on the one hand. As he writes, his life "after childhood has two main stories: the story of the hustler and the story of the rapper, and the two overlap as much as they converge." On the other hand, he believes that the hustler's story, particularly his own, has connected with audiences on a global scale because the experience of the young black male as hustler is also part of "the ultimate human story, the story of struggle, which is what defines us all."[36] A bit hyperbolic perhaps, but it nonetheless complicates his own story and that of young black males in the United States whose lives are often determined by birth and circumstance, and this has certainly found resonance with the socio-economic struggles of others in any number of geographical locations around the world.

Jay-Z is a curious mash-up of Jack Johnson and Muhammad Ali, at once repugnant and heroic, egomaniacal and generous of spirit. The comparison between boxing and rap is not lost on him, and he in fact sees the former as a perfect metaphor for the latter. In his view, just as boxing "takes the most primal type of competition and transforms it into a sport, battling in hip-hop took the very real competitive energies on the street—the kind of thing that could end in some real life-and-death shit—and transformed them into art."[37] Jay-Z's evolutionary arc has also seen him move from a bad nigger figure to something more resembling the bad man figure, calling attention to problems as diverse as water shortages in Africa and the human suffering caused by Hurricane Katrina in New Orleans. He has, after having attained riches beyond even his own wildest fantasies, increasingly looked for ways in which to, as he puts it, be helpful.

In more than eleven studio albums beginning with 1996's *Reasonable Doubt*, the references that Jay-Z makes in his music to the gangsta/Mafioso life of hustling and drug dealing are so nuanced and artful that they appear no more ominous than a Robert De Niro gangster film, except that he is dealing in the register of the real rather than weaving the fictions of screenwriters. Jay-Z portrays himself as an entrepreneur whose beginnings as a street corner crack dealer are the stuff of Horatio Alger, no less part of the mythical American Dream than corporate robber barons or big city crime bosses. A high school dropout, Jay-Z put a new spin on the intelligent hoodlum when he showed he could step from the streets to the stage to the boardroom, for a time holding the position as CEO of Def Jam Records. His part-ownership in the New Jersey Nets basketball team in addition to numerous other high-profile business ventures have bestowed on him the kind of mainstream credibility and prestige usually reserved for captains of Fortune 500 companies.

Reasonable Doubt takes a not always glamorous stroll through a hustler's life, all swagger and bravado in songs like "Can't Knock the Hustle" and "Can I Live" but exposing the human costs to one's humanity in others like "Regrets" and "D'Evils." There is a real depth of vulnerability beneath the macho posturing of the hard man evoked in many of these lyrics. Exposing that frailty, opening a window so others could see inside his soul without flinching, was a risky move for a performer who embodies the hard man persona, but it helped Jay-Z recast the hip-hop gangsta/thug as not merely a monster on the rampage (a role Tupac was sometimes all too willing to play), or a besieged man misunderstood (how the Notorious B.I.G. ultimately portrayed himself), but as an underdog who was not going to take it lying down, or, as he frames it in "Can't Knock the Hustle's" closing lines, "all these blacks got is sports and entertainment/until we even, thievin'/as long as I'm breathin'/ can't knock the way a nigga eatin."' In *Decoded* he describes the arrival of crack cocaine as "a total takeover. Sudden and complete,"[38] a generational catastrophe that saw adolescents his age serving (selling) crackheads the age of his parents, wearing automatic weapons like fashion accessories and engaging in broad-daylight shootouts over money and turf.

On his second album *In My Lifetime Vol. 1*, Jay-Z shows his hand in case anybody hearing *Reasonable Doubt* wasn't keeping up, connecting the dots between hustling street dope and spitting dope rhymes on "Rap Game/Crack Game." At times he borders on recklessness, rapping in "Real Niggaz" about clocking eightballs[39] on the corner, but it's all between the lines, coded in dense metaphor and street slang, modern-day work songs about the urban slavery of street-level hustling. Jay-Z the dope dealer and street performer embodies the brutal courage of the hard man because he risks his body in performance on the streets in a base and potentially demeaning art where his natural enemies are police, drug fiends, and rival drug dealers. Because he pushes poison on neighborhood streets knowing the powerful addictive nature of crack in particular, he arguably plays the role of the bad nigger, interested only in enriching himself and his cronies. He justifies this by arguing that he is only selling dope to dope fiends whom he does not respect anyway because they deserve none. "Crackheads," he writes, "they got no respect." Even if they were neighborhood elders, friends, and family, "once they started smoking, they were simply crackheads, the lowest on the food chain in the jungle, worse than prostitutes and almost as bad as snitches."[40]

Jay-Z the stage performer, on the other hand, transposes the physically risky act of dope peddling into the verbal aesthetic of rhyming, which carries its own risks. Because he does not write down his rhymes, Jay-Z puts himself at risk in performance because he is always essentially freestyling, the *lingua franca* of battle rapping. If flow, narrative, and drama are all part of the art of rhyming, all infused by the experiential and situational dimensions of a performer's life and daily activities, Jay-Z has crafted a vision that is coherent, almost philosophical, deeply personal, and universal in its scope. He rhymes about the narrative arc of his own life, the experiences that have made him who he is, the situations and daily drama of the hustler's life that he has used as the raw materials of aesthetic performance. His rhythmic flow is unorthodox, athletic, and dexterous, often using multiple meters or mixing them all up, jumping over bar lines as if they were prison bars trying to pen him in. It is a style carefully considered, and which he is able to penetrate and insightfully articulate for himself, writing that "sometimes the flow chops up the beat, breaks the beat into smaller units, forces in multiple syllables and repeated sounds and internal rhymes." He compares musical time and a rapper's flow to life and any individual's experience of it, an almost Zen-like metaphor that makes rhyming if not a transcendental practice (though it could be), then certainly one able to provide a space of deep introspection and the possibility of transformation. "If the beat is time," he offers, "flow is what we do with that time, how we live through it. The beat is everywhere, but every life has to find its own flow."[41] For Jay-Z, two separate flows of life—full-time hustler and part-time rapper—eventually merged into a unitary and singularly unique experience that has become the basis for his art. In his memoir, he writes that he "loved rhyming for the sake of rhyming, purely for the aesthetics of the rhyme itself—the challenge of moving around couplets and triplets, stacking double entendres, speed rapping," but that "when I hit the streets for real, it altered my ambition. I finally had a story to tell. And I felt obligated, above all, to be honest about that experience."[42]

In telling his own story, Jay-Z arguably tells the stories of many others who might be experientially like him in terms of social background and life chances, and who might also aspire to be like him, which is to say, to escape the dead end poverty of lives lived in not so quiet desperation. If hip-hop in the post-old school period had largely painted pictures of poverty, violence, and hustling, Jay-Z has sought the interiority of feeling and the actualization of human experience that Robert Plant Armstrong articulates in terms of the affecting presence, and of exteriorizing that experience. If his art resonates with authenticity, if his street credibility remains intact after a decade and a dozen platinum albums, it is because it gets inside "the interior space of a young kid's head, his psychology," and humanizes the often dehumanizing experience of being black and impoverished, of hustling street drugs for spare change and being willing to kill or die for it because the alternatives appear no better. To create entertaining art from such narratives that retains enough universality to find mass appeal is no small feat. Jay-Z's art is "rooted in the truth of that experience," something he feels he owes "to all the hustlers I met or grew up with who didn't have a voice to tell their own stories—and to myself."[43] If Jay-Z's oeuvre appears more or less variations on a theme, he is often trying to deepen his understanding of his own existential predicament and that of others who identify with him, and in this way he is no less than any other artist working within the confines of a particular aesthetic framework—whether it be rondo form, the short story, or metered poetry—and the techniques it requires. The example he offers is that of a sonnet, which has a recurring theme and a set structure, but of which there are volumes of variations by hundreds of romantic poets. "It's the same with braggadocio in rap," Jay-Z observes. "When we take the most familiar subject in the history of rap—why I'm dope—and frame it within the sixteen-bar structure of a rap verse, synced to the specific rhythm and feel of the track, more than anything it's a test of creativity and wit," and where "there are always deeper layers of meaning buried in the simplest verses."[44]

Braggadocio aside, Jay-Z has offered intimate and candid portraits of his life in song, powerfully, for example, in "Renegade," where he opens up about growing up in a broken home ("My pops left me an orphan, my momma wasn't home") and the desperation to escape dire poverty ("I had to hustle, my back to the wall, ashy knuckles/pockets filled with a lot of lint, not a cent") by hustling in the street, an arena where he applied himself to a dangerous business and earned a hardcore rap artist's most precious possession, the street credibility of having risked his body in performance. Like the bad nigger of black folklore, he played the outlaw, renegade as he would have it, a kind of antiheroic figure and a powerful masculine actor who succeeded against the odds and lived to rap about it. Jay-Z now sees himself in legendary terms, justifiably so perhaps since he changed the rap game in a number of ways, walking the line between the urban street and the corporate world while retaining the respect of both. He is not the first rapper from the street to succeed in corporate America—Snoop Dogg has been pitching brand-name products for more than two decades—but Jay-Z is the first street hustler turned mogul to succeed at the level to which he has attained as a hit maker, tastemaker, and pop culture icon. His last nine solo studio albums, beginning with his third in 1998, *Vol. 2 . . . Hardknock Life*, have climbed to the top of *Billboard* magazine's 200 pop album chart as well as the R&B chart. The release in 2009 of his eleventh album, *The Blueprint 3*, amounted to a victory lap, reminiscing old moves over new beats and reminding everybody how much he has helped take the hip-hop brand from the inner-city street ("oversized clothes and chains we off that/Niggaz still making it rain we off that") to Wall Street ("used to rock a throwback, ballin' on the corner/now I rock a Teller suit, lookin' like a owner") and amassing a fortune estimated at $450 million by *Forbes* magazine, which also predicts that by the end of the decade, Jay-Z will become hip-hop's first billionaire.[45]

Jay-Z's *The Blueprint 3* also gave him more No. 1 albums on *Billboard* magazine's pop charts than Elvis Presley, the man many consider to be the most important figure in the history of American popular music. The significance of that accomplishment can only be comprehended in the context of where he came from, what he overcame to get where he is, and the odds against his doing so without being killed or going to prison. Jay-Z's Horatio Alger embodies more than opportunistic entrepreneurship and the perhaps ruthless character it takes to rise to the top of the drug trade, but the idea of "hardcore smart," the rough and tumble kind of practical knowledge one acquires from the street trying to survive. In making the leap from nefarious to legitimate largely on his own terms, Jay-Z, like Muhammad Ali in the 1960s and 1970s, transformed not only his representation of himself but constructed a compelling new model of black masculinity that may have begun in brute acts but ultimately transcended them, unapologetically and with his dignity intact. Like Ali, Jay-Z escaped the "prison writ large" that polices and contains black male subjectivities by staring down white patriarchal hypocrisy and the limitations of American democracy. And, like Ali, he has lived long enough to see history stand with him.

In the song "Blue Magic" from his 2007 album *American Gangsta*, Jay-Z makes the connections between U.S. government complicity in the events that led to the explosion of crack cocaine on inner-city streets and the intrusion of narratives of drug-related violence into hip-hop culture when he rhymes "Blame Reagan for making me into a monster/Blame Oliver North and Iran-Contra/I ran contraband that they sponsored/Before this rhyming stuff we was in concert." Hyperbole aside, Jay-Z's awareness of what are now largely substantiated allegations does not mean that he excuses his own actions, but rather that he also indicts the malevolence of democratic institutions that have at various times in the history of the United States aligned themselves against the survival of the black community generally and black men in particular. The deeper causes of the crack cocaine epidemic, he writes in *Decoded*, "were in policies concocted by a government that was hostile to us, almost genocidally hostile when you think about how they aided or tolerated the unleashing of guns and drugs on poor communities, while at the same time cutting back on schools, housing, and assistance programs. And to top it all off, they threw in the so-called war on drugs, which was really a war on us."[46]

Nonetheless, Jay-Z's brutality and risk taking as a hard man has always fit more the pattern of the bad nigger than the bad man, championing only his own ambition and the struggle to escape grinding underclass poverty by grinding out rocks until he could move up to pushing real weight, kicking it all back into the chance of making a shot for himself to go straight as a rapper. Like the black outcasts in Jean Genet's *Les Negres* who sought authenticity through becoming wholly and excessively what they were—thieves, murderers, prisoners, the guilty, Negroes, niggers—Jay-Z and many like him drew themselves up in defiant if risky and destructive behavior with the realization that "the world don't like us/is that not clear." Consequently, after the crack explosion, the hustler's life became the meta-narrative of hip-hop when young black men made the connection between hustling dope and hustling dope beats—you could use the one to finance the other and hopefully graduate from one game to the next. As Jay-Z recalls, "a lot of people came to hip-hop like that, not out of a pure love of music, but as a legit hustle, another path out of the 'hood."[47] Jay-Z would appear to have few regrets in this regard judging by the line from his song "What We Talking About," also from *The Blueprint 3:* "As far as street guys we was dealin' crack/That's just how the game goes I don't owe nobody jack."

The reality has always been more complicated, and perhaps part of Jay-Z's genius and appeal is that he has managed to complicate the lives and struggles of young black males whom others are quick to read as no better than two-dimensional. Part of Jay-Z's personal narrative has always been about carrying the weight of regret, the ability to live with the consequences of bad choices and to keep moving forward. It is a theme he has articulated in some way since *Reasonable Doubt*, an album he ended with a song entitled "Regrets" ("This is the number one rule for your set/In order to survive, you gotta learn to live with regrets") and to which he gives perhaps its most eloquent rendering in *Decoded*, where one of the annotations to that song suggests a full awareness of the contradictions that haunt his humanity: "I wanted to end [*Reasonable Doubt*] with regret, that last feeling you have before you go to sleep, or feel when you wake up and look at yourself in the bathroom mirror."[48]

As a successful entrepreneur, Jay-Z can now—as other robber barons before him—afford the luxury of philanthropy. In this regard, he has begun to assume more the position of the bad man who looks after a community of others outside his circle. Besides raising money for victims of Hurricane Katrina, he joined UNICEF and MTV in 2006 to make the video documentary *Diary of Jay-Z: Water for Life* to raise awareness about the problem of severe water shortages in Africa, and put on free concerts to get young people involved in the 2008 presidential campaign behind the candidacy of Barack Obama. Besides employing hundreds of people through his various enterprises that include the multimedia entertainment conglomerate Roc Nation, his efforts to help build a new stadium for the New Jersey Nets basketball team and bring them to Brooklyn may also be seen as beneficial to the community (his part-ownership has been touted in promotional ads raising the team's public profile) though it profits him handsomely as a business venture. Perhaps few begrudge Jay-Z his success given his undeniable talent and business acumen, but his path to fame and riches remains problematic since it does not take into account the number of dead crackheads he has left in his wake or the number of young black males who will try to follow his path and fail.

Jay-Z and other African American hardcore rap performers who work a brute trade have transformed the dynamics, contradictions, and often tragic ironies of their own lives and life experiences into ritual play and entertainment that many adolescent males find as alluring as other forms of violence-oriented entertainment in popular culture. Nonetheless, the downside certainly is that hardcore rap music and its street-oriented cultural milieu construct a grotesque theater of the absurd where the boundary between the real and performance is ever shifting and quite arbitrary, and where there is often little difference between the stage, the studio, and the street. Because hardcore rap performers *do* construct their personas and narratives in the register of the real, this has tended to bestow upon them the credibility that goes with authenticity, even if that authenticity explores black rage as the nihilistic brutality of street violence, drugs, and gangbanging. Ghetto narratives and 'hood tales involving a legion of bad nigger figures have come to be seen as having universal appeal without the entanglement of politics and polemics associated with socially conscious bad men types who descend from the Native Tongues lineage. The racial politics of Public Enemy ultimately proved bad for business, so that "by the turn of the century, to be labeled a 'conscious' or 'political' rapper by the music industry was to be condemned to preach to a very small choir"[49] and to a relatively small share of hip-hop's hugely profitable mainstream commercial market. This is not to say that many hardcore rappers, young black males from the street with few life chances who *have* risked their bodies in performance, are not aware of the existential dilemma in which they find themselves—to hustle bricks or hustle rhymes—even though success at the latter is often contingent upon success at the former. The fact that they *can* self-reflexively transform their real-life narratives into artifice and art suggests that they are conscious social actors who know their stories are more real than most, and that this is what gives them appeal and credibility.

Importantly, what hardcore styles of rap in particular have helped to do is reinforce the powerful ways in which language, emotion, music, blackness, and the body intersect at dangerous crossroads that are circulated in a contemporary context of global exchange that "retains residual contradictions of centuries of colonialism, class domination, and racism."[50] Ideas of blackness and masculinity derived from hip-hop music and culture all circulate as commodities in a global marketplace that does not necessarily reflect relations of reciprocity and mutuality when participants in that dialogue "speak from positions of highly unequal access to power, opportunity, and life chances."[51] The ways in which hardcore styles of rap are perceived and consumed have arguably had a deleterious effect on how black people and black culture are viewed not only in the United States but in other parts of the world even though this in itself is not new. Modernist literature, art, and music in the West have "consistently spectacularized difference, titillating 'respectable' audiences with sensational portrayals of 'primitive,' 'exotic' and 'oriental' outsiders"[52] who are nonetheless perceived as frightening exactly because they are objectified and rendered in terms of the grotesque. The problem is certainly complicated when those being portrayed are also participants in the construction of their own spectacularization and objectification. In this case it is fair to ask whether the selling of stereotypes of difference by those who *are* different constitutes the selling out of innocents who see no compensatory benefits from such Faustian deals with the devil.

A larger issue, perhaps, is whether Jay-Z and other artists who have made their names in a vile trade must ultimately bear the burden of what I call a "Bert Williams problem." What I mean is that, even though these artists are lavishly paid and many of them admired by fans and respected by peers, and while they have opened up enormous doors of commerce and opportunity for those with the talent and grit to follow them, the question of whether their cultural productions and philanthropy do enough to counterbalance the empty space in the representation of black masculinities left in their wake remains a serious one. The most egregious consequences of perpetuating historically pejorative meta-narratives of black males—of reinserting the bad nigger into contemporary popular culture, of making hustling appear to be a viable life choice even in the face of nothing better—are likely to last beyond their own careers and well into the future. Few people outside black music historians and serious fans of hardcore rap may have ever heard the name Schoolly D, yet his influence on the direction of hip-hop music and popular culture continues to be lasting and profound a quarter century on. In the final chapter I discuss the predictable consequences of such cultural productions in terms of what other social actors choose to emulate, as well as some perhaps alternative routes.

Notes

1. Roberts, 177.
2. Roberts, 6.
3. Gilmore, 102.
4. In 2009, the U.S. Congress approved a resolution, first introduced in 2004, urging President Barack Obama to grant a posthumous pardon to Johnson for his 1913 conviction under the Mann Act, also known as the White Slave Traffic Act. Senator John McCain of Arizona was the lead sponsor of the Senate resolution, which states in part that the pardon would "expunge a racially motivated abuse of the prosecutorial authority of the Federal Government from the annals of criminal justice in the United States." As of this writing, President Obama has not granted the pardon.
5. Jefferson, 92.
6. Jefferson, 84.
7. Jefferson, 94.
8. Jefferson, 94.
9. Lott, 118.
10. Roberts, 215.
11. Messerschmidt, 6.
12. Messerschmidt, 6.
13. Messerschmidt, 6.
14. Messerschmidt, 43.
15. Messerschmidt, 46.
16. Monson, 419.
17. L. Tucker, 18.
18. Lively, 226.
19. Lively, 232.
20. Lively, 241.
21. Lively, 237.
22. Lively, 238.
23. Samuels, 242.
24. The convictions of Poindexter and North were overturned on appeal. Weinberger and others were later pardoned during the administration of President George H. W. Bush.
25. On April 17, 1986, the Associated Press published a news article entitled "U.S. Concedes Contras Linked to Drugs, But Denies Leadership Involved."
26. On July 23, 1998, Justice Department Inspector General Michael Bromwich issued a report showing Reagan administration officials were aware of cocaine traffickers in the Contra operation. A report issued on October 8, 1998, by the CIA inspector general gave evidence that money from drug trafficking was used by Oliver North at the National Security Administration for Contra operations. Gary Webb was found dead in 2004 from two gunshot wounds to the head. His death was officially ruled a suicide. (Source: The National Security Archive, The Gelman Library, George Washington University, Washington, D.C.)
27. See Nick Schou's 2006 book *Kill the Messenger: How the CIA's Crack Cocaine Controversy Destroyed Journalist Gary Webb* (New York: National Books, 2006).
28. Levitt and Dubner, 100.
29. Levitt and Dubner, 103.
30. Levitt and Dubner, 103.
31. Levitt and Dubner, 212.
32. Levitt and Dubner, 122.
33. Levitt and Dubner, 122.
34. As of this writing (December 4, 2010, which happens to be Jay-Z's forty-first birthday), the book had risen to the third position on *The New York Times* list of bestselling hardcover nonfiction works.
35. Carter, 10.
36. Carter, 18–19.
37. Carter, 71.
38. Carter, 12.
39. Clockers, and clocking, refer to street-level crack dealing by organized teams who put in long hours distributing "work" (drugs) to customers. An eightball is an eighth of an ounce of cocaine.

40. Carter, 12–13.
41. Carter, 12.
42. Carter, 17.
43. Carter, 17.
44. Carter, 26.
45. Forbes 400. *The Richest People in America.* 2010 Edition. Special issue.
46. Carter, 158.
47. Carter, 130.
48. Carter, 265.
49. Chang, 137.
50. Lipsitz, 5.
51. Lipsitz, 4.
52. Lipsitz, 5.

PART 10

The Gender of Politics and the Politics of Gender

The realm of the political—of states and governments, welfare and warfare, taxes and services, elected and electorate—has always been gendered. What governments *do* is gendered—whether it is diplomacy with other nations, engaging in warfare, or administering justice and collecting revenues (all considered masculine) as opposed to ensuring fairness in the legal and political process, spending on social services, health care, education, or families and providing a social safety net—that is, *caring* for its citizens (all coded as feminine).

Just as political institutions are gendered, so too are the politicians and those who elect them. Voters are categorized into smaller constituencies, and gender turns out to be an increasingly important one. Women not only represent more than half the electorate, but an increasingly independent one. Did you know that a century ago, the campaign against woman suffrage argued that allowing women to vote would be unfair to single men? You see, we believe in "one man, one vote" but allowing women to vote would be like giving married men two votes, since those critics couldn't conceive that a woman could possibly even consider voting differently than her husband!

The essays in this section approach the gender of politics at all these levels. Georgina Waylen provides a more general overview of the interplay between gender and politics. Carol Cohn explores the gendered state, and the ways in which defense intellectuals enacted gender scripts in deciding their battle strategies. And Ann C. McGinley offers an astute analysis of three of the more visible women on the current political stage.

Gender Matters in Politics

GEORGINA WAYLEN

ALTHOUGH often ignored by both practitioners and academics alike, gender matters in both politics as a practice and politics as a subject of study. As Karen Beckwith has claimed:

> [Gender is] conventionally understood as sets of socially constructed meanings of masculinities and femininities . . . these meanings emerge from stereotypes about male and female behavior; from characteristics and behaviors conventionally associated with women and men; from normative assumptions about appropriate behaviors of men and women; from assumptions about biological difference; and from social structures of power and difference.[1]

The importance of gender in politics can easily be demonstrated anecdotally through a few contemporary examples. If we look at some of the key issues that divide American politics today—whether it is reproductive rights most controversially in the form of abortion, or same-sex marriage—we can see that many of the 'culture wars' are fought over the hugely gendered issues of sexuality and bodily autonomy. Or to take another case, as we have seen recently in France as well as in other parts of Europe, the veil (and a number of other debates around multiculturalism) is another arena where women's bodies and the attendant claims to emancipate women are also a symbolic battleground. Finally, in a somewhat different vein, the recent rhetoric in the United Kingdom that 'we are all in it together' obscures the very differentiated impact of the current spending cuts and austerity programmes. It is clear that some groups are affected far more adversely than others, and many women who make up a large proportion of public sector workers and the majority of lone parents and poor pensioners have been particularly hard hit and affected in different ways to men.

This article aims to demonstrate more systematically how both the practice and study of politics are gendered in significant ways, but also how both have changed over last thirty years. It will then highlight some of the challenges that remain, and end by outlining some of the key themes that should be part of any ongoing agenda to improve our understanding of the important ways in which politics is gendered.

Fundamental to this endeavour is the realisation that we cannot look at the practice and the discipline of politics as separate from one another. The challenges facing both politics as a practice and politics as an academic discipline with regard to gender issues are intertwined. This has always been the case and particularly so after the advent of second wave feminism in late 1960s/early 1970s. The development of much of the academic work on gender and politics was fundamentally informed by second wave feminism and its aftermath. For the majority of gender scholars, the 'personal is political'—their academic interests are intertwined and inseparable from their political commitment. Their endeavour is therefore one of 'critical scholarship,' similar to other scholars within a progressive tradition and encapsulated by Robert Cox when he famously argued that scholarship is 'always *for* someone and *for* some purpose.'[2] This does not mean a critical scholarship that is not rigorous and methodologically robust, even if it does not adhere to a model of social science that

Georgina Waylen, "Gender Matters in Politics." *The Political Quarterly* 83 (January 2012): 24–32.

is 'scientific' or correspond to an idealised conception of science.

The starting point of many gender and politics scholars echoes Theda Skocpol's sentiment that the aim of research is to look at real world problems and puzzles; in this case, to understand gender inequality and how to tackle it.[3] As such, the methods chosen to undertake this endeavour need to fit the problem that is being explored. These can be quantitative or qualitative or, as is increasingly common, a mixture of both quantitative and qualitative methods. So most gender and politics scholars are pluralists and believe that rational choice bargaining models have their place, as does regression analysis, even if they do not personally use them, as there is no template of how to do research with predetermined models or methods.

Politics as a Discipline and a Practice

Our starting point is the big changes both in politics as practice and politics as discipline over last thirty years. We now see more women as prominent politicians, heads of state and of international bodies in Europe, Africa and Latin America, ranging from Angela Merkel in Germany to Dilma Roussef, an ex-guerrilla and recently elected president of Brazil, and Christine Lagarde at the International Monetary Fund. The parity cabinet (2004/08) of Zapatero's socialist government in Spain contained equal numbers of male and female ministers and outraged the defence establishment with the appointment of a heavily pregnant woman as defence minister. There have also been some very distinguished and influential women political scientists (in 2009, the political scientist Elinor Ostrom became the first woman to win the Nobel Prize for economics). And academia as a whole has recently made some concerted efforts to create more of a level playing field with regard to women. It would be impossible to deny that there have been significant efforts and achievements, both in terms of increasing women's political representation and improving the opportunities for women scholars in academia in general.

However, both are still male-dominated even today. In the United Kingdom in 2011 there are 504 male, but only 144 women, MPs in Westminster (women currently make up only 22 per cent of the House of Commons). This is, however, the highest figure ever as the Conservatives doubled their number of women MPs to 49 (16 per cent of their total) and 31 per cent of Labour MPs are women after 2010 election (even if the number of female Liberal Democrat MPs declined from nine to seven). The last election also saw a large increase in the numbers of black and minority ethnic (BME) MPs. There are now 27 BME MPs (or 4.6 per cent of the total) of which nine are women (who comprise 33 per cent of all BME MPs and are made up of two Conservative and seven Labour MPs), so both main parties have a relatively larger proportion of female BME MPs than they do women MPs in general. However, the United Kingdom is still joint 51st in global league table of women's representation and the current coalition cabinet contains relatively few women ministers.

While important, it is not just a question of 'sheet numbers'—namely increasing the numbers of women in either sphere—that is not enough in itself. More profound changes are needed to both politics as a practice and politics as a discipline to make them more gender equitable. To facilitate this, it is important to understand what it is about politics as an academic discipline and politics as a practice and the ways in which the two interact that result in this overrepresentation of men.

If we first think about the nature of politics as a discipline, we can see that traditionally it has been based on very narrow definitions of what counts as politics. These core assumptions have their roots in the work of political theorists like Locke, who based many of their ideas on the analytical separation of the public and the private spheres—namely that citizens/heads of household (for which read 'men') were the ones who were active in the public sphere. This subsumed women (and also children) into the household / family within a private sphere where 'every man's home is his castle' and in which he can do as he pleases, free from the interference of the state.[4]

The notion of a separation of the public and private spheres has had a lasting impact on the real world. Women's roles and the assumptions made about their roles in the private sphere still impact on their roles in the public sphere. This does not play out in the same way for men. Very different assumptions are still made, for example, about men's caring responsibilities and what might be an appropriate job and working patterns. It continues to affect notions of what counts as politics and the political, which is still predominantly 'high politics' in the public sphere; who is seen as a suitable person to be involved in politics; and what are appropriate issues—often narrowly defined—that exclude certain activities and actors and embody particular notions of masculinity and femininity.

These ideas have again affected what has been deemed suitable subject matter for the discipline of politics. They have sometimes impacted too on methods that are used, privileging models that are based on assumptions about the individual as a supposedly 'rational' actor using a restrictive definition of 'rationality' and a notion of the individual more reminiscent of economics. And even although this individualist rational actor model has been increasingly criticised—not just by feminist scholars, but also by many economists—it remains pervasive. We are still living with the legacy of all these factors—the artificial separation of the public and private, the privileging of 'high politics' and the adoption of certain models of the individual that has made politics as a discipline somewhat different to sociology and anthropology and the other social sciences which find it easier to incorporate the private sphere and, as such, have also found it easier to take gender on board and include women in their disciplines.

If we turn to politics as practice, we see that these underlying assumptions are also reflected in the ways in which politics is practised. This has been the case whether it is the Tory party candidate selection committees that in the past were unashamed at looking askance at women aspiring to be candidates, accusing them of neglecting their homes and husbands (as revealed in Lovenduski and Norris' ground-breaking study in the mid-1990s).[5] Or that, for years, domestic violence was thought of as something with which the police should not interfere as it lay outside state jurisdiction in the realm of the private sphere. As recently as the 1960s it was commonplace for incidents to be considered 'only a domestic' and therefore not worthy of police action.

Those notions were profoundly shaken by second wave feminism with its slogan the 'personal is political.' Second wave feminism challenged the definitions of what activities and issues are legitimately seen as political. Of course, the women's movement, as it was known then, was part of the social movements, such as the civil rights and anti-war movements, that were challenging the status quo in 1960s and early 1970s, but it is also important to remember that the emergence of the women's movement itself was in part a reaction to the sexism within those other movements. The net result was to begin a rethink of our understanding of politics, what it means and how to do it.

Understanding Gender and Politics

To return to politics as discipline, we can see that much of the early gender and politics scholarship reflected these pressing real world issues and concerns and, as such, developed two major strands of research. The first aimed to show the importance of women's activism outside of the conventional political arena, thereby helping to redefine and broaden what counts as 'political.' The second strand focused on putting women back into analyses of conventional politics. Gender research highlighted different aspects of women's activism and women's movements defined in the broadest sense. One important avenue has shown the impact of the diverse activities and ideas that are often thought of as feminist. It demonstrated how feminist movements put important issues onto the political agenda. For example, it looked at the women's peace movement, epitomised by the Greenham Common Women in the mid-1980s, and also at the campaigns around abortion and reproductive choice, domestic violence and pornography. Second, gender research highlighted the successful policy outcomes that resulted from feminist campaigns to get reform, such as the criminalisation of rape in marriage. Finally, it examined the often autonomous organisations that provided important services such as women's refuges and rape crisis centres.

However, researchers did not just focus on what we might think of as 'middle-class' feminists and activists. They also looked at other groups of organised women who would not necessarily be associated with feminism, such as the Asian women strikers at Grunwick in West London in the late 1970s, and as we have recently seen portrayed in the film *Made in Dagenham*, women in the 1968 Fords machinists strike. The women machinists went on strike to get their work sewing car seat covers re-graded from the 'unskilled' 'B' category (where they received only 85 per cent of the male 'B' rate) in which it had been placed by Ford management (and condoned by the trade unions).

The activities of the diverse women's movements organising in other contexts apart from these First World ones have also been highlighted, examining, for example, women's organising in transitions to democracy. Although initially ignored by many democratisation scholars, a range of women's movements played an important part in the breakdown of some non-democratic regimes, often bringing about the 'end of fear' as some of the first protesters on the streets. Perhaps the best known are human rights protesters such as the Madres of the Plaza de Mayo in Argentina, who, at great personal risk, demonstrated publicly to demand the return of their missing children (and in some cases, grandchildren) who had been 'disappeared' by the repressive military regime. These movements also included feminist organisations. Feminists in Chile, for example, held one of the first demonstrations against the Pinochet regime to celebrate International Women's Day in 1983 and campaigned using the slogan 'democracy in the home and in the country.'[6]

In addition to their important role in the broader opposition movements against dictatorship, organised women also tried to ensure that the outcomes of some transitions would bring positive change, such as increased political representation for women and the provision of greater rights in the post-transition period. In both the Chilean and South African transitions, women, organised as women, attempted to influence the developing political processes, but with varying results. More recently we have seen similar efforts in Tunisia and Egypt. Egyptian women organised after only one woman was appointed to the transitional government and a clause was inserted into the draft constitution that appeared to preclude women from becoming president.

If we turn to the second strand of gender research, we see that initially gender scholars also focused on putting women back into the study of conventional politics. They challenged the widely held stereotypes about women's political activity and behaviour in the conventional political arena. Scholars looked at women's political behaviour and the differences between theirs' and that of men without either unthinkingly assuming that the two were the same or seeing women as somehow a deviant version of the male norm. So, for example, classic early gender work on voting behaviour demonstrated that when education, age and background are controlled for, men and women vote at same rates, thereby disproving earlier beliefs that the women's rate was lower than the men's.

However, women and men do often exhibit differences in their political attitudes and behaviour, but not necessarily in the ways that had been assumed (for example, for a long time it had been thought that women were inherently more right wing than men). Men and women do tend to line up on issues in different ways, but not necessarily on a straight forward left-right split (such as on law and order). Recent opinion polls in the United Kingdom, for example, showed that while 52 per cent of men initially supported bombing of Libya, only 35 per cent of women did.[7] Women also exhibit higher levels of support for welfare spending and are more worried than men about impact of cuts, particularly in education and health. At the last British general election, maybe unsurprisingly, men were more likely to vote Conservative than women, who were more likely to vote Liberal Democrat or Labour. In the 25–34 age group this 'gender gap' was extremely stark. The Conservatives had an 18 per cent lead among 25–34 year-old men, while in contrast Labour had an 11 per cent lead among women in the same age group.[8]

Not unexpectedly perhaps, a lot of emphasis has also been put by gender scholars on looking at women's representation—particularly in legislatures. They have focused on analysing and explaining the differing levels of women's representation, including so-called 'descriptive representation' and the strategies that can be introduced to increase the number of women in legislatures, and particularly on measures such as electoral quotas. Attention has subsequently turned to look more at 'substantive representation' and the question of how far women MPs can (or even should) represent 'women's interests' however these are defined (which is always a thorny and controversial issue for gender scholars); and at the level of women MPs needed (the 'critical mass') to achieve this substantive representation of women. More recently, in part reflecting real world changes, there has been more interest in women in the executive, such as the New Labour women ministers in the core executive in the United Kingdom.[9]

As a consequence of the efforts of activists and academics, we now know a lot about women's movements and the impact of women activists in a wide array of political arenas—for example, in bringing about changes in norms, such as the recognition of women's rights as human rights and anti-domestic violence measures, on a global level. We have also seen the introduction of a raft of equality measures. Equality legislation, gender mainstreaming and women's policy agencies (WPAs) have been established in most of the world and endorsed by international and regional bodies like the European Union and the United Nations. Electoral quotas, too, are now wide-spread globally (adopted in roughly half the world's parliaments) and although controversial, it is clear that if they are well designed, actually implemented and enforced (unlike in France and Brazil), they are one of the most effective ways to 'fast track' increases in women's representation.

The Remaining Challenges

There is still much that remains to be done both to politics as a practice and the study of politics. First, there has been increased contestation around issues associated with gender equality in politics as practice. As far back as the early 1990s an 'unholy alliance' emerged at the Cairo population conference when President Bush, the Vatican and the Islamic lobby united to fight against moves to improve women's reproductive rights. In addition to the very differentiated impact of current austerity measures by gender (as well as by race, class and disability), the current British coalition government has abolished the Women's National Commission as part of its 'bonfire of the quangos'; made big cuts to the single equality body, the Equality and Human Rights Commission; and ignored the gender equality duty introduced by the previous Labour government in its 2010 emergency budget (later condoned by courts). In 2011 it began consulting about abolishing the Equality Act altogether as part of its drive to cut 'red tape.' These changes are all happening in the context of an increasingly sexualised culture in which issues of violence, rape, street harassment and pornography have increased and taken on new forms. Yet the seeming decline in feminism that had been much vaunted until recently appears to be reversing with evidence of a resurgence of interest, particularly among younger women, with the emergence of new forms of activism, blogs, demonstrations and actions taking advantage of technologies such as social media. The 'slutwalks' that took place all over the world in the summer of 2011 following remarks made by a senior policeman to Canadian law students are further evidence of this.

Much also remains to be done to improve politics as a discipline. Although gender is now accepted as part of the discipline of politics, the gender and politics scholarship still runs largely parallel to and ignored by the majority of scholars. The best that usually happens is that there is one gender lecture or chapter in a book separate from the 'real business' of the discipline that remains unchanged. However, there are also a number of important challenges facing gender scholarship itself. The efficacy of its analyses could be improved if it broadened its focus in several ways. First, as many have argued, too little attention was given initially to issues of intersectionality. Much of the pioneering gender scholarship was primarily focused on the issues and concerns of white, middle-class women. Scholars were then forced to pay more attention to race, class, sexuality and disability by vocal black, working-class, lesbian and postcolonial feminists. Men's and women's voting behaviour, for example, can only be understood if you also look at a range of factors that include race, class and age, and not just gender. Analyses now are, on the whole, better than they were, but there is still some way to go.

Second, and again this is not a new insight, more attention needs to be given to men and masculinity, although this lack is understandable given the early focus on 'putting women back in.' Men and masculinity should now be problematised more.

Third, gender scholarship has sometimes been too narrowly focused on gender equality policies and bodies. This is not to deny the excellent work that has been done on WPAs and equality measures, but this has sometimes been at the expense of examining how wider policies and institutions are gendered and the implications of this. Perhaps not surprisingly, this focus has also not been of much interest to the wider discipline or encouraged more attention to be given to the gender and politics scholarship, which if we want gender scholarship to play a bigger role within the discipline as a whole, is surely important.

Finally, there has been a tendency to be overly focused on actors. No one would deny that actors, and certain actors in particular, are hugely important in both the conventional or nonconventional political arenas, but sometimes the research has been overly concerned with counting the numbers of women ('descriptive representation') first in legislatures, and now in some of the recent work on women in executives. Or it has occasionally been marred by a certain degree of wish fulfilment/celebration. Feminist scholars understandably have been looking for significance in the actions of women activists or legislators, underpinned by a belief that they either are/or should be doing things in 'women's interests,' and this has sometimes driven the underlying research questions and research focus.

We therefore need more sophisticated analyses to satisfactorily explain some of the important real world puzzles in which we are interested—in particular, why is it that certain outcomes are not as they were hoped for or expected? Why, for example, have some women's movements not had the successes they were anticipating in terms of policy results after successful mobilisations? Or why have WPAs/state feminism also not been able to effect the transformations that had been hoped for by those who set up the machineries, despite all their efforts? Or, indeed, why has the introduction of quotas and increases in women's representation not been as transformative as had been hoped for by some of their supporters? And why it is that the outcomes of some transitions to democracy have been more positive in gender terms than others? Why was there initial disillusionment in Chile when it appeared that women's movements, despite their high levels of mobilisation and attempts to influence the transition, had not achieved many of their goals?

The Way Forward

I end with some suggestions about the way forward to deal with some of these challenges. We need a more sophisticated understanding of actors, and to move more fully away from a preoccupation with 'sheer numbers.' This has already been happening with the increasing discussion of 'critical actors,' who are of course men as well as women, in a range of locations. To go back to the case of the Ford machinists mentioned earlier, we need also to explore the key role played by Barbara Castle as Secretary of State for Employment both in resolving that dispute and in creating the resulting Equal Pay Act that was passed in 1970. How influential was her role in ensuring that change occurred? We also need better analyses of structures and institutions and their interaction with actors or, at the very least, how structures shape actors' goals and strategies. I am advocating a return to the old conundrum of structure and agency and their inter-relationship.

We also need better analyses of institutions. In common with much of social science, there has been an institutional turn in gender and politics. Feminist Institutionalists are developing a wider understanding of institutions as gendered structures and an improved understanding of how they operate in gendered ways. Underlying this development is a belief that if we understand institutions as rules, norms and practices, then we need to know how both formal and informal rules, norms and practices are gendered. In particular, one of the key questions for all institutionalists, as well as feminist ones, is how to explain institutional change. How and why does change occur (or not occur)? Linked to that, how is it that institutions can remain the same? We need to explain institutional continuity—or, more accurately, institutional reproduction. How do institutions actually sustain and reproduce themselves? This can help us to understand why attempts to change institutions do not have the desired results or why the creation of new institutions does not always fulfil the hopes of their designers.

If we take the example of one relatively new institution—the Scottish Parliament—it is clear that after a lot of input from women activists, the institutional designers made conscious efforts to make it more gender friendly with a less adversarial style both in its design and procedures, more family friendly working hours and conditions, as well as an electoral system that might lead to the election of more women than in Westminster. This initially did result in relatively high levels of women's representation, but according to Fiona Mackay what we have seen is a 'nested newness.'[10] The institution was not created with a blank slate. Westminster still formed the default position for Scottish parliamentary practice and process. For example, First Minister's Questions, modelled on Prime Minister's Questions (PMQs), were introduced later on to promote a sense of theatricality that was felt to be lacking. And despite the new formal rules, old practices such as Labour party candidate selection procedures slipped back in, contributing to a reduction in the number of women MSPs. We need to understand more fully how and why this could happen.

Feminist institutionalists are trying to investigate different forms of institutional change using approaches derived from some of the latest work by new institutionalist and, in particular, historical institutionalist research.[11] Whether it is of the rapid exogenous kind witnessed when new institutions displace old ones, as we have seen, for example, in some post conflict settlements, or of a more gradual endogenous kind, when actors use or convert existing institutions for new purposes, research like this is often difficult to do. It needs approaches with which political scientists are often unfamiliar (and often rather sceptical about) in order to unravel how longstanding pre-existing informal institutions may undermine formal rule changes. We also need to investigate the roles played by the sometimes seemingly irrelevant rituals and practices; and many of these rules, norms and practices are often hard to discern because they are so taken for granted as to render them almost invisible.

Overall it is vitally important that we improve our understanding of how both politics as a practice and politics as a discipline are gendered; and to do this we need to improve our analyses of actors, institutions and the interaction between them. This will help us to change both the practice and the discipline of politics for the better.

Notes

1. K. Beckwith, 'Comparative politics and the logics of a comparative politics of gender', *Perspectives on Politics*, vol. 8, no. 1, 2010, p. 160.
2. R. Cox, 'Critical political economy', in B. Hettne, ed., *International Political Economy: Understanding Global Disorder*, London, Zed Press, 1995, p. 31.
3. T. Skocpol, 'Doubly engaged social science', in J. Mahoney and D. Rueschememyer, eds, *Comparative Historical Analysis in the Social Sciences*, Cambridge, Cambridge University Press, 2003, pp. 407–28.
4. C. Pateman, 'Feminist critiques of the public/private dichotomy', in S. Benn and G. Gaus, eds, *The Public and Private in Social Life*, London, Croom Helm, 1983, pp. 281–303.
5. P. Norris and J. Lovenduski, *Political Recruitment: Gender, Race and Class in British Parliament*, Cambridge, Cambridge University Press, 1995.
6. G. Waylen, 'Women and democratization: conceptualizing gender relations in transition politics', *World Politics*, vol. 46, no. 3, 1994, pp. 573–88.
7. Com Res Poll, 25–27 March 2011.
8. IPSOS MORI General Election Outcome, 2010.
9. C. Annesley and F. Gains, 'The core executive: gender, power and change', *Political Studies*, vol. 58, no. 5, 2010, pp. 909–29.
10. F. Mackay 'Institutionalising the "new politics" in post devolution Scotland: nested newness and the limits of gendered institutional change'. Paper presented at ECPG, Budapest, 2009.
11. M. L. Krook and F. Mackay, eds, *Gender, Politics and Institutions: Towards a Feminist Institutionalism*, Basingstoke, Palgrave Macmillan, 2011.

Wars, Wimps, and Women: Talking Gender and Thinking War

CAROL COHN

I start with a true story, told to me by a white male physicist:

> Several colleagues and I were working on modeling counterforce attacks, trying to get realistic estimates of the number of immediate fatalities that would result from different deployments. At one point, we remodeled a particular attack, using slightly different assumptions, and found that instead of there being thirty-six million immediate fatalities, there would only be thirty million. And everybody was sitting around nodding, saying, "Oh yeah, that's great, only thirty million," when all of a sudden, I heard what we were saying. And I blurted out, "Wait, I've just heard how we're talking—Only thirty million! Only thirty million human beings killed instantly?" Silence fell upon the room. Nobody said a word. They didn't even look at me. It was awful. I felt like a woman.

The physicist added that henceforth he was careful to never blurt out anything like that again.

During the early years of the Reagan presidency, in the era of the Evil Empire, the cold war, and loose talk in Washington about the possibility of fighting and "prevailing" in a nuclear war, I went off to do participant observation in a community of North American nuclear defense intellectuals and security affairs analysts—a community virtually entirely composed of white men. They work in universities, think tanks, and as advisers to government. They theorize about nuclear deterrence and arms control, and nuclear and conventional war fighting, about how to best translate military might into political power; in short, they create the discourse that underwrites American national security policy. The exact relation of their theories to American political and military practice is a complex and thorny one; the argument can be made, for example, that their ideas do not so much shape policy decisions as legitimate them after the fact. But one thing that is clear is that the body of language and thinking they have generated filters out to the military, politicians, and the public, and increasingly shapes how we talk and think about war. This was amply evident during the Gulf War: Gulf War "news," as generated by the military briefers, reported by newscasters, and analyzed by the television networks' resident security experts, was marked by its use of the professional language of defense analysis, nearly to the exclusion of other ways of speaking.

My goal has been to understand something about how defense intellectuals think, and why they think that way. Despite the parsimonious appeal of ascribing the nuclear arms race to "missile envy," I felt certain that masculinity was not a sufficient explanation of why men think about war in the ways that they do. Indeed, I found many ways to understand what these men were doing that had little or nothing to do with gender. But ultimately, the physicist's story and others like it made confronting the role of gender unavoidable. Thus, in this paper I will explore gender discourse and its role in shaping nuclear and national security discourse.

I want to stress, this is not a paper about men and women, and what they are or are not like. I will not be claiming that men are aggressive and women peace loving. I will not even address the question of how men's and women's relations to war may differ, nor the different propensities they may have to committing acts of violence. Neither will I pay more than passing attention to the question which so often crops up in discussions of war and gender, that is, would it be a more peaceful world if our national leaders were women? These questions are valid and important, and recent feminist discussion of them has been complex, interesting, and contentious. But my focus is elsewhere. I wish to direct attention away from gendered individuals and toward gendered discourses. My question is about the way that civilian defense analysts think about war, and the ways in which that thinking is shaped not by their maleness (or, in extremely rare instances, femaleness), but by the ways in which gender discourse intertwines with and permeates that thinking.

Let me be more specific about my terms. I use the term *gender* to refer to the constellation of meanings that a given culture assigns to biological sex differences. But more than that, I use gender to refer to a symbolic system, a central organizing discourse of culture, one that not only shapes how we experience and understand ourselves as men and women, but that also interweaves with other discourses and shapes *them*—and therefore shapes other aspects of our world—such as how nuclear weapons are thought about and deployed.

So when I talk about "gender discourse," I am talking not only about words or language but about a system of meanings, of ways of thinking, images and words that first shape how we experience, understand, and represent ourselves as men and women, but that also do more than that; they shape many other aspects of our lives and culture. In this symbolic system, human characteristics are dichotomized, divided into pairs of polar opposites that are supposedly mutually exclusive: mind is opposed to body; culture to nature; thought to feeling; logic to intuition; objectivity to subjectivity; aggression to passivity; confrontation to accommodation; abstraction to particularity; public to private; political to personal, ad nauseam. In each case, the first term of the "opposites" is associated with male, the second with female. And in each case, our society values the first over the second.

I break it into steps like this—analytically separating the *existence* of these groupings of binary oppositions, from the association of each group with a gender, from the valuing of one over the other, the so-called male over the so-called female, for two reasons: first, to try to make visible the fact that this system of dichotomies is encoding many meanings that may be quite unrelated to male and female bodies. Yet once that first step is made—the association of each side of those lists with a gender—gender now becomes tied to many other kinds of cultural representations. If a human activity, such as engineering, fits some of the characteristics, it becomes gendered.

My second reason for breaking it into those steps is to try to help make it clear that the meanings can flow in different directions; that is, in gender discourse, men and women are supposed to exemplify the characteristics on the lists. It also works in reverse, however; to evidence any of these characteristics—to be abstract, logical or dispassionate, for example—is not simply to be those things, but also to be manly. And to be manly is not simply to be manly, but also to be in the more highly valued position in the discourse. In other words, to exhibit a trait on that list is not neutral—it is not simply displaying some basic human characteristic. It also positions you in a discourse of gender. It associates you with a particular gender, and also with a higher or lower valuation.

In stressing that this is a *symbolic* system, I want first to emphasize that while real women and men do not really fit these gender "ideals," the existence of this system of meaning affects all of us, nonetheless. Whether we want to or not, we see ourselves and others against its templates, we interpret our own and others' actions against it. A man who cries easily cannot avoid in some way confronting that he is likely to be seen as less than fully manly. A woman who is very aggressive and incisive may enjoy that quality in herself, but the fact of her aggressiveness does not exist by itself; she cannot avoid having her own and others' perceptions of that quality of hers, the meaning it has for people, being in some way mediated by the discourse of gender. Or, a different kind of example: Why does it mean one thing when George Bush gets teary-eyed in public, and something entirely different when Patricia Shroeder does? The same act is viewed through the lens of gender and is seen to mean two very different things.

Second, as gender discourse assigns gender to human characteristics, we can think of the discourse as something we are positioned *by.* If I say, for example, that a corporation should stop dumping toxic waste because it is damaging the creations of mother earth (i.e., articulating a valuing and sentimental vision of nature), I am speaking in a manner associated with women, and our cultural discourse of gender positions me as female. As such I am then associated with the whole constellation of traits—irrational, emotional, subjective, and so forth—and I am in the devalued position. If, on the other hand, I say the corporation should stop dumping toxic wastes because I have calculated that it is causing $8.215 billion of damage to eight nonrenewable resources, which should be seen as equivalent to lowering the GDP by 0.15 percent per annum (i.e., using a rational, calculative mode of thought), the discourse positions me as masculine—rational, objective, logical, and so forth—the dominant, valued position.

But if we are positioned *by* discourses, we can also take different positions *within* them. Although I am female, and this would "naturally" fall into the devalued term, I can choose to "speak like a man"—to be hard-nosed, realistic, unsentimental, dispassionate. Jeanne Kirkpatrick is a formidable example. While we can choose a position in a discourse, however, it means something different for a woman to "speak like a man" than for a man to do so. It is heard differently.

One other note about my use of the term *gender discourse:* I am using it in the general sense to refer to the phenomenon of symbolically organizing the world in these gender-associated opposites. I do not mean to suggest that there is a single discourse defining a single set of gender ideals. In fact, there are many specific discourses of gender, which vary by race, class, ethnicity, locale, sexuality, nationality, and other factors. The masculinity idealized in the gender discourse of new Haitian immigrants is in some ways different from that of sixth-generation white Anglo-Saxon Protestant business executives, and both differ somewhat from that of white-male defense intellectuals and security analysts. One version of masculinity is mobilized and enforced in the armed forces in order to enable men to fight wars, while a somewhat different version of masculinity is drawn upon and expressed by abstract theoreticians of war.

Let us now return to the physicist who felt like a woman: what happened when he "blurted out" his sudden awareness of the "only thirty million" dead people? First, he was transgressing a code of professional conduct. In the civilian defense intellectuals' world, when you are in professional settings you do not discuss the bloody reality behind the calculations. It is not required that you be completely unaware of them in your outside life, or that you have no feelings about them, but it is required that you do not bring them to the foreground in the context of professional activities. There is a general awareness that you *could not* do your work if you did; in addition, most defense intellectuals believe that emotion and description of human reality distort the process required to think well about nuclear weapons and warfare.

So the physicist violated a behavioral norm, in and of itself a difficult thing to do because it threatens your relationships to and your standing with your colleagues.

But even worse than that, he demonstrated some of the characteristics on the "female" side of the dichotomies—in his "blurting" he was impulsive, uncontrolled, emotional, concrete, and attentive to human bodies, at the very least. Thus, he marked himself not only as unprofessional but as feminine, and this, in turn, was doubly threatening. It was not only a threat to his own sense of self as masculine, his gender identity, it also identified him with a devalued status—of a woman—or put him in the devalued or subordinate position in the discourse.

Thus, both his statement, "I felt like a woman," and his subsequent silence in that and other settings are completely understandable. To have the strength of character and courage to transgress the strictures of both professional and gender codes *and* to associate yourself with a lower status is very difficult.

This story is not simply about one individual, his feelings and actions; it is about the role of gender discourse. The impact of gender discourse in that room (and countless others like it) is that some things get left out. Certain ideas, concerns, interests, information, feelings, and meanings are marked in national security discourse as feminine, and are devalued. They are therefore, first, very difficult to *speak,* as exemplified by the physicist who felt like a woman. And second, they are very difficult to *hear,* to take in and work with seriously, even if they *are* said. For the others in the room, the way in which the physicist's comments were marked as female and devalued served to delegitimate them. It is almost as though they had become an accidental excrescence in the middle of the room. Embarrassed politeness demanded that they be ignored.

I must stress that this is not simply the product of the idiosyncratic personal composition of that particular room. In other professional settings, I have experienced the feeling that something terribly important is being left out and must be spoken; and yet, it has felt almost physically impossible to utter the words, almost as though they could not be pushed out into the smooth, cool, opaque air of the room.

What is it that cannot be spoken? First, any words that express an emotional awareness of the desperate human reality behind the sanitized abstractions of death and destruction—as in the physicist's sudden vision of thirty million rotting corpses. Similarly, weapons' effects may be spoken of only in the most clinical and abstract terms, leaving no room to imagine a seven-year-old boy with his flesh melting away from his bones or a toddler with her skin hanging down in strips. Voicing concern about the number of casualties in the enemy's armed forces, imagining the suffering of the killed and wounded young men, is out of bounds. (Within the military itself, it is permissible, even desirable, to attempt to minimize immediate civilian casualties if it is possible to do so without compromising military objectives, but as we learned in the Persian Gulf War, this is only an extremely limited enterprise; the planning and precision of military targeting does not admit of consideration of the cost in human lives of such actions as destroying power systems, or water and sewer systems, or highways and food distribution systems.) Psychological effects—on the soldiers fighting the war or on the citizens injured, or fearing for their own safety, or living through tremendous deprivation, or helplessly watching their babies die from diarrhea due to the lack of clean water—all of these are not to be talked about.

But it is not only particular subjects that are out of bounds. It is also tone of voice that counts. A speaking style that is identified as cool, dispassionate, and distanced is required. One that vibrates with the intensity of emotion almost always disqualifies the speaker, who is heard to sound like "a hysterical housewife."

What gets left out, then, is the emotional, the concrete, the particular, the human bodies and their vulnerability, human lives and their subjectivity—all of which are marked as feminine in the binary dichotomies of gender discourse. In other words, gender discourse informs and shapes nuclear and national security discourse, and in so doing creates silences and absences. It keeps things out of the room, unsaid, and keeps them ignored if they manage to get in. As such, it degrades our ability to think *well* and *fully* about nuclear weapons and national security, and shapes and limits the possible outcomes of our deliberations.

What becomes clear, then, is that defense intellectuals' standards of what constitutes "good thinking" about weapons and security have not simply evolved out of trial and error; it is not that the history of nuclear discourse has been filled with exploration of other ideas, concerns, interests, information, questions, feelings, meanings and stances which were then found to create distorted or poor thought. It is that these options have been *preempted* by gender discourse, and by the feelings evoked by living up to or transgressing gender codes.

To borrow a term from defense intellectuals, you might say that gender discourse becomes a "preemptive deterrent" to certain kinds of thought.

Let me give you another example of what I mean—another story, this one my own experience:

One Saturday morning I, two other women, and about fifty-five men gathered to play a war game designed by the RAND Corporation. Our "controllers" (the people running the game) first divided us up into three sets of teams; there would be three simultaneous games being played, each pitting a Red Team against a Blue Team (I leave the reader to figure out which color represents which country). All three women were put onto the same team, a Red Team.

The teams were then placed in different rooms so that we had no way of communicating with each other, except through our military actions (or lack of them) or by sending demands and responses to those demands via the controllers. There was no way to negotiate or to take actions other than military ones. (This was supposed to simulate reality.) The controllers then presented us with maps and pages covered with numbers representing each side's forces. We were also given a "scenario," a situation of escalating tensions and military conflicts, starting in the Middle East and spreading to Central Europe. We were to decide what to do, the controllers would go back and forth between the two teams to relate the other team's actions, and periodically the controllers themselves would add something that would ratchet up the conflict—an announcement of an "intercepted intelligence report" from the other side, the authenticity of which we had no way of judging.

Our Red Team was heavily into strategizing, attacking ground forces, and generally playing war. We also, at one point, decided that we were going to pull our troops out of Afghanistan, reasoning it was bad for us to have them there and that the Afghanis had the right to self-determination. At another point we removed some troops from Eastern Europe. I must add that later on my team was accused of being wildly "unrealistic," that this group of experts found the idea that the Soviet Union might voluntarily choose to pull troops out of Afghanistan and Eastern Europe so utterly absurd. (It was about six months before Gorbachev actually did the same thing.)

Gradually our game escalated to nuclear war. The Blue Team used tactical nuclear weapons against our troops, but our Red Team decided, initially at least, against nuclear retaliation. When the game ended (at the end of the allotted time) our Red Team had "lost the war" (meaning that we had political control over less territory than we had started with, although our homeland had remained completely unviolated and our civilian population safe).

In the debriefing afterwards, all six teams returned to one room and reported on their games. Since we had had absolutely no way to know why the other team had taken any of its actions, we now had the opportunity to find out what they had been thinking. A member of the team that had played against us said, "Well, when he took his troops out of Afghanistan, I knew he was weak and I could push him around. And then, when we nuked him and he didn't nuke us back, I knew he was just such a wimp, I could take him for everything he's got and I nuked him again. He just wimped out."

There are many different possible comments to make at this point. I will restrict myself to a couple. First, when the man from the Blue Team called me a wimp (which is what it felt like for each of us on the Red Team—a personal accusation), I felt silenced. My reality, the careful reasoning that had gone into my strategic and tactical choices, the intelligence, the politics, the morality—all of it just disappeared, completely invalidated. I could not explain the reasons for my actions, could not protest, "Wait, you idiot, I didn't do it because I was weak, I did it because it made sense to do it that way, given my understandings of strategy and tactics, history and politics, my goals and my values." The protestation would be met with knowing sneers. In this discourse, the coding of an act as wimpish is hegemonic. Its emotional heat and resonance is like a bath of sulfuric acid: it erases everything else.

"Acting like a wimp" is an *interpretation* of a person's acts (or, in national security discourse, a country's acts, an important distinction I will return to later). As with any other interpretation, it is a selection of one among many possible different ways to understand something—once the selection is made, the other possibilities recede into invisibility. In national security discourse, "acting like a wimp," being insufficiently masculine, is one of the most readily available interpretive codes. (You do not need to do participant observation in a community of defense intellectuals to know this—just look at the "geopolitical analyses" in the media and on Capitol Hill of the way in which George Bush's military intervention in Panama and the Persian Gulf War finally allowed him to beat the "wimp factor.") You learn that someone is being a wimp if he perceives an international crisis as very dangerous and urges caution; if he thinks it might not be important to have just as many weapons that are just as big as the other guy's; if he suggests that an attack should not necessarily be answered by an even more destructive counterattack; or, until recently, if he suggested that making unilateral arms reductions might be useful for our own security. All of these are "wimping out."

The prevalence of this particular interpretive code is another example of how gender discourse affects the quality of thinking within the national security community, first, because, as in the case of the physicist who "felt like a woman," it is internalized to become a self-censor; there are things professionals simply will not *say* in groups, options they simply will not argue nor write about, because they know that to do so is to brand themselves as wimps. Thus, a whole range of inputs is left out, a whole series of options is foreclosed from their deliberations.

Equally, if not more damagingly, is the way in which this interpretive coding not only limits what is *said,* but even limits what is *thought.* "He's a wimp" is a phrase that *stops* thought. When we were playing the game, once my opponent on the Blue Team "recognized the fact that I was a wimp," that is, once he interpreted my team's actions through the lens of this common interpretive code in national security discourse, he *stopped thinking;* he stopped looking for ways to understand what we were doing. He did not ask, "Why on earth would the Red Team do that? What does it tell me about them, about their motives and purposes and goals and capabilities? What does it tell me about their possible understandings of *my* actions, or of the situation they're in?" or any other of the many questions that might have enabled him to revise his own conception of the situation or perhaps achieve his goals at a far lower level of violence and destruction. Here, again, gender discourse acts as a preemptive deterrent to thought.

"Wimp" is, of course, not the only gendered pejorative used in the national security community; "pussy" is another popular epithet, conjoining the imagery of harmless domesticated (read demasculinized) pets with contemptuous reference to women's genitals. In an informal setting, an analyst worrying about the other side's casualties, for example, might be asked, "What kind of pussy are you, anyway?" It need not happen more than once or twice before everyone gets the message; they quickly learn not to raise the issue in their discussions. Attention to and care for the living, suffering, and dying of human beings (in this case, soldiers and their families and friends) is again banished from the discourse through the expedient means of gender-bashing.

Other words are also used to impugn someone's masculinity and, in the process, to delegitimate his position and avoid thinking seriously about it. "Those Krauts are a bunch of limp-dicked wimps" was the way one U.S. defense intellectual dismissed the West German politicians who were concerned about popular opposition to Euromissile deployments. I have heard our NATO allies referred to as "the Euro-fags" when they disagreed with American policy on such issues as the Contra War or the bombing of Libya. Labeling them "fags" is an effective strategy; it immediately dismisses and trivializes their opposition to U.S. policy by coding it as due to inadequate masculinity. In other words, the American analyst need not seriously confront the Europeans' arguments, since the Europeans' doubts about U.S. policy obviously stem not from their reasoning but from the "fact" that they "just don't have the stones for war." Here, again, gender discourse deters thought.

"Fag" imagery is not, of course, confined to the professional community of security analysts; it also appears in popular "political" discourse. The Gulf War was replete with examples. American derision of Saddam Hussein included bumper stickers that read "Saddam, Bend Over." American soldiers reported that the "U.S.A." stenciled on their uniforms stood for "Up Saddam's Ass." A widely reprinted cartoon, surely one of the most multiply offensive that came out of the war, depicted Saddam bowing down in the Islamic posture of prayer, with a huge U.S. missile, approximately five times the size of the prostrate figure, about to penetrate his upraised bottom. Over and over, defeat for the Iraqis was portrayed as humiliating anal penetration by the more powerful and manly United States.

Within the defense community discourse, manliness is equated not only with the ability to win a war (or to "prevail," as some like to say when talking about nuclear war); it is also equated with the willingness (which they would call courage) to threaten and use force. During the Carter administration, for example, a well-known academic security affairs specialist was quoted as saying that "under Jimmy Carter the United States is spreading its legs for the Soviet Union." Once this image is evoked, how does rational discourse about the value of U.S. policy proceed?

In 1989 and 1990, as Gorbachev presided over the withdrawal of Soviet forces from Eastern Europe, I heard some defense analysts sneeringly say things like, "They're a bunch of pussies for pulling out of Eastern Europe." This is extraordinary. Here they were, men who for years railed against Soviet domination of Eastern Europe. You would assume that if they were politically and ideologically consistent, if they were rational, they would be applauding the Soviet actions. Yet in their informal conversations, it was not their rational analyses that dominated their response, but the fact that for them, the decision for war, the willingness to use force, is cast as a question of masculinity—not prudence, thoughtfulness, efficacy, "rational" cost-benefit calculation, or morality, but masculinity.

In the face of this equation, genuine political discourse disappears. One more example: After Iraq invaded Kuwait and President Bush hastily sent U.S. forces to Saudi Arabia, there was a period in which the Bush administration struggled to find a convincing political justification for U.S. military involvement and the security affairs community debated the political merit of U.S. intervention. Then Bush set the deadline, January 16, high noon at the OK Corral, and as the day approached conversations changed. More of these centered on the question compellingly articulated by one defense intellectual as "Does George Bush have the stones for war?" This, too, is utterly extraordinary. This was a time when crucial political questions abounded: Can the sanctions work if given more time? Just what vital interests does the United States actually have at stake? What would be the goals of military intervention? Could they be accomplished by other means? Is the difference between what sanctions might accomplish and what military violence might accomplish worth the greater cost in human suffering, human lives, even dollars? What will the long-term effects on the people of the region be? On the ecology? Given the apparent successes of Gorbachev's last-minute diplomacy and Hussein's series of nearly daily small concessions, can and should Bush put off the deadline? Does he have the strength to let another leader play a major role in solving the problem? Does he have the political flexibility to not fight, or is he hellbent on war at all costs? And so on, ad infinitum. All of these disappear in the sulfuric acid test of the size of Mr. Bush's private parts.

I want to return to the RAND war simulation story to make one other observation. First, it requires a true confession: *I was stung by being called a wimp.* Yes, I thought the remark was deeply inane, and it infuriated me. But even so, I was also stung. Let me hasten to add, this was not because my identity is very wrapped up with not being wimpish—it actually is not a term that normally figures very heavily in my self-image one way or the other. But it was impossible to be in that room, hear his comment and the snickering laughter with which it was met, and not to feel stung, and humiliated.

Why? There I was, a woman and a feminist, not only contemptuous of the mentality that measures human beings by their degree of so-called wimpishness, but also someone for whom the term *wimp* does not have a deeply resonant personal meaning. How could it have affected me so much?

The answer lies in the role of the context within which I was experiencing myself—the discursive framework. For in that room I was not "simply me," but I was a participant in a discourse, a shared set of words, concepts, symbols that constituted not only the linguistic possibilities available to us but also constituted me in that situation. This is not entirely true, of course. How I experienced myself was at least partly shaped by other experiences and other discursive frameworks—certainly those of feminist politics and antimilitarist politics; in fact, I would say my reactions were predominantly shaped by those frameworks. But that is quite different from saying "I am a feminist, and that individual, psychological self simply moves encapsulated through the world being itself"—and therefore assuming that I am unaffected. No matter who else I was at that moment, I was unavoidably a participant in a discourse in which being a wimp has a meaning, and a deeply pejorative one at that. By calling me a wimp, my accuser on the Blue Team positioned me in that discourse, and I could not but feel the sting.

In other words, I am suggesting that national security discourse can be seen as having different positions within it—ones that are starkly gender coded; indeed, the enormous strength of their evocative power comes from gender. Thus, when you participate in conversation in that community, you do not simply choose what to say and how to say it; you advertently or inadvertently choose a position in the discourse. As a woman, I can choose the "masculine" (thoughtful, rational, logical) position. If I do, I am seen as legitimate, but I limit what I can say. Or, I can say things that place me in the "feminine" position—in which case no one will listen to me.

Finally, I would like to briefly explore a phenomenon I call the "unitary masculine actor problem" in national security discourse. During the Persian Gulf War, many feminists probably noticed that both the military briefers and George Bush himself frequently used the singular masculine pronoun "he" when referring to Iraq and Iraq's army. Someone not listening carefully could simply assume that "he" referred to Saddam Hussein. Sometimes it did; much of the time it simply reflected the defense community's characteristic habit of calling opponents "he" or "the other guy." A battalion commander, for example, was quoted as saying "Saddam knows where we are and we know where he is. We will move a lot now to keep him off guard."[1] In these sentences, "he" and "him" appear to refer to Saddam Hussein. But, of course, the American forces had *no idea* where Saddam Hussein himself was; the singular masculine pronouns are actually being used to refer to the Iraqi military.

This linguistic move, frequently heard in discussions within the security affairs and defense communities, turns a complex state and set of forces into a singular male opponent. In fact, discussions that purport to be serious explorations of the strategy and tactics of war can have a tone which sounds more like the story of a sporting match, a fistfight, or a personal vendetta.

> I would want to suck him out into the desert as far as I could, and then pound him to death.[2]
>
> Once we had taken out his eyes, we did what could be best described as the "Hail Mary play" in football.[3]
>
> [I]f the adversary decides to embark on a very high roll, because he's frightened that something even worse is in the works, does grabbing him by the scruff of the neck and slapping him up the side of the head, does that make him behave better or is it plausible that it makes him behave even worse?[4]

Most defense intellectuals would claim that using "he" is just a convenient shorthand, without significant import or effects. I believe, however, that the effects of this usage are many and the implications far-reaching. Here I will sketch just a few, starting first with the usage throughout defense discourse generally, and then coming back to the Gulf War in particular.

The use of "he" distorts the analyst's understanding of the opposing state and the conflict in which they are engaged. When the analyst refers to the opposing state as "he" or "the other guy," the image evoked is that of a person, a unitary actor; yet states are not people. Nor are they unitary and unified. They comprise complex, multifaceted governmental and military apparatuses, each with opposing forces within it, each, in turn, with its own internal institutional dynamics, its own varied needs in relation to domestic politics, and so on. In other words, if the state is referred to and pictured as a unitary actor, what becomes unavailable to the analyst and policy-maker is a series of much more complex truths that might enable him to imagine many more policy options, many more ways to interact with that state.

If one kind of distortion of the state results from the image of the state as a person, a unitary actor, another can be seen to stem from the image of the state as a specifically *male* actor. Although states are almost uniformly run by men, states are not men; they are complex social institutions, and they act and react as such. Yet, when "he" and "the other guy" are used to refer to states, the words do not simply function as shorthand codes; instead, they have their own entailments, including assumptions about how men act, which just might be different from how states act, but which invisibly become assumed to be isomorphic with how states act.

It also entails emotional responses on the part of the speaker. The reference to the opposing state as "he" evokes male competitive identity issues, as in, "I'm not going to let him push me around," or, "I'm not going to let him get the best of me." While these responses may or may not be adaptive for a barroom brawl, it is probably safe to say that they are less functional when trying to determine the best way for one state to respond to another state. Defense analysts and foreign policy experts can usually agree upon the supreme desirability of dispassionate, logical analysis and its ensuing rationally calculated action. Yet the emotions evoked by the portrayal of global conflict in the personalized terms of male competition must, at the very least, exert a strong pull in exactly the opposite direction.

A third problem is that even while the use of "he" acts to personalize the conflict, it simultaneously abstracts both the opponent and the war itself. That is, the use of "he" functions in very much the same way that discussions about "Red" and "Blue" do. It facilitates treating war within a kind of game-playing model, A against B, Red against Blue, he against me. For even while "he" is evocative of male identity issues, it is also just an abstract piece to be moved around on a game board, or, more appropriately, a computer screen.

That tension between personalization and abstraction was striking in Gulf War discourse. In the Gulf War, not only was "he" frequently used to refer to the Iraqi military, but so was "Saddam," as in "Saddam really took a pounding today," or "Our goal remains the same: to liberate Kuwait by forcing Saddam Hussein out."[5] The personalization is obvious: in this locution, the U.S. armed forces are not destroying a nation, killing people; instead, they (or George) are giving Saddam a good pounding, or bodily removing him from where he does not belong. Our emotional response is to get fired up about a bully getting his comeuppance.

Yet this personalization, this conflation of Iraq and Iraqi forces with Saddam himself, also abstracts: it functions to substitute in the mind's eye the abstraction of an implacably, impeccably evil enemy for the particular human beings, the men, women, and children being pounded, burned, torn, and eviscerated. A cartoon image of Saddam being ejected from Kuwait preempts the image of the blackened, charred, decomposing bodies of nineteen-year-old boys tossed in ditches by the side of the road, and the other concrete images of the acts of violence that constitute "forcing Hussein [*sic*] out of Kuwait."[6] Paradoxical as it may seem, in personalizing the Iraqi army as Saddam, the individual human beings in Iraq were abstracted out of existence.

In summary, I have been exploring the way in which defense intellectuals talk to each other—the comments they make to each other, the particular usages that appear in their informal conversations or their lectures. In addition, I have occasionally left the professional community to draw upon public talk about the Gulf War. My analysis does *not* lead me to conclude that "national security thinking is masculine"—that is, a separate, and different, discussion. Instead, I have tried to show that national security discourse is gendered, and that it matters. Gender discourse is interwoven through national security discourse. It sets fixed boundaries, and in so doing, it skews what is discussed and how it is thought about. It shapes expectations of other nations' actions, and in so doing it affects both our interpretations of international events and conceptions of how the United States should respond.

In a world where professionals pride themselves on their ability to engage in cool, rational, objective calculation while others around them are letting their thinking be sullied by emotion, the unacknowledged interweaving of gender discourse in security discourse allows men to not acknowledge that their pristine rational thought is in fact riddled with emotional response. In an "objective" "universal" discourse that valorizes the "masculine" and deauthorizes the "feminine," it is only the "feminine" emotions that are noticed and labeled as emotions, and thus in need of banning from the analytic process. "Masculine" emotions—such as feelings of aggression, competition, macho pride and swagger, or the sense of identity resting on carefully defended borders—are not so easily noticed and identified as emotions, and are instead invisibly folded into "self-evident," so-called realist paradigms and analyses. It is both the interweaving of gender discourse in national security thinking *and* the blindness to its presence and impact that have deleterious effects. Finally, the impact is to distort, degrade, and deter roundly rational, fully complex thought within the community of defense intellectuals and national security elites and, by extension, to cripple democratic deliberation about crucial matters of war and peace.

Notes

1. Chris Hedges, "War Is Vivid in the Gun Sights of the Sniper," *New York Times,* February 3, 1991, A1.
2. General Norman Schwarzkopf, National Public Radio broadcast, February 8, 1991.
3. General Norman Schwarzkopf, CENTCOM News Briefing, Riyadh, Saudi Arabia, February 27, 1991, p. 2.
4. Transcript of a strategic studies specialist's lecture on NATO and the Warsaw Pact (summer institute on Regional Conflict and Global Security: The Nuclear Dimension, Madison, Wisconsin, June 29, 1987).
5. Defense Secretary Dick Cheney, "Excerpts from Briefing at Pentagon by Cheney and Powell," *New York Times,* January 24, 1991, A 11.
6. Scarry explains that when an army is described as a single "embodied combatant," injury, (as in Saddam's "pounding"), may be referred to but is "no longer recognizable or interpretable." It is not only that Americans might be happy to imagine Saddam being pounded; we also on some level know that it is not really happening, and thus need not feel the pain of the wounded. We "respond to the injury... as an imaginary wound to an imaginary body, despite the fact that that imaginary body is itself made up of thousands of real human bodies" (Elaine Scarry, *Body in Pain: The Making and Unmaking of the World* [New York: Oxford, 1984], p. 72).

Hillary Clinton, Sarah Palin, and Michelle Obama: Performing Gender, Race, and Class on the Campaign Trail

ANN C. McGINLEY

Introduction

In *Our First Unisex President?: Black Masculinity and Obama's Feminine Side*,[1] Frank Rudy Cooper posits that President Obama consciously performed a feminine identity[2] in order to navigate the tricky waters of race and gender in the presidential election.[3] Cooper notes that white popular culture perceives black masculinity as bipolar: there are "good blacks" and "bad blacks."[4] According to white popular culture, the "Bad Black Man is animalistic, sexually depraved, and crimeprone."[5] His counterpart, the "Good Black Man distances himself from black people and emulates white views."[6]

Because of the image of the Bad Black Man, black men must take care not to show excessive anger.[7] Obama is known for his "cool," a somewhat feminine identity performance that comforts white citizens and distances him from the "dangerous" Bad Black Man. His conciliatory empathic style and willingness to negotiate with "evil" foreign powers made him appear more feminine that his female rival, Hillary Clinton, who performed a more masculine demeanor and espoused a tough stance toward Iran.

Although Obama's more feminine presentation downplayed white fear, it was also risky to his candidacy because it raised the question of whether he is masculine enough for the job.[8] Ironically, perhaps it was his blackness that imbued Obama with sufficient masculinity to successfully walk the tightrope between being too masculine and too feminine, too black and too white. Cooper theorizes that Obama's success may actually have a gender- and race-bending effect, by removing stigma from "the feminine" and opening space for all persons, especially men who do not conform to masculine gender norms, to perform their identities in unconventional ways.[9]

While Cooper's essay does not directly address women in the political spotlight, its focus on Obama's feminization provokes the question of how white women and women of color can successfully perform their gender and racial identities in the public arena. The 2008 Presidential campaign highlighted three strong, interesting, and very different women—Hillary Clinton, Sarah Palin and Michelle Obama—who negotiated identity performances in the political limelight. Because of their diverse backgrounds, experience,[10] and ages, an examination of how these three women performed their identities and the public response to them offers a rich understanding of the changing nature of gender, gender roles, age, sexuality and race in our culture. This study suggests that Professor Cooper's optimism that Obama's race and gender performances may have removed the stigma from "the feminine" may be misplaced, at least when it comes to women aspiring to high public office. Indeed, a review of the public's reaction to the gender, race, and class performances of these three women confirms that women aspiring to high

This chapter was originally published by the Denver University Law Review at Ann C. McGinley, "Hillary Clinton, Sarah Palin, and Michelle Obama: Performing Gender, Race, and Class on the Campaign Trail." *Denver University Law Review* 86 (2009).

public office continue to suffer intense public scrutiny of their gender performances.

Part I provides background for my analysis of these three women's identity performances and the public reactions to them. It discusses contemporary theories of identity performance, gender and leadership. Part II applies the theory and research to the public careers of Hillary Clinton, Sarah Palin and Michelle Obama and observes that although women still face significant obstacles in the public arena, there may be more acceptance of women as political candidates than in the past. The essay concludes that the candidacies of Hillary Clinton and Sarah Palin and the public appearance of Michelle Obama as a successful career woman, who is also a wife of the winning candidate, have moved women one step further toward equality in the national political scene. Moreover, the public may be more willing to consider women's identities to include a mix of both traditional family values and competence in one's career. By the same token, women's identities as aspiring political leaders continue to be problematic, and require women to negotiate a double bind: if they are too feminine, they are deemed incompetent. If they are too masculine, they are considered not likeable.

I. Identity, Gender and Leadership

This part explains the theory of identity performance at work—how individuals work their identities in workplaces. It then applies identity performance theory to the political arena, exploring the differences between performing one's identity at work and in political campaigns. Finally, it discusses research on gender and leadership that demonstrates that women in leadership positions are judged more harshly than their male counterparts. Because this is true, it is considerably more difficult for women leaders to navigate and perform their identities.

A. Performing and Negotiating Identities in Workplaces

In *Working Identities*, Devon Carbado and Mitu Gulati explain that individual identities are not fixed, but are negotiated and performed.[11] For example, a person negotiates between his sense of self or self identity and his attributed identity, how others perceive him. In order to achieve certain reactions from others, an individual may perform identity in different ways. For example, in a firm that values hard work, an employee may work late, mention to colleagues how tired she is because she has worked late so many evenings, or leave her office light on so it appears that she is there even after she leaves the office.[12] Carbado and Gulati posit that all individuals perform identity, but they demonstrate that when outsiders[13] perform their identities at work, they risk working against some stereotypes but confirming others.[14] For example, if a workplace values hard work, creativity and a quick intelligence, a black law firm associate may find performing his identity difficult. If he chooses to counter the stereotype that blacks are lazy by working diligently, his behavior may confirm in the minds of his employers the stereotype that blacks are not as intelligent or as quick as whites.[15]

All of these behaviors by outsiders entail not only public performances but also internal negotiations with the self about how much an employee is willing or able to perform an identity desired by the firm without losing a sense of self.[16] Because members of outsider groups "perceive themselves as subject to negative stereotypes, they are also likely to feel the need to do significant amounts of 'extra' identity work to counter those stereotypes."[17]

Even while attempting to conform to institutional values, an outsider might compromise herself and confirm negative stereotypes. If the workplace values collegiality, for example, a young woman may choose to go out to bars after work with her colleagues, even though she sees herself as a loner or a homebody. This identity performance, however, may confirm the stereotype that women are sexual objects, and interested in having affairs with co-workers, especially if she joins in sexual banter or willingly goes to a strip club with her colleagues in order to fit in. Unlike a man who engages in the same behavior, the woman is viewed negatively because the firm defines collegiality in terms of what it perceives to be appropriate male behavior. Because societal norms continue to govern our judgments, a woman performing similar behavior runs the risk of disrespect.

Stereotypes are comparative measurements to the standard bearer: the white, middle class, heterosexual male. When we judge a black man as not hard-working or a Korean woman as too hard-working, the judgment is based on the view that the ideal worker[18]—the white, middle class, heterosexual male—works the proper amount. But the irony is that even if it were possible to engage in exactly the same behavior as their white, heterosexual, male counterparts, outsiders may fail to meet community norms. In cases where the amount of work performed is measured, stereotypes about outsiders would likely color insiders' perceptions of how much the outsiders worked. Stereotypes involving more qualitative judgments than the number of hours that a person works are even more difficult and risky to defeat. Professor Cooper makes this point when he explains that in order to avoid the stereotype of the Bad Black Man, President Obama performs his identity as less masculine, more feminine and community-oriented.[19] Obama learned early in life that in order to accomplish his goal of living within the white society, he had to give comfort to whites and allay their fears that he may be an aggressive black male.[20]

B. Performing Political Identities During Presidential Campaigns

People perform their identities in the workplace; in the political arena, too, all politicians attempt to perform their identities to please the electorate. During the long campaigns for President and Vice President, this is a complicated endeavor because unlike workplaces that have certain identifiable preferences and norms that remain fairly constant over time, the electorate represents a variety of different groups with different values whose views often change in reaction to ongoing current events. A candidate must perform an identity that is sufficiently constant to convey an air of confidence and imperviousness, but also sufficiently flexible to appeal to different constituencies and to respond to changing events. As events change, a candidate must adapt, performing identity in slightly different ways, while avoiding a charge that he or she is an opportunist. Getting "stuck" in an identity that is perceived to be inflexible and out of date, while simultaneously acting in erratic fashion as some claim that John McCain did, can be deadly to a campaign.

Because the roles of President and Vice President are gendered male and raced white, and because there has never been a woman or minority President or Vice President, an outsider running for these offices encounters obstacles that go beyond those faced by a heterosexual white male in negotiating and performing identity as a political candidate. Voters often claim to vote based on the candidates' personal characteristics rather than on the issues.[21] Because of stereotypes about the proper roles of men and women, and the normal cognitive process of categorizing, these voters will likely judge the candidates' personal characteristics through a distorted lens. This lens can lead to biased evaluations of the candidates even though the voter is unaware of the error.[22]

C. Gender Roles and Leadership

Notwithstanding sociologists' and feminist scholars' conclusion that gender roles are learned behaviors,[23] people generally view gender as naturally derived from biological sex, and expect others to behave in a manner that conforms to their biological sex. Women in leadership positions and doing jobs that are traditionally male are judged much more harshly than men. In "Goldberg" studies, for example, a participant evaluates resumes reflecting equivalent education and experience designated with men's and women's names. When the job is identified as requiring "male" characteristics, participants consistently rank the men's resumes more highly than the women's, even though the resumes are identical.[24]

Gender roles and social incongruity explain these disparate results. Gender roles are widely held beliefs about the attributes of men and women and the roles they play in society. They are based on descriptive and injunctive norms: descriptive norms describe how women and men behave while injunctive norms are consensual expectations about how men or women should behave.[25]

Most descriptive and injunctive norms about the sexes pertain to communal and agentic[26] behavior. Women are described as communal and are expected to act in others-oriented ways. The descriptive norm sees women as followers and as inappropriate leaders.[27] The injunctive norm forbids women from behaving in agentic ways; women who behave agentically are rated worse than men who engage in the same behavior.[28] Men are described as agentic and expected to exhibit aggression, ambition, dominance, independence, and self-confidence.[29] Women, on the other hand, are considered to be untrustworthy and are disliked in leadership roles, especially if their agentic style "entails exerting control and dominance over others."[30]

Role congruity theory considers congruity or incongruity between the gender role and leadership roles.[31] Studies demonstrate that people see leadership roles as primarily agentic, and therefore requiring masculine traits.[32] Women are typically at a disadvantage when applying for or working in leadership positions because their gender role conflicts with the qualities needed to perform the job. Male group members evaluate women's work as less competent than that of men, even when the work is equally competent.[33] Moreover, women receive less attention at work for the same idea expressed the same way as men do.[34]

When there is clear evidence that a woman is a good leader, she still experiences a disadvantage due to a conflict between leadership qualities and her gender role.[35] Even when women are perceived as successful,[36] both men and women rank them as less likeable than men based on their success at a "man's job."[37]

This research demonstrates the difficulties caused by gender role incongruity that women experience when they work in men's jobs or take on leadership positions. The public perceives these positions as requiring masculine traits, and masculine traits are considered to be superior to feminine traits.[38] By the same token, the public responds negatively to a woman who is too masculine. Because of these restraints, a woman who seeks a leadership position may try to perform her identity in a way that demonstrates her strength and ability to perform the requirements of the position without appearing too masculine. This is a difficult performance that, to date, has proved elusive to women running for President or Vice President. It is complicated by the changing societal views of women and their roles in the family and the workplace and by the public's and the media's hyper-vigilance of women's appearance and dress.

II. Applying the Research to Hillary Clinton, Sarah Palin, and Michelle Obama

This part looks at specific examples of Hillary Clinton, Sarah Palin and Michelle Obama, three women who have attempted to negotiate the tricky waters of gender and authority, and how the public reacted to their gender and race performances.

A. Hillary Clinton

Hillary Clinton was an accomplished lawyer and partner in a well-known law firm, graduate of prestigious Wellesley College and Yale Law School, first lady of Arkansas, law professor, and mother of one child in 1992 when her husband, Bill Clinton, announced his candidacy for President of the United States. Earlier, in 1975, when she married Bill Clinton in Arkansas, Hillary Rodham retained her own surname, a practice that was common among feminists of her age in order to avoid losing their identity and independence. Because of a chilly reception in Arkansas to her use of her birth name, presumably because she was too independent of her husband, she soon switched her name to Hillary Clinton.

Hillary Rodham graduated from law school in 1973, a time when women began to attend law school in significant numbers. She was among the first generation of women to enjoy the benefits of the civil rights laws' guarantees of equal employment and educational opportunities for women.[39] Despite the legal protections, "second wave" feminists[40] like Hillary Clinton had to fight for equal rights in employment. Many women believed that they had to work harder than their male counterparts to earn respect. Because these women were path breakers at work, many downplayed their roles as mothers and wives and sexual partners. These women performed their identities at work as efficient, hard workers because of the fear that colleagues would not take them seriously if they viewed them first as mothers and wives and second as professionals. While the second wave feminists matured during an era of more sexual freedom than their mothers, those who entered the professions performed their identities at work as asexual beings in order to avoid being treated as sexual objects by their male counterparts. Included in this asexual performance was work clothing that deemphasized their sexuality.

Clinton, the first career woman to serve as first lady, had significant problems performing her gender on the national scene. From almost the moment she appeared on the political scene as Bill Clinton's wife, Hillary suffered the public's disregard. Much of the reaction to Hillary stemmed from deep-seeded unconscious and conscious biases against independent women who perform their gender identities in professional and independent ways, and are not sufficiently submissive to their husbands.[41] Hillary Clinton's identity performance was a threat to men and to those women who had made a choice to live in more traditional marriages. These women viewed their work lives outside the home, if they worked outside the home at all, as secondary to their husbands' careers, and they spent a large percentage of their time caring for their husbands and children.

Hillary Clinton also made some serious political mistakes in Bill Clinton's campaign, which contributed to the public's dislike of her. Early in the campaign, Hillary performed her identity in a way that showed disrespect for other women's choices and that made men uncomfortable. She disparaged non-working mothers when she asked sarcastically whether she should have stayed home and baked cookies instead of working as a lawyer.[42] Many members of the public interpreted this comment as demonstrating Clinton's lack of empathy with stay-at-home moms who struggled to manage their households and care for their children. Clinton added salt to the national wound by stating that she was not like Tammy Wynette, the famous country singer who sang "Stand by Your Man."[43]

Once she became the first lady, Hillary Clinton's high-powered education and career as a corporate lawyer and her husband's insistence that she was an equal partner in the White House, combined with her disastrous attempt to redesign the health care system, led to even greater unpopularity. The public perceived her as arrogant and condescending, masculine and too rough around the edges. Distancing herself from her feminine side in order to demonstrate her strength, Clinton was the butt of ridicule and scorn. Her popularity ratings plummeted.

It was not until she suffered the humiliating experience of her husband's public infidelity that she became more popular. Thus, as a victim, and specifically as a woman victim, Hillary became more human and more likeable. This response to Hillary Clinton's personal problems is ironic given that she had struggled to perform her identity to demonstrate her strength and invulnerability. It was her feminine vulnerability that raised her popularity in the ratings. Nonetheless, while this vulnerability was an attractive trait in a first lady, it may not have been attractive in a candidate for the Senate or the Presidency. For this reason, Hillary Clinton performed her gender in order to command respect and attention without inviting scorn. Like Obama's mission, this is a tricky assignment. Clinton downplayed her femininity and emphasized her toughness in order to compensate for being a woman, and to earn respect for her competence and experience. Masculinities research demonstrates that men and women value masculinity more than femininity, so it makes sense that a woman candidate should put forth a masculine image.[44] By the same token, it is dangerous to do so because people do not like women who are too masculine.[45] Hillary Clinton, therefore, found herself in a double bind: Either act more feminine and be judged incompetent or act masculine and be considered unlikeable.

As a senator, Clinton gained respect of her colleagues, but the public was initially very cool to her Presidential campaign. As is typically demonstrated by the leadership research, the populace considered her competent, but not necessarily likeable, because she was a woman acting as a leader in a masculine job. She came across as a genderless policy wonk. She had a slight rise in New Hampshire when she showed her feminine side by breaking down on the campaign trail, and a significant rise in popularity when she found her voice half-way through the primaries. Instead of humorless and shrill, Clinton now was strong and she empathized with the economic problems of Middle America. This was a very risky balancing act like the one in which Barack Obama had to engage. Like Obama, who was criticized for "playing the race card" when he mentioned that he did not look like the other men on the paper currency, an allusion to his race,[46] Hillary was criticized for "playing the gender card" when she talked about the "all-boys' club of politics" to students at Wellesley.[47] The public, evidently, did not want the candidates to make the electorate confront its unconscious racial and gender biases. A silent pact between the electorate and the candidates required the candidates to perform their identities and to design their candidacies to appear "beyond gender" and "beyond race." Nonetheless, gender and race were constant subtexts of the campaigns.

Hillary Clinton was able to retain her strength, but soften and feminize her image by expressing concern for families in the industrial states who were in tough economic straits. But she also used Barack Obama as a foil in performing her identity. She avoided a too-feminine appearance and sought to demonstrate strength by criticizing Barack Obama and portraying him as inexperienced and not tough enough to do the job. In this way, as Professor Cooper mentions, Hillary was often considered the tougher and more masculine candidate in the democratic primary.

Throughout her career, Hillary Clinton suffered criticism for her dress and appearance. During her campaign for President, she was criticized for her pant suits, a symbol of women's empowerment since the 1960's.[48] This criticism demonstrates the bind that women often face when they appear in public. The public evaluates women's competence and authority based partially on their clothing.[49] Community norms for women's dress and appearance are stricter than those for men's. While men are more often rated as "average" in looks, their female counterparts are rated more frequently as "above average" and "below average."[50] This double standard creates an additional burden on women running for public office. A sixty year old woman who apparently struggles with her weight, Clinton may not have gained public approval for her clothes even if she had dressed in high style feminine clothing. The pant suit was her uniform, like the men's suits were their uniforms. Men, however, are considered more powerful and sexy as they age, while women lose their appeal as their waists thicken and their hair turns grey. Clinton showed her masculine toughness by wearing pants, while distinguishing herself as feminine by choosing pant suits of many brilliant colors.

Hillary Clinton's experience demonstrates that "second wave" brand of feminism is dead, at least when it comes to public acceptance of a woman candidate running for high public office. As a candidate, Clinton was considered unattractive when she emphasized her asexuality, toughness and competence, while downplaying her softer side—the considerable empathy she has for children and families. As she demonstrated more empathy, she became more acceptable to the public. Thus, the double bind played itself out in Hillary Clinton's campaign. While she did not negotiate the tricky waters perfectly, she learned as her campaign progressed to appear more feminine and less as a woman acting tough.

B. Sarah Palin

Unlike Hillary Clinton, the nation has known Sarah Palin for only a short time. When John McCain announced her as his running mate, the curiosity about Sarah Palin, a moose-hunting, conservative, forty-four year old woman who had served as Alaska's Governor for two years, was intense. Palin electrified the Republican Convention during her acceptance speech in which she consciously performed her gender and class identities and walked a fine line between being assertive and masculine and retaining her femininity. She performed her female gender by dressing in a feminine but professional way, wearing her hair long around her shoulders and by emphasizing her role as a mother of five children. She made deferential comments about her husband—that he was her "guy." She acted as the supportive wife in praise of her running mate, John McCain. But as she smiled in a feminine manner, she adopted a tough, masculine style, lambasting Barack Obama, and talking about his community organizing in a disparaging and condescending manner. She jokingly referred to herself as a "hockey mom" stating that the only difference between a hockey mom and a pit bull is lipstick. In pit bull style, Palin repeatedly attacked Barack Obama. After her attack and her speech were over, Palin carefully resumed her feminine performance, holding her infant son on stage as her other four children and her husband surrounded her. Her lipstick still shone through.

Throughout the campaign and after losing the election, Palin performed her gender and class. During the Vice Presidential candidates' debate, Palin asked Vice Presidential candidate Joe Biden if she could call him "Joe," winked at the audience, made overt entreaties to the "Joe-six packs" who were watching, and attacked Joe Biden repeatedly. Palin continued the fierce attacks on Obama in masculine style, accusing him of "palling around with terrorists" and questioning his patriotism. In contrast, she simultaneously presented herself as a maverick, a mother and a wife. Upon losing the election, Palin performed her gender by inviting reporters to interview her while she prepared dinner in the kitchen of her home.

Sarah Palin is an appealing personality because of her good looks, her quick smile, her careful grooming and her ability to use her gender to soften an extraordinary toughness. She is also appealing in a populist way, a Western woman who is a member of the National Rifle Association, who knows how to gut a moose and prefers moose stew to more delicate foods. But her femininity is not at risk because she makes clear her pro-life stance and her lived experience of giving birth to an infant, knowing that he had Down Syndrome. Thus, Palin performs her femininity in the most important arena—in her role as mother. While she has tough traits and practices, she is not threatening because she has not broken with her "natural" role. She is still a feminine woman in dress and lifestyle, in her role as mother, in her belief in her family, and in her deference to her man. Her pit bull manner on the job can be "cute" and non-threatening but effective because, in the end, she defers to her god, her running mate, her pastor and her husband. Even when faced with the challenge of a seventeen year-old daughter who was pregnant out of wedlock, Palin performed in a post-feminist and yet traditional way. She welcomed the new infant into her family and supported her daughter while simultaneously rejecting the possibility of an abortion.[51]

Palin's gender performance starkly contrasts with that of Hillary Clinton. While Hillary Clinton used a gender strategy of gender denial and avoidance, Palin, in subtle and not so subtle ways, emphasized her gender. Hillary Clinton offered a tough, masculine approach, downplaying her role as wife and mother and her sexuality. Even when she was younger, Clinton wore clothing that deemphasized her sexuality, and during her campaign for the presidency, she was criticized for her various colored pant suits and flat shoes. Sarah Palin, too, offered a tough approach, but it cannot be characterized as too masculine. She emphasized her role as mother and wife. She placed her family front and center. She dressed in designer jackets and tight, pencil-thin skirts with very high heels, wore her hair long or in a feminine upsweep, and displayed a significant amount of makeup. She was perceived as sexy by many who viewed her candidacy. In sum, Sarah Palin fully embraced her gender, and broke from the "second wave" feminist approach of downplaying gender.[52]

Palin's candidacy soon began to demonstrate weakness because of her lack of experience on the national scene, her lack of foreign policy knowledge, her perceived lack of curiosity, and the contradiction between her "down-home" style and her clothing expenditures.[53] She suffered severe criticism from liberals and conservatives, men and women.[54] The criticism is legitimate if directed at her lack of understanding of foreign affairs, especially because John McCain is advancing in years. By the same token, some argued that her experience was superior to Barack Obama's, and that she was treated worse than he, in part, because she is a woman.

Because of the obvious flaws in Palin's candidacy apart from gender, it is impossible to determine whether and to what extent her gender performance affected her candidacy, either positively or negatively. We do know, however, that Palin's candidacy sparked intense and protracted debate. Palin's style raises the question of whether a woman who performs her gender in a family-conscious, sexy fashion will simultaneously be able to prove to the electorate that she is competent, tough and skilled enough to serve as President of the United States. If so, Palin's popularity would signal a sea change in gender politics. It would confirm the death of "second wave" feminism's focus on gender androgyny and independence as symbols of competence and ability. Instead, it would likely show that a muted sexuality, combined with a willingness to conform to gender norms regarding motherhood may be attractive in a woman candidate so long as she also engages in masculine performances when necessary. The reaction to Palin's candidacy may indicate that women must accept the double bind and simultaneously negotiate a "split personality" where they at times emphasize their femininity and at other times their masculinity.[55] Palin's success resulted largely from her failure to challenge gender norms while strategically emphasizing femininity or masculinity as needed.

C. Michelle Obama

The public did not evaluate Michelle Obama as a political candidate because she did not run for political office herself. Nonetheless, the reaction to Michelle Obama's gender performance adds insight to changing gender roles and the importance of gender, age, and racial identity to the public. Like Hillary Clinton, Michelle Obama is an accomplished professional, career woman. A graduate of Princeton University and Harvard Law School, she worked at a prestigious law firm in Chicago, eventually moving to a job as an executive at a hospital. There was, however, less attention paid to Michelle Obama's career success during the campaign than to that of Hillary Clinton when Bill Clinton ran for the White House. This lack of media focus on Michelle Obama's accomplishments may indicate that America is more comfortable with women with careers today than it was sixteen years ago when Hillary and Bill Clinton surfaced on the national political scene. Moreover, Michelle Obama appears to be more relaxed and comfortable in her own gender skin than Hillary Clinton was. Hillary Clinton, who is a generation older than Michelle Obama, may have felt an anxiety and a need to prove herself as a professional, a need that is much less common with younger women today.

Notwithstanding her relatively relaxed demeanor at the time of the election, Michelle Obama's introduction to national politics was not smooth. At first, she was considered too outspoken and too critical of her husband, and perhaps not as domesticated as many of the public would like. She openly expressed ambivalence about his running for the presidency, discussed the tensions in their marriage because of his schedule, and admitted he had morning breath, snored, and left his dirty socks on the floor.[56] She received negative press attention when, referring to her husband's success in the primaries, she stated "for the first time in my adult life I am really proud of my country."[57] Reaction to this comment quickly turned to racial politics. She was characterized as an "angry" and "militant" woman, and one commentator mentioned that he did not want to do a "lynching" of Michelle Obama until the facts were clear.[58] Another article characterized her campaign opponents as depicting Michelle Obama "as an unpatriotic angry black woman nursing racial grievances despite her successful life story."[59] As Professor Verna Williams describes the criticism, "Mrs. Obama was an authentically and stereotypically Black woman: angry, sassy, unpatriotic, and uppity."[60]

Although a descendent of slaves and the daughter of working class parents from the South side of Chicago, Michelle Obama, according to her political enemies, had no right to criticize her country. In essence, many appeared to criticize her for her lack of gratitude to the country.[61] If she had not backed off and adopted a more pleasing, submissive stance, Michelle Obama may have ruined her husband's chances for the presidency, tainting him, as "too black."[62] Ironically, however, it may be that Michelle Obama's open and strong statements, especially those about her husband, actually helped her husband by feminizing him and reducing the chance that he would appear too aggressive or dangerous to the public.

By the time of the Democratic Convention at the end of August 2008, Michelle Obama had tamed her image. No longer was she the outspoken, critical wife. Now, she performed her identity as the supportive spouse who drew a touching picture of her husband's driving them home from the hospital with their new baby. The main focus on Michelle Obama ever since has been on her traditional roles as wife and mother and on her unique fashion style. Scores of articles have been written about her fashion sense, her down-to-earth yet stylish clothing, and the attention she has paid to selecting a school and creating a home in the White House for her children.[63]

Even though the country may be more comfortable with Michelle Obama as a traditional first lady and mother and wife of a traditional family, the fact is that she is a very accomplished career woman. Although she does not emphasize her accomplishments, neither she nor the press has hidden her career successes. Given her high-powered background, many have wondered what role she will play as first lady.[64] While it is unclear exactly what Michelle Obama's role will be, it seems highly unlikely that Michelle Obama will limit her sphere to that of the traditional mother and wife. Michelle Obama, however, appears to have learned the lesson that Hillary Clinton learned the hard way: to tread carefully into the gendered political arena. In fact, Michelle Obama, like Hillary Clinton and Sarah Palin, may have achieved her popularity by enacting a "split personality" once she and her backers realized the backlash created by her outspoken independence earlier in the campaign. Her comments over the past few months seem more traditionally female and they emphasize her role as wife and mother. She may, however, in the future show her more independent masculine side as she takes on policy issues of military families.

Conclusion

The stories of Hillary Clinton, Sarah Palin and Michelle Obama raise many questions about whether the country is ready to accept women as equal players in the highest political offices. Clinton lost her bid to a strong candidate, but she received more votes than any other woman in the history of the nation. And, her ability to connect with blue collar workers in the industrial states of the Northeast and Midwest demonstrates that the voters were able to overcome their unconscious or conscious biases that rate women as less qualified than men to lead. Contrary to the research results, many appeared to find Clinton both competent and likeable as her candidacy progressed, and she connected with voters on economic issues.

Palin's candidacy eventually imploded because of her lack of experience and readiness to be president, but the initial excitement about her candidacy suggests that the electorate may accept a woman who performs her identity by proudly displaying her family and acknowledging her roles as wife and mother. If Palin's failed candidacy demonstrates that the country will not accept women as tokens, but will apply the same standards of knowledge, competence and experience to women as to men, that is a good message.

Although she did not run for high office, Michelle Obama's experience during the campaign and after indicates that the country still wishes to see a traditional family in the White House. Her ultimate popularity, however, may result not only from her performance as a traditional wife and mother, but also from the comfortable manner in which she appears to embrace both her family and her professional lives.

If the country is ready for a woman President, the important question is whether the country will accept women without requiring performances that volley back and forth between feminine warmth and masculine toughness. Hillary Clinton's, Sarah Palin's and Michelle Obama's experiences indicate that, even today, women have to perform their identities in particular ways. They still suffer from the double bind, and must negotiate the fine line of acceptable identity behaviors. One thing we do know: "second wave" feminism is dead, rejected not only by men but also by women in the electorate. To the extent that "second wave" feminism imposed rigid restrictions on women to behave like men, perhaps this is not a bad thing. But to the extent that a masculine style is comfortable or natural for a particular woman, the new order may represent a rigid restriction as well. Moreover, with the demise of feminism, what is left? Will the electorate give women the opportunity to be themselves? This is unlikely, even if we could agree upon what "being oneself" would mean.

Notes

1. Frank Rudy Cooper, *Our First Unisex President?: Black Masculinity and Obama's Feminine Side*, 86 DENV. U. L. REV. 633 (2009).
2. Two types of identity include one's self identity and attributed identity, the impressions others have of a person. Identity is not a fixed phenomenon, but is created through negotiation (with oneself and others) and performance. Everyone works identity. Devon W. Carbado & Mitu Gulati, *Working Identity*, 85 CORNELL L. REV. 1259, 1261 n.2, 1263 (2000).
3. *See generally* Cooper, *supra* note 1.
4. Frank Rudy Cooper, *Against Bipolar Masculinity: Intersectionality, Assimilation, Identity Performance, and Hierarchy*, 39 U.C. DAVIS L. REV. 853, 857–59 (2006).
5. *Id.* at 857.
6. *Id.*
7. Cooper, *supra* note 1, at 654.
8. *Id.* at 633–34.
9. *Id.*
10. Hillary Clinton has served in three different public roles over a period of sixteen years. She served as first lady to Bill Clinton's Presidency, Junior Senator from New York, and candidate for President of the United States. She is now about to embark on a new role as Secretary of State.
11. Carbado & Gulati, *supra* note 2, at 1260–61, 1261 n.2.
12. *Id.* at 1260.
13. For this purpose, "outsiders" include white women, persons of color, and gays and lesbians. *Id.* at 1268.
14. *Id.* at 1262, 1270.
15. *Id.* at 1292.
16. *Id.* at 1264.
17. *Id.* at 1262.
18. JOAN WILLIAMS, UNBENDING GENDER 64–66 (2000) (describing the "ideal worker" norms in the workplace).
19. Cooper, *supra* note 1, at 636.
20. *Id.*
21. Carol Polsky, *Looking Past Economy*, NEWSDAY, Nov. 1, 2008, at A14; Posting of Stuart O'Neill to Democratic Daily, http://thedemocraticdaily.com/2008/10/10/mccain-trading-in-his-character-to-chase-the-news-cycle/ (Oct. 10, 2008, 4:45 p.m. EST) (using the title "McCain Trading In His Character To Chase The News Cycle").
22. Ann C. McGinley, *Viva la Evolucion!: Recognizing Unconscious Motive in Title VII*, 9 CORNELL J. L. & PUB. POL'Y 415, 421–46 (2000) (describing unconscious bias in decision making).
23. *E.g.*, Judith Lorber, *Beyond the Binaries: Depolarizing the Categories of Sex, Sexuality and Gender*, 66, SOC. INQUIRY 143, 146 (1996) ("[G]ender . . . is a social institution that establishes patterns of expectations for individuals, orders the social processes of everyday life, is built into the major social organizations of society such as the economy, ideology, the family, and politics, and is also an entity in and of itself.").
24. Alice H. Eagly & Steven J. Karau, *Role Congruity Theory of Prejudice Toward Female Leaders*, 109 PSYCHOL. REV. 573, 582, 587 (2002).
25. *Id.* at 574.
26. An "agentic" person is one who takes control and leads. *Id.*
27. *Id.* at 576.
28. *Id.* at 576–90.
29. *Id.*
30. Alice H. Eagly et al., *Transformational, Transactional, and Laissez-Faire Leadership Styles: A Meta-Analysis Comparing Women and Men*, 129 PSYCHOL. BULL. 569, 573 (2003).
31. *Id.* at 575.
32. *Id.*
33. *See* Martha Foschi et al., *Gender and Double Standards in the Assessment of Job Applicants*, 57 SOC. PSYCHOL. Q. 326, 337 (1994).
34. *See* VIRGINIA VALIAN, WHY SO SLOW?: THE ADVANCEMENT OF WOMEN 131 (1998).
35. *See* Eagly & Karau, *supra* note 24 at 575–76.
36. *Id.* at 575.

37. Madeline E. Heilman et al., *Penalties for Success: Reactions to Women Who Succeed at Male Gender-Typed Tasks*, 89 J. APPL. PSYCHOL. 416, 426 (2004).
38. *See* R.W. CONNELL, MASCULINITIES 15–16 (2d ed. 2005) (explaining that Alfred Adler and others posited that the polarity between masculine and feminine traits saw female traits as inferior).
39. Title VII of the Civil Rights Act of 1964, which went into effect in 1965, made it unlawful to discriminate against an applicant or employee because of her sex. Title VII of the Civil Rights Act of 1964, Pub. L. No. 88–352, 78 Stat. 241 (1964) (codified as amended at 42 U.S.C. § 2000e-2(a) (2006)). It was amended in 1972 in order to make state governments subject to the Act. Title VII of the Civil Rights Act of 1964, Pub. L. No. 92–261, 86 Stat. 103 (1972) (codified as amended at 42 U.S.C. § 2000e-2(e) (2006)). Title IX of the Civil Rights Act of 1964 made it unlawful to discriminate in education because of sex. Title IX of the Civil Rights Act of 1964, Pub. L. No. 88–352, 78 Stat. 241 (1964) (codified as amended at 42 U.S.C. § 2000c-6 (2006)). In 1972, the 1964 Civil Rights Act was amended to apply to public employers and universities. Title IX of the Civil Rights Act of 1964, Pub. L. No. 92–261, 86 Stat. 103 (1972) (codified as amended at 42 U.S.C. § 2000c-6 (2006)).
40. "Second Wave Feminism" is the term used to describe the feminist movement of the late 1960's and the 1970's. STANFORD ENCYCLOPEDIA OF PHILOSOPHY, TOPICS IN FEMINISM 2.1 (Mar. 15, 2004), http://plato.stanford.edu/entries/feminism-topics/#FemBelFemMov. I use the term in quotation marks in the text because it ignores the waves of abolitionist and post-abolition feminism.
41. *See generally* VALIAN, *supra* note 34 (discussing the effect of unconscious bias on women's success and the psychological studies supporting her conclusions).
42. Jack Hitt, *Bill and Hill and History; Southern Consort: A Guided Tour of His Good Ol' Soul*, WASH. POST, Oct. 21, 1993, at C1 ("The reason Hillary's remark—'I could have stayed home and baked cookies'—provoked such a projectile vomiting of rage below Washington is because she so openly represents a full rejection of Southern womanhood.").
43. *See* Gwen Ifill, *The 1992 Campaign: Democrats Trapped in a Spotlight, Hillary Clinton Uses It*, N.Y. TIMES, Feb. 3, 1992, at A12.
44. *See, e.g.*, Emmanuel Reynaud, *Holy Virility: The Social Construction of Masculinity, in* FEMINISM & MASCULINITIES 136, 142–44 (Peter Murphy ed., 2004) (arguing that man imposes femininity on women in order to establish his power and to produce the opposite of his own freedom and independence).
45. *See, e.g.*, Heilman et al., *supra* note 37, at 426.
46. *See* Cynthia Tucker, *Cards on the Table: Like it or Not, Race a Factor in '08*, ATLANTA J.-CONST., Aug. 6, 2008, at 18A.
47. Kerry Howley, *Hillary Never Played the Gender Card*, CHICAGO SUN-TIMES, Nov. 18, 2007, at B3.
48. Frank James, *Thank YLS for Clinton Pantsuits*, http://www.swampolitics.com/news/politics/blog/2008/06/by_frank_james_how_many.html (noting that Ives St. Laurent designed the pantsuit in the 1960's for working women, and that it has been a symbol of women's empowerment since its design); *see also* Robin Givhan, *Wearing the Pants*, WASH. POST, Dec. 9, 2007, at A24, *available at* http://tinyurl.com/cd61rz (noting that Clinton wore skirts and jackets as first lady, and wears pantsuits in the campaign to show toughness, but she also notes the variety of colors Clinton's pantsuits were the allowed her to stand out among her rivals).
49. *See* Katharine T. Bartlett, *Only Girls Wear Barrettes: Dress and Appearance Standards, Community Norms, and Workplace Equality*, 92 MICH. L. REV. 2541, 2553 (1994) (citing studies by Sandra M. Forsythe).
50. *See id.* at 2564.
51. Imagine the consternation if Obama's family had similar problems. The stereotype of black families with unwed mothers would likely have defeated his presidency.
52. Since her return to Alaska, Palin continues to perform her gender identity as mother and new grandmother publicly. The web page for the Alaska Governor has an announcement of the birth of her 17 year-old daughter, Bristol's, baby. *Governor Welcomes Her First Grandchild Tripp Easton Mitchell Johnston*, http://gov.state.ak.us/news.php?id=1593 (last visited Jan. 19, 2009). The web page also contains a link to a site about Palin's

infant son who has Down Syndrome. Alaska Governor Sarah Palin, http://gov.state.ak.us/trig.html (last visited Jan. 19, 2009).

53. *See* Andy Barr, *Tarnished Pols Look to Burnish Images*, POLITICO, Nov. 16, 2008, *available at* http://www.politico.com/news/stories/1108/15645.html; Kate Zernike & Monica Davey, *Win or Lose, Many See Palin as Future of the Party*, N.Y. TIMES, Oct. 29, 2008, at A21.

54. *See, e.g.*, Liam Julian, *Palin Must Connect on an Intellectual Level—But Will She? Can She?*, ORLANDO SENTINEL, Oct. 30, 2008, at A 15 (noting that conservatives George Will, Peggy Noonan and David Brooks criticized Palin for her lack of experience and seriousness).

55. I am indebted to Frank Rudy Cooper for the concept of the "split personality."

56. *See* Patricia J. Williams, *The Power of One*, 8 BLACK RENAISSANCE/RENAISSANCE NOIRE 42, 45 (Winter/Spring 2008); Margery Eagan, *Marriages Give Clues to Candidates' True Colors—Or Do They?*, BOSTON HERALD, Jan. 1, 2008, at 4; Andrew Herrmann, *Fame Puts Squeeze on Family Life: Many Hurdles as Obamas Seek Balance*, CHICAGO SUN TIMES, Oct. 19, 2006, at 6.

57. *The Belle of Capitol Hill*, IRISH TIMES, Nov. 8, 2008, at 5.

58. *See* Don Frederick & Andrew Malcolm, *Top of the Ticket Campaign '08: Race for the White House; How Deep Did Romney End Up Digging into his Pocket?*, L.A. TIMES, Feb. 24, 2008, at A16; *see also* Michael Graham, *Michelle, No Belle!*, BOSTON HERALD, Feb. 21, 2008, at 19.

59. Maria Puente, *What Kind of First Lady Will She Be?*, USA TODAY, Dec. 18, 2008, at 1A.

60. Verna L. Williams, *The First (Black) Lady*, 86 DENV. U. L. REV. 833, 834 (2009) (footnotes omitted).

61. *See, e.g.*, Stuart Taylor, Jr., *Obama's Wife and Spiritual Advisor*, NAT'L JOURNAL, Apr. 5, 2008 (criticizing Michelle Obama for her comments and her lack of gratitude).

62. Social science research demonstrates that politically active first ladies receive more negative press coverage. *See* Gregory S. Parks & Quinetta M. Roberson, *Michelle Obama: Intersectionality, Implicit Bias, and Third-Party Associative Discrimination in the 2008 Election*, http://ssrn.com/abstract=1248302 (posted on SSRN on Aug. 22, 2008).

63. *See, e.g.*, Marie Puente, *Excitement Builds Over Obama's Fashion Sense*, USA TODAY, Dec. 18, 2008, at 2A; Angela Burt-Murray, *Let Michelle Obama's Real Self Shine*, CNN.COM, Dec. 11, 2008, http://www.cnn.com/2008/POLITICS/12/11/burt-murray.michelle.obama/.

64. *See, e.g.*, Burt-Murray, *supra* note 63.

PART II

The Gendered Body

Perhaps nothing is more deceptive than the "naturalness" of our bodies. We experience what happens to our bodies, what happens *in* our bodies, as utterly natural, physical phenomena.

Yet to the social scientist nothing could be further from the truth. Our bodies are themselves shaped and created, and interpreted and understood by us, in entirely gendered ways. How we look, what we feel, and what we think about how our bodies look and feel, are the products of the ways our society defines what bodies should look like and feel. Thus, for example, cultural standards of beauty, musculature, and aesthetics are constantly changing—and with them our feelings about how we look stacked up against those images.

Take, for example, women's notions of beauty. Feminist writer Naomi Wolf argued that "the beauty myth"—constantly shifting and unrealizable cultural ideals of beauty—traps women into endless cycles of diets, fashion, and consumer spending that render them defenseless. Fortunes are made by companies that purvey the beauty myth, reminding women that they do not measure up to these cultural standards and then provide products that will help them try. By such logic, women who experience eating disorders are not deviant nonconformists, but rather

Viewed historically, the discipline and normalization of the female body—perhaps the only gender oppression that exercises itself, although to different degrees and in different forms, across age, race, class, and sexual orientation—has to be acknowledged as an amazingly durable and flexible strategy of social control. In our own era, it is difficult to avoid the recognition that the contemporary preoccupation with appearance, which still affects women far more powerfully than men, even in our narcissistic and visually oriented culture, may function as a backlash phenomenon, reasserting existing gender configurations against any attempts to shift or transform power relations.[4] Surely we are in the throes of this backlash today. In newspapers and magazines we daily encounter stories that promote traditional gender relations and prey on anxieties about change: stories about latch-key children, abuse in day-care centers, the "new woman's" troubles with men, her lack of marriageability, and so on. A dominant visual theme in teenage magazines involves women hiding in the shadows of men, seeking solace in their arms, willingly contracting the space they occupy. The last, of course, also describes our contemporary aesthetic ideal for women, an ideal whose obsessive pursuit has become the central torment of many women's lives. In such an era we desperately need an effective political discourse about the female body, a discourse adequate to an analysis of the insidious, and often paradoxical, pathways of modern social control.

Developing such a discourse requires reconstructing the feminist paradigm of the late 1960s and early 1970s, with its political categories of oppressors and oppressed, villains and victims. Here I believe that a feminist appropriation of some of Foucault's later concepts can prove useful. Following Foucault, we must first abandon the idea of power as something possessed by one group and leveled against another; we must instead think of the network of practices, institutions, and technologies that sustain positions of dominance and subordination in a particular domain.

Second, we need an analytics adequate to describe a power whose central mechanisms are not repressive, but *constitutive:* "a power bent on generating forces, making them grow, and ordering them, rather than one dedicated to impeding them, making them submit, or destroying them." Particularly in the realm of femininity, where so much depends on the seemingly willing acceptance of various norms and practices, we need an analysis of power "from below," as Foucault puts it; for example, of the mechanisms that shape and proliferate—rather than repress—desire, generate and focus our energies, construct our conceptions of normalcy and deviance.[5]

And, third, we need a discourse that will enable us to account for the subversion of potential rebellion, a discourse that, while insisting on the necessity of objective analysis of power relations, social hierarchy, political backlash, and so forth, will nonetheless allow us to confront the mechanisms by which the subject at times becomes enmeshed in collusion with forces that sustain her own oppression.

This essay will not attempt to produce a general theory along these lines. Rather, my focus will be the analysis of one particular arena where the interplay of these dynamics is striking and perhaps exemplary. It is a limited and unusual arena, that of a group of gender-related and historically localized disorders: hysteria, agoraphobia, and anorexia nervosa.[6] I recognize that these disorders have also historically been class- and race-biased, largely (although not exclusively) occurring among white middle- and upper-middle-class women. Nonetheless, anorexia, hysteria, and agoraphobia may provide a paradigm of one way in which potential resistance is not merely undercut but *utilized* in the maintenance and reproduction of existing power relations.[7]

The central mechanism I will describe involves a transformation (or, if you wish, duality) of meaning, through which conditions that are objectively (and, on one level, experientially) constraining, enslaving, and even murderous, come to be experienced as liberating, transforming, and life-giving. I offer this analysis, although limited to a specific domain, as an example of how various contemporary critical discourses may be joined to yield an understanding of the subtle and often unwitting role played by our bodies in the symbolization and reproduction of gender.

The Body as a Text of Femininity

The continuum between female disorder and "normal" feminine practice is sharply revealed through a close reading of those disorders to which women have been particularly vulnerable. These, of course, have varied historically: neurasthenia and hysteria in the second half of the nineteenth century; agoraphobia and, most dramatically, anorexia nervosa and bulimia in the second half of the twentieth century. This is not to say that anorectics did not exist in the nineteenth century—many cases were described, usually in the context of diagnoses of hysteria[8]—or that women no longer suffer from classical hysterical symptoms in the twentieth century. But the taking up of eating disorders on a mass scale is as unique to the culture of the 1980s as the epidemic of hysteria was to the Victorian era.[9]

The symptomatology of these disorders reveals itself as textuality. Loss of mobility, loss of voice, inability to leave the home, feeding others while starving oneself, taking up space, and whittling down the space one's body takes up—all have symbolic meaning, all have *political* meaning under the varying rules governing the historical construction of gender. Working within this framework, we see that whether we look at hysteria, agoraphobia, or anorexia, we find the body of the sufferer deeply inscribed with an ideological construction of femininity emblematic of the period in question. The construction, of course, is always homogenizing and normalizing, erasing racial, class, and other differences and insisting that all women aspire to a coercive, standardized ideal. Strikingly, in these disorders the construction of femininity is written in disturbingly concrete, hyperbolic terms: exaggerated, extremely literal, at times virtually caricatured presentations of the ruling feminine mystique. The bodies of disordered women in this way offer themselves as an aggressively graphic text for the interpreter—a text that insists, actually demands, that it be read as a cultural statement, a statement about gender.

Both nineteenth-century male physicians and twentieth-century feminist critics have seen, in the symptoms of neurasthenia and hysteria (syndromes that became increasingly less differentiated as the century wore on), an exaggeration of stereotypically feminine traits. The nineteenth-century "lady" was idealized in terms of delicacy and dreaminess, sexual passivity, and a charmingly labile and capricious emotionality.[10] Such notions were formalized and scientized in the work of male theorists from Acton and Krafft-Ebing to Freud, who described "normal," mature femininity in such terms.[11] In this context, the dissociations, the drifting and fogging of perception, the nervous tremors and faints, the anesthesias, and the extreme mutability of symptomatology associated with nineteenth-century female disorders can be seen to be concretizations of the feminine mystique of the period, produced according to rules that governed the prevailing construction of femininity. Doctors described what came to be known as the hysterical personality as "impressionable, suggestible, and narcissistic; highly labile, their moods changing suddenly, dramatically, and seemingly for inconsequential reasons... egocentric in the extreme... essentially asexual and not uncommonly frigid"[12]—all characteristics normative of femininity in this era. As Elaine Showalter points out, the term *hysterical* itself became almost interchangeable with the term *feminine* in the literature of the period.[13]

The hysteric's embodiment of the feminine mystique of her era, however, seems subtle and ineffable compared to the ingenious literalism of agoraphobia and anorexia. In the context of our culture this literalism makes sense. With the advent of movies and television, the rules for femininity have come to be culturally transmitted more and more through standardized visual images. As a result, femininity itself has come to be largely a matter of constructing, in the manner described by Erving Goffman, the appropriate surface presentation of the self.[14] We are no longer given verbal descriptions or exemplars of what a lady is or of what femininity consists. Rather, we learn the rules directly through bodily discourse: through images that tell us what clothes, body shape, facial expression, movements, and behavior are required.

In agoraphobia and, even more dramatically, in anorexia, the disorder presents itself as a virtual, though tragic, parody of twentieth-century constructions of femininity. The 1950s and early 1960s, when agoraphobia first began to escalate among women, was a period of reassertion of domesticity and dependency as the feminine ideal. *Career woman* became a dirty word, much more so than it had been during the war, when the economy depended on women's willingness to do "men's work." The reigning ideology of femininity, so well described by Betty Friedan and perfectly captured in the movies and television shows of the era, was childlike, nonassertive, helpless without a man, "content in a world of bedroom and kitchen, sex, babies and home."[15] The housebound agoraphobic lives this construction of femininity literally. "You want me in this home? You'll have me in this home—with a vengeance!" The point, upon which many therapists have commented, does not need belaboring. Agoraphobia, as I. G. Fodor has put it, seems "the logical—albeit extreme—extension of the cultural sex-role stereotype for women" in this era.[16]

The emaciated body of the anorectic, of course, immediately presents itself as a caricature of the contemporary ideal of hyper-slenderness for women, an ideal that, despite the game resistance of racial and ethnic difference, has become the norm for women today. But slenderness is only the tip of the iceberg, for slenderness itself requires interpretation. "C'est le sens qui fait vendre," said Barthes, speaking of clothing styles—it is meaning that makes the sale.[17] So, too, it is meaning that makes the body admirable. To the degree that anorexia may be said to be "about" slenderness, it is about slenderness as a citadel of contemporary and historical meaning, not as an empty fashion ideal. As such, the interpretation of slenderness yields multiple readings, some related to gender, some not. For the purposes of this essay I will offer an abbreviated, gender-focused reading. But I must stress that this reading illuminates only partially, and that many other currents not discussed here—economic, psychosocial, and historical, as well as ethnic and class dimensions—figure prominently.[18]

We begin with the painfully literal inscription, on the anorectic's body, of the rules governing the construction of contemporary femininity. That construction is a double bind that legislates contradictory ideals and directives. On the one hand, our culture still widely advertises domestic conceptions of femininity, the ideological moorings for a rigorously dualistic sexual division of labor that casts woman as chief emotional and physical nurturer. The rules for this construction of femininity (and I speak here in a language both symbolic and literal) require that women learn to feed others, not the self, and to construe any desires for self-nurturance and self-feeding as greedy and excessive.[19] Thus, women must develop a totally other-oriented emotional economy. In this economy, the control of female appetite for food is merely the most concrete expression of the general rule governing the construction of femininity: that female hunger—for public power, for independence, for sexual gratification—be contained, and the public space that women be allowed to take up be circumscribed, limited. Figure 1, which appeared in a women's magazine fashion spread, dramatically illustrates the degree to which slenderness, set off against the resurgent muscularity and bulk of the current male body-ideal, carries connotations of fragility and lack of power in the face of a decisive male occupation of social space. On the body of the anorexic woman such rules are grimly and deeply etched.

On the other hand, even as young women today continue to be taught traditionally "feminine" virtues, to the degree that the professional arena is open to them they must also learn to embody the "masculine" language and values of that arena—self-control, determination, cool, emotional discipline, mastery, and so on. Female bodies now speak symbolically of this necessity in their slender spare shape and the currently fashionable men's-wear look. (A contemporary clothing line's clever mirror-image logo, shown in Figure 2, offers women's fashions for the "New Man," with the model posed to suggest phallic confidence combined with female allure.) Our bodies, too, as we trudge to the gym every day and fiercely resist both our hungers and our desire to soothe ourselves, are becoming

Figure 1.

more and more practiced at the "male" virtues of control and self-mastery. Figure 3 illustrates this contemporary equation of physical discipline with becoming the "captain" of one's soul. The anorectic pursues these virtues with single-minded, unswerving dedication. "Energy, discipline, my own power will keep me going," says ex-anorectic Aimee Liu, recreating her anorexic days. "I need nothing and no one else.... I will be master of my own body, if nothing else, I vow."[20]

The ideal of slenderness, then, and the diet and exercise regimens that have become inseparable from it offer the illusion of meeting, through the body, the contradictory demands of the contemporary ideology of femininity. Popular images reflect this dual demand. In a single issue of *Complete Woman* magazine, two articles appear, one on "Feminine Intuition," the other asking, "Are You the New Macho Woman?" In *Vision Quest*, the young male hero falls in love with the heroine, as he says, because "she has all the best things I like in girls and all the best things I like in guys," that is, she's tough and cool, but warm and alluring. In the enormously popular *Aliens,* the heroine's personality has been deliberately constructed, with near-comic book explicitness, to embody traditional nurturant femininity alongside breathtaking macho prowess and control; Sigourney Weaver, the actress who portrays her, has called the character "Rambolina."

In the pursuit of slenderness and the denial of appetite the traditional construction of femininity intersects with the new requirement for women to embody the "masculine" values of the public arena. The anorectic, as I have argued, embodies this intersection, this double bind, in a particularly painful and graphic way.[21] I mean *double bind* quite literally here. "Masculinity" and "femininity," at least since the nineteenth century and arguably before, have been constructed through a process of mutual

Figure 2.

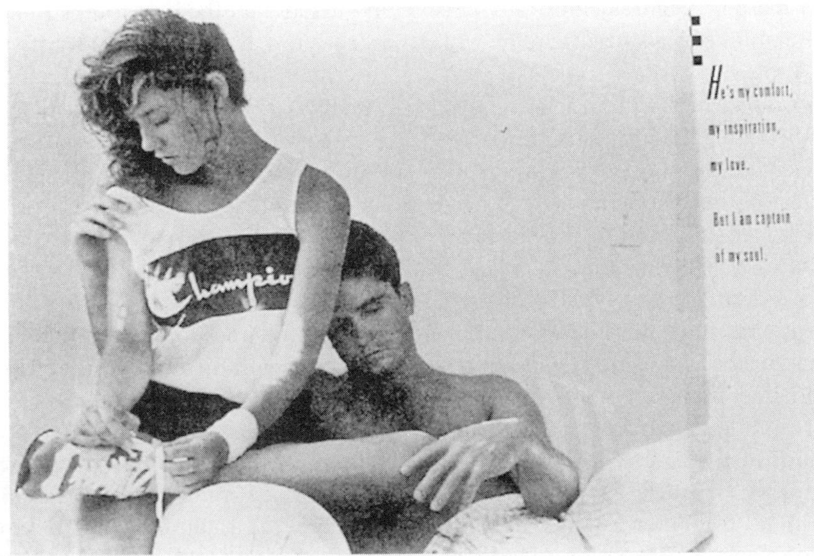

Figure 3.

exclusion. One cannot simply add the historically feminine virtues to the historically masculine ones to yield a New Woman, a New Man, a new ethics, or a new culture. Even on the screen or on television, embodied in created characters like the *Aliens* heroine, the result is a parody. Unfortunately, in this image-bedazzled culture, we find it increasingly difficult to discriminate between parodies and possibilities for the self. Explored as a possibility for the self, the "androgynous" ideal ultimately exposes its internal contradiction and becomes a war that tears the subject in two—a war explicitly thematized, by many anorectics, as a battle between male and female sides of the self.[22]

Protest and Retreat in the Same Gesture

In hysteria, agoraphobia, and anorexia, then, the woman's body may be viewed as a surface on which conventional constructions of femininity are exposed starkly to view, through their inscription in extreme or hyperliteral form. They are written, of course, in languages of horrible suffering. It is as though these bodies are speaking to us of the pathology and violence that lurks just around the corner, waiting at the horizon of "normal" femininity. It is no wonder that a steady motif in the feminist literature on female disorder is that of pathology as embodied *protest*—unconscious, inchoate, and counterproductive protest without an effective language, voice, or politics, but protest nonetheless.

American and French feminists alike have heard the hysteric speaking a language of protest, even or perhaps especially when she was mute. Dianne Hunter interprets Anna O.'s aphasia, which manifested itself in an inability to speak her native German, as a rebellion against the linguistic and cultural rules of the father and a return to the "mother-tongue": the semiotic babble of infancy, the language of the body. For Hunter, and for a number of other feminists working with Lacanian categories, the return to the semiotic level is both regressive and, as Hunter puts it, an "expressive" communication "addressed to patriarchal thought," "a self-repudiating form of feminine discourse in which the body signifies what social conditions make it impossible to state linguistically."[23] "The hysterics are accusing; they are pointing," writes Catherine Clément in *The Newly Born Woman;* they make a "mockery of culture."[24] In the same volume, Hélène Cixous speaks of "those wonderful hysterics, who subjected Freud to so many voluptuous moments too shameful to mention, bombarding his mosaic statute/law of Moses with their carnal, passionate body-words, haunting him with their inaudible thundering denunciations." For Cixous, Dora, who so frustrated Freud, is "the core example of the protesting force in women."[25]

The literature of protest includes functional as well as symbolic approaches. Robert Seidenberg and Karen DeCrow, for example, describe agoraphobia as a "strike" against "the renunciations usually demanded of women" and the expectations of housewifely functions such as shopping, driving the children to school, accompanying their husband to social events.[26] Carroll Smith-Rosenberg presents a similar analysis of hysteria, arguing that by preventing the woman from functioning in the wifely role of caretaker of others, of "ministering angel" to husband and children, hysteria "became one way in which conventional women could express—in most cases unconsciously—dissatisfaction with one or several aspects of their lives."[27] A number of feminist writers, among whom Susie Orbach is the most articulate and forceful, have interpreted anorexia as a species of unconscious feminist protest. The anorectic is engaged in a "hunger strike," as Orbach calls it, stressing that this is a political discourse, in which the action of food refusal and dramatic transformation of body size "expresses with [the] body what [the anorectic] is unable to tell us with words"—her indictment of a culture that disdains and suppresses female hunger, makes women ashamed of their appetites and needs, and demands that women constantly work on the transformation of their body.[28]

The anorectic, of course, is unaware that she is making a political statement. She may, indeed, be hostile to feminism and any other critical perspectives that she views as disputing her own autonomy and control or questioning the cultural ideals around which her life is organized. Through embodied rather than deliberate demonstration she exposes and indicts those ideals, precisely by pursuing them to the point at which their destructive potential is revealed for all to see.

The same gesture that expresses protest, moreover, can also signal retreat; this, indeed, may be part of the symptom's attraction. Kim Chernin, for example, argues that the debilitating anorexic fixation, by halting or mitigating personal development, assuages this generation's guilt and separation anxiety over the prospect of surpassing our mothers, of living less circumscribed, freer lives.[29] Agoraphobia, too, which often develops shortly after marriage, clearly functions in many cases as a way to cement dependency and attachment in the face of unacceptable stirrings of dissatisfaction and restlessness.

Although we may talk meaningfully of protest, then, I want to emphasize the counterproductive, tragically self-defeating (indeed, self-deconstructing) nature of that protest. Functionally, the symptoms of these disorders isolate, weaken, and undermine the sufferers; at the same time they turn the life of the body into an all-absorbing fetish, beside which all other objects of attention pale into unreality. On the symbolic level, too, the protest collapses into its opposite and proclaims the utter capitulation of the subject to the contracted female world. The muteness of hysterics and their return to the level of pure, primary bodily expressivity have been interpreted, as we have seen, as rejecting the symbolic order of the patriarchy and recovering a lost world of semiotic, maternal value. But *at the same time*, of course, muteness is the condition of the silent, uncomplaining woman—an ideal of patriarchal culture. Protesting the stifling of the female voice through one's own voicelessness—that is, employing the language of femininity to protest the conditions of the female world—will always involve ambiguities of this sort. Perhaps this is why symptoms crystallized from the language of femininity are so perfectly suited to express the dilemmas of middle-class and upper-middle-class women living in periods poised on the edge of gender change, women who have the social and material resources to carry the traditional construction of femininity to symbolic excess but who also confront the anxieties of new possibilities. The late nineteenth century, the post–World War II period, and the late twentieth century are all periods in which gender becomes an issue to be discussed and in which discourse proliferates about "the Woman Question," "the New Woman," "What Women Want," "What Femininity Is."

Collusion, Resistance, and the Body

The pathologies of female protest function, paradoxically, as if in collusion with the cultural conditions that produce them, reproducing rather than transforming precisely that which is being protested. In this connection, the fact that hysteria and anorexia have peaked during historical periods of cultural backlash against attempts at reorganization and redefinition of male and female roles is significant. Female pathology reveals itself here as an extremely interesting social formation through which one source of potential for resistance and rebellion is pressed into the service of maintaining the established order.

In our attempt to explain this formation, objective accounts of power relations fail us. For whatever the objective social conditions are that create a pathology, the symptoms themselves must still be produced (however unconsciously or inadvertently) by the subject. That is, the individual must invest the body with meanings of various sorts. Only by examining this productive process on the part of the subject can we, as Mark Poster has put it, "illuminate the mechanisms of domination in the processes through which meaning is produced in everyday life"; that is, only then can we see how the desires and dreams of the subject become implicated in the matrix of power relations.[30]

Here, examining the context in which the anorexic syndrome is produced may be illuminating. Anorexia will erupt, typically, in the course of what begins as a fairly moderate diet regime, undertaken because someone, often the father, has made a casual critical remark. Anorexia *begins in*, emerges out of, what is, in our time, conventional feminine practice. In the course of that practice, for any number of individual reasons, the practice is pushed a little beyond the parameters of moderate dieting. The young woman discovers what it feels like to crave and want and need and yet, through the exercise of her own will, to triumph over that need. In the process, a new realm of meanings is discovered, a range of values and possibilities that Western culture has traditionally coded as "male" and rarely made available to women: an ethic and aesthetic of self-mastery and self-transcendence, expertise, and power over others through the example of superior will and control. The experience is intoxicating, habit-forming.

At school the anorectic discovers that her steadily shrinking body is admired, not so much as an aesthetic or sexual object, but for the strength of will and self-control it projects. At home she discovers, in the inevitable battles her parents fight to get her to eat, that her actions have enormous power over the lives of those around her. As her body begins to lose its traditional feminine curves, its breasts and hips and rounded stomach, begins to feel and look more like a spare, lanky male body, she begins to feel untouchable, out of reach of hurt, "invulnerable, clean and hard as the bones etched into my silhouette," as one student described it in her journal. She despises, in particular, all those parts of her body that continue to mark her as female. "If only I could eliminate [my breasts]," says Liu, "cut them off if need be."[31] For her, as for many anorectics, the breasts represent a bovine, unconscious, vulnerable side of the self. Liu's body symbolism is thoroughly continuous with dominant cultural associations. Brett Silverstein's studies on the "Possible Causes of the Thin Standard of Bodily Attractiveness for Women"[32] testify empirically to what is obvious from every comedy routine involving a dramatically shapely woman: namely, our cultural association of curvaceousness with incompetence. The anorectic is also quite aware, of course, of the social and sexual vulnerability involved in having a female body; many, in fact, were sexually abused as children.

Through her anorexia, by contrast, she has unexpectedly discovered an entry into the privileged male world, a way to become what is valued in our culture, a way to become safe, to rise above it all—for her, they are the same thing. She has discovered this, paradoxically, by pursuing conventional feminine behavior—in this case, the discipline of perfecting the body as an object—to excess. At this point of excess, the conventionally feminine deconstructs, we might say, into its opposite and opens onto those values our culture has coded as male. No wonder the anorexia is experienced as liberating and that she will fight family, friends, and therapists in an effort to hold onto it—fight them to the death, if need be. The anorectic's experience of power is, of course, deeply and dangerously illusory. To reshape one's body into a male body is *not* to put on male power and privilege. To *feel* autonomous and free while harnessing body and soul to an obsessive body-practice is to serve, not transform, a social order that limits female possibilities. And, of course, for the female to become male is only for her to locate herself on the other side of a disfiguring opposition. The new "power look" of female body-building, which encourages women to develop the same hulklike, triangular shape that has been the norm for male body-builders, is no less determined by a hierarchical, dualistic construction of gender than was the conventionally "feminine" norm that tyrannized female body-builders such as Bev Francis for years.

Although the specific cultural practices and meanings are different, similar mechanisms, I suspect, are at work in hysteria and agoraphobia. In these cases too, the language of femininity, when pushed to excess—when shouted and asserted, when disruptive and demanding—deconstructs into its opposite and makes available to the woman an illusory experience of power previously forbidden to her by virtue of her gender. In the case of nineteenth-century femininity, the forbidden experience may have been the bursting of fetters—particularly moral and emotional fetters. John Conolly, the asylum reformer, recommended institutionalization for women who "want that restraint over the passions without which the female character is lost."[33] Hysterics often infuriated male doctors by their lack of precisely this quality. S. Weir Mitchell described these patients as "the despair of physicians," whose "despotic selfishness wrecks the constitution of nurses and devoted relatives, and in unconscious or half-conscious self-indulgence destroys the comfort of everyone around them."[34] It must have given the Victorian patient some illicit pleasure to be viewed as capable of such disruption of the staid nineteenth-century household. A similar form of power, I believe, is part of the experience of agoraphobia.

This does not mean that the primary reality of these disorders is not one of pain and entrapment. Anorexia, too, clearly contains a dimension of physical addiction to the biochemical effects of starvation. But whatever the physiology involved, the ways in which the subject understands and thematizes her experience cannot be reduced to a mechanical process. The anorectic's ability to live with minimal food intake allows her to feel powerful and worthy of admiration in a "world," as Susie Orbach describes it, "from which at the most profound level [she] feels excluded" and unvalued.[35] The literature on both anorexia and hysteria is strewn with battles of will between the sufferer and those trying to "cure" her; the latter, as Orbach points out, very rarely understand that the psychic values she is fighting for are often more important to the woman than life itself.

Textuality, Praxis, and the Body

The "solutions" offered by anorexia, hysteria, and agoraphobia, I have suggested, develop out of the practice of femininity itself, the pursuit of which is still presented as the chief route to acceptance and success for women in our culture. Too aggressively pursued, that practice leads to its own undoing, in one sense. For if femininity is, as Susan Brownmiller has said, at its core a "tradition of imposed limitations,"[36] then an unwillingness to limit oneself, even in the pursuit of femininity, breaks the rules. But, of course, in another sense the rules remain fully in place. The sufferer becomes wedded to an obsessive practice, unable to make any effective change in her life. She remains, as Toril Moi has put it, "gagged and chained to [the] feminine role," a reproducer of the docile body of femininity.[37]

This tension between the psychological meaning of a disorder, which may enact fantasies of rebellion and embody a language of protest, and the practical life of the disordered body, which may utterly defeat rebellion and subvert protest, may be obscured by too exclusive a focus on the symbolic dimension and insufficient attention to praxis. As we have seen in the case of some Lacanian feminist readings of hysteria, the result of this can be a one-sided interpretation that romanticizes the hysteric's symbolic subversion of the phallocentric order while confined to her bed. This is not to say that confinement in bed has a transparent, univocal meaning—in powerlessness, debilitation, dependency, and so forth. The "practical" body is no brute biological or material entity. It, too, is a culturally mediated form; its activities are subject to interpretation and description. The shift to the practical dimension is not a turn to biology or nature, but to another "register," as Foucault puts it, of the cultural body, the register of the "useful body" rather than the "intelligible body."[38] The distinction can prove useful, I believe, to feminist discourse.

The intelligible body includes our scientific, philosophic, and aesthetic representations of the body—our cultural *conceptions* of the body, norms of beauty, models of health, and so forth. But the same representations may also be seen as forming a set of *practical* rules and regulations through which the living body is "trained, shaped, obeys, responds," becoming, in short, a socially adapted and "useful body."[39] Consider this particularly clear and appropriate example: the nineteenth-century hourglass figure, emphasizing breasts and hips against a wasp waist, was an intelligible *symbolic* form, representing a domestic, sexualized ideal of femininity. The sharp cultural contrast between the female and the male form, made possible by the use of corsets and bustles, reflected, in symbolic terms, the dualistic division of social and economic life into clearly defined male and female spheres. At the same time, to achieve the specified look, a particular feminine *praxis* was required—straitlacing, minimal eating, reduced mobility—rendering the female body unfit to perform activities outside its designated sphere. This, in Foucauldian terms, would be the "useful body" corresponding to the aesthetic norm.

The intelligible body and the useful body are two arenas of the same discourse; they often mirror and support each other, as in the above illustration. Another example can be found in the seventeenth-century philosophic conception of the body as a machine, mirroring an increasingly more automated productive machinery of labor. But the two bodies may also contradict and mock each other. A range of contemporary representations and images, as noted earlier, have coded the transcendence of female appetite and its public display in the slenderness ideal in terms of power, will, mastery, the possibilities of success in the professional arena. These associations are carried visually by the slender superwomen of prime-time television and popular movies and promoted explicitly in advertisements and articles appearing routinely in women's fashion magazines, diet books, and weight-training publications. Yet the thousands of slender girls and women who strive to embody these images and who in that service suffer from eating disorders, exercise compulsions, and continual self-scrutiny and self-castigation are anything *but* the "masters" of their lives.

Exposure and productive cultural analysis of such contradictory and mystifying relations between image and practice are possible only if the analysis includes attention to and interpretation of the "useful" or, as I prefer to call it, the practical body. Such attention, although often in inchoate and theoretically unsophisticated form, was central to the beginnings of the contemporary feminist movement. In the late 1960s and early 1970s the objectification of the female body was a serious political issue. All the cultural paraphernalia of femininity, of learning to please visually and sexually through the practices of the body—media imagery, beauty pageants, high heels, girdles, makeup, simulated orgasm—were seen as crucial in maintaining gender domination.

Disquietingly, for the feminists of the present decade, such focus on the politics of feminine praxis, although still maintained in the work of individual feminists, is no longer a centerpiece of feminist cultural critique.[40] On the popular front, we find *Ms.* magazine presenting issues on fitness and "style," the rhetoric reconstructed for the 1980s to pitch "self-expression" and "power." Although feminist theory surely has the tools, it has not provided a critical discourse to dismantle and demystify this rhetoric. The work of French feminists has provided a powerful framework for understanding the inscription of phallocentric, dualistic culture on gendered bodies, but it has offered very little in the way of concrete analyses of the female body as a locus of practical cultural control. Among feminist theorists in this country, the study of cultural representations of the female body has flourished, and it has often been brilliantly illuminating and instrumental to a feminist rereading of culture.[41] But the study of cultural representations alone, divorced from consideration of their relation to the practical lives of bodies, can obscure and mislead.

Here, Helena Mitchie's significantly titled *The Flesh Made Word* offers a striking example. Examining nineteenth-century representations of women, appetite, and eating, Mitchie draws fascinating and astute metaphorical connections between female eating and female sexuality. Female hunger, she argues, and I agree, "figures unspeakable desires for sexuality and power."[42] The Victorian novel's "representational taboo" against depicting women eating (an activity, apparently, that only "happens offstage," as Mitchie puts it) thus functions as a "code" for the suppression of female sexuality, as does the general cultural requirement, exhibited in etiquette and sex manuals of the day, that the well-bred woman eat little and delicately. The same coding is drawn on, Mitchie argues, in contemporary feminist "inversions" of Victorian values, inversions that celebrate female sexuality and power through images exulting in female eating and female hunger, depicting it explicitly, lushly, and joyfully.

Despite the fact that Mitchie's analysis centers on issues concerning women's hunger, food, and eating practices, she makes no mention of the grave eating disorders that surfaced in the late nineteenth century and that are ravaging the lives of young women today. The practical arena of women dieting, fasting, straitlacing, and so forth is, to a certain extent, implicit in her examination of Victorian gender ideology. But when Mitchie turns, at the end of her study, to consider contemporary feminist literature celebrating female eating and female hunger, the absence of even a passing glance at how women are *actually* managing their hungers today leaves her analysis adrift, lacking any concrete social moorings. Mitchie's sole focus is on the inevitable failure of feminist literature to escape "phallic representational codes."[43] But the feminist celebration of the female body did not merely deconstruct on the written page or canvas. Largely located in the feminist counterculture of the 1970s, it has been culturally displaced by a very different contemporary reality. Its celebration of female flesh now presents itself in jarring dissonance with the fact that women, feminists included, are starving themselves to death in our culture.

This is not to deny the benefits of diet, exercise, and other forms of body management. Rather, I view our bodies as a site of struggle, where we must *work* to keep our daily practices in the service of resistance to gender domination, not in the service of docility and gender normalization. This work requires, I believe, a determinedly skeptical attitude toward the routes of seeming liberation and pleasure offered by our culture. It also demands an awareness of the often contradictory relations between image and practice, between rhetoric and reality. Popular representations, as we have seen, may forcefully employ the rhetoric and symbolism of empowerment, personal freedom, "having it all." Yet female bodies, pursuing these ideals, may find themselves as distracted, depressed, and physically ill as female bodies in the nineteenth century were made when pursuing a feminine ideal of dependency, domesticity, and delicacy. The recognition and analysis of such contradictions, and of all the other collusions, subversions, and enticements through which culture enjoins the aid of our bodies in the reproduction of gender, require that we restore a concern for female praxis to its formerly central place in feminist politics.

Acknowledgments

Early versions of this essay, under various titles, were delivered at the philosophy department of the State University of New York at Stony Brook, the University of Massachusetts conference on Histories of Sexuality, and the twenty-first annual conference for the Society of Phenomenology and Existential Philosophy. I thank all those who commented and provided encouragement on those occasions. The essay was revised and originally published in Alison Jaggar and Susan Bordo, eds., *Gender/Body/Knowledge: Feminist Reconstructions of Being and Knowing* (New Brunswick: Rutgers University Press, 1989).

Notes

1. Mary Douglas, *Natural Symbols* (New York: Pantheon, 1982), and *Purity and Danger* (London: Routledge and Kegan Paul, 1966).
2. Pierre Bourdieu, *Outline of a Theory of Practice* (Cambridge: Cambridge University Press, 1977), p. 94 (emphasis in original).
3. On docility, see Michel Foucault, *Discipline and Punish* (New York: Vintage, 1979), pp. 135–69. For a Foucauldian analysis of feminine practice, see Sandra Bartky, "Foucault, Femininity, and the Modernization of Patriarchal Power," in her *Femininity and Domination* (New York: Routledge, 1990); see also Susan Brownmiller, *Femininity* (New York: Ballantine, 1984).
4. During the late 1970s and 1980s, male concern over appearance undeniably increased. Study after study confirms, however, that there is still a large gender gap in this area. Research conducted at the University of Pennsylvania in 1985 found men to be generally satisfied with their appearance, often, in fact, "distorting their perceptions [of themselves] in a positive, self-aggrandizing way" ("Dislike of Own Bodies Found Common Among Women," *New York Times*, March 19, 1985, p. C1). Women, however, were found to exhibit extreme negative assessments and distortions of body perception. Other studies have suggested that women are judged more harshly than men when they deviate from dominant social standards of attractiveness. Thomas Cash et al., in "The Great American Shape-Up," *Psychology Today* (April 1986), p. 34, report that although the situation for men has changed, the situation for women has more than proportionally worsened. Citing results from 30,000 responses to a 1985 survey of perceptions of body

image and comparing similar responses to a 1972 questionnaire, they report that the 1985 respondents were considerably more dissatisfied with their bodies than the 1972 respondents, and they note a marked intensification of concern among men. Among the 1985 group, the group most dissatisfied of all with their appearance, however, were teenage women. Women today constitute by far the largest number of consumers of diet products, attenders of spas and diet centers, and subjects of intestinal by-pass and other fat-reduction operations.

5. Michel Foucault, *The History of Sexuality.* Vol. 1: *An Introduction* (New York: Vintage, 1980), pp. 136, 94.

6. On the gendered and historical nature of these disorders: the number of female to male hysterics has been estimated at anywhere from 2:1 to 4:1, and as many as 80 percent of all agoraphobics are female (Annette Brodsky and Rachel Hare-Mustin, *Women and Psychotherapy* [New York: Guilford Press, 1980], pp. 116, 122). Although more cases of male eating disorders have been reported in the late eighties and early nineties, it is estimated that close to 90 percent of all anorectics are female (Paul Garfinkel and David Garner, *Anorexia Nervosa: A Multidimensional Perspective* [New York: Brunner/Mazel, 1982], pp. 112–13). For a sophisticated account of female psychopathology, with particular attention to nineteenth-century disorders but, unfortunately, little mention of agoraphobia or eating disorders, see Elaine Showalter, *The Female Malady: Women, Madness and English Culture, 1830–1980* (New York: Pantheon, 1985). For a discussion of social and gender issues in agoraphobia, see Robert Seidenberg and Karen DeCrow, *Women Who Marry Houses: Panic and Protest in Agoraphobia* (New York: McGraw-Hill, 1983). On the history of anorexia nervosa, see Joan Jacobs Brumberg, *Fasting Girls: The Emergence of Anorexia Nervosa as a Modern Disease* (Cambridge: Harvard University Press, 1988).

7. In constructing such a paradigm I do not pretend to do justice to any of these disorders in its individual complexity. My aim is to chart some points of intersection, to describe some similar patterns, as they emerge through a particular reading of the phenomenon—a political reading, if you will.

8. Showalter, *The Female Malady*, pp. 128–29.

9. On the epidemic of hysteria and neurasthenia, see Showalter, *The Female Malady;* Carroll Smith-Rosenberg, "The Hysterical Woman: Sex Roles and Role Conflict in Nineteenth-Century America," in her *Disorderly Conduct: Visions of Gender in Victorian America* (Oxford: Oxford University Press, 1985).

10. Martha Vicinus, "Introduction: The Perfect Victorian Lady," in Martha Vicinus, *Suffer and Be Still: Women in the Victorian Age* (Bloomington: Indiana University Press, 1972), pp. x–xi.

11. See Carol Nadelson and Malkah Notman, *The Female Patient* (New York: Plenum, 1982), p. 5; E. M. Sigsworth and T. J. Wyke, "A Study of Victorian Prostitution and Venereal Disease," in Vicinus, *Suffer and Be Still,* p. 82. For more general discussions, see Peter Gay, *The Bourgeois Experience: Victoria to Freud.* Vol. 1: *Education of the Senses* (New York: Oxford University Press, 1984), esp. pp. 109–68; Showalter, *The Female Malady,* esp. pp. 121–44. The delicate lady, an ideal that had very strong class connotations (as does slenderness today), is not the only conception of femininity to be found in Victorian cultures. But it was arguably the single most powerful ideological representation of femininity in that era, affecting women of all classes, including those without the material means to realize the ideal fully. See Helena Mitchie, *The Flesh Made Word* (New York: Oxford, 1987), for discussions of the control of female appetite and Victorian constructions of femininity.

12. Smith-Rosenberg, *Disorderly Conduct*, p. 203.

13. Showalter, *The Female Malady*, p. 129.

14. Erving Goffman, *The Presentation of the Self in Everyday Life* (Garden City, N.Y.: Anchor Doubleday, 1959).

15. Betty Friedan, *The Feminine Mystique* (New York: Dell, 1962), p. 36. The theme song of one such show ran, in part, "I married Joan . . . What a girl . . . what a whirl . . . what a life! I married Joan . . . What a mind . . . love is blind . . . what a wife!"

16. See I. G. Fodor, "The Phobic Syndrome in Women," in V. Franks and V. Burtle, eds., *Women in Therapy* (New York: Brunner/Mazel, 1974), p. 119; see also Kathleen Brehony, "Women and Agoraphobia,"

in Violet Franks and Esther Rothblum, eds., *The Stereotyping of Women* (New York: Springer, 1983).

17. In Jonathan Culler, *Roland Barthes* (New York: Oxford University Press, 1983), p. 74.
18. For other interpretive perspectives on the slenderness ideal, see "Reading the Slender Body" in this volume; Kim Chernin, *The Obsession: Reflections on the Tyranny of Slenderness* (New York: Harper and Row, 1981); Susie Orbach, *Hunger Strike: The Anorectic's Struggle as a Metaphor for Our Age* (New York: W. W. Norton, 1985).
19. See Susan Bordo, "Hunger as Ideology," in Bartholomae, David and Anthony Petrosky, eds. *Ways of Reading: An Anthology for Writers*. 6th Edition. (Boston: Bedford/St. Martins, 2002), pp. 138-171, for a discussion of how this construction of femininity is reproduced in contemporary commercials and advertisements concerning food, eating, and cooking.
20. Aimee Liu, *Solitaire* (New York: Harper and Row, 1979), p. 123.
21. Striking, in connection with this, is Catherine Steiner-Adair's 1984 study of high-school women, which reveals a dramatic association between problems with food and body image and emulation of the cool, professionally "together" and gorgeous superwoman. On the basis of a series of interviews, the high schoolers were classified into two groups: one expressed skepticism over the superwoman ideal, the other thoroughly aspired to it. Later administrations of diagnostic tests revealed that 94 percent of the pro-superwoman group fell into the eating-disordered range of the scale. Of the other group, 100 percent fell into the noneating-disordered range. Media images notwithstanding, young women today appear to sense, either consciously or through their bodies, the impossibility of simultaneously meeting the demands of two spheres whose values have been historically defined in utter opposition to each other.
22. See "Anorexia Nervosa" in this volume.
23. Dianne Hunter, "Hysteria, Psychoanalysis and Feminism," in Shirley Garner, Claire Kahane, and Madelon Sprenger, eds., *The (M)Other Tongue* (Ithaca: Cornell University Press, 1985), p. 114.
24. Catherine Clément and Hélène Cixous, *The Newly Born Woman,* trans. Betsy Wing (Minneapolis: University of Minnesota Press, 1986), p. 42.
25. Clément and Cixous, *The Newly Born Woman,* p. 95.
26. Seidenberg and DeCrow, *Women Who Marry Houses*, p. 31.
27. Smith-Rosenberg, *Disorderly Conduct*, p. 208.
28. Orbach, *Hunger Strike,* p. 102. When we look into the many autobiographies and case studies of hysterics, anorectics, and agoraphobics, we find that these are indeed the sorts of women one might expect to be frustrated by the constraints of a specified female role. Sigmund Freud and Joseph Breuer, in *Studies on Hysteria* (New York: Avon, 1966), and Freud, in the later *Dora: An Analysis of a Case of Hysteria* (New York: Macmillan, 1963), constantly remark on the ambitiousness, independence, intellectual ability, and creative strivings of their patients. We know, moreover, that many women who later became leading social activists and feminists of the nineteenth century were among those who fell ill with hysteria and neurasthenia. It has become a virtual cliché that the typical anorectic is a perfectionist, driven to excel in all areas of her life. Though less prominently, a similar theme runs throughout the literature on agoraphobia.
    One must keep in mind that in drawing on case studies, one is relying on the perceptions of other acculturated individuals. One suspects, for example, that the popular portrait of the anorectic as a relentless over-achiever may be colored by the lingering or perhaps resurgent Victorianism of our culture's attitudes toward ambitious women. One does not escape this hermeneutic problem by turning to autobiography. But in autobiography one is at least dealing with social constructions and attitudes that animate the subject's own psychic reality. In this regard the autobiographical literature on anorexia, drawn on in a variety of places in this volume, is strikingly full of anxiety about the domestic world and other themes that suggest deep rebellion against traditional notions of femininity.
29. Kim Chernin, *The Hungry Self: Women, Eating, and Identity* (New York: Harper and Row, 1985), esp. pp. 41–93.
30. Mark Poster, *Foucault, Marxism, and History* (Cambridge: Polity Press, 1984), p. 28.
31. Liu, *Solitaire*, p. 99.
32. Brett Silverstein, "Possible Causes of the Thin Standard of Bodily Attractiveness for Women," *International Journal of Eating Disorders* 5 (1986): 907–16.

33. Showalter, *The Female Malady*, p. 48.
34. Smith-Rosenberg, *Disorderly Conduct*, p. 207.
35. Orbach, *Hunger Strike*, p. 103.
36. Brownmiller, *Femininity*, p. 14.
37. Toril Moi, "Representations of Patriarchy: Sex and Epistemology in Freud's Dora," in Charles Bernheimer and Claire Kahane, eds., *In Dora's Case: Freud—Hysteria—Feminism* (New York: Columbia University Press, 1985), p. 192.
38. Foucault, *Discipline and Punish*, p. 136.
39. Foucault, *Discipline and Punish*, p. 136.
40. A focus on the politics of sexualization and objectification remains central to the anti-pornography movement (e.g., in the work of Andrea Dworkin, Catherine MacKinnon). Feminists exploring the politics of appearance include Sandra Bartky, Susan Brownmiller, Wendy Chapkis, Kim Chernin, and Susie Orbach. And a developing feminist interest in the work of Michel Foucault has begun to produce a post-structuralist feminism oriented toward practice; see, for example, Irene Diamond and Lee Quinby, *Feminism and Foucault: Reflections on Resistance* (Boston: Northeastern University Press, 1988).
41. See, for example, Susan Suleiman, ed., *The Female Body in Western Culture* (Cambridge: Harvard University Press, 1986).
42. Mitchie, *The Flesh Made Word*, p. 13.
43. Mitchie, *The Flesh Made Word*, p. 149.

Beards, Breasts, and Bodies: Doing Sex in a Gendered World

RAINE DOZIER

Gender is ubiquitous and, along with race and class, orders most aspects of daily life. "Talking about gender for most people is the equivalent of fish talking about water" (Lorber 1994, 13). Because transsexuals, transgendered people, and others at the borders of gender and sex are fish out of water, they help illuminate strengths and weaknesses in common conceptions of gender. This project clarifies the relationship between sex, gender, and sexual orientation through interviews with female-to-male transsexuals and transgendered people.[1] The interviewees challenge the underlying assumption in much of gender literature that sex, gender, and sexual orientation align in highly correlated, relatively fixed, binary categories. Instead, these categories are a process of differentiation and constructed meaning that is bound in social context.

Sex, Gender, and Sexuality

In the United States, the term "gender" is increasingly used as a proxy for the term "sex" (Auerbach 1999). My own small rebellion against this tendency is to respond literally. When asked to indicate sex, I reply female; when asked for gender, I reply male. Perhaps I am doing little to change concepts of gender and sex,[2] but at least I am on mailing lists that target my diverse interests! At the same time that the public seems to be increasingly using "gender"

Raine Dozier, "Beards, Breasts, and Bodies: Doing Sex in a Gendered World" from *Gender & Society* 19, no. 3 (June 2005): 297–316.

as proxy for "sex," gender theorists are more clearly delineating the relationship between sex and gender. However, because gender and sex are seemingly inexplicably connected in most aspects of social life, theorists have difficulty in retaining these delineations throughout their work.

Intellectuals have been creating, critiquing, and advancing concepts of gender for the past 30 years. Generally, gender is defined as the socially constructed correlate of sex. The concept of gender as socially constructed has been theorized extensively and illustrated in a variety of arenas from the playground to the boardroom (Fausto-Sterling 2000; Kanter 1977; Kessler 1990; Lorber 1994; Messner 2000; Thorne 1993; West and Zimmerman 1987). However, many definitions positing gender as an ongoing accomplishment rely on sex as the "master status" or "coat rack" on which gender is socially constructed (Nicholson 1994). Although there is a general consensus that gender is socially constructed, theorists have too often relied on sex as its initiating point.

Delphy (1993) critiqued the overreliance on sex in defining gender. She claimed that illustrating the social construction of gender by describing the cross-cultural variation in men's and women's behavior and social roles only reinforces the notion that gender originates in sex. The description of cross-cultural variation further entrenches the notion of "gender as the *content* with sex as the *container*" (Delphy 1993, 3). Both Nicholson (1994) and Delphy (1993) challenged the view that gender derives from sex and, in a sense, posited the opposite: That "gender is the knowledge that establishes meanings for bodily differences" (Scott 1988, 2). Gender, then, is the concept that creates and defines sex differences.

Typically, sex is assigned based on genital inspection at birth, but biological sex is a complex constellation of chromosomes, hormones, genitalia, and reproductive organs. The study of intersexed and sex-reassigned children illustrates that social notions of sex are employed when biological sex is ambiguous (Fausto-Sterling 2000; Kessler 1990). Because sex is an organizing principle of most societies, people are forced to be one or the other, even when "only a surgical shoehorn can put them there" (Fausto-Sterling 1993, 24). Given this, sex is both a physical attribute and socially constructed.

West and Zimmerman (1987) grappled with the social aspect of sex by adding a category to the sex, gender, and sexuality framework. They defined "sex category" as socially perceived sex and claimed that "recognition of the analytical independence of sex, sex category, and gender is essential for understanding the relationships among these elements and the interactional work involved in 'being' a gendered person in society" (West and Zimmerman 1987, 127). However, the categories of sex category, gender, and sexuality are not just analytically, but also practically, distinct. West and Zimmerman ultimately identified gender as the performance one is accountable for based on sex category's leaving little room for feminine men and masculine women. "In virtually any situation, one's sex category can be relevant, and one's performance as an incumbent of that category (i.e., gender) can be subjected to evaluation" (West and Zimmerman 1987, 145). We are left with the ironic conclusion that gender is socially constructed yet is rigidly defined by sex category—an inadequate framework for the explanation of atypical gender behavior.

Lorber (1994, 1999) attempted to uncouple masculinity and femininity from sex category by developing subcategories of gender including gender status (being taken for a man or woman), gender identity (sense of self as a man or woman), and gender display (being feminine and/or masculine). Even with this delineation, Lorber, like West and Zimmerman (1987), consistently slipped into assumptions of the "natural" link between categories. For instance, she claimed transsexuals and "transvestites" do not challenge the gender order because "their goal is to be feminine women and masculine men" (Lorber 1994, 20). As well, she described socialization as a woman or man as "produce[ing] different feelings, consciousness, relationships, skills—ways of being that we call feminine or masculine" (Lorber 1994, 14). This account fails to explain the behavior and identity of trans people for two reasons. First, it assumes the intransigence between the categories man/

masculine and woman/feminine, which is not the experience of transsexuals and transgendered people. Not all men, constructed or biological, are masculine or wish to be. Second, Lorber asserted that being treated as a man or woman in social interaction creates a masculine or feminine consciousness. This assertion fails to explain how people grow up to have a gender identity contrary to that expected from their socialization. Lorber's work is important in defining gender as an institution that creates and reinforces inequality, but it also illustrates how easily sex and gender (masculinity and femininity) become elided when sex is used as the initiating point for gendering individuals.

Just like sex and gender, sexuality can also be defined as socially constructed. Sexual behaviors and the meanings assigned to them vary across time and cultures. For instance, Herdt's (1981) study of same-sex fellatio in a tribe in Papua, New Guinea, found that this behavior did not constitute homosexuality or pedophilia, although it might be defined as both in the United States. In the United States, same-sex behavior is assumed to occur only in individuals with a gay or bisexual orientation, yet the AIDS epidemic forced educators and epidemiologists to acknowledge the lack of correlation between identity and behavior (Parker and Aggleton 1999). Schippers (2000) documented a lack of correlation between sexual orientation and sexual behavior in her study of alternative hard rock culture in the United States. Seeing sexual behavior and its meaning as highly reliant on social context helps explain the changing attractions and orientation of female-to-male transsexual and transgendered people (FTMs) as they transition.

Sex, gender, and sexuality, then, are all to varying degrees socially interpreted, and all contribute to an overarching concept of gender that relies on both perceived sex and behaviors and their attribution as masculine or feminine.

A growing number of scholars are writing particularly about FTMs and female masculinities. The longest-term contributor has been Devor (1989, 1997, 1998, 2004). Adding to Devor's work in recent years have been Cromwell (1999), Halberstam (1998), Prosser (1998), and Rubin (2003). Although transsexuals are increasingly represented in academic research, concepts of gender, sex, and sexuality are rarely explored. Gender theorists have often examined transsexuality through the lens of gender (Kessler and McKenna 1978; Nicholson 1994; West and Zimmerman 1987); less often have transsexual theorists interrogated gender through the lens of transsexuality. Using transsexuality as a standpoint to complicate and critique gender has been more common in nonacademic writing (Bornstein 1995; Califia 1997; Feinberg 1998).

Most work in the social sciences regarding transsexuals has focused largely on male-to-female transsexuals (Bolin 1988; Ekins 1997; Lewins 1995). Work by social scientists is important because it can help transform individual, personal experiences into broader social patterns and illuminate the role of social interaction and institutions. The limited research on FTMs offers a unique construction to social science research regarding transsexuality. Devor (1997) documented the lives of 46 FTMs using extensive quotes, allowing FTMs to speak about their lives, their upbringing, and their experiences with transitioning. Although this work is an incredibly detailed recording of the life experiences of FTMs, Devor avoids interpreting or theorizing about the experiences of FTMs and the potential meanings they have for the field of gender studies.

Prosser (1998) took to task the loss of materiality and "the body" in postmodern work regarding transsexuals. Prosser reminded theorists that gender is not simply conceptual but real, and experienced in the body (see Devor 1999). Although Prosser's critique of postmodern thought around transsexuality is extremely important, my interviews indicate that he may overemphasize the importance of the body in transsexual experience. Particular body characteristics are not important in themselves but become important because of social interpretation.

Cromwell (1999) eloquently summarized notions of gender and sexuality and described them as being located in either essentialist or constructed frameworks. He criticized both and claimed that exclusively constructionist explanations rely on the primacy of social interaction, implying that gender identity does not exist when individuals are alone. He claimed that trans people are important to study because, through them, it is evident that even if socially constructed, there is an underlying, unwavering gender identity. Most important though, Cromwell asserted that trans people's construction of identities, bodies, and sexualities as different rather than deviant subverts the dominant gender/sex paradigm. Rubin (2003) concurred with Cromwell's view of the paradox that gender identity is socially constructed yet at the same time embodied and "absolutely real" (Cromwell 1999, 175). Prosser (1998), Cromwell, and Rubin all challenge aspects of gender theory that do not mesh with the experiences of transsexuals and transgendered people. The body is a very real aspect of the (trans)gendered experience and expression, and even though gender identity is socially constructed, it takes on a solidity and immutability that is not dependent on social interaction.

With this emerging academic work regarding transsexuality, the need to examine how transsexuality and transgenderism complicate the gender field has arisen. Questions such as the following have become increasingly compelling:

> What is the impact of changing sex on the individual's social and sexual behaviors? How does an individual's sex affect other people's interpretation of his or her behavior? As sex changes, how does social interaction change?

By investigating the changing behaviors and interactions of FTMs as they transition, this article illustrates important connections between gender and perceived sex and contributes to the social scientific understanding of transsexuality. Examining the experience of FTMs clarifies that masculinity and femininity are not inextricably linked with male and female and that perceived sex is important in interpreting behavior as masculine or feminine. This project also adds to social scientific work on transsexuality by using transsexuality as a standpoint to critique gender in a systematic, empirically based manner. As well, it supports recent academic work regarding FTMs (Cromwell 1999; Prosser 1998; Rubin 2003) by illustrating the importance of the body to gender and gender identity and helps to increase the representation of FTMs in the social scientific literature on transsexuality.

Study Design and Sample

For this project, I interviewed 18 trans-identified people, all born female, the majority residing in Seattle, Washington. I sought informants in a variety of ways. I contacted friends and acquaintances with contacts in the trans community and introduced myself to people I knew to be trans, soliciting interviews. I also attended the National Gay and Lesbian Task Force conference, Creating Change, in Oakland, California, in November 1999, recruiting two informants and attending two trans-specific workshops, one regarding families and the other regarding relationships. I relied on snowball sampling to recruit the majority of the interviewees. Although this small sample is not random, the interviewees were able to provide a great deal of information regarding the relationship between perceived sex and gendered behavior.

Respondents ranged in age from 20 to 45 and had begun living as trans between the ages of 18 and 45 (see Table 1). I say this with some hesitation because many FTMs privately identify as trans for years before transitioning or being out about their identity. In this case, I am defining "living as trans" v being referred to as "he" consistently, publicly and/or in their subcultural network. With this definition, three of the respondents were not living as trans even though they identified as transgendered.

Fourteen of the respondents were white, one was African American, two were Latino, and one was Chinese American. Only one respondent did not previously identify as lesbian or bisexual. After transitioning, defining sexual orientation becomes more complicated since sex, and sometimes sexual preference, changes. Assigning sexual orientation requires assigning people to categories based on the sex of the sexual participants. Since many FTMs report being newly attracted to men after transitioning, it appears that their orientation has changed even though, in a sense, they remain homosexual (previously a lesbian, now gay). However, if they are still primarily involved with lesbians or with feminine women, it is difficult to say their orientation has changed when only their perceived sex is different. As well, if an individual is primarily attracted to feminine people, but after transitioning dates feminine men as well as feminine women, his gendered sexual preference has not changed, so it is unclear whether this describes a change in sexual orientation. Because of these complexities, the table records the reported sexual preference as closely as possible without relying on usual categories of sexual orientation.

Even though they were raised in a variety of locations, the great majority of respondents currently live in urban areas. The sample is probably not representative of the trans population in the United States because it is overwhelmingly urban and emphasizes FTMs who have chosen not to assimilate into mainstream, heterosexual culture. These people, it seemed, might be better positioned to comment on changes in the trans community regarding notions of sex, gender, and sexuality because they have access to greater numbers of

Table 1. Sample Characteristics

Pseudonym	Age	Race/ Ethnicity	Current Sexual Preference	Time from Beginning of Physical Transition	Transition Status
Aaron	34	White	Bio women, bio men, FTMs	1 year	Hormones
Billy	30	White	Bio men, FTMs	6 years	Hormones, chest surgery
Brandon	20	African American	FTMs, male-to-female transsexuals, bio women		Nontransitioned
Dick	27	White	Bisexual	2 years	Hormones, chest surgery
Jessica	22	White	Mainly bio women, femmes		Nontransitioned
Jay	27	Chinese American	Bio women		Nontransitioned
Joe	38	Latino	Bio women, FTMs	8 years	Hormones, chest surgery
Kyle	25	White	Bio women		Nontransitioned
Luke	25	White	Mainly bio women		Nontransitioned
Max	21	White	Bio women, femmes	1 year	Hormones, chest surgery
Mick	38	White	Lesbians	2 years	Chest surgery
Mitch	36	White	Bio women, femmes	4 years	Hormones, chest surgery
Pete	34	White	Queer, bisexual	3 years	Hormones, chest surgery
Rogelio	40	Latino/Black	Bio women	6 years living as trans, 1 year taking hormones	Hormones
Sam	30	White	Bio women, bio men, FTMs	4 years	Hormones, chest surgery
Ted	29	White	Pansexual	1 year	Hormones
Terry	45	White	Unknown because of recent transition	3 months	Hormones
Trevor	35	White	Bio women, femmes	1 year	Hormones, chest surgery

Note: Bio women = biological women; bio men = biological men; FTMs = female-to-male transsexual and transgendered people.

trans people and are more often engaged with others about trans issues.

At the time of the interviews, five of the informants were nonoperative and not taking hormones. Only one seemed certain he never wanted medical intervention, and that was due to a compromised immune system. Of these five, none have seriously considered taking hormones, but four expressed a strong desire for chest surgery that involves removal of the breasts and repositioning of the nipples if necessary. Two could not have surgery for financial reasons and one for medical reasons, and one was hesitant for family and political reasons.[3]

Only 1 of the 18 interviewees had had chest surgery, was not taking hormones, and had no further plans for medical intervention. Twelve of the 13 taking hormones had had chest surgery or were planning to do so. The remaining individual was not considering chest surgery due to concerns about keloids due to his dark skin.[4] He expressed frustration at how little information was available to darker-skinned transmen about the potential effects of surgery.

I interviewed FTMs using a general set of questions regarding their experiences with the medical community, the trans community, their families, and their relationship to masculinity. I did not set out to prove a preformulated hypothesis regarding the relationship between sex, gender, and sexual orientation; nor did I predetermine the ideal number of respondents. Instead, in a manner derived from grounded theory, I interviewed respondents until I started to hear common patterns in their comments and stories. Ekins (1997, 3), utilizing grounded theory in his exploration of identity processes for female-to-male transsexuals, described grounded theory as that "which demands intimate appreciation of the arena studied, but which writes up that intimate appreciation in terms of theoretical analyses." Grounded theory expands our understanding of qualitative research; it relies not only on documentation of interviews but also on the standpoint of the researcher and her or his intimate relationship with the topic of interest. For this reason, I reveal myself as transgendered, born female, with no immediate plans to transition. By "transition," I mean to live as a man by taking hormones and acquiring whatever surgeries necessary. This position as both transgendered and not transitioned gives me a keen interest in the relationship between sex, sex category (perceived sex), and gender and perhaps a voyeuristic interest in hearing what it is like to "cross over"—the difference between internal identity as a man and social interaction when perceived as one. I believe being trans identified gave me easier access to trans people and made it easier for interviewees to confide in me not only because they felt more at ease but because I had familiarity with common cultural terms, customs, and issues.

Findings

The perceived sex of individuals, whether biological or not, influences the meaning assigned to behavior and the tenor of social and sexual interaction. FTMs illustrate the reliance on both sex and behavior in expressing and interpreting gender. Perceived sex and individual behavior are compensatory, and both are responsible for the performance of gender: When sex is ambiguous or less convincing, there is increased reliance on highly gendered behavior; when sex is obvious, then there is considerably more freedom in behavior. For this reason, sex is not the initiating point for gender. Instead, sex, whether biological or constructed, is an integral aspect of gender. "If the body itself is always seen through social interpretation then sex is not something that is separate from gender but is, rather, that which is subsumable under it" (Nicholson 1994, 79).

As I listened to interviewees, the tension and balance between behavior and appearance, between acting masculine and appearing male, became evident. In general, interviewees confirmed Nicholson's (1994) assertion that (perceived) sex is an important aspect of the construction of gender and that perceived sex is a lens through which behavior is interpreted. However, particular sex characteristics such as a penis or breasts are not as crucial to the perception of sex as their meanings created in both social and sexual interaction.

Generally, after taking hormones, interviewees were perceived as men regardless of behavior and regardless of other conflicting sex signifiers including breasts and, in the case of one interviewee, even when nine months pregnant.[5] The physical assertion of sex is so strong through secondary sex characteristics that gender identity is validated. Interviewees find certain sex characteristics to be particularly important to their social identity as male: "I think it's all about facial hair. It's not about my fetish for facial hair, but socially, when you have facial hair, you can pass regardless of what your body looks like. I mean, I was nine months pregnant walking around and people were like, 'Ooh, that guy's fat' " (Billy).

Another interviewee also finds facial hair to be particularly important to initial gender/sex attribution. In reply to the question, "For you, what is the most important physical change since transitioning," he responds, "Probably facial hair, because nobody even questions facial hair.... I've met FTMs that have these huge hips. I mean this guy, he was [shaped] like a top, and he had a full beard. Nobody questioned that he had huge hips, so that is the one key thing. And probably secondary is a receding hairline. Even with a high voice, people accept a high voiced man" (Joe).

As the interviewees became socially recognized as men, they tended to be more comfortable expressing a variety of behaviors and engaging in stereotypically feminine activities, such as sewing or wearing nail polish. The increase in male sex characteristics creates both greater internal comfort with identity and social interactions that are increasingly congruent with sex identity. As a result, some FTMs are able to relax their hypermasculine behavior.

> I went through a phase of thinking every behavior I do is going to be cued into somehow by somebody. So, I've got to be hypervigilant about how many long sentences I say, does my voice go up at the end of a sentence, how do I move my hands, am I quick to try and touch someone.... And I got to a point where I said, This is who I am.... There are feminine attributes and there are masculine attributes that I like and I am going to maintain in my life.... If that makes people think, "Oh you're a fag," well great, all my best friends are fags.... But when I was first coming out, it was all about "I've got to be perceived as male all the time, no matter what." That bone-crushing handshake and slapping people on the back and all of that silliness. I did all that. (Rogelio)

Like Rogelio, Pete finds transitioning gave him the freedom to express his feminine side: "It was very apparent how masculine a woman I was... and now it's like I've turned into this flaming queen like 90 percent of the time. And so my femininity, I had an outlet for it somehow, but it was in a kind of gay way. It wasn't in a womanly kind of way, it was just femininity. Because I don't think that female equals femininity and male equals masculinity" (Pete).

Sex category and gendered behavior, then, are compensatory; they are both responsible for the social validation of gender identity and require a particular balance. When sex is ambiguous or less convincing, there is increased reliance on highly gendered behavior. When sex category is obvious, then there is considerably more freedom in behavior, as is evident when talking to FTMs about the process of transitioning.

For two interviewees, gay men are particularly valuable role models in deconstructing traditional masculinity and learning to incorporate "feminine" behavior and expression into a male identity:

> So, those fairly feminine men that I have dated have been very undeniably male, but they haven't been a hundred percent masculine all the time, and I think I've learned from my relationships with them to sort of relax. Lighten up a little; nail polish isn't going to kill anybody. I think that I'm more able to be at peace with all of the aspects of myself.... [Now] I'm not going to go out of my way to butch it up. I'm male looking enough to get away with it, whereas when I did that kind of stuff before I transitioned people were like, "Well, you're not butch enough to be a man." (Billy)

FTMs transition for many reasons, but aligning external appearance with internal identity and changing social interaction were the chief reasons given by my interviewees. "Doing gender" (West and Zimmerman 1987) in a way that validates identity relies on both internal and external factors. Being able to look like one feels is key to the contentment of many FTMs. More than interacting with the social world as a man, comfort in one's body can be a chief motivator for FTMs, especially when seeking chest surgery. "I'd say that having a flat chest really seems right, and I really like that. I can throw a T-shirt on and feel absolutely comfortable instead of going [hunching shoulders]. And when I catch my reflection somewhere or look in the mirror, it's like, 'Oh, yeah' instead of, 'Oh, I forgot,' and that's been the most amazing thing… recognizing myself" (Trevor).

Some interviewees believed they would be content to live without any medical treatment or with chest surgery but not hormones as long as they were acknowledged as transgendered by themselves and their social circle. Even for those who were able to achieve a reasonable level of internal comfort, social interaction remained an ongoing challenge. Feeling invisible or not being treated in congruence with their gender identity motivated them to take hormones to experience broader social interaction appropriate to their gender identity. Some FTMs reported the desire to be seen as trans by other FTMs as an important factor in their decision to transition. For others, being called "ma'am" or treated as a woman in public was particularly grating. Being "she'd" was a constant reminder of the incongruence between social identity and internal gender identity.

> And the longer I knew that I was transgendered, the harder it got to live without changing my body. It's like the acknowledgment wasn't enough for me, and it got to a point where it was no longer enough for the people who knew me intimately to see my male side. It just got to be this really discordant thing between who I knew I was and who the people in my life knew I was… because I was perceived as a woman socially. I was seen as a woman and was treated differently than how I was treated by my friends and the people that I loved…. So finally after a couple of years… I finally decided to take hormones. (Billy)

The potential impact on social interaction is key to the decision to transition. Although for some FTMs, gaining comfort in their body is the crucial element in decision making, for most interviewees, the change in social interaction is the motivating factor. Being treated as a man socially is important enough to risk many other things including loss of family, friends, and career. For other interviewees, though, not wanting to be treated as a man in all social situations motivated them not to transition. "In some ways, I wouldn't really want to give up my access to woman's space, and I think that would be a big reason why I wouldn't do it because I like being around women. I don't feel like I'm women identified, but I'm women centered. So in that sense, I wouldn't want to give up being able to spend a lot of time with women in different contexts that I might lose if I passed as a man" (Jay).

Some interviewees also worried that appearing as a biological man would make them no longer identifiable as trans or queer, making them invisible to their communities. As well, for some of those not transitioning, the potential loss of friends and family outweighed their desire to transition.

As expected, social interaction changed radically after transitioning, but sometimes in ways not anticipated. Whether these changes were positive or negative, expected or not, they still provided FTMs with social validation of their gender identity and the clear message that they were passing.

Changing Interaction

Many transmen found being perceived as a man enlightening. The most often noted changes to social interaction included being treated with more respect, being allowed more conversational space, being included in men's banter, and experiencing an increase in women's fear of them. Some FTMs realized that they would be threatening to women at night and acted accordingly while others were surprised to realize that women were afraid of them. "I remember one time walking up the hill; it was like nine o'clock, and this woman was walking in front of me, and she kept looking back, and I thought, 'What the hell is wrong with that girl?' And then I stopped in my tracks. When

I looked at her face clearly under the light, she was afraid. So I crossed the street" (Joe).

For many FTMs, becoming an unquestioned member of the "boys' club" was an educational experience. The blatant expressions of sexism by many men when in the company of each other was surprising to these new men.

> I was on one of the school shuttles on campus and it was at a time when there weren't a lot of people on. There was a male bus driver, myself, and a young woman on the bus, and she had long blonde hair, a very pretty girl. She got off the bus, and there was just me and the bus driver, and the bus driver was reading me as a guy and totally being a sexist pig. I did not know how to deal with it or how to respond, let alone call him on his shit because I wasn't particularly, at this point, feeling like I wanted to get read or anything. So I basically just nodded my head and didn't say anything. (Ted)

One nontransitioned FTM who is usually taken for a man at work also feels pressure to conform and to ward off suspicion by either ignoring or contributing to sexist and homophobic comments when among coworkers. This is in direct contrast to Pete's experience, who became known as an outspoken advocate for women and minorities at his job after transitioning: "I feel like I'm one of the guys, which is really kind of odd. In some ways, it's really affirming, and in some ways, it's really unsettling. In Bellevue [his former job], it was a joke. 'Pete's here, so you better shut up.' Because they're sexist, they're homophobic, they're racist. And I would say, 'This is not something I think you should be talking about in the lunch room.' So I was constantly turning heads because I'm kind of an unusual guy" (Pete).

Acting like a "sensitive new age guy" did not challenge Pete's masculinity or essential maleness but simply defined him as "kind of an unusual guy." He was able to assume this role because his gender was established and supported through his unquestionably male appearance.

Interviewees found that their interactions with both men and women changed as they transitioned. After transitioning, a few FTMs, like the previously quoted interviewee, maintained strong feminist ideals and worked hard to change to appropriate behavior for a feminist man. This was an effort as behavioral expectations for men and butch lesbians differ radically, and what may be attributed to assertiveness in a masculine woman becomes intolerable in a man:

> I found that I had to really, really work to change my behavior. Because there were a lot of skills that I needed to survive as a butch woman in the world that made me a really obnoxious guy. There were things that I was doing that just were not okay. Like in school, talking over people. You know when women speak, they often speak at the same time with each other and that means something really different than when a guy speaks at the same time. And so it wasn't that I changed, it was that people's perceptions of me changed and that in order to maintain things that were important to me as a feminist, I had to really change my behavior. (Billy)

The perception that behavior had not really changed, but people's assignation of meaning to that behavior had, was common in the interviews. That is, what is masculine or feminine, what is assertive or obnoxious, is relative and dependent on social context. And the body—whether one appears male or female—is a key element of social context. These interviews suggest that whether a behavior is labeled masculine or feminine is highly dependent on the initial attribution of sex.

Besides gaining information as insiders, FTMs also felt they gained permission to take up more space as men. Many FTMs transition from the lesbian community, and most in this sample had been butch identified. As a result, they were used to having what they perceived to be a comfortable amount of social space even though they were women. As they transitioned, however, they were surprised at how much social privilege they gained, both conversationally and behaviorally. Terry, a previously high-profile lesbian known for her radical and outspoken politics, reported, "I am getting better service in stores and restaurants, and when I express an opinion, people listen. And that's really weird because I'm not a shy person, so having people sort of check themselves and make more conversational space than they did for me before is really kind of unsettling" (Terry).

As well as being allowed conversational space, many of these new men received special attention and greater respect from heterosexual women because their behavior was gender atypical yet highly valued. They were noticed and rewarded when confronting sexist remarks, understanding women's social position, and performing tasks usually dominated by women. Billy reports an experience in a women's studies class where he was the only man siding with the female students' point of view: "A woman came up to me after class and said, 'Wow, you know you're the most amazing feminist man I've ever met.' I just did not have the heart to ruin that for her. I was just like, you know, there are other guys out there who are capable of this, and it's not just because I'm a transsexual that I can be a feminist" (Billy). The ability to shop for clothes for their girlfriends was cited by two interviewees as a skill much admired. They reported excessive attention from saleswomen as a result of their competence in a usually female-dominated area:

> One other thing I have noticed about women, and in particular saleswomen in stores, is that they're always shocked that I can pick out good clothing items either for myself or for someone else, and I don't really need help with that. And I get flirted with constantly by saleswomen, I think largely because they get that I get how to shop. So, they see this guy that's masculine and secure in himself and he's not having to posture, and he can walk up with an armload of women's clothes that he's been picking out.... She [the saleswoman] says, "Wow, I want a boyfriend like you." So I get a lot of that. (Mitch)

These accounts underscore the relationship between behavior and appearance. When FTMs are perceived as men, their gender-atypical behavior is not sanctioned or suspect but admired and rewarded. Their perceived status as male allows their masculinity to remain intact even in the face of contradictory evidence. This contrasts with the experience of one FTM not taking hormones who is usually taken for a butch lesbian. Saleswomen at Victoria's Secret treated him rudely when he shopped for lingerie for his girlfriend until he made a greater effort to pass as a man. When passing as a man, he received markedly better service.

Not all FTMs gain social status by being perceived as men. It is a common assumption, bordering on urban legend, that transitioning brings with it improved status, treatment, and financial opportunities. However, having a paper trail including a previous female name and identity can severely compromise job prospects, especially in a professional position.

> The reality is we are on the bottom of the economic totem pole. And it does not matter what our educational background is. We could be the most brilliant people on the planet and we're still fucked when it comes to the kinds of jobs that we've gotten or the kinds of advances that we've gotten in the job market. Here I am, I've been out of law school for nearly 10 years, and I'm barely scraping by. And if I go in and apply for a job with a firm, well yeah, they may really like me, but once they start doing any investigating on my background, my old name comes up. (Mitch)

The assumption of a rise in status after sex reassignment also rests largely on the assumption of whiteness. Through my limited sample and conversations with friends, it appears that becoming a Black man is often a step down in status. Rogelio talks about the change in his experience as he becomes more consistently taken for a man:

> I am a Black male. I'm the suspect. I'm the one you have to be afraid of. I'm the one from whom you have to get away, so you have to cross the street, you have to lock your doors. You have to clutch whatever you've got a little closer to your body.... It's very difficult to get white FTMs to understand that.... [As a Black person], if I go into a store, I am followed. Now I am openly followed; before it was, "Oh, let's hide behind the rack of bread or something so that she won't see us." Now it's, "Oh, it's a guy, he's probably got a gun; he's probably got a knife. We have to know where his hands are at all times." (Rogelio)

Although it is an unpleasant experience, he reports that at least he knows he is consistently passing as a man by the rude treatment he receives from other men in social situations.

Another group of FTMs also experiences being perceived as male as a liability, not a privilege. Even though FTMs can have feminine behavior without calling their maleness into question, feminine behavior does lead to an increase in gay bashing and antigay harassment. FTMs who transitioned from being very butch to being perceived as male generally experienced a radical decline in harassment. Two of these butches were even gay bashed before transitioning because they were perceived to be gay men. With additional male sex characteristics, however, they were no longer perceived to be feminine men. For these men, the transition marked a decline in public harassment and intimidation. However, for more feminine FTMs, the harassment increased after transitioning. Appearing as small, feminine men made them vulnerable to attack. This interviewee reported a marked increase in violence and harassment after transitioning:

> I get gay bashed often. That's my biggest fear right now is male-on-male violence.... Once I just got over pneumonia. I was downtown and I was on my way to choir, and some guy looked at me, and I was wondering why he was staring. I looked at him and I looked away. He called me a faggot because I was staring. He said, "Stop looking at me, faggot," and he chased me seven blocks. At first I thought he was just going to run me off, but I kept running and he was running after me as fast as he could and everybody was standing around just kind of staring. And I became really panicked that no one was ever going to help if I really needed it. People yell "faggot" at me all the time. (Dick)

One interviewee experienced about the same level of violence and harassment before and after transitioning. Unfortunately, he was attacked and harassed as a gay man as often before as after transitioning. On one occasion before transitioning, he was followed home and badly beaten by two men who forced their way into his house believing that they were assaulting a gay man: "If I'm with my partner I'm read as straight so I don't have to worry about being jumped as a gay guy, but if I am at a queer event and my partner's not around or if I'm just by myself.... But I've just gotten to a point where I'm like, 'Fuck it.' At least now that I am on hormones, I have a little more strength to fight back" (Ted).

In sum then, FTMs are motivated to change their physical presentations for two reasons: First, to become more comfortable with their bodies and achieve greater congruence between identity and appearance and, second, to change social interaction so that it better validates their gender identity, both subculturally and in the wider social world. This strategy to change social interaction is very effective. All FTMs who transitioned noticed a marked change in their social interactions. Not all of these changes in interaction were positive, however. First, the recognition that women are treated poorly compared to men was a shock. Second, being identified as a man was a liability when one was Black or appeared feminine. In other words, the assumption of an increase in privilege only consistently applied to masculine, non-Black men. Even then, the liabilities of being found out, especially on the job, remained.

Sexual Orientation and Gender Identity

Sexual behavior is another site that more clearly explicates the relationship between sex and gender. Sexual orientation is based not solely on the object of sexual and erotic attraction, but also on the sex category and gender performance created in the context of sexual interaction. The performance of gender is crucial in the sexual arena for two reasons: First, because sexuality is expressed through the body, which may or may not align with an individual's gender identity and, second, because heterosexual intercourse can symbolize the social inequalities between men and women. Altering the body alters the sexual relationships of FTMs by changing their gender/sex location in sexual interaction.

Many FTMs change sexual orientation after transitioning or, at the least, find that their object attraction expands to include both sexes. Devor (1997) found a large increase in the number of FTMs who, after transitioning, were sexually attracted to gay men. Why do many transmen change sexual orientation after transitioning? Even the earliest sexuality studies such as the Kinsey report (Kinsey, Pomeroy, and Martin 1948) provide evidence that individuals' attractions; fantasies, and behaviors do not always align with their professed sexual orientation. Currently, a diverse gay culture and the increased ease of living a gay lifestyle have created a wide variety of options for people with attractions to the same or both sexes (Seidman 2002). As well, coinciding with a rise in gay and lesbian cultures in the 1960s and 1970s was a heightened feminist consciousness. For some feminists, sexual relationships with men are problematic because of the power dynamic and broader cultural commentary enacted in heterosexual relations. Bisexual women sometimes find the dynamic untenable and choose to identify as lesbians. Aaron, a previously bisexual woman, confirms:

> I do have an attraction to men; however, when I was a straight woman, I totally gave up going out with men because I was a strong female person and had a lot of problems interacting with men, even in the anarchist community, the punk community. They like tough girls, this strong riot girl persona, and yet when you're in the relationship with those same people, they still have those misogynistic, sexist beliefs about how you're supposed to interact in bed, in the relationship. I just never fit into that mold and finally said, "Fuck you guys; I'm not going there with you," and just came out as a dyke and lived happily as a dyke.... What I realize coming into the transgendered community myself was that it made so much sense to become transgendered, to become visually male, and to be able to relate to men as a man because then they would at least visually see me as part of who I am in a way that they could not see me when I was female.... That's really exciting for me.... I can still relate to femmes who are attracted to transmen. I can still relate to butches. I can still relate to straight women... but I also get back being able to relate to men, and that's definitely a gift. (Aaron)

In another example, Dick was primarily involved with men and briefly identified as a lesbian before transitioning. He found sexual orientation and gender identity to be inexplicably entangled as he struggled to clarify his identity. When he was a woman and in a long-term relationship with a man, he began to identify as queer. He assumed that his male partner was incongruent with his queer orientation. Over time, he realized that the sex of his partner was not as crucial to his queer identity as was the gender organization of the relationship. Identifying as queer was an attempt to express the desire for interaction congruent with gender identity rather than expressing the desire for a partner of a particular sex.

> [Transitioning] makes a difference because it's queer then, and it's not locating me as a straight woman, which is not going to work. The way that I came out as queer, I thought it was about sexuality but it's really about gender. I was in a relationship with a man who I had been with for a couple of years... and then I started figuring out this thing about queerness, and I could not put my finger on it and I couldn't articulate it, but I knew that I couldn't be in a relationship with him.... But what I figured out a lot later was that it wasn't about not wanting to be with a guy; it was about not wanting to be the girl. (Dick)

Heterosexuality, then, is a problem for these FTMs not because of object choice but because of the gendered meaning created in intimate and sexual interaction that situates them as women. Most of the FTMs in the sample who changed sexual orientation or attractions after transitioning did not previously identify as bisexual or heterosexual. Two key changes allowed them to entertain the idea of sexual involvement with men. First, the relationship and power dynamic between two men is very different from that between a man and a woman. Second, in heterosexual interactions previous to transitioning, the sexual arena only reinforced FTMs' social and sexual position as women, thus conflicting with their gender identity. After transitioning, sexual interaction with men can validate gender identity:

> So, it's okay for me to date men who were born men because I don't feel like they treat me weird. I couldn't stand this feminization of me, especially in the bedroom. Now I feel like I actually have a sex drive. Hormones didn't make me horny, the combination

of me transitioning and taking hormones made me have maybe a normal sex drive. (Dick)

I've never totally dismissed men as sexual partners in general, but I knew that I'm very much dyke identified. But I think being masculine and having a male recognize your masculinity is just as sexy as a woman recognizing your masculinity, as opposed to a man relating to you as a woman. (Trevor)

I do not wish to imply that many lesbians are simply repressed bisexuals or heterosexuals using sex reassignment to cope with their sexual attraction toward men. Instead, I am arguing that the sexual interaction between FTMs and men is decidedly different from heterosexual interaction. The type of male partner generally changes as well—from straight to gay. For many FTMs, their change in sexual orientation and the degree of that change were a welcome surprise. Some appreciated the opportunity to interact with men on a sexual level that felt free of the power dynamics in heterosexual relations. Others were happy to date other FTMs or biological men as a way of maintaining their queer identity. Several interviewees who transitioned from a lesbian identity did not like appearing heterosexual and identified as queer regardless of their object choice because their body and gender status disrupted the usual sexuality paradigm. Still, they struggled with their invisibility as queer after transitioning. "Being with an FTM, we're the same, it's very queer to me.... A lot of times, I'm bugged if I walk down the street with a girl and we seem straight.... I think that's the worst part about transitioning is the queerness is really obliterated from you. It's taken away. I mean you're pretty queer, somebody walking down the street with a guy with a cunt is queer, but it's invisible" (Joe).

In his work with male-to-female transsexuals, Lewins (1995) discussed the relationship between gender and sexual orientation in the context of symbolic interactionism. The sexual arena is a site for creating and validating sex and gender identity because "when we desire someone and it is reciprocated, the positive nature of continuing interaction reaffirms and, possibly for some, confirms their gender identity" (Lewins 1995, 38). Sexual interaction, depending on the sexual orientation of the partner, is key to validating the male identity of FTMs. Whether that partner is a heterosexual or bisexual woman or a gay man, the interaction that involves the FTM as male confirms gender identity.

Conclusion

Trans people are in the unique position of experiencing social interaction as both women and men and illustrate the relativity of attributing behavior as masculine or feminine. Behavior labeled as assertive in a butch can be identified as oppressive in a man. And unremarkable behavior for a woman such as shopping or caring for children can be labeled extraordinary and laudable when performed by a man. Although generally these new men found increased social privilege, those without institutional privilege did not. Becoming a Black man or a feminine man was a social liability affecting interaction and increasing risk of harassment and harm. Whether for better or worse, being perceived as a man changed social interaction and relationships and validated gender identity.

In addition to illustrating the relativity of assignation of meaning to behavior, these interviews illustrate the relativity of sexual orientation. Sexual orientation is based not exclusively on object attraction but also on the gendered meanings created in sexual and romantic interaction. Sexual orientation can be seen as fluid, depending on both the perceived sex of the individuals and the gender organization of the relationship.

This study of a small group of FTMs helps clarify the relationship between sex and gender because it does not use sex as the initiating point for gender and because most respondents have experienced social interaction as both men and women. Much sociological theory regarding gender assumes that gender is the behavioral, socially constructed correlate of sex, that gender is "written on the body." Even if there are case studies involving occasional aberrations, gender is generally characterized as initiating from sex. With this study, though, the opposite relationship is apparent. Sex is a crucial aspect of gender, and the gendered meaning assigned to behavior is based on sex attribution. People are not simply held accountable for a gender performance based on their sex (see West and Zimmerman 1987); the gendered meaning of behavior is dependent on sex attribution. Whether behavior is defined as masculine or feminine, laudable or annoying, is dependent on sex category. Doing gender, then, does not simply involve performing appropriate masculinity or femininity based on sex category. Doing gender involves a balance of both doing sex and performing masculinity and femininity. When there is no confusion or ambiguity in the sex performance, individuals are able to have more diverse expressions of masculinity and femininity. This balance between behavior and appearance in expressing gender helps explain the changing behavior of FTMs as they transition as well as the presence of men and women with a diversity of gendered behaviors and display.

Notes

1. Interviewees do not necessarily identify as female-to-male transsexual and transgendered people (FTMs). There are many terms that more closely describe individuals' personal identity and experience including "trans," "boy dyke," "trannyboy," "queer," "man," "FTM," "transsexual," and "gender bender." For simplicity and clarity, I will use "FTM" and "trans" and apologize to interviewees who feel this does not adequately express their sex/gender location.
2. See Lucal (1999) for an excellent discussion regarding interpersonal strategies for disrupting the gender order.
3. Politically, some feminist FTMs express discomfort at becoming members of the most privileged economic and social class (white men).
4. A keloid is thick, raised, fibrous scar tissue occurring in response to an injury or surgery; it occurs more often in darker-skinned individuals.
5. After taking testosterone, an individual appears male even if he or she discontinues use. The interviewee who became pregnant discontinued hormones to ovulate and continue his pregnancy, then began hormones again after childbirth.

References

Auerbach, Judith D. 1999. From the SWS president: Gender as proxy. *Gender & Society* 13: 701–703.

Bolin, Anne. 1988. *In search of Eve: Transsexual rites of passage*. South Hadley, MA: Bergin & Garvey.

Bornstein, Kate. 1995. *Gender outlaw: On men, women, and the rest of us*. New York: Vintage.

Califia, Patrick. 1997. *Sex changes: The politics of transgenderism*. San Francisco: Cleis Press.

Cromwell, Jason. 1999. *Transmen and FTMs: Identities, bodies, genders, and sexualities*. Urbana: University of Illinois Press.

Delphy, Christine. 1993. Rethinking sex and gender. *Women's Studies International Forum* 16: 1–9.

Devor, Holly [Aaron Devor]. 1989. *Gender blending: Confronting the limits of duality*. Bloomington: Indiana University Press.

———. 1997. *FTM: Female-to-male transsexuals in society*. Bloomington: Indiana University Press.

———. 1998. Sexual-orientation identities, attractions, and practices of female-to-male transsexuals. In *Current concepts in transgender identity*, edited by Dallas Denny. New York: Garland.

———. 1999. Book review of "Second skins: The body narratives of transsexuality" by Jay Prosser. *Journal of Sex Research* 36:207–208.

Devor, Aaron H. 2004. Witnessing and mirroring: A fourteen stage model of transsexual identity formation. *Journal of Gay and Lesbian Psychotherapy* 8:41–67.

Ekins, Richard. 1997. *Male femaling: A grounded theory approach to cross-dressing and sex-changing*. New York: Routledge.

Fausto-Sterling, Anne. 1993. The five sexes: Why male and female are not enough. *Sciences* 33 (2): 20–24.

———. 2000. *Sexing the body: gender politics and the construction of sexuality*. New York: Basic Books.

Feinberg, Leslie. 1998. *Trans liberation: Beyond pink or blue*. Boston: Beacon.

Halberstam, Judith. 1998. *Female masculinity*. Durham, NC: Duke University Press.

Herdt, Gilbert. 1981. *Guardians of the flutes: Idioms of masculinity*. New York: McGraw-Hill.

Kanter, Rosabeth Moss. 1977. *Men and women of the corporation*. New York: Basic Books.

Kessler, Suzanne J. 1990. The medical construction of gender: Case management of intersexed infants. *Signs: Journal of Women in Culture and Society* 16:3–27.

Kessler, Suzanne J., and Wendy McKenna. 1978. *Gender: An ethnomethodological approach*. New York: John Wiley.

Kinsey, Alfred C., Wardell B. Pomeroy, and Clyde E. Martin. 1948. *Sexual behavior in the human male*. Philadelphia: W. B. Saunders.

Lewins, Frank. 1995. *Transsexualism in society: A sociology of male-to-female transsexuals*. Melbourne: Macmillan Education Australia.

Lorber, Judith. 1994. *Paradoxes of gender*. New Haven, CT: Yale University Press.

———. 1999. Embattled terrain: Gender and sexuality. In *Revisioning gender*, edited by Myra Marx Ferree, Judith Lorber, and Beth Hess. Thousand Oaks, CA: Sage.

Lucal, Betsy. 1999. What it means to be gendered me: Life on the boundaries of a dichotomous gender system. *Gender & Society* 13:781–97.

Messner, Michael A. 2000. Barbie girls versus sea monsters: Children constructing gender. *Gender & Society* 14:765–84.

Nicholson, Linda. 1994. Interpreting gender. *Signs: Journal of Women in Culture and Society* 20:79–105.

Parker, Richard, and Peter Aggleton. 1999. *Culture, society and sexuality: A reader*. Los Angeles: UCLA Press.

Prosser, Jay. 1998. *Second skins: The body narratives of transsexuality*. New York: Columbia University Press.

Rubin, Henry. 2003. *Self-made men: Identity and embodiment among transsexual men*. Nashville, TN: Vanderbilt University Press.

Schippers, M. 2000. The social organization of sexuality and gender in alternative hard rock: An analysis of intersectionality. *Gender & Society* 14:747–64.

Scott, Joan. 1988. *Gender and the politics of history*. New York: Columbia University Press.

The Rise of Recreational Burlesque: Bumping and Grinding Towards Empowerment

KAITLYN REGEHR

American Burlesque is a historical movement dating back to the late nineteenth century that has recently made a resurgence into modern day culture. The form of performance, which in 1934 Fiorello LaGuardia the mayor of New York described as involving "cock-eyed philosophies of life" and "ugly sex situations" (Tracey 2003), has of late been adopted as a recreational activity. This phenomenon has embraced historic seductive performance styles and iconic sexualized images of women, such as the Ziegfeld Follies and pin-up girls, and is credited with converting them into modern forms of empowerment. Searching for community, physical and emotional well-being, and increased self-esteem, women are seeking to draw upon the bold strength of the audacious burlesquers of the past.

"ReVamped" is a Canadian reality television show in which a group of women move into a house with a burlesque choreographer, who teaches them the art of burlesque, working on confidence, self-awareness and historical concepts of beauty.

Kaitlyn Regehr, "The Rise of Recreational Burlesque: Bumping and Grinding Towards Empowerment." *Sexuality & Culture* 16. (June 2012): 134–57.

The eight women have all been through difficult relationship breakups leaving them (to a greater or lesser extent) with lowered self-esteem, and in some more severe cases, a misplaced sense of identity, because who or what they used to define themselves as has ceased to exist in their lives. The participants range in age from 21 to 49. They have varying amounts of dance training, and come from across Canada from major metropolitan areas to towns of 500 people. At the completion of 6 weeks of burlesque bootcamp, each individual performs in a solo burlesque act, broadcast on national television, in their new "empowered" state. This study examines the experiences of women on the television show "ReVamped." Through reviewing video-footage and transcripts of filmed interviews and participant observation, the study examines the relationship between burlesque dancing and empowerment through the experiences of these individuals.

Several authors and researchers contend that dance is a viable therapeutic modality to enhance emotional and cognitive health. The American Dance Therapy Association (ADT Association 2011), for instance, suggests that the psychotherapeutic use of movement can heighten cognitive, social and physical integration of the individual. While dance/movement therapy differs from recreational dancing and is conducted by a trained professional in a specialized environment, many studies support the use of recreational dance as a valid instrument for the improvement of emotional health. Studies have focused on such topics as ballroom dance for the treatment of geriatric depression (Haboush et al. 2006), calypso dancing as a form of women's empowerment (Thorington Springer 2008), and aerobic dance to enhance positive affect in undergraduate students (Bartholomew and Miller 2002). Although, as Haboush et al. (2006) suggest, recreational dancing does not systematically include the expression of emotions as emphasized in dance/movement therapy, it is a physical activity that can have potential benefits.

When considering both professional and recreational burlesque, questions of empowerment versus objectification often arise. Whitehead and Kurz's study *Empowerment and the Pole: A Discursive Investigation of the Reinvention of Pole Dancing as a Recreational Activity* is one of the few academic papers to date that examines the modern integration of what has traditionally been exotic dance into women's fitness (Whitehead and Kurz 2009). This study repeatedly questions women who participate in research focus groups and semi-structured interviews, when they refer to pole dancing aerobics as "empowering." Although the suggestion that the authors can detect *real empowerment* over women who practice *(un)real empowerment* is questionable, the concern regarding objectification is valid and leads to an important conversation.

The common apprehension in studies of striptease or other performance forms in which women display their bodies in a sexual fashion is the historical implications of objectification. Sheila Jeffreys, in her study *Keeping Women Down and Out: The Strip Club Boom and the Reinforcement of Male Dominance*, asserts that striptease instills male dominance and that "all women living in a society where strip clubs flourish (such as ours) are likely to be affected by them in a variety of ways" (Jeffreys 2008: p. 164). Others counter by suggesting that it is men who are the financially exploited, weak and passive participants in strip clubs, succumbing to the sexual control of the female performer (Dodds 1997; Frank 2002). Yet both arguments are potentially reconcilable. Dancing can be exploitative and destructive for women, while it can also be experienced as liberating and rewarding. Barton concludes that "with sexual and the sexist as closely intertwined as they are in our culture, it is difficult to assess what is truly freeing and what is subtly undermining of a woman's long term happiness" (Barton 2002: p. 600). What has not been discussed in the literature is the applicability of this argument to recreational burlesque in which women actively choose to engage without financial gain. Can engaging in recreational burlesque be empowering?

Empowerment itself is a controversial concept. Ozer and Bandura (1990: p. 472) suggest that empowerment methods "achieve their effects by equipping people with requisite knowledge, skills, and resilient self-beliefs of efficacy to alter aspects of their lives over which they can exercise some control." According to Richard Breeding in his study *Empowerment as a Function of Contextual Self Understanding*, the development of empowering personal characteristics is associated with developing greater self-awareness (Breeding 2008). Empowerment, however, seems to be a word that can span any field and can be defined as anything from emotional self-worth to legal authority. A library database search for articles with the word empowerment in the title, revealed over 14,000 articles. For instance, a study of the empowerment of female dairy farmers in India defines empowerment as "the process of building a woman's capacity to be self-reliant and to develop her sense of inner strength" (Shefner-Rogers et al. 1998: p. 323). Judi Chamberlin, who writes from the "National Empowerment Center" in the United States, found when doing a study on empowerment in mental health that almost every type of mental health program claimed to "empower" clients (Chamberlin 2011). However, she noted that there seemed to be very few operational definitions of the term and even less evidence that the programs that used the term were in any measurable way different from those that do not.

A term that is closely affiliated with empowerment is *self-efficacy*. Albert Bandura, originator of the term and prominent scholar in the area, defines self-efficacy as a person's belief in their ability to successfully perform a particular task (Bandura 1977); that is, the individual's capabilities to mobilize the motivation and courses of action needed to exercise control over events (Ozer and Bandura 1990). A sense of personal efficacy is the root of human agency. Regardless of other factors serving as guides or motivators, the foundational belief that one has the power to produce a desired effect as a result of one's actions is the core incentive for overcoming difficulties (Benight and Bandura 2004). Self-efficacy beliefs regulate and dictate human functioning concerning whether the individual thinks in self-enhancing or self-debilitating ways, how well they motivate themselves, their quality of emotional life, their relationships both romantic and otherwise, and the choices they make at important decision points which sets life's courses (Benight and Bandura 2004). Ozer and Bandura (1990) assert that self-efficacy can be enhanced through four possible processes: (1) mastery of experiences; (2) social persuasion; (3) changes in emotional states; and (4) modeling of coping strategies. Positive outcomes attained through personal action or achievement heightens self-efficacy. In addition, Bandura asserts that positive self-efficacy can be strengthened by reducing "negative emotional proclivities and correct misinterpretations of bodily status" (Bandura 1995: pp. 4–5).

This study explores whether women engaging in recreational burlesque training describe their experience as empowering, and how they, as individual participants in the performance, define and operationalize the concept of empowerment. It examines the concept of empowerment and self-efficacy in relationship to the female form, and will attempt to unearth the vast complexities within such discussions.

Burlesque in a Historical Context

On February 8th, 1869, the *News Clipper*, America's principal theatrical trade paper, printed the following classified advertisement:

> Miss Lydia Thompson, the Celebrated Burlesque, will arrive in New York on August or September. Applications for engagements to be made to Mr. Alex Henderson, Prince of Wales Theatre, Liverpool (Allen 1991: p. 3)

After tremendous success in London, on October 7, 1868, Miss Lydia Thompson and her touring troupe, the "British Blondes," opened at the Metropolitan Theatre in New York (Pullen 2005), thus launching the tradition of the American Burlesque. Lydia Thompson appeared on stage invariably dressed as a male character, such as Robinson Crusoe or Robin Hood, yet clothed in such a way as to clearly show her feminine form. In the documentary film *The Anatomy of Burlesque*, John Kenrick, New York University theatre historian, notes that "On top of having the tights, these women looked at the men in the audience, were audacious to them, were sexually enticing, said very suggestive things" (Tracey 2003). Lydia Thompson and her troupe posed a threat in the form of a gender revolution (Pullen 2005), acting simultaneously as a threat to patriarchal structures and yet paradoxically having considerable appeal to bourgeoisie men (Allen 1991). As Robert Allen suggests in his commentary *Horrible Prettiness: Burlesque and American Culture*, "The history of burlesque since 1869 demonstrates the transgressive power of the union of charismatic female sexuality and invasive insubordination, as well as strategies employed by patriarchal culture to disengage, marginalize, and/or contain these two aspects of public, commercial gender representation" (p. 281). Ironically, despite public perception of the lewdness of burlesque, the early forms did not involve any nudity.

In 1893, the Chicago World's Fair exhibited a performer by the name of "Little Egypt" who performed an aggressive variant of belly dancing called the "cooch" dance. From then on, every burlesque show required a pseudo "cooch" dance performer operating under such names as "Little Cairo" or "Little Alexandria" (Tracey 2003). Coinciding with this fascination of the exotic, Oscar Wilde wrote his 1891 play *Salome*. At the end of the play, when Salome is to perform for Herod, Wilde simply writes in parentheses one brief sentence "Salome dances the Dance of the Seven Veils" (Wilde 1891). From this brief stage direction. *Salomania* was born (Keft-Kennedy 2005). As author of *Salome and Her Sisters*, Toni Bentley describes women bought Salome outfits, cigarette cartons adorned with the image of Salome, and Salome figurines (Tracey 2003). Salome was a pop icon of the time "women's newly realized social and sexual freedoms were crystallized in dance in the figure of Salome" (Studlar 1997: p. 106). Striptease then entered burlesque, as some performers added the removal of parts of their costumes as an allusion to the *Dance of the Seven Veils* (Allen 1991).

By the late 1920s, Minsky Brothers had taken a working class form of entertainment and created an upscale multi-million dollar operation. In 1930, a *New York Times* theatre critic wrote a profile titled "*Burlesque with a Ph.D.: Those Up and Coming Entrepreneurs, the Brothers Minsky Finally Tell All*." (Shteir 2004: p. 133). The article suggested that the Minskys were the "first citizens of Second Avenue" and that they not only brought burlesque to Hudson Street but they also ennobled it. The Minskys brought burlesque to historic Broadway theatres and made the entertainment of the working class a profitable "high class" operation.

In January 1934, Fiorello LaGuardia assumed the office of Mayor of New York harboring a "fierce hatred of the commercialized vice." He is reported to have asserted "Cock-eyed philosophies of life, ugly sex situations, cheap jokes and dirty dialogue are not wanted. Decent people don't like this sort of stuff and it is our job to see to it that they get none of it" (Shteir 2004: p. 156). Including the words *Minsky* and *Burlesque* on a marquee became illegal in New York City. Consequently, burlesque was reduced to traveling shows. By the mid-1960s, burlesque had for the most part died out. As Dixie Evans, a 77-year-old former burlesque traveling dancer explains "now what do they gotta do to get those people, they gotta take it all off . . . society changed and it happened in the late 1950s burlesque went out" (Tracey 2003).

In the 1960s, competition with x-rated movies, topless bars and men's magazines resulted in many burlesque theatres resorting to interspersing adult movies with the performances of strippers (Shteir 2004). Despite these efforts, it was clear that the world had changed and, on the morning of December 28, 1969 in Kansas City, one of the last burlesque houses in America closed its doors (Shteir 2004).

Allen (1991) suggests that, although it is possible to view nineteenth century burlesque as a "woman-centered form of theatrical expression with strong progressive, anti-patriarchal leanings" (p. 282), it can also simply be viewed as one of many forms of exploitation of women's bodies throughout history. Others assert that burlesque confronts conceptions regarding sexual and gender boundaries within the mainstream, thus confounding perceptions that performing women are dichotomized into the categories of victims or capitalists (Shteir 2004). The latter argument is very much in line with the spirit of the burlesque revival of this past decade. This counter culture community simultaneously ironically mocks, whilst also nostalgically embracing, historic seductive performance styles and iconic sexualized images of women (i.e. Ziegfeld Follies and pin-up girls). Groups encompassing a wide range of women have found expression in burlesque, including Big Burlesque, which refers to itself as the "the original fat bottom review" (MacAllister 2011), and Queer Femme Follies: "Where dykes are proud to be flirty and feminine" (Flemming 2007). Within this movement, which is often referred to as "nouveau burlesque," individuals have found communities and performance-based media to explore their sexuality. The nouveau burlesque movement has been closely affiliated with women's empowerment, a claim that has sparked a heated debate amongst feminist scholars. Some scholars view nouveau burlesque as positive, suggesting that such performances provide a physical display of women taking ownership of their sexuality. Others, however, feel differently:

> Let's not kid ourselves that this is liberation. The women who buy the idea that flaunting your breasts in sequins is power—I mean, I'm for all that stuff—but let's not get so into the tits and ass that we don't notice how far we haven't come. Let's not confuse that with real power. I don't like to see women fooled. Erica Jong in Interview with Ariel Levy (2005: p. 76)

The current study is not concerned with nouveau burlesque, but rather is interested in the revival of traditional burlesque dance and how it is being redefined and used by women as a form of exercise and recreation. The women that are the focus of this paper are not involved in professional or semi-professional performance communities, nor are they involved in public displays of disrobing.

Research Method

This qualitative study explored the experience of empowerment in women undergoing an intensive 6-week "ReVamping." Specifically, this research has the following objectives:

1. To document the views of women engaging in a 6-week intensive burlesque training program;
2. To understand the current resurgence of burlesque;
3. To explore women's subjective views and experiences of empowerment and self-efficacy through burlesque.

The Case

Qualitative research is a naturalistic inquiry (Lincoln and Guba 1985), and while the setting for this research is by no means natural or without complications, the phenomenon of "reality" television has ironically become a common occurrence. Over the past decade, scholars have identified reality television as a concentrated environment where female participants play an active role in the exploitation of their own sexuality (Nowatzki and Morry 2009; Stern 2005). Viewers are offered a plethora of programs that focus around heavy drinking and women in bikinis. Stern's 2005 study, which interviewed young MTV viewers, revealed that female viewers are aware of the exploitation in the programming, yet view the programs as somewhat based in reality. Furthermore, although the women interviewed were critical of the young women featured on the shows, they themselves would consider applying to be contestants (Stern 2005). Nowatzki and Morry (2009) also touch upon reality television and media, and identify that, although there has always been a pressure on women's physical appearance, the current abundance of sexual material in mainstream media (including reality television) has enforced an expectation on women to be sexual and beautiful.

There is a large distinction, however, that must be made between reality programming targeting the 12- to 24-year-old mixed gender demographic on MTV, and ReVamped, the program in question. ReVamped is a health and wellness show that is targeted at women in their mid-twenties into their mid-fifties. The goal of the show is to explore emotional recovery for women after a relationship break-up using the sensual movements of burlesque to improve self-esteem. The show's aim is to promote confidence in women following the end of a relationship. It looks to encourage independence from the men (as these were all heterosexual women) whom these women had previously utilized to define themselves.

In the season of the show that is the focus of this study, the participants were flown in from across Canada to a small city in southern Ontario in order that they might be removed from possible distractions and contact with their former partner. Here, the participants moved into a large house in which a state-of-the-art gym and dance studio had been constructed specifically for the show. The dance studio was also equipped with iconic burlesque props that might be used to inspire the women. In addition to daily burlesque dance classes, the women had daily sessions with a fitness trainer and nutrition expert, and spent time with a specialist in women's sexuality and relationships. The house was equipped with a private video diary room for women who did not feel comfortable documenting the entirety of their progress with interviewers and preferred to record their experiences individually. At the completion of the 6 weeks, there was a cabaret performance in which the women performed one group dance number and individual solo dances. The individual solos were choreographed to capitalize on the women's strengths and body type with a goal of boosting their confidence. While filming, efforts were made to provide a female-only environment during the dance classes.

Data Collection: Sources of Data

While all data reviewed for this study was filmed for television, the names of the women have been changed in this analysis.

1. *Transcripts of Video Interviews with the Producer:* Each woman participated in lengthy interviews with the producer at three separate times: prior to the beginning of the show; at mid-point in the filming; and at the end of the filming. These interviews were filmed in order that segments could be used on air.
2. *Transcripts of Daily Debriefing Interviews:* The women did daily on-camera debriefing interviews about their feelings of the events of the day. The filmed interviews were transcribed verbatim.
3. *Video Footage of Dance Classes:* All dance classes over the 6-week period were recorded by three cameras to provide different perspectives.
4. *Participant-Observation:* Daily discussions, informal interactions, and dance instructions were held over the 6-week period. These discussions and interactions were recorded by the three camera crews for the purposes of televising the discussions.

Trustworthiness

Trustworthiness is a concept used to address the credibility and reliability of qualitative inquiry (Creswell 2007). The intention of trustworthiness in a qualitative study is to support the project and to uphold that the inquiry's findings are "worth paying attention to" (Lincoln and Guba 1985: p. 290). Ensuring trustworthiness in this study was achieved through: (1) prolonged engagement; (2) triangulation of data; (3) noting exceptions to major findings; (4) peer debriefing; and (5) rich, thick description.

Prolonged engagement involves a building of trust with participants and becoming immersed in the culture (Creswell 2007). In this study, I spent a 6-week intensive period with participants, where they engaged in daily burlesque classes and discussions about their experiences. In addition to my time spent as a participant observer (Murchison 2010), I spent weeks reviewing transcripts and video footage.

Triangulation of data refers to the process by which researchers make use of multiple and different sources of data and methods of data collection (Creswell 2007; Murchison 2010). These multiple sources of data lead to an analysis of common themes or perspectives that are expressed in different manners or domains. In this study, this was achieved through observations in classes, and by review of written and video documentation of classes, interactions and interviews.

Noting exceptions, also called negative case analysis (Denzin and Lincoln 2005), involves the researcher identifying outliers and exceptions to common themes. That is, in which circumstances do the summarized themes not apply? These negative cases allow the researcher to refute, challenge or amend their own interpretations (Olesen 2005). In this study, examples of women who did not fit into the theme or interpretation are included in the results and discussion.

Peer debriefing occurs when the researcher seeks to externally check the research process and findings through the discussion with colleagues (Lincoln and Guba 1985; Murchison 2010). The role of the peer debriefer is to challenge the researcher's assumptions. Multiple discussions were had during the process with the creative team and with colleagues who have expertise in documentary film and women's studies. These colleagues provided alternative views and interpretations to my own, which are incorporated into this analysis.

Rich, thick description entails detailed description of the participants and settings under study. This allows readers to determine whether the findings can be transferred to other situations because of shared characteristics (Creswell 2007). This paper provides a description of the environment, the process and the participants, and has many direct quotes from the women that were filmed for the show.

Observations and Analysis

"Comes With Baggage" . . . The Beginning

This section reports themes derived from a review of footage of the participants from dance class over the first 3 weeks of filming, the initial on-camera interview with the producer, and observations of the women's statements and behavior in the first week of filming. Themes that arose were *"damaged goods"* that included low self-worth and lack of control; *"not comfortable in my own skin"* that reflected body image issues; and *"been a long time since I've been in front of a mirror,"* a look at the physical manifestation of insecurities. From this examination of the women at the beginning of this study, the question that inevitably arises is "*Why Burlesque*?"

Why Burlesque? . . . I Want to Be "Me" Again

Before commencing this process all participants were asked a variety of questions by the producer, one of which was "Why do you wish to spend 6 weeks training as a burlesque dancer?" One woman, Crystal, responded *"To feel like a woman again! To feel value in me, as in my own skin. To find what is under this snake skin."* Similarly another woman, Alison, replied *"My goal is to regain Alison."* Joanne stated, *"I want to become me again. . . . My goal is to become emotionally strong and have a feeling of self-worth."* Joanne from Peachland, British Columbia, had never been a burlesque dancer nor had she ever performed on stage aside from a ballet dance recital as a child, and yet she believed that training as a burlesque dancer would allow her to "become me again." In this statement, there is somehow a notion that the freed body acting upon impulses is the true self, and that the bawdy movements of burlesque are a departure from the current state and are thus liberating.

Many would suggest that the sexualized woman is placed in a position of little power. From this perspective, Joanne's attempt to "be emotionally strong and have a feeling of self-worth" through burlesque is simply evidence that she is engaging in "self-objectification" by subscribing to feminine ideals as defined by the male gaze (Fredrickson and Roberts 1997). Self-objectification as defined by Fredrickson and Roberts is the process in which women begin to internalize the external and value themselves based on physical appearance (Strelan et al. 2003). In this context, the women engaging in burlesque dance training could be viewed as simply reenacting women's historically subordinate position within the symbolic order of our society (Dodds 1997). As Broadway historian John Kenrick explains, although scholars have continuously fought for burlesque to be viewed as respectable by depicting the dancers as artists and asserting that the comedy has influenced our modern day sitcoms, the issue remains that "men went to watch women get undressed . . . [the dancers] offered you as much skin as they could get away with" (Tracey 2003).

By contrast, many scholars who have done work with exotic dancers suggest that burlesque and striptease are in fact inversions of the everyday world (Barton 2002; Dodds 1997; Frank 2002). These scholars contend that, at times, the performers are placed in a position of power by becoming sexually assertive and taking control of the offer, thereby reducing the audience to the passive state of voyeurism (Dodds 1997). The burlesque artist is thus a challenge to the dominant order (Kroker and Kroker 1987). Thus, for women in this study, and in particular Joanne, who came from an abusive relationship, it is possible that practising burlesque with a group of women does offer individuals a safe environment for self-exploration and emotional support.

Damaged Goods

Yet another layer of complexity in the conceiving of women's bodies within the question of empowerment is the variability of experience and emotional health of the individual women. All the women engaged in the television show had recently been through difficult relationship breakups. Before participating in the experience, they answered questions regarding their sense of self-worth post-breakup and prior to shooting. Joanne, when asked the question, "How do you feel about yourself and see yourself today?" stated, *"I feel like I have a sign on me that says" "comes with baggage" or "damaged goods."* She went on to express that *"I feel like I have lost my inner light, my joy of life, things, people, me."* Ottana stated, *"I see myself as being invisible, under-appreciated, and not noticed."* One woman, Jess, goes as far as to sympathize with her ex-boyfriend for having dumped her. This participant suggests that *"ever since I broke up with my ex, I'm just kind of "blah" about myself. I can understand why he broke up with me completely."*

Their answers to questions revealed a general sense of a lack of control. Many of the women reported that the breakup had not simply affected their lives romantically but in fact on a more general level throughout many aspects of their lives. Jess stated, *"I couldn't believe how upset I was. I left school because I couldn't handle the breakup. It took over my life and I wasn't able to study and I failed my finals."* Joanne explains that, *"I even had to take time off work."* Furthermore, she expressed feeling *"scatterbrained, zombie-like, forgot how to do every-day things sometimes."*

According to Social Cognitive Theory (SCT), perceived self-efficacy mirrors feelings of control over one's own environment and life activities (Luszczynska et al. 2009). Self-efficacy makes a difference in how people feel (Bandura 1977) and may be a substantial factor in the outcome of emotional states, symptoms of mental disorders, disability, pain and a variety of health-related outcomes (Luszczynska et al. 2009). Beliefs about one's own abilities help to overcome difficulties arising after a traumatic event (Benight and Bandura 2004). Although few studies have explored the potential impact of a woman's feelings of self-efficacy by allowing her to gain comfort with her own sexuality and sensuality, it seems logical that the relationship may exist between these two constructs. Luszczynska and colleagues postulate that, if negative emotions about the self and low self-esteem are present, self-efficacy perceptions are reduced, leaving the individual feeling less capable of mastering situations in which they are placed (Luszczynska et al. 2009). Thus, it seems reasonable that the more a woman perceives herself to be unappealing "invisible, under-appreciated, and not noticed," the less likely she is to view herself as capable of dealing with life's stressors, thereby decreasing her probability of attaining success.

Comfortable in My Own Skin

Body image, or the perception of one's own appearance, is recognized to be an integral factor in predicting self-esteem (Steese et al. 2006). Women in this study speak of their physical self. Joanne stated, "*I feel like I am not as attractive as I should be. I don't feel youthful any more. I used to feel SO youthful and vibrant. That is gone.*" Ottana also speaks of this concept of "sexy" stating, "*These days, I don't feel like my old self, I don't feel sexy. . . . I want to feel sexy for myself, to myself. I want to look in the mirror and see sexy.*" Here, Ottana seems to use "sexy" as synonymous with confident. Joanne also equates "sexy" with confident, explaining:

> *My concept of sexy is mostly I think attitude, feeling comfortable in your own skin, liking who you are. Being able to smile and mean it, not a fake smile . . . , I think sexy is a lot of things and I think if you're confident, I mean, sexy is also how you carry yourself.*

It is somewhat reassuring that participants do not seem to perceive "sexy" as a quantitative entity but rather understand it to be linked to their emotional self-worth. If feeling sexy is equated with self-worth, increasing confidence through recreational burlesque may indeed be empowering. Nevertheless, these women are at risk of tying their self-worth to dominant views of what "sexy" is. Many scholars have described the images of the modern sexually empowered woman as simply the same slim, white, heterosexual patriarchal ideal, repackaged and remarketed for the 3rd wave and post-feminist generation (Evans et al. 2010; Strelan et al. 2003).

Been a Long Time Since I've Been in Front of a Mirror

Dance classes allowed for a visual examination of the participants' comfort with their physical selves. Dance class during the filming of the show began with isolations of various parts of the body. The women were asked to exaggerate their movements to the full extent of their range of movement. This exaggeration of movement is an attempt to break the tension of a first burlesque class. Some of the women displayed substantial tightness in their shoulders. Crystal felt extremely uncomfortable opening up her shoulders. She openly stated that holding her shoulders in a caved formation gave her the sense that people were less likely to notice her. Due to the posture to which Crystal had become accustomed, she required private instruction to gain more fluidity in her back. When she was encouraged to open up her shoulders, she expressed feeling extremely vulnerable and became emotional. Joanne, who had undergone breast augmentation explained, *"My breast augmentation was a gift from him to me,"* also carried tension in her upper body. However, she had become so reliant on the silicon as a projected form of confidence, that she rarely found any need to use her upper back and shoulders as a source of movement.

When moving into the lower body and most specifically the hips, the instructor breaks down movements very technically. This way, in the beginning stages of the work, the participants can focus on the technicalities rather than "being sexy," a rather impossible and constricting concept to force upon women. One participant, Alison, became so embarrassed by hip rotations that she blushed and needed to turn away from the mirror. She noted, *"I haven't danced in a really long time, probably 18 years. So it's been a long time since I've been in front of a mirror. So I've changed a lot since then, I'm a little more self-conscious, so that'll take a bit of getting used to."* Another, Jess, similarly explained that she simply did not like mirrors, stating, *"we're not all comfortable with ourselves like that yet. So it's just very tense, weird."*

The mirror is particularly relevant here as it became a central figure within the study. Not only literally, since the mirror is a prominent fixture in the dance studio, but symbolically as well. Participants seemed to utilize the mirror as a measurement tool reflecting their insecurities and body image issues. I will discuss the mirror in greater detail below.

"I Might Not Look Sexy But I Feel a Little More Sexy" . . . Halfway Through Shooting

This section reports themes that were derived from a review halfway through the women's process. The information has been compiled using footage of the participants' group and solo dance classes, the halfway point on-camera interview with the producer, and observations of the women's statements and behavior during filming. Themes in this section are *"looking in the mirror," "me and the ex,"* and *"Eve Meringue's solo routine."*

Looking in the Mirror

By 3 weeks into the work, some of the women were still finding dance class to be a somewhat uncomfortable and exposing experience. Carla, who was probably most concerned with her weight, explained her continuous struggle with the concept of "being sexy." She explained, *"I find if I'm looking in the mirror, it's even harder. So if I avoid the mirror, I tend to be a little more sexy. I might not look sexy but I feel a little more sexy. So that's probably my biggest struggle, the dancing."* A study that observed women's exercise classes in mirrored and un-mirrored environments concluded, unsurprisingly, that women who had negative body image issues found taking classes in front of a mirror detrimental to their feeling state. However, changes in self-efficacy were unrelated to whether the exercise environment was mirrored or un-mirrored (Martin Ginis et al. 2003). In the present study, as the women continued with classes and began to see improvements in their abilities in class and subsequently their self-esteem, the mirror became less of a detrimental presence in the room and seemed to become an instrument of self-reflection.

Michelle, a woman in her mid-twenties, explained, "*I don't want to look at myself as a little girl doing big girl stuff anymore, like I want to be like a woman, like a full woman.*" Michelle, who is actually a hip-hop instructor, noted the following:

> *Well, (the burlesque instructor) has helped me be confident like as a dancer, definitely just to, you know, show more of my face. And like as a hip-hop dancer, I'm like, I'm very grounded and like mean and aggressive but you don't necessarily have to do that all the time. . . . , she's kind of helped me bring that new dimension to performing and you know, feeling confident with what my face looks like.*

Michelle used her new found comfort in what her "face looks like" as an indicator of her confidence as a whole. Michelle described her background as a hip-hop dancer as requiring her to project her energy into the floor, with shoulders and face focusing downward. By contrast, the burlesque training asked her to open her chest and project her energy outward. To fulfill the choreography requirements, Michelle needed not only to be comfortable with being looked at but she also needed to gain the confidence in herself to actively look back and engage with the audience. *Looking* is a consistent theme within burlesque history. Reports of Lydia Thompson's "British Blonds" upon arriving in New York in the late nineteenth century commented upon the performer's sheer audacity at both being looked at and looking. This confidence in "looking" in fact threatened to spark a gender revolution against 1870s American cultural norms (Pullen 2005).

The act of looking, or more specifically being looked at, is similarly a common topic within objectification theory. Liss et al. (2010) discuss the positive and negative implications of women enjoying the male gaze or male sexual attention. These authors suggest that, while women may enjoy the positive reinforcement from men through being admired or revered, such attitudes comply with and reinforce the current gender hierarchy in which women are valued as sexual objects. Therefore, although women may feel empowered, their actions may actually serve to help in enabling negative consequences of objectification (Liss et al. 2010).

In recreational burlesque, generally there are no men present in the classes, rarely do these women develop their skills to the level that would allow for public performance, and many participants even state they never show what they learn in class to their partners. However, what distinguishes this study is the reality television element. Although the program ReVamped airs on a women's network that targets female viewers, we must assume that men from the participants' lives would be surely be tuning in. Thus, eventual broadcast of the burlesque classes adds an additional complexity. Yet another factor that is problematic within this discussion is the presence of the ex-boyfriend/husband. Producers allowed women to invite their ex-partners to the final performance. As will be discussed later, women who did invite the men from their previous relationship gave a variety of reasons, including marking a life milestone, shedding the past, and "sweet revenge." While some participants may have determined their progress based on the ex's reaction, for others self-gaze became an essential measure of emotional health and healing:

> *I can now look in the mirror and go, I can see me as Crystal, as a person and not labeled as Crystal, as his wife and if he's disappointed in me today, then I look in the mirror and I'm disappointed in myself. Just owning myself again and just feeling like, okay, I don't need his permission. . . . I'm going to start just looking in the mirror and just seeing me for me.*

Me and the Ex

The term "me," as evidenced in the above quote by Crystal, seems to be a great distinguisher between the women. By the halfway point, some of the individuals continued to chart their success based on how their "ex" would respond to their progress, rather than from the standpoint of "me." Jess, for example, stated:

> *At the finale when my ex sees me dancing, I think he will be kind of stunned in a way because I'm dancing like really out of my element, it's like totally not me . . . I'm pretty modest in the way that I am. So I think he'll be surprised about that . . . And he'll probably regret it. I think he regrets it now that he broke up with me because well, look it, his loss. I'm on national television and he's going to cry.*

Similarly, Michelle explained, *"I want my ex's jaw to drop on the floor. I want him to be super shocked and just wowed by how far out of the box that I'm performing."* Others also continued to feel judged from afar. Carla expressed, *"So at the finale, I know kind of how my ex is going to react because I know him so well . . . he's just not that type of guy to like complement you or anything like that."*

Three weeks into the filming of the television show, all but one of the women confessed to wanting their ex to be able to see her at the end of the 6 weeks, as they were certain that they would feel more confident and project this confidence in their performance. Only four of the women said they continued to think about their ex. The other four participants said that their time spent worrying about their past relationship had greatly minimized. Crystal stated that,

> *My ex and I definitely have been in contact. And things that I've discovered and learned just in the last few weeks, made me realize it's so many things that, a lot of issues that we had was, it's his problem, it's no longer my problem. And I have to now know that and own that. Not everything is my problem.*

Alison, when asked by the producer if she had a different perspective on things 3 weeks into the process, responded, ". . . . *I'm working on forgiving myself for putting myself in that situation and allowing the things to happen that did."*

As suggested by Ozer and Bandura, self-efficacy can be enhanced through four possible processes, one of which is social persuasion (Ozer & Bandura 1990). That is, self-efficacy in part derives from how your performance is reflected by others. Joanne suggests that the women as a group created a supportive environment in which they were able to encourage each other and give positive feedback on each other's progress. This positive social persuasion only seemed to increase as the women's relationships became stronger and the pressure of the performance drew closer.

Most of the women commented that much of the experience involved being reliant on the other participant. A large portion of their emotional recovery was derived from the support of each other. One of the women explained, *"So far, I've learned so much about myself, especially with the ladies and I see so much of what I did wrong in the ladies because they went through the same thing."* Joanne explained a situation where she began to cry during gym class:

> *I was like, where is this emotion coming from. But I think maybe that's part of the healing too. You know, just being in a safe place and being able to cry and not really having to have a reason why you're doing it. It's just okay. And the other women look at you and go, hmm, alright, they put their arm around you and it's okay and they don't ask you why you're crying. It's okay, it doesn't matter why you're crying, you need to cry, you cry.*

However, it should be noted that not all of the individuals shared this sentiment. As Crystal noted:

> *You want everybody to get along but it's just not always possible for everybody to get along, at every moment of the time. Especially when each one of us has come from different walks of life and just different, we're all at just different pages in our world. And it's like trying to read all these pages all at once, you know, it just can't be done.*

Eve Meringue's Solo Routine

By the midway point through the burlesque training, the participants were working towards the finale show. The preparation for the performance involved individual sessions during which the participants created a burlesque persona. During persona work, the choreography was geared to the individual's specific body type, personality and skill set, hopefully allowing the individual a greater sense of competence. As Joanne stated:

> *Oh, I love my solo dance. My character is the muse and so it's like the model that an artist is going to paint. I'm here, you're so lucky to paint me and I'm wonderful. It's weird. It can almost be conceited. But that's how burlesque works, you know. Just, it's sensual and it's awesome and it's just, it's me, it is me.*

The performative nature of the task allowed Joanne to experience something she would normally view as "conceited," now as confidence. In this respect, the character is able to take responsibility for any criticism of vanity.

Crystal, who would be performing a traditional fan dance, was nervous about her slow and sensual piece of choreography. Although she revealed very little of her body in the dance, Crystal perceived the choreography to be more exposing than a modern striptease. Here, Crystal spoke about her persona Eve Meringue as being able to take on things she would deem to be inappropriate for herself.

> *Well, Eve Meringue's solo routine, has this big beautiful fan of feathers, wow. She's really going to come out in this one. She's going to have to . . . I think that my routine has a sense of intimacy . . . I feel very, in a vulnerable state for that . . . I think that slow seductive side of me has been put away for a very long time. So it'll be interesting to tap into that part of me again. It's there, it's just not something that I've displayed . . . I always keep talking about that whole let it go moment. Yeah, for Eve Meringue to come out, it's, I'm going to have to let it all go at this point.*

Crystal utilized her burlesque persona to unleash a different aspect of herself much like women buying Salome costumes in the early twentieth century. These women used the iconic image of the Salome's femme fatale to grant themselves the liberty to move and behave in a way that they would normally deem unacceptable (Keft-Kennedy 2005). For many turn of the century burlesque dancers, the myth of Salome's sensually exotic power and emasculating potential could be exploited in such a way that enabled the "middle-class white body of a dancer" (Keft-Kennedy 2005: p. 29). The exploitation of orientalism and the Middle Eastern belly dance was ideologically necessary to maintain their off-stage sense of propriety. The dancer's embodiment of the sexually uncontrollable Salome was constructed as a socially acceptable role play game for the western women (Keft-Kennedy 2005). She was allowed to explore the "otherness" of the Orient whilst maintaining her place within the secure construction of western gender roles (Keft-Kennedy 2005). Crystal continued in the burlesquer tradition of enjoying such liberties deemed inappropriate within "normative" cultural discourse but permitted under the guise of performance. By saying *"I always keep talking about that whole let it go moment. Yeah, for Eve Meringue to come out,"* she is unknowingly awaiting the privileges granted to performers throughout burlesque history. Carla similarly utilizes her burlesque persona "Mica May" to give her a confidence she would not allow herself under other circumstances.

> *I think Mica May would be confident, strong, you know, like a strong performer, all eyes on her, that kind of, you know, maybe a little bit of attitude. Yeah, I think that's going to be Mica May.*

For Carla, Mica May represents an idealized version of self. When asked if Mica May has similar characteristics to Carla, she replied:

> *I wouldn't say that's like Carla. . . . I'm so nervous and I get butterflies and then when it, I'm actually going to do it, like when I start doing it, it's like, okay, bam, I just do it and want to do it to the best I can. And so maybe for the finale, that'll come out, of me. And we'll, you know, it'll be Mica May with my little attitude too. Well, I'm hoping, hope I don't stumble and fall.*

The Grand Finale

This section reports themes that were derived from a review at the conclusion of the women's process. The information has been compiled using footage of the Finale performance, the women's final on-camera interview with the producer, and observations of the women's filmed statements and behavior backstage and after their performance. Themes in this section are *"it's OK for me to be alone," "sexy's back,"* and *"is the feeling sustainable?"*

It's OK for Me to Be Alone

Prior to performing, the participants were asked backstage to reflect upon the 6-week experience. Many of the women described their feelings towards their ex or the breakup of the relationship that initiated everything. The ex, a looming figure throughout the whole process, had become a symbol of low self-esteem, degradation and a weakened version of self. This is not to say, however, that the participants felt they now needed a new partner to complement their new found confidence. As Ottana explained:

> *The biggest thing that I discovered was that it's okay for me to be alone. I don't need a partner at the moment. I do want to be with somebody, but I've discovered that I'm not ready mentally and emotionally and, I think I'm just going to attack my problems now as opposed to go around them and try and avoid them. I'm going to deal with those first and, and then bring somebody in my life or in my son's life.*

Joanne, a woman who began this process stating that she felt completely "out of control" of her life due to her past relationship, explained that she doesn't *"even think about the ex at all."* Joanne continued this sentiment stating:

> *Unless I'm asked about him. And I don't even think about him, not one bit. And that feels good. And I'm dancing and I'm getting in better shape. . . . And emotionally, I just, I still cry sometimes but not like I used to. It's, it's amazing, I just, I feel like I'm back to who I was before I met him.*

Some of the participants chose to invite their former partners to the performance. This choice for some was conceived out of a need to prove superiority post-breakup. For others, however, it seemed to mark a life milestone of sorts. Crystal, having met her husband at the age of 17, contemplated the complexity of their relationship and a desire for him to mark this occasion with her based on their past intimacy and understanding. She explained that he is really the only person who can appreciate her growth and bear witness to the change.

> *My ex-husband is coming to the finale. And I'm actually excited to see him. He's known me for half my life and there is no, you know, he knows, there's no way I would have ever been able to do this. I did this for me, I did all of this for me. And I think he would appreciate it in the end to go, good job. And it's not like I need his approval or anything like that. This is about me.*

Crystal's sentiments are understandable, as performance requires viewers. As this entire process culminates in a performance, it is reasonable to expect that the participants may have specific ideas about who makes up their viewership. Kaeppler asks within performance "who are these viewers and what do these viewers see and understand?" (Kaeppler 1999: p. 22). In Crystal's case, it is important for her viewer to fully understand her development.

Sexy's Back

It is perhaps helpful to look at Joanne's progress here to fully appreciate the change within the individual. In an interview, Joanne discussed her progress over the past 6 weeks:

> *When I came here, I was, felt like a wounded little bird that had no confidence, no belief in myself, wasn't really sure if I could pull off the dance, wasn't really sure how in shape I was capable of getting in. The emotions I was going through were so heavy that I really didn't see the light at the end of the tunnel. And now, I think I'm at the light at the end of the tunnel. It's great. I mean, I am confident in myself. I hope to get more confident than I feel right now but so far, this is good.*

Other participants similarly noted changes within themselves due to the burlesque training. Ottana explained:

> *Yeah, I, when I started, I actually felt like I had lost the part of me that was actually sexy. I felt invisible. And now, doing the dances, the ladies are*

complimenting me all the time, that I look good and this and that. It's helped a lot. Especially the dances, it's just, it just, you, you have to feel sexy to be able to do the routine, so. If you don't feel sexy, you can't actually perform as well as you should. So yeah, I definitely think sexy's back.

Thorington Springer in her study of Calypso dance explains that, if only for a brief moment, the female performer grants both herself and the women in the audience the ability to embrace their "sexual selves" and "appreciate the erotic power of their bodies" without feelings of shame (Thorington Springer 2008: p. 114). She explains that, because erotic power has been confused with the pornographic, we deny the experience of the "erotic power" within us (Thorington Springer 2008). Thorington Springer goes on to discuss Andre Lorde who explains that, "The very word erotic comes from the Greek word eros, the personification of love in all aspects . . . " When I speak of the erotic, then I speak of it as an assertion of the life force of women; of that creative energy empowered, the knowledge and the use of which we are now reclaiming in our language, our history, our dancing . . . " (Lorde 1984: p. 55).

When interviewed after walking off stage, Crystal, having performed a traditional fan dance, similarly brought up this concept of "sexy":

I think I have my sexy back! This dancing and this moving and you know, just, just letting that part of me go to be able to enjoy being sexy and enjoy doing the dance moves but yet, feeling it inside and go, you know what? This actually looks pretty good. Hey, I really like this move, you know. But believing in it. So yeah, kind of a little bit feeling, feeling sexy.

"Sexy," as we have previously discussed, has become synonymous with "confident," in the women's excited conversations when exiting the stage. The performance becomes a space for a woman to vent, opening her fans wide, caressing herself on the wooden boards of a crowded smoky theatre. As Thorington Springer explains in her description of Calypso, the dance affords women the opportunity to "misbehave" and "break away," allowing them to disregard their preconceptions of womanhood and the desire of "respectability" (Thorington Springer 2008: p. 117). Sexy, mature and self-assured all seem to be the physical image of confidence to which the women had been aspiring. Michelle, after performing her solo dance in her role of Maven á la Mode "The Heroine" a World War II fighter pilot, spoke in these terms:

I feel like a very confident person and I feel like I have a completely different perspective on the world and how to live my life . . . I feel like a sexy mature woman. And even that, in itself, it was hard for me to say that, it was hard for me to acknowledge that. Because the real thing was I didn't believe it.

Is the Feeling Sustainable?

It is somewhat difficult to distinguish the women's unanimous positive response to the experience as truth, from the inevitable adrenalin rush they would have experienced while performing. Crystal writes in a Facebook wall post *"ReVamped is a life changing experience!"*

However, even now, less than a year after the study was conducted, we are still too close to the actual event to look seriously at the sustainability of these feelings. It is for this reason that the comments of participants from Season 1 of the television series who went through this process two and a half years ago are instructive. Kim, an individual who went on to file for divorce and buy a home for herself and her three-year-old daughter, explains her feelings one-year post-shooting.

Right after ReVamped I felt stronger, physically and emotionally, more empowered and much more confident than I ever have in my life. To take on a dance . . . and feel so comfortable with it so quickly already begins a process within your "self" of change . . . I felt so confident and sure of myself after Revamped that I went on to make life changing decisions for myself that I was not able to make before embarking on the ReVamped journey.

Then, when Kim was asked if she felt that this feeling had been sustained, she replied:

The feeling has definitely been sustained. I don't believe that there is anything about the ReVamped experience that I didn't take a piece of home with me and integrate into my life . . . Specifically I have embraced trying new things and trusting myself and my feelings. Burlesque inspired a lot of different feelings in me, but none more so then strength and the trust I now have for me. . . .

These comments are very much in line with four possible processes of enhancing self-efficacy as described by Bandura and Ozer. Firstly, a mastery of experience, then acknowledged by social persuasion, and finally changes in emotional states (Ozer and Bandura 1990). Bandura explains that human accomplishments and positive well-being require an optimistic sense of personal efficacy. There are moments throughout the women's performance where they are encouraged to be audacious, engage with the audience, and dare to be looked at. Thus, they are engaging with the liberating and transformative nature of dance/performance. They are browsing the aisles of historical seduction, whilst powerfully engaging with a sensual sense of self. What leaves to be seen is whether the emotional advances they made over 6 weeks, transfer to other areas of their lives.

Conclusion

American Burlesque is a historical movement that dates to the late nineteenth century and has had a resurgence in our culture in several forms and variations. This recent revival of burlesque has been popularized into the mainstream. Modern-day burlesque has embraced historic seductive performance styles and iconic sexualized images of women and converted them into forms of modern empowerment. Within these movements, women have found communities and performance based mediums to embrace their sexuality. This redefinition of burlesque has been closely affiliated with empowerment and self-efficacy. Over a 6-week period, eight participants in a reality TV show were filmed as they trained as burlesque dancers. This study sought to examine the relationship between burlesque dancing and empowerment. Observed here was the concept of empowerment and self-efficacy and how it relates to a woman's body and sensuality through movement.

Self-efficacy refers to a person's belief in their ability to successfully perform a particular task. That is, the individual's capabilities to mobilize personal motivation. Ozer and Bandura suggest that self-efficacy can be enhanced through four possible processes: (1) mastery of experiences; (2) social persuasion; (3) changes in emotional states; and (4) modeling of coping strategies. Within the burlesque training, 3 out of 4 of these processes were operationalized (Ozer and Bandura 1990). Firstly, the mastery of experiences was to be accomplished through learning a new skill and successfully performing a solo burlesque number on stage. Second, social persuasion involved deriving a sense of success through the group camaraderie and the enthusiasm of the audience. Finally, the changes in emotional state were expressed by the women at the finale.

Not everybody would agree that this study examined true change or a genuine enhancement of self-efficacy. Whitehead and Kurz (2009) concluded their study of recreational pole dancing by stating that although the women experienced the activities as liberating and empowering on an individual level, the movement may secure societal level oppression in covert ways. Other authors have similarly expressed concerns that third wave feminist and post-feminist notions of sexual empowerment are simply familiar forms of oppression in a new guise (Strelan et al. 2003). The question remaining is: do we have the right to determine this experience? Just as the participants in Kurtz and Whitehead's study perceived themselves to be empowered, the women in this study expressed that they felt that they had enhanced self-efficacy and had a greater sense of empowerment. Controversies center around respecting women's choices, rights to sexual agency and reported enjoyment of sexual culture on one end of the spectrum, whilst also observing the re-objectification of the female form and women's active participation in re-sexualization of women on the other (Evans et al. 2010). It is possible, however, that these two polarities are somewhat reconcilable. Peterson (2010), in her study of the experiences of adolescent girls, argues that there is not one singular sexual empowerment. Rather, she suggests sexual empowerment is a continuum with multiple degrees and dimensions.

Largely absent from the literature that pits the notions of empowerment and exploitation related to exotic dance against each other is the impact on the individual. In Bernadette Barton's paper *Dancing on the Mobius Strip; Challenging the Sex War Paradigm*, she discusses the debate between empowerment and exploitation within research about sex workers. She states that sex workers find those who theorize about them as having little interest in them other than as a potential symbol for a cause (Barton 2002). In quoting a sex worker, Barton writes, *"When I read some stuff written by so-called "feminist allies" it feels like they are fighting over our bodies. Some of them are "pro-prostitution," as if it could be that easy. Then there are the others who say that prostitution is evil because it contributes to violence against women. . . . It's like prostitutes are just these bodies who are somehow connected to something bad and evil or something good and on the cutting edge of revolution. They just turn us into symbols"* (p. 587). Barton concludes that both sides of such a debate make defensible claims. Although this study does not concern the physical act of sex nor does it concern itself with professionals, we are looking at a sexualized dance form as empowerment. The women in this study did describe themselves as empowered through participation in a show in which they were taught burlesque dancing.

It is hard to determine the degree to which the findings of this study were biased due to the contrived nature of the reality TV environment. Firstly, there may have been a selection bias for contestants. Producers say they tried to involve a variety of women with a variety of body types, from different walks of life and with diverse levels of confidence and willingness to perform on stage in order to create "tension" and "drama" on the show. For example, stage fright or body image issues would provide "good story points" for the network. However, one must assume that anyone with true stage fright, performance anxiety or severe body image issues would be unlikely to apply to the program in the first place. Secondly, all discussions between the participants and directors, producers and on-air talent were filmed. No one was allowed to engage in a discussion with the women without a camera present, in order to ensure there would be no potential "story point" omitted. Therefore, the participants may have felt inhibited by the cameras or felt the need to perform for the camera.

Finally, it is essential to note the potential pressures for the women to convince themselves of a positive outcome. The women did invest 6 weeks away from their lives in order to participate in the television program. They had little contact with family and friends during this time. This investment of time and effort may have swayed an individual to convince herself that the experience had been worthwhile and beneficial. The participants were also aware that the network had invested tremendous amounts of money in the television show. However, while this may potentially have resulted in bias, network satisfaction seems unimportant to the group. In fact, at one point, the group wanted one individual to be removed from the show because they were unable to get along with her and denied producers any interviews or verbal communication until their demands were met. The participants did seem to be interested in the millions of viewers that would be watching the program. It is possible that the participants may have assumed that viewers would be hoping for a positive outcome.

It is likely that this would have been a more beneficial experience for contestants if it were not televised. That having been said, it would be rare to operate a 6-week retreat where women are removed from their lives in order to participate in such an experience in many other circumstances.

We may assume then that, although the women all stated that they were empowered by the experience, perhaps there are degrees of empowerment, as proposed by Peterson (2010). Lamb (2010) suggests in a study about sexuality in adolescent girls that, although feminist scholars may have notions or apprehensions of how to express a "healthy sexuality," it is possible that (in this case) adolescents should not be expected to address that ambivalence for us. This researcher does not suggest that adult women do not have greater responsibilities to society than adolescents, but it does touch upon a substantial question. If there are negative forms of sexual expression, such as behavior in which women actively re-produce objectification and the male gaze, what is our responsibility to offer women alternate forums that we deem as "good" or positive sexual outlets? Lerum and Dworkin (2009), in response to the APA's 2007 Task Force on the Sexualization of Girls, identify that feminists have had a long history battling for equality for women. Yet, they concede, "*Sounding the alarms on sexualization without providing space for sexual rights results in a setback for girls and women and for feminist theory*" (Lerum and Dworkin 2009: p. 260).

Some media images and message undoubtedly have influence on women as a group to the great detriment of some women. Sexuality has historically been, and will continue to be, complex. Nevertheless, one of the goals of contemporary feminism is to ensure sexual agency, sexual health and right to sexual exploration. In the context of recreational burlesque, the objective is to provide a safe environment where these goals can be achieved.

References

ADT Association. (2011). *What is dance/movement therapy?* Retrieved June 6, 2011, from http://www.adta.org/Default.aspx?pageId=378214.

Allen, R. (1991). *Horrible Prettiness: Burlesque and American Culture*. North Joanneina: University of North Joanneina Press.

Bandura, A. (1977). *A social learning theory*. New York: Prentice Hall.

Bandura, A. (1995). *Self-efficacy in changing societies*. Cambridge, UK: Cambridge University Press.

Bartholomew, J., & Miller, B. (2002). Affective responses to an aerobic dance class: The impact of perceived performance. *Research Quarterly for Excersize and Sport, 73*(3), 301–309.

Barton, B. (2002). Dancing on the Mobius Strip: Challenging the sex war paradigm. *Gender and Society, 16*(5), 585–602.

Benight, C., & Bandura, A. (2004). Social Cognitive Theory of posttraumatic recovery: The role of perceived self-efficacy. *Behaviour Research Therapy, 42*, 1129–1148.

Breeding, R. (2008). Empowerment as a function of contextual self-understanding; the effect of work interest profiling on career decision self-efficacy and work locus of control. *Rehabilitation Counseling Bulletin, 51*(2), 96–106.

Chamberlin, J. (2011). *A working definition of empowerment*. Retrieved June 7, 2011, from http://www.power2u.org/articles/empower/working_def.html.

Creswell, J. (2007). *Qualitative inquiry and research design: Choosing among five traditions* (2nd ed.). Thousand Oaks, CA: Sage.

Denzin, N., & Lincoln, Y. (2005). *Handbook of qualitative research* (3rd ed.). Thousand Oaks, CA: Sage.

Dodds, S. (1997). Dance and erotica: The construction of the female stripper. In H. Thomas (Ed.), *Dance in the city* (pp. 218–233). London: MacMillan Press.

Evans, A., Riley, S., & Shankar, A. (2010). Technologies of sexiness: Theorizing women's engagement in sexualization of culture. *Feminism & Psychology, 20*, 114–131.

Flemming, L. (2007). Queer femme follies: these queer burlesque dancers are fighting their own sexual revolution, where dykes are proud to be flirty and feminine in fishnet. *Curve*.

Frank, K. (2002). *G-strings and sympathy*. London: Duke University Press.

Fredrickson, B., & Roberts, T. (1997). Objectification theory: Toward understanding women's lived experiences and mental health risks. *Psychology of Women Quarterly, 21*, 173–206.

Haboush, A., Floyed, M., Carton, J., LaSota, M., & Alvarez, K. (2006). Ballroom dance lessons for geriatric depression: An exploratory study. *The Arts in Psychotherapy, 33*, 89–97.

Jeffreys, S. (2008). Keeping women down and out: The strip club boom and the reinforcement of male dominance. *Journal of Women in Culture and Society, 34*(1), 152–173.

Kaeppler, A. (1999). The mystique of fieldwork. In T. Buckland (Ed.), *Dance in the field: Theory, methods and issues in dance ethnography* (pp. 13–40). London: Macmillan Press.

Keft-Kennedy, V. (2005). How does she do that?: Belly dancing and the horror of a flexible woman. *Women's Studies, 34*, 279–300.

Kroker, A., & Kroker, M. (1987). *Body invaders: Panic sex in America*. New York: St. Martin's Press.

Lamb, S. (2010). Feminist ideals for a healthy female adolescent sexuality: A critique. *Sex Roles, 62*, 294–306.

Lerum, K., & Dworkin, S. (2009). "Bad girls rule": An interdisciplinary feminist commentary on the report of the APA Task Force on the Sexualization of Girls. *Journal of Sex Research, 46*, 250–263.

Levy, A. (2005). *Female chauvinist pig: Women and the rise of raunch culture*. New York: Free Press.

Lincoln, Y., & Guba, E. (1985). *Naturalistic inquiry*. New York: Sage.

Liss, M., Erchull, M., & Ramsey, L. (2010). Empowering or oppressing?: Development and exploration of the enjoyment of sexualization scale. *Personality and Social Psychology Bulletin, 37*, 55–68.

Lorde, A. (1984). Uses of the erotic: The erotic as power. In A. Lorde (Ed.), *Sister outsider: Essays and speeches* (pp. 53–59). Berkeley, CA: Crossing Press.

Luszczynska, A., Benight, C., & Cieslak, R. (2009). Self-efficacy and health-related outcomes of collective trauma: A systematic review. *European Psychologist, 14*(1), 51–62.

MacAllister, H. (2011). *Big Burlesque: The original fat-bottom review*. Retrieved June 7, 2011, from http://www.bigburlesque.com/.

Martin Ginis, K., Jung, M., & Gauvin, L. (2003). To see or not to see: Effects of exercising in mirrored environments on sedentary women's feeling states and self-efficacy. *Health Psychology, 22*(4), 354–361.

Murchison, J. (2010). *Ethnography essentials*. San Francisco: Jossey-Bass.

Nowatzki, J., & Morry, M. (2009). Women's intentions regarding, and acceptance of, self-sexualizing behavior. *Psychology of Women Quarterly, 33*, 95–107.

Olesen, V. (2005). Feminisms and models of qualitative research. In N. Denzin & Y. Lincoln (Eds.), *Handbook of qualitative research* (3rd ed., pp. 158–174). Thousand Oaks, CA: Sage.

Ozer, E., & Bandura, A. (1990). Mechanisms governing empowerment effects: A self-efficacy analysis. *Journal of Personality and Social Psychology, 58*(3), 472–486.

Peterson, Z. (2010). What is sexual empowerment? A multidimensional and process-oriented approach to adolescent girls' sexual empowerment. *Sex Roles, 62*, 307–313.

Pullen, K. (2005). *Actresses and whores: On stage and in society*. Cambridge, UK: Cambridge University Press.

Shefner-Rogers, C., Rao, N., Rogers, E., & Wayangankar, A. (1998). The empowerment of women dairy farmers in India. *Journal of Applied Communication Research, 26*, 319–337.

Shteir, R. (2004). *Striptease: The untold history of the girly show*. Oxford: Oxford University Press.

Steese, S., Dollette, M., Phillips, W., Hossfeld, E., Matthews, G., & Taormina, G. (2006). Understanding Girls' circle as an intervention on perceived social support, body image, self-efficacy, locus of control and self-esteem. *Adolescence, 41*(161), 56–74.

Stern, D. (2005). MTV, reality television and the commodification of female sexuality in the real world. *Media Report to Women, 33*(2), 13–22.

Strelan, P., Mehaffrey, S., & Tiggemann, M. (2003). Self-objectification and esteem in young women: The mediating role of reasons for exercise. *Sex Roles, 48*, 89–95.

Studlar, G. (1997). Out-Salomeing Salome: Dance, the new woman, and the fan magazine Orientalism. In M. Bernstine & G. Studlar (Eds.), *Visions of the east: Orientalism in film* (pp. 99–130). New Brunswick, NJ: Rutgers University Press.

Thorington Springer, J. (2008). Roll it gal: Alison Hinds, female empowerment, and calypso. *Meridians: Feminism Race and Transnationalism, 8*(1), 93–129.

Tracey, L. L. (Writer). (2003). *The anatomy of Burlesque: Magnolia movies and white pines pictures*.

Whitehead, K., & Kurz, T. (2009). Empowerment and the pole: A discursive investigation of the reinvention of pole dancing as a recreational activity. *Feminism & Psychology, 19*(2), 224–244.

Wilde, O. (1891). *Salome*. New York: Dover Publications Inc.

PART

12

Gendered Intimacies

"Man's love is of man's life a thing apart," wrote the British Romantic poet, Lord Byron. " 'Tis woman's whole existence." Nowhere are the differences between women and men more pronounced than in our intimate lives, our experiences of love, friendship, and sexuality. It is in our intimate relationships that it so often feels like men and women are truly from different planets.

The very definitions of emotional intimacy bear the mark of gender. As Francesca Cancian argues, the ideal of love has been "feminized" since the nineteenth century. No longer is love the arduous pining nor the sober shouldering of familial responsibility; today, love is expressed as the ability to sustain emotional commitment and connection—a "feminine" definition of love.

But there are signs of gender convergence. Women, it appears, find themselves more interested in pursuing explicitly sexual pleasures, despite their "Venutian" temperament that invariably links love and lust. Beth A. Quinn navigates that always-controversial gray zone between "girl-watching" and intrusive harassment in a way that enables us to understand better how street harassment is not designed to engage women but to intimidate them.

The Feminization of Love

FRANCESCA M. CANCIAN

A feminized and incomplete perspective on love predominates in the United States. We identify love with emotional expression and talking about feelings, aspects of love that women prefer and in which women tend to be more skilled than men. At the same time we often ignore the instrumental and physical aspects of love that men prefer, such as providing help, sharing activities, and sex. This feminized perspective leads us to believe that women are much more capable of love than men and that the way to make relationships more loving is for men to become more like women. This paper proposes an alternative, androgynous perspective on love, one based on the premise that love is both instrumental and expressive. From this perspective, the way to make relationships more loving is for women and men to reject polarized gender roles and integrate "masculine" and "feminine" styles of love.

The Two Perspectives

"Love is active, doing something for your good even if it bothers me," says a fundamentalist Christian. "Love is sharing, the real sharing of feelings," says a divorced secretary who is in love again. In ancient Greece, the ideal love was the adoration of a man for a beautiful young boy who was his lover. In the thirteenth century, the exemplar of love was the chaste devotion of a knight for another man's wife. In Puritan New England, love between husband and wife was the ideal, and in Victorian times, the asexual devotion of a mother for her child seemed the essence of love. My purpose is to focus on one kind of love: long-term heterosexual love in the contemporary United States.

What is a useful definition of enduring love between a woman and a man? One guideline for a definition comes from the prototypes of enduring love—the relations between committed lovers, husband and wife, parent and child. These relationships combine care and assistance with physical and emotional closeness. Studies of attachment between infants and their mothers emphasize the importance of being protected and fed as well as touched and held. In marriage, according to most family sociologists, both practical help and affection are part of enduring love, or "the affection we feel for those with whom our lives are deeply intertwined."[1] Our own informal observations often point in the same direction: if we consider the relationships that are the prototypes of enduring love, it seems that what we really mean by love is some combination of instrumental and expressive qualities.

Historical studies provide a second guideline for defining enduring love, specifically between a woman and a man. In precapitalist America, such love was a complex whole that included work and feelings. Then it was split into feminine and masculine fragments by the separation of home and workplace. This historical analysis implies that affection, material help, and routine cooperation all are parts of enduring love.

Consistent with these guidelines, my working definition of enduring love between adults is a relationship wherein a small number of people are affectionate and emotionally committed to each

---

Francesca M. Cancian, "The Feminization of Love" from *Signs* 11, no. 4 (Summer 1986): 692–709.

other, define their collective well-being as a major goal, and feel obliged to provide care and practical assistance for each other. People who love each other also usually share physical contact; they communicate with each other frequently and cooperate in some routine tasks of daily life. My discussion is of enduring heterosexual love only; I will for the sake of simplicity refer to it as "love."

In contrast to this broad definition of love, the narrower, feminized definition dominates both contemporary scholarship and public opinion. Most scholars who study love, intimacy, or close friendship focus on qualities that are stereotypically feminine, such as talking about feelings. For example, Abraham Maslow defines love as "a feeling of tenderness and affection with great enjoyment, happiness, satisfaction, elation and even ecstasy." Among healthy individuals, he says, "there is a growing intimacy and honesty and self-expression."[2] Zick Rubin's "Love Scale," designed to measure the degree of passionate love as opposed to liking, includes questions about confiding in each other, longing to be together, and sexual attraction as well as caring for each other. Studies of friendship usually distinguish close friends from acquaintances on the basis of how much personal information is disclosed, and many recent studies of married couples and lovers emphasize communication and self-disclosure. A recent book on marital love by Lillian Rubin focuses on intimacy, which she defines as "reciprocal expression of feeling and thought, not out of fear or dependent need, but out of a wish to know another's inner life and to be able to share one's own."[3] She argues that intimacy is distinct from nurturance or caretaking and that men are usually unable to be intimate.

Among the general public, love is also defined primarily as expressing feelings and verbal disclosure, not as instrumental help. This is especially true among the more affluent; poorer people are more likely than they to see practical help and financial assistance as a sign of love. In a study conducted in 1980, 130 adults from a wide range of social classes and ethnic backgrounds were interviewed about the qualities that make a good love relationship. The most frequent response referred to honest and open communication. Being caring and supportive and being tolerant and understanding were the other qualities most often mentioned. Similar results were reported from Ann Swidler's study of an affluent suburb: the dominant conception of love stressed communicating feelings, working on the relationship, and self-development. Finally, a contemporary dictionary defines love as "strong affection for another arising out of kinship or personal ties" and as attraction based on sexual desire, affection, and tenderness.

These contemporary definitions of love clearly focus on qualities that are seen as feminine in our culture. A study of gender roles in 1968 found that warmth, expressiveness, and talkativeness were seen as appropriate for women and not for men. In 1978 the core features of gender stereotypes were unchanged although fewer qualities were seen as appropriate for only one sex. Expressing tender feelings, being gentle, and being aware of the feelings of others were still ideal qualities for women and not for men. The desirable qualities for men and not for women included being independent, unemotional, and interested in sex. The only component perceived as masculine in popular definitions of love is interest in sex.

The two approaches to defining love—one broad, encompassing instrumental and affective qualities, one narrow, including only the affective qualities—inform the two different perspectives on love. According to the androgynous perspective, both gender roles contain elements of love. The feminine role does not include all of the major ways of loving; some aspects of love come from the masculine role, such as sex and providing material help, and some, such as cooperating in daily tasks, are associated with neither gender role. In contrast, the feminized perspective on love implies that all of the elements of love are included in the feminine role. The capacity to love is divided by gender. Women can love and men cannot.

Some Feminist Interpretations

Feminist scholars are divided on the question of love and gender. Supporters of the feminized perspective seem most influential at present. Nancy Chodorow's psychoanalytic theory has been especially influential in promoting a feminized perspective on love among social scientists studying close relationships. Chodorow's argument—in greatly simplified form—is that as infants, both boys and girls have strong identification and intimate attachments with their mothers. Since boys grow up to be men, they must repress this early identification, and in the process they repress their capacity for intimacy. Girls retain their early identification since they will grow up to be women, and throughout their lives females see themselves as connected to others. As a result of this process, Chodorow argues, "girls come to define and experience themselves as continuous with others; . . . boys come to define themselves as more separate and distinct."[4] This theory implies that love is feminine—women are more open to love than men—and that this gender difference will remain as long as women are the primary caretakers of infants.

Scholars have used Chodorow's theory to develop the idea that love and attachment are fundamental parts of women's personalities but not of men's. Carol Gilligan's influential book on female personality development asserts that women define their identity "by a standard of responsibility and care." The predominant female image is "a network of connection, a web of relationships that is sustained by a process of communication." In contrast, males favor a "hierarchical ordering, with its imagery of winning and losing and the potential for violence which it contains." "Although the world of the self that men describe at times includes 'people' and 'deep attachments,' no particular person or relationship is mentioned. . . . Thus the male 'I' is defined in separation."[5]

A feminized conception of love can be supported by other theories as well. In past decades, for example, such a conception developed from Talcott Parsons's theory of the benefits to the nuclear family of women's specializing in expressive action and men's specializing in instrumental action. Among contemporary social scientists, the strongest support for the feminized perspective comes from such psychological theories as Chodorow's.

On the other hand, feminist historians have developed an incisive critique of the feminized perspective on love. Mary Ryan and other social historians have analyzed how the separation of home and workplace in the nineteenth century polarized gender roles and feminized love. Their argument, in simplified form, begins with the observation that in the colonial era the family household was the arena for economic production, affection, and social welfare. The integration of activities in the family produced a certain integration of expressive and instrumental traits in the personalities of men and women. Both women and men were expected to be hard working, modest, and loving toward their spouses and children, and the concept of love included instrumental cooperation as well as expression of feelings. In Ryan's words, "When early Americans spoke of love they were not withdrawing into a female byway of human experience. Domestic affection, like sex and economics, was not segregated into male and female spheres." There was a "reciprocal ideal of conjugal love" that "grew out of the day-to-day cooperation, sharing, and closeness of the diversified home economy."[6]

Economic production gradually moved out of the home and became separated from personal relationships as capitalism expanded. Husbands increasingly worked for wages in factories and shops while wives stayed at home to care for the family. This division of labor gave women more experience with close relationships and intensified women's economic dependence on men. As the daily activities of men and women grew further apart, a new worldview emerged that exaggerated the differences between the personal, loving, feminine sphere of the home and the impersonal, powerful, masculine sphere of the workplace. Work became identified with what men do for money while love became identified with women's activities at home. As a result, the conception of love shifted toward emphasizing tenderness, powerlessness, and the expression of emotion.

This partial and feminized conception of love persisted into the twentieth century as the division of labor remained stable: the workplace remained impersonal and separated from the home, and married women continued to be excluded from paid employment. According to this historical explanation, one might expect a change in the conception of love since the 1940s, as growing numbers of wives took jobs. However, women's persistent responsibility for child care and housework, and their lower wages, might explain a continued feminized conception of love.

Like the historical critiques, some psychological studies of gender also imply that our current conception of love is distorted and needs to be integrated with qualities associated with the masculine role. For example, Jean Baker Miller argues that women's ways of loving—their need to be attached to a man and to serve others—result from women's powerlessness, and that a better way of loving would integrate power with women's style of love.[7] The importance of combining activities and personality traits that have been split apart by gender is also a frequent theme in the human potential movement. These historical and psychological works emphasize the flexibility of gender roles and the inadequacy of a concept of love that includes only the feminine half of human qualities. In contrast, theories like Chodorow's emphasize the rigidity of gender differences after childhood and define love in terms of feminine qualities. The two theoretical approaches are not as inconsistent as my simplified sketches may suggest, and many scholars combine them; however, the two approaches have different implications for empirical research.

Evidence on Women's "Superiority" in Love

A large number of studies show that women are more interested and more skilled in love than men. However, most of these studies use biased measures based on feminine styles of loving, such as verbal self-disclosure, emotional expression, and willingness to report that one has close relationships. When less biased measures are used, the differences between women and men are often small.

Women have a greater number of close relationships than men. At all stages of the life cycle, women see their relatives more often. Men and women report closer relations with their mothers than with their fathers and are generally closer to female kin. Thus an average Yale man in the 1970s talked about himself more with his mother than with his father and was more satisfied with his relationship with his mother. His most frequent grievance against his father was that his father gave too little of himself and was cold and uninvolved; his grievance against his mother was that she gave too much of herself and was alternately overprotective and punitive.

Throughout their lives, women are more likely to have a confidant—a person to whom one discloses personal experiences and feelings. Girls prefer to be with one friend or a small group, while boys usually play competitive games in large groups. Men usually get together with friends to play sports or do some other activity, while women get together explicitly to talk and to be together.

Men seem isolated given their weak ties with their families and friends. Among blue-collar couples interviewed in 1950, 64 percent of the husbands had no confidants other than their spouses, compared to 24 percent of the wives. The predominantly upper-middle-class men interviewed by Daniel Levinson in the 1970s were no less isolated. Levinson concludes that "close friendship with a man or a woman is rarely experienced by American men."[8] Apparently, most men have no loving relationships besides those with wife or lover; and given the estrangement that often occurs in marriages, many men may have no loving relationship at all.

Several psychologists have suggested that there is a natural reversal of these roles in middle age, as men become more concerned with relationships and women turn toward independence and achievement; but there seems to be no evidence showing that men's relationships become more numerous or more intimate after middle age, and some evidence to the contrary.

Women are also more skilled than men in talking about relationships. Whether working class or middle class, women value talking about feelings and relationships and disclose more than men about personal experiences. Men who deviate and talk a lot about their personal experiences are commonly defined as feminine and maladjusted. Working-class wives prefer to talk about themselves, their close relationships with family and friends, and their homes, while their husbands prefer to talk about cars, sports, work, and politics. The same gender-specific preferences are expressed by college students.

Men do talk more about one area of personal experience: their victories and achievements; but talking about success is associated with power, not intimacy. Women say more about their fears and disappointments, and it is disclosure of such weaknesses that usually is interpreted as a sign of intimacy. Women are also more accepting of the expression of intense feelings, including love, sadness, and fear, and they are more skilled in interpreting other people's emotions.

Finally, in their leisure time women are drawn to topics of love and human entanglements while men are drawn to competition among men. Women's preferences in television viewing run to daytime soap operas, or if they are more educated, the high-brow soap operas on educational channels, while most men like to watch competitive and often aggressive sports. Reading-tastes show the same pattern. Women read novels and magazine articles about love, while men's magazines feature stories about men's adventures and encounters with death.

However, this evidence on women's greater involvement and skill in love is not as strong as it appears. Part of the reason that men seem so much less loving than women is that their behavior is measured with a feminine ruler. Much of this research considers only the kinds of loving behavior that are associated with the feminine role and rarely compares women and men in terms of qualities associated with the masculine role. When less biased measures are used, the behavior of men and women is often quite similar. For example, in a careful study of kinship relations among young adults in a southern city, Bert Adams found that women were much more likely than men to say that their parents and relatives were very important to their lives (58 percent of women and 37 percent of men). In measures of actual contact with relatives, though, there were much smaller differences: 88 percent of women and 81 percent of men whose parents lived in the same city saw their parents weekly. Adams concluded that "differences between males and females in relations with parents are discernible primarily in the subjective sphere; contact frequencies are quite similar."[9]

The differences between the sexes can be small even when biased measures are used. For example, Marjorie Lowenthal and Clayton Haven reported the finding, later widely quoted, that elderly women were more likely than elderly men to have a friend with whom they could talk about their personal troubles—clearly a measure of a traditionally feminine behavior. The figures revealed that 81 percent of the married women and 74 percent of the married men had confidants—not a sizable difference.[10] On the other hand, whatever the measure, virtually all such studies find that women are more involved in close relationships than men, even if the difference is small.

In sum, women are only moderately superior to men in love: they have more close relationships and care more about them, and they seem to be more skilled at love, especially those aspects of love that involve expressing feelings and being vulnerable. This does not mean that men are separate and unconcerned with close relationships, however. When national surveys ask people what is most important in their lives, women tend to put family bonds first while men put family bonds first or second, along with work. For both sexes, love is clearly very important.

Evidence on the Masculine Style of Love

Men tend to have a distinctive style of love that focuses on practical help, shared physical activities, spending time together, and sex. The major elements of the masculine style of love emerged in Margaret Reedy's study of 102 married couples in the late 1970s. She showed individuals statements describing aspects of love and asked them to rate how well the statements described their marriages. On the whole, husband and wife had similar views of their marriage, but several sex differences emerged. Practical help and spending time together were more important to men. The men were more likely to give high ratings to such statements as: "When she needs help I help her," and "She would rather spend her time with me than with anyone else." Men also described themselves more often as sexually attracted and endorsed such statements as: "I get physically excited and aroused just thinking about her." In addition, emotional security was less important to men than to women, and men were less likely to describe the relationship as secure, safe, and comforting.[11] Another study in the late 1970s showed a similar pattern among young, highly educated couples. The husbands gave greater emphasis to feeling responsible for the partner's well-being and putting the spouse's needs first, as well as to spending time together. The wives gave greater importance to emotional involvement and verbal self-disclosure but also were more concerned than the men about maintaining their separate activities and their independence.

The difference between men and women in their views of the significance of practical help was demonstrated in a study in which seven couples recorded their interactions for several days. They noted how pleasant their relations were and counted how often the spouse did a helpful chore, such as cooking a good meal or repairing a faucet, and how often the spouse expressed acceptance or affection. The social scientists doing the study used a feminized definition of love. They labeled practical help as "instrumental behavior" and expressions of acceptance or affection as "affectionate behavior," thereby denying the affectionate aspect of practical help. The wives seemed to be using the same scheme; they thought their marital relations were pleasant that day if their husbands had directed a lot of affectionate behavior to them, regardless of their husbands' positive instrumental behavior. The husbands' enjoyment of their marital relations, on the other hand, depended on their wives' instrumental actions, not on their expressions of affection. The men actually saw instrumental actions as affection. One husband who was told by the researchers to increase his affectionate behavior toward his wife decided to wash her car and was surprised when neither his wife nor the researchers accepted that as an "affectionate" act.

The masculine view of instrumental help as loving behavior is clearly expressed by a husband discussing his wife's complaints about his lack of communication: "What does she want? Proof? She's got it, hasn't she? Would I be knocking myself out to get things for her—like to keep up this house—if I didn't love her? Why does a man do things like that if not because he loves his wife and kids? I swear, I can't figure what she wants." His wife, who has a feminine orientation to love, says something very different: "It is not enough that he supports us and takes care of us. I appreciate that, but I want him to share things with me. I need for him to tell me his feelings."[12] Many working-class women agree with men that a man's job is something he does out of love for his family,[13] but middle-class women and social scientists rarely recognize men's practical help as a form of love. (Indeed, among upper-middle-class men whose jobs offer a great deal of intrinsic gratification, their belief that they are "doing it for the family" may seem somewhat self-serving.)

Other differences between men's and women's styles of love involve sex. Men seem to separate sex and love while women connect them, but paradoxically, sexual intercourse seems to be the most meaningful way of giving and receiving love for many men. A twenty-nine-year-old carpenter who had been married for three years said that, after sex, "I feel so close to her and the kids. We feel like a real family then. I don't talk to her very often, I guess, but somehow I feel we have really communicated after we have made love."[14]

Because sexual intimacy is the only recognized "masculine" way of expressing love, the recent trend toward viewing sex as a way for men and women to express mutual intimacy is an important challenge to the feminization of love. However, the connection between sexuality and love is undermined both by the "sexual revolution" definition of sex as a form of casual recreation and by the view of male sexuality as a weapon—as in rape—with which men dominate and punish women.

Another paradoxical feature of men's style of love is that men have a more romantic attitude toward their partners than do women. In Reedy's study, men were more likely to select statements like "we are perfect for each other." In a survey of college students, 65 percent of the men but only 24 percent of the women said that, even if a relationship had all of the other qualities they desired, they would not marry unless they were in love.

The common view of this phenomenon focuses on women. The view is that women marry for money and status and so see marriage as instrumentally, rather than emotionally, desirable. This of course is at odds with women's greater concern with self-disclosure and emotional intimacy and lesser concern with instrumental help. A better way to explain men's greater romanticism might be to focus on men. One such possible explanation is that men do not feel responsible for "working on" the emotional aspects of a relationship, and therefore see love as magically and perfectly present or absent. This is consistent with men's relative lack of concern with affective interaction and greater concern with instrumental help.

In sum, there is a masculine style of love. Except for romanticism, men's style fits the popularly conceived masculine role of being the powerful provider. From the androgynous perspective, the practical help and physical activities included in this role are as much a part of love as the expression of feelings. The feminized perspective cannot account for this masculine style of love; nor can it explain why women and men are so close in the degrees to which they are loving.

Negative Consequences of the Feminization of Love

The division of gender roles in our society that contributes to the two separate styles of love is reinforced by the feminized perspective and leads to political and moral problems that would be mitigated with a more androgynous approach to love. The feminized perspective works against some of the key values and goals of feminists and humanists by contributing to the devaluation and exploitation of women.

It is especially striking how the differences between men's and women's styles of love reinforce men's power over women. Men's style involves giving women important resources, such as money and protection that men control and women believe they need, and ignoring the resources that women control and men need. Thus men's dependency on women remains covert and repressed, while women's dependency on men is overt and exaggerated; and it is overt dependency that creates power, according to social exchange theory. The feminized perspective on love reinforces this power differential by leading to the belief that women need love more than do men, which is implied in the association of love with the feminine role. The effect of this belief is to intensify the asymmetrical dependency of women on men. In fact, however, evidence on the high death rates of unmarried men suggests that men need love at least as much as do women.

Sexual relations also can reinforce male dominance insofar as the man takes the initiative and intercourse is defined either as his "taking" pleasure or as his being skilled at "giving" pleasure, either way giving him control. The man's power advantage is further strengthened if the couple assumes that the man's sexual needs can be filled by any attractive woman while the woman's sexual needs can be filled only by the man she loves.

On the other hand, women's preferred ways of loving seem incompatible with control. They involve admitting dependency and sharing or losing control, and being emotionally intense. Further, the intimate talk about personal troubles that appeals to women requires of a couple a mutual vulnerability, a willingness to see oneself as weak and in need of support. It is true that a woman, like a man, can gain some power by providing her partner with services, such as understanding, sex, or cooking; but this power is largely unrecognized because the man's dependency on such services is not overt. The couple may even see these services as her duty or as her response to his requests (or demands).

The identification of love with expressing feelings also contributes to the lack of recognition of women's power by obscuring the instrumental, active component of women's love just as it obscures the loving aspect of men's work. In a culture that glorifies instrumental achievement, this identification devalues both women and love. In reality, a major way by which women are loving is in the clearly instrumental activities associated with caring for others, such as preparing meals, washing clothes, and providing care during illness; but because of our focus on the expressive side of love, this caring work of women is either ignored or redefined as expressing feelings. Thus, from the feminized perspective on love, child care is a subtle communication of attitudes, not work. A wife washing her husband's shirt is seen as expressing love, even though a husband washing his wife's car is seen as doing a job.

Gilligan, in her critique of theories of human development, shows the way in which devaluing love is linked to devaluing women. Basic to most psychological theories of development is the idea that a healthy person develops from a dependent child to an autonomous, independent adult. As Gilligan comments, "Development itself comes to be identified with separation, and attachments appear to be developmental impediments."[15] Thus women, who emphasize attachment, are judged to be developmentally retarded or insufficiently individuated.

The pervasiveness of this image was documented in a well-known study of mental health professionals who were asked to describe mental health, femininity, and masculinity. They associated both mental health and masculinity with independence, rationality, and dominance. Qualities concerning attachment, such as being tactful, gentle, or aware of the feelings of others, they associated with femininity but not with mental health.[16]

Another negative consequence of a feminized perspective on love is that it legitimates impersonal, exploitive relations in the workplace and the community. The ideology of separate spheres that developed in the nineteenth century contrasted the harsh, immoral marketplace with the warm and loving home and implied that this contrast is acceptable. Defining love as expressive, feminine, and divorced from productive activity maintains this ideology. If personal relationships and love are reserved for women and the home, then it is acceptable for a manager to underpay workers or for a community to ignore a needy family. Such behavior is not unloving; it is businesslike or shows a respect for privacy. The ideology of separate spheres also implies that men are properly judged by their instrumental and economic achievements and that poor or unsuccessful men are failures who may deserve a hard life. Levinson presents a conception of masculine development itself as centering on achieving an occupational dream.[17]

Finally, the feminization of love intensifies the conflicts over intimacy between women and men in close relationships. One of the most common conflicts is that the woman wants more closeness and verbal contact while the man withdraws and wants less pressure. Her need for more closeness is partly the result of the feminization of love, which encourages her to be more emotionally dependent on him. Because love is feminine, he in turn may feel controlled during intimate contact. Intimacy is her "turf," an area where she sets the rules and expectations. Talking about the relationship, as she wants, may well feel to him like taking a test that she made up and that he will fail. He is likely to react by withdrawing, causing her to intensify her efforts to get closer. The feminization of love thus can lead to a vicious cycle of conflict where neither partner feels in control or gets what she or he wants.

Conclusion

The values of improving the status of women and humanizing the public sphere are shared by many of the scholars who support a feminized conception of love; and they, too, explain the conflicts in close relationships in terms of polarized gender roles. Nancy Chodorow, Lillian Rubin, and Carol Gilligan have addressed these issues in detail and with great insight. However, by arguing that women's identity is based on attachment while men's identity is based on separation, they reinforce the distinction between feminine expressiveness and masculine instrumentality, revive the ideology of separate spheres, and legitimate the popular idea that only women know the right way to love. They also suggest that there is no way to overcome the rigidity of gender roles other than by pursuing the goal of men and women becoming equally involved in infant care. In contrast, an androgynous perspective on love challenges the identification of women and love with being expressive, powerless, and nonproductive and the identification of men with being instrumental, powerful, and productive. It rejects the ideology of separate spheres and validates masculine as well as feminine styles of love. This viewpoint suggests that progress could be made by means of a variety of social changes, including men doing child care, relations at work becoming more personal and nurturant, and cultural conceptions of love and gender becoming more androgynous. Changes that equalize power within close relationships by equalizing the economic and emotional dependency between men and women may be especially important in moving toward androgynous love.

The validity of an androgynous definition of love cannot be "proven"; the view that informs the androgynous perspective is that both the feminine style of love (characterized by emotional closeness and verbal self-disclosure) and the masculine style of love (characterized by instrumental help and sex) represent necessary parts of a good love relationship. Who is more loving: a couple who confide most of their experiences to each other but rarely cooperate or give each other practical help, or a couple who help each other through many crises and cooperate in running a household but rarely discuss their personal experiences? Both relationships are limited. Most people would probably choose a combination: a relationship that integrates feminine and masculine styles of loving, an androgynous love.

Notes

1. See John Bowlby, *Attachment and Loss* (New York: Basic Books, 1969), on mother-infant attachment. The quotation is from Elaine Walster and G. William Walster, *A New Look at Love* (Reading, Mass.: Addison-Wesley Publishing Co., 1978), 9. Conceptions of love and adjustment used by family sociologists are reviewed in Robert Lewis and Graham Spanier, "Theorizing about the Quality and Stability of Marriage." in *Contemporary Theories about the Family,* ed. W. Burr, R. Hill, F. Nye, and I. Reiss (New York: Free Press, 1979), 268–94.
2. Abraham Maslow, *Motivation and Personality,* 2d ed. (New York: Harper & Row, 1970), 182–83.
3. Zick Rubin's scale is described in his article "Measurement of Romantic Love." *Journal of Personality and Social Psychology* 16, no. 2 (1970): 265–73; Lillian Rubin's book on marriage is *Intimate Strangers* (New York: Harper & Row, 1983), quote on 90.
4. Nancy Chodorow, *The Reproduction of Mothering* (Berkeley: University of California Press, 1978), 169. Dorothy Dinnerstein presents a similar theory in *The Mermaid and the Minotaur: Sexual Arrangements and Human Malaise* (New York: Harper & Row, 1976). Freudian and biological dispositional theories about women's nurturance are surveyed in Jean Stockard and Miriam Johnson, *Sex Roles* (Englewood Cliffs, N.J.: Prentice-Hall, Inc., 1980).
5. Carol Gilligan, *In a Different Voice* (Cambridge, Mass.: Harvard University Press, 1982), 32, 159–61; see also L. Rubin, *Intimate Strangers.*
6. I have drawn most heavily on Mary Ryan, *Womanhood in America,* 2d ed. (New York: New Viewpoints, 1978), and *The Cradle of the Middle Class: The Family in Oneida County, N.Y., 1790–1865* (New York: Cambridge University Press, 1981); Barbara Ehrenreich and Deidre English, *For Her Own Good: 150 Years of Experts Advice to Women* (New York: Anchor Books, 1978); Barbara Welter, "The Cult of True Womanhood: 1820–1860," *American Quarterly* 18, no. 2 (1966): 151–174.
7. Jean Baker Miller, *Toward a New Psychology of Women* (Boston: Beacon Press, 1976). There are, of course, many exceptions to Miller's generalization, e.g., women who need to be independent or who need an attachment with a woman.
8. Daniel Levinson, *The Seasons of a Man's Life* (New York: Alfred A. Knopf, 1978), 335.
9. Bert Adams, *Kinship in an Urban Setting* (Chicago: Markham Publishing Co., 1968), 169.
10. Marjorie Lowenthal and Clayton Haven, "Interaction and Adaptation: Intimacy as a Critical Variable." *American Sociological Review* 22, no. 4 (1968): 20–30.
11. Margaret Reedy, "Age and Sex Differences in Personal Needs and the Nature of Love." (Ph.D. diss. University of Southern California, 1977). Unlike most studies, Reedy did not find that women emphasized communication more than men. Her subjects were upper-middle-class couples who seemed to be very much in love.
12. Lillian Rubin, *Worlds of Pain* (New York: Basic Books, 1976), 147.

13. See L. Rubin, *Worlds of Pain;* also see Richard Sennett and Jonathan Cobb, *Hidden Injuries of Class* (New York: Vintage, 1973).
14. Interview by Cynthia Garlich, "Interviews of Married Couples" (University of California, Irvine, School of Social Sciences, 1982).
15. Gilligan (n. 5 above), 12–13.
16. Inge Broverman, Frank Clarkson, Paul Rosenkrantz, and Susan Vogel, "Sex-Role Stereotypes and Clinical Judgments of Mental Health," *Journal of Consulting Psychology* 34, no. 1 (1970): 1–7.
17. Levinson (n. 8 above).

Sexual Harassment and Masculinity: The Power and Meaning of "Girl Watching"

BETH A. QUINN

Confronted with complaints about sexual harassment or accounts in the media, some men claim that women are too sensitive or that they too often misinterpret men's intentions (Bernstein 1994; Buckwald 1993). In contrast, some women note with frustration that men just "don't get it" and lament the seeming inadequacy of sexual harassment policies (Conley 1991; Guccione 1992). Indeed, this ambiguity in defining acts of sexual harassment might be, as Cleveland and Kerst (1993) suggested, the most robust finding in sexual harassment research.

Using in-depth interviews with 43 employed men and women, this article examines a particular social practice—"girl watching"—as a means to understanding one way that these gender differences are produced. This analysis does not address the size or prevalence of these differences, nor does it present a direct comparison of men and women; this information is essential but well covered in the literature.[1] Instead, I follow Cleveland and Kerst's (1993) and Wood's (1998) suggestion that the question may best be unraveled by exploring how the "subject(ivities) of perpetrators, victims, and resistors of sexual harassment" are "discursively produced, reproduced, and altered" (Wood 1998, 28).

This article focuses on the subjectivities of the perpetrators of a disputable form of sexual harassment, "girl watching." The term refers to the act of men's sexually evaluating women, often in the company of other men. It may take the form of a verbal or gestural message of "check it out," boasts of sexual prowess, or explicit comments about a woman's body or imagined sexual acts. The target may be an individual woman or group of women or simply a photograph or other representation. The woman may be a stranger, coworker, supervisor, employee, or client. For the present analysis, girl watching within the workplace is centered.

The analysis is grounded in the work of masculinity scholars such as Connell (1987, 1995) in that it attempts to explain the subject positions of the interviewed men—not the abstract and genderless subjects of patriarchy but the gendered and privileged subjects embedded in this system. Since I am attempting to delineate the gendered worldviews of the interviewed men, I employ the term "girl watching," a phrase that reflects their language ("they watch girls").

I have chosen to center the analysis on girl watching within the workplace for two reasons. First, it appears to be fairly prevalent. For example, a survey of federal civil employees (U.S. Merit Systems Protection Board 1988) found that in the previous 24 months, 28 percent of the women surveyed had experienced "unwanted sexual looks or gestures," and 35 percent had experienced "unwanted sexual teasing, jokes, remarks, or questions." Second, girl watching is still often normalized and trivialized as only play, or "boys will be boys." A man watching girls—even in his workplace—is frequently accepted as a natural and commonplace activity, especially if he is in the presence of other men.[2] Indeed, it may be required (Hearn 1985). Thus, girl watching sits on the blurry edge between fun and harm, joking and harassment. An understanding of the process of identifying behavior as sexual harassment, or of rejecting this label, may be built on this ambiguity.

Girl watching has various forms and functions, depending on the context and the men involved. For example, it may be used by men as a directed act of power against a particular woman or women. In this, girl watching—at least in the workplace—is most clearly identified as harassing by both men and women. I am most interested, however, in the form where it is characterized as only play. This type is more obliquely motivated and, as I will argue, functions as a game men play to build shared masculine identities and social relations.

Multiple and contradictory subject positions are also evidenced in girl watching, most notably that between the gazing man and the woman he watches. Drawing on Michael Schwalbe's (1992) analysis of empathy and the formation of masculine identities, I argue that girl watching is premised on the obfuscation of this multiplicity through the objectification of the woman watched and a suppression of empathy for her. In conclusion, the ways these elements operate to produce gender differences in interpreting sexual harassment and the implications for developing effective policies are discussed.

Previous Research

The question of how behavior is or is not labeled as sexual harassment has been studied primarily through experimental vignettes and surveys.[3] In both methods, participants evaluate either hypothetical scenarios or lists of behaviors, considering whether, for example, the behavior constitutes sexual harassment, which party is most at fault, and what consequences the act might engender. Researchers manipulate factors such as the level of "welcomeness" the target exhibits and the relationship of the actors (supervisor-employee, coworker-coworker).

Both methods consistently show that women are willing to define more acts as sexual harassment (Gutek, Morasch, and Cohen 1983; Padgitt and Padgitt 1986; Powell 1986; York 1989; but see Stockdale and Vaux 1993) and are more likely to see situations as coercive (Garcia, Milano, and Quijano 1989). When asked who is more to blame in a particular scenario, men are more likely to blame, and less likely to empathize with, the victim (Jensen and Gutek 1982; Kenig and Ryan 1986). In terms of actual behaviors like girl watching, the U.S. Merit Systems Protection Board (1988) survey found that 81 percent of the women surveyed considered "uninvited sexually suggestive looks or gestures" from a supervisor to be sexual harassment. While the majority of men (68 percent) also defined it as such, significantly more men were willing to dismiss such behavior. Similarly, while 40 percent of the men would not consider the same behavior from a coworker to be harassing, more than three-quarters of the women would.

The most common explanation offered for these differences is gender role socialization. This conclusion is supported by the consistent finding that the more men and women adhere to traditional gender roles, the more likely they are to deny the harm in sexual harassment and to consider the behavior acceptable or at least normal (Gutek and Koss 1993; Malovich and Stake 1990; Murrell and Dietz-Uhler 1993; Popovich et al. 1992; Pryor 1987; Tagri and Hayes 1997). Men who hold predatory ideas about sexuality, who are more likely to believe rape myths, and who are more likely to self-report that they would rape under certain circumstances are less likely to see behaviors as harassing (Murrell and Dietz-Uhler 1993; Pryor 1987; Reilly et al. 1992).

These findings do not, however, adequately address the between-group differences. The more one is socialized into traditional notions of sex roles, the more likely it is for both men and women to view the behaviors as acceptable or at least unchangeable. The processes by which gender roles operate to produce these differences remain underexamined.

Some theorists argue that men are more likely to discount the harassing aspects of their behavior because of a culturally conditioned tendency to misperceive women's intentions. For example, Stockdale (1993, 96) argued that "patriarchal norms create a sexually aggressive belief system in some people more than others, and this belief system can lead to the propensity to misperceive." Gender differences in interpreting sexual harassment, then, may be the outcome of the acceptance of normative ideas about women's inscrutability and indirectness and men's role as sexual aggressors. Men see harmless flirtation or sexual interest rather than harassment because they misperceive women's intent and responses.

Stockdale's (1993) theory is promising but limited. First, while it may apply to actions such as repeatedly asking for dates and quid pro quo harassment,[4] it does not effectively explain motivations for more indirect actions, such as displaying pornography and girl watching. Second, it does not explain why some men are more likely to operate from these discourses of sexual aggression contributing to a propensity to misperceive.

Theoretical explanations that take into account the complexity and diversity of sexual harassing behaviors and their potentially multifaceted social etiologies are needed. An account of the processes by which these behaviors are produced and the active construction of their social meanings is necessary to unravel both between- and within-gender variations in behavior and interpretation. A fruitful framework from which to begin is an examination of masculine identities and the role of sexually harassing behaviors as a means to their production.

Method

I conducted 43 semistructured interviews with currently employed men and women between June 1994 and March 1995. Demographic characteristics of the participants are reported in Table 1. The interviews ranged in length from one to three hours. With one exception, interviews were audiotaped and transcribed in full.

Participants were contacted in two primary ways. Twenty-five participants were recruited from "Acme Electronics," a Southern California electronic design and manufacturing company. An additional 18 individuals were recruited from an evening class at a community college and a university summer school class, both in Southern California. These participants referred 3 more individuals. In addition to the interviews, I conducted participant observation for approximately one month while on site at Acme. This involved observations of the public and common spaces of the company.

At Acme, a human resources administrator drew four independent samples (salaried and hourly women and men) from the company's approximately 300 employees. Letters of invitation were sent to 40 individuals, and from this group, 13 women and 12 men agreed to be interviewed.[5]

The strength of organizationally grounded sampling is that it allows us to provide context for individual accounts. However, in smaller organizations and where participants occupy unique positions, this method can compromise participant anonymity when published versions of the research are accessed by participants. Since this is the case with Acme, and since organizational context is not particularly salient for this analysis, the identity of the participant's organization is sometimes intentionally obscured.

Table 1. Participant Demographic Measures

Variable	Men n		Men %	Women n		Women %	Total n		Total %
Student participants and referrals	6		33	12		67	18		42
Racial/ethnic minority	2		33	2		17	4		22
Mean age		27.2			35			32.5	
Married	3		50	3		25	6		33
Nontraditional job	1		17	4		33	5		28
Supervisor	0		0	6		50	6		33
Some college	6		100	12		100	18		100
Acme participants	12		48	13		52	25		58
Racial/ethnic minority	2		17	3		23	5		20
Mean age		42.3			34.6			38.6	
Married	9		75	7		54	16		64
Nontraditional job	0		0	4		31	4		16
Supervisor	3		25	2		15	5		20
Some college	9		75	9		69	18		72
All participants	18		42	25		58	43		100
Racial/ethnic minority	4		22	5		20	9		21
Mean age		37.8			34.9			36.2	
Married	12		67	10		40	22		51
Nontraditional job	1		6	8		32	9		21
Supervisor	3		17	8		32	11		26
Some college	15		83	21		84	36		84

The strength of the second method of recruitment is that it provides access to individuals employed in diverse organizations (from self-employment to multinational corporations) and in a range of occupations (e.g., nanny, house painter, accounting manager). Not surprisingly, drawing from college courses resulted in a group with similar educational backgrounds; all participants from this sample had some college, with 22 percent holding college degrees. Student samples and snowball sampling are not particularly robust in terms of generalizability. They are, nonetheless, regularly employed in qualitative studies (Chen 1999; Connell 1995) when the goal is theory development—as is the case here—rather than theory testing.

The interviews began with general questions about friendships and work relationships and progressed to specific questions about gender relations, sexual harassment, and the policies that seek to address it.[6] Since the main aim of the project was to explore how workplace events are framed as sexual harassment (and as legally bounded or not), the term "sexual harassment" was not introduced by the interviewer until late in the interview.

While the question of the relationship between masculinity and sexual harassment was central, I did not come to the research looking expressly for girl watching. Rather, it surfaced as a theme across several men's interviews in the context of a gender reversal question:

> It's the end of an average day. You get ready for bed and fall to sleep. In what seems only a moment, the alarm goes off. As you awake, you find your body to be oddly out of sorts.... To

> your surprise, you find that you have been transformed into the "opposite sex." Even stranger, no one in your life seems to remember that you were ever any different.

Participants were asked to consider what it would be like to conduct their everyday work life in this transformed state. I was particularly interested in their estimation of the impact it would have on their interactions with coworkers and supervisors. Imagining themselves as the opposite sex, participants were forced to make explicit the operation of gender in their workplace, something they did not do in their initial discussions of a typical workday.

Interestingly, no man discussed girl watching in initial accounts of his workplace. I suspect that they did not consider it to be relevant to a discussion of their average *work* day, even though it became apparent that it was an integral daily activity for some groups of men. It emerged only when men were forced to consider themselves as explicitly gendered workers through the hypothetical question, something they were able initially to elide.[7]

Taking guidance from Glaser and Strauss's (1967) grounded theory and the methodological insights of Dorothy Smith (1990), transcripts were analyzed iteratively and inductively, with the goal of identifying the ideological tropes the speaker used to understand his or her identities, behaviors, and relationships. Theoretical concepts drawn from previous work on the etiology of sexual harassment (Bowman 1993; Cleveland and Kerst 1993), the construction of masculine identities (Connell 1995, 1987), and sociolegal theories of disputing and legal consciousness (Bumiller 1988; Conley and O'Barr 1998) guided the analysis.

Several related themes emerged and are discussed in the subsequent analysis. First, girl watching appears to function as a form of gendered play among men. This play is productive of masculine identities and premised on a studied lack of empathy with the feminine other. Second, men understand the targeted woman to be an object rather than a player in the game, and she is most often not the intended audience. This obfuscation of a woman's subjectivity, and men's refusal to consider the effects of their behavior, means men are likely to be confused when a woman complains. Thus, the production of masculinity through girl watching, and its compulsory disempathy, may be one factor in gender differences in the labeling of harassment.

Findings: Girl Watching as "Hommo-Sexuality"

> *[They] had a button on the computer that you pushed if there was a girl who came to the front counter. . . . It was a code and it said "BAFC"—Babe at Front Counter. . . . If the guy in the back looked up and saw a cute girl come in the station, he would hit this button for the other dispatcher to [come] see the cute girl.*
>
> *—Paula, police officer*

In its most serious form, girl watching operates as a targeted tactic of power. The men seem to want everyone—the targeted woman as well as coworkers, clients, and superiors—to know they are looking. The gaze demonstrates their right, as men, to sexually evaluate women. Through the gaze, the targeted woman is reduced to a sexual object, contradicting her other identities, such as that of competent worker or leader. This employment of the discourse of asymmetrical heterosexuality (i.e., the double standard) may trump a woman's formal organizational power, claims to professionalism, and organizational discourses of rationality (Collinson and Collinson 1989; Gardner 1995; Yount 1991).[8] As research on rape has demonstrated (Estrich 1987), calling attention to a woman's gendered sexuality can function to exclude recognition of her competence, rationality, trustworthiness, and even humanity. In contrast, the overt recognition of a man's (hetero)sexuality is normally compatible with other aspects of his identity; indeed, it is often required (Connell 1995; Hearn 1985). Thus, the power of sexuality is asymmetrical, in part, because being seen as sexual has different consequences for women and men.

But when they ogle, gawk, whistle and point, are men always so directly motivated to disempower their women colleagues? Is the target of the gaze also the intended audience? Consider, for example, this account told by Ed, a white, 29-year-old instrument technician.

> When a group of guys goes to a bar or a nightclub and they try to be manly. . . . A few of us always found [it] funny [when] a woman would walk by and a guy would be like, "I can have her." [pause] "Yeah, OK, we want to see it!" [laugh]

In his account—a fairly common one in men's discussions—the passing woman is simply a visual cue for their play. It seems clear that it is a game played by men for men; the woman's participation and awareness of her role seem fairly unimportant.

As Thorne (1993) reminded us, we should not be too quick to dismiss games as "only play." In her study of gender relations in elementary schools, Thorne found play to be a powerful form of gendered social action. One of its "clusters of meaning" most relevant here is that of "dramatic performance." In this, play functions as both a source of fun and a mechanism by which gendered identities, group boundaries, and power relations are (re)produced.

The metaphor of play was strong in Karl's comments. Karl, a white man in his early thirties who worked in a technical support role in the Acme engineering department, hoped to earn a degree in engineering. His frustration with his slow progress—which he attributed to the burdens of marriage and fatherhood—was evident throughout the interview. Karl saw himself as an undeserved outsider in his department and he seemed to delight in telling on the engineers.

Girl watching came up as Karl considered the gender reversal question. Like many of the men I interviewed, his first reaction was to muse about premenstrual syndrome and clothes. When I inquired about the potential social effects of the transformation (by asking him, Would it "be easier dealing with the engineers or would it be harder?") he haltingly introduced the engineers' "game."

> KARL: Some of the engineers here are very [pause] they're not very, how shall we say? [pause] What's the way I want to put this? They're not very, uh [pause] what's the word? Um. It escapes me.
>
> RESEARCHER: Give me a hint?
>
> KARL: They watch women but they're not very careful about getting caught.
>
> RESEARCHER: Oh! Like they ogle?
>
> KARL: Ogle or gaze or [pause] stare even, or [pause] generate a commotion of an unusual nature.

His initial discomfort in discussing the issue (with me, I presume) is evident in his excruciatingly formal and hesitant language. The aspect of play, however, came through clearly when I pushed him to describe what generating a commotion looked like: " 'Oh! There goes so-and-so. Come and take a look! She's wearing this great outfit today!' Just like a schoolboy. They'll rush out of their offices and [cranes his neck] and check things out." That this is as a form of play was evident in Karl's boisterous tone and in his reference to schoolboys. This is not a case of an aggressive sexual appraising of a woman coworker but a commotion created for the benefit of other men.

At Acme, several spatial factors facilitated this form of girl watching. First, the engineering department is designed as an open-plan office with partitions at shoulder height, offering a maze-like geography that encourages group play. As Karl explained, the partitions offer both the opportunity for sight and cover from being seen. Although its significance escaped me at the time, I was directly introduced to the spatial aspects of the engineers' game of girl watching during my first day on site at Acme. That day, John, the current human resources director, gave me a tour of the facilities, walking me through the departments and offering informal introductions. As we entered the design engineering section, a rhythm of heads emerged from its landscape of partitions, and movement started in our direction. I was definitely aware of being on display as several men gave me obvious once-overs.

Second, Acme's building features a grand stairway that connects the second floor—where the engineering department is located—with the lobby. The stairway is enclosed by glass walls, offering a bird's eye view to the main lobby and the movements of visitors and the receptionists (all women). Robert, a senior design engineer, specifically noted the importance of the glass walls in his discussion of the engineers' girl watching.

> There's glass walls around the upstairs right here by the lobby. So when there's an attractive young female... someone will see the girl in the area and they will go back and inform all the men in the area. "Go check it out." [laugh] So we'll walk over to the glass window, you know, and we'll see who's down there.

One day near the end of my stay at Acme, I was reminded of his story as I ventured into the first-floor reception area. Looking up, I saw Robert and another man standing at the top of the stairs watching and commenting on the women gathered around the receptionist's desk. When he saw me, Robert gave me a sheepish grin and disappeared from sight.

Producing Masculinity

I suggest that girl watching in this form functions simultaneously as a form of play and as a potentially powerful site of gendered social action. Its social significance lies in its power to form identities and relationships based on these common practices for, as Cockburn (1983, 123) has noted, "patriarchy is as much about relations between man and man as it is about relations between men and women." Girl watching works similarly to the sexual joking that Johnson (1988) suggested is a common way for heterosexual men to establish intimacy among themselves.

In particular, girl watching works as a dramatic performance played to other men, a means by which a certain type of masculinity is produced and heterosexual desire displayed. It is a means by which men assert a masculine identity to other men, in an ironic "hommo-sexual" practice of heterosexuality (Butler 1990).[9] As Connell (1995) and others (Butler 1990; West and Zimmerman 1987) have aptly noted, masculinity is not a static identity but rather one that must constantly be reclaimed. The content of any performance—and there are multiple forms—is influenced by a hegemonic notion of masculinity. When asked what "being a man" entailed, many of the men and women I interviewed triangulated toward notions of strength (if not in muscle, then in character and job performance), dominance, and a marked sexuality, overflowing and uncontrollable to some degree and natural to the male "species." Heterosexuality is required, for just as the label "girl" questions a man's claim to masculine power, so does the label "fag" (Hopkins 1992; Pronger 1992). I asked Karl, for example, if he would consider his sons "good men" if they were gay. His response was laced with ambivalence; he noted only that the question was "a tough one."

The practice of girl watching is just that—a practice—one rehearsed and performed in everyday settings. This aspect of rehearsal was evident in my interview with Mike, a self-employed house painter who used to work construction. In locating himself as a born-again Christian, Mike recounted the girl watching of his fellow construction workers with contempt. Mike was particularly disturbed by a man who brought his young son to the job site one day. The boy was explicitly taught to catcall, a practice that included identifying the proper targets: women and effeminate men.

Girl watching, however, can be somewhat tenuous as a masculine practice. In their acknowledgment (to other men) of their supposed desire lies the possibility that in being too interested in women the players will be seen as mere schoolboys giggling in the playground. Taken too far, the practice undermines rather than supports a masculine performance. In Karl's discussion of girl watching, for example, he continually came back to the problem of men's not being careful about getting caught. He referred to a particular group of men who, though "their wives are [pause] very attractive—very much so," still "gawk like schoolboys." Likewise, Stephan explained that men who are obvious, who "undress [women] with their eyes" probably do so "because they don't get enough women in their lives. Supposedly." A man must be interested in women, but not too interested; they must show their (hetero)sexual interest, but not overly so, for this would be to admit that women have power over them.

The Role of Objectification and (Dis)Empathy

As a performance of heterosexuality among men, the targeted woman is primarily an object onto which men's homosocial sexuality is projected. The presence of a woman in any form—embodied, pictorial, or as an image conjured from words—is required, but her subjectivity and active participation are not. To be sure, given the ways the discourse of asymmetrical sexuality works, men's actions may result in similarly negative effects on the targeted woman as that of a more direct form of sexualization. The crucial difference is that the men's understanding of their actions differs. This difference is one key to understanding the ambiguity around interpreting harassing behavior.

When asked about the engineers' practice of neck craning, Robert grinned, saying nothing at first. After some initial discussion, I started to ask him if he thought women were aware of their game ("Do you think that the women who are walking by...?"). He interrupted, misreading my question. What resulted was a telling description of the core of the game:

> It depends. No. I don't know if they enjoy it. When I do it, if I do it, I'm not saying that I do. [big laugh]...If they do enjoy it, they don't say it. If they don't enjoy it—wait a minute, that didn't come out right. I don't know if they enjoy it or not [pause]; that's not the purpose of us popping our heads out.

Robert did not want to admit that women might not enjoy it ("that didn't come out right") but acknowledged that their feelings were irrelevant. Only subjects, not objects, take pleasure or are annoyed. If a woman did complain, Robert thought "the guys wouldn't know what to say." In her analysis of street harassment, Gardner (1995, 187) found a similar absence, in that "men's interpretations seldom mentioned a woman's reaction, either guessed at or observed."

The centrality of objectification was also apparent in comments made by José, a Hispanic man in his late 40s who worked in manufacturing. For José, the issue came up when he considered the topic of compliments. He initially claimed that women enjoy compliments more than men do. In reconsidering, he remembered girl watching and the importance of intent.

> There is [pause] a point where [pause] a woman can be admired by [pause] a pair of eyes, but we're talking about "that look." Where, you know, you're admiring her because she's dressed nice, she's got a nice figure, she's got nice legs. But then you also have the other side. You have an animal who just seems to undress you with his eyes and he's just [pause], there's those kind of people out there too.

What is most interesting about this statement is that in making the distinction between merely admiring and an animal look that ravages, José switched subject position. He spoke in the second person when describing both forms of looking, but his consistency in grammar belies a switch in subjectivity: you (as a man) admire, and you (as a woman) are undressed with his eyes. When considering an appropriate, complimentary gaze, José described it from a man's point of view; the subject who experiences the inappropriate, violating look, however, is a woman. Thus, as in Robert's account, José acknowledged that there are potentially different meanings in the act for men and women. In particular, to be admired in a certain way is potentially demeaning for a woman through its objectification.

The switch in subject position was also evident in Karl's remarks. Karl mentioned girl watching while imagining himself as a woman in the gender reversal question. As he took the subject position of the woman watched rather than the man watching, his understanding of the act as a harmless game was destabilized. Rather than taking pleasure in being the object of such attention, Karl would take pains to avoid it.

> So with these guys [if I were a woman], I would probably have to be very concerned about my attire in the lab. Because in a lot of cases, I'm working at a bench and I'm hunched over, in which case your shirt, for example, would open at the neckline, and I would just have to be concerned about that.

Thus, because the engineers girl watch, Karl feels that he would have to regulate his appearance if he were a woman, keeping the men from using him in their game of girl watching. When he considered the act from the point of view of a man, girl watching was simply a harmless antic and an act of appreciation. When he was forced to consider the subject position of a woman, however, girl watching was something to be avoided or at least carefully managed.

When asked to envision himself as a woman in his workplace, like many of the individuals I interviewed, Karl believed that he did not "know how to be a woman." Nonetheless, he produced an account that mirrored the stories of some of the women I interviewed. He knew the experience of girl watching could be quite different—in fact, threatening and potentially disempowering—for the woman who is its object. As such, the game was something to be avoided. In imagining themselves as women, the men remembered the practice of girl watching. None, however, were able to comfortably describe the game of girl watching from the perspective of a woman and maintain its (masculine) meaning as play.

In attempting to take up the subject position of a woman, these men are necessarily drawing on knowledge they already hold. If men simply "don't get it"—truly failing to see the harm in girl watching or other more serious acts of sexual harassment—then they should not be able to see this harm when envisioning themselves as women. What the interviews reveal is that many men—most of whom failed to see the harm of many acts that would constitute the hostile work environment form of sexual harassment—did in fact understand the harm of these acts when forced to consider the position of the targeted woman.

I suggest that the gender reversal scenario produced, in some men at least, a moment of empathy. Empathy, Schwalbe (1992) argued, requires two things. First, one must have some knowledge of the other's situation and feelings. Second, one must be motivated to take the position of the other. What the present research suggests is that gender differences in interpreting sexual harassment stem not so much from men's not getting it (a failure of the first element) but from a studied, often compulsory, lack of motivation to identify with women's experiences.

In his analysis of masculinity and empathy, Schwalbe (1992) argued that the requirements of masculinity necessitate a "narrowing of the moral self." Men learn that to effectively perform masculinity and to protect a masculine identity, they must, in many instances, ignore a woman's pain and obscure her viewpoint. Men fail to exhibit empathy with women because masculinity precludes them from taking the position of the feminine other, and men's moral stance vis-à-vis women is attenuated by this lack of empathy.

As a case study, Schwalbe (1992) considered the Thomas-Hill hearings, concluding that the examining senators maintained a masculinist stance that precluded them from giving serious consideration to Professor Hill's claims. A consequence of this masculine moral narrowing is that "charges of sexual harassment... are often seen as exaggerated or as fabricated out of misunderstanding or spite" (Schwalbe 1992, 46). Thus, gender differences in interpreting sexually harassing behaviors may stem more from acts of ignoring than states of ignorance.

The Problem with Getting Caught

But are women really the untroubled objects that girl watching—viewed through the eyes of men—suggests? Obviously not; the game may be premised on a denial of a woman's subjectivity, but an actual erasure is beyond men's power! It is in this multiplicity of subjectivities, as Butler (1990, ix) noted, where "trouble" lurks, provoked by "the unanticipated agency of a female 'object' who inexplicably returns the glance, reverses the gaze, and contests the place and authority of the masculine position." To face a returned gaze is to get caught, an act that has the power to undermine the logic of girl watching as simply a game among men. Karl, for example, noted that when caught, men are often flustered, a reaction suggesting that the boundaries of usual play have been disturbed.[10]

When a woman looks back, when she asks, "What are you looking at?" she speaks as a subject, and her status as mere object is disturbed. When the game is played as a form of hommosexuality, the confronted man may be baffled by her response. When she catches them looking, when she complains, the targeted woman speaks as a subject. The men, however, understand her primarily as an object, and objects do not object.

The radical potential of sexual harassment law is that it centers women's subjectivity, an aspect prompting Catharine MacKinnon's (1979) unusual hope for the law's potential as a remedy. For men engaged in girl watching, however, this subjectivity may be inconceivable. From their viewpoint, acts such as girl watching are simply games played with objects: women's bodies. Similar to Schwalbe's (1992) insight into the senators' reaction to Professor Hill, the harm of sexual harassment may seem more the result of a woman's complaint (and law's "illegitimate" encroachment into the everyday work world) than men's acts of objectification. For example, in reflecting on the impact of sexual harassment policies in the workplace, José lamented that "back in the '70s, [it was] all peace and love then. Now as things turn around, men can't get away with as much as what they used to." Just whose peace and love are we talking about?

Reactions to Anti-Sexual Harassment Training Programs

The role that objectification and disempathy play in men's girl watching has important implications for sexual harassment training. Consider the following account of a sexual harassment training session given in Cindy's workplace. Cindy, an Italian American woman in her early 20s, worked as a recruiter for a small telemarketing company in Southern California.

> [The trainer] just really laid down the ground rules, um, she had some scenarios. Saying, "OK, would you consider this sexual harassment?" "Would you..." this, this, this? "What level?" Da-da-da. So, um, they just gave us some real numbers as to lawsuits and cases. Just that "you guys better be careful" type of a thing.

From Cindy's description, this training is fairly typical in that it focuses on teaching participants definitions of sexual harassment and the legal ramifications of accusations. The trainer used the common strategy of presenting videos of potentially harassing situations and asking the participants how they would judge them. Cindy's description of the men's responses to these videos reveals the limitation of this approach.

> We were watching [the TV] and it was [like] a studio audience. And [men] were getting up in the studio audience making comments like "Oh well, look at her! I wouldn't want to do that to her either!" "Well, you're darn straight, look at her!"

Interestingly, the men successfully used the training session videos as an opportunity for girl watching through their public sexual evaluations of the women depicted. In this, the intent of the training session was doubly subverted. The men interpreted scenarios that Cindy found plainly harassing into mere instances of girl watching and sexual (dis) interest. The antiharassment video was ironically transformed into a forum for girl watching, effecting male bonding and the assertion of masculine identities to the exclusion of women coworkers. Also, by judging the complaining women to be inferior as women, the men sent the message that women who complain are those who fail at femininity.

Cindy conceded that relations between men and women in her workplace were considerably strained after the training ("That day, you definitely saw the men bond, you definitely saw the women bond, and there was a definite separation"). The effect of the training session, rather than curtailing the rampant sexual harassment in Cindy's workplace, operated as a site of masculine performance, evoking manly camaraderie and reestablishing gender boundaries.

To be effective, sexual harassment training programs must be grounded in a complex understanding of the ways acts such as girl watching operate in the workplace and the seeming necessity of a culled empathy to some forms of masculinity. Sexually harassing behaviors are produced from more than a lack of knowledge, simple sexist attitudes, or misplaced sexual desire. Some forms of sexually harassing behaviors—such as girl watching—are mechanisms through which gendered boundaries are patrolled and evoked and by which deeply held identities are established. This complexity requires complex interventions and leads to difficult questions about the possible efficacy of any workplace training program mandated in part by legal requirements.

Conclusion

In this analysis, I have sought to unravel the social logic of girl watching and its relationship to the question of gender differences in the interpretation of sexual harassment. In the form analyzed here, girl watching functions simultaneously as only play and as a potent site where power is played. Through the objectification on which it is premised and in the nonempathetic masculinity it supports, this form of girl watching simultaneously produces both the harassment and the barriers to men's acknowledgment of its potential harm.

The implications these findings have for antisexual harassment training are profound. If we understand harassment to be the result of a simple lack of knowledge (of ignorance), then straightforward informational sexual harassment training may be effective. The present analysis suggests, however, that the etiology of some harassment lies elsewhere. While they might have quarreled with it, most of the men I interviewed had fairly good abstract understandings of the behaviors their companies' sexual harassment policies prohibited. At the same time, in relating stories of social relations in their workplaces, most failed to identify specific behaviors as sexual harassment when they matched the abstract definition. As I have argued, the source of this contradiction lies not so much in ignorance but in acts of ignoring. Traditional sexual harassment training programs address the former rather than the later. As such, their effectiveness against sexually harassing behaviors born out of social practices of masculinity like girl watching is questionable.

Ultimately, the project of challenging sexual harassment will be frustrated and our understanding distorted unless we interrogate hegemonic, patriarchal forms of masculinity and the practices by which they are (re)produced. We must continue to research the processes by which sexual harassment is produced and the gendered identities and subjectivities on which it poaches (Wood 1998). My study provides a first step toward a more process-oriented understanding of sexual harassment, the ways the social meanings of harassment are constructed, and ultimately, the potential success of antiharassment training programs.

Notes

1. See Welsh (1999) for a review of this literature.
2. For example, Maria, an administrative assistant I interviewed, simultaneously echoed and critiqued this understanding when she complained about her boss's girl watching in her presence: "If he wants to do that in front of other men... you know, that's what men do."
3. Recently, more researchers have turned to qualitative studies as a means to understand the process of labeling behavior as harassment. Of note are Collinson and Collinson (1996), Giuffre and Williams (1994), Quinn (2000), and Rogers and Henson (1997).
4. Quid pro quo ("this for that") sexual harassment occurs when a person with organizational power attempts to coerce an individual into sexual behavior by threatening adverse job actions.
5. This sample was not fully representative of the company's employees; male managers (mostly white) and minority manufacturing employees were underrepresented. Thus, the data presented here best represent the attitudes and workplace tactics of white men working in white-collar, technical positions and white and minority men in blue-collar jobs.
6. Acme employees were interviewed at work in an office off the main lobby. Students and referred participants were interviewed at sites convenient to them (e.g., an office, the library).
7. Not all the interviewed men discussed girl watching. When asked directly, they tended to grin knowingly, refusing to elaborate. This silence in the face of direct questioning—by a female researcher—is also perhaps an instance of getting caught.
8. I prefer the term "asymmetrical heterosexuality" over "double standard" because it directly references the dominance of heterosexuality and more accurately reflects the interconnected but different forms of acceptable sexuality for men and women. As Estrich (1987) argued, it is not simply that we hold men and women to different standards of sexuality but that these standards are (re) productive of women's disempowerment.
9. "Hommo" is a play on the French word for man, *homme*.
10. Men are not always concerned with getting caught, as the behavior of catcalling construction

workers amply illustrates; that a woman hears is part of the thrill (Gardner 1995). The difference between the workplace and the street is the level of anonymity the men have vis-à-vis the woman and the complexity of social rules and the diversity of power sources an individual has at his or her disposal.

References

Bernstein, R. 1994. Guilty if charged. *New York Review of Books*, 13 January.

Bowman, C. G. 1993. Street harassment and the informal ghettoization of women. *Harvard Law Review* 106:517–80.

Buckwald, A. 1993. Compliment a woman, go to court. *Los Angeles Times*, 28 October.

Bumiller, K. 1988. *The civil rights society: The social construction of victims*. Baltimore: Johns Hopkins University Press.

Butler, J. 1990. *Gender trouble: Feminism and the subversion of identity*. New York: Routledge.

Chen, A. S. 1999. Lives at the center of the periphery, lives at the periphery of the center: Chinese American masculinities and bargaining with hegemony. *Gender & Society* 13:584–607.

Cleveland, J. N., and M. E. Kerst. 1993. Sexual harassment and perceptions of power: An under-articulated relationship. *Journal of Vocational Behavior* 42 (1): 49–67.

Cockburn, C. 1983. *Brothers: Male dominance and technological change*. London: Pluto Press.

Collinson, D. L., and M. Collinson. 1989. Sexuality in the workplace: The domination of men's sexuality. In *The sexuality of organizations*, edited by J. Hearn and D. L. Sheppard. Newbury Park, CA: Sage.

———. 1996. "It's only Dick": The sexual harassment of women managers in insurance sales. *Work, Employment & Society* 10 (1): 29–56.

Conley, F. K. 1991. Why I'm leaving Stanford: I wanted my dignity back. *Los Angeles Times*, 9 June.

Conley, J., and W. O'Barr. 1998. *Just words*. Chicago: University of Chicago Press.

Connell, R. W. 1987. *Gender and power*. Stanford, CA: Stanford University Press.

———. 1995. *Masculinities*. Berkeley: University of California Press.

Estrich, S. 1987. *Real rape*. Cambridge, MA: Harvard University Press.

Garcia, L., L. Milano, and A. Quijano. 1989. Perceptions of coercive sexual behavior by males and females. *Sex Roles* 21 (9/10): 569–77.

Gardner, C. B. 1995. *Passing by: Gender and public harassment*. Berkeley: University of California Press.

Giuffre, P., and C. Williams. 1994. Boundary lines: Labeling sexual harassment in restaurants. *Gender & Society* 8:378–401.

Glaser, B., and A. L. Strauss. 1967. *The discovery of grounded theory: Strategies for qualitative research*. Chicago: Aldine.

Guccione, J. 1992. Women judges still fighting harassment. *Daily Journal*, 13 October, 1.

Gutek, B. A., and M. P. Koss. 1993. Changed women and changed organizations: Consequences of and coping with sexual harassment. *Journal of Vocational Behavior* 42 (1): 28–48.

Gutek, B. A., B. Morasch, and A. G. Cohen. 1983. Interpreting social-sexual behavior in a work setting. *Journal of Vocational Behavior* 22 (1): 30–48.

Hearn, J. 1985. Men's sexuality at work. In *The sexuality of men*, edited by A. Metcalf and M. Humphries. London: Pluto Press.

Hopkins, P. 1992. Gender treachery: Homophobia, masculinity, and threatened identities. In *Rethinking masculinity: Philosophical explorations in light of feminism*, edited by L. May and R. Strikwerda. Lanham, MD: Littlefield, Adams.

Jensen, I. W., and B. A. Gutek. 1982. Attributions and assignment of responsibility in sexual harassment. *Journal of Social Issues* 38 (4): 121–36.

Johnson, M. 1988. *Strong mothers, weak wives*. Berkeley: University of California Press.

Kenig, S., and J. Ryan. 1986. Sex differences in levels of tolerance and attribution of blame for sexual harassment on a university campus. *Sex Roles* 15 (9/10): 535–49.

MacKinnon, C. A. 1979. *The sexual harassment of working women*. New Haven, CT: Yale University Press.

Malovich, N. J., and J. E. Stake. 1990. Sexual harassment on campus: Individual differences in attitudes and beliefs. *Psychology of Women Quarterly* 14 (1): 63–81.

Murrell, A. J., and B. L. Dietz-Uhler. 1993. Gender identity and adversarial sexual beliefs as predictors of attitudes toward sexual harassment. *Psychology of Women Quarterly* 17 (2): 169–75.

Padgitt, S. C., and J. S. Padgitt. 1986. Cognitive structure of sexual harassment: Implications for university policy. *Journal of College Student Personnel* 27:34–39.

Popovich, P. M., D. N. Gehlauf, J. A. Jolton, J. M. Somers, and R. M. Godinho. 1992. Perceptions of sexual harassment as a function of sex of rater and incident form and consequent. *Sex Roles* 27 (11/12): 609–25.

Powell, G. N. 1986. Effects of sex-role identity and sex on definitions of sexual harassment. *Sex Roles* 14: 9–19.

Pronger, B. 1992. Gay jocks: A phenomenology of gay men in athletics. In *Rethinking masculinity: Philosophical explorations in light of feminism*, edited by L. May and R. Strikwerda. Lanham, MD: Littlefield Adams.

Pryor, J. B. 1987. Sexual harassment proclivities in men. *Sex Roles* 17 (5/6): 269–90.

Quinn, B. A. 2000. The paradox of complaining: Law, humor, and harassment in the everyday work world. *Law and Social Inquiry* 25 (4): 1151–83.

Reilly, M. E., B. Lott, D. Caldwell, and L. DeLuca. 1992. Tolerance for sexual harassment related to self-reported sexual victimization. *Gender & Society* 6:122–38.

Rogers, J. K., and K. D. Henson. 1997. "Hey, why don't you wear a shorter skirt?" Structural vulnerability and the organization of sexual harassment in temporary clerical employment. *Gender & Society* 11:215–38.

Schwalbe, M. 1992. Male supremacy and the narrowing of the moral self. *Berkeley Journal of Sociology* 37:29–54.

Smith, D. 1990. *The conceptual practices of power: A feminist sociology of knowledge*. Boston: Northeastern University Press.

Stockdale, M. S. 1993. The role of sexual misperceptions of women's friendliness in an emerging theory of sexual harassment. *Journal of Vocational Behavior* 42 (1): 84–101.

Stockdale, M. S., and A. Vaux. 1993. What sexual harassment experiences lead respondents to acknowledge being sexually harassed? A secondary analysis of a university survey. *Journal of Vocational Behavior* 43 (2): 221–34.

Tagri, S., and S. M. Hayes. 1997. Theories of sexual harassment. In *Sexual harassment: Theory, research and treatment*, edited by W. O'Donohue. New York: Allyn & Bacon.

Thorne, B. 1993. *Gender play: Girls and boys in school*. Buckingham, UK: Open University Press.

U.S. Merit Systems Protection Board. 1988. *Sexual harassment in the federal government: An update*. Washington, DC: Government Printing Office.

Welsh, S. 1999. Gender and sexual harassment. *Annual Review of Sociology* 1999:169–90.

West, C., and D. H. Zimmerman. 1987. Doing gender. *Gender & Society* 1: 125–51.

Wood, J. T. 1998. Saying makes it so: The discursive construction of sexual harassment. In *Conceptualizing sexual harassment as discursive practice*, edited by S. G. Bingham. Westport, CT: Praeger.

York, K. M. 1989. Defining sexual harassment in workplaces: A policy-capturing approach. *Academy of Management Journal* 32:830–50.

Yount, K. R. 1991. Ladies, flirts, tomboys: Strategies for managing sexual harassment in an underground coal mine. *Journal of Contemporary Ethnography* 19:396–422.

The Glass Partition: Obstacles to Cross-Sex Friendships at Work

KIM ELSESSER AND LETITIA ANNE PEPLAU

Cross-sex friendships can be difficult to develop and maintain under any circumstances (O'Meara, 1989). Issues stemming from male-female differences in friendship norms and interests, sexual attraction, and concerns that a cross-sex friendship may be misperceived as sexual all pose potential challenges (Martin, 1997; Swain, 1992). Within the workplace, where friendships are particularly important for career development (Kram & Isabella, 1985), physical proximity and job requirements may facilitate cross-sex friendship formation. On the contrary, other organizational influences such as fear that a cross-sex friendship may be misperceived as a romantic relationship or fear of sexual harassment charges may decrease interactions between cross-sex co-workers, limiting the pool of potential friends. The present analysis of interviews with professionals investigates the impact of the workplace on the development and maintenance of these friendships.

Workplace friendships are important because they can provide benefits which promote career success. Lincoln and Miller (1979) defined friendship networks in organizations as 'systems for making decisions, mobilizing resources, concealing or transmitting information, and performing other functions closely allied with work behavior and interaction' (p. 196). Friends in the workplace provide information, networking, and support that are invaluable for both job performance and satisfaction (Kram & Isabella, 1985; Lincoln & Miller, 1979).

Bridge and Baxter (1992) found that work friends provided career support in three forms. Friends provided information access, serving 'as a second pair of eyes and ears for one another.' Friends also provided work-related assistance, helping each other accomplish their job tasks. Third, friends gave psychological support to one another, 'providing understanding, empathy and comfort' (Bridge & Baxter, 1992: 216).

While friendships with peers are important, relationships with those more senior in the organization can also be valuable to the careers of junior employees. Sometimes these mentor relationships are formally initiated and managed by the organization, but more often they are informal relationships similar to friendships (Ragins & Cotton, 1999). Mentors can provide advice and information, offer protection, and promote the mentee's career by making his or her accomplishments more visible (Burke, 1984; Kram & Isabella, 1985; Mobley et al., 1994).

Given the substantial advantages that friendships in the workplace offer, those not able to form friendships are at a career disadvantage. A preference for same-sex friendships restricts an individual's pool of potential friends. This may have the most impact for women in male-dominated work environments who need to befriend men in order to develop both peer friendships and mentor-like relationships. Extending the previous research on cross-sex friendships to the workplace may therefore illuminate an important barrier to women's career advancement.

Cross-Sex Friendships

To date, research on barriers to the development of cross-sex friendships has typically been conducted

Kim Elsesser and Letitia Anne Peplau, "The Glass Partition: Obstacles to Cross-Sex Friendships at Work." *Human Relations* 59 (August 2006): 1077–100.

outside the context of work. Nonetheless, this research suggests several important factors that may be relevant to workplace friendships. First, gender differences in recreational interests and preferred topics of conversation result in a preference for same-sex friends (Martin, 1997; Swain, 1992). In addition, gender differences in norms and expectations of friendships could cause problems for cross-sex friends. For example, men often disapprove of their same and cross-sex friends crying while women approve of this behavior (Felmlee, 1999).

Sexual attraction toward a potential friend can spur the initiation of a cross-sex friendship. However, in situations where a romantic or sexual relationship is inappropriate or where one partner prefers a non-romantic friendship, sexual undercurrents often jeopardize cross-sex relationships (Kaplan & Keys, 1998; Monsour, 1992; Swain, 1992; Werking, 1997). Finally, friends are concerned that a platonic cross-sex friendship will be misconstrued by third parties as romantic (Monsour et al., 1994; O'Meara, 1989; Swain, 1992).

Workplace Environment

Since little research has examined cross-sex friendship in the workplace, the effects of organizational influences on these friendships remain unknown. Certain aspects of the work environment may facilitate cross-sex friendship development while others may hinder the development of new friendships.

Many workplaces encourage teamwork (Beyerlein et al., 1995) which leads to greater interaction between employees. Therefore, the workplace potentially provides an environment where men and women can work closely together to achieve common goals. Consequently, the workplace offers co-workers proximity, familiarity, and common interests, all of which have been shown to promote liking and friendship (Berscheid & Reis, 1998). This suggests that cross-sex friendships may be easier to develop within the workplace than outside of work.

Other current workplace trends may inhibit cross-sex friendship. For example, since workplace romances are often discouraged, some may want to avoid any possibility that their co-workers misperceive a friendship as a romance. Even co-workers who are participants in workplace romances typically attempt to keep their romance a secret (Anderson & Hunsaker, 1985). Unlike friendships and other work-sanctioned relationships, workplace romances can be disruptive to the organization and typically lead to negative gossip (Bowes-Sperry & Tata, 1999; Mainiero, 1986; Powell & Graves, 2003). The romantic label can be particularly damaging when the alleged couple are not peers in the organization. For example, Powell (2001) found that when those perceived to be in a romantic relationship are not peers, and the subordinate is female, other employees tend to believe that the relationship is utilitarian (where sex is traded for career advancement). Once a relationship is deemed utilitarian, outsiders may question the basis for work-related rewards from the higher-level participant. To date, there is no research on how this fear of third-party misperception of cross-sex friendship impacts friendships at work.

Similarly, the increased awareness of sexual harassment within organizations may impact cross-sex friendship development. A recent survey by the Society for Human Resources Management (SHRM) found that 97 percent of organizations had sexual harassment policies, and 62 percent had formal training in dealing with sexual harassment (SHRM, 1999). However, little research has addressed how increased awareness of sexual harassment has impacted interactions between cross-sex co-workers. One survey of university professors found that 68 percent were concerned about being unjustly accused of sexual harassment, and 45 percent had modified their behavior toward students due to that concern (Nicks, 1996). In addition, Gutek (1997) suggests that 'the adversarial nature of the formal complaint procedures has had the effect of polarizing men and women in the workplace' (p. 196).

Finally, an examination of the literature on social networks and mentor relationships provides material relevant to cross-sex friendships at work. The preference of men to associate with other men has been well-established in the literature on social networks (see McPherson et al., 2001 for a review).

Among managers, men tend to have more gender homophilous networks than do women (Ibarra, 1992, 1995). The causes for same-gender preference in these work networks have included similarity (individuals choose to be close to those who are similar to themselves) and contact (people are most likely to come into contact with others like themselves).

Research on cross-sex mentor relationships (typically male mentor and female protégé) indicates they can be more difficult to develop than same-sex mentor relationships. Cross-sex mentor pairs socialize less outside of work than same-sex mentor pairs, and report their relationships are harder to initiate due to fear that the prospective mentor or other co-workers would misconstrue their friendliness as sexual interest (Ragins & Cotton, 1999). These same concerns may apply to cross-sex friendship development in the workplace.

The purpose of this exploratory study was to investigate friendships within the professional workplace and to examine what impact, if any, the workplace environment has on cross-sex friendship formation. Structured interviews were combined with a questionnaire in order to obtain a broad range of descriptions of friendship development within organizations. We focused exclusively on professionals in this study as one example of how the work environment impacts cross-sex friendships. It will be left to future research to explore how other categories of workers' cross-sex friendships are affected by their organizations.

Method

Structured telephone interviews were conducted with 41 professionals from 30 different organizations. A sample of 21 women and 20 men were recruited. E-mail messages describing the study were sent to personal contacts of the first author requesting their participation, and these contacts were encouraged to forward the e-mail to other potential participants. Although personal contacts of the author represented 39 percent of the sample, these professionals were unaware of the study objectives or the author's research prior to participation. All interviews were conducted by the primary investigator who is female. In addition, questionnaires were sent to participants to supplement the interview.

To be eligible for the study, participants had to be professionals in organizations with at least 50 employees and had to be employed by their organization for at least six months. Participants were from various geographical regions of the US with the majority from New York City (54 percent) and Los Angeles (19 percent). Professions which typically require at least a bachelor's degree were considered 'professional' for purposes of this study. Occupations covered a wide range of professions including lawyers, computer programmers, investment bankers, management consultants and managers. Ages ranged from 23 to 59 years with a mean age of 31.7 years (SD = 8.47). Eighteen percent of participants described themselves as senior level managers in their organizations, 57 percent as mid-level, 20 percent as entry-level, and five percent as other. Fifteen percent of respondents were married, 15 percent were living with their romantic partner, and the remaining 70 percent were single. No questions were asked about the race, ethnicity or sexual orientation of respondents.

Since this study explored the impact of sexual harassment policies on cross-sex friendships, it is important to note that these professionals were all employed by organizations that had sexual harassment policies. The majority (56 percent) were employed by organizations which offered formal sexual harassment training or video programs that employees had to attend. Others received pamphlets, memos, or guidelines which had to be read and signed annually. These professionals heard about sexual harassment frequently, with 43 percent formally hearing from their organizations about sexual harassment at least once a year (and as frequently as once a month). Only one participant had never heard about sexual harassment from his organization, and he had only been employed with his organization for six months.

Participants were told that the interviews would focus on friendships at work. For purposes of this study, participants were asked to use the following definition of a friend:

> A friend is defined as someone you make an effort to talk to outside of what is required to complete your duties at work. That would not include people with whom you only exchange greetings, but would include those with whom you have short conversations that are not required by your job.

Respondents were first asked general questions about their friendships at work. Each participant was asked to discuss the benefits of friendships at work, the initiation of friendships at work compared to outside of work, and their three closest friends from work. The professionals were then asked specifically about their cross-sex friendships, and how these friendships were similar to or different from their same-sex friendships at work. Finally, participants were asked if they ever thought about sexual harassment issues when interacting with the opposite sex.

When the interview was concluded, participants completed a questionnaire about their organization. In the questionnaire, they rated their perception of the magnitude of certain obstacles to initiating cross-sex friendships at work. Consistent with prior research on cross-sex friendships, these items covered fear of sexual interpretation of the friendly overtures, third-party concerns and gendered differences in friendship. Some items were specific to the workplace (e.g. 'Fear friendliness will be misinterpreted as sexual harassment'), while others would apply both inside and outside of the workplace (e.g. 'Jealousy from a romantic partner'). Participants rated how large an obstacle each item was for them in starting cross-sex friendships with peers and also how large an obstacle it was in starting cross-sex friendships with their superiors and subordinates. Participants rated these potential obstacles on a scale from 1 (representing no obstacle at all) to 9 (an insurmountable obstacle). Most participants completed the interview and questionnaire within 40 minutes.

Interviews were transcribed, and a qualitative analysis using multiple readings of transcripts was used to identify the major concepts that emerged from the interview. A process of open coding was then applied (Strauss & Corbin, 1990). Codes were generated from a microanalysis involving a line by line reading of the transcripts. The codes were noted next to each response on the transcripts. The code labels were reviewed and more abstract categories, applying to several specific responses, were determined. To identify possible differences between men and women, transcripts for each group were read separately to determine categories that were more dominant in each group. In addition, we completed exploratory data analysis to uncover patterns in the quantitative data.

Results

The primary goal of analyzing interview and questionnaire data was to investigate obstacles to the formation of cross-sex friendships at work. Before turning to this topic, however, we briefly consider respondents' views on initiating friendships, benefits of workplace friendships, their perceptions of the ease of making friends at work, and the gender patterning of respondents' workplace friendships.

Friendships at Work

Participants were asked about their three closest friendships at work and how these friendships were initiated. The most common theme that emerged was having a similar interest or goal. The similarities mentioned were both work-related (worked on the same projects together) and non-work related (interests in current events, sports, family, members of the opposite sex and jokes). Other themes that emerged for why the friendships began include physical proximity (e.g. having desks or offices in close proximity to one another), a previous relationship with the person (e.g. went to college together) and a formal work relationship (e.g. boss/subordinate, mentor/mentee, or interviewer/interviewee).

Consistent with previous research, all respondents were able to identify benefits they received from their friends at work when asked specifically about these benefits during the interview. Although the specific benefits cited were varied, respondents commonly emphasized that friends provided many forms of assistance and that informal social interactions with friends make the work setting more enjoyable.

Friends were also seen as providing valuable information and assistance. One man, an urban planner, reported that his friends at work help him 'gather information, not just about how the company works, but who is doing what to whom and when, and what the real story was.' Friends were thought to aid with networking and information flow that is critical to career success. A female computer programmer provided a typical description of the benefits of friends at work:

> It gives you a network, it does help in learning what's going on in other areas of the organization . . . It could be things that help you do your job better when you hear about things that you might not have heard about from your manager or people you work with directly.

Professionals often felt more comfortable turning to friends rather than other co-workers or supervisors for advice, information, and assistance.

Friends were described as helpful, even essential, to one's career. Friends were characterized as allies who 'look out for you.' A male manager commented, 'Friends are necessary for survival . . . because your enemies are going to kill you, it's a jungle out there.'

In addition to providing information and assistance, friends also made the workplace more enjoyable on a day-to-day basis. Conversations with friends were seen as offering a break in the monotony of the work day. As a male investment banker explained:

> It allows you to work longer, because you don't have to be focused on doing the same job all day long. You can have breaks which consist of conversations about other topics which allows you to get some mental relief or rest time from work issues so that you can then go back to them.

Friends also provided someone to listen to complaints. A female information technology consultant noted that:

> Being able to share some of your grievances or what you like about your job with somebody who is able to understand . . . especially in our line of work, it's really complicated what we do, so when you try to talk about work with somebody else, you have to explain, but when you're with people at work they understand.

In sum, friends were seen as a vital ingredient in a professional's work life.

The professionals we interviewed perceived the workplace as providing many opportunities for making new friends. In interviews, when asked to compare the initiation of friendships at work with those outside of work, most respondents (80 percent) reported that it was easier for them to initiate friendships at work. The workplace provided mutual interests and occasions for informal conversations that could lead to friendship. As one woman technology consultant explained, 'you spend approximately eight hours a day, five days a week with a certain group of people at work so there's a rather high probability of making friends at work.'

The workplace presumably offers opportunities for both same-sex and cross-sex friendships to develop. In some ways, the shared goals and interests of co-workers might help to overcome the obstacles to cross-sex friendships found outside of work, where gender differences in interests and leisure activities may limit opportunities for cross-sex friendships. In the current research, the majority of professionals came from predominantly male organizations. Consequently, it might be expected that both men and women would be more likely to report having men as friends. This was not the case. When asked to list their three closest friends at work, 69 percent of the friends chosen were same-sex and only 31 percent were cross-sex.

An overview of barriers to cross-sex friendship is provided by participants' numerical ratings of nine potential obstacles presented to them in the questionnaire (see Table 1). Participants were asked to rate each potential obstacle to cross-sex friendships on a scale of 1 (no obstacle at all) to 9 (an insurmountable obstacle). The variance in responses indicate that these barriers do impact cross-sex friendships for some employees. In order to determine when the barriers to cross-sex friendship are greatest, differences in mean ratings were examined with respect to marital status, age and organizational size (all three of which emerged as themes from the qualitative portion of the analysis). Ratings of obstacles for cross-sex friendships between peers were also compared to those between superiors and subordinates. No significant differences were found between the ratings of male and female participants.

Mean comparisons revealed that participants who were married (M = 2.4, SD = 1.6) rated sexual tension in friendship as less of a barrier to cross-sex friendship between peers than single participants (M = 3.8, SD = 1.5), $t(39)$ = 2.033, p = .04. No other significant differences were found between the ratings of married and single participants. With respect to age, participants under 30 years old (M = 3.3, SD = 1.7) were less likely to rate jealousy from a romantic partner as an obstacle to a cross-sex friendship between subordinates and superiors (M= 4.8, SD = 1.95), $t(39)$ = 2.5, p = .01. No other mean differences between older and younger participants were significant at the .05 level. For organizational size, mean comparisons revealed those who were in larger organizations (between 50 and 100 people) rated jealousy from a romantic partner (M = 4.5, SD = 1.9), sexual tension in friendship (M = 3.0, SD = 1.7) and comfort with same-sex friends (M = 3.3, SD = 1.9) as a greater obstacle to cross-sex friendships between peers than those in smaller organizations (M = 3.1, SD = 1.7), $t(39)$ = 2.1, p = .04; (M = 1.7, SD = 1.0), $t(39)$ = 2.3, p = .03; and (M = 1.9, SD = 0.8), $t(39)$ = 2.3, p = .03 respectively. In addition, those in large organizations (M = 4.4, SD = 2.1) rated jealousy from a romantic partner as more of an obstacle to cross-sex friendships between superiors and subordinates than those in smaller organizations (M = 2.8, SD = 2.0), $t(39)$ = 2.1, p = .04.

Table 1. Ratings of Potential Obstacles to Cross-Sex Friendships at Work

	Friendships with Peers Mean (S.D.)			Friendships with Subordinates and Superiors Mean (S.D.)		
Potential Barrier	**Men**	**Women**	**All**	**Men**	**Women**	**All**
Fear of sexual interpretation of friendship						
Fear friendliness will be misinterpreted as sexual harassment	3.7 (2.0)	2.9 (1.6)	3.3 (1.8)	4.5 (2.1)	3.7 (2.1)	4.1 (2.1)
Sexual tension in friendship	2.6 (1.6)	2.7 (1.7)	2.6 (1.6)	2.6 (1.6)	3.1 (1.9)	2.9 (1.7)
Fear friendliness will be misinterpreted as sexual or romantic interest	4.1 (1.7)	3.4 (1.6)	3.7 (1.7)	4.6 (2.3)	3.9 (2.1)	4.2 (2.2)
Fear of sexual harassment charges	3.3 (1.8)	4.2 (2.3)	3.8 (2.1)	4.3 (2.0)	4.6 (2.4)	4.4 (2.2)
Fear of third party concerns						
Other coworkers misinterpret friendship	3.9 (1.8)	3.5 (1.9)	3.7 (1.8)	4.8 (1.9)	4.2 (2.2)	4.5 (2.1)
Jealousy from romantic partner	3.7 (1.9)	4.4 (1.9)	4.1 (1.9)	3.8 (2.1)	4.1 (2.3)	4.0 (2.2)
Gendered preferences in friendship						
Different interaction styles of men and women	3.4 (1.6)	3.2 (1.7)	3.3 (1.7)	3.2 (1.6)	3.8 (1.9)	3.5 (1.8)
Different interests	2.9 (1.5)	3.2 (2.0)	3.0 (1.7)	2.9 (1.4)	3.8 (2.1)	3.4 (1.8)
More comfortable with same-sex friends	2.5 (1.2)	3.2 (2.1)	2.9 (1.8)	2.8 (1.5)	3.8 (2.2)	3.4 (1.9)

There are no significant differences between ratings between peers and ratings between subordinates and superiors at p < .05. There are no significant differences between ratings by men and by women at p < .05.

Finally, the obstacles may have a greater impact on cross-sex friendships between subordinates and superiors than those between peers. With the exception of jealousy of spouses, mean ratings for all other obstacles to cross-sex friendships between superiors and subordinates exceeded mean ratings for friendships between peers. On each individual item, mean comparisons indicated that the differences between ratings for peers and superiors/subordinates were not significant at the .05 level. However, using the binomial expansion, the probability that eight of the nine mean ratings for subordinates and superiors randomly would be greater than the respective mean ratings for peers if there was no true mean difference is .017.

In the following sections, we used interview data to consider in greater depth professionals' concerns that other co-workers will misperceive the nature of a cross-sex friendship, concerns that a potential cross-sex friend will misinterpret a friendly overture, and fears related to possible accusations of sexual harassment. We also examined the differential impact of these obstacles in relationships with friends versus acquaintances.

Concern that Other Co-Workers Will Misperceive Cross-Sex Friendships

In interviews, professionals expressed concern that their co-workers would misperceive a cross-sex friendship as romantic. Although this third party issue also affects cross-sex friendships outside the office, the workplace exacerbates such concerns. In the workplace, sexual and romantic relationships between co-workers are often deemed inappropriate. Further, in the work environment, privacy is limited, and individuals can often easily observe the behavior of their co-workers.

A female recruiter described her apprehensions about being observed with a male co-worker friend and suggested that the size of an organization may impact this concern:

> When I go out with my one male friend I always wonder what people are thinking. . . . You can really shoot yourself in the foot if you're forging personal relationships that go beyond friendships with members of the opposite sex. Sometimes I do feel it's a little bit different here, because it's a smaller audience. And what you're doing here is more closely scrutinized than it would be with a larger organization.

Marital status may be another factor in third party judgment of relationships. Married women and men believed that their cross-sex friendships were not questioned, because their co-workers knew they were married. A single, female attorney described how this third party scrutiny was particularly aimed at single employees:

> If you're not married or you're not dating someone seriously, people in the office will always think there is something going on between opposite-sex friends. So you have to get over, get used to that, just work through it.

Similarly, a male management consultant conveyed how his friendship was misinterpreted:

> My good friend, the one that I walk around with at lunch and stuff, she got engaged a couple of years ago, and this guy saw us walking around together, saw that she was engaged, and assumed that I was who she was engaged to. So, I think people have probably wondered whether there was any kind of romantic relationship going on because we hung out so much. Although that was the only time anyone ever said something about it, it was obvious that was what they thought.

In total, 30 percent of participants reported in interviews that they had a co-worker question them about a cross-sex friendship. This suspicion from co-workers creates self-consciousness for those involved in cross-sex friendships.

Concern That a Potential Cross-Sex Friend Will Misinterpret Friendliness

The professionals in this study also worried that a potential cross-sex friend might misinterpret their friendly gestures as sexual or romantic interest. The first concern focused on features of the work culture that discourage any type of sexual attraction in the workplace. Men were more likely than women to mention these concerns, and they expressed how their concern was greater in the workplace where misinterpretation can result in sexual harassment allegations. The following male engineering consultant described how the heightened awareness of sexual harassment issues in the workplace may make his cross-sex friendships take longer to develop:

> There is certainly an atmosphere of awareness in this day and age about what type of behavior is acceptable between opposite-sex relationships so those friendships that weren't initiated by activities relating directly to work would probably take longer to nurture than they would if you had some direct interaction on a daily basis, because there is that element that you feel like you're seeking that person out in a non-work sort of way.

A second concern expressed by both men and women was more interpersonal. Professionals mentioned the awkwardness of dealing with a misunderstanding and the discomfort of repeatedly seeing someone at work who had previously made such an interpretation. These concerns made some professionals wary of cross-sex friendships and led others to end these relationships. As one female management consultant explained, 'I always feel that it [being friends] ends up being something where maybe someone gets the wrong idea, and then you can't be friends anymore.' Similarly, a female technology consultant described how she ended a cross-sex friendship when there was a misinterpretation:

> I just stopped being friends with him. Usually I just would either try and bring up the fact that I have a boyfriend in casual conversation so the other person gets the message that I'm not interested, or really try and be less friendly than I might normally be, so that the person doesn't interpret that. Or just stop being friends with them at all.

In summary, 25 percent of professionals linked their fears of misinterpretation to aspects of the workplace. They sought to refrain from anything that could be misconstrued because of an 'atmosphere of awareness' of sexual harassment issues at work or because 'it's ingrained in you that you don't.' Professionals also describe the awkwardness that surrounds misinterpretations and how this awkwardness often results in the termination of friendships.

Not all of the professionals interviewed were afraid of appearing romantically interested in their co-workers. Four professionals described instances of flirtation with co-workers, and this ability to flirt made initiating cross-sex friendships easier for them. One female attorney suggested that the work environment was a particularly safe place to flirt with her male colleagues:

> I think they're different though, the same-sex [friendships], especially in the legal field, we have all these lawyers' lunches and it tends to be like we're women in this together. Where with the guys it would be, more like it would be outside of work, flirting a little bit, and joking around. . . . I think that to me, as a single person, and all these single guys here, it helps start it [cross-sex friendship] definitely cause you know you can flirt with them, but there's always, oh we work together so it wouldn't work out anyway.

In summary, the professionals we interviewed had differing views about flirting and sexual attraction in the workplace. Most of the participants who discussed this issue seemed to accept the idea that sexual attraction should be minimized at work and sought to avoid being falsely perceived as romantically linked to a co-worker. A smaller set of participants, both men and women, suggested that flirtation and even mutual romantic attractions in this environment might promote cross-sex friendships.

Heightened Awareness about Sexual Harassment

A third common obstacle to cross-sex friendship centered on issues directly related to sexual harassment. Men, in particular, mentioned how they had to think about what they said before speaking to women because they feared their comments could be misinterpreted. In interviews, 75 percent of male participants mentioned that they think about sexual harassment issues when interacting with women at work. They discussed how they must watch what they say with women and cannot share the same stories and jokes with women that they can with men. Humor and joking were mentioned most frequently by men as something that could not be shared with women at work. Those same comments among same-sex friends go unedited and unnoticed. One male management consultant explained how fears of offending a woman can inhibit friendship:

> If I make an off-color joke or something like that, I'm more likely to do that with a male than a female. Not that I go around telling dirty jokes all the time, but if I get a funny e-mail or something like that, that I find humorous, I would certainly segregate by gender who I'd send that to, if I were to pass it on. So is it harder to develop a real friendship. I have to have comfort that, even though I am not necessarily operating strictly within the professional decorum boundaries, that's not going to reflect back on me professionally through that person's eyes. And it's easier to get a feel for that with a same-sex person.

By contrast, women were not afraid of sharing jokes and humor with men. Instead, women reported sensing men's discomfort and noticing their exclusion by men. In interviews, only five percent of women felt as though they had to watch what they say around men at work, but 66 percent of the women mentioned that men at work seemed inhibited in their conversations with women. A woman consultant summarized how she feels the need to put men at ease:

> I think a lot of times [cross-sex friendships] are harder to make because I feel like sometimes, [men] don't feel like they can relax when women are around as much. They feel like they have to be careful what they say, and they have to be careful what jokes they tell in front of the women in the office. Whereas when they're just all men they can joke around and talk about things they wouldn't want to talk about when women were around so it's harder to break that barrier, but once that barrier has been broken, then I guess it's easier for me to be closer with them. . . . I try to make the men feel like I understand them, that I'm not offended by all their stupid jokes and things like that. I guess after they understand that I'm not like every woman that's going to sue them for sexual harassment or something, then it's fine.

Similarly, a woman attorney noted the discomfort of male partners in her firm:

> My own experience when I worked with certain male partners, I think when they worked with male associates they would be more free to, as some attorneys do, probably a lot senior management do, to swear or act in a certain way. You felt as though they didn't feel comfortable doing that in front of you which was fine, but then you felt that also they just didn't feel comfortable, they felt uncomfortable with you entirely. You could tell they were trying to think about how they should act which made it a kind of uncomfortable relationship. You wanted to say, hey, act how you want, I don't really care, I'm very easy going, just do whatever. You could just sense that they felt they had to act differently and that it made them just prefer to not be alone with you in an office and not have to, you know, they would rather work with a male associate.

A recurrent theme in the interviews was that the same behavior might be interpreted differently by a same-sex versus other-sex co-worker. Consider a situation in which an employee compliments a co-worker on her new dress. If the compliment comes from a woman, it might initiate the development of a friendship. A woman hospital manager described how she began her relationship with one of her closest same-sex friends at work: 'In the building, she's the closest one to my age, it just automatically started by commenting on each other's outfits or accessories or something.'

In contrast, when a male manager offered a similar compliment to a woman at work, he was questioned by the human resources department for alleged sexual harassment:

> Then the next question [from the human resources department] was 'Have you ever complimented this person on her clothes?' And then all the sudden I said, 'Oh, where are you going with this? First of all, this is a person who did wear very nice clothes, but otherwise, believe me I had no interest in her whatsoever, but if I said that's a nice suit or something, nothing was meant by that.' Quite specifically, I know that sometimes that comment can be a euphemism for nice tight sweater, but this is not a case of a woman who had a shapely figure or

> wore revealing clothes, she wore tailored stuff and there was no turn-on there, so anything that was interpreted, it had to be entirely on her part.

As a result of the questioning and accusations, this man was more reserved and hesitant in talking to women about certain topics. In short, concerns linked to sexual harassment can contribute to a preference for same-sex friends at work.

Obstacles Affect Interactions with Acquaintances More Than Close Friends

In discussing how concern about sexual harassment impacts their cross-sex friendships, a noticeable distinction was made between close friendships and less established friendships. In interviews, when asked specifically what they talk about with their three closest friends at work, no participants reported concern over sexual harassment and none said they restricted their conversational topics even when the close friend was a cross-sex friend. However, it was in response to interview questions about all of their cross-sex friends at work (e.g. at work, is there anything that makes opposite-sex friendships either easier or more difficult to start than same-sex friendships?) that the conversational concerns began to emerge. The discrepancy may be explained by the closeness of the friend. The conversational concerns may not apply to close cross sex friends, but only to those they knew less well. As one man, a technology consultant, described:

> My closer friends that are opposite sex, now that I've gotten to know them, I don't really temper my discussions, but with people that aren't one of my couple best friends at work, I pretty much don't even talk to them about anything other than work or I try to temper what I say.

Similarly, women did not report that their closest male friends exhibited the discomfort they described of their more distant friends. As previously pointed out by the female technology consultant,

> . . . once that barrier has been broken, then I guess it's easier for me to be closer with them [male co-workers]. . . . I guess after they understand that I'm not like every woman that's going to sue them for sexual harassment or something then it's fine.

Discussion

The professionals in this study reported receiving substantial benefits from their friends at work. In addition to making the workday more enjoyable, friends provided valuable advice, information, and assistance. Although it was easier for the professionals to meet people and make friends at work than outside work, the participants reported the majority of their closest friends at work were of the same sex. Even women working in predominantly male organizations tended to form more friendships with women than with men.

Although many factors undoubtedly contribute to this pattern of same-sex friendships at work, several were particularly noteworthy. Similar interests played a role in the friendship development of the professionals in this study, and gender differences in interests may lead to a preference for same-sex friends (Martin, 1997; Swain, 1992). However, within the workplace, co-workers share a common interest in the work they perform, which facilitates friendship development. The majority of the participants' closest friendships in the present study were launched as a result of cooperating on a work project. Although gendered interests may still pose some obstacle to friendships within the workplace, they most likely create a more substantial barrier to friendships outside of work.

Instead, barriers to cross-sex friendship at work centered around aspects of the work environment that discourage romantic entanglements among co-workers and seek to prevent sexual harassment. Professionals were concerned that their co-workers might misperceive a platonic cross-sex friendship as an inappropriate sexual liaison. While misperception is also a concern of cross-sex friends outside of the workplace, it may present a greater barrier inside the organization, where co-workers speculate about the motives of the perceived romantic partners (Bowes-Sperry & Tata, 1999; Mainiero, 1986; Powell & Graves, 2003). In addition, men reported concern that women at work might misinterpret a friendly overture as sexual harassment, or that women would take offense at their jokes or topics of conversation. Women were concerned that men felt uncomfortable in their presence and therefore might avoid them. These concerns appeared to be more common in interactions with acquaintances and casual friends than among close friends and between senior and subordinate pairs than between peers.

On a positive note, the findings of this study suggest that sexual harassment policies are working. Men reported they joke less in front of women and are less likely to perform behaviors that may be interpreted as harassment. Women concur that men joke less around them, and that men are less likely to be alone in an office with a woman. Certainly these behaviors create a workplace with a less hostile environment for women. However, an additional, unintended consequence of increased sexual harassment awareness is that it may make cross-sex friendships harder to develop. Consistent with research that indicates that women perceive more behaviors as harassing, the male participants restricted their behavior around women, but not around men, increasing contact among men (Berryman-Fink & Riley, 1997; Solomon & Williams, 1997). Furthermore, the same interactions that were deemed inappropriate for cross-sex communication were utilized to develop same-sex friendships. For example, male employees described initiating friendships by joking with other men, but not women. A male participant who complimented a woman on her clothes is charged with harassment, while a female participant reported offering clothing compliments to other women to start friendships. If co-workers believe that same-sex friends will not label their behavior as harassing, they may have a larger range of behaviors to utilize in initiating same-sex friendships.

The Glass Partition

Along with obstacles associated with cross-sex friendships outside of the organization, organizational practices that heighten workers' fears about sexual harassment and proper conduct on the job may create barriers that inhibit male and female employees from crossing the gender line to form cross-sex friendships. We label these barriers to cross-sex friendship in the workplace the 'glass partition.' Much like the glass ceiling which prevents women from reaching the top levels of corporations, the glass partition may differentially disadvantage women who work in predominantly male organizations. As participants in this study clearly indicated, friends can be invaluable to success on the job.

Factors that limit a worker's range of friends based on gender place greater restrictions on women than on men. For example, women in male-dominated professions need to befriend men in order to obtain the information and networking necessary for career success. Men in these professions, however, have sufficient numbers of same-sex co-workers and senior managers to befriend.

Obstacles to cross-sex friendships may also limit women's ability to establish friendships with senior employees which could evolve into mentor relationships. The present research suggests that the barriers to cross-sex friendship may be greater for friendships between superiors and subordinates. Since men often hold the most powerful positions in corporations (e.g. in 2002, 84 percent of the corporate officers in Fortune 500 companies were men [Catalyst, 2002]), women who are not able to forge friendships with men in their workplace may be left with less powerful mentors or no mentors at all. This may be particularly true for women who are senior within their organization and must seek out mentors at the top levels of the organization.

Although some have suggested same-sex mentor relationships may be more effective than cross-sex relationships, the research is inconclusive as to whether same-sex mentor relationships or cross-sex mentor relationships are more beneficial to the protégé (see Powell, 1999, for review). However, because of their power in the organizations, male mentors may have the ability to provide more valuable support to both their male and female protégés. For example, Dreher and Cox (1996) found that both male and female MBA graduates with male mentors were able to attain greater compensation than those with female mentors. Once again, women who have more difficulty establishing friendships or mentor relationships with men in the organization have a career disadvantage.

By contrast, the glass partition may have less impact for men in female-dominated environments, where women outnumber men. Williams (1989, 1992, 1995) suggests that men who enter female-dominated professions, such as nursing, befriend the men who are often at the supervisory levels of these professions. That is, since many female-dominated professions often have men at higher levels of management, the men entering these professions have other, more senior men with whom they can establish friendships or mentor relationships. These relationships with senior men create what Williams labeled a 'glass escalator' for men in these fields, allowing them to advance their careers more quickly than their female co-workers. However, this preference for same-sex friends may prevent the women in female-dominated professions, which are still predominantly managed by men, from establishing valuable friendships with management and senior personnel.

Possible moderators of the impact of the glass partition on cross-sex friendship include the closeness of the friendship, the relative status of those in the organization, the marital status of the friends and the size of the organization. First, the discomfort with cross-sex co-workers may impact acquaintance relationships more than close friendships. Although close friendships can create a strong bond between individuals, there are significant advantages to acquaintance-type relationships. Granovetter (1973, 1974) found that people with whom an individual shares a close bond are likely to be in the same network as the individual and therefore provide redundant contacts and information. Acquaintances, or what Granovetter labels weak ties, can be more advantageous than closer ties because they bring individuals into new networks and provide less redundant information and contacts than the closer ties. For example, several studies have found those who used weak ties to find new jobs obtained better jobs than those who used only strong ties (Bian, 1997; Lin & Dumin, 1986). In addition, closer friendships evolve from acquaintances in the organizations, so barriers to the establishment of weak ties may ultimately hinder the development of close friendships.

Second, the glass partition may have a greater impact on cross-sex friendships between superiors and subordinates than those between peers. Senior employees may be more concerned about befriending cross-sex junior employees, because misperceptions may have consequences for both employees' careers. If the cross-sex friendship is misperceived as romantic then others may speculate that the relationship is utilitarian or that inequities exist in the workplace (Bowes-Sperry & Tata, 1999; Powell, 2001). Also, since sexual harassment often involves one party with greater power in the organization (Tangri et al., 1982), the more senior employee may have a greater fear that friendly gestures will be misperceived as harassment.

The relationship between marital status and the glass partition is less clear. Some barriers may have less impact for married people whose 'off-limits' status reduces the likelihood that their friendliness will be misperceived as sexual interest, and thus allows them more freedom in establishing friendships. However, sexual attraction can aid in the development of cross-sex friendships (Rose, 1985), and some single participants reported their ability to flirt broke down barriers to cross-sex friendship.

The effect of organizational size on the glass partition remains equally unresolved. A small organization may foster more frequent contact facilitating friendship development, but third-party concerns may be greater in a small organization where everyone can observe their co-workers' behaviors. Future research should further investigate the relationship between the glass partition, marital status and organization size.

It is important to note that these barriers to cross-sex friendships are not insurmountable. With the exception of one male participant, all participants in the study had at least one cross-sex friendship at work. The glass partition merely suggests that it may be more difficult to establish cross-sex friendships than same-sex friendships. With over 112 million women in the US workforce (US Census Bureau, 2003), and men holding the most powerful positions in many corporations (Catalyst, 2002), phenomena which create even small barriers to cross-sex friendships could have a large impact on the career advancement of women (Prentice & Miller, 1992). Although a substantial number of cross-sex friendships develop in the workplace, future researchers of the glass partition are cautioned to examine not only these friendships that were able to overcome barriers, but also to consider potential friendships that were never initiated due to the glass partition.

Limitations

As a first study of cross-sex friendship at work, the goal of this research was exploratory. As a result the research was limited in several ways. Due to the difficulty in recruiting busy professionals for lengthy interviews, the sample was relatively small. However, the sample of professionals came from diverse organizations and different regions of the country. It is also important to note that this study examined cross-sex friendships in large professional organizations. It is possible that employees in smaller organizations or in non-professional work environments may have different experiences. In addition, different organizational cultures may differentially impact the barriers to cross-sex friendship. A systematic investigation of organizational culture and cross-sex friendship would be useful.

No information was requested about the sexual orientation of the participants or of their cross-sex friends. It is possible that homosexuals and heterosexuals face different barriers to same-sex and cross-sex friendships at work. One woman in this study mentioned that a gay male work friend was 'no threat whatsoever' and that her friendship with him was similar to her same-sex friendships. However, lesbians and gay men may encounter more barriers to same-sex friendship than cross-sex friendship in the workplace. Future research examining sexual orientation and workplace friendship would be useful.

Although the gender make-up of the participants' organizations was assessed, no information was collected on the gender makeup of the participant's work role. Although men and women often work in the same organization, work roles or jobs are often segregated by sex (see Padavic & Reskin, 2002, for review). Having similar work roles may also lead workers to prefer same-sex friends. It will be left to future research to examine the impact of gender segregated work roles on the glass partition.

Future Directions for the Organization

Although some barriers to cross-sex friendships will exist regardless of organizational policies, there may be directions the organization can take to diminish the impact of the glass partition. For example, sexual harassment policies that were initiated to make the workplace a more hospitable environment for women may, inadvertently, have increased barriers to cross-sex friendship at work. Sexual harassment has been a serious problem faced by women at work, and efforts to prevent harassment and to make the work-place more welcoming to women are commendable. Fortunately, results of this study suggest that an awareness of harassment has successfully influenced men to reduce their in appropriate joking and conversation in front of women in the workplace. However, male employees may continue to utilize this inappropriate behavior to bond with other men in the workplace, leaving the female employees feeling ostracized. It is therefore time for those who train employees about sexual harassment to see beyond the legal liability and consider the behavioral consequences of these programs. For example, employees should understand that jokes and offensive language and behavior that are not appropriate for cross-sex interactions are also not appropriate for same-sex interactions in the workplace. In addition, if sexual harassment regulations were less ambiguous, employees might not need to fear misinterpretation of their well-intentioned actions.

Future investigations could also explore other organizational changes that could help break down the glass partition. Powell (2001) has suggested that the implementation of organizational training on handling workplace romances may reduce the negative reactions from co-workers. This may have the additional benefit of reducing the anxiety that surrounds cross-sex friendships that may appear romantic. Finally, if organizations encouraged social interaction and facilitated friendship among men and women at work, perhaps social, cross-sex interactions would not be perceived as unusual.

References

Anderson, C.I. & Hunsaker, P. Why there's romancing at the office and why it's everyone's problem. *Personnel*, 1985, 62(2), 57–63.

Berscheid, E. & Reis, H.T. Attraction and close relationships. In D.T. Gilbert, S.T. Fiske & G. Lindzey (Eds), *Handbook of social psychology*. Boston, MA: McGraw-Hill, 1998, pp. 193–281.

Berryman-Fink, C. & Riley, K.V. The role of gender and feminism in perceptions of sexual and sexually harassing communication. *Women's Studies in Communication*, 1997, *20*, 24–44.

Beyerlein, M., Johnson, D. & Beyerlein, S. *Advances in interdisciplinary studies of work teams: Knowledge work in teams, Vol. 2.* Stamford, CT: JAI Press, 1995.

Bian, Y. Bringing strong ties back in: Indirect ties, network bridges, and job searches in China. *American Sociological Review*, 1997, *6*, 366–85.

Bowes-Sperry, L. & Tata, J. A multiperspective framework of sexual harassment. In G.N. Powell (Ed.), *Handbook of gender and work*. Thousand Oaks, CA: Sage, 1999, pp. 263–80.

Bridge, K. & Baxter, L. Blended relationships: Friends as work associates. *Western Journal of Communication*, 1992, *56*, 200–25.

Burke, R. Mentors in organizations. *Group and Organization Studies*, 1984, *9*, 353–72.

Catalyst. *Catalyst census of women corporate officers and top earners*. New York: Catalyst, 2002.

Dreher, G. & Cox, T. Race, gender and opportunity: A study of compensation attainment and the establishment of mentoring relationships. *Journal of Applied Psychology*, 1996, *81*, 297–308.

Felmlee, D. Social norms in cross-gender friendships. *Social Psychology Quarterly*, 1999, *62*, 53–67.

Granovetter, M. The strength of weak ties. *American Journal of Sociology*, 1973, *78*, 1360–80.

Granovetter, M. *Getting a job: A study of contact and careers*. Cambridge, MA: Harvard University Press, 1974.

Gutek, B. Sexual harassment policy initiatives. In W. O'Donohue (Ed.), *Sexual harassment: Theory, research and treatment*. Needham Heights, MA: Allyn & Bacon, 1997, pp. 185–98.

Ibarra, H. Homophily and differential returns: Sex differences in network structures and access in an advertising firm. *Academy of Management Review*, 1992, *18*, 56–87.

Ibarra, H. Race, opportunity, diversity of social circles in managerial networks. *Academy of Management Journal*, 1995, *38*, 673–703.

Kaplan, D. & Keys, C. Sex and relationship variables as predictors of sexual attraction in cross-sex platonic friendships between young heterosexual adults. *Journal of Social and Personal Relationships*, 1998, *14*, 191–206.

Kram, K. & Isabella, L. Mentoring alternatives: The role of peer relationships in career development. *Academy of Management Journal*, 1985, *28*, 110–32.

Lin, N. & Dumin, M. Access to occupations through social ties. *Social Networks*, 1986, *8*, 365–85.

Lincoln, J. & Miller, J. Work and friendship ties in organizations: A comparative analysis of relational networks. *Administrative Science Quarterly*, 1979, *24*, 181–98.

Mainiero, L.A. A review and analysis of power dynamics in organizational romances. *Academy of Management Review*, 1986, *11*, 750–62.

Martin, R. 'Girls don't talk about garages!': Perceptions of conversation in same- and cross-sex friendships. *Personal Relationships*, 1997, *4*, 115–30.

McPherson, M., Smith-Lovin, L. & Cook, J.M. Birds of a feather: Homophily in social networks. *Annual Review of Sociology*, 2001, *27*, 415–44.

Mobley, G., Jaret, C., Marsh, K. & Lim, Y. Mentoring, job satisfaction, gender and the legal profession. *Sex Roles*, 1994, *31*, 79–96.

Monsour, M. Meanings of intimacy in cross- and same-sex friendships. *Journal of Social and Personal Relationships*, 1992, *9*, 277–95.

Monsour, M., Harris, B., Kurzweil, N. & Beard, C. Challenges confronting cross-sex friendships: 'Much ado about nothing?' *Sex Roles*, 1994, *31*, 55–77.

Nicks, S.D. Fear in academia: Concern of unmerited accusations of sexual harassment. *The Journal of Psychology*, 1996, *130*, 79–82.

O'Meara, J. Cross-sex friendship: Four basic challenges of an ignored relationship. *Sex Roles*, 1989, *21*, 525–43.

Padavic, I. & Reskin, B. *Women and men at work*. Thousand Oaks, CA: Pine Forge Press, 2002.

Powell, G. *Handbook of gender and work*. Thousand Oaks, CA: Sage, 1999.

Powell, G. Workplace romances between senior-level executives and lower-level employees: An issue of work disruption and gender. *Human Relations*, 2001, *54*, 1519–44.

Powell, G. & Graves, L. *Women and men in management*. Thousand Oaks, CA: Sage, 2003.

Prentice, D.A. & Miller, D.T. When small effects are impressive. *Psychological Bulletin*, 1992, *112*, 160–4.

Ragins, B. & Cotton, J. Mentor functions and outcomes: A comparison of men and women in formal and informal mentoring relationships. *Journal of Applied Psychology*, 1999, *84*, 529–50.

Rose, S. Same and cross-sex friendships and the psychology of homosociality. *Sex Roles*, 1985, *12*, 63–74.

Society for Human Resource Management (SHRM). Press release from the society for human resource management. Available at: [http://www.shrm.org/press/releases/990 315.htm], 1999.

Solomon, D.H. & Williams, M.L. Perceptions of social-sexual communication at work: The effects of message, situation and observer characteristics on judgments of sexual harassment. *Journal of Applied Communication Research*, 1997, *25*, 196–216.

Strauss, A. & Corbin, J. *Basics of qualitative research: Grounded theory procedures and techniques*. Newbury Park, CA: Sage, 1990.

Swain, S. Men's friendships with women. In P. Nardi (Ed.), *Men's relationships*. Newbury Park, CA: Sage, 1992, pp. 153–71.

Tangri, S., Burt, M. & Johnson, L. Sexual harassment at work: Three explanatory models. *Journal of Social Issues*, 1982, *38*, 33–54.

US Census Bureau. *American community survey: 2003 data profile*. Washington, DC: US Census Bureau, 2003.

Werking, K. *We're just good friends: Women and men in nonromantic relationships*. New York: Guilford Press, 1997.

Williams, C.L. *Gender differences at work: Women and men in nontraditional occupations*. Berkeley: University of California Press, 1989.

Williams, C.L. The glass escalator: Hidden advantages for men in the 'female' professions. *Social Problems*, 1992, *39*, 253–67.

Williams, C.L. *Still a man's world: Men who do women's work*. Berkeley: University of California Press, 1995.

PART 13

The Gender of Sexuality

We've long understood that sex was gendered. He and she had different sexualities, different experiences of pleasure, different motivations for sex. Half of the sexual jokes we have in our stock of stupid jokes are about the differences between men's and women's sexualities. And they follow a distinct pattern: he wants sex all the time, is constantly going for it, constantly ready for it, and is sexually "organized" to have lots of sex with lots of different people with little or no emotional connection to them. She, by contrast, doesn't really like sex, requires a deep emotional commitment before she'll consent, and is far more conservative in her sexual repertoire.

This gives rise to most of the conventional Mars and Venus stereotypes about gender and sex. She trades sex to get love, he trades love to get sex. Sex is a competition, and women and men engage in a battle of the sexes, a war between the sexes even, in which he attempts to conquer, to break down her resistance, and she decides if she will surrender, capitulate. In this model, she gives, he gets. And if she gives, she loses, and he wins.

But empirically, the reality is far from that stereotypic model. And we think that's a good thing. Frankly, we think that adversarial model is also a recipe for bad sex. The real story of our sexual lives is that these stereotypic constructions have begun to erode to the point where women and men are converging—in their motivations to have sex, in what they like, and with whom they want to have it. Women's and men's sexualities are increasingly similar. Neither Martian nor Venusian, our sexualities are decidedly Earthbound (though the experience itself can send us to the moon!).

The essays in this section address that convergence—and the inequalities that persist. Breanne Fahs and Eric Swank look at what predicts women's sexual satisfaction and sexual activity (and it has little to do with his shoe size). Jane Ward approaches the question from an entirely different perspective, looking at the navigation of identity among guys who have sex with other guys, but consider themselves resolutely heterosexual.

Finally, in a report from the largest study of campus "hooking up" sexual culture, Paula England and her colleagues suggest that while women and men are both doing an increasing amount of hooking up, those behaviors may mean different things to college women and men.

Hooking Up and Forming Romantic Relationships on Today's College Campuses

PAULA ENGLAND, EMILY FITZGIBBONS SHAFER, AND ALISON C. K. FOGARTY

The "sexual revolution" of the 1960s and 1970s marked a sea change in public attitudes toward sexuality. Prior to this, premarital sex had been taboo. The norm was often broken, but most women who had sex before marriage did so only with the man they were going to marry. Women who had nonmarital sex were so stigmatized that the discovery of a premarital pregnancy was seen as a crisis that often led to a "shotgun" marriage. The sexual revolution rendered premarital sex acceptable, at least in a relationship. Not all groups accepted the new norm, but its mainstream acceptance can be seen by how common cohabitation before marriage became; by the early 1990s, well over half of marriages were preceded by cohabitation (Bumpass and Lu 2000).

The pre-1970s sexual norms went together with a particular gender system. Women's virginity was seen as more important than men's, men were seen as the leaders in politics and the economy, and men were supposed to be the initiators in dating, proposals of marriage, and sexuality. Women's primary adult role was that of wife and mother, and men's primary role *in* the family was accomplished precisely by his role *outside* the family as a breadwinner. Men were seen as the heads of their family.

The "gender revolution" shook some of this up, with the most important change being the increase in women's employment and career orientation. In 1960, 41% of American women between 25 and 54 years of age were in the labor force, but this figure had climbed to 74% by 2000. Today, more women than men are graduating from college, and while college majors are still substantially segregated by sex, more women than previously are entering traditionally male fields in management and the professions (England and Li 2006).

In the aftermath of these two "revolutions," what do dating, sexuality, and relationships look like on today's college campuses? We report here on a study we undertook to answer this question. As undergraduate readers of this article know, casual dating is no longer as common as "hooking up" among college students. So our first goal is simply to clarify the definition and characteristics of the new social form, the "hook up." Our second goal is to probe how meanings and behavior in hook ups or relationships are structured by gender.

Our Study

We collected quantitative and qualitative data on college students. In this report, we limit ourselves to heterosexual students because we are interested in how gender structures their romantic and sexual relations. The quantitative data come from an online survey of over 4,000 undergraduate students at several universities who answered fixed-response questions suitable for statistical analysis. Questions covered their experiences of and attitudes toward hooking up, dating, and relationships. Participating universities include University of Arizona, Indiana University, Stanford University, University of California at Santa Barbara, and State University of New York at Stony Brook.[1] Statistics presented later in this paper are from the data from the online survey.

The second part of our study makes use of qualitative data gathered from in-depth face-to-face discussions with students at Stanford, where the authors work. We conducted focus groups in large Sociology classes in 2004 and 2006.[2] In 2004, 270 undergraduates in a class taught by the first author interviewed one fellow undergraduate student (not in the class) about experiences with relationships, hooking up, and dating. Based on what we learned from the large number of 2004 face-to-face interviews, 25 more elaborate interviews were carried out by a trained team of undergraduate and graduate student interviewers during 2006, with a random sample of Stanford seniors as the target.[3] In all the qualitative interviews, interviewers worked from an interview guide delineating the topics to cover, and were trained to add probe questions so as to encourage respondents to tell relevant stories in their own words. All quotes below are from these two sets of interviews of Stanford undergraduates.

The Hook Up: A New Social Form

The hook up has replaced the casual date on college campuses today, students told us. The term "hook up" is ambiguous in definition. But, generally, students use it to refer to a situation where two people are hanging out or run into each other at an event (often a party), and they end up doing something sexual, usually after going to one person's room. In some cases the sexual behavior is intercourse, but not in the majority of cases. (Sexual behavior that doesn't include intercourse is not seen as "having sex," as students typically use the term.) A hook up carries no expectation that either party has an interest in moving toward a relationship, although in some cases such an interest is present either before or after the hook up. By their senior year, while 24% of respondents have never hooked up, on average they have had 6.9 hook ups (the median is 5), and 28% have had 10 or more. Hook ups often happen after a good bit of drinking. The median number of drinks men had drunk the night of their last hook up was 6, whereas women had consumed 4.[4]

We asked respondents to the online survey to tell us about their most recent hook up, thinking that asking about a specific and fairly recent event would allow more accurate recall. While the most recent event may be atypical for any one respondent, with a large sample, as we have, what is typical should emerge from the statistics. Figure 1 shows what sexual activity occurred during respondents' most recent hook ups. The categories are arrayed so that a hook up is categorized by the behavior the couple engaged in that entailed going "farthest," as students generally see it. (For example, if a couple had oral sex and had intercourse, they would be categorized in the "intercourse" category.[5]) As Figure 1 shows, 31% made out and touched but didn't have any genital contact, 16% had some hand/genital contact, 15% had oral sex, and 38% had intercourse on their most recent hook up.[6]

While a hook up implies no commitment to hook up again, we found that it was not uncommon to hook up with the same person more than once, as Figure 2 shows. When students reported about their most recent hook up, we asked them how many previous times they had hooked up with this same person. About half of hook ups were the first time with this person. Only 11% were second hook ups, 8% were third, 6% were fourth, and so on, until we come to the last category for those who had hooked up 10 or more times with this person. Fully 16% of these hook ups involved someone the student had hooked up with 10 or more times. When students hook up regularly with the same person outside of a romantic relationship, it is sometimes called "friends with benefits," "fuck buddies," or, simply, "a regular hook up." Although we don't show the statistics here, when couples have hooked up more times, they are more likely to have intercourse on the hook up.

The hook up is clearly a product of the increased permissiveness that came with the sexual revolution. Its mainstream adoption among college students shows a change to norms that permit some amount of sexual behavior that is casual. The sexual behavior in hook ups is not seen to have affection, an exclusive romantic relationship, or even an interest in such a relationship as a prerequisite. Although the idea that hooking up is acceptable is

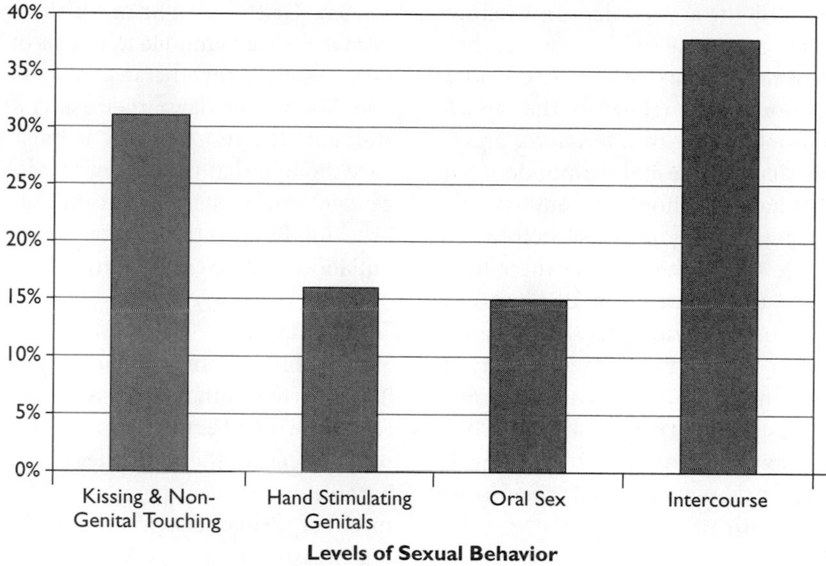

Figure 1. Percent of Hook Ups Involving Levels of Sexual Behavior.

Note: Categories to the right may also include behaviors in those to the left, but not vice versa. N = 2,904 undergraduates, reporting on their most recent hook up.

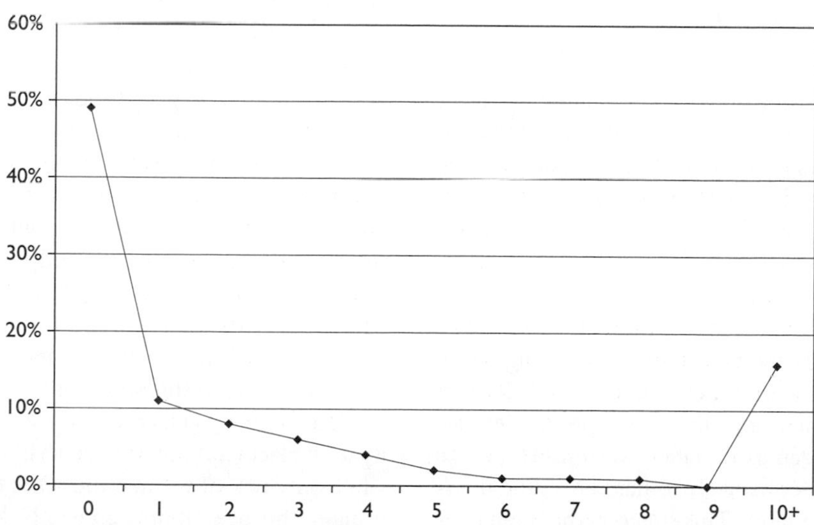

Figure 2. The Number of Previous Hook Ups a Student Reported with His or Her Most Recent Hook Up Partner.

Note: N = 2,510 undergraduates, reporting on their most recent hook up.

quite pervasive, students are divided on whether it is okay to have intercourse (which is what they mean when they talk about "having sex") on a casual hook up. Some see oral sex as the typical limit for casual hook ups, with intercourse signifying a pretty big step. As one male respondent put it, "She was very happy to hook up, but actually having sex was gonna really mean something to her." Another male said, "There are all these little lines . . . gradations, then there's a *big* line between oral sex and intercourse." Widespread acceptance of hooking up can coexist with a large minority of both men and women who disapprove of casual sex in part because the term "hook up," while always entailing some casual sexual behavior, is ambiguous enough that it does not necessarily entail "sex" in the sense of intercourse.

Gender and the Hook Up

Hook ups are "gendered" in three important ways. First, men initiate more of the interaction, especially the sexual action. Second, men have orgasms more frequently than women. Men's sexual pleasure seems to be prioritized. Third, a sexual double standard persists in which woman are more at risk than men of getting a bad reputation for hooking up with multiple partners.

Initiation

Most hook ups start at parties or hanging out in (often coed) dorms. To get things started, one of the two partners has to initiate talking or dancing. Our survey asked who did this: him, her, or both equally. In about half the cases, initiation of talking or dancing was deemed equal. But where one of the two was reported to have initiated talking or dancing it was more likely the man. When we asked who initiated the sexual interaction, things were much more gendered. Less than a third thought both had initiated equally, and a preponderance of cases were seen as initiated by men.[7] Hook ups were almost twice as likely to happen in the man's room as the woman's.[8] This suggests that men have initiated the move from the party or public area of the dorm into the room in order to facilitate sexual activity.[9] These patterns of male initiation may mean that men are more eager for hook ups than women. Or they might mean that both men and women feel accountable to norms of how gender is to be displayed that dictate male, not female, initiation.[10] In the "old days," men asked women on dates and initiated most sexual behavior. One might have thought that the gender revolution would degender scripts of initiation on dates or in sexual behavior. But this transformation hasn't happened; initiation is nowhere near equal.

The Orgasm Gap

Since hook ups are defined by some sexual activity occurring, with no necessary implication of any future, we might expect people to judge them by the sexual pleasure they provide. Orgasm is one good barometer of sexual pleasure (although we recognize that sexual behavior can be pleasurable without orgasm). Our survey asked students whether they had an orgasm on the most recent hook up and whether they thought their partner did. Figure 3 shows men's and women's reports of their own orgasm on their most recent hook up, depending on what sexual behavior occurred. (Here we omit hook ups that involved no more than kissing and nongenital touching, since virtually none of them led to orgasm.) What is notable is how much more often men have orgasms on hook ups than women. When men received oral sex and did not engage in intercourse, they had an orgasm 57% of the time, but women only experienced orgasm a quarter of the time they received oral sex and did not engage in intercourse. Men who engaged in intercourse but who did not receive oral sex had an orgasm 70%; however, intercourse without receiving oral sex led to orgasm for women only 34% of the time. Even when women received oral sex *and* had intercourse, they had orgasms just under half the time on these hook ups, while men had orgasms about 85% of the time in this situation.

Of all hook ups (regardless of what sexual activity took place) 44% of men experienced an orgasm while only 19% of women did. One factor contributing to this overall orgasm gap is that couples are more likely to engage in behavior that prioritizes male pleasure and orgasm. One key example of this is nonreciprocal oral sex. Figure 4 shows that in hook ups where there was some oral sex but no

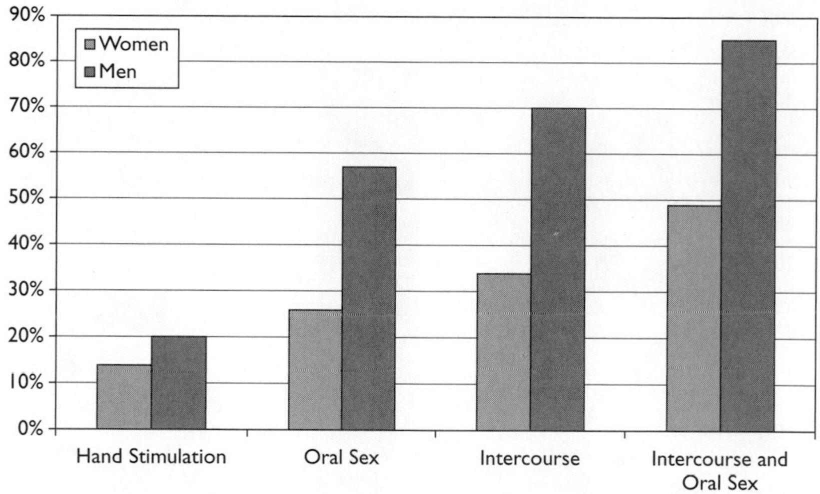

Figure 3. Men's and Women's Report of Whether They Had an Orgasm in Hook Ups Involving Various Sexual Behaviors.

Note: Statistics include only men's report of men's orgasm and women's report of women's orgasm. Women's orgasm for hook ups involving oral sex include only those where she received oral sex, whether he did or not. Men's orgasm for hook ups involving oral sex include only those where he received oral sex, whether she did or not. Hand stimulation (of genitals) was treated analogously. Each category excludes any case where the couple also engaged in behaviors in the categories to the right. N = 2,693 undergraduates, reporting on their most recent hook up.

intercourse, the oral sex was reciprocal less than 40% of the time. In 45% of the cases, men were the only ones to receive oral sex, whereas it was only 16% of the cases where only women received it. Thus, when oral sex is not reciprocal, men are on the receiving end three times as often as women. Even when men do give women oral sex, they are either unable to or do not make it a priority to bring the woman to orgasm (refer back to Figure 3).

Moreover, men often believe their partner had an orgasm when she really didn't, if we believe that each sex accurately reports their own orgasm. Figure 5 compares women's and men's reports of the *woman's* orgasm on the most recent hook up. It shows, for example, that when women receive cunnilingus, they report an orgasm about a quarter of the time, but men who performed cunnilingus on their partners report the woman to have had an orgasm almost 60% of the time—a huge disparity. A large disparity exists between men and women's reports of women's orgasm from intercourse as well. For example, when the couple had intercourse (but the women did not receive oral sex), women reported orgasm 34% of the time, but 58% of men reported the woman to have had an orgasm in this situation. Although the figure doesn't show these statistics, women's reports of men's orgasms lines up quite well with men's own reports. Of course, male orgasm, usually accompanied with ejaculation, is fairly easy to identify.

Why are men so misinformed about their female partner's orgasms on hook ups? Being drunk and lack of communication may contribute to misperception. Another factor is that women sometimes fake orgasms. One woman reported doing this "to make that person feel good, to make them feel like they've done their job." She also said that sometimes it was "just really to end it," continuing, "a lot of people say they've faked it just because they're like bored with it."

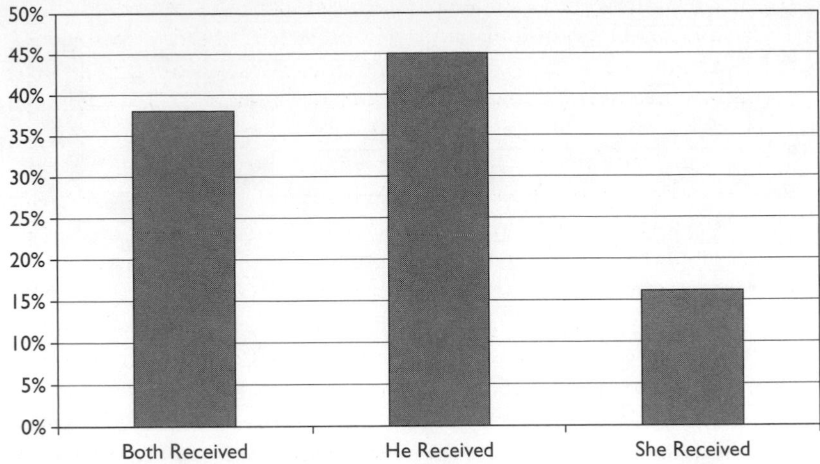

Figure 4. Who Received Oral Sex in Hook Ups Where Oral Sex Occurred But Intercourse Did Not.

Note: N = 443 undergraduates, all of whom engaged in some form of oral sex (giving or receiving) in their most recent hook up but did not engage in intercourse. "He received" means that only he received oral sex; "she received" means that only she received oral sex.

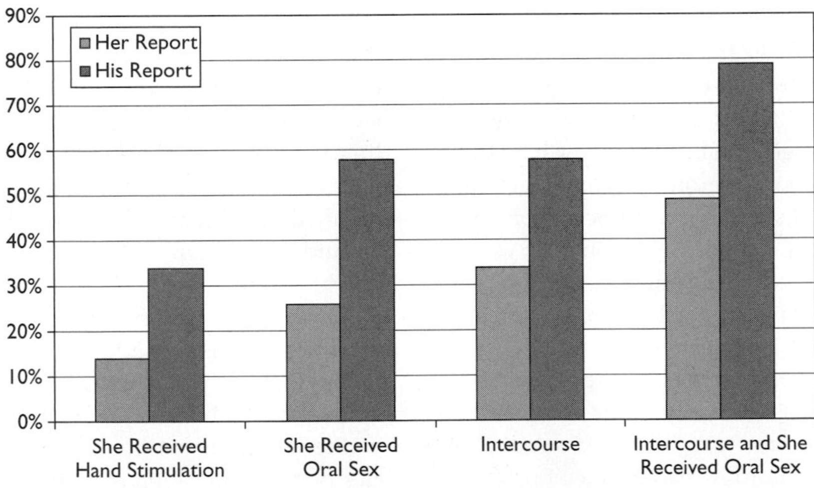

Figure 5. Men's and Women's Perceptions of the *Woman's* Orgasm in Hook Ups Involving Various Sexual Behaviors.

Note: All categories to the right of "She Received Hand Stimulation" may also include her receiving hand stimulation. Oral sex and intercourse, however, occur only in each category as labeled. Statistics for hook ups involving oral sex or hand stimulation for her (she received) include such cases whether or not these occurrences entailed oral sex or hand stimulation for him. N = 2,630 undergraduates, reporting on their most recent hook up.

Despite the orgasm gap, if we ask students how much they enjoyed the hook up overall, and how much they enjoyed the sexual part of it, men and women give very similar and largely positive responses. Women's lesser rate of orgasm doesn't translate into lower reported satisfaction on average. Perhaps women are evaluating hook ups on a standard of what seems possible to them in their social world. Social psychologists often find that groups that recurrently have lower rewards (for example, pay from jobs) focus on within-group rather than between-group comparisons, which leads them to develop a lesser sense of entitlement. Expecting less, they tend not to be disappointed when they get less (Major 1987).

But not all women accept nonreciprocal oral sex and the orgasm gap as "natural." Some try to assert their wants and are critical of men's lack of concern for their orgasm. One woman said, "When I... meet somebody and I'm gonna have a random hook up... from what I have seen, they're not even trying to, you know, make a mutual thing." She went on to say that in cases like this, she doesn't even bother to fake orgasm. Referring to nonreciprocal oral sex, another complained, "He did that thing where... they put their hand on the top of your head... and I hate that!... Especially 'cause there was no effort made to, like, return that favor." One woman who is assertive about her sexual wants said, "(I)n my first relationship... it was very one way... and that just didn't do much for me in terms of making me feel good about myself... so... I hate it when a guy is like take your head and try and push it down, because I then just switch it around to make them go down first usually. And some guys say no and then I just say no if they say no."

Some men conceded that if they see a hook up as a one time thing, they aren't concerned about women's orgasm. One said, "I mean like if you're just like hooking up with someone, I guess it's more of a selfish thing...." Another said, "If it's just a random hook up.... Say, they meet a girl at a party and it's a one night thing, I don't think it's gonna matter to them as much." Other men said they tried but were often unsure what worked and whether the woman had had an orgasm.

The Sexual Double Standard

Decades ago, the double standard took the form of an expectation of virginity before marriage for women but not men. One might have thought that the emphasis on equal opportunity of the gender revolution would have killed the double standard. While the expectation that women be virgins before marriage is now a thing of the past in most social groups,[11] women are still held to a stricter standard than men when it comes to sex. But today, the difference is in how men versus women who hook up a lot are viewed. In focus groups, students told us that women who hook up with too many people, or have casual sex readily, are called "sluts" by both men and women. While some men who hook up a lot are called "man whores," such men also encounter accolades from other men for "scoring" more. Women are held to a stricter standard, but it is fairly vague exactly what that standard is.

As an illustration of the double standard, Figure 6 shows that when students in our online survey were asked if they had ever respected someone less because that person hooked up with the respondent, 34% of men but only 22% of women answered yes. When asked if they ever hooked up with someone who they think respected them less because of the hook up, 55% of women but only 21% of men said yes. Thus, men disrespect their partners for hooking up with them more than women do, and women seem to know this (and even exaggerate it).[12]

One male respondent illustrates the double standard when he says "I definitely see some girls out there just wanting to hook up.... Sometimes they're called 'slutty'... I guess it's... less stigmatic for a guy to go out and be, like, 'I'm gonna go get some ass' than for a girl..." He dissociates himself from the double standard but attributes it to his friends when he says, "I mean not myself—... women are sexual creatures too; they can do what they want. But... they... see this girl and go... there's no way I can date her, but... she's hot for a hook up." Indeed, in focus groups students said that men would sometimes decide that a woman was relationship material because she wouldn't hook up with them the first time they were together. This presents women who want relationships with a real dilemma: the main

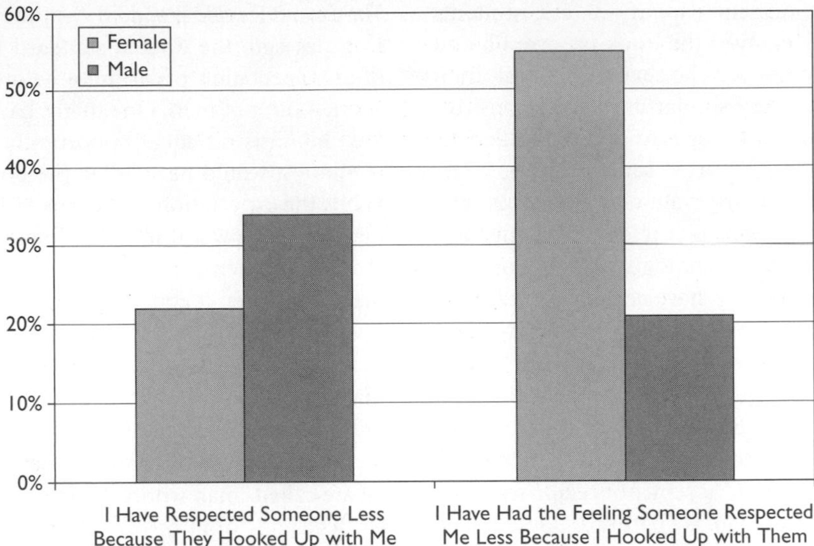

Figure 6. Percentage of Students Who, After a Hook Up, Have Ever Respected Someone Less or Felt a Partner Respected Them Less, by Gender.

Note: N = 2,931 and 2,928 undergraduates, respectively.

path into relationships today is through hook ups, but through hooking up they also risk men's thinking that they aren't relationship material.

Gender, Dating, and Exclusive Relationships

By their senior year, 71% of students report that they've been in a relationship that lasted at least six months while in college. Hook ups have not replaced relationships, but they have altered the pathway into relationships and may have largely replaced casual dating. One woman bemoaned this, saying, "(S)ometimes I wish that this environment here were... more conducive to just like casual dating, because... it's difficult to go on actual dates without... already being in a relationship...." A male student said, "So there's no such thing as casually going out to... gauge the other person.... I mean you can hang out.... But we're only dating once we've decided we like each other... and want to be in a relationship."

Thirty to forty years ago a common college pattern involved casually dating a number of people. Dating did not necessarily imply an interest in a relationship with the person. But sometimes a succession of dates led to a relationship simultaneous with a progression of sexual activity.[13] Today, college students generally use the term "dating" to refer to a couple who has already decided they are in an exclusive relationship. (This is also called "going out," or being "official" or "exclusive.") "Dating" is different than going on a "date." Dates may be between people who are not already in a relationship. While less common than decades back, dates are sometimes present in the sequence leading to relationships. Indeed, because casual dating has become less common, dates may be more indicative of relational intent today than decades ago. Among respondents in our online survey, by their senior year, students had been on an average of 4.4 dates (the median is 3).[14] This is less than the number of times seniors had hooked up (a mean of 6.9 and median of 5), but shows that dates are not completely dead. What has changed is the typical sequence. Dates often come after a hook up, and thus after some sexual behavior. They often have the function of expressing an interest in a possible relationship. When reporting on those with just the person with whom they had their most recent relationship of at least six months, 4% had at least one hook up but no dates, 26% had at least one date but no hook ups, while the majority, 67%, had at least one of each before it became a relationship. In cases where there were both dates and hook ups, our qualitative data suggest that the hook ups usually came first.

Many hook ups never lead to either another hook up or a relationship, and some lead only to more hook ups with the same person. But, as we've just seen, some lead to a relationship ("dating") via the pathway of one or more dates. Who initiates these dates? The gender revolution seems to have changed attitudes but not behavior in this area. When asked about their attitudes, students approve heartily of women asking men on dates (well over 90% of both men and women agreed that it is okay). Yet it rarely happens; as Figure 7 shows, asked about their most recent date with someone with whom they weren't already in a relationship, 87% claimed that the man had asked the woman out on this date. Focus groups suggested that asking a woman on a date is a way that men signal their interest in a possible relationship.

Who pays on these dates? Asked about their most recent date with someone with whom they were not already in a relationship, two-thirds said the man paid, and less than 5% said the woman did. The remainder was evenly split between reporting that no money was spent and that they split the cost. Indeed, in qualitative interviews, when women report some event that might have been considered a date or not, they sometimes use the fact that he paid as evidence that it was a real date. One woman described such a situation this way: "It also kind of threw me that he like insisted on paying because I didn't really think of it as like a date.... I thought we were just hanging out.... I think I sort of knew that maybe he was thinking it was a date, but I definitely offered to pay for my meal... And he was like, 'No, no, no.' "

Relationships are often made "official" or exclusive via "the talk"—where one of the two people seek to define the relationship more clearly. This may happen after a few hook ups followed by hanging out or some dates. Some students call this a "DTR" or "define the relationship" talk. Others just call it "the talk." In the old days, it would be the man who would ask a woman to "go steady" or "be pinned" or who would propose marriage. We sought to ascertain who initiates the talk to define things as a relationship on today's campuses. In focus groups and in-depth interviews, the consensus was that these

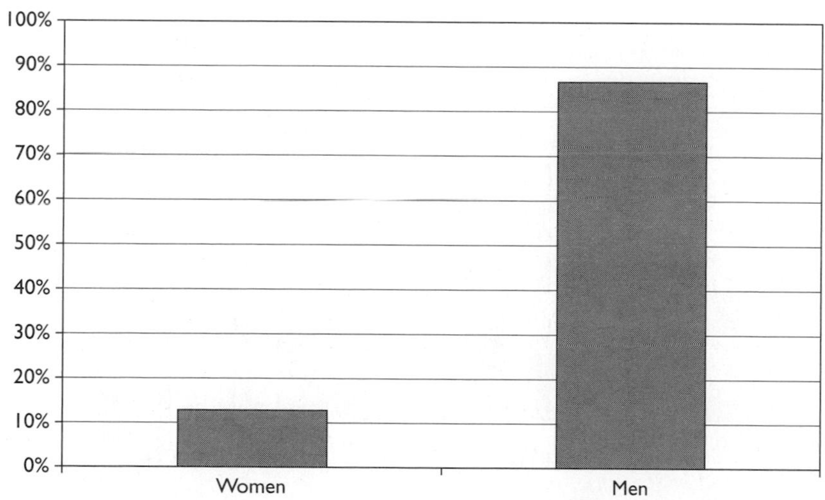

Figure 7. Who Asked Whom Out on Student's Most Recent Date.

Note: N = 2,870 undergraduates, reporting on their most recent date with someone with whom they were not already in an exclusive relationship.

talks are more often initiated by the woman who wants to know where she stands with the guy after several hook ups. As one female interviewee said, "I feel like it's . . . the stereotypical girl thing to do, like . . . the guy feels like the girl is boxing him into a relationship." To confirm this statistically, we asked students in the survey how it became "clear that this person was your boy/girlfriend." About half of men and women say that the man initiated it, while about a fifth say that the woman did. Most of the rest say they "just knew." Thus, at least in the cases where a relationship ensued, it was typically not the woman initiating the talk. Of course, this is not inconsistent with the possibility that women initiate more talks overall, but get shut down by men who don't want relationships. To find out about those DTRs that didn't lead to relationships, we also asked how many times the student ever initiated a talk to try to define a relationship as exclusive but had the partner respond that s/he didn't want a relationship. The distribution of male and female responses was very similar, with "never" the most frequent category. This suggests that, counter to the stereotype students themselves seem to have, women do *not* initiate such talks more than men. At this point in our research, we aren't sure what to make of this discrepancy between the generalizations students make in focus groups, and what they report about their own experiences in the survey.

Whether or not women initiate more talks to define relationships, the larger question is whether women are more interested in relationships than men. Our attitudinal data suggest that they are, while men express a more recreational view of sex, although the two sexes overlap substantially. As Figure 8 shows, asked if they had been interested in a relationship with the person they hooked up with *before* the hook up, 47% of women but only 35% of men said they had at least some interest. Asked about their feelings of interest in a relationship right after the hook up, almost half the women but only 36% of the men had at least some interest in a relationship with this person. We think this indicates more interest in relationships among women. But there are other possible interpretations. It is possible that women's responses are different than men's because social pressures lead the two genders in the opposite direction of reporting bias. That is, women may feel they are supposed to limit hook ups to those in whom they have a relational interest, while men feel they are supposed to be ready for sex all the time. Alternatively, women may want

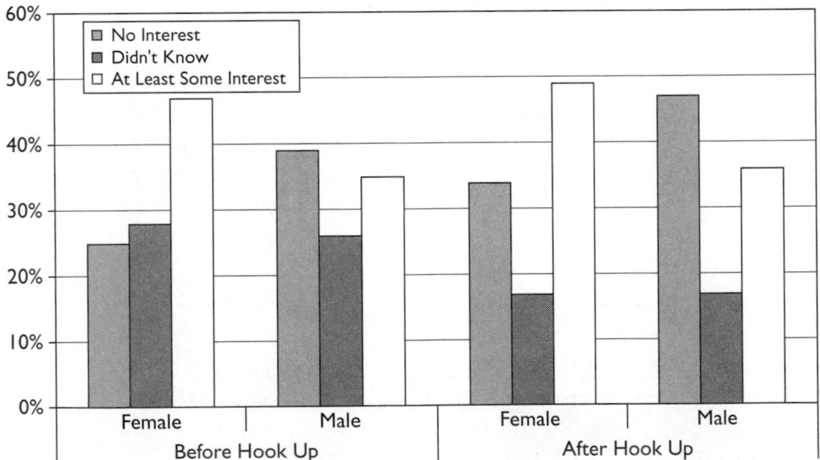

Figure 8. Women's and Men's Interest in a Relationship with This Partner Before and After Their Most Recent Hook Up.

Note: N = 2,144 and 2,903 undergraduates, respectively, reporting on their interest before and after their most recent hook up.

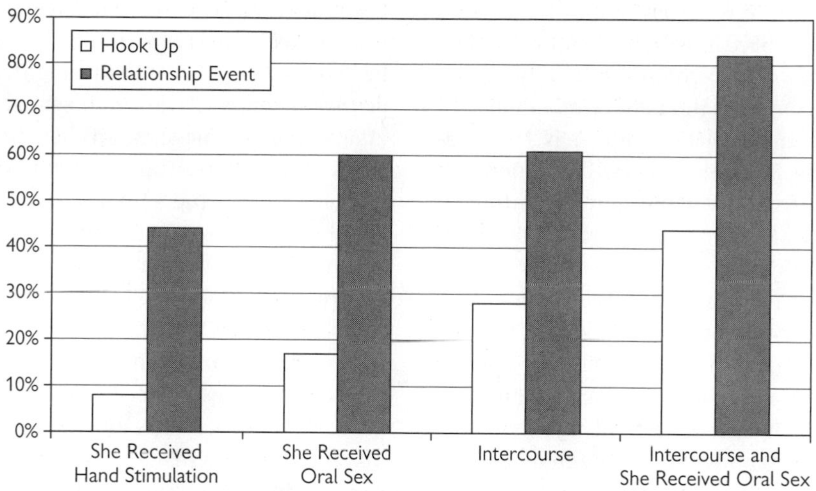

Figure 9. Women's Report of Own Orgasm in Last Hook Up That Was a First Hook Up with a Particular Partner and Last Relationship Sexual Event.

Note: N = 1,865 and N = 1,276 female undergraduates, respectively, reporting (white bar) on their sexual behavior and orgasm on their most recent hook up (only includes those that were first-time hook ups with that partner) and reporting (gray bar) on their sexual behavior and orgasm the last time they did anything sexual with a person with whom they had been in a relationship for at least six months.

relationships not because they like them more, but because they believe more strongly that sex should be relational, or because they know they will be judged more harshly than men for nonrelational sex. Indeed, given the statement, "I would not have sex with someone unless I was in love with them," 49% of women agreed but only 34% of men.[15]

One advantage of relationships for women is that most women have a better chance of orgasm when having sex with a regular partner. In our survey, we asked those in a relationship about the last time they did something sexual with their partner, so we could compare what happens in those situations to what happens on first-time hook ups. Figure 9 shows that women are much more likely to orgasm with a regular relationship partner than when hooking up with someone for the first time. ("For the first time" here refers to the first time with this partner.) First-time hook ups in which women received oral sex but did not have intercourse led to orgasm for women only 17% of the time, but, within a relationship, oral sex without intercourse led to orgasm 60% of the time. When couples had intercourse, women had orgasm about 28% of the time in first-time hook ups but over 60% of the time in relationships. Although we don't show these statistics in the figure, the analogous percents for men are 52% and 89%; so relationships are also better for men than first-time hook ups with a given partner, although the gain is not quite as great as for women.

If the higher rates of orgasm in a relationship come mainly from communication and "practice" with this particular partner, then we might expect this advantage to be present in "friends with benefits" or "regular hook up" situations as well, even where there is not a professed romantic relationship. We don't show statistics on this in the figure, but there is evidence of this. Where couples had intercourse, women's orgasm rates were 28% in first-time hook ups and 60% in a relationship as shown in Figure 9; in hook ups where they had previously hooked up at least ten times with this person, women's rate was 54%, not quite as good as the 60% in relationships but much better than in first-time hook ups. Perhaps the genuine caring in relationships explains their added advantage for orgasms.[16] Of course, relationships may have disadvantages as well as advantages. Both men and women lose autonomy while gaining intimacy, and women may be expected to redefine themselves more than men.[17]

Talking about why she has orgasm more easily in a relationship, one woman said, "I'm more comfortable with the person." The same male student we quoted above about men not caring about the woman's orgasm in one-time hook ups said this: "If you're with somebody for . . . more than just that one night, I think . . . it is important for guys. . . . And I think if you're in a long-term relationship, like I know I feel personally responsible."

Two Partial Revolutions and Today's College Scene

What is happening on college campuses today reflects the two large-scale social changes that some have dubbed revolutions: the sexual revolution and the gender revolution. But it simultaneously reveals many aspects of the gender system left relatively untouched by these revolutions. The sexual revolution was pushed along by the availability of the birth control pill starting in the 1960s, and by the legalization of abortion with a Supreme Court decision in 1973. Both made it more possible to have sex without fear of having an unwanted birth. Unquestionably, norms about premarital sex have become more permissive, and the new social form of the hook up is one result. We have shown that hooking up is now quite mainstream among college students, however vague the norms surrounding it are.

The gender revolution also contributed to sexual permissiveness. As more women decided to train for careers, this pushed up age at marriage, which made sex before marriage more likely. More directly, the feminist idea that women should be free to pursue careers—even in traditionally male fields—may have spilled over into the idea that women as well as men had a right to sexual freedom. Clearly women have won the right to be nonvirgins at marriage in most social groups. But beyond this gain, what is striking to us is how little gender revolution we see in sexual and romantic affairs. The double standard has not changed to a single "equal opportunity" standard for men and women. Rather, the standard, vague though it is, has shifted to a less restrictive line for each sex but remained dual; women who hook up a lot or have sex too easily are more at risk of a bad reputation than are men. One might have thought that the gender revolution would lead to women asking men out on dates. Instead, the casual date not preceded by a hook up has almost died. In both hook ups and the dates that sometimes come after them, men are initiating much of the action. The gender initiating the action seems to be getting more of the sexual rewards, particularly in hook ups, where women give men oral sex more than vice versa, and even when women receive oral sex or have intercourse, they have orgasms much less often than men. Equal opportunity for women appears to have gone farther in the educational and career world than in the college sexual scene.

Notes

1. In almost all cases, respondents were recruited through classes. The numbers of respondents at the universities were: U. Arizona 309, Indiana U. 1,616, Stanford U. 925, U. California Santa Barbara 745, and SUNY-Stony Brook 628. We also collected a small number of responses from students at the Evergreen State College in Olympia, Washington (27) and Ithaca College (69). These are included in the results reported here. Overall, we had 2,779 women and 1,550 men, a total of 4,329 respondents. Our sample is not a probability sample from any of the participating colleges, so cannot be said to be strictly representative of college students at these institutions.
2. What we learned in the focus groups informs our discussion. We took notes in these groups, but did not record them. Therefore, we use no direct quotes from these sessions.
3. We started from a random sample of 118 seniors provided by the Registrar. Data collection is

ongoing, but this preliminary analysis uses the 25 interviews that have been conducted and transcribed to date. Given the low response rate so far, and the fact that the other larger group of 270 interviews conducted in 2004 obtained respondents through a convenience sample (students chose an acquaintance to interview), the qualitative data should not be considered representative. The data should, however, reveal most of the range of behaviors and meanings present in the undergraduate culture.

4. The mean number of drinks on the most recent hook up was 6.7 for men and 3.9 for women. Extreme outliers affect means more than medians.
5. Classifying hand stimulation of genitals as "going less far" than oral sex is somewhat arbitrary, but we did so because we believe students see oral sex as "going farther," and also because the data show that, as practiced by college students, hand stimulation of genitals leads to orgasm less often than oral sex. Our rankings imply no value judgment about which practices are better; we are trying to rank order practices as students see them in terms of which are seen as "going farther."
6. There were a few cases where the couple had anal sex but not vaginal intercourse; we classified these as intercourse. While about a quarter of women say they have ever had anal sex, a very small per cent engage in this on any one occasion, which is why we did not include the practice in our classification.
7. While both men and women are more apt to report male than female initiation, the disparity is actually much greater in women's reports. This suggests that some events that women see as male initiation are seen by men as female initiation, or that women are more reluctant to report initiating because it is more stigmatized for them.
8. Twenty-four percent of men reported hooking up in the woman's room, while 44% said it was in their own room. Similarly, 25% of women said it was in their own room, while 42% said it was in the guy's room. The remainder of cases were in some other room.
9. Students also told us that male roommates are more accepting of hook ups occurring in the room, and even feel under pressure to help their roommates "score" by allowing them to use the room. In all-male focus group discussions, men were candid about the challenge of coming up with a pretext for getting the young woman to his room. Sometimes suggesting that they watch a movie on a DVD serves this function.
10. For a discussion of the theoretical perspective called "doing gender" that posits such gender display, see West and Fenstermaker 1993. The idea is that people are accountable to norms and conform their behavior to them even if they have not deeply internalized the belief that this is how it should be.
11. This standard is still emphasized among Mexican immigrants to the U.S., according to Gonzáléz-López (2005). Although most of the women she interviewed were not virgins when they married, the norm was that women should be, while men were expected to have their first sexual experience with a sex worker. Since the 1980s, fundamentalist Christian groups have encouraged youth to take a pledge to remain virgins till marriage, as discussed by Bearman and Brückner (2001). While endorsing many other forms of gender differentiation and male leadership, fundamentalist Christians generally encourage a single standard of virginity before marriage for both men and women.
12. Responses to another question showed a fascinating pattern in which each sex appears to have a double standard favoring their own sex, but men having a much harsher double standard against women than women have against men. Our survey asked students if they agree or disagree with the statement: "If women hook up or have sex with lots of people, I respect them less." They were given the same item about men. While 58% of female respondents agreed that they respected women less if they hook up or have sex with lots of people, they agreed by a somewhat wider margin (69%) that they respect men less who do this. Among men, however, only 41% agreed when asked about men but 67% agreed concerning women. Despite women's answer on the survey suggesting that they hold men a more exacting standard than women, focus groups said that women talk a lot amongst themselves about whether other women are "slutty."
13. For a history of courtship and dating in America, see Bailey 1988.

unwillingness of MSMs to recognize and/or celebrate their essential nature, or 'who they really are.' At the cultural level, and akin to 'culture of poverty' arguments used to pathologize African Americans, mainstream down low and MSM discourses imply that homophobia stems from essential, ethno-racial cultures of sexual repression.

As I will argue, however, a more productive reading of homophobia views the disavowal of gay identity and culture as one of the constitutive elements of heterosexual subjectivity—or a primary means of expressing heterosexual selfhood in a sexually binary world. While down low discourse implies that same-sex sexuality reveals a homosexual selfhood and that homophobia is an expression of culture, this article explores the theoretical insights that emerge from a reversal of this logic, or from viewing gay and straight as cultural spheres, and homophobia as a subjectifying practice (or a struggle to construct heterosexual selfhood).

Based on examination of an online community in which white 'str8'-identified men assert that sex with other white men *bolsters* their heterosexual masculinity, I highlight the heterosexual and racialized meanings that white MSMs attach to their same-sex behaviors. I argue that while some men who have sex with men prefer to do so within gay/queer cultural worlds, others (such as the 'straight

dudes' described here[2]) indicate a greater sense of belonging or cultural 'fit' with heterosexual identity and heteroerotic culture. For the latter group, homophobia, or the need to strongly disidentify with gay men and gay culture, is less a symptom of the *repression* of a 'true self', but rather an attempt to *express* a 'true self'—or one's strong sense of identification with heteropatriarchal white masculinity—in the context of having sex with men.

More specifically, this study points to the role of whiteness—including white archetypes and images—in the process of establishing heterosexual 'realness,' or believable straight culture. In contrast with the media's recent efforts to locate tensions between sexual identity and practice within African American and Latino cultures, my findings suggest that whiteness is also a commonly used resource for bridging the gap between heterosexual identification and same-sex desire. Previous research has pointed to various institutional contexts in which straight-identified men have sex with men, such as 'tearooms,' prisons, and the military (Humphreys, 1978; Kaplan, 2003; Schifter, 1999). These studies have demonstrated how men leverage hyper-masculinity, socioeconomic success, and the 'need' for quick and easy sex to preserve heterosexual identity and moral 'righteousness' (to use Humphrey's term). Building upon this research, the present study considers how *race* (including racial identification) and *racialized culture* (including racialized images, clothing, language and 'style') are also used to bolster claims to heterosexuality and to reframe sex between men as a hetero-masculine and 'not-gay' act. Similar to the assertion of feminist theorists that gender is always an intersectional accomplishment—or a construction that takes forms in and through race, class, and sexuality (Bettie, 2002; Hill Collins, 2004; Hull et al., 1982)—I show that the appearance of 'authentic' hetero-sexuality is also accomplished in interaction with race, socioeconomic class, and gender. While recent research has begun to critically explore these intersections for men of color (González, 2007), this article marks the often-invisible significance of race and culture for white dudes who have sex with dudes.

Race, Culture, and the Social Construction of Heterosexuality

While other research has examined the historical relationship between racial ideologies and the invention of homosexuality (Ferguson, 2004; Somerville, 2000), limited attention has been given to the role of race in the routine and daily accomplishment of heterosexuality and homosexuality. In this article, I argue that the ongoing construction of authentic or believable male heterosexuality is reliant upon racial codes that signify 'normal' straight male bonding, 'average' heterosexual masculinity, and lack of interest in gay culture. Whiteness—and more specifically the use of white masculine archetypes for example frat boys, surfers, skaters, jocks, and white 'thugs'—can play a central role in the production of an authentic and desirable heterosexual culture distinct from gay male culture.

In this article I do not make claims about the 'actual' sexual and racial identities of men who place advertisements for sex online, instead I am interested in the sexualized and racialized *cultures* these advertisements draw upon and reproduce. Indeed, a growing body of queer scholarship has pointed to the significance of *culture* in the construction and regulation of the heterosexual/homosexual binary. Following Foucault's assertion that 'homosexuality threatens people as a "way of life," rather than a way of having sex,' Halberstam (2005) has argued that 'queer subjects' might be redefined as those who 'live (deliberately, accidentally, or of necessity) during the hours when others sleep and in the spaces (physical, metaphysical, and economic) that others have abandoned,' including, 'ravers, club kids, HIV-positive barebackers, rent boys, sex workers, homeless people, drug dealers, and the unemployed' (2005: 10). Halberstam expands the boundaries of queerness to include subjects often not thought of as queer, and in a distinct but similarly motivated move, other queer scholars have 'disidentified' with mainstream or 'homonormative' lesbian and gay politics and its focus on monogamy, domesticity, and prosperity (Duggan, 2003; Muñoz, 1999). Queer, in each of these approaches, is less about sexual practices than about a 'way of life' that defies the rules of normative, respectable adult citizenship. Transcending long-held debates about whether to privilege sexual identification or sexual practice in the study of sexuality, this conceptualization of queerness is de-linked from both. Instead, because queer sexual culture or 'way of life' is what most violates social norms, *culture* becomes the material of queer resistance.

This article offers support for the argument that the lines between queerness and normativity are marked less by sexual practices and identities than by cultural practices and interpretive frames. In contrast with recent work that has expanded queer subjectivity or disavowed 'normal' gays and lesbians, I take a different empirical approach by demonstrating how whiteness and masculinity interact to offer *heterosexual culture* to white men who have sex with men. At the end of this article, I return to the question of culture and to my own queer disidentification with the hetero-erotic culture produced by str8 dudes online.

Method: Studying Dude-Sex

The 'Casual Encounters' section of Craigslist-Los Angeles (craigslist.org) is an online community bulletin board in which predominantly white 'str8 dudes' solicit sex with other white str8 dudes.[3] Exemplifying the arguments about culture described earlier, sex acts themselves are not meaningful indicators of sexual identification for str8 dudes on Craigslist. Instead, ads placed by str8 dudes suggest that it is willingness to identify with or consume 'perverted' queer culture that makes others queer, and conversely, it is str8 dudes' mastery of 'normal' heterosexual culture that makes them straight. This study builds upon an earlier pilot project, where I examined how beer, straight pornography, references to violent sex with women, 'dude speak' and other symbols of hypermasculinity were used to construct and authenticate heterosexuality on Craigslist (Ward, 2007). In that project, the ads constructed a str8 dude erotic culture that was decidedly *not* gay, often homophobic, and distinct from the erotic culture of the 'Men Seeking Men' section of Craigslist (which included ads posted by men on the 'DL' and 'straight-acting' gay men seeking 'same'). In contrast with the earlier pilot project, my focus here is on the role of race in the construction of heterosexuality among white, str8-identified men who seek sex with other str8 men.

As stated earlier, studies of sexuality have frequently invoked the notion of a 'real' sexual self, one that can be identified by interviewing research subjects about their 'actual' sexual practices, desires, and identifications. The notion of 'the real' has become particularly salient for researchers of online blogs and chat rooms—sites in which people may *represent* themselves in one way (man, woman, gay, straight, Black, white), but *actually be* another. From the perspective that there is a distinct dichotomy between the representational and the real, it is important to note that the study at hand reveals how 'str8 dudes' represent themselves in their Craigslist ads, but does not reveal how they identify, what they actually do, or how they think about what they do 'in real life' (or 'IRL,' the abbreviation used in cyberspace).[4] (This is significant, as I will show, in terms of racial identification, not just sexual identity.) Reflecting the method of cultural analysis more broadly, this study demonstrates how a heterosexual *culture* is constructed online without making any claims about the 'true' heterosexuality of the men who post ads on Craigslist. However, if genders and sexualities are *always* performed and accomplished within particular cultural contexts (Butler, 1990; West and Zimmerman, 1987), we might view the identities claimed online as equally 'revealing' or 'reliable' sources of knowledge about the gendered and racialized construction of sexualities. This article points to the gendered and racialized strategies that are used to construct 'authentic' heterosexuality in cyberspace; yet given that 'cyberspace . . . implicates the real outside the machine,' these strategies are likely to inform (and be informed by) other realms as well (Rodriguez, 2003: 119).

As I will argue, the production of heterosexual culture on Craigslist is accomplished not only through what is arguably a 'homophobic' and hyper-masculine rejection of queer culture; it is also dependent upon racial archetypes and images that invoke 'real' heterosexual white masculinity. For this study, I collected and analyzed all ads placed on Craigslist Los Angeles by 'str8' self-identified men during May through July of 2006.[5] Of the resulting 125 'Casual Encounters' ads collected and analyzed, 71 per cent made reference to race—either the racial identification of the person placing the ad or a specific racial preference for a sex partner. Among the ads that made reference to race, 86 per cent were placed by men who either identified themselves as white, or included a photo of themselves in which they appeared to be white (though I recognize that the latter is a flawed indicator of racial identity and that race itself is socially and historically constructed).[6] In order to capture all ads placed by straight-identified men seeking men, I searched for ads containing either the terms 'DL' or 'str8,' the latter of which was more commonly used on Craigslist. In 'Casual Encounters,' self-identified white men placed approximately 85 per cent of the ads, regardless of whether the term 'str8' or 'DL' was used.

As I will describe later, the sociopolitical landscape of Southern California is clearly significant to the construction of white hetero-masculinity on Craigslist Los Angeles, as many ads reference Southern California masculine archetypes (e.g. surfers, skaters, sun-tanned frat boys and others). I selected Southern California as the site of my analysis because of my own location in Los Angeles and my familiarity with the local neighborhoods, regional slang, and other references that appear in 'Casual Encounters' ads. While my focus on Los Angeles limits the generalizability of the study, it also allows for consideration of the ways in which racial, gendered, and sexual authenticity are locally and regionally constructed. Future research may benefit from a comparative approach.

Regular Dudes, Casual Encounters

Before describing how whiteness was deployed in Casual Encounters, I begin with a general description of str8 dudes' heteroerotic culture. In contrast with the logic that gay and straight are at opposite ends of a behavioral and biologically-determined binary, the str8 dudes who post on Craigslist construct 'gay' as a chosen identity that is not particularly linked to who is having sex, or what sexual acts are involved. Instead, being gay is about *how* sex is done—the language that is used, the type of 'porn' films that are watched, the beverages consumed, and the motivation that drives the sex itself. The following ads, representative of dozens of others, illustrate how str8 dudes lay claim to 'straightness' while soliciting sex with other men:

> *Straight Dude Drunk and Horny . . . Any str8 bud wanna jack? – 27.* Here's the deal. Went out drinking and clubbing, thought I'd hook up with a chick, but didn't pan out. I'm buzzed, horny, checking out porn. Is there any other straight dude out there who would be into jacking while watching porn? . . . I'd rather hook up with a chick, but none of the CL [Craigslist] chicks ever work out.
>
> *What happened to the cool bi/str8 dude circle jerks? – 33.* What happened to a group of masc[uline] dudes just sitting around stroking,

watching a game, drinking some brews, jerking, showing off, swapping college stories, maybe playing a drinking game and see what comes up?

Str8 guy wants to try BJ tonight – 27. Ok, I'll make this short. I'm up late tonight. I have a girlfriend. But I'm at home by myself now. I watch porn and I like when the women suck on big cocks. I've been thinking about it, and I think I'd like to suck one. I'm not attracted to guys so I'd rather not look at you much. Just suck your cock. I have a Polaroid and would like to take a pic with cum on my face. But this is really only for tonight cuz I'm horny! . . . I am Caucasian and prefer Caucasian.

$300 Bucks Cash If You're STR8 & Goodlooking!! – 27. Hey, are you str8, good-looking and broke? Are you Under 30 and hella cool? Like watching porn and talking bout pussy? You're in luck. 300 bucks every time we hangout. Be under 30. Honestly STR8. I'm mostly str8, great looking chill bro.

Str8 jackoff in briefs outside male bonding edging stroke – 34. I am a tall blond built packin' jockman with a big bulge in my jockeys. Dig hanging in just our briefs man to man in the hot sun workin' my bulge freely . . . If you are into jackin' and being free to be a man, let's hang. If you have a pool or a yard to layout and jack freely smoke some 420 [marijuana] and just be men, hit me up. No gay sex, I am looking for legit male bonding, masturbating in the hot sun only.

Unlike in similar websites for gay men, women are a central part of str8 dudes' erotic discourse. As these ads illustrate, str8 dudes often describe sex between dudes as a less desirable, but 'easy,' alternative to sex with women, or suggest that dude-sex is a means of getting the kind of sex that all straight men want from women, but can only get from men—uncomplicated, emotionless, and guaranteed. Str8 dudes get drunk, watch heterosexual porn, talk about 'pussy,' and maintain a clear emotional boundary between each other that draws upon the model of adolescent friendship, or the presumably 'harmless,' 'proto-sexual' circle jerk. References to being 'chill bros' and 'male bonding' help to reframe dude-sex as a kind of sex that bolsters, rather than threatens, the heterosexual masculinity of the participants. Only those who are 'man enough' and 'chill enough' will want dude-sex or be able to handle it.

In some cases, misogyny and references to violence against women are used to reinforce the link between dude-sex and heterosexual male bonding:

Whackin Off to Porn: STR8 porn. Gang bang. STR8, bi-curious masculine white guy lookin' for a masculine guy. Get into stroking bone with a bud, talkin' bout pussy and bangin' the bitch.

Any Straight/Bi Guys Want to Help Me Fuck My Blow up Doll???: Come on guys . . . we can't always pick up the chick we want to bone right??? So let's get together and fuck the hell out of my hot blow-up doll. Her mouth, her pussy, and her ass all feel GREAT. Just be cool, uninhibited, horny, and ready to fuck this bitch. It's all good here . . . lates.

Such ads suggest that dude-sex is a sexual and often violent expression of heterosexual masculinity and heterosexual culture, distinct from gay male culture in which misogyny typically manifests as the invisibility, rather than the objectification, of women (Ward, 2000). Marilyn Frye (1983), in her analysis of drag queens, argues 'What gay male affectation of femininity seems to be is a serious sport in which men may exercise their power and control over the feminine, much as in other sports . . . But the mastery of the feminine is not feminine. It is masculine.' I draw on Frye's analysis to suggest that while dude-sex makes use of and 'masters' homosexual or non-normative sex practices, this deployment of non-normative sexuality in the service of 'str8' culture is perhaps not best understood as 'queer.'

White Dudes, Race, and Class

Str8 dudes draw on the imagery of male bonding and the symbols of straight male culture, including references to sports, beer, fraternity membership, smoking pot and being 'chill,' 'buds,' or 'bros.' Yet 'dude speak' and 'dude style' is not simply masculine and heterosexual, it is also racialized. Recent studies of Black and Latino men on the down low have emphasized the importance of shared urban culture, and particularly hip hop, to the construction of down-low masculinity and sexuality

(González, 2007). González explains that *culture* (and not public or politicized identity) is what is at stake for Latinos on the down low: 'gay is not an option; Hip Hop is' (2007). Here I argue that *racial cultures* are also a central player in how white str8 dudes make sense of their str8 sexuality. In some cases, white dudes appropriate the symbols of Black and Latino down-low masculinity; in other cases, they foreground symbols of white masculinity (surfers, frat guys, jocks and so on) or synthesize the former with the latter.

Appropriating Hip Hop Masculinity: White Bros and Thugs on the DL

White str8 dudes—like a growing number of young white men in general—bolster their masculinity through the appropriation of terms and gestures used by Black and Latino men, especially within rap lyrics and culture. Writers critical of the mainstreaming and white ownership of rap have pointed to the ways in which its consumption by white youth has bled into other forms of racial and cultural appropriation (Kitwana, 2005). Young white men, in particular, have turned to rap for a new model of masculinity, male rivalry/violence, and heterosexual male bonding—resulting in white males giving each other 'daps,' wearing hip hop clothing, and 'affectionately' referring to one another using the term 'nigga' (Kitwana, 2005). While the appropriation of Black culture is rarely this explicit on Craigslist, str8 dudes nonetheless construct a masculine and heterosexual culture through a complex synthesis of white masculinity (e.g. surfer dudes) and masculinities of color (e.g. bros, thugs, and the DL). Str8 dudes commonly use phrases identified by African American studies scholars as 'Black slang,' such as 'sup?', 'hit me up,' and 'thugged out' (Smitherman, 2000), such as in the following ads:

> *23 y/o white dude party in Hollywood* – Hey guys, I'm partyin right now at home and have plenty of stuff to share . . . I'm lookin to meet a cool str8 thugged out white dude around my age, who would wanna come over, kick back, watch a lil porn, smoke a lil, and stroke off together. I might even be down to deepthroat some cock so if you love getting awesome head you should definitely hit me back! I'm lookin for someone chill & masculine so hit me up if this sounds like you . . . LATE
>
> *Str8 curious on the DL. Lookin' to chill – 23.* Sup? Just looking to chill with another str8/ bi dude, into young or older bros type . . . to mess around, not into perverted shit. Also not into fatty, femm guys. If you're a guy, please be in shape. I'm sort of skinny, curious here and haven't really acted on it. Just regular sane dude. Discretion a must. Aiite, late.

In an effort to convey that the sexual encounter will be casual, meaningless, and embedded in heterosexual male culture, white str8 dudes rely upon 'urban' slang derived from Black culture to represent heterosexuality. However, as with many forms of cultural appropriation, the slang used by str8 dudes is fast becoming associated with whites, and white masculinity in particular. For instance, according to the American Heritage Dictionary, 'bro,' a term commonly used by str8 dudes, is a slang term for 'brother' with etymological roots in African American vernacular English. However, its popular and contemporary usage by young white men in California has transformed its local and contextual meaning. Bloggers on urbandictionary.com, for example, define 'bros' as: 'white frat guys,' 'stupid white trash guys,' and 'usually white young males, found commonly in places like San Bernardino County in California, as well as Orange County.'

It may be most accurate to describe the racialized heterosexuality of str8 dudes as a kind of Eminem-inspired white working-class 'thuggery,' constructed through an in-your-face reclamation of 'white trash' and homophobic, or anti-gay, sexuality. While some ads express desire for 'average' working-class men (e.g. 'carpenters, carpet layers, plumbers, construction workers, mechanics, truckers, cable guys, delivery guys, overall just a hard working guy as I am. NO GAYS sorry'), others eroticize aggressive 'white trash' masculinity, such as in the following ad (with original photo, cropped to protect anonymity):

> *Str8 fuck a guy in his briefs, masc(uline) man to man fuck, hiv neg only*. Hey fucks. I need to fuckin

lay the pipe in some tight manhole today. I am hiv neg fuck with rubbers only. I want to have a hot packin guy in some tighty whities bent over and on all fours takin my dick like a champ. No fems or tweeking pnp ['party and play'] dudes. I hate that shit. Only 420 and a hot packin butt. Hit me up with your pix and your contact info.

Ads such as this amplify the appearance of heterosexuality through a synthesis of working-class culture, whiteness, and what is arguably the subtle appropriation of Black masculinity through hip hop slang ('hit me up') and 'thug' masculinity. Other ads produced similar images of 'rough' white masculinity through reference to skinheads and other archetypes of white male rebellion historically rooted in white racist, sexist and homophobic violence—'lookin for str8, bi, surfr, sk8r, punk, military, truckers, skinhead, rough trade . . . I'll give you the best head ever, buddy.'

Though being on the DL has been sensationalized in the media as a rejection of white gay culture specific to Black men living 'otherwise heterosexual lives' (Denizet-Lewis, 2003), a few white str8 dudes on Craigslist claimed DL identity as their own (though 'str8' was used far more commonly):

STR8 DUDES . . . White boy lookin for a NO CHAT suck . . . u lemme suck u . . . – 29. Hot dude on ur dick . . . u fuck my throat and bust it. . . . we never talk. Come over, kick back, pull ur cock out and get a kick ass wet deepthroat BJ. Love to deepthroat a hot str8 dude on the DL . . . bust ur nut and split. I'm a very goodlooking in shape white dude . . . totally on the DL . . . just wanna suck a hot str8 dude off, take ur nut . . . that's all. My place is kewl.

SECRET SERVICE HEAD – 28. Sup? Looking for bi/ str8 bud who is just looking to crack a nut . . . Just walk in kick back watch a porn and get blown . . . Cum and go . . . That's all I am looking for . . . Be white, under 30, masculine and discreet. This is on the DL . . . Have a girlfriend . . . but new to town.

Black gay writer and activist Keith Boykin has argued that there is a racist stigma and double standard associated with the 'down low.' Referring to the white characters in the hit film *Brokeback Mountain*, Boykin contends,

> the reason why we don't say they're on the down low is simple—they're white. When white men engage in this behavior, we just call it what it is and move on. But when black men do it, then we have to pathologize it into something evil called the 'down low'. (Boykin, blog on keithboykin.com, May, 2006)

Indeed, the stereotypical image of the DL is that of partnered, heterosexual, masculine Black men having quick and deceitful sexual relations unconnected to mainstream gay culture. As such, the DL is a useful shorthand available to white str8 dudes wishing to affirm their own heterosexuality, as well as to invoke the perhaps fetishized imagery of deceitful, immoral, or 'evil' sex (to use Boykin's term).

Surfers, Skaters, and Frat Guys: Archetypes of White Heterosexual Masculinity

Archetypes of youthful, white, heterosexual masculinity are also popular among str8 dudes on Craigslist, who commonly include a list of desired 'male types' in their ads. Many str8 dudes express an explicit preference for other white dudes, and this preference is strengthened by naming specific forms of hegemonic masculinity, such as jocks, skaters, surfers, and frat dudes (Connell, 2005):

Any HOT White jocks lookin to get sucked off??? – 23. Hey guys, I'm just a chill good looking dude

> heading down to the area for a BBQ and I'm looking for any other HOT Str8 or bi white dudes looking to get sucked off. Just sit back and relax and get drained. I'm especially into sucking off hot jocks, skaters, surfers, and frat dudes. If you're hot and if you're into a hot no strings blow job, then hit me up.
>
> *Seeking a MASCULINE JACK OFF BUD to STR8 PORN – 29.* Hot masculine white dude here . . . looking for another hot white dude to come by my place, and work out a hot load side by side. Straight Porn only. Prefer str8, surfer, etc. Not usually into gay dudes.

In such ads, the heterosexual culture of dude-sex is established by drawing upon available typologies of white heterosexual masculinity. Others make reference to specific white ethnicities, such as one ad seeking 'blondes, Italian(s), Jewish types, fat dick heads, hairy, white and/or Latin dudes . . . suit and tie types.'[7] Just as the appropriation of Black and white working-class masculinities helps construct an authentic 'heteroerotic' culture, so too does the image of a normative middle-class or professional whiteness (i.e. dudes who go to college, participate in sports, wear suit and ties, and so on). In both cases, race and socioeconomic class play a central role in making heterosexuality legible in the context of men's sexual seduction of other men.

In addition to naming racialized archetypes, some ads include long and detailed accounts of the exact clothing, dialogue, sex acts, and erotic mood required to maintain the heteroeroticism of dude-sex. For instance, the following ad was placed by a 'str8 guy' who 'lives a very str8 life' seeking someone to enact a 'role play' in exchange for $400. The ad included a much longer script from which I have excerpted only a small segment:

> . . . You come to the hotel in loose shorts with no underwear on, a tank top and flip flops, and when you get there we just kick back and maybe have a few beers and shoot the shit to get to know each other a little bit and feel more comfortable, then we start talking about our girlfriends and girls that we have fucked before or the best blow jobs we have had, etc., the whole time acting like we are just good friends that are horny. I am kind of dumb and don't have a lot of experience with chicks and you want to teach me and help me learn more. You then tell me that you are getting really horny thinking about all the hot sex you have had and ask me if I have any porn we can watch. I put one on and as we watch the porn, you are constantly grabbing your dick and playing with it as it gets harder and harder . . . Then you sit down right next to me and you say, 'dude, you gotta hear this story about this one chick that I made suck my dick until I blew my load in her,' then you tell me the story about it. While you are telling me the story you act it out with me . . .

While whiteness is not explicitly named in the role-play, the script mirrors the white surfer/frat dude fetishism common in the 'Casual Encounters' section of Craigslist-Los Angeles. As stated in a web article on 'frat fashion' (published by the New York hipster website blacktable.com in 2005): 'From out of the shower or off the lacrosse field and right into happy hour, flip-flops take [frat guys] every place they want to go. Flip-flops suggest sand and SoCal-cool [southern-California-cool] . . . !' Thus, some of the ad's references—such as the 'costume' of flip flops, shorts and a tank top—possibly hint at white surfer/frat masculinity, exemplifying the ways in which erotic fantasies may be implicitly or unintentionally racialized. Yet the glorification of surfers and frat dudes also illustrates the way in which the racialized construction of heterosexual and homosexual cultures are locally or regionally specific. Many of the references to white masculinity on Craigslist-Los Angeles—surfers, bros, dudes—appear to be rooted in southern California lifestyles, or at least the imagination of them.

Less Str8, More DL: Desiring Black Men?

In addition to self-identifying with the DL, a small number of white str8 dudes expressed desire for 'no strings' sex with 'hung' Black men on the DL. These ads, in contrast with the ads in which white dudes used Black slang and style to seduce one another, produced a distinct cultural effect. While many 'white on white' ads implied sameness, reciprocity or egalitarianism (let's stroke together, watch porn together, 'work out a hot load side by side' and so on), 'white seeking Black' ads typically emphasized difference, hierarchy, and service. The majority of such ads were placed by white men looking to perform 'blow jobs' for big, muscular Black men. Many of the ads in 'Casual Encounters' mention the importance of being 'hung,' but ads seeking Black men placed particular emphasis on the relationship between race and body size (e.g., 'big BLACK cock,' 'nice big meaty Black guys'):

> *Discreet White Deep Throat 4 DL Black – Size Matters – 44.* Discreet 44 yr old white guy lookin' to service hot Black guys on the DL. I'm hairy, good shape. I'm lookin' for very hung Black guys who love to kick back, watch porn and get their cocks serviced. I really like to deep throat big BLACK cock. If you are interested, hit me back with your stats and a pic if you have one . . . I really love very tall skinny men, hung huge.
>
> *Looking to suck off big black men, on the DL* – White guy here looking to suck off big muscular black guys. I like them big, over 250lbs and muscular. No strings attached. Hoping to meet some men on the DL. Got my own place, it's private and discreet, no strings, no hassles, etc. Just want to suck off some nice big meaty black guys.

Ads placed by white guys seeking Black men on the DL were less likely to focus on authenticating heterosexuality through reference to women, straight porn, and friendship (male bonding, 'being buddies') and more likely to focus on 'the DL' as preformulated code for impersonal sex across racial difference.

White submission and Black dominance was also a central theme in these ads. In the following ad, an image is included that reverses the master/slave relationship (a dominant Black male, and a shackled white male) and has likely been taken from BDSM-themed gay porn:

> *Muscled Guy Looking for Str8 or Bi to Service on the Down Low* – Meet me at the construction site. I will be there waiting for you [in the?] dark, service you and leave anonymous . . . Send pic must be hot like me.

While race is not mentioned in the text of this ad, the figure of the dominant Black male (and the submissive white male body) is used to represent

Source: Craigslist

the queerer—or less normal and natural—white fantasy of the down low. This and similar ads suggest that in the Black–white encounter, Black men are always dominant; they receive sexual service, but they don't provide it. Friendship, equity, and 'normal and natural male bonding' are represented as either undesirable or impossible across racial lines. In some ads, class differences also pervade the encounter. In the foregoing ad, the 'construction site'—in contrast to the reference to white 'suit and tie types'—invokes manual labor and the type of job more likely to be held by men of color. The DL requires anonymity, discretion, and meeting in 'dark' places like the construction site. In the Craigslist representation of the Black–white encounter, cross-racial sex is not an organic expression of 'male bonding' or 'just being men.' Instead, the presence of (or desire for) race and class difference produces a darker, less natural and less straight encounter.

Because of its association with men of color and the closet (or hidden homosexuality), the term 'DL' was less likely to be associated with authentic white heterosexuality in 'Casual Encounters' ('str8' was preferred by white dudes) and was more likely to be used by men of color in the 'Men Seeking Men' section of Craigslist. In fact, though beyond the scope of this study (which focuses on white men), I noticed during data collection that ads placed by men of color appeared more frequently in the 'Men Seeking Men' section than in the 'Casual Encounters' section. I can only speculate about why men of color would not have chosen to post ads in 'Casual Encounters,' but it seems likely that they were deterred by the predominance of white dudes seeking other white dudes. Conversely, it makes sense that white dudes uninterested in gay identification would be drawn to 'Casual Encounters,' given that its moniker makes no reference to gender identity (or identity at all), while 'Men Seeking Men' makes gender identity primary.

While reference to the symbols of Black masculinity and style helped in the production of authentic heterosexuality, reference to actual sexual contact with Black men generally did not. Instead, cross-racial sex was permeated with difference and inequality, becoming itself somewhat queer. This finding mirrors the findings of the study more broadly—for straight-identified white men seeking men, maintaining a heteroerotic culture was largely reliant upon specifically white forms of heterosexual masculinity (including those that appropriate some elements of Black culture).

Discussion: Disavowing Str8 Dudes

Str8 dudes who seek sex with men draw upon a wide variety of conceptual resources to assert a heterosexual male identity, including the use of racialized archetypes and images intended to signify authentic heterosexuality. While other research has highlighted the ways in which racial binaries were used to construct the heterosexual/homosexual binary in the late 19th century (Somerville, 2000), the ads placed on 'Casual Encounters' suggest that race continues to play a central role in the daily accomplishment of heterosexual 'realness,' particularly when authenticity is likely to be called into question. This deployment of race to signify heterosexuality included both cross-racial identifications and the preservation of white racial boundaries. In some cases, white str8 dudes appropriated the symbols/language of Black heterosexual masculinity to construct a culture of male bonding that is arguably recognizable as the antithesis of gay male culture. In other cases, white str8 dudes invoked the 'DL' as a means of eroticizing deceitful and 'evil' sex or expressing desire for closeted Black men looking to be 'serviced.'

However, most commonly, white str8 dudes drew on archetypes of white heterosexual masculinity to provide evidence of being an average, normal dude. The majority of white str8 men who posted in 'Casual Encounters' expressed a preference for men like themselves, or men who fit the paradigmatic image of the straight middle-class white male (i.e. frat dudes, suit and tie types, surfers, skaters, and so on). While being gay has often been stereotyped as a 'white thing' (Muñoz, 1999), the figure of the '*straight* white man' symbolizes both financial and cultural power as well as the average man, the 'everyman,' the 'regular dude.' Given the ways in which systems of white racial dominance construct whiteness as natural, invisible, and non-racialized (Frankenberg, 2001; Lipsitz, 1998), sex between white men is likely to be experienced as deracialized and 'natural,' possessing none of the 'difference' or racial fetishism expressed in cross-racial sexual encounters. Thus, for white str8 dudes, whiteness played a key role in producing evidence of normal/average male heterosexuality. This may be because desire for the ostensibly deracialized (but white) 'everyman' is less threatening than the desire for men of color, who are coded as both hypermasculine and hypersexual within US popular culture (Hill Collins, 2004).

However, despite the ways in which the emphasis on whiteness may be experienced as the absence of racial fetish, the erotic culture of 'Casual Encounters' was rife with white fetishism. In addition to simply declaring oneself a white str8 dude, detailed descriptions of white male bodies, white male lifestyles ('looking for surfers, [and other] LA-types'), and white male bonding helped to create and maintain the heteroerotic culture of dude-sex. Surfers, for example, were a particularly desired type, not because of the importance of surfing skills or the desire to actually surf together, but more likely because of the white, hetero-masculine script associated with southern California surf lifestyle—flip flops, chillin', just being bros and talking about chicks. In sum, racial markers are not used only to identify one's physical 'type,' they also provide an entire cultural universe from which to draw heterosexual costumes, scripts, and countless other codes for heterosexual masculinity.

At a broader level, this and other studies indicate that racial categories are always already sexualized and that sexuality categories are always already raced (González, 2007; Muñoz-Laboy, 2004; Somerville, 2000). Though I have focused on the intersections of whiteness and heterosexuality, my aim is not to position whiteness simply as one of several possible and equivalent examples of the racialization of heterosexuality. Instead, the ads on Craigslist suggest that in a culture constituted by both a racial and sexual binary (white/other and heterosexual/other), whiteness and heterosexually become 'natural' bedfellows. Both whiteness and heterosexuality simultaneously signify the 'really, really normal, nothing out of the ordinary' subject. For the str8 dudes on Craigslist, it appears that the most average and normal of male heterosexualities is white heterosexuality, even when it engages in same-sex practices and appropriates Black culture. In the context of white male bonding, Black bodies disrupt the staging of normalcy and occupy a distinctly queerer space 'down low.'[8] Building on sociological analyses of hegemonic and marginalized masculinities (Connell, 2005), future research might also reveal the range and hierarchy of heterosexualities by conceptualizing white heterosexuality as 'hegemonic' and heterosexualities of color as 'marginalized.'

In addition to highlighting the racialization of heterosexuality and heteroerotic culture, the ads placed by str8 dudes also confirm the importance of giving as much consideration to sexual *culture* as has been given to sexual practice. When queer feminist colleagues and I first read an ad placed by a str8 dude in 'Casual Encounters'—'nothing gay here at all, just two guys, watching hot porn, stroking until the point of no return'—we marveled at the suggestion that the ad was anything but gay. Later, I marveled that my colleagues and I had been so invested in owning (as queer) a cultural space that is so decidedly intent on identifying with heterosexuality. In Casual Encounters, sex practices are not useful guides for delineating the boundaries of queer and non-queer, or establishing political alliances with queer stakeholders. While the white str8 dudes who post ads in Casual Encounters express their desire for sex with other men, their desire takes form within the context of heterosexual identification and heterosexual erotic culture (in other words, the use of heterosexual pornography, the disavowal of gay culture, misogynistic discussions of women and their bodies, insistence on 'normal' heterosexual male bonding as the organizing principle of the sexual encounter).

To de-queer the sex described on Craigslist is to give up the epistemological pleasure of self-righteous knowing, owning, outing and naming. In the face of homophobia and heterosexism, honing one's 'gaydar' and revealing that '*we are everywhere*' have been among few queer luxuries. Yet as others have argued (Halberstam, 2005;

Duggan, 2003), political solidarity built primarily around sex acts misrecognizes what is most threatening, and subversive, about queerness. Queer *culture*—including a collective rejection of the rules associated with normal, adult, reproductive sexuality and (nonconsensual) heterosexual power relations—may better help scholars and activists determine the meaning of queer. On the one hand, str8 dudes exemplify sexual rule-breaking and the defiance of respectable sex behavior. On the other hand, their reliance on misogyny and homophobia to interpret and organize their sexual practices suggests a greater degree of cultural alignment with heterosexual traditions of same-sex sexuality, in which male sexual bonding is interconnected with violence against women and gay men. This complexity reveals the permeability of the categories 'straight' and 'queer,' which signify not only the divide between normal and abnormal sexual practices but also the divide between normal and abnormal interpretive frames for understanding these practices. Str8 dudes have abnormal sex, but they invest in ideologies of racial and sexual normalcy. Thus, str8 dudes' 'erotic culture of normalcy' also suggests the need to rethink the ways in which repression and 'internalized homophobia' are mapped onto all straight-identified same-sex behaviors. Rather than a symptom of repression, passivity, or lack of self-awareness, str8 dudes' rejection of queerness may be more accurately understood as agentic acts of identification with heterosexual culture.

This article has pointed to the value of viewing queer and straight as cultural spheres that people choose to inhabit in large part because they experience a cultural and political fit. Such an approach highlights the *intersections* of queer and straight cultures, identities, and practices, and suggests that some intersections may be formed by queer sexual practices and straight cultural and political investments. Redefining queer and non-queer as cultural affiliations also implies that queer 'rights' serve to protect not everyone who engages in same-sex sexuality, but all those who cannot or will not invest in hegemonic str8 culture—gender freaks, kids in gay–straight alliances, and all people who are or are willing to be part of this thing we call 'queer.'

Acknowledgements

This research was supported in part by a Wayne F. Placek Investigator Development Award from the American Psychological Foundation. The author wishes to thank the special issue editors, Salvador Vidal-Ortiz and Karl Bryant, for their thoughtful guidance and feedback on several drafts of this work. Thanks also to Rachel Luft, Kat Ross, and the *Sexualities* reviewers for their helpful comments.

Notes

1. MSM is a term first adopted by epidemiologists to classify men who have sex with men, regardless of whether they identify as gay, bisexual, or heterosexual.
2. 'Dude' is a vernacular term used by young white men in the USA to refer to one another. It was originally popularized by young, primarily white, surfers and skaters (or skateboarders) in California, but has since achieved popularity throughout the USA. 'Jock' is a slang term used to refer to young male athletes, and 'frat' is an abbreviation for a college fraternity.
3. There is disagreement on the web regarding the meaning of the term 'str8.' In some online communities, 'str8' functions simply as internet slang for 'straight,' and it has also been used as an abbreviation for 'straight' in rap lyrics. However, others, such as contributors to 'urbandictionary.com,' argue that 'str8' is used almost exclusively by gay and bisexual men 'in the closet.'
4. See González (2007) for a discussion of the distinction between 'cyberdata' and real time observations in 'cyberethnography.'
5. This study received approval from the University of California Internal Review Board for the use of human subjects. Though Craigslist is a public site, I have made every effort to protect the anonymity of the men whose personal ads I have used. Any specific identifying information (e.g. name of a small and specific neighborhood, physical descriptions, contact information) has been removed from the ads.
6. I note here that the association between light skin and whiteness is not specific to the research context, but is an aspect of racial hegemony that arguably exists independent of data selection methods and over-determines the analysis of visual images.

7. Some white dudes on Craigslist named 'Latin' men as a desired type. It is unclear whether these ads positioned 'Latin'—like Jewish and Italian—as a form of white ethnicity or a category of racial otherness. I note that within the racial discourses of the state, such as in the US census, Latinos are conceptualized as racially white. Reflecting broader racial politics, it is possible that including Latinos in the category of 'white dudes' on Craigslist is a racial strategy used by whites to expand and solidify the category of whiteness.
8. Thank you to Rachel Luft for clarifying this point.

References

Bettie, Julie (2002) *Women Without Class: Girls, Race, and Identity*. Berkeley: University of California Press.

Blacktable.com (2005) 'That Was Then, This is Now: Frat Fashions, They Are a Changin', *Black Table* 28 July, URL (accessed 5 May 2008): http://blacktable.com/fratguys050728.htm

Boykin, Keith (2005) *Beyond the Down Low: Sex, Lies, and Denial in Black America*. New York: Carroll & Graf.

Boykin, Keith (2006) 'The White Down Low', 23 May, URL (accessed 5 May 2008): http://www.keithboykin.com/arch/2006/05/23/the_white down

Butler, Judith (1990) *Gender Trouble: Feminism and the Subversion of Identity*. New York: Routledge.

Connell, R. W. (2005) *Masculinities* (2nd edition). Berkeley: University of California Press.

Craigslist.org (2006) 'Casual Encounters', ads posted by 'str8' self-identified men, May through July 2006 (particular ads no longer available). Home page URL (accessed April 2008): www.craigslist.org

Denizet-Lewis, Benoit (2003) 'Double Lives on the Down Low', *The New York Times Sunday Magazine* 3 August, URL (accessed May 2008): http://query.nytimes.com/gst/fullpage.html?res=9F0CE0D61E3FF930A3575BC0A9659C8B63.

Diaz, Rafael (1997) *Latino Gay Men and HIV: Culture, Sexuality, and Risk Behavior*. New York: Routledge.

Duggan, Lisa (2003) *The Twilight of Equality? Neoliberalism, Cultural Politics, and the Attack on Democracy*. New York: Beacon Press.

Ferguson, Roderick (2004) *Aberrations in Black: Toward a Queer of Color Critique*. Minneapolis: University of Minnesota Press.

Foucault, Michel (1978) *The History of Sexuality: An Introduction*. New York: Vintage Books.

Frankenberg, Ruth (2001) 'The Mirage of Unmarked Whiteness', in B. B. Rasmussen, E. Klinenberg, I. J. Nexica and M. Wray (eds) *The Making and Unmaking of Whiteness*, pp. 72–96. Durham, NC: Duke University Press.

Frye, Marilyn (1983) 'Lesbian Feminism and the Gay Rights Movement: Another View of Male Supremacy, Another Separatism', in Marilyn Frye *The Politics of Reality: Essays in Feminist Theory*, pp. 128–51. New York: Crossing Press.

González, M. Alfredo (2007) 'Latinos on Da Down Low: The Limitations of Sexual Identity in Public Health', *Latino Studies*. 5(1): 25–52.

Halberstam, Judith (2005) *In a Queer Time and Place: Transgender Bodies, Subcultural Lives*. New York: New York University Press.

Hill Collins, Patricia (2004) *Black Sexual Politics: African Americans, Gender, and the New Racism*. New York: Routledge.

Hull, Gloria, Bell Scott, Patricia and Smith, Barbara (eds) (1982) *All the Women Are White, All the Blacks Are Men, But Some of Us Are Brave: Black Women's Studies*. New York: Feminist Press.

Humphreys, Laud (1978) *Tearoom Trade: Impersonal Sex in Public Places* (2nd edition). Chicago, IL: Aldine Transaction.

Kaplan, Danny (2003) *Brothers and Others in Arms: The Making of Love and War in Israeli Combat Units*. New York: Harrington Park Press.

Katz, Jonathan (1996) *The Invention of Heterosexuality*. New York: Plume.

King, J. K. (2004) *On the Down Low: A Journey Into the Lives of 'Straight' Black Men Who Sleep With Men*. New York: Broadway.

Kitwana, Bakari (2005) *Why White Kids Love Hip Hop: Wangstas, Wiggers, Wannabes, and the New Reality of Race in America*. New York: Basic Civitas Books.

Lipsitz, George (1998) *The Possessive Investment in Whiteness: How White People Profit from Identity Politics*. Philadelphia, PA: Temple University Press.

Mukherjea, Ananya and Vidal-Ortiz, Salvador (2006) 'Studying HIV Risk in Vulnerable Communities: Methodological and Reporting Shortcomings in the Young Men's Study in New York City', *The Qualitative Report* 11(2): 393–416, URL (accessed 5 May 2008): http://www.nova.edu/ssss/QR/QR11-2/mukherjea.pdf

Muñoz, Jose (1999) *Disidentifications: Queers of Color and the Performance of Politics*. Minneapolis: University of Minnesota Press.

Muñoz-Laboy, Miguel (2004) 'Beyond "MSM": Sexual Desire among Bisexually-Active Latino Men in New York City'. *Sexualities* 7(1): 55–80.

Rodriguez, Juana Maria (2003) *Queer Latinidad: Identity Practices, Discursive Spaces*. New York: New York University Press.

Schifter, Jacobo (1999) *Macho Love: Sex Behind Bars in Central America*. New York: Harrington Park Press.

Sedgwick, Eve Kosofsky (1992) *Epistemology of the Closet*. Berkeley: University of California Press.

Smitherman, Geneva (2000) *Black Talk: Words and Phrases from the Hood to the Amen Corner*. New York: Mariner Books.

Somerville, Siobhan (2000) *Queering the Color Line: Race and the Invention of Homosexuality in American Culture*. Durham, NC: Duke University Press.

Urbandictionary.com (1999–2008) Slang dictionary, URL (accessed April 2008): http://www.urbandictionary.com

Ward, Jane (2000) 'Queer Sexism: Rethinking Gay Men and Masculinity', in Peter Nardi (ed.) *Gay Masculinities*, pp. 152–75. Thousand Oaks: SAGE Publications.

Ward, Jane (2007) 'Straight Dude Seeks Same: Mapping the Relationship Between Sexual Identities, Practices, and Cultures', in Mindy Stombler, Dawn M. Baunauch, Elisabeth O. Burgess and Denise Donnelly (eds) *Sex Matters: The Sexuality and Society Reader* (second edition), pp. 31–7. New York: Allyn & Bacon.

West, Candace and Zimmerman, Don (1987) 'Doing Gender', *Gender & Society* 1(2): 125–51.

Social Identities as Predictors of Women's Sexual Satisfaction and Sexual Activity

BREANNE FAHS AND ERIC SWANK

Introduction

While much research has examined sexual problems and dysfunction, far less research has examined sexual satisfaction, particularly as it relates to social identities. This study addressed two understudied areas of sexuality research. First, research on sexual satisfaction and sexual activity has typically argued that high sexual satisfaction explicitly correlates with high sexual activity (Blumstein & Schwartz, 1983; Peplau, Fingerhut, & Beals, 2004; Waite & Joyner, 2001) or that high sexual satisfaction is thought to itself *imply* high sexual activity (Haavio-Mannila & Kontula, 1997; Mansfield, Koch, & Voda, 2000; Young, Denny, Luquis, & Young, 1998). Little research has examined differences between women with regard to sexual satisfaction and sexual activity as two distinct, possibly misaligned, dimensions of sexuality. Instead, existing research has often either conflated sexual activity and sexual motivation (Hiller, 2005), thereby reductively assuming that sexual activity is universally pleasurable and rewarding, or it has combined satisfaction and activity as definitive markers of healthy sexual functioning.

Second, there are running debates about what predicts women's sexual satisfaction (Henderson, Lehavot, & Simoni, 2009; Schwartz & Young, 2009). While several studies have explored the role of psychological factors that promote sexual satisfaction (Haavio-Mannila & Kontula, 1997; Strelan, Mehaffey, & Tiggemann, 2003), we focused on how sexual satisfaction relates to social hierarchies like race, class, education, and other gendered systems. Accordingly, this study examined whether membership in privileged or stigmatized social statuses enhanced or inhibited women's sexual satisfaction.

The purpose of this study was twofold: first, we questioned whether sexual satisfaction and sexual activity were part of the same phenomenon among women; second, we examined the ways that social identity variables like race, class, gender, level of education, age, and sexual identity predicted women's reported levels of sexual satisfaction and sexual activity.[1] In particular, this study examined the social statuses of U.S. women who were most likely to report a divergence or mismatch between sexual satisfaction and sexual activity in order to illuminate the role of social status in predicting these aspects of women's sexual lives.[2]

Sexual Satisfaction

The question of how to measure sexual satisfaction has long befuddled sex researchers, as much debate exists whether orgasm or the more abstract self-reported satisfaction measures more accurately represent satisfaction. Discussions of wanting, pleasure, and bodily satisfaction permeate the recent sex literatures (Crawford, Diener, Wirtz, Lucas, & Oishi, 2002; Fine & McClelland, 2006). Further, debates about what constitutes sexual function and dysfunction, and how researchers define sexual satisfaction, reveal how gender norms are integral to understanding sexual satisfaction (Bridges & Horne, 2007; McClelland, 2010; Tiefer, 2004).

Breanne Fahs and Eric Swank, "Social Identities as Predictors of Women's Sexual Satisfaction and Sexual Activity." *Archives of Sexual Behavior* 40 (October 2011): 903–14.

Given this methodological complexity, it is not surprising that research on women's sexual satisfaction has yielded mixed results both about what constitutes satisfaction and what predicts satisfaction. Still, one consistent finding is that gender matters: women are less sexually satisfied than men (Haavio-Mannila & Kontula, 1997), and women also think about sex less, masturbate less, have fewer orgasms with partners, and fantasize less when compared with men (Baumeister & Tice, 1998; Laumann, Gagnon, Michael, & Michaels, 1994; Oliver & Hyde, 1993; Petersen & Hyde, 2010; Sprecher & Regan, 1996). These gender discrepancies may stem from women's learned tendencies toward self-objectification, that is, conceptualizing their worth according to externally-perceivable traits and socially approved definitions of beautiful bodies. Self-objectification behaviors have been linked with eating disorders, depression, body shame, sexual dissatisfaction, and difficulty initiating sex (Frederickson & Roberts, 1997; Strelan et al., 2003). Women with poor body image reported more self-consciousness and rated the importance of physical attractiveness much higher (Ackard, Kearney-Cooke, & Peterson, 2000; Weaver, 2006). Those with positive body image were less likely to internalize media images, were less depressed, and were more likely to have positive views of sexuality (Walker-Hill, 2000). These factors are a likely culprit in women's decreased satisfaction and activity compared to men.

When examining differences between women, satisfied women reported more sexual assertiveness, earlier first sexual intercourse, and had nonreligious childhoods (Haavio-Mannila & Kontula, 1997). They also reported less anxiety about the meaning of sex along with fewer intrusive thoughts (Purdon & Holdaway, 2006). Also, satisfied women had more satisfying romantic relationships, felt more intimacy with partners (Birnbaum, 2007; Pinney, Gerrard, & Denney, 1987; Smith, 2007; Sprecher, Barbee, & Schwartz, 1995), and reported more reciprocal feelings of love and more intense orgasms with partners (González, Viáfara, Caba, Molina, & Ortiz, 2006; Sprecher, 2002). Satisfied women also reported more self-disclosure to their partners about what brings them pleasure (MacNeil & Byers, 2005), embraced more non-traditional gender roles (Pedersen & Blekesaune, 2003), and started out their relationships with more satisfaction (McNulty & Fisher, 2008).

Most research links women's satisfaction to frequency of orgasm during partnered sexual activity. Some studies suggest that half of women orgasm frequently or always (Hunt, 1974; Raboch & Raboch, 1992), yet in studies highlighting social identities, these numbers diverge depending on women's social locations. For example, Janus and Janus (1993) found that 56% of women ages 18–26, 67% of age 27–38, 66% of age 39–50, and 50% of age 65 or over reported frequent orgasm during sex. Other studies reported the percentage of women who frequently experience orgasm ranges from around 25–60% depending on age, race, and class backgrounds (Haavio-Mannila & Kontula, 1997; Hurlbert, Apt, & Rabehl, 1993; Schwartz & Young, 2009). Several recent studies found that older women reported much lower frequencies of orgasm compared to younger women (Lutfey, Link, Rosen, Wiegel, & McKinlay, 2009; Wilkins & Warnock, 2009), revealing the importance of examining social identities as predictors of satisfaction and activity.

Social Identities and Sexuality

People's locations in the social order typically convey a litany of privileges, opportunities, obligations, and restrictions about their social roles. Although the social science literature has established that disadvantaged identities—women, people of color, sexual minorities, lower socioeconomic status groups, and so on—regularly face institutionalized discrimination in most familial, work, judicial, educational, and housing situations (Acker, 2006; Jackman, 1994; McCall, 2001; Pyke, 1996), questions remain about how issues of sexual satisfaction relate to race, class, education, and other social identity differences.

While all women do not report equal levels of satisfaction, researchers disagree about which social identities support or inhibit greater sexual satisfaction. Women in lower social status groups reported less sexual satisfaction than higher status women

(Martin & Purkiss, 2001), particularly with regard to race, socioeconomic status, education, sexual identity, marital status, and age. Studies have linked working-class backgrounds to less interest in marital sex (Rubin, 1994), more restrictive views of sexuality (Gordon, Schroeder, & Abrams, 1990), and greater premarital sexual experience compared to middle-class women (Janus & Janus, 1993). Upper-income women reported the most premarital sexual experience compared to both working-class and middle-class women (Janus & Janus, 1993). Though studies of work status do not directly correlate with socioeconomic status, research has shown that fatigue from long work hours, work-related stress, or dissatisfaction with work strongly predicted less satisfaction and less sexual frequency for both employed women and stay-at-home women (Call, Sprecher, & Schwartz, 1995). One study, however, found that socioeconomic class did not predict differences in women's sexual behavior or attitudes (Weinberg, Lottes, & Gordon, 1997).

Correlations between race and sexuality also point to some interesting, and conflicting, results. Most studies have found strong similarities between black women and white women (Chadiha, Veroff, & Leber, 1998; Henderson-King & Veroff, 1994; Kalof & Wade, 1995; Oggins, Veroff, & Leber, 1993), except that black women more often endorsed nontraditional relationships (Kalof & Wade, 1995) and engaged more often in premarital sex (at all socioeconomic levels) (Fisher, 1980). Along racial lines, black and white women had more permissive sexual attitudes than Latina and Asian-American women (Fugère, Escoto, Cousins, Riggs, & Haerich, 2008) and Latina women faked orgasm less often than white women (Bryan, 2002). Compared to white women, black women also reported more desire but less sexual activity than white women (Huang et al., 2009). Henderson-King and Veroff (1994) found that, for black women, income was negatively correlated with sexual satisfaction, indicating that more financial resources strained their satisfaction.

Marital status and presence of children also influence sexual satisfaction, as married or cohabitating participants reported significantly more sexual and emotional satisfaction, and higher levels of physical satisfaction, than did single participants (Waite & Joyner, 2001), though married couples had sex less often than cohabiters (Call et al., 1995). Similarly, women with children reported less spontaneous sexual encounters and less sexual frequency (DeJudicibus & McCabe, 2002; Hyde, DeLamater, Plant, & Byrd, 1996), but largely had satisfying relationships with plenty of affection and warmth (Ahlborg, Dahlof, & Hallberg, 2005). Women with children also prioritized emotional intimacy and commitment over physical arousal and excitement when compared to women without children (Means, 2001).

Age and life stage seem to also influence sexual satisfaction and orgasm experiences. While teenage sexuality has been shown to predict later sexual dissatisfaction (Seldin, Friedman, & Marin, 2002), other studies found that early sexual experience predicted sexual satisfaction and more frequent orgasm as adults (Haavio-Mannila & Kontula, 1997). Studies of midlife sexuality have consistently connected older age with decreased sexual response, particularly for desire, arousal, enjoyment, frequency of sex, and orgasm (Call et al., 1995; Lutfey et al., 2009; Mansfield et al., 2000; Tomic et al., 2006). However, for coupled heterosexuals, better marital adjustment buffered the increase in sexual dysfunction that typically came with age (Hawton, Gath, & Day, 1994).

Level of educational attainment might also influence satisfaction and activity. Women with the highest education had the most sexual partners (twice as many as other groups) and the most sexual experience (including oral sex and masturbation) before marriage (Janus & Janus, 1993). In addition, Haavio-Mannila and Kontula (1997) found that sexual satisfaction correlated positively with level of education. Krull (1994) associated more education with more liberal views, more sexual promiscuity, and positive attitudes toward sexuality, though a recent study correlated higher education with "lower passion" for a partner (Tomic et al., 2006).

Hypotheses and Research Questions

As shown in the literature, women's sexual satisfaction, activity, desire, and motivation may change in response to cultural expectations, gendered belief systems, partnered relationships, and internalized ideas about normative sexuality. Social identities like race, class, gender, age, education, and sexual identity probably alter women's relationship to their sexuality, though the literature yields highly inconsistent findings about how social identities correlate with sexual satisfaction and sexual activity. Though most sex research assumes that high sexual satisfaction correlates with high sexual activity, and that women are motivated primarily by the pursuit of pleasure, this research tests these premises by interrogating sexual satisfaction and sexual activity as separate, but related, factors in women's lives.

This study also examined how women's social identities might predict a match or mismatch with regard to sexual satisfaction and sexual activity. In other words, which of women's social identities predict *both* satisfaction *and* more frequent sex? Which social statuses predict women being *not* satisfied *and* having more frequent sex? Or, which women are satisfied but *not* having sex very often? And finally, which social groupings of women report little satisfaction *and* little sexual activity?

Specifically, we hypothesized that sexual satisfaction and sexual activity would not always be aligned, and that many women would report misalignment on these dimensions (e.g., high sexual satisfaction and low sexual activity or low sexual satisfaction and high sexual activity). In particular, because conformity to a partner's expectations for frequent sexual activity could be itself motivating yet not particularly pleasurable, we hypothesized that some women would report feeling unsatisfied despite frequent sexual activity. Conversely, because periods of less sexual activity are normative in sexual relationships, we also hypothesized that some women would report feeling satisfied with infrequent sexual activity. Because social identities clearly influence women's sexuality, we hypothesized that social identities would directly affect women's sexual satisfaction and sexual activity.

More specifically, though the literature suggested conflicting results about the relationship between social identities and sexual satisfaction/frequency, we predicted that lower status women would report lower sexual satisfaction compared to higher status women. Because high status is typically correlated with greater resources and more social validation, high status groups were hypothesized to report more satisfaction overall.

Method

Participants

This study analyzed data from the National Health and Social Life Survey (NHSLS), a representative, national probability sample of approximately 3,432 U.S. adults. This survey had a 78.6% response rate, and was conducted as a face-to-face survey with an additional shorter pencil and paper instrument for items that could be considered shameful or embarrassing for some people. These data were collected in 1992 with the explicit goal "to undertake a broad investigation of sexual conduct in the age of AIDS . . . and to represent as much of the U.S. adult population as possible" (Laumann et al., 1994, p. 53). The NHSLS is the only national probability sample to date that addresses in detail the issues of sexual desire, sexual dysfunction, fantasy, and a diverse group of non-procreative sexual behaviors. The richness of the survey, and the sensitivity with which these kinds of questions were asked, made it a good instrument for examining the interaction among demographics, sexual attitudes, and sexual behavior.

Because the current study focused on the sexuality of women, we used a subsample of 1,473 women from the original 3,432 participants in the NHSLS. This sample included nationally-representative populations of women, and accounted proportionally for racial diversity, differences in sexual orientation, marital status, and other important demographic features such as age and socioeconomic class.[3]

SPSS version 13 was used throughout this study. In order to maximize the study's generalizability, weights were applied for all analyses and inference tests, in order to make the analyses and computations of statistics comparable to what would be seen in the population that the sample was drawn from. Specifically, weights[4] were used to correct for any differences by Census region (Northeast,

Midwest, South, West), gender (male, female), household size (one, two, three, four, five or more), age (in four intervals: 18–24, 25–34, 35–44, 45–59), and race/ethnicity (in four categories: white, black, Hispanic, other) based on the 1990 census.

Measures

Two groupings of items ("sexual satisfaction" and "sexual activity") were used to measure different dimensions of female sexualities. The four dimensions that defined "sexual satisfaction" included: physical pleasure, emotional satisfaction, feelings and emotions about sex, and frequency of orgasm. The two dimensions that defined "sexual activity" included: frequency of sexual activity and sexual variety. The sexual satisfaction composite index had an alpha coefficient of 0.75, while the alpha coefficient for the sexual variety variables was 0.71.

We measured sexual satisfaction based on both subjective and objective criteria, attending to prominent debates within sexuality literatures about what constitutes satisfaction (McClelland, 2010). In line with previous research (Lawrance & Byers, 1995; Sprecher & Cate, 2004), we imagine satisfaction to include dimensions of positive affect about the sexual exchange, positive expectations about future sexual events, and positive bodily reactions to sex. As such, each of these dimensions is represented in our definitions of sexual satisfaction.[5]

Participants' scores were summed and standardized for both satisfaction and activity. The physical pleasure, emotional satisfaction, and feelings and emotions about sex dimensions were derived from questions about the participants' "most recent sexual partner." As a result, women who did not have *any* past sexual partners (approximately 82 women, or 5.2% of the population) were excluded. The frequency of orgasm variable asked directly about women's orgasm history in the past 12 months; 222 women (or 12.9%) were excluded from the analysis because they had no sexual partners in the past 12 months,[6] reducing our sample to 1,473 women.

For the reported physical pleasure variable, participants were asked, "How physically pleasurable did you find your relationship with your partner to be?" Participants rated their responses on a 6-point scale ranging from 0 (not at all pleasurable) to 5 (extremely pleasurable).

For the reported emotional satisfaction variable, participants were asked, "How emotionally satisfying did you find your relationship with your partner to be?" Participants rated their responses on a 6-point scale ranging from 0 (not at all satisfying) to 5 (extremely satisfying).

For the feelings and emotions about sex variable, participants were asked, "I would like to ask you how sex with your partner made you feel. Please tell me if sex with your partner made you feel: satisfied, sad, loved, anxious or worried, wanted or needed, taken care of, scared or afraid, thrilled or excited, guilty." For each of these nine items, participants answered "yes" or "no." "Yes" responses on positive items received 1 point each (e.g., "yes" on "taken care of" would be coded as a "1"). The negative items were reverse coded (e.g., "no" on "scared" would be coded as a "1"), so that participants received one total score for all positive emotions about sex. Cumulative scores ranged from 0 (all negative feelings and no positive feelings) to 9 (all positive feelings and no negative feelings).

For the frequency of orgasm variable, participants were asked, "When you and your partner had sex during the past 12 months, did you always, usually, sometimes, rarely, or never have an orgasm, that is come or come to climax?" Participants rated their responses on a 6-point scale ranging from 0 (never) to 5 (always).

For the frequency of sex component, participants were asked a single question: "About how often did you have sex during the past 12 months?" Participants rated their answers on an 8-point scale ranging from 0 (not at all) to 7 (four times or more per week).

For the sexual variety dimension, participants were asked to report whether they had *ever* engaged in nine sexual behaviors (e.g., anal sex, group sex, etc.). Participants responded "yes" or "no" to each question. These answers were then summed, and participants were placed on a 10-point scale ranging from 0 (no sexual behaviors) to 9 (all sexual behaviors).

After creating scores for sexual satisfaction and sexual activity, we first performed a principal component analysis on the six dependent measures to determine whether sexual satisfaction and sexual activity would explain a large proportion of the variation between the participants. We predicted that the four sexual satisfaction variables would be highly correlated with each other, and that the two sexual variety variables would be inversely correlated with each other. Our analysis found that sexual satisfaction and sexual activity explained 49.32% of the variation between participants on the six dependent variables. The sexual satisfaction factor explained 34.54% of variance, while the sexual variety factor explained 14.78% of the total variance.

Nine social identity variables were expected to predict different patterns of female sexual satisfaction and activity. These social identity categories included: marital status, education, socioeconomic class, age, sexual identity, racial/ethnic identity, geographical "coming of age" location, employment status, and whether participants had children.

Marital status was examined as a dichotomous variable by dividing women into two groups: Married = 1, and Single/Divorced/Widowed/Separated = 0.

When asked about level of education, participants rated their responses on a 9-point scale ranging from 0 (8th grade or less) to 8 (other advanced degree).

To determine socioeconomic class, participants were asked, "What (is/was) your usual wage rate, before taxes at this [current] job?" Total family annual income was calculated and participants were scored on a scale ranging from lowest income to highest income. Income was measured on a 9-point scale ranging from 0 ($0 per year) to 8 (over $75,000 per year).

Race was measured through a dichotomous dummy variable. Participants were divided into two groups: those who identified as "White," and, as a second group, those who identified as any other kind of racial or ethnic category, including Black, Hispanic, Asian/Pacific Islander, Alaskan Native/Native American, Biracial, or Other.

Sexual identity was coded in a binary fashion, as participants were divided into two categories, heterosexual and sexual minority, based on their answers to three questions: "Are you attracted to other women?"; "Have you ever done anything sexual with another woman?"; and "What is your sexual orientation?" Participants who answered "Yes" to either of the first two questions, and/or those who identified themselves as bisexual or homosexual were scored as "sexual minority" while those who answered "No" to both of the first questions *and* identified as heterosexual were scored as "sexual majority." Though this does not necessarily mean that all of those within the sexual minority group self-identified as homosexual or bisexual, it nonetheless reveals openness toward same-sex sexual relationships.

To assess participants' metropolitan backgrounds, they were asked about their geographical location at age 14. Responses were placed into two categories: those who lived "in a suburb near a large city" and "in a large city (over 250,000)" were deemed metropolitan, while other responses were considered non-metropolitan (e.g., "on a farm," "in a small city or town (under 50,000)," and "in a medium-sized city (50,000–250,000)."

To trace employment status, participants' work hours were divided into two groups: those who reported working full-time or part-time, and those who reported not working.

To determine whether participants were parents, participants were divided into two groups: those with children/those without children. Location of children (i.e., whether children resided in the home) was not considered.

Procedure

Using sexual satisfaction and sexual activity, we performed a hierarchical cluster analysis using Ward's method to divide participants into four clusters based on their values on the two dependent variables. To account for the appropriate weights of each individual variable within the dependent variables, factor scores (based on the regression model) were used to perform this hierarchical cluster analysis. This analysis divided participants into four clusters based on their values for sexual satisfaction and sexual activity.[7] Cluster analysis assigns each participant to a particular cluster of participants who share similar responses on the dependent variables (e.g., participant #1 would be assigned to the cluster of women with high satisfaction and low activity). This technique highlighted the social identities most common to each cluster, as it compared the qualities of women who belonged to the separate clusters. Ward's method of cluster analysis is a type of cluster analysis that is especially efficient at maximizing between-group differences by using analysis of variance (ANOVA) techniques.

For our analysis, participants' overall *z*-scores (factor scores) assigned them to a particular cluster using Ward's method. This analysis produced four distinct clusters based on the initial Ward calculations (i.e., high satisfaction/high activity; low satisfaction/high activity; high satisfaction/low activity; and low satisfaction/low activity).

After establishing the four clusters, we then compared the clusters using ANOVA, multiple pairwise comparisons, and χ^2 tests for our specified independent variables. Multivariate analysis of variance (MANOVA) was not emphasized for these analyses because MANOVA can only be used for continuous variables and therefore cannot be applied to dichotomous or categorical variables, and because MANOVA assumes a single underlying dimension in the data and therefore does not accurately reflect the complexities that can be illuminated in univariate analyses. Instead of using MANOVA on the continuous variables, we chose to conduct one-way ANOVA tests on these variables in order to more fully explore the range of results. For each ANOVA, we performed six pairwise comparisons, using the Bonferroni correction to prevent inflation of Type 1 errors.[8] As such, this analysis did not single out specific independent variables as singularly predictive of either dependent variable (satisfaction or activity). The distinctiveness of each cluster emerged from a combination of variables derived from multiple one-way ANOVAs, pairwise comparisons, and χ^2 tests.

Results

Participants in this study varied widely in terms of all major demographic categories (see Table 1 for complete description). Notably, 60.4% of participants were married, 20.9% graduated from college (5.7% had an advanced degree), 27.8% had a total household income of $50,000 or above, 91.8% identified with an organized religion (with 44.3% attending at least 2–3 times per month), 77.7% were white, 96.8% identified as heterosexual, 29.9% lived in large cities or suburbs at age 14, 63.4% reported working on a regular basis, and 72.9% had at least one child.

Four clusters from the dependent variables were generated from the cluster analysis in order to allow us to look specifically at the relationship between social identity categories and the intersections between sexual activity and sexual satisfaction. The high satisfaction/high activity cluster had 16.1% (237 participants). The low satisfaction/high activity cluster had 8.7% (128 participants). The high satisfaction/low activity cluster had 59.0% (869 participants). Finally, the low satisfaction/low

Table 1. Social Identity Variables: Estimated Means and ANOVA Results

Variable	HS-HA M (SD)	LS-HA M (SD)	HS-LA M (SD)	LS-LA M (SD)	*F*-test
Education	2.37 (1.04)^a	2.35 (1.01)^a	2.70 (1.05)^b	3.05 (.99)^c	$F(1, 12) = 76.87$***
Class	4.92 (2.14)^b	4.05 (2.36)^a	5.29 (2.10)^b	5.11 (2.36)^b	$F(3, 1238) = 11.11$***
Age	38.84 (11.16)^b	33.66 (11.75)^a	35.65 (10.03)^a	35.14 (10.16)^a	$F(3, 1468) = 8.88$***

All variables, with the exception of age, are reported on a five-point scale, with 1 representing lower scores on that variable, while 5 represents higher scores

HS-HA high satisfaction, high activity, *LS-HA* low satisfaction, high activity, *HS-LA* high satisfaction low activity, *LS-LA* low satisfaction, low activity

^{a,b,c} Superscript numbers indicate clusters that are similar in terms of the reported means. For each row, numbers with different letters were significantly different

*** $p < .001$

activity cluster had 16.2% (239 participants). This suggests that the majority of women (59.0% and 8.7%) reported a mismatch between their sexual satisfaction and their sexual activity, and that this latter group (low satisfaction/high activity) was, importantly, engaging in frequent sexual activity without satisfaction. Alternatively, these findings suggest that 32.3% of women reported a match between satisfaction and activity (16.1% and 16.2%). However, the vast majority of women (67.7%) were mismatched on dimensions of sexual satisfaction and sexual activity.

All social identity variables reached significance ($p < .001$). Table 1 shows the results of the one-way ANOVAs comparing the derived clusters in terms of means on the continuous social identity variables of interest. Differences worth noting are marked with superscript numbers to indicate which clusters were significantly different from the other clusters. For example, the education variable yielded three statistically distinct groups, with high satisfaction/high activity women and low satisfaction/high activity women representing one group (means of 2.35 and 2.50), while high satisfaction/low activity women represented a second distinct group (mean of 2.70), and low satisfaction/low activity women represented a third distinct group (mean of 3.05). This is meant to indicate not only that a significant difference exists between the clusters, but to also point out which particular clusters differ from each other. For example, in the social class variable, the distinctive group was only low satisfaction and high activity (mean of 4.05 compared to means of 5.12 and 4.92). Statistically significant differences ($p < .05$) were found for all of these variables, including education, socioeconomic class, and age. In making sense of these findings, women with low satisfaction/high activity tended to be less educated, had lower socioeconomic status, and were younger than high satisfaction/low activity women.

Table 2 shows the results of the χ^2 tests comparing the derived clusters in terms of means on the categorical social identity variables of interest. Statistically significant differences ($p < .05$) were found for many of these variables, including marital status (and specific variation within the category of "single" on the marital status variable, such as single, divorced, widowed, or separated), racial/ethnic identity, sexual identification, geographical location, and children. Statistical trends ($p < .10$) were noted for employment status. Most notably, women with low satisfaction/high activity, when compared with high satisfaction/low activity women, tended to be unmarried or divorced, more urban, and less of them worked or had children.

Table 2. Social Identity Variables: χ^2 Results

Variable	HS-HA (%)	LS-HA (%)	HS-LA (%)	LS-LA (%)	χ^2
Marital status					
Married	77.4	39.4	73.1	48.3	109.83***
Never married	13.0	35.5	16.3	30.5	119.40***
Divorced	6.1	16.3	6.6	13.9	
Widowed	2.2	1.1	1.4	1.3	
Separated	1.3	8.7	2.6	6.0	
White	69.0	60.6	82.2	84.7	50.02***
Heterosexual	100	100	99.0	84.6	144.21***
Metropolitan	29.8	28.3	26.4	37.1	25.11**
Work	57.5	62.1	64.7	69.3	7.64*
Children	83.3	69.7	78.0	62.8	34.12***

HS-HA high satisfaction, high activity, *LS-HA* low satisfaction, high activity, *HS-LA* high satisfaction low activity, *LS-LA* low satisfaction, low activity

*** $p < .001$, ** $p < .01$, * $p < .05$

Additionally, women with lower levels of satisfaction and activity included white women, women who worked full-time, and those who resided in larger metropolitan areas.

As predicted, a substantial number of women reported that sexual satisfaction and sexual activity were not aligned. Moreover, these incongruencies related closely to women's social identities. Most notably, lower status women clustered most heavily in the low satisfaction/high activity cluster, though they were also represented in the low satisfaction/low activity cluster. Higher status women clustered most heavily in the high satisfaction/low activity cluster, though they also appeared in the high satisfaction/high activity cluster. In particular, the assortment of features that predicted low satisfaction/high activity—or engaging in sex despite not enjoying it—included women who were unmarried, less educated, working-class, younger, nonwhite, unemployed, and did not have children.

Discussion

When addressing our dependent variables, the most central finding was that sexual satisfaction and sexual activity were more often not aligned, highlighting how women's social location related to sexual satisfaction and sexual activity. The finding that low status groups clustered in the low satisfaction/high activity cluster (8.2%) suggests that low social status predicts frequent, less satisfying sex rather than no sex at all. This suggests that many women may have felt pressured or coerced into sex on a regular basis despite lack of sexual desire. Perhaps this group prioritized their partners' satisfaction over their own (Nicolson & Burr, 2003). Conversely, the low satisfaction/low activity cluster (16.2%) engaged in low frequency of sex while also not feeling very satisfied. This suggests that far more women—nearly twice the amount—disengage from sex when not feeling satisfied. Also, women may choose not to couple or their partners might have lower sexual desire so they have sex less often together.

Our explanatory analysis also highlighted some other insights. When considering issues of social status as it relates to satisfaction and activity, the data worked as predicted. Low status women engaged in frequent, less satisfying sex more than high status women. Compared to the other low satisfaction cluster, which included a diverse mix of low status groups (e.g., unmarried, more likely homosexual or bisexual) and high status groups (e.g., highly educated, upper-class, mostly white, primarily urban), the low satisfaction/high activity group included the most low status groups.

When examining the reasons for this divide, several possibilities come to light. Perhaps low status women lack knowledge or education about sexuality, subscribe to more traditional gender roles, or inhibit sexual satisfaction. These results could reflect qualities about low status women's partners, particularly attitudes toward sexuality and gender, as well as sexual histories (e.g., younger men generally have less sexual experience). Also, because women typically couple with partners of the same age, social class, and racial backgrounds, possibly their partners have internalized the hyper-aggressive and domineering aspects of hegemonic masculinity (Connell, 2005; Pyke, 1996). These results may also reveal power imbalances in couples and the larger society, as women (particularly low status women) have less social power than men. As The New View group has argued (Kleinplatz, 2001; Tiefer, 2001), occupying lower social status in the public realm can blend into matters of sexual satisfaction in their personal lives (e.g., pay inequities, working long hours), as these factors can hinder the conditions that make sex enjoyable. Lower status women may lack resources to escape sexually unsatisfying relationships, particularly in terms of financial, legal, and familial constraints. Disadvantaged women may be resigned or accustomed to engaging in sexual activities they do not enjoy.

Lower status women may face structural inequalities, but they may also have a strong desire to please their (male) partners, face internal pressures to perform sexually, feel like sex is something one *should* do, do not expect to be satisfied from sex, are undereducated about how to derive sexual satisfaction from partnered sex, and feel the need to support the male partner's pleasure or sexual needs. Low satisfaction/high activity women may have sex more often with cohabitating boyfriends and one-night stands, which could potentially yield lower satisfaction scores. Other research could examine why the high satisfaction/low activity cluster tends to include high status groups. Perhaps these women do not have frequent access to a partner, are more okay with infrequent sexual encounters, or have learned how to maximize their opportunities for sex by prioritizing their satisfaction. Further, given that the most educated women reported low satisfaction and low activity more often, this could reflect time constraints, an ability of educated women (and all women with more power) to refuse unwanted sex, or lack of eroticizing educated or "successful" women compared with more traditional women.

Women in the high satisfaction/high activity cluster, relative to other clusters, had a notable assortment of features that predicted dependent relationships with a male partner[9]: married or widowed, less educated, older in age, heterosexual, did not work outside the home, and had children. Economically-speaking, these women may have less ability to assert autonomy and power in their relationships due to educational and income factors. Also, married women more often engaged in frequent sexual activity than unmarried women, as consistently available partners predicts sexual activity (though unmarried cohabiters were not distinguished in our analysis). Their older age may predict traditional views of gender, though these findings bode well for the association between age and satisfaction. That said, older cohorts of women in 1992 came of age before the second wave of feminism, so they may have lower expectations for "good lovers" compared to younger women. Frequent, satisfying sex is something expected from them in their roles as traditional wives, and they seem willing and able to fulfill these roles.

Issues of self-reporting must be considered when examining women's ideas about their sexuality. Research has shown that both men (in their perceptions of) and women (in their reported experience of) over-report frequency of female orgasm (Laumann et al., 1994). Pressure to orgasm is particularly strong in relationships characterized by traditional gender roles. Laumann et al. also noted that, though they made concerted efforts to maximize accurate self-reporting, many people over- or under-reported certain aspects of their sexuality, due to emotional factors (shame, guilt, embarrassment, pride), social factors (pressure to seem "normal," religious or familial norms, gender roles), and other factors.

Several features of these results, however, make sense when considering them at face value. For example, those who have very narrowly defined social roles (high satisfaction/high activity women) reported high satisfaction and high activity, as they can successfully fulfill these social roles. Those women who worked *and* had children—women taxed for their time and likely more exhausted—clustered most often in the high satisfaction/low activity. This does not, however, necessarily indicate dissatisfaction with their sexual relationships (Ahlborg et al., 2005). Longitudinal data would better reveal whether women change clusters over time depending on their children's age or the changing demands of their career. Logically, the majority of women (59.0%) would cluster in high satisfaction/low activity, given prominent social trends to pursue the dual roles of career and motherhood. Also, celibacy or low sexual frequency may be *positive* for women, particularly when over-taxed with other responsibilities.

Limitations and Future Directions

This study was limited by the fact that these data were collected in 1992; sexual norms may have changed significantly since then. This dataset, however, was the only nationally-representative probability sample of its kind that sufficiently addressed issues of desire, satisfaction, orgasm, and pleasure across all populations in the United States, making it generalizable to all populations of women. In addition, because this study utilized secondary data analysis, this prevented the addition of other questions about women's sexual experiences. Also, the very low number of participants who identified themselves as lesbian or bisexual (less than 2%) represented a serious limitation, as diversity in sexual identity could not be adequately addressed. These numbers may not accurately reflect women's lived experiences with same-sex eroticism, particularly as these norms evolve (e.g., high rates of women performing as bisexual at parties to feel socially normative—see Fahs, 2009). Other measurement limitations affected our findings as well, in that most satisfaction questions failed to address women's entire sexual biography throughout their lifetime. Also, our measures of activity may conflate variety and frequency even though these may represent different behaviors. Likewise, our measure of social class focused on family income, which may have disguised women's stay-at-home status or changing occupational roles. Also, a dichotomous racial identity variable does not fully explore differences and nuances between women of color in this sample (e.g., Latina, Asian-American, Native-American, African-American, biracial, etc.).

This study suggests that conceptualizing satisfaction and activity as possibly different dimensions of women's sexual experience helps better illuminate the relationship between social identity, sexual satisfaction, and sexual activity. It suggests that many women (upwards of 65%) had divergent satisfaction and activity, contrary to the portrayal of female sexuality in most sexual health and popular literatures. The specific group of women with low satisfaction and high activity provided a framework for questioning the coupling of satisfaction and activity by suggesting that low status women engage in less satisfying, frequent sex. Certain questions arise: Why do women with less social power experience less sexual satisfaction? Moreover, why would some continue to engage in frequent bouts of less satisfying sex? On the other hand, the high satisfaction/low activity finding suggests that many women feel satisfied by having infrequent sexual activity, which may call into question the common clinical constructions of more sex = more satisfaction (Tiefer, 2001).

This study might also inspire a new round of multivariate relationships, as researchers could better explore the inter-correlations among race, education, income, and marital status. Also, future research could examine how these findings translate for men. Some of the basic questions could include: Does a gender gap exist in levels of sexual satisfaction? Do men experience a similar degree of mismatch on sexual satisfaction and sexual activity? How would education correlate with sexual satisfaction for men, given different values placed upon monetary success and upward mobility for men? Would lower status men be overrepresented in the low satisfaction/high activity cluster? Given research on the value men place on sexual frequency (McNulty & Fisher, 2008), would men show similar results to women?

Future research could examine the implications of these findings for the clinical literatures and the sex therapy literatures. If infrequent sexual activity often correlates with high sexual satisfaction, this nuances the claim that over 40% of women are "sexually dysfunctional" (Shifren, Monz, Russo, Segreti, & Johannes, 2008) by suggesting that, despite low desire or other "dysfunctions," women may not be particularly bothered by those issues. Research should ask women what they want to change about their sexuality, or what would improve satisfaction; too much research focuses exclusively on frequencies of behavior instead of subjective accounts of women's sexuality.

Of central importance to sex research is the examination of the interplay among social identities, political beliefs, sexual satisfaction, sexual behavior, and sexual ideologies. How can we make sexual relationships more egalitarian, not only between genders, but also between races, classes, ages, and sexual identities? The framing of sexuality as a social justice issue needs more attention, not only within the field of sex research but also within psychological, sociological, and political science fields in general. Longitudinal research that addresses evolving and changing social norms could illuminate the ways in which social norms shift throughout time, particularly for different identity groups. Additional research on women's sexual partners and perception gaps between couples could also prove useful in exploring the relationship between satisfaction and activity. Finally, further research about the ways that women's sexuality interacts with social norms and ideologies—including gender beliefs, openness to alternative lifestyles, fluidity of sexual identity, and political beliefs about pornography, abortion, homosexuality, and feminism—could more fully situate sexual satisfaction and sexual activity in their sociopolitical contexts.

Notes

1. To clarify, the term "social status" deals with a person's location in a social hierarchy while a "social identity" refers to an individual's self-concept derived from perceived membership in a social group or a given status (Tajfel & Turner, 1986). Additionally, ascribed social statuses like race and gender are mostly determined at birth while achieved social statuses are obtained through some sort of actions (e.g., getting married or having children).
2. Note that "mismatch" simply refers to a divergence and does not imply that sexual satisfaction and sexual activity should always be aligned; rather, "mismatch" readily describes the differentness of these variables.
3. Interviews were conducted without matching interviewer/interviewee on key demographic features like race and gender, as there were no significant results for "matching" interviewers and interviewees (DeLamater & MacCorquodale, 1979). Some notable (and standard) exclusions to the original survey, due to difficulty reaching these participants by phone, included: persons not living in a "household," prison populations, military personnel, and Spanish-speaking (non-English-speaking) populations. The NHSLS did cover over 95% of the adult population aged 18–59. This survey also included an oversample of Blacks and English-speaking Hispanics (both groups = 273 cases).
4. Frankel, the chief statistician, noted that the weight first adjusts for oversampling, and then a multidimensional "balancing procedure" is applied, which adjusts for any differences as needed. He also noted that the weight combines a sampling weight (for the oversampling of certain groups), an eligibility weight (for the household size), and a poststratification weight (primarily for differential nonresponse). The weights were scaled to sum to the actual sample size, so the average weight is 1.0 (Laumann et al., 1994).
5. Previous research has shown that frequency of orgasm is strongly correlated with sexual satisfaction (Edwards & Booth, 1994; Haavio-Mannila & Kontula, 1997; McClelland, 2010; Philippsohn & Hartmann, 2009; Sprecher, 2002; Waite & Joyner, 2001; Young et al., 2000), though Laumann et al. (1994) and McClelland (2010) argued that orgasm should not be used as the sole measure of satisfaction. As Laumann et al. (1994) said, "One can usefully draw an analytic distinction between the two aspects of sexual satisfaction [physical and emotional pleasure], even as we recognize that the two are likely to be highly interdependent. . . . [I]f women do not expect orgasm to be a regular outcome of sexual activity, they are less likely to consider its absence of deprivation" (p. 118). While orgasm can be considered an "objective" measure of sexual response, it also may include a variety of subjective confounds as well (e.g., participant's wish to be considered normative, shame about faking orgasm, etc.). To enhance our measurement of these subjective dimensions, our feelings and emotions about sex variable inquired about participants' specific emotions about sex with their partner rather than solely measuring emotional satisfaction based on a single item. In total, we included Laumann et al.'s original two measures of sexual satisfaction (physical and emotional satisfaction) along with frequency of orgasm and feelings/emotions about sex in order to address recent debates in the field as well as maximally represent the different dimensions of sexual satisfaction available in the Laumann et al. dataset.
6. Excluded women did not differ significantly from the women in the sample on many major demographic characteristics (e.g., racial identity, sexual identity, education), but did differ significantly on marital status (those with no partners were, of course, less likely to have married, $p < .001$). The women excluded from the analysis who did not have a sexual partner within the past 12 months did not differ from the women in the sample on many major demographic characteristics except racial identity (those with no partners in the past year were more likely to be white, $p < .05$), and marital status (those with no partners in the past year were less likely to be married, $p < .001$).
7. The primary goal of cluster analysis was to derive a small set of clusters of observations, such that between-cluster differences were maximized, and within-cluster differences were minimized.

8. Though not a central part of these analyses, MANOVA results for Table 1 showed a significance of $p < .001$.
9. High satisfaction/high activity women were actually 100% heterosexual, so we can refer to all of their partners as men.

References

Ackard, D. M., Kearney-Cooke, A., & Peterson, C. B. (2000). Effect of body image and self-image on women's sexual behaviors. *International Journal of Eating Disorders, 28*, 422–429.

Acker, J. (2006). Inequality regimes: Gender, class, and race in organizations. *Gender & Society, 20*, 441–464.

Ahlborg, T., Dahlof, L. G., & Hallberg, L. (2005). Quality of the intimate and sexual relationship in first-time parents six months after delivery. *Journal of Sex Research, 42*, 167–174.

Baumeister, R., & Tice, D. (1998). *The social dimension of sex*. Boston: Allyn and Bacon.

Birnbaum, G. E. (2007). Attachment orientations, sexual functioning, and relationship satisfaction in a community sample of women. *Journal of Social and Personal Relationships, 24*, 21–35.

Blumstein, P. W., & Schwartz, P. (1983). *American couples: Money, work, and sex*. New York: William Morrow.

Bridges, S. K., & Horne, S. G. (2007). Sexual satisfaction and desire discrepancy in same sex women's relationships. *Journal of Sex and Marital Therapy, 33*, 41–53.

Bryan, T. S. (2002). Pretending to experience orgasm as a communicative act: How, when, and why some sexually experienced college women pretend to experience orgasm during various sexual behaviors. *Dissertation Abstracts International, 63*, 2049.

Call, V., Sprecher, S., & Schwartz, P. (1995). The incidence and frequency of marital sex in a national sample. *Journal of Marriage and Family, 57*, 639–652.

Chadiha, L. A., Veroff, J., & Leber, D. (1998). Newlywed's narrative themes: Meaning in the first year of marriage for African American and white couples. *Journal of Comparative Family Studies, 29*, 115–130.

Connell, R. W. (2005). *Masculinities*. Berkeley: University of California Press.

Crawford, E., Diener, E., Wirtz, D., Lucas, R. E., & Oishi, S. (2002). Wanting, having, and satisfaction: Examining the role of desire discrepancies in satisfaction with income. *Journal of Personality and Social Psychology, 83*, 725–734.

DeJudicibus, M. A., & McCabe, M. P. (2002). Psychological factors and the sexuality of pregnant and postpartum women. *Journal of Sex Research, 42*, 139–149.

DeLamater, J., & MacCorquodale, P. (1979). *Premarital sexuality: Attitudes, relationships, behavior*. Madison: University of Wisconsin.

Edwards, J., & Booth, A. (1994). Sexuality, marriage, and well-being: The middle years. In A. S. Rossi (Ed.), *Sexuality across the life course* (pp. 233–259). Chicago: University of Chicago Press.

Fahs, B. (2009). Compulsory bisexuality? The challenges of modern sexual fluidity. *Journal of Bisexuality, 9*, 1–19.

Fine, M., & McClelland, S. I. (2006). Sexuality education and desire: Still missing after all these years. *Harvard Educational Review, 76*, 297–338.

Fisher, S. (1980). Personality correlates of sexual behavior in Black women. *Archives of Sexual Behavior, 9*, 27–35.

Frederickson, B. L., & Roberts, T. (1997). Objectification theory: Toward understanding women's lived experiences and mental health risks. *Psychology of Women Quarterly, 21*, 173–206.

Fugère, M. A., Escoto, C., Cousins, A. J., Riggs, M. L., & Haerich, P. (2008). Sexual attitudes and double standards: A literature review focusing on participant gender and ethnic background. *Sexuality and Culture, 12*, 169–182.

González, M., Viáfara, G., Caba, F., Molina, T., & Ortiz, C. (2006). Libido and orgasm in middle-aged women. *Maturitas, 53*, 1–10.

Gordon, B. N., Schroeder, C. S., & Abrams, J. M. (1990). Age and socialclass differences in children's knowledge of sexuality. *Journal of Clinical Child Psychology, 19*, 33–43.

Haavio-Mannila, E., & Kontula, O. (1997). Correlates of increased sexual satisfaction. *Archives of Sexual Behavior, 26*, 399–419.

Hawton, K., Gath, D., & Day, A. (1994). Sexual function in a community sample of middle-aged women with partners: Effects of age, marital, socioeconomic, psychiatric, gynecological, and menopausal factors. *Archives of Sexual Behavior, 23*, 375–395.

Henderson, A., Levahot, K., & Simoni, J. (2009). Ecological models of sexual satisfaction among lesbian/bisexual and heterosexual women. *Archives of Sexual Behavior, 38*, 50–65.

Henderson-King, D. H., & Veroff, J. (1994). Sexual satisfaction and marital well-being in the first years of marriage. *Journal of Social and Personal Relationships, 11*, 509–534.

Hiller, J. (2005). Gender differences in sexual motivation. *Journal of Men's Health & Gender, 2*, 339–345.

Huang, A. J., Subak, L. L., Thorn, D. H., Van Den Eeden, S. K., Ragins, A. I., Kuppermann, M., et al. (2009). Sexual function and aging in racially and ethnically diverse women. *Journal of the American Geriatrics Society, 57*, 1362–1368.

Hunt, M. (1974). *Sexual behavior in the 1970s*. Oxford: Playboy Press.

Hurlbert, D. F., Apt, C., & Rabehl, S. M. (1993). Key variables to understanding female sexual satisfaction: An examination of women in nondistressed marriages. *Journal of Sex and Marital Therapy, 19*, 154–165.

Hyde, J. S., DeLamater, J. D., Plant, E. A., & Byrd, J. M. (1996). Sexuality during pregnancy and the year postpartum. *Journal of Sex Research, 33*, 143–151.

Jackman, M. R. (1994). *The velvet glove: Paternalism and conflict in gender, class, and race relations*. Berkeley: University of California Press.

Janus, S. S., & Janus, C. L. (1993). *The Janus report on sexual behavior*. New York: John Wiley & Sons.

Kalof, L., & Wade, B. H. (1995). Sexual attitudes and experiences with sexual coercion: Exploring the influence of race and gender. *Journal of Black Psychology, 21*, 224–238.

Kleinplatz, P. J. (2001). A critique of the goals of sex therapy, or the hazards of safer sex. In P. J. Kleinplatz (Ed.), *New directions in sex therapy: Innovations and alternatives* (pp. 109–132). New York: Routledge.

Krull, C. D. (1994). Level of education, sexual promiscuity, and AIDS. *Alberta Journal of Education Research, 40*, 7–20.

Laumann, E. O., Gagnon, J. H., Michael, R. T., & Michaels, S. (1994). *The social organization of sexuality: Sexual practices in the United States*. Chicago: University of Chicago Press.

Lawrance, K., & Byers, E. S. (1995). Development of the interpersonal exchange model of sexual satisfaction in long term relationships. *Canadian Journal of Human Sexuality, 1*(3), 123–128.

Lutfey, K. E., Link, C. L., Rosen, R. C., Wiegel, M., & McKinlay, J. B. (2009). Prevalence and correlates of sexual activity and function in women: Results from the Boston Area Community Health (BACH) Survey. *Archives of Sexual Behavior, 38*, 514–527.

MacNeil, S., & Byers, E. S. (2005). Dyadic assessment of sexual self-disclosure and sexual satisfaction in heterosexual dating couples. *Journal of Social and Personal Relationships, 22*, 169–181.

Mansfield, P. K., Koch, P. B., & Voda, A. M. (2000). Midlife women's attributes for their sexual response changes. *Health Care for Women International, 21*, 543–559.

Martin, K., & Purkiss, J. (2001, August). *Is sexual dysfunction a social problem?: Examining race, class, and gender*. Paper presented at the meeting of the American Sociological Association, Anaheim, CA.

McCall, L. (2001). Sources of racial wage inequality in metropolitan labor markets: racial, ethnic, and gender differences. *American Sociological Review, 66*, 520–541.

McClelland, S. I. (2010). Intimate justice: A critical analysis of sexual satisfaction. *Social and Personality Psychology Compass, 4*, 663–680.

McNulty, J. K., & Fisher, T. D. (2008). Gender differences in response to sexual expectancies and changes in sexual frequency: A short-term longitudinal study of sexual satisfaction in newly married couples. *Archives of Sexual Behavior, 37*, 229–240.

Means, M. C. (2001). An integrative approach to what women really want: Sexual satisfaction. *Dissertation Abstracts International, 61*, 4417.

Nicolson, P., & Burr, J. (2003). What is "normal" about women's (hetero) sexual desire and orgasm? A report of an in-depth interview study. *Social Science and Medicine, 57*, 1735–1745.

Oggins, J., Veroff, J., & Leber, D. (1993). Perceptions of marital interaction among black and white newly weds. *Journal of Personality and Social Psychology, 65*, 494–511.

Oliver, M. B., & Hyde, J. S. (1993). Gender differences in sexuality: A meta-analysis. *Psychological Bulletin, 114*, 29–51.

Pedersen, W., & Blekesaune, M. (2003). Sexual satisfaction in young adulthood: Cohabitation, committed dating, or unattached life? *Acta Sociologica, 46*, 179–193.

Peplau, L. A., Fingerhut, A., & Beals, K. P. (2004). Sexuality in the relationships of lesbians and gay men. In J. H. Harvey, A. Wenzel, & S. Sprecher (Eds.), *Handbook of sexuality in close relationships* (pp. 349–369). Mahwah, NJ: Lawrence Erlbaum Associates.

Petersen, J. L., & Hyde, J. S. (2010). A meta-analytic review of research on gender differences in sexuality, 1993–2007. *Psychological Bulletin, 136*, 21–38.

Philippsohn, S., & Hartmann, U. (2009). Determinants of sexual satisfaction in a sample of German women. *Journal of Sexual Medicine, 6*, 1001–1010.

Pinney, E. M., Gerrard, M., & Denney, N. W. (1987). The pinney sexual satisfaction inventory. *Journal of Sex Research, 23*, 233–251.

Purdon, C., & Holdaway, L. (2006). Non-erotic thoughts: Content and relation to sexual functioning and sexual satisfaction. *Journal of Sex Research, 43*, 154–162.

Pyke, K. D. (1996). Class based masculinities: The interdependence of gender, class, and interpersonal power. *Gender & Society, 10*, 527–549.

Raboch, J., & Raboch, J. (1992). Infrequent orgasms in women. *Journal of Sex and Marital Therapy, 18*, 114–120.

Rubin, L. (1994). *Families on the fault line: America's working class speak about the family, the economy, race, and ethnicity*. New York: Harper Collins.

Schwartz, P., & Young, L. (2009). Sexual satisfaction in committed relationships. *Sexuality Research and Social Policy, 6*, 1–17.

Seldin, D. R., Friedman, H. S., & Marin, L. R. (2002). Sexual activity as a predictor of life-span mortality risk. *Personality and Individual Differences, 33*, 409–426.

Shifren, J. L., Monz, B. U., Russo, P. A., Segreti, A., & Johannes, C. B. (2008). Sexual problems and distress in United States women: Prevalence and correlates. *Obstetrics and Gynecology, 112*, 970–978.

Smith, V. C. (2007). In pursuit of "good" sex: Self-determination and the sexual experience. *Journal of Social and Personal Relationships, 24*, 69–85.

Sprecher, S. (2002). Sexual satisfaction in premarital relationships: Association with satisfaction, love, commitment, and stability. *Journal of Sex Research, 39*, 190–196.

Sprecher, S., Barbee, A., & Schwartz, P. (1995). "Was it good for you too?": Gender differences in first sexual intercourse experiences. *Journal of Sex Research, 32*, 3–15.

Sprecher, S., & Cate, R. M. (2004). Sexual satisfaction and sexual expression as predictors of relationship satisfaction and stability. In J. H. Harvey, A. Wenzel, & S. Sprecher (Eds.), *The handbook of close relationships* (pp. 235–256). Mahwah, NJ: Lawrence Erlbaum.

Sprecher, S., & Regan, P. C. (1996). College virgins: How men and women perceive their sexual status. *Journal of Sex Research, 33*, 3–15.

Strelan, P., Mehaffey, S. J., & Tiggemann, M. (2003). Self-objectification and esteem in young women: The mediating role of reasons for exercise. *Sex Roles, 48*, 89–95.

Tajfel, H., & Turner, J. C. (1986). The social identity theory of inter-group behavior. In S. Worchel & L. W. G. Austin (Eds.), *Psychology of intergroup relations* (pp. 7–24). Chicago: Nelson-Hall.

Tiefer, L. (2001). Feminist critique of sex therapy: Foregrounding the politics of sex. In P. Kleinplatz (Ed.), *New directions in sex therapy: Innovations and alternatives* (pp. 29–49). Philadelphia: Brunner-Routledge.

Tiefer, L. (2004). *Sex is not a natural act and other essays*. Boulder, CO: Westview Press.

Tomic, D., Gallicchio, L., Whiteman, M. K., Lewis, L. M., Langenberg, P., & Flaws, J. A. (2006). Factors associated with determinants of sexual functioning in midlife women. *Maturitas, 53*, 144–157.

Waite, L. J., & Joyner, K. (2001). Emotional satisfaction and physical pleasure in sexual unions: Time horizon, sexual behavior, and sexual exclusivity. *Journal of Marriage and the Family, 63*, 247–264.

Walker-Hill, R. (2000). An analysis of the relationship of human sexuality knowledge, self-esteem, and body image to sexual satisfaction in college and university students. *Dissertation Abstracts International, 60*, 4560.

Weaver, A. D. (2006). The relationships among body image, body mass index, exercise, and sexual functioning in heterosexual women. *Psychology of Women Quarterly, 30*, 333–339.

Weinberg, M. S., Lottes, I. L., & Gordon, L. E. (1997). Social class background, sexual attitudes, and sexual behavior in a heterosexual undergraduate sample. *Archives of Sexual Behavior, 26*, 625–642.

Wilkins, K. M., & Warnock, J. K. (2009). Sexual dysfunction in older women. *Primary Psychiatry, 16*, 59–65.

Young, M., Denny, G., Luquis, R., & Young, T. (1998). Correlates of sexual satisfaction in marriage. *Canadian Journal of Human Sexuality, 7*, 115–127.

PART

14

The Gender of Violence

As a nation, we fret about "teen violence," complain about "inner city crime" or fear "urban gangs." We express shock at the violence in our nation's public schools, where metal detectors crowd the doorways, and knives and guns commingle with pencils and erasers in students' backpacks. Those public school shootings leave us speechless and sick at heart. Yet when we think about these wrenching events, do we ever consider that, whether white or black, inner city or suburban, these bands of marauding "youths" or these troubled teenagers are virtually all young men?

Men constitute 99 percent of all persons arrested for rape; 88 percent of those arrested for murder; 92 percent of those arrested for robbery; 87 percent for aggravated assault; 85 percent of other assaults; 83 percent of all family violence; 82 percent of disorderly conduct. Men are overwhelmingly more violent than women. Nearly 90 percent of all murder victims are murdered by men, according to the United States Department of Justice (Uniform Crime Reports 1991, 17).

From early childhood to old age, violence is perhaps the most obdurate, intractable gender difference we have observed. The National Academy of Sciences (cited in Gottfredson and Hirschi; 1990) puts the case most starkly: "The most consistent pattern with respect to gender is the extent to which male criminal participation in serious crimes at any age greatly exceeds that of females, regardless of source of data, crime type, level of involvement, or measure of participation." "Men are always and everywhere more likely than women to commit criminal acts," write the criminologists Michael Gottfredson and Travis Hirschi (1990, 145). Yet how do we understand this obvious association between masculinity and violence? Is it a biological fact of nature, caused by something inherent in male anatomy? Is it culturally universal? And in the United States, what has been the association between gender and violence? Has that association become stronger or weaker over time? What can we, as a culture, do to prevent or at least ameliorate the problem of male violence?

Our concern throughout this book has been to observe the construction of gender difference and gender inequality at both the individual level of identity and the institutional level. The readings here reflect these concerns.

To argue that men are more prone to violence than women are does not resolve the political question of what to do about it. It would be foolish to resignedly throw up our hands in despair that "boys will be boys." Whether you believe this gender difference in violence derives from different biological predispositions (which I regard as dubious because these biological impulses do not seem to be culturally universal) or because male violence is socially sanctioned and legitimated as an expression of masculine control and domination (a far more convincing explanation), the policy question remains open. Do we organize society so as to maximize this male propensity toward violence, or do we organize society so as to minimize and constrain it? The answers to this question, like the answer to the questions about alleviating gender inequality in the family, in our educational institutions, and in the workplace, are more likely to come from the voting booth than from the laboratories of scientists. As a society, we decide how much weight to give what few gender differences there are, and how best to alleviate the pain of those who are the victims of gendered violence.

The essays included here overturn or challenge the common stereotypes in arresting ways. Angela Stroud examines men's fascination with concealed handguns and its relationship to masculinity. Betsi Little and Cheryl Terrance look at the way gender stereotypes play out in domestic violence situations in lesbian couples. And Carleen M. Thompson and her colleagues examine gender differences in that most gendered of behaviors: stalking. Even though the overwhelming majority of stalkers are male, the differences between women and men are quite telling.

References

U.S. Department of Justice, Uniform Crime Reports, 1991. Washington, DC: Dept of Justice.

Michael Gottfredson and Travis Hirschi, *A General Theory of Crime* (Stanford: Stanford University Press, 1990).

Good Guys with Guns: Hegemonic Masculinity and Concealed Handguns

ANGELA STROUD

An estimated six million people in the United States possess a concealed handgun license (Stuckey 2010), which means they have the legal right to carry a concealed firearm in most public places. Like gun use generally, the vast majority of concealed handgun license holders are men, and men are more likely than women to support concealed handgun licensing (Carroll 2005; Jones 2005). This study explores how gender dynamics shape the motives of men who are licensed to carry concealed handguns.

Previous studies have argued that guns are symbols of masculinity (Connell 1995; Gibson 1994; Melzer 2009). Stange and Oyster (2000, 22) explain, "In [men's hands], the gun has served a symbolic function that exceeds any practical utility. It has become the symbol par excellence of masculinity: of power, force, aggressiveness, decisiveness, deadly accuracy, cold rationality." Because of these associations, it seems logical that men could use them to perform masculinity. However, the only studies of how men actually use guns have focused on criminals (Kimmel and Mahler 2003; Stretesky and Pogrebin 2007). In this study, I investigate how masculinity motivates law-abiding men in their use of concealed handguns.

To understand the relationship between carrying a concealed firearm and masculinity, I conducted 20 in-depth interviews with men in Texas who currently have a concealed handgun license. Of the nearly one million licenses issued in the state between 1995 and 2009, 81 percent were to men and 19 percent were to women (Texas Department of Public Safety [DPS] 1995–2010a). Though Texas has a "Wild West" image in popular culture, its firearm laws can be considered "middle of the road." Texas' permitting process requires a person to be at least 21 years old, pass state and federal background checks, attend a licensing course, submit two sets of fingerprints, and remit a fee to the state. Moreover, the firearm must remain concealed or the license holder can be charged with a weapons crime.

In this study, I use the concept of hegemonic masculinity to examine motives of men who have a concealed handgun license. Hegemonic masculinity is Connell's (1995) term for the discursive practices and embodied dispositions that legitimize male domination. I argue that by having a license, economically privileged white men are able to define themselves in contrast to femininity and to alternative versions of masculinity that are vilified or ridiculed. In so doing, they shore up white male privilege in society.

My research suggests that some men see their gun carrying as central to what it means to be a good husband and father who is able to protect his wife and children from danger. For older men, who fear that they are losing their ability to physically dominate others, concealed firearms can act as a totem to boost their confidence in their interactions with men. Men also justify their need for a license by positioning themselves in contrast to vilified forms of masculinity. While these men see their own gun carrying as noble and just, they attribute violence and aggression to others, particularly Black and Latino men. Hegemonic masculinity provides a framework for understanding

Angela Stroud, "Good Guys with Guns: Hegemonic Masculinity and Concealed Handguns." *Gender & Society* 26 (April 2012): 216–38.

these discursive practices, and connecting the use of concealed handgun licenses to continued male domination in society.

Literature Review

The literature on firearm use and gender has focused on three main themes: how firearms contribute to cultural constructions of masculinity (Gibson 1994; Jeffords 1994); how organizations such as the National Rifle Association (NRA) utilize masculine tropes to mobilize members (Connell 1995; Melzer 2009; O'Neill 2007); and how masculinity is implicated in violent acts in which firearms are used (Kimmel and Mahler 2003; Stretesky and Pogrebin 2007). Each of these themes is important for understanding why men want to carry a concealed firearm.

The first theme in the literature on firearm use and gender explores the relationships between firearms, violence, and masculinity in fantasy life. James Gibson (1994) argues that movies celebrating war and the warrior ethos, such as the *Rambo* series, emerged on the cultural landscape as a response to the U.S. defeat in Vietnam. The warrior ethos was an extension of the larger cultural shift that linked masculinity to masculinity and physical toughness (Jeffords 1994). The body is central to how this operates because "to be fully, appropriately masculine, a male person must exhibit physical control of his space and be able to act on objects and bodies in it" (Crawley, Foley, and Shehan 2008, 59). This post-Vietnam ethos ushered in a more militarized version of masculinity that helped to popularize the use of guns for personal defense, led to a proliferation of paramilitary organizations, and contributed to the popularity of simulated war games such as paintball (Gibson 1994).

The willingness to engage in violence is central to meanings of masculinity (Messerschmidt 2000) because "real men" must show others that they are not afraid (Kimmel 2010). Yet few men have culturally legitimate occasions to express this violence, making simulated scenarios ideal settings to engage in violence fantasies. They promote a "New War ethos" where power, force, and might are celebrated as socially necessary when used to protect "good people" from evil. In this worldview, firearms endow "good guys" with the strength, power, and moral right needed to defend the world from "bad guys."

As Gibson suggests, the fantasy of using guns to fight "bad guys" is not only an acceptable form of violence in U.S. culture, it is also celebrated. But unlike Gibson's subjects, the vast majority of people who carry a concealed firearm will never be in a position to enact this New War ethos—even as a playful performance. Furthermore, according to Connell and Messerschmidt (2005, 883), exalted versions of masculinity need not be based in reality, and might instead "express widespread ideals, fantasies, and desires" that justify masculinity's dominance over femininity. In the case of carrying a concealed firearm, an object that is particularly useful for communicating strength, it is important to ask how fantasies of domination allow men to construct masculine selves, whether or not their guns are actually fired.

The second theme in the literature on gender and firearms focuses on the gun lobby's role in linking gun use with hegemonic masculinity (Connell 1995; Melzer 2009; O'Neill 2007). Connell argues that the gun lobby is engaged in masculinity politics, "those mobilizations and struggles where the meaning of masculine gender is at issue and with it, men's position in gender relations" (1995, 205). The gun lobby has been active in producing meanings of masculinity as it works to expand gun rights, even in the face of public outcry over the danger of guns. Connell argues that the gun lobby is able to defeat opponents of gun control by explicitly appealing to discourses of masculinity. By evoking concepts like security, family values, or individual freedom, the gun lobby works to make masculinity "a principal theme, not taken for granted as background" (1995, 205).

Scott Melzer (2009) utilizes Connell's framework to analyze how the National Rifle Association (NRA) exploits popular understandings of guns as masculine symbols to mobilize its members. Melzer attended NRA conventions, analyzed the history of the organization, and interviewed its members to understand how the NRA has used masculinity discourses to become the most powerful lobby in the United States. He argues that gun ownership is associated in NRA discourse with self-reliance, rugged individualism, and a strong work ethic, a constellation of traits that Melzer refers to as "frontier masculinity." He writes that "guns and masculinity have long been inseparable" (2009, 30) thanks to mythologized narratives of the American frontier. These narratives appeal to working-and middle-class white men who are threatened by the civil rights and feminist movements. According to Melzer, the predominantly white male membership of the NRA is motivated to act in defense of guns because they symbolize individual freedom.

The NRA's magazine *The American Rifleman* is the most popular of the organization's monthly publications. Kevin O'Neill (2007) examines how the magazine's section "Armed Citizen" relays stories of violent crimes thwarted by private citizens using guns. For example, the author cites one story that tells of a man whose children rushed into his room in the middle of the night to tell their father that two men were breaking into their home. The father, who was disabled, grabbed a handgun, shot one of the intruders and held him at gunpoint until the police arrived. O'Neill finds that most of the victims in these stories are women, the elderly, or in some way disabled or in failing health. He argues that these "classically vulnerable" people heighten the narrative structure of the stories, because as otherwise helpless victims, they are able to "achieve masculinity" with firearms. According to O'Neill, the NRA uses discourses that simultaneously construct masculinity and terror, and they produce an "especially vigilant kind of citizen who is distinctly masculine in character" (2007, 459). Though defensive gun uses are statistically rare events,[1] the NRA is able to use its monthly publication to circulate stories of "real-life heroes" who use guns to defend the defenseless.

The literature on the NRA illustrates how this powerful lobby links gun use with hegemonic masculinity: Gun users heroically defend the defenseless (O'Neill 2007) and they care deeply about "American virtues," particularly individual freedom (Melzer 2009) and family values (Connell 1995). These NRA discourses "provide a cultural framework that may be materialized in daily practices and interactions" and thus represent what Connell and Messerschmidt (2005, 850) call a "regional" hegemonic masculinity. Though it is important to understand how masculinities emerge in particular contexts, what Connell and Messerschmidt (2005) call the "local level," dominant culture frames and shapes the possibilities for enacting preferred versions of masculinity in everyday life. In this article, I explore how this regional discourse is materialized in the daily practices and interactions of men who are licensed to carry concealed handguns.

The third set of studies on guns and gender examine how some men actually use firearms. However, these studies have focused on the commission of violent crimes and on what Connell might label "alternative" or "marginal" masculinities (Connell 1995). Some researchers consider criminal behavior an attempt by some marginal men to accomplish masculinity when they lack alternative resources to do so (Britton 2011; Messerschmidt 1993).

In this vein, Kimmel and Mahler (2003) analyze random school shootings in the United States. All of those shootings were perpetrated by boys and young men and "all or most of the shooters had tales of being harassed—specifically gay-baited—for inadequate gender performance" (Kimmel and Mahler 2003, 1440). By using firearms to commit acts of violence, these boys attempted to move from margin to center, from being the wimp who was picked on to the aggressor who dominated and controlled others. Similarly, Stretesky and Pogrebin (2007) interviewed gang members serving prison time for violent crimes. The authors found that the reputations of both the gang and the individual gang member were determined by their willingness to defend their honor and to be seen as masculine. The primary way this was accomplished was by using firearms. The authors write, "Guns provide gang members with a sense of power" and guns "help gang members project a tough image" (Stretesky and Pogrebin 2007, 90). Because guns are so lethal, they imbue their users with traits associated with masculinity—control and power.

Taken together, the literature on guns and masculinity reveals a gaping hole that has implications for how we understand both the way guns factor into cultural constructions of masculinity and how hegemonic masculinity operates. On the regional level, guns factor heavily in displays of masculine violence that are celebrated in action films through fantasies of "good guys" killing "bad guys" (Gibson 1994). The gun lobby taps into and expands this discourse by tying guns to American virtues (Connell 1995; Melzer 2009; O'Neill 2007). But the only analyses that examine how real men use guns to construct masculinity have focused on criminal uses by men who embody marginalized masculinities (Kimmel and Mahler 2003; Stretesky and Pogrebin 2007). Thus, while on the regional level it is clear that guns are discursively linked to hegemonic masculinity, it is unclear how men on the local level might use guns to construct versions of masculinity that are celebrated in culture.

Race and class are central to hegemonic masculinity (Connell and Messerschmidt 2005), but have been virtually ignored in the literature on guns and masculinity. This elision is significant particularly because the image of the ideal gun user constructed by the NRA emerges alongside controlling images of Black masculinity that frame Black males as "threats to white society" (Collins 2006, 75). As a symbol that at once signifies violence and protection, gun use will likely take on different meanings when analyzed at the intersection of race, class, and gender.

The men that are the focus of my study are positioned quite differently from the marginalized men in the literature: Instead of being defined as "criminals," they consider themselves law-abiding men and are licensed by the state to carry concealed guns. Furthermore, they are predominantly white and upper middle class and thus are socially privileged. To fully explore the significance of their gun carrying, it is important not only to interrogate the meanings they give the practice, but to understand the extent to which they are able to position themselves in relationship to the larger discourses around guns and hegemonic masculinity.

The following questions emerge from this literature: How do law-abiding men use concealed firearms to signify masculinity? How are race, class, and gender implicated in the production of hegemonic masculinity? This study extends the literature on masculinities and guns by examining the gendered meanings of concealed firearm carry by law-abiding men. It also extends the literature on hegemonic masculinity by utilizing a race/class/gender focus in examining dynamics of power between local and regional levels of analysis.

Methods

I conducted in-depth interviews with 20 men who are licensed to carry a concealed handgun. To develop a sample, I first contacted concealed handgun licensing instructors, four of whom agreed to be interviewed. Those initial contacts referred me to others. Seventeen of the interviews were face-to-face and were conducted in Texas; three respondents were interviewed over the phone (and recorded using a telephone recording device). Sixteen of the respondents identified as white, two identified as white and Hispanic/Latino, and two identified as Hispanic/Latino (see Table 1). All but two of the respondents were married, and they ranged in age from 26 to 66 with a median age of 44.

Though it is difficult to discern the extent to which my sample mirrors the population of men with a concealed handgun license in Texas, it is clear that the majority of license holders are white men. Between 1995 and 2010, 81 percent of the nearly one million licenses issued in Texas were to men, 88 percent of whom were white (Texas DPS 1995–2010b). Because the fees associated with getting a license are typically between $200 and $250, it is likely that the expenses associated with licensing make concealed handgun license cost-prohibitive for Texans with low incomes. Nearly all of the respondents in my sample had high household incomes, though two refused to answer this question. Four of the course instructors I interviewed said that most of their students are middle-class, college-educated professionals.

Because firearms are aligned with conservative politics (Melzer 2009), I had some apprehension about being accepted into the networks of license instructors and holders. All interview participants wanted to know if I was "pro-gun" and if I

Table 1. Demographic Characteristics of Respondents

Name[a]	Sex	Age	Race/Ethnicity	Education	Estimated Income
Adam	M	36	White	High school degree	$61–80,000
Alex	M	26	White	High school	$21–40,000
Bill	M	38	White	Technical (military)	$101,000 +
Chris	M	63	White	College degree	$41–60,000
David	M	66	White	Advanced degree	$21–40,000
George	M	40	Hispanic	College degree	$101,000 +
Gil	M	65	White	High school degree	$101,000 +
Greg	M	57	White	High school degree	$101,000 +
Jack	M	46	White	College degree	$101,000 +
Jeff	M	48	Latino and White	College degree	$81–100,000
John	M	44	White	Advanced degree	NA
Joseph	M	45	White and Hispanic	Associate's degree	$81–100,000
Larry	M	54	White	Associate's degree	NA
Leo	M	52	Hispanic	Advanced degree	$101,000 +
Mark	M	34	White	High school degree	$61–80,000
Mike	M	36	White	College degree	$101,000 +
Nick	M	46	White	Trade school	$81–100,000
Paul	M	34	White	Technical (military)	$61–80,000
Richard	M	38	White	College degree	$101,000 +
Steven	M	30	White	Advanced degree	$101,000 +

a. All names are pseudonyms.

shot firearms. Though I do not own a gun, I am not opposed to them. As a part of this research project, I have regularly visited local guns ranges and rented guns for target practice. When I told participants this, it seemed to put them at ease and signaled to them that my intention with this research is not to bolster an antigun position, but is instead to learn about their experiences as concealed handgun license holders.

Interviews lasted between one to two hours and were conducted at locations chosen by the respondents. Sites included a gun range, the respondent's office, coffee shops, restaurants, and a church. During the interviews research participants were first asked to describe their background experiences, including their earliest memories with guns, whether either of their parents were gun users, and at what age they received their first gun. I then asked what motivated them to get a license and whether they have friends or acquaintances who are license holders. The third set of questions involved their firearm-carrying practices, including whether they carry a gun every day, if they avoid places where carrying a gun is restricted, and if they have ever had to pull their gun from its holster. The fourth section included questions that asked participants their views on gun free zones and gun rights. I digitally recorded and transcribed each interview, then read through each transcript to identify themes.

Through my analysis of the interviews, three primary themes emerged in men's explanations of why they want to carry a firearm in public: (1) to protect their wives and children from violent crime; (2) to compensate for lost physical strength as they age; and (3) to make them feel more secure in places they feel vulnerable. I will argue that each of these themes is connected to fantasies of violence and heroic defense that contribute to hegemonic masculinity.

Family Defender

Defending the family is significant in men's accounts of carrying a concealed firearm. Nearly all of the men I interviewed are married, and ten have children living at home. In almost every case, the men I interviewed explained their gun use as deeply tied to defending their families. Adam, 36, says that he first bought a gun around the age of 21 because, having just finished college, he could afford to live only in "lower income neighborhoods where there's more crime and there's more shootings and violence." Adam described that neighborhood as "a bad part of Houston" and said he used his gun only for protection in his home and was never very serious about self-defense. All this changed when he and his wife were expecting a child. He explains his perspective: "I'm the dad. I think my role is that I have to protect my family. That's my number one duty as a dad: to provide . . . food, shelter, and protection for my wife and my child. I mean that's what being a dad is." I asked Adam if that is a role he is trying to learn or if it's one a man automatically assumes when he gets married. He responded,

> I think you automatically assume it when you get married. And, then especially when you have a kid. And I don't know if that's my belief, or it's just the way I grew up or whatever. But you know, when you get married, you're supposed to do certain things. You know, you have roles. And I know that in today's society [pause] a lot of people like to think well, men and women, they're the same and you know, the women work and so do the men and all that stuff. Which, to some extent, I agree. But there's other certain inherent parts of being a man and being a woman that you have certain roles. I can't have a baby! You know, physically I can't have a baby and physically I'm stronger than my wife. And, it's just up to me to protect her, in every situation. And if, you know, if we were ever attacked or accosted or something then, then it's up to me to protect her until she can, you know, be safe.

Adam became very animated about what he termed "his role" in his family and seemed exasperated by the suggestion that men and women are equals in all senses. Adam sees his wife and child as dependent on him for their safety. Rooting his argument in bodily differences makes the distinction seem natural and inevitable (Connell 1995; Hollander 2001).

Like many respondents, Adam says that a gun is a superior tool for self-defense because it doesn't matter if a criminal is larger or stronger than he is; with a gun, he can defend himself. This is what is meant when guns are referred to as "equalizers." Presumably, this logic would also apply to women and would suggest that there is nothing inevitable about Adam, and the other men who made such statements, occupying the role of the family protector. Instead of stemming from a natural consequence of him being "the dad," Adam utilizes discourses that link masculinity to physicality and aggression and femininity to vulnerability (Hollander 2001) to place his wife and children in positions of dependence.

Mark, a very tall and physically imposing man, is 34 and married with two small children. Standing 6 feet 10 inches, his first jobs after college were in personal security. Mark says he never felt particularly vulnerable until he and his wife were expecting their first child. Mark describes developing a deep-seated need to ensure that his family is protected. He says, "You know, I've got a newborn child that is relying on me to not only protect him, but to protect myself and his mother." As his perspective shifted toward a focus on defending his family, Mark not only obtained a concealed handgun license, he also pursued advanced training in handgun self-defense tactics. He now carries a gun everywhere he goes—including the gym and his own home—whether it is legal or not. Like Adam, he suggests that becoming a father was a transitional moment for how he thinks about vulnerability and self-defense. Both men went from only having guns in the home to wanting to carry a gun in public because, as fathers, they feel it is their duty to protect their family.

Though Mark says that he carries a gun to protect his family, he also explains that he spends much of his time apart from them. Mark says that he would love for his wife to carry a firearm because "if something happens to me, you know, if I get shot, she can take it and use it. If I'm not there. If she's by herself." He elaborates by saying,

"I can't be with [my kids] 24 hours a day. She can't be either, but you know, she's more . . . likely to be there than I am." In this explanation Mark wants his wife to be armed not because she would also become a family defender but because he cannot always be with his family. Like Mark, many of the other married men I interviewed said that they wish their wives would carry a concealed handgun, but in contrast to how they see their role as fathers, they do not see their wives as bad mothers because they are not licensed. Moreover, their wives' refusal to be armed further emphasizes that it is a father's job to protect his family.

When I asked Mark if he is ever stressed about his wife's safety when he is not with her, he replied, "No, I mean . . . she's a good girl. She can take care of herself [laughs]. But you know, it's been in the back of my mind always. You . . . gotta kinda balance the practicality versus the, the uh [long pause] oh, what's the word? The paranoia." There is a disconnect between how Mark explains his need for a concealed firearm—because crime can happen to anyone, anywhere—and his general comfort with the fact that his wife does not carry a gun. His contradictory response underscores how, in addition to simply being a tool for self-defense, Mark's possession of a concealed handgun license signifies that he is a good father and husband.

The men I talked to consider themselves law-abiding, virtuous, and brave defenders of their families—matching the image of the ideal gun owner perpetrated by the NRA (Connell 1995; Melzer 2009; O'Neill 2007). But paradoxically, carrying a concealed firearm does not actually enable them to defend their families. Though Mark suggested that as his family's breadwinner, his defense is integral to his family's security, he nevertheless minimized the threat to his wife and children when he is away from them. In fact, the fathers I interviewed recognize that their wives are more likely than they are to be in a position to use a gun in defense of the family. This contradiction suggests that while carrying a concealed gun may symbolize their fatherly role, it may not actually translate into an ability to protect their wives and children from harm.

Though they may never be in a position to carry out heroic fantasies of masculine bravery, their concealed handgun suggests to them that they could. By signifying that their wives and children are dependent on them for protection (whether or not this is actually true), the men I interviewed are discursively positioning themselves as brave leaders of their families; thus, their concealed handgun license is very useful as a symbol that allows men to construct hegemonic masculinity. In many respects, it is an ideal symbol because it signifies to them that they are good fathers and husbands, even when they are away from their wives and children.

The Aging Male Body

Few respondents younger than 40 said that they needed a gun primarily to defend themselves; however, five of the 12 respondents 40 and older explained that age factored into why they have a concealed handgun license. For example, Jeff, 48, is an affable gun enthusiast. He regularly participates in shooting competitions and carries a firearm with him whenever he can. Like many respondents, Jeff reports that he cannot carry his gun at work. When I asked him how that makes him feel, he replied, "Vulnerable. [Laughs]. As I'm being reminded, like today at my orthopedist, trying to get my knee fixed, I'm not as young as I used to be. And [pause] I don't, I don't want to have to dance with somebody if they want to do me violence." Jeff explains that with a gun he does not have this sense of vulnerability and instead feels relaxed knowing he has "a superior ability to deal with a situation harshly if I have to." He then tells the following story:

> Years ago I was practicing martial arts regularly. And a friend of mine at the office—a good friend of mine—was just always real aggressive. And, he had his usual fifteen pots of coffee that day, and got vulgar like he always did, and I think . . . he said, "I'll kick your ass" or something like that. I just turned around and smiled at him. And he said, "Oh man, I'm sorry. I didn't mean it. I was just joking." I said, "I know. I know you were joking, don't worry about it" [laughs]. Then we laughed it off. And he was very visibly shaken. I wasn't gonna do anything to him, but he knew and I knew that I could've. No big deal.

Jeff felt proud that his officemate feared him. Though he is older now, and not able to do martial arts, carrying a firearm gives him the same sense of confidence. Jeff's firearm supplies him with a virility that his aging body has surrendered. He says he feels "calm and relaxed" when he's carrying a gun and that when he is armed, if someone threatens him, he can just smile back, rather than worrying about how to handle the situation. Without having to show his firearm to others. Jeff's gun makes him feel at ease, confident he can handle any confrontation.

Gil, 66, lives in a major metropolitan city in the Southwest. He says he carries a firearm because "I refuse to be a victim. I refuse to put myself in the position where . . . someone can exercise that kind of control over me." Gil relayed a story about a time when he felt physically threatened and did not have his firearm with him. He was coming out of a sporting arena in a major metropolitan city. "We were goin' into the parking ramp to get our vehicle. And there were a bunch of [long pause] young [pause] punks." Gil struggled to find the words to describe the group of people he was approaching. "It was pretty uncomfortable for about five minutes, until I was certain that they were goin' somewhere else and not to us." When I asked if the group of people were being hostile toward him, he replied, "Well . . . let's just say I was uncomfortable." And, after a long pause, he said, "I think we've all had that experience in a public place." Because sports arenas are gun-free zones, Gil could not carry his gun and had left it in his car. When I asked him how his behavior would have been different if he had his gun on him, Gil said he would have been more confident. "In what ways?" I asked. He replied,

> Confident in that I can take care of myself. You know, at my age, I'm not gonna win many kung fu fights with an assailant [laughs]. And, you know, 34 years ago if someone wanted to mix it up, I probably would've been okay taking my chances. But you get to a certain age and you've got some problems. You know, dealing on a physical level. And you don't run as fast [laughs]. You know what I mean?

Gil then said, "You know the old saying 'Don't piss off an old guy because he'll probably just kill ya'? [Laughs]." This joke was an abrupt response to the admission that Gil no longer sees himself as physically strong. It seemed intended to convey that, though getting older has taken its toll, if provoked, he could still defend himself.

Another example of how firearms can compensate for lost capacities as bodies age comes from Larry, 54. When we met, Larry arrived on a Harley motorcycle and was wearing a black bandanna and black leather vest. A tall, stout man, he sported a goatee. Throughout the interview Larry projected a very tough, almost threatening persona. When Larry told me he carried a gun long before he had a license to do so legally, I asked him if that was because he had experienced a violent incident or if it was because of a "generalized fear that something could happen." Larry quickly dismissed the notion that he feared violent crime. Instead, Larry says, he's realistic: "Most people have this delusion that the world's this warm happy place, and for most of them, it is. But that's only because nothing's happened to them yet." Similar to the New War ethos Gibson (1994) studied, Larry has constructed a worldview in which there is a perpetual struggle between forces of good and evil. This worldview justifies Larry's tough and aggressive, thoroughly masculine, self-presentation. Later in the interview, I asked him if he had ever felt physically threatened when he was not armed. Again, Larry dismissed the idea that he would feel threatened, attributing it to his military training in hand-to-hand combat:

> If I've got a stake or a pool cue, I will own your ass. As far as not having anything? When I was a little bit younger and in a little bit better shape, I was comfortable with up to three people. So, no, I didn't particularly feel threatened. If worse gets to worst, I can grab one person, they will scream like a little girl before it's all over with and the other two people will not want to get that close.

In this moment, and in many others during the interview, Larry seemed purposive in communicating to me that being tough and capable of violence are important attributes in a man, attributes he has always had. He is both willing to engage in violence and capable of domination, traits deeply tied to masculinity (Messerschmidt 2000; Messner

1992). However, he also admits that growing older has taken a toll on his body. Because he was so quick to dismiss suggestions that he might feel vulnerable or threatened, and because he feels like he can dominate other men without a gun, I asked Larry, "So, then, why do you carry [a gun]?" He responded, "Because you never know."

Michael Kimmel (1996, 6) has argued, "Manhood is less about the drive for domination and more about the fear of others dominating us, having power or control over us." Though men like Larry might scoff at the notion that he carries a gun because of fear, he is motivated by a desire to prevent his domination at the hands of another man. Getting older has meant that these men have begun to lose access to a fundamental aspect of masculinity: the capacity to physically dominate others (Crawley, Foley, and Shehan 2008). Carrying a gun allows them to recoup the sense of dominance that stems from having an ability to fight back. Unlike subordinate men who are unable or unwilling to fight, "real" men are able and ready to defend themselves, a position that allows them to claim dominance and assert hegemonic masculinity. It is striking how elaborate the fantasies of potential domination can be. Larry describes an imaginary fight scene with a group of three men; Gil wishes he were armed when a group of young men, who did not physically threaten him, walked by him in a parking garage; and Jeff uses a gun to essentially recapture a kung fu warrior fantasy.

Though these men say that their guns are simply tools to prevent victimization, they are also symbols of virility, and, thus carrying one impacts how they see themselves as men. This helps to explain the appeal of concealed firearms for some men: not that they are communicating to others their ability to dominate them, but that they are reassuring themselves that they will "not be a victim." Gil makes this clear when he says, "You know, none of us want to be victims. [It's] not that any of us are cowboys or going out there looking for a fight, but nobody wants to be a victim." Rather than serving as tools of aggression, for these men, having a concealed gun means that they will never have to "scream like a little girl." The gun functions as a totem of masculinity, giving them calm assurance that they can defend themselves against attack—despite their aging bodies.

Dangerous Neighborhoods

When I asked the men I interviewed how they make decisions about whether or not to carry a gun, eleven said they carry a gun wherever it is legally allowed and nine said they make decisions based on where they are going. For example, they will carry a firearm if they go somewhere they have never been; if they are traveling out of town; or if they go to a part of town with a reputation for being dangerous. "Bad parts of town" were always marked as areas with high poverty and often, though not always explicitly, as areas that are predominantly Black or Latino. When I asked Adam if he regularly carries a gun he said no, because he now lives in a safe city. Adam sets this in contrast to his experiences growing up in Houston, parts of which he describes as a "war zone." Adam says he always carries a gun when he travels to Houston because, unlike his current city, where the "bad parts of town" are relegated to one side of the city and the "nice" parts of town are on the other, Houston isn't "zoned." Adam says his friends who live in Houston carry their firearms daily because

> the gas station right down the street is totally different than the gas station one mile down the road. I mean you can have the one that's right by your house is fine and you've got no problems, there's no people hanging out there drinkin' beer and acting crazy. But you decide not to go to that one and you just drive down the street and all of a sudden it's like, you know, Compton down there.

Adam invokes "Compton" as a euphemism for race; it is code for a space he sees as predominantly poor, Black, dangerous, and scary. Like many white Americans, Adam links blackness with criminality (Feagin 2010). Because of Houston's uncertain racial landscape, he feels compelled to be armed.

Respondents' perceptions of danger were often loaded with similarly racialized notions of criminality and vulnerability. For example, Jack, a 46-year-old licensing instructor, blames Hurricane Katrina evacuees from New Orleans for what he perceives to be a steady increase in violent crime in

Texas. Jack carries at least one gun on him whenever possible. When I asked him if he has ever had the occasion to use his gun, he told the following story:

> I got lost and ended up in a predominantly Black neighborhood. [A man in] an old beat-up truck in front of me was driving around and he stops . . . in the middle of the road where I couldn't go around him. And he gets out, so I pulled my weapon out and put it right where he couldn't see it just below the door. Rolled my window down about an inch and he comes back and he asks me some stupid question about how to get to the freeway and I told him, "Don't know, can't help you." And he's like, "Thanks, God bless you," or something, gets in his truck and leaves. I don't know if that was legitimate or what, but I wasn't going to take the chance.

Explanations of threat that link perceived criminality to Black men create a "racialized fear of crime" (Davis 2007) whereby feelings of vulnerability are heightened when whites make contact with the racial Other. Jack is able to use his firearm to quell this sense of vulnerability, and to protect himself should the need arise.

When I asked Adam if he has ever had a situation where he thought he might have to use his gun, he says, "Let's say you pull up to a convenience store and there's some certain people outside that make you feel a little nervous. Then you've got your gun there." Later Adam elaborates:

> You pull up and there's, you know, three guys out there, gangster guys, just kind of hanging around at midnight in front of the convenience store. . . . So you make your decision: Do I leave? Or do I protect myself? . . . So when it's just you outside and them outside, you know, I would just kind of grab my gun and stick it in the back of my pants and pump my gas and be on my way.

The use of the term "gangster" coupled with his previous comment about "Compton" suggests that Adam is describing encountering a group of Black men. He feels threatened by this group, unsure if he should get out of his car. By putting a gun in his waistband, he does not let his fear of the criminal other restrict his behavior; he does not shirk from whatever conflict he imagines might ensue.

Another example comes from Mike, 36. We met at a café in a predominantly white, upper-middle-class part of town. Despite claims that he carries wherever he can, Mike was not carrying a firearm when we met; he had left it in his truck. As we talked he said, "I don't feel strange sitting here and not having it. I think if I did have it, it would probably make me a little bit more aware of my surroundings." I was taken aback by this comment, having assumed that the power a firearm bestows would allow a person to relax. Mike explains:

> When I have it with me, I'm paying a lot more attention to people . . . somebody walks in, looks like they're lookin' for trouble. Somebody that doesn't fit. You know, not to play the, uh, race card or anything, but there aren't too many Black people around here. So if you . . . walk into a place and you don't really fit in. Like if I went over to [a predominantly Black part of town] and walked into Martin Luther King, Jr., church on Sunday morning, I'm betting I'd be one of the few white guys. And people would probably look at me and go, well what's this white guy doing here?

Mike's explanation of how race factors into the way he imagines risk is cloaked in discourses of "color blind racism" (Bonilla-Silva 2001). Equating the experience of a Black man's being seen as a potential criminal to Mike's being seen as oddly out of place in a church minimizes racial inequality. Yet race plays a profound role in how Mike imagines risk. In this predominantly white space, Mike feels safe enough to not bother bringing his gun in; however, he suggests this safety could be disrupted if a Black man were to come into the store.

Three of the four men in my sample who identified as Hispanic/ Latino did not differ dramatically from the rest of the sample in how they talked about the link between race and crime. For instance, Joseph, a 45-year-old license holder who identifies as white on forms, but says that his father is Hispanic, explained that he used his "Hispanic appearance" to intimidate others when he lived in a high-crime neighborhood that was predominantly Black and Latino. He said that looking "pure white" would have made him a target. The only person in the sample who resisted racist constructions of threat was George, a 44-year-old licensing instructor who is Mexican American and lives in a predominantly Hispanic city along the Texas–Mexico border. He says that he grew up with guys who are now involved in the drug trade and that he tries to not have a "black and white" view of who is a threat. George says, "Some of the nicest guys I know . . . have tattoos from [head to toe]. Some of the meanest guys I know are the stereotypical middle-aged . . . white male professionals [who are] hot-headed, hot-tempered, on edge, on the defense all the time." Of the 20 men I interviewed, George was the only one who did not rely on a racialized fear of crime. It is significant that George was the only person interviewed who was reared and currently lives in a region that is not predominantly white/Anglo. It seems his perceptions of criminality were not developed according to the white racial frame (Feagin 2010).

R. W. Connell (1995, 80) writes that "in a white supremacist context, Black masculinities play symbolic roles for white gender construction." In this case, many of the men I interviewed identified Black men and areas of town marked as poor and predominantly Black or Latino as threatening. Indeed, race is conflated with social class, such that Mike sees it as impossible that a Black man would have a legitimate reason to enter a café in a wealthy part of town.

It is significant that in the previous descriptions of fear-inducing events none of the respondents describe being physically confronted or overtly threatened by the Black men they encounter. Instead, they report that simply coming into contact with Black men induces a desire to be armed. The men I interviewed project violence, aggression, and criminal intent onto the Black men they encounter. These characterizations are a form of "gendered racism" that are used both to "validate inequality [and] also to contrast Black masculinity with white masculinity as a hegemonic ideal" (Harvey-Wingfield 2007, 198). The men I interviewed construct their sense of masculinity in contradistinction to what Black masculinity represents to them: They presume the men they see are criminals, thus they are armed in defense. They imagine the men they see will be violent; thus they are prepared to respond. Whiteness is critical to these dynamics not because these men see it as an evident marker of status, but because (to them) whiteness signifies nothing at all.

Discussion

Concealed handguns, by definition, are not visible to others. Moreover, the vast majority of license holders will never fire their guns in public. Despite this, concealed handguns prove profoundly meaningful in the reproduction of hegemonic masculinity. For some of the men I interviewed, carrying a concealed gun in public allows them to position themselves as defenders of their families, and as embodiments of the American virtues of self-reliance, strength, and courage (Connell 1995; Melzer 2009; O'Neill 2007). Having a license is critical to how this operates because only people without a criminal record can obtain one, and only with a license can someone carry a gun legally. Being law-abiding is the lynchpin that distinguishes "good guys" from "bad guys" (Gibson 1994).

Ironically, although men say they need a gun to defend their families, they are often away from their wives and children and thus would be unable to carry out their role of the defender should the need arise. Second, men who say it's their job to defend their families because they are physically stronger than their wives are among the same people who say that guns are needed for self-defense because as "equalizers" they reduce whatever physical differences might exist between a perpetrator of violent crime and themselves. Third, these men say that they wish their wives would be armed (a claim that is not surprising given that the threat of ever-present victimization is precisely what justifies the need for a concealed handgun license). These contradictions suggest that concealed handguns function as props for doing masculinity by asserting the "father/husband as protector." The consequence is that it heightens the extent to which women are presumed to be vulnerable, in need of protection by the men in their lives (Hollander 2001). Having a concealed handgun license is a material practice that sustains their belief in essential gender differences by enabling men to fantasize about being the defenders of their families.

The men I interviewed also have elaborate fantasies of potential violence at the hands of other men. As they age, some begin to see themselves as less capable of self-defense. Because the body's capacity for aggression and violence is central to what it means to be masculine (Crawley, Foley, and Shehan 2008), some older men feel that their masculinity is diminished. According to Kimmel (2010, 120), this gets to the root of men's fear, a fear that others might "unmask us, emasculate us, reveal to us and the world that we do not measure up, that we are not real men." With a concealed handgun, the capacity for aggression and domination is restored. As Jeff explained, this can boost a man's sense of confidence, as he is able to regain access to the muscular version of masculinity and the capacity to dominate other, weaker men that is celebrated in American culture (Gibson 1994; Jeffords 1994).

No figure makes these men feel more physically vulnerable than the specter of the Black criminal. They ascribe a violent masculinity to men of color, and construct a sense of self in contradistinction. Because they assume that the Black men they encounter are potentially armed and dangerous, they want to carry a concealed handgun. Having a gun allows them to maintain a confidence that they are capable of responding to any threat, like Adam at the gas station: Should he get out of his car or drive off? Will he stand up to the threat or shirk from it?

It has been established that gang members—and other marginal men—can brandish and shoot guns to assert control and dominance over other men (Stretesky and Pogrebin 2007). The men I interviewed use guns in a similar way, but with profoundly different implications. When gang members use guns, they may be empowered in that instance by their masculine performance of domination, but it is also a sign of their marginalization. Indeed, the men Stretesky and Pogrebin (2007) interviewed were all incarcerated. In contrast, the men I interviewed are among the most privileged in society and already have access to culturally celebrated versions of masculinity: Most of them are white and middle- or upper-middle class, and all of them are heterosexual. Their state-issued license to carry a concealed handgun, a license that is expensive and available only to those who can afford it and who are not legally restricted, gives them an added level of privilege: It gives them a symbol around which they construct both an empowered and culturally celebrated masculinity.

This work extends the literature on guns and masculinity by illustrating how dynamics between masculinities of privilege and marginalization lead to qualitatively different meanings for the same object. Criminals use guns to do masculinity (Kimmel and Mahler 2003; Stretesky and Pogrebin 2007), and so do law-abiding men. Unlike boys who shoot their classmates in a desperate attempt to be seen as "manly" (Kimmel and Mahler 2003), or gang members, for whom masculine bravado is a valuable currency (Stretesky and Pogrebin 2007), the men I interviewed gain access to aspects of masculinity that are celebrated at the regional level of culture by media and the gun lobby (Connell 1995; Gibson 1994; Jeffords 1994; Melzer 2009; O'Neill 2007). That these men are able to tap into these discourses—to cast themselves in the light of versions of masculinity celebrated by dominant culture—reveals the extent to which they are privileged. By contrast, Black and Latino men are assigned masculine traits of dominance, aggression, and violence, but this happens in a cultural context in which their skin color makes them suspect and they are assumed to be criminals (Collins 2006).

The implications of this study suggest the need for further research. The literature on hegemonic masculinity would benefit from closer attention to how dominant culture shapes and frames the discursive strategies that men have available to construct masculinities. One topic that should be addressed is the experiences of men of color who have concealed handgun licenses. How do Black men who are legally armed deal with the assumption that they are criminals? To fully understand how gender shapes the experience of carrying a concealed handgun, the case of women license holders must be considered. Does carrying a concealed handgun give women access to dominance in the way that it does for men? I am currently conducting interviews with women who have a concealed handgun license to understand how they explain their interest in carrying a firearm in public.

The men that I interviewed explain their desire for concealed firearms in light of versions of masculinity that are celebrated in culture: They want to be good fathers and husbands, they want to be able to fight back if attacked, and, unlike dangerous criminals, they are interested only in self-defense. Thus, their concealed handguns signify to them that they are "good guys," men who will use violence if necessary, but only to fight "bad guys."

Acknowledgment

I would like to thank Dana Britton for her guidance with an earlier version of this article and the anonymous reviewers of Gender & Society for their helpful comments. I also owe a debt of gratitude to Christine Williams for her tireless efforts in helping me to clarify my ideas and improve my writing.

Note

1. It is impossible to determine the exact number of defensive gun uses (DGUs) that occur in a given year, and estimates vary from 600,000 to 2.5 million (Cook and Ludwig 1998). While Kleck and Gertz (1995, 180) argue that there is "little legitimate scholarly reason to doubt that defensive gun use is very common in the U.S.," many scholars provide evidence that does just that. For example, Cook and Ludwig (1998) argue that reported incidents of DGUs are wracked with methodological problems that lead to highly inflated numbers. McDowall, Loftin, and Presser (2000) argue that reported DGUs often involve scenarios where the defender had no way of knowing the motives of their alleged offenders and so could not reasonably argue that their gun stopped a criminal act. Though the overall number is debated, what is known is that the vast majority of DGUs happen at home, while DGUs in public, the type that CHLs are intended for, are rare (Cook and Ludwig 1998).

References

Bonilla-Silva, Eduardo. 2001. *White supremacy and racism in the post civil rights era*. Boulder, CO: Rienner.

Britton, Dana. 2011. *The gender of crime*. Lanham, MD: AltaMira Press.

Carroll, Joseph. 2005. Gun ownership and use in America. *Gallup Poll*, 22 November.

Collins, Patricia H. 2006. A telling difference: Dominance strength and Black masculinities. In *Progressive black masculinities?*, edited by A. Mutua. New York: Routledge.

Connell, R. W. 1995. *Masculinities*. Cambridge, UK: Polity.

Connell, R. W., and J. W. Messerschmidt. 2005. Hegemonic masculinity: Rethinking the concept. *Gender & Society* 19:829–59.

Cook, Phillip J., and Jens Ludwig. 1998. Defensive gun uses: New evidence from a national survey. *Journal of Quantitative Criminology* 14:111–31.

Crawley, Sara L., Lara J. Foley, and Constance L. Shehan. 2008. *Gendering bodies*. Lanham, MD: Rowman and Littlefield.

Davis, Angela. 2007. In *Race, ethnicity, and gender: Selected readings*, edited by Joseph F. Healey and Eileen O'Brien. Thousand Oaks, CA: Pine Forge Press.

Feagin, J. R. 2010. *Racist America: Roots, current realities, and future reparations*. Hoboken, NJ: Taylor & Francis.

Gibson, James. 1994. *Warrior dreams: Paramilitary culture in post-Vietnam America*. New York: Hill and Wang.

Harvey-Wingfield, Adia. 2007. The modern mammy and the angry Black man: African American professionals' experience with gendered racism in the workplace. *Race, Gender, and Class* 14:196–212.

Hollander, Jocelyn. 2001. Vulnerability and dangerousness: The construction of gender through conversations about violence. *Gender & Society* 15:83–109.

Jeffords, Susan. 1994. *Hard bodies: Hollywood masculinity in the Reagan era*. New Brunswick, NJ: Rutgers University Press.

Jones, Jeffrey M. 2005. Public wary about broad concealed firearm privileges. *Gallup Poll*, 14 June.

Kimmel, Michael. 1996. *Manhood in America: A cultural history*. New York: Free Press.

Kimmel, Michael. 2010. Masculinity as homophobia: Fear, shame, and silence in the construction of gender identity. In *Privilege*, edited by Michael S. Kimmel and Abby L. Ferber. Boulder, CO: Westview.

Kimmel, M., and M. Mahler. 2003. Adolescent masculinity, homophobia, and violence: Random school shootings, 1982–2001. *American Behavioral Scientist* 46:1439–58.

Kleck, Gary, and Marc Gertz. 1995. Armed resistance to crime: The prevalence and nature of self-defense with a gun. *Journal of Criminal Law and Criminology* 86:150–87.

McDowall, David, Colin Loftin, and Stanley Presser. 2000. Measuring civilian defensive firearm use: A methodological experiment. *Journal of Quantitative Criminology* 16:1–19.

Melzer, Scott. 2009. *Gun crusaders: The NRA's culture war*. New York: New York University Press.

Messerschmidt, James W. 1993. *Masculinities and crime: Critique and reconceptualization of theory*. Lanham, MD: Rowman and Littlefield.

Messerschmidt, James W. 2000. *Nine lives: Adolescent masculinities, the body, and violence*. Boulder, CO: Westview Press.

Messner, Michael. 1992. *Power at play: Sports and the problem of masculinity*. Boston: Beacon Press.

O'Neill, Kevin Lewis. 2007. Armed citizens and the stories they tell: The National Rifle Association's achievement of terror and masculinity. *Men and Masculinities* 9:457–75.

Stange, Mary Zeiss, and Carol K. Oyster. 2000. *Gun women: Firearms and feminism in contemporary America*. New York: New York University Press.

Stretesky, P.B., and M.R. Pogrebin. 2007. Gang-related gun violence: Socialization, identity, and self. *Journal of Contemporary Ethnography* 36:85–114.

Stuckey, Mike. 2010. Record numbers now licensed to pack heat. Msnbc.com, April 24, 2010, http://www.msnbc.msn.com/id/34714389/ns/us_news-life.

Texas Department of Public Safety. 1995–2010a. Demographic information by race/sex: License applications: Issued (calendar year).

Texas Department of Public Safety. 1995–2010b. Active license counts (calendar year).

Perceptions of Domestic Violence in Lesbian Relationships: Stereotypes and Gender Role Expectations

BETSI LITTLE AND CHERYL TERRANCE

During the past two decades, the issue of domestic violence has come to be recognized as a serious social issue (Burke, Jordan, & Owen, 2002; Pitt, 2000; Seelau & Seelau, 2005). Although researchers have investigated perceptions of battered women in general, little research has examined perceptions of lesbians in violent relationships (Burke et al., 2002; Letellier, 1994; Seelau & Seelau, 2005). Challenging assumptions that domestic violence is primarily a heterosexual issue, studies suggest that domestic violence within lesbian relationships occurs nearly as often as it does in heterosexual relationships (Koss, 1990; Letellier, 1994; Pitt, 2000; Turell, 2000). Despite this, when compared to violence against women in heterosexual relationships, violence within lesbian relationships is less likely to be reported by victims to authorities, less likely to be prosecuted within the

Betsi Little and Cheryl Terrance, "Perceptions of Domestic Violence in Lesbian Relationships: Stereotypes and Gender Role Expectations." *Journal of Homosexuality* 57 (March 2010): 429–40.

legal system, and generally disregarded by helping agencies as well as the general public (Connolly, Huzurbazar, & Routh-McGee, 2000; Renzetti, 1989; Turell, 2000).

The dismissal of lesbian violence may in part stem from gender-based stereotypes that situate the roles of men and women in oppositional terms and support heterosexual-based assumptions concerning intimate relationships (Balsam, 2001). How gender and heterosexist-based stereotypes impact claims of victimization advanced by lesbian victims is unclear. However, to date, little research has examined how victims of domestic violence within lesbian partnerships are perceived. In light of preexisting norms dictating appropriate female behaviors and stereotypical beliefs concerning lesbians, this study examined attributions of blame and responsibility for violence within a lesbian relationship.

Prevalence

Establishing rates of lesbian domestic violence is difficult due to negative attitudes that lead to the dismissal of claims as well as differing data collection methods and operational definitions of domestic violence (Pitt & Dolan-Soto, 2001). Because domestic violence can include physical, emotional, and economic control as well as the threat of being "outed," rates reported from surveys of lesbians in the context of domestic violence vary from 9% to 60% (Bologna, Waterman, & Dawson, 1987; Brand & Kidd, 1986; Lie & Gentlewarrier, 1991; Lie, Schilit, Bush, Montagne & Reyes, 1991; Lockhart, White, Causby, & Isaac, 1994; Loulon, 1987; Waldner-Haugrud, Gratch, & Magruder, 1997; Wood, 1987). Further, because there is lack of acknowledgment that lesbian domestic violence does occur within relationships, in part due to a lack of reporting within the lesbian community (Turell, 2000), official reports may underrepresent the prevalence of violence within lesbian relationships.

According to the most recent statistics (Bureau of Justice, 2003) gathered from local, state, and federal law enforcement agencies as well as social service agencies, 7% of women (3.9 million) are physically abused by their partners and 37% (20.7 million) are verbally or emotionally abused (Burke et al., 2002). Considering even the lowest reported prevalence rate within lesbian relationships, lesbian battering appears to present as much of a pervasive problem as it is within heterosexual couples (e.g., Burke & Follingstad, 1999; Letellier, 1994; Pitt, 2000, Renzetti, 1989, 1999; Turell, 2000). Despite the prevalence of violence within lesbian relationships, the issue of lesbian battering is often dismissed, which may in part reflect expectations that construct "legitimate" victim status. Such expectations may stem from gender-based stereotypes concerning men and women's roles within society.

Gender-Based Stereotypes

Gender-based stereotypes support expectations regarding "appropriate" behavior for men and women (Hilton & von Hipple, 1990, 1996). Society constructs gender in oppositional terms: what men are, women are not, and vice versa (Renzetti, 1999). It is women's "nature" to be passive and dependent, while men are most often described as assertive (Hegstrom & McCarl-Nielsen, 2002). Indeed, while men are socialized to be competitive, assertive, autonomous, self-confident, and to have the tendency to not express intimate feelings (Maccoby, 1990), women on the other hand, are socialized to be nurturing, warm, and emotionally expressive (Noller, 1993). Such stereotypes in turn may support expectations regarding victims of domestic violence; that is, stereotypes delineating the roles of men and women are reflected within characteristics typically ascribed to domestic violence victims and offenders. Thus, within the context of heterosexual domestic violence, women are perceived as the "legitimate" recipients of abuse and men are seen as the perpetrators (Terrance & Parisien, 2006). Gender-based stereotypes extend beyond individuals and further serve to define intimate relationships within heterosexual terms (Corley & Pollack, 1996). Specifically, intimate relationships become equated with male-female relationships (Corley & Pollack, 1996; Kite & Deaux, 1987; Storms, Stivers, Lambers, & Hill, 1981; Viss & Burn, 1992).

Interestingly, these stereotypes are inversely associated with one's sexual orientation. While heterosexual women are described as feminine, lesbians are perceived as masculine. Because of this, beliefs about gay men and lesbians represent a special case of gender stereotypes (Storms et al., 1981; Viss & Burn, 1992). The association between one's gender and sexual orientation can be so robust that, when it has been demonstrated to be untrue, alternate explanations for the inconsistency are generated by the observer (Merrill, 1996; Perilla, Frndak, Lillard, & East, 2003; Storms et al., 1981). Further, the perceived association between gender and sexual orientation supports the contention that gender-based stereotypes support expectations that prescribe partner preference. As Ponse (1978) notes, gender and sexual partner choice are presumed to be related in a highly consistent manner such that, given one of the elements, the rest are expected to follow.

Considered within the context of lesbian partnerships, a lesbian couple would be perceived as having one masculine and one feminine partner that adopt the dominant and submissive gender-based stereotypes, respectively, in the relationship (Peplau, 1983; Tripp, 1975). This assignment of masculine and feminine roles in a lesbian relationship is not necessarily accurate (Cardell, Finn, & Marecek, 1981; Kurdek, 1988). Indeed, lesbian couples are self-reportedly less gender-typed when compared to heterosexual couples (Cardell et al., 1981). However, observers may not have firsthand knowledge of what constitutes a lesbian couple and, therefore, rely on heterosexual-based assumptions concerning intimate relationships. The reliance on assumptions regarding homosexual relationships has implications for perceptions of domestic violence allegations within lesbian partnerships. Indeed, perceptions of what it means to be a "legitimate" victim can directly contradict the stereotype of what it means to be a lesbian.

Method

Participants

Two hundred eighty-seven undergraduate psychology students (men = 101; women = 186; self-described heterosexuals = 281, self-described homosexuals = 4, self described other = 1, no sexual orientation given = 1) were drawn from among undergraduate psychology students at a Midwestern university and ranged in age from 18 to 28 years old ($M = 19.66$, $SD = 1.79$). Participants' ethnic and racial background was not assessed; however, they were drawn from a student body population where the majority (87%) identifies as White/non-Hispanic American. After gathering consent forms prior to the commencement of the study, no other identifying information was gathered. Participants volunteered to participate in exchange for extra course credit that was claimed by credit slip handed to the student to be redeemed in the appropriate courses. The study was conducted in accord with American Psychological Association standards on ethical treatment of participants, and institutional review board (IRB) of the University of North Dakota requirements.

Materials

Vignettes

The scenario was adapted from the vignette used in Harris and Cooke's (1994) study. Briefly, this vignette described a situation in which the police were called to investigate a domestic disturbance between two women. Upon arriving at the location of the reported dispute, which appeared to have ended, the officers found the victim on the living room couch bleeding and with a black eye.

The alleged victim reported returning home from work later than usual. As she was late, she decided to prepare leftovers from the previous night for dinner and then sat down to watch the news. When the alleged offender returned from home 10 minutes later to find the victim watching television, a verbal argument ensued. The victim then went into the kitchen to prepare dinner. The offender followed the victim into the kitchen, grabbed her by the arm and slapped her, knocking her to the floor, and kicked her several times. The offender subsequently left the house. Upon her return, she was informed by one of the officers that her partner was charging her with assault.

For each level of the condition, the names of the victim and offender in the vignette remain unchanged; however, the occupation of each reflected the gender characteristics as designated by the condition.

Photographs

Participants viewed two photographs in Microsoft PowerPoint format, one of the alleged victim and one of the accused batterer. The photos, consisting of close-cropped, head shots of White/non-Hispanic women apparently taken in someone's home, were presented together, side by side, for the duration of the study. Target pictures were selected on the basis of a pilot study that combined extreme scores on an attribute measure derived from Deaux and Lewis (1983) that assessed traits (e.g., independent, emotional), roles (e.g., financial provider, takes care of home) and occupation (e.g., engineer, nurse worker, telephone operator). Attractiveness and likeability were assessed during the selection of the photographs and failed to differ. The two most extreme pictures, defined as masculine or feminine in appearance, were selected on the basis.

Perception of Violence Questionnaire

Participants were asked to respond to a questionnaire using a 5-point Likert scale with endpoints defined by the wording of the item (i.e., not serious-very serious; not violent-very violent). The 20 items on this questionnaire tapped into seven measures reflecting perceptions of the incident.

- *Victim blameworthiness.* Evaluation of victim blameworthiness consisted of participants' responses on a single item, assessing the degree to which the victim should be blamed for the incident of abuse. Higher scores reflect more blame assigned to the victim.
- *Accused blameworthiness.* Evaluation of the accused blameworthiness consisted of participants' responses to a single item, assessing the degree to which the accused should be blamed for the incident of abuse. Higher scores reflect more blame assigned to the accused.
- *Plausibility of the claim.* Ratings of the extent to which participants perceived the incident as plausible consisted of participants' mean response on two items (r = .55) evaluating the extent to which they perceive the incident as probable and realistic. Higher scores reflect higher perception of the incident seen as plausible.
- *Dangerousness of the situation.* Ratings of the extent to which participants perceived the incident as dangerous, consisted of participants' mean response on four items ($\propto$ = 0.75), assessing how serious, severe, and violent the incident was and the likelihood that the respondent would have contacted the police if they themselves witnessed the incident. Higher scores reflected higher perception of dangerousness.

Procedure

In accordance with IRB requirements, participants' informed consent was sought both verbally and in writing. Participants who consented to participate were randomly assigned to one of four domestic violence batterer-victim conditions that varied the appearance (masculine vs. feminine) of both the batterer-victim: masculine victim-feminine batterer, masculine victim-masculine batterer, feminine victim-feminine batterer, and feminine victim-masculine batterer. After reading the police report regarding a domestic violence incident, participants were provided with photos of the victim and asked to fill out the Perceptions of Violence questionnaire. When participants had completed the questionnaire, they were debriefed orally as well as in written format, thanked for their time and dismissed.

Results

Perceptions of Violence Questionnaire

Dangerousness of the Situation

A 2 (Victim Appearance: Masculine vs. Feminine × 2 (Offender Appearance: Masculine vs. Feminine) × 2 (Participant Gender) analysis of variance (ANOVA) revealed a significant main effect for gender, $F(1,229) = 18.93$, $p < .05$, such that women ($M = 3.67$, $SD = .72$) rated the incident as more dangerous than men ($M = 3.29$, $SD = .79$).

Plausibility of the Claim

A 2 (Victim) × 2 (Offender) × 2 (Participant Gender) ANOVA revealed a three-way interaction between victim appearance, offender appearance, and gender, $F(1,269) = 13.12$, $p < .05$. This interaction was broken down into two-way interactions between victim appearance and offender appearance as a function of gender. Only the two-way interaction for women attained significance, $F(1, 150) = 10.29$, $p < .05$.

Simple main effects of offender appearance at each level of victim appearance revealed significance for both the masculine-appearing victim, $F(1, 150) = 6.83$, $p < .05$, and the feminine-appearing victim, $F(1, 150) = 5.68$, $p < .05$. Female participants viewed the masculine-appearing victim as having a more plausible claim when the offender was depicted as feminine ($M = 3.80$, $SD = .73$) than when the offender was depicted as masculine ($M = 3.22$, $SD = 1.10$). Conversely, female participants rated the feminine-appearing victim as having a more plausible claim when the offender was depicted as masculine ($M = 3.93$, $SD = 1.03$) than when the offender was depicted as feminine ($M = 3.36$, $SD = 1.13$).

Victim Blame

A 2 (Victim Appearance) × 2 (Offender Appearance) × 2 (Participant Gender) ANOVA revealed a significant main effect for victim, $F(1,266) = 5.41$, $p < .05$. The victim who appeared more feminine ($M = .77$, $SD = 1.26$) was blamed less than the victim who was portrayed as more masculine in appearance ($M = 1.16$, $SD = 1.28$).

Accused Blameworthiness

A 2 (Victim Appearance) × 2 (Offender Appearance) × 2 (Participant Gender) ANOVA revealed an interaction of offender appearance by gender, $F(1,276) = 6.23$, $p < .05$. Simple main effect of offender appearance at each level of gender revealed significance only for female participants, $F(1,181) = 4.55$, $p < .05$. The feminine-appearing offender ($M = 4.18$, $SD = .99$) was rated by female participants as more to blame than the masculine-appearing offender ($M = 4.04$, $SD = 1.14$), $t(154) = 1.34$, $p < .05$.

Discussion

The purpose of the present study was to evaluate the impact of gender and heterosexist-based stereotypes within the context of domestic violence occurring within a lesbian relationship. More specifically, this study examined the extent to which the victim would be blamed for her own abuse when she was portrayed as either masculine or feminine in appearance and the degree to which these perceptions would be influenced by the masculine or feminine appearance of the offender.

Overall, results suggest that perceptions of victims of domestic violence are influenced by pervasive expectations about behaviors and characteristics (i.e., feminine) of lesbians in relationships. However, these beliefs appear to be mitigated not only by the gendered appearance of the victim and offender, but the gender of the observer as well.

In regards to level of blame, both men and women rated the feminine-appearing victim as less blameworthy than the masculine-depicted victim. This result is not surprising in light of gender-based stereotypes that support that men, and in turn, masculine individuals, are supposed to be stronger and more aggressive than women or feminine individuals (Corley & Pollack, 1996). Consequently, masculine individuals are perceived as being able to protect themselves in an attack. It could be that the masculine-appearing victim was violating this stereotype and, therefore, was perceived as more blameworthy.

One of the most consistent findings in the present study concerned the heterosexual-based assumptions that female participants seem to hold. The characterization of the victim in combination with the physical appearance of her abuser had an impact on how she was perceived. This was demonstrated most significantly when considering the plausibility of the claim. Surprisingly, the masculine victim was viewed as having a more plausible claim by women when the offender was depicted as feminine. It may be the case that female participants perceived the feminine-appearing offender as violating gender-based norms prescribing appropriate (i.e., nonaggressive) behavior for women to a greater degree than the masculine appearing offender and were thus more sympathetic to the claims advanced by the masculine victim.

At the same time, however, female participants viewed the feminine-appearing victim as having a more legitimate claim when the offender was depicted as masculine. Again, as gender-based stereotypes characterize intimate relationships in heterosexist terms, such that the passive role is assigned to the women and the aggressive role is assigned to men, it may be the case that this scenario was viewed by female participants as most consistent with gender-based norms. Overall, women viewed the victim as having a more legitimate claim when the offender was depicted as masculine.

Beliefs such as these serve only to reduce the legitimacy of any victim's claim of abuse in a relationship that does not fit this ideal. Additionally, it was only women endorsing this heterosexist ideology in regard to lesbian relationships. Indeed, men failed to differ on claims of victimization despite the gender depiction of the victim or the offender. In comparison to women, men rated all claims as less plausible and less dangerous. This suggests a dismissal of claims and a perception of the abuse as mutual combat. Future research examining the impact of adherence to gender-role ideology would be helpful in terms of delineating the impact of attitudes toward women and perceptions of violence within lesbian relationships.

Finally, victim and offender appearance were not the only contributing factors and perceptions of lesbian domestic violence. Gender also played an important role in the degree to which the offender was blamed for the incident. Specifically, female participants blamed the feminine depicted offender more for the incident than the masculine depicted offender. Blaming the feminine appearing offender more may be again, due to the fact that she was perceived as violating the traditional gender-based expectations for women in general (i.e., by being aggressive). Indeed, previous research has found that women who are seen as aggressive are liked less and, therefore, blamed more for the abuse (Terrance & Parisien, 2006). Women may be especially sensitive to this belief and may resort to other justifications for the abuse when perpetrated by a characteristically feminine offender as opposed to a masculine offender. Among women, it may be that the justification for a masculine offender is that she is already perceived as aggressive and dominant. For a feminine-appearing offender, that justification does not work and, therefore, there must be something about the offender that makes her more blameworthy.

The perceived level of danger in this domestic violence scenario also varied as a function of participant gender. Female participants tended to rate the incident as more dangerous than male participants. This may in part be due to the more prevalent threat that women face in regards to becoming a victim of domestic violence (Pitt, 2000). It may be the case that, for women, the plight of the battered woman is more salient, whereas, the perceived threat of being a battered man is more remote. It may be then that women rate domestic violence as more serious irrespective of the appearance of the victim or offender.

Further exploration of factors that influence victim blame and perceptions of lesbian domestic violence would be helpful. A future study could evaluate participants' preexisting stereotypes of lesbians and beliefs about appropriate gender roles within a relationship. An additional direction for future research would be exploration of the perceptions of lesbian domestic violence within a community of gay and lesbian people. Although this study's participant pool consisted of mostly self-identified heterosexuals, it would be beneficial to study the community in which this violence occurs, the implication being that often times lesbians will seek out other lesbians and gay-friendly organizations for help. One cannot assume that these resources would be stereotype free.

As with any research, methodological limitations should be noted. The use of photos may be a confounding variable. Although measures were employed to help reduce effects (i.e., no significant differences in rating of attractiveness), there is no doubt that individual perceptions of attractiveness can play a role in perceptions of guilt (Efran, 1974; Stewart, 1980, 1985; Darby & Jeffers, 1988). Despite that the photographs were rated independently and not within the context of a lesbian domestic violence scenario, these photographs were not identical in features common to physical attractiveness, such as symmetry. These were photographs of real women, not computer generated, and, therefore, all confounds could not be eliminated, but none were found. Additional limitations stem from the demographic makeup of the sample. College-aged students from a predominantly White, Christian, Midwestern region limits the generalizablity of these results.

These limitations notwithstanding, this study found support for the contention that gender and heterosexual-based expectations can influence the standing of a victim of lesbian domestic violence. These stereotypes may have implications for the legitimacy with which claims of domestic violence advanced by lesbians are perceived. These expectations may undermine or distort claims of domestic violence advanced by lesbians, therefore limiting the resources that may be offered to lesbian victims of domestic violence.

References

Balsam, K. (2001). Nowhere to hide: Lesbian battering, homophobia, and minority stress. *Women and Therapy, 23*(3), 25–37.

Bologna, M., Waterman, C., & Dawson, L. (1987). Violence in gay male and lesbian relationships: Implications for practitioners and policy makers. Paper presented in July at the Third National Conference for Family Violence Researchers, Durham, NH.

Brand, P. A., & Kidd, A. H. (1986). Frequency of physical aggression in heterosexual and female homosexual dyads. *Psychological Reports, 59*, 1307–1313.

Bureau of Justice. (2003). Bureau of Justice Statistics Intimate Partner Violence, 1993–2001. In *Intimate Partner Violence*. Retrieved November 8, 2006, from http://www.ojp.usdoj.gov/bjs/abstract/ipv01.htm

Burke, L., & Follingstad, D. (1999). Violence in lesbian and gay relationships: Theory, prevalence, and correlational factors. *Clinical Psychology Review, 19*(5), 487–512.

Burke, T., Jordan, M., & Owen, S. A cross-national comparison of gay and lesbian domestic violence. *Journal of Contemporary Criminal Justice, 18*(3), 231–257.

Cardell, M., Finn, S., & Marecek, J. (1981). Sex-role identity, sex-role behavior and satisfaction in heterosexual, lesbian and gay male couples. *Psychology of Women Quarterly, 5*(3), 488–494.

Connolly, C., Huzurbazar, S., & Routh-McGee, T. (2000). Multiple parties in domestic violence situations and arrest. *Journal of Criminal Justice, 28*, 181–188.

Corley, T., & Pollack, R. (1996). Do changes in the stereotypic depiction of a lesbian couple affect heterosexuals' attitudes toward lesbianism? *Journal of Homosexuality, 32*(2), 1–17.

Darby, B., & Jeffers, D. (1988). The effects of defendant and juror attractiveness on simulated courtroom trial decisions. *Social Behavior and Personality, 16*(1), 39–50.

Deaux, K., & Lewis, L. (1983). Structure of gender stereotypes: Interrelationships among components and gender label. *Journal of Personality and Social Psychology, 46*(5), 991–1004.

Efran, M. (1974). The effect of physical appearance on the judgment of guilt, interpersonal attraction, and severity of recommended punishment in a simulated jury task. *Journal of Research in Personality, 8*(1), 45–54.

Harris, R., & Cooke, C. (1994). Attributions about spouse abuse: It matters who the batterers and victims are. *Sex Roles, 4*(7–8), 553–565.

Hegstrom, J., & McCarl-Nielsen, J. (2002). Gender and metaphor: Descriptions of familiar persons. *Discourse-Processes, 33*(3), 219–234.

Hilton, J., & von Hippel, W. (1990). The role of consistency in the judgement of stereotype-relevant behaviors. *Personality and Social Psychology Bulletin, 16*(3), 430–448.

Hilton, J., & von Hippel, W. (1996). Stereotypes. *Annual Review of Psychology, 47*, 237–71.

Kite, M., & Deaux, K. (1987). Gender belief systems: Homosexuality and the implicit inversion theory. *Psychology of Women Quarterly, 11*, 83–96.

Koss, M. P. (1990). The women's health research agenda: Violence against women. *American Psychologist, 45*, 374–380.

Kurdek, L. (1988). Perceived social support in gays and lesbians in cohabitating relationships. *Journal of Personality and Social Psychology, 54*(3), 504–509.

Letellier, P. (1994). Gay and bisexual male domestic violence victimization: Challenges to feminist theory and responses to violence. *Violence and Victims, 9*(2), 95–107.

Lie, G., & Gentlewarrier, S. (1991). Intimate violence in lesbian relationships: Discussion of survey findings and practice implications. *Journal of Social Service Research, 15*, 41–59.

Lie, G., Schlit, R., Bush, J., Montagne, M., & Reyes, L. (1991). Lesbians in currently aggressive relationships: How frequently do they report aggressive past relationships? *Violence and Victims, 6*, 121–135.

Lockhart, L., White, B., Causby, V., & Isaac, A. (1994). Letting out the secret: Violence in lesbian relationships. *Journal of Interpersonal Violence, 9*(4), 469–492.

Loulon, J. (1987). *Lesbian passion: Loving ourselves and each other*. San Francisco: Spinsters, Aunt Lute.

Maccoby, E. (1990). The role of gender identity and gender constancy in sex-differentiated development. *New Directions for Child Development, 47*, 5–20.

Merrill, G. (1996). Ruling the exceptions: Same-sex battering and domestic violence theory. In C. M. Renzetti & C. H. Miley (Eds.), *Violence in gay and lesbian domestic partnerships* (pp. 9–21). New York: Harrington Park Press/Haworth Press.

Noller, P. (1993). Gender and emotional communication in marriage: Different cultures or differential social power? *Journal of Language and Social Psychology, 12*(1–2), 132–152.

Peplau, L. (1983). Research on homosexual couples: An overview. *Journal of Homosexuality, 8*(2), 3–8.

Perilla, J., Frndak, K., Lillard, D., & East, C. (2003). A working analysis of women's use of violence in the context of learning, opportunity, and choice. *Violence Against Women, 9*(10), 10–45.

Pitt, E. (2000). Domestic violence in gay and lesbian relationships. *Journal of the Gay and Lesbian Medical Association, 4*(4), 195–196.

Pitt, E., & Dolan-Soto, D. (2001). Clinical considerations in working with victims of same-sex domestic violence. *Journal of the Gay and Lesbian Medical Association, 5*(4), 163–169.

Ponse, B. (1978). Identities in the lesbian world. *Dissertations Abstracts International, 38*(1-A), 504.

Renzetti, C. (1989). Building a second closet: Third-party responses to victims of lesbian partner abuse. *Family Relations, 38*, 157–163.

Renzetti, C. (1999). The challenge to feminism posed by women's use of violence in intimate relationships. In S. Lamb (Ed.), *New versions of victims: Feminists struggle with the concept*. New York: New York University Press.

Seelau, S., & Seelau, E. (2005). Gender-role stereotypes and perceptions of heterosexual, gay and lesbian domestic violence. *Journal of Family Violence, 20*(6), 363–371.

Stewart, J. (1980). Defendant's attractiveness as a factor in the outcome of criminal trials: An observational study. *Journal of Applied Social Psychology, 10*(4), 348–361.

Stewart, J. (1985). Appearance and punishment: The attraction-leniency effect in the courtroom. *Journal of Social Psychology, 125*(3), 373–378.

Storms, M., Stivers, M., Lambers, S., & Hill, G. (1981). Sexual scripts for women. *Sex Roles, 7*(7), 699–707.

Terrance, C., & Parisien, A. (2006). Evaluating claims of domestic violence: In search of a "legitimate" victim. Poster presented at the annual American Psychology Law Society Conference, St. Petersburg, FL.

Tripp, C. (1975). *The homosexual matrix*. New York. McGraw Hill.

Turell, S. (2000). A descriptive analysis of same-sex relationship violence for a diverse sample. *Journal of Family Violence, 15*(3), 281–293.

Viss, D., & Burn, S. (1992). Divergent perceptions of lesbians: A comparison of lesbian self-perceptions and heterosexual perceptions. *Journal of Social Psychology, 132*(2), 169–177.

Waldner-Haugrud, L., Gratch, L., & Magruder, B. (1997). Sexual coercion in gay/lesbian relationships: Descriptive and gender differences. *Violence and Victims, 12*, 87–98.

Wood, D. (1987). *A statistical analysis of dominance, possessiveness and violence in same-sex and opposite-sex dating relationships*. Unpublished master's thesis, University of Texas, Arlington, TX.

Are Female Stalkers More Violent Than Male Stalkers? Understanding Gender Differences in Stalking Violence Using Contemporary Sociocultural Beliefs

CARLEEN M. THOMPSON, SUSAN M. DENNISON, AND ANNA STEWART

Introduction

While there may be an assumption that males perpetrate more stalking violence than females (e.g., Mullen et al. 2000), there is limited evidence to support this. In fact, the majority of research indicates that males and females perpetrate comparable rates of stalking violence (e.g., Harmon et al. 1998, US forensic psychiatric referrals; Meloy and Boyd 2003, cross-national mental health and law enforcement cases; Thomas et al. 2008, Australian citizens) and there is some evidence that females perpetrate higher rates of moderate violence (Sinclair and Frieze 2002, US students). These findings are inconsistent with patriarchal views often applied to stalking violence. However, there is a co-existing belief among young western cultures that males should not be physically violent against females. Accordingly, violence perpetrated by males against females is viewed as more unacceptable and damaging than violence perpetrated by females against males. Although these attitudes have not been investigated in stalking research, it is possible that they are associated with comparable or elevated rates of female-perpetrated stalking violence.

This study constitutes the first attempt to examine gender differences in stalking violence using self-reports of moderate and severe physical violence and to explore how sociocultural beliefs may account for these differences/similarities. The present research will investigate these variables in a sample of Australian university students to contribute to a better understanding of the interplay between gender, sociocultural beliefs and stalking violence perpetration. Two overarching research questions will be investigated: (1) Do male and female relational stalkers perpetrate different rates of moderate and severe stalking violence? and (2) What sociocultural beliefs may account for these gender differences/similarities?

Stalking violence encompasses physical violence perpetrated by a stalker against their target or a third party during the course of stalking. Violence has been estimated to occur in between 30% and 40% of stalking cases (Mullen et al. 1999, Australian forensic psychiatric referrals; Roberts 2005, UK students; Rosenfeld and Harmon 2002, US forensic psychiatric referrals; Spitzberg and Cupach 2007, cross-national meta-analysis). These figures are alarming given that conservative estimates suggest that approximately one million women and nearly 400,000 men in the United States of America (USA) are victims of stalking each year (Tjaden and Thoennes 1998). If one third of these escalate to violence, almost half a million adults will be subjected to stalking violence annually in the USA alone. Although stalking that escalates to violence is not necessarily more frightening or damaging than non-violent stalking (Mullen et al. 2000), violence has been demonstrated to exacerbate

Carleen M. Thompson, Susan M. Dennison, and Anna Stewart, "Are Female Stalkers More Violent Than Male Stalkers? Understanding Gender Differences in Stalking Violence Using Contemporary Sociocultural Beliefs." *Sex Roles* 66 (2012): 351–65.

the psychological impact of stalking (Thomas et al. 2008, Australian citizens) in addition to causing physical injuries (e.g., Brewster 2002, US victims; Pathe and Mullen 1997, Australian victims). Consequently, it is important to understand how gender and sociocultural beliefs influence stalking violence perpetration to gain a better understanding of the nature and causes of this phenomenon.

Gender Differences in Stalking Violence

Although male gender is typically identified as a risk factor for violence (Mullen et al. 2000), there is currently little evidence to suggest that male *stalkers* perpetrate higher rates of violence than their female counterparts. Although a British study indicated that male stalkers perpetrated higher rates of severe violence than female stalkers (e.g., James and Farnham 2003), the majority of studies have reported no gender differences in the perpetration of stalking violence, including studies conducted in Australia (e.g., Purcell et al. 2001; Purcell et al. 2005; Thomas et al. 2008), USA (e.g., Harmon et al. 1998; Meloy et al. 2001; Rosenfeld and Harmon 2002; Schwartz-Watts and Morgan 1998) and cross-national samples (e.g., Meloy and Boyd 2003, USA, Australia & Canada). Moreover, one study conducted in the USA reported higher rates of violence by female stalkers than male stalkers (Dutton and Winstead 2006).

Furthermore, it is possible that those studies examining gender differences in stalking violence underestimate rates of stalking violence perpetrated by females to males. To date, this phenomenon has largely been examined in studies of self-identified victims (e.g., Purcell et al. 2005, Australian psychologists), forensic or clinical populations (e.g., James and Farnham 2003, UK forensic psychiatric referrals; Purcell et al. 2001, Australian forensic psychiatric referrals), or studies requiring targets to experience fear (e.g., Thomas et al. 2008, Australian citizens). These studies may not be representative of stalking behaviour perpetrated by females against males as males are less likely to (a) self-identify as stalking victims (see Tjaden et al. 2000, US community; Williams et al. 2007), (b) report stalking behaviour to the police (e.g., Bjerregaard 2002, US students; Haugaard and Seri 2000, US students; Hills and Taplin 1998, Australian community) and (c) experience and/or report feeling fearful (e.g., Budd et al. 2000, UK community; Davis et al. 2002, US community; Dietz and Martin 2007; Hills and Taplin 1998, Australian community). Accordingly, victim and legally-defined samples typically comprise disproportionate numbers of male stalkers (i.e., between 80%–90%., e.g., James and Farnham 2003, UK forensic psychiatric referrals; Thomas et al. 2008, Australian citizens) and females victims (i.e., 70–90%., e.g., Sheridan and Davies 2001, UK victims; Thomas et al. 2008, Australian citizens). This gender asymmetry has been upheld across victim and legally-defined samples in Australia (Purcell et al. 2002), USA (Tjaden and Thoennes 1998), UK (Budd et al. 2000) and Germany (Dressing et al. 2007). Analogous gender patterns have been identified in the intimate partner violence literature whereby males' intimate partner violence victimisation is thought to be underestimated for similar reasons (e.g., Cercone et al. 2005, US students; Fontes 2007; Sarantakos 1999, Australian review; Stewart and Maddren 1997, Australian police officers; Tjaden and Thoennes 2000, US community). Consequently, it is possible that female-to-male stalking behaviour may be underestimated in victim and legally-defined samples even when this behaviour escalates to violence. This may result in comparable rates of stalking violence or even higher rates of male-perpetrated stalking violence than female-perpetrated stalking violence in these samples. Studies investigating victim and legally-defined samples for stalking violence in Australian (e.g., Purcell et al. 2001), American (e.g., Rosenfeld and Harmon 2002) and cross-national samples (e.g., Meloy and Boyd 2003) have typically reported comparable rates of stalking violence. Additionally, higher rates of *male-perpetrated* stalking violence was reported in a British sample of stalkers referred to a forensic psychiatric service (James and Farnham 2003).

Studies investigating the frequency of *relational* stalking behaviours perpetrated by university students and community members that omit the fear requirement are not influenced by targets' responses or subjective experiences. These studies have reported gender symmetry in *stalking behaviour* across Australian (Dennison and Stewart 2006) and US samples (e.g., Dutton and Winstead 2006; Haugaard and Seri 2004; Sinclair and Frieze 2002; Spitzberg et al. 1998). The few studies that have investigated *stalking violence* using this methodology have utilised student samples from the USA and have reported either comparable (Sinclair and Frieze 2002) or higher rates of *female-perpetrated violence* (Dutton and Winstead 2006). Dutton and Winstead (2006) did not offer an explanation for why females may perpetrate more stalking violence and this research finding is yet to be replicated. Nevertheless, similar trends have been reported in intimate partner violence research whereby community and student surveys indicate that females perpetrate higher, or at least comparable, rates of intimate partner violence even though victim and legally-defined samples typically comprise disproportionate numbers of male perpetrators (see Archer 2000, cross-national meta-analysis; de Vries Robbe et al. 1996, Australian emergency patients; Headey et al. 1999, Australian community; Sarantakos 1999, review of Australian and international research; Stewart and Maddren 1997, Australian police officers). Therefore, it is possible that community and student perpetration surveys identify hidden rates of both female-perpetrated stalking and violence, at least in the context of relational stalking. This study examines gender differences in relational stalking violence perpetration in a sample of university students in an attempt to uncover these hidden rates.

Hidden gender differences in stalking violence may also be identified by differentiating the severity of the violence perpetrated. When Sinclair and Frieze (2002, US students) examined gender differences for mild aggression in relational stalking, no gender differences were identified. However, their classifications also incorporated non-physical violence such as verbal abuse, threats and property damage. This may have masked potential differences for females perpetrating more attempted (16%) and actual moderate *physical* violence (9%; i.e., slapping, a single punch, grabbing, pushing or shoving), than their male counterparts (2% and 2%, respectively). This is consistent with intimate partner violence research across Western countries that indicates that women perpetrate elevated rates of minor forms of intimate partner violence, such as slapping and pushing or shoving (e.g., Archer 2002, cross-national meta-analysis; Krahe and Berger 2005, German community; Williams and Frieze 2005b, US community). Given the overlaps between stalking and intimate partner violence (see Dennison and Thomson 2005; Melton 2007) and the trends identified in Sinclair and Frieze's (2002, US students) research, *it is possible that women perpetrate more moderate stalking violence than their male counterparts.*

Gender differences are more ambiguous for severe stalking violence. No gender differences were identified in a sample of university students from the USA (Sinclair and Frieze 2002). However, men were reported to perpetrate elevated rates of serious violence in a British sample of forensic psychiatric cases (James and Farnham 2003). Similar ambiguity has been reported in the intimate partner violence literature (Cercone et al. 2005, US students; de Vries Robbe et al. 1996, Australian emergency patients; Headey et al. 1999, Australian community; Krahe and Berger 2005, German community; Williams and Frieze 2005b, US community). This study investigates gender differences across both moderate and severe stalking violence to clarify ambiguous findings and thus contribute to a better understanding of this phenomenon.

This study examines gender differences in relational stalking violence perpetration in an Australian sample of university students. Although gender differences are examined in the Australian cultural context, there is no reason to believe that Australian findings will contradict research conducted in samples from the USA and the UK given the similarity of findings regarding (a) gender differences in stalking violence in studies of victim and legally defined samples (e.g., James and Farnham 2003, UK forensic psychiatric referrals; Purcell et al. 2001, Australian forensic psychiatric referrals; Rosenfeld and Harmon 2002, US forensic psychiatric referrals; Thomas et al. 2008, Australian citizens) (b) discrepancies in gender differences for stalking *behaviours* across samples sources and stalking definitions (Budd et al. 2000,

UK community members; Dennison and Stewart 2006, Australian students; Haugaard and Seri 2004, US students; Purcell et al. 2002, Australian citizens; Tjaden and Thoennes 1998, US community members) and (c) discrepancies in gender differences for intimate partner violence across samples sources (for example see Archer 2000, cross-national; Ferrante et al. 1996, Australia; Headey et al. 1999, Australia).

Sociocultural Beliefs

The finding that females perpetrate similar rates of stalking violence, and potentially higher rates of moderate violence, than their male counterparts is inconsistent with traditional views of violence as a male perpetrated phenomenon (see Herzog 2007). Researchers frequently present cultural patriarchal beliefs as a useful explanatory framework to understand stalking, intimate partner violence and more recently, stalking violence (e.g., Brewster 2003; Davis et al. 2000; Morewitz 2003). According to this explanatory framework stalking violence is a gendered phenomenon perpetrated by males against females as a means to exercise power and control over women (Brewster 2003). Here, violence against women is perceived to be justified in a range of contexts, including sustaining, establishing or reestablishing power and control (Brewster 2003). While this explanatory framework has been demonstrated to be useful for understanding some stalking violence (e.g., Brewster 2003, US victims; Davis et al. 2000, US students; Morewitz 2003, US protection orders), it cannot account for the potentially high rates of female-perpetrated stalking violence.

Another sociocultural belief prevalent in young western societies is that men should not physically assault women (see Archer 2000; 2002, cross-national meta-analyses; Indermaur 2001, Australian community), the 'chivalry norm.' Accordingly, violence perpetrated by males against females is viewed to be unacceptable and potentially more damaging than violence perpetrated by females against males (Archer 2000; Williams and Frieze 2005a). However, violence perpetrated by females against males may be trivialised and deemed more acceptable than the reverse (see Archer 2000; Fontes 2007; Kernsmith 2005). To illustrate, a female university student commented "even if I hit him [i.e., her intimate partner] my hardest there is no way I could hurt him" (Miller and Simpson 1991, p. 352, US students). Likewise, a male in this sample stated that "no woman would be arrested for hitting her partner" (Miller and Simpson 1991, p. 352, US students). Consequently male victims of female violence may be expected to exhibit greater physical and emotional strength than female victims (Fontes 2007). It is likely that these beliefs are associated with expected gender differences in the impact of violence, whereby females are perceived to be more vulnerable and males are perceived to be stronger and more capable of defending themselves (Fontes 2007; Kernsmith 2005; Miller and Simpson 1991). Consistent with this, research suggests that community members and university students view male stalking victims and domestic violence victims as more capable of defending themselves (Cass 2007, US students; Dennison and Thompson, forthcoming, Australian community members; Sheridan et al. 2003, UK students) and female stalking victims and domestic violence victims having a greater need for police assistance (Cass 2007, US students; Dennison and Thompson, forthcoming, Australian community members; Phillips et al. 2004, US students; Sheridan et al. 2003, UK students). This explanatory framework can account for the findings that male victims may be underrepresented in victim and legally-defined samples because male victims of stalking and stalking violence may experience less fear, be less likely to identify themselves as a victim and more reluctant to report the behaviour to the police. Although much of the aforementioned research was conducted in the USA (See Archer 2000; Fontes 2007; Kernsmith 2005), evidence of similar sociocultural beliefs have been documented in Australian studies of domestic violence (e.g., Dennison and Thompson, forthcoming; Indermaur 2001) and stalking (Dennison 2007).

Although the chivalry norm has not been applied to stalking violence, this sociocultural belief has four implications for stalking violence.

First, *males may be more inhibited from perpetrating stalking violence* due to the social stigma and the anticipated severity of the consequences associated with male-to-female violence. *Females, on the other hand, may be less inhibited from perpetrating stalking violence* because the effects of such violence can be minimised and they may have less fear of reprisal.

Second, *support for justifications for violence are likely to differ according to the perpetrator's gender*. As violence perpetrated by males against females is viewed to be more unacceptable and damaging, while violence perpetrated by females against males may be trivialised, there is likely to be greater support for female-perpetrated stalking violence in comparison to male-perpetrated stalking violence. Moreover, *females who are more supportive of female-perpetrated relational violence may be more likely to perpetrate violence in the context of relational stalking*. Third, as violence perpetrated by males against females is viewed to be more damaging than the reverse, *violent female stalkers may perceive that the impact of their behaviour is less serious than violent male stalkers*, including whether the stalker perceives that his/her behaviour frightens, intimidates or harms the target. Fourth, if the harm caused by male stalking violence is perceived to be greater than female stalking violence and if females perceive that their violence is relatively harmless, *violent male stalkers may be more likely to intend to frighten, intimidate or harm their target than their female counterparts*. This study will investigate each of these implications to contribute to a better understanding of the interplay between gender, sociocultural beliefs and stalking violence.

Two overarching research questions are investigated:

(1) *Do male and female relational stalkers perpetrate different rates of moderate and severe stalking violence?* Given the trends identified in Sinclair and Frieze's (2002) research that females perpetrate more attempted and actual moderate *physical* violence than their male counterparts, it was hypothesised that female relational stalkers with perpetrate more moderate violence than their male counterparts (Hypothesis 1). Due to inconsistent findings for gender differences in severe stalking violence, no hypothesis was proposed for gender differences in the perpetration of severe violence.

(2) *What sociocultural beliefs may account for these gender differences/similarities?* Four hypotheses were tested for the second research question on the basis of the implications of the chivalry norm. Hypothesis 2 predicts that participants will be more accepting of females' justifications for using relational violence than males' justifications for using relational violence. Hypothesis 3 predicts that violent stalkers will have greater support for justifications for using violence than their non-violent counterparts. Specifically, (a) violent female stalkers will have greater support for justifications for females using violence than their non-violent counterparts (b) violent male stalkers will have greater support for justifications for males using violence than their non-violent counterparts. Hypothesis 4 predicts that violent male relational stalkers will have greater intentions to frighten, intimidate or harm the target than their female counterparts. Hypothesis 5 predicts that violent male relational stalkers will be more likely to believe that their behaviour frightened, intimidated or harmed the target than their female counterparts. Findings for hypotheses 2 and 3b also test the applicability of patriarchal beliefs, whereby support for justifications for male-perpetrated violence is consistent with patriarchal beliefs that such violence can be used as a means to establish, sustain or reestablish power and control.

The present study examines self-reported stalking violence perpetration in a sample of university students from Queensland, Australia. This research methodology was adopted to identify potentially hidden rates of stalking violence that may not be evident in victim and legally-defined samples. Gender differences in stalking violence and associated sociocultural beliefs will be examined in the context of stalking that occurs after relationship terminations and in the pursuit of relationships. This context was selected as (a) this context is most relevant to the sociocultural beliefs reviewed previously (b) much stalking behaviour and stalking violence occurs in the context of relationship dissolutions or relationship pursuits (e.g., Pathe and Mullen 1997, Australian victims; Purcell et al. 2002, Australian community; Tjaden et al. 2000, US community) and (c) as this study is largely informed by intimate partner violence literature, the links between intimate partner violence research and stalking are likely to have the biggest overlaps in this context.

Method

Participants

Seven hundred and twelve graduate and undergraduate students from Griffith University in Queensland, Australia participated in the present research (28.2% male, 71.8% female). Only those participants classified as relational stalkers (N=293, 41.2%), however, were included in the current study (24.2% male, 75.8% female). Although females were more likely to be classified as relational stalkers (n=222, 43.4%) than their male counterparts (n=71, 35.3%), χ^2 (1, N=712)= 3.93, p=.047, φ=.07, the phi co efficient indicates that the strength of this association was weak. The ages of relational stalkers ranged from 17 to 49 years (M=23.5 years, Mdn = 21 years, SD=6.0, missing n=2). The mean age of males was 23.1 years (SD=5.9), and the mean age of females was 23.7 years (SD=6.1), t (289)= −.61, p=.54. Most of the relational stalkers were either single (n=131, 44.7%) or in a dating relationship (n=82, 28.0%). Relatively few relational stalkers were married (n=24, 8.2%), in a defacto relationship (n=44, 15.0%) or divorced/separated/widowed (n=12,4.1%). There was no significant variability between males and females in relation to marital status (χ^2 [4, N=293]=4.22, p=.38, Cramer's V=.12). Participants were treated in accordance with the ethical requirements of the Griffith University Human Research Ethics Committee and the ethical principles of the National Health and Medical Research Council.

Materials

The present study was part of a larger project examining violence in relational stalking (see Thompson 2009). A self-report questionnaire was utilised to assess participants' engagement in relational stalking, stalking violence and other factors associated with this behaviour. Only the relevant portions of the questionnaire will be described, including scales used to assess gender differences in (a) relational stalking, (b) stalking violence, and (c) sociocultural beliefs, including a scale measuring justifications for relational violence and questions measuring assessments of target fear (scale items are available in Thompson 2009).

The entire questionnaire took between 30 and 60 min to complete, depending on the answers supplied by the participant. Two versions of the questionnaire were available; a web-based version (n=619; 86.9%) and a paperbased version (n=93; 13.1%). Consistent with much previous research (e.g., Knapp and Kirk 2003; Richman et al. 1999), none of the independent or dependent variables significantly differed across questionnaire formats.

Relational Stalking

To measure participants' perpetration of relational stalking, participants were asked whether they had *ever* engaged in any of 25 behaviours that they *knew were unwanted* after they had *broken up with an intimate partner* or had been *rejected by someone they wanted a relationship with* (scored never, once, two or more, five or more, or ten or more times). The behaviours included in the list were largely derived from Spitzberg and Cupach's (1997) Relational Pursuit: Pursuer Short Form (unpublished measure). To be consistent with behaviours typically used in stalking legislation and research (e.g., Brewster 2003; Criminal Code [Stalking] Amendment Act 1999 [Queensland]; Davis et al. 2000; Dennison and Stewart 2006; James and Farnham 2003; Purcell et al. 2000; Sheridan et al. 2001a, b), this scale was amended to exclude some items (e.g., making exaggerated expressions of affection), combine similar items and to include some additional behaviours (e.g., unwanted telephone calls). Examples of the items incorporated in the checklist include following him/her around and stealing or damaging his/her possessions (amended scale is available in Thompson 2009). Those participants who had engaged in behaviours towards multiple people were asked to select one person who "had the biggest impact on them" and complete the checklist again for this person only. This ensured that the data were obtained for relational stalking perpetrated against one person, as opposed to an accumulation of behaviours perpetrated against multiple people. The relational stalking checklist had a Cronbach's alpha co-efficient of .83.

Participants who perpetrated five or more intrusions from the relational stalking checklist were defined as relational stalkers. The number of intrusions perpetrated by participants was calculated by adding the frequency score for each type of stalking behaviour. For example, two different stalking behaviours each performed five times resulted in a total score of '10 or more' intrusions. The decision to use a threshold of five or more intrusions was informed by research conducted by Thompson and Dennison (2008, Australia) that compared cut-points of two, five and ten or more intrusions on sample size and severity of behaviour. This research indicated that two or more stalking intrusions were relatively normal, perpetrated by two thirds of the sample (Thompson and Dennison 2008). Ten or more intrusions resulted in a more restrictive sample (i.e., 22.4%) and higher rates of threats and violence than the sample attained with a cut-point of two (see Thompson and Dennison 2008). However, many participants perpetrated threats and violence but did not engage in at least ten intrusions and most legal definitions require a minimum of just two intrusions. A cut-point of five or more intrusions balanced these issues. This cut-point classified 40% less participants as stalkers than a cut-point of two intrusions, limiting relatively common behavioural patterns. At the same time this cut-point identified 50% more violent participants than a cut-point of 10. As the present study focuses on violence, it was deemed more purposeful to select a larger sample that included more violent behaviour, but was not too encompassing. Therefore, relational stalking is operationally defined in the present research as *five or more unwanted intrusions perpetrated against any one person after the dissolution of an intimate relationship, or in the pursuit of an intimate relationship* (see Thompson and Dennison 2008).

Stalking Violence

To assess violence, participants who had engaged in relational stalking behaviours were asked whether they had ever *attempted to, or actually did*, a range of physically violent acts to the person to whom the unwanted behaviours were targeted towards, or towards someone for whom this person cared, during the course of stalking (scored never, once, two or more, five or more, or ten or more times). The violence checklist was an amended version of two subscales from the Revised Conflict Tactics Scale (CTS2; Straus et al. 1996), the physical assault and sexual coercion subscales. Additional violent acts commonly reported in stalking violence research were incorporated in the checklist, including running the target's car off the road (original scale is available in Straus et al. 1996; amended scale is available in Thompson 2009). The physical violence checklist included two sub-scales, a moderate violence sub-scale (e.g., slapping and grabbing) and a severe violence sub-scale (e.g., choking and kicking). The severity of behaviours was classified according to the CTS2 and the probable severity of the consequences of the behaviour. Relational stalkers were classified into three mutually exclusive categories; 'not violent,' 'moderately violent' or 'severely violent.' Participants were classified according to the most severe form of violence they perpetrated. The Cronbach's alpha coefficient was .78 for the moderate violence subscale and .68 for the severe violence subscale.

Sociocultural Beliefs

Justifications for Using Relational Violence

Justifications for using relational violence was measured using an amended version of Mazerolle's

(1999) Intimate Partner Violence Justification Scale (IPVJS). The scale assessed participants' agreement with justifications for using violence against an intimate partner (scored agree/disagree). While the original scale only measures justifications for males using relational violence, the scale was presented twice to assess justifications for males (i.e., participants' agreement with nine justifications for violence perpetrated by men against their intimate partner) and justifications for females (i.e., participants' agreement with nine justifications for violence perpetrated by women against their intimate partner). For example, participants were asked if they agreed with the statement "It is okay for a man to hit or slap his partner if his partner stays out past midnight without telling him where she/he is" (original scale available in Mazerolle 1999; amended scale available in Thompson 2009). Scores were then calculated by adding the number of items participants agreed with across the respective scales. IPVJS had a Cronbach's alpha co-efficient of .78 for justifications for male-perpetrated relational violence and .81 for justifications for female-perpetrated relational violence.

Assessments of Target Fear

Assessments of fear were measured using two non-standard questions devised for the present research. To measure the participants' intention to cause fear and harm, participants were asked "Did you intend to frighten, intimidate or harm this person?" (scored yes/no). To measure perceived target fear or harm, participants were asked "Do you think your behaviour did frighten, intimidate or harm this person?" (scored yes/no).

Procedure

Participants were recruited between July 2006 and May 2007 through several sampling techniques, including (1) research participation schemes in three undergraduate criminology courses, (2) a university-wide student e-mail, (3) an advertisement on the university computer laboratory homepage, and (4) attending five undergraduate lectures to invite student participation. All participants entered a draw to win one of three $100 cash prizes for their participation. Where applicable, students also obtained credit points for undergraduate courses for their participation.

Participants were told that the purpose of the study was to examine the behaviours and tactics used by individuals after breaking up from an intimate relationship or in the pursuit of a new intimate relationship. At no time was the behaviour labelled 'stalking'. This decision was made to circumvent error that may arise from individuals' preconceived notions of what constitutes stalking.

Results

Analyses

In the present study, gender differences were examined in relation to (1) stalking violence (2) justifications for using relational violence (3) intentions to frighten, intimidate or harm the target and (4) perceived target fear, intimidation or harm. Chi-square analyses were used to examine between subject differences. For chi-square analyses with variables with greater than two possible outcomes, cells with adjusted residuals exceeding absolute 2.0 were deemed to significantly differ (Cooksey 2007). When the assumptions of chi-square analyses were violated due to expected frequencies below 5, exact tests were utilised (Brace et al. 2006) to provide preliminary support or rejection of hypotheses. Fisher's exact tests were used for 2×2 tables (reported as 'Fisher's exact test *p*') and standard exact tests were used for tables with more levels of analysis (reported as 'exact *p*'). McNemar's tests were conducted to test within subject differences across dichotomous variables (Norusis 2000). Analyses were conducted using the statistical package SPSS for Windows, Version 15.0.

The Nature of Stalking Perpetration in the Sample

Most relational stalkers engaged in more than the minimum of five intrusions (n=256; 87.4%), whereby the average number of intrusions committed was 16.8 (Mdn=11; SD=15.9; range=1–118). Participants classified as relational stalkers primarily targeted persons of the opposite gender

(n=271, 92.5%). Same-gender relational stalking was reported by similar proportions of males (n=6; 8.5%) and females (n=16; 7.2%). The majority of relational stalkers reported behaviour that followed the dissolution of an intimate relationship (n=264; 90.1%). Approximately 10% of relational stalkers reported behaviours that occurred in the pursuit of an intimate relationship (n=29, 9.9%), for example pursuing relationships with acquaintances, casual dates, friends or work colleagues.

The vast majority of respondents classified as relational stalkers reported neither police involvement nor the issuance of a restraining order or a domestic violence order (n=289, 98.6%). Only three respondents disclosed that their behaviour had been reported to the police and three respondents disclosed that their behaviour resulted in the issuance of a restraining order or a domestic violence order.

Stalking Violence Perpetration

Of the 293 relational stalkers, 44.4% (n=130) reported the actual or attempted perpetration of violence during the course of stalking. The median number of violent acts was three (M=6.1; SD=8.3; range=1–60). Most of the violence reported in the sample was moderate violence perpetrated in the absence of severe violence (n=75; 57.7%). Over 40% of stalking violence perpetrated was severe (n=55; 42.3%), most of which was perpetrated in conjunction with moderate violence (n=51; 92.7%).

Research Question 1: Do Male and Female Relational Stalkers Perpetrate Different Rates of Stalking Violence (i.e., No Violence, Moderate Violence or Severe Violence)?

Stalking violence varied significantly across gender, χ^2 (2, N=293)=6.33, p=.042, Cramer's V=.15. Consistent with hypothesis 1, females (n=64, 28.8%) were more likely to perpetrate actual or attempted moderate violence than their male counterparts (n=11, 15.5%; adjusted residuals=2.2 and −2.2, respectively). No hypothesis was proposed for gender differences for severe violence. Males (n=12, 16.9%) and females (n=43, 19.4%) did not significantly differ in the perpetration of actual or attempted severe violence (adjusted residuals= −.5 and .5, respectively).

Research Question 2: What Sociocultural Beliefs May Account for These Gender Differences/Similarities?

Four hypotheses were tested for the second research question on the basis of the implications of the chivalry norm. Hypotheses 2 and 3 tested gender differences in support for males' justifications for using relational violence versus females' justifications for using relational violence. Hypotheses 3 and 4 tested gender differences in intended and perceived target fear, intimidation and harm.

Hypothesis 2: Participants Will Be More Accepting of Females' Justifications for Using Relational Violence Than Males' Justifications for Using Relational Violence

The majority of participants did not believe that men were justified to use violence against their partner under any of the nine circumstances assessed (n=223, 76.1%). A smaller proportion of participants did not believe that women were justified to use violence against their partner under any of the nine circumstances assessed (n=120, 41.0%). Due to highly skewed data for justifications for both females (M=1.5, SD=1.9, range=1–9) and males (M=.4, SD=1.0, range=1–9) using violence, both variables were recoded into dichotomous variables for this and all subsequent analyses, scored as supportive of no justification for intimate violence (scored 0) or supportive of one or more justification for intimate violence (scored 1). Consistent with hypothesis 2, participants were more supportive of justifications for females using violence against their partners than males using violence against their partners (*McNemar's Test*, N=293, p<.001; see Table 1). This finding was upheld across non-violent stalkers (*McNemar's Test*, N=163, p<.001), moderately violent stalkers (*McNemar's Test*, N=75, p<.001) and severely violent stalkers (*McNemar's Test*, N=55, p<.001) as well as across both males (*McNemar's*

Test, N=71, p<.001) and females (*McNemar's Test*, N=222, p<.001).

Hypothesis 3a: Violent Female Stalkers Will Have Greater Support for Justifications for Females Using Violence Than Their Non-Violent Counterparts

Due to the dichotomisation of justifications for using violence, it was only possible to investigate the relationship between any support for justifications for using relational violence and associated levels of stalking violence. Consistent with hypothesis 3a, there was a significant relationship between support for justifications for females using relational violence and females' levels of stalking violence (χ^2 [2, N=222]=6.5,p=.038, Cramer's V=.17, see Table 1). Specifically, severely violent female stalkers reported the greatest support for females using relational violence (74.4%; adjusted residual=2.5). There was no significant difference between non-violent female stalkers (53.9%; adjusted residual= −1.0) and moderately violent female stalkers (51.6%; adjusted residual= −1.1) and these rates fell below those reported by severely violent stalkers. Therefore, hypothesis 3a was partially supported with the exception of no significant difference between non-violent female stalkers and moderately violent female stalkers. There was no relationship between support for justifications for males using relational violence and females' levels of stalking violence (χ^2 [2, N=222]=2.5, p=.288, Cramer's V=.11, see Table 1).

Hypothesis 3b: Violent Male Stalkers Will Have Greater Support for Justifications for Males Using Violence Than Their Non-Violent Counterparts

As was the case with hypothesis 3a, the dichotomisation of justifications for using violence meant that it was only possible to investigate the relationship between any support for justifications for using relational violence and associated levels of stalking violence. Due to a small sample of male relational stalkers, exact tests were conducted. Contrary to hypothesis 3b, there was no significant relationship between support for justifications for males using relational violence and males' levels of stalking (χ^2 [2, N=71]=4.06, exact p=.139, Cramer's V=.24, see Table 1). However, the relationship between support for justifications for males using relational violence and males' levels of moderate violence approached significance (adjusted residual=1.9), with 63.6% of moderately violent male stalkers supporting justifications for males using relational violence compared to 31.3% of non-violent male

Table 1. The Number of Relational Stalkers Who Supported One or More Justifications for Male Relational Violence and Female Relational Violence

Gender	Stalking Group	Support for Male Relational Violence n (%)	Support for Female Relational Violence n (%)
Male	Non-Violent Stalkers	15 (31.3)	26 (54.2)
	Moderately Violent Stalkers	7 (63.6)	9 (81.8)
	Severely Violent Stalkers	5 (41.7)	11 (91.7)
	Total	27 (38.0)	46 (64.8)
Female	Non-Violent Stalkers	20 (17.4)	62 (53.9)
	Moderately Violent Stalkers	11 (17.2)	33 (51.6)
	Severely Violent Stalkers	12 (27.9)	32 (74.4)
	Total	43 (19.4)	127 (57.2)
Total		70 (23.9)	173 (59.0)

Figures represent the number of participants who supported one or more justifications for violence. The remaining participants supported no justifications for violence.

stalkers and 41.7% of severely violent male stalkers. An examination of the relationship between males' support for female-perpetrated relational violence and males' stalking violence indicated that more violent behaviour was associated with greater levels of support (non-violent stalkers=54.2%, moderately violent stalkers=81.8%, severely violent stalkers=91.7%), χ^2 (2, N=71)=7.58, exact p=.02, Cramer's V=.33.

Hypothesis 4: Violent Male Relational Stalkers Will Have Greater Intentions to Frighten, Intimidate or Harm the Target Than Their Female Counterparts

Few relational stalkers reported that they intended to frighten, intimidate or harm the target (n=26; 8.9%). Due to the low endorsement of such intentions, Fisher's exact tests were conducted. Consistent with hypothesis 4, male moderately violent stalkers were more likely to report an intent to frighten, intimidate or harm the target (n=4; 36.4%) than their female counterparts (n=4; 6.3%), Fisher's exact test, p=.01, φ= −.35. Contrary to hypothesis 4, male severely violent stalkers were no more likely to report an intent to frighten, intimidate or harm the target (n=3; 25.0%) than their female counterparts (n=11; 25.6%), Fisher's exact test, p=1.00, φ=.01. A similarly small proportion of male (n=2; 4.2%) and female (n=2; 1.7%) non-violent stalkers reported that they intended to frighten, intimidate or harm the target, Fisher's exact test, p=.58, φ=−.07.

Hypothesis 5: Violent Male Relational Stalkers Will Be More Likely to Believe That Their Behaviour Frightened, Intimidated or Harmed the Target Than Their Female Counterparts

Few relational stalkers believed they frightened, intimidated or harmed the target (n=59; 20.1%). Consistent with hypothesis 5, male moderately violent stalkers were more likely to believe they frightened, intimidated or harmed the target (n= 6; 54.5%) than their female counterparts (n=10; 15.6%), Fisher's exact test, p=.009, φ= −.34 and male severely violent stalkers were more likely to believe they frightened, intimidated or harmed the target (n=10; 83.3%) than their female counterparts (n=16; 37.2%), χ^2 [1, N=55]=8.0, p=.005, φ= −.38. Male non-violent stalkers were no more likely to believe they frightened, intimidated or harmed the target (n=7; 14.6%) than their female counterparts (n=10; 8.7%), χ^2 (1, N=163)=1.3, p=.262, φ=−.09, however, there was a trend in the expected direction.

Discussion

This study investigated gender differences in stalking violence in a sample of student relational stalkers. Two overarching research questions were investigated: (1) Do male and female relational stalkers perpetrate different rates of moderate and severe stalking violence? and (2) What sociocultural beliefs may account for these gender differences/similarities? This is the first stalking study to systematically examine these gender differences using self-reports of the perpetration of moderate and severe physical violence. This study also constitutes the first attempt to interpret these gender differences/similarities in the context of sociocultural beliefs that view male-perpetrated violence as more unacceptable than female-perpetrated violence. Contrary to the assumption that males perpetrate more stalking violence than their female counterparts (e.g., Mullen et al. 2000), female relational stalkers perpetrated elevated rates of moderate violence and there were no gender differences for severe violence. Consistent with sociocultural beliefs that view male-perpetrated violence as more unacceptable than female-perpetrated violence, both male and female relational stalkers were more supportive of justifications for female-perpetrated relational violence than male-perpetrated relational violence, Consistent with sociocultural beliefs that view male-perpetrated violence as more harmful than female-perpetrated violence, males who perpetrated moderate or severe stalking violence were also more likely to believe that their behaviour frightened, intimidated or harmed the target than their female counterparts. There was little support for justifications for male-perpetrated relational violence in this sample.

Stalking violence was common in the present study, whereby close to half of the student relational stalkers reported actually or attempting to perpetrate violence during the course of stalking. As 99% of relational stalking behaviour in the present study had not been reported to the police, the relational stalking and associated violence measured in this study primarily comprises 'hidden' behaviour that has not been addressed in the criminal justice system. These hidden rates of relational stalking and violence may differ from those attained from the criminal justice system. Despite this, the rate of violence attained in the present study is consistent with stalking violence research conducted in Australia, USA and UK, including that from forensic and clinical samples, which typically report prevalence rates of between 30% and 50% (James and Farnham 2003, UK forensic psychiatric referrals; Mullen et al. 1999, Australian forensic psychiatric referrals; Rosenfeld and Harmon 2002, US forensic psychiatric referrals; Spitzberg and Cupach 2007, cross-national metaanalysis). The fact that the majority of violence perpetrated was moderate in nature is also consistent with stalking violence research conducted in Australia (McEwan et al. 2009), USA (Rosenfeld and Harmon 2002) and UK (James and Farnham 2003). Interestingly, however, this was due to elevated rates of moderate violence amongst females only (moderate violence =29%; severe violence =19%). Males, on the other hand, perpetrated similar rates of moderate and severe violence (16% and 17%, respectively).

The value of differentiating the severity of violence was confirmed in the present study, with gender differences varying across moderate and severe violence. Consistent with intimate partner violence research (e.g., Archer 2002, cross-national meta-analysis; Williams and Frieze 2005a, US community sample), female stalkers were more likely to perpetrate moderate stalking violence than male stalkers (such as slapping, throwing something at the target and pushing and shoving). In fact actual/attempted moderate violence was common amongst females. Since almost all severe violence was perpetrated in conjunction with moderate violence, almost half of the female stalkers perpetrated moderate violence either alone or in conjunction with severe violence. Although this is the first stalking study to examine significant gender differences in the perpetration of moderate *physical* violence, similar trends have been identified in previous research using a US student sample (Sinclair and Frieze 2002).

There were no gender differences in the perpetration of severe violence. This is consistent with trends reported in Sinclair and Frieze's (2002) research regarding extreme harm in a sample of students from the USA. Furthermore, although findings vary, a number of studies have reported similar rates of severe intimate partner violence across gender (e.g., Headey et al. 1999, Australian community; Krahe and Berger 2005, German community). The gender symmetry in the present study is inconsistent with James and Farnham's (2003) stalking violence research. However, this research was conducted in a British sample of forensic psychiatric cases. It was previously argued that legal samples may underestimate female-to-male stalking and stalking violence. As the present research has utilised a university sample and a behavioural definition of relational stalking, it is possible that sampling methods can account for these conflicting results. Alternatively, the definition of serious violence utilised by James and Farnham (2003) was largely contingent on the violence inflicting serious injuries on the victim, which was not measured in the present study. It is possible that severely violent male stalkers in the present study inflicted more serious injuries than their female counterparts. The severe violence reported in James and Farnham's (2003) research (e.g., murder, attempted murder, wounding) was also likely more serious than that attained in the present study. Therefore, gender differences may be more pronounced at the extreme end of the severe violence continuum.

Together, these findings provide no support for the assumption that males perpetrate higher rates of violence (e.g., Mullen et al. 2000). Instead, females were more likely to perpetrate moderate violence, whereby this form of violence was relatively normal among female stalkers. Therefore the application of sociocultural beliefs that explain stalking violence as a male-perpetrated phenomenon will provide an incomplete understanding of the relationship between stalking violence and gender. However, sociocultural beliefs that can also account for female-perpetrated stalking violence, like the chivalry norm, may have greater explanatory power. This study examined the relationship between gender and stalking violence in relation to support for justifications for using relational violence, intentions to cause fear and harm and perceived fear and harm.

There was little support for justifications for using relational violence in the present study, despite moderate rates of stalking violence perpetration. This is consistent with research investigating community attitudes towards violence and intimate partner violence in Western countries (e.g., Anderson et al. 2006, US students; Indermaur 2001, Australian community). Non-violent, moderately violent and severely violent relational stalkers were all more supportive of relational violence perpetrated by females than relational violence perpetrated by males. These attitudes were consistent across both male and female relational stalkers. The fact that identical situations were interpreted as more or less acceptable on the basis of the perpetrators' gender gives credence to the proposition that young Western cultures support a sociocultural belief that is more disapproving of violence perpetrated by males towards females than females towards males (Archer 2000, 2002; Fontes 2007). Furthermore, severely violent female stalkers were more likely to support justifications for female-perpetrated relational violence than moderately violent and non-violent female stalkers. While there was no difference between non-violent and moderately violent female stalkers, support for these justifications was high in both of these groups. It is plausible that those females perpetrating stalking itself may have more support for female-perpetrated violence than non-stalkers due to the intrusiveness of this phenomenon. Therefore it is possible that acceptance of female-perpetrated violence disinhibits females from engaging in stalking and stalking violence. This is consistent with the chivalry norm.

The differential support for female-perpetrated relational violence and male-perpetrated relational violence, and the low level of support for justifications for male-perpetrated relational violence, also indicates that there was little evidence of patriarchal beliefs that support males being justified in using violence against their partners. Additionally, preliminary evidence suggested males' support for justifications for violence in general (i.e., male and female) was associated with moderate and severe stalking violence, rather than justifications for male violence only. In fact between 80%–90% of violent male stalkers reported support for justifications for female-perpetrated relational violence. Again, this preliminary finding provides little evidence that violent stalkers foster patriarchal views in this sample. However, due to a small sample of males in the present study these findings are only preliminary. It is important that future research re-examines the relationship between males' support for justifications for relational violence and moderate and severe stalking violence.

The examination of participants' perceptions of the impact of their behaviour provides further support for the applicability of aspects of the chivalry norm. While participants who perpetrated more violent behaviour perceived their behaviour to have more of an impact on the target, both moderately and severely violent males believed their behaviour caused more fear, intimidation and harm than their female counterparts. In fact, very few female stalkers believed that their behaviour frightened the target or caused harm, even when females perpetrated severe violence.

It is possible that gender differences in perceptions of fear/ harm are a reflection of differences in actual fear or harm displayed by targets as a function of the perpetrator-target gender composition. This argument is consistent with research that suggests that male perpetrators of intimate partner violence inflict greater injuries than female perpetrators (Archer 2000, cross-national meta-analysis). Moreover, male victims of stalking and intimate partner violence may experience less fear than their female counterparts (e.g., Bjerregaard 2002, US students; Budd et al. 2000, UK community; Cercone et al. 2005, US students; Davis et al. 2002, US community; Dietz and Martin 2007; Pathe and Mullen 1997, Australian victims; Tjaden and Thoennes 2000, US community). Alternatively, males may be reluctant to display fear/harm due to social norms that suggest that males should display strength both physically and emotionally, particularly in response to female violence (Fontes 2007).

It is also plausible that gender differences in perceptions of fear/harm reflect perceived gender differences in victim impact, as opposed to actual victim impact. Consistent with this, research suggests that stalking and intimate partner violence perpetrated by females against males is trivialised as males are perceived to be stronger and more capable of defending themselves (Dennison and Thompson, forthcoming, Australian community; Miller and Simpson 1991, US students; Molidor and Tolman 1998, US students). Stalking and intimate partner violence perpetrated by males against females, on the other hand, is interpreted as more threatening and fear-provoking (Dennison 2007, Australian community; Phillips et al. 2004, US students; Sheridan et al. 2003, UK students). Consequently, perpetrators may interpret the impact of their behaviour in accordance with these social perceptions. Importantly, while these findings are consistent with the chivalry norm, these findings may also be explained by patriarchal sociocultural beliefs that view women's violence as less impactful due to patriarchal stereotypes of women as weak, submissive and of lower status (Brewster 2003).

Preliminary findings regarding perpetrators' intentions to cause fear or harm also provide support for the chivalry norm. Female moderately violent stalkers were less likely to intend to frighten, intimidate or harm the target than their male counterparts; however, males' and females' intentions did not differ for severe violence. Additionally, males' intent to cause fear/harm were actually higher for moderate violence than severe violence, although this may be a product of the small sample size. Nevertheless, it appears that males' intentions are at least comparable across moderate and severe violence. Each of these findings can be interpreted using the chivalry norm. Due to a perception of female perpetrated violence as trivial and likely to cause low levels of fear/harm in general, females may believe that moderate violence will have very little effect, particularly on males. Therefore, moderate violence may not be perpetrated to cause fear, intimidation or harm. Instead, females with these intentions may be more likely to perpetrate severe violence. It is important that the intentions of moderately violent female stalkers are examined to provide a better understanding of the causes of this phenomenon and, in turn, drive preventive strategies. As male moderately and severely violent stalkers are both considered more threatening and more likely to cause fear/harm, males may be more likely engage in either of these behaviours with the intent to cause fear, intimidation or harm. Importantly, due to a small sample of males and the low endorsement of intentions to cause fear or harm, these findings are only preliminary. Future research should reexamine gender differences in intentions to cause fear or harm using larger sample sizes. Further investigations are also required to examine whether low endorsement of intentions to cause fear/harm are due to participants' reluctance to report such intentions or the fact that violent stalkers have alternative intentions (see Dennison and Thomson 2005).

Limitations and Future Research

The present study contributes to the growing body of research that attempts to elucidate the extent and nature of gender differences in stalking violence. However, these findings need to be interpreted according to the limitations of this study. First, the present sample is not representative of relational stalkers in the community. The student sample was relatively young, highly educated and comprised a disproportionately small number of male stalkers. Consequently, future research should replicate this research in a more representative community sample with greater numbers of male participants. Second, the student sample utilised in this research is older than student samples typically used to examine relational stalking. However, there were only 19 participants aged over 35 years (6%) and the results did not differ when these participants were excluded. Third, due to small numbers of male participants exact tests were used to analyse hypotheses 3b and 4 (i.e., violent male stalkers will have greater support for justifications for males using violence than their non-violent counterparts and violent male relational stalkers will have greater intentions to frighten, intimidate or harm the target than their female counterparts). Consequently, the findings for these hypotheses are preliminary only and should be investigated in samples with sufficient numbers of male participants. Only then will it be possible to confidently support these hypotheses.

Fourth, it is impossible to estimate the proportion of stalking in the present study that could be prosecuted as unlawful stalking. This is difficult to address given the complexities associated with simulating legislative criteria in operational definitions of stalking used in self-report perpetration studies (see Thompson and Dennison 2008). Fifth, the sample was restricted to stalking behaviours perpetrated following a relationship termination or in the pursuit of a relationship. It is possible that the current findings are applicable to relational stalking but not necessarily stalking in other contexts. That is, females may be more reluctant to perpetrate stalking violence in non-relational contexts. Future research should examine gender differences in non-relational stalking using community samples and investigate whether sociocultural beliefs are applicable across types of stalking.

Sixth, although there may be little support for male-perpetrated relational violence in student samples of stalkers (and potentially community samples) due to contemporary sociocultural beliefs that view male-perpetrated violence as more unacceptable and harmful than female-perpetrated violence. Patriarchal beliefs that support males being justified in using violence against their partners may be more prevalent in stalking cases sampled from victim services, refuges or intimate partner violence intervention programs (e.g., Brewster 2003, US victims). Similar trends have been identified in the intimate partner violence literature (e.g., Archer 2000, cross-national meta-analysis; de Vries Robbe et al. 1996, Australian emergency patients; Headey et al. 1999, Australian community; McHugh 2005; Tjaden and Thoennes 2000). For example, common couple forms of domestic violence predominate surveys of community members and university students, whereas patriarchal terrorism is more prevalent in samples from victim services, refuges or intimate partner violence intervention programs (see Archer 2000, cross-national meta-analysis; McHugh 2005; Tjaden and Thoennes 2000). Therefore, similar to the intimate partner violence literature, both the chivalry and patriarchal explanations may be valid in the contexts of relational stalking and should be considered in future research.

In the present research gender differences and sociocultural beliefs were examined in an Australian cultural context. However, there is no reason to believe that these findings will contradict research conducted in samples from the USA given the similarity of findings across Australia and USA in relation to gender differences in stalking, stalking violence, intimate partner violence and sociocultural beliefs. Nevertheless, as this study constitutes the first attempt to apply these sociocultural beliefs to gender differences in stalking violence, it is important that this study is replicated in other cultural contexts, as well as in additional Australian samples.

Conclusion

In the present study, female relational stalkers perpetrated elevated rates of moderate violence; however, there were no gender differences for severe violence. These findings were interpreted according to a sociocultural belief supported in this sample that female-perpetrated violence is less damaging and more justifiable than male-perpetrated violence. This norm may promote particularly high rates of moderate violence among female relational stalkers as this behaviour has greater social support than male-perpetrated violence. Additionally, as female-perpetrated moderate violence is perceived to have an especially low impact on victims it may be particularly easy for females to justify. Possibly due to the perceived minimal impact of female-perpetrated moderate violence, very few females (5%) engaging in this behaviour intended to cause fear/harm. If victims share the perceptions that female-perpetrated moderate violence is innocuous this behaviour may not be reported to the police and thus may be undetected in forensic samples. The gender symmetry attained for severe violence is in contrast to the assumption that males perpetrate more violence, including stalking violence, than females. It is possible that this was due to such behaviour simultaneously being inhibited in males and disinhibited in females, whereby male-perpetrated severe violence was perceived to be particularly damaging as well as socially unacceptable.

These findings have several implications. (1) If male victims of stalking violence are less fearful, and/or they believe females are justified to use violence against them, they may be less likely to report their victimisation to the police. Consequently, gaining a comprehensive understanding of stalking violence requires an investigation of both legal and community and student samples. (2) If police officers also hold sociocultural beliefs that are more accepting of violence perpetrated by females against males than violence perpetrated by males against females, police officers may be less likely to respond to male victimisation, especially with female perpetrators (for example see Kamphuis et al. 2005, European cross-national police officers; Sheridan et al. 2003, UK students; Stewart and Maddren 1997, Australian police officers). These potential biases should be investigated and, if necessary, strategies devised to minimise gender biases in criminal justice responses. (3) As the majority of research addressing violence intervention and prevention programs are tailored towards male perpetrators, the frequency of female-perpetrated violence in the present study suggests that there is a need to ensure stalking violence intervention and prevention programs are applicable across gender. (4) If moderate violence perpetrated by females is rarely perpetrated with the intention to cause fear/harm, it is important to understand the intentions of these individuals to gain a better understanding of the nature and causes of stalking violence.

References

Anderson, C. A., Benjamin, A. J., Wood, P. K., & Bonacci, A. M. (2006). Development and testing of the Velicer Attitudes Towards Violence Scale: Evidence for a four-factor model. *Aggressive Behavior, 32*, 122–136.

Archer, J. (2000). Sex differences in aggression between heterosexual partners: A meta-analytic review. *Psychological Bulletin, 126*, 651–680.

Archer, J. (2002). Sex differences in physically aggressive acts between heterosexual partners: A meta-analytic review. *Aggression and Violent Behavior, 7*, 313–351.

Bjerregaard, B. (2002). An empirical study of stalking victimization. In K. E. Davis, I. H. Frieze, & R. D. Maiuro (Eds.), *Stalking: Perspectives on victims and perpetrators* (pp. 112–137). New York: Springer Publishing Company.

Brace, N., Kemp, R., & Snelgar, R. (2006). *SPSS for psychologists: A guide to data analysis using SPSS for windows (versions 12 and 13)*. New York: Palgrave Macmillan.

Brewster, M. P. (2002). Stalking by former intimates: Verbal threats and other predictors of physical violence. In K. E. Davis, I. H. Frieze, & R. D. Maiuro (Eds.), *Stalking: Perspectives on victims and perpetrators* (pp. 292–311). New York: Springer Publishing Company.

Brewster, M. P. (2003). Power and control dynamics in prestalking and stalking situations. *Journal of Family Violence, 18*, 207–217.

Budd, T., Mattinson, J., & Myhill, A. (2000). *The extent and nature of stalking: Findings from the 1998 British Crime Survey*: Home Office Research, Development and Statistics Directorate.

Cass, A. (2007). *Individual perceptions of stalking: An examination of the influence of gender and the victim/offender relationship*. (Doctoral dissertation). Retrieved from Dissertation Abstracts International. (Publication No. AAT 3277835)

Cercone, J. J., Beach, S. R. H., & Arias, I. (2005). Gender symmetry in dating intimate partner violence: Does similar behavior imply similar constructs? *Violence and Victims, 20*, 207–218.

Cooksey, R. W. (2007). *Illustrating statistical procedures: For business, behavioural and social science research*. Prahan: Tilde University Press.

Davis, K. E., Ace, A., & Andra, A. (2000). Stalking perpetrators and psychological maltreatment of partners: Anger-jealousy, attachment insecurity, need for control, and break-up context. *Violence and Victims, 15*, 407–425.

Davis, K. E., Coker, A. L., & Sanderson, M. (2002). Physical and mental health effects of being stalked for men and women. *Violence and Victims, 17*, 429–443.

de Vries Robbe, M., March, L., Vinen, J., Horner, D., & Roberts, G. (1996). Prevalence of domestic violence among patients attending a hospital emergency department. *Australian and New Zealand Journal of Public Health, 20*, 364–368.

Dennison, S. M. (2007). Interpersonal relationships and stalking: Identifying when to intervene. *Law and Human Behavior, 31*, 353–367.

Dennison, S. M., & Stewart, A. (2006). Facing rejection: New relationships, broken relationships, shame and stalking. *International Journal of Offender Therapy and Comparative Criminology, 50*, 324–337.

Dennison, S. M., & Thompson, C. M. (forthcoming). Intimate Partner Violence: The Effect of Gender and Contextual Factors on Community Perceptions of Harm, and Suggested Victim and Criminal Justice Responses. *Violence and Victims*.

Dennison, S. M., & Thomson, D. M. (2005). Criticisms or plaudits for stalking laws? What psycholegal research tells us about proscribing stalking. *Psychology, Public Policy and Law, 11*, 384–406.

Dietz, P. E., & Martin, P. Y. (2007). Women who are stalked: Questioning the fear standard. *Violence Against Women, 13*, 750–776.

Dressing, H., Gass, P., & Kuehner, C. (2007). What can we learn from the first community-based epidemiological study on stalking in Germany? *International Journal of Law and Psychiatry, 30*, 10–17.

Dutton, L. B., & Winstead, B. A. (2006). Predicting unwanted pursuit: Attachment, relationship satisfaction, relationship alternatives, and break-up distress. *Journal of Social and Personal Relationships, 23*, 565–586.

Ferrante, A., Morgan, F., Indermaur, D., & Harding, R. (1996). *Measuring the extent of domestic violence*. Sydney: Hawkins Press.

Fontes, D. L. (2007). Male victims of domestic violence. In J. Hamel & T. Nicholls (Eds.), *Family interventions in domestic violence: A handbook of gender-inclusive theory and treatment* (pp. 303–318). New York: Springer Publishing Company.

Harmon, R. B., Rosner, R., & Owens, H. (1998). Sex and violence in a forensic population of obsessional harassers. *Psychology, Public Policy and Law, 4*, 236–249.

Haugaard, J. J., & Seri, L. G. (2000). Stalking and other forms of intrusive contact in adolescent and young-adult relationships. *Kansas City Law Review, 69*, 227–238.

Haugaard, J. J., & Seri, L. G. (2004). Stalking and other forms of intrusive contact among adolescents and young adults from the perspective of the person initiating the intrusive contact. *Criminal Justice and Behavior, 31*, 37–54.

Headey, B., Scott, D., & De Vaus, D. (1999). Domestic violence in Australia: Are men and women equally violent? *Australian Social Monitor, 2*, 57–62.

Herzog, S. (2007). An empirical test of feminist theory and research: The effects of gheterogeneous gender-role attitudes on perceptions of intimate partner violence. *Feminist Crimninology, 2*, 223–244.

Hills, A. M., & Taplin, J. L. (1998). Anticipated responses to stalking: Effect of threat and target-stalker relationship. *Psychiatry, Psychology and Law, 5*, 139–146.

Indermaur, D. (2001). Young Australians and domestic violence. *Trends & Issues in Crime and Criminal Justice, 195*, 1–6.

James, D. V., & Farnham, F. R. (2003). Stalking and serious violence. *The Journal of the American Academy of Psychiatry and the Law, 31*, 432–439.

Kamphuis, J. H., Galeazzi, G., De Fazio, L., Emmelkamp, P. M. G., Farnham, F. R., Groenen, A., et al. (2005). Stalking—perceptions and attitudes amongst helping professions. An EU cross-national comparison. *Clinical Psychology and Psychotherapy, 12*, 215–225.

Kernsmith, P. (2005). Treating perpetrators of domestic violence: Gender differences in the applicability of the theory of planned behavior. *Sex Roles, 52*, 757–770.

Knapp, H., & Kirk, S. A. (2003). Using pencil and paper, internet, and touch-tone phones for self-administered surveys: Does methodology matter? *Computers in Human Behavior, 19*, 117–134.

Krahe, B., & Berger, A. (2005). Sex differences in relationship aggression among young adults in Germany. *Sex Roles, 52*, 829–838.

Mazerolle, P. (1999). *Omaha Intimate Partner Violence Study: Final Report*. Ohio: Cincinnati.

McEwan, T., Mullen, P. E., Mackenzie, R., & Ogloff, J. R. P. (2009). Violence in stalking situations. *Psychological Medicine, 39*, 1469–1478.

McHugh, M. C. (2005). Understanding gender and intimate partner abuse. *Sex Roles, 52*, 717–724.

Meloy, J. R., & Boyd, C. (2003). Female stalkers and their victims. *Journal of the American Academy of Psychiatry and Law, 31*, 211–219.

Meloy, J. R., Davis, B., & Lovette, J. (2001). Risk factors for violence among stalkers. *Journal of Threat Assessment, 1*(1), 3–16.

Melton, H. C. (2007). Closing in: Stalking in the context of intimate partner abuse. *Sociology Compass, 1*(2), 520–535.

Miller, S. L., & Simpson, S. S. (1991). Courtship violence and social control: Does gender matter? *Law & Society Review, 25*, 335–366.

Molidor, C., & Tolman, R. M. (1998). Gender and contextual factors in adolescent dating violence. *Violence Against Women, 4*, 180–194.

Morewitz, S. J. (2003). *Stalking and violence: New patterns of trauma and obsession*. New York: Kluwer Academic/Plenum Publishers.

Mullen, P. E., Pathe, M., Purcell, R., & Stuart, G. W. (1999). Study of stalkers. *American Journal of Psychiatry, 156*, 1244–1249.

Mullen, P. E., Pathe, M., & Purcell, R. (2000). *Stalkers and their victims*. Cambridge: Cambridge University Press.

Norusis, M. J. (2000). *SPSS 10.0 Guide to data analysis*. New Jersey: Prentice Hall.

Pathe, M., & Mullen, P. E. (1997). The impact of stalkers on their victims. *British Journal of Psychiatry, 170*, 12–17.

Phillips, L., Quirk, R., Rosenfeld, B., & O'Connor, M. (2004). Is it stalking? Perceptions of stalking among college undergraduates. *Criminal Justice and Behavior, 31*, 73–96.

Purcell, R., Pathe, M., & Mullen, P. E. (2000). *The incidence and nature of stalking victimisation*. Paper presented at the Stalking: Criminal Justice Responses Conference, Sydney.

Purcell, R., Pathe, M., & Mullen, P. E. (2001). A study of women who stalk. *American Journal of Psychiatry, 158*, 2056–2060.

Purcell, R., Pathe, M., & Mullen, P. E. (2002). The prevalence and nature of stalking in the Australian community. *Australian and New Zealand Journal of Psychiatry, 36*, 114–120.

Purcell, R., Powell, M. B., & Mullen, P. E. (2005). Clients who stalk psychologists: Prevalence, methods, and motives. *Professional Psychology: Research and Practice, 36*, 537–543.

Richman, W. L., Kiesler, S., Weisband, S., & Drasgow, F. (1999). A meta-analytic study of social desirability distortion in computer-administered questionnaires, traditional questionnaires, and interviews. *Journal of Applied Psychology, 84*, 754–775.

Roberts, K. A. (2005). Women's experience of violence during stalking by former romantic partners: Factors predictive of stalking violence. *Violence Against Women, 11*, 89–114.

Rosenfeld, B., & Harmon, R. B. (2002). Factors associated with violence in stalkers and obsessional harassment cases. *Criminal Justice and Behavior, 29*, 671–691.

Sarantakos, S. (1999). Husband abuse: Fact or fiction. *Australian Journal of Social Issues, 34*, 231–252.

Schwartz-Watts, D., & Morgan, D. W. (1998). Violent versus nonviolent stalkers. *Journal of the American Academy of Psychiatry and Law, 26*, 241–245.

Sheridan, L., & Davies, G. M. (2001). Violence and the prior victim-stalker relationship. *Criminal Behaviour and Mental Health, 11*, 102–116.

Sheridan, L., Davies, G. M., & Boon, J. (2001a). The course and nature of stalking: A victim perspective. *The Howard Journal of Criminal Justice, 40*, 215–234.

Sheridan, L., Davies, G. M., & Boon, J. (2001b). Stalking: Perceptions and prevalence. *Journal of Interpersonal Violence, 16*, 151–167.

Sheridan, L., Gillett, R., Davies, G. M., Blaauw, E., & Patel, D. (2003). 'There's no smoke without fire': Are male ex-partners perceived as more 'entitled' to stalk than acquaintance or stranger stalkers? *British Journal of Psychology, 94*, 87–98.

Sinclair, H. C., & Frieze, I. H. (2002). Initial courtship behaviour and stalking: How should we draw the line? In J. A. Davis, I. H. Frieze, & R. D. Maiuro (Eds.). *Stalking: Perspectives on victims and perpetrators* (pp. 186–211). New York: Springer Publishing Company.

Spitzberg, B. H., & Cupach, W. R. (2007). The state of the art of stalking: Taking stock of the emerging literature. *Aggression and Violent Behavior, 12*, 64–86.

Spitzberg, B. H., Nicastro, A. M., & Cousins, A. V. (1998). Exploring the interactional phenomenon of stalking and obsessive relational intrusion. *Communication Reports, 11*, 33–47.

Stewart, A., & Maddren, K. (1997). Police officers' judgements of blame in family violence: The impact of gender and alcohol. *Sex Roles, 37*, 921–933.

Straus, M. A., Hamby, S. L., Boney-McCoy, S., & Sugarman, D. B. (1996). The revised conflict tactics scale (CTS2): Development and preliminary psychometric data. *Journal of Family Issues, 17*, 283–316.

Thomas, S. D. M., Purcell, R., Pathe, M., & Mullen, P. E. (2008). Harm associated with stalking victimization. *Australian and New Zealand Journal of Psychiatry, 42*, 800–806.

Thompson, C. M. (2009). *Developing and testing an integrated theoretical model of stalking violence.* (Doctoral dissertation). Available from Australasian Digital Theses Program. (Record No. 280553)

Thompson, C. M., & Dennison, S. M. (2008). Defining Relational Stalking in Research: Understanding Sample Composition in Relation to Repetition and Duration of Harassment. *Psychiatry, Psychology and Law, 15*, 482–499.

Tjaden, P., & Thoennes, N. (1998). *Stalking in America: Findings from the national violence against women survey:* National Institute of Justice Centers for disease control and prevention.

Tjaden, P., & Thoennes, N. (2000). Prevalence and consequences of male-to-female and female-to-male intimate partner violence as measured by the National Violence Against Women Survey. *Violence Against Women, 6*, 142–161.

Tjaden, P., Thoennes, N., & Allison, C. J. (2000). Comparing stalking victimisation from legal and victim perspectives. *Violence and Victims, 15*, 7–22.

Williams, S. L., & Frieze, I. H. (2005a). Courtship behaviors, relationship violence, and breakup persistence in college men and women. *Psychology of Women Quarterly, 29*, 248–257.

Williams, S. L., & Frieze, I. H. (2005b). Patterns of violent relationships, psychological distress, and marital satisfaction in a national sample of men and women. *Sex Roles, 52*, 771–784.

Williams, S. L., Frieze, I. H., & Sinclair, H. C. (2007). Intimate stalking and partner violence. In J. Hamel & T. Nicholls (Eds.), *Family interventions in domestic violence: A handbook of gender-inclusive theory and treatment* (pp. 109–123). New York: Springer Publishing Company.